GOOD GARDENS GUIDE 2002

EX LIBRIS

THE
GOOD
GARDENS
GUIDE 2002

EDITED BY PETER KING

BLOOMSBURY

Text copyright © Peter King 2002

This paperback edition published 2002

The moral right of the author has been asserted

Managing Editor: Katherine Lambert
Botanical Editor: Lizzie Boyd
Disk Editor: Anita Owen
Maps: Neil Hyslop
Index: Angie Hipkin
Design: Michelle Radford

Bloomsbury Publishing Plc,
38 Soho Square, London WID 3HB

A CIP catalogue record is available from the British Library

ISBN 0 7475 5652 0

10 9 8 7 6 5 4 3 2 1

Typeset by Hewer Text Ltd, Edinburgh
Printed in Great Britain by Clays Limited, St Ives plc

Contents

THE GARDENS

Illustrations: All the colour photographs in the *Guide* were chosen by
Andrew Lawson from his portfolio. The cover illustrates the laburnum walk
at Barnsley House, Gloucestershire, planted by the late Rosemary Verey
and described by Andrew Lawson at her memorial service in July 2001
as 'one of the icons of the gardening world'.

Introduction and Acknowledgements

This is the thirteenth annual edition of the *Guide*, containing a considerable number of gardens which were not in the 2001 book, as well as some deletions of those that, for one reason or another, it was not appropriate to repeat. All the gardens described are open to the public and there is an emphasis on those that are open frequently or 'by appointment' over several months of the year. Some owners are only able or willing to open once or twice, and certain gardens of this kind are included on merit; we hope that such owners may be encouraged to open more frequently if they can.

Our thanks to everyone who has helped with the preparation of the *Guide* – to owners, custodians, professional gardening staff, and many others. In particular, we thank our inspectors and those who advised them. Some of those who have given advice do not wish to be listed and, although anonymous, they have been every bit as valuable. We are also obliged to staff of The National Trust, The National Trust for Scotland and English Heritage for their co-operation. The names which follow include inspectors and past inspectors (but not all of them) and advisors: Barbara Abbs, Jane Allsopp, Diana Atkins, Rosie Atkins, David Baldwin, Susan Barnes, Mr and Mrs Basten, Kerry Bate, Kenneth and Gillian Beckett, Lavender Borden, Kathryn Bradley-Hole, Hilary Bristow, Cecil Brown, Adam Caplin, Dr Joan Carmichael, Richard and Imogen Carter Jonas, Brian and Gillian Cassidy, Lady Cave, Liz Challen, Anne Chamberlain, Sir Jeremy and Lady Chance, Annabel Chisholm, Jeremy Cockayne, Sarah Coles, Anne Collins, E. Anne Colville, Beatrice Cowan, Simon Cramp, Jo, Penelope, Rosie and Trixie Currie, Wendy Dare, Margreet Diepeveen-Bruins Slot, Marilyn Dodd, Rosemary Dodgson, Daphne Dormer, Lady Edmonstone, Matthew Fattorini, Daphne Fisher, Michael and Freda Fisher, Adrian and Audrey Gale, Lucy Gent, Alison Gregory, Elizabeth Hamilton, Stewart Harding, Camilla Harford, Anne Harrison, Sunniva Harte, Lance Hattatt, Tara Heinemann, Jane Henson, Ronald Higgins, Steve Hipkin, Judith Hitchings, Hilary Hodgson, Mariana Hollis, Caroline Holmes, Jackie Hone, Sophie Hughes, Pam Hummer, Jill Husselby, David Jacques, Judith Jenkins, Valerie Jinks, Vanessa Johnston, Rosemarie Johnstone, Belinda Jupp, Mary Keen, Jo Kenaghan, Margaret Knight, Jean Laughton, Virginia Lawlor, Andrew Lawson, Anne E. Liverman, Tony Lord, Malcolm Lyell, Charles Lyte, Janet Macnutt, Michael Mallett, Rhian de Mattos, Pat McCrostie, Anna McKane, Christopher McLaren, Deirdre McSharry, Bettine Muir, Dr Charles Nelson, Hugh Palmer, Lucinda Parry, John and Carol Pease, Victoria Petrie-Hay, Lady Pigot, Stephen Player, Jocelyn Poole, Heather Prescott, Lorna Ramsay, Finola Reid, Anne Richards, Tim Rock, Christopher Rogers, Dorothy Rose, Jane Russell, Alison Rutherford, Sarah Rutherford, Peter de Sausmarez, Kathy Sayer, George and Jane Scott, Barbara Segall, Marjorie Sime, Jill Skeet, Gillian Sladen, Dr Gordon Smith, Michael Smith, Lady Smith-Ryland, Elaine Snazell, Margaret Soole, Marlene Storah, Vera Taggart, Sally Tamplin, Bill Tobias, Caroline Todhunter, Michael Tooley, Annetta Troth, Marie-Françoise Valery, Jackie Ward, Jennifer Wates, Sue Watts, Myra Wheeldon, Susan Whittington, Cynthia Wickham, John Wilks. The editor also expresses his appreciation of the dedicated assistance of Lizzie Boyd, Angie Hipkin, Katherine Lambert, Anita Owen and Wendy Turner.

How to Use the Guide

The *Guide* is **arranged by counties**. Within each of these the gardens are listed alphabetically by the normal name of the garden/house. The index at the end of the book can also be used to find a garden whose name only is known to the reader.

Maps at the beginning of each county section have numbers which refer to those given against each garden entry. Gardens in neighbouring counties may be close enough to the named county to be visited at the same time, so these are indicated by a flower symbol on the maps. Turn to the relevant county map to find the names of these nearby gardens. For detailed information about how to reach gardens use the data given in the garden entry itself.

Readers who do not have a specific garden in mind may like to take the following **procedure to discover gardens** in their particular area which are available for viewing:

1. Choose the county or neighbouring counties which will be your target area.
2. Search out (in these counties) the gardens which are open all year round, i.e. those marked with ○.
3. Having listed these gardens, pay particular attention to ★★ and then ★ gardens on the list.
Alternatively, readers can concentrate on the starred gardens, checking which of these are open on the days available to the visitor.

Symbols: These are intended to convey some useful information at a glance.

NEW entries new for 2002; ○ open all year; ◑ open most of year; ◐ open for main season; ● open on a certain number of days and/or by appointment; ☕ teas/light refreshments; ✕ meals; 🧺 picnics permitted; WC toilet facilities; <u>WC</u> toilet facilities, inc. disabled; ♿ garden partly wheelchair accessible; 🐕 dogs permitted on lead; 🌿 plants for sale; 🛍 shop; ♞ events held; ❀ children-friendly.

This list is repeated in various places throughout the book and further explanation of symbols is given under **Detailed Use of the *Guide*** (below).

Detailed use of the *Guide*
(information listed in order used in entry)

Garden name The name of the garden, or the building with which it is associated.

Stars To help give the reader the opinion which inspectors and editors have formed about the status of certain gardens, over 100 properties have been marked with ★★ to indicate that in our opinion these are amongst the finest gardens in the world in terms of design and content. Many are of historic importance, but some of recent origin. Readers will appreciate that direct comparisons cannot be made between a vast estate like Chatsworth with its staff of professional gardeners and a tiny plantsman's garden behind a terraced house, although both may be excellent of their kind. Those gardens which are of very high quality, though not perhaps as outstanding as the ★★ ones, are given a single ★. The latter will be worth travelling a considerable distance to see, and sometimes the general ambience of the property as a whole will make the visit especially rewarding. The bulk of the gardens in the *Guide* are not given a mark of distinction, but all have considerable merit and will be well worth visiting when in the region. Some of them will have distinctive features of design or plant content, noted in the description, which will justify making a special journey. To give readers an idea of scale, we estimate that some 5000 properties in the UK are open to the public on announced dates in the year, plus public parks and green spaces. We list well over 1000, of which over 100 have ★★ status, that is about ten per cent of the total listed by us, but two and a half per cent of the total open. On the maps, those gardens given ★★ status are distinguished from the others by being boxed in bold.

Address This is the address supplied by the owner or some other reputable source. In the index, gardens with street numbers are listed at the beginning rather than under the initial letter of the street name.

Telephone/Fax/E-mail/Website Except where owners have specifically requested them to be excluded, telephone numbers to which enquiries may be directed are given for each property. To maintain the support and co-operation of private owners, it is suggested that the telephone, fax and e-mail be used with discretion. Where group visits are proposed, owners should be advised in advance and arrangements preferably confirmed in writing. Telephone code numbers are given in brackets. Visitors calling the Republic of Ireland from Britain should phone 00353 followed by the code (Dublin is 1) followed by the subscriber's 6-figure number. Northern Ireland and the Channel Islands follow the mainland system. France has 9-figure numbers prefixed by 0033, Belgium by 0032 and Netherlands by 0031.

Many gardens now have their own websites, and we include these by owners' request. Other useful websites for garden visitors are: CADW (Welsh Historic Monuments) (www.cadw.wales.gov.uk); Duchas (www.heritageireland.ie); English Heritage (www.english-heritage.org.uk); Historic Houses Association (www.hha.org.uk); Historic Royal Palaces (www.hrp.org.uk); Historic Scotland (www.historic-scotland.gov.uk); Landmark Trust (www.landmarktrust.co.uk); The National Gardens Scheme (www.ngs.org.uk); The National Trust (www.nationaltrust.org.uk); The National Trust for Scotland (www.nts.org.uk); The Royal Horticultural Society (www.rhs.org.uk).

Owners' names given are those available at the time of going to press. In the case of The National Trust, some properties may be the homes of tenants of the Trust. Some other gardens are owned or managed by other trusts.

Location, travel and parking This information has been supplied by owners or inspectors and is aimed to be the best available to those travelling by car. No specific details are given where to park because it is assumed that most owners make some convenient arrangement for visitors' cars. However, if special circumstances apply (i.e. if parking is a long walk away) this is usually mentioned under Other Information. The unreliability of train and bus services makes it unrewarding to include many details, particularly as most garden visits are made on Sundays. However, a number of properties can be reached by public transport.

Opening dates and times (see also symbols as opening indicators, below). Dates and times given of access to house (if open) and to garden are usually the best available at the moment of going to press, but some may have been changed subsequently. Some owners unavoidably cannot give their opening information before we go to press. The details given are the most helpful we can present. The dates and times given for all entries are inclusive – that is, an entry such as May to Sept means that the garden is open from 1st May to 30th Sept inclusive, and 2 – 5pm also means that visits will be effective during that period, although some gardens may close to visitors beforehand, and it is wise to arrive at least half an hour before closing time. Please note that many owners will open their gardens to visitors by appointment. They will often arrange to give a personally conducted tour on these occasions.

Gardens in Great Britain which are open by courtesy of the owners for one of many charities are included where the gardens are of special interest even if, as on some occasions, they are open in this way on only one day in the year. However, many such gardens are also open at other specific times, such as for local charities or church restoration funds, and it is not generally possible to give dates for all these locally-publicised openings. Readers should note that other nearby gardens, not listed in this guide for one reason or another, may well be open at similar times to those of listed gardens.

Entrance fees As far as is known, these are correct at time of going to press, but changes may be made without notice. Where there are variations, these will be upwards, but the amount of increase is usually small. Children are often charged at a lower rate, but are expected to be accompanied by an adult. Charges for parties are often at special rates. National Trust charges are explained in their literature with special concessions for members. The Trust is tightening its admissions policy: members who arrive without their membership card will have to pay the full entrance charges. Accompanied children are normally admitted by the Trust at half price and this is why no specific charge for children is usually listed for Trust properties. Figures for the Republic of Ireland are given in Euros – the official currency from 1st January 2002. The Royal Horticultural Society, in addition to its own properties, has a 'free access' scheme to a wide range of other British gardens. RHS members will find details in the *Handbook*; otherwise consult the website (www.rhs.org.uk).

Other information This section gives helpful information notified to us which we pass on to the reader. It includes: extra attractions in or near the garden (eg a museum or nursery); facilities outside the garden but nearby (eg toilet facilities); facilities which are limited either by availability (eg teas on charity open days only), or by location (eg picnics in park only); warnings (eg no coaches), and helpful hints (eg possible for wheelchairs but some gravel paths).

Disclaimer

The information given is believed to be correct at the time of going to press but changes do occur, properties are sold or ownership changed, times of opening varied. In 2002, the Queen's Jubilee celebrations (1st to 4th June) replace the end-May Bank Holiday. It may be wise to check with garden owners concerning these particular dates. There may also be closures of over-visited properties, or limitations imposed on opening times, such as timed tickets. Prices of entry may be changed without notice.

It has not been possible for *Guide* inspectors to visit every garden which was open to the public at some time in the year. In general, inspections have been made on an anonymous basis to ensure objectivity.

Symbols

NEW New garden for 2002

○, ◑, ◐, ● **Opening times** These symbols indicate gardens are open as follows: ○ means open throughout the year; ◑ indicates open most of the year; ◐ shows open more or less throughout the season from Easter to October for several days (i.e. more than two or three) each week; and ● applies to those gardens open on a certain number of days and/or by appointment.

🍵, ✕, 🧺 **Refreshments**: a guide only. Where the symbol 🍵 is given, this means that the owners have arranged to serve a simple tea or light refresh-ments on the property, or near at hand, at reasonable prices during opening hours. The symbol ✕ indicates that meals are served. 🧺 means that picnics are permitted, although probably in certain areas only .

WC, <u>WC</u> Toilet facilities The symbol WC indicates that access to a toilet or toilets is provided, while <u>WC</u> means that the toilet facilities are also suitable for disabled visitors. Where neither symbol is given, no specific toilets are available and enquiries will have to be directed to staff or owners.

♿ **Wheelchair suitability** Inspectors have told us where they believe a garden is partly or wholly negotiable by someone in a wheelchair and the symbol indicates this. This comment refers to the garden only and if a house or other building is also open, it may or may not be suitable for wheelchairs.

🐕 **Dogs** If dogs on lead are allowed in the property (although often in restricted areas), a symbol is given.

🌿 **Plants for sale** The symbol means that plants are for sale. Often these are grown on the property, but some owners now buy in plants from a commercial source for re-sale.

🏛 **Shop** The symbol refers to shops on the premises, such as National Trust shops, those selling souvenirs, etc.

🎪 **Events** The symbol indicates that events may be held during, or additional to, normal garden opening times. Those wishing either to participate in, or to avoid, events should check before travelling.

🧒 **Children-friendly** Some owners pay particular attention to expanding the attractions for the whole family.

No symbol means either that a certain facility is not available at a garden or that we have not been notified of it. However, it is worth checking under Other Information for details of partial availability.

Two-Starred Gardens

BUCKINGHAMSHIRE
Ascott; Cliveden; The Manor House, Bledlow; Stowe; Waddesdon; West Wycombe

CAMBRIDGESHIRE
Anglesey Abbey; Christ's College; University Botanic Garden

CHESHIRE
Ness Botanic Gardens; Tatton Park

CORNWALL
Caerhays; Heligan; Pine Lodge; Trebah; Tresco; Trewithen

CUMBRIA
Holehird; Holker; Levens

DERBYSHIRE
Chatsworth

DEVON
Castle Drogo; Coleton Fishacre; Knights-hayes; Marwood Hill; Rosemoor

DORSET
Cranborne Manor; Forde Abbey

ESSEX
The Beth Chatto Gardens

GLOUCESTERSHIRE
Barnsley House; Hidcote; Kiftsgate; Sezincote; Westbury Court; Westonbirt Arboretum

HAMPSHIRE
Exbury; Longstock Park Water Gardens; Mottisfont Abbey; Sir Harold Hillier Gardens and Arboretum; Ventnor Botanic Garden

HERTFORDSHIRE
Benington Lordship; Gardens of the Rose; Hatfield House;

KENT
Goodnestone Park; Hever Castle; Sissinghurst

LANCASHIRE
Gresgarth Hall

LONDON AREA
Chiswick House; Hampton Court; Royal Botanic Gardens, Kew

NORFOLK
East Ruston Old Vicarage

NORTHAMPTONSHIRE
Cottesbrooke

NORTHUMBERLAND
Belsay Hall

OXFORDSHIRE
Blenheim Palace; Oxford Botanic Garden; Rousham; Westwell Manor

SHROPSHIRE
Hodnet Hall; Wollerton Old Hall

SOMERSET
Greencombe; Hadspen

STAFFORDSHIRE
Biddulph Grange

SUFFOLK
Helmingham Hall; Somerleyton Hall

SURREY
Painshill; RHS Wisley; The Savill Garden; Sutton Place; The Valley Gardens

SUSSEX (East)
Great Dixter; Sheffield Park

SUSSEX (West)
Leonardslee; Nymans; Wakehurst Place

WILTSHIRE
Iford Manor; Stourhead

YORKSHIRE
Castle Howard; Newby Hall; Studley Royal and Fountains Abbey

IRELAND
Butterstream; Castlewellan Arboretum; The Dillon Garden; Earlscliffe; Glenveagh Castle; Ilnacullin; Mount Congreve; Mount Stewart; Mount Usher; Rowallane

SCOTLAND
Arduaine; Castle Kennedy; Castle of May; Crarae; Crathes Castle; Culzean; Drummond Castle; House of Pitmuies; Inverewe; Little Sparta; Logan Botanic Garden; Manderston; Mount Stuart; Royal Botanic Garden Edinburgh; Younger Botanic Garden

WALES
Bodnant; Clyne Gardens; Powis Castle

FRANCE
Château de Brécy; Château de Canon; Parc Floral des Moutiers, Le Vasterival

BELGIUM
Annevoie

NETHERLANDS
Paleis Het Loo

Where to Stay

This section to help those seeking accommodation while garden visiting has three main categories. Accommodation is listed for England, Ireland, Scotland and Wales with the suffixes (H) for hotel, (P) for pub/inn, (BB) for bed and breakfast. First, there are those hotels which themselves have particularly fine gardens and therefore feature in the main text of the *Guide*. They are listed here by county with the appropriate reference. Second, there are hotels with gardens, some of which may also have particular distinction. Next we have listed a number of pubs/inns which feature in *The Good Pub Guide*. Finally we list a range of B&Bs, taken from Mrs Sue Colquoun's publication called *Bed and Breakfast for Garden Lovers*. Those readers who wish to obtain her full list may do so by sending a 22cm × 11cm self-addressed envelope with 4 first-class stamps to: *BBGL*, Handywater Farm, Sibford Gower, Banbury, Oxfordshire OX15 5AE. Their website is www.bbgl.co.uk.

A number of National Trust tenants offer bed and breakfast accommodation. Addresses are given in their booklet, *Bed & Breakfast 2001*, probably reprinting in 2002. Their list carries a note that the Trust takes no responsibility for standards. Another (posher) organisation renting self-catering properties is The Landmark Trust, which has a mouth-watering brochure. In Ireland, other estimable hotels and B&Bs are listed in two recommended booklets, *Friendly Homes of Ireland* and *The Hidden Ireland*, both available from the Tourist Board, P.O. Box 5451, Dublin 2.

Bedfordshire
Knife and Cleaver (P), Houghton Conquest. Tel: (01234) 740387

Berkshire
Meadow House (BB) *(see entry)*
White Hart (P), Hampstead Marshall. Tel: (01488) 658201

Bristol Area
White Hart (P), Littleton upon Severn. Tel: (01454) 412275

Buckinghamshire
Cliveden (H) *(see entry)*
Five Arrows (H), Waddesdon. Tel: (01296) 651727.
Hartwell House Hotel (H), Aylesbury. Tel: (01296) 747444.
Stag and Huntsman (P), Hambleden. Tel: (01491) 571227.
Walnut Tree (P), Fawley. Tel: (01491) 638360.

Cambridgeshire
Leeds Arms (P), Eltisley. Tel: (01480) 880283

Cheshire
Bears Head (P), Brereton Green. Tel: (01477) 535251.
Nunsmere Hall (H), Oakmere. Tel: (01606) 889100.
Sutton Hall (H), Macclesfield. Tel: (01260) 253211.

Cornwall
Long Cross (H) *(see entry)*
Meudon (H), Mawnan Smith. Tel: (01326) 250541.(Garden open at weekends)
Trengilly Wartha (P), Constantine. Tel: (01326) 340332.
The Well House (H), St Keyne. Tel: (01579) 342001.

Cumbria
Leeming House Hotel (H), Watermillock. Tel: (017684) 86622.
Linthwaite House Hotel (H), Bowness-on-Windermere. Tel: (015394) 88600.
The Mortal Man (H), Troutbeck. Tel: (01229) 860291.

Sharrow Bay Country House (H), Pooley Bridge. Tel: (018536) 301.
The Trout (P), Cockermouth. Tel: (01900) 823591.

Derbyshire
The Clock Warehouse (P), Shardlow. Tel: (01332) 792844.
Horsleygate Hall (BB), Holmesfield. Tel: (0114) 289 0333
Riber Hall (H), Matlock. Tel: (01629) 582795.
Underleigh House (H), Hope.

Devon
Avenue Cottage (BB) (see entry)
Blue Ball (P), Sidford. Tel: (01395) 514062.
Buckland-Tout-Saints Hotel (H), Kingsbridge. Tel: (01548) 853055.
The Cider House (BB), Yelverton. Tel: (01822) 853285.
Combe House (H), Gittisham. Tel: (01404) 42756.
Docton Mill (BB) (see entry)
Endsleigh House (H) (see entry)
Gidleigh Park (H) (see entry)
The Knoll House, Studland Bay. Tel: (0191) 450450.
Whitechapel Manor (H), South Molton. Tel: (01769) 573377.

Dorset
Chedington Court (H), Chedington. Tel: (01935) 891265
Friars Way (BB), Upwey. Tel: (01305) 813243.
The Knoll House (H) (see entry)
Langton Arms (P), Tarrant Monkton. Tel: (01258) 830225.
The Manor (H), West Bexington. Tel: (01308) 897616.
The Museum (P), Farnham. Tel: (01725) 516261.
Plumber Manor (H), Sturminster Newton. Tel: (01258) 472507.
Priory (H), Wareham. Tel: (01929) 551666.
Summer Lodge (H), Evershot. Tel: (01935) 83424.

Durham
Morritt Arms (P), Greta Bridge. Tel: (01833) 627232.

Essex
The Queen's Head (P), Littlebury. Tel: (01799) 522251.
The Rose (P), Peldon. Tel: (01206) 735248.

Gloucestershire
Burleigh Court Hotel (H), Burleigh. Tel: (01453) 883804.
Calcot Manor (BB), Tetbury. Tel: (01666) 890391.
Crown of Crucis (P), Ampney Crucis. Tel: (01285) 851806.
Halewell Close (H), Withington. Tel: (01242) 890238.
The Lygon Arms (H), Broadway. Tel: (01386) 852255.
Upper Court (H), Kemerton. Tel: (01386) 725351.
Village Pub (P), Barnsley. Tel: (01285) 740421.
Wesley House (H), Winchcombe. Tel: (01242) 602366.
The Wild Duck (P), Ewen. Tel: (01285) 770310.

Hampshire
Esseborne Manor (H), Hurstbourne Tarrant. Tel: (01264) 736444.
Lainston House Hotel (H), Sparsholt. Tel: (01962) 863588.
Tylney Hall Hotel (H) (see entry)
The Vine (P), Stockbridge. Tel: (01264) 810652.

Herefordshire
Broxwood Court (BB), Nr Pembridge. Tel: (01544) 340245.
Darkley House (see entry).
Cottage of Content (P), Carey. Tel: (01432) 840242.
The Green Man (P), Fownhope. Tel: (01432) 860243.
Hope End Hotel (H), Ledbury. Tel: (01531) 633613.

Hertfordshire

Brocket Arms (P), Ayot St Lawrence. Tel: (01438) 850250.
Hanbury Manor (H) (see entry)
West Lodge Park Hotel (H) (see entry for The Beale Arboretum)

Kent

The Crown (P), Groombridge. Tel: (01892) 864742.
The Dering Arms (H), Pluckly. Tel: (01223) 840371.
Maycotts (BB), Tonbridge. Tel: (01892) 723983
Vine Farm (BB), Headcorn. Tel: (01622) 890203.

Lancashire

Parkers Arms (P), Newton. Tel: (01200) 446236.
The Ridges (BB) (see entry)

Leicestershire

Neville Arms (P), Medbourne. Tel: (01858) 565288.

Lincolnshire

Black Horse (P), Donington on Bain. Tel: (01507) 343640.
The George (P), Stamford. Tel: (01780) 755171.

London Area

Grim's Dyke (H), Old Redding. Tel: (0181) 954 4227.

Norfolk

Beeches Hotel (H) (see entry for The Plantation Garden)
Buckinghamshire Arms (H), Blickling. Tel: 01263) 732133.
Congham Hall (H) (see entry)
Manor Hotel (P), Titchwell. Tel: (01485) 210221.
Morston Hall (H), Morston. Tel: (01263) 741041.
Rose and Crown (P), Snettisham. Tel: (01485) 541382.
The Victoria (P), Holkham. Tel: (01328) 710469.

Northamptonshire

Olde Coach House (P), Ashby St Ledgers. Tel: (01788) 890349.
Red Lion (P), East Haddon. Tel: (01604) 770223.

Northumberland

Lord Crewe Arms (P), Blanchland. Tel: (01434) 675251.
Manor House (P), Carterway Heads. Tel: (01207) 255268
Warren House Hotel (H), Waren Mill. Tel: (01668) 214581

Nottinghamshire

Griff Inn (P), Drakeholes. Tel: (01777) 817206.

Oxfordshire

The Feathers (P), Woodstock. Tel: (01993) 812291.
The Lamb (P), Burford. Tel: (01993) 823155.
Le Manoir aux Quat' Saisons (H), Great Milton. Tel: (01844) 278881.
Upper Court Barn (BB), Chadlington. Tel: (01608) 676375.

Rutland

Fox and Hounds (P), Exton. Tel: (01572) 812403.

Shropshire

Hawkstone Park Hotel (H) (see entry for Hawkstone Historic Park and Follies)
The Hundred House (P), Norton. Tel: (01952) 730353

Somerset

Bull Terrier (P), Croscombe. Tel: (01749) 343658.
Brewers Cottage (BB). Tel: (01460) 281395
Charlton House Hotel (H), Shepton Mallet. Tel: (01749) 342008
Hunstrete House (H), Chelwood. Tel: (01761) 490490.
The Old Rectory (BB), Stanton Prior. Tel: (01761) 471942.
Ralegh's Cross (P), Brendon Hills. Tel: (01984) 40343

The Ship (P), Porlock. Tel: (01643)
862507.
Ston Easton (H) (see entry)

Staffordshire
The Greyhound (P), Warslow. Tel:
(01298) 84249.
Olde Dog and Partridge (P), Tutbury.
Tel: (01283) 813030.

Suffolk
The Angel (P), Lavenham. Tel:
(01787) 247388.
The Crown (P), Bidleston. Tel:
(01449) 740510.
Hintlesham Hall (H), Hintlesham. Tel
(01473) 652334.
Sun House (BB) (see entry)
The Swan (P), Lavenham. Tel: (01787)
247477.

Surrey
Drummond Arms (P), Albury. Tel:
(01483) 202039.
Great Fosters (H) (see entry)
Langshott Manor (H) (see entry)
Nutfield Priory (H), Redhill. Tel:
(01737) 822066.
The Plough (P), Coldharbour. Tel:
(01306) 711793.

Sussex, East
Bates Green Farm (BB) (see entry)
Cleveland House (H), Winchelsea.
Tel: (01797) 226256.
The Griffin (P), Fletching. Tel: (01825)
722890.
The Gun (P), Gun Hill. Tel: (01825)
872361.
King John's Lodge (see entry).
Lye Green House (BB), Lye Green,
Tel: (01892) 652018.
Netherfield Place (H), Battle. Tel:
(01424) 774455.
The Ram (P), Firle. Tel: (01273)
858222.
The Studio, Fletching. Tel: (01825)
723128.
The Warren House (H), Crowbor-
ough. Tel: (01892) 663502.

Sussex, West
Amberley Castle (H), Arundel. Tel:
(01798) 831992.
Gravetye Manor (H) (see entry)
The Half Moon (P), Kirdford. Tel:
(01403) 820223.
Ockenden Manor (H), Cuckfield. Tel:
(01444) 416111.
73 Sheepdown Drive (BB), Petworth.
Tel: (01798) 342269
South Lodge Hotel (H), Lower Beed-
ing. Tel: (01403) 891711.
Three Horseshoes (P), Elsted. Tel:
(01730) 825746.

Warwickshire
Howard Arms (P), Ilmington. Tel:
(01608) 682226.
Red Lion (P), Little Compton. Tel:
(01608) 674397.
Welcombe Hall (H), Nr Stratford-
upon-Avon. Tel: (01892) 295252.

Wiltshire
Compasses (P), Chicksgrove. Tel:
(01722) 714318.
The Garden Lodge (BB), Chittoe. Tel:
(01380) 850314.
Goulters Mill (BB), Gibb. Tel: (01249)
782555
The Harrow (P), Little Bedwyn. Tel:
(01672) 870871.
The Horseshoe (P), Ebbesbourne
Wake. Tel. (01722) 780474.
Landford Wood (BB), Salisbury. Tel:
(01794) 390220.
The Rattlebone (P), Sherston. Tel:
(01666) 840871.
Red Lion (P), Axford. Tel: (01672)
520271.
Red Lion (P), Kilmington. Tel: (01985)
844263.
Sturford Mead (BB), Warminster.
Tel: (01373) 832039.
Woolley Grange (H), Woolley Green.
Tel: (01225) 864705.

Worcestershire
The Elms, (H) Abberley.
Tel: (01299) 896666.

Grafton Manor, (H) Bromsgrove. Tel: (01527) 579007

Luggers Hall (BB), Broadway. Tel: (01386) 852040

Yorkshire

Abbey Inn (P), Byland Abbey. Tel: (01347) 868204.

Devonshire Arms (P), Cracoe. Tel: (01756) 730237.

Middlethorpe Hall (H), York. Tel: (01904) 641241.

Millgate House (BB) (see entry)

Ireland

Abbey Hotel (H), Roscommon. Tel: (903) 26505.

Adare Manor, Adare, Co. Limerick. Tel: (61) 396566.

Annesbrook, Duleck, Co. Meath. Tel: (41) 23293.

Ardnamona (BB), (see entry).

Ashbrook, Co. Londonderry. Tel: (01504) 349223.

Assolas Country House (H), Kanturk, Co. Cork. Tel: (29) 50015.

Avondale House, Scribblestown, Co. Dublin. Tel: (1) 838 6545.

Ballymaloe (H) (see entry)

Ballyvolane House (H), Castlelyons, Co. Cork. Tel: (25) 36349.

Bantry House (see entry).

Blanchville House (H), Dunbell, Co. Kilkenny. Tel: (56) 27197.

Blessingbourne (H), Fivemiletown.

Caragh Lodge (H), Caragh Lake, Co. Kerry. Tel: (66) 61411/69115.

Cariglass Manor (H), Longford. Co. Longford. Tel: (43) 451165.

Cashel Palace Hotel (H), Co. Tipperary. Tel: (62) 62707

Castle Leslie, Co. Monaghan. Tel: (47) 88109

Clonalis House, Castlerea, Co. Roscommon. Tel: (907) 20014.

Deer Park Hotel (H), Howth. Tel: (18) 332 624.

Delphi Lodge, Leenane, Co. Galway. Tel: (95) 42211.

Dunloe Castle (H) (see entry)

Enniscoe House (H), Castlehill, Co. Mayo. Tel: (96) 31112.

Glin Castle (H) (see entry)

Great Southern Hotel (H), Killarney, Co. Kerry. Tel: (64) 31262.

Gregans Castle (H), Ballyvaughan, Co. Clare. Tel: (65) 77005.

Hilton Park (BB) (see entry)

Hunter's Hotel (H), Rathnew, Co. Wicklow. Tel: (404) 40106.

Killyreagh, Tormlaght, Enniskillen, Co. Fermanagh. Tel: (028) 6638 7221.

Kilmokea (see entry).

Lismacue House, Bansha, Co. Tiperary. Tel: (62) 54106.

Lisnavagh (see entry)

Lorum Old Rectory, Bagenalstown, Co. Carlow. Tel: (0503) 75282.

Magheramorne House Hotel (H), Larne, Co. Antrim. Tel: (01574) 279444

Marlfield House (H), Gorey, Co Wexford. Tel: (55) 21124.

The Mustard Seed at Echo Lodge (H), Ballingarry, Co. Limerick. Tel: (69) 68508.

Newport House (H), Newport, Co Mayo. Tel: (98) 41222.

The Park Hotel (H), Kenmare, Co. Kerry. Tel: (64) 41200.

Powerscourt (see entry)

Red House, Ardee, Co. Louth. Tel: (41) 53523.

Rosleague Manor (H), Letterfrack, Co. Galway. Tel: (95) 41101.

Temple House, Ballymote, Co. Sligo. Tel: (71) 83329.

Tullanisk, Birr, Co. Offaly. Tel: (509) 20572.

Tyrella House, Downpatrick, Co. Down. Tel: (01396) 851422.

Waterford Castle, Ballinakill, Co. Waterford. Tel: (51) 78203.

Scotland

Airds Hotel (H), Port Appin. Tel: (01631) 730236.

Ardanaiseig Hotel (H) (see entry)

Ardrannoch, Ledaig (BB), Tel: (01631) 720241.

Arisaig House (H), Beasdale. Tel: (01687) 450622.

Balbirnie Hotel Hotel (H), Markinch. Tel: (01592) 610066.

Balfour Castle (H), Shapinsay, Orkney. Tel: (01856) 711282.

Cambo (BB) (see entry)

Ceilidh Place (P), Ullapool. Tel: (01854) 612103.

Connoisseur Scotland (H), Edinburgh. Tel: (0131) 220 2729.

Creebridge House (P), Creebridge. Tel: (01671) 402121.

Creggans (P), Strachur. Tel: (01369) 86279.

Cringletie House Hotel (H), Peebles. Tel: (01721) 730233.

The Crown (P), Portpatrick. Tel: (01776) 810261.

Ferry Boat (P), Ullapool. Tel: (01854) 612366.

Fisherman's Tavern (P), Bloughty Ferry. Tel: (01382) 775941

Galley of Larne (P), Ardfern. Tel: (01852) 500284.

Glenborrodale Castle (H), Ardnamurchan. Tel: (01972) 500266.

Glenfeochan House (H), Kilmore. Tel: (01631) 770273.

Greywalls (H), Muirfield. Tel: (01620) 842144.

Kilberry Inn (P), Kilberry Tel: (010001) 770223

Kildrummy Castle (H) (see entry)

Killiecrankie Hotel (P), Pitlochry. Tel: (01796) 473220.

Kilravock Castle (H), Croy. Tel: (01667) 493258.

Kinnaird, Dunkeld (H). Tel: (01796) 482440.

Knockinaam Lodge (H), Portpatrick. Tel: (01776) 810471.

Lion and Unicorn (P), Thornhill. Tel: (01786) 850204/850707.

Loch Melfont Hotel (P), Arduaine. Tel: (01852) 200233.

Murray Arms (P), Gatehouse of Fleet. Tel: (01557) 814207.

Plockton Hotel (P), Plockton. Tel: (01599) 544.

Prestonfield House (H), Edinburgh. Tel: (0131) 668 3346.

Riverside (P), Canonbie. Tel: (013873) 71512/71295.

Skaebost House Hotel (P), Skaebost, Skye. Tel: (01470) 532202.

Tibbie Shiels Inn (P), St Mary's Loch. Tel: (01750) 42231

11 Warriston Crescent (BB), Edinburgh. Tel: (0131) 556 0093.

Wheatsheaf (P), Swinton. Tel: (01890) 860257.

Wales

Abbey Hotel (P), Llanthony. Tel: (01873) 890487.

The Bear (P), Crickhowell. Tel: (01873) 810408.

Bodysgallen Hall (H) (see entry)

Halfway Inn (P), Aberystwyth. Tel: (01970) 880631.

The Harp (P), Old Radnor. Tel: (01544) 421655.

The Lion (P), Tudweiliog. Tel: (01758) 770244.

Llanerch (P), Llandrindod Wells. Tel: (01597) 822086.

Nantygilwch, Llaw-y-glyn, Nr Caersws, Powys. Tel: (01686) 430423.

Plas Penhelig (H) (see entry)

Portmeirion (H) (see entry)

Radnorshire Arms (P), Presteigne. Tel: (01544) 267406.

Trewern Arms (P), Nevern. Tel: (01239) 820395.

Tyddyn Llan (H), Llandrillo. Tel: (01490) 440264.

Ynyshir Hall (H) (see entry)

Channel Islands

Mille Fleurs (self-catering) (see entry)

Glossary of Garden Terms

Arbour Any sheltered covered area open to one side which usually contains a seat. Arbours can be surrounded by masonry, hedging or by trellis work covered with climbing plants such as roses.

Allée or Alley A path either cut through a thick shrubbery or woodland or closely surrounded by a hedge or wall.

Bath house A rectangular sunken pool for cold water bathing, with seating approached by steps.

Belvedere A high point on a building, or a summerhouse, which commands a beautiful view.

Bosket or _bosquet_ A block of very closely planted trees.

Canal An ornamental water basin made in the form of an elongated rectangle. It can either be excavated into the ground or confined above ground within masonry walls.

Clair-voyée A gap in a wall or hedge which extends the view by allowing a glimpse of the surrounding countryside.

Exedra An area of turf within a semi-circular hedge which is usually used to display ornaments or locate a semi-circular seat; or the seat itself.

Eye-catcher A building such as a tower, temple, obelisk, etc. or sometimes merely a bench, large urn or an outstanding long-lived plant designed to beckon the eye towards a particularly rewarding view.

Finial An ornament such as an urn or a pointed sculptural form used to cap features like gateposts, the tops of spires, the top corners of buildings, etc.

Folly A decorative building with no serious function except perhaps to lure attention along a vista or to improve the composition of the garden 'picture'.

Gazebo Dog latin for 'I will gaze', used to describe a building usually sited on a high terrace from which the surrounding countryside can be enjoyed.

Grotto/Nymphaeum An artificial garden feature made to simulate an underground cavern and usually dimly lit from a single small natural light source such as the cave mouth or an oval occulus pierced through the roof or wall. When rather dank and simply lined with natural rock, a grotto can be a good example of art echoing nature. But when formally shaped and lined with statuary and a sophisticated encrusting of shellwork a grotto can become a nymphaeum and an example of art inspired by, and improving upon, nature. Such features are usually made by excavating into a natural hillside or are constructed on level ground then covered with earth to form a mound. Occasionally (as at Woburn Abbey) a grotto can be made as an extension to the house, so offering a cool area in hot weather. Other functions of grottos are to shock and surprise visitors, play upon their perception of the garden or provoke a fruitful melancholy.

Ha-ha A deep ditch separating the garden from the landscape beyond. It allows the unscreened view to be enjoyed from the house but is profiled in such a way that livestock cannot enter the garden.

Knot garden Geometric patterns of low-growing hedge plants such as box or shrubby germander which are made to appear as though they intertwine like knotted cord. The areas between the hedges are filled with plants or decorative gravels.

Mount An artificial hill usually surmounted by an arbour from which landscapes both inside and beyond the garden can be enjoyed from a different perspective.

Obelisk A tall, thin vertical column diminishing in width as it rises and frequently tapered to a pyramid. Large-scale examples have been built to commemorate great events or notable people and frequently to act as eye-catchers in great landscape schemes. Smaller _treillage_ versions have been used to beckon for attention in smaller gardens or to act as vertical frames for climbing plants.

Pagoda A feature in a few great landscape gardens based on Buddhist multistorey towers of spiritual significance. In Britain they first were introduced during the eighteenth-century craze for things Chinese.

Palisade A tall hedge of deciduous trees or shrubs with interlaced branches.

Palladian bridge A bridge with a classical superstructure, usually open-sided with columns supporting a roof.

Parterre An intricately-patterned formal garden which usually includes other features such as statuary, water basins and fountains, much larger than a knot garden.

Patte d'oie Literally 'goose foot'; a series of usually three formal paths or grand avenues leading fanwise from a single point through densely-planted trees.

Pergola A framework of columns supporting beams which is usually clad with climbing plants such as roses, clematis or wisteria. If their parallel rows of columns are joined by cross beams and the cover of summer foliage, pergolas can become tunnels.

Pleaching Training the branches of a line of trees horizontally by pruning and attaching them to canes and wires, so that the remainder can be intertwined as they grow to form a screen of foliage.

Pylon A tower which is narrower at its squared-off top than at its base.

Ribbon bed A very narrow band of bedding plants which the Victorians were fond of using to border their lawns.

Rotunda Strictly a circle of classical columns on a raised circular plinth supporting a domed roof. Instead of a solid dome it may be topped with an open ironwork dome. Sometimes loosely called a kiosk.

Rustic work Garden features such as garden houses, fences or seats made from unbarked tree branches - frequently embellished with such decoration as patterns made from sectioned pine cones.

Souterrain An underground chamber usually in a grotto.

Stilt hedge Clipped trees, such as limes, which have all branches removed for several feet above the ground to reveal a line of bare trunks like stilts.

Tapis vert A long strip of lawns between paths or canals.

Théâtre de verdure Similar to but usually more spacious than an exedra, a turf 'stage' with a backcloth of trimmed hedge and sometimes other hedges disposed like the wings of a theatre.

Treillage Architectural features such as arbours, obelisks or ambitious screens made out of trellis.

Trompe-l'oeil A feature designed to deceive the eye, such as a path which narrows as it recedes from a viewpoint to exaggerate the perspective and make the garden seem larger.

Notes on Great Gardeners

Sir Charles Barry (1795 – 1860) A highly successful architect (Houses of Parliament etc), he popularised the formal Italian style of gardening in the mid-nineteenth century, creating impressive designs incorporating terraces, flights of steps, balustrading, urns, fountains and loggias. His most notable gardens were at Trentham Park, Dunrobin Castle, Cliveden, Shrubland Hall and Harewood.

Charles Bridgeman (d. 1738) Famous for the way in which he exploited the outstanding features of the sites for which he designed gardens, Bridgeman provides the link between the rigid formality of much of seventeenth-century garden design and the apparent freedom of the landscape movement pioneered by William Kent and 'Capability' Brown. While retaining features such as geometric parterres close to the house and straight *allées*, he also incorporated wilderness and meadow areas linked by meandering paths. By his use of the ha-ha he made vistas of the surrounding landscape part of his designs. Apart from work for royal patrons in gardens such as Richmond and Kensington Gardens (where he was responsible for the Round Pond and the Serpentine), Bridgeman carried out important works at Blenheim, Claremont, Rousham, Cliveden and Stowe.

Lancelot 'Capability' Brown (1716 – 83) Having worked as head gardener and clerk of works at Stowe early in his career, Brown became familiar with the work of Bridgeman and Vanbrugh and helped to execute the designs of William Kent and James Gibbs. Their influence was particularly noticeable in the buildings he designed for his later schemes. However, he was much more radical than any of them, discarding formality when creating very natural-looking landscapes for his clients. Banishing all flowering plants and vegetables he confined them in walled gardens well away from the house and by using ha-has to prevent the ingress of cattle he made the surrounding meadow land appear to run right up to the house walls. Making lakes by excavation and damming streams, he used the excavated soil to create slopes elsewhere which he clad with distinctive clumps of often quite large specimens of native trees to provide the type of park which seemed to flow naturally into the countryside and suited the hunting requirements of the sporting eighteenth-century squirearchy. To many people it seems that Brown strove to bring the rolling landscapes of his native Northumberland to his client's parks in the flatter Midlands and South. Examples of his work in the *Guide* are: Audley End, Berrington, Blenheim, Bowood, Broadlands, Burghley, Burton Constable, Cadland, Charlecote, Chatsworth, Claremont, Corsham, Euston, Harewood, Highclere, Holkham, Leeds Castle, Longleat, Petworth, Ripley, Sheffield Park, Sledmere, St John's College (Cambridge), Sutton Place, Syon, Temple Newsam, Trentham, University Arboretum (Oxford), Warwick Castle, Weston, Wimpole Hall, Wrest Park.

Percy Cane (1881 – 1976) He began as a writer in *My Garden Illustrated* which he owned from 1918 - 20; he also owned *Garden Design* from 1930 - 39. During this latter period he developed an influential international practice, and was a star performer at Chelsea Flower Shows in the thirties, where his curvy borders, now a common feature, were regarded as innovatory. Falkland Palace, Scotland and Dartington, Devon, show his imaginative horticultural skills at their best.

Brenda Colvin (1897 – 1981) Highly influential landscape architect who worked on large-scale projects such as land reclamation schemes and urban design. A founder member of the Landscape Institute, she became its president from 1951 to 1953, and her 1947 book *Land and Landscape* became a standard work. Clipsham (Rutland) is an example of her work.

Dame Sylvia Crowe (1901 – 98) Responsible for many large-scale projects such as the master planning for new towns like Warrington and Washington as well as being consultant on landscaping for the new towns of Harlow and Basildon. She became an acknowledged expert on the sympathetic integration of development schemes, such as the construction of power stations, with the surrounding landscape. She designed the roof garden for the Scottish Widows Fund in Edinburgh and a park in Canberra, Australia. She was President of the Landscape Institute 1957 -59. Examples of her work in the *Guide* are at Blenheim, Cottesbrooke and Lexham Hall.

Margery Fish (1888 – 1969) An informed plantswoman and influential lecturer and author who was a great partisan of the nineteenth century designer William Robinson's naturalistic approach to gardening. This she developed in her own garden at East Lambrook Manor in Somerset which became a haven for endangered garden plants. Her style for the garden which mixed semi-formal features with traditional planting has been influential.

Charles Hamilton (1704 – 86) Under the influence of William Kent between 1738 and 1773, when he was obliged to sell the estate at Painshill Park in Surrey to pay his debts, Hamilton created one of Britain's most picturesque landscape gardens which is now in the process of being restored. As well as being a talented designer, he was an exemplary plantsman, incorporating many exotics in his schemes, particularly those from North America. He also designed a cascade and grotto at Bowood and advised on work at Holland Park and Stourhead.

Henry Hoare II (1705 – 85) He was the scholarly member of the banking family and greatly influenced the design of the great landscape garden at Stourhead in Wiltshire. A friend of Charles Hamilton, Lord Burlington and William Kent, he shared their naturalistic approach towards landscaping.

Gertrude Jekyll (1843 – 1932) By both her writings and the examples of her work (much of it accomplished in partnership with the architect Sir Edwin Lutyens) during the last years of the last century and the first quarter of this, she has probably had as much influence on the appearance of British gardens as any other designer. As someone trained initially as a painter and an embroiderer, her great strength was in carefully considered and subtle use of plant colour. Finding inspiration in the happy informality of cottage gardens, she created large interwoven swathes of plants rather than confining them to precise 'spotty' patterns and in so doing she changed our attitude towards the way in which borders should be planted. One of the best examples of Gertude Jekyll's work with Edwin Lutyens is the restored Hestercombe Gardens. Other examples, also in the *Guide*, are Barrington, Castle Drogo, Castle Tor, Folly Farm, Goddards, Hatchlands, Knebworth, Upton Grey Manor House, Munstead Wood, Tylney, Vann and Yalding.

Sir Geoffrey Jellicoe (1900 – 96) Shortly after becoming an architect, Jellicoe made an extensive study of Italian gardens with J.C. Shepheard, which led to their producing in 1925 what has become a classic book, *Italian Gardens of the*

Renaissance. The publication of *Gardens and Design* in 1927 confirmed his understanding of basic principles and helped to bring him interesting commissions such as the design of a formal garden at Ditchley Park in Oxfordshire. After World War II he was given much public work, including an extensive water garden in Hemel Hempstead town centre, the Cathedral Close in Exeter, the Kennedy Memorial at Runnymede and a large theme park at Galveston in Texas. Among his work for private clients, the gardens at Sutton Place and at Shute House are notable. His witty designs have a strong architectural quality. In the past his late wife Susan suggested the planting for many of his schemes and she shared the authorship of the authoritative *The Landscape of Man*, published in 1975, which discussed in great detail the history and art of landscape design. His work may also be seen at Cliveden, Cottesbrooke, Mottisfont, Sandringham and Sutton Place.

Lawrence Johnston (1871 – 1948) One of the most outstandingly stylish twentieth-century gardeners, Johnston was an American who spent much of his youth in Paris and built two great gardens in Europe which influenced the design of a great many others, such as that of Harold Nicolson and Vita Sackville-West at Sissinghurst. He began to make the garden at Hidcote Manor in Gloucestershire in 1905 where he pioneered the creation of a series of sheltered and interconnected garden 'rooms', each of which surprised by its different content and treatment. Close to Menton in Southern France, at a property called La Serre de la Madone, Johnston could include in his planting schemes many southern-hemisphere plants which were not hardy enough to survive at Hidcote and allow his formal schemes to be softened by the terracotta, orange trees and bougainvilleas of the Mediterranean.

Inigo Jones (1573 – 1652) Best known as a prolific architect, Jones brought formal Palladian ideas, acquired on two visits to Italy, to garden design at Arundel House in Sussex, Wilton House in Wiltshire and Lincoln's Inn in London. Apart from his own work, he strongly influenced William Kent (see below), who edited a book of his designs.

William Kent (1685 – 1748) This former apprentice coach painter from Hull twice made the Grand Tour of Italy with his most influential patron, Lord Burlington. Heavily influenced by the paintings of Claude and Salvator Rosa, he later tried to introduce the type of romantic landscape encountered in their canvases into his gardens, freeing them from much of the formality which had dominated previous British gardening. His work at Rousham, Holkham Hall, Chiswick House, Claremont and Stowe had a great influence on Lancelot 'Capability' Brown, Charles Hamilton of Painshill Park and Henry Hoare of Stourhead. See also in the *Guide* his work at Euston Hall and Gunnersbury Park.

Norah Lindsay (1866 – 1948) A disciple of Gertrude Jekyll and a friend of Lawrence Johnston, she made the famous garden at the Manor House at Sutton Courtenay. Her style tended towards the theatrical and romantic, and gained favour with the then Prince of Wales (for whom she worked at Fort Belvedere) and Lord Lothian of Blickling Hall. Her work may also be seen at Mottisfont.

George London (d. 1714) and **Henry Wise (1653 – 1738)** Towards the end of the seventeenth century, London took Wise as partner in his Brompton Park Nursery (now the South Kensington Museum area). London travelled, giving advice to great estates like Chatsworth, specialising in French-style layouts with plenty of clipped trees and shrubs. His design skills were preeminent for about 30 years. Wise, although involved in several projects for the Royals, stayed at home managing the 100-acre nursery. He was 'perfectly well skill'd in Fruit' such as oranges and lemons, and also saw that there was a plentiful supply of the fashionable bays and box. Wise moved to Blenheim in 1705. They planted Chelsea Hospital, Kensington Palace, Hampton Court, Longleat, Chatsworth, Melbourne Hall and Castle Howard.

John Claudius Loudon (1783 – 1843) A prolific author who founded the very successful *Gardener's Magazine* and published a popular and comprehensive *Encyclopedia of Gardening* (first published in 1822 and regularly updated), he had a considerable influence on the design of the middle- and small-sized villa gardens being made in their thousands by the burgeoning middle class. Initially a partisan of picturesque designs, he later favoured more formal arrangements and latterly advocated the adoption of the so-called gardenesque style in which each plant was isolated and displayed to its best advantage – an approach still favoured in the beds of many of our parks. Much of his design work has been lost, but there are good surviving examples in Derby Arboretum and Gunnersbury Park.

Sir Edwin Lutyens (1869 – 1944) A fine architect who between 1893 and 1912 created approximately 70 gardens in partnership with Gertrude Jekyll. Her subtle planting always softened and complemented the strong architectural nature of his garden designs. And they in their turn splendidly integrated the house in the garden and its site. A fine example of the work of the partnership is at Hestercombe in Somerset, now fully restored, where Lutyens' genius for using classical masonry forms in a highly imaginative and individual way is wonderfully displayed. Other examples of his work in the *Guide* are Abbotswood, Ammerdown, Castle Drogo, Folly Farm, Goddards, Heywood, Irish National War Memorial Park, Knebworth, Misarden, Munstead Wood and Parc Floral des Moutiers.

Thomas H. Mawson (1861 – 1933) A Lancastrian who trained in London and set up a landscape practice in Windermere in 1885, Mawson's reputation grew quickly and he was chosen by many of the rich northern industrialists to landscape the gardens of their Lakeland holiday homes. His distinctive designs earned him many commissions, and his garden and town-planning schemes were adopted as far afield as Greece and Canada. Examples of his work in the *Guide* may be seen at Brockhole, Dyffryn, Graythwaite, Hill Garden (London), Holker, Little Onn, Rivington, Thornton, Tirley Garth and Wightwick.

William E. Nesfield (1793 – 1881) In a long and adventurous life he was a soldier and talented watercolour painter specialising in the depiction of cascades in Europe and America before becoming a landscaper when he was over 40. He was persuaded by his brother-in-law, the famous architect Anthony Salvin, to use his talent for making pictures to help him design gardens. While his work was eclectic and the style he chose for his gardens usually reflected that of the houses which they surrounded, he was responsible for the reintroduction of the parterre as a garden feature in the nineteenth century. One of the best can still be seen at Holkam Hall in Norfolk. At the Royal Botanic Gardens at Kew, as well as a parterre, he made a pond and created the vistas from the Palm House. He is believed to have worked at 260 estates during his career. Those in the *Guide* include Alton, Blickling, Cliveden, Dorfold, Holkham, Rode, Shugborough, Somerleyton and Trentham.

Russell Page (1906 – 85) Trained as a painter he quickly became absorbed by garden design and between 1935 and 1939 worked in asssociation with Sir Geoffrey Jellicoe. After the war he gained an international reputation and worked on many projects in Europe and America, including the garden at the Frick Gallery in New York and the Battersea Festival Gardens in London. He encapsulated many of his ideas about garden design in *The Education of a Gardener*, first published in 1962. Examples of his work in the *Guide* are at Longleat and Port Lympne.

James Paine (1716 – 89) Distinguished designer of garden buildings including the bridge at Chatsworth in Derbyshire, Gibside Chapel in Newcastle-upon-Tyne and the Temple of Diana at Weston Park in Shropshire.

Sir Joseph Paxton (1803 – 65) Gardener at Chatsworth in Derbyshire for 32 years from 1826, where he made the great fountain and the great conservatory in which he pioneered ideas later used in the design of the Crystal Palace. One of the earliest designers of public parks including those at Birkenhead and Halifax, he was also influential as a writer and was one of the founders of *The Gardener's Chronicle*. Other examples of his work in the *Guide* are at Birkenhead, Capesthorne, Darley, Somerleyton and Tatton.

Harold Peto (1854 – 1933) A talented architect who worked for the partnership which later employed young Edwin Lutyens who undoubtedly influenced his style. A lover of Italianate formal gardens, one of Peto's best works was his own garden at Iford Manor in Wiltshire, but his canal garden at Buscot Park in Oxfordshire and at Ilnacullin, the garden on Garinish Island, Ireland, are also notable achievements. Other examples of his work in the *Guide* are at Easton Lodge, Greathed, Heale, Wayford and West Dean.

Humphry Repton (1752 – 1818) The most influential eighteenth-century landscaper after the death of Lancelot Brown, he was a great protagonist of Brown's ideas but he did tend to favour thicker planting than Brown, and the buildings he used to draw the eye into the landscape were rustic rather than classical. However, he restored formality to gardens in the form of terracing with flights of steps and balustrading near the house. His success in selling his ideas to clients was due to the production of excellent 'before and after' pictures of their parks, demonstrating the effects to be obtained if his schemes were adopted. These pictures with an explanatory text were bound into books which later became known as Repton's 'Red Books' because red was the colour of their binding. Repton was notable for his energy, producing over 400 Red Books and working on such fine estates as Holkham Hall, Sheffield Park, Cobham Hall, Woburn Abbey and Sheringham Park, which is his best-preserved work. Other examples of his work in the *Guide* are at Ashridge, Attingham, Bayfield, Catchfrench, Corsham, Endsleigh, Hatchlands, Holkham, Kenwood, Longleat, Rode and Ston Easton.

William Robinson (1838 – 1935) An Irishman who settled in England and became one of the most prolific writers and influential designers of his epoch. By his teaching and his example he liberated gardeners from the prim rigidity which had begun to dominate garden design in the mid-nineteenth century. Instead of the tightly-patterned bedding displays which the Victorians had adopted in order to show off the host of annual bedding plants which the explorers were sending home, he advocated a very free and natural attitude towards the creation of herbaceous and mixed beds. It was Robinson's attitudes towards planting which early inspired Gertrude Jekyll. He founded a weekly journal, *The Garden* (later absorbed into *Homes and Gardens*), and wrote *The English Flower Garden* which ran to 15 editions during his life and more later. Examples of his work in the *Guide* are at Gravetye Manor, High Beeches, Killerton, Leckhampton College (Cambridge) and Shrubland Park.

Lanning Roper (1912 – 83) A Harvard graduate from New Jersey who adopted Britain as his home and became one of the most popular landscapers in the 30 years after World War II. His best schemes, such as that at Glenveagh in Ireland, involved a subtle handling of plants combined with interesting formal features. One of his most controversial designs is the ornamental canal in the R.H.S. garden at Wisley. Other examples of his work in the *Guide* are at Anglesey Abbey, Broughton, Fairfield, Lower Hall, Old Rectory (Orford), Trinity College (Dublin) and Trinity Hospice (London).

Vita Sackville-West (1892 – 1962) With her husband, Harold Nicolson, she made two notable gardens in Kent. The first, at Long Barn, Sevenoaks, was based on a Nicolson design which she planted during and after World War I. The second and more famous, at Sissinghurst Castle, was begun in 1932 and developed during the rest of her life. The Nicolsons were friendly with Lawrence Johnston, and their attitude to gardening was influenced by the ideas which he exploited at Hidcote. Another example of her work may be seen at Alderley, also in Gloucestershire. Although she was the propagandist of the pair, some think that her husband's conception of structure made a great contribution to twentieth-century garden design.

William Shenstone (1714 – 63) An early partisan of picturesque gardening who bankrupted himself making a fine landscape garden of his own, Shenstone wrote an essay entitled 'Unconnected thoughts on gardening' which analysed picturesque gardening and contained advice from which hundreds of landscapers have subsequently benefitted.

Sir John Vanbrugh (1644 – 1726) A considerable dramatist and spectacular architect of palaces like Blenheim in Oxfordshire and Castle Howard in Yorkshire. Although he did not generally design landscapes, he ensured that his houses were magnificently sited and often created buildings for their gardens, such as the bridge at Blenheim and for landscapes made by other designers such as Stowe in Buckinghamshire, and Claremont in Surrey.

Ellen Willmott (1858 – 1934) She made a famous garden at Warley Place in Essex, part of which became a reserve for the Essex Naturalists' Trust in 1978, though little of her garden remains. She became renowned for her knowledge of plants, her patronage of plant hunters (notably Ernest Wilson), the book she published on roses, and her prickly temperament. One of her influential achievements was the garden at Boccanegra on the Italian Riviera.

Henry Wise see **George London** and **Henry Wise**

Thomas Wright (1711 – 86) Astronomer and adviser on about 30 gardens owned by great men of the time – including Badminton, Shugborough and Stoke Gifford. His variety of styles included primitive, Chinese, Gothic and classical, and he designed elaborate flower gardens when flower beds (other than parterres) were not common.

BEDFORDSHIRE

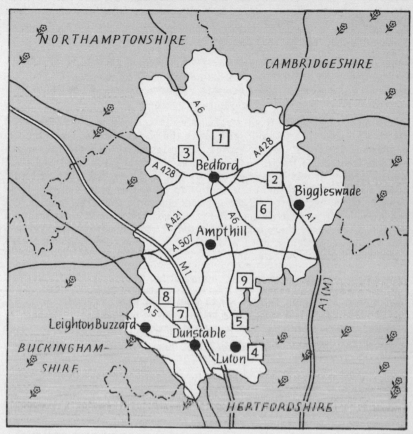

Broadfields

**Keysoe Row East, Keysoe, Bedford MK44 2JD. Tel: (01234) 376326;
Website: www.teagardens.ndo.co.uk**

*Mr and Mrs Chris Izzard • Leave Bedford on B660 Kimbolton road. After 10m,
turn right at Keysoe crossroads by White Horse pub, then ½ m on right • Open
28th May to mid-Sept, Sun to Fri, 2 – 5pm (telephone for details), and by appt
• Entrance: donation to charity* ● ☕ **WC** ♿ ⟋ ⚘ ⚘

This three-acre garden, the creation of a passionate amateur, is notable for its
formal planting-out with wonderful standard fuchsias and clipped box trees,
but has a variety of other pleasures: vistas with heathers, mature trees, shrubs,
conifers for winter interest and beautifully grown begonias and bedding
plants. There is also a model kitchen garden. It is worth pausing in Bedford

to enjoy a riverside stroll in the *Embankment Gardens*, a charming Victorian set piece adjoining Russell Park near the town centre.

The Lodge 2

Sandy SG19 2DL. Tel: (01767) 680551

Royal Society for the Protection of Birds • 7m E of Bedford, 1m E of A1 off B1042 Sandy – Potton road • Open all year, daily, dawn to dusk • Entrance: £2.50, OAPs £1.50, children free (2001 prices). RSPB members free ○ ☕ 🍴 WC ♿ 🏛

One of over 100 reserves established by the RSPB throughout the country, where birds can be seen from woodland walks and nature trails. The RSPB Memorial Garden is a tranquil spot where the names of those who have left bequests to the Society are honoured. The reserve, with a Victorian terrace and fine trees set in lawns, has seven acres of formal garden and two small walled gardens. It was developed in the 1930s by Sir Malcolm Stewart, who added a terraced fish pond on the south side. Its mature trees include a large weeping birch, Wellingtonias, acers, sweet chestnuts and large conifers. On the house is a huge wisteria and *Campsis radicans*. Azalea-lined walks lead to a woodland heath, and there is a well-planted vista of old cedar trees. There is also a wildlife garden, a joint project between the RSPB and the Henry Doubleday Research Association.

The Manor House ★ 3

Church Road, Stevington, Bedford MK43 7QB. Tel: (01234) 822064; Fax: (01234) 825531; E-mail: kathy_brown@tinyworld.co.uk; Website: www.kathybrownsgarden.homestead.com

Kathy Brown • 5m NW of Bedford off A428, through Bromham. In Stevington, turn right at crossroads; garden is on left after ¼ m • Open 28th April, 23rd June, 3rd July, 2 – 6pm, and for parties by appt • Entrance: £3, children free ● ☕ WC ♿ 🌱 🏛 ✂

This is a garden of exuberant imagination and reworked classic gardening themes: for example, a fine French-style, formal garden with clipped hedges and patterns in box punctuated by two fountains, one a splendid modern one. The manor house itself is set off by a mound-strewn lawn and some old trees, but everything else has been created in the last ten years. Pots and containers of all sorts – some will make you blink and wonder if you really saw an iguana! Rectangular areas are subdivided into patterns of succulents and grasses, with gravels of different colours providing foils for the plants in the newest areas. The owner is known for her recipes for growing plants in containers, so there are confections of roses, violets, diascias, succulents, etc.

Seal Point ★ 4

7 Wendover Way, Luton LU2 7LS. Tel: (01582) 611567

Mrs Danae Johnston • In NE of Luton. Turn N off Stockingstone Road into Felstead Way and take second turning on left • Open by appt for individuals and groups • Entrance: £2.50 ● ☕ 🍴 🌱 ✂

This small, sloping town garden with a Japanese theme goes from good to better, with interesting plant combinations (for example *Aeonium* 'Schwarz-kopf' associated with *Clematis florida* 'Sieboldii'), and gorgeous colour schemes. A hardy standard fuchsia is now over 3 metres high, and 20 or more different grasses are integrated into the borders. There is something unusual at every turn: a wildlife copse, a tiny bonsai garden, three pools (one with a waterfall), yin and yang beds, amusing topiary, original ornaments, and much more.

Stockwood Park 5

Stockwood Craft Museum, Farley Hill, Luton LU1 4BH. Tel: (01582) 738714

Borough of Luton • Leave M1 at junction 10 for Luton. Take Farley Hill (Chapel Street) turn off A505 Dunstable road out of Luton. Signposted from A1081 • Open April to Oct, Tues – Sat, 10am – 5pm, Sun and Bank Holidays, 10am – 6pm; Nov to March, Sat and Sun, 10am – 4pm. Guided tours available by appt • Entrance: free • Other information: Craft museum in stable block ☾ ➎ ✗ 🎋 WC ♿ 🚻 ☕

A series of period gardens – medieval, seventeenth-century knot, cottage and Victorian – laid out within the walled gardens of the old house, designed by Robert Burgoyne, ably assisted by Peter Ansell, the head gardener. In the park is a landscape garden with sculpture by Ian Hamilton Finlay, whose work gives a convincing continuity to the landscape tradition by its location alongside the original ha-ha. Another of his sculptures is a curved inscribed wall, and his modern fragments of 'antique' buildings, partly buried, suggest the eight-eenth-century ideal of a harmonious blend of planting, architecture and sculpture.

The Swiss Garden 6

Old Warden Park, Biggleswade SG18 9EA. Tel: (01767) 626255

Bedfordshire County Council • Take A1 to Biggleswade and follow signposts from A1 Biggleswade roundabout. Also signposted on A600 Shefford – Bedford road. Entrance in Old Warden • Open March to Sept, daily, 1 – 6pm (Sun and Bank Holiday Mons opens 10am); Jan, Feb and Oct, Sun only, 11am – 3pm (but open 1st Jan). Guided tours available • Entrance: £3, concessions £2, family ticket £8, season ticket £12, concessions £8. Special rates for parties • Other information: Restaurant in grounds of Shuttleworth Mansion. Disabled parking. Two wheelchairs available for loan ☾ WC ♿ 🚗 🚻 ☕

This romantic 10-acre landscape garden is said to have been created in 1820 by the third Lord Ongley for his Swiss mistress. It was neglected for 40 years from 1939, then leased by the council and restored. Innumerable rustic iron bridges cross over miniature ponds. Beside the little Swiss cottage sheets of spring bulbs flower beneath azaleas, rhododendrons and spring-flowering shrubs. The gloom of the grotto and the dazzling light of the fernery provide a dramatic contrast.

Toddington Manor ★ 7

Toddington LU5 6HJ. Tel: (01525) 872576; Fax: (01525) 874555

Sir Neville and Lady Bowman-Shaw • 1m W of M1 junction 12, 1m NW of Toddington. Signposted from village • Open May to Aug, Tues – Sat, 1 – 5pm (last admission 4pm). Please telephone for confirmation • Entrance: £3.50, OAPs £2.50, children £2 • Other information: Rare breeds of sheep, goats and pigs. Vintage tractor collection ● ● ● WC ● ● ● ●

Each area of the garden is themed individually, but great care is taken to maintain an atmosphere of stylish elegance. The glorious double herbaceous borders, 100 metres long, are split by a stone-paved walk bordered by hostas, ferns and bluebells. Inside the walled garden are dramatic sweeps of peonies, delphiniums and grasses, complemented by spacious lawns and old walls draped with roses, clematis and fruits. The neighbouring rose garden is filled with the scent of yellow and white Floribunda roses and philadelphus. A stream flows through here, running underground to feed the larger ponds. By the two greenhouses, complete with their own stream, is an extensive herb garden. Beyond the walls a wildflower meadow, orchards and woods contribute a wonderful display of natural beauty.

Woburn Abbey 8

Woburn MK17 9WA. Tel: (01525) 290666; Fax: (01525) 290271

The Marquess of Tavistock and Trustees of Bedford Estates • From M1 junction 13 follow signs • Open Jan to 23rd March, Sat and Sun only, 10.30am – 4pm; 24th March to 20th Sept, daily, 10am – 4.30pm; 30th Sept to 26th Oct, Sat and Sun, 10.30am – 4pm • Entrance: £6 per car. Abbey and park £8, OAPs £7, children (12–16) £3.50, under 12 free • Other information: Pottery and antiques centre ● ● × ● WC ● ● ●

Humphry Repton, who designed the park and 42 acres of garden, considered Woburn to be one of his finest achievements. Today, huge magnificent sweeping lawns are meticulously mown in diamonds and stripes lining up with the house. Rare water lilies float on the lovely ponds, and in the spring there are over 100 varieties of daffodils and narcissi, with fritillaries and orchids naturalised in the grass. The many fine trees include cedars, redwoods and tulip trees, plus rarities such as *Eucommia ulmoides* and *Acer triflorum* and champion trees like the swamp cypress. A National Collection of viburnums may be held here. The private gardens, which are open to the public at stated times, contain a large hornbeam maze. They also have formal gardens, good herbaceous borders, massed beds of 'Iceberg' roses edged with lavender, a most successful rose garden designed by Anita Pereire, a camellia house and a collection of statues. Ten different types of deer roam freely in their park, which is landscaped down to the Shoulder-of-Mutton pond, with fine groups of trees. A wonderful, historic site.

Wrest Park 9

Silsoe, Bedford MK45 4HS. Tel: (01525) 860152

English Heritage • 10m S of Bedford, ¾ m E of Silsoe off A6 • Gardens open April to Sept, Sat, Sun and Bank Holidays only, 10am – 6pm; Oct, Sat and Sun only, 10am – 5pm (last admission 1 hour before closing) • Entrance: £3.50, OAPs £2.60, children (5–15) £1.80 ❶ 💷 ▦ WC ﹠ ⬇ ⬛ ⬤

Superb! – a French château set in 'one of the most unappreciated and little visited landscapes in England', according to *Country Life*. It is one of the few places where it is possible to see an early-eighteenth-century formal garden in the manner of Bridgeman: the Great Garden, made for the 1st Duke of Kent. Bridgeman's layout dominates the main axis of the grounds – a canal, many *allées* cut through thick blocks of woodland, and giant urns set in grassy glades. 'Capability' Brown also worked here, creating a naturalistic river to surround the grounds at their perimeter. The woods on either side of the Long Water are intersected by avenues and dotted with 'incidents of delight'. The Thomas Archer pavilion stands at the end of the Long Water, and the Bath House was built as a romantic classical ruin. Water catches the eye in every direction. The house (not open) was built in the French style, fronted by terraces and parterres. The large orangery was designed by Cléphane. Walls are host to fan-trained Judas trees with thick trunks; two wide borders are rather besieged by rabbits.

RESEARCHING GARDEN HISTORY

The Register of Parks and Gardens of Special Historic Interest is an authoritative record of the nation's historic landscapes, which was initiated by the Garden History Society in the 1970s' and taken over by English Heritage in the '80s. Over the past three years, it has been substantially revised and upgraded. Just over half of it has been completed, parks and gardens have been added, and threatened landscapes 'spot-listed', extending the coverage from 1365 to 1400 of the nation's most important landscapes. Each entry is documented in a description of the site's historical evolution, accompanied by specially drawn paper maps which delineate the historical boundaries of the park or garden and chronicle its development.

The *Register* is available for public consultation at English Heritage's National Monuments Record Centre in Swindon (open Tues – Fri, 9.30am – 5pm). Copies of individual entries or complete county registers can also be purchased and supplied by post. For more information contact NMR Enquiry & Research Services (Tel: (01793) 414600; Fax (01793) 414606; E-mail: nmrinfor@english-heritage.org.uk). Additionally, each local planning authority will have a copy of the relevant descriptions and maps within their jurisdictions. Be sure to telephone in advance of a visit.

BERKSHIRE

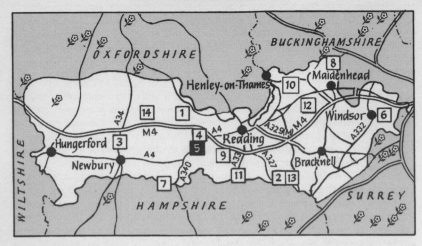

Some gardens have postal addresses in one county and are physically situated in another. If in doubt, a check in the index will direct the reader to the page on which the garden appears.

Two-starred gardens are marked on the map with a black square.

Ashdown House

(see Oxfordshire)

Basildon Park 1

Lower Basildon, Reading RG8 9NR. Tel: (0118) 984 3040

The National Trust • Between Pangbourne and Streatley, 7m NW of Reading on W side of A329; leave M4 at junction 12 and continue to Theale roundabout, then take Pangbourne road • House open 23rd March to 3rd Nov, Wed – Sun, 12 noon – 5.30pm • Park open April to Oct, Wed – Sun and Bank Holiday Mons, 12 noon – 5.30pm • Entrance: House and garden £4.30. Park only, £1.80, children 90p, family £4.50 • Other information: Parking 400 metres from house ◑ 🍽 ✕ <u>WC</u> ♿ ⬥ 🪑 ⓟ ✿

Within the park, with very old trees which frame a glimpse of the Thames, is a small formal garden with herbaceous borders. The early-nineteenth-century pleasure grounds, which are being restored, include a thatched 'Umbrello', probably based on an original design by J.B. Papworth.

Blencathra 2

Finchampstead, Wokingham RG40 3SS. Tel: (0118) 973 4563

Dr and Mrs F.W. Gifford • 3m S of Wokingham, 1m W of A321 near Crowthorne Station, at NW end of Finchampstead Ridges (B3348). Entrance

300 metres down joint private drive • Open for charity 21st April, 19th May, 2 – 6pm, 9th June, 2 – 5pm, and by appt for individuals and parties • Entrance: £2.50, accompanied children free ◐ ♨ WC & ⬧

The owners started this 11-acre garden in 1964, when they purchased an unmanaged woodland site and built their house. Their enthusiasm for fresh ideas is inspiring. With minimal budget and help – none professional – the low-maintenance garden has evolved. Established shrubs, lawns and specimen trees surround the house, whose design blends well with the plantings. Features include woodland areas on either side of the drive and an extensive water garden, including three lakes, a stream and small 'bog' areas. Spring bulbs, especially bluebells, together with rhododendrons and many conifers, ensure colour and interesting features in all seasons. White Knights (see entry) is nearby.

Chieveley Manor 3

Chieveley, Newbury RG20 8UT. Tel: (01635) 248208; Fax: (01635) 248070

Mr and Mrs C.J. Spence • 4m N of Newbury, ½ m from M4 junction 13 via A34. In Manor Lane by church • Open 30th July, 2 – 6pm • Entrance: £1, children free ◐ ♨ WC & ⌾℺

The fine garden, which features a walled garden and a swimming pool garden, complements its manor house. Two good herbaceous borders include purple sage beds interspersed with geraniums, and another at the front of the house has a new repeat planting of shrubs and herbaceous perennials. Interesting shrubs and roses. There are fine views over the paddock area from the stud with its imposing cedar tree.

Englefield House 4

Englefield, Theale, Reading RG7 5EN. Tel: (0118) 930 2221;
E-mail: benyon@netcomuk.co.uk; Website: www.englefield.co.uk

Sir William and Lady Benyon • 5m W of Reading. Entrance on A340, near Theale • Open all year, Mon; also April to Sept, Tues – Thurs; all 10am – 6pm • Entrance: £3, children free ◑ ⬚ WC & ⌾ ♨ ℺

The seven-acre garden descends dramatically from the hill above the house through open woodland with a wide variety of interesting and unusual trees and shrubs and a water garden bordering the stream. On the lower levels, stone balustrades and staircases make a background for deep borders and small enclosed gardens of differing character, including a children's garden with four little joke fountains. A walled kitchen garden produces many varieties of fruit, vegetables, herbs and flowers. The whole area is enclosed by a deer park, with fine views over the lake and surrounding countryside.

Folly Farm ★ 5

Sulhamstead, Reading RG7 4DF. Tel: (Contact: Janet Findon) (01635) 841541

7m SW of Reading, 2m W of M4 junction 12. Turn onto A4 and left at road signed 'Sulhamstead' at Mulligan's Fish Restaurant 1m after Theale

*roundabout; entrance ¾ m on right • Open all year, Mon, Wed, Fri, 9.30am –
12 noon, for groups of 10 to 25 • Entrance £6, incl. coffee and biscuits* ◐

Historically, this is one of the country's most important twentieth-century
gardens – a sublime example of the Lutyens and Jekyll partnership in its
vintage years before World War I. The intimate relationship of house and
garden personifies Lutyens' genius for design and craftsmanship. A complex
arrangement of spaces and courts is linked by herringbone-patterned brick
paths, enhancing the vernacular origins of an attractive Edwardian country
house. The gardens retain much of their original character, although changes
of ownership have inevitably compromised some of the original objectives.
The mixed borders are mainly shrub roses, which look wonderful in the
second half of June, with old-fashioned herbaceous plants in between giving
colour as late as August. The formal sunken rose garden surrounded by a high
yew hedge is notable for its masterful design on several levels, and this has
been substantially replanted in subtle colours. An original Jekyll bed of irises
now contains ornamental grasses, and the previously neglected kitchen garden
has been made over by a team of organic vegetable growers. Other features
include a formal entrance court, barn court, Dutch-inspired canal garden,
flower parterre and a tank cloister. The working range of three tropical stove
houses is now bursting with medal-winning treasures.

Frogmore Gardens   6

Windsor SL4 2JG.

*H.M. The Queen • At Windsor Castle. Entrance via signed car park on B3021
between Datchet and Old Windsor. Pedestrian access only from Long Walk •
House open as garden in Aug • Garden open several days in May, 10am –
7pm, and in Aug, 10am – 5.30pm. Telephone for details (01753) 868286 ext.
2347 • Entrance: house, gardens and mausoleum £5.20, OAPs £4.20, children
£3.20 (children under 8 not admitted) (2001 prices)* ◐

Set amid the extensive Home Park of Windsor Castle, Frogmore House is
surrounded by 30 acres of landscaped and picturesque gardens. Fine and unusual
trees include a remarkable incense cedar planted in 1857. The house dates from
the 1680s and was purchased in 1792 for Queen Charlotte, consort of George III.
It then passed through a succession of royal owners, becoming a favoured retreat
of Queen Victoria and later of King George V and Queen Mary; its sense of peace
drew Prince Albert and Queen Victoria to break with royal tradition and to
choose a corner of the garden to build a mausoleum for themselves. Other
architectural features include a charming wisteria-covered Gothick ruin by
Wyatt, Queen Victoria's tea house and an Indian kiosk brought from Lucknow
after the Mutiny. (Unfortunately, the limited opening means that the public will
not see what must be one of the garden's chief glories, the 200,000 spring bulbs
planted in Queen Mary's time.) The formal layout at the Castle, called the East
Terrace, laid out by Sir Geoffrey Wyatville for George IV, is now open to the
public. It has a somewhat municipal air, quite different from the private garden
for the royal family behind its walls, or the gardens in the Great Park, begun after
1931, or, for that matter, Frogmore itself.

Meadow House 7

**Ashford Hill, Thatcham RG19 8BN. Tel/Fax: (0118) 981 6005;
E-mail: harriet@rosejones.freeserve.co.uk**

*Antony and Harriet Jones • 8m SE of Newbury. From B3051 take turning at
SW end of village to Wolverton Common. After 350 metres turn right down track
to house • Garden open for NGS 30th May, 13th June, 4th, 18th July, 11am –
4pm, and at other times by appt. Parties of up to 40 welcome • Entrance: £2.50,
children free • Other information: Park cars in meadow and coaches at top of
lane. Plants for sale in nursery* ● 🔥 ⚘ ℮

Essentially a plantsman's creation – a modest country house garden of just
under two acres with lawn sweeping down to a small lake supporting ducks
and waterside planting. The nursery and greenhouse are screened by a tall
trellis smothered with wisteria, clematis, rambler roses and honeysuckle.
Woodland is underplanted with hostas, primulas, camellias and 'Annabelle'
hydrangeas. The borders contain mixed shrubs, unusual herbaceous perennials
and shrub roses.

Odney Club 8

Odney Lane, Cookham, Maidenhead SL6 9ST. Tel: (01628) 530011

*John Lewis Partnership • Between Beaconsfield and Maidenhead, off A4094
near Cookham Bridge • Open one Sun in April, 2 – 6pm • Entrance: £2,
children free* ● 🍵 🛍 WC 🔥 ⚘

This huge 120-acre site along the Thames, well cared-for and continuously
developing, makes a full afternoon visit. It was a favourite with Stanley
Spencer, who often visited to paint the magnolia which featured in his work.
There is a magnificent wisteria walk, and also specimen trees, herbaceous
borders, small side gardens, and terraces with spring bedding plants.

The Old Rectory ★ 9

Burghfield, Reading RG30 3TH. Tel: (0118) 983 3200

*Mr A.R. Merton • 5m SW of Reading. Turn S off A4 to Burghfield village and
right after Hatch Gate Inn • Open 17th Feb, 7th April, 5th May, 2nd June, 7th
July, 1st Sept, 11am – 4pm, and for parties by appt in writing • Entrance: £2,
parties £2.50 per person* ● 🍵 🛍 WC 🔥 ⚘ ℮

This garden has achieved wide renown, and its maturity and the amazing
generosity of plants skilfully planted are remarkable in a site started from
scratch in 1950. The late Mrs Merton, who described herself as 'a green-
fingered lunatic', collected plants from all over the world, notably some rare
items from Japan and China. The terrace has a fine display most of the year, and
the herbaceous border and beds are impressive, with collections of hellebores,
pinks, violas, peonies, snowdrops, old roses and much else besides. In the
spring there are drifts of daffodils and rather rare cowslips and so many other
plants to see that it is well worth making a visit month by month if you live
within reasonable range. Something here for every type of gardener.

The Savill Garden

(see Surrey)

Scotlands ★ 10

Cockpole Green, Wargrave, Reading RG10 8QP. Tel: (01628) 822648

Mr Michael and The Hon. Mrs Payne • 4m E of Henley-on-Thames, off A4 at Knowl Hill, halfway between Warren Row and Cockpole Green • Open for various charities and NGS, and by appt • Entrance: £2.50, children free • Other information: Picnics permitted on Cockpole Green ● ◐ ▤ WC ♿ ◁ ◒

The attractive chalk-and-flint house, formerly a seventeenth-century barn, is surrounded by a series of courtyards, one with a lily pool. To the west is an oval swimming pool, guarded by yew hedges and the lead statue of a drummer boy. A herb garden with patterned paving and box, roses, lavender and choice vegetables such as artichokes is overlooked by a gazebo. To the east, a lawn sweeps down to woodland and pond gardens, with the Repton-style summerhouse signalling the merging of the landscaped water garden with natural woodland. Mown grass paths lead to a waterfall with large rocks. Fine specimen catalpa, cedars, Spanish chestnut and copper beech mark the boundary of the four-acre site.

Swallowfield Park 11

Swallowfield, Reading RG7 1TG. Tel: (0118) 988 3815; Fax: (0118) 988 3930

Country Houses Association Ltd • 5m S of Reading in Swallowfield. Entrance in Church Road • Open May to Sept, Wed and Thurs, 2 – 5pm • Entrance: House and gardens £2.50, children £1; larger parties by appt ◐ ◐ ♿ ◁ ♨

Twenty-five acres of garden, all maintained to the highest standard. In the six-and-a-half-acre walled garden (much of it built by Thomas Pitt, grandfather of the Prime Minister), there are colourful herbaceous borders, scented roses, a small orchard and a laburnum-and-wisteria-covered pergola. In other parts of the grounds are fine lawns and specimen trees, many of them brought to the park in the nineteenth century. One of Charles Dickens' dogs is buried in the dogs' cemetery. Visitors are encouraged to walk past the croquet lawn (often in use) and a large decoy pond to the banks of the River Loddon, which forms the northern boundary.

Virginia Water

(see VALLEY GARDENS, Surrey)

Waltham Place ★ 12

White Waltham, Maidenhead SL6 3JH. Tel: (01628) 825517;
Website: www.waltham-place.org.uk

Mr and Mrs N.F. Oppenheimer • 3½ m S of Maidenhead. From M4 junction 8/9, take A404M and follow signs to White Waltham. Take left turn to Windsor and Paley Street. Parking signed at top of hill • Open April to Sept, Mon – Fri (but closed Bank Holiday Mons), 2 – 7pm, and for parties by appt all year (Tel:

(01628) 824605) • *Entrance: £3.50, children £1* • *Other information: Organic meals available for groups by prior arrangement* • ◐ ▭ ▤ WC ↳ ⬳ ⌖

Forty acres of organic garden, including kitchen garden and orchards, integrated within a 100-acre organic farm with parkland meadows. A variety of garden areas includes several walled gardens, rabbit-proof long borders, a butterfly garden, a *potager*, a Japanese garden, a knot garden, a lake, and woodland underplanted with rhododendrons, camellias and bluebells. Henk Gerritsen, owner of the renowned Priona Gardens in Holland (see entry), is transforming the gardens in the style pioneered by the new generation of Dutch designers, combining native and cultivated plants into naturalistic flowerbeds within the existing structure of hedges and seventeenth-century walls.

White Knights   13

The Ridges, Finchampstead, Wokingham RG40 3SY. Tel: (0118) 973 3274

Mrs Heather Bradly • *9m SE of Reading between A327 and A321, midway along Finchampstead Ridges on B3348. Turn in through white gateposts on right between Crowthorne station and war memorial* • *Open by appt only* • *Entrance £2.50* • *Other information: Refreshments available. Guide dogs only* ◐ ▭ ↳ ⌖

The present owners have created a large garden designed to look interesting throughout the year with minimum upkeep. The beds around the house are mainly planted with dwarf conifers of all hues and many varieties of heathers. A noble wisteria covers the south-facing wall. A Japanese garden complete with flowing water and tea house in the Zen tradition, a Mediterranean area with cacti, both hardy and overwintered in the greenhouse, and a Chinese courtyard alongside the swimming pool graced by a fountain give the garden an international flavour. Indoors, a model of a Tudor village will appeal to all ages.

Wyld Court Rainforest   14

Hampstead Norreys, Nr Newbury RG18 0TN. Tel: (01635) 202444;
Fax: (01635) 202440; E-mail: enquiries@livingrainforest.org;
Website: www.livingrainforest.org

Wyld Court Rainforest • *7m NE of Newbury. Follow signs from M4 junction 13* • *Open daily except 25th, 26th Dec, 10am – 5.15pm (last admission ¾ hour before closing)* • *Entrance: £4.50, concessions £3.50, children (5 – 14) £2.50, children (3 – 4) £1 (2001 prices)* ○ ▭ ▤ WC ↳ ⌖ ⚒ ♨ ⚲

A remarkable 1860-square-metre glasshouse with a fine collection of exotic plants, splendidly grown, which educates visitors in the beauty and diversity of the rainforest. A feature is the tasteful and imaginative way in which the plants are displayed in a carefully studied interior landscape with paths at various levels, allowing them to be enjoyed from above. There are two distinct environments – an area known as Lowland which mimics conditions of lowland rainforest, and an area called Amazonica which emphasises life in the forest canopy. In each is a representative collection of the animals to be found there, chosen to illustrate the symbiotic relationship between animals and plants in their natural environment.

BIRMINGHAM AREA

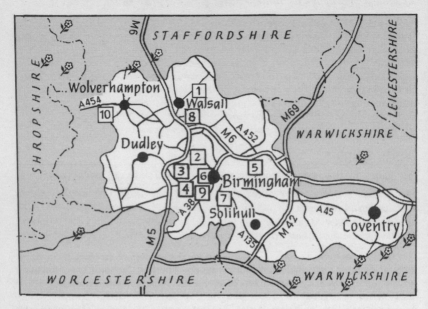

Ashover 1

25 Burnett Road, Streetly B74 3EL. Tel: (0121) 353 0547

Mr and Mrs Martin Harvey • 8m N of Birmingham. Take A452 towards Streetly then B4138 alongside Sutton Park. Turn left at shops into Burnett Road • Open for NGS 26th May, 14th July, 11th Aug, 1.30 – 5.30pm, and by appt • Entrance: £2, children 50p • Other information: Teas on NGS open days only
NEW ● 🌱

This is a garden for all who love colour – a third of an acre cleverly planted for year-round interest, from bulbs and azaleas in the spring through roses, clematis, lilies and herbaceous plants, both traditional and unusual, in summer and autumn. Colour-themed beds and an attractive water feature catch the eye and close planting constantly challenges the interest of the discerning visitor. The layout brings surprises round every turn, making it appear larger than it actually is, and a luxuriant feel is generated by the variety, quality and quantity of plants amassed here.

9 Augustus Road 2

Edgbaston B15 3NB. Tel: (0121) 455 8258

Mr and Mrs David Orchard • Take A456 (Hagley road) out of city for 1½ m. Turn left at traffic lights into Norfolk Road, left again at next lights into Augustus Road. After Gilchrist Drive on left, turn left into drive behind holly hedge; house is last in block of four • Open 23rd June, 2 – 6pm, and other Suns in June/July by appt • Entrance: by donation to charity ◑ ⚘

This small town garden makes full use of the space available. On different levels, it has a lawn, a small fountain, a vegetable plot and a new scree bed with grasses and alpines which will give pleasure throughout the year. There is colour at all seasons from a great variety of perennials, shrubs, climbers and a succession of flowering plants. Acers and collections of hostas, grasses and sempervivums contribute to the interesting foliage effects.

The Birmingham Botanical Gardens and Glasshouses ★　　3

Westbourne Road, Edgbaston B15 3TR. Tel: (0121) 454 1860;
E-mail: admin@bham-bot-gdns.demon.co.uk;
Website: www.bham-bot-gdns.demon.co.uk

2m from city centre. Approach from Hagley Road or Calthorpe Road, following tourist signs • Open all year, daily, 9am – 7pm, or dusk if earlier (opens 10am on Sun) • Entrance: £4.80 (£5.20 on summer Suns), OAPs, disabled, students and children £2.60. Parties £4 per person (£2.30 for concessions) (2001 prices) • Other information: Manual and electric wheelchairs available free of charge
○ ☕ ✕ 🛍 WC ♿ ⚘ � 🌻

This 15-acre ornamental garden will appeal both to the keen plantsperson and to the everyday gardener. In addition to the unusual plants in the tropical and the Mediterranean houses, there is a sub-tropical house and an arid house, a small display of carnivorous plants, aviaries with parrots and macaws, peacocks and a waterfowl enclosure. Less rarified gardeners will enjoy the beautiful old trees, the border devoted to E.H. Wilson plants, the raised alpine bed and the sunken rose garden beside the Lawn Aviary. The rock garden contains a wide variety of alpine plants, primulas, astilbes and azaleas. There are also herbaceous borders, a quaint cottage-style garden, a herb garden and model domestic-theme gardens, plus a plantsman's area. An attractive courtyard houses the National Collection of bonsai. The recently developed alpine yard has examples of the many ways to grow plants in a variety of raised beds and containers. A children's playground and adventure trail make this a pleasant place for a family outing. Bands play on summer Sundays and Bank Holidays.

Cannon Hill Park　　4

Moseley B13 8RD. Tel: (0121) 442 4226

Birmingham City Council • 2m from city centre opposite Edgbaston Cricket Ground • Park open all year, daily, 7.30am – dusk. Glasshouse open 10am – 4pm • Entrance: free • Other information: Midland Art Centre in park contains bookshop, gallery, theatre and restaurant and toilet facilities ○ ☕ ✕ 🛍 WC ♿ ⚘ 🚽 🌻 ⚲

Eighty acres of park with formal beds and a wide range of herbaceous plants, shrubs and trees. The glasshouse houses a collection of tropical and sub-tropical plants. There are nature trails and a children's area, and boating, miniature golf, bowls and tennis are also on offer. A model of the Elan Valley is set in the garden area.

Castle Bromwich Hall Gardens ★ 5

Chester Road, Castle Bromwich B36 9BT. Tel/Fax: (0121) 749 4100

Castle Bromwich Hall Gardens Trust • 4m E of city centre. 1m from junction 5 of M6 northbound. Southbound leave M6 at junction 6 and follow A38 and A452. Signposted • Open 31st March to Oct, Tues – Thurs, 1.30 – 4.30pm, Sat, Sun and Bank Holiday Mons, 2 – 6pm. Guided tours daily • Entrance: £3, OAPs £2, children £1 ◐ ☕ WC ♿ ⇦ ✿ 🏛 ♟

The hall, built at the end of the sixteenth century, was sold to Sir John Bridgeman in 1657, and his wife created the garden with expert help. It fell into decay, and now a series of formal connecting gardens is being restored to give them the appearance and content of a garden of 1680–1740. The perimeter wall, summerhouse and greenhouse have been rebuilt. There are fan- and espalier-trained fruit trees and an orchard, a kitchen garden, ponds, classical parterres, an archery lawn, a holly maze, a wilderness and historic borders. A formal vegetable garden is planted with historic and unusual vegetables, such as white carrots and blue 'Congo' potatoes. Ten acres in all.

City Centre Gardens 6

Cambridge Street B1 2NP.

Birmingham City Council • Off Cambridge Street, to rear of theatre and Symphony Hall on Broad Street • Open all year, daily during daylight hours • Entrance: free ○ 🛍 ♿ ✎

Approximately half an acre of rough ground remaining after building demolition and subsequently used as a car park has been converted into a garden for all seasons. The flowering year begins with the earliest spring bulbs, but there is something for gardeners to discover and enjoy throughout the year. The layout is formal, the planting skilful and exuberant, with a great variety of shrubs, perennials, roses and some annuals, many less usual and all blending harmoniously. Climbers cover the walls and fences, and the general effect on a summer's day is of colour and perfume.

16 Prospect Road 7

Moseley B13 9TB. Tel: (0121) 449 8457

Mr and Mrs Londesborough • Coming into Birmingham on A435, turn right in Kings Heath just after Safeway supermarket and pedestrian lights, up Poplar Road to roundabout, second left into School Road, second right into Prospect Road • Open 21st April, 14th July, 2 – 6pm, and by appt all year • Entrance: £2 on open days, £1 by appt ◐ ☕ WC ✿

In this plantsman's garden the journey of discovery begins with a conservatory full of tender perennials, continues with a display of grasses, colour-filled pots and troughs of alpines on the terrace, and proceeds along winding paths between beds stocked with a remarkable variety of usual and unusual plants showing colour at all seasons. At each turn of the path different plants lead the eye on to a fresh discovery.

15 St Johns Road   8

Pleck, Walsall WS2 9TJ. Tel: (01922) 441027. E-mail: sid@allen0.fsnet.co.uk

Mr and Mrs Allen • 10m NW of Birmingham. From M6 junction 10, head towards Walsall on A454 Wolverhampton road, and turn right into Pleck Road (A4148). St Johns Road is fourth right • Open one Sun for NGS, and by appt • Entrance: £1.50, children free NEW ● ⚘ ⚲

This comparatively small garden is landscaped so as to appear larger. It contains a wide range of delights, from a tropical area near the house, past a pool and a varied collection of trees, shrubs, climbers (73 different clematis) and flowers, to a Japanese feature at the far end, where a stream runs under a little bridge leading to a tea house. The smaller trees include acers, and there are shrubs, grasses, ferns, hostas, perennials and clematis blooming through the season, with annuals adding splashes of colour. It has been created by garden-makers who not only choose unusual and interesting specimens but also understand how to raise and maintain them in good health and display them to their best advantage.

University Botanic Garden ★   9

Winterbourne, 58 Edgbaston Park Road, Edgbaston B16 3TT.
Tel: (0121) 414 4944; E-mail: Unibotanic@bham.ac.uk;
Website: www.botanic.bham.ac.uk

University of Birmingham School of Continuing Studies • Off A38 Bristol road leading out of city. On university campus • Open all year, Mon – Fri (but closed Bank Holiday Mons and some university holidays), 11am – 4pm • Entrance: £2 • Other information: Events at weekends ● 🖻 WC &

The six acres of garden belonging to a Grade II listed Arts and Crafts house owe much to the landscape style developed by Edwin Lutyens and Gertrude Jekyll. Its wide range of plants and different features make it of interest to the ordinary gardener as well as the botanist. Geographical beds show typical trees and shrubs from Europe, Australasia, the Americas, China and Japan. The pergola is covered with clematis and roses and there are extensive herbaceous borders backed by brick walls covered with climbers. A miniature arboretum contains interesting specimens, including acers, conifers and a *Ginkgo biloba*, together with hedges of yew (*Taxus baccata*) and copper beech. In the Commemorative Garden is a black mulberry planted to mark the 100th anniversary of Birmingham's status as a city. The range of plants continues with the sandstone rock garden, troughs, rhododendrons, heathers and alpines. Unusual features include a nut walk containing several varieties of *Corylus avellana* trained over an iron framework, and a crinkle-crankle wall. A special feature is the walled garden laid out with beds of roses showing the history of the European rose. There are also water gardens, rock and scree gardens, a meadow, a bog garden and a Japanese tea house.

Wightwick Manor 10

Wightwick Bank, Wolverhampton WV6 8EE. Tel: (01902) 761400

The National Trust • 3m W of Wolverhampton off A454. Turn by Mermaid Inn up Wightwick Bank • House open Thurs and Sat, 1.30 – 5pm. Timed tickets • Garden open March to Dec, Wed, Thurs and Sat, Bank Holiday Suns and Mons, 11am – 6pm, and other weekdays by appt. Pre-booked parties accepted Wed and Thurs • Entrance: £2.50, children free (house and garden £5.50, concessions £2.80) • Other information: Possible for wheelchairs but sloping site. Braille guide available ☕ 🍴 ♿ WC ♿ 🐕 ♿ 🍷

This 17-acre garden, designed by Alfred Parsons and Thomas Mawson, surrounds an 1887 house strongly influenced in its design by William Morris and his Movement, which contains a collection of Pre-Raphaelite paintings. Large trees form a delightful framework, the main feature of which is the magnificent octagonal arbour in the centre of the rose garden, hung with climbing roses and clematis. This was based on designs in the 1906 Thomas Mawson catalogue. Through an old orchard is a less formal area with pools surrounded by shrubs and rhododendrons. There are herbaceous borders, two rows of barrel-shaped yews and beds containing plants from gardens of famous men. It is a surprise when, round a corner, one comes across a line of boulders from Scotland and the Lake District, left when the great glaciers melted in the last Ice Age. The peach house and the rose garden have been restored, the Mathematical Bridge, giving access to the Bridge Garden filled with spring bulbs, is now reconstructed, and there is a new mixed border.

GUIDANCE ON SYMBOLS

Wheelchair users: The symbol ♿, denoting suitability for wheelchairs, refers to the garden only – if there is a house open, it may or may not be suitable. Additionally, some areas in the garden may not be accessible by wheelchair, or may require assistance.

Dogs: 🐕 indicates that there is somewhere on the premises where dogs may be walked, preferably on a lead. The garden itself is often taboo – parkland, or even the car park, are frequently indicated for the purpose.

Picnics: 🧺 means that picnics are allowed, but usually in certain restricted areas only. It does not give visitors the all-clear to feast where they please!

Children-friendly: the symbol ⚘ suggests that there are activities specifically designed for children, such as an adventure playground, or that the garden itself is a place they would instinctively enjoy.

BRISTOL AREA

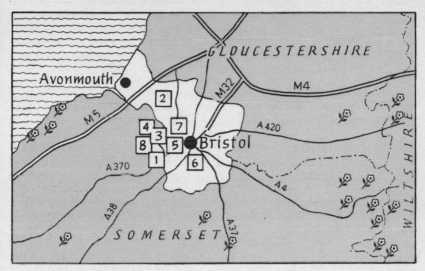

Ashton Court Estate 1

Long Ashton BS41 9JN. Tel: (0117) 963 9174;
E-mail: heritage_estates@bristol.city.gov.uk

Bristol City Council • SW of city off A369 • Open daily, 8am – dusk • Entrance: free ○ 🍵 ✕ 🗑 WC ♿ 🐕 🎪 ⚲

The house dates from the early fifteenth century with the addition of a remarkable seventeenth-century wing, and some features of this period are incorporated in the predominantly Victorian gardens. The terraced lawn is bounded by an early eighteenth-century wall; steps lead down to the sunken garden with redwood trees and a pond. The pets' graves of the Smyth family overlook the ha-ha. A rose garden now graces an area that used to be greenhouses. The picturesque landscaped park, attributed to Humphry Repton, with its curving drive, tree belt and clumps, has a rare survival (one indebted to Bristol City Council for its maintenance) in the form of two deer parks. Nearby Clarkencombe Wood has ancient dramatic oaks.

Blaise Castle House ★ 2

Henbury BS10 7QS. Tel: (0117) 950 6789

Bristol City Museum • 4m N of city, W of Henbury, N of B4057 • House and first-floor museum open April to Oct, Sat – Wed, 10am – 5pm • Entrance: free pedestrian access to green • Other information: Visitors requested not to picnic or invade privacy of cottage owners ○ 🗑 WC ♿ 🐕 🚻 ⚲

Blaise Hamlet is a picturesque village owned by The National Trust in the form of a green surrounded by nine cottages with private gardens, designed by John

Nash with George and John Repton in 1809 for the pensioners of John Harford's estate. The village pump and sundial of 1812 remain. Jasmines, ivies and honeysuckles were planted around the cottages to reflect their picturesque names ('Jessamine', 'Rose Briar'), with ornamental shrubs added to the woodland setting. A spectacular drive can be taken from Henbury Hill to the entrance lodge of Blaise Castle House – another charming *cottage orné* is halfway. The driveway into the gorge and up to the house passes a Robber's Cave and the Lovers' Leap. The view is exceptional. Near the house are the ornamental dairy and elegant orangery, both by Nash. Not far away is *Algars Manor*, Iron Acton, which has a remarkable collection built up by Dr Naish and his wife. Private visits welcome – telephone (01454) 228372.

Bristol Zoo Gardens 3

Clifton BS8 3HA. Tel: (0117) 973 8951;
E-mail: information@bristolzoo.org.uk; Website: www.bristolzoo.org.uk

Bristol Zoo Gardens • Signposted from M5 junctions 17 and 18 and from city centre • Open daily except 25th Dec, 9am – 5.30pm (4.30pm in winter) • Entrance: £8.40, concessions £7.40, children (3 – 14) £4.80. Special rates for parties of 15 or more ○ 💭 ✕ 🍽 WC ♿ 🍴 ⛛ ☕

Set up in 1835 as a garden as well as a zoo, the gardens will satisfy those with Victorian tastes for splashes of colour. Displays range from formal to informal, and botanically interesting plants are highlighted. The terrace bedding gives a 'rich tapestry of vibrant colours in an individual style using the choicest of plants'. The bedding is complemented by herbaceous borders, a lake, rose and rock gardens, indoor displays and numerous interesting trees and shrubs. All is well contrived and maintained with evident love and care. Two National Collections, actinidias and caryopteris, are held here.

Emmaus House 4

Retreat and Conference Centre, Clifton Hill, Clifton BS8 4PD.
Tel: (0117) 907 9950; E-mail: emmaushouse@msn.com;
Website: www.emmaus-house.co.uk

Sisters of La Retraite • From city centre take A4018 to Clifton, then A4176 past Zoo, and turn left into Clifton Down Road. Follow through to Regent Street; house is at bottom of drive on right • Open five times a year and on weekdays by prior appt • Entrance: £2, OAPs £1, children free (2001 prices) ◗ 💭 ✕ WC ⚲ ⛛

Covering one and a half acres, the gardens lie hidden from the road behind two imposing eighteenth-century merchants' houses. Walking down from the front entrance and around the side of the property the visitor enters a succession of separate gardens set on different levels, all carefully linked and with extensive views towards the harbour and beyond. They have been considerably altered in recent years, but the Victorian kitchen garden is substantially intact, supplying fruit and vegetables to the house. The old greenhouses are still in use, containing apricots and a 150-year-old Black

Hamburg vine. A formal herb garden framed by clipped box pyramids surrounds an ornamental fishpond. This leads down to a Zen Garden, where large stones and running water are imaginatively used to represent the Zen concepts of life and rebirth. At a lower level, the visitor enters the Secret Garden containing many old apple trees and underplanted with spring bulbs. Then, continuing round the houses, the courtyard garden is enclosed by high walls with macleayas and vigorous euphorbias.

Goldney Hall 5

Lower Clifton Hill, Clifton BS8 1BH. Tel: (0117) 903 4873

University of Bristol • *In city centre at top of Constitution Hill, Clifton* • *Open 28th April, 2 – 5pm, and three other days for charity – telephone from details* • *Entrance: £1, guided tours £2* ◐ ✕ WC ⅃

The eighteenth-century garden (or what remains) is a thrilling discovery in the middle of the city. Perched on a hillside, it is full of surprises, not least the small formal canal with an orangery at its head. From the largely nineteenth-century house the visitor is led through the shadows of an *allée* of yews to a dank grotto entrance whose façade is a striking example of early but sophisticated Gothick. The grotto itself is astonishingly elaborate: water really gushes through it and the walls are liberally encrusted with shells and minerals. Passing through the grotto and out by narrow labyrinthine passages, suddenly there is a terrace, a broad airy grass walk with magnificent views over the old dock. At the far end of the terrace is a Gothick gazebo, and towering above the other end a castellated tower. Goldney also has follies, a parterre and a herb garden packed into its nine acres.

The Red Lodge 6

Park Row BS1 5LJ. Tel: (0117) 921 1360

Bristol City Council • *In city centre* • *House open* • *Garden open June and July, Sat – Wed, 10am – 5pm. Opening hours vary so telephone (0117) 922 3571 for information* • *Entrance: free* ◐

This is a good reconstruction of the early seventeenth-century garden of a merchant's town house, with old varieties of roses, shrubs and other plants, trelliswork re-created from a seventeenth-century design, and a knot garden based on a plasterwork pattern in the house. A list of plant names is available for a small charge. Georgian *Queen Square* in the city is also undergoing major restoration with lottery funding. If you drive 6m south of Bristol on the A37 you reach *Blackmore and Langdon's Nursery*, open daily, a pleasure at any time, but particularly when the delphiniums are blooming.

9 Sion Hill 7

Clifton, Bristol BS8 4BA. Tel: (0117) 973 2761

Mr and Mrs R.C. Begg • *In city, 100 metres from Clifton Suspension Bridge* • *Open by prior appt* • *Entrance: £2* ◐ ⌖ ⚭

This is not a typical town garden. On the contrary, twenty years of profuse planting have produced an overall impression of peace and plenty on a scale which belies the garden's true size. Entering through a working conservatory, a small grassed area dominated by a vigorous black mulberry tree (planted by the owners and for once not in King James's time) and surrounded by densely planted borders, leads to a central path whose axis is established by the 'temple', an ivy-clad terracotta architectural finial, from which paths radiate to various points. The timber pergola, unusual in spanning the entire width of the garden, is smothered in roses and clematis. The play of light and shade provides a constantly changing effect. Looking back from the house, the garden is terminated by a seven-metre-high wall which acts as a backdrop to a splendid Kanzan cherry tree. A town garden full of interesting ideas – the subtle placing of pots of various kinds is particularly successful.

University Botanic Garden   8

Bracken Hill, North Road, Leigh Woods BS8 3PF. Tel: (0117) 973 3682; Fax: (0117) 974197

University of Bristol • Cross Suspension Bridge from Clifton, turn first right (North Road) and go ¼ m up on left • Open all year, Mon – Fri except public holidays, 9am – 5pm. Parties welcome at other times by appt – contact Superintendent for details • Entrance: free, but guided tours for parties £3 per person • Other information: Plants for sale on two NGS dates in June and Sept. Friends of UBG (subscription £20) have out-of-hours access and members-only plant sales ○ WC &

The Botanic Garden relocated to this site in 1959 and is an interesting garden for the keen plantsman. Large collections of New Zealand and South African flora as well as comprehensive collections of aeonium, cistus, hebe, paeonia, pelargonium, salvia and sempervivum are all cultivated in the attractive five-acre garden. There are collections of native trees and shrubs and plants peculiar to the Avon Gorge, plus conservation collections of rare native south-west species. Glasshouses contain ferns, orchids, bromeliads, cacti and succulents, insectivorous plants and tender bulbs. Plants and borders are well labelled and arranged with various themes, such as poisonous, dye, economic, medicinal, sand dune and woodland. A garden of Chinese medicinal herbs has recently been planted.

2003 GUIDE
The 2003 *Guide* will be published before Christmas 2002. Reports on gardens for consideration are welcome at all times of the year, but particularly by early summer (June 2002) so that they can be inspected that year.

All descriptions and other information are as accurate as possible at the time of going to press, but circumstances change and, if in doubt, it is wise to telephone before making a long journey.

BUCKINGHAMSHIRE

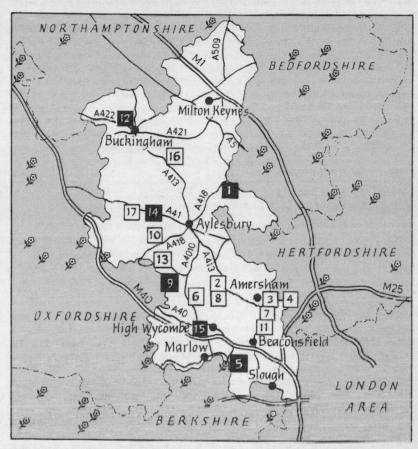

Two-starred gardens are marked on the map with a black square.

Ascott ★★ 1

Wing, Leighton Buzzard LU7 0PS. Tel: (01296) 688242;
Fax: (01296) 681904; E-mail: ascottinfo@scottestate.co.uk;
Website: www.ascottestate.co.uk

The National Trust • ½ m E of Wing, 2m SW of Leighton Buzzard on S of A418 •
House and gardens open 2nd to 30th April, 6th Aug to 13th Sept, daily except Mon;
2 – 6pm (last admission 5pm). Gardens only open May to 31st July, Wed and last
Sun in month, plus 18th, 25th, Sept 2 – 6pm (last admission 5pm). Parties must
pre-book • Entrance: £4, children £2 (house and garden £5.60, children £2.80)
(2001 prices) • Other information: Parking 220 metres from house ◑ 🍴 ♿ ⚲

Thirty acres of Victorian gardening at its very best, laid out with the aid of Sir Harry Veitch and overlaid with designs and planting by Arabella Lennox-Boyd. It is notable for its formidable collection of mature trees of all shapes and colours, set in rolling lawns. Fascinating topiary includes an evergreen sundial with a yew gnomon and the inscription 'Light and shade by turn but love always' in golden yew. Wide lawns slope away to magnificent views across the Vale of Aylesbury, glimpsed between towering cedars. Formal gardens include the Madeira Walk with sheltered flower borders, and the bedded-out Dutch garden. More topiary has been added, and there are new plantings of magnolias. The Long Walk has been reconstructed as a serpentine walk with new beech hedging leading to the lily pond, and a wild garden planted in Coronation Grove. Two stately fountains were created by Thomas Waldo Story – one a large group in bronze, the other a slender composition in marble. Interesting all year, spring gardens feature massed carpets of bulbs.

Blossoms 2

Cobblers Hill, Great Missenden HP16 9PW. Tel: (01494) 863140

Dr and Mrs Frank Hytten • 8m N of High Wycombe. From Great Missenden follow Rignall Road towards Butlers Cross. After about 1m turn right into Kings Lane and up to top of Cobblers Hill. At T-junction turn right at yellow stone marker in hedgerow. After 50 metres turn right again • Open for NGS by appt only • Entrance: £1.50 ● 💬 &

The five-acre garden has a good variety of trees: an acre of beech woodland, underplanted with bluebells and other spring-flowering bulbs, an old apple orchard, and collections of eucalyptus, acers and salix and other specimen trees such as *Euodia hupehensis* (syn. *Tetradium danielli*) and a magnificent ivy-leaved beech. Interesting features include rock and cutting gardens, a small lake with an island, and sculpture by the owner and friends; two other water gardens and a paved well garden with sundial are linked by woodland paths.

Campden Cottage ★ 3

51 Clifton Road, Chesham Bois, Amersham HP6 5PN. Tel: (01494) 726818

Mr and Mrs P. Liechti • On A416 between Amersham and Chesham. Turn into Clifton Road by Catholic church (opposite primary school). Close to traffic lights at pedestrian crossing • Open 3rd March, 14th April, 12th May, 9th June, 14th July, 18th Aug, 8th Sept, 6th Oct, 2 – 6pm, and by appt for parties (no coaches) • Entrance: £1.50, accompanied children free • Other information: School car park available for parking on open days by arrangement ● 🌿

The masterful design takes advantage of a magnificent weeping ash, and displays both the owner's fine collection of rare and unusual plants and her skill in putting together interesting associations of colour, shape and foliage. The sunny York-stone terrace, with its large and ever-increasing collection of terracotta pots, planted for seasonal colour, contrasts pleasingly with the more formal area of yew hedge, walled border and extended lawns. The busiest open day is in March for the well-known collection of hellebore species and hybrids, but the garden is worth visiting month by month to keep in touch with all developments.

Chenies Manor House ★   4

Chenies, Rickmansworth, Hertfordshire WD3 6ER. Tel: (01494) 762888

Lt Col. and Mrs MacLeod Matthews • Off A404 between Amersham and Rickmansworth. If approaching via M25, take junction 18 • House open (extra charge) • Garden open April to Oct, Wed, Thurs and Bank Holidays, 2 – 5pm • Entrance: £3, children £1.25 (2001 prices) ◐ ✕ WC ⅃ ♨ ⏟ ⓠ

The owners have created several extremely fine linked gardens in keeping with their fifteenth/sixteenth-century brick manor house. The gardens are highly decorative and maintained to the highest standards. Planted for a long season of colour and using many old-fashioned roses and cottage plants, there is always something to enjoy here: the formal topiary in the 'white' garden, collections of medicinal and poisonous plants in a 'physic' garden, a parterre, an historic turf maze, an intricate yew maze area over two metres high, and a highly productive kitchen garden. On her visits here, Queen Elizabeth I had a favourite tree and the 'Royal Oak' survives.

Cliveden ★★   5

Taplow, Maidenhead, Berkshire SL6 0JA. Tel: (01628) 605069

The National Trust • 6m NW of Slough, 2m N of Taplow off A4094 • House (three main rooms) open April to Oct, Thurs and Sun, 3 – 6pm (last admission 5.30pm) • Woodlands open all year, daily, 11am – 4pm (close 6pm Jan to 14th March); Estate and gardens open 13th March to 1st Nov, daily, 11am – 6pm; Nov and Dec, daily, 11am – 4pm. Closed Jan and Feb • Entrance: £5.50, family ticket £13.75 (house £1 extra, entry by timed ticket) • Other information: Refreshments in Conservatory Restaurant, 14th March to end Oct, Wed – Sun and Bank Holiday Mons. Dogs allowed in specified woodlands only. Open-air theatre festival in summer ◐ ⬛ ✕ ⬛ WC ⅃ ⏟ ⓠ ⚲

The original house was built in 1666 by the Duke of Buckingham in the grand manner overlooking the River Thames, which flows at the foot of a steep slope (the cliff of 'Clif-den') below. The present house (now a luxury hotel) was designed by Sir Charles Barry, together with a terrace which incorporates a famous balustrade brought by the 1st Viscount Astor from the Villa Borghese in Rome in the 1890s. The water garden, secret garden and herbaceous borders are attractive at the appropriate times of year; the formal gardens below the house and the Long Garden, fountains, temples and statuary are pleasing throughout the year. Amongst famous designers who have worked on the grounds are Bridgeman (walks and amphitheatre), Leoni (Octagon Temple), John Fleming (parterre), and Jellicoe (secret garden). The Trust has restored Jellicoe's secret garden of 1959, re-laying paths to his abstract design and replanting with herbaceous perennials and grasses. Other renovations include the Long Garden and the partere. An inner avenue of limes has been planted north of the house, and the Yew Walk steps have been restored. It is easy to underestimate the horticultural features, although it is true to say that visitors will probably remember most the stunning views to and from the house and parterre. Nearby *Dorneywood Gardens* is a National Trust property used as an official residence for a Secretary of State. Write for an appointment to The Secretary, Dorneywood, Burnham SL1 8PY. Do not miss the colourful gardens in The Street, a row of discreetly renovated sixteenth-century cottages.

Gracefield 6

Main Road, Lacey Green, Princes Risborough HP27 0QU. Tel: (01844) 345560

Mr and Mrs B.C. Wicks • Take A4010 High Wycombe – Aylesbury road. In Bradenham turn right by Red Lion towards Walters Ash. Turn left at T-junction to Lacey Green. Brick and flint house is beyond church facing Kiln Lane • Open 6th May for NGS, and for parties by written appt May to Aug • Entrance: £2, children free • Other information: Park at village hall. Lunches and teas on open day only ● ▣ & ℘

A steeply terraced water garden is a fine feature in this one-and-a-half-acre garden. Plants for the flower arranger; new designs for paved terraces and trough gardens; collections of clematis and shrub roses. Specimen trees include a special malus, M. 'Marshal Oyama', giving fantastic crab apple jelly. The owners are self-confessed plantaholics and have thoughtfully labelled many specimens in this unusual collection.

Halfpenny Furze 7

Mill Lane, Chalfont St Giles HP8 4NR. Tel: (01494) 872509

Mr and Mrs R. Sadler • 5m NE of Beaconsfield off A413, ¼ m past mini-roundabout to Chalfont St Giles • Open with two other gardens one day in May, and by appt • Entrance: £2 (£3 for all three gardens on open day) • Other information: Teas on open day only ● WC & ℘

Created over the years since 1956, this plantsman's garden contains a wide collection of shrubs and trees providing colour nearly all year. To the north of the house, magnolias, rhododendrons and hydrangeas flourish in a woodland garden on soil made suitably by the needles from a dense larch wood clear-felled some sixteen years ago. South of the house, the circular lawn is surrounded by mixed borders of perennials and shrubs, including three different azaras, a fine *Cornus kousa*, a *Hoheria lyallii* and a well-grown *Magnolia highdownensis* (*M. wilsonii*). Grass paths radiate to areas of particular interest, including a Mediterranean garden.

Hughenden Manor 8

High Wycombe HP14 4LA. Tel: (01494) 755573; Fax: (01494) 474284

The National Trust • 1½ m N of High Wycombe on A4128 • House open as garden • Park and woodland open all year. Garden open March, Sat and Sun only; April to 3rd Nov, Wed – Sun and Bank Holiday Mons, 12 noon – 5pm, house 1 – 5pm (last admission ½ hour before closing). No parties on Sat, Sun or

Bank Holidays. Parties must pre-book at other times • Entrance: £1.50, children 75p (manor and garden £4.40, children £2.20, family ticket £11. Party rates on application) (2001 prices) ◗ ☕ ✕ 🍴 **WC** & ⟨⟩ ♨ ⛪ 🔦 ⚲

A High-Victorian garden created by Mrs Disraeli in the 1860s and recently restored. Particularly pleasing is the human scale of house and gardens. The five acres include lawns, terraced garden with sub-tropical planting scheme, formal brightly coloured annual bedding (Mrs Disraeli's guests commented at the time on the blinding colour schemes she chose) and woodland walks. Orchard with old varieties of apples and pears. The unusual chimaera shrub *Laburnocytisus* 'Adamii' combines yellow and mauve flowers of *Laburnum anagyroides* and mauve sprays of *Cytisus purpureus* in late spring/early summer. The additional Victorian flower beds, usually at their best in July, have been restored.

The Manor House ★★ 9

Bledlow, Princes Risborough HP27 9PB.

Lord and Lady Carrington • 8m NW of High Wycombe, ½ m E of B4009 in middle of Bledlow • Manor House Garden open 5th May, 23rd June, 2 – 6pm, and May to Sept for groups by written appt. Lyde Garden open all year, daily • Entrance: Manor House Garden, £4.50, children free. Lyde Garden free • Manor House Garden: ◗ **WC** & *Lyde Garden:* ○

With the help of landscape architect Robert Adams, Lord and Lady Carrington have created an elegant English garden of an exceptionally high standard. The highly productive and colourful walled vegetable garden has York-stone paths and a central gazebo. Formal gardens are enclosed by tall yew and beech hedges. Mixed flower and shrub borders feature many roses and herbaceous plants around immaculately manicured lawns. A garden approached through a yew and brick parterre, incorporating several modern sculptures (displayed with a wit typical of their owners), planned around existing mature trees on a contoured and upward-sloping site with open views, is now thoroughly established, with its trees and lawns fulfilling the original landscaping designs. The Lyde Garden, across the lane, is a magnificent wild water garden of great beauty and tranquillity, supporting a variety of species plants. A note of caution: although the Manor House garden is children-friendly, in the Lyde Garden they need watching on the difficult slopes.

Nether Winchendon House 10

Nether Winchendon, Aylesbury HP18 0DY. Tel: (01844) 290101

Mr and Mrs R. Spencer Bernard • 7m SW of Aylesbury, 5m NE of Thame. Near church in Nether Winchendon • Open 2 days for NGS, and at other times by appt • Entrance: £2, children under 15 free (2001 prices) ◗ ☕ **WC** & ♨

The gardens surround a romantic brick and stone Tudor manor which is approached by an unusual line of dawn redwoods (*Metasequoia glyptostroboides*) planted in 1973, continuing a centuries-old tree planting tradition by the Spencer Bernard family. Small orchards on either side of the house combine with fine specimen trees, including mature acers, catalpas, cedars, paulownias,

liquidambars and, dominating the lawns at the back of the house, an eighteenth-century variegated sycamore and a late-1950s' oriental plane of almost
equal height. There are also well-kept lawns, shrub and flower borders, and
walled gardens, including a productive kitchen garden.

Spindrift   11

Jordans, Beaconsfield HP9 2TE. Tel: (01494) 873172

*Norma Desmond-Mawby • 1m NE of Beaconsfield, N of A40 in Jordans village.
At far side of green turn right into cul-de-sac next to school • Open by appt •
Entrance: £2, children (under 12) 20p • Other information: Park in school
playground on open days* ● ⬛ ✕ 📖 WC ♿ ⏏ 💡 ⚲

A series of linked 'secret gardens' on different levels, with fine trees and
hedges, sets off a wide range of unusual plants and shrubs. A miniature version
of Monet's flower garden has been created recently and features iris, poppies,
peonies and arches with climbing nasturtiums. A model fruit and vegetable
garden is terraced on a hillside, and there are three greenhouses with vines.
Large collection of hostas and hardy geraniums. Nearby is a small orchid
nursery, *Butterfields*. It is at Harvest Hill, Bourne End. Telephone (01628) 525455
ahead of visit as there are no special facilities.

Stowe Landscape Gardens ★★   12

Buckingham MK18 5EH. Tel: (01280) 822850

*The National Trust • 3m NW of Buckingham via Stowe Avenue off A422
Buckingham – Brackley road • House (Stowe School) may be open in holidays.
Check before visiting • Garden open 2nd March to 27th Oct, 1st to 23rd Dec,
Wed – Sun, but open Bank Holiday Mons, 10am – 5pm (last admission 4pm,
but 3pm in Dec). Closed 25th May • Entrance: £4.80, family ticket £12 (house,
NT members must also pay, £2). All parties must pre-book • Other information:
Refreshments for parties must be pre-booked through Property Manager. Picnics
permitted in Grecian Valley only. Self-drive powered 2-seater batricars available,
must be pre-booked* ◐ ⬛ ✕ 📖 WC ⏏ 🛍 💡 ⚲

This is garden restoration on an heroic scale. In the nineteenth century the
landscape at Stowe was diversified into distinct 'scenes', each with a character of
its own. The aim now is to reinstate them. Initially the Trust had £10m to
complete the project, including £1m from a mystery donor. The public will have
free access to the parkland 365 days a year and greater access to the house. The
concept is brilliantly planned, using the Trust's considerable management and
computer resources to reinstate lost plantings or remove recent redundant
additions. The work on the buildings alone deserves whatever medal the country
gives to citizens who do fine work for posterity. Stowe has had enormous
influence on garden design – starting from the mid-seventeenth century under
a succession of distinguished designers including the owner, Viscount Cobham,
Vanbrugh, Bridgeman, Kent, 'Capability' Brown, and then the new owner Lord
Temple, who thinned out Brown's plantings after 1750. There are two ways of
visiting Stowe. One is just to enjoy the wonderful views, the water, the trees and

the buildings and sculpture; the other is to try to step back in time and understand what was meant by political/philosophical design which led to the landscape movement. This is exemplified at its finest by Stowe, influencing not only Britain but the gardening world at large. Whichever approach is adopted, the views are breathtaking and it is wise to allow a minimum of two hours to walk round, preferably with a map. Visitors must understand that the site has been a school since 1923, and that while the staff did their best to keep things going, what is now happening is a wondrous change of a quite different order. The Trust has also acquired the home farm and deer park with two large lakes, 320 acres in all, adjoining Stowe. The land was part of the original deer park and is an integral part of the designed landscape; It includes the Wolfe obelisk, the Gothick Umbrello and a superb set of 1790s' farm buildings. This acquisition ensures that a substantial area of the park will be available for open access on foot without charge throughout the year. The Trust has also restored the Chinese house and returned it to Stowe in memory of the late Gervase Jackson-Stops, its advisor for twenty years. When it was last seen at Stowe, the building was on a platform in the lake in the Elysian Fields; it stands now in a small grove in the Pheasantry. A short walk away, the bases for the seven Saxon deities have been built and three copies installed on their respective 'months'. More statues will be replaced with the original or modern casts as funds permit. Planting continues – for example, 8000 trees and shrubs flanking one side of the Grecian Valley.

Turn End ★ 13

Townside, Haddenham, Aylesbury HP17 8BG. Tel: (01844) 291383/291817

Mr and Mrs P. Aldington • 7m SW of Aylesbury. From A418 turn to Haddenham. From Thame Road turn at Rising Sun into Townside. Turn End is 250 metres on left • Open several days during summer – telephone for details. Parties by appt at other times • Entrance: £2, children (under 14) 50p. • Other information: No parking at garden. Teas on charity days only ● WC ⓓ ⬮ ⬮ ⬮

Peter Aldington's RIBA-award-winning development of three linked houses (now listed) is surrounded by a series of garden rooms evolved over the last thirty years. A sequence of spaces, each of individual character, provides focal points at every turn. There is a fishpond courtyard, a shady court, a formal box court, an alpine garden, hot and dry raised beds and climbing roses. A wide range of plants is displayed to good effect against a framework of mature trees. This one-acre plantsman's garden, created within a village-centre site, is the subject of Jane Brown's book, *A Garden and Three Houses*.

Waddesdon Manor ★★ 14

Waddesdon, Aylesbury HP18 0JH. Tel: (01296) 653211; house bookings with charge, garden tours and events (01296) 653226;
Website: www.waddesdon.org.uk

The National Trust • 6m NW of Aylesbury on A41, 11m SE of Bicester. Entrance in Waddesdon village • House (inc. wine cellars) open 27th March to 3rd Nov, Wed – Sun and Bank Holiday Mons, 11am – 4pm (timed ticket system in operation from 10am; recommended last admission 2.30pm). No children under 5, except babies in front slings • Grounds (inc. gardens, aviary, restaurant and shops) open 27th Feb to 22nd Dec, Wed – Sun and Bank Holiday Mons, 10am – 5pm • Entrance: £3, children £1.50 (house and grounds £10, children £7.50) (2001 prices) • Other information: Parking for disabled. Guide dogs only ◐ 🐕‍ ✕ 🖼 WC ♿ 🌳 🏛 🍴 ℺

Baron Ferdinand de Rothschild's remarkable château (built 1874–1889), which houses a formidable art collection, is set in an appropriately grand grounds with fountains, vistas, terraces and walks. The gardens contain an extensive collection of Italian, French and Dutch statuary. An ornate, semi-circular aviary of six-teenth-century French style, erected in 1889, provides a distinguished home to many exotic birds. The area in front of it was designed by Lanning Roper. A new rose garden, laid out as a circle with eight beds filled with a wide range of fragrant varieties, also contains marble benches and a fourteenth-century well-head. The grounds today benefits from its 100-year old plantings of native yews, limes and chestnuts with a liberal sprinkling of exotic pines, cedars, Wellingtonias and cypresses. The gardens continue to undergo changes, with old features being restored and new ones added. The extensive parterre and fountains, intended to be viewed from the south side of the house, have undergone the most extensive restoration of all, requiring over 100,000 plants in the main summer display alone. John Sales describes the south parterre as 'the central jewel of a rich Victorian scheme'. He recounts that one of the original head gardeners to the Rothschilds used to quote an aphorism describing how the rich showed their wealth by the size of their bedding-out plant list: 10,000 for a squire, 20,000 for a baronet, 30,000 for an earl and 50,000 for a duke. Waddesdon is truly regal. The latest bedding feature is a design of two vibrantly coloured rainbows created by the fashion designer Oscar de la Renta and boldly placed in the Victorian parterre garden at the south front of the house. Parterres of this complexity used to demand a large staff but Lord Rothschild has called on experts who bed plants by computer. Elsewhere the exterior lighting scheme has won awards and can be enjoyed from the gardens on special evenings. Wildflower Valley is a major summer attraction with thousands of wild flowers, including cowslips, ox-eye daisies and a range of orchids, which are encouraged to seed. Close by, over 20,000 camassias and colchicums have been naturalised into grassland and in the woodland garden.

West Wycombe Park ★★ 15

West Wycombe HP14 3AJ. Tel: (01628) 488675

The National Trust • 2m W of High Wycombe, at W end of West Wycombe, S of A40 Oxford road • House open June to Aug, Sun – Thurs, 2 – 6pm (weekday entry by timed ticket, last admission 5.15pm) • Grounds open April to Aug, Sun – Thurs and Bank Holiday Mons, all 2 – 6pm (last admission 5.15pm) • Entrance: £2.70 (house and grounds £4.30, family ticket £12) ◑ WC ♿ 🍴 ℺

The park was largely created by the second Sir Francis Dashwood and was influenced by his experiences on the Grand Tour, which included visits to Asia Minor and Russia. The first phase involved the creation of the lake with meandering walks, completed by 1739. Numerous classical temples and statues were added subsequently, as well as the delightful little flint and wooden bridges which span the streams. Later still, in the 1770s, the park was enlarged; Nicholas Revett was employed to design even more temples and follies, including a particularly fine music temple on an island. Thomas Cook, a pupil of 'Capability' Brown, was entrusted with the planting of trees and alterations to the landscape. There are splendid vistas, especially towards the lake which is in the shape of a swan. This is not the place to visit if you seek flower gardens and rose beds, but those who know a little about Dashwood's Hell Fire Club will enjoy seeing the other side of his nature.

Wotton House   16

Wotton Underwood, Aylesbury HP18 OSB.

Mrs April Gladstone • 8m W of Aylesbury off A41 • Open to groups by application in writing ☻

This remarkable landscape garden (250 acres) with over a dozen follies and other attractions shares a history with the Grenvilles of Stowe (see entry). Derelict after World War II, it has, under two generations of the Brunner family in the latter half of the twentieth century, been painstakingly restored. Much, however, remains to be done. George London's early-eighteenth-century design is still evident, with the remains of his three avenues, two of them double, radiating from the house. South of the house is London's walled garden with a terrace, an orangery below it, a double staircase with a shell niche between its wings, and a pavilion, formerly the coach house. The unchanged wider view remains splendid, and was shaped by 'Capability' Brown between 1750 and 1767. His main work was to remodel the contours and create a large lake, connecting it to a smaller, existing lake by a serpentine canal. Note the two Tuscan pavilions overlooking the water and the bridges. The Island grotto, the Turkey Building, strikingly handsome and the Rotunda are contemporary, but not Brown's handiwork. In all, a remarkable and little-known survival. A few miles further west, S of A41, is *Bernwode Plants*, Kingswood Lane, Ludgershall. Described as one of the best nurseries not listed in *The Plant Finder*, it specialises in herbaceous perennials (2000 different kinds). [Open March to Oct, daily except Mon (but open Bank Holiday Mons), 10am – 6pm.]

CAMBRIDGESHIRE

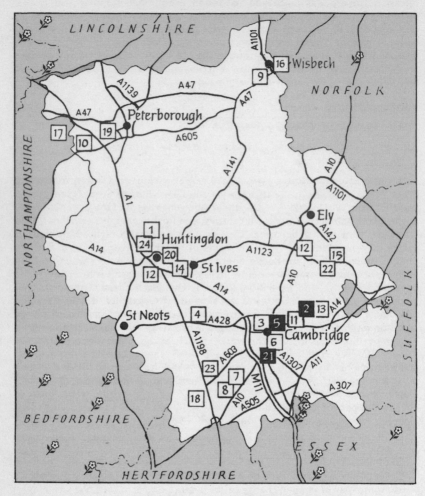

Two-starred gardens are marked on the map with a black square.

Abbots Ripton Hall ★ 1

Abbots Ripton, Huntingdon PE28 2PQ. Tel: (01487) 773555; Fax: (01487) 773545

Lord and Lady De Ramsey • 2m N of Huntingdon, approached from B1090 • Open probably 19th May, 23rd June, 7th, 21st July, 4th Aug for charities, 2 – 5pm, and for private visits by appt • Entrance: £3 on charity days; £6 (including plant guide) for private visits ● ☕ WC ♿ ✿ ✿

This superb garden was designed in the 1950s by Humphrey Waterfield with contributions by Lanning Roper and Tony Venison. Fine lake, fishing hut like a Chinese pavilion, and a grey-leaved border with alpines and sun-loving perennials. Modern but rustic octagonal summerhouse, Doric loggia, and several timber bridges, including one of Chinese style. There is a circular rose garden: a ring of historic roses backed by grey foliage of sea buckthorn with a circular lawn at its centre. The spectacular herbaceous borders stretching from the eighteenth-century house are backed by columns of yew and philadelphus and punctuated by a circle of Gothick trellising. Look out for the biggest Huntingdon elm in the country. The two follies are by Peter Foster, who also designed some of the bridges.

Anglesey Abbey Gardens and Lode Mill ★★   2

Lode, Cambridge CB5 9EJ. Tel/Fax: (01223) 811200;
E-mail: aayusr@smtp.ntrust.org.uk;
Website: www.nationaltrust.org.uk/angleseyabbey

The National Trust • 6m NE of Cambridge off A14, on B1102 • House open 20th March to 27th Oct, Wed – Sun and Bank Holiday Mons (but closed 29th March), 1 – 5pm (last admission 4.30pm) • Garden open 20th March to 27th Oct, Wed – Sun and Bank Holiday Mons and daily 1st July to 1st Sept (but closed 29th March), 10.30am – 5.30pm (last admission 4.30pm). Winter Walk open 2nd Jan to 17th March and 30th Oct to 22nd Dec, Wed – Sun, 10.30am – 4pm • Entrance: £3.85, winter £3.25 (house, garden and Lode Mill: £6.25). Charge is made for tours with Head Gardener • Other information: Four electric wheelchairs available. Gravel surfaces on Winter Walk paths. Lode Mill machinery working first Sat of month ◐ 🍽 ✕ <u>WC</u> ⓺ 🌿 🏤 🔌 ⚲

The Abbey's setting is one of England's finest twentieth century gardens. You will need a whole day – many whole days – to absorb this place, its separate gardens, the parade of sculptures, trees and open spaces, and the changeful seasons. Avenues of mature trees lead the wanderer to intimate gardens enclosed by meticulous hedges; smooth lawns give way to meadows awash with cowslips, lady's bedstraw and ox-eye daisies; visitors will unexpectedly come upon dramatic vistas lined by superb trees, or glimpse the peaceful River Lode and Lode Mill. A semi-circular garden with a deep encircling herbaceous border is a highlight for the summer; the bold, imaginative planting of perennials is splendid, plumes of seakale and spires of delphinium mingling with mysterious sages. In another garden, 4500 hyacinths bloom in spring while dark-foliaged dwarf dahlias take their place in late summer. Narcissus gazes at his reflection surrounded by scented white- and yellow-blossomed shrubs. A curved border of randomly planted late-summer dahlias may not be to everyone's taste, but what garden is ever entirely perfect? This place is almost so, and is maintained with great panache. It is vast, too – 100 acres. The mile-long Winter Walk, underplanted with thousands of early small bulbs, features a serpentine walk and other paths, including a recently rediscovered Victorian one. A grove of giant redwoods marks the start of the walk, a forest of white-stemmed birches underplanted with the black-stemmed *Cornus alba* 'Kesselring' its conclusion.

Cambridge College Gardens 3

Most colleges are helpful about access to their gardens, although the Masters' or Fellows' Gardens are often strictly private or rarely open. Specific viewing times are difficult to rely on because some colleges prefer not to have visitors in term time or on days when a function is taking place. The best course is to ask at the porters' lodge or to telephone in advance. However, some college gardens will always be open to the visitor, by arrangement with porters. Several now charge for entry.

Amongst the College Gardens of particular interest are the following: *Christ's* (see entry). *Clare* (see entry). *Downing College*: Spacious neo-classical campus (founded 1800), covering 6 acres, with lawns and trees; much recent tree planting. Fine old cedars of Lebanon and an interesting tulip tree in the Master's Garden [Open most days and for charity at least one day a year]. *Emmanuel*: large gardens with herb garden designed by John Codrington. Also memorable for its fine trees, including a Caucasian wing nut, swamp cypress, dawn redwood and the splendid plane tree, cloaked to the ground, in the Fellows' Garden. Informal shrubberies and herbaceous borders skirt the lawns, and there is a pond with a restrained piece of modern sculpture nearby [Open daily, 9am – 5pm; College Gardens and Fellows' Garden open one day in summer]. *Jesus*: a must for those interested in sculpture to see the Flanagan Venetian horse. Sensitive planting elsewhere, and do not miss the head in the cloisters. The new St Radegund's garden has planting derived from the sixth-century saint's garden in Poitiers, France [Open daily, 9am – 4.30pm, but closed May to mid-June]. *King's*: one of the greatest British architectural experiences, set off by fine lawns. Spring bulbs [College and Chapel open daily until 6.30pm, but grounds closed mid-April to mid-June, 9.30am – 4.30pm, and closed over Christmas period &]. Fellows' Garden with magnificent old specimen trees [Open one day in summer for NGS, 2 – 6pm]. *Leckhampton* (part of *Corpus Christi*) at 37 Grange Road: laid out by William Robinson, originally seven acres with two acres added [Open one day for charity ♨ WC]. *Magdalene*: Fellows' Garden [Open daily, 1 – 6pm. Closed May and June &]. *Pembroke*: extensive and varied garden, including orchard and winter bed, with notable range of unusual plants, most of which benefit from shelter provided by various walls. Lobster claw (*Clianthus puniceus*) cheek by jowl with tassel bush (*Garrya elliptica*), pomegranates and trumpet vine (*Campsis* x *tagliabuana*) form a mini-botanic garden. Good selection of herbaceous perennials. [Open daily during daylight hours. Closed May and June &]. *Peterhouse*: varied, smallish gardens and interesting octagonal court with hot and cool sides. Extensive naturalised daffodils in spring [Open Mon – Fri, 1 – 5pm. Closed late May to early June &]. *Robinson*: Warden and Fellows' Garden, Grange Road [Open daily, 10am – 6pm]. 10 acres surround this modern college, formerly grand Edwardian villas. Memorable trees, wild garden. *St John's*: huge park-like garden with eight acres of grass, fine trees and good display of bulbs in spring. Wilderness (nearly three acres) introduced by 'Capability' Brown has spring bulbs including, from June to July, the spectacular Turk's cap lily (martagon lily). In the Master's Lodge Garden are quantities of *Arabus turnata*, probably the only specimens in the country. Rose garden [Open Mon – Fri, 10am – 5pm], Sat and Sun, 9.30am – 5pm. *Trinity*: a garden and grounds of 45 acres with good trees. [Grounds open daily although restricted access with charge for entry, March to

Sept; opening times from Porter's Lodge. Fellows' Garden open one day, 2 – 6pm]. Nearby is *Little St Mary's Church*: wild and natural garden developed since 1925 [Open all year].

Childerley Hall 4

Dry Drayton, Cambridge CB3 8BB. Tel: (01954) 210271

Mr and Mrs John Jenkins • 6m W of Cambridge on A428 opposite Caldecote turn • Open mid-May to mid-July by appt • Entrance: £2 ●

The hall lies between the sites of the two vanished villages of Great and Little Childerley, and the drive leading to the house, chapel and four-acre garden is nearly a mile and a half through flat open country, making it seem particularly still and remote. To one side is an ornamental Tudor moat and a yew hedge crowned by topiary birds. The south front of the house is on a raised terrace. From here the main garden, sunken and surrounded by raised grass walks, can be viewed. The corners of these walks were originally Tudor mounts. Here, flourishing in the boulder clay, are 350 shrub and species roses: planted beside straight paths, in the winding wilderness, and in the white rose garden. Modern and historic roses grow together in harmony and with abandon, and there is a further selection of roses in the kitchen garden.

Christ's College ★★ 5

St Andrew's Street, Cambridge CB2 3BU. Tel: (01223) 334900

In city centre • Open mid-June to Sept, Mon – Fri, 9.30am – 12 noon; Oct to May, Mon – Fri during term, also out of term in winter, 2 – 4pm. Closed Bank Holidays, Easter Week and 23rd Dec to 2nd Jan ● **WC** & ●

First impressions are telling, and the court beyond the porter's lodge is a spectacle that proclaims excellence. The summer display of fuchsias and petunias in window boxes and tubs is tasteful, refined and peaceful. Tubs of hydrangeas welcome visitors into the immaculate gardens beyond. The well-planned herbaceous borders are augmented with panache by bedded-out plants. On a mound in the far corner the venerable mulberry, contemporary with Milton, sheds its fruit onto the exemplary lawn. There are many other lovely trees, including Indian bean trees (*Catalpa bignonioides*) in full bloom in mid-summer, and the cypress grown from seed from the tree on Shelley's grave in Rome. Charles Darwin's garden with canal intrigues the visitor with its false perspective.

Clare College Fellows' Gardens 6

**Trinity Lane, Cambridge CB2 1TL. Tel: (01223) 333200;
Fax: (01223) 333219; Website: www.clare.cam.ac.uk**

In city centre. Entry from Queens Road and Trinity Lane • College open • Garden open April to Sept, daily inc. Bank Holidays (except on graduation, May Ball and special events days), 10am – 4.30pm. Also one Sun in June, 5.30 – 7.30pm, with wine, and one afternoon in August for Red Cross with tea • Entrance: College and garden £2 ◑ ℺

Reached by crossing the oldest bridge over the Cam (from the college itself), or (from Queens Road) by walking along the avenue laid out in 1690. Between the college buildings and the bridge are two gardens – to the north the private Master's Garden and to the south the Scholars' Garden, where the planting relies on silver, blue, purple and white. Professor E.N. Willmer designed the present, well-regarded planting scheme for the Fellows' Garden. The fine trees are mainly the legacy of his predecessors. At the garden's heart, concealed by hedges, is a formal pool. The double herbaceous borders have a yellow and blue theme, while along the northern boundary is a ribbon of silver with a mass of white flowers, including some that show up well against walls and hedges. Summer bedding is used to insert oranges and reds in island beds by the river.

Crossing House Garden ★ 7

78 Meldreth Road, Shepreth, Royston, Hertfordshire SG8 6PS.
Tel: (01763) 261071

Mr and Mrs Douglas Fuller • 8m SW of Cambridge, ½ m W of A10 • Open all year, daily, dawn – dusk • Entrance: by collecting box ○ WC ⬦

Highly recommended, a delightful, eccentric place which proves that plantsmanship is alive and well in Cambridgeshire. A small garden, started by the present owners over 30 years ago, it is crammed full of plants and is an eye-opener about what can be achieved in a small space. There are little pools, excellent dwarf box edging, an arbour in clipped yew, rockeries and a lawn, and three tiny glasshouses full of orchids and alpines. In all there are estimated to be about 5000 different plants here, so a visit at any time of year will be rewarding. Docwra's Manor (see below) is about 250 metres away.

Docwra's Manor 8

2 Meldreth Road, Shepreth, Royston, Hertfordshire SG8 6PS.
Tel: (01763) 261473/261557/260235

Mrs John Raven • 8m SW of Cambridge, ½ m W of A10. Opposite war memorial • Open all year, Wed, Fri, 10am – 4pm, and first Suns of April to Oct, 2 – 5pm, and at other times by appt. Parties welcome • Entrance: £3, accompanied children under 16 free. Extra charge for guided and out-of-hours parties • Other information: Park in village hall car park ○ 🍴 WC ⴠ ✂

'Simply a garden as reasonably varied as could be' – that was John and Faith Raven's original intention when they bought a manor house with an ancient lineage and one and a half acres of land in 1954, and this they have triumphantly achieved. It is a fascinating garden, now expanded by a further acre, divided into unexpected compartments by buildings, walls and hedges, and containing many choice plants. Seedlings are left where they appear, so the effect is wild in parts; other areas are more formal, with hosts of roses, spurges, clematis, eryngiums and philadelphus. John Raven (1914–80), a lecturer in classics and an eminent field botanist, wrote about the plants he and his wife grew here in *A Botanist's Garden* (1971; re-issued). The Crossing House garden (see above) is within easy walking distance.

Elgood's Brewery 9

North Brink, Wisbech PE13 1LN. Tel: (01945) 583160; Fax: (01945) 587711

Elgood's Brewery • In Wisbech, at W end of North Brink • Brewery open for tours, Wed – Fri, 2pm. £4.50 inc. tasting • Garden open May to Oct, Wed, Thurs, Fri and Sun and Bank Holiday Mons, 1 – 5pm • Entrance: £2.50, OAPs and children £2 • Other information: Guide dogs only ◑ ➌ WC ❧ ⚜ ⚲ ℺

Wisbech is an elegant market town and among its delights are several splendid Georgian terraces. North Brink, along the River Nene, is arguably the most spectacular. Peckover House (see entry) is near the eastern end of the Brink, while the brewery dominates the western end. Behind the brewery is a large enclosed garden, now restored, with some superlative trees. The *Ginkgo biloba* near the public entrance catches the eye first. A few paces away stands a tulip tree (*Liriodendron tulipifera*) the like of which you will rarely see; in June every shoot bears a flower, a cup of orange and jade. Other dignitaries are a mulberry, a variegated sycamore, a weeping willow, a tree of heaven (*Ailanthus altissima*) and an oak. The deep pool has become home to a colony of great crested newts. Paths have been reinstated, and colourful herbaceous borders, a rose garden, a herb garden, a maze and a rockery planted. Onto this new planting the trees look down with grace and dignity.

Elton Hall 10

Peterborough PE8 6SH. Tel: (01832) 280468 (during office hours)

Mr and Mrs William Proby • 8m W of Peterborough in Elton, just off A605 • Hall open • Garden open 3rd, 4th June, and Weds in June; July and Aug, Wed, Thurs, Sun and Bank Holiday Mons; all 2 – 5pm. Hall and garden open for tours by appt at other times • Entrance: £3 (hall and garden £5, accompanied children under 16 free) ➌ ➌ ✕ WC ♿ ❧ ⚜ ⚲ ℺

Steps cloaked in aubretia and lavender, guarded by two sphinxes, ascend to the low castellated mansion, parts of which date from 1475. By the steps is a knot parterre in box, elegantly wrought, and in front a smooth lawn that rises to meet the surrounding pasture. A sunken pool, enveloped in a billow of whites and blues with some purple, is the first feature visitors see as they enter the garden through an archway. Take the gravel path that encircles the lawn, which has an ornamental well-head offset in the middle, and wander past the immaculately clipped low yew hedges and tumps of golden yew, and the short ha-ha, to the restored rose garden, full of old-fashioned roses – summer scents and colours. The distant sound of water will eventually beckon you on, across a hornbeam-lined avenue punctuated with pyramids of box, into an informal silvery shrubbery, under a fine *Paulownia tomentosa*, to discover a new Gothick orangery set in an ornamental garden.

Hardwicke House 11

High Ditch Road, Fen Ditton, Cambridge CB5 8TF. Tel: (01223) 292246

Mr J. Drake • 3½ m E of Cambridge off A14, ½ m from centre of Fen Ditton. From A1303 Newmarket road turn N by borough cemetery • Open one day in late May for NGS, and by appt (if you are unable to keep appt please let owner know). Closed Aug • Entrance: £2.50, children 50p ● ♨

Fenland gardens need shelter, and shelter is provided here by tall hedges, some of beech, some of conifers, with elderly pruned apple trees in between. The compartments are all different. Closely mown paths radiate through rougher grass providing vistas; the main one is lined by birch trees alternating with yellow-blossomed *Rosa* 'Cantabrigiensis'. In late spring and early summer the garden is awash with columbines and cranesbills and filled with the fragrance of old roses; in autumn there are colchicums in abundance, while hellebores and daffodils provide spring colour. Unusual plants are scattered around, and a National Collection of aquilegias is here.

Island Hall 12

Post Street, Godmanchester PE29 2BA. Tel: (01480) 459676

Mr C. and Lady Linda Vane Percy • In centre of Godmanchester • Open 26th May for NGS and Suns in July, 1 – 5pm; parties by appt, May to July, Sept • Entrance: £2 • Other information: refreshments on NGS day only ● ▣ ⚱

The garden is in two parts, separated by a mill-race yet linked by a Chinese-style wooden bridge erected in 1988. The Island was the pleasure garden in Victorian times – today it has tall trees, mainly horse-chestnuts, underneath which cow-parsley and other wild flowers are being encouraged. There are lovely views across the River Ouse to Portholme Meadow. Returning via the bridge, another vista embraces two fine cedars of Lebanon, one of which stands in front of the eighteenth-century house. On the terrace is a formal parterre with clipped variegated box hedges, box spirals and yew pyramids; the Mill Garden has a sundial ensconced in another parterre spilling over with white shrubby cinquefoil, white Scotch roses and columbines.

21 Lode Road ★ 13

Lode, Cambridge CB5 9ER.

Richard Ayres • 6m NE of Cambridge. From A14 take B1102 to Lode • Open for charity 22nd, 23rd June, 6th, 7th July, 11am – 6pm • Entrance: £1.50 • Other information: Parking facilities at village hall. Possible for wheelchairs but narrow paths ● ▣ ♿

The owner's use of foliage in variety – glittering, golden, ferny, fulsome, silvery – and his placing of shrubs and trees to their best advantage are magisterial. The yellows and blues of the flowers, with occasional flashes of scarlet and crimson, and the subtle whites, form a brilliant tapestry through which the paths weave and wind, opening new views at every turn. Everything is compact – there is no sense of boundaries – and everything immaculate.

The Manor   14

**Hemingford Grey, Huntingdon PE18 9BN. Tel: (01480) 463134;
Fax (01480) 465026**

*Diana Boston • 4m SE of Huntingdon off A14. Access off river tow path •
House open by appt only • Garden open all year, daily • Entrance: £2, children
50p • Other information: Park in High Street* ○ ⇔ ℘

A storybook garden for children of any age – but there is much more than a
garden here, for the wonderful moated Norman manor (c. 1130) is perhaps the
oldest continuously inhabited house in England. It was the home of Lucy
Boston from 1939 and the setting for her *Green Knowe* children's books. She
designed the garden, intermixing old-fashioned roses with herbaceous perennials, creating parallel herbaceous borders, a formal rose garden and topiary
in the form of chess pieces. Trees in the lawns are underplanted with autumn
crocuses. At the Norman front are ancient yews and a superb copper beech
that has layered itself. Parts of the garden are left wild deliberately.

Netherhall Manor   15

Tanner's Lane, Soham. Tel: (01353) 720269

*Timothy Clark • 6m SE of Ely on A142; pass church and war memorial and
take second road on left. From Newmarket turn right in Soham at second road
after cemetery • Open 31st March, 5th May, 4th, 11th Aug for NGS, 2 – 5pm •
Entrance: £1* ◑ ▭

An elegant garden, touched with antiquity, and for those fond of old-fashioned
plants a veritable joy. In spring the garden blazes with Victorian hyacinths, crown
imperials and old primroses, followed by the only display of florists' tulips and
florists' ranunculus in the country. In high summer, the beds contain collections of
nineteenth-century variegated pelargoniums. Entering through a courtyard with
formal box-edged beds and a handsome fountain, visitors first glimpse the formal
aconite garden later filled with old fuchsias; behind is the organic vegetable garden.
To the right is a colonnade of lichen encrusted columns linked by a balustrade on
which pots of seasonal flowers are displayed; summer is gold and silver tricolour
pelargoniums, yellow and golden-brown calceolarias, heliotropes and double
lobelias. Old apples, specimen trees, vast clumps of violets and hepatica and, most
remarkably, the double-flowered ornamental blackberry (*Rubus ulmifolius* 'Bellidi-
florus') trained against the gable wall, make this a most diverting garden.

Peckover House   16

**North Brink, Wisbech PE13 1JR. Tel/ Fax: (01945) 583463;
E-mail: aprigx@smtp.ntrust.org.uk**

*The National Trust • In centre of Wisbech on N bank of River Nene • House
open as garden, but Wed, Sat and Sun only, plus Thurs in July and Aug •
Garden open 23rd March to Oct, Sat – Thurs and Bank Holiday Mons, 12.30
– 5pm • Entrance: £2.50 (house and garden £4) • Other information: 1 electric
wheelchair available by prior application* ◐ ▭ ✗ <u>WC</u> ♿ ℘ ⏚ ♀ ⚲

The red-brick town house was built in 1722, whereas the elongated, two-acre garden has a distinctly late-Victorian ambience. Stepping from the house onto the croquet lawn, you are surrounded by greenery, mature trees and ever-green shrubs. In summer, bedding plants add colour and the scent of a host of roses will draw you westwards, passing a (reconstruction) formal pool, into compartments variously planted with flowering shrubs, perennials and those perfumed roses. Topiary peacocks overlook a second pool and summerhouse. Lilies, peonies, hydrangeas and 'Mrs Sinkins' pinks provide a succession of bloom in the walled garden, at the end of which is the orangery, full to bursting with flowering pot plants and three mature, fruiting orange trees. Further on, a new border, dominated by dark red, is maturing, backed by espalier pear trees. Vegetables and cut flowers are grown for the tea room and house. Everything is neat and tidy, bearing out the claim that this garden is 'the product of prudent tidiness, a period piece'. Elgood's Brewery (see entry) is close by.

South Farm 17

Shingay, Royston, Hertfordshire SG8 0HR. Tel: (01223) 207581

Mr P. Paxman • 6m NW of Royston off A1198, via Wendy • Open two days in June for NGS, and May to July for private visits by appt • Entrance: £2.50 (joint entrance with Brook Cottage and other properties) on charity days
● ● ● WC & ♨

The main flower garden is enclosed and protected by a tall cypress hedge, pierced frequently by gates that allow you to glimpse the long fields of wheat. The hedge even has a *trompe-l'oeil* cut into it – not a bad use for the loathsome 'Leylandii'. A lily pond in one corner is awash with sedges and monkey flowers and around it an informal garden with such beauties as *Rosa chinensis* 'Mutabilis'. Familiar flowers abound: Jacob's-ladders, day lilies, loosestrife, plume poppies. On the other side of the farmhouse is a pool terrace and an exotic conservatory and a 1000-metre-square vegetable garden, enclosed by espalier fruit trees and totally netted. Each rotation plot is subdivided by gravel paths, parterre-style, into about 15 beds in which grow over 150 varieties of vegetables and fruit. Beyond is a small wildflower meadow, and more wheat. A happy, not-too-tidy garden – the lucky ducks and their companion 'rare breeds' have some well-trained humans to keep it for them. Nearby is a private nature reserve with a three-acre lake, which is open to the public. *Brook Cottage* (Mr and Mrs Charvil), four minutes' walk away, is a much smaller garden with a crystal-clear stream – a real cottage garden with vegetables and poultry as well as honeysuckle and horsetails.

Thorpe Hall 18

Longthorpe, Peterborough PE3 6LW. Tel: (01733) 330060

Sue Ryder Care • In Longthorpe, on W edge of Peterborough between A47 and A605 • Ground floor of house open for some events • Garden open all year, daily except 25th, 26th Dec and 1st Jan, 10am – 5pm • Entrance: by donation
○ WC & ♨ ⊞ ♀ ✿

A wooden door lets the visitor out of the courtyard into the L-shaped garden comprising a series of parterres and borders. Two elegant Georgian pavilions, far apart, are linked by a long vista which is interrupted as it pierces a third pavilion. A boldly planted herbaceous border and a restrained, lavender-hedged rose garden around an oval pond occupy parts of a longer axis. On the shorter axis is an architectural Victorian parterre planted with a strange mixture of perennials, including ornamental grasses, clipped bay laurel, box and yew, and bedded-out plants. The south court is planted with Cromwellian plants, the east border with 1850s' plants, while the west end has rose gardens typical of the 1920s and '30s. What has been achieved so far is pleasing and worthwhile, providing a diverting small garden with echoes of former grandeur, especially in its Grade-II-listed pavilions, ancient yews and spreading cedar trees.

Turf Maze   19

The Green, Hilton, Huntingdon. Tel: (01480) 830137 (Mr P. Blake);
E-mail: peter@blake45.freeserve.co.uk

Parish of Hilton • On green in centre of village • Open April to Nov • Entrance: free • Other information: Parking at parish hall 🕐 🗑 🐟 ✎

Mazes are mysterious things, believed by some to be linked to fertility rites. This turf one, scheduled as an ancient monument, was created by one William Sparrow in 1660. It is circular, compact and intricate, and at its centre is an obelisk with Latin and English inscriptions about Mr Sparrow and his maze. Then go on to Fenstanton (2m NE of Hilton) and inside the medieval parish church on the north wall of the chancel you will find a memorial to the famous landscape gardener Lancelot 'Capability' Brown, who owned the manor house and is buried in the churchyard.

University Botanic Garden ★★   20

Cambridge CB2 1JF. Tel: (01223) 336265

University of Cambridge • In S of city, on E side of A1309 (Trumpington Road). Entrance off Bateman Street • Open all year except 25th Dec to 1st Jan inclusive: summer 10am – 6pm, winter 10am – 4pm • Entrance: charge for March to Oct, Mon – Fri, and weekends and Bank Holidays all year; Nov to Feb, Mon – Fri, free ○ 🍽 🗑 WC ♿ 👜 ⚘ ✎

This diverse and impressive garden covers 40 acres, and admirably fulfils its three purposes – research, education and amenity. A visit at any time is worthwhile, even in winter when the winter garden, especially on a sunny day, is dramatic. The various dogwoods with red, black, green and yellow-ochre stems contrast with *Rubus biflorus*, while the pale pink trunk of the birch *Betula albo-sinensis* var. *septentrionalis* is stunning. As this is primarily a research institute, there is a splendid collection of native trees, including willows, poplars and junipers, and an illuminating display of rare and endangered British species, together with historic systematic beds and a rock garden. There are 'exotic' rockeries, too, both sandstone and limestone, so that plants with similar requirements can be seen growing together. Exotic trees include pawpaw (*Asimina triloba*), and good specimens of madroña (*Arbutus andrachne*), *Tetracentron sinense* and dawn redwood (*Metasequoia glyptostroboides*). The glasshouse range is always fascinating, and in winter the tropical section can be a welcome retreat. It contains a green-flowered jade vine (*Strongylodon macrobotrys*), cycads, tropical economic plants and much more. In the alpine house, plants are changed regularly as they come into flower. A recent addition is the Dry Garden, which investigates how design and plant selection can reduce the need for watering in a typical city garden. Nearby is another novelty, a linear bed showing arable weed flora changes in UK agricultural history. The Genetic Garden is a new display which illustrates how the amazing diversity of flowering plants results from genetic variation due to mutation.

Wicken Fen Cottage   20

Lode Lane, Wicken, Ely CB7 5XP. Tel: (01353) 720274; Fax: (01353) 720274

The National Trust • 9m SE of Ely, 3m SW of Soham, S of A1123, signed Wicken Fen National Nature Reserve • Fen Cottage open April to Sept, Sun, 2 – 5pm • Entrance: Fen Cottage and Nature Reserve £3.70 • Other information: Light refreshments, toilet facilities and shop in Reserve visitor centre opposite, open Tues – Sun, 10am – 5pm (closed occasionally in winter) ● ■ ▦ WC ◁▷ ▦ ▮

A simple, effective garden with jumbles of foxgloves, hollyhocks, Shasta daisies, clary and golden yarrow in midsummer, a few roses, some butcher's broom, a patch of fruit and vegetables and lots of nettles – unpretentious, in keeping with the rural cottage. You can just peep over the garden hedge on your way to Wicken Fen National Nature Reserve, which is one of the wild treasures of Cambridgeshire.

Wimpole Hall   21

Arrington, Royston, Hertfordshire SG8 0BW. Tel: (01223) 207257; Fax: (01223) 207838; Website: www.wimpole.org

The National Trust • 7m SW of Cambridge, signed off A603 at New Wimpole • Hall open 23rd March to 3rd Nov as garden, but open 1 – 5pm (Bank Holiday Mons opens 11am) • Garden open 23rd March to 3rd Nov, Tues – Thurs, Sat, Sun and Bank Holiday Mons, 10.30am – 5pm (Tues – Sun in July and Aug); Nov to March, Sat, Sun, 11am – 4pm. Pre-booked guided tours for parties with head gardener. Park walks open all year • Entrance: £2.50 (hall and garden £6.20, children £2.80) (2001 prices) • Other information: Pre-booked self-drive vehicles available for disabled visitors ◐ ■ ✕ WC ♿ ⚘ ▦ ▮ ◔

The colossal landscaped park follows almost every fashion in landscaping during the eighteenth and nineteenth centuries; Charles Bridgeman (1720s), Lancelot 'Capability' Brown (1760s) and many others worked here. Today, their handiwork is in part immaculate, in part preserved, but elsewhere decrepit and in the process of restoration. Restoration of the walled garden is progressing well too, and the glasshouses have been rebuilt. The parterre before the north front of the house is planted in Victorian style. In the park vast avenues lead to the cardinal points of the compass, past lakes, bridges, a splendid 1770 folly which can be seen in the distance from the parterre, trees at all stages from ancient to newly planted, and rare breeds of cattle and sheep everywhere. To reach the folly an hour is needed; other marked walks take longer. A new walks leaflet is available.

Wytchwood 22

Owl End, Great Stukeley, Huntingdon PE28 4AQ.

Mr and Mrs David Cox • 2m N of Huntingdon off B1043. In Great Stukeley, turn at village hall into Owl End • Open one day for charity • Entrance: £2, children 50p • Other information: Parking at village hall ● ✕ & ⌀

Cascades of petunias and an ornamental wheelbarrow filled with annuals are striking preludes to the garden proper. The brightly planted borders have manicured, matching golden cypress columns as backdrops. Even the magnolia has been clipped. A small pool, and a blue spruce in a heather bed frame the patio. A few steps further on and Wytchwood becomes altogether different. There is an acre of mown grass with large uncut islands full of wild grasses and native plants softly waving in the breeze, especially attractive to amphibians, butterflies and dragonflies. After the cliché of the front garden, which some will dislike but most will thoroughly enjoy, the restraint of the meadow islands, filled with lady's bedstraw and poppies, set with rowans and birches, is inspired.

A TOTALLY INDEPENDENT PUBLICATION
The *Guide* makes no charge for entries, which are written by our own inspectors. The factual details are supplied by owners. This is a totally independent publication and its only revenue comes from sales of copies in bookshops.

POSTCODE PLANTS DATABASE
It is often difficult to find out which plants are local to an area. The Postcode Plants Database locates the names of flowers, trees, butterflies and birds for each of Britain's 26 million home addresses. Simply by typing in the first four characters of their postcode, householders, schools, garden centres and councils, can obtain tailor-made lists of local plants which are both hospitable and garden-worthy. Also included are the names of butterflies and birds most likely to visit gardens in each area. The lists come from innovative software, developed by Royal Mail and *FLORA-for-FAUNA* in conjunction with the Natural History Museum, which searches through hundreds of distribution maps of fauna and flora in the British Isles.

CHESHIRE

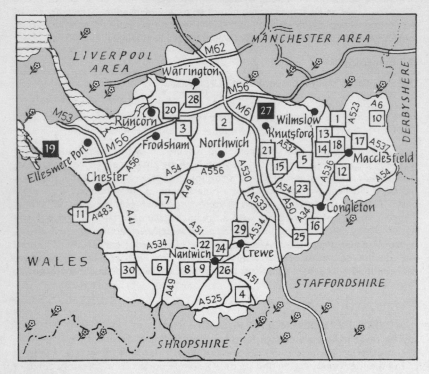

We have included some gardens with Cheshire postal addresses in the Manchester Area for convenience. So before planning a day out in Cheshire it is worthwhile consulting pages 289–293.

Two-starred gardens are marked on the map with a black square.

Adlington Hall 1

**Adlington, Macclesfield SK10 4LF. Tel: (01625) 820875;
E-mail: enquiries@adlingtonhall.com; Website: www.adlingtonhall.com**

Mrs C.J.C. Legh • 5m N of Macclesfield off A523. Signed in Adlington • Hall and garden open to parties by appt • Entrance: hall and garden £4.50, children £1.75, parties of 20 or more £4 per person (2001 prices) ● ● ✕ WC ◁ ●

An attractive woodland park, mostly landscaped in the eighteenth century in the style of 'Capability' Brown. To the porticoed Georgian south front of the house a gravelled carriage-sweep encircles an oval lawn with a sundial at its centre, then leads through a pair of iron gates to a short avenue of limes dating from 1688; a path then bears eastwards to the shell house, a small brick building of 1794 embellished with shells in the mid-nineteenth century. The wood to the west of the house offers pleasant walks, especially one along the small river bank. In the centre, close to the bridge, is a temple to Diana, and various follies in the eighteenth-century wilderness have been restored. Formal gardens created in front of the early Elizabethan north front of the house include a maze and rose garden and a herbaceous border. East of the house across a cobbled area is a formal pool with a large statue of Father Tiber.

Arley Hall and Gardens ★ 2

Arley, Great Budworth, Northwich CW9 6NA. Tel: (01565) 777353/777284; E-mail: enquiries@arleyestate.zuunet.co.uk; Website: www.arleyestate.zuunet.co.uk

Viscount Ashbrook • 5m W of Knutsford off A50, 7m SE of Warrington off A559. Signed from M6 junctions 19 and 20 and M56 junctions 9 and 10 • Hall open (times vary) • Garden open Easter to Sept, Tues – Sun and Bank Holiday Mons, 11am – 5pm, (unlikely to open weekends in April; check before travelling • Entrance: £4.50, reductions for OAPs and children (hall extra) (2001 prices) • Other information: Arley Garden Festival 29th and 30th June, 10am – 5pm ◑ 🍵 ✕ 🐀 WC ఉ 🐕 ℘ 🎃 ♀

One of the few remaining landed estates in Cheshire, this is the ancestral home of the Warburtons; the present hall dates from 1840. The gardens cover 12 acres. It is thought that one of the earliest herbaceous borders in England was planted here in 1846, and the 'garden room' concept may have been adopted from Elvaston (see entry in Derbyshire). Bounded by old brick walls and yew hedges, there is a special predilection for topiary, as evidenced in the splendid avenue of pleached limes which forms the approach to the house, and the remarkable ilex avenue clipped to the shape of giant cylinders. The walled garden, once a kitchen garden, now contains a variety of cordoned fruit trees, shrubs and herbaceous plants. There is also a collection of hybrid and species shrub roses, a rock garden planted with azaleas and rhododendrons, and the Grove, featuring over 200 varieties of rhododendrons, exotic trees and shrubs.

Bluebell Cottage Gardens (Lodge Lane Nursery)) 3

Lodge Lane, Dutton, Nr Warrington WA4 4HP. Tel/Fax: (01928) 713718; Website: www.bluebellcottagegardens.co.uk

Rod and Diane Casey • 4m SE of Runcorn, 6m NW of Northwich, S of A533. Signposted • Nursery open mid-March to mid-Sept, Wed – Sun and Bank Holiday Mons, 10am – 5pm. Gardens, meadow and woodland open May to Aug, Fri, Sat, Sun and Bank Holiday Mons, 10am – 5pm. Parties by appt • Entrance: Gardens, meadow and woodland £2, children free ◑ WC ఉ ℘ ♀

Set around an old cottage, the gardens include three acres of woodland, three acres of wildflower meadow and a large well-run nursery. Clustered around the cottage are a number of small gardens divided by hedges and trellises covered in climbers. Each is devoted to a different theme: herb garden, yellow garden, raised vegetable garden, the mandatory area of grasses and a patio with a large collection of pelargoniums and other tender perennials grown in pots. In a larger open area to the side of the house a scree bed runs down to a pool backed by a well-planted herbaceous border. Beds of penstemons and asters provide colour at the tail end of the year. A plantperson's garden with over 3000 different varieties on display.

Bridgemere Garden World 4

Bridgemere, Nantwich CW5 7QB. Tel: (01270) 521100; Fax: (01270) 520215; Website: www.bridgemere.co.uk

On A51 7m SE of Nantwich. Signed from M6 junctions 15 and 16 • Open all year, daily except 25th, 26th Dec, 9am – dusk (summer 8pm, winter 5pm) • Entrance: free ○ 🍴 ✕ <u>WC</u> & 🌿 ♨ ⚱ ℃

The 25-acre garden centre claims to be one of Europe's largest. There are some 5000 different plants for sale, pots and water features. The main area of interest is over 20 different gardens. These include The Hill (containing dwarf or slow-growing plants), cottage, rhododendron and azalea, winter, rock and water gardens, a French rose garden and a folly garden, a Victorian garden and the re-created 'best in show' garden from the Tatton Park Flower Show, patio areas, and silver-grey, autumn, herbaceous and annual borders. All this plus woodlands and lawns.

Capesthorne Hall and Gardens ★ 5

Macclesfield SK11 9JY. Tel: (01625) 861221; Fax: (01625) 861619; E-mail: info@capesthorne.com; Website: www.capesthorne.com

Mr W.A. Bromley Davenport • 7m S of Wilmslow, 1m S of Monks Heath on A34 • House open as gardens but 1.30 – 3.30pm only • Gardens open April to Oct, Wed, Sun and Bank Holidays, 12 noon – 5pm • Entrance: gardens and chapel £4, OAPs £3, children (5–18) £2 (hall extra charge)(2001 prices) • Other information: Lunches, teas and suppers by arrangement. Dogs and picnics in park only ◐ 🍴 <u>WC</u> & ♨ ℃

A fine historic park which illustrates the English style of eighteenth- and nineteenth-century landscape design, with belts of trees enclosing a broad sweep of park and the house as the focal element. The gardens are best enjoyed by following the suggested woodland walks, because the outstanding features are the range of mature trees and the views and plants associated with the series of man-made lakes. There is much, too, to interest those with a taste for the history of gardens – for example, the site of a conservatory built by Sir Joseph Paxton, and a pair of outstanding Rococo Milanese gates. The formal lakeside garden was designed in the 1960s by Vernon Russell-Smith.

Cherry Hill 6

Malpas SY14 7EP.

Mr and Mrs Miles Clarke • 6m NW of Whitchurch, 2m W of Malpas off A41. From B5069 turn N at Cuddington Heath towards Chorlton and continue for 1m; garden is on left • Open one day in June for NGS, 2 – 6pm, and by appt • Entrance: £2.50, children under 16 £1 ◑ 🍴 📷 <u>WC</u> & ⬦ ℃

A pleasant mix of the formal and informal. The formal is to be found within an old walled garden divided into different areas, all with a strong geometric design. A path through the centre leads under a rose-covered pergola, through a double border of peonies, under another rose pergola and finally to a double herbaceous border, where soft blues and pinks are picked out by a purple prunus hedge. On one side of the walk is a rectangle of lawn bisected by a rill surrounded by lavender, shrub roses and cherry trees, with a rose-covered arbour looking over a knot garden. On the other side of the walk is a neatly kept *potager*, a fine old greenhouse and a collection of shrub roses. Outside the formal area a long sweep of lawn drops away from the house with the magnificent backdrop of the Welsh hills to a trout pool with specimen ducks and black swans. A woodland walk leads to the pavilion and cricket ground.

Cheshire Herbs   7

Fourfields, Forest Road, Tarporley CW6 9ES. Tel: (01829) 760578

Libby and Ted Riddell • 9m E of Chester, on A49 close to crossroads with A54 • Open daily except 24th Dec to 3rd Jan, 10am – 5pm • Entrance: free ○ WC
& ⟨⟩ ✿ ⊞

This is principally a nursery stocking some 400 varieties of herbs, but there is also a small garden in a lawned area enclosed by a yew hedge. It is a circular knot garden small enough to be emulated by most gardeners; the raised bank around it reminds us that such gardens are best seen from a higher level. Beyond is a larger area of beds, again circular in pattern, containing many herbs and planted in an informal manner. There is also a polytunnel full of large tubs of plants. The aroma here and in other parts of the nursery makes a visit more than worthwhile.

Cholmondeley Castle Gardens ★   8

Cholmondeley Castle, Malpas SY14 8AH. Tel: (01829) 720383

The Marquess of Cholmondeley • On A49 between Tarporley and Whitchurch • Open April to Oct, Wed, Thurs, Sun and Bank Holiday Mons, 11.30am – 5pm, and on other days by prior appt for parties of 20 or more • Entrance: £3, children £1.50 (2001 prices) ◐ ☞ ✕ ▤ WC ⟨⟩ ✿ ⊞ ☗

Although the family has lived at Cholmondeley since the twelfth century, the present castle (not open) dates from the early nineteenth century. The park and gardens were laid out in the nineteenth century and have been extensively replanted since the 1960s. The site is magnificent, with the castle straddling a hill-top and a view across parkland to two meres full of wildfowl, and the garden's attractive setting is enhanced by mature trees and interesting plants. The Temple Garden – containing two islands in the small lake, a rock garden, two waterfalls and many colourful moisture-loving plants – is particularly satisfying, and there are new grass beds between the Temple Garden and the house. The grass round the tea room is filled with wild orchids and backed by a good planting of rhododendrons – indeed rhododendrons and azaleas feature throughout. The rose garden has an interesting mixture of old and new species.

Dorfold Hall 9

Chester Road, Acton, Nantwich CW5 8LD. Tel: (01270) 625245

Mr R. Roundell • 1m W of Nantwich, S of A534 • Hall open • Garden open April to Oct, Tues and Bank Holiday Mons, 2 – 5pm • Entrance: £5, children £3 ◖ &

The hall, impressive from the front, is approached along an avenue of limes with open parkland to each side and a large pool just to the west. The approach was laid out by William Nesfield. To the rear or south of the house is a large lawn, at the east side of which a statue of Shakespeare stands between two herbaceous borders. Beyond a low wall another large lawn has views across a ha-ha to flat countryside. A broad grass walk leads eastwards to a dell, where the present owner has planted rhododendrons and other acid-loving shrubs amongst mature trees around a small stream. To the west is another grassed area with specimen trees and two fine gates.

Dunge Valley Gardens 10

Windgather Rocks, Kettleshulme, Whaley Bridge, High Peak SK23 7RF.
Tel: (01663) 733787; E-mail: gardens@dungevalley.co.uk;
Website: www.dungevalley.co.uk

David and Elizabeth Ketley • 12m SE of Stockport in Kettleshulme. Signed from B5470 Macclesfield – Whaley Bridge road • Open April to Aug, Tues – Sun, but open Bank Holiday Mons; March, Sat and Sun (plant sales only); all 10.30am – 6pm • Entrance: £3, children 50p, season ticket £4.50 • Other information: Mini-buses up to 12 seats only. Telephone for appt at other times to buy plants at Hardy Plant Nursery ◖ ☕ ✗ WC ✿

Nestling in a small valley high up in the Peak District, every view is provided with a marvellous backdrop by the surrounding hills. Alpines grow around the terrace, and beds of diverse herbaceous plants and shrubs surround the old stone farmhouse. From here a number of walks spread out. One leads into the rhododendron dell, where amongst a great variety of rhododendrons and azaleas there are also acers, magnolias and other shrubs. There are perennials, too, mainly moisture-lovers as a small stream keeps this area damp. Another walk, also planted with rhododendrons, goes around the side of the valley and joins the stream further up; seats have been positioned carefully at the best viewpoints back down the valley. Shrub and species roses are plentiful, giving further interest after the rhododendrons have finished.

Eaton Hall ★ 11

Eccleston, Chester CH4 9ET. Tel: (01244) 684400

The Duke of Westminster • 4m S of Chester off A483 Chester – Wrexham road • Gardens probably open three Sundays in spring and summer, 1.30 – 5.30pm • Entrance: £2.50, children £1 (2001 prices) • Other information: Chapel open ◕ ☕ WC &

The gardens and parkland surrounding the modern hall are vast. There are several fine features: well-kept herbaceous beds, two laburnum tunnels and many stone statues and urns. A long, narrow greenhouse contains camellias, and a deep bed backing against the walled garden is planted for dramatic effect with hot-coloured perennials and shrubs such as cotinus and dark-flowering buddleia. There is also a large lake covered with water lilies, and a small Gothic-style cottage with stone and brick paths, set within its own small garden of herbs. Close to the house is the imposing Italian garden surrounded by a high yew hedge; a large dragon fountain stands at the centre of a pool, and there are beds of annuals and more statues. Arabella Lennox-Boyd has been working on the garden for several years.

Gawsworth Hall 12

Macclesfield SK11 9RN. Tel: (01260) 223456; Fax (01260) 223469

Mr and Mrs T. Richards • 3m S of Macclesfield off A536. Signposted • Hall open • Garden open Easter to mid June, Sun – Wed and Bank Holiday Mons; mid-June to Aug, daily; Sept to early Oct, Sun – Wed; all 2 – 5pm • Entrance: hall, park and garden £4.50, children under 16 £2.10, parties of 20 or more £3 per person (2001 prices) • Other information: Open-air theatre in garden mid-June to mid-Aug ◑ ☕ WC ♿ ⬛ ♀

The hall is approached by a drive leading between two lakes to the north end, where there is a large yew tree and lawns sloping down to one of the rhododendron-fringed lakes. A formal garden on the west side has beds of modern roses edged with bright annuals and many stone ornaments, including a sundial and a circular pool with a fountain. Stone steps lead to a sunken lawn and mixed beds. To the south is another lawned garden surrounded by a high yew hedge and herbaceous borders. A grassed area containing mature trees lies to the west of these formal areas, from where there is a view of the medieval tilting ground and the site of the Elizabethan pleasure gardens. A path back to the house passes a small conservatory containing classical statues.

Hare Hill Gardens 13

Hare Hill, Over Alderley, Macclesfield SK10 4QB. Tel: (01025) 828981

The National Trust • 5m NW of Macclesfield, N of B5087 between Alderley Edge and Prestbury at Greyhound Road • Open April to Oct, Wed, Thurs, Sat, Sun and Bank Holiday Mons, 10am – 5.30pm. Special opening for rhododendrons and azaleas 10th to 30th May, daily, 10am – 5.30pm. Parties by written appt • Entrance: £2.50, children £1.25. £2 per car refundable on entry to garden • Other information: Picnics at lakeside only ◑ WC ♿

There are two distinct areas here: a walled garden, once used for growing vegetables, and surrounding it a large woodland garden. Climbing plants around the walls include vines, roses, ceanothus and wisteria, and in the centre are rose beds with statues; a seat set into the north wall is surrounded by a white trellis pergola. The woodland garden contains over 50 varieties of holly, many fine rhododendrons and magnolias, spring-flowering bulbs and some roses climbing high into their host trees; a central pond is spanned by two wooden bridges.

Henbury Hall ★ 14

Macclesfield SK11 9PJ.

Mr S.Z. de Ferranti • 2m W of Macclesfield on A537 • Open one day for NGS • Entrance: £2.50, children £1 ● ● WC

The hall was built in 1986 based on Palladio's Villa Rotunda, and the French limestone goes well with its parkland setting. To the north the land slopes down to a lake with ornamental bridges at each end. The 12 acres are well landscaped and planted with many mature trees, azaleas and rhododendrons. Further north the land rises again, and beyond more banks of trees and shrubs is a walled garden with a double herbaceous border and a laburnum arch. Close by is a unique design of tennis court and a large modern conservatory housing a swimming pool, a fernery and a grotto. At the other side of the walled garden a cottage has recently been renovated in the Gothic style.

Jodrell Bank Arboretum 15

Jodrell Bank Science Centre and Arboretum, Macclesfield SK11 9DL.
Tel: (01477) 571339; Fax: (01477) 571695;
E-mail: visitorcentre@jb.man.ac.uk; Website: www.jb.man.ac.uk/scicen/

Manchester University • On A535 between Holmes Chapel and Chelford, 5m NE of M6 junction 18. Signposted • Open mid-March to Oct, daily, 10.30am – 5.30pm; Nov to mid-March, Tues to Sun, 11am – 4.30pm. Closed several days over Christmas and New Year – telephone to check • Entrance: £4.90, OAPs £3.50, children £2.50 (under 4 free, but not admitted to Planetarium), family £14.50 (2001 prices) ● ● ✕ ● WC ● ● ●

The arboretum, begun in 1972 largely at the instigation of Professor Sir Bernard Lovell, is set in a flat landscape with all views to the west dominated by the massive radiotelescope. The large collection of trees covers 35 acres and includes National Collections of malus and sorbus. There is also a collection of hornbeams and shrubs such as berberis, fine specimens of *Ulmus minor* (syn. *U. elegantissima*) 'Jacqueline Hillier' and the cut-leaved form of the common walnut (*Juglans regia* 'Laciniata'). Broad grass walkways lead among the trees, and small natural ponds are dotted around the garden. There are also beds of shrub roses, heathers and azaleas. A new apple orchard is based on varieties that originated in Cheshire. A day out for the family and good value when all the attractions are considered.

Little Moreton Hall 16

Congleton CW12 4SD. Tel: (01260) 272018; Fax: (01260) 292802;
E-mail: mlmsca.smtp@ntrust.org.uk

The National Trust • 4m SW of Congleton on E side of A34 between Congleton and Newcastle-under-Lyme • Open 31st March to 4th Nov, Wed – Sun, Bank Holiday Mons and Good Friday, 11.30am – 5pm (last admission 4.30pm); 10th Nov to 22nd Dec, Sat and Sun, 11.30am – 4pm • Entrance: £4.40, children £2.20, family £11, group entry, £3.50 per person (hall and gardens); joint ticket with Biddulph Grange (see entry in Staffordshire) £6.75, children

£3.30, family £16.50 • Other information: Wheelchair and scooter for loan. Guide dogs and hearing dogs permitted, but other dogs in areas outside moat only ◑ 🍽 ✕ <u>WC</u> ঙ ⌘ 🖐 ♀

The hall is one of the best-known and most astonishing timber-framed buildings in the country, and its gardens are pleasant in their own quiet way. Largely the creation of the Trust and a fitting complement to the house, they cover about an acre and are set within a moat. The hall has a central cobbled courtyard and is surrounded by herbaceous borders; a gravel walk follows the inside perimeter of the moat. To the west is a large lawn with fruit trees and an old grassed mound, to the north a yew tunnel and a knot garden laid out under the guidance of Graham Stuart Thomas following a seventeenth-century model – a simple design of gravel and lawn separated by a low box hedge. Behind the knot garden, four beds have been planted with medieval and culinary herbs and a selection of seventeenth-century vegetables.

Lodge Lane Nursery

(see BLUEBELL COTTAGE)

Mellors Gardens   17

Hough Hole House, Sugar Lane, Rainow, Macclesfield SK10 5UW. Tel: (01625) 573251

Mr and Mrs A. Rigby • From Macclesfield take B5470 Whaley Bridge road. In Rainow turn off to N opposite church into Round Meadow, then turn first left into Sugar Lane and follow down to garden • Open 3rd June, 26th Aug for charity, 2 – 5pm, and by appt for parties (10 persons min.) • Entrance: £1.50, children free ◑ WC

Where can you pass through the Valley of the Shadow of Death, climb Jacob's Ladder, see the Mouth of Hell and visit the Celestial City, all within the space of ten minutes? Here, in a valley in a rugged but attractive part of the Peak District, in the second half of the nineteenth century, James Mellor, much influenced by Swedenborg, designed a unique allegorical garden which attempts to re-create the journey of Christian in Bunyan's *Pilgrim's Progress*. There are many small stone houses and other ornaments to represent features of the journey. Most areas are grassed, with stone paths running throughout; at one end a large pond is overlooked by an octagonal summerhouse. Excellent guide book.

The Mount   18

Andertons Lane, Whirley, Macclesfield SK11 9PB.

Mr and Mrs Nicholas Payne • 2m W of Macclesfield off A537. Turn into Pepper Street opposite Blacksmith's Arms, and left into Church Lane which becomes Andertons Lane. The Mount is 200 metres further on. Signposted • Open one day a year for NGS, and by appt at other times for parties of 10 or more. Parties by written appt • Entrance: £3, children 50p ◑ 🍽 WC ঙ ⌘

The two-acre garden, originally planted in the 1920s but enlarged, improved and replanted over the past 16 years by the present owners, is a fine setting for the Regency house. Each distinct area has its own individual style. The terraced garden has an Italian feel, with a swimming pool, many architectural features and brightly planted terracotta pots. The shade garden is more informal, with rhododendrons, azaleas and camellias underplanted with hostas and other shade-lovers. A lawned area has an herbaceous border; opposite is another small border planted entirely with astilbes, and a conservatory containing a climbing pelargonium. In one corner of the garden an area of grass has been cut to different heights, forming patterns and paths leading to an obelisk looking across the Cheshire plain towards Wales.

Ness Botanic Gardens ★★   19

Neston Road, Ness, Wirral, CH64 4AY. Tel: (0151) 353 0123;
Website: www.merseyworld.com./nessgardens/

University of Liverpool • 10m NW of Chester, 2m off A540 between Ness and Burton • Open daily except 25th Dec: March to Oct, 9.30am – 5pm; Nov to Feb, 9.30am – 4pm • Entrance: admission charge • Other information: Guide dogs only ○ ⬛ ✕ 🗎 WC ⬥ ⬩ 🏛 ⬤

Mr A. Bulley began gardening on this site in 1898, using seeds from plants collected for him by George Forrest, the noted plant hunter. His daughter, Lois Bulley, who gave the gardens to the University in 1948, was described in her *Times* obituary as 'an exceptional human being, born into wealth, which she rejected, a member of the Labour Party, Communist Party and Cheshire County Council, a Quaker, a fighter against racism and for social justice and equality, especially for women, a philanthropist with a shrewd business brain, a national benefactor of applied plant biotechnology and horticultural research'. Ness Gardens extend to over 60 acres. Those who have experience of the north-west winds blowing off the Irish Sea will marvel at the variety and exotic nature of the plant life. The secret is in trees planted as shelter belts. The aim has been to provide interest from spring, through the herbaceous and rose gardens of summer, to the heather and sorbus collections of autumn. There are in addition areas of specialist interest, such as the native plant garden, which houses plants raised from seed or cuttings from wild plants and is used for propagation or the re-stocking of natural habitats. With the creation of an academic chair at the gardens in 1991 there has been a positive move to increase on-site research. Specialisms include sorbus, betulas, salix, rhododendrons and primulas. Maps, coloured guides and interest trails are available.

Norton Priory Museum and Gardens ★   20

Tudor Road, Manor Park, Runcorn WA7 1SX. Tel: (01928) 569895;
E-mail: info@nortonpriory.org; Website: www.nortonpriory.org

The Norton Priory Museum Trust • From M56 junction 11 turn for Warrington and follow Norton Priory signs. From all other directions follow signs to Runcorn then Norton Priory signs • Gardens open Nov to March, daily, 12 noon – 4pm; April to Oct, weekdays, 12 noon – 5pm, Sat, Sun and Bank Holiday Mons, 12 noon – 6pm. Walled garden open March to Oct by prior arrangement •

Entrance: £3.75, OAPs and children £2.50, family £9.80 • Other information: Museum open. Teas and snacks in Museum ○ 🍽 🛍 <u>WC</u> & ⟳ 🌿 🍴 🔔 🐾

This is a garden of distinct halves. The woodland garden, covering 30 acres and containing many fine mature trees, surrounds the remains of the twelfth-century Augustinian priory. The stream glade is the most attractive area, planted with azaleas, candelabra primulas and astilbes; a water-lily tank has a statue of Coventina (goddess of wells and streams) at its centre. There are many modern sculptures dotted around both parts of the garden. At some distance to the north of the woodland garden is the clearly signposted walled garden, built in the mid-eighteenth century as a vegetable garden and redesigned on more ornamental lines. A rose walk runs down the centre – two broad borders contain a large variety of shrub roses, an orchard has many varieties of pear, plum, greengage and quince (the National Collection of *Cydonia oblonga*, tree quince, is held here). There is also a vegetable garden and a distinctive herb garden. Along the south-facing wall a series of brick arches, covered with vines and honey-suckle and sheltering two large figs, is fronted by beds of perennials, strongly planted with kniphofias, euphorbias, salvias and geums. Indeed the walled garden is a good illustration of the twin strengths of the garden as a whole – a bold, coherent design and its great variety of plants.

Peover Hall 21

Over Peover, Knutsford WA16 6SW.
Tel: (01565) 632358 (Tour Guide, I. Shepherd)

Mr R. Brooks • 4m S of Knutsford off A50 at Whipping Stocks Inn, down Stocks Lane, signposted • Hall open April to Oct, Mon only except Bank Holiday Mons, 2 – 5pm • Gardens open April to Oct, Mon and Thurs, 2 – 5pm • Entrance: £3, children £2 (hall, stables and garden £4.50, children £3) • Other information: Teas on Mon only. Possible for wheelchairs but many grass paths. Dogs in park only, on lead. Plants for sale on special occasions only ◑ **WC**

Peover Hall (pronounced Peever) and its 15-acre gardens are surrounded by a large expanse of flat parkland laid out in the early eighteenth century, but the gardens are mainly Edwardian. On the north side of the Elizabethan house a broad grass walk leads from the forecourt through an avenue of pleached limes to a summerhouse overlooking a small circular lawn; both are enclosed by a high yew hedge. On the west side of the gardens is a wooded area containing many rhododendrons and a particularly attractive grassy dell. Clustered around the south and west of the hall are small formal gardens – rose, herb, white and pink – separated by brick walls and yew hedges, some containing yew topiary. The lily-pool garden has a summerhouse with a tiled roof supported by Doric columns. Fine Carolean stables and a church to visit.

Queen's Park, Crewe 22

Victoria Avenue, Wistaston Road, Crewe CW2 7SE. Tel: (01270) 569176

Crewe and Nantwich Borough Council • 2m W of town centre, S of A530 • Open all year, daily, 9am – sunset • Entrance: free • Other information: Parking off Queen's Park Drive ○ 🍽 🛍 <u>WC</u> & ⟳ 🔔

The well-landscaped Victorian park, created in 1878, is oval in shape and covers 48 acres, with large grassed areas and a wide variety of mature trees. From the ornate entrance with two Gothick lodges and a clock tower, a drive leads through an avenue of birches to the centre of the park, where a café, overlooks the large boating lake surrounded by banks of trees and shrubs. From the west of the park a stream runs through a lightly wooded valley to join the lake. A path linking the entrance to this valley passes some raised beds of heathers and under a laburnum tunnel. There is also a scented garden for the disabled. It merits a high grade for the quality of landscaping, the trees and the Victorian buildings, but in essence it is a large municipal park where the fight against vandalism and litter is fought hard.

The Quinta ★   23

Swettenham, Congleton CW12 2LD.

Sir Bernard Lovell and Cheshire Wildlife Trust • 5m NW of Congleton, E of A535 Holmes Chapel – Alderley Edge road, near Tremlow Green in Swettenham, next to church • Open daily, 2 – 6pm, and for parties on weekdays by appt • Entrance: £2 • Other information: Teas on Sun openings only ☕

Sir Bernard Lovell began planting this garden in 1948 to satisfy his love of trees. It now contains a large variety of trees and shrubs. There are good collections of pines and birches, five of the six varieties of wingnut and an oriental plane directly descended from the Hippocratic tree on the island of Cos. Most areas are informally planted and interspersed with grassed glades; several avenues pass up and down the garden, including one of limes planted in 1958 to celebrate Sir Bernard's Reith lectures. Across the more recently planted areas to the west of the garden a walk (one mile from the car park and back), taking in some marvellous views across the Dane Valley (SSSI), leads to the 39 steps that descend into the wooded valley of a small brook.

Reaseheath College   24

Reaseheath, Nantwich CW5 6DF. Tel (01270) 625131; Fax (01270) 625665

Reaseheath College • 1½ m N of Nantwich on A51 • Open for College Open Days in May and 22nd, 29th May, 5th June, 1 – 5pm for NGS • Entrance: by donation. Guided tours available. Prices on application ☕ 🍽 🏪 WC ✿ ♿ ♟

The attractive gardens must provide the College's students with constant inspiration. From the old brick hall a large lawn sweeps southwards to a lake, flanked on one side by a heather garden and on the other by a rockery. The lake is spanned by a wooden bridge and stocked with a variety of water lilies and marginals. On the south side is a woodland garden with many fine trees, including a large cut-leaf beech. Underplanting is of primulas, hostas, azaleas and other shade-loving plants. To the west of the lake another lawned area has island beds with a variety of small trees, shrubs and perennials. Other interests include a new garden with water features, a herb garden, a model fruit garden, a range of glasshouses and a nursery.

Rode Hall 25

Church Lane, Scholar Green, via Stoke on Trent ST7 3QP. Tel: (01270) 882961; Fax: (01270) 882962

Sir Richard and Lady Baker Wilbraham • 5m SW of Congleton between A34 and A50 • House open as garden from 1st April, Wed and Bank Holidays only. Also for parties by appt at other times • Garden open 6th to 24th Feb (for snowdrops), 12 noon – 4pm; 1st April to 26th Sept, Tues – Thurs and Bank Holidays, 2 – 5pm; plus 12th May for NGS, 2 – 5pm. Also for parties by appt at other times • Entrance: £2.50, OAPs £1.50 (house and garden £4, OAPs £2.50. Special parties at other times £7, including tea) ◑ ☕ WC ⬧ ⌗

A long drive leads through parkland to an attractive red brick house with fine stable buildings. The gardens lie to the north and east, with many areas remaining as planned by Repton in 1790. The rose garden and formal areas were designed by Nesfield in 1860; these are mainly lawn, with gravel paths and clipped yews, and good views from here of the surrounding countryside and Repton's lake. In a dell to the west is a woodland garden with hellebores and flowering shrubs, rhododendrons, azaleas and some fine climbing roses. Old stone steps lead up the opposite side of the dell to a grotto and early-nineteenth-century terraced rock garden. A small stream is dammed at the open end of the dell with the resulting pond surrounded by marginals; a path leads from here to the lake. The two-acre Georgian walled kitchen garden is at its best in June, July and August. The ice-house in the park is also worth a visit.

Stapeley Water Gardens 26

London Road, Stapeley, Nantwich CW5 7LH. Tel: (01270) 623868; Fax: (01270) 624919; E-mail: www.stapeleywg@btinternet.com; Website: www.stapeleywatergardens.com

Mr R.G.A. Davies • 1m SE of Nantwich on A51. Signed from M6 junction 16 • Open all year, daily except 31st March, 25th Dec. Opening and closing times vary from 9am/10am and 4pm/8pm • Entrance: Display gardens free. The Palms Tropical Oasis £3.85, OAPs £3.40, children £2.15, parties of 15 or more £3.40 per person, OAPs £2.85, children £1.85. Season tickets available • Other information: Wheelchairs available ○ ☕ ✕ WC ♿ ⌗ 🍴 🔦 ⚲

Two acres of garden shopping under cover form the world's largest water garden centre. Within it a few areas are attractive gardens in their own right. At the back are many pools containing the largest display of aquatic plants and the land around is landscaped with lawns and shrub borders. Another area has small demonstration gardens. Across the car park is The Palms Tropical Oasis. This huge greenhouse has none of the architectural merit of a Victorian palm house, but the main hall is impressive, with a long rectangular pool flanked by huge palm trees, a display from the Manchester Museum of the World of Frogs, and other exhibits. Those with an interest in water gardens might comment that this is a bleak description – think of the giant *Victoria amazonica* water lily from Brazil, the rare breeding sting-rays, the *Nymphaea gigantea* from Australia. Ooh-aah! And an angling centre for the non-horticultural.

Tatton Park ★★ 27

Knutsford WA16 6QN. Tel: (01625) 534400

Cheshire County Council/The National Trust • 10m SE of Warrington. Signed from M6 and M56 • House open April to Oct, 12 noon – 4pm • Gardens open April to Sept, daily, 10.30am – 6pm, Oct to 25th March 2003, daily, except 25th Dec, 11am – 4pm • Entrance: gardens £3, children £2, family £8, park £3.60 per car, Discovery Saver Ticket (to any two attractions excluding park entry) £4.60, children £2.60 (2001 prices) • Other information: RHS Flower Show 17th to 21st July ○ 💭 ✕ wc ⛓ ⌗ 🏛 🕯

The gardens cover 50 acres and warrant extensive exploration; however, time your visit time carefully if you don't like crowds. Near the entrance is the orangery, built in 1820 by Lewis Wyatt and recently restored to his original 1818 plan, which contains orange trees, lemon trees and plants of the period. Next door is Paxton's huge fernery of 1850. This has large New Zealand tree ferns in its distinctively Victorian interior. To the east, passing a large L-shaped herbaceous and shrub border, the Edwardian rose garden is formal in design with a pool at its centre and fine stone paths and ornaments around. To the south lie informally planted areas, an arboretum with many conifers and rhododendrons, and a lake containing water lilies and a good variety of marginals. On the west side of the lake is a unique Japanese garden built in 1910 by workers brought especially from Japan, and now restored and new features created. Visitors now sees a wonderful two-dimensional picture as they walk up the western side of the garden. Azaleas are colourful in their season. The nearby Broadwalk leads to the Choragic Monument. To the south of the house is the Italian garden, possibly designed by Paxton and best viewed from the top floor of the house. A Lottery grant to restore the walled kitchen gardens has initiated a huge programme of work, which should be completed in 2002. The garden also contains a maze and is surrounded by 1000 acres of attractive parkland. The RHS Flower Show, a major event in the horticultural calendar, takes place here.

Walton Hall Gardens 28

Walton Lea Road, Higher Walton, Warrington WA4 6SN. Tel: (01925) 601617; Fax: (01925) 861868; E-mail: waltonhall@warrington.gov.uk; Website: www.warrington.gov.uk

Warrington Borough Council • 2m SW of Warrington on S side of A56 in Walton • Open all year, daily, 8am – dusk • Entrance: free • Other information: Pay-and-display car park. Plants for sale on Suns only. Heritage centre, children's zoo and play area, pitch and putt, crazy golf, bowls ○ 💭 🍽 wc ⛓ ⌒ 🏛 🕯 ⚲

The gardens are dominated by the dark brick Victorian mansion with its distinctive clock tower. To one side of the building a large pool containing carp and terrapins is backed by an impressive rockery well planted with azaleas, rhododendrons, birches and other small shrubs and trees. Water cascades down the rocks to a pool planted with water lilies and marginals, including a clump of gunneras. Behind the hall is a series of formal gardens separated by yew hedges and low stone walls and containing beds of bright tulips and annuals. Beyond some large beech trees, modern roses are set out in formal beds. The walk back down the west side of the garden passes through light woodland with a collection of camellias and some fine acers and magnolias. The council keeps these gardens in good condition; a Ranger Service organises public events.

85 Warmingham Road 29

Coppenhall, Crewe CW1 4PS. Tel: (01270) 582030

Mr and Mrs A. Mann • 3m N of Crewe off A530 between Warmingham and Leighton Hospital near White Lion Inn • Open probably March to July by appt for parties of up to 40 • Entrance: £2, children free ● ● WC ⚘ ♞

Two-thirds of an acre with a small woodland, a large herbaceous border and a good display of hellebores and snowdrops. Many and various alpines are to be found here. In the first section of the garden, paths run among lushly planted beds lightly shaded by trees. There are perennials and small shrubs as well as a collection of lilies. A small pond in the centre is planted with marginals such as golden sedge. Beyond this area is a lighter, more open section containing gravel screes, a rock garden and a peat bed. Diascias, violas and geraniums abound. There are also two greenhouses, one with a good collection of cacti and succulents.

The Well House 30

Tilston, Malpas SY14 7DP. Tel: (01829) 250332

Mrs S.H. French-Greenslade • 12m S of Chester on A41. Turn right after Broxton roundabout, then on Malpas road through Tilston. Garden is at antique shop • Open one day for NGS, 2 – 5.30pm, and March to July by appt • Entrance: £2, children 25p (2001 prices) • Other information: Plants for sale sometimes ● ● WC ⚒ ♞

A one-acre garden set around a small natural stream, well worth visiting both for the range of plants grown and the natural landscaping of the site. Close to the house is a geometric layout of beds containing perennials such as campanulas and alstroemerias, backed by a rose-covered pergola and with a sundial at the centre. There is also an area devoted to rock plants and a patio on which a large number of plants are grown in containers – an inspiration for those with small gardens. Another area has plants chosen for foliage colour, including yellow robinia, purple berberis and silver pyrus. Moisture-lovers, including many ferns, line the stream that divides the garden, and a bridge leads across to a small hexagonal summerhouse. The land rises steeply from the stream, giving views back over the garden, and another fine view can be had from the balcony, where tea may be taken.

CORNWALL

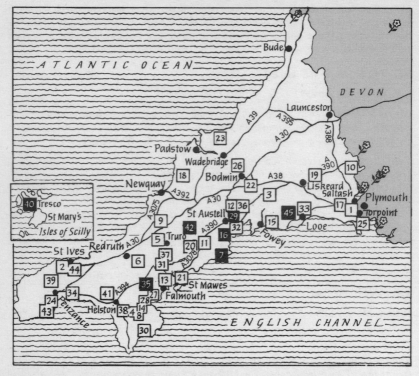

Two-starred gardens are marked on the map with a black square.

Antony ★ 1

Torpoint PL11 2QA. Tel: (01752) 812364

The National Trust and Trustees of Carew Pole Garden Trust • 2m W of Torpoint on A374, 16m SE of Liskeard. From Plymouth use Torpoint car ferry • House open as formal garden • Formal garden open 26th March to 1st Nov, Tues – Thurs and Bank Holiday Mons; also June to Aug, Sun, all 1.30 – 5.30pm (last admission 4.45pm). Woodland garden open March to Oct, Tues – Thurs, Sat, Sun and Bank Holiday Mons, 11am – 5.30pm • Entrance: £3; combined gardens only £3.60 (house and formal garden £4.20, children £2.10, pre-booked parties £3.50 per person, family ticket £10.50) (2001 prices) ◑ ☕ ✕ 🍴 <u>WC</u> ♿ 🏛*

Antony is a little off the beaten track, but it is well worth the effort to visit one of the country's finest early-eighteenth-century houses, in a truly magnificent natural setting. The house and adjacent formal gardens now belong to the Trust, while the woodland gardens, which lie between the parkland and the

River Lynher and are also open, belong to the family trust. The formal gardens, with a terrace round the house, wide lawns, extensive vistas, yew hedges and old walls, are of the highest quality. Eighteenth-century statues, modern sculpture and topiary are features of the yew walk and of the formal compartments of the summer garden; the latter includes a pleached lime hedge, mixed shrub and herbaceous borders with roses, and a knot garden. The woodland gardens have a separate car park, and the printed garden guide is numbered from here. There are fine walks along the river banks. The woodland gardens, also known as the wilderness – the central section – include Jupiter Hill and a late-Georgian bath house and are planted with superb camellias, magnolias and rhododendrons, with scented rhododendrons outstanding in May. In the neighbouring woodland walk there is a ruined fifteenth-century dovecote and Richard Carew's sixteenth-century Fishful Pond. Few years go by without some stylish addition to the gardens and parkland. Last year was no exception. A standing stone of purest Cornish granite was erected on top of Jupiter Hill in memory of Sir Richard Carew Pole's parents, who created the woodland gardens before he himself, as befits the new President of the Royal Horticultural Society, set his own mark on the gardens we see today. The National Trust garden contains a National Collection of hemerocallis (610 cultivars) and the woodland gardens contain the National Collection of Camellia japonica (300 cultivars).

Barbara Hepworth Museum and Sculpture Garden 2

Barnoon Hill, St Ives TR26 1AD. Tel: (01736) 796226

Administered by The Tate Gallery • In centre of St Ives. Signposted • Open all year, Tues – Sun, and Mons in July and Aug, 10.30am – 5.30pm • Entrance: museum and sculpture garden £3.75, OAPs £2 ○ **WC**

The sculpture garden, within walking distance of the new St Ives Tate Gallery (itself well worth a visit), represents a permanent exhibition of Hepworth's work and has been awarded special historic interest status by English Heritage. It is distinctly Mediterranean in atmosphere, interconnected by intricate pathways; native trees and semi-tropical flowers enhance the setting. She lived and worked in the house (restored after the fire in which she died in 1996), designed the garden with the South African composer Priaulx Rainier, and placed the sculptures herself. It is, as the art critic Richard Cork has said, a marvellous expression of her total aesthetic.

Boconnoc 3

The Stewardry, Boconnoc, Lostwithiel PL22 0RG. Tel: (01208) 872546

Mr and Mrs J.D.G. Fortescue • Between Lostwithiel and Liskeard, S of A390. Well-signed on open days between Lostwithiel and Middle Taphouse • Open for various charities 28th April, 5th, 12th, 19th, 26th May, 2 – 5pm • Entrance: £2, children free ● ▬ **WC** & ⬧ ⚘ 🏛 ♛ ⚭

The extensive grounds, with great landscape effects, were first laid out by Thomas Pitt, Lord Camelford, in the eighteenth century. The magnificent woodland garden, covering some 20 acres, contains fine flowering shrubs and many large and unusual trees. It is best seen by taking a walk along the well-kept paths. Not far away in Lostwithiel is the *Duchy of Cornwall Nursery*, reputed to be the best garden centre in the county (Tel: (01208) 872668).

Bosahan ★ 4

Manaccan, Helston TR12 6JL. Tel: (01326) 231351

Mr and Mrs R.J. Graham-Vivian • 10m SE of Helston, 1m NE of Manaccan • Open by appt for parties of 6 or more • Entrance: £4 per person • Other information: Coach companies must confirm dates in advance ● 💺 WC ⬧ 🌿

This valley garden of five acres, started 100 years ago, leads down to the Helford river and will give pleasure to the keen plantsman for its mature and more recently planted trees and shrubs, including some New Zealand and South American varieties and many palms (*Trachycarpus fortunei*). A giant magnolia stands near the house. Spring colour is provided by masses of camellias, rhododendrons, azaleas and magnolias, along with bog plants in the water garden. Walking down through the gardens, the visitor comes to a valley leading to more mature specimens, including pittosporums and dicksonias. Fine views from the top of the valley.

Bosvigo ★ 5

Bosvigo Lane, Truro TR1 3NH. Tel/Fax: (01872) 275774; Website: www.bosvigo.com

Mr Michael and Mrs Wendy Perry • ¾ m W of Truro. From A390, turn into Dobbs Lane adjacent to Sainsbury foodstore roundabout. Entrance is 500 metres down lane on left, just after sharp left bend • Open March to Sept, Thurs – Sat, 11am – 6pm • Entrance: £3, children £1, under-5s free • Other information: Rare and unusual plants for sale at nursery ◖ WC 🌿

An immaculately maintained garden of great artistry and imagination. The three acres surrounding the Georgian house consist of several delightful enclosed and walled areas. The hot garden displays red, yellow and orange flowers, the Vean Garden white and yellow, and the walled garden many rare plants. Flowers and foliage are grouped with boldness or subtlety to enchanting effect. Not a typical Cornish garden (rhododendrons and camellias are banned), it is at its best in summer when the mainly herbaceous plants start their display. A few miles away is the recently opened 60-acre *Tregothnan Estate*, private garden of the Boscawen family. For the first time in its 400-year history, organised visits are being arranged under the guidance of the head gardener. Previously unknown except by *cognoscenti* or family, it is home to part of the Edinburgh Royal Botanic Garden's collection of rare and endangered conifers and to the collection of rhododendrons, rare trees and the earliest outdoor planting of camellias in this country made by the sixth Viscount Falmouth and his brother. Although not open to the public on a regular basis, individuals can join parties already booked (Tel: (01872) 520325).

Burncoose Gardens   6

Gwennap,Redruth TR16 6BJ. Tel: (01209) 860316; Fax: (01209) 860011;
E-mail: burncoose@eclipse.co.uk; Website: www.burncoose.co.uk

*Burncoose and Southdown Nurseries • On A393 Redruth – Falmouth road
between Lanner and Ponsanooth. Signposted • Open daily except 25th Dec,
8.30am – 5pm (Sun opens 11am) • Entrance: £2 , children free* [NEW] ○ ☕
🍴 WC ♿ ☂ 🌿 🛍 🔦 ⚲

This woodland garden, belonging to the Williams family of Caerhays Castle
(see entry), was laid out originally at the turn of the twentieth century; it is
now allied to the Burncoose Nurseries. It contains many fine camellias,
magnolias, rhododendrons, acers and other spring shrubs and ornamental
trees. Though the woodland extends to more than 30 acres, accessible by a
network of paths, the main planted areas lie either side of the main drive and
beside the pond. The devastating storm of December 1979 made room for
much new planting, now maturing.

Caerhays Castle Garden ★★   7

Caerhays, Gorran, St Austell PL26 6LY. Tel: (01872) 501310;
Fax: (01872) 501870; E-mail: estateoffice@caerhays.co.uk;
Website: www.caerhays.co.uk

*Mr F.J. Williams • 10m S of St Austell. On coast by Porthluney Cove between
Dodman Point and Nare Head • House open 18th March to 26th April, Mon –
Fri (excluding Bank Holidays), 1 – 4pm • Garden open 11th March to 31st
May, daily, 10am – 5.30pm, and for charity 31st March, 14th April, 6th May,
10am – 4.30pm • Entrance: £4.50, children £1.50 (on charity open days £2.50,
children free). House and garden £8, groups (minimum 15 persons) £3.50 •
Other information: Car park by beach; short walk to garden entrance* ● ☕ 🍴
WC ☂ 🌿

Unsurpassed in spring and one of the greatest of all Cornish and British gardens,
this has an international reputation which is well deserved. Principally a woodland garden, it stretches up and around the extensive hillside above the romantic
early-nineteenth-century castle. It can lay claim to a superlative collection of
camellias and rhododendrons and an unrivalled collection of magnolias. All of
these, as well as many other fine shrubs and trees, are not only huge themselves,
but bear flowers of a remarkable size and depth of colour. Many of the plants were
raised from material brought back by famous plant hunters or sent recently from
China; it was at Caerhays that the famous 'Williamsii' camellias were originally
propagated, and the National Collection of magnolias is held here. Half a day is
required to do justice to the garden at its peak.

Carwinion   8

Mawnan Smith, Falmouth TR11 5JA. Tel: (01326) 250258

*Mr and Mrs H.A.E. Rogers • 5m SW of Falmouth. From Mawnan Smith, take
left road by Red Lion. 500 metres up hill on right is white gate marked*

'Carwinion' • Open all year, daily, 10am – 5.30pm • Entrance: £2.50, children free (2001 prices) ○ 🍴 🏠 WC ♿ ⬦ 🐕

Twelve acres of wild woodland garden leading down to the Helford River, containing the most comprehensive collection of bamboos in the country, and large gunneras, and rhododendrons. There are some impressive camellias in the attached *Towan Camellia Nursery*. The most interesting part of the lower woodland area is on the right bank of the stream.

Chyverton ★ 9

Zelah, Truro TR4 9HD. Tel: (01872) 540324; Fax: (01872) 540648

Mr N. Holman • 12m NE of Redruth, 1m W of Zelah on A30. At end of bypass, turn N at Marazanvose; entrance is $\frac{1}{2}$ m on right • Open by appt only, preferably Feb to Sept, usually by personally conducted tour • Entrance: £5 (parties, minimum 20, £4) • Other information: Lunch or tea by arrangement for groups ● WC ⬦ ♘

Chyverton is one of the greatest and most magical of woodland gardens. It covers perhaps 140 acres, depending on the distinction between garden and woods, and is maintained virtually single-handedly by the owner, and without the use of chemical sprays. It has benefited from 70 years of unbroken planting, hence the outstanding collection of magnolias in particular, but also of rhododendrons, camellias, ferns and many other plants of the greatest interest; all thrive in an unspoilt setting which is certainly not over-manicured, aptly described by the owner as a 'magic jungle'. Many of the plants have been sent by collectors or botanical institutes, or direct from their native habitat. The garden surrounds the 1730s' house, which has a contemporary copper beech nearby, and stretches under mature trees along the floor of the adjacent valley. It is divided into 29 separate 'rooms', some of them given added interest by a collection of modern statues. A recent addition is a herbaceous border by the house.

Cotehele ★ 10

St Dominick, Saltash PL12 6TA. Tel: (01579) 351346

The National Trust • 8m SW of Tavistock, 4m SE of Gunnislake, 1m W of Calstock. Turn at St Anne's Chapel • House open 23rd March to 3rd Nov, daily except Fri (but open Good Friday), 11am – 5pm • Garden open daily, 10.30am – dusk • Mill open daily except Fri (but open Good Friday and Fris in July and Aug), 1pm – 5.30pm (6pm in July and Aug; 4.30pm in Oct) • Entrance: garden and mill £3.60 (house, garden and mill £6.40, pre-booked parties £5.40 per person) • Other information: Presentation of estate history given in Film Room. Picnics and dogs in woodland only ○ 🍴 ✕ 🏠 WC ♿ 🐕 🎁 🍺

There are two separate parts to this 14-acre garden. The upper gardens around the beautiful sixteenth-century house are largely formal, with courtyards, herbaceous borders, walls, yew hedges, fine lawns, a pool and a formally planted terrace falling away before the house. There is also a daffodil meadow, a grove of acers and an orchard. This area is probably at its peak in the late spring and early summer. The second part, the woodland valley garden, lies in the view below the formal terrace. Here beneath large conifers and hardwoods are many colourful flowers, shrubs and ornamental trees; rhododendrons and azaleas are especially striking in spring. Nearby a nineteenth-century river quay has fine views.

Creed House   11

Creed, Grampound TR2 4SL. Tel: (01872) 530372

Mr and Mrs W.R. Croggon • Mid-way between St Austell and Truro. Take A390 to Grampound, then road in main street signed 'To Creed'. After 1m, opposite Creed church, turn left. Entrance to house and garden on left • Open all year, daily, 10am – 5.30pm, and 12th May for NGS and 9th June for charity, 2 – 5.30pm • Entrance: £2.50, children free • Other information: Teas, toilet facilities and plant sales on charity open days only ○

The seven-acre garden, devotedly restored and developed over the last three decades by the present owners, surrounds a handsome Georgian former rectory and has views of the countryside through mature trees; below the lawn the delightful fish pond is a focal point. The fine trees and shrubs include camellias, magnolias and rhododendrons. A walled garden with summer planting is being developed behind the house, and there is a woodland walk above. For maximum enjoyment use the garden guide to be found beside the front door, and view the historical photographic montage in the stable-block garage.

Eden Project   12

Bodelva, St Austell PL24 2SG. Tel: (01726) 811911; Fax: (01726) 811912; Website: www.edenproject.com

1½ m off A391 NE of St Austell, or by Luxulyan Road, St Blazey Gate on A390 E of St Austell, or from A30 (all signposted). Open all year, daily, 10am – 6pm (last admission 5pm). Closed 24th and 25th December • Entrance: £9.50, OAPs £7.50, students £5, children 5-14 £4, under 5 free, family ticket £22 (2001 prices) ☕ ✕ WC ♿ 🌿 🏛 🍽 ⚲

This spectacular project – not a garden, rather an extremely successful educational theme park of botany and ecology – has been created from a vast disused china clay pit. It contains two huge, transparent geodesic lean-to conservatories and a landscaped area with a large waterfall and flowing river planted with species from Amazonia, West Africa, Malaysia and Oceania. These two 'biomes' provide a humid tropical and a warm temperate Mediterranean environment respectively, each planted accordingly. £80 million and worth every penny. It is a stunning experience for the whole family – indeed there are special events for children. Of course, some planting areas are not yet fully developed, and some imaginative activity will be required. However, while it is wise to time a visit carefully in terms of anticipated temperatures, public holidays or weekends, this visit to Cornwall is unmissable.

Fox Rosehill Gardens 13

Melville Road, Falmouth TR11 4DB. Tel: (01326) 319377

Carrick District Council • From A39 follow signs to beaches and hotels • Open all year, daily, 8am – dusk • Entrance: free • Other information: Plant sale in early June ○ 🍽 🚻 🎧 🍷

A truly remarkable long-established small park of two acres, famous for its many exotic trees and shrubs, including an *Embothrium coccineum* (Chilean firebush) and a *Syragus romanzoffiana* (queen palm). Most of the shrubs and trees, set amongst paths and two lawns, are labelled. A delight for the ordinary visitor and of great interest to the plantsman.

Glendurgan Garden ★ 14

Mawnan Smith, Falmouth TR11 5JZ. Tel: (01326) 250906

The National Trust • 4m SW of Falmouth, ½ m SW of Mawnan Smith on road to Helford Passage • Open 16th Feb to 2nd Nov, Mon to Fri and Bank Holiday Mons, 10.30am – 5.30pm (last admission 4.30pm). Closed 29th March • Entrance: £3.75, family £9.25, booked parties £3.25 ◑ 🍵 WC 🍷 🏛 ℀

One of the great sub-tropical gardens of the South-West. Forty acres in extent, it was originally planted by Alfred Fox in the 1820s in a valley with wonderful views of the Helford river, and the village of Durgan at its foot. The woodland valley contains many specimen trees and conifers, including gigantic tulip trees, a swamp cypress and the fastest-growing tree recorded in any Trust garden, a *Populus* 'Androscoggin' which has reached 24 metres in 14 years. Sub-tropical plants such as tree ferns, palms, bananas and the bird of paradise flower thrive here. Camellias, rhododendrons and magnolias, including a fine *Magnolia campbellii* 'Alba', flower in spring and early summer, as do primroses, bluebells, foxgloves, aquilegias and many wild flowers. In summer there are drimys, eucryphias, embothriums and hydrangeas. The 1833 laurel maze has a summer house at its heart, and there is also a Giant Stride for children. Fine views.

Headland 15

Battery Lane, Polruan–by–Fowey PL23 1PW. Tel: (01726) 870243; E-mail: hilljap@aol.com

John and Jean Hill • 8m E of St Austell off A3082. Passenger ferry from Fowey and 10-minute walk up hill. Or car ferry from Fowey to Bodinnick and follow signs for Polruan (3m). Ignore first car park, turn left for second car park, overlooking harbour. Turn left (on foot) down St Saviour's Hill • Open for charity 2nd May to 12th Sept, Thurs only, 2 – 6pm • Entrance: £2, children £1 • Other information: Beach for swimming ◑ 💜 WC

This unique garden, set on a steep cliff face with fine sea views, has been developed with great courage and ingenuity by the present owners. The narrow interlocking paths and archways reveal hidden areas and intimate seats on many different levels, which maximise the feeling of space. Despite the salt spray and gales, a fine collection of temperate, alpine, antipodean and sub-tropical plants with a sheltered aspect gives a colourful display, especially in summer. A path lined with trees and a steep flight of steps lead to a small sandy beach. This is a garden of tremendous character, but definitely not for the disabled, and small children should be supervised.

Heligan ★★ 16

Pentewan, St Austell PL26 6EN. Tel (01726) 845100; Fax: (01726) 845101; E-mail: info@heligan.com; Website: www.heligan.com

The Lost Gardens of Heligan • 5½ m S of St Austell off A390. Take B3273 signed 'Mevagissey' past Pentewan • Open all year, daily except 24th, 25th Dec, 10am – 6pm (last admission in summer 4.30pm; 3.30pm in winter). Guided tours by arrangement • Entrance: £6, OAPs £5.50, children (5–15) £3, family (2 adults and 3 children) £17 ○ 🍷 ✕ 🍴 WC ♿ 🚭 🐾 🛍 🔦 ♈

Started in the seventeenth century but neglected since 1914, the restoration of this 80-acre garden, is, rightly, a well-known story. A massive amount of work has been completed, though much remains to be done. The gardens consist of two principal parts. Around the house are more formal gardens, including an impressive walled flower garden, gardens in courtyards and other secluded compartments, fountains and sundials. Though the work is not yet complete, all is kept extremely tidy. The large lawn is enclosed by massive, mainly red, rhododendrons, some collected by Sir Joseph Hooker. The Jungle, some 10-minutes walk away, is a wild, beautiful and overgrown valley, in the process of being cleared, where rhododendrons, bamboo, ferns and moss-covered palms flourish. Beyond, the Lost Valley has two large lakes and an old mill pond. The Eden Project (see entry), also initiated by Tim Smit, is nearby.

Ince Castle 17

Saltash PL12 4QZ. Tel: (01752) 842249

Viscount and Viscountess Boyd of Merton • 3m SW of Saltash off A38 at Stoketon Cross. Turn at sign for Trematon and then for Elmgate • Open 17th March, 21st April, 12th May, 9th June, 21st July, 2 – 5pm, and for parties by appt • Entrance: £2.50, children under 14 free • Other information: Due to very narrow lanes, no large coaches. Picnics in car park only ● 🍷 ♿ 🚭 ♈

Five acres of formal and informal gardens are knit together here by strong design and the personalities of its two generations of creators. The formal areas and lawns, enhanced with statues and planted with summer flowers, are set round the castle, with dramatic views over the Lynher River and a background of mature trees. Daffodils and other bulbs create colour early in the year, while the woodland areas, with paths and an oval open space, contain camellias, rhododendrons, azaleas and other fine shrubs. The summer-house is decorated internally with shells collected during the 1960s. The castle itself is romantic and at the end of a very long drive.

The Japanese Garden and Bonsai Nursery 18

St Mawgan, Newquay TR8 4ET. Tel: (01637) 860116; Fax: (01637) 860887;
E-mail: rob@thebonsainursery.com; Website: www.thebonsainursery.com

*Mr and Mrs Hore • 6m NE of Newquay, signed from A3059 and B3278 •
Open all year, daily (closed 25th Dec to 1st Jan), 10am – 6pm (5.30pm in
winter) (last admission 1 hour before closing time) • Entrance: £2.50, children
£1 (bonsai nursery free) • Other information: Tea house does not serve
refreshments. Toilet facilities nearby. Guide dogs permitted* ○ ♿ 🌿 ▦

This Japanese garden has an authentic feel, and it is a surprise to find it in
Cornwall. It covers one and a half acres along a shady stream and has small
ponds, a stroll garden, a Zen garden and a tea house. Among the Japanese
plants are bamboos, camellias, dwarf rhododendrons and *Acer palmatum*. In all,
120 named varieties of specialist plants.

Ken Caro 19

Bicton, Liskeard PL14 5RF. Tel: (01579) 362446

*Mr and Mrs K.R. Willcock • 5m NE of Liskeard. Turn off A390 at Butcher's Arms,
St Ive, take Pensilva road to next crossroads, then road signed 'Bicton' • Open 14th
April to 29th Aug, Sun – Thurs, 2 – 6pm • Entrance: £3, children £1* ◑ WC 🌿

These four acres are planted in two sections. One consists of a series of small
enclosed areas interconnected by well-kept paths, and contains shrubs, conifers, rhododendrons and flowers, all well labelled, and an aviary. Some rare
shrub specimens include *Eucryphia* x *nymansensis* and *Lomatia ferruginea*. In contrast to the enclosed area, the second part is open to pleasing views of the
surrounding landscape. Beds with a fine collection of roses are well kept, and
there is a large fish pond. A good visit for plantsman and gardener alike.

Ladock House 20

Ladock, Nr Truro TR2 4PL. Tel: (01726) 882274

*Mr G.J. and Lady Mary Holborow • 7m E of Truro on B3275. Entrance by
church • Open 28th April, 2 – 5pm, and for groups by appt • Entrance: £2.50,
children free* 💷 WC ♿ 🍴 ☕

The Georgian former rectory is set in six and a half acres of garden and
woodland, all reclaimed and planted during the past 25 years. Spacious lawns
are embellished with shrubs and flower beds, and a spring garden has clearings
in wooded areas planted with rhododendrons, azaleas and camellias. On the
other side of a park-like field are drifts of bluebells and another shrub garden.

Lamorran House ★ 21

Upper Castle Road, St Mawes TR2 5BZ. Tel: (01326) 270800;
Fax (01326) 270801

*Mr and Mrs R. Dudley-Cooke • Above St Mawes turn right at garage.
Signposted at Castle. Continue for ½ m, and house is on left set behind line of*

pine trees • *Open April to Sept, Wed, Fri and first Sat of each month, 10.30am – 5pm, and at other times by appt* • *Entrance: £3.50, children free* • *Other information: Coaches by prior appt* ◑ WC ⑤

This four-acre garden on a south-facing slope above the sea enjoys a most favoured microclimate that supports wonderful collections of plants from the southern hemisphere, sub-tropical plants flourishing in the lower sections of the garden, temperate plants higher up. The latter include rhododendrons, evergreen azaleas and viburnums, many of which surround small lawns. Paths in an intricate pattern zigzag down the steep hillside between enclosed compartments, some designed in Japanese or Italian style, and all with fine views over the sea to St Anthony's Head. There are many imaginative neo-classical statues and columns, and streams and pools permeate the whole slope. The planting is so dense and comprehensive that the paths, though there is often little space between them, are well screened from each other and so appear to magnify the total area. The immaculate upkeep of the garden enhances the overall effect. Nearby, in the grounds of *St Mawes Castle*, is another sub-tropical garden, with good views.

Lanhydrock ★ 22
Bodmin PL30 5AD. Tel: (01208) 73320

The National Trust • *2½ m SE of Bodmin off A38 and A30, or off B3268* • *House open 23rd March to 3rd Nov, Tues – Sun and Bank Holiday Mons, 11am – 5.30pm (5pm in Oct)* • *Garden open, daily, 10am – 6pm (5pm in Oct)* • *Entrance: garden and grounds £3.70, children £1.85; (house, garden and grounds £6.80, children £3.40, family ticket (2 adults and up to 3 children) £17, pre-booked parties of 15 or more £5.80 per adult, £2.90 per child) (2001 prices)* • *Other information: Parking 600 metres from garden but disabled may park adjacent to garden* ○ ☕ ✕ 🍴 WC ⑤ ♨ 🎪 ❦

Although the collection of trees was started as early as 1634, the bones of this superb 30 acre garden, in a dramatic woodland and parkland setting, were put in place in 1857 by the 1st Baron Robartes. The architect of his choice was George Gilbert Scott, who had been brought in to restore and extend the seventeenth-century house, and to redesign the garden. The formal gardens remain largely as he conceived them. Behind the original seventeenth-century gatehouse is a formal lawn with 29 topiary yews in the shape of truncated cones and with rose beds in between, and, beside the house, a Victorian parterre is flanked by six similar yews and with spring and summer bedding plants. The herbaceous circle is planted for both spring and autumn. A shady stream fringed by water-loving plants runs off the hill behind the house. The Higher Garden is planted with large groups of 'Cornish Red' and other rhododendrons, many camellias, azaleas, magnolias and *Viburnum plicatum*. The hillside woods have fine walks beneath mature trees underplanted with large-leaved rhododendrons and bluebells, though for some visitors the heavily gravelled paths introduce an artificial element.

Long Cross Victorian Gardens 23

Trelights, Port Isaac PL29 3TF. Tel: (01208) 880243;
Website: www.longcrosshotel.co.uk

*Mr and Mrs D.J. Crawford • 7m N of Wadebridge just N of Trelights off B3314
near St Endellion church. Signposted • Open all year, daily • Entrance: £1.50,
children under 14 50p, season ticket £2* ○ 🍴 ✕ WC ♿ ⏏ 🌿 ⚲

The gardens are in the grounds of an hotel and cover three acres. They have a
genuine and rather magical Victorian atmosphere, while not pretending to be
a plantsperson's garden; the layout resembles a maze of quite formal hedges
with small groups of shrubs. At the centre is a small pond, with a fountain and
an island bearing neo-classical statuary. A pleasant place to stroll, with many
secluded alcoves, often with seats or statues. The hedges are of different
textures, including laurel, cotoneaster and escallonia. Good amusements for
children.

Morrab Subtropical Garden 24

Penzance. Tel: (01736) 362341 ext. 6647 (Garden Manager)

*Penwith District Council • In centre of Penzance. Entrances in St Mary's
Terrace, Morrab Road and Coulson's Place • Open all year, daily, dawn – dusk
• Entrance: free* ○ 🍴 🛍 WC ♿ ⏏ ⚲

The three-acre garden designed by Reginald Upcher, a well-known garden
architect in his day, remains exactly in accordance with his plan. The land was
bought by Penzance Corporation in 1888 and the garden opened in 1889. It
contains two ponds, a large, highly ornamental fountain and a magnificent
bandstand, and many rare trees and plants, including a *Cordyline australis* (New
Zealand cabbage palm), a *Dicksonia antarctica* (tree fern) and a *Clethra arborea* (lily-
of-the-valley tree). The exceptional climate allows camellias to bloom as early
as mid-November. The garden is in two sections, the main one joined to a
smaller area beside the Morrab Library.

Mount Edgcumbe House and Country Park ★ 25

Cremyll, Torpoint PL10 1HZ. Tel: (01752) 822236; Fax: (01752) 822199

*Cornwall County Council and Plymouth City Council • Access from Plymouth by
Cremyll ferry (pedestrian) to park entrance or Torpoint ferry (vehicle) via A374
and B3247. Access from Cornwall A38 to Trerulefoot roundabout then A374
and B3247 • House open as Earl's Garden • Park and formal gardens open all
year, daily, 8am – dusk. Earl's Garden open April to Sept, Wed – Sun and
Bank Holiday Mons, 11am – 4.30pm • Entrance: Park and formal gardens free.
Earl's Garden and house £4.50, concessions £3.50, children under 15 £2.25,
family £10, season £7.50, groups £3.50 per person • Other information: Coaches
must pre-book* ○ 🍴 ✕ 🛍 WC ♿ ⏏ 🌿 🏛 ⚲ ⚲

The gardens and Grade I landscaped park were created by the Mount
Edgcumbe family in the eighteenth century. They were praised by William

Kent and Humphry Repton. There are two main areas of interest in the 865-acre site. Surrounding the house is the Earl's Garden, an informal terrace and shrub garden containing a rare eighteenth-century shell grotto and re-established late Victorian flower beds. The gardens at the lower end of the old tree-lined avenue include a formal Italian garden, complete with orange trees, slightly less formal English and French gardens, and gardens commemorating the Edgcumbe family's connection with America and New Zealand; in the amphitheatre is a national collection of camellias. Fine views.

Pencarrow ★ 26

Washaway, Bodmin PL30 3AG. Tel: (01208) 841369; Fax: 01208 841722; E-mail: pencarrow@aol.com; Website: www.pencarrow.co.uk

The Molesworth-St Aubyn family • 4m NW of Bodmin. Signed from A389 Bodmin – Wadebridge road and B3266 at Washaway • House open 31st March to Oct, Sun – Thurs, 11am – 4pm • Garden open 4th March to Oct, daily, 9am – 6pm • Entrance: £2.50, children free (house and garden £5, children £2.50, parties of 20 or more £4 per person) (2001 prices) • Other information: Dogs near house only. Craft gallery ◐ ▣ ✕ 🍴 WC ⅃ ⅏ ⅌ ♨ ⅋ ⅌

Pencarrow lies at the end of an impressive one-mile drive, planted with flowering shrubs, conifers and hardwoods. The setting of the magnificent Palladian mansion is superb, with formal gardens on two sides, a rock garden above, and wide and beautiful lawns in front of mature trees; these include an open beech grove. The trees are underplanted with shrubs, including azaleas and huge mounds of 'Cornish Red' and other rhododendrons. There is a fine view over the formal garden with its circular lawn from the main façade of the house. The parklands and woodlands, which extends to 50 acres, contain many varieties of rhododendrons and camellias, and a woodland walk leads to a lake covered with water lilies.

Penjerrick 27

Budock, Falmouth TR11 5ED. Tel: (01872) 870105

Mrs R. Morin • 3m SW of Falmouth between Budock and Mawnan Smith. Entrance opposite Penmorvah Manor Country Hotel • Open March to Sept, Wed, Fri and Sun, 1.30 – 4.30pm • Entrance: £2, children £1 • Other information: Parking for one coach only, at gate. Plants for sale on charity days only ◐ ⅏

A 15-acre garden set in parkland created by the Fox family in the late eighteenth century, famous as the home of the 'Barclayi' and 'Penjerrick' rhododendron hybrids. The upper garden with its large sloping lawns is planted with rhododendrons, camellias, tree ferns and bamboos and many rare trees. The wilder lower garden has ponds enhanced by tree ferns.

Penwarne   28

Mawnan Smith, Falmouth TR11 5PH. Tel: (01326) 250585/250325

Mr and Mrs H. Beister • 3¼ m SW of Falmouth and 1¼ m N of Mawnan Smith off Falmouth – Mawnan Smith road • Open one or two days – write or telephone for details • Entrance: £2, children 50p • Other information: Coaches by prior arrangement only ● 📷 WC ⬦ ♋

Many large trees, including *Cryptomeria japonica*, beeches and oaks, form a backcloth to this woodland garden planted about 1900 as the setting for a fine Georgian house. The old walled garden has roses, clematis and lilies and there are banks of azaleas, rhododendrons, camellias and magnolias, together with shrubs from New Zealand. The pool and stream running through the garden provide areas for primulas and tree ferns. Fruit trees and bushes, bamboos, many new plantings.

Pine Lodge Garden and Nursery ★★   29

Cuddra, Holmbush, St Austell PL25 3RQ. Tel: (01726) 73500;
Fax: (01726) 73500; E-mail: sclemo@talk21.com;
Website: www.pine-lodge.co.uk

Mr and Mrs R. Clemo • Just E of St Austell off A390 between Holmbush and turning for Tregrehan. Signposted • Open 25th March to Oct, 10am – 5pm. Guided tours for parties of 20 or more by appt all year • Entrance: £4, children £2 ◐ 🍴 WC ♿ ✿ 🍵

The 30-acre estate comprises gardens within a garden which hold a wide range of some 5500 plants, all of them labelled. Complementing the rhododendrons, magnolias and camellias so familiar in Cornish gardens are Mediterranean and southern-hemisphere plants grown for year-round interest. Features include herbaceous borders, a fernery, a formal garden, a woodland walk and shrubberies. A large wildlife pond, an ornamental pond with cascades (stocked with koi carp), a lake with an island (home to black swans and many waterfowl) and marsh gardens add the important element of water. Trees are also a speciality, with an acer glade, a collection of 80 different conifers in a four-acre pinetum, and an arboretum. A Japanese garden will soon be completed. Holder of National Collection of grevilleas. Plants for sale in the nursery include some raised from seed collected on plant hunting expeditions every year since 1985. A new sculpture is set in the courtyard and another in the parkland leading down to the lake.

Poldowrian   30

Coverack, Helston TR12 6SL. Tel: (01326) 280468

Mrs P.S. Hadley • Take B3293 Helston – St Keverne road. 2m after Goonhilly Earth Station, turn right at National garage at Zoar. Take second right signed 'Gwenter', then second left at Poldowrian sign • Open April to July by appt only • Entrance: by donation to charity (£2.50 min) ● 📷 ⬦ ♋

This is a four-acre woodland garden, well pathed, leading to unspoilt coast. The area has remains which date from the Neolithic Age, such as an ancient roundhouse, and a museum of pre-history. The trees and shrubs include two Japanese umbrella pines, Norway maples, camellias, hydrangeas and rhododendrons, and there are many woodland flowers. Other features are a pond with an island in the middle, and a bog garden.

Polgwynne   31

Feock, Truro TR3 6SG. Tel: (01872) 862612

Mrs P. Davey • 5m S of Truro. Take A39, then B3289 to first crossroads. Continue on past garage on right following signposts to Feock. At T-junction turn left down steep hill and house is situated at bottom on right • Open 28th April, 26th May, 30th June, 2 – 5pm, and by appt all year round • Entrance: £2.50 for charity, children free • Other information: Refreshments and plants for sale on open days only ● ▆ WC & ⟨⟩ ℘ ℺

A three-and-a-half-acre garden in a beautiful setting with fine views and woodlands extending to the shore of Carrick Roads. It contains many unusual shrubs and fine trees, including what is reputed to be the largest female *Ginkgo biloba* in Britain. Pleasing early-Victorian greenhouses stand in the large vegetable garden.

Porthpean House   32

Porthpean, St Austell PL26 6AX. Tel: (01726) 72888

Mr and Mrs C. Petherich • 1½ m S of St Austell. Take A390 and then road signed Porthpean, past Mount Edgcumbe Hospice, turn left down Porthpean Beach Road. House is white building at bottom of hill just before car park • Open 7th, 21st April, 12th May for charity, 2 – 5pm, and at other times by appt • Entrance: £2, children free • Other information: Teas for parties only ● ▆ WC & ⟨⟩ ℘ ℺

The three-acre garden was first developed by Maurice Petherick some 40 years ago. It contains a special collection of camellias, also many azaleas and rhododendrons. The grounds have access to the beach and from the main lawn there is a magnificent view of St Austell Bay; on spring days cherry blossoms stand out sharply against the blue of the sea. There is also a nursery garden with Victorian greenhouses.

St Martin's Manor   33

St Martin–by–Looe, Looe PL13 1NX Tel: 01503 262825

Dr Kenneth Olson • 1m NW of Looe off B3253 Plymouth road. Go down small lane almost opposite Looe Garden Centre to St Martin's Church; garden is adjacent • Open by appt only • Entrance: £2.50, children (over 6) £1 [NEW] ●
WC ⟨⟩ ℘

The garden is that rarity, a plantsman's delight that is also beautifully designed and planted, reflecting the creativity of its owner. Its four acres are on a hillside and surround a Georgian rectory. Much of the lower garden, including the pond, is visually enclosed, while the upper part has views of the countryside. The borders are closely planted with rare shrubs and perennials, and ferns and many tender plants are concentrated round the pound. Attractive all through the year, the garden is at its peak in mid-June to August.

St Michael's Mount ★ 34

Marazion, Penzance TR17 0EF. Tel: (01736) 710507; Fax: (01736) 711544

The National Trust • ½ m from shore at Marazion, ½ m S of A394. Access by ferry or across causeway • Castle and gardens open 25th March to Oct, Mon – Fri, 10.30am – 5.30pm (last admission 4.45pm), and most weekends from June to Sept for charity, when NT members are asked to pay for admission. Nov to March, essential to telephone for opening arrangements in advance. Entrance: April and May gardens only £2.50 (otherwise castle and gardens £4.50, family ticket £12, pre-booked parties of 20 or more £4.10 per person) • Other information: Parking in Marazion ◑ ⬛ ✕ WC ⌘ ♿

A unique and extraordinary 20-acre maritime garden created in terraces just above the sea at the foot of a 90-metre perpendicular cliff. Here, in spite of apparent total exposure to gales and salt spray, sub-tropical species abound. The walled garden was planned in the eighteenth century by two young ladies, St Aubyn ancestors; the family still lives in the castle. A remarkable example of microclimate effect is in itself a fascinating study for the keen gardener. Planting has been done amongst granite boulders, some weighing hundreds of tons. There are yuccas, geraniums, euryops, hebes, phormiums, fuchsias, puyas and in spring sheets of wild narcissi. Kniphofias grow wild in bracken – great splashes of colour. The climb to the castle is steep and rough and can be difficult for the elderly or handicapped; sensible shoes are advised.

Trebah ★★ 35

Mawnan Smith, Falmouth TR11 5JZ. Tel: (01326) 250448;
E-mail: mail@trebah-garden.co.uk; Website: www.trebah-garden.co.uk

Major and Mrs J.A. Hibbert (Trebah Garden Trust) • 4m W of Falmouth. Signed from A39/A394 Junction at Treliever Cross roundabout, 500 metres W of Glendurgan Garden • Open all year, daily, 10.30am – 5pm • Entrance: £4.50, OAPs £4, disabled and children (5–15) £2.50, RHS members and children under 5 free, NT members free Nov to Feb (reduced rates Nov to Feb) • Possible for wheelchairs but paths steep in places • Other information: Powered wheelchairs available ○ ⬛ ✕ ▦ WC ⌘ ⬥ ♿ ⬛ ♀ ♋

The most remarkable feature of Trebah is the spectacular view over the massive clumps of rhododendrons, tree ferns, bananas and bamboos and into the ravine, which runs between tall trees down to the Helford River. The garden is about 25 acres in all and contains many interesting and beautiful mature trees and shrubs. An extensive collection of colourful sub-tropical Mediterranean plants, a stream and some carp ponds occupy the upper reaches, while in the lower parts is a lake, a vast plantation of gunnera, and acres of blue and white hydrangeas giving summer colour. Superbly maintained throughout, but in no way over-manicured.

Tregrehan ★ 36
Par PL24 2SJ. Tel/Fax: (01726) 814389

*The Carlyon Estate/Mr T. Hudson • On A390 Lostwithiel – St Austell road.
Entrance opposite Britannia Inn • Open mid-March to mid-June, Wed – Sun
and Bank Holiday Mons, 10.30am – 5pm; mid-June to Aug, Wed, 2 — 5pm •
Closed 31st March • Entrance: £3.50, children free. Guided tours for groups by
prior arrangement* ◑ ☕ WC & ℘ 👤 ℀

Woodlands occupy most of the 20 acres here, planted with interesting
conifers, hardwoods and many fine rhododendrons and camellias, and underplanted with a variety of shade-lovers; the bluebell walk is beautiful in spring.
There are lovely views of the recently cleared valley with its young plantings
from South America and New Zealand. The nineteenth-century walled garden
is the central focus, with a magnificent Victorian glasshouse range, an arch of
Acer palmatum and a variety of flourishing climbers, many of them summer-
flowering.

Trelissick ★ 37
Feock, Truro TR3 6QL. Tel: (01872) 862090

*The National Trust • 4m S of Truro on B3289 above west end of King Harry
Ferry • Garden open 16th Feb to 3rd Nov, Mon – Sat, 10.30am – 5.30pm,
Sun, 12.30 – 5.30pm or dusk if earlier • Entrance: £4.50, children £2.25,
family ticket £11.20, pre-booked parties £3.80 per person (2001 prices). Parking
charge (refundable) • Other information: Wheelchairs and Batricar available.
Theatrical events during season and autumn and winter evens programme.
Cornwall Garden Show on site 1st to 4th May* ◑ ☕ ✕ 🍽 WC & ℘ 🛍

This beautiful spring garden, which also has many summer flowering shrubs,
covers 30 acres and is set in the middle of 500 acres of park and farm land, with
fine panoramic views down Carrick Roads to the open sea. In its infancy
compared to many similar Cornish gardens, the plantings and layout date only
from the 1920s. It has fine open lawns, particularly in the area known as the
Caradon, and is renowned both for its collection of camellias, magnolias and
rhododendrons and for its large collection of hydrangeas and other tender and
exotic plants. The woodland walks, surrounded by shrubs, reveal attractive
views of the water below.

Trelowarren 38
Mawgan, Helston TR12 6AF. Tel: (01326) 221224; Fax: (01326) 221440

*Sir Ferrers Vyvyan • House open Wed, 2 – 4pm • Grounds open Easter to Sept,
daily, 10am – 5pm • Entrance: £1.50 car parking charge (2001 prices)* NEW ●
☕ ✕ 🍽 WC & ⏵ ℘ 🛍 👤 ℀

The estate is said to have been the model for Du Maurier's *Frenchman's Creek*. Sir
Richard Vyvyan, who took over in 1754, converted the Gothic house, landscaped the park and laid out the pleasure grounds under the direction of

Dionysius Williams. He also began the plantations of beech, chestnut and firs –
his successor, who inherited in it 1820, more than doubled the size of the
estate and put picturesque theories into effect. The present owner is undertaking the restoration of this interesting eighteenth-century Rococo garden.

Trengwainton Garden ★ 39

Penzance TR20 8RZ.
Tel: (01765) 362297 (General Enquiries); (01637) 875404 (Coach Bookings)

*The National Trust • 2m NW of Penzance on B3312, or ½ m N of A3071 •
Open 17th Feb to 3rd Nov, Sun – Thurs (but open Good Friday), 10.30am –
5.30pm (5pm in Feb, March and Oct) (last admission ½ hour before closing) •
Entrance: £3.60, family £9, pre-arranged groups of 15 or more £2.90 per person
(2001 prices) • Other information: Teas at Trengwainton Farm, weather
permitting* ◐ ☕ 🍽 WC ⬆ ☂ 🏛

Trengwainton, the 'House of the Spring', was acquired by the Bolitho family in
1867. It will appeal to both the plantsman and the ordinary gardener for its
magnificent collections of magnolias, rhododendrons and camellias and its
series of walled gardens with many tender and exotic shrubs and plants that
would not survive in less mild areas of England. The stream garden alongside
the drive, backed by a beech wood, provides masses of colour from candelabra
primulas, lilies, lysichitums and other bog plants. Many of the rhododendrons
were raised from seed collected by Kingdon Ward's expedition to NE Assam
and the Mishmi Hills of Burma. New Zealand tree ferns, pittosporums from
China, Japanese maples, embothriums, olearias, acacias, eucryphias, and Chatham Island forget-me-nots are just a few of the beautiful plants to be seen
during the spring and summer. The woodland walk also now features an
ornamental pond. There are magnificent views of the hills leading down to the
sea and St Michael's Mount.

Tresco Abbey ★★ 40

Tresco, Isles of Scilly TR24 0QQ. Tel: (01720) 424105; Fax: (01720) 422868
(Garden Curator: Mike Nelhams)

*Mr R.A. Dorrien-Smith • On Island of Tresco. Travel by helicopter from
Penzance Heliport to Tresco Heliport (reservations (01736) 363871 and (01720)
422970) or from St Mary's by launch • Open all year, daily, 10am – 4pm •
Entrance: £5, children free, weekly tickets (7 days) £10 (2001 prices) • Other
information: Possible for wheelchairs but some paths very steep. Wheelchairs
available at gate* ○ ☕ 🍽 WC ♿ ☂ 🏛 🅿

One of the most spectacular of all Britain's 'sub-tropical' gardens on an island
which lies in the warming Gulf Stream. Usually protected from Atlantic gales,
this was not the case in 1990, and as a result of the devastation several thousand
trees have been replanted and massive clearance work done with financial
assistance from English Heritage. Robin Lane Fox calls this 'a paradise...one of
the most important recoveries in British garden history', and the amazing fact
is that it is tended by a mere four full-timers. The garden, set around the ruins

of two castles, is arranged on several terraces mounting a hillside linked by flights of steps. They serve as a home for myriad exotic plants like proteas from South Africa, the tender geranium G. *maderense* from Madeira and trees and shrubs from the North Island of New Zealand and Australia which could not thrive out-of-doors in many places on the British mainland. This 17-acre garden is both formal and informal. Many of the plants are self-seeded. The grounds also house the Valhalla collection of ship figureheads from the National Maritime Museum.

Trevarno Estate and Gardens and The National Museum of Gardening ★ 41

Trevarno Manor, Helston TR13 0RU. Tel: (01326) 574274; Fax: (01326) 574282

Mr M. Sagin and Mr N. Helsby • 3m NW of Helston off A394 or B3302 • Open all year, daily except 25th, 26th Dec, 10.30am – 5pm • Entrance: Gardens £3.50, concessions £3, children 5 – 14 £1.25, under 5 free (house and garden £4.50, concessions £3.95, children 5 – 14, under 5 free) ○ 💬 ✗ 🗒 WC ઙ 🔊 ⌖ 🎋 ☕ ✎

A vast restoration is taking place in a 60-acre woodland area, accessible throughout by well-kept paths. Here one can enjoy spectacular views, rare trees, shrubs and spring flowers. In other areas visitors will discover a lake, cascade, rockery, grotto and pinetum. (The large lake with a Victorian boat is now easy to approach since a further clearing of the earth around it.) The walled Georgian gardens are to be replanted and a sunken Italian garden has been remodelled and restored to its original design. A large glasshouse containing vines planted in 1830 is likewise to be restored, while a large garden conservatory with a central fountain acts as a delightful tea room. A small museum has been built to exhibit what is believed to be the most comprehensive collection of gardening tools, implements, memorabilia and ephemera in the country.

Trewithen ★★ 42

Grampound Road, Truro TR2 4DD. Tel: (01726) 883647; Fax: (01726) 882301

Mr and Mrs A.M.J. Galsworthy • On A390 between Truro and St Austell • Walled garden open when house open • House open April to July, Mon, Tues, 2 – 4pm; rest of gardens open March to Sept, Mon – Sat, 10am – 4.30pm (also Suns in April and May) • Entrance: £3.50, children £2, parties of 20 or more £3.20 per person (house £3.50, children £2), joint ticket (house and garden) £6 (2001 prices) ◑ 💬 🗒 WC ઙ 🔊 ⌖

Trewithen is one of the greatest of all Cornish and British gardens. It covers 30 acres, mainly of woodland, and is known internationally for its great collections of magnolias, camellias and rhododendrons, and for many other rare trees and shrubs. The most magnificent feature is the long lawn in front of the house, flanked by sinuous borders of mature rhododendrons, magnolias, acers and other shrubs and ornamental trees, and backed by mature hardwoods. To the west the shrub beds and paths are sheltered by beeches and other woodland trees. A deep sunken garden contains acers, camellias and tree ferns. There is a walled garden (not always open) with a pond, and a pergola. Many hybrid rhododendrons and camellias originated here, some of them named by George Johnstone, the garden's founder, after members of his family.

Trewoofe House   43

Lamorna, Penzance TR19 6PA. Tel: (01736) 810269

Mr and Mrs H.M. Pigott • 6m SW of Penzance. Take B3315 from Penzance via Newlyn towards Lamorna. At top of hill take sharp right turn signed Trewoofe • Open May to Sept by appt; May, Wed, 2 – 5pm; June, Wed, Sun, 2 – 5pm • Entrance: £2, children under 16 free • Coaches and group visits by appt ● WC & ♨ ♀

This two-acre garden, situated at the head of the Lamorna valley, is planted informally with shrub and herbaceous beds that give colour all year round. An ancient mill leat runs through it, enabling a bog garden to be developed with a wide variety of moisture-loving plants. The garden is on two levels, linked by two bridges over the leat and using local granite. There is a small fruit garden with cordon- and espalier-trained trees, and a conservatory with semi-tender climbers.

Trewyn Garden   44

St Ives TR26 1AQ. Tel: (01736) 362341 ext. 3322 (Garden Manager)

Penwith District Council • In St Ives, near Barbara Hepworth Museum (see entry) • Open all year, daily • Entrance: free • Other information: Special wheelchair slope in main section ○ & ♨

The garden is divided into three sections: a main garden with a superbly kept lawn, bright flowers and well-matured deciduous trees as well as numerous palms, a shrubbery, and a series of flower beds and a lawn leading to pensioners' flats – in all about one acre. About 150 metres away from Trewyn Garden is the Memorial Garden, under the same management (though not suitable for wheelchairs and locked at night) – a rest haven, well furnished with benches, and with attractive flower beds. Another pleasant garden open all year, although connected with the *Tregenna Castle Hotel*, is a public garden (Tel: (01736) 795254). It has several areas: a woodland, a well-stocked lavender garden and a rare plants section which includes Canary Island foxgloves and echium species. Pleasant seating. Though the trees hide the view from the garden, there are fine views towards St Ives Bay. In all, 72 acres.

CUMBRIA &
THE ISLE OF MAN

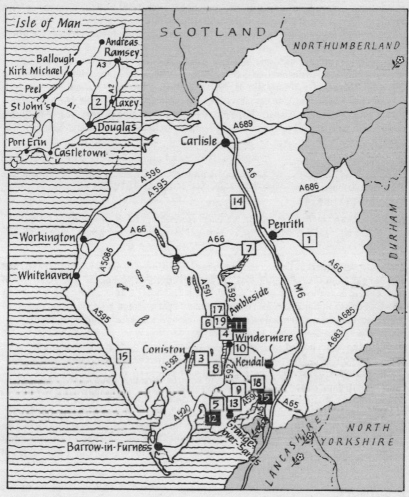

Two-starred gardens are marked on the map with a black square.

Acorn Bank Garden and Watermill

Temple Sowerby, Penrith CA10 1SP. Tel: **(017683) 61893**; Fax: **(017683) 61467**

The National Trust • 6m E of Penrith off A66 N of Temple Sowerby • Garden open March to Oct, 10am – 5pm (last admission 4.30pm) • Entrance: £2.50, children £1.20, family £6.20, pre-booked parties £1.80 per person ◐ 🍵 🍴 wc ♿ ⟨⟩ ✿ 🛍 💡

The 'acorn bank' is the ancient oakwood sloping down to the Crowdundle Beck behind the house. In spring it is a carpet of daffodils and narcissi in many varieties planted profusely in the 1930s, and there are some 60,000 Lenten lilies. The walled gardens are then also a mass of blossom from the old varieties of apple, medlar, pear and quince, carpeted with wild tulips, anemones and narcissi. The orchard trees include later-blossoming apple varieties. Along the three sheltering walls are herbaceous and shrub borders, backed by good clematis and other climbers. A bed of species roses flanks the steps to a picturesque sunken garden, with a pond and alpine terraces. Through a gateway lies a splendid walled herb garden – a well-tended collection of some 250 medicinal and culinary herbs. For those interested in alpines, it is worth taking the A686 over the spectacular Hartside fell to *Hartside Nursery Garden* about 14m away near Alston. [Open daily in summer, weekdays, 9am – 4.30pm, weekends and Bank Holidays, 12.30 – 4pm, otherwise by appt. Tel: (01434) 381372.]

Ballalheannagh ★   2

Glen Roy, Lonan, Isle of Man IM4 7QB. Tel: (01624) 861875; Fax: (01624) 86114

Maureen Dadd • On E of island in Glen Roy, 2m inland from Laxey • Open March to Oct, daily, 10am – 5pm, Nov to Feb variable (all dates under review – telephone to check) • Entrance: £2.50, children free ○ ♨

Take a steep-sided valley, a ladder, some seedlings of exotic rhododendrons and forget all about digging pits to accommodate the roots. Just stick them into crevices among the mosses and ferns and wait a few years, never giving up. Outcome – paradise for plant-lovers. You expect to find a garden like Ballalheannagh in Cornwall or Kerry – but this is the middle of the Isle of Man. No visitor with an interest in gardening who is marooned on that island need fear boredom, for this is a botanical garden, not in name, but surely in content. Steep winding paths cling to the valley sides, and crystal water cascades below, carrying the bells of pieris to the Irish Sea. The lower portion contains lofty rhododendrons, while the upper parts of the valley have newer plantings that will certainly delight in years to come. Here are eucalyptus, drimys, epacris, epigaea, megacarpaea and betula (species with evocative names like *Betula tatewakiana*), and a host of others too, and the native mosses and ferns are a wonderful sight. The garden has been extended to more than 20 acres, with four miles of gravel walks and new oriental features, plus a millennium window.

Brantwood   3

Coniston LA21 8AD. Tel: (015394) 41396

Brantwood Trust • On E side of Coniston Water off B5285, signposted. Coniston Launch provides hourly service to Brantwood and other points around lake. Steam yacht 'Gondola' sails regularly from Coniston Pier • House open • Garden open 12th March to 11th Nov, daily, 11am – 5.30pm; winter season Wed – Sun, 11am – 4.30pm, but closed 25th and 26th Dec • Entrance: garden £2,

house and garden £4.50 (students £3), children under 16 £1 (2001 prices)
◑ ▣ ✕ WC ⬦ ⚲ ⛪ ☕ ⚲

A superb site with wonderful views, atmosphere and history. The rocky hillside behind the house is threaded with a wandering network of paths created by John Ruskin to delight the eye and please the mind. A succession of small, individual gardens threads the landscape, exploring the many themes that fascinated the artist social and visionary. This 'living laboratory' of ideas is being revived by Sally Beamish and her small team. Ruskin's own Professor's Garden, the woodland pond and harbour walk are maturing beautifully. An extensive collection of British native ferns surrounds an ice-house and several waterfalls. A British herb garden is now open, and work has begun on the allegorical Zig-zaggy Garden and the Victorian viewing terrace. The restoration of the main structure of this old garden will be completed in 2003.

Brockhole ★ 4

Lake District Visitor Centre, Windermere LA23 1LJ. Tel: (015394) 46601

Lake District National Park Authority • 1½ m N of Windermere on A591 • Grounds and gardens open all year, daily, 10am – dusk • Entrance: parking fee only: private cars £3 for 3 hours, £4 all day; minibuses and coaches free if pre-booked • Other information: Centre open April to Nov, with slide theatre and exhibition. Cruises from jetty ○ ▣ ✕ ▤ WC ♿ ⬦ ⚲ ⛪ ☕ ⚲

A garden blessed with the Lakeland combination of western aspect and water to the hills beyond, in this case notably the Langdale Pikes. To frame this view Mawson worked closely (c.1900) with his architect colleague Gibson. The ornamental terraces drop through rose beds, herbaceous borders and shrubbery to a wildflower meadow flanked by mature woodland. The original kitchen and herb garden has been restored; other special features are herbaceous plants, tender shrubs and rarities and the constantly changing colour from spring rhododendrons and azaleas through to late Chilean hollies, maples and eucryphias. In Troutbeck, between Windermere and Ambleside, is High Cross Lodge, a small fellside garden planted with rhododendrons, foliage and tender plants. Open by appt – write to Mr and Mrs Sydney Orchant, High Cross Lodge, Bridge Lane, Troutbeck LA23 1AA.

Charney Well ★ 5

Hampsfell Road, Grange-over-Sands LA11 6BE. Tel: (015395) 34526 Fax: (015395) 35765; E-mail: christopher@charneywell.com / richard@charneywell.com; Website: www.charneywell.com

Richard Roberts and Christopher Holliday • Travelling W on A590, take B5277 to Grange-over-Sands. Continue up main street past railway station up hill of shops to mini-roundabout and turn right; at crossroads turn right, then left up Hampsfell Road. Park in town centre. Garages painted gorse-yellow • Open 22nd, 23rd June 11am — 4.30pm for NGS, and for private groups (minimum 20 persons) 17th to 28th June (excluding NGS open days) • Entrance: £2
● ▣ ⚲

This remarkable half-acre garden has been developed by the owners over the past 13 years. It is on a steep limestone slope and surrounded on three sides by high limestone walls with magnificent views over Morecambe Bay. The sheltered situation and almost frost-free microclimate has made it possible to fill the site with tender exotica. Yuccas and grasses are planted in the rockery. Amongst the profusion, ceanothus, pittosporum, corokia, *Melianthus major* and *Fatsia japonica* thrive; a National Collection of phormiums is held here. This is an unexpected jewel in the crown of Lakeland gardens.

Copt Howe 6

Chapel Stile, Great Langdale, Ambleside LA22 9JR. Tel: (015394) 37685 (Infoline)

Professor R.N. Haszeldine • 3m W of Ambleside on B5343 • Open 29th March to 1st April, 5th to 8th, 26th to 28th May, 12 noon – 5pm, for NGS; also many days mid-April to Sept (telephone for recorded weekly information). Private visits and parties by appt • Entrance: £2.50, children free ● ▨ ⬥ ✥

This plantsman's fellside woodland two-acre garden, with magnificent views of the Langdale Pikes and interesting geological features, has an exceptionally wide range of rare acid-loving plants from many mountainous countries, including expedition plants from the Himalayas, China, Tibet, Japan, Bhutan, Tasmania, New Zealand and North and South America. The extensive collections includes acers, camellias, azaleas, quercus, fagus, large and dwarf conifers, pieris, kalmias, tilias, bamboos, cercis and cercidiphyllums; among herbaceous plants are many bulbous species with orchids and species lilies, *Tropaeolum tuberosum, T. tricolor* and *T. speciosum*. The varied plantings extend to alpine troughs, streams and woodland with mountain primulas, nomocharis, trilliums, hepaticas, hellebores, cardiocrinum, *Myosotidium hortensia* and many species of meconopsis, including *M. punicea*. Dramatic spring, early summer and autumn colours.

Dalemain Historic House and Gardens ★ 7

Dalemain Estate Office, Dacre, Penrith CA11 0HB. Tel: (017684) 86450; Fax: (017684) 86223; Website: www.dalemain.com

Mr and Mrs R.B. Hasell-McCosh • On A592 3m W of Penrith on Ullswater road • House open 11am – 4pm • Garden open 24th March to 13th Oct, Sun – Thurs, 10.30am – 5pm • Entrance: £3 (house and garden £5, children (6–16) £3, family (2 adults plus own children) £14.50. Special prices for pre-booked parties) • Other information: Wheelchair and electric scooter available by prior arrangement. Dogs outside garden only, on lead ◑ ⬤ ✕ ▨ WC ⬥ ✥ ⬛ ⚐

Dalemain has evolved in the most natural way from a twelfth-century pele tower with its kitchen garden and herbs. The Tudor-walled knot garden is there, as are the Stuart terrace (1680s) and the walled orchard where apple trees like 'Nonsuch' and 'Keswick Codling', planted in 1728, still bear fruit. The gardens were re-established by the late Mrs Sylvia McCosh during the 1960s and '70s with shrubs, a collection of over 100 old-fashioned roses, and other rarities, together with richly planted herbaceous borders along the terraces and around the orchard; maintained since then under the direction of her daughter-in-law, Mrs Jane Hasell-McCosh, they continue to improve. The wild garden on the lower ground features an outstanding display of Himalayan blue poppies in early summer and a walk past the Tudor gazebo into woods overlooking the Dacre Beck. Some thoughtful planting in the woodland augurs well for the future. A plantsman's garden with an artist's appreciation of form, texture and colour.

Graythwaite Hall ★   8

Ulverston, Graythwaite LA12 8BA. Tel: (015395) 31248

Graythwaite Estate • 4m N of Newby Bridge on W side of Lake Windermere •
Open April to June, daily, 10am – 6pm • Entrance: £2, children free
❶ 🍴 WC ♿ ☕

Essentially a spring garden landscaped by the late Victorian Thomas Mawson in partnership with Dan Gibson in a beautiful parkland and woodland setting. Azaleas and rhododendrons lead to cultivars of late spring-flowering shrubs. Formal terraced rose garden. The finely wrought sundials and gate by Gibson, the Dutch garden and the stream and pond all add charm to this serene garden. For topiary admirers, Mawson employed interesting effects to contrast with his more billowy plantings. Notable are the battlemented yew hedge and some yew globes with golden yew in the top half and green in the bottom. While in Hawkshead, those interested in sculpture in nature should visit the *Grizedale Sculpture Trail*, organised by the Forestry Commission (Tel: (01229) 86029). The first piece was placed there over 20 years ago and there are now 80 sculptures.

Halecat   9

Witherslack, Grange-over-Sands LA11 6RU. Tel: (015395) 52536;
Fax: (015395) 52215 (Contact: Mrs K. Willard)

Mrs M. Stanley • 14m SW of Kendal, off A590. Signposted • Garden open all
year, daily, 9am – 4.30pm (Sun opens 12.30pm) • Entrance: free • Other
information: Plants, especially hydrangeas, for sale in adjoining nursery ○

These two acres are the front garden of the mid-nineteenth-century house which stands at the head of a small valley with distant views of Arnside Knott and the Forest of Bowland. Mrs Stanley has created this pleasing, personal garden over the past 45 years as a series of terraces and squares, and the limestone quarried from the borders has been used to build the retaining walls and the perimeter wall separating the garden from the surrounding woodland. An azalea bed has been made on the bottom terrace by removing rock and filling the beds with peat from a nearby bog. The mixed borders are well maintained and filled with many shrubs, clematis, herbaceous plants, and shrub and climbing roses. Look out for unusual wooden animals, especially the bear. The gazebo with stained glass quarries was designed by Francis Johnson.

High Cleabarrow 10

Windermere LA23 3ND. Tel: (015394) 42808

Mr and Mrs R. T. Brown • 3m SE of Windermere off B5284 (opposite Windermere Golf Course)• Open for groups by appt only, April to Oct • Entrance: £2, children under 12 free • Other information: Teas by prior arrangement [NEW] ☀ ☕ WC ♿ ☸

A plantsperson's garden of approximately two acres, created by the owners and continually evolving. Set in a shallow bowl sloping gently down to a pond with waterside planting, it is sheltered at the rim by woodland; terraces and herbaceous borders have been created on the slope. The combination of shrubs, mixed borders, a rose garden, alpines, hostas and hellebores make it a garden for all seasons; azaleas, rhododendrons and hydrangeas create a magnificent display among the trees on the rocky outcrop. There are paths for exploring the terraces and borders and viewing the many interesting and unusual plants.

Holehird ★★ 11

Patterdale Road, Windermere LA23 1NP. Tel: (015394) 46008

Lakeland Horticultural Society • 1m N of Windermere on A592 Paterdale road • Open all year, daily, sunrise – sunset. Garden guides available April to Oct, 11am – 5pm • Entrance: by donation (minimum £2 appreciated) • Other information: Annual plant sale first Sat in May in local school ○ ☕ WC

Run by members of a society dedicated to promoting 'knowledge on the cultivation of plants, shrubs and trees, especially those suited to Lakeland conditions', this garden is maintained to an exceptionally high standard. It lies on a splendid hillside site alongside the house with a natural water course and rock banks looking over Windermere to the Langdale Pikes. The Society has nine acres of attractive gardens and trial areas. Much of the earlier planting has been preserved, including many fine specimen trees. Highlights are the summer-autumn heathers, winter-flowering shrubs, alpines and National Collections of astilbes, hydrangeas and polysticum ferns. The walled garden, now accessible for wheelchairs, has fine herbaceous borders, herbs and climbers. The site has now expanded to encompass the lower Victorian terrace of the estate and includes the original Victorian garden furnishings. The views of the fells from the terrace are breathtaking, and there are many mature shrubs in this sheltered area. A new alpine house contains outstanding displays, and the Victorian greenhouses have been restored.

Holker Hall ★★ 12

Cark-in-Cartmel, Grange-over-Sands LA11 7PL. Tel: (015395) 58328; Website: www.holker-hall.co.uk

Lord and Lady Cavendish • 4½ m W of Grange-over-Sands, 4m S of Haverthwaite on B5278 • Hall open. Extra charge • Garden open April to Oct, daily except Sat, 10am – 6pm (last admission 4.30pm) • Entrance: wide variety

of entrance prices on offer depending on visitor requirements – telephone or contact website for details. • *Other information: Dogs on leads in grounds only. Holker Garden Festival 31st May to 2nd June* ◑ 🍺 ✕ 🦐 wc ⚅ 𝒫 🏛 🛈 ♒

Set in 125 acres of parkland, the award-winning 25 acres of woodland walks and formal gardens at Holker (pronounced Hooker) have been constantly developed by the family ever since Lord George Cavendish established his 'contrived natural landscape' over 200 years ago. The woods now contain many rare and beautiful specimens, usually tagged and chronicled in the excellent guide to the garden walks. The National Collection of styracaceae is maintained here. Other features are the impressive cascade, evocative of the Villa d'Este, and a beautifully contrived transformation of the croquet lawn into summer gardens. This combination of formal beds and inventive planting makes a wonderful Italianate-cum-English garden that typifies the spirit of the place. There is also a sunken garden, which was formerly the rose garden and contains many sub-tropical plants due to its sheltered position within the garden and to the garden's position within the Gulf stream. Mawson's pergola and balustrade survive. Of particular note are the Elliptical Garden, the rhododendron and azalea walk and the northern meadow. Replanting and redesign ensure that the gardens are constantly changing.

Holme Cragg   13

**Blea Cragg Bridge, Witherslack, Grange–over–Sands LA11 6RZ.
Tel: (015395) 52366**

Mr J. Watson • *14m SW of Kendal, off A590. From A590, follow signs to Witherslack. Past telephone kiosk in Witherslack, turn first left, first left again and follow signs to Newton (past Halecat) for 1¼ m over small bridge to third gate on left* • *Open all year, daily* • *Entrance: by donation to Cumbria Wildlife Trust* • *Other information: Coaches must pre-book* ○ 🦐 wc ⬲

This is an amateur's and a plantsman's garden which has made magnificent use of natural features of the site. Every rocky outcrop is clothed in alpines, sedums, sempervivums and saxifrages. Azaleas and rhododendrons are an important feature, as are the irises and candelabra primulas around the pond. The shaded areas are filled with the blue of the Himalayan meconopsis, a grass bank is covered with double and single Welsh poppies in colours from deep orange to pale yellow, and there is an interesting natural wildflower area. Rhododendrons are followed by shrub roses and later the foliage of acers provide colour interest. Well worth a visit after Halecat (see entry), with which it provides interesting contrasts and comparisons.

Hutton–in–the–Forest   14

**Penrith CA11 9TH. Tel: (017684) 84449; Fax: (017684) 84571;
E-mail: hutton-in-the-forest@talk21.com**

Lord and Lady Inglewood • *6m NW of Penrith on B5305 (M6 junction 41)* • *House open 29th, 31st March, 1st April and 3rd, 4th June; then 2nd May to 29th Sept, Thurs, Fri, Sun and Bank Holiday Mons, 12.30 – 4pm* • *Gardens open all year, daily except Sat, 11am – 5pm. Private parties by arrangement from April. Monthly tours with head gardener • Entrance: £2.50, children free (house and grounds £4.50, children (7–16) £2.50, family ticket £12) • Other information: Electric scooter available for disabled (donation requested). Light lunches and teas when house open. Other meals on request* ◑ 🍺 📷 WC ♿ ⟨⟩ 🏵 🌱 🐾

This garden, a compelling setting for the appealing house, which ranges across the centuries from a thirteenth-century pele tower to Salvin's handsome addition, is itself a mixture of features from the seventeenth to the twentieth century. It has great visual appeal, with a magnificent view from the seventeenth-century terraces now embellished with Victorian topiary. The beautiful walled garden, dating from the 1730s, is divided into compartments and has excellent herbaceous borders, trained fruit trees and roses. The backdrop of the house, the surrounding yew hedges and compartments and well-filled herbaceous borders combine to make a dramatic composition. Some of the mature woodland trees were planted by Henry Fletcher, an ancestor of the owners, in the early eighteenth century. A woodland walk has many fine specimen trees identified in a leaflet. Other features include a seventeenth-century dovecot and an eighteenth-century lake.

Levens Hall ★★   15

Kendal LA8 0PD. Tel: (015395) 60321; Fax: (015395) 60669;
E-mail: email@levenshall.fsnet.co.uk; www.levenshall.co.uk

Mr C. H. Bagot • 5m S of Kendal on A6 (M6 junction 36) • House open as garden, but 12 noon – 5pm • Garden open April to mid-Oct, Sun – Thurs, 10am – 5pm • Entrance: £4.50, children £2.20 (house and garden £6, children, £3). Party rates available (2001 prices) ◑ 🍺 📷 WC ♿ 🌿 🏵

James II's gardener, Guillaume Beaumont, designed this famous topiary garden in 1694; it is one of very few to retain its original trees and design. The impeccably clipped yews and box hedges are set off by colourful spring and summer bedding and borders. The primroses in the seventeenth-century garden may be the start of a permanent collection. To celebrate the tercentenary of the gardens in 1994 a new area, the Fountain Garden, has been created with lime avenues meeting at the pool. Indeed there is much to see in addition to the topiary. Massive walls of beech hedge open to vistas over parkland. One avenue leads to the earliest English ha-ha. There is a picturesque herb garden behind the house. The record of only 10 head gardeners in 300 years, and the affectionate care by the Bagot family, account for the rare harmony of this exceptional garden, which clearly still has a stylish hand at the helm. Further developments include the installation of two pairs of clematis gates, a green-oak ticket booth disguised as a garden pavilion, and a pair of gates with hearts as handles – celebrating the old legend that a gambler acquired the property in the seventeenth century by turning over the ace of hearts.

Muncaster Castle ★ 16

Ravenglass CA18 1RQ. Tel: (01229) 717614; Fax: (01229) 717010;
E-mail: info@muncastercastle.co.uk; Website: www.muncastercastle.co.uk

Mr and Mrs Gordon-Duff-Pennington • 15m S of Whitehaven on A595 • Castle open 11th March to 4th Nov, Sun – Fri, 12 noon – 5pm, or dusk if earlier • Gardens, owl centre and meadow vole maze open all year, daily, 10.30am – 6pm • Entrance: inclusive price for all 4 attractions, £6.50, children £4 (under 5s free), family ticket (2 adults, 2 children) £18, parties of 12 or more £5.50, children £3 per person, garden family ticket £15 • Other information: Wheelchairs available for pre-booking ○ 🍲 ✕ 🛏 WC ♿ ⟨⟩ 🌶 🏠 ♀

The castle is set against the splendid backdrop of Scafell and the hills, with a wide open view from the terrace. The acid soil and the Gulf Stream warmth provide ideal conditions for one of the finest collections of species rhododendrons in Europe, substantially from plant-hunting expeditions to Nepal in the 1920s (Kingdon Ward, Ludlow and Sheriff). There are excellent azaleas, camellias, magnolias, hydrangeas and maples, plus many unusual trees (e.g. nothofagus species). The gardens are at their best in May and June but intensive new planting is ensuring constant pleasure for visitors in all seasons. Extensive clearing and replanting continues and will take time to mature; this has been made possible by a £2½ m Heritage Lottery Fund grant – matched by the owners. The Sino-Himalayan Walk is now complete and maturing at an encouraging rate. Foot-and-mouth has brought one benefit: a new wild walk has been created opening up the estate for visitors. One section, which takes two and half hours and ends appropriately enough at the tea rooms, embraces a wide spectrum of sea, estuary and coastline views. The other reveals Ruskin's famous 'Gateway to Paradise', with glorious sights of the Fells. An imaginative case of snatching victory from the jaws of defeat and a long-term benefit to the locality to boot.

Rydal Mount 17

Ambleside LA22 9LU. Tel: (015394) 33002; Fax: (015394) 31738;
E-mail: Rydalmount@aol.com

Rydal Mount Trust • 1m N of Ambleside on A591 • House open • Gardens open March to Oct, daily, 9.30am – 5pm; Nov to Feb, daily except Tues, 10am – 4pm • Entrance: £1.75 (house and garden £4, OAPs £3.25, students £3, children (5–15) £1.50, parties of 10 or more pre-booked £2.75 per person, non-booked £3.25 per person. Reciprocal discounts with Dove Cottage and Wordsworth's House) • Other information: Limited parking with awkward entry/exit ○ 🛏 WC ⟨⟩ 🏠 ♀

The carefully maintained grounds of Wordsworth's house still follow the lines of his own plan, and it is easy to imagine the poet wandering along the upper terrace walk ('the sloping terrace') and down through winding, shaded paths to the lawns, or across a terrace to the ancient mound with its distant glimpse of Windermere. Apart from its poetic association the garden is also a visual delight, with good herbaceous borders, shrubs and unusual trees (e.g. the fern-leaf beech). Dora's Terrace, named after the poet's daughter, is now open. An addition to the spring display is the bank of dancing daffodils in nearby Dora's Field. Wordsworth's other house at Cockermouth has a pleasant town garden, but it is only worth it if the house, too, is to be visited.

Sizergh Castle ★   18

Kendal LA8 8AE. Tel: (015395) 60070

The National Trust • 3½ m S of Kendal on A590 (M6 junction 36) • Castle and garden open 24th March to Oct, 12.30 – 5.30pm (last admission 5pm) • Entrance: £2.50, children £1.20 (castle and garden £5, children £2.50, family £12.50, parties of 15 or more £4 per person) • Other information: Manual wheelchair and powered buggies available. Guided walks ◗ ☕ 🧺 <u>WC</u> ⅙ 🐾 🏬 🎪 ⚘

An exceptionally varied garden with colour from early spring daffodils to summer borders and climbers, culminating in glorious autumn tints (the vine-clad tower all fiery red is a memorable spectacle). Other features encountered along shady paths are the herbaceous border, the terrace wall, with half-hardy shrubs and climbers not expected this far north, and the south garden with many species roses, including Musk and Moss roses. The replanting of the rock garden is completed, with excellent results. Of special interest are the maples and hardy ferns, and the restored 'Dutch' garden with its new avenue of 'Shirotae' flowering cherries, part of the 16-acre garden round the pele tower. There are also wildflower banks with native limestone flora, including six species of orchids, and a water garden and lake.

Stagshaw   19

Ambleside LA22 0HE. Tel/Fax: (015394) 46027

The National Trust • ½ m S of Ambleside on A591 • Open April to June, daily, 10am – 6.30pm, July to Oct, by appt (s.a.e. to NT Property Office, St Catherine's, Patterdale Road, Windermere LA23 1NH) • Entrance: £1.50 • Other information: Limited parking, access dangerous ◕

Created by the Trust's former Regional Agent, the late Cubby Acland, this is a carefully blended area of azaleas and rhododendrons among camellias, magnolias and other fine shrubs with unusual underplanting on a west-facing hillside of oaks looking over the head of Lake Windermere. A large area of pink erythroniums. Rather difficult of access, with the volume of traffic on A591 making the exit especially dangerous, but worth the effort.

SYMBOLS

[NEW] entries new for 2002; ○ open all year; ◐ open most of year; ◗ open during main season; ◕ open rarely and/or by appt; ☕ teas/light refreshments; ✗ meals; 🧺 picnics permitted; **WC** toilet facilities; <u>WC</u> toilet facilities, inc. disabled; ⅙ partly wheelchair-accessible; 🐾 dogs on lead; 🐾 plants for sale; 🏬 shop; 🎪 events held; ⚘ children-friendly.

DERBYSHIRE

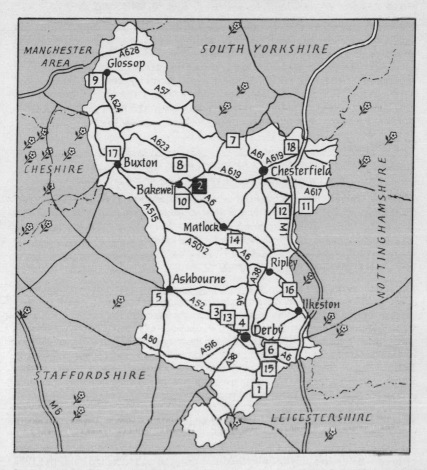

Some gardens have postal addresses in one county and are physically situated in another. If in doubt, a check in the index will direct the reader to the page on which the garden appears.

Two-starred gardens are marked on the map with a black square.

Calke Abbey   1

Ticknall DE73 1LE. Tel: (01332) 863822 (office); Fax: (01332) 865272;
E-mail: eckxxx@smtp.ntrust.org.uk

*The National Trust • 10m S of Derby, off A514 at Ticknall • House open
probably 1 – 5.30pm • Park open all year daily. Garden and church open 23rd
March to 3rd Nov, Sat – Wed and Bank Holiday Mons, 11am – 5.30pm •*

Entrance: £3.10, children £1.50 (house and garden £5.40, children £2.70, family £13.50). £2.60 vehicle charge entry to park ◐ ⬛ ✕ WC ♿ ⚐

Previously owned by the Harpur Crewe family, Calke has a long history and with a sympathetic approach could be another Trust jewel. The vinery in the physic garden has been restored, as have the tomato house, frames, pits, and an auricula theatre. The gardeners are growing flowers, fruit and old varieties of vegetables in the two walled compartments formerly kept for flowers and physic herbs. The third and biggest compartment is the old kitchen garden, now disused, overlooked by an orangery, and housing a head gardener's office of 1777. An orchard of old local apple varieties is of particular interest.

Chatsworth ★★   2

Bakewell DE45 1PP. Tel: (01246) 582204; Fax: (01246) 583536;
E-mail: visit@chatsworth-house.co.uk; Website: www.chatsworth.org

The Duke and Duchess of Devonshire • 4m E of Bakewell, 10m W of Chesterfield on B6012, off A619 and A6 • House open • Garden open 20th March to 27th Oct, daily, 11am – 6pm (last admission 5pm) • Entrance: £4, OAPs and students £3, children £1.75, family £9.50 (house and garden £7, OAPs and students £5.70, children £3, family £17.25) (2001 prices). Parking charge for cars only ◐ ⬛ ✕ 🍽 WC ♿ ⬭ 🐾 ♿ ☕

The 100 acres of garden at Chatsworth have developed over 400 years and many areas still reflect the garden fashions of each century. The seventeenth-century gardens of London and Wise remain only as the cascade, the canal pond to the south and the copper 'willow tree' with water pouring from its branches. During the eighteenth century 'Capability' Brown destroyed much of the formal gardens to create a landscaped woodland park. Notable is the vista he created from the Salisbury Lawn to the horizon, which remains unchanged, as does the lawn itself since no liming or fertiliser has been used, allowing many varieties of wild flowers, grasses, moss and sedges to thrive. From the twentieth century come the orange borders and blue and white borders, the terrace, display greenhouse, rose garden and old conservatory garden, which has lupin, dahlia and Michaelmas daisy beds, and a yew maze planted in 1963. In the arboretum and pinetum the suffocating rhododendrons, laurels and sycamores have been removed, and many new trees planted. The double rows of pleached red-twigged added in 1952 and the 1953 serpentine beech hedge are both now rewarding features. Paxton's work still gives pleasure: there is the large rockery, some rare conifers, the magnificent 84-metre water jet from the Emperor Fountain. Alas, the Great Conservatory was a casualty of the 1914–18 war and metre-wide stone walls in the old conservatory garden are all that remain to give an idea of its size. The epitome of a cottage garden has been created near another recent addition, up the yew stairs to a 'bedroom' where the four-poster is of ivy and the dressing-table of privet, which future generations may regard as a folly. The kitchen garden has been resited and redesigned – it has been called 'indelibly British'. The first major piece of garden statuary to be placed in the garden for 150 years, 'War Horse' by Dame Elisabeth Frink, is sited at the south end of the canal, while Angela Connor's water sculpture 'Revelation' has been described by *Country Life* as 'terrific'.

Dam Farm House ★ 3

Yeldersley Lane, Ednaston, Ashbourne DE6 3BA. Tel: (01335) 360291

Mrs S.D. Player • 5m SE of Ashbourne on A52. Opposite Ednaston village turn, gate is 500 metres on right • Open April to Oct by appt only (also some Suns for NGS) • Entrance: £3, children free • Other information: Teas on charity open days only ● ▭ ▦ WC & ⌖ ⌀

This wonderful garden, created from a farmyard – hence its stone troughs used as planters – owes its existence to the dedication of Jean Player, whose knowledgeable eye for good plants of all kinds – perennials, shrubs and roses –is evident throughout. It is this planting that gives the garden, including the vegetable garden, its special character. The drive through the arboretum is punctuated by a high deciduous tapestry hedge which shields the scree bed, filled with choice alpines. Climbers are used abundantly for clothing walls, trees, pergolas, even spilling down over high retaining walls. There is also an expanding arboretum. One of the best gardens in Derbyshire.

Derby Arboretum 4

Arboretum Square, Derby DE23 8FN. Tel: (01332) 716644

Derby City Council • Between Reginald Street and Arboretum Square with entrances on either side of Royal Crown Derby Factory • Open all year, daily • Entrance: free ○ ▦ **WC** & ⌖

The first specifically designed urban arboretum in Britain, this was commissioned in 1839 from John Claudius Loudon, whose original plans involved the planting of 1000 trees. A useful leaflet now lists 40 varieties, many from around the world, all individually numbered, and also describes other parks in Derby, including the well-known *Markeaton Park*. While in the city, try to visit the refurbished market place, where there is a splendid water sculpture by William Pye, of free-falling water over a bronze cascade – it will give you the sensation of walking behind a waterfall.

Dove Cottage Gardens 5

Clifton, Ashbourne DE6 2GL. Tel: (01335) 343545

Mr and Mrs S.G. Liverman • 1½ m SW of Ashbourne off A515. In Clifton turn right at crossroads then first left down lane (signed Mayfield Yarns). House is 200 metres on left by River Dove • Open by appt for party bookings (10 persons min.) and certain Suns May to Aug for charity, 1 – 5pm • Entrance: Parties £3 per person for guided tour and for charity £2, children free ● ▭ WC ⌀

It is only to be expected that this richly stocked cottage garden is above the average, for it has had the benefit of being developed and nurtured by an owner who is a qualified horticulturist. There are several hardy plant collections, including alliums, campanulas, euphorbias, geraniums and variegated plants; hardy perennials are being nurtured in a dry woodland area.

Elvaston Castle Country Park ★ 6

**Borrowash Road, Elvaston, Derby DE72 3EP. Tel: (01332) 571342;
Fax: (01332) 758751; E-mail: derbyshirecountycouncil@elvastoncastle.fsnet.co.uk**

*Derbyshire County Council • 6m SE of Derby on B5010 between Borrowash
(A6005) and Thulston (A6). Signed from A6 and A52 • Park and museum
possibly under new tenancy, so telephone before travelling • Entrance: free.
Parking charge* ◐ ▆ ✕ ▆ WC ♿ ⬥ ⬛ ℺

The estate's historic Grade-II-listed gardens were designed by William Barron
in the early nineteenth century and include the Italian, parterre and old
English gardens, all of which were enclosed within 11 miles of hedges. It is
probable that these were the first 'garden rooms', which influenced others
when, twenty years after their establishment, they were opened to the public.
Discover the extensive topiary, tree-lined avenues and large ornamental lake,
search out the golden gates, boat house and Moorish temple, and wonder at
the distinctive cedars of Lebanon – William Barron transplanted mature trees
as high as 13 metres from as early as 1831, using his unique transplanting
machines, one of which is housed at the Royal Botanic Gardens, Kew. For
those who find a park out of scale with their own smaller gardens, a tiny
'romantic' garden nearby, *White Gate* at Arleston Meadows, is recommended.
The owner, Mrs Judy Beba-Thompson, welcomes private visits and small
parties by prior appointment (Tel: (01332) 763653).

Fanshawe Gate Hall 7

**Holmesfield S18 7WA. Tel: (0114) 289 0391;
Website: www.fanshawegate.org.uk**

*Mr and Mrs John Ramsden • 6m NW of Chesterfield, 6m SW of Sheffield, 1m E
of Holmesfield. Follow B6054 and turn first right after Robin Hood pub • Open
for charity 7th, 14th, 21st July, 11am – 5pm, and for groups by appt June and
July • Entrance: £1.50* ◐ ▆ WC ♿ ⬥ ℘ ℺

A popular garden with visitors on charity open days. The owners, who moved
here over 40 years ago, have tried to choose plants appropriate to the age of
the stone property (some 700 years). Topiary, mixed borders, a variegated
border, an Elizabethan garden and a sixteenth-century dovecot are features of
this two-acre garden. The upper walled garden displays herbaceous plants,
shrubs, ferns, water features and roses, while the lower courtyard has a knot
garden and a herb border. A millennium parterre is being developed in the
upper courtyard, and the orchard replanted with old varieties of English fruit
trees. A *potager* is planned for the vegetable garden.

Fir Croft 8

Froggatt Road, Calver, Hope Valley S32 3ZD.

*Dr S.B. Furness • 4m N of Bakewell, between Power filling station and A625/B6001
junction • Open 28th April, 19th May, 2nd June, 16th June, 2 – 5pm • Entrance:
By donation • Other information: Plants for sale at adjoining nursery* ◐ ℘

The owner is a botanist and botanical photographer who has put his expertise into an extensive alpine garden – a 'must' to visit for those interested in alpine and scree gardens, particularly as the garden, started from scratch in 1985, now contains one of the largest collections of alpines in the UK.

Gamesley Fold Cottage 9

10 Gamesley Fold, Glossop SK13 6JJ. Tel: (014578) 67856;
Website: www.gamesleyfold.fsnet.co.uk

Mrs G. Carr • Off A626 Glossop – Marple road near Charlesworth. Turn down lane opposite St Margaret's School • Open for NGS; also 3rd June, 26th Aug, and May to Oct for groups by appt • Entrance: £2, children free ● ♿ WC ♨

Although all gardeners will find much of interest here, those who like native or 'wild' flowers will be particularly impressed. The loosely planted beds are crammed with primulas, violets, campions and poppies, many of them self-seeded. Mixed in is a good variety of perennials, notably campanulas, euphorbias, geraniums, verbascums, meconopsis and others that go well with their wild neighbours. There is also a vegetable garden, an orchard and woodland. Wildlife abounds within the garden, especially butterflies lured here by the flowers, trees and shrubs; looking outward are extensive views of the surrounding countryside and hills.

Haddon Hall ★ 10

Bakewell DE45 1LA. Tel: (01629) 812855; Website: www.haddonhall.co.uk

Lord Edward Manners • 2m SE of Bakewell, 6½ m N of Matlock on A6 • House open • Garden open April to Sept, daily, 10.30am – 5pm, Oct, Mon – Thurs, 10.30am – 1.30pm • Entrance: hall and gardens £5.90, OAPs £5, children £3, family (2 adults and 2 children) £15, parties £5 per person, school parties £2.75 per child (no garden-only ticket) (2001 prices). Parking charge for cars, coaches free ◑ ♿ ✕ WC ♿

The medieval castle and gardens of seventeenth century origin – reconstructed this century – stand on a limestone bluff. The gardens are mainly on the south side and are laid out in a series of stone-walled terraces with the River Wye at their foot. The thick stone walls of the house and terrace walls face south and west and look well as a background for the extensive collection of climbing and rambling roses. The plants, shrubs and roses all have legible labels. A garden for the active and fit, but worth the effort.

Hardwick Hall ★ 11

Doe Lea, Chesterfield S44 5QJ. Tel: (01246) 850430

The National Trust • 6½ m NW of Mansfield, 9½ m SE of Chesterfield. Approach from M1 junction 29 then A6175 • House open 27th March to 27th Oct, Wed, Thurs, Sat, Sun, Bank Holiday Mons and Good Friday, 12.30 – 5pm or sunset if earlier (last admission 4.30pm) • Garden open 27th March to 27th Oct, daily, 11am – 5.30pm. Country park open all year, daily, dawn –

dusk • Entrance: £3.40, children £1.70 (house and garden £6.40, children £3.20). Reduction for parties of 15 or more • Other information: Refreshments in Great Kitchen on days hall is open. Limited access for wheelchairs ◑ WC ⓷ ⌗

This famous Elizabethan mansion house was built by Bess of Hardwick and designed by Robert Smythson in the late sixteenth century. Mature yew hedges and stone walls provide necessary shelter to an otherwise exposed escarpment site. The borders of the South Court have spring-flowering shrubs to give colour for a longer period than herbaceous plants can provide. The West Court's herbaceous borders have strong, hot colours graduating to soft hues and are mainly late summer- and autumn-flowering. The herb garden is outstanding. The south-east quarter is now an orchard, and the north-east orchard has been progressively replanted with old varieties and crab apples. The grass is left long for the naturalised daffodils and wild flowers.

The Herb Garden

12

**Hall View Cottage, Hardstoft, Pilsley, Chesterfield S45 8AH.
Tel: (01246) 854268**

Mrs Raynor • 3m SW of M1 junction 29, 6m SE of Chesterfield on B6039 Holmewood – Tibshelf road • Garden open probably mid-March to mid-Sept, daily except Tues, 10am – 5pm • Entrance: £1, children free • Other information: Tea room closed Mon and Tues ◑ 🍵 WC ⓷ ⌁ ⌗

A rich herb garden in a rural setting with a now-established parterre. Three speciality gardens have been added: a physic garden, a scented pot-pourri garden and a lavender garden. The large range of herbs for sale includes some rare and unusual species. This garden is only a short distance from the other excellent herb garden at Hardwick Hall (see entry).

Kedleston Hall ★

13

Kedleston, Derby DE22 5JH. Tel: (01332) 842191

The National Trust • 4½ m NW of Derby on Derby – Hulland road between A6 and A52. Signposted • Hall open 23rd March to 3rd Nov, Sat – Wed, 12 noon – 4.30pm • Park open 23rd March to 3rd Nov, daily, 10am – 6pm; Nov to 17th Mar, Sat and Sun only, 10am – 4pm. Garden open 23rd March to 3rd Nov, Sat – Wed, 10am – 6pm • Entrance: park (Thurs and Fri only) £2 per vehicle; park and garden £2.40, children £1.10 (hall, park and garden £5.20, children £2.60, family ticket £13.20) • Other information: Coaches must pre-book by writing to Property Manager. Electric stairclimber and batricar available ◑ 🍵 ✕ WC ⓷ ⌗ 🍴

The extensive gardens do not compete with this neo-classical Robert Adam palace – the ancient home of the Curzon family – but are of mature parkland where the eye is always drawn to the house. The rhododendrons when in flower are worth seeing in their own right, otherwise visit the gardens as a pleasurable way not only to view Adam's magnificent south front but also the hexagonal-domed summerhouse, the orangery, the Venetian-windowed fishing house, the bridge across the lake, the aviary and slaughterhouse (now a loggia) and the main gateway. The formal gardens have a sunken rose garden.

The Sulphur Bath House, one of the earliest eighteenth-century landscape park features, where a small spa used to operate, has been restored but is not accessible to the public.

Lea Gardens   14

Long Lane, Lea, Matlock DE4 5GH. Tel: (01629) 534380; Fax: (01629) 534260

Mr and Mrs Tye • 5m SE of Matlock E off A6 • Open 20th March to 30th June, daily, 10am – 5pm, and rest of year by appt • Entrance: £3, children 50p (season ticket £5) • Other information: Coaches by appt ◑ ☕ WC �& ◁�﹥ ⌀ 🍽 ⚘ ♽

This garden has a comprehensive collection of rhododendrons, azaleas, alpines and conifers, all brought together in a beautiful woodland setting. John Marsden Smedley started his rhododendron garden in 1935, inspired by his visits to Bodnant and Exbury. Under the Tye family the collection now comprises some 550 varieties of rhododendrons and azaleas in a much-increased area. The excellent booklet includes a visitor route.

Melbourne Hall Gardens ★   15

Melbourne DE73 1EN. Tel: (01332) 862502

Lord Ralph Kerr • 8m S of Derby between A514 and A453, off B587 in Melbourne • House open, Aug, daily except 5th, 12th, 19th, 2 – 5pm (last admission 4.15pm). £3, OAPs £2.50, children £1.50 • Open April to Sept, Wed, Sat, Sun and Bank Holiday Mons • Entrance: £3, OAPs and children £2 ◑ ☕ ✕ WC �& 🍽

There has been little alteration to the Rt Hon. Thomas Coke's formal plan, so this is a visual record of a complete late seventeenth-/early eighteenth-century design laid out by London and Wise in the style of Le Nôtre. It is in immaculate condition with avenues culminating in exquisite statuary and fountains, including a lead urn of The Four Seasons by van Nost, whose other lead statuary stands in niches of yew. A series of terraces runs down to a lake, the Great Basin. A grotto has an inscription thought to be that of Byron's troublesome mistress Caroline Lamb. Unique in English gardens is the Birdcage iron arbour of 1706, which can be seen from the house along a long walk hedged with yews. Also in Melbourne, on the site of the fourteenth-century castle, is *Castle Farm*, a garden of interesting plants, open for private visits and groups by appointment; telephone (01332) 864421.

210 Nottingham Road   16

Woodlinkin, Langley Mill, Nottingham NG16 4HG. Tel: (01773) 714903

Mr and Mrs R. Brown • 12m NW of Nottingham, 4m N of Ilkeston on A610 • Open 16th June, 2 – 5pm • Entrance: £1.50 ◉

A plantsman's half-acre with an emphasis on shrub roses – the garden is packed with many good examples – and some rarer shrubs and trees. Geraniums, hellebores and hostas provide prolonged interest in the herbaceous section.

Pavilion Gardens 17

St John's Road, Buxton SK17 6XN. Tel: (01298) 23114

High Peak Borough Council • Near town centre • Open all year, daily •
Entrance: free • Other information: Refreshments in complex ○ 🍽 ✕ 📷 <u>WC</u>
♿ 🐕 🏛 💡 📷

Twenty-three acres of landscaped municipal park, woodland and two ornamental lakes, this updated pleasure garden of 1871 has the distinction of having
been laid out by Edward Milner, Paxton's chief assistant at Crystal Palace. The
gardens are well maintained and the pleasing 1875 octagon (now a conference
centre) is a graceful backdrop. The conservatory is well stocked but many find
the colour schemes of the bedding plants harsh; there are, however, band
concerts to soothe shattered nerves. In the nearby Crescent, examples of the
arcane art of well-dressing may be seen during summer. A Heritage grant has
aided a refurbishment programme costing £4m over five years.

Renishaw Hall 18

Renishaw, Sheffield S21 3WB. Tel: (01246) 432042; Fax: (01246) 430760;
E-mail: info@renishawhall.free-online.co.uk; Website: www.sitwell.co.uk

Sir Reresby and Lady Sitwell • 6m SE of Sheffield, 5m NE of Chesterfield on
A616. From M1 at junction 30, take A616 towards Sheffield for 3m through
Renishaw • Open 29th March to Sept, Fri – Sun, also 1st April, 6th, 27th May,
26th Aug, all 10.30am – 4pm. • Entrance: £3, OAPs £2.50 • Other
information: Sitwell museum, costume museum, art gallery, performing arts
gallery and craft workshops ◑ 🍽 ✕ <u>WC</u> ♿ 🐕 💷 🏛 💡

For nearly 20 years Renishaw had 'the most northerly vineyard in western
Europe'. Also astonishing to see at this northerly latitude and on top of a hill
are enormous specimens of ceanothus, *Acacia dealbata*, *Cytisus battandieri* and
Fremontodendron californicum, and other rare, slightly tender specimen shrubs.
Sir George Sitwell spent much of his life in Italy and this is the style he re-
created at Renishaw nearly 100 years ago, all vividly described in Osbert
Sitwell's memoirs. The statues, terraces and the sound of splashing water,
enhance to the Italianate atmosphere, and the present incumbents have added
a stupendous water jet to increase the effect. They have also increased the
number of different gardens (10 in all), divided and protected by yew hedges
and columns, enlarged the borders, introduced innovative planting (Sir
George had rejected Miss Jekyll's designs as being too colourful) and linked
the garden to the wood with new planting and paths. A nature trail leads into
an avenue of camellias and on to the classic temple, Gothick lodge, old sawmill,
cave and lakes. A cliffside walk is planned.

DEVON

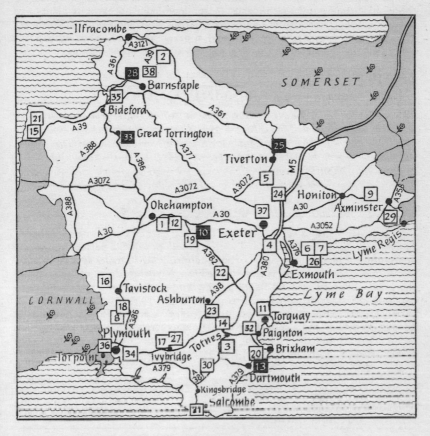

Two-starred gardens are marked on the map with a black square.

Andrew's Corner

Belstone, Okehampton EX20 1RD. Tel: (01837) 840332;
E-mail: Edwina-robin.hill@virgin.net

Mr and Mrs R.J. Hill • 3m E of Okehampton off A30, signed to Belstone then Skaigh • Open 15th, 22nd April, 5th, 19th May, 2nd, 9th June, 2.30 – 6pm, and by appt at other times • Entrance: £1.50, children free • Other information: Teas on open days only ● ☕ ♿ ⚘ ✎

High above sea level on north Dartmoor, facing the Taw valley and the high moor, in only one and a half acres (amazing that it is not larger) grows a wide variety of plants of all sorts not normally seen at such an altitude. The sense of space is achieved by the division of the garden into different levels by rhododendrons and trees, each area having its own microclimate, and all with glimpses through to other areas and to the wider landscape. Colour in spring comes from bulbs and meconopsis, in summer from herbaceous plants and lilies, in autumn from maples (many grown from seed) and gentians. There are drystone walls (a speciality of the area), a paved area and ponds with water plants; among the stone and paving are lewisias and other alpines.

Arlington Court 2

Arlington, Barnstaple EX31 4LP. Tel: (01271) 850296

The National Trust • 7m NE of Barnstaple on A39 • House and carriage collection open as garden, but 11am – 5pm. Carriage driving school open March to Nov by appt • Garden open 23rd March to 3rd Nov, daily except Tues, 10.30am – 5pm; July and Aug, daily except Tues, 10.30am — 6pm; 4th Nov to 22nd March 2003, during daylight hours • Entrance: garden and carriage museum £3.40, children £1.70 (house, carriage collection and garden £5.40, children £3.70, family ticket £13.50, parties of 15 or more £4.60 per person, children £2.30) (2001 prices) ◐ 🍽 ✕ 🍴 WC ሌ ⟨⟩ 🏕 ♿

The Georgian house is set in a largely informal garden extending to 30 acres. The mild, damp climate, combined with acid soil, provides a perfect home for a wide range of plants, particularly rhododendrons, with many species of tree-like proportions; hydrangeas also thrive here. In spring, drifts of bulbs carpet the grass, followed by wild flowers. The wilderness pond is surrounded by rhododendrons, contrasting with the formal and symmetrical terraced Victorian garden with its annual bedding. There is also a double herbaceous border, a rockery and a conservatory. The one-acre walled kitchen garden is being restored, and the Victorian lean-to greenhouse has been rebuilt to the original design. A few miles SE of Barnstable on A377, in Pixie Lane, Umberleigh, *Glebe Cottage Plants* (the nursery owned by Chelsea gold-medal winner Carol Klein) stocks a mouth-watering range of rare and newly introduced perennials. [Open all year, Wed – Fri. Tel: (01769) 540554.]

Avenue Cottage Gardens 3

Ashprington, Totnes TQ9 7UT. Tel/Fax: (01803) 732769

Mr R.C.H. Soans and Mr R.J. Pitts • 3m S of Totnes. Take A381 from Totnes towards Kingsbridge, turn left to Ashprington. Facing Durant Arms in Ashprington turn left uphill past church; gardens are 300 metres on right • Open April to Sept, Tues – Sat, 11am – 5pm, and by appt • Entrance: £2, children 25p by collecting box ◐ 🍴 WC ⟨⟩

These were originally part of the eighteenth-century landscape gardens of Sharpham House, separated 60 years ago. They are approached down a splendid avenue of Turkey oaks dating from 1844. Many of the rhododendrons and azaleas planted in the last century are enormous and magnificent, but as parts of the garden had become very overgrown over the years a clearing programme was started. The owners are always delighted to point out some of their more unusual treasures.

Bickham House 4

Kenn, Exeter EX6 7XL. Tel: (01392) 832671; Fax: (01392) 832825

Mr and Mrs John Tremlett • 6m S of Exeter on A38 before junction with A380. Leave dual carriageway at Kennford Services and follow signs to Kenn, then take first right and follow lane for ³/₄ m to end of no-through road • Open 14th, 16th, 17th April, 12th, 14th, 15th May, 9th, 11th, 12th June, 14th, 16th, 17th July, 11th, 13th, 14th Aug, 8th, 10th, 11th Sept, 2 – 5pm, and at other times by appt • Entrance: £2, children 50p ● ♨ 🍴 WC ♿ ✿

Six acres of garden in a peaceful wooded valley, overlooking a small lake. The house has been in the family since it was built in 1682, but the garden has been extensively remodelled in the last few years, and new features are being added all the time. There are lawns and fine trees, spring-flowering shrubs and many naturalised bulbs and a box-hedged parterre around a lily pond. In the mixed borders great attention is paid to colour co-ordination. The one-acre walled garden with rose beds, a formal herb garden and a highly productive flower and vegetable section is full of colour and interest throughout the year; an avenue of palm trees leads to a new summerhouse. Colourful too is the small water garden. There is also a conservatory, leading into an enclosed cobbled area with raised beds and a wall fountain. A mown path circles the lake, which is home to wild duck, geese and other waterfowl.

Bickleigh Castle 5

Tiverton EX16 8RP. Tel: (01884) 855363

Mr M.J. Boxall • 4m S of Tiverton off A396. At Bickleigh Bridge take A3072 and follow signs • Castle and exhibitions open • Garden open Easter to Sept, Wed, Sun and Bank Holiday Mons only, 2 – 5.30pm (last admission 4.30pm) • Entrance: castle, garden £4, children (5–15) £2, family ticket £10, parties by appt ◑ ♨ ♿

Situated in the valley of the Exe around the ancient buildings, which are historically fascinating with much to see, the castle became the home of the Carew family, Sir George Carew being the Vice Admiral of the *Mary Rose*. Beyond the eighteenth-century Italian wrought-iron gates is a large mound planted in the 1930s with every known variety of rhododendron. There is a 300-year-old wisteria and many more mature trees, including *Ginkgo biloba*, magnolias, a Judas tree and a tulip tree. Iris and water lilies in moat. The gardens are undergoing a five-year programme of restoration.

Bicton College 6

East Budleigh, Budleigh Salterton EX9 7BY. Tel: (01395) 562353; Fax: (01395) 567502

2m N of Budleigh Salterton on A376 • Open all year, daily except 25th Dec to 1st Jan, 10.30am – 4.30pm • Entrance: £2, children free (2001 price) • Other information: Parking beyond student car park, short walk to garden ○ ♨ ⬦ ✿

The gardens of this Georgian house form the horticultural department of Bicton College, and as such contain a large number of plants laid out for both study and general interest – truly a plantsman's paradise. As well as the fascinating herbaceous beds there is an arboretum of interest at all times of the year and an old walled garden, all approached by an avenue of araucarias (monkey puzzle trees). Amongst the plants which provide both information and effect are National Collections of agapanthus and pittosporums. Large area of parkland and a lake. Ten miles to the north is *Escot Place*, Ottery St Mary, described as 'one of Devon's most important stately homes'. Here the latest project of Ivan Hicks, the creator of the Garden in Mind at Stanstead Park (see entry in West Sussex), is evolving in 220 acres of traditional woodland garden. Telephone (01404) 822188 for more information, or visit the website at www.escot-devon.co.uk.

Bicton Park Botanical Gardens ★ 7

East Budleigh, Budleigh Salterton EX9 7BJ. Tel: (01395) 568465;
Fax: (01395) 568374; email: info@bictongardens.co.uk;
Website: www.bictongardens.co.uk

*Bicton Park • 2m N of Budleigh Salterton on B3178 • Open daily, 11am –
5pm. Closed 25th Dec • Entrance: £4.75, children (3–15) £2.75, family £12.75,
concessions £3.75* ○ 💹 ✕ 🍴 WC 🚻 🐕 🎈 🎪 ♿ ⚲

There is much to see here in the Grade-I-listed 60 acres. The formal and informal gardens date from 1734, largely landscaped in the style of Le Nôtre. There is a stream garden with a 150-year-old mulberry, azaleas, camellias, flowering cherries and a peony border (herbaceous and tree), an American garden established in the 1830s, and a hermitage garden with a lake and water garden. The pinetum, first planted in 1838 and extended in 1910 to take the collection of the famous botanist and explorer 'Chinese' Wilson, has some rare conifers, including a Mexican juniper, yuccas, Korean thuya and Tasmanian cedar. Perhaps Bicton's greatest glory is the palm house, built between 1815 and 1820, one of the oldest in the country and recently refurbished; inside, Kentia palms up to seven metres, tree ferns and bromeliads, and outside an Assam tea plant. There are also geranium and fuchsia houses and a tropical and a temperate house for bananas, coffee trees and bougainvilleas. The new Museum of Garden History has combined with the existing Museum of Country Life to make one of the largest museums in the West Country. Nearby are Sidmouth's *Connaught Gardens*, originally designed in the 1930s, combine breathtaking views across its beautiful and mercifully still unspoilt bay, stunningly colourful traditional bedding displays and a large and varied collection of unusual and tender shrubs and plants; also herbaceous borders with new varieties introduced on a regular basis, all immaculately kept – very different from the expected seaside public garden. Meandering paths lead from sheltered walled areas to the clifftop walk, with seats everywhere.

Buckland Abbey 8

Yelverton PL20 6EY. Tel: (01822) 853607

*The National Trust and Plymouth City Council • 6m S of Tavistock, 11m N of
Plymouth. Turn off A386 ¼ m S of Yelverton • Open 23rd March to 3rd Nov,
daily except Thurs, 10.30am – 5.30pm; mid-Feb to March, 4th Nov to 22nd*

Dec, Sat and Sun; all 2 – 5pm (last admission ¾ hour before closing). Closed 23rd Dec to 21st Feb • Entrance: £2.40, children £1.20 (abbey and grounds £4.60, children £2,30, family (2 adults, 2 children), £11.50) (2001 prices) • Other information: Possible for wheelchairs but steep site. Motorised buggy usually available ☀ 🍴 ✕ WC ♿ 🌿 🏭 🍴 ♒

The garden is largely a twentieth-century creation. There is a box hedge parterre between the 30-metre-long medieval barn and the abbey, its pockets filled with over 50 different herbs, reputedly inspired by Vita Sackville-West. *Magnolia delavayi* and *M. grandiflora* grow against the abbey walls. A line of ailing yews on the north border of the lawn has been replaced by an Elizabethan garden, and a thyme area has recently been created. Delightful estate walks, and glorious views of Devon and Cornwall.

Burrow Farm Gardens ★   9

Dalwood, Axminster EX13 7ET. Tel: (01404) 831285;
Website: www.burrowfarmgardens.co.uk

Mr and Mrs John Benger • 4m W of Axminster off A35 Honiton road. After 3½ m turn N near Shute garage onto Stockland road. Garden is ½ m on right • Open April to Sept, daily, 10am – 7pm • Entrance: £3, children 50p, parties (discount rate) by appt ◑ 🍵 🍽 WC ♿ 🐕 🌿 ♒

These lovely gardens, created from pasture land, are the inspiration of Mary Benger and her family, who are still developing the six-acre site. Foliage effect has been admirably achieved with a colourful array of azaleas and rhododendrons. A former Roman clay pit is graded from top to bottom through mature trees and shrubs to an extensive bog garden with a marvellous show of candelabra primulas and native wild flowers during the early part of the season. In summer the pergola walk, with its old-fashioned roses and herbaceous borders, is a picture. A courtyard garden and a terraced garden feature late-flowering herbaceous plants. The rill garden has ponds, a classical summerhouse and a ha-ha laid out in a formal design, luxuriantly and informally planted with trees, shrubs and herbaceous plants. The setting and sense of grandeur are more typical of gardens of greater repute. Magnificent views. Nearby is Homelea Farm, where *R&D Plants* has an inventive list of herbaceous and woodland plants. [Open by appt in Feb for hellebores, then daily March to Oct, 9am – 5pm, but closed for lunch. Tel: (01460) 220206.]

Castle Drogo ★★   10

Drewsteignton EX6 6PB. Tel: (01647) 433306; Fax: (01647) 433186

The National Trust • 5m S of A30 or 4m NW of Moretonhampstead on A382; follow signs from Sandy Park • Shop • Castle open 23rd March to 3rd Nov, Sat – Thurs, 11am – 5.30pm • Garden open all year, daily, 10.30am – dusk • Entrance: £2.80 (reduced rate Nov to Feb, but castle extra). Reduced rate for parties by appt (2001 prices) • Other information: Coaches by appt only. Disabled parking. Access for wheelchairs by arrangement at reception. Scented plants for visually handicapped. Croquet equipment for hire ◑ 🍴 ✕ 🍽 WC 🌿 🏭 🍴 ♒

The last castle to be built in England (begun 1910) was designed by Sir Edwin Lutyens. The plans for the planting of the garden were by George Dillistone of Tunbridge Wells. Apart from the evergreen oaks above the magnificent views over the Teign Gorge, and a valley planted with rhododendrons, magnolias, camellias, cornus and maples, there is a series of formal terraces and borders with walls of granite, sharp-edged yew hedges with rose beds and arbours of yew and *Parrotia persica* (the iron tree). In the main formal gardens, with galleries round a sunken centre, paths are serpentine (an Indian touch typical of Lutyens, who built New Delhi in the 1920s while he was supervising here), and herbaceous borders are full of old varieties of crocosmia (montbretia), lychnis, campanulas, iris and red-hot pokers. Under the granite walls are perennials – euphorbias, hellebores, alchemillas and veronicas – planted with spring bulbs. Steps lead to a second terrace with yuccas and wisterias and herb borders; more steps to shrub borders of lilacs, azaleas, magnolias and lilies; and finally comes a splendid circular lawn surrounded by a tall yew hedge at the top, a huge green circle and a perfect stage set for croquet. In Chagford, off A30 via Whiddon Down, are *Stone Lane Gardens*, an informally landscaped five-acre arboretum containing a national collection of wild-origin alder and birch from all over the world. An annual sculpture exhibition is held from May to September. [Open mid-June to mid-Sept, daily, 2 – 6pm, but telephone (01647) 231311 first to check.]

Castle Tor   11

Oxlea Road, Wellswood, Torquay TQ1 2HF. Tel: (01803) 214801

Mr G. Creighton • In Torquay. From Higher Lincombe Road, turn E into Oxlea Road. Entrance is 200 metres on right with eagle-topped pillars • Open by appt only • Entrance: free ◐

In the 1920s the then owner of Castle Tor approached Sir Edwin Lutyens and asked him to design a smaller version of Castle Drogo; being too busy himself, Sir Edwin nominated his pupil, Frederick Harrild, and the result is this fascinating architectural garden with magnificent views over Lyme Bay and Tor Bay. Gertrude Jekyll's ideas about garden colour – no violent juxtapositions or circular beds full of salvias – were incorporated, and the whole is framed in terraces of Somerset limestone and cubic green walls of yew hedges; topiary is fashioned from both green and golden yew. There are architectural-type follies: a pillared orangery with a domed roof, a tower with portcullis and gatehouse, and best of all a long ornamental water course or small canal.

Cleave House   12

Sticklepath, Okehampton EX20 2NL. Tel: (01837) 840481 Fax: (01837) 840482; E-mail: bowdenhostas@eclipse.co.uk; Website: www.hostas-uk.com

Ann and Roger Bowden • 3½ m E of Okehampton on old A30 towards Exeter. House is in Sticklepath on left just past small right turn for Skaigh • Open 1st, 2nd June, 10.30am – 5pm • Entrance: £1.50 ◐ **WC** ♨

For the Bowdens hostas are not just a business, they are an abiding passion. Their one-acre garden, tucked away at the heart of a small Devon village, boasts some delightful mixed planting – both trees and shrubs – but hostas are the dominant feature. A few varieties, notably the brightly coloured, have been imported from the United States. This Mecca for the hosta enthusiast includes demonstration beds resplendent with over 600 different varieties, displaying fascinating variations in both colour and size. The collection has been designated an NCCPG reference (of modern hybrids).

Coleton Fishacre Garden ★★ 13

Brownstone Road, Kingswear, Dartmouth TQ6 0EQ. Tel: (01803) 752466; Fax: (01803) 753017; Website: www.nationaltrust.org.uk

The National Trust • 3m E of Dartmouth, 3m S of Brixham off B3205. 2½ m from Kingswear, take Lower Ferry Road and turn off at toll house • House open as garden, 11am – 4.30pm • Garden open March, Sun, 11am – 5pm; then 23rd March to 3rd Nov, Wed – Sun and Bank Holiday Mons, 10.30am – 5.30pm • Entrance: £3.80, children £1.90, pre-booked parties of 15 or more £3.10 per person (house and garden £4.80, children, £2.40, family ticket £12, pre-booked parties £4.10, children £2) (2001 prices) ◐ ▆ ▩ WC ⅌ ⛫ ● ⚲

Oswald Milne, a pupil of Edwin Lutyens, designed the house and the architectural features of this garden for Rupert and Lady D'Oyly Carte; the house was completed and the garden begun in 1926. The exceptionally mild setting is a Devon combe, sloping steeply to the cliff tops and the sea, and sheltered by belts of Monterey pines and holm oaks. The streams and ponds make a humid atmosphere for the moisture-loving plants like the magnificent bamboos and mimosas, and many other sub-tropical plants. There is a collection of unusual trees like dawn redwood, swamp cypress and Chilean myrtle, and dominating all a tall tulip tree and tree of heaven (*Ailanthus altissima*) the same age as the house. The Paddock Woodland Walk runs from the Gazebo Walk near the house, through woodland to a main viewing area. Formal walls and terraces make a framework round the house for a large number of sun-loving tender plants. There are various water features, notably a stone edged rill and a circular pool in the herbaceous-bordered walled garden. A brilliant garden.

Dartington Hall ★ 14

Dartington, Totnes TQ9 6EL. Tel/Fax: (01803) 862367; E-mail: gardens@dartingtonhall.org.uk; Website: www.dartington.u-net.com

Dartington Hall Trust • 2m NW of Totnes, E of A384 • Open all year, daily, dawn – dusk. Parties by appt only • Entrance: by donation £2, guided tours by arrangement £4 • Other information: Coaches by appt ○ ✗ WC ⅁ ⅌ ⛫ ● ⚲

In 1925, Leonard and Dorothy Elmhirst purchased the then-declining Dartington Hall estate, to launch their great experiment in rural regeneration. Over the years many notable garden designers have influenced the restoration, including the American Beatrix Farrand, who was responsible for transforming the courtyard and opening up the woodland walkways. There are three walks, each using bay, yew and holly as background plantings for the collections of camellias, magnolias and rhododendrons. Percy Cane introduced such features as the glade, the azalea dell and the impressive magnolia steps. More recently, Preben Jacobsen re-designed the herbaceous border and Philip Booth was commissioned to create the Japanese garden. The overall effect is strongly architectural, with the fourteenth-century tiltyard and its terraces at the heart.

Docton Mill ★   15

Lymebridge, Elmscott, Hartland EX39 6EA. Tel: (01237) 441369;
Website: www.doctonmill.co.uk

Mr and Mrs J. Borrett • 12m N of Bude, 14m W of Bideford off A39. From north Devon travel via Hartland to Stoke or from north Cornwall to West Country Inn, then turn left signed Elmscott towards Lymebridge in Spekes Valley • Open March to Oct, daily, 10am – 6pm • Entrance: £3.50, OAPS £3, children £1 • Other information: coaches by appt ◑ 🅿 ♿ WC ⬥ ⌘ ℺

The garden was created from a derelict water mill of Saxon origin in 1980 by the previous owners, who embarked upon a large-scale clearance of the waterways. There are ponds, leats, footbridges over the river and many smaller streams as it is only 1500 metres from Spekes Mill Mouth coastal waterfall and the beach. A stream and a bog garden is planted with ligularias, primulas and ferns. The whole purpose has been to make everything as natural as possible. In spring there are displays of narcissi, camellias, primulas, azaleas and magnolias with bluebells; in summer the garden abounds in roses, mostly old shrub roses. There is a hedge of 'Felicia' and 'Pax' hybrid musk roses and a climbing 'Felicia' – a rarity. Roses are underplanted with perennial geraniums, and these are also used on the rockery (which is wet clay and north-facing and not suitable for alpines) together with hebes and dwarf conifers. A new planting of magnolias (25 species) has transformed the old donkey paddock, and a woodland garden is being planted in the spring of 2002.

Endsleigh House and Gardens   16

Milton Abbot, Tavistock PL19 0PQ. Tel: (01822) 870248; Fax: (01822) 870502

Endsleigh Charitable Trust • 4m NW of Tavistock on B3362 • Gardens open April to Sept, daily, 11am – 5pm • Entrance: £3 (ticket machine) • Other information: Lunch and tea at hotel by arrangement ◑ 🅿 WC ♿ ⬥ ⌘

Endsleigh was built, starting in 1811, for the 6th Duke of Bedford from designs by architect Jeffry Wyatville and landscape gardener Humphry Repton. The house is a good example of a *cottage orné* and was used as a fishing and hunting lodge by the Duke. It is now a quiet country house hotel. The house and the immediate garden have tight views overlooking the almost stream-like character of the upper Tamar, wooded on either bank. The garden has been restored to re-establish the nineteenth-century vision, and an uneasy truce established between the rich wilderness that has invaded Repton's landscape and the slow process of ongoing authentication. Rare tree species in the arboretum have largely survived the storms of the late 1980s. Buzzards and cormorants command the sky.

Fardel Manor 17

Ivybridge PL21 9HT. Tel: (01752) 892353; Fax: (01752) 894962

Dr A.G. Stevens • 1¼ m NW of Ivybridge off A38, 2m SE of Cornwood, 200 metres off railway bridge • At time of going to press house is on market, so check before travelling • Entrance: £1.50, children 50p • Other information: Teas and plants available on July open day only ● WC &

A five-acre, all-organic garden, maintained with conservation and wildlife in mind. Small courtyards and a walled garden cluster around the fourteenth-century manor, with an orangery, herbaceous borders, a formal pond and a shrub garden. There are also enclosed fruit and vegetable gardens and an orchard with a wildflower meadow. A two-and-a-half-acre arboretum was planted during the 1980s, and a stream and lake with ornamental and native plantings create a habitat for waterfowl of all kinds.

The Garden House ★ 18

Buckland Monachorum, Yelverton PL20 7LQ. Tel: (01822) 854769; Fax: (01822) 855358; E-mail: office@thegardenhouse.org.uk; Website: www.thegardenhouse.org.uk

The Fortescue Garden Trust • 10m N of Plymouth, 2m W of Yelverton off A386 • Open March to Oct, daily, 10.30am – 5pm • Entrance: £4, OAPs £3.50, children £1 ◑ ▬ ✕ ▤ WC ♨

A garden in the 'new naturalism' style, providing colour and interest from spring through summer and into autumn. Largely north-facing and nearly 150 metres above sea level, it has to contend with up to 150 centimetres of rain *per annum*. Its origins are deep in the past, but in gardening terms its story began when Mr and Mrs Lionel Fortescue arrived in 1945 to breathe life into the derelict walled garden, which surrounds the ruins of a medieval vicarage and includes a thatched barn and a tower. Through years of painstaking restoration, the walled garden has become one of the finest of its type in the country. In 1978 Keith and Ros Wiley came here and continued the work. Their modification and planting programme since the 1980s has been quite remarkable. Eight acres of pasture and paddock have been transformed by the planting of more than 3000 trees and shrubs, more than 1000 herbaceous plants and thousands of spring bulbs. A wisteria wood is now maturing and landscaping work for a two-acre water-meadow garden is continuing.

Gidleigh Park ★ 19

Chagford TQ13 8HH. Tel: (01647) 432367; Fax: (01647) 432574; E-mail: gidleighpark@gidleigh.co.uk; Website: www.gidleigh.com

Kay and Paul Henderson • Off A382 11m SE of Okehampton. In Chagford Square turn right into Mill Street by Lloyds TSB. In 150 metres fork right (virtually straight across junction). Go to end of the road – about 2m • Open all year except Bank Holidays, Mon – Fri • Entrance: £6 (inc. coffee or tea with biscuits) • Other information: Lunches and teas served in hotel ○ ▬ ✕ WC ◁

Gidleigh Park, the acclaimed hotel and restaurant, is set in 45 acres of magnificent and secluded grounds on the north bank of the River Teign, within the Dartmoor National Park. The woodland garden and parkland were created between 1850 and 1930. Since 1980, under the direction of head gardener Keith Mansfield, the owners have undertaken an extensive pro- gramme of restoration. Among the many interesting features is a delightful water garden rebuilt and planted in 1986, and extended significantly into the woodland in 1997. Visitors can take this in on their way round the Boundary Walk — a 45-minute stroll through natural mixed woodland, underplanted with azaleas and rhododendrons. The Teign is never far away, tumbling over granite boulders, past spring displays of rhododendrons. The mock-Tudor house gives way to a terrace resplendent with summer colour, while a parterre and herb garden add a touch of formality. There is an interesting avenue of young pleached limes adjacent to the front lawn, and one must mention the croquet lawns, the very upmarket golf 'putting garden' and the pavilion — the final decadent flourishes.

Greenway House   20

Greenway Road, Galmpton, Churston Ferrers, Brixham TQ5 0ES.
Tel: (01803) 842382 (Greenway Gardens)

The National Trust • *4m W of Brixham. From A3022 Paignton — Brixham road, take road to Galmpton, then towards Greenway Ferry. Vehicles strictly limited. Parking spaces for cars and mini-coaches must be pre-booked (Tel: (01803) 842382). No parking in lanes outside property. Please either take Dartmouth — Dittisham 'Red and Yellow' ferry (Tel: (01803) 833206) or drive to Goodrington park and ride, take steam train to Churston station, then walk down Greenway Road (20 mins); or use bus service 106 Paignton — Galmpton (Tel: (09018) 802288) and walk as above • Garden open 6th March to 5th Oct, Wed — Sat, 10.30am — 5pm • Entrance: £3.50, children £1.75 • Other information: Plants for sale in nursery* ● 🍵 📗 WC ⟨⟩ 🌳 🧺 🔍

The 30-acre ancient Devon garden is set on the bank of the tree-lined Dart river which has woodland walks. There are many indigenous trees over 150 years old and a giant tulip tree. In the walled garden are many camellias, 30 varieties of magnolias, ceanothus, wisterias and abutilons. The banks of primroses and bluebells make it magical in spring. In the natural glades are foxgloves, white iris, herb Roberts, pennyworts, ivies and hart's tongue and male ferns. The house (Agatha Christie's home for many years) and the area immediately around it are not open.

Hartland Abbey   21

Nr Bideford, EX39 6DT. Tel: (01237) 441264/234;
Fax: (01237) 44126/(01884) 8611344 (Administrator);
E-mail: stucley@care4free.net; Website: www.hartlandabbey.com

Sir Hugh and Lady Stucley • *15m SW of Bideford off A39 Bideford — Bude road. Follow signs to Hartland; drive through village, take road to Hartland Quay. Signposted • House, gardens and grounds open 31st March, 1st April;*

then April to Sept, Wed, Thurs, Sun and Bank Holiday Mons (plus July and Aug, Tues); all 2 – 5.30pm • Garden and grounds open April to Oct, daily except Sat, 2 – 5.30pm, and at other times by appt • Entrance: gardens and grounds £3, children 50p (house, gardens and grounds £5, OAPs £4.50, children £1.50) ◑ ➤ ▨ WC ♿ ⬳ ⅋ ⬛ ♞

Once an Augustinian monastery, the abbey is set across a narrow sheltered valley. Because of the gales, gardens were not created around the house – although a row of 100-year-old bay trees survives – but were planted either side of the valley with azaleas, rhododendrons, camellias, hydrangeas, gunneras and many other shrubs and trees. Some of the paths in the bog garden were designed by Gertrude Jekyll, who used to be a guest at the abbey, and the Victorian fernery, also thought to be by her, has been replanted. The series of eighteenth-century walled gardens, set in a south-facing, gently sloping valley five minutes' walk away, are carpeted in spring with bluebells, primroses and violets, filled with vegetables, herbaceous plants, roses and clematis, plus self-seeded giant echiums. The walk to the Atlantic, over a mile away, gives stunning views of the rugged coastline.

Higher Knowle   22

Lustleigh, Newton Abbot TQ13 9SP. Tel: (01647) 277275;
Fax: (0870) 1315914; E-mail: d.quicke@connectfree.co.uk

Mr and Mrs D.R.A. Quicke • 13m NW of Torquay, 8m NW of Newton Abbot, 3m NW of Bovey Tracey on A382 towards Moretonhampstead. After 2½ m, turn left at Kelly Cross for Lustleigh; after ¼ m left then right at Brookfield along Knowle Road; after ¼ m steep drive on left • Open 31st March to 2nd June, Sun and Bank Holiday Mons, 2 – 6pm, for NGS, and by appt between these dates • Entrance: £2.50, children free ● WC ⬳

A three-acre woodland garden surrounding a stone house built in 1914 with many Lutyens-style features by his pupil Fred Harrild as architect. Situated on a steep hillside with spectacular views to Dartmoor, the sheltered garden usually avoids late frosts and is home to tender plants. The old oak wood is carpeted with primroses and bluebells in the spring, with mature Asiatic magnolias providing a fine display in late March, followed by camellias, new hybrid magnolias, many rhododendrons and azaleas, and tall embothriums. Giant Dartmoor granite boulders add much natural sculpture to the woodland walks, which include a water garden. Plants are labelled. Not far away is *Pleasant View Nursery*, near Denbury, which also has a show garden for National Collections of abelias and salvias [Open May to Sept, Wed and Fri, 2 – 5pm].

Hill House Nursery and Garden ★   23

Landscove, Ashburton, Newton Abbot TQ13 7LY. Tel: (01803) 762273;
E-mail: sacha@garden.demon.co.uk; Website: www.garden.demon.co.uk

Mr and Mrs Raymond Hubbard and Mr Matthew Hubbard • 17m SW of Exeter. From Plymouth-bound A38, take second exit signed 'Ashburton', then left signed 'Landscove 2½ m', or from A384 Totnes – Buckfastleigh road follow signs to Landscove. Signposted • Open all year, daily, 11am – 5pm. Booking required for parties • Entrance: free • Other information: Tea room open March to Sept only ○ ☕ ✕ 🧺 WC ⬦ 🌢

Hill House, once a Victorian vicarage next to its church – both by John Loughborough Pearson – is known to enthusiasts as the garden created by Edward Hyams and filled by him with rare, exotic and tender plants. Since the 1980s it has been restored by the present owners, plantsmen Raymond and Matthew Hubbard, both as a private garden and a family-run nursery. Hyams' small eighteenth-century Grecian temple has been restored. The pond has by it a pretty conservatory also designed by him, and containing a grape vine, passion flowers and a lemon tree. An integral feature of the garden is the commercial nursery, which offers both everyday plants and tender, exotic and rare varieties.

Killerton ★ 24

Broadclyst, Exeter EX5 3LE. Tel: (01392) 881345

The National Trust • 7m NE of Exeter, on W side of B3181 • House and costume museum open 9th March to 2nd Sept, daily except Tues, 11am – 5.30pm (last admission ½ hour before closing) • Park and garden open all year, 10.30am – dusk • Entrance: £3.70 (2001 price) • Other information: Tea room limited opening in winter. Motorised buggies with drivers available for disabled. Dogs in park only, on lead ○ ☕ 🧺 WC ♿ ⬦ 🌢 🏛 🌡 ♺

This large hillside garden surrounded by woods, park and farmland extends to over 6000 acres. It was created by John Veitch in the 1770s and later involved the famous Victorian gardening writer William Robinson. The actual garden area of 18 acres is a haven of delight. It will provide pleasure and interest to all but particularly to the tree and shrub enthusiast. Many of the plants for sale were propagated here. Besides the avenue of beeches, there are Wellingtonias (the first plantings in England), Lawson cypresses, oaks, maples and many fine broadleaved trees. Trees and shrubs introduced by Veitch are now reaching an imposing size. Terraced beds and extensive herbaceous borders provide summer colour. Killerton has a rhododendron collection with 95 different species, many brought back from China and Japan. There is also an early-nineteenth-century summerhouse, the Bear's Hut, an ice-house and rock garden. The handsome chapel has its own three-acre grounds containing many other fine trees, notably the largest tulip tree in England. Nearby is *Little Upcot*, Marsh Green, a two-acre plantsman's garden, open by appointment (Tel: (01404) 822797).

Knightshayes ★★ 25

Bolham, Tiverton EX16 7RQ. Tel: (01884) 254665 (Property Manager); Tel/Fax: (01884) 253264 (Garden Office)

The National Trust • 16m N of Exeter, 2m N of Tiverton. Turn off A396 at Bolham • Gardens open 16th March to 3rd Nov, daily, 11am – 5.30pm. House open 23rd March to 3rd Nov, daily except Fri, 11am – 5.30pm (open Good

Friday); Oct, 11am – 4.30pm; • *Entrance: house and gardens, £5.40, children £2.70; gardens only £3.80, children £1.90 (2001 prices)* • *Other information: Dogs in park and Impey Walk only, on lead* ◑ 🍵 ✕ 🏠 WC ⅗ ⟨⟩ 🌱 🏛 🍴 ❀

This wonderful garden is the setting for a Victorian house designed by William Burges. His flamboyant style is seen in the stables with their fairytale Gothick tower. The garden was transformed from the 1950s by Sir John and Lady Amory. The terraces have shrub roses, tree peonies and herbaceous plants in soft colours and silvers. Yew encloses a paved garden planted in pink, purple and grey with two standard wisterias. Battlemented hedges frame the pool garden with a backdrop of *Acer pseudoplatanus* 'Brilliantissimum'. The Garden in the Wood is a magical place sheltering magnolias, rhododendrons, cornus, hydrangeas and many rare and tender plants. Drifts of pink erythroniums, white foxgloves and cyclamen appear in their seasons.

Lee Ford 26

Budleigh Salterton EX9 7AJ. Tel: (01395) 445894; Fax: (01395) 441100

Mr and Mrs N. Lindsay-Fynn • *3½ m E of Exmouth on B3178 Budleigh Salterton – Knowle road* • *Open for charity, but by prior application; parties by appt* • *Entrance: £2.50, OAPs £2, children £1.50. Pre-booked parties of 20 or more £2 per person* • *Other information: Coffee or teas for parties by arrangement* ● 🏠 WC ⅗ ⟨⟩

Inspired by the Savill Gardens (see entry in Surrey), the present owner's father developed this woodland garden in the 1950s. Although at its peak in spring, with acres of daffodils followed by rhododendrons, azaleas and magnolias, there is now plenty to see later in the year. Following much recent landscaping, the formal garden round the house merges into the woodland rising above it, with curving beds full of new planting that includes collections of hydrangeas and fuchsias, together with many grasses and a bog garden. In the woodland, with its fine tall trees and distant views of the sea, the mown glades are surrounded by masses of azaleas, species and *ponticum* rhododendrons, some rare, and there is a large collection of camellias, including white varieties which are often in flower on Christmas Day. The nineteenth-century walled garden is still run as a traditional vegetable garden, with flowers for cutting and greenhouses. There is also a conservatory, an Adam pavilion and a little herb garden.

Lukesland 27

Harford, Ivybridge PL21 0JF. Tel: (01752) 893390

Mr and Mrs B.N. Howell • *1½ m N of Ivybridge off A38, on Harford road. On E side of Erme valley* • *Open 14th April to 16th June, Wed, Sun and Bank Holiday Mons, 2 – 6pm* • *Entrance: £3.20, children free. Other information: coaches by appt* ● 🍵 WC ⅗ ⟨⟩ ❀

More a botanical park than a garden – on entering the grounds you could be forgiven for believing you were in the foothills of the Himalayas. Lying on the hem of Dartmoor, Lukesland is Victorian in both origin and taste. The house was built in 1862 in the Victorian Gothic style by W.E. Matthews. The delightfully secluded valley of the Addicombe Brook is the setting here for 15 acres of flowering shrubs, trees and carpets of wild flowers – a gem of its kind. Although recent planting has ensured a greater variety of all-year interest, it is in spring that the profusion of rhododendrons, camellias and azaleas show the garden at its resplendent best. The magnificent *Magnolia campbellii*, over 21 metres tall, is one of the many fine specimen trees. The pocket-handkerchief tree, planted in 1936, is thought to be one of the largest in the country. Addicombe Brook, which tumbles and gurgles its way over ponds and waterfalls, is criss-crossed by a series of delightful bridges which enable the visitor to wander at leisure amid scenes of great tranquillity. James McAndrew undertook the first major landscaping of the garden in the 1880s. The present owner and his family have carried out further planting, including a fine pinetum, and in the construction of more ponds and bridges, all in the spirit of the original. Also near Ivybridge, on A38, is *Endsleigh Garden Centre*, worth a visit. [Open daily, 9am – 6pm (Suns 10am – 4.30pm).]

Marwood Hill ★★ 28

Marwood, Barnstaple EX31 4EB. Tel: (01271) 342528

Dr J.A. Smart • 4m NW of Barnstaple off A361. Signposted • Open all year, daily except 25th Dec, dawn – dusk • Entrance: £3, accompanied children under 12 free • Other information: Teas on Sun and Bank Holidays or for parties by arrangement ○ 💭 🍴 WC ⬦ ♨ ℺

With its wonderful collection of plants and its delightful setting, this 20-acre garden is of special interest to the connoisseur but could not fail to give pleasure to any visitor. Five thousand different varieties of plants covering collections of willows, ferns, magnolias, eucryphias, rhododendrons and hebes, and a fine collection of camellias in a glasshouse. There is also a large planting of eucalyptus and betulas. Other features include a pergola draped with 12 varieties of wisteria, raised alpine scree beds, and three small lakes with an extensive bog garden and National Collections of astilbes, clematis, *Iris ensata*, and tulbaghias.

The Moorings 29

Rocombe, Lyme Regis, Dorset DT7 3RR. Tel: (01297) 443295

Mrs E. Marriage • 2m NW of Lyme Regis. Take A3070 out of Lyme Regis, turn right to Rocombe and Rhode Hill. After ½ m fork left (unsuitable for HGVs). Fourth house on right, drive is beyond house • Visitors welcome any time, but please telephone or call in advance • Entrance: £1, accompanied children free 🌑 WC ⬦

Especially rewarding to visit in spring and autumn, the garden lies on a sheltered, steep, west-facing slope. Impressively, most of the newly planted arboretum trees have been grown from seed; there is a collection of eucalyptus, many unusual pines including umbrella and maritime pines (grown from seed gathered in the south of France) and nothofagus, including *N. obliqua* and *N. procera*, and the woodland is underplanted with snowdrops, daffodils and bluebells. *Hibiscus paramutabilis*, a hardy shrub with large flowers in August, is very rare in this country; there are camellias and a 10-metre-high magnolia, and a buddleia flowering rose-red in June. A point of interest is the collection of many different species of fern.

The Old Rectory 30

Woodleigh, Loddiswell TQ7 4DG. Tel: (01548) 550387

Mr H.E. Morton • $3\frac{1}{2}$ m N of Kingsbridge off A381, E of Kingsbridge – Wrangaton road at Rake Cross (1m S of Loddiswell), $1\frac{1}{2}$ m from Woodleigh itself • Open by appt only • Entrance: £2, children 20p ● & ℀

The three-acre woodland garden and walled garden were rescued from neglect nearly 40 years ago. In the woodland are several individual glades of mature trees, underplanted with magnolias, azaleas, camellias and rhododendrons. Evergreens and shrubs are planted for scent and winter effect, and the wild garden is most colourful in spring with crocus and daffodils, while the walled garden is designed with summer in mind. The garden is a haven for wildlife; no chemicals are used and it is managed without outside help.

Overbecks Museum and Garden ★ 31

Sharpitor, Salcombe TQ8 8LW. Tel: (01548) 842893

The National Trust • $1\frac{1}{2}$ m S of Salcombe, SW of South Sands • Museum open 24th March to Sept, daily except Sat, 11am – 5.30pm; Oct, Sun – Thurs, 11am – 5pm • Garden open all year, daily • Entrance: £2.90 (museum and garden £4.10) • Other information: No coaches ○ 🍺 🍴 WC ℀ ♿ ℀

Palms stand in this exotic garden high above the Salcombe estuary, giving a strongly Mediterranean atmosphere. The mild maritime climate enables it to be filled with exotics such as myrtles, daturas, agaves and the rare example of a large camphor tree, *Cinnamomum camphora*. The Himalayan *Magnolia campbellii*, over 100 years old and 12 metres high and wide, is a sight to see in February and March. The steep terraces were built in 1901 and lead down through fuchsia trees, huge fruiting banana palms and myrtle trees to a wonderful *Cornus kousa*. In the centre of the garden are four large beds packed with herbaceous perennials, many of which are rare and tender. They are spectacular from July through to September: *Myosotidium hortensia* (hydrangea-like) with flowers as clear as blue china, phormiums, and tender roses among the rocks. The new parterre of classical design is enlivened in season by orange and lemon trees.

Paignton Zoo Environmental Park 32

Totnes Road, Paignton TQ4 7EU. Tel: (01803) 697500; Fax: (01803) 523457

The Whitley Wildlife Conservation Trust • 1m W of centre of Paignton on Totnes Road • Open all year, daily except 25th Dec, from 10am (closing times vary according to season) • Entrance: £7.70, OAPs £6.20, children £5.50 (2001 prices). Rates for parties available ○ 🍺 ✗ 🍴 WC & ♿ 🍷 ℀

Those with mixed views on zoos may be won over by Paignton; it is in the forefront of animal and plant conservation and one of the zoos worldwide involved in the breeding of endangered species. As well as the healthy and happy animals there are the plants. Over 100 acres in size, this was the first zoo in the country to combine animals and a botanic garden, laid out 60 years ago and added to over the years. There are six habitat areas: wetland, desert, savannah, forest, tropical forest and Devon woodland. In addition an arboretum is being developed to a 25-year programme. The choice of plants has been dictated by their harmlessness to teeth and beaks and their ability to provide shade and perching, swinging and basking places. There are geographical collections of plants in the paddocks, and plants also make the fences safer. Hardy Chinese plants surround the baboon rocks. National Collections of sorbarias and buddleias are held here. One of the large glasshouses contains a desert exhibit with plants from arid areas. A tropical display area, complete with birds and reptiles, gives visitors the experience of this very different environment.

RHS Garden Rosemoor ★★ 33

Great Torrington EX38 8PH. Tel: (01805) 624067

The Royal Horticultural Society • 7m SE of Bideford, 1m SE of Great Torrington on A3124 • Garden open all year, daily except 25th Dec, 10am – 6pm (closes 5pm Oct to March) • Entrance: £4.50, children £1 ○ 💷 ✕ 🍴 WC ⑤ 🌿 🏛 🕯 ⚘

Lady Anne Berry created the original garden here and her eight acres contain over 3500 plants from all over the world, many of which she collected. Rosemoor was the Society's first regional garden, second in importance only to Wisley, with which it has a certain stylistic affinity. The 40 acres include a new formal garden with 2000 roses in 200 varieties, colour-theme gardens, herb garden, *potager*, cottage garden, foliage garden, winter garden, alpine terrace, three model gardens and extensive herbaceous borders. The new foliage garden designed by Tom Stuart-Smith displays a wide range of plants grown mainly for their leaves, particularly grasses. The eighteenth-century gazebo from the grounds of Palmer House, Great Torrington has been reconstructed in the south arboretum, giving fine views across the garden and the valley. Elsewhere are stream and bog gardens and a large walled fruit and vegetable garden. National Collections of ilex (over 100 kinds) and cornus are planted throughout. Lectures, talks, garden walks and demonstrations are held all year; there are also many events (telephone for full programme). Free guides for children.

Saltram House 34

Plympton, Plymouth PL7 1UH. Tel: (01752) 333500; Fax: (01752) 336474

The National Trust • 3m E of Plymouth. From A379 turn N to Billacombe. After 1m turn left to Saltram • House open 23rd March to 3rd Nov, daily except Fri (but open Good Friday) • Garden open, daily except Fri; Feb and March, 11am – 4pm (telephone for details); April to Oct, 11am – 5pm • Entrance: £3 (house and garden £6). Parking £1.50 (2001 prices) ◐ 💷 ✕ 🍴 WC ⑤ 🚭 🌿 🏛 🕯 ⚘

The original garden dates from the 1740s, with Victorian and twentieth-century overlays; there are three eighteenth-century buildings – a castle or belvedere, an orangery (due to the mild climate the orange and lemon trees are moved outside in the summer) and a classical garden house named Fanny's Bower after Fanny Burney, who came here in 1789 in the entourage of George III. There is a long lime avenue underplanted with narcissi in spring and *Cyclamen hederifolium* in autumn, and a central glade with specimen trees like the stone pine and Himalayan spruce. Set against rolling lawns are several walks with magnolias, camellias, rhododendrons and Japanese maples which, with other trees, make for dramatic autumn colour. Tree walk guide available.

Tapeley Park ★   35

Instow EX39 4NT. Tel: (01271) 342558

Mr H.T.C. Christie • 2m N of Bideford S off A39 Barnstaple – Bideford road • House open for pre-booked parties. Additional £2 per person • Gardens open probably mid-March to Oct, daily except Sat, 10am – 5pm • Entrance: £3.50, OAPs £3, children £2. Special rates for parties ◑ 🍴 🏛 WC ♿ ⏳ 🌿 ⛺ 🌼

The mellow red-brick William and Mary house bestrides the narrow estuary of the River Torridge. It was the nobility of its elevated setting that inspired a much later hand – the architect John Belcher – to create a triple cascade of Italian terraces at the beginning of the twentieth century. These have now been restored to startling effect by Mary Keen, with planting of longitudinal bands of colour emphasising the length and formality of the terraces. The way from the house to the lake winds down a beautiful woodland walk; the water is backed by magnificent *Thuja plicata*, said to be the oldest in the country. Within the gardens are a set of small buildings, which include a circular shell-lined grotto, a brick ice-house, a Georgian dairy, a handsome neo-Grecian lodge and a fine 1855 obelisk. The eighteenth-century walled kitchen garden is very much a working area, and there is a new organic garden producing fruit, vegetables, nuts and herbs. The wild garden houses farm animals and an adventure playground. For plantsmen there are fine plants and exotics *Abelia floribunda*, sophoras and feijoas from Brazil. For those interested in landscape design there is ornamental water, yew hedges, an ilex tunnel, giant beeches and oaks. A garden for all tastes and all seasons, and a house owned by a family with a fascinating history – the Christies of Glyndebourne in Sussex. Mary Keen was also responsible for the new gardens around the rebuilt opera house at *Glyndebourne* itself, where Christopher Lloyd and head gardener Chris Hughes are also reinvigorating the existing planting schemes.

Tudor Rose Tea Rooms and Garden   36

36 New Street, The Barbican, Plymouth PL1 2NA.

Plymouth Corporation • In old town centre • Open all year, daily, 10am – 6pm • Entrance: free ○ 🍴 ✕ WC ♿ ⏳ ☕

An integral part of an area of Plymouth that is being refurbished, this is an interesting reconstruction of the type of Tudor garden that would have existed behind the house in this ancient street. As far as possible only plants which grew in Elizabethan England have been established. Elsewhere in Plymouth the Corporation commemorates great Victorian seaside gardening with colourful carpet bedding, hanging baskets and tubs.

University of Exeter ★ 37

Streatham Estate, Prince of Wales Road, Exeter EX4 4PX. Tel: (01392) 263059; Fax: (01392) 264547

University of Exeter • On N outskirts of Exeter on A396, turn E on to B3183 • Gardens open all year, daily • Entrance: free • Other information: Coaches by appt only ○ ⌇

There is much to see on a one-mile tour of these extensive gardens based on those created in the 1860s by an East India merchant millionaire who inherited a fortune made by blockade-running in the Napoleonic Wars. The landscaping and tree planting was carried out by Veitch, whose plant collectors (E.H. 'Chinese' Wilson among them) went all over the world, and at that time many of the trees were unique in Europe. There is a series of lakes with wildfowl, dogwoods, birches, hazels and alders, callistemon shrubs (bottle brushes), wingnut trees (*Pterocarya stenoptera*) brought from China in 1860, and a maidenhair tree (*Gingko biloba*) sacred in Buddhist China. Rockeries have collections of alpines; there is a banana tree (*Musa basjoo*), a large *Gunnera chilensis* and palm trees introduced by Robert Fortune in 1849. Formal gardens and bedding plants lead to a sunken, scented garden. Exeter will house the National Collection of azaras, evergreens from Chile with scented yellow flowers. There are, of course, rhododendrons, magnolias, camellias in a woodland walk; also roses, eucalyptus and *Opuntia humifusa*, the prickly pear cactus flowering in summer. A useful nursery is *St Bridgets*, of Old Rydon Lane and Clyst St Mary, Exeter.

Woodside 38

Higher Raleigh Road, Barnstaple EX31 4JA. Tel: (01271) 343095

Mr and Mrs M. Feesey • Off A39 Barnstaple – Lynton road, turn right 300 metres above fire station • Open 7th July, 1 – 5.30pm, for charity, and at other times by appt • Entrance: £1.50, children 50p

South-facing semi-woodland with intensive shrub planting and many ornamental grasses, bamboos and monocots (the owner is the author of a RHS handbook on ornamental grasses). Much is shaded and peaceful with good protection for tender shrubs. A collection of New Zealand flora and acid-loving shrubs; also raised beds and troughs, ornamental trees and conifers – all with emphasis on form and foliage colour.

DORSET

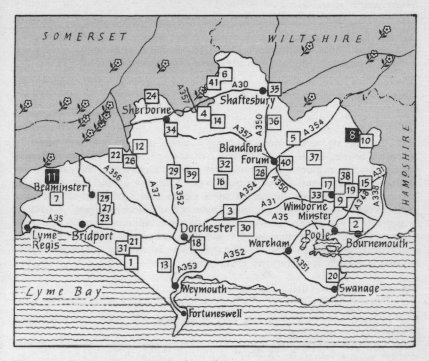

Two-starred gardens are marked on the map with a black square.

Abbotsbury Sub-Tropical Gardens ★   1

Abbotsbury, Weymouth DT3 4LA. Tel: (01305) 871387;
E-mail: info@abbotsbury-tourism.co.uk; Website: www.abbotsbury.tourism.co.uk

Ilchester Estates • 9m NW of Weymouth, 9m SW of Dorchester off B3157 • Open Murch to Oct, daily, 10am – 6pm; Nov to Feb, daily except 25th, 26th Dec and 1st Jan, 10am – dusk • Entrance: £4.90, OAPs £4.70, children £3.50 (2001 prices). Party bookings discount available ○ ▭ ✕ ▤ WC ⟁ ⟲ ⟐ ⬚ ⛾ ⚲

Proximity to the sea helps to provide the microclimate which makes Abbotsbury so special. Within its 20 acres there is much of interest to the plant-sperson in the many rare species on display, while those less specialised will derive pleasure from the banks of colour and the shaded walks – particularly in the spring, but also at other seasons. People travel a long way to visit these gardens – often called 'sub-tropical', but probably technically better described as 'wet Mediterranean'. The visitor centre, shop and colonial teahouse are an bonus for the many coach parties that come both for gardens and the nearby swannery (not to be missed when open); there is also a woodland trail and a children's play area. The redesigned plant sales area, while not extensive, has a range of healthy stock on display. There are several events in the evenings – Shakespeare, opera, etc.

Arnmore House   2

57 Lansdowne Road, Bournemouth BH1 1RN. Tel: (01202) 551440; E-mail: david@mdmusic.com; Website: www.mdmusic.com/arnmore

Mr and Mrs David Hellewell • *On B3064 just S of hospital* • *Open all year, by appt* • *Entrance: £2, children free* ◑ ᕒ

This highly individual garden has been created over the past 25 years by its owner and reflects his interests as a composer who also has a strong feeling for Chinese art. Ease of maintenance has also been a priority as Mrs Hellewell is disabled. Shape, colour and texture are all-important, with many unusual specimen trees, topiary and box parterres. Trees and shrubs, many chosen for year-round colour and grown in pots, have been pruned and trained to give the desired effect. The formal parterre consists of neat diagonals of *Buxus sempervirens* complemented by clipped balls of *B.s.* 'Aureovariegata'. A booklet is available. If you are an agapanthus fan, you can by appointment, all year, visit Dr and Mrs Slade's garden at *46 Roslin Road South*, also in Bournemouth; a plantsman's third-of-an-acre walled garden with many rare and unusual items as well as a kitchen garden and greenhouses.

Athelhampton House Gardens ★   3

Athelhampton, Dorchester DT2 7LG. Tel: (01305) 848363; Fax: (01305) 848135; E-mail: enquiry@athelhampton.co.uk; Website: www.athelhampton.co.uk

Patrick Cooke • *5m NE of Dorchester, 1m E of Puddletown off A35 at Northbrook junction* • *House and gardens open March to Oct, daily except Sat, Dec to Feb, Sun; all 10.30am – 5pm or dusk if earlier* • *Entrance: £3.95, children free (house and garden £5.50, OAPs £5.20, children £1.50, parties of 12 or more £4.20 per person) (2001 prices)* • *Other information: Picnics in riverside area only* ◑ ▦ ✕ ▧ WC ᕒ ⚘ ▥ ⬤ ◔

The four gardens and two pavilions of the Tudor manor house were designed for Alfred Cart de La Fontaine in 1891, and the late Robert Cooke extended the garden with great sensitivity. Courts and walls follow the original plan with beautiful stone and brickwork arches. Visitors will take away with them an abiding memory of water, water everywhere, and some of the most stylish architectural topiary in England. The River Piddle, girdling the garden in its own right, is busily harnessed within it to service pools, fountains and a long canal studded with water lilies. Major features are a fifteenth-century circular dovecot on the lawn facing the west wing of the house, and the pleached lime circular grove behind the Pyramid Garden. Here, twelve massive yews are fashioned to echo the obelisks on the raised terrace walk, which has charming pavilions standing at each end. The toll house to the south has been restored. The planting, including tulips, rambling roses, clematis and jasmine, is big-boned, low-key and sophisticated. A remarkable, unforgettably atmospheric interpretation of the late-medieval ideal.

Cartref   4

Station Road, Stalbridge, Sturminster Newton DT10 2RG. Tel: (01963) 363705

Mrs Nesta Ann Smith • 10m SW of Shaftesbury. From A30 at Henstridge traffic lights turn S for 1m to Stalbridge. Turn left opposite post office; house is 80 metres on right • Open two days for NGS, and April to Sept by appt • Entrance: £2, children free ● ⬤ 📧 WC ⬡

If one is to question what makes a good garden, a visit to this quarter acre behind an unassuming semi-detached village house has the answer for inveterate collectors. In this comparatively small area, winding paths, lawn and small woodland are crammed with clearly labelled rarities, each tree is a framework for interesting climbers, and the microclimate encourages plants such as *Cytisus battandieri*, *Poncirus trifoliata* and terrestrial orchids. The owner is happy to talk about the plants from provenance to maintenance; her vast knowledge is gleaned from experience gained by working in well-known nurseries under such masters as Jim Archibald and the hosta expert, Eric Smith. Many of the varieties are for sale.

Chettle House   5

Chettle, Blandford Forum DT11 8DB. Tel: (01258) 830209; Fax: (01258) 830380; Email: Patrick.bourke@talk21.com

Mr and Mrs P. Bourke • 6m NE of Blandford on A354, turn left to Chettle • House open • Garden open 31st March to end July, Sun only; Aug daily except Fri. Groups by appt at other times • Entrance: £3, children free. Discount entry with Larmer Tree Gardens (see entry in Wiltshire) ◐ ⬤ 📧 WC ♿ 🐕 ⚲

Beyond the wide lawns framing this impressive Queen Anne house (designed by Thomas Archer of rounded style and inverted scrolls fame), vistas appropriate to that period are preserved, with a vineyard on the south slope. Lavish herbaceous borders contain many chalk-loving plants (some rare), including no fewer than 20 varieties of honeysuckle, a buddleia collection, and some fine clematis. The owners are always on the lookout for the unusual, and plants seen in the garden are sometimes available for sale in the plant centre. The tranquil site is approached through mature trees where a number of different horse chestnut species may be seen. There is an elegant church in the grounds.

Chiffchaffs   6

Chaffeymoor, Bourton, Gillingham SP8 5BY. Tel: (01747) 840841

Mr and Mrs K.R. Potts • 3m E of Wincanton. Leave A303 (Bourton bypass) at sign marked 'Bourton' and continue to end of village • Garden open April to Oct, Wed and Thurs; also 3rd, 31st March, 7th, 21st, 28th April, 5th, 12th May, 2nd, 9th, 23rd June, 14th July, 25th Aug, 8th Sept, 6th Oct; all 2 – 5pm. Also by appt • Entrance: £2, children 50p • Other information: Refreshments and toilet facilities for groups only ◐ 📧 ⚲

An impressive avenue of flowering cherries leads to the house and garden, full of colour and interest, immaculately maintained, with an invitation to more pleasures at each turn of the path. The terraces and viewpoints afford glimpses of open country around, and the varied and colourful beds and borders are delightful. There is a noteworthy collection of dwarf bulbs, dwarf rhododendrons and old-fashioned roses, a wide range of herbaceous plants, and interesting underplanting in the woodland area. 12 acres in all. The well-stocked nursery has a wide variety of healthy-looking plants. Further along the lane is *Snape Cottage*, a half-acre garden with a selection of old-fashioned and unusual perennials with special emphasis on plant history, nature conservation and cottage-garden flowers.

The Coach House ★ 7

Bettiscombe, Bridport DJ6 5NT. Tel: (01308) 868560;
E-mail: hobhouse@compuserve.com; Website: www.penelopehobhouse.com

Mrs P. Hobhouse • 5m W of Beaminster off B3164 Broadwindsor – Birdsmoorgate road. Take narrow lane S signed to Shave Cross and Bettiscombe • Open for garden tours for parties by appt only • Entrance: fee by arrangement ◗

The owner has used her well-known professional skills to transform a simple walled garden and small field into areas of elegance which reflect her particular concern for structural plants and her painter's eye for colour associations. Formal beds, laid on gravel, are packed with interest, and lavish climbers adorn trellises and old brick walls. Grass avenues through wildflower planting in the former field are punctuated with urns; secluded arbours have been established to satisfy visitors wishing to observe this inspirational garden from a quiet corner. This is a garden which plantspersons should make every effort to see.

Cranborne Manor Garden ★★ 8

Cranborne, Wimborne Minster BH21 5PP. Tel: (01725) 517248;
Fax: (01725) 517862; E-mail: gardencentre@cranborne.co.uk;
Website: www.cranborne.co.uk

Viscount and Viscountess Cranborne • 10m N of Wimborne on B3078. Entrance via garden centre • Garden probably open March to Sept, Wed only, 9am – 5pm, and some weekends for charity – telephone to check dates • Entrance: £3, OAPs £2.50 • Other information: Garden centre, open all year ◗ 💷 WC ⚘ 🏛

Tradescant established the basic framework in the early seventeenth century, but little is left of the original plan. Neglected for a long period, the garden has been revived in the last three generations and now includes several smaller areas surrounded by tall clipped yew hedges, a walled white garden at its best in midsummer, wide lawns (again yew-lined) and extensive woodland and wild areas. Best of all is the high-walled entrance courtyard to the south, approached through an arch between the two Jacobean gatehouses. Here the plant selection along the lengthy borders is delightfully imaginative, providing the perfect introduction to what has been called 'the most magical house in

Dorset' (not least for the garden which surrounds it). The excellent nursery garden specialises in traditional rose varieties, but also carries a wide selection of other plants, particularly clematis and herbaceous perennials. Another garden with an interesting historical pedigree, but an entirely different experience, is to be found at nearby *Ashley Park Farm*, Damerham. Created by a dedicated conservationist, there are unusual trees and shrubs in attractive woodland walks, ponds and a wildflower meadow, a farm and wild fowl and rare sheep. [Open for NGS and by appt. Tel: (01725) 518200.]

Dean's Court   9

Wimborne Minster BH21 1EE.

Sir Michael and Lady Hanham • In centre of Wimborne off B3073 • Open for NGS, Bank Holiday Suns and Mons March to June, Aug, also 9th, 23rd June, 21st July, 15th Sept, 2 – 6pm (but opens 10am Mons) • Entrance: £2, OAPs £1.50, children 50p (2001 prices) ● ➤ WC ⟨ ᨹ

A mellow brick house set in 13 acres of parkland containing a number of interesting and very large trees. A swamp cypress towers near the house, also a 28-metre tulip tree which flowers from June to July. The many fine specimens include Wellingtonias, Caucasian wing nut, Japanese pagoda tree, blue cedars and horse chestnuts. There are few formal beds, but a courtyard contains an unusually comprehensive herb garden with over 250 different plants. The walled kitchen garden, in which many of the old varieties of vegetable are grown by chemical-free methods, is extensive and obviously successful. A monastic stewpond where the medieval monks bred their carp can still be seen in this peaceful haven.

Edmondsham House   10

Edmondsham, Cranborne, Wimborne Minster BH21 5RE. Tel: (01725) 517207

Mrs J. Smith • 1m S of Cranborne. From A354 turn at Sixpenny Handley crossroads to Ringwood and Cranborne • House open Easter Sun, Bank Hol Mons, also April and Oct, Wed, 2 – 5pm • Garden open April to Oct, Wed and Sun, 2 – 5pm. Also by appt • Entrance: £1.50, children 50p (house and garden £3, children £1, under 5 free) (2001 prices) • Other information: Refreshments April and Oct, Wed only ◑ ▦ WC ᨹ

The visitor should allow time for a tour of the interesting family house and dairy before venturing out into the large walled kitchen garden. No chemical fertilisers or pesticides are used here. Admire the beds of Russian comfrey, rhubarb, Jerusalem artichokes and asparagus, the herb gardens and the fruit cage before taking the path to the lean-to peach house. The Pit House is a sunken greenhouse, restored in 1990. The arch of the walled garden leads to Cowleaze, the paddock and later the drive and the dell. The pond (dry in hot summers) has an island of *Sasa palmata* and a dawn redwood (*Metasequoia glyptostroboides*). (The 'dawn' is the common name and refers to the Dawn of Time.) An unusual circular grass hollow is said to have been a cockpit, one of only a very few 'naturalised' areas of the sort in the country. The massed spring bulbs together with the many spring-flowering shrubs make this the best season, but the peaceful, mellow atmosphere pervades the garden throughout the year. Allow time to visit the church to look for the clumps of mistletoe and two unusual trees, *Magnolia acuminata* (cucumber tree) and *Paulownia tomentosa* (foxglove tree).

Forde Abbey ★★   11

Chard, Somerset TA20 4LU. Tel: (01460) 221290 (Infoline); E-mail: forde.abbey@virgin.net; Website: www.fordeabbey.co.uk

Mr M. Roper • 7m W of Crewkerne, 4m SE of Chard off A30 • House open April to Oct, Tues, Wed, Thurs, Sun and Bank Holidays, 1 – 4.30pm • Garden open all year, daily, 10am – 4.30pm • Entrance: £4.20, OAPs £3.95, children under 15 free. Parties of 20 or more £3.75 per person (house and garden £5.40, OAPs £5.10, children under 15 free. Parties of 20 or more £4.50 per person – telephone 01460 220231 for bookings) (2001 prices) ○ ◗ ✕ ▤ WC & ◁▷ ♨ ⌂ ▾ ⚲

This unique and fascinating former Cistercian abbey, inhabited as a private house since 1649, is set in a varied and pleasing garden. Old walls and colourful borders, wide sloping lawns, lush ponds and cascades, graceful statuary and huge mature trees combine to create an atmosphere of timeless elegance. There is something here for every gardener to appreciate: the bog garden displays a large collection of primulas and other Asiatic plants; the shrubbery contains a variety of magnolias, rhododendrons and other delightful specimens. The rock garden was revolutionised by the late Jack Drake, and a fine arboretum has been built up since 1947; at the back of the abbey is an extensive kitchen garden and a nursery selling rare and unusual plants which look in fine health. Allow plenty of time as the grounds extend to 30 acres in all.

Frankham Farm   12

Ryme Intrinsica, Sherborne DT9 6JT. Tel: (01935) 872304

Mr and Mrs R.G. Earle • Off A37 Yeovil – Dorchester road. 3m S of Yeovil turn left; garden is 1/4m on left • Open 3 days for NGS, and by appt • Entrance: £2, children free NEW ◑ ◗ &

In spring and early summer, visitors to this charming garden can be assured of plenty of colour. Developed since the 1960s, the flat site of over two acres (enjoyable easy walking) includes extensive plantings of roses and clematis. Well-stocked herbaceous borders frame a fine view of adjacent fields, with grass walks meandering through woodland and wild garden planted with spring bulbs and shrubs making a pleasing contrast. A striking group of white floxgloves under eucalyptus leads from the neat kitchen garden into a small plantation of unusual trees where the Chilean firebush (*Embothrium coccineum*) and *Aesculus pavia* thrive alongside rhododendrons, azaleas and camellia. Farm buildings form an attractive backdrop. This is a high-quality, very English garden in a tranquil setting.

Friars Way 13

Church Street, Upwey, Weymouth DT3 5QE. Tel/Fax: (01305) 813243;
E-mail: friarsway@hotmail.com

*Les and Christina Scott • 4m N of Weymouth off A354. In Upwey opposite
church • Open for parties and private visits by appt • Entrance: £1.80* ● ✿

This half-acre garden on a steeply sloping, south-facing alkaline site is a
treasure house of unusual plants. Visitors are greeted by a high rock wall
planted to give colour from spring to late autumn. Walls, terracing and
meandering gravel paths enhance the setting for the choicest of plants. An
old apple tree provides dry shade for plants which thrive in such conditions. A
scented garden contains perfumed roses, together with daphnes, lavenders,
thymes and nepetas. There is a small wildlife pond with appropriate planting,
and a hot dry area planted with various cistus where the colours of larger
shrubs are highlighted by underplanting with perennials such as *Knautia
macedonica* and *Aster* x *frikartii* 'Mönch'. Over 100 varieties of geraniums. A
border with plants relating to the seventeenth century (when the cottage was
built) has been developed. After visiting the royal watering hole of Weymouth,
travel 4m S to *Portland Castle*, one of the best-preserved of Henry VIII's historic
forts, where English Heritage has commissioned a new garden – a circular
walled space within the walled Governor's Garden.

Frith House 14

Stalbridge, Sturminster Newton DT10 2SD. Tel: (01963) 250232

*Urban Stephenson • 12m SW of Shaftesbury, between Milborne Port and Stalbridge,
1m S of A30, or turn west by Stalbridge post office, 2m along narrow lane, lodge on
left • Open for parties in coaches or cars by appt only • Entrance: £1.50 children free
• Other information: Plants occasionally for sale* ● 🍴 **WC** ♿ ⬦ ✿

In an open valley surrounded by unspoilt pastoral views, this friendly Edwardian house lies beneath a shelterbelt of woodland and looks south across
sweeping lawns studded with orchard trees and fine old cedars. The four-acre
grounds are very well maintained, in particular the immaculately trimmed
yew hedges and the shrub borders within sunny walled areas. Below the
terrace is a bed filled with a striking array of 20-year-old scarlet 'Frensham'
roses; there is also an excellent kitchen garden, and shady avenues to enjoy on
the woodland walk. Further down are two lakes, fed by a stone conduit, which
have been developed as an ornamental area of shrubs and water plants.
Pleasant grassy walks surround the lakes, where crayfish are bred.

Highbury 15

Woodside Road, West Moors, Ferndown BH22 0LY. Tel: (01202) 874372;
Fax: (01202) 874370

*Mr Stanley Cherry • 8m N of Bournemouth off B3072. In Woodside Road, last
road at N end of West Moors • Open April to Sept by appt • Entrance: 75p (pre-
booked parties for house and garden £1 per person inc. teas)* ● **WC**

A woodland garden of half-an-acre in a mature setting, surrounding an interesting Edwardian house (1909), which may also be visited. There are unusual plants and shrubs with ground cover.

Ivy Cottage ★ 16

Aller Lane, Lower Ansty, Dorchester DT2 7PX. Tel/Fax: (01258) 880053

Anne and Alan Stevens • 12m NE of Dorchester, 10m W of Blandford in centre of triangle between A352, A354 and A3030. Take turning near Fox Inn, Ansty • Open May to Sept, Thurs, 10am – 5pm, and to parties by appt at other times • Entrance: £2.25 ● ● WC ⚘

Mrs Stevens trained and worked as a professional gardener before coming to her cottage over 30 years ago. Although chalk underlies the surrounding land, this one-and-three-quarter-acre garden is actually on greensand; it has springs and a stream that keep it well watered and is therefore an ideal home for plants such as primulas, irises, gunneras, and in particular trollius and moisture-loving lobelias. Other delights are a thriving and ordered vegetable garden (which hardly ever needs a hose), large herbaceous borders giving colour all year round, drifts of bulbs and other spring plants surrounding specimen trees and shrubs, and three most interesting raised beds for alpines. Wildlife, especially birds, are actively encouraged. This garden has justifiably been featured in print and on television, and merits a wide detour. Just up the road is *Aller Green*, a typical peaceful Dorset cottage garden of approximately one acre in an old orchard setting. The two share some charity opening days with a combined admission charge, and both cottages are particularly worth seeing in their autumn colours.

Kingston Lacy ★ 17

Wimborne Minster BH21 4EA. Tel: (01202) 883402

The National Trust • 1½ m NW of Wimborne on B3082 • House open late March to early Nov, Sat – Wed and Bank Holiday Mons, 12 noon – 5.30pm (last admission 4.30pm) • Park and garden open late March to early Nov, daily, 11am – 6pm; Nov to 23rd Dec, Fri, Sat, Sun, 11am — 4pm; Feb, March, Sat, Sun, 11am – 4pm. Additional opening for snowdrops – telephone for details • Entrance: garden and park: £3, children £1.50 (house, garden and park: £6.50, children £3, family (2 adults and up to 3 children) £17, parties of 15 or more £5 per person, children £2.50 • Other information: volunteer driven buggy on house-open days. Dogs in park only, on lead ● ● ✕ ● WC ⚅ ⚘ ⚘ ⚘ ⚘

This 32-acre formal garden, with nine acres of lawn, also has a wonderful lime avenue planted in 1668, which leads to the Nursery Wood containing a fine collection of rhododendrons and azaleas. The terrace displays urns, vases and lions in bronze and marble, and there are six interesting marble wellheads or tubs for bay trees; also an Egyptian obelisk and a sarcophagus. The parterre was laid out in 1899 for Mrs Henrietta Bankes in memory of her husband and is still planted in the seasonal schemes designed for her. During the summer they are filled with salmon-pink *Begonia semperflorens and Heliotropum* 'Marine', during the spring with wallflowers and forget-me-nots. The Victorian fernery, planted with 25 different types of fern and the National Collection of *Anemone nemorosa*, leads to the once-fine cedar walk, where one of the trees was planted by the Duke of Wellington in 1827 and others by visiting royalty. Spectacular roses include 'Bonica', 'Cardinal Hume', 'Nozomi' and 'Amber Queen'. The garden also contains the National Collection of convallarias. There is a circular woodland walk, including children's play equipment. In spring, many areas are covered in snowdrops, daffodils and bluebells.

Kingston Maurward Gardens ★   18

Dorchester DT2 8PY. Tel: (01305) 215003; E-mail: administration@kms.ac.uk; Website: www.kmc.ac.uk

Kingston Maurward Gardens • E of Dorchester off A35. Turn off at roundabout at end of bypass • Open mid-March to Oct, daily, 10am – 5.30pm. Guided tours by appt • Entrance: £3.75, children £2, under 3 free. Family season tickets available (gardens and farm animal park) ◑ 🍴 ✕ 🏛 WC ♿ 🌿 🏬 🐕 ⚲

The original parkland encompasses 35 acres of specimen trees, water features and woodland, and overlooks the water meadows of the Frome Valley. The formal gardens to the west of the house were laid out between 1910 and 1915 by the Hanbury family, who also owned La Mortola in Italy. The splendid stone terraces, balustrading, steps and yew hedges have been used to create many intimate gardens and carefully planned vistas. Extensive refurbishment of the stone features has taken place, with the statuary on long loan from the Palace of Westminster and the Grecian temple recarved from the original design. The gardens contain a large collection of roses, herbaceous perennials and half-hardy plants, including National Collections of penstemons and salvias. Large drifts of spring bulbs, cyclamen and autumn crocus surround fine specimen trees. There is a tree trail with 65 different species represented, and the original large lake has a nature trail around its margin, giving superb views of the gardens and water meadows. The garden is entered through the animal park, which has an interesting collection of unusual breeds, set in a beautiful wooded paddock overlooking Stinsford Church of Hardy fame. The author's birthplace, *Hardy's Cottage*, a National Trust property with a small garden and a walk through the woods, is nearby. [Open 5th Jan to 22nd Dec, daily, 10am – 5.30pm (or dusk if earlier)] In Dorchester itself is a stylish public park, *Borough Gardens*, late-nineteenth century in style and atmosphere, with colourful displays of summer bedding, an impressive clock and fountain. A paddling pool, tennis courts and a bowling green provide exercise for all ages.

Knoll Gardens and Nursery ★   19

Hampreston, Wimborne Minster BH21 7ND. Tel: (01202) 873931; Fax: (01202) 870842; Web: www.knollgardens.co.uk

Mr Neil Lucas • Between Wimborne and Ferndown, off Ham Lane (B3073). Leave A31 at Canford Bottom roundabout. Signed 1½ m • Gardens open daily April to September 10am – 5pm; Oct to March, Sun – Thurs, 10am – 5pm (or

dusk if earlier; closed 25th Dec to 1st Jan • Entrance: £4, OAPs £3.50, students £3, children (5–15) £2, family (2 adults and 2 children) £9.75. Reductions for parties of 15 or more ◐ 🍵 WC ♿ 🌱 🏢 ♿ ♋

Twenty-five years ago this was a private botanic garden, but it is now laid out in an informal English setting with mature specimen trees and shrubs giving a relaxed and intimate atmosphere. Although only a little over four acres, the many different areas, winding pathways and constantly changing views give an impression of a much larger area. The owners continue to develop the garden and its plant collections, particularly with hardy perennials and grasses. The summer garden has a collection of exotic-looking tender perennials, the water garden has several waterfalls and the newly designed Dragon Garden boasts a fine collection of modern perennials and penstemons around a central pool full of large koi carp. There are areas planted for dry shade and for moisture and a gravel garden for drought-tolerant plants. The 'Living Gardens' project, in partnership with Dorset Wildlife Trust, promotes the wildlife value of private gardens. National Collections of deciduous ceanothus and phygelius. The nursery offers a mail order service by post and through the website.

Knoll House Hotel   20

Studland Bay BH19 3AH. Tel: (01929) 450450; E-mail: info@knollhouse.co.uk; Website: www.knollhouse.co.uk

Ferguson family • 2m NE of Swanage between Studland and Sandbanks ferry • Hotel open Easter to Oct • Garden open 18th, 19th May for NGS, and for hotel guests at all times • Entrance: £2.50, children free (2001 price) ◐ 🍵 WC ♿ 🌱 ♋

The house is now part of a family-run hotel with an interesting history and approximately 100 acres of grounds. The gardens, including eight acres at Studland Bay House across the road, have magnificent views over the bay to the Isle of Wight, and are surrounded by National Trust land, a nature reserve and Purbeck Heritage Coast. Following storm damage, the family replanted extensively and imaginatively, and the glades and clearings now impart a sense of intimacy, with carefully placed seating creating peaceful arbours for quiet reflection. There is a delightful azalea walk, magnificent rhododendrons and specimen trees.

Langebride House   21

Long Bredy, Dorchester DT2 9HU. Tel: (01308) 482257

Mrs Greener • Off A35 Dorchester – Bridport road, turn S to Long Bredy • Open two Suns for NGS, and at other times by appt • Entrance: £3 • Other information: teas on NGS open days only ◐ ♿

This garden has so many desirable features it is impossible to avoid making a list: 200-year-old copper beech rising from wide, lush lawns, underplanted with carpets of spring bulbs; a thriving enclosed vegetable garden of manageable size, backing onto a sloping grass area with colourful mixed borders along the tile-topped walls; a rising slope to the mixed wild woodland behind, where favourite trees have been planted in groups to allow for culling as they enlarge; a formal yew-lined lawn with pond, fountain and old stone features, from which steps descend through sloping shrubberies towards the front of the house. A miniature area of greensand allows a patch of acid-loving plants to provide contrast. A long line of pleached limes runs parallel with the bi-colour beech hedge along the road. There is also a sloping orchard, a tennis court with a tall rockery behind as a viewing point and sun-trap, beds and borders, trellises for climbing plants and low stone walls for those that prefer to hang. All around, thousands of bulbs hide in waiting for the spring explosion which, in the owner's opinion, is the best season to visit.

Leigh Farm 22

Halstock, Nr Yeovil BA22 9QU. Tel: (01935) 891848

Mrs L.J. Lauderdale • 2m S of Yeovil on Dorchester road turn right towards Sutton Bingham and Halstock. In Halstock turn right signed 'Halstock Leigh'; house is 1¾ m on right • Open for NGS • Entrance: £2, children 50p NEW ○ 🍵 & �

Five years ago the owners left their acclaimed cottage garden in Wiltshire to tackle this acre on the southern slopes of a deep valley, approached down a narrow lane well outside the village. The remarkable borders reflect Mrs Lauderdale's skill at colour co-ordination. A pretty rose garden, ponds and a small tree plantation feature.

Loscombe House 23

Bridport DT6 3TL. Tel: (01308) 488361

Mr and Mrs Andrewes • 3m N of Bridport, 2m SE of Beaminster, 1m E of A3066. In Melplash take Loscombe turn opposite Half Moon Inn and after ½ m turn right at Loscombe sign. Continue 2m to bottom of lane • Open April to Sept, Sat – Tues, 11am – 6pm • Entrance: free (donations to RNIB welcome) 🍵 🛒 &

Once a 'lost combe', this is Dorset at its most rural. Set in a four-acre site, the garden has a background of hills which drop down close to the boundary. Hillside tree-planting undertaken in 1970 has now developed into woodland, improved from 1984 when the valley bog was drained. An attractive flowing stream is a focus, with grass paths winding among well-maintained and decorative shrubs and perennials, including roses, clematis and hostas, sustained by the microclimate within this sheltered site. A delightful, peaceful scene, far indeed from the madding crowd.

The Manor House 24

Sandford Orcas, Sherborne DT9 4SB. Tel: (01963) 220206

Sir Mervyn Medlycott, Bt • 2½ m N of Sherborne, turning off B3148, next to village church • House open • Garden open 1st April, 10am – 6pm, then May and July to Sept, Sun, Mon, 10am – 5pm. Also by appt for parties at other

*times • Entrance: £1.50 (house and garden £3, children £1.50). Reduced rates
for pre-booked parties of 10 or more* ◑ 🪑 WC ⬧ ℀

Looked at purely as a garden, this is not exceptional. An old, flagged path
slopes up between bordered lawns towards an open field. The stone walls at
either side are attractive, and where they stop the eye travels on into the
countryside beyond. There is a herb garden with a pleasant view across a lower
lawn along the south side of the house. At the end of this lawn another
viewpoint back towards the south front allows the attractive planting below
the herb garden to show at its best. Roses and other climbing plants clinging to
the honey-grey walls harmonise well with this gracious setting. It is the house,
ancient and redolent of its long history, which permeates the scene and
transforms the garden.

Mapperton ★ 25

Beaminster DT8 3NR. Tel: (01308) 862645; Fax: (01308) 863348;
E-mail: office@mapperton.com; Website: www.mapperton.com

*The Earl and Countess of Sandwich • 5m NE of Bridport, 2m SE of Beaminster
• House open to parties of 15 or more by appt • Plants for sale • Garden open
March to Oct, daily, 2 – 6pm (opens 1pm Wed, Thurs, Sat). Garden tours
available by prior appt • Entrance: £3.50, children (5–18) £1.50, under 5 free.
Tour with gardener can be arranged in advance • Other information: Lunches
available Wed, Thurs, Sat from 12 noon* ◑ ☕ 🪑 WC ♿ 🌿 🏛 ♨

A garden with a difference, running down a gradually steepening valley
dominated by the delightful sixteenth/seventeenth-century manor house.
Terraces in brick and stone descend through formal Italian-style borders
towards a summerhouse, which itself stands high above two huge fish ponds.
On all sides there is topiary in yew and box. Beyond the ponds, the valley
becomes a shrubbery and arboretum, most of it planted since the 1950s. Some
statuary depicting animals and birds, both natural and stylistic. Numerous
ornaments (many supplied by a local firm founded in 1885) provide interest
and surprise.

Melbury House 26

Melbury Sampford, Dorchester DT2 0LF. Tel: (01935) 83699 (Garden Office)

*Mr James and The Hon. Mrs Townshend • 13m NW of Dorchester on A37
Yeovil – Dorchester road. Signposted • Open 16th, 30th May, 13th, 27th June,
11th, 25th July, 15th Aug, 2 – 5pm • Entrance: £3, OAPs and children £2 •
Other information: Guided walks on normal open days at no charge at 2.30pm,
and by arrangement for parties of up to 15 at £3.50 per person* ◕ ☕ WC 🌿

This historic house (not open to the public) is approached by a long drive
through open parkland. Visitors are directed to the west side and enter
through the large walled garden, a good part still maintained as a productive
kitchen garden. A walk through the western part of the arboretum leads to
the bottom of the south lawn with fine views of the house and across the lake
to the deer park. The main part of the arboretum with its massed spring bulbs

lies to the east in the Valley Garden, overlooked by the ancient family church (open). Herbaceous borders along the south of the house lead to a colourful walled flower garden. Recent seasons have seen much replanting so this garden will be a source of continuous interest. *Frampton Roses* nursery (Tel: (01300) 320453) is 5m away off the A356 Dorchester road.

Melplash Court 27

Melplash, Bridport DT6 3UH. Tel: (01308) 488418; Fax: (01308) 488687

Mr and Mrs T. Lewis • 5m N of Bridport on A3066 • Open one day in May for NGS, 2 – 6pm, and by appt • Entrance: £3 ● ● WC & ⊲⊳ ⅋ ℺

The elegant sixteenth-century house, set among the Dorset hills with the sea over the horizon, is approached through an avenue of mature trees. The owners have respected plans for the garden as laid out by the previous owner, Lady Diana Tiarks, but have extensively restored and extended the area so that new planting is a feature without disturbing the general concept. On the whole, muted colours are preferred and expressed in a wonderful variety of foliage, particularly on the banks above the stream garden. Each section, including the outstanding Japanese garden, is a surprise as the visitor progresses via walled areas into carefully planned bedding that dramatises the sloping contours. A walled kitchen garden features knots where again leaf shape, in the form of rhubarb, leek, cabbage, angelica, creates attractive patterns. Maintenance is first class and the overall effect impressive.

Millmead 28

Winterbourne Stickland DT11 0NT. Tel: (01258) 880814

Michele Barker • 4m SW of Blandford. After Shire House pub, turn right down West Street, signed 'Winterbourne Houghton', then first left after 30mph sign • Open for NGS and by appt • Entrance: £2, children 50p [NEW] ● ⅋ ℺

This 1/3-acre site is a showcase for its owner, a talented garden designer. Situated in the picturesque Winterbourne valley it has been developed around a modern village house, with garden rooms that belie its sloping nature, each demonstrating good use of colour, architectural features and vistas through to each area. The modern trend for pebbles, pillars and coloured furniture is predominant, with clever use of screening and some arresting blue and purple planting. Any gardener wishing to renovate a small patch would benefit from a visit, learning from good structure and strong contrasts.

Minterne 29

Minterne Magna, Dorchester DT2 7AU. Tel: (01300) 341370

Lord Digby • 9m N of Dorchester, 2m N of Cerne Abbas on A352 • Open March to 10th Nov, daily, 10am – 7pm • Entrance: £3, children (accompanied only) free ◑ WC ⊲⊳

The garden has an interesting collection of Himalayan rhododendrons and azaleas, spring bulbs, cherries and maples. There are many rare trees, and one and a half miles of walks with palm trees, cedars, beeches, etc. Alas, no labelling to help the amateur. The first half of the walk can be disappointing in midsummer, although evidence remains of some spectacular spring colour and tree colour in autumn should be special. At the lower end of the valley the stream with its lakes and waterfalls is surrounded by splendid tall trees, among which the paths wind back towards the house. The lakes contain many water lilies and ducks have been introduced to deal with the duckweed. A restful and attractive atmosphere.

The Moorings

(see Devon)

Moreton Gardens   30

Moreton DT2 8RF. Tel: (01929) 405084

Richard and Liz Frampton-Hobbs • 7m E of Dorchester off B3390 • Open March to Sept, daily, 10am – 5pm. Groups and coaches welcome • Entrance: £2.50, accompanied children under 16 free ◑ 🍽 WC ♨ ♿ 🐾

This tranquil three-acre garden has been re-created in an old setting along the banks of a flowing stream in a picturesque village associated with Lawrence of Arabia – he is buried in the cemetery. The presence of water, the gentle undulations of the site, and the imaginative design and planting schemes result in a delightful scene in which the visitor is led from one pleasant vista to another. Although the new planting is well established, and the rose beds in particular make a great show, in future years the design will greatly benefit from fast-maturing trees; a pergola and eye-catching fountains provide a good structural framework. The extensive plant centre reflects the number of attractive plants to be seen in the garden itself.

The Old Rectory   31

Litton Cheney, Dorchester DT2 9AH. Tel: (01308) 482383; Fax: (01308) 482261

Mr and Mrs Hugh Lindsay • 9m W of Dorchester, 1m S of A35, beside Litton Cheney church • Open probably 31st March, and on other days for charity in May and June, 2 – 6pm, and April to June by appt • Entrance: £2.50, children free ● 🍴 WC ♿ ⬤ 🐾 ♧

The house rests comfortably below the church and is approached by a gravel drive which circles a small lawn; a thatched summerhouse stands to one side like a massive beehive. The small walled garden has outhouses and a large barn on two sides and borders around three, prolifically stocked with well-chosen and favourite plants in specific colour bands. A steep path leads down into the four acres of natural woodland, a surprisingly extensive area of mature trees with many springs, streams and ponds – never a water shortage here, even in the driest of summers. This area was reclaimed by the current owners, who are adding new young trees and shrubs as well as successfully encouraging many spring-flowering plant colonies, mostly native. Climbing back up to the house, the visitor arrives at the belvedere giving views over trees to farmland on the other side of the valley. Spring and autumn are the best times to see this garden, from which Reynolds Stone, the wood-engraver, drew inspiration.

The Old Rectory   32

Pulham, Dorchester DT2 7EA. Tel (01258) 817595

Mr and Mrs N Elliott • 13m N of Dorchester, 8m SE of Sherborne on B3143. Turn E at Pulham crossroads and continue to church • Open for NGS, and for groups by appt • Entrance: £2, children free NEW ● ● ●

A well maintained three-acre garden with superb views, developed around a fine eighteenth-century house. Plants, sometimes rare and often for sale, are attractively placed within box parterres sheltered by yew hedging and mature trees. Beyond the formal areas lie a further four and a half acres of recently planted woodland and shrubbery, with pleasant walks. There are also two ponds and a small arboretum.

The Priest's House Museum   33

23–27 High Street, Wimborne Minster BH21 1HR. Tel: (01202) 882533

The Priest's House Museum • In centre of Wimborne • Museum open • Garden open April to Oct, Mon – Sat, 10.30am – 5pm; also June to Sept, Sun, 2 – 5pm, (but closed 31st July). Preferable to check before travelling • Entrance: £2.20, OAPs £1.75, children £1 (museum and garden) • Other information: Refreshments in summer only ● ● WC ● ● ● ●

In the heart of this small town lies a walled garden, hidden from the busy shopping thoroughfare by the frontage of the Museum. Both are well worth a visit. The 100-metre-long garden is laid out with some formal beds but mostly lawn, herbaceous and herb borders. There are a few unusual plants. In late spring the wisteria on the back of the house is particularly appealing. Sit on one of the seats dotted around and enjoy the peaceful atmosphere in this well-cared-for garden staffed by volunteers who are only too pleased to answer questions about the plants.

Sherborne Castle   34

**Sherborne DT9 5NR. Tel: (01935) 813182; Fax: (01935) 816727;
Website: www.sherbornecastle.com**

The Wingfield Digby family • Signed from Sherborne • Castle and garden open April — Oct, Tues, Wed, Thurs, Sat, Sun and Bank Holiday Mons, 11am – 6pm (last admission 4.30pm) (Castle open Sat 2.30pm) • Entrance: £3, children (maximum of 4) 15 and under free (castle and grounds £5.75, OAPs £5.25, children (maximum of four) under 15 free, parties of 15 or more £5 per person, children 15 and under free), private viewing for parties of 15 or more £8.50, children £4.25 (2001 prices) ● ● ● WC ● ● ● ●

As they are seen today, the castle grounds are based on landscaping under-taken in the late eighteenth century by 'Capability' Brown for the sixth Lord Digby, when the lake was created out of the then-flowing River Yeo, and the famous hanging gardens enjoyed by Sir Walter Raleigh and his wife Bess a century earlier were lost forever. Sweeping acres of deer park surround the castle, and masonry salvaged from the crumbling ruin of the old castle, destroyed during the Civil War in 1645, gave rise to fine stable blocks, courtyards and nearby Castleton Church. A charming walled flower garden has been designed within one of the courtyards near the Orangery, but the main attraction lies surely in the site's unique history, the colourful scene of water against graceful sloping lawns, and the ancient ruin visible across the lake. As Alexander Pope wrote with enthusiasm to a friend: 'This is so peculiar and its situation of so uncommon kind, that it merits a more particular description.' A visit to the delightful and comprehensive *Castle Gardens Plant Centre*, established in the original walled kitchen garden of the Castle and accessible from the main road, is worth a detour.

Shute House ★ 35

Donhead St Mary, Shaftesbury SP7 9DG. Tel: (01747) 828866

Mr and Mrs John Lewis • 5m NE of Shaftesbury, off A30. Near Donhead St Mary church • Open weekdays by appt for parties of 20 to 40 • Entrance: charge ● ⚹

The handsome historic house is surrounded by a garden of many springs and ponds — the source of a river. The marvellous site faces south, overlooking a slope to farmland. Behind, mysterious shrubberies have a magical hold on the visitor, who is led by paths through groves of camellias and rhododendrons into knot gardens and borders and by placid pools and canals. The late Sir Geoffrey Jellicoe designed the musical cascade that tumbles down the slope over projecting copper Vs set in concrete — an inspired statement of the Modern Movement of the 1930s. This famous feature is being revived and replanted, while other structural features are being created by the present owners, who it appears are respecting Jellicoe's overall design 'while introducing their own sense of fun'. It remains to be seen how this will come off, but Suzy Lewis is the renowned Esther Merton's daughter.

Springhead 36

Fontmell Magna, Shaftesbury SP7 0NU. Tel: (01747) 811853/811206

The Springhead Trust • 5m S of Shaftesbury, 6m N of Blandford Forum on A350 • Open by appt only • Entrance: £3, children free ● ⚏ WC ⚐

Although the *raison d'être* of Springhead is the promotion of ecology, education and the arts, its magical garden is also developing fast under the daughter of the original owners, Rolf and Marabel Gardiner, who created here in the 1930s a centre for rural regeneration. Day and residential courses are held in the house, which is based on several cottages on the site of an old mill and overlooks a sweeping view of the lake. At the far end emerge the springs of absolutely clear water which give the place its name and its spirit – it is indeed a haven of peace and privacy, nestling in a small green valley below the Cranborne Chase. The upper garden surrounds the lake, informal planting (including a fine copper beech framing wild flowers and magnolias in the spring) giving way to a more formal area along the banks. Further down the stream, in the lower garden, Neal's Yard Remedies are growing herbs organically. Wildlife abounds. A walk leads up to the chalk down glorious with wild flowers and orchids in the summer, and with spectacular views all year.

Stanbridge Mill   37

Gussage All Saints. Tel: (01258) 841185

James Fairfax • 7m N of Wimborne on B3078 Cranborne road • Open for NGS 12th June, otherwise by appt only • Entrance: £2.50, children 50p NEW ● ⅄

Designed in its initial stages by Arabella Lennox-Boyd with sensitive later additions by the present gardener, the 50-acre site greets the summer visitor by clouds of white ox-eye daisies either side of the drive. This wild theme is paramount throughout. Extensive water meadows, now tamed, harvest an abundance of wild flowers; grass drives meander alongside streams towards an elegant thatched summerhouse – an ideal point from which to view this pleasing profusion. The house itself, once a water mill, is surrounded by more formal areas, although the millstream remains a key part of the design. A particular feature is the Mound Garden, from where tiers of hedges – ranging from diminutive box through yew and beech to pleached lime – lead up to a higher level with a magnificent swimming pool and a pavilion. All is rectangular, with clever planting edged by neat box. A striking white-flowered *allée* lies beneath a series of iron archways; as one emerges into the wider landscape, crossing a wisteria walk alongside herbaceous borders stretch for some 60 metres. Everything is well maintained and shown off to perfection by paving and steps created in patterns by up-ended tiles, flints and bricks.

Stapehill Abbey, Crafts and Gardens   38

278 Wimborne Road West, Stapehill, Nr. Wimborne BH21 2EB.
Tel: (01202) 861686

Mr and Mrs J. Pickard (Managers) • On old A31 Wimborne Ferndown road, ½ m E of Canford Bottom roundabout • Abbey open • Garden open 13th April to Sept, daily, 10am – 5pm; Oct to March, daily except Mon and Tues (but closed 21st Dec to 31st Jan) 10am – 4pm • Entrance: £7, OAPs and students £6.50, children (4–16) £4.50, family ticket £18.50 (2001 prices) • Other information: Guide dogs only. Craft workshops ○ ⬤ ▦ WC ⅄ ⚘ ⌂ ⬤ ⚲

Formerly home for 200 years to Cistercian nuns, this lovely old abbey has now been restored and the grounds transformed into award-winning gardens, including a Victorian cottage garden, a wisteria walk, a tropical house, a lake, a woodland walk and picnic area, a large rock garden with waterfall and pools and a new Japanese garden. A number of craft shops in the abbey offer demonstrations of traditional crafts on most days. The restaurant is in the former refectory, off a lovely walled terrace so one can eat out of doors in summer. The Country World museum has a good collection of tractors etc, and overlooks the farmyard. Nearby is the long-established *Trehane Camellia Nursery*, with a vast range of camellias, magnolias and other acid lovers. [Open Mon – Fri, 9am – 4.30pm; spring weekends, 10am – 4pm.]

Sticky Wicket ★ 39

Buckland Newton, Dorchester DT2 7BY. Tel: (01300) 345476

Peter and Pam Lewis • 11m from Dorchester and Sherborne, 2m E of A352, or take B3143 from Sturminster Newton. At T-junction midway between church and school • Open June to Sept, Thurs, 10.30am – 8pm, and for parties by appt (write for details) • Entrance: £2.50, children £1.50 ● ⬛ & ⌾

One of the four garden areas has a design of concentric circles and radiating paths, which has enabled the creation of many separate beds showing different planting styles. A fragrant and colourful display is mingled with ornamental grasses. The garden is designed to attract birds, butterflies and bees and to provide seed heads. There is a small pond and a wet area which is also attractive to wildlife, an informal white garden with late-summer interest and a wildflower meadow. This is very much the garden of conservationist-minded plant lovers and is not suitable for most children; if the progress of recent years is maintained it is destined to become outstanding.

Stour House 40

41 East Street, Blandford Forum DT11 7DU. Tel: (01258) 452914

Mr T.S.B. Card • In Blandford, 100 metres before Market Place on one-way system • Open 24th March, 28th April, 2 – 5pm; 7th July, 11th Aug, 2 – 6pm; 15th Sept, 20th Oct, 2 – 5pm • Entrance: £2, children 20p; group visits welcome ● ⬛ WC & ⌾

The secret garden of a Georgian town house, well worth a visit, appealing to both formal and informal tastes. It is remarkable for its extent (two and a half acres) and its planting, with a surprise beyond the River Stour and a delightful island joined to the garden by a modern mathematical bridge. The island has beautiful mature trees, both native and introduced species, and many younger varieties. The garden is dominated by a herbaceous border running its full length, planted by the owner over the past 15 years. Parallel to it are paths through a long-established orchard and kitchen garden. New axes have been introduced and sculptures skilfully placed within created settings.

Weston House 41

Buckhorn Weston, Gillingham SP8 5HG. Tel: (01963) 371005

Mr and Mrs E.A.W. Bullock • 4m W of Gillingham, 4m SE of Wincanton. From A30 turn N to Kington Magna, continue towards Buckhorn Weston and after railway bridge take left towards Wincanton. House is second on left • Open

by appt mid-May, June, July, Sept for charity; groups welcome • Other
information: Teas by arrangement • Entrance: £1.50, children free
● WC &. ⇦ ℺

Since 1985 the Bullocks have transformed a neglected rubble-strewn plot and
paddock into a one-and-a-half acre garden vibrant with colour, designed
around an exceptional collection of old-fashioned and English roses: currently
95 varieties are on display, all clearly labelled. Near the house stone walls
enveloped in climbers create a colourful backdrop to mixed borders. An
archway of white rambler roses frames a York-stone path edged with standard
'Polar Star' roses underplanted with blue and white. Hot colours in borders
and a herb collection entice butterflies. Beyond the well-kept lawn, mown
paths lead visitors to the meadow area with pond and wild flowers as well as a
lovely view of the Blackmore Vale. The rough-cut grass is interspersed with
some unusual trees; there is also a new plantation of old-fashioned roses.
Throughout the summer this garden is full of interest and colour in a design
which links the formal garden, trees, wild flowers and grasses with the
countryside beyond.

GARDENING FOR THE DISABLED

- The Gardening for the Disabled Trust (Charity No. 255066) collects
  donations to assist people with improvements to their gardens, or to
  supply equipment which will enable them to continue to garden.
  Information from Mrs Angela Parish, Frittenden House, Nr Cranbrook
  TN17 2DG; Fax (01580) 852120; E-mail: apparish@hotmail.com.
- Thrive is a national charity promoting the use of garden and horti-
  culture as a therapy for restricted or disabled gardeners (Tel: (0118) 988
  5688; Website: www.carryongardening.org.uk).
- For details of The Disabled and Older Gardeners' Association, write to
  Growing Point, Herefordshire College of Agriculture, Holme Lacy,
  Hereford (Tel: (01432) 870316). For details of workshops etc. telephone
  Susan van Laun (Tel: (01531) 636226).
- Demonstration gardens to assist the disabled are on view at a number
  of properties open to the public and are also featured in the *Guide*. They
  include: Battersea Park (for an appt with the Horticultural Therapy
  Unit telephone (020) 7720 2212), Broadview Garden and Capel Manor.
- Open days for the disabled are also held from time to time at other
  gardens described in the *Guide*, including Dolly's Garden and Hillsborough Walled Garden.

DURHAM

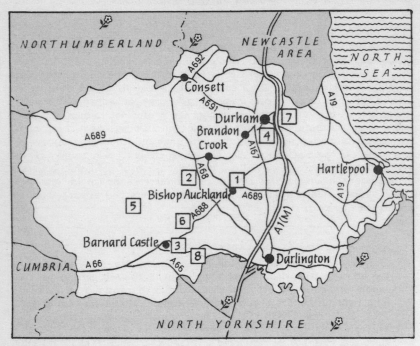

Some gardens have postal addresses in one county and are physically situated in another. If in doubt, a check in the index will direct the reader to the page on which the garden appears.

Auckland Castle Deer Park   1

Auckland Castle, Bishop Auckland DL14 7NR. Tel: (01325) 462966 (Smiths–Gore Chartered Surveyors)

The Church Comissioners for England (leased to Wear Valley District Council) • Leave A1(M) at junction signed 'Bishop Auckland'. Follow A689 W through Rushyford past Windlestone Hall and Coundon into Bishop Auckland • Castle state rooms and St Peter's Chapel open May to 16th July, Sept, Fri, Sun and Bank Holiday Mons; 17th July to Aug, daily except Sat; all 2 – 5pm • Entrance: Deer park free (state rooms, chapel and gardens within inner wall £3.50, OAPs £2.50, children under 12 free) • Other information: Symbols relate to castle only – no facilities in park ○ 🍴 🏪 WC ♿ 🏛 ♟

A remarkable survival of an eighteenth-century deer house enclosed within part of the original park in the well-wooded valleys of the Coundon Burn and Gaunless River, a tributary of the River Wear. Visitors enter the park through the Gothick gateway crowned by a turreted clock and weather vane, designed by Sir Thomas Robinson with touches of Thomas Wright, and walk past the entrance to the castle, glimpsed through a *clairvoyée*. Suddenly, through Bishop Barrington's screen of 1796, designed by James Wyatt, they see the twelfth-century banqueting hall converted into a chapel by Bishop Cosin in the late seventeenth century. The inner and outer park covers 160 acres, with the remainder of the 800-acre deer park leased to local farmers and the golf club. Within them, the river traces a meandering course among precipitous bluffs and craggy outcrops. It has been canalised in places with a weir dating from the eighteenth century. There are avenues of Austrian pine and sweet chestnut and circular stands of trees, groves of ancient alders and clumps of holly trees amongst which dog roses climb. The gnarled and ancient hawthorns are also a feature. A listed ornamental building, a scheduled ancient monument under the guardianship of English Heritage, exists within the park: the deer house, designed in 1757 for Bishop Trevor by Thomas Wright, the Wizard of Durham, to provide shelter for the deer and wild cattle that roamed the park.

Bedburn Hall Gardens   2

Hamsterley, Bishop Auckland DL13 3NN. Tel: (01388) 4888231

Mr I. Bonas • 9m NW of Bishop Auckland. W of A68 at Witton-le-Wear. 3m SE of Wolsingham off B6293 • Open as advertised on certain days in summer, 2 – 6pm, and at other times by appt • Entrance: £2, children 50p • Other information: Teas and plants for sale on NGS open day only ● 🍵 🏠 WC 🚻 ⚘ 🐾 ❧

A medium-sized terraced garden, largely developed by the present owner, beautifully situated by Hamsterley Forest. It is dominated by a lake with associated rhododendrons and bamboos. A well-established conservatory contains passion flowers and other exotics. Lilies and fuchsias are a speciality. 2000 saw the planting of a 17-metre lavender bed and a fruit cage of similar size.

The Bowes Museum Garden   3

Barnard Castle DL12 8NP. Tel: (01833) 690606

Durham County Council • In Barnard Castle about ¼ m E of market place • Garden open all year, daily, dawn – dusk, except during occasional events when access to gardens may be restricted • Entrance: free (museum and gardens £4, OAPs and children £3) ○ 🍵 ✕ 🏠 WC 🚻 ⚘ 🏛 🌂 ❧

In front of the museum to the south side, beneath a stone balustrade, a traditional herbaceous border announces a formal parterre, laid out in 1981 to complement the style of the building designed in 1869 by Jules Pellechet for John Bowes. The raised beds of the parterre are edged with box, which if laid out would stretch for over one and a half miles. There are 20 acres of grounds, planted with 56 different species of tree. A double avenue starts behind the east lodge and follows the park perimeter; the trees mark a carriageway which led from the main gate to the first site of the Bowes chapel. The low terrace wall and enclosed garden and tennis courts are on the site of this chapel, now a picnic area, and the yew trees survive from this scheme. The trees continue as a windbreak round the whole of the northern edge of the grounds, with exotics such as Wellingtonias planted in front of the native species. The mound behind the car park has been designed as a retreat, with arbours, shrubs and statues (removed from the Houses of Parliament during restoration work in the 1970s). A 15p leaflet, *A Walk through the Grounds*, lists all the trees. The museum has an important collection of European art.

East Durham and Houghall Community College 4

Houghall, Durham DH1 3SG. Tel: (0191) 386 1351

1m SE of Durham city S of A177 Durham – Stockton-on-Tees road. Or leave A1(M) at A177 signed Peterlee and continue towards Durham • Open all year, daily, 1 – 4pm • Entrance: free ○ 🍴 WC ♿ ▧

These campus grounds have been developed over the last 35 years as the county's main horticultural educational and training facility. They comprise some 24 acres of sports fields and ornamental features and contain one of the largest collections of hardy plants in north-east England. The gardens are in a frost pocket, where some of the lowest temperatures in the country are recorded annually. Ornamental features include a water garden, woodland garden, alpine house, display greenhouses, rock garden, raised beds, troughs, narcissi naturalised under trees, heather garden and arboretum. Since this is a working college the visitor may see empty beds and much work in progress. The College is holder of National Collections of sorbus and meconopsis.

Eggleston Hall Gardens 5

Eggleston, Barnard Castle DL12 0AG. Tel/answerphone: (01833) 650115; Fax: (01833) 650971

Mrs R. Gray (Managers: Gordon Long and Malcolm Hockham) • 18m NW of Darlington, 5m NW of Barnard Castle on B6278 • House not open but available for private functions – telephone (01833) 450553 • Garden open daily except 25th Dec, 10am – 5pm • Entrance: £1, season tickets £5, guided tours for parties £1 per person • Other information: Catering and guides for parties by arrangement ○ 🍴 ✕ 🍽 WC ♿ ⬐ ▧ ⬚ 🛈 ⚲

The house was designed by Ignatius Bonomi in the early nineteenth century for the antiquarian William Hutchinson. The lodge entrance, also by Bonomi, gives access to the gardens; Doric gate piers, a much later wrought-iron gate bought from The Great Exhibition by William Gray, and the lodge itself, with its pedimented, columned porch in warm stone greet the visitor. There are enjoyable walks along the stream with many unusual plants. The winding paths within the main garden continue to hold excitement, rounding corners to reveal colourful vistas which change with the seasons. The old churchyard, with gravestones dating from the seventeenth century, is now open to the public; curving stone steps have been built to lead into it from the main garden. Sadly the church was left to become a ruin, but interesting plantings have been made among the gravestones and within the roofless area inside the church walls, which can only get better as the plants mature. This area has a microclimate, so less hardy plants can be grown there. Three old greenhouses and several modern glasshouses and polytunnels hold plants of interest. In the sales area, celmisias are still a speciality, and soon the beautiful variegated lilac *Syringa emodi* will also be available. Organic vegetables and plants, trees, shrubs and perennials are for sale within the walled garden.

Raby Castle Gardens 6

Staindrop, Darlington DL2 3AH. Tel: (01833) 660202; Fax: (01833) 660169; Website: www.rabycastle.com

The Rt Hon. The Lord Barnard • 1m N of Staindrop on A688 Barnard Castle – Bishop Auckland road • House open 1 – 5pm (extra charge) • Garden open May and Sept, Wed and Sun only; June to Aug, daily except Sat; Bank Holidays (including Easter), Sat until following Wed; all 11am – 5.30pm • Entrance: £3, OAPs/children £2, season ticket £12, OAPs/children £10 • Other information: Dogs in park only, on lead ◑ ☕ ▦ WC ⅖ ⚘ ⛪ ♀ ☙

One of the country's most impressive medieval castles, once the seat of the Nevills and home to Lord Barnard's family for over 350 years, is set in a 200-acre deer park and has an interesting walled garden. This formal garden, dating from the mid-eighteenth century, was designed by Thomas Wright (the Wizard of Durham) for the 2nd Earl of Darlington and has a wide array of trees, shrubs and herbaceous plants. Thomas White advised on the landscaping along with Joseph Spence. The garden walls built from locally hand-made bricks have flues which used to enable sub-tropical fruits to be grown on the south terrace. The famous white Ischia fig tree, brought to Raby in 1786, still survives. Rose garden, shrub borders, original yew hedges, lakes and ornamental pond.

University Botanic Garden 7

Hollingside Lane, Durham DH1 3TN. Tel: (0191) 374 2670

Durham University • 1m from city centre, E of A1050. Accessible from A1(M). From S leave A177 and drive NW through Bowburn and Shincliffe to Durham. From N leave at A690 and drive SW to Durham. Garden off Hollingside Lane • Garden open all year. Glasshouses open daily, 9am – 4pm. Visitor centre open March to Oct, daily, 10am – 5pm; Nov to Feb, daily except Christmas week and bad weather, 11am – 4pm • Entrance: £1, concessions 50p • Other information: Wheelchair and map of wheelchair route available ○ ☕ WC ⅖ ⚘ ⛪

Established in 1970 as a centre for botanical study, this is now one of the few botanical gardens in the north of England. Of special interest are woodland walks with exotic trees from the Americas and the Himalayas. There is little in the way of herbaceous borders because throughout the garden trees and herbaceous plants are grown together as they would be found in the wild. There are, however, individual features devoted to heathers and conifers and to woodland plants, plus a North American arboretum, a Himalayan valley and a gazebo garden overshadowed by a huge monkey puzzle tree. Newly completed is an alpine/scree garden. The greenhouses contain tropical and Mediterranean plants and cacti, further details of which are available at the visitor centre. Near this centre is the Prince Bishop's Garden, comprising sculptures originally designed for the 1990 Gateshead Garden Festival; the six figures of some of County Durham's famous sons were carved by Colin Wilburn from elm trees, felled because of Dutch elm disease. While this has potential to be a very interesting botanical garden, some improvement in maintenance in specific areas will be required. Eighteen acres in all.

Westholme Hall   8

Winston, Darlington DL2 3QL. Tel: (01325) 730442

Mr and Mrs J.H. McBain • 10m W of Darlington on B6274 between Staindrop and Winston • Open day in July for charity, 2 – 6pm – telephone for dates. Parties by arrangement • Entrance: £2, children 50p ● ➡ 🍴 WC & ⬦ ⚘

The Jacobean house and the garden (which was laid out in 1890) are reached by a short drive of limes with mature hollies on the north side. To the south is parkland. Immediately inside the garden enclosure (about five acres), there are lawns: on the right an old tree supports a 'Félicité et Perpétue' rose and a 'Comtesse de Bouchaud' clematis. From the front door in the south elevation an axial line leads to a stone-flagged bridge over a stream, the Westholme Beck – a tributary of the Alwent Beck – and thence to the River Tees. A stone retaining wall parallel to and south of the house forms the backing for a grass walk running east-west; then a grass slope descends to a wide croquet lawn with bold plantings of rhododendrons and thence to grass walks with cherries and specimen trees. Cross the stream that bisects the garden and there is a paddock and more walks through maturing woodland; one vista through what will one day become an avenue of beeches is closed by a massive stone plinth. Elsewhere in the garden the long grass terrace walk is terminated by a wall and an urn. Stone parapets were salvaged from the Streatlam Park demolition sale of the 1930s, and now adorn this garden. There is a delightful shrub rose garden to the west of the house, partly sunken and overlooked by a summerhouse, with a good collection of Albas, Bourbons, etc. At Headlam Hall, about five miles east, excellent lunches and dinners are available.

HOW TO FIND THE GARDENS
Directions to each garden are included in the entry. This information has been supplied by the owners and garden inspectors. It is aimed to be the best available to those travelling by car, and has been compiled to be used in conjunction with a road atlas.

Some gardens can be approached by public transport, but alas these are few and far between. The unreliability of train and bus services makes it unrewarding to include details, particularly as many garden visits are made on Sundays. However, properties that can be reached by public transport feature in National Trust guides and the NGS Yellow Book, which sometimes give details.

ESSEX

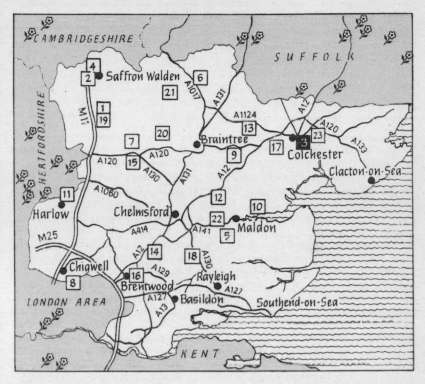

Two-starred gardens are marked on the map with a black square.

Amberden Hall ★ 1

Widdington, Saffron Walden CB11 3ST. Tel: (01799) 540402; Fax: (01799) 542827

Mr and Mrs D. Lloyd • 6m S of Saffron Walden, E of B1383 near Newport. Follow signs to Mole Hall Wildlife Park. Hall is ½ m past park on right • Open by appt only • Entrance: £2.50, children free (2001 prices) ● **WC** ⏃ 🕭

Lovely old walls covered in a variety of climbers, some of them rare, enclose this medium-sized garden set at one side of a fine house. The colour-themed borders are cleverly designed so that not all of the garden is visible at once. A *leylandii* hedge has been clipped and the sides corrugated. There is a good vegetable garden with raised beds to make it easier to cope with heavy clay soil. The garden has been extended beyond the walls with an ivy *allée* – this has two viburnum hedges with poles rising out of them supporting different ivies. More recent additions are a secret garden inside a dismantled barn, a bog garden, a moss garden and a woodland walk.

Audley End   2

Saffron Walden CB11 4JF. Tel: (01799) 522399

English Heritage • 1m W of Saffron Walden on B1383 • House open as grounds but different opening and closing times • Garden open April to Sept, Wed – Sun and Bank Holiday Mons, 11am – 6pm; 3rd to 31st Oct, Wed – Fri, 11am – 4pm, Sat and Sun, 11am — 5pm. Last admissions 1 hour before closing time • Entrance: £4, OAPs £3, children under 16 £2, family £10 (house and grounds £6.75, OAPs £5.10, children under 16 £3.40, family ticket £16.90) • Other information: Picnics in park only ◑ 💭 ✕ 🍴 WC ♿ ⬟ 🌀 🏛 ♟ ⚲*

The Jacobean house has always been a gem but now visitors can enjoy an early version of the parterre garden restored to the plans developed by Lord Braybrooke and his wife c. 1830, advised by William Sawrey Gilpin. The design was inspired by the classic seventeenth-century French parterres, with sheltering shrubberies which relate to contemporary (1830) interiors, but the overall effect is rather Victorian. English Heritage has introduced the whole repertory of the flower garden of the period – irises, martagon lilies, roses, peonies and astrantias, violas, hypericums – all planted in some 170 beds. Restoration has taken 10 years and has been completed without interfering with the surrounding 'Capability' Brown landscape park, which features a circular temple, bridge and Lady Portsmouth's Column by Adam, also a cascade constructed in the same year on the site of an ancient mill dam. There are fine plane, oak and tulip trees, and a pond garden, laid out in 1868, containing many scented old roses and sub-tropical bedding, with a Pulhamite rock garden at one end. The whole is immaculately maintained. The walled kitchen garden, which includes a 52-metre-long vine house, a full set of service buildings, gardeners' bothy and orchard house, is now open to the public for the first time in 250 years. Known as Lady Portsmouth's Garden, it has been developed into a working organic kitchen garden laid out in the Victorian style – a restoration by the Henry Doubleday Research Association. It includes new fruit trees on the walls, a mile of box edging, and a splendid variety of Victorian vegetables, which are also for sale in season. A Twenty-First-Century Garden opened in 2001.

The Beth Chatto Gardens ★★   3

Elmstead Market, Colchester CO7 7DB. Tel: (01206) 822007;
Fax: (01206) 825933; Website: www.bethchatto.co.uk

Mrs Beth Chatto • ¼ m E of Elmstead Market on A133 • Open March to Oct, Mon – Sat, 9am – 5pm; Nov to Feb, Mon – Fri, 9am – 4pm. Closed Sun and Bank Holidays • Entrance: £3, accompanied children free • Other information: Parties by arrangement ◯ 💭 WC ♿ 🌀

Beth Chatto designed these gardens in the 1960s from a neglected hollow which was either boggy and soggy or exceedingly dry. She, more than anyone else, has influenced gardeners by her choice of plants for any situation, and her ability to show them off to perfection. Her planting is a lesson to every gardener on how to use both leaf and flower to best advantage. The large gravel garden which she planted to replace the old car park is maturing well as a home for beautiful plants which can thrive in very dry conditions. In the last few years some of the earliest borders have been renewed, and part of the Mediterranean garden has been given over to scree beds – a setting for the smaller plants in the form of five irregular islands. The other major change has taken time to evolve: the creation of four large ponds, each slightly lower than the other, at the heart of the garden. To enter these gardens is 'to walk into another climate'. On the perimeter of the garden, a patch of woodland garden nurtures shade-loving plants. The beautifully designed and photographed handbook (£3) includes a fully descriptive catalogue with notes on the Chatto philosophy, a full page on the gravel garden and a free price list. Adjoining is the excellent *Unusual Plants* nursery. All compulsory visiting.

Bridge End Gardens 4

Bridge Street, Saffron Walden CM6 1AN. Tel: (01799) 510444 (Tourist Information Office)

In town centre. Entrance in Bridge Street and Castle Street • Gardens open all year, daily. Yew hedge maze open by pre-booked key from Tourist Information Office, No. 1 The Market Place • Entrance: free but £10 refundable key deposit
○ **WC** ♋

The early Victorian gardens were started by Atkinson Francis Gibson. The yew hedge maze, planted in 1840 in the Italian Renaissance style, has 610 metres of pathways, originally embellished with statues and columns and entered by richly ornamented iron gates. After some fifty years of neglect, restoration began in 1984; the maze was replanted with 1000 yews and officially opened in 1991. Other features include a rose garden and a Dutch garden with elaborate topiary and a viewing platform. On the common nearby is the ancient *Turf Maze of Saffron Walden*, a circular labyrinth of medieval Christian design, 29 metres in diameter with only four outer bastions. It is probably the largest of its kind in the world and one of only eight in England. Not far away, at Ashdon, *Beeches Nurseries* sell a range of rare and exciting plants. [Open all year, daily except Christmas and New Year. Telephone (01799) 584362.]

Cameo Cottage 5

Chapel Lane, Purleigh, Chelmsford CM3 6PY. Tel: (01621) 828334

Mrs Joan Cook • 9m SE of Chelmsford, S of Maldon between B1010 and B1012. Locate hill that leads to church. Facing hill, turn right, take first left (Howe Green Road), then first right by black house (Chapel Lane). Cameo Cottage is first house on right • Open by appt for individuals and groups • Entrance: £1.50 ● 🏠 ♋

Set around a cottage, the early part of which dates from the seventeenth century, this one-acre cottage garden is immediately captivating. It is entirely filled with plants that tumble and spill gloriously around a maze of narrow paths and small courtyards, yet the apparent informality is restrained within particular colour schemes, forming the cameos that give the cottage its name. Additional depth and texture are provided by a variation in levels and numerous raised troughs made by the owner's late husband. A diverted field ditch has allowed the creation of a bog garden. This is an enthralling place for the plantsman as it contains many rare treasures among more familiar herbaceous varieties. It is also known as a garden for all seasons, providing interest from February onwards. American visitors will be interested to learn that George Washington's great-great-grandfather was rector of Purleigh from 1633 to 1643; the church itself dates back to the thirteenth century.

Cracknells ★   6

Great Yeldham CO9 4PT. Tel: (01787) 237370

Mr and Mrs T. Chamberlain • 10m N of Braintree, on A1017 between Halstead and Haverhill • Open by appt • Entrance: by donation to collecting box ☻

Mr Chamberlain started contouring this large plot even before he started building his house. The landscape rolls away from the house down to the lake, also excavated at the start. This is not a garden in the accepted sense but 'a garden picture painted with trees', to use his own words. He has gathered together an impressive collection from all over the country. Here is the rare cut-leaf beech, *Fagus sylvatica heterophylla*, and its purple- and pink-leaved forms, 'Rohanii' and 'Roseomarginata', as well as the variegated tulip tree, *Liriodendron tulipifera* 'Aureomarginatum'. There are also collections of birches, acers, sorbus and oaks. If you are a lover of trees, make your pilgrimage.

Easton Lodge, The Gardens   7

Easton Lodge, Little Easton, Great Dunmow CM6 2BB. Tel: (01371) 876979; Fax: (01371) 876979; E-mail: enquiries@eastonlodge.co.uk; Website: www.eastonlodge.co.uk

Mr and Mrs B. Creasey • 11m W of Baintree, 1m N of Great Dunmow on B184. Signposted • Open Feb to Oct, Fri – Sun and Bank Holiday Mons, 12 noon – 6pm, and at other times by appt. • Entrance: £3.80, OAPs £3.50, children under 12 £1.50. Discount for parties • Other information: Teas at weekends only ☻ 🍴 ✕ 📷 ⟡ 🌿 ♿ ♀

The Lodge, in the old west wing of Easton Lodge, is all that has survived. 'Darling Daisy', Countess of Warwick, who was the mistress of Edward VII, spent vast sums on making the wonderful garden and grounds and on entertaining Edward VII. Originally designed in 1903 by Harold Peto, parts of the garden were described as some of his most outstanding work. The house was demolished and the garden abandoned in 1950, but restoration work has been done. The pavilion was restored in 1996 with a grant from Essex County Council, and the *allée* to the lake has been mown. In spring the snowdrops are worth seeing. It is a lovely place to walk around, but it needs vast sums spent on it and a substantial work-force.

7A Ellesmere Gardens   8

Redbridge, Ilford IG4 5DA. Tel: (020) 8550 5464

Cecilia Gonzalez • Travelling E, off A12 Eastern Avenue between Redbridge roundabout (M11 interchange) and Gants Hill roundabout • Open by appt only (garden only takes two at a time) • Entrance: £2.50 ◐

A charming split-level courtyard garden, only six metres square, and a treasure trove of unusual plants. The upper level is filled with containers,the lower with dense tropical planting. The owner knew little about gardening when she moved here in the early 1980s and the site was covered with paving stones, most now removed. The number of species here is remarkable but all growth is restricted and imaginative use is made of container planting.

Feeringbury Manor   9

Coggeshall Road, Feering, Colchester CO5 9RB. Tel: (01376) 561946; Fax: (01376) 562481

Mr and Mrs Giles Coode-Adams • 6m E of Braintree between Coggeshall and Feering • Open 4th April to 27th July, Thurs, Fri, 8am – 4pm, and by appt • Entrance: £2.50 ◑ WC & ⬧ ℞

This is a garden distinguished by detailed planting. There are bog-loving plants by two ponds and a stream as well as plants that prefer dry soil. The season is prolonged with interesting bulbs and climbers such as sweet peas and clematis, the latter a speciality. Notable, too, are the sculptured gates by Ben Coode-Adams.

Folly Faunts House   10

**Goldhanger, Maldon CM9 8AP.
Tel: (01621) 788213 (Home), (01621) 788611 (Office); Fax: (01621) 788754**

Mr and Mrs J.C. Jenkinson • On B1026 between Maldon and Colchester • Open for charity several days in summer, 2 – 5pm, and for parties (min. 6) at other times by appt • Entrance: £2.50 • Other information: Teas and plants for sale on charity open days only ◐ 🍴 WC & ⬧ ℞

The 20-acre garden, created round an eighteenth-century manor house since 1963, is divided into compartments, each with a different theme, and has a wide variety of unusual trees and shrubs. The plantings around the informal and formal ponds are a special feature. The 16 acres of park and woodland, divided by five double avenues, provide attractive walks.

The Gibberd Garden ★   11

Marsh Lane, Gilden Way, Harlow CM17 0NA. Tel: (01279) 442112

Gibberd Garden Trust • E of Harlow between A414 and B183. From M11 junction 7 take A414 to Harlow, follow signs to Old Harlow onto B183 (Gilden Way) and continue for 1m. Marsh Lane is on left • Open April to Sept, Sat, Sun and Bank Holiday Mon, 2 – 6pm; June to Aug, 12.30 – 6pm • Entrance:

£3, concessions £2, children free (2001 prices) • *Other information: Lunches available June to Aug* ● 💭 WC &.

This is the extremely individual creation of the architect and art collector Sir Frederick Gibberd. Considered an outstanding example of twentieth-century garden design, the nine-acre sloping site comprises a series of rooms designed to display his remarkable collection of modern sculpture and architectural artefacts. However, there is no rigidity of structure; tranquillity as well as drama is provided by glades, groves and *alles* as they open up vistas or focus on statuary. A waterfall and quiet pools have been incorporated into a small brook which borders the east of the property and towards which run lushly planted channels of water. At one end of the brook stands a moated castle. There are also natural ponds, a tree house, a labyrinth and a gazebo. Sir Frederick died in 1984, but the garden is now in the enthusiastic hands of the Gibberd Garden Trust, which is aiming to realise his wish that it be kept open to the public in perpetuity. Hugh Johnson states that this 'must certainly be one of the most important [gardens] in the history of the twentieth century'.

Glen Chantry ★ 12

Wickham Bishops CM8 3LG. Tel/Fax: (01621) 891342

Mr and Mrs W.G. Staines • *9m NE of Chelmsford off A12, 2m SE of Witham. Turn left off B1018 towards Wickham Bishops. Pass golf course, cross River Blackwater bridge and turn left up Ishams Chase by Blue Mills* • *Open 5th April to 5th Oct, Fri and Sat, 10am – 4pm* • *Entrance: £2, children 50p* • *Other information: D.I.Y. teas* ◑ 💭 WC & 🌿

A large undulating garden, started in 1977. The huge, informally shaped beds are filled with an imaginative mixture of bulbs, hostas, peonies, grasses, brunneras, white martagon lilies, crambes and shrub roses. The centres of some beds are raised, and this gives an excellent shape to the planting. Other features include large rock gardens, a stream with waterfalls leading to ponds with rodgersias, iris and good foliage plants and an attractive white garden. Overall, the plantings and colour schemes are really spectacular.

Hill House 13

Chappel, Colchester CO6 2DX. Tel: (01787) 222428

Mr and Mrs R. Mason • *8m W of Colchester on A1124 between Colchester and Earls Colne* • *Open by appt* • *Entrance: by donation to charity* ●

This large garden is now moving towards maturity. Designed by the owners on formal lines and using yew hedging and walls to create vistas, it has a lime avenue sited to lead the eye out into the country. A mixed planting of tough native trees, sorbus and hawthorn, etc., has been established as a windbreak. A small courtyard with a raised pool, reminiscent of a London plot, has been planted with green-leaved plants and white flowers only. Another feature is a pond with two black swans. The bones of the garden are in place including urns, statues and seats, and all the colour and secondary planting has now been introduced. Further land has been acquired giving a fine view over the Colne Valley and Chappel Viaduct, and hedges and trees are being established here.

Ingatestone Hall 14
Ingatestone CM4 9NR. Tel: (01277) 353010

Lord Petre • 7m SW of Chelmsford on A12. From Ingatestone main street, take Station Lane at SW end. Signposted • House open • Garden open 30th March to Sept, Sat, Sun and Bank Holiday Mon; also 17th July to 6th Sept, Wed – Fri, all 1 – 6pm • Entrance: £4, OAPs and students £3.50, children £2 ◑ ▇ WC ⅋ ✿ ⅏ ⅋

There have been buildings here since 950 AD, and the present house was built in the 1540s. A large stewpond, contemporary with the house, provided fish and fresh-water mussels; it is now bordered by huge gunneras and shady walks. The walled garden has magnificent standard roses and a lily pond. There is a nut walk and a grass walk, but the lime walk is haunted by Bishop Benjamin Petre's dog, which saved his life when he was set upon in 1740 and still patrols. The extensive, immaculate lawns have specimen trees: mulberries, *Magnolia grandiflora* and weeping beeches. The house is well worth a visit.

Langthorns Plantery 15
High Cross Lane West, Little Canfield, Dunmow CM6 1TD. Tel: (01371) 872611

Mr and Mrs David Cannon • 5m E of M11 junction 8, on A120 • Plantery open daily, 10am – 5pm • Garden open by appt (telephone or ask at the plantery) • Entrance: free ● ⬷ ✿

The owners, avid collectors of unusual plants, propagate in the nursery, which stocks one of the widest ranges of good-quality plants in the country: over 1200 varieties of herbaceous perennials, many unusual forms of tricyrtis, geraniums and salvias; 1300 varieties of shrubs and conservatory plants, alpines, clematis and honeysuckles. The garden has now been revamped and is open to the public on a limited basis.

The Magnolias 16
18 St John's Avenue, Brentwood CM14 5DF. Tel: (01277) 220019; Website: www.themagnolias.co.uk

Mr and Mrs R.A. Hammond • From A1023 turn S to A128. After 300 metres turn right at traffic lights, over railway bridge. St John's Avenue is third on right • Open 17th, 24th, 31st March, 7th, 21st, 28th April, 5th, 19th, 26th May, 16th June, 14th July, 18th Aug, 15th Sept, 27th Oct, 11am – 5pm. Parties by appt • Entrance: £1.50, children 50p ● ✿

The garden may be overgrown and unpruned, but the owners are fine plantsmen. The front garden (7 1/2 x 6 metres) has impressive trees and shrubs – *Carpenteria californica* with white-flowered *Solanum jasminoides* growing through it, *Cercis canadensis*, *Sophora microphylla* and *Cytisus battandieri*. A dark path leads to a long narrow garden with seven ponds, and mature trees and plantings, including trilliums, *Embothrium coccineum* (Chilean firebush), *Magnolia campbellii* which finally flowered after thirty years, and several *Cornus* 'Norman Hadden'.

Olivers 17

Olivers Lane, Colchester CO2 0HJ. Tel: (01206) 330575; Fax: (01206) 330366; E-mail: gay.edwards@virgin.net

Mr and Mrs David Edwards • 3m SW of Colchester off B1022 Maldon road. Follow signs to Colchester Zoo. From zoo continue $\frac{3}{4}$ m towards Colchester and at roundabout turn right. After $\frac{1}{4}$ m turn right again into Olivers Lane. From Colchester pass Shrub End church and Leather Bottle pub then turn left at second roundabout • Open 5th, 6th May and by appt for individuals and parties • Entrance: £2.60, children free ● ● ● WC ⅙ ⅍ ℺

The moment visitors arrive at the attractive Georgian-fronted house and step down onto the large York-stone terrace, beautifully planted in soft sympathetic colours, they are entranced. All around are 20 acres of garden and woodland. From the terrace one can see down over the lawn, fine borders, pools and woods to a natural meadow (cut only to encourage wild flowers and grasses) and to trees bordering the river. A 'willow pattern' bridge crosses the first of a succession of pools dropping down to an ancient fish pond. *Taxodium distichum*, metasequoia and ginkgo flourish by the pools. There are yew hedges and a delightful woodland walk, where mature native trees shelter rhododendrons, azaleas and shrub roses in the rides.

RHS Garden Hyde Hall 18

Rettendon, Chelmsford CM3 8ET. Tel: (01245) 400256; E-mail: hydehall@rhs.org.uk; Website: www.rhs.org.uk

The Royal Horticultural Society • 7m SE of Chelmsford, signed from A130 • Open April to Oct, daily, 11am – 6pm (closes 5pm in Sept and Oct) • Entrance: £3, children (6–16) £1. Parties of 10 or more £2.50 per person (2001 prices) • Other information: Guide dogs only ◑ ● ✕ ● WC ⅙ ⅍ ⚏ ♀

The hilltop garden, which is being more than doubled in area to some 20 acres, is perched above the East Anglian wheatfields in a truly Tuscanesque manner. Notable are the beds of species roses with white peonies and naturalised *Eremurus robustus* growing through them. There is much else to see: a colour-themed herbaceous border; an informal pond; a spring garden of massed hellebores and many bulbs; a formal enclosed rose garden with pillars behind a broad planting of alliums and half-hardy salvias. This is on a double crossfall which poses a severe problem. It is against all classical garden design principles, but still produces a stunning display. The National Collection of viburnums is here. Three thousand young trees have been planted, the upper and lower ponds are being opened up and replanted, and the terrace (entered through a massive oak pergola adorned with clematis and wisteria) is being enlarged. The development of a 12-acre malus field at the entrance is currently a major project, including a winding, shallow 'riverbed', an ash and oak avenue with a central pool, display and shrub beds and a shrub rose garden. The new dry shingle garden is on fertile alkaline clay with huge glacial boulders from Scotland, and grows things like the self-seeding *Eremurus robustus*, *Erigeron karvinskianus* and much more. Hyde Hall is primarily a teaching garden, but the individual sections and plantings are outstanding.

R. and R. Saggers ★   19

**Waterloo House, High Street, Newport, Saffron Walden CB11 3PG.
Tel: (01799) 540858**

*R. and R. Saggers • 8m N of Bishop's Stortford, on B1383 through Newport •
Open all year, daily except Mon (but open Bank Holiday Mons), 10am – 5pm.
Closed Sun, Jan, Feb, March, Aug • Entrance: free • Other information: Possible
for wheelchairs but gravel paths* ○ WC & ◁▷ 🌳 ⛲

This small, immaculately kept nursery has a charming town garden running down to a stream between flint walls. The nursery stocks old-fashioned roses and rare and unusual plants, grown and propagated by Mr Saggers. Almost everything on sale is grown in the wide borders in front of the flint walls. As well as the many exciting shrubs and herbaceous plants, there is a good range of statuary, lead urns, Whichford pots and armillary sundials.

Saling Hall ★   20

Great Saling, Braintree CM7 5DT.

*Mr and Mrs Hugh Johnson • 6m NW of Braintree, halfway between Braintree
and Dunmow on A120 turn N at Saling Oak • Open for NGS May to July,
Wed, 2 – 5pm. Parties on weekdays by written appt • Entrance: £2.50, children
free* ● WC ◔

Hugh Johnson's wonderful garden is essentially for tree lovers. The huge elms died, and he turned the 12 acres of chalky boulder clay into an arboretum of genera that thrive on alkaline clay or gravel. A marvellous collection of pines, quercus, sorbus, aesculus, robinias, prunus, tilia, fraxinus, fagus, salix and betulas leads the eye to a classical Temple of Pisces. Many rarities like *Carpinus fangiana*, *Eriobotrya japonica*, *Staphylea pinnata*, an unknown weeping juniper, incense cedars from Oregon seed and unusual pines on the east slope. The walled garden faces south-west. Fruit trees are trimmed into mushroom shapes to contrast with a file of clipped cypress and a matching file of Irish junipers and pyramid box bushes. The borders are informal, with grey and blue plants of rather typical Mediterranean associations – agapanthus, euphorbias, etc. The disciplined planting in the various sections creates a distinct atmosphere in each. There is a vegetable garden, a Japanese garden, a water garden, a valley garden and a strange menhir in its private glade. The old moat with its cascade boasts some substantial carp.

Shore Hall ★   21

Cornish Hall End, Braintree CM7 4HW. Tel: (01799) 586411;
Fax: (01799) 586106; E-mail: dswete@shorehall.com;
Website: www.shorehall.com

*Mr and Mrs Peter Swete • 10m NW of Braintree off B1057, 2½ m NE of
Finchingfield, ½ m W of Cornish Hall End on Great Sampford road • Open
several dates for NGS – telephone for details. Parties on weekdays only by appt •
Entrance: £2.50 • Other information: Teas on Sun open days only* ◐ WC ♫ ⊞

An immaculate, beautifully planted garden, with miles of wonderful mowing.
There is a formal rose garden with flagged paths, another (newish) formal
garden with timber edging and patterns of vegetables interplanted with
variegated strawberries, leeks and red and green lettuces; adding an element
of height are roses over arches and gooseberries and euonymus grown as
standards. In the borders fine plants abound, and a feature of the planting are
shrubs mixed with pink and grey. The hall itself sells excellent metal obelisks,
rose arches, flower baskets and flower supports. A catalogue is available.

Stone Pine ★   22

Hyde Lane, Danbury, Chelmsford CM3 4LJ. Tel: (01245) 223232

*Mr and Mrs David Barker • 4m E of Chelmsford from Runsell Green, 1m S of
A414 leaving Danbury towards Maldon • Open by appt • Entrance: by donation
to collecting box* ◐ 📗 WC

This small garden, owned by a former Chairman of the Hardy Plant Society, is
filled with choice and unusual varieties. The area of grass is minimal and paths
wind around borders crammed with trees, acers being particularly popular,
and shrubs. Surprising plants appear around each corner, like the rarely seen
Paris quadrifolia. Mr Barker is also knowledgeable on lilies, hemerocallis, irises
and grasses. National Collections of epimediums and Japanese anemones.

Tye Farm   23

Colchester Road, Elmstead Market, Colchester CO7 7AX. Tel: (01206) 822400

*Mr and Mrs C. Gooch • 2m E of Colchester on A133, ½ m W of Elmstead
Market • Open to groups by appt • Entrance: £2* ◐ WC ♿

This one-acre garden is cleverly planted with hedges to make compartments to
break the prevailing wind. The shrubs and perennials complement one another, and there are over 60 varieties of old and modern roses. Look for the
gold area in the small walled kitchen garden. There is a formally planted, box-
edged area for herbs. The conservatory contains many unusual plants.

Warwick House

(see EASTON LODGE, THE GARDENS)

GLOUCESTERSHIRE

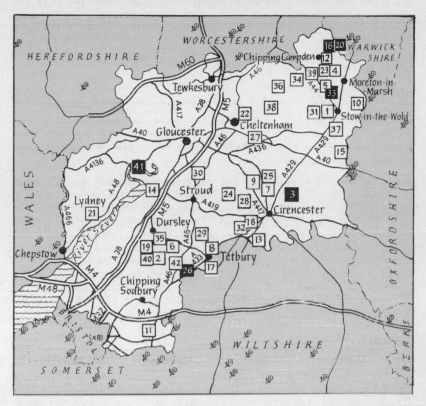

Some gardens have postal addresses in one county and are physically situated in another. If in doubt, a check in the index will direct the reader to the page on which the garden appears.

Two-starred gardens are marked on the map with a black square.

Abbotswood ★   1

Stow-on-the-Wold GL54 1EN. Tel: (01451) 830173

Dikler Farming Co • 1m W of Stow on B4077 • Open several Suns in May and June for charity, 1.30 – 6pm • Entrance: £2, children free • Other information: Coaches must drop passengers at top gate and park in Stow ● ● WC & ◁

The house is in one of the most beautiful of Cotswold settings. From the car park it is approached via a descending stream and pools towards woodland carpeted in spring with flowers and bulbs, including one of the largest displays of fritillaries in season. The woods continue above and beyond the house and have been planted with rhododendrons, flowering shrubs and specimen trees. Near the house are terraces and formal gardens, including a box-edged rose garden and a water garden. Extensive heather plantings. The gardens round the house are by Lutyens. Note especially his lily pool running up to the house; there is a jet of water there which, if the angle of the sun is right, shimmers spectacularly. Alas, other vertical features by Lutyens were removed by an earlier owner, though the planting remains faithful to his design.

Alderley Grange ★   2

Alderley GL12 7QT. Tel: (01453) 842161

Mr Guy and The Hon. Mrs Acloque • 2m S of Wotton-under-Edge. Turn NW off A46 Bath – Stroud road at Dunkirk • Open during June by appt • Entrance: £3, children free ● WC ♿

A garden of exceptional beauty and character in a tranquil walled setting, renowned for its collection of aromatic plants and scented flowers. Designed by the late Alvilde Lees-Milne, it is believed to be the last garden in which Vita Sackville-West had a hand, Alderley Grange was acquired by the present owners in 1974 and has been immaculately maintained and developed with discretion and style. The fine house and a mulberry tree date from the seventeenth century; a pleached and arched lime walk leads to a series of enclosed gardens. There is a notable hexagonal herb garden with many delightful perspectives of clipped, trained or potted shrubs and trees, and abundant plantings of old roses. Many tender and unusual plants flourish in this cherished and exquisite space.

Barnsley House ★★   3

Barnsley, Nr Cirencester GL7 5EE. Tel: (01285) 740561; Fax: (01285) 740628; Website: www.opengarden.co.uk

Mr and Mrs Charles Verey • 4m NE of Cirencester on B4425 in Barnsley • Open 1st Feb to 21st Dec, Mon, Wed – Sat (but closed 29th March), 10am – 5.30pm. Coaches and guided tours by appt • Entrance: £5, OAPs £3.50, children free. Open garden membership £12.50 (includes season ticket). Guided tours extra ☾ WC ♿ 🌿 🛍 🍴

A highly influential garden in its day, comprising many garden styles from the past, carefully blended by Rosemary and David Verey after they inherited the house from David's father, the Rev. Cecil Verey, in 1951. The 1697 Cotswold stone house is set in the middle of the four-acre garden, surrounded on three sides by a 1770 stone wall. Borders create vistas and divide the garden into areas of distinct and individual character, and great attention is paid to colour and texture. The kitchen garden, with its numerous small beds, ornate paths, box hedges, trained fruit trees, etc., and the laburnum, allium and wisteria walk, best mid-May to mid-June, are especially renowned. Although management of the garden passed to Rosemary's elder son in 1999, she continued to watch over it until her much-lamented death in 2001. Barnsley was her unique creation, and for the present generation of gardeners will remain her memorial, but it will be rewarding to watch it evolve over the coming years. Just W of the B4425 near Aldworth is *Lodge Park*, the uniquely interesting hunting lodge built expressly for deer coursing for John 'Crump' Dutton of Sherborne Park in the 1650s. The course survives, and the lodge has been restored by the National Trust. [Open Fri – Mon, 11am – 4pm.]

Batsford Arboretum ★ 4

Batsford Park, Moreton-in-Marsh GL56 9QB. Tel: (01386) 701441; Fax: (01386) 701827

The Batsford Foundation • $1\frac{1}{2}$ m NW of Moreton-in-Marsh on A44 to Evesham. Opposite entrance to Sezincote (see entry) • Arboretum open mid-Feb to mid-Nov, daily; mid-Nov to mid-Feb, Sat, Sun and 26th Dec, 10am – 5pm • Entrance: £4, OAPs £3, children £1 (2001 prices) • Other information: Aquatic Centre, Falconry Centre (2001 prices) ◐ 🍵 ✕ 🥪 WC 🐕 🌿 ⚱ 🔦 🦆

Over 1500 different species and varieties of trees, shrubs and bamboos in 55 acres of typical Cotswold countryside, plus an unusual collection of exotic shrubs and bronze statues from the Far East, originally collected for the garden by Lord Redesdale. It was expanded by the first Lord Dulverton in the 1960s. There are fine collections of magnolias, Japanese cherries and spring bulbs, and excellent autumn colour. A 'swampery' combines elements of a bog and a stumpery. Good views of the house (not open).

Bourton House ★ 5

Bourton-on-the-Hill, Moreton-in-Marsh GL56 9AE. Tel: (01386) 700754; E-mail: cd@bourtonhouse.com; Website: www.bourtonhouse.com

Mr and Mrs R. Paice • 2m W of Moreton-in-Marsh on A44 • Open 23rd May to Oct, Thurs and Fri; also 2nd, 3rd, 4th June, 25th, 26th Aug; all 10am – 5pm • Entrance: £3.50, children free • Other information: Parking across road ◐ 🍵 🥪 WC 🌿 ⚱

This exceptionally handsome eighteenth-century Baroque Cotswold village house with fine views is enhanced by a medium-sized garden largely created under the present ownership. The diminutive geometrical *potager* is a particular delight. Well-kept lawns, quiet fountains, a knot garden and Cotswold stone walls set off a number of herbaceous borders in which the choice and arrangement of plants and shrubs make skilful use of current fashions in garden design. Each year there are new interests – the raised pond in the top garden, a topiary walk, and long terraces on the main lawn now planted with low-growing shrubs, perennials and roses. The plantation in the field opposite is roaring along and a pleasure to roam, and a gallery of local arts, crafts and design has opened in the tithe barn. The cocoon-like shade-house is a flourishing environment for novel shade-loving plants. Nearby Sezincote and Batsford, and Hidcote and Kiftsgate (see entries) are less than half an hour away and make Bourton House a sensible location to include while touring in this part of Gloucestershire.

Brackenbury 6

Coombe, Wotton-under-Edge GL12 7NF. Tel: (01453) 842238

Mr and Mrs Peter Heaton • 1m NE of Wotton-under-Edge off B4058. From church go ½ m on Stroud road, turn right (signed 'Coombe'). From Stroud, go 300 yards past Wotton sign, turn left (signed 'Coombe') and garden is on right • Open for NGS 26th May, 30th June, 28th July, 26th Aug, 2 – 6pm • Entrance: £2, children free ● ▆ WC ☺

This terraced garden with multi-layer planting is clearly designed by a plantsman with designer tastes. Foliage is a feature. Good mixed borders, a cottage garden, a pool, 1000 different hardy perennials and 200 different shrubs are all fitted into two-thirds of an acre. The vegetable garden is laid out on the deepbed system. It is worth a visit in June and July just to see the National Collection of erigerons.

Cerney House Gardens 7

North Cerney, Cirencester GL7 7BX. Tel: (01285) 831300/831205; Fax: (01285) 831676

Sir Michael and Lady Angus • 3½ m N of Cirencester off A435 Cheltenham road. Turn left opposite Bathurst Arms, follow road up hill past church, signed 'Bagendon', and turn in through gates on right • Open April to Sept, Tues, Wed and Fri, 10am – 5pm, and one Sun in May for charity. Open at other times and for parties by appt • Entrance: £3, children £1 • Other information: Lunches and high teas by arrangement. Picnics in car park only ◖ ▆ WC ♿ ☺ ▥ ☕

Around the house, remodelled by Decimus Burton in 1791, goats and sheep graze and wild flowers flourish in their meadow. The pleasantly unmanicured garden is not for those who like everything tickety-boo – the plants are happy and unrestrained, and dead-heading is not a priority. There are lawns, shrubs and trees around the house, and behind it a three-and-a-half-acre sloping walled garden restored since the mid-1980s with riotous herbaceous borders, vegetables, many old-fashioned roses, clematis and a delightful children's story-book pig (a Gloucester Old Spot, of course) beneath the apple trees nearby. A woodland walk is carpeted with snowdrops in February and bluebells in May. Behind the house is a colourful rockery with a waterfall. The herb garden, the geranium and thyme bank, and the pink border beside the swimming pool are now well established, and there is a genera-garden leading down to the pond, and a tree trail. Garden labels are packed with information, particularly those in the new beds to the side of the house which tell the stories of plant-hunters and famous nurserymen. The locality is rich in Roman history, with Chedworth Roman Villa a few miles away. The nearby twelfth-century church is well worth a visit.

The Chipping Croft 8

The Chipping, Tetbury GL8 8EY. Tel: (01666) 503570/503178

Dr and Mrs P. Taylor • In town centre proceed between The Snooty Fox and Barclays past parking in Chipping Square. Garden is at bottom on left behind

wall with tall trees, entrance in driveway to courtyard • *Open by appt* •
Entrance: £2.50 ● ⟁ ℺

This is a most unusual town garden because of its size and character. Entering
through a courtyard leading to a terrace, sunken patio and large lawn
bordered by mature trees and a wooded walk. It extends to about two acres
and is on three levels. At one time, the mostly Queen Anne house was used as a
school, and since 1985 Dr Taylor has transformed a hard-surfaced playground
area into a courtyard with a small rectangular raised pool and a conservatory.
He has replanted extensively, constructed a summerhouse/potting shed and
added new steps connecting the various levels. Three formal terrace gardens
contain a variety of cottage-garden flowers as well as unusual plants, vegetables and herbs, with the kitchen garden proper laid out as a *potager* on a
higher level. Beneath the terraces is a wide walk with borders either side and
arches covered with roses, honeysuckle and clematis leading back to the
house.

Cotswold Farm 9

Duntisbourne Abbots, Cirencester GL7 7JS. Tel: (01285) 821857;
E-mail: mdbirchall@aol.com

Mark and Iona Birchall • *5m NW of Cirencester off A417. From Cirencester
turn left signed 'Duntisbourne Abbots', then at once right, right again after 300
yards, under the new dual carriageway, and house drive is opposite. From
Gloucester 1m past Highwayman Inn, turn left signed 'Duntisbourne Abbots/
Services' right at once, and the drive is 300 yards on left* • *Open 23rd June,
18th Aug, and by appt at other times (good notice appreciated)* • *Entrance: £3*
● ● WC ℺

A mature garden planted in grand style and sustained with sensitive artistry
surrounding a fine old house in a superb Cotswold setting. The terrace was
designed by Norman Jewson in 1938. The formal walled gardens have a pool
and are planted with shrub, bush and climbing roses, alpines, lavender and a
collection of scented flowers. There are also established plantings of shrubs,
herbaceous perennials and many small treasures overlooking an unspoilt
wooded valley. A charmed garden redolent of another age in a remote and
lovely situation.

Daylesford House ★ 10

Daylesford, Moreton–in–Marsh GL56 0YH. Tel: (01608) 659888

Sir Anthony and Lady Bamford • *Off A436 between Stow-on-the-Wold and
Chipping Norton* • *Open one day for NGS, and by appt on weekdays for parties
only* • *Entrance: £5 per person* ● WC ઇ

Like nearby Sezincote, Daylesford House was designed by Samuel Pepys
Cockerell. Warren Hastings, the first Governor-General of India, bought
the estate in 1785. He was interested in gardening and built the large walled
garden before the house was completed, stocking it with exotic plants and
fruits; a yak he had brought back from India roamed around the extensive

grounds. John Davenport was employed to design the layout of the garden, the lakes and the Gothick orangery. The garden is a delight, with its magnificent lawns, lakes complete with swans and Canada geese, woodland walks (carpeted with violets, primroses and many other wild flowers in spring, bluebells in May and wild orchids in the summer). There is a delightful orangery full of unusual shrubs, a trellised rose garden and a decorative formal fruit and vegetable walled garden with an orchid house, a peach house and working glasshouses, reworked by Rupert Golby. The Secret Garden is in its infancy; it will be rewarding to see it when the tender exotics mature and counter-balance the rather assertive water features. Elsewhere the new planting is subtle, sophisticated, relaxed – a magical place.

Dyrham Park   11

Chippenham SN14 8ER. Tel: (0117) 937 2501

The National Trust • 8m N of Bath, 12m E of Bristol on A46. Take M4 junction 18 in direction of Bath • House (including Victorian domestic areas) open 23rd March – 3rd Nov, daily except Wed and Thurs, 12 noon – 5.30pm (last admission 4.45pm) • Garden open as house, 11am – 5.30pm. House and garden closed 5th to 8th July • Park open all year except 25th Dec, daily, 11am – 5.30pm or dusk if earlier • Entrance: park only £2, children £1; park and garden £3, children £1.50; house, garden and park £7.90, children £3.90, family ticket £19 • Other information: Possible for wheelchairs on terrace but park steep in places. All cars in car park at East Lodge, bus link to house and garden. Dogs in dog walking area only, on lead • Garden: ◑ 🍽 ✕ 🛍 WC ♿ 🧺 ☕ ⚲ *Park:* ○ 🛍 ⚲

Only a tiny fragment of the extensive London and Wise Baroque garden shown in the view by Kip in 1712 survives. The terraces were all smoothed out in the late eighteenth century to form an 'English' landscape with fine mature beech, Spanish chestnut, Lucombe oak, red oak and black walnut. Avenues of elms survived until the mid-1970s when they were wiped out by Dutch elm disease; they have since been replanted with limes. The cascade in the garden on the west side is still working and one can make out the form of the original garden and enjoy the terrace and Talman's orangery, all 30 metres now splendidly transformed and wonderfully scented. The views towards Bristol and the elegance of the 'natural' landscape, with the house and church tucked into the hillside, make this an outstanding example of English landscape gardening. In all, 263 acres of ancient parkland.

The Ernest Wilson Memorial Garden   12

Leasbourne, High Street, Chipping Campden. Tel: (01386) 840884 (Dick Smith)

N of A44 between Evesham and Stow-on-the-Wold and S of Stratford-upon-Avon off A46 E of Broadway • Open all year, daily except 25th Dec, 9am – dusk • Entrance: free, but contributions welcome (donation box) ○ ♿ ⟁ ⚲

Because of its position near Hidcote, Kiftsgate and Charlcote, the town is a popular holiday stopping-off point, so it is fortuitous that it has a garden to appeal to horticulturally minded visitors. It was opened in 1984 in memory of 'Chinese' Wilson, who was born in Chipping Campden in 1876. The famous collector is estimated to have introduced 1200 species of trees and shrubs during his career, and the garden has several of his finds, including *Acer griseum* (the paperbark maple), *Davidia involucrata* (the pocket-handkerchief tree), and the plant for which he wished to be remembered, *Lilium regale*. It is a peaceful oasis, with seats and shade, backed by the beautiful church tower. Other gardens in Chipping Campden and neighbouring Broad Campden are open on certain days, and for the past few years a charity has arranged for some 20 gardens to open over a June weekend. This will probably become an annual event. The choice of gardens appears to have been dictated by a desire for quantity rather than quality, and in general their appeal will be to those who like what is now called the traditional Cotswold style.

Ewen Manor 13

Ewen, Cirencester GL7 6BX. Tel: (01285) 770206

Lady Gibbs • 4m S of Cirencester off A429. Turn at signpost for Ewen, 1m • Open 8th May to 8th July, Wed – Thurs, and probably two days in April and May for charity • Entrance: £2 • Other information: Teas on charity days only ● 📷 WC & ⚐ ℺

In the late 1940s this was a run-down manor garden which had in part been used as a Dig-for-Victory patch. The Georgian house had been moved here from across the Thames 200 years earlier. Backed by magnificent trees, it now contains a series of gardens with architectural features, and everywhere the planting is profuse. There are views across the pattern-mown lawn to the circular summerhouse with its conical Cotswold stone-tiled roof, and to the 215-year-old cedars of Lebanon in the woodland area all around. The main herbaceous border is backed by a high yew hedge, behind which is a large rectangular lily pool surrounded by masses of hellanthemums, overlooked by the garden room, once the stables, with its plant-filled terrace and pots. Daffodils and spring bulbs.

Frampton Court 14

Frampton-on-Severn GL2 7EU.
Tel: (01452) 740267 (Home); (01452) 740698 (Office); Fax: (01452) 740698

Mrs Peter Clifford • SW of Gloucester, 2m from M5 junction 13. Signposted. Left hand side of village green, entrance through imposing gates in long wall between two large chestnut trees • House open all year by appt with guided tours by owner. £5 per person • Garden open all year by appt • Entrance: £2 • Other information: Refreshments in village hall on selected days ● ☕ 📷 WC & ⚐ ♨ ℺

Home of the remarkable Clifford family of female artists, who created the *Frampton Flora* (1830-1860), the elegant 1730s' house stands on land owned by the family since the twelfth century. It was designed by John Strahan in the style of Vanbrugh; the interior has exquisite woodwork and furnishings. The five-acre grounds are maintained with a minimum of labour and contain a lake, fine trees and a formal water garden of Dutch design, believed to have been built by the architects of the larger Westbury Court Garden (see entry) on the other side of the Severn. The Strawberry Hill Gothic orangery of 1750 (not always open but available for holiday letting), where the ladies are believed to have executed their work, stands reflected in the still water, planted with lilies and flanked by a mixed border. This garden is open in association with that of *Frampton Manor*, also occupied by Cliffords, where a boldly planted walled garden with many old roses is set off splendidly by a fine fifteenth-century timbered house.

Great Rissington Farm 15

Great Rissington GL54 2LH. Tel: (01451) 820322

The Hon. John and Mrs Donovan • 4m SE of Stow-on-the-Wold, 6m NW of Burford off A424 onto Barrington road. From Stow, turn right after sign to 'Barn Business Centre' at lodge. From Burford pass sign left to Great Rissington and turn left at lodge • Open May and June, Tues, 2 – 5.30pm • Entrance: £2, children free ●

Arriving at this sixteenth-century Cotswold house and its two acres, the visitor is assured of a warm welcome from the enthusiastic owner-gardeners. Three small walled gardens are filled with a large collection of roses and herbaceous plants; a long, partly shaded border runs behind. A wide border on the edge of the lawn has a bold planting of large shrubs, and on the far side is a small spinney, partially cleared and being replanted with interesting new trees and shrubs. This is a most exciting garden with lovely design and great potential, complemented by splendid views over surrounding country-side.

Hidcote Manor Garden ★★ 16

Hidcote Bartrim, Chipping Campden GL55 6LR. Tel: (01386) 438333; Fax: (01386) 438817; E-mail: hidcote_manor@smtp.ntrust.org.uk

The National Trust • 3m NE of Chipping Campden. Signposted • Garden open 23rd March to May, Aug to 3rd Nov, daily except Thurs and Fri (but open Good Friday); June, July, daily except Fri; all at 10.30am – 6.30pm (except Oct, closes 4.30pm) (last admission 1 hour before closing). Infoline: (01684) 855370 for regularly updated details. Parties by written appt only. Liable to overcrowding on Bank Holiday Mons and fine Suns. • Entrance: £5.80, children £2.90, family (2 adults and up to 3 children) £14.50. No party concessions • Other information: Coaches by prior arrangement only ◑ ☕ ✕ WC ও ৶ ♨ ♀ ✃

One of the most famous gardens in Britain – famous especially for its highly disciplined formal outdoor rooms, many of them filled with wonderfully dramatic plantings. It was created in the early years of the twentieth century by Lawrence Johnston, an American with a strong sense of design and great planting skills. He made many new introductions and rediscovered many forgotten plants, some of which he collected himself; several varieties now bear the Hidcote name. The Trust has, since its acquisition in 1948, done its utmost to retain the spirit of the Johnston original, but its researches and some new evidence suggests that his planting legacy may have been eroded over the years. The plan now is to make a gradual return to Johnston's own stated vision of 'a wild garden in a formal setting'. His plant house may be re-created and other features reinstated. As always, a garden to watch. *Note:* For those lucky enough to be visiting the South of France, Lawrence Johnston's other garden, *La Serre de la Madone* in Menton, has undergone considerable restoration after being bought by a public conservation body, and is now open to the public.

Hodges Barn ★   17

Shipton Moyne, Tetbury GL8 8PR. Tel: (01666) 880202

Mrs Charles Hornby • 3m S of Tetbury, 3m NW of Malmesbury, just outside Shipton Moyne on Malmesbury side • Open 7th, 8th April, 12th, 13th May, 9th, 10th June, 1st, 2nd, 5th July, 10am — 5pm and at other times by appt, groups welcome • Entrance: £4. children free ● 🍴 WC & ⬥ ℗

In 1499 this was built as a dovecot or columbarium to a large house nearby, the latter burnt down in 1556. It was converted to a home in 1938 and bought by the Hon. Mrs Arthur Strutt, the late Mr Hornby's grandmother, in 1946. She set about creating the basic structure of the garden with good stone walls and topiary, and had planted most of the trees before her death in 1973. Another influence was the once-famous Pusey House, near Faringdon, owned by Mr Hornby's parents, who supplied some of the fine plants at Hodges Barn. It is an extensive eight-acre garden, with plenty of interest for everyone – above all those who like roses (there are well over 100 different varieties). The spring garden, the water garden, the little wild woodland, the large cleared wood, the topiary and the splendid lawns are all enjoyable. The plantings reflect a preoccupation with colour, scent and variety, uninhibited by a desire to prevent one flower or shrub from growing into another. Note the planting in gravel along some of the many beds, and the tapestry hedges. This is a garden which reeks of enthusiasm – long may it continue.

Hullasey House   18

Tarlton, Cirencester GL7 6PA. Tel: (01285) 770132

Mr and Mrs Jonathan Taylor • 5m SW of Cirencester off A433. In Tarlton, follow lane marked 'Church'; drive is few 100 yds on right • Open 15th, 16th, 17th June, 2 – 5pm for charity; also May to July, Mons, by appt • Entrance: £2, children free ●

Mrs Taylor has achieved a well-established, medium-sized traditional Cotswold garden here in little more than five years, overcoming the problem of a windy situation. With spectacular views, the front of the house is a formal area with sweeping lawn and octagonal box-edged beds in purple, mauve, white and silver. The luxuriant herb garden is contained within a walled parterre, with fruit trees, yet more roses and a miniature camomile lawn. There is a splendid walled garden with an exuberant mixture of herbaceous plants and roses of every description, rambling around and beside the walls and over arches, intertwined with honeysuckle. Beyond is the spring garden, planted with wild daffodils and scillas, and the wild rose garden.

Hunts Court   19

North Nibley, Dursley GL11 6DZ. Tel: (01453) 547440

Mr and Mrs T.K. Marshall • 2m NW of Wotton-under-Edge near North Nibley. Turn E off B4060 in Nibley at Black Horse Inn and fork left after ¼ m • Garden open all year, Tues – Sat, 9am – 5pm, but closed 29th March, Aug, and 25th Dec to 2nd Jan 2003. Also open 1st April, 6th May, 3rd June and some Suns for NGS, 2 – 6pm. Telephone for details • Entrance: £2, OAPs £1.50, children free • Other information: Teas on Suns only ☽ WC ﾒ ⚘ ℞

A must for those with a love of old roses. June sees in excess of 400 varieties – species, climbing and shrub – filling the borders, cascading over rails, pergolas and trees and spilling out over the informal grass paths which weave a passage through rare shrubs and herbaceous perennials. Summer is inevitably dominated by roses, but this is not to deny interest in other seasons, for this is a garden to provide something of note for the greater part of the year. A more formal sundial garden, recently developed, the beds intersected with gravel paths provides a home for hardy geraniums, penstemons and diascias. In another area mown paths draw the eye towards the Cotswold escarpment which commands the eastern landscape. In the adjoining nursery many of the plants growing in the garden are for sale, and the owner is on hand with advice.

Kiftsgate Court ★★   20

Chipping Campden GL55 6LW. Tel/Fax: (01386) 438777;
E-mail: kiftsgte@aol.com; Website: www.kiftsgate.co.uk

Mr and Mrs J.G. Chambers • 3m NE of Chipping Campden and near Mickleton, very close to Hidcote, which is signposted • Open April, May, Aug and Sept, Wed, Thurs, Sun and Bank Holiday Mons, 2 – 6pm; June and July, Wed, Thurs, Sat, Sun, 12 noon – 6pm (Note: opening times not identical to Hidcote's) • Entrance: £4, children £1 • Other information: Coaches by appt only ◑ ⬛ WC ⚘

The house was built in the late nineteenth century on this magnificent site surrounded by three steep banks. The garden was largely created by the present owner's grandmother, who with her husband moved there after World War I. Her work was carried on by her daughter, Diany Binny, who made a few alterations but followed the same colour schemes in the borders, and by her grand-daughter Anne Chambers, who continues to perfect her vision. In spring, the white sunken garden is covered with bulbs, and there is a fine show of daffodils along the drive. June and July are the peak months for colour and scent, but the magnificent old and species roses are the glory of this garden, home of *Rosa filipes* 'Kiftsgate'. Other features are perennial geraniums, a large wisteria and many species of hydrangea, some very large. In autumn, Japanese maples glow in the bluebell wood. Unusual plants are sometimes amongst those available for sale. This garden should not be missed, not only because of its proximity to Hidcote, but because of its profusion of colour and apparent informality. This said, most visitors had thought of Kiftsgate as trapped in a time warp, when, lo and behold, the owners add a flower-free water garden. Jane Owen says this 'adds an unexpected *frisson*'. She descrigbed it thus: 'It is a stark, minimalist affair of white stone, water, turf, sculpture and yew. The 4-metre-high yew hedges surrounding the water garden are a legacy of the area's previous incarnation as a clay tennis court, which had begun to disintegrate. Within, a rectangular pool is outlined in white paving slabs, which look like Portland stone but are, in fact, reconstituted stone by Haddonstone. The inky darkness of the water is maintained by the black-painted pool. In contrast, symmetrical white stone steps seem to float across it to a rectangle of mown turf in the centre. Beyond, water trickles from 24 cast-bronze and gold-leaf philodendron leaves on steel stems that sway in the breeze, created by the sculptor Simon Allison.'

Lydney Park Gardens 21

Lydney GL15 6BU. Tel: (01594) 842027

Viscount Bledisloe • 20m SW of Gloucester. N of A48 between Lydney and Aylburton • Gardens open 24th March to 2nd June, Sun, Wed and Bank Holiday Mons; also 2nd to 5th April, 28th to 31st May, 2nd June; all 11am – 6pm. Parties and guided tours by appt • Entrance: £3 (£2 on Weds), accompanied children 50p (2001 prices) • Other information: Picnics in deer park only. Roman site and New Zealand museum ● ● ● ● WC ◁▷ ✿ ⚑ ◔

The park dates from the seventeenth century, and although it has been in the hands of one family since 1723, a new house was built in 1875 and the old one demolished. An area near the house has an interesting collection of magnolias, and a picturesque sight is the bank of daffodils and cherries, splendid in season. From 1955 a woodland garden was developed in the wooded valley, behind and below the house, with the aim of achieving bold colour at different times between March and June. Near the entrance to the main part of the gardens is a small pool surrounded by azaleas and a collection of acers. From here the route passes through carefully planted groups of rhododendrons and past a folly, brought from Venice. This overlooks a valley and bog garden. Criss-crossing the hillside are rare and fine rhododendrons and azaleas, including an area planted with unnamed seedlings. Enormous effort has gone into the plant design, colour combination and general landscaping, and those who are enthusiastic about rhododendrons, azaleas and all varieties of shrubs and trees will find enough to enjoy for a whole day. Nearby is the Roman camp and museum containing the famous bronze Lydney dog, while the park has a fine collection of trees and a herd of fallow deer. Guide book with map available.

13 Merestones Drive   22

Cheltenham GL50 2SU. Tel: (01242) 578678

Mr Dennis Moorcraft • In Cheltenham. From A46, follow signs to GLOSCAT (technical college). Turn off The Park to Merestones Drive • Open 2nd, 16th June, 2 – 5pm, for NGS, and by appt • Entrance: £1.50 ● ⬎ ⌀ ℀

Merestones Drive, a suburban *cul-de-sac*, gives not the slightest hint of the pleasures and surprises to be found at the end of it. Bordered by mature trees and with a small brook running through, the garden has an enormous variety of unusual plants, shrubs and trees, many propagated from seed brought back from the owner's travels abroad and now growing in profusion beside brick paths and terraces and/or in the dry shade under the trees. Species roses riot into and over the trees alongside the drive. There is a small scree garden. Ferns are a speciality, and there are 160 different varieties of hosta. In less than a decade, the owner has created a richly diverse plantsperson's garden.

Mill Dene   23

Blockley, Moreton-in-Marsh GL56 9HU. Tel: (01386) 700457;
Fax: (01386) 700526; email: wendy@milldene.co.uk;
Website: http://www.gardenvisit-cotswolds.co.uk

Mr and Mrs B.S. Dare • 3m W of Moreton-in-Marsh on A44. Follow brown tourist-signs from Bourton-on-the-Hill • Open April to Oct, Mon – Fri (inc. most Bank Holiday Mons), 10am – 6pm, and by appt. Parties welcome for tours • Entrance: £2.50, children £1. Special rates for parties ◑ ⬛ ✕ WC ⌀ ⬤

Wendy Dare has made the most of her attractive and unusually situated 2½ - acre garden, built around the mill pond and stream and climbing in steep terraces, each with its own character and colour scheme, to the newly planted *potager* and fruit garden at the top. With a rose walk and cricket lawn on the way, scented plants are a priority, and there are splendid views of the Cotswold hills and surrounding picturesque village. Quirky surprises include a grotto and *trompe-l'œil*. The house offers B&B. Up to a dozen other gardens are open on two days for charity in this popular hillside village and are well worth a visit, though some stamina is required. Nearby is *Peartrees*, a small cottage garden full of Mrs Beckwith's treasures, open by appointment (telephone (01386) 700464).

Misarden Park Gardens ★   24

Miserden, Stroud GL6 7JA. Tel: (01285) 821303; Fax: (01285) 821530.

Major M.T.N.H. Wills • 3m NW of Cirencester, 3m off A417. Signposted • Open April to Sept, Tues, Wed and Thurs, 10am – 5pm. Parties by appt • Entrance: £3.50 (inc. printed guide), children free. Reduction for parties of 20 or more. Guided tour extra • Other information: Adjacent nursery open daily except Mon ◑ WC ♿ ⌀ ℀

This lovely, timeless English garden, which commands spectacular views over the Golden Valley, has most of the features one expects of a garden started in the seventeenth century. There are extensive yew hedges, a York-stone terrace, a Lutyens loggia overhung with wisteria, and a good specimen of *Magnolia* x *soulangeana*. The south lawn sports splendid grass steps. West of the house the ground ascends to the nursery in a series of grassed terraces. Two good herbaceous borders lead to a new parterre of tulips, alliums, hebes and lavender, and a rill and summerhouse have been added. There are many fine specimen trees, and the spring show of blossom and bulbs is notable. The seventeenth-century manor house is not open.

Moor Wood   25

Woodmancote, Cirencester GL7 7EB. Tel: (01285) 831397; Fax: (01285) 831859

Mr and Mrs Henry Robinson • 3½ m N of Cirencester off A435. At North Cerney turn uphill signed 'Woodmancote'. In Woodmancote go through white gates on left beside lodge • Parking at end of drive • Open probably 26th and 30th June, 2 – 6pm, and by appt • Entrance: £2.50, children free • Other information: Teas on open days only ●

With its attractive valley setting, this is the perfect home for a National Collection of rambler roses – 120 in all, crawling over every wall surrounding the gardens of this Cotswold family house and its cottages and stables. Since 1984 the owners have been gradually building up the collection and restoring the gardens, a continuing process. There are two acres of cottage gardens, formal lawn and borders, shrubs, orchard and terraced garden. What was the old walled vegetable garden is now a mass of wild flowers, all contributing to a delightfully natural atmosphere in keeping with the surrounding farmland.

The National Arboretum, Westonbirt ★★   26

Westonbirt, Tetbury GL8 8QS. Tel: (01666) 880220; Fax: (01666) 880559

The Forestry Commission • 3m SW of Tetbury on A433, 5m NE of A46 junction • Grounds open all year, 10am – 8pm (or dusk if earlier) • Entrance: £4.25, OAPs £3.50, children £1 (2001 prices) • Other information: Cafe and visitor centre closed Christmas week ○ ▆ ✕ ▆ WC ⓗ ⬤ ✎ ⛪ ⓨ ⚲

This is perhaps the finest arboretum in Britain. Started in 1829 by Robert Stayner Holford, it was expanded and improved by successive generations of the same family until it was taken over by the Forestry Commission in 1956. Numerous grass rides divide the trees into glades used for special plantings, such as the famous collection of Japanese maples. Westonbirt is noted for its vast range of stunning mature specimen trees. The Forestry Commission is continuing with planting, for example the Hillier Glade with ornamental cherries. Across the valley from the original arboretum is Silkwood, with collections of native, Asian and American species that in spring are carpeted with primroses, wood anemones and bluebells. There are in excess of 18,000 numbered trees and 17 miles of paths. Colour is best in May (rhododendrons, magnolias, etc.) and October (Japanese maples, fothergillas, etc.). From mid-November until Christmas the garden is illuminated at weekends with hundreds of twinkling lights after dark, and many champion trees are floodlit. Westonbirt plans to institute a festival of garden design, inspired by Chaumont in France, where show gardens will be planted early in the year, giving them time to develop a modest maturity before the public arrive. Exhibitions of modern sculpture are also planned.

The Old Barn 27

Upper Dowdeswell, Cheltenham GL54 4LT. Tel: (01242) 820858

Dawn and Jamie Adams • 5m E of Cheltenham off A40. Turn right after reservoir to Dowdeswell. Turn right at crossroads at top of hill past church and after 200 yds turn right again into Upper Dowdeswell. Park outside Manor on left and walk short distance to garden • Open all year for private visits by appt • Entrance: £2.50, children free NEW ⅃ ⅏

Dawn Adams, a garden designer, has cleverly combined style and naturalism in this beautifully kept three-quarter-acre hillside woodland garden, which perfectly complements its fine Cotswold setting with splendid views towards the Malvern hills. Developed from a field over the past twenty years and following gently sloping contours, individual areas are bounded by immaculate beech and yew hedges and stone walls. Planted for year-round appeal with many unusual species, there are traditional colour-themed borders, a rose-and-clematis-covered pergola, a croquet lawn, a fruit garden and a white garden – something of interest in and around every corner. Snowdrops and bluebells, auriculas and hellebores flower in profusion in their seasons. A one-acre woodland walk with a profusion of wild flowers overlooks the Severn Vale with spectacular views to the Malvern Hills.

The Old Rectory 28

Duntisbourne Rouse, Daglingworth, Cirencester GL7 7AP.
E-mail: Dunt@keengardener.com

Charles and Mary Keen • 3m NW of Cirencester off A417. From Daglingworth take narrow valley road for the Duntisbournes. After ½ m house is on right next to church • Open on several Mons for NGS and also by written appt for parties of 10 or more • Entrance: £3, children free. Parties negotiable • Other information: Light refreshments available in winter ◉

In an exceptional natural setting next to the Saxon church admired by John Betjeman, overlooking the little River Dunt, the Old Rectory was once the home of Katherine Mansfield's sister, Jean Renshaw. This is, however, by no means a typical Cotswold garden. Since 1993, Mary Keen, garden writer and designer, has created an unusual garden of many moods and different levels, full of year-round interest and surprising variety. Its one and a half acres combine informality within a formal framework of box and yew, as well as areas of lawn, orchard and meadow in miniature, a kitchen garden and a conservatory ablaze with unusual pelargoniums. An auricula cupboard and topiary. Unusual perennials, half-hardies and winter plants are specialities.

Owlpen Manor 29

Uley, Dursley GL11 5BZ. Tel: (01453) 860261

Mr and Mrs N. Mander • 6m SW of Stroud, 3m E of Dursley off B4066, 1m E of Uley. Signposted • House open • Garden open April to Sept, Tues – Sun and Bank Holiday Mons, 2 – 5pm • Entrance: £2.75 (house and garden £4.50, children £2) ◑ 💻 ✕ 🧺 WC

Situated in a remote Cotswold valley, the small hillside garden at Owlpen is an unusually complete survival of an early formal manorial garden, described by the late Sir Geoffrey Jellicoe as possibly the loveliest domestic garden in England, largely retaining its original form. Formal seventeenth-century gardens are laid out on seven hanging terraces with topiary yews, box parterres, old roses, and steep steps leading down to the mill pond. Making use of the old records, the gardens are being extended among open lawns, suggesting a plan of the early eighteenth century.

Painswick Rococo Garden ★ 30

Painswick GL6 6TH. Tel: (01452) 813204; Fax: (01452) 814888
Website: www.rococogarden.co.uk

Painswick Rococo Gardens Trust • ½ m from Painswick on B4073. Signposted • Open 12th Jan to Nov, Wed – Sun (and open 16th April); then May to Sept, daily; all 11am – 5pm • Entrance: £3.60, OAPs £3.30, children £1.80 • Other information: Coaches by appt ◐ 💻 ✕ 🧺 WC ⬦ 🌿 🛒 🍴 ◯

A great deal of time, money and effort is going into the continuing restoration (almost complete redevelopment) of this rare Rococo survival. Much of the work is now completed with new plantings becoming established. At present, the best features are the eighteenth-century garden buildings, the views into beautiful surrounding countryside, and the marvellous snowdrop wood spanning a stream that flows from a pond at the lower end. This must be one of the best displays of naturalised snowdrops in England. There are some splendid beech woods and older specimen trees. Wild flowers are allowed complete freedom. Rococo gardening was an eighteenth-century combination of formal geometric features with winding woodland paths, revealing sudden incidents and vistas – in essence, a softening of the formal French style, apparent from about 1715 onwards in all forms of art. The basis for Painswick's present restoration is a painting of 1748 by Thomas Robins (1716–1778) for Benjamin Hyett, who created the garden in the grounds of the house built by his father in 1735. To celebrate the 250 years of its existence, Painswick's owners have planted a yew hedge maze, designed by Angela Newing, in adjoining farmland; something to look forward to as it matures. In total it is a large estate and visitors (who should be fit for some steep inclines) must allow three-quarters of an hour even for a brisk walk round its many beauties.

Rockcliffe   31

Lower Swell, Stow-on-the-Wold GL54 2JW

Mr and Mrs Simon Keswick • 3m W of Stow-on-the-Wold on B4068 • Open 6th, 12th, 18th, 19th June, 11am – 5pm • Entrance: £3, children under 15 free ● WC ❧

Tranquil Cotswold pastures with grazing sheep are the perfect setting for this immaculately cared-for eight-acre garden which Mrs Keswick has created in the last 20 years. The walled and box-edged kitchen garden has pleached hornbeams, espaliered medlars and herbaceous borders, and to the side of it an intriguing bird topiary yew avenue flanking the path through the wildflower orchard which leads up to the site of the proposed dovecot. At the front of the house is a box parterre and well-kept lawns with a delightful pastoral view beyond the ha-ha. The sunken garden has a lily pond surrounded by variegated *Cornus controversa* to reflect in the water. The main herbaceous border leads on through a succession of yew-enclosed pink, blue, white and silver gardens, with vistas at every turn. The swimming-pool garden is exceptionally pretty, with rose-clad walls and hardy geraniums: the pump-house is covered with bright pink *Rosa* 'Zéphirine Drouhin', with blue *Nepeta* x *faassenii* all around – a simple but stunning effect.

Rodmarton Manor ★   32

Rodmarton, Cirencester GL7 6PF. Tel: (01285) 841253; Fax: (01285) 841298; E-mail: simon.biddulph@farming.co.uk

Mr and Mrs Simon Biddulph • 6m SW of Cirencester, 4m NE of Tetbury off A433, halfway between Cirencester and Tetbury • House open as garden, and for pre-booked guided group visits at other times • Garden open 6th May to Aug, Wed, Sat and Bank Holiday Mons, 2 – 5pm. Guided tours available – telephone for details • Other information: Garden also open in snowdrop season – telephone for details • Entrance: £3, accompanied children under 14 free (house and garden: parties of 20 or more £6 per person, children £3) • Other information: Coaches use holly (west) drive. Tea and biscuits by prior arrangement (£2.50 per person) ◑ ▣ WC ໐

Rodmarton Manor and its garden, designed by Ernest Barnsley for the Biddulphs from 1909, is an excellent example of the English Arts and Crafts Movement at its best and has been featured in numerous books and magazines over the years. The drive lies between impeccably clipped tapestry hedges, and the garden, which retains virtually all its original features, comprises a series of outdoor rooms, each with its own character, bordered by fine hedges of yew, beech, holly and box, for which it is famous. In front of the house is the terrace and topiary garden, the recently replanted trough garden, a sunken garden and white borders leading to the cherry orchard, which has a wide variety of snowdrops in early spring, as well as shrubs and roses. There is a good rockery, a wild garden with a hornbeam avenue, and many attractive vistas. The large working kitchen garden features both culinary and ornamental plants, old apple arches, a new collection of old-fashioned and scented roses, and a row of sinks. Several areas have been replanted since 1991 when the present owners moved into the manor, including parts of the leisure garden and the four large herbaceous borders, which are now quite magnificent. The shrubbery has been renovated. Beautifully kept, this garden is full of romance and excitement. Helpful and interesting booklet available.

Sezincote ★★ 33

Moreton-in-Marsh GL56 9AW.

Mr and Mrs D. Peake • 1½ m W of Moreton-in-Marsh on A44 just before Bourton-on-the-Hill • House open May to July, Sept, Thurs, Fri, 2.30 – 6pm (no children in house) • Garden open Jan to Nov, Thurs, Fri and Bank Holiday Mons, 2 – 6pm (or dusk if earlier), and 7th July for charity • Entrance: £3.50, children £1, children under 5 free (house and garden £5) • Other information: Teas on charity open day only ○ WC

The entrance to Sezincote is up a long dark avenue of holm oaks that opens into the most English of parks, with a distinct feeling of Repton influence – fine trees and distant views of Cotswold hills. Turning the last corner is the surprise, for there is that fascinating rarity, an English country house built in the Moghul architectural style by Samuel Pepys Cockerell. The form of the garden has not changed since Repton's time, but the more recent planting was carried out by Lady Kleinwort with help from Graham Stuart Thomas, and on her return from India in 1968 she laid out the Paradise Garden in the south garden, with canals and Irish yews. Behind this is the curved orangery, home to many tender climbing plants. The house is sheltered by great copper beeches, cedars, yews and limes, which provide a fine backdrop for the exotic shrubs. Streams and pools are lined with great clumps of bog-loving plants, and the stream is crossed by an Indian bridge, adorned with Brahmin bulls. The garden, planted for year-round interest, is particularly strong on autumn colours. Graham Stuart Thomas's instructive guidebook is highly recommended. Nearby is Compton Lane Nurseries, open March to Sept, Wed, Thurs and Sat, 10am – 5pm (Tel: (01608) 674578).

Snowshill Manor ★ 34

Broadway WR12 7JU. Tel: (01386) 852410; Fax: (01386) 852410; E-mail: snowshill@smtp.ntrust.org.uk

The National Trust • 3m S of Broadway off A44 • House open 29th March to 3rd Nov, Wed – Sun and Bank Holiday Mon; July, Aug, Mon, Wed – Sun, 12 noon – 5pm. Timed ticket system. Entry to house may be restricted 4th Sept to 3rd Nov. Please telephone to confirm opening arrangements • Garden open 24th March to 3rd Nov, Wed – Sun and Bank Holiday Mons; July, Aug, Mon, Wed – Sun, 11am – 5.30pm • Entrance: gardens £3.50 (house and gardens £6, children £3, family ticket £15) • Other information: Coaches and school parties by written appt only. No entry from Snowshill village. Car park 500 metres from manor with entry via footpath; motorised buggy available ◑ ✕ 🏛

From a design by M.H. Baillie-Scott, the owner Charles Wade transformed a 'wilderness of chaos' on a Cotswold hillside into an interconnecting series of outdoor 'rooms' in Hidcote style from the 1920s onwards. Wade was a believer in the Arts and Crafts rustic ideal and the garden, like the house, expresses his eccentricities. Seats and woodwork are painted 'Wade blue', a powdery dark blue with touches of turquoise which goes well with the Cotswold stone walls. The simple cottage style conceals careful planting in shades of blue, mauve and purple. Organic gardening is employed here.

Stancombe Park ★   35

Stancombe, Dursley GL11 6AU. Tel: (01453) 542815

Mrs Barlow • Between Wotton-under-Edge and Dursley on B4060 • Open by appt for parties • Entrance: £3, children 50p ◗ ▱ ▨ WC

People still rush to view the most curious park and garden south of Biddulph Grange (see entry in Staffordshire), built in the 1840s. Set on the Cotswold escarpment, it has all the ingredients of a Gothick best-seller. A narrow path drops into a dark glen, roots from enormous oaks, copper beeches and chestnuts trip your feet, ferns brush your face, walls drip water, and ammonites and fossils loom in the gloom. Rocks erupt with moss. Egyptian tombs trap the unwary. Tunnels turn into grottos. Even plants live in wire cages. Folly freaks are in their element, though it has to be admitted that some people do not find it gloomy since the droughts have stopped the springs; indeed the secret garden can be light and friendly when it is not raining. Everyone has a good time in this Victorian curiosity turned romantic vision turned horror movie. But some think this description far too negative, and only appropriate on drizzly days. There is another side to Stancombe – a pretty rose garden, twentieth-century follies around the house, patterned borders and extensive gardens with 'wonderful design and use of colour' created by the owner and by the designer Nada Jennett.

Stanway House   36

Winchcombe, Cheltenham GL54 5PQ. Tel: (01386) 584469

Lord Neidpath • 1m E of B4632 Cheltenham – Broadway road, 4m NE of Winchcombe • House open • Garden open Aug and Sept, Tues and Thurs, 2 – 5pm. Tours for parties at other times by appt • Entrance: £1.50 (house and garden £3, OAPs £2.50, children £1) (2001 prices) ◗ ▱ WC ⅁ ⬧

Stanway is a honey-coloured Cotswold village with a Jacobean 'great house' which has changed hands just once since 715AD. It was much frequented by Arthur Balfour and 'The Souls' in the latter years of the nineteenth century. The garden rises in a series of dramatic terraced lawns and a rare, picturesque 'grasswork' to the pyramid, which in the eighteenth century stood at the head of a 190-metre-long cascade descending to a formal canal on a terrace above the house. This was probably designed by Charles Bridgeman, and exceeded in length and height (36 metres) its famous rival at Chatsworth (see entry in Derbyshire). Inside the house is a fascinating painting recording the cascade as it looked in the eighteenth century. The canal, the upper pond behind the pyramid, a short section of the cascade, and the upper fall below the pyramid were restored in 1998, and a 70-foot-high single-jet fountain added in the middle of the canal. The medieval pond in the Lower Garden, recently restored, has enhanced the beauty of the fourteenth-century tithe barn. It is hoped soon to restore the pyramid itself, a banqueting house from which guests on a summer evening could watch the sluices being opened and the water falling down towards the house. A high walk along the hillside above the cascade reveals the splendid park trees and the good progress made with water features. A magical place.

Stone House 37

Wyck Rissington GL54 2PN. Tel: (01451) 810337; Fax: (01451) 810340

Mr and Mrs Andrew Lukas • 1½ m S of Stow-on-the-Wold off A429 just NE of Bourton-on-the-Water. Last house in village, past church on opposite side of road • Open one day for NGS, and at other times by appt • Entrance: £3 • Other information: Teas by prior arrangement. Plant fair 27th May ◕ WC ✿

This is a plantsman's garden which is the perfect antidote to all those daffodil-lined Cotswold lanes, as it avoids horticultural clichés all year round. Note, for example, the bold use of euphorbias. Its two acres are filled with unusual bulbs, shrubs and herbaceous perennials, including an abundance of aquilegias and hostas. There is a crab apple walk, rose borders and a herb garden. A spring-fed stream flowing into the River Dikler bubbles throughout; the area of sloping, box-edged lawns leading down from a terrace via rounded Lutyens-esque brick steps to the water's edge is especially charming. The overall design is sensitive, making full use of the sloping site and the views out across a ha-ha to unspoilt countryside; major elements such as a swimming pool and tennis court are cunningly concealed. The annual plant fair is prized for its wide range of good and unusual plants, with some of the stands manned by professional nurserymen fresh from Chelsea triumphs. The attractive village has an unusual church with a fine tower, where Gustav Holst was organist for a period at the princely annual stipend of £4.

Sudeley Castle ★ 38

Winchcombe, Cheltenham GL54 5JD. Tel: (01242) 602308; Fax: (01242) 602959; E-mail: marketing@sudeley.org.uk

Lord and Lady Ashcombe • 8m NE of Cheltenham off B4632 at Winchcombe • Castle open April to Oct, daily, 11am – 5pm • Gardens open March to Oct, daily, 10.30am – 5.30pm • Private guided tours in and out of season by arrangement • Entrance: castle and gardens £6.20, concessions £5.20, children £3.20; party rates for 20 or more £5.20, £4.20, £3.20; season ticket £17, family season ticket £34 (2001 prices) ◑ ☕ ✕ WC ♿ ✿

There has been a house on this magnificent site, with views of the surrounding Cotswold hills at every turn, for over 1000 years, and today the emphasis is on tourism, with pleasant facilities and special exhibitions. The extensive grounds contain ten integrated but individual gardens, notably the Queen's Garden with its outstanding collection of old-fashioned roses, surrounded by immaculately clipped double yew hedges. These were laid out in the nineteenth century by an ancestor of the present owners on the site of the original Tudor parterre. In recent years Jane Fearnley-Whittingstall guided the restoration of this area, as well as designing the knot garden and newly planted buddleia walk, featuring 23 different varieties. The gardens surrounding the ruins of the banqueting hall and the tithe barn, with its carp pond, are exceptionally lovely, with old climbing roses and (should you be lucky enough to avoid the coachloads) a romantic atmosphere. There is a white garden, a secret garden recently replanted by Charles Chesshire, a mulberry garden and a small Victorian kitchen garden, managed in collaboration with the Henry Double-day Research Association to produce seed for propagation.

Upton Wold 39

Northwick Estate, Moreton-in-Marsh GL56 9TR. Tel: (01386) 700667;
Fax: (01386) 700196; E-mail: northwick.estate@virgin.net

Mr and Mrs I.R.S. Bond • 5m NW of Moreton-in-Marsh on A44. Pass Batsford, Sezincote and Bourton House (see entries), continue up Bourton hill, pass Troopers Lodge Garage at A424 junction, and drive is 1m further on right • Open two days for NGS, 2 – 6pm, and for private visits May to July, by appt 10am – 6pm • Entrance: NGS openings £3, children free; May to July openings £4 ● 💭 WC ⚲ ℺

One would never know, travelling along the busy A44, that four fine gardens lie along this stretch of a few miles, the newest and best concealed of these being the garden set around a small seventeenth-century manor house hidden in a wold. The owners arrived here in the 1970s and have created, from scratch, what is now one of the most distinguished of typical Cotswold gardens. The view from the south-east faade of the house (not open) stretches out across a lawn and ha-ha to the valley. To the left is a long border, through which is the entrance to the pond and wild garden (fritillaries bursting through in season). The walk on the opposite side of the central lawn is bordered by a tunnel of yew. Beyond this the ground slopes up through the Hidden Garden and hedged croquet lawn to a long level area which hosts an ornamental fruit garden, fine vegetable garden and greenhouses. Imaginative planting is everywhere (note the owners' passion for standards), with parti-cular care taken to provide pleasing views from the house windows, such as the bank of old roses below the dovecot. Lots of interest for the plant enthusiast in this charming garden.

The Urn Cottage 40

19 Station Road, Charfield, Wotton-under-Edge GL12 8SY.
Tel: (01453) 843156; Website: www.lesleyrosser.co.uk

Mr A.C. and Dr L.A. Rosser •3m E of M5 junction 14. In Charfield turn off main road at the Railway Tavern; house is 400yds on left, a short walk from parking • Open 6th April to 27th July and Sept, Sat, 2 – 6pm; Open for NGS 6th May, 8th Sept, and for groups by appt • Entrance: £2.50, children £1
NEW ● 💭 WC ⚲ ℺

This splendidly varied garden around an old stone cottage has been entirely created by the owners since 1982. The trees they planted for shelter have now matured and frame beautiful views of the Cotswolds from its edge-of-village setting. Dr Rosser is a horticultural consultant and lecturer, and her expertise is evident in the skilful design and planting of this attractive ¾ -acre garden. Her preference for well-behaved plants results in a wide and remarkably healthy looking selection, all maintained to a high standard. Long-season interest is achieved throughout the garden, from the stylish schemes around the house to a shady stream-side and even a patch of volcanic rock. A small vegetable garden is cleverly terraced with wooden railway sleepers, and interesting sculptures are imaginatively displayed.

Westbury Court Garden ★★ 41

Westbury–on–Severn GL14 1PD. Tel: (01452) 760461

The National Trust • 9m SW of Gloucester on A48, close to church • Open March to June, Wed – Sun and Bank Holiday Mon; July to Aug, daily; Sept to 27th Oct, Wed — Sun; all at 10am – 6pm. Individuals at other times by appt and parties of 15 or more by written appt • Entrance: £3, children £1.50 • Other information: Braille plan available ◑ 🖺 WC ♿ 🔦 ℀

A remarkable seventeenth-century Dutch water garden and, as such, one of the rarest types to have survived more or less intact in this country – an assembly of *allée*, canal, *clairvoyée* and vista, all carefully restored and maintained to a high standard. A contemporary Tall Pavilion dominates a long canal which is flanked by clipped yew hedges regularly spaced with pyramids and holly balls. Parallel to this is a T-shaped canal with Neptune bestriding a dolphin in the centre of the arm. There is an elaborate seventeenth-century seat in the 'bowling green', a central area which appears, from the Kip engraving, to have been a vegetable garden. To the north-east is a charming gazebo, one side of which overlooks a small, walled enclosure where species of plants to be found growing in England prior to 1700 grow now in box-edged beds. Beyond is the parterre: beds of simple shape containing box topiary; this in turn is surrounded by the quincunx, a formal arrangement of small trees and clipped evergreens. A specimen of *Quercus ilex* is thought to be one of the oldest in the country, with a girth of eight metres at a point of one-and a half metres above ground. The historic houses on this site were destroyed, one as late as the 1950s, and there is now a home for elderly people here. If you then feel inclined for a completely different experience, take the *Forest of Dean Sculpture Trail*, on the B4226 between Cinderford and Coleford. Further to the north, on the Herefordshire border is *Cinderdine Cottage*, where Daphne Chappell has over 100 varieties of snowdrops. [3m NE of Newent off B4215, south of Dymock; look for sign Ryton/Ketford; cottage is on right after ¾ m. Open frequently in February and March and at other times throughout the year, including every Tues. Telephone (01531) 890265 for details.]

Westonbirt Arboretum

(see THE NATIONAL ARBORETUM, WESTONBIRT)

Westonbirt School Gardens 42

Tetbury GL8 8QG. Tel: (01666) 880333; Fax: (01666) 880364;
E-mail: debbiesg@westonbirt.gloucs.sch.uk; Web: www.westonbirt.gloucs.sch.uk

*Westonbirt School • 3m SW of Tetbury on A433 opposite Westonbirt Arboretum •
Open two days for NGS, 2 – 4.30pm, and at other times by appt • Entrance:
£2, children 25p (2001 prices) • Other information: Teas when open for events
only* ● & ⬦ 🌢 ℺

The house, modelled on Wollaton Hall, Nottinghamshire, was built by the
eminent Victorian plant collector Robert Stayner Holford. A pioneer collector
of trees, shrubs and flowers from around the world, he had already started to plant
trees when he inherited the estate from his father in 1839, and the spectacular
gardens which we see today had started to take shape before the house was
completed in 1872. After his death in 1892 his son George, who had also inherited
his father's love of horticulture, becoming one of the most successful amateur
gardeners of his time, continued the development of both arboretum and garden.
He was particularly keen on orchids and exotics. The garden is designed to have
leisurely walks and a few surprises. Sweeping lawns and terraces lead down to the
fountain pool, with views across the ha-ha, which hides the road, to farmland
beyond. The other axis leads from the church to the sunken garden, with its pond
and statue of Mercury. An Italian garden with architectural features, a knot garden
and a pergola walk complete the formal eastern side of the house, while the other
side is more informal, with irregular groups of trees and shrubs (many rare and
exotic), a lake, grotto and rockery. Fascinating illustrated booklet.

2003 GUIDE
The 2003 *Guide* will be published before Christmas 2002. Reports on
gardens for consideration are welcome at all times of the year, but
particularly by early summer (June 2002) so that they can be inspected
that year.
   All descriptions and other information are as accurate as possible at the
time of going to press, but circumstances change and, if in doubt, it is wise
to telephone before making a long journey.

FEEDBACK
Readers are invited to advise the *Guide* of any gardens which in their
opinion should be listed in future editions, and where possible arrangements will be made to review such suggestions. Readers who would like
to add information about gardens listed are warmly invited to write to
the *Guide* with their comments, which may be used in future editions
without attribution. Please send letters to the publishers, Bloomsbury
Publishing, 38 Soho Square, London W1D 3HB. All letters are acknowledged by the editor.

HAMPSHIRE &
THE ISLE OF WIGHT

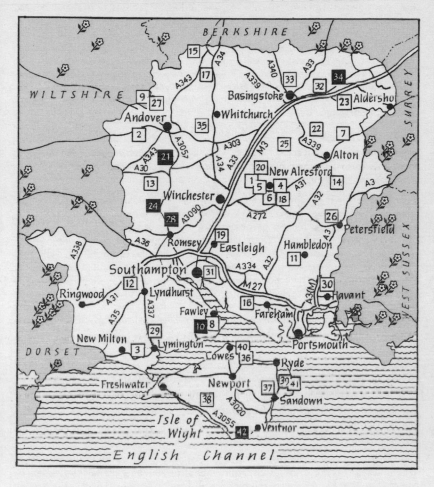

Gardens on the Isle of Wight will be found at the end of the Hampshire section.
Two-starred gardens are marked on the map with a black square.

Abbey Cottage   1

Rectory Lane, Itchen Abbas, Winchester SO21 1BN. Tel: (01962) 779575

*Col. Patrick Daniell • 3m NE of Winchester on B3047, 1m E of Itchen Abbas •
Open 7th April, 5th, 6th May, 25th, 26th Aug, 12 noon – 5pm, and by appt
at other times. Parties welcome • Entrance: £2.50* ● ➽ 🖥 WC ☂ ⚘ ✂

A variety of levels above the cottage, each aligned with interlinking vistas, results in a series of gardens within an old walled kitchen garden, leading into each other by means of steps, slopes and corridors, and culminating with a meadow of bulbs and young specimen trees. Within the one and a half acres is an orchard, a pond and skilfully planted borders; walls of every aspect are clothed with climbers. In places the articulation of this immaculate garden seems contrived, but there is much of inspiration and interest throughout the year, including *Magnolia* x *loebneri* 'Merrill', stunning against the yew hedge, bulbs and daphnes in spring, clematis, shrub and climbing roses in summer and *Sorbus vilmorinii* in autumn. *Juniper chinensis* 'Aurea' and *Cornus alternifolia* 'Argentea' are also very striking.

Amport House 2

Armed Forces Chaplaincy Centre, Amport, Andover SP11 8BG.

4m W of Andover, S of A303 • *Open by written appt only to Rev. Peter Howson or Jim Wilson* • *Entrance: £2* • *Other information: Light refreshments by arrangement* ● ● WC ♿

This little-known garden of the Lutyens/Jekyll partnership has a great water terrace on two levels, with rills, a central oval mirror pond and square lily pools, and is said to be the prototype for the water gardens at New Delhi. Since Lutyens found the Victorian house designed by Sir William Burn unattractive, he sought to distract the eye to his terraced gardens and waterways. Note his hallmark arrangement of millstone and diaper paving. Other features are herbaceous borders, a sunken rockery, pleached limes, a splendid Victorian parterre with the Winchester coat of arms, parkland and a ha-ha. A few miles E of Andover, on B3400 Whitchurch road, is Mr and Mrs Beeson's one-acre eco-friendly garden, *Forest Edge*, brimming with wild flowers, many native species and wildlife galore.

Apple Court 3

Hordle Lane, Hordle, Lymington SO41 0HU. Tel: (01590) 642130

Mrs Diana Grenfell and Mr Roger Grounds • *200 metres N of A337 between Lymington and New Milton along Hordle Lane opposite Royal Oak* • *Open Mar to Sept, daily, except Wed, 10am – 1pm, 2 – 5pm* • *Entrance: £2, children 50p* • *Other information: Plants for sale in adjoining nursery* ◑ 🍽 WC ♿ ⚘

The garden is a showcase for a National Collection of day lilies and of hostas, which are displayed under a pergola where the varied greens are livened by purple heuchera and punctuated by pots filled with grasses. The day lily garden is at its peak in July and August, when the flowers, mostly American introductions, are mixed with agapanthus, crocosmias, kniphofias and phormiums, and has a frothy rectangle of ornamental grasses at its centre. The white garden has a different drama – a square of yew hedging holds an oval border of white flowers and silvery-leaved grasses viewed through an inner oval of pleached hornbeam box which frames them like a series of lit pictures. The effect is architectural, like entering a square with a circular colonnade. Three rectangular ponds are connected by cascading rills, and there is also a fern path and herbaceous borders lined with rose-covered rope swags.

Bramdean House ★ 4

Bramdean, Alresford SO24 0JU. Tel: (01962) 771214; Fax: (01962) 771095

Mr and Mrs H. Wakefield • 9m E of Winchester on A272 in middle of Bramdean • Open 31st March, 14th April, 12th May, 16th June, 14th July, 11th Aug, 8th Sept, 2 – 5pm, for NGS and at other times by appt • Entrance: NGS days £2.50, other days £4, children free ● ➧ WC ⌖

The mellow brick eighteenth-century house is well protected from the main road by a huge undulating yew and box hedge. The six-and-a-half-acre garden on chalk slopes away from the house and is divided into three parts. One contains the famous mirror-image herbaceous borders, and surrounding beds have a large array of usual and unusual plants, shrubs and small trees. Fine wrought-iron gates lead through into the walled working kitchen garden, cultivated entirely by hand, and containing fruit and vegetables grown for the house, old-fashioned sweet peas, perpetual carnations, a peony walk and a trial area for plants. Ornamental flower beds along a central path lead through a second wrought-iron gate into the orchard area, featuring fruit trees under-planted with massed daffodils and terminated by a blue-doored apple house and belfry. To the east are interesting shrubs and trees and castellations of yew. In spring there are carpets of aconites, snowdrops, crocuses and other early bulbs.

Brandy Mount House 5

Brandy Mount, Alresford SO24 9EG. Tel: (01962) 732189;
E-mail: baron1@brandymount.co.uk; Website: www.brandymount.co.uk

Mr and Mrs M. Baron • In town centre. First right in East Street before Sun Lane • Open 2nd, 3rd, 6th Feb, 11am – 4pm; 3rd March, 7th April, 5th May, 2 – 5pm (telephone to check), and by appt in snowdrop season • Entrance: £2, children free • Other information: No vehicular access. Parking in station car park and Broad Street. Teas available except in Feb. Children must be supervised ● ➧ ⌖ ⌖ ⌖ ⌖

This one-acre informal garden of trees, shrubs and lawns is essentially for the plantsman. Michael Baron is on hand to guide the visitors through his National Collections of snowdrops and daphnes, and there is also a wide variety of hellebores, pulmonarias and species peonies. You may wish to discuss the problems of growing shrubs on dry chalk soil and see a variety of alpine primulas, geraniums and lilacs. Amongst the rare plants in borders and spot beds are cardamine (dentaria), *Narcissus bulbocodium* and *Fritillaria pyrenaica*.

48 Broad Street 6

New Alresford, Alresford SO24 9AN. Tel: (01962) 732441

Mr and Mrs David Ashdown • In town centre • Open by appt to individuals and parties • Entrance: £2.50 ●

This town garden turns a long and narrow plot into a journey of light and dark through varied passes and rooms. Near the house are pots, paving, *Trachelo-*

spermum jasminoides and the silver-leaved *Elaeagnus angustifolia* grown as a standard with *Clematis viticella* 'Etoile Violette' weaving through it. Next comes the lawn, sculpture and box-edged beds of lilies, perennials and roses. Then you reach miniature woodland and a new geometric garden in shades of lavender with slate chippings which has yet to mature. The transition to Hampshire countryside is completed by a nut walk leading to a view of fields and a glimpse of Alresford pond. Everywhere there is the sound of water bubbling from low fountains.

Bury Court   7

Bentley, Farnham, Surrey GU10 5LZ. Tel: (01420) 520351; Fax: (01420) 22382

Marina Christopher and John Coke • 5m SW of Farnham, 1½ m N of Bentley on road signed 'Crondall' • Open May to Oct, Thurs, 10am – 6pm • Entrance: £1 (2001 price) ◑ ◙ ✕ <u>WC</u> &

The walled garden is the work of the Dutch designer Piet Oudolf and displays a typical combination of naturalism, originality and elegance which has won him prizes at the Chelsea Flower Show. Surrounded by walls of brick and stone, curved oast houses and other buildings, with a glimpse of the countryside beyond, the asymmetrical geometric beds are dominated by robust perennials, various grasses and many species of cistus. The herbaceous borders are outstanding in mid- and late summer, a time when they might well be flagging. With cambered cobble paths, two water tanks, a gravel bed, several beds of small bushes and some hedging, it is a fine exemplar of Oudolf at his best.

Cadland House ★   8

Fawley, Southampton SO45 1AA.

Mr and Mrs Maldwin Drummond • 16m SE of Southampton off A326/B3053 • Open May to end July, Sept and Oct, by written appt for parties of 20 or more • Entrance: £3 • Other information: Teas by arrangement. House also open by arrangement ◑ ◙ <u>WC</u> & ⟜

A unique landscape garden of eight acres overlooking the Solent, designed by 'Capability' Brown in 1776 for the banker Robert Drummond and now restored to the original plan using period plants. A path with tiered shrubs (roses, brooms, philadelphus, *Lavandula stoechas*, laurels, *Ptelea trifoliata*) winds from the modern house (replacing the original three-roomed *cottage orné* designed by Henry Holland), along the shore and back through a lime walk and Georgian flower border. Broad vistas alternate with carefully orchestrated glimpses of the sea. There is a kitchen garden with fruit houses, and a walled garden with a red border, a cool border and rare plants (*Astelia chathamica, Pileostegia viburnoides*, tender acacias). The National Collection of leptospermums is held here.

Conholt Park ★ 9

Chute, Nr Andover SP11 9HA

Prof Caroline Tisdall • 5m NW of Andover off A342. Turn N at Weyhill church and continue 5m through Clanville and Tangley Bottom. Turn left for Conholt; house is ½ mile on right just off Chute causeway • Garden open 23rd June, 14th July, 2 – 6pm • Entrance: £2.50, children free • Other information: Hardy's plants for sale ● ● WC

Surrounding the Regency house is a ten-acre garden created over the past few years. Spacious lawns, towering cedars and fine views are grace-notes providing a dignified setting for a variety of individual spaces, including rose, secret, winter and Shakespeare gardens, an Edwardian Ladies' Walk and a laurel millennium maze. The walled kitchen garden has a good glasshouse, a sunken pool, tunnels of runner beans, herbs and flowers. Future plans include a meadow rose garden with the roses allowed free growth through an existing meadow – something which has been done in France but rarely over here.

Exbury Gardens ★★ 10

Exbury, Southampton SO45 1AZ. Tel: (023) 8089 1203/8089 9422;
Fax: (023) 8089 9940; Website: www.exbury.co.uk

Mr E.L. de Rothschild • 15m S of Southampton. From M27 junction 2 take A326 then B3054. 2½ m SE of Beaulieu, after 1m turn right for Exbury. Signposted • Open 23rd Feb to 3rd Nov, 10am – 5.30pm (or dusk if earlier) (last admission 5.30pm) • Entrance: main-season £5, OAPs £4.50 (£1 on Tues, Wed and Thurs), children (10–15) £4, parties of 15 or more £4.50 per person. Seasonal discounts (2001 prices) ● ● ✕ ● WC & ⬦ ● ● ● ●

Established between the wars by Lionel de Rothschild, these gardens of rhododendrons and azaleas are the most outstanding of their kind in the south. Winding paths meander over 200 acres and proceed under a light canopy of trees, mostly oak and pine, over a bridge and beside ponds to the Beaulieu river. Many rhododendrons and azaleas, such as *R. yakushimanum* and *R.* (Hawk Group) 'Crest', were introduced here and are to be found growing beside purple Japanese maples and candelabra primulas. At times the colour associations seem careless – harsh orange beside blush, metallic magenta beside pale blue – but a glade of towering white blooms, pink in bud, more than makes up for this. In March early rhododendrons, camellias and the daffodil meadow flower; in April the rock garden, miniature mountain scenery with screes and valleys, is at its peak with alpine rhododendrons among 'Skyrocket' junipers. May is the high season. In June and July the modern rose garden is a mass of colour and the garden of herbaceous grasses is full of interest, while the 'winter garden' (seen in autumn) has thick sinuous trunks of *Rhododendron sinogrande* and *Magnolia macrophylla*. The most recent addition is the Summer Lane Garden, which opened in 2001 with the steam railway. Its contemporary design was inspired by Piet Oudolf, combining huge swathes of herbaceous plants, grasses, bulbs and wild flowers, and including an apple and pear orchard.

Fairfield House ★ 11

East Street, Hambledon, Portsmouth PO7 4RY. Tel: (023) 9263 2431

Mrs Peter Wake • 10m SW of Petersfield in Hambledon • Open two days in April and June for NGS, and by appt. Suitable for parties • Entrance: £2.50, children 50p • Other information: Teas on open days and by arrangement only
● ● WC & ⟳ ✿ ℺

This magnificent collection of species and old roses, climbers and ramblers, together with some modern roses, was established by Peter Wake nearly thirty years ago with advice from Lanning Roper, and continues to flourish under the care of Marion Wake. The roses are planted informally on five acres, divided by yew hedges and brick walls, around the white Regency house. The lower stems of the species and larger shrub roses like 'Wolly Dodds' rose and *Rosa* x *alba* 'Maxima' are contained within stakes from which they rise and flower as if from giant urns. It is worth noting that none of these roses is sprayed. On the spreading lawns are mature cedars, limes and copper beeches, as well as more recently planted sorbus, malus, robinia, *Ptelea trifoliata*, tulip tree and fern beech, indicating the range of trees which can grow on a thin chalk soil.

Furzey Gardens ★ 12

Minstead, Lyndhurst SO43 7GL. Tel: (023) 8081 2464; Fax: (023) 8081 2297

Mrs M.M. Cole (Administrator) • 8m SW of Southampton, 1m S of A31, 2m W of Cadnam and end of M27, 3½ m NW of Lyndhurst • Gardens open daily except 25th and 26th Dec, 10am – 5pm (earlier in winter) • Entrance: summer: £3.50, OAPs £2.80, children £1.50, families £9; winter: £1.50, OAPs £1, children 50p, families £3. Reductions for parties by arrangement • Other information: Art and craft galleries. Sixteenth-century cottage open daily (some weekends in winter) ○ ● ▧ WC & ✿ ⊞ ℺

The eight acres of this well-maintained woodland garden were laid out by Hew Dalrymple in the early 1920s. In early March the acacia tree in full fragrant bloom, a group of *Corylopsis pauciflora* dripping with pale yellow flowers, species daffodils, *Magnolia stellata* and banks of heathers make a visit worthwhile. Among the plants which revel in the sandy acid soil of the New Forest are the ubiquitous rhododendrons and azaleas, the Chilean fire bush (*Embothrium coccineum*) flowering bright scarlet in May, and a host of shrubs and trees from Australasia. There is also a lake and water garden with yellow skunk cabbage, ferns, etc. Introduced in 2000 was a new sensory garden. Sir Arthur Conan Doyle is buried in the churchyard of the fine village church.

The Garden Gallery (Grandfathers) 13

Broughton, Nr Stockbridge SO20 8AZ. Tel:(01794) 301144;
E-mail: gardengallery@compuserve.com; Website: www.gardengallery.uk.com

Mr and Mrs G Bebb • Open May to Sept for groups of 10 or more by appt only • Entrance: £5 NEW ●

Swooping down from the busy A30 outside Stockbridge into the remote and meandering village of Broughton, you realise how rich the soil must be here. The gardens are bursting with rude health; and this one does not disappoint. A series of enclaves, each one different but all stylishly informal in their planting, encircle the characterful old house (not open). Water features include fountains and an ornamental pool, and modern sculptures for sale are encountered at every turn, although they are eclipsed in early summer by the *Rosa* 'Nevada' luxuriating in a sheltered corner. A peaceful and light-hearted place. Stockbridge itself, with handsome houses and an unusually wide main street crossed by the Test, is worth visiting; the room above the projecting porch of the eighteenth-century hostelry is the meeting place of one of England's most famous angling clubs.

Gilbert White's House and Garden 14

The Wakes, Selborne, Alton GU34 3JH. Tel: (01420) 511275; Fax: (01420) 511040

Oates Memorial Trust • 4½ m S of Alton, 8m N of Petersfield on B3006 • House open • Garden open daily Jan to 24th Dec, 11am – 5pm. Additional evening opening for parties • Entrance: £4, OAPs and students £3.50, children £1. Special rates for parties • Other information: Public car park behind Selborne Arms. Unusual plant fair 15th, 16th June and other non-horticultural events later ☾ ☕ WC ☈ ⚘ 🏛 🍴 ⚒

Here the naturalist Gilbert White wrote his classic *The Natural History of Selborne* (published 1788). The sundial and ha-ha beyond the lawn, with its splendid views of the beech-clad hangar, were there in his day. A copy of the amusing wooden cut-out of the Hesperian Hercules which he set up in the 'Hanger' in 1758 (12½ feet high, compared with the 30-foot version at Vaux-Le-Vicomte and Caserta) has been created by sculptor David Swinton and re-installed in the garden. The quincunx, a square pattern of five cypresses on a mound, was also originally conceived by White. Borders and beds near the house contain many plants from his time including hollyhocks (which were called 'hollyoaks'), sweet Williams, pinks, species foxgloves, santolina, martagon lilies and old roses, Gallicas, Damasks, etc. Later additions include a laburnum tunnel, a herb garden, a fine tulip tree planted in 1910 and some yew topiary. The garden is being restored to its eighteenth-century form with historic varieties of fruit, vegetables, herbaceous plants, annuals and wild flowers. An article in *Hortus* says that both for plant lists and descriptions of layout, this is one of the best-documented eighteenth-century gardens and that praise-worthy efforts to re-invent it include the quincunx, features such as a revolving wine barrel, the orchard, old fruit bushes, a typical vegetable garden of White's time including his favourite melons – and much more.

Hazelby House ★ 15

North End, Nr Newbury RG20 0AZ. Tel: (01635) 255414

Mr and Mrs P Hungerford • 5m S of Newbury from M4 junction 13. Take A34 to Newbury, then turn left to Ball Hill, and after 3m take left turning off Kintbury Rd • Open by appt • Entrance: £5, children £2.50 ☾ 🏛 WC

Twenty-five years ago there was only a vegetable patch here – now there is a most impressive garden, planned on the Sissinghurst system of 'rooms'. The pergola is wreathed with the pale 'Paul's Himalayan Musk' rose, jasmine and grape vines. Doorways in the hedges open onto two lily pools (one of pink water lilies and one of white), a rose garden heavily underplanted with herbaceous perennials, and a long herbaceous border between beech hedges. A grass bank then leads down to the small lake with an islet showing a splash of colour from climbing roses, where a garden started some seven years ago is being steadily extended to include a woodland walk. Meadows surround the intensively cultivated garden, and there are 20 acres of shaded woodland.

Heathlands ★ 16

47 Locks Road, Locks Heath, Southampton SO31 6NS. Tel: (01489) 573598; Fax: (01489) 557884; E-mail: john.burwell@btinternet.com.uk

Dr John Burwell • 5m W of Fareham. Leave M27 at junction 9. Locks Road runs due S from A27 at Park Gate • Open 17th March, 14th April, 12th May, 25th Aug, 2 – 5.30pm • Entrance: £2, children free ● 🍴 & ⬧ ⚘ ⚲

A row of paulownias, grown from seed by the owner, is a memorable sight in May and raises the expectations of any visitor to this remarkable garden on the outskirts of Southampton. The lawn stretches through spring bulbs to a more wooded area. To the north a pond with small herbaceous border is separated from the kitchen garden by a yew hedge sporting topiary balls and a peacock, its tail in low relief, its head and crown rising above the hedge line. The kitchen garden has four bay cones and Worcesterberries grown espalier-fashion. A huge holly drum is one of over 1000 different plants, including the architectural *Yucca gloriosa* and *Phormium tenax*, ferns, pieris, *Rhododendron sinogrande*, corylopsis, and a National Collection of Japanese anemones. There is also a part-yew walk focusing on an obelisk, a secret garden with tiny pool, and a conservatory.

Highclere Castle and Gardens 17

Highclere, Newbury RG20 9RN. Tel: (01635) 253210/253204

The Earl and Countess of Carnarvon • 4½ m S of Newbury, W of A34 • House open as garden • Garden probably open July to early Sept (telephone for exact dates), daily, 11am – 5pm (Sat closes 3.30pm) (last admission 1 hour before closing) • Entrance: £3, children £1.50 (castle and gardens £6, OAPs/students £5, children (5–14) £3, season ticket £25, parties of 20 or more £4.75 per person, children £3) (2001 prices) ◑ 🍴 ✕ 🖼 WC ⚘ ♿ 🔦

At first glance it seems that the Houses of Parliament have flown and settled in a parkland setting of lawns and cedars. Not surprising, since Highclere Castle (1840) was designed by the same architect, Sir Charles Barry, who remodelled a Georgian mansion to create a fine Victorian home for the 3rd Earl of Carnarvon. Three follies, a rotunda beside the lake, a roofless temple called Jackdaw's Castle, and Heaven's Gate on Sidown Hill opposite the castle are remnants of the garden before 'Capability' Brown remodelled the grounds in

1774 to give a gloriously simple vista of valley and hills. Tucked out of sight is the walled garden and the flower garden, designed by the late James Russell.

Hillier Gardens

(see THE SIR HAROLD HILLIER GARDENS AND ARBORETUM)

Hinton Ampner ★ 18

Hinton Ampner, Bramdean, Alresford SO24 0LA. Tel: (01962) 771305; Fax: (01962) 793101

The National Trust • 8m E of Winchester, 1m W of Bramdean on A272 • House open. Telephone for details • Garden open 17th, 24th March; then 30th March to Sept. Telephone for details • Entrance: £4, children (5–16) £2. Parties of 15 or more must pre-book • Other information: Coaches must use entrance through village. Plants usually for sale ◑ 🍽 WC & ⚘

Approached through parkland, this quintessentially English garden has been well restored in recent years. It was created by Ralph Dutton, later Lord Sherborne, who inherited the estate in 1935. A dramatic series of terraces with downland views descends to the south, and from the cross-axis of each terrace you see – as if by happy chance – urns, a temple, an obelisk or a silhouetted statue of Diana luring you to the garden's limits. The route leads through a series of secret gardens. Huge, immaculately trimmed topiary mushrooms give a surreal *Alice in Wonderland* effect. The features are interesting, the planting self-assured, ranging from an avenue of domed yews to a water-lily pond, a garden of hexagons and a dell with philadelphus, lilies, cotinus etc. In August, furnished with blue and white agapanthus, *viticella* clematis, species salvias and *Romneya coulteri*, the garden stays resplendent. The Trust claims the property as 'one of its undiscovered secrets'.

53 Ladywood ★ 19

Eastleigh SO50 4RW. Tel: (023) 806 15389

Mr and Mrs D. Ward • Leave A33/M3 at junction 12 signed A335 to Eastleigh, turn right at roundabout into Woodside Avenue, second right into Bosville, fifth right into Ladywood • Open for NGS on three Suns, 11am – 5.30pm, and by appt April to Sept • Entrance: £2, children 75p • Other information: Parking in Bosville only ● ⚘

This suburban garden, four metres square, containing 1800 different labelled plants, is subdivided into several more miniscule areas: a water garden with water hawthorn (*Aponogeton distachyos*) and water lilies, a scree garden, a shade garden with hostas and variegated plants and a tiny oval lawn. Among the healthy plants are alpines, erodiums, hardy geraniums galore, the white *Clematis* 'Henryi', roses, grasses, the miniature *Philadelphus* 'Manteau d'Hermine', all sensitively arranged with good colour associations and contrasts, eg the black viola 'Molly Sanderson' and black grass *Ophiopogon planiscapus* emerging from pale shingle.

Lake House   20

Northington, Alresford SO24 9TG.

Lord Ashburton • 3m NW of Alresford off B3046. Follow signs for Northington and the Grange, and turn sharp left before entrance to Grange • Open probably two Suns for NGS • Entrance: £3, children free ◐ 🕭 WC ⬯

Lord Ashburton's modern single-storied house is situated in the old kitchen garden of the ruined Grange. A wall has been pierced to give views of lake and parkland. An adjacent walled garden is filled with herbaceous borders and herringbone-pathed, box-edged plots growing old roses and perennials, as well as a rose-and-wisteria pergola and an avenue of Irish yews leading to a moon gate. This opens to a scenic walk round the lake, with views of the neo-classical shell of the Grange, a nineteenth-century cascade and ruined 'castle', and an arched bridge in oriental style. Near the house are conservatory, terrace, pots and small herb garden. The Grange, formerly home to the Ashburton family and now in the guardianship of English Heritage, may be visited at any time.

Longstock Park Water Gardens ★★   21

Longstock, Stockbridge SO20 6EH. Tel: (01264) 810894

John Lewis Partnership (Leckford Estate Ltd) • 2m N of Stockbridge. From A30 turn N on A3057. Signposted • Open April to Sept, first and third Sun of each month, 2 – 5pm, and by appt for parties • Entrance: £3, children 50p • Other information: Refreshments and plants for sale at nursery ◐ ☕ 🕭 WC ♿ 🌿 ⯊

The seven acres of these superb water gardens, created by John Spedan Lewis in 1948, are fed from the River Test and surrounded by acid-loving trees and shrubs. They form an archipelago connected by narrow bridges and causeways. Gunnera, the swamp cypress (*Taxodium distichum*) surrounded by stilts, royal fern, giant white lily (*Cardiocrinum giganteum*) and Japanese angelica tree (*Aralia elata*) are just some of the plants reflected in the clear waters moving with gold carp, and a walk along the paths gives a succession of views followed by more intimate spaces. Aquatics include 48 different water lilies. Do not miss a visit to *Longstock Park Nursery* nearby (also open daily), set in a walled garden with climbing plants, and the fine herbaceous border reached through a gate in its wall. This runs parallel to a pergola planted with roses and an exquisite and extensive collection of *viticella* clematis. A National Collection of buddleias, with over 100 varieties, may be seen by request.

The Manor House ★   22

Upton Grey, Basingstoke RG25 2RD. Fax: (01256) 861035;
E-mail: uptongrey.garden@lineone.net;
Website: www.website.lineone.net/~uptongrey.garden

Mr and Mrs J. Wallinger • 6m SE of Basingstoke in Upton Grey, on hill immediately above church • Open April to Oct, Mon – Fri (but closed Bank

*Holidays), by appt only • Entrance: £4 (includes guide/leaflet) • Other
information: Teas available if notice given* ● 🐷 WC ♿ 🏛

Over the past 17 years this garden has been meticulously restored by Mrs Ros
Wallinger to the original 1908 Gertrude Jekyll planting plans, copies of which
are on display, and the tender care invested makes it more than a unique
museum piece. Here are formal beds with lilies, peonies and roses edged with
lamb's ears, drystone walls clothed with plants, terraces, pergola and yew
hedging, as well as Jekyll's only surviving restored wild garden with pond,
daffodils and rambling roses. A living example of many Jekyll theories, it is
worth noting her use of colour, with hot reds moving through yellows to
distant greys and blues, the proportions of the steps, and the relation of the
house (designed in grand vernacular style with hung tiles, etc by Ernest
Newton for Charles Holme, founder and owner of *The Studio* magazine) to
the garden. This is claimed to be the most authentic Jekyll garden reconstruction, supported by a useful booklet and plant list.

Marycourt 23

43 High Street, Odiham, Hook RG29 1LF. Tel: (01256) 702100

*Mr and Mrs M.N. Conville • 7m E of Basingstoke, 7m W of Aldershot off A287
1½ m from M3 junction 5 • Open 30th June, 7th July, 2 – 6pm, 10th July,
9am – 6pm, for NGS, and by appt • Entrance: £2, children free* ● 🍴 WC ♿
🔖 ☕

The large, long town garden is approached from the drive in the High Street.
Splendid mixed borders (alpines, clematis, honeysuckles, roses, shrubs, bulbs,
phormiums, perennials) along the walls open out to a riot of primary colours
(ligularias, heleniums, bergamot, achilleas) beside the swimming pool. The
detail and the variety of plants in the alkaline soil of this garden is remarkable;
note particularly the half-hardy plants. Near the grass tennis court, with its
copper beech and climbing roses, are over 20 varieties of ivy, grown as ground
cover, in pots, as shrubs and, best of all, 'Paddy's Pride' draping a shed. Blue
and white beds are planted with agapanthus, white roses and delphiniums and
edged with lavender. Hostas grown with Solomon's seal and *Lilium regale* in a
tunnel of overhanging apple trees are most effective.

Mottisfont Abbey Garden ★★ 24

Mottisfont, Romsey SO51 0LP. Tel: (01794) 340757

*The National Trust • 15m NW of Southampton, 4¼ m NW of Romsey, ½ m W
of A3057 • Garden open 23rd March to 6th Nov, Sat – Wed; July and Aug,
Sat – Thurs; all at 11am – 6pm or dusk if earlier; for rose season 8th to 23rd
June, daily, 11am – 8.30pm (last admission 1 hour before closing) (check
recorded message on (01794) 341220, June only, for state of roses) • Entrance:
£6, children £3, family ticket (2 adults and two children 5–18) £15. No
reduction for parties • Other information: Coaches must pre-book. Picnics in
grounds only. Four-seater golf buggy available. No smoking in walled garden
during rose season* ◑ 🐷 ✕ 🍴 WC ♿ 🔖 🏛 🍷

This famous collection of historic roses, based on the design and selection by Graham Stuart Thomas, was established in 1972 in the original walled kitchen garden, quartered with paths and box hedging – a formal design given additional interest by fine herbaceous borders, a central pond and a fountain. Here are the Albas, Damasks and Gallicas of the Middle Ages, cabbage and moss roses, and the earliest Chinas, Bourbons, hybrid perpetuals, French nineteenth-century Gallicas and Albas as well as Rugosas, and ramblers up walls, arches and stands – in all, a National Collection of 300 old-fashioned roses (also a few species and New English roses), now being renovated. The best time to visit is on midsummer evenings, when the coaches have gone. Sweeping lawns around the house, cedars, the largest London plane tree (*Platanus* x *hispanica*) in the country, a magically deep and bubbling pool, and a spring running down to the River Test provide a tranquil contrast to the heady and scented delights of the roses. The simple but effective design of grass terraces, yew octagon and pollarded lime walk is the work of the late Sir Geoffrey Jellicoe, while Norah Lindsay contributed the small lavender- and box-edged parterre infilled with spring bulbs and summer annuals. A few miles SW of Mottisfont is *March End*, Doctor's Hill, Sherfield English – an inspiration for actual and aspiring organic gardeners, and proof that productivity and attractive design can go hand in hand. [Open several days in June for NGS, plus Organic Gardeners' Weekend. Telephone (01794) 340255 for details.]

Moundsmere Manor 25

Preston Candover, Basingstoke RG25 2HE. Tel: (01256) 389207

Mr and Mrs Andreae • 6m S of Basingstoke on B3046. Manor gates on left just after Preston Candover sign • Open 7th July, 2 – 5pm • Entrance: £2, children 50p • Coaches by appt ◗

The 'Wrenaissance' house was inspired by Hampton Court and designed in 1908 by Sir Reginald Blomfield (1856–1942). To its south lies Blomfield's formal garden, with herbaceous borders backed by yew hedges and buttresses at either side, then yew avenues, and at the centre a sunken garden edged with roses and a central pool in which the house is pleasingly reflected from the far end. There is also a pinetum and good hothouses with streptocarpus, abutilons, figs, etc. This is Edwardian gardening on a grand scale, characteristically architectural, and exemplifies Blomfield's theories in *The Formal Garden in England*, in which he attacks the informal style supported by William Robinson. Other examples of Blomfield's work can also be found at Athelhampton House (Dorset) and Godinton Park (Kent) (see entries).

Petersfield Physic Garden 26

16 High Street, Petersfield.

Hampshire Gardens Trust • Behind 16 High Street • Open daily except 25th Dec, during daylight hours • Entrance: free (donations welcome) • Other information: Teas or wine for pre-booked parties by arrangement ○ **WC** ⅍ ✍

This small secluded garden, planted since 1990 with plants known in the seventeenth century, is a welcome amenity in the centre of Petersfield. It has a knot garden, an orchard, roses, box, topiary and a herb garden with plants labelled according to their traditional uses.

Redenham Park ★ 27

Redenham, Nr Andover, SP11 9AQ. Tel: (01264) 772511; Fax: (01264) 772616

Sir John and Lady Clark • 4m NW of Andover on A342 • Open 1st, 2nd Sept for charity, and for groups by appt • Entrance: £3.50 NEW ◐

The perfect setting for a Jane Austen novel, this classic five-acre garden embraces its early-nineteenth-century ashlar-faced house. Views of parkland with sheep and cedars are followed by an enclosed paved rose garden with a circular pond (home to zantedeschia and white iris) and a fountain, and then herbaceous borders leading to a pleached lime walk and a moon gate. There are also fine borders, sculptural clipped yews, a tapestry hedge of copper- and green-leaved beech bordering the croquet lawn, and a low pear and apple espalier in a walled garden, with walls and paths dripping in June with scented roses. The walled kitchen garden is immaculate, and the mass of exotic fowls includes an ebony cock and hens.

Selborne

(see GILBERT WHITE'S HOUSE AND GARDEN)

The Sir Harold Hillier Gardens and Arboretum ★★ 28

Jermyns Lane, Ampfield, Romsey SO51 0QA. Tel: (01794) 368787;
Fax: (01794) 368027; www.hillier.hants.gov.uk

Hampshire County Council • 3m NE of Romsey, 9m SW of Winchester, ³/₄ m W of A3090 along Jermyns Lane. Signed from A3090 and A3057 • Open all year except 25th, 26th Dec, 10.30am – 6pm (Nov to March 5pm or dusk) • Entrance: £4.25, OAPs £3.75, children under 16 free, parties of 10 or more £3.25 per person (Nov to March reduced rates) • Other information: Plants for sale and shop in adjacent nursery ○ ☕ ✕ 🍽 WC ⅙ ♿ ♨

Administered by Hampshire County Council since 1977, this enormous collection of trees and shrubs was begun in 1953 by the late Sir Harold Hillier, using his house and garden as a starting point. It extends to 180 acres and includes approximately 12,000 different species and cultivars, with many rarities. With a total of 40,000 plants it is impossible not to be impressed or to learn something about what, where and how to plant. Eleven National Collections are held here, including quercus and hamamelis. Seasonal-interest maps and labelling will lead the visitor to herbaceous, scree, heather and bog gardens. Amongst the trees and shrubs *Eucalyptus nitens* and *E. niphophila*, *Magnolia cylindrica* and the acers are worthy of note. The winter garden, on the site of the old rose garden, is claimed to be the largest such in the UK, specialising in plants at their best from November to March. Much more than an arboretum, this attractively laid-out garden will be enjoyed at many levels and can only increase in interest as the immense collection of young trees gains in maturity. Nearby at *Broadlands* there is a 'Capability' Brown landscape. It is also worth the detour into Winchester to view *Queen Eleanor's Garden*, the re-creation of a small medieval plot designed by Dr Sylvia Landsberg behind the Great Hall of Winchester Castle, and the *Dean Garnier Garden*, a secluded site with scented plants and fine views, reached by stairs from an oak door in the east wall of Winchester Cathedral.

Spinners ★   29

School Lane, Boldre, Lymington SO41 5QE. Tel: (01590) 673347

Mr and Mrs P.G.G. Chappell • 1½ m N of Lymington. Follow county signs on A337 between Brockenhurst and Lymington • Open 14th April to 14th Sept, Tues – Sat, 10am – 5pm (Sun and Mon by appt); mid-Sept to March nursery and part of the garden open on same days. Telephone for details • Entrance: £2 • Other information: Plants for sale in nursery ◑ 🏵 WC ℘ 🕯

This informal woodland garden on the acid soil of the New Forest, created by the Chappells and praised by Roy Lancaster and other plantsmen, is remark-able for its plant associations and the owners' careful choice of scale. Nothing is over-large or dwarfs the smaller pleasures. In spring the sun shines through the canopy of trees, lighting camellias and dwarf rhododendrons, exochordas, magnolias, *Cornus kousa* and the brilliant coral leaves of *Acer palmatum* 'Shishio Improved'. Admire at ground level the carpets of cyclamen, *Erythronium revolutum* like pale pink stars, and the white and strange maroon trilliums (a National Collection held here). Beside the spring near the house the yellow-greens of ferns and variegated iris synchronise with white and yellow skunk cabbage. Ferns, primulas and hostas thrive in the bog garden, and good autumn colouring comes from *Nyssa sinensis* and other trees.

Staunton Country Park   30

Middle Park Way, Havant PO9 5HB. Tel: (023) 9245 3405;
Fax: (023) 9249 8156

Hampshire County Council and eight other public bodies • 2m N of Havant on B2149. Signposted • Open daily: summer 10am – 5pm; winter 10am – 4pm • Entrance: £3.90, OAPs £3.50, children £2.90, family ticket £11.40 ○ 🍽 ✕ 🏵 WC ♿ ⚘ ℘ 🏛 🕯 ☞

Formerly the Leigh estate, belonging to the nineteenth-century horticulturist and adventurer Sir George Staunton. The walled garden has a crinkle-crankle wall to the south, and within it lies the largest restoration of Victorian greenhouses in the country, costing over £1 million. Here are the passion flowers, pepper vines and exotics grown by Staunton, including the giant *Victoria amazonica* lily in its original circular pool. The great house has gone and the park is split by a main road, but fine specimen trees remain, as well as the Gothic library and follies such as the shell house and the beacon, also the terrace and the lakes, the Chinese bridge, and the remains of the lake fort where Staunton used to fire guns and fly the imperial yellow flag of China. Don't miss the ornamental Regency farm, stocked, as in the 1800s, with peacocks, deer, pigs, sheep, goats and horses.

The Tudor House Museum 31

Tudor House, Bugle Street, Southampton SO14 2AD. Tel: (023) 8033 2513;
Fax: (023) 8033 9601; Website: www.southampton.gov.uk/leisure/heritage

*Southampton City Council • Near Docks in Bugle Street, off Town Quay Road •
Museum open • Garden open all year, Tues – Fri, 10am – 12 noon, 1 – 5pm,
Sat, 10am – 12 noon, 1 – 4pm, Sun, 2 – 5pm • Entrance: free* ○ **WC** ૐ ⊞ ☙

This delightful museum, with its dark polished floors and gallery, includes a
garden designed by Dr Sylvia Landsberg. It incorporates many features from
Tudor gardens, such as heraldic beasts on poles, a camomile seat, a knot garden
with twisting lines of santolina, germander and box, a skep for bees, a fountain
surrounded by camomile and hyssop, an arbour hung with vines, and many
herbs, labelled with details of their associations and uses. With its old walls and
buildings, this is a peaceful corner in the heart of the city.

Tylney Hall Hotel ★ 32

Rotherwick, Hook RG27 9AZ. Tel: (01256) 764881

*Access from M3 junction 5 (take A287 via Newnham) or from M4 junction 11
(take B3349 via Rotherwick) • Open for meals to non-residents and also open to
public 12th May, 9th June, 7th July for NGS • Entrance: £2, children free
(2001 prices) • Other information: On garden open days main hotel closed except
to guests with reservations, but refreshments available to garden visitors. Plants
for sale on June open day* ☾ ⬛ ✕ WC ⚘ ⚘

An Edwardian period piece. The elaborate brick house with gardens stretching to
67 acres was built in 1900 by Seldon Wornum for Sir Lionel Phillips, a South
African diamond merchant. Wornum and Weir Schultz designed the gardens,
with an Italian terrace and fountain overlooking the boathouse lake, a Dutch
garden, a fine avenue with Wellingtonias and splendid vistas framed by trees to
the north and south. Schultz obtained designs from Gertrude Jekyll for the water
garden, where two rivulets fell from one lake to another. When the house
became a school in 1984, hard tennis courts were built on the Italian terrace, the
lakes became choked and balustrades and statuary were lost, but it is now a hotel,
and the gardens have been restored by head gardener Paul Tattersdill and five
under-gardeners. A fountain plays again on the Italian terrace, the boathouse lake
is cleared and its bridge rebuilt, the water fountains are restored with rivulets,
lakes and bogside planting, the kitchen garden has regained its rose pergola, the
orchards stock 20 varieties of apple, and the vistas with their mature trees now
look better than in the photographs of earlier days. Fine specimen trees.

The Vyne 33

Sherborne St John, Basingstoke RG24 9HL. Tel: (01256) 881337

*The National Trust • 4m N of Basingstoke between Sherborne St John and
Bramley on A340; turn E at NT signs • House and garden open Feb and Mar,
Sat, Sun, 11am – 4pm; 23rd March to 3rd Nov, daily except Thur and Fri,
11am – 6pm (house closes 5pm) • Entrance: £3 (house and garden £6.50,*

children, £3.25, family ticket £16.25). Parties of 15 or more for house and garden £5.50 per person, Mon – Wed only • Other information: Picnics in car park only ◑ 💭 ✗ <u>WC</u> ⑁ ⊞ ⚑

Classic English parkland of lawn, cedars, oaks and occasional clipped yews beside Wey Brook, widened here into a lake, complements the brick house with its handsome Corinthian portico added by John Webb, a harmonious *mélange* of sixteenth-, seventeenth- and eighteenth-century styles. The galleried Tudor chapel houses important stained glass windows depicting young Henry VIII and Catherine of Aragon, and rare encaustic floor tiles dating from around 1500. The garden house, also by John Webb, previously a dovecot, has the ground plan of a Greek cross. Small herbaceous beds to the west and a newly designed and planted summerhouse garden. From the wild garden and woodland walk, the house may be seen to advantage across the water. A serene place.

West Green House Garden ★★ 34

West Green, Hartley Wintney, Hook RG27 8JB. Tel/Fax: (01252) 844611

Miss Marylyn Abbott • 10m NE of Basingstoke, 1m W of Hartley Wintney, 1m N of A30 • Open 27th April to Aug, Thurs – Sun and Bank Holiday Mons, Sept, Sat, Sun; all 11am – 5pm • Entrance: £4 ◑ 💭 ✗ WC ⑁ 🌢 ⊞ ⚑

Nestling in a wooded corner of Hampshire is the attractive 1720s' manor house, where busts of gods, emperors and dukes look down from the walls onto two major gardens. The inner gardens, enclosed by eighteenth-century walls, are all devoted to parterres. One is filled with water lilies, another is of classical design with box topiary, and a third enacts the whimsy of *Alice in Wonderland* with the story's characters in ivy and box topiary surrounded by roses of red and white. The main walled garden is planted in subtle hues of mauve, plum and blue, contained in beds that have been faithfully restored to their original outlines. A decorative *potager* is centred around berry-filled fruit cages where herbs, flowers and unusual vegetables are designed into colourful patterns. All this is surrounded by a second garden, a neo-classical park studded with follies, birdcages and monuments hidden beside a tree-fringed lake, especially attractive in spring when carpeted with snowdrops, crocus and fritillaries. A grand water garden, the Nymphaeum, spills down rills and steps from a devil's mouth into serene ponds. Work continues with planting aimed at resolving the landscape lacuna between the lake and the Nymphaeum, leading to a woodland planting and a new white and grey garden. A green theatre, a picturesque orangery and long *allées* of green all add to this fine restoration that has been undertaken by the well-known Australian gardener Marylyn Abbott, who purchased a 99-year lease from the National Trust to remake this enchanted place after some years of neglect (and worse).

White Windows ★ 35

Longparish, Andover SP11 6PB. Tel/Fax: (01264) 720222

Mrs Jane Sterndale-Bennett • 5m E of Andover. Turn off A303 to Longparish on B3048 • Open two days for charity, 2 – 6pm, and by appt April to Sept, Wed, 2 – 6pm • Entrance: £2 ◑ WC ⑁ 🌢

Jane Sterndale-Bennett is the former Chairman of the Hardy Plant Society and crams a wealth of hardy perennials into the undulating beds of her immaculate garden. Three mini-gardens stretch in sequence from the house, each giving informal but theatrical views to adjacent areas. The fragrant white columbine grows among a mass of glaucous foliage, including *Artemisia ludoviciana* 'Valerie Finnis', and grasses like *Elymus (Leymus) hispidus* and *Carex comans*. Gold, variegated and purple-leaved shrubs, as well as unusual trees like *Malus transitoria* with its hawthorn-like leaves, make this a garden of interest throughout the year.

ISLE OF WIGHT

Barton Manor   36

Whippingham, East Cowes PO32 6LB. Tel: (01983) 528989

Robert Stigwood • From East Cowes take A 3021, 500 metres beyond Osborne House on left • Garden open for themed charity days, probably 1st June, 7th July and 1st Sept, 10am – 5pm • Entrance: £3, OAPs £2, children £1 • Other information: Coaches welcome. Guide dogs only ● 🖶 🦽 WC ♿ ♿

Prince Albert's original design included fine trees and the cork grove. The grand terraces were added by Edward VII. There is also a secret garden planted with azaleas and roses and impressive herbaceous borders. In 1968 Hillier's laid out an intriguing water garden on the far side of the lake, home to carp and waterfowl, on what was originally Queen Victoria's skating rink. The present owner (a keen conservationist) has spared no effort in restoring and maintaining the estate. National Collections of red hot pokers (kniphofias) and watsonias are here. The most recent addition to the estate is a rose hedge maze which is the largest such attraction on the island – it is now tall enough to get lost in. Another former royal residence, Osborne (see entry), is nearby.

Morton Manor   37

Brading, Sandown PO36 0EP. Tel: (01983) 406168;
Website: www.warbirdart.demon.co.uk

J.B., J. and J.A. Trzebski • 3m from Ryde on A3055. Turn right at Brading traffic lights, signposted 100 metres up hill • Manor open (guided tours) • Garden open April to Oct, daily except Sat, 10am – 5.30pm • Entrance: £4.25, OAPs £3.75, children (6–16) £1.75. Parties of 15 or more £3.25 per person (house and garden) (2001 prices) • Other information: Vineyard and winery ● 🖶 ✕ 🦽 WC ♿ ♿ ♿ ♿ ♿

The history of Morton goes back to the thirteenth century. The Elizabethan sunken garden is surrounded by a 400-year-old box hedge and old-fashioned roses and shaded by a magnificent *Magnolia grandiflora*. The terraces are nineteenth-century with extensive herbaceous borders and a huge London plane. Masses of spring bulbs are followed by rhododendrons and traditional herbaceous displays. Among the wide range of fine trees is an Indian bean (*Catalpa bignonioides*) and a *Cornus kousa*; particularly lovely In early June is *Robinia hispida*.

There are also 90 different varieties of Japanese maple, and several varieties of acer imported from New Zealand are now on sale. Another feature is a pagoda covered with the vine variety 'Baco'. Little remains of the old walled garden, but in the corner behind the herbs are the restored bee boles; also a turf maze made for children, and a vineyard growing seven varieties of grape.

NorthCourt ★   38

Shorwell, Newport PO30 3JG. Tel: (01983) 740415; Fax: (01983) 740409; Website: www.wightfarmholidays.co.uk/northcourt

Mr and Mrs J. Harrison • 4m S of Newport on B3323. Entrance on right after rustic bridge, opposite thatched cottage • Open one Sun in May, 2 – 5.30pm for NGS, and one evening in June, 6 – 8pm (pre-booked guided tour). Telephone for details. Special openings for pre-booked parties of 10 or more • Entrance: approx. £2.50 (varies according to charity) ◐ 💷 WC ♿

Fifteen acres of wooded grounds surround a Jacobean manor house, with varied gardens consisting of seventeenth-century landscaped terraces leading down to the stream and water gardens, herbaceous borders, woodland walks, a sunken rose garden and a walled kitchen garden. Terraces with a south-easterly aspect have been made into a maritime garden with far-reaching views of the sea. The garden specialises in more tender plants – abutilons, salvias, diascias and argyranthemums all thrive here, especially in the new Mediter-ranean garden. The 'secret walled garden' at the top has been cleared and planted in sub-tropical style. The cottage garden of *Little Northcourt* is full of hidden delights. The owners welcome bed and breakfast guests, and suggest May and June when the gardens are at their very best. Swinburne, the poet, stayed and wrote at the big house. 3m W on B3399, the National Trust's *Mottistone Manor* has good views of the Channel and a herb garden.

Nunwell House   39

Coach Lane, Brading PO36 0JQ. Tel: (01983) 407240

Col. and Mrs J.A. Aylmer • 3m S of Ryde, signed off A3055 in Brading into Coach Lane • House open, tours 1.30pm, 2.30pm, 3.30pm • Garden open 2nd, 3rd June, then July to 4th Sept, Mon – Wed, 1 – 5pm • Entrance: £2.50 (house and garden £4, OAPs and students £3, accompanied children under 10 £1) ◑ 🍴 WC

Nunwell House stands in six acres of gardens with wonderful views across the park to Spithead. The rose garden (a bowling green in the seventeenth century) is set at the top of a slope in front of the walled garden, which is now replanted with a double herbaceous border. The Long Walk leads down past the side of the house, where stand two very handsome paulownias, to the front. Among the varied shrubs and plants in the borders are several pretty *Lavatera* 'Barnsley', a notable acanthus, an enormous *Elaeagnus* x *ebbingei* and a *Cotoneaster* x *watereri* 'Cornubia'. There is also a 45-metre run of *Rosa* 'Frensham' and a *Cornus kousa*, and on the front of the house are three large myrtles. A steep flight of steps bordered by lavender leads up to the woods. To the rear of the house is an arboretum laid out by Vernon Russell-Smith in 1963. Restoration by the present owners is nearing completion.

Osborne House 40

East Cowes PO32 6JY. Tel: (01983) 200022 or 281784 or 281784

English Heritage • 1m SE of East Cowes off A3021 • House open as grounds, 10am – 5pm • Grounds open April to Sept, daily, 10am – 6pm; Oct, daily, 10am – 5pm. Pre-booked guided tours of house and terrace garden only, Nov to 9th Dec, 3rd Feb to 28th March, Sun, Mon, Wed, Thurs • Entrance: £3.80, OAPs £2.90, children £1.90 (house and grounds £7.20, OAPs 5.40, children £3.60, family ticket £18) (2001 prices) ◐ ☕ ✕ 🗐 WC ♿ 🐾 🏛 ☝ ℺

Built by Queen Victoria in 1845–51 as a family retreat, the royal apartments are open to the public. The gardens, designed jointly by Victoria and Albert in the formal Italianate style, are now being restored and replanted to the original designs. Old cultivars have been used for the 'Victorian' bedding on the terraces, and the borders have been replanted with plants of the period. The park and gardens are notable for their magnificent trees. The Swiss Cottage chalet, in what were the royal children's gardens, has nine plots, each with 14 beds, planted with old varieties of soft fruit, flowers and vegetables, with a carriage ride to and fro, and the children's gardening tools, wildflower meadow and orchard, and Queen Victoria's bathing machine on show. The one-acre walled garden has been restored sympathetically by Rupert Golby using historic plants within a modern design to celebrate the lives of Queen Victoria and Prince Albert. The plantings in the walled garden fully exploit the island climate, enhanced by the protective walls of the garden. The usual wall-trained fruit of vines, figs, pears, plums and cherries are complemented by an olive, an orange and a lemon tree and the edible flowers of the acca. Drifts of multiple plantings span the length and width of the garden, ensuring a continuous display of striking colour throughout the summer, and broad rows of herbaceous plants are offset by extensive plots of annually sown flowers, herbs and vegetables. The glasshouse built by Prince Albert and Thomas Cubitt is restored, and house collections of plants from South Africa. The frequent use of entwined V and A motifs in the furnishings of the house is also used in the garden, on ironwork arches, garden benches and terracotta pots.

Pitt House 41

Love Lane, Bembridge PO35 5NF.

L.J. Martin • Near village centre and Maritime Museum • Open June to Aug, Thurs, 2 – 5pm • Entrance: £2, OAPs and children 75p ◐ ♿

Four acres with lovely views of the Solent through the trees. On a lower level from the house is a delightfully shady dell with a waterfall, ponds and water plants. In the main part of the garden are pergolas hung with roses and honeysuckle, and a Victorian greenhouse with two magnificent yellow daturas. Interesting trees include a crinodendron and a paulownia.

Ventnor Botanic Garden ★★   42

The Undercliffe Drive, Ventnor PO38 1UL. Tel: (01983) 855397,
Fax: (01983) 856756; E-mail: simon@vbgl.demon.co.uk;
Website: www.botanic.co.uk

*Isle of Wight Council • SW of Ventnor. Signed from A3055 • Garden open all year,
daily. Temperate house open Jan to 2nd March, Sat, Sun, 10am – 4pm; 3rd March
to 27th Oct, daily, 10am – 5pm; 28th Oct to Dec, except 25th Dec, Sat, Sun, 11am
– 4pm • Entrance: charge for car park but gardens and temperate house free •
Guided tour for groups by appt, £3 per person* ○ ● ✕ 🗎 wc ᵬ ⬳ 🌿 🎴 🎭

Twenty-two acres, moderately sheltered from the south and north by *Quercus ilex*
and escallonias. The shelterbelt, which was decimated in the 1987 and 1990 gales,
has been replanted. Many tender plants (including olives, *Berberis asiatica* and *Acer
sikkimensis* from the Himalayas, *Cestrum elegans* from Mexico, *Pittosporum daphniphyl-
loides* from China) all flourish in the mild climate. Banana plants from Japan and *Citrus
ichangensis* are but a few of the rare plants displayed to maximum effect in
surroundings which are now designed as a Victorian sub-tropical garden. The
magnificent temperate house has a worldwide collection of plants from the warm
temperate zones, together with written and pictorial displays. There is an
Australian section, a central bed of flowers from southern Africa, an island section
concentrating on vulnerable and endangered species. New planting includes an
extensive New Zealand garden, a Mediterranean terrace and, recently, a Japanese
terrace. The medicinal garden, which contains plants used in folk medicine around
the world, is outstanding. *Teucrium chamaedrys* (germander) makes an effective low
hedge in the small formal area. The garden is particularly well supplied with seats
throughout. New attractions planned include a visitors' centre (where exhibitions
will be held), a gift shop and restaurant. The plant sales area is well laid out with
many unusual varieties. *Deacon's Nursery*, Godshill [open Oct to March, Sat only] has
a large variety of fruit trees and bushes together with hops and nut trees. Their
catalogue contains over 200 varieties of apples. A few miles inland is the ruined shell
of the eighteenth-century *Appuldurcombe House*, now owned by English Heritage,
which stands in grounds by 'Capability' Brown. [Open April to Oct, 10am – 6pm.]

OPENING DATES AND TIMES

Times of access given are the best available at the moment of going to press,
but some may have been changed subsequently. *Note:* In 2002 the late-May
Bank Holiday is replaced by the Queen's Jubilee celebrations (1st to 4th June).
It may be wise to check with garden owners concerning these particular
dates. In the entries, the times given are inclusive: that is, an entry such as May
to Sept means that the garden is open from 1st May to 30th Sept inclusive, and
2–5 pm means that entry will be effective during that period. Please note that
many owners will open their gardens to visitors by appointment. They will
often arrange to give a personally conducted tour on these occasions.
Unavoidably some owners cannot give their opening times before we go
to press. In such cases we attempt to give the best guidance we can.

HEREFORDSHIRE

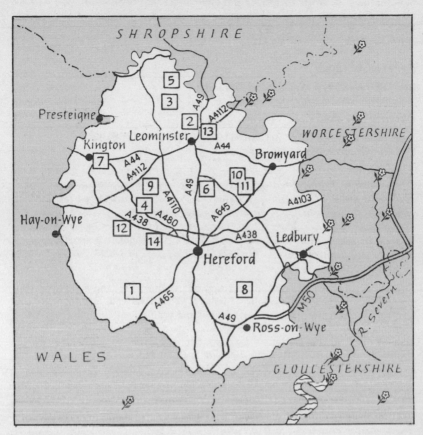

Abbey Dore Gardens

1

Abbey Dore, Hereford HR2 0AD. Tel: (01981) 240419

*Mrs C.L. Ward • 11m SW of Hereford off A465 • Open April to Sept, daily
except Mon and Wed, 11am – 6pm, and by appt • Entrance: £3, children 50p*
◗ ☕ WC ♿ ⚘

Six acres in all, incorporating a large part of the original Abbey Dore Court
Garden and all of Huntsman's Cottage Garden. Two acres are left wild, to
delight both the garden specialist and casual visitor, laid out with flair and
imagination. A new area, incorporated in 2001, focuses on a gazebo. The
purple, gold and silver borders, created twelve years ago at the suggestion of
Graham Stuart Thomas, are unusual and retain year-round interest. They lead
to a wild riverside walk, and across the River Dore a meadow is planted with

rare trees and shrubs. A walled orchard, with old fruit trees and wide borders punctuated with white foxgloves and cimicifugas, has been developed with an eye for colour and form. Hellebores, peonies and astrantias are specialities. The plants for sale are equally inspirational, with many of the more unusual cultivars available.

Arrow Cottage

(see THE LANCE HATTATT DESIGN GARDEN)

Berrington Hall   2

Leominster HR6 0DW. Tel: (01568) 615721; Fax: (01568) 613263; E-mail: berrington@smtp.ntrust.org.uk

The National Trust • 4m N of Leominster, W of A49 • House and garden open 23rd March to 3rd Nov, Sat – Wed (but open Good Friday), house 1 — 5pm, garden 12 noon — 5pm (closes 4.30pm Oct, Nov). Park walk open July to 3rd Nov, 1 — 5pm. Parties of 15 or more by written appt • Entrance: £3 (house and grounds £4.40, children £2.20, family ticket £11) • Other information: Two wheelchairs and batricar available for pre-booking. Telephone for wheelchair access to restaurant. Picnics in car park and play area in walled garden ◑ ● ✕ WC ⑆ 🏛 ♔ ℃

The late-eighteenth-century house designed by Henry Holland is set in mature grounds landscaped by 'Capability' Brown, with a park walk leading down to a pool designed by him. The gardens are well maintained and formally organised, with many shrubs plus a woodland walk with unusual trees, some recently planted. The walled garden is a young orchard of 50 varieties of pre-1900 apples. Children will enjoy the eye-spy trail, orienteering course, and the living willow tunnel in the play area. Croft Castle (see entry) is nearby.

Croft Castle   3

Leominster HR6 9PW. Tel: (01568) 780246

The National Trust • 5m NW of Leominster off B4362 • Castle closed during 2002 • Garden open 23rd March to 3rd Nov, Wed – Sun and Bank Holiday Mon, 11am – 5pm (last admission ½ hour before closing). Parties of 15 or more by written appt. Parkland open all year • Entrance: £3, children £1.50. Car parking charge £2 per car, £10 per coach (refundable on entry to garden) • Other information: Picnics in car park only. Braille guides available. Dogs in parkland only, on leads ◑ ● WC ⑆ ♔ ℃

The Welsh Marches castle dates from the fourteenth century and commands a spectacular landscape of open countryside. It is well kept and pleasant to walk through but lacks interest for the specialist, except for the walled garden which is in good condition. The park is notable for its fine avenue of Spanish chestnuts, possibly 350 years old, and for its venerable pollarded oaks. There are charming walks in the Fishpool valley. Berrington Hall (see entry) is nearby.

Darkley Gardens 4

Norton Canon, Nr Weobley HR4 7BT. Tel: (01544) 318121

Jill and Malcolm Ainslie • 10m NW of Hereford off A480. Follow signs to Norton Wood and Hurstley. Gardens 1m on left-hand side • Open mid-May to Sept, Thurs, Sun, 1 – 5pm and by appt • Entrance: £3, children free [NEW] ● WC 🌿 ☕

This peaceful traditional garden is tucked away down a quiet lane, with views across to the Black Mountains. The many herbaceous borders are carefully colour-themed: a yellow bed with hemerocallis and euphorbias, a pink bed of roses and geraniums under a silver pear tree, a striking purple bed of heucheras and deep-coloured penstemons. A pretty arch of golden hops leads through to a well-kept *potager*, while the walled garden adjoining provides a tranquil retreat with bubbling water and scented thyme paths. The garden is host to 150 varieties of clematis, many of them in the clematis walk, which leads to a wilder pond area, the domain of a charming family of call ducks. A friendly and very English garden.

Elton Hall 5

Elton, Ludlow, Shropshire SY8 2HQ. Tel: (01568) 770218; Fax: (01568) 770753

Mr and Mrs James Hepworth • 5m SW of Ludlow between B4361 and A4110. From Ludlow cross River Teme at Ludford Bridge and take first right signed to 'Wigmore' • Open for societies and groups by appt • Entrance: £2, children £1 • Other information: Plant fair – consult local press for details ● 🍵 ♿ 🌿 🍴

A must for those who appreciate a slightly eccentric touch to their gardens, and an opportunity to see a relatively young four-acre garden developing. Within the eccentricities (tortoise fort, Moorish sheep palace) lie a new kitchen garden and several herbaceous borders filled, amongst others, with National Collections of echinaceas and rudbeckias, offset by rich colourings of wine and purple-coloured foliage plants. A hermitage, brick-built gazebos, Doric columns and gracious urns, not to mention elephants and wigwams, add to the entertainment of it all.

Hampton Court 6

Hope under Dinmore, Leominster HR6 0PN. Tel: (01568) 797777

The Van Kampen Gardens at Hampton Court Estates (Herefordshire) Ltd • 5m S of Leominster, on A417 near junction with A49 between Leominster and Hereford • Open, daily, 24th March to 26th Oct, 11am – 5pm • Entrance: £4, OAPs £3.50, children £2, family ticket £10. Prices may vary on event days – telephone for details ● 🍵 ✕ WC ♿ 🚻 🍴

This magnificent garden has only been in creation since 1996. Surrounding a fifteenth-century Grade-I-listed building, already fully restored by the American owners, the grounds have been designed on a suitably grand scale by Simon Dorrell. The kitchen garden is currently being brought back into cultivation and will produce organic vegetables and fruit, grown in decorative *potager* style. The water garden is a large, geometrically laid out walled enclosure, with a pair of octagonal pavilions surrounded by canals and ornamental water steps; the lushly planted borders create an effective contrast to their crisp formality. An intricate yew maze, incorporating the owners' initials, surrounds a viewing tower, from which a dark subterranean tunnel leads to a thatched hermitage, beside a cascade and sunken pool. These contrasts – light and dark, high and low viewpoints, formal and wild planting schemes – all add to the sense of playfulness and enjoyment. A nineteenth-century wisteria arch leads to a formal, Dutch-inspired water garden, calm and tranquil. Large lawns surround the romantic, crenellated house, and a ha-ha allows an uninterrupted view of cattle grazing in the park beyond. The quality of workmanship from the gardeners, carpenters, stonemasons, bricklayers and blacksmith involved in this huge project is quite breath-taking. A splendiferous place, which deserves repeated visits to watch the grand scheme unfold.

Hergest Croft Gardens ★ 7

Kington HR5 3EG. Tel/Fax: (01544) 230160; E-mail: banks@hergest.kc3.co.uk; Website: www.hergest.co.uk

W.L. Banks • 14m W of Leominster, $\frac{1}{2}$ m W of Kington off A44 • Open April to Oct, daily, 1.30 – 6pm • Entrance: £4, children under 16 free, season ticket £15, parties of 20 or more £3.50 per person (2001 prices) ◑ ☕ 🍴 WC ♿ ⟨⊳ ⚘ 🏛 🔦 ⚲

This has been the family home of the Banks family since 1896, and the garden design was much influenced by the writings of William Robinson and Gertrude Jekyll. Miles Hadfield rated the tree and shrub collection very highly, and the autumn colour from maples and birches is a great feature. There is an excellent kitchen garden. Half a mile through the park is a delightful woodland containing vast sheets of rhododendrons nine metres high. By following the path at the top of the dingle you can look down on scenes not far removed from those of their native habitat. Wellington boots are usually necessary, not least in crossing the park in which many sheep safely graze. Fifty acres in all. A few miles to the north is *Bryan's Ground*, a much-visited garden which for several years has been included in the *Guide*. David Wheeler and Simon Dorrell plan to re-open the garden in 2003.

How Caple Court 8

How Caple, Ross-on-Wye, Hereford HR1 4SX. Tel: (01989) 740626; Fax: (01989) 740611; E-mail: how.caple@clara.co.uk; Website: www.how.caple.clara.co.uk

Mr and Mrs Roger Lee • 10m S of Hereford on B4224. Turn right at crossroads in How Caple • Open Easter to Oct, daily, 10am – 5pm, and for parties by appt • Entrance: £2.50, children under 16 free ○ ☕ 🍴 WC ⟨⊳ ⚘ 🏛

Sitting high above a valley through which the River Wye flows, the house and its 11-acre Edwardian gardens are set in parkland with a wooded backcloth. Formal terraces have yew hedges and contain statuary and pools, including a large one surrounded by a curious pergola. The Florentine garden and its water supply have been restored, and the owners are completing a spectacular set of water steps below. Much of the Edwardian planting has been re-established and the informal planting in the valley is beginning to mature. The stable yard has a small area set aside for the sale of plants such as unusual shrubs, old roses and dried flowers.

The Lance Hattatt Design Garden ★   9

Ledgemoor, Weobley HR4 8RN. Tel: (01544) 318468

Mr and Mrs L. Hattatt • 10m NW of Hereford between A4110 and A480, 1½ m E of Weobley • Open April to Sept, Wed – Sun, 2 – 5pm • Entrance: £3 • Other information: Unsuitable for children ◑ ▧ WC ⚘

The clever lay-out of this garden makes it seem much larger than its two-acre site. A series of well-defined areas, each named (Midas, for example, is planted with golden foliage plants), offers the visitor a kaleidoscope of contrasting shapes, colours and moods. A long, peaceful rill of water, punctuated by pots of agapanthus, terminates in a simple and elegant fountain. Elsewhere, old shrub roses flower in informal profusion. Luxor is the most recently planted area, where clipped yews, in maturity, will form large pyramids and tables, surrounded by curtain walls of pleached hornbeams.

Lower Hope   10

Ullingswick HR1 3JF. Tel: (01432) 820557; E-mail: cliverichards@crco.co.uk

Mr and Mrs Clive Richards • 7m NE of Hereford. At roundabout on A465 near Burley Gate take A417 towards Leominster. After 2m turn right, signed 'Pencombe and Lower Hope'; garden is about ½ m on left. Signposted • Open 7th April, 26th May, 7th July, 11th Aug, 6th Oct, 2 — 6pm, for charity • Entrance: £3, children £1 • Other information: Guide dogs only ● ▧ WC ⚘ ☕ ♿

This eight-acre garden is dazzlingly colourful and immaculately maintained. Bog gardens boast impressive gunneras and swathes of candelabra primulas. The swimming-pool garden, with its palm trees and air of quiet seclusion, feels positively Mediterranean. A laburnum walk is magnificent in early summer. The many large island beds are sheets of bright flowers and coloured foliage, and interesting sculptures are artfully placed within the grounds. A large and magnificent glasshouse has been added, where melons, palms, orchids and other exotic plants flourish. The fields surrounding this exuberant garden are grazed by pedigree Hereford cattle and Suffolk sheep.

Lower Hopton Farm   11

Stoke Lacy, Bromyard HR7 4HX. Tel: (01885) 490294

Mr and Mrs Giles Cross • 10m NE of Hereford off A465 Bromyard – Hereford road • Open for individuals and parties of 20 or more only, by personal introduction, to be confirmed in writing • Entrance: By donation – guideline individuals £10 per person, parties £6 per person (minimum £100) ● ▧

This five-acre garden, created from a field since 1992, is a testament to the skill and vision of Mrs Cross (the garden designer Veronica Adams), who tends it single-handedly. Rare plants abound. There are over a hundred named cultivars of snowdrops, unusual coloured roses – grey, green, buff – and splendid, towering cardiocrinums. The moated island holds rare shrubs and ferns, and unusual varieties of peony, hellebore and magnolia, among many other treasures. The prize in this collection is the ethereal, mauve-white giant bell-flower (*Ostrowskia magnifica*), flowering happily in a sunny border. These wonderful rarities are seamlessly woven into an imaginative design, with subtle colour schemes and light, humorous touches: two clipped yew giraffes are growing well, and a topiary fox peers out from a border. An elegant gazebo gives a view upstream to a series of small waterfalls, with climbing roses cascading from overhanging trees, and 'Paul's Himalayan Musk' towering over all. A new area, planted with white Judas trees, arching white wisteria and 'Débutante' roses leads to a small fountain. A tunnel of airy robinias heralds a garden of old shrub roses, and a lacquer-red Chinese bridge adds an exotic note, leading to an area of pink and lime-green plants – a refreshing colour combination. The cleverly created 'ruin' provides a sheltered spot for tender perennials. Despite heavy plant losses from the floods and frosts of spring 2001, this garden is a triumph of creativity and much hard work – a most rewarding and inspiring place to visit.

Monnington Court   12

Monnington-on-Wye HR4 7NL. Tel: (01981) 500698

John and Angela Bulmer • 9m W of Hereford, off A438. Turn left opposite Portway pub, follow lane to end • Open 6th to 8th July, and for groups by appt only • Entrance: £3.50 NEW ◐ ☕ WC ♿

The 20 acres around this historic house are full of surprises and delights: black swans swim on the large, man-made lake, peacocks show off their fine plumage and all around are many interesting sculptures, both abstract and figurative – Mrs Bulmer is the internationally acclaimed sculptor Angela Conner. Monnington Walk, a mile-long avenue of pine and yew trees, leads to the house. This is also the Foundation Farm of the Morgan horse in Britain, a beautiful, old-fashioned looking breed which originated in the United States. Not for the garden specialist, but a fascinating and enjoyable place to visit nonetheless.

The Picton Garden

(see Worcestershire)

Stockton Bury Gardens   13

Kimbolton, Leominster HR6 0HB. Tel: (01568) 613432

Mr G. Fenn and Mr R. Treasure • 1m N of Leominster. From A49, turn right onto A4112 Kimbolton road. Garden is 300 metres on right. Signposted • Open April to mid-Oct, Wed – Sun and Bank Holiday Mons, 12 noon – 5pm • Entrance: £3.50 • Other information: Garden unsuitable for children ◐ ☕ ✕ WC ♿ 🐾

This garden is the epitome of the true plantsman's garden. The expanding four-acre site is divided into different areas framed by brick and stone walls and yew hedges, all containing a wealth of unusual and rarely seen clematis, shrubs, climbers and herbaceous plants. Six years ago a delightful grotto, made in true Georgian spirit with seashells and mirrors, is now merging well with the dingle surrounding it. Beyond, a wild woodland garden has been created to greet the millennium. The plant sales area is not to be missed, with offspring of many of the rare plants seen in the garden for sale.

The Weir Garden   14

Swainshill, Hereford HR4 8BS. Tel: (01981) 590509 (Infoline)/(01684) 855372

The National Trust • 5m W of Hereford on A438 • Open 19th Jan to 10th Feb, Sat, Sun, 11am – 4pm; 13th Feb to 3rd Nov, Wed – Sun and Bank Holiday Mon, 11am – 6pm • Entrance: £3, children £1.50, family ticket £7.50 • Other information: No coaches ◐ ℀

Mass upon mass of naturalised daffodils and other bulbs, and a spectacular setting along the banks of the River Wye, make this a memorable experience in the spring. Informal terracing, a small rock garden and, later in the year, colonies of wild flowers, are the principal charms of this understated garden. It is pleasant to walk and relax in, to enjoy the proximity of the river and to delight in the far-reaching views of the Black Mountains. Some of the paths are steep, especially those with the most spectacular views across the river – sensible shoes are a good idea.

GUIDANCE ON SYMBOLS

Wheelchair users: The symbol ♿, denoting suitability for wheelchairs, refers to the garden only – if there is a house open, it may or may not be suitable. Additionally, some areas in the garden may not be accessible by wheelchair, or may require assistance.

Dogs: ☜ indicates that there is somewhere on the premises where dogs may be walked, preferably on a lead. The garden itself is often taboo – parkland, or even the car park, are frequently indicated for the purpose.

Picnics: ⬛ means that picnics are allowed, but usually in certain restricted areas only. It does not give visitors the all-clear to feast where they please!

Children-friendly: the symbol ℀ suggests that there are activities specifically designed for children, such as an adventure playground, or that the garden itself is a place they would instinctively enjoy.

HERTFORDSHIRE

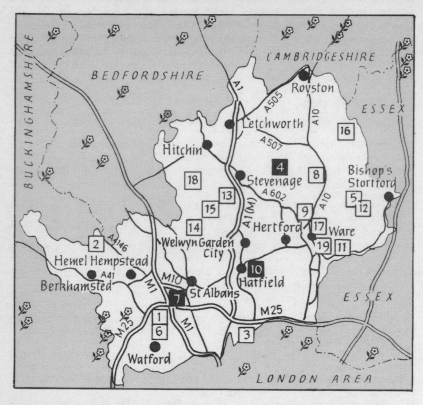

Two-starred gardens are marked on the map with a black square.

The Abbot's House 1

10 High Street, Abbots Langley WD5 0AR. Tel: (01923) 264946

Peter and Sue Tomson • 5m N of Watford, in Abbots Langley. Approach via M25 junction 19 (from W) and 21A (from E) or M1 junction 6 • Garden open 5th May, 16th June, 2 – 5pm; 12th June, 6 – 8.30pm. Groups welcome by appt • Entrance: £2, children free • Other information: Plants for sale in nursery
● ☕ WC ♿ ⚘ ❀

One and three quarter acres of plantsman's garden full of delights: *Mahonia gracilipes, Itea ilicifolia, Hoheria sexstylosa* 'Stardust' and *Halesia carolina*, and many outstanding shrub and tree specimens, some of which must be tender. The sunken garden has plants thriving between the brickwork. There is also a Mediterranean semi-formal garden, a shrub border with contrasting foliage, borders of differing colour schemes, an annual and wildflower meadow and a conservatory.

Ashridge Management College 2

Berkhamsted HP4 1NS. Tel: (01442) 843491

Ashridge (Bonar Law Memorial) Trust • 3½ m N of Berkhamsted (A41), 1m S of Little Gaddesden off A4146 • Open 29th March to Sept, Sat, Sun and Bank Holiday Mons, 2 – 6pm • Entrance: £2, OAPs and children £1 ● WC & ⬠

A total of 150 acres comprising 90 acres of garden with the rest woodland. The nineteenth-century design was influenced by Humphry Repton, whose Red Book for the garden was presented to the 7th Earl of Bridgewater in 1813. Following the death of Repton the gardens were laid out by Sir Jeffry Wyatville, retaining many of Repton's suggested small gardens. An orangery with an Italian garden and fountain leads round to the south terrace, which is dominated by clipped yews approximately 100 years old, and spring and summer bedding. The main lawn in front of the terrace links many small gardens and has within it a group of ancient yews and a large oak planted by Princess (later Queen) Victoria. The circular Rosarie is sited virtually where Repton intended. The Monk's Garden and Holy Well comprises box laid out to represent an armorial garden depicting the four families closely associated with the property. The conservatory dates from 1864 and was used as a fernery. The grotto is constructed of Hertfordshire pudding-stone, and the *souterrain* leading from it of flints hung on an iron framework. This follows the original boundary between Hertfordshire and Buckinghamshire. Crossing the main lawn brings visitors to a sunken garden formerly used as a skating pond. Beyond a disused moat is an avenue of Wellingtonias planted in 1858 and underplanted with rhododendrons, leading to the arboretum with many specimen trees and a Bible garden featuring a circle of incense cedars.

The Beale Arboretum 3

West Lodge Park, Cockfosters Road, Hadley Wood EN4 0PY.
Tel: (020) 8216 3900; E-mail: headoffice_beales@compuserve.com;
Website: www.bealeshotels.co.uk

The Beale family • Leave M25 at junction 24 and take road S towards Cockfosters (A111). West Lodge Park is 1m further on left • Open April to Oct, Wed, 2 – 5pm; also 19th May, 2 – 5pm, and 20th Oct, 12 noon – 4pm, for NGS. Organised parties of 10 or more, including tour and luncheon or tea, by appt all year • Entrance: £2, children free • Other information: Possible for wheelchairs but undulating gravel paths ● ⬚ ✗ WC &

The late Edward Beale bought West Lodge Park Hotel in 1945 with the intention of enriching its fine eighteenth-century park with many more trees and creating the important arboretum which it has now become. Today, there are 10 acres of arboretum with some fine rare trees. These, together with the three acres of more formal garden, the lake, the many azaleas and rhododendrons, and the impressive four-star hotel, make a visit to this little-known gem, only 12 miles from central London, memorable. Certainly if he were to visit the property today, as he did in 1675, the diarist John Evelyn would still be able to say that it was 'a very pretty place – the garden handsome', although he would probably fail to recognise the strawberry tree which was believed to be there at the time of his visit and which has become one of the largest in England.

Benington Lordship ★★ 4

Benington, Stevenage SG2 7BS. Tel: (01438) 869668; Fax: (01438) 869622; E-mail: rhbott@beningtonlordship.co.uk; Website: www.beningtonlordship.co.uk

Mr and Mrs C.H.A. Bott • 5m E of Stevenage • Open Feb/March for snowdrops (telephone end of Jan for recorded message on opening dates); April to Sept, Wed and Bank Holiday Mons, 12 noon – 5pm; also April to Aug, Sun, 2 – 5pm. Check opening times before making journey • Entrance: £3, children free ● ♨ 🍴 WC ⚘ ☕

Surrounding the manor house, Norman gatehouse and Victorian folly is a romantic hill-top garden of timeless charm, with wonderful views over the lake and open countryside. The massive herbaceous double borders are filled with a glorious mixture of foliage and colour, backed on one side by the kitchen garden wall and a sloping bank planted with a wonderful informal mixture of foliage and flowering plants. The kitchen garden is ornamental as well as functional, with borders of gold and silver and another filled with penstemons. A great deal of grass is not cut until July, allowing the snowdrops, scillas, garlics and cowslips to seed.

Bromley Hall 5

Standon, Ware SG11 1NY. Tel: (01279) 842422

Mr and Mrs A.J. Robarts • 6m W of Bishop's Stortford near A120 and A10 on Standon – Much Hadham road • Open 2nd, 23rd June, 2 – 5.30pm, for charity, and for groups by appt • Entrance: £3, children free ● ♨ WC ⚘

Mrs Robarts has created this four-acre garden entirely herself over the past 30 years, and improvements and alterations are going on all the time. It is both an architectural garden, making good use of walls and hedges, statuary and seats, and a plantsman's garden. Mr Robarts looks after the vegetable garden, and it is immaculate. The wide border on the edge of the drive, backed by a tall hedge, is a well-designed mixture of shrub and foliage planting with unusual and elegant perennials.

Cheslyn House 6

54 Nascot Wood Road, Watford WD1 3SL. Tel: (01923) 235946 (Watford Council)

Managed by Watford Council • In north Watford off A411 Hemel Hempstead road or Langley Road, near M25 junction 19 • Open daily except 25th, 26th Dec, 1st Jan, dawn – dusk. Pre-booked tours with resident gardener available for parties • Entrance: free ○ 🍴 WC ⚘ ☞

This three-and-a-half-acre garden has woodland, lawns, a bog garden and pond, herbaceous borders, a rock garden and an aviary, all bequeathed in 1965 by Mr and Mrs Colbeck, well-travelled collectors who chose and planted the fine trees. Among these are *Sequoiadendron giganteum, Catalpa bignonioides*, a particularly good *Diospyros kaki* and a large *Eucryphia* x *nymansensis* 'Nymansay', spectacular in late-summer bloom. The woodland, a haven for wildlife, is well planted with mature rhododendrons, azaleas, camellias and pieris, and there are drifts of spring and autumn bulbs amongst the trees. A renovation programme is presently underway to include structural features and plantings. The herbaceous borders have been redesigned and replanted and feature a collection of hemerocallis.

Gardens of the Rose ★★   7

Chiswell Green, St Albans AL2 3NR. Tel: (01727) 850461; Fax: (01727) 850360; E-mail: mail@rnrs.org.uk; Website: www.roses.co.uk

Royal National Rose Society • 2m S of St Albans on B4630. Signposted • Open June to Sept: Mon – Sat, 9am – 5pm, Sun and Bank Holiday Mon, 10am – 6pm • Entrance: £4, disabled £3.50, children (6–16) £1.50, parties £3.50 per person ◑ 🍷 ✕ 🍽 WC ♿ ⏦ 🌿 ⚜ 🍵 ⚘

The Royal National Rose Society's gardens provide a splendid display of one of the best and most important collections of roses in the world. There are some 30,000 rose trees and at least 1700 varieties, including Hybrid Teas, Floribundas and climbing roses of every kind, miniature roses and ground-cover roses. Some are thought to differ little from those admired by writers in classical times. (Note: Hybrid Teas and Floribundas are now known as large-flowered and cluster-flowered roses respectively.) Part of the gardens is the trial grounds for roses from all over the world, and the British Clematis Society assesses new clematis here as well. The Society has introduced many other plants which harmonise with roses to give a more natural effect, including clematis and hardy geraniums. H.M. The Queen Mother is particularly fond of old roses and the garden named for her contains a fascinating collection of Gallicas, Albas, Damasks, Centifolias, Portland and Moss roses. Here can be seen what is thought to be the original red rose of Lancaster and white rose of York. Among the Gallicas is the *Rosa mundi* said to have been named for Fair Rosamund, the mistress of Henry II. Plans have been approved for the extension of the garden to some 65 acres, which will be planted for all seasons and will be open for most of the year.

Great Munden House   8

Dane End, Ware SG11 1HU. Tel: (01920) 438244

Mr and Mrs D. Wentworth-Stanley • 7m N of Ware off A10. Turn off W of Puckeridge bypass • Open for small parties by appt only, with refreshments • Entrance: £3 for NGS ◑ 🍷 WC 🌿

The charming three-and-a-half-acre garden, beautifully planned, immaculately kept and containing a great variety of plants, is situated down the side of a valley with a backdrop of wheat fields and trees. Beech hedges act as necessary windbreaks, as the wind funnels down the valley. The mixed borders are imaginatively planted with shrubs, shrub roses and excellent foliage plants. A paved pond area is surrounded by silver plants, with a *Juniperus virginiana* 'Skyrocket' in each corner. Many climbing roses ramble through old apple trees, and there is an additional pond area with shade-loving plants and hostas, as well as a well-planned kitchen garden and herb garden.

Hanbury Manor Hotel 9

Ware SG12 0SD. Tel: (01920) 487722; Fax: (01920) 487692

Hanbury Manor Hotel • *2m N of Ware on A10* • *Garden open all year* • *Entrance: free (charge on charity days)* • *Other information: Refreshments, toilet facilities and shop in hotel* ○ & ◁▷

Edmund Hanbury inherited the property in 1884. He replaced the old house with a Jacobean-style mansion designed by Sir Ernest George. The Hanbury family were gifted horticulturists and the original gardens, now part of the hotel complex, were widely acclaimed both for their species trees and orchid houses. Today, a colourful pre-Victorian walled garden with a listed moon gate has extensive herbaceous borders, herb garden and fruit houses. The original pinetum with its centuries-old sequoias still stands, and major restoration work has seen the revival of the period rose gardens and bulb-planted orchard. A more recent secret garden in a woodland setting is well worth a visit.

Hatfield House, Park and Gardens ★★ 10

Hatfield AL9 5NQ. Tel: (01707) 287010; Fax: (01707) 287033;
E-mail: curator@hatfield-house.demon.co.uk;
Website: www.hatfield-house.co.uk

The Marquess of Salisbury • *2m from A1(M) junction 4 off A414 and A1000, opposite Hatfield railway station* • *Open 30th April to Sept. House: daily 12 noon – 4pm (guided tours weekdays only). Park, West Gardens, restaurant and shops: daily 11am – 5.30pm. East Gardens also open Fri (Connoisseurs' Day)* • *Entrance: Park and gardens £4.50, children £3.50. Park only £2, children £1 (house, park and gardens £7, children £3.50; Connoisseurs' Day house, park and gardens £10.50, park and gardens £6.50)* • *Other information: Dogs in park only* ◑ ◖ ✕ ▣ WC & ♨ ♨ ♨ ⚲

Laid out originally in the early seventeenth century by Robert Cecil and planted by John Tradescant the Elder, the garden underwent various changes in the following centuries, particularly in the Victorian era, but during the past three decades it has enjoyed a splendid transformation at the hands of the Marchioness of Salisbury. She began the work of restoration with an imaginative and bold stroke – a new garden as the setting for the Old Palace. From there she went from strength to strength. Not all her re-created gardens are open (the maze, for example, is a protected space) but all, including the splendid East Gardens, can be viewed on Fridays (Connoisseurs' Day). Lady Salisbury is well known for her creative work on other private gardens such as Castletown and Highgrove, but here at Hatfield are many splendours, such as the recently completed south-front inner courtyard. The plantings are her particular skill – see the mop-headed *Quercus ilex* imported especially for the garden, and the wild garden around the New Pond (formed in 1607), landscaped and planted since the devastation by two hurricanes. Amongst the many features are the varied knot gardens and a charming herb garden in the scented garden, all planted by Lady Salisbury in the early 1980s following her own designs, and sited, like those in Tudor times, to be viewed from above, filled with plants used from the fifteenth to seventeenth centuries. There is an annual midsummer festival, part-country fair, part-garden party and part-flower show, which gives an opportunity to visit all the gardens. Those interested in so-called wild gardens should spend time in the Wilderness and note that its splendours have not been achieved by throwing flower seeds about but by planting up to 20,000 bulbs a year. The whole 42 acres is gardened organically.

Hill House ★   11

63 Cappell Lane, Stanstead Abbots, Ware SG12 8BX. Tel: (01920) 870013

Mr and Mrs R. Pilkington • Between Hertford and Harlow. From A10 turn E onto A414, and at roundabout take B181 for Stanstead Abbots. At end of High Street turn left and first right past church • Open 2nd, 9th June, 2 – 5.30pm, and at other times by appt • Entrance: £2.50, children 50p ● ▣ WC ☺ ℗

Set on a south-facing slope with a magnificent view overlooking the Lee valley, here are nine acres of very varied garden including woodland, a controlled wild garden, a bog garden, a fine herbaceous border and a highly recommended Victorian conservatory. The beds are immaculate, the lawns and walls extensive, and the range of plants impressive.

Hopleys ★   12

Much Hadham SG10 6BU. Tel: (01279) 842509; Fax (01279) 843784

Mr A. Barker • 5m SW of Bishop's Stortford off B1004. 50 metres N of Bull pub in Much Hadham • Open March to Dec, Mon, Wed – Sat, 9am – 5pm, Sun, 2 – 5pm, and also on special days for charities • Entrance: £1.50, children under 16 free • Other information: Teas available May to Oct, Sun only, otherwise self-service refreshments ☺ ▤ WC ⅋ ℗

The owner and his parents have been working on this four-acre plantsman's garden for many years, and it has been expanding annually. The pool and bog area are now well established, there are numerous borders filled with shrubs and hardy plants, most of which are for sale in the nursery, and the conifer bed is a graphic illustration of the different sizes and shapes of mature specimens. Much Hadham has two other properties of interest to gardeners. In Bourne Lane (Tel: (01279) 842685) is the headquarters of *Andrew Crace*, who designs and sells a wide range of fine garden furniture and bronze and stone ornaments; and *Dane Tree House* is the home of the *Henry Moore Foundation*. Moore lived here for 40 years and his collection, studios and workshops remain very much as they were in his lifetime, in a parkland with many native trees and particularly fine ancient hedgerows. Larger works are placed in the surrounding fields with sheep grazing round them – as he intended them to. [Open April to Sept, Tues – Thurs, mornings only by appointment or 2.30pm for tour. Tel: (01279) 843333.]

Knebworth House ★   13

Knebworth, Nr Stevenage SG3 6PY. Tel: (01438) 812661

The Hon. Henry Lytton Cobbold • 2m S of Stevenage off B656. Access from A1(M) junction 7 • House open as garden, 12 noon to 5pm • Garden open 23rd March to 7th April, 1st to 9th June, 6th July to 3rd Sept, daily; 13th April to 26th May, 15th to 30th June, 7th to 29th Sept, Sat, Sun and Bank Holiday Mons only; all 11am – 5.30pm. • Entrance: £5.50, family (4 persons) £19 (house and gardens £7, OAPs and children £6.50) (2001 prices) • Other information: Guided tours available. Dogs in park only, on lead ◑ 🍵 ✕ 🖼 WC ⬦ 🌳 ⛪ 🎖 ℺

As the historic home of the Lytton family, the garden evolved from a simple Tudor green and orchard to Sir Edward Bulwer Lytton's elaborate Victorian design of the mid-1800s. Edwin Lutyens redesigned the garden at the beginning of the twentieth century with twin avenues of pollarded lime trees leading to the rose garden, lily ponds and herbaceous borders with tall yew hedges behind. Beyond lie the Green Garden, the Gold Garden, the Brick Garden with a blue and silver theme, and a pergola. To one side is a pets' cemetery, to the other a malus (crab apple) walk. Other features are the maze (replanted in 1995), the ponds, and the Gertrude Jekyll herb garden, designed in 1907 but not laid out until 1982. The Wilderness with its woodland walk is a carpet of daffodils in spring followed by blue alkanet, foxgloves and other wild flowers. The redeveloped walled garden has a collection of culinary herbs and vegetables. In all there are 25 acres of garden to explore. A few miles north at Hitchin are the rose gardens of *R. Harkness & Co Ltd* [open all year, Mon – Sat, 10am – 5.30pm, Sun and Bank Holiday Mons, 10am – 4.30pm].

Mackerye End House   14

Harpenden AL5 5DR.

Mr and Mrs David Laing • 3m NE of Harpenden. From A1 junction 4 follow signs for Wheathampstead. Then follow B653 past Wheathampstead, turn right by Indian restaurant • Open 23rd June, 11am – 5pm • Entrance: £3, concessions £1.50, children £1 (entry includes access to three other gardens open in hamlet of Mackerye End) ◔ 🍵 ✕ WC ♿ 🌳 ℺

The Grade-I-listed manor house (1550) is set in 11 acres of park and garden. Its Victorian walled garden, filled with wonderful peonies of all shades, is now divided by magnificent yew hedges. There is a path maze, a cutting garden, a new garden enclosed by a pergola walk of old English roses and vines, a paved walk around the house with camellias and magnolias, and a patio with a large ginkgo tree. The rough grass in front of the house has a mass of wild daffodils and a vast tulip tree planted in the seventeenth century.

The Manor House   15
Ayot St Lawrence, Welwyn AL6 9BR. Tel: (01438 820943)

*Mrs A. Duncan • 6m NW of Welwyn Garden City, between B653 and B651.
Bear right into village from Bride Hall Lane, past Brocket Arms on right. A pair
of brick gates on bend leads to drive • Open by appt only • Entrance: charge*
NEW ☕ WC &

This is a new garden made by the present owner. The house was empty for six
years and the garden derelict; now it is immaculately kept. A lovely walled
garden with massed *Geranium* 'Johnson's Blue', espaliered fruit trees and an *Acer
palmatum*. A huge dark-flowered *Magnolia* x *soulangeana* and many other delights. A most exciting garden.

Pelham House   16
Brent Pelham, Buntingford SG9 0HH. Tel: (01279) 777473

*David Haselgrove • 7m NW of Bishop's Stortford, east of Brent Pelham on B1038
Buntingford – Newport Road • Open 31st March, 21st April, 12th May, 12 noon
– 5pm, and by appt at other times • Entrance: £2.50* NEW ● ☕ WC ℘

The garden is the creation of the present owner, plantsman, avid plant hunter
and keen member of the Alpine Society. He has won his battle with an
extremely unprepossessing site – a cold and windswept clay field – and
achieved a most interesting and ambitious garden. Raised beds are a feature,
and among the noteworthy plants are hellebores, erythroniums, trilliums, a
host of lovely orchids, euphorbias, *Daphne cneorum*, *Cornus kousa*, excellent
magnolias and a collection of betula species. Where the land has been drained,
masses of bee orchids have sprung to life.

Scotts Grotto   17
Scotts Road, Ware SG12 9JQ. Tel: (01920) 464131;
Website: www.scotts-grotto.org

*East Hertfordshire District Council • In Ware, off A119 Hertford road • Open
April to Sept, Sat and Bank Holiday Mons only, 2 – 4.30pm. Party visits by
prior arrangement • Entrance: £1 donation suggested* ● ℘

This eighteenth-century folly, restored by the Ware Society and described by
English Heritage as 'one of the finest in the country', is decorated with exotic
shells and lined with flints. It is truly grotto-esque, with a council chamber,
committee room, consultation room and several passages. Take a torch!

St Paul's Walden Bury ★   18
Whitwell, Hitchin SG4 8BP. Tel: (01438) 871218

*Mr and Mrs Simon Bowes Lyon • 5m S of Hitchin, $\frac{1}{2}$ m N of Whitwell on
B651 • Open probably four Suns in April, May or June, 2 – 7pm, and to
groups at other times by appt • Entrance: £2.50, children 50p, groups £5 per
person* ● ☕ WC & ⬧

The formal landscape garden has retained intact its original design of 1730, one of the few to survive. It covers an area of 40 acres. The long mown rides or *allées* are lined with clipped beech hedges and fan out from the eighteenth-century house – the heart of the layout – through *bosquets* to temples, statues, ponds and a medieval church. In one of the *bosquets* is an elegant green theatre. The Bowes Lyon family have lived at St Paul's for more than 250 years, and it was here that H.M. Queen Elizabeth the Queen Mother spent her childhood. Interesting plants are grouped in small gardens of differing character, woodland is underplanted with shrubs, and spring bulbs abound. The lake, with its temple and wonderful vistas, is well worth walking to.

Van Hage's Nursery ★   19

Great Amwell, Ware SG12 9RP. Tel: (01920) 870811;
Website: www.vanhage.co.uk

Van Hage's Nursery • At M25 junction 25, take A10 towards Cambridge, A1170 towards Ware. On outskirts of Ware • Open daily except 31st March, 25th, 26th Dec: Mon – Sat, 9am – 6pm (opens 9.30am on Mon); Sun, 10.30am – 4.30pm • Entrance: free ○ ☕ ✗ WC & ⌂ ⛪ ♟ ℁

A superbly run nursery with top-class plants. Exotica such as topiary elephants and bonsai trees, imaginative tubs with catmint and lilies, and excellent indoor plants including wonderful orchids. With its wide range of garden furniture and accessories, this is a Harrods of the gardening world.

GARDENING FOR THE DISABLED
- The Gardening for the Disabled Trust (Charity No. 255066) collects donations to assist people with improvements to their gardens, or to supply equipment which will enable them to continue to garden. Information from Mrs Angela Parish, Frittenden House, Nr Cranbrook TN17 2DG; Fax (01580) 852120; E-mail: apparish@hotmail.com.
- Thrive is a national charity promoting the use of garden and horticulture as a therapy for restricted or disabled gardeners (Tel: (0118) 988 5688; Website: www.carryongardening.org.uk).
- For details of The Disabled and Older Gardeners' Association, write to Growing Point, Herefordshire College of Agriculture, Holme Lacy, Hereford (Tel: (01432) 870316). For details of workshops etc. telephone Susan van Laun (Tel: (01531) 636226).
- Demonstration gardens to assist the disabled are on view at a number of properties open to the public and are also featured in the *Guide*. They include: Battersea Park (for an appt with the Horticultural Therapy Unit telephone (020) 7720 2212), Broadview Garden and Capel Manor.
- Open days for the disabled are also held from time to time at other gardens described in the *Guide*, including Dolly's Garden and Hillsborough Walled Garden.

KENT

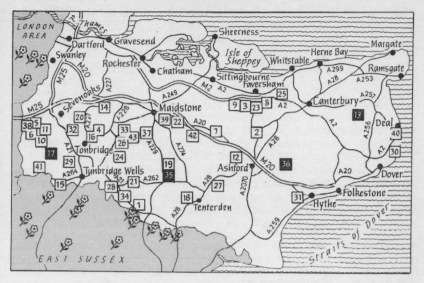

We have included some gardens with Kent postal addresses in the London section for convenience. So before planning a day out in Kent it is worthwhile consulting pages 250–288.

Two-starred gardens are marked on the map with a black square.

Bedgebury National Pinetum and Forest Gardens ★   1

Goudhurst, Cranbrook TN17 2SL. Tel: (01580) 211781 (Shop)

Forestry Commission ● 10m SE of Tunbridge Wells off A21, on B2079 Goudhurst – Flimwell road ● Arboretum open all year, daily, 10am – 5pm (gates close 7pm), (4pm in winter) ● Entrance: £2.50, OAPs £2, children £1.20, family (2 adults and 2 children) £7. Exact money sometimes required ○ 🍵 ✕ 🧺 WC 🐕 🎑 🛍 🔦

The modern pinetum was founded in 1921, but some of the larger specimen trees dating from 1850 are still flourishing. Its conifer collection has been listed as the best in the world by the International Dendrological Research Institute based in America and Hungary. As well as conifers, it has many deciduous trees, including rare oaks and maples, and a wide range of rhododendrons flowers from January to August. The Japanese garden contains trees from wild-collected seed, and an American garden is proposed with less common trees and shrubs from the southern states of North America. The pinetum has five National Collections: Lawson cypresses, Leyland cypresses, junipers, yews and red cedars.

Beech Court 2

Challock, Ashford TN25 4DJ. Tel: (01233) 740735; Fax: (01233) 740842

Mr and Mrs Vyvyan Harmsworth • 5m N of Ashford, W of A251/A252 crossroads, off The Lees • Open 30th March to 3rd Nov, Tues – Fri, 10am – 5pm, Sat, Sun and Bank Holiday Mons, 12 noon – 6pm. At other times by appt • Entrance: £3.50, OAPs £3, children £1, parties of 12 or more £2.50 per person ◑ 🍴 🧺 WC ♿ 🐾 ⚜ 🌢 ⚘

One hundred and fifty metres above sea level in a pocket of acidic clay on the edge of the North Downs, this 10-acre woodland garden was designed with Inverewe (see entry in Scotland) in mind and has many acres of rhododendrons, azaleas, hydrangeas and viburnums. Spring colour from the rhododendrons, azaleas and acers is augmented by bulbs. Summer interest is provided by roses, philadelphus and hydrangeas, and the many specimen trees give good autumn colour. Mature acers and various oaks, a rose walk, buddleia avenue and viburnum avenue encourage a natural feeling of tranquillity in this garden of meandering paths and surprising vistas. A small sunken pond has well-planted margins and is set in a lawn edged with herbaceous plants.

Belmont ★ 3

Belmont Park, Throwley, Faversham ME13 0HH. Tel: (01795) 890202; E-mail: belmontadmin@cwcom.net

Harris (Belmont) Charity • 4m SW of Faversham, 1½ m W of A251 Faversham – Ashford road. From A2 or M2 junction 6, take A251 S towards Ashford. Signed at Badlesmere • House open • Garden open April to Sept, Sat, Sun and Bank Holiday Mons, 2 – 5pm • Entrance: £2.75, children £1 (house, clock museum and gardens £5.25, children £2.50) ◑ 🍴 🧺 WC ♿ 🗣 🐾 ⚜

The eighteenth-century house by Samuel Wyatt has been the seat of the Harris family since 1801 and, though somewhat off the beaten track down winding lanes, it is well worth a visit. It was built at a time when beautiful country-house architecture was required to blend in with equally beautiful and well-planned surroundings, exemplified here by 40 acres of formal and informal gardens blending with the 150 acres of parkland to give marvellous vistas of aged and noble trees. There is also a yew walk and a pinetum. The walled garden includes borders, a pool, a rockery; note also the shell grotto and folly. In 2001 the two-acre kitchen garden was restored and replanted, and in 2002 the surrounding area is being transformed with grasses, wild flowers and nut trees; it will contain a formal garden based on a Hindu design, thus perpetuating the Harris family's long connection with India.

Broadview Gardens 4

Hadlow, Tonbridge TN11 0AL. Tel: (01732) 850551; Fax: (01732) 853207

Hadlow College • 8m SW of Maidstone, 3m NE of Tonbridge, on A26 • Open 1st April to 1st Nov, Mon – Sun, 10am – 5pm • Entrance: £2 ◑ 🍴 WC 🐾 ⚜ 🌢 ⚘

This series of gardens in the grounds of Hadlow College was opened to the public in early 1997. Within an area of 40 acres are many new design and planting ideas. The visitor enters an area of sub-tropical plants with four different varieties of musa, canna lilies, stooled paulownia and golden catalpa. A 100-metre-long herbaceous border is bordered by an avenue of fastigiate oaks. There is an experimental garden with a modern steel wave sculpture and a low-maintenance gravel garden. The cottage garden has a wall of golden hop contrasting with the very dwarf trained fruit trees. In the sensory garden a water rill at waist height falls over cobbles and raised beds. The contrast between the Heaven and Hell gardens is achieved by planting the former with scented herbs and subtly varied foliage colour, while in the latter the hot colours of flowers and foliage convey an oppressive atmosphere, heightened by a black 'river' of *Ophiopogon planiscapus* 'Nigrescens' (lily turf). The seating alcoves in Hell are unusual, being lopsided and enclosed in intertwined willow stems. A half-acre Japanese garden has all the oriental elements and appropriate planting. There is a one-acre lake edged with bog plants and an area vibrant with colour in the autumn. The garden also contains National Collections of hellebores and Japanese anemones.

Chart's Edge 5

Westerham TN16 1PL.

Mr and Mrs Bigwood • S of M25 and A25, ½ m S of Westerham on B2026 towards Chartwell • Open 5th, 19th May, 7th July, 2 – 5pm • Entrance: £2, children free ◐ ☕ WC ⬦ ▨

The removal of some mature trees during storms over the last 10 years has opened up areas of this seven-acre garden to provide sweeping lawns, space for some interesting trees and the reclamation of some of the original Victorian features. Whilst a large part of the planting, especially many trees and rhododendrons, dates from the '60s, there are unusual later plantings. Recent additions include a *Paulownia tomentosa*, a cut-leaf beech and a weeping form of *Morus alba*. A 30-metre-long raised herbaceous border containing a wide selection of plants leads down to the atmospheric dell garden with acers, ferns, hostas and other bog plants. An interesting feature here, built into the hillside, is a Victorian grotto lined with flint; adjoining is a brick-lined room with steps leading down to what was probably a bath with a lead pipe. Around the house are borders with roses, a large well-planted rockery, a terrace with views over the North Downs framed by two *Acer palmatum* var. *dissectum*, and an old mulberry.

Chartwell 6

Westerham TN16 1PS. Tel: (01732) 866368 (Infoline); Fax: (01732) 868193

The National Trust • S of M25 between junctions 5 and 6, 2m S of Westerham off B2026 • House open • Garden open 23rd March to 3rd Nov, Wed – Sun and Bank Holiday Mons; also Tues in July and Aug; all 11am – 5pm (last admission 4.15pm) • Entrance: house and garden £5.60, children £2.80, family £14 ◑ ☕ ✕ WC ㉓ ⬦ 🏭 ⚲ ✑

Within this garden on a hill, with vast views over the Weald of Kent, the first feature to greet the visitor is a melodious waterfall. This enters the fish pool above the swimming pool (the latter constructed by Sir Winston Churchill). Well-established trees along a path lead the way to a walled rose garden, its perimeter planted with herbaceous plants such as hostas, peonies and penstemons. A cloud of shrub roses perfumes the terrace, and ceanothus, white potentillas and dark red double Rugosa roses invite the visitor on towards the house, one wing of which is covered by a huge *Hydrangea petiolaris*. The south wall has a large *Magnolia grandiflora*. A vine-covered pergola leads to a gazebo and viewpoint. A series of smaller terraces, one planted with silver-foliage plants, and a Golden Rose walk bordered by clipped beech hedges. Maintenance and labelling are excellent, but remember that Churchill bought Chartwell for 'that view'.

Church Hill Cottage Gardens ★ 7

Charing Heath, Ashford TN27 0BU. Tel/Fax: (01233) 712522

Mr and Mrs M. Metianu • From M20 junction 8 (from Maidstone) or junction 9 (from Folkestone) join A20; ½ m W of Charing, turn S from A20 dual-carriageway section to Charing Heath and Egerton. Fork right after 1m at Red Lion pub, take next right and gardens are 250 metres on right • Garden open 21st March to Sept, daily except Mon (but open Bank Holiday Mons), 10am – 5pm. Coaches by appt • Entrance: £2, children free • Other information: Nursery open Feb to Oct ◑ 🍴 WC & ♨ ℺

In these tranquil one and a half acres surrounding a sixteenth-century cottage there is a strong sense of design in the curves of borders and island beds, but they are so well matched by the fine and well-developed planting that the whole seems natural. Established birches form a central point. Beds are varied, some with colour themes, others with shrubs underplanted with a wide range of unusual hardy plants and bulbs in season. Of particular interest to the plantsman are the large collections of dianthus and violas, which include between 30 and 40 types of old forms dating from the sixteenth to the eighteenth century. The woodland area has enlarged by the addition of two fine fern and hosta beds.

Copton Ash Gardens 8

105 Ashford Road, Faversham ME13 8XW. Tel: (01795) 535919

Drs Tim and Gillian Ingram • 1m S of Faversham. Just N of M2 junction 6 on A251 Faversham – Ashford road • Garden open several days for NGS and by appt. Nursery open March to Oct, Tues – Sun, 2 – 6pm, and by appt, but check before travelling • Entrance: £1.50, accompanied children free ◑ 🍴 & ♨

Despite its position close to the M2 there is a pleasant atmosphere at Copton Ash. This a plantsman's garden created since 1978 on the site of an old cherry orchard. About one and a half acres in extent, it accommodates some 3000 species in herbaceous borders and island beds with specimen plantings. There is a collection of fruit varieties, alpines are grown in raised beds, and experiments are underway to examine the hardiness of species from Australia, New Zealand and South America. Helpfully, many plants and shrubs and the fruit varieties are labelled. From the garden, Tim Ingram has developed a specialist nursery with an emphasis on plants for dry situations, including cistus and umbellifers. Belmont and Longacre (see entries) are nearby. So is *Brogdale Horticultural Trust*, which holds the National Collection of fruit – over 4000 varieties.

Doddington Place Gardens 9

Doddington, Sittingbourne ME9 0BB. Tel: (01795) 886101

Mr R. Oldfield • 6m S of Sittingbourne. From A20 turn N at Lenham, from A2 turn S at Teynham. Signposted • Open Easter day to September, Tues, Wed, Thurs and Bank Holidays, 10.30am – 5pm, Sun, 2 – 6pm, and other days for parties by appt • Entrance: £3.50, children over 5 75p, groups £3 per person • Other information: Picnics in park only ◑ ☕ ✕ WC ⅖ ⬷ 🌳 🏛 🍴

Ten acres of landscaped grounds in part designed by Markham Nesfield in the nineteenth century and further developed in the 1910s, 1960s, 1990s and 2001. The main attractions here are the views of open countryside and the spaciousness which offers pleasant walks. Other features are a rather fine Edwardian rock garden, excellent yew hedging (some cut to resemble undulating mountain scenery), a new *allée* and, in season, the woodland garden's collection of rhododendrons and azaleas. The two-storey Gothic folly was built in 1997.

Edenbridge House 10

Main Road, Edenbridge TN8 6SJ. Tel: (01732) 862122; Fax: (01732) 867385

Mrs M.T. Lloyd • 1½ m N of Edenbridge on B2026 • Open April to Sept, Tues and Thurs, 2 – 5pm; 14th April, 5th May, 2 – 6pm, 15th May, 1 – 5pm, 9th June, 2 – 6pm, 12th June 6 – 9pm, 7th July 2 – 6pm, 18th Sept, 1 – 5pm, 22nd Sept, 2 – 6pm, all for NGS; and by appt for parties • Entrance: £2.50 (2001 price) • Other information: Refreshments on charity open days only ◑ 🍴 WC ⅖ ⬷ 🌳 ↺

This five-acre garden, originally made in the 1920s, is set on a south-facing slope. The part-sixteenth-century house is surrounded on three sides by a wide terrace on which a large variety of tender plants – datura, *Punica granatum*, *Streptosolen jamesonii* and *Cestrum elegans* – flourishes in pots. A walled courtyard to one side of the house contains a parterre filled with scented herbs and violas. *Itea ilicifolia*, *Clerodendrum bungei*, wisteria, jasmine and a *Magnolia grandiflora*, together with roses, drape the walls. Garden rooms are linked to the house by a lawn containing a fountain pool guarded by elegant drum-shaped golden yews. A small stream, crossed by two wisteria-clad bridges, meanders down to a small lower pool. The banks of the stream are edged with rocks and planted with moisture-loving plants. There is a large kitchen garden, a soft-fruit cage and an apple and cherry orchard. Part of the kitchen garden has been turned into an arboretum and planted with a selection of trees and shrubs to give a wide range of colour: *Amelanchier canadensis*, liquidambar, *Ginkgo biloba*,

Acer platanoides 'Crimson King' and *Gleditsia triacanthos* 'Sunburst'. A 21-metre-long peach house now contains plumbago, passiflora and a large *Cobaea scandens alba*. This is a plantsman's garden, with year-round interest provided by displays of early spring bulbs, colourful summer herbaceous borders and the foliage colours of autumn. A gravel garden which is hot and sheltered, with the added benefit of a boggy area, has hostas, bamboos, various grasses, ferns, including a tree fern, spiky agaves and palms.

Emmetts Garden ★   11

Ide Hill, Sevenoaks TN14 6AY. Tel: (01732) 868381; Fax (01732) 750490

The National Trust • 1½ m S of A25 and M25 Junction 5, 1½ m N of Ide Hill off B2042 Edenbridge – Sundridge road • Open 31st March to May, Wed – Sun and Bank Holiday Mons; June to Oct, Sat, Sun, Wed and Bank Holiday Mon; all 11am – 5.30pm (last admission 4.30pm) • Entrance: £3.40, children £1.70, family £8.50 • Other information: Buggy available from car park to entrance ◐ .
🍴 🍽 WC ♿ 🔄 🏧 ☼

Set on the top of Ide Hill, the garden gives a superb view over the Weald of Kent and provides an impressive setting for this plantsman's collection of trees and shrubs. It is a garden to visit at any time of the year, but is particularly fine in spring, with its bluebell woods and flowering shrubs. First planted by Frederick Lubbock, the owner from about 1890 until his death in 1926, it is noted especially for its rhododendrons and azaleas. It follows the late-nine-teenth-century style of combining exotics with conifers to provide a 'wild' garden; the plants are all listed in the guidebook. Extending the interest throughout the season are a rose garden, a rock garden and extensive planting of acers for autumn colour. The enforced clearance of some trees and shrubs after the gales of 1987 has enabled new planting to keep the traditions of the garden and also to expand it – the rock garden in particular is becoming established. It is still a wonderful site and a fascinating garden.

Godinton House and Gardens   12

Ashford TN23 3BP. Tel/Fax: (01233) 620773; Fax: (01233) 632652

The Godinton House Preservation Trust • 1½ m NW of Ashford in Godinton Lane at Potter's Corner (opposite Hare and Hounds pub) • House open 30th March to 6th Oct but Fri – Sun only • Garden open 16th March to 6th Oct, Thurs – Mon, 2 – 5.30pm (or dusk if earlier) • Entrance: £2, children £1 (house and garden £5, children £2) • Other information: Coaches by appt only. Garden tours available by prior arrangement. Refreshments for booked groups and when house is open ◐ 🍴 🍽 WC ☼

The house reopened in 1999 after major restoration. The outstanding feature of the garden is the great boundary hedge planted to Blomfield's original design and one of the largest in the country; it has been cut back to encourage new growth and will re-establish itself within a few years. The longest yew hedge, shaped to reflect the gables of the house, encloses Blomfield's first formal garden with its lawns, pond, terraces, topiary and the box-hedged Pan

Garden. The wild garden is famous for its show of daffodils, and the fine trees here include a huge tulip tree and two of the largest 'Tai Haku' cherry trees in Britain. In the walled garden, delphinium borders have been established in partnership with the Delphinium Society, and 25 varieties of *Clematis montana* have been planted amongst the wall-trained fruit trees. A quarter is planted with a cornfield wildflower mix, the rest given over to flowers. The rose garden has been replanted, as has the architectural Italian garden adjoining the walled garden, where restored statuary is on display.

Goodnestone Park ★★ 13

Goodnestone, Nr Wingham, Canterbury CT3 1PL. Tel: (01304) 840107

Lady FitzWalter • *5m E of Canterbury. A2 to Dover, turn left at junction B2046 for Wingham/Aylesham, then E after 1m* • *House open by appt for pre-booked parties* • *Garden open 25th March to 25th Oct, Mon, Wed – Fri, 11am – 5pm, Sun, 12 noon – 6pm. Closed Tues and Sat* • *Entrance: £3.30, OAPs £3, students £1.50, children under 12 50p, family ticket (2 adults and 2 children) £5 (guided tours £4.50 per person)* • *Other information: Teas available April to Sept only* ◑ 🍵 🖼 WC ♿ 🌱 🍴 🌂

Goodnestone (pronounced Gunston) Park is a 14-acre garden in a rural setting. Built in 1700 by Brook Bridges, the Palladian-style house was rebuilt and enlarged by his great-grandson, Sir Brook Bridges, 3rd Baronet, whose daughter Elizabeth married Jane Austen's brother, Edward. In her letters Jane makes frequent reference to Goodnestone and her Bridges cousins. There are pleasant vistas within the garden and good views out to open countryside. The garden ranges from the mid-eighteenth-century parkland with fine trees and cedars to the walled area behind the house, which dates from the sixteenth and seventeenth centuries. The garden tour leads along a broad terrace in front of the house, planted with a parterre for the millennium. Behind the house a small woodland garden, laid out in the 1920s, gives pleasant walks and welcome shade. Here are rhododendrons, camellias, magnolias and hydrangeas among many others. A cedar walk leads, between spring borders on the left and a red and grey border on the right, to a walled garden overlooked by the church tower. Old roses mingle with mixed underplanting, and walls bear clematis, jasmine and climbing roses.

Great Comp ★ 14

Platt, Borough Green, Sevenoaks TN15 8QS. Tel: (01732) 882669/886154; Website: www.greatcomp.co.uk

Great Comp Charitable Trust • *From M20 junction 2, take A20 towards Maidstone. At Wrotham Heath take B2016. Signposted* • *Open April to Oct, daily, 11am – 6pm* • *Entrance: £3.50, children £1. Annual ticket £10, OAPs £7* ◑ 🍵 🖼 WC ♿ 🌱 🍴 🌂

A half-day is likely to be required to do justice to this imaginatively planned seven-acre garden, which offers all-year interest. Although the setting for an early-seventeenth-century house, it has only been created since 1957 by Mr

Roderick Cameron and the late Mrs Joyce Cameron out of the neglected earlier garden, rough woodland and paddock. Long grass walks intersect the beds and borders, creating ever-changing views to tempt visitors to stray from their intended route. Focal points and interest are created by statuary, a temple and ruins built from the tons of ironstone dug up over the years. There are woodland areas, herbaceous borders, a heather garden, a rose garden, formal lawns and a new Italianate garden, designed to set off a collection of Mediterranean plants. Hellebores, especially *H. orientalis*, are a feature,. The *Taxus baccata* at the front of the house was planted in 1840. Other specimen trees include a young dawn redwood (*Metasequoia glyptostroboides*) and a Californian redwood (*Sequoia sempervirens* 'Cantab'). A music festival is held here each year, with recitals in the former stables.

Groombridge Place ★ 15

Groombridge, Tunbridge Wells TN3 9QG. Tel: (01892) 863999; Fax: (01892) 863996; E-mail: office@groombridge.co.uk; Website: www.groombridge.co.uk

4m SW of Tunbridge Wells. Take A264 towards East Grinstead. After 2m take B2110 to Groombridge • Open April to Oct, daily, 9am – 6pm • Entrance: £7.50, OAPs, students and children £6.50, family ticket £25 (2001 prices) • Other information: Canal boat rides, birds of prey. ◑ WC

This mid-seventeenth-century moated house (not open to the public) is set at the bottom of a valley with enclosed formal gardens sloping up to the north: the Drunken Garden with topiary of drum yews and junipers leaning at angles; the Oriental Garden containing some very old gnarled cut-leaf acers; the Draughtsman's Garden (the eponymous film was filmed in the garden) and the White Rose Garden. These areas are subdivided by topiaried yews, a nut walk and a 'bowling alley'. There are many magnificent trees, such as the four nineteenth-century Wellingtonias to the west of the house. Beside the moat is a parterre knot from which a door in the wall leads into the Secret Garden – a small shady area planted with candelabra primulas alongside a stream flowing through mossy rocks. Dotted around are information boards giving details of the garden's historical and literary associations. Peacocks wander freely. A walk up through the vineyard gives access to the Enchanted Forest, through the Chime Walk and on up to the wooded hillside with magnificent views across the Weald. Several theme gardens designed by Ivan Hicks, plus an imaginative Spring of Life by Myles Challis, are to be found along the walk which then brings the visitor back beside the canal to the formal gardens and the Golden Key Maze.

115 Hadlow Road 16

Tonbridge TN9 1QE. Tel: (01732) 353738

Mr and Mrs Richard Esdale • 1m N of Tonbridge. From High Street take A26 signed Maidstone. House is 1m on left in service road • Open 14th July, 24th Aug, 2 – 6pm, and by appt • Entrance: £2 ◕

A third-of-an-acre terraced suburban garden with many interesting specimen trees such as *Catalpa bignonioides* 'Aurea', *Acer negundo* 'Flamingo', *A. japonicum*

'Aureum', golden elm and *Sorbus cashmiriana*. Herbaceous border, clematis, hardy fuchsias, ferns, grasses (*Stipa gigantea*), alpines, roses, shrubs and summer bedding provide additional colour, and a small pool with a fountain contains water-loving plants. There is a small, well-stocked fruit and vegetable garden.

Hever Castle and Gardens ★★ 17

Hever, Edenbridge TN8 7NG. Tel: (01732) 865224; Fax: (01732) 866796;
E-mail: mail@hevercastle.co.uk; Website: www.hevercastle.co.uk

Broadlands Properties Ltd • 3m SE of Edenbridge, between Sevenoaks and East Grinstead off B2026 • Castle opens 12 noon • Gardens open March to Nov, daily, 11am – 6pm (last admission 5pm). Pre-booked guided tours available for both castle and gardens for parties • Entrance: £6.30, OAPs £5.40, children (5– 14) £4.20, family (2 adults, 2 children) £16.80; castle and gardens £8, OAPs £6.80, children (5–14) £4.40, family £20.40. Rates for parties of 15 or more available (2001 prices) ☽ ☕ ✕ 🖼 <u>WC</u> ♿ ⟁ 🐾 🎖 🍴 ✎

The gardens were laid out between 1904 and 1908 to William Waldorf Astor's designs. One thousand men were employed, 800 of whom dug out the 35-acre lake; steam engines shifted rock and soil to create apparently natural new features, and teams of horses moved mature trees from Ashdown Forest. Today the gardens have reached their maturity and are teeming with colour and interest throughout the year. Amongst the many superb features is an outstanding four-acre Italian garden, the setting for a large collection of classical statuary. Opposite is a magnificent pergola, supporting camellias, wisteria, crab apple, Virginia creeper and roses. It fuses into the hillside beyond, which has shaded grottos of cool damp-loving species such as hostas, astilbes and polygonums. Less formal areas include the rhododendron walk, Anne Boleyn's orchard and her walk, which extends along the full length of the grounds and is particularly attractive in autumn; in keeping with the Anne Boleyn connection a so-called Tudor herb garden has been added, and the Sunday Walk nearby runs beside a stream past newly created borders in mature woodland. The 110 metre herbaceous border has been re-created and the water maze on Sixteen-acre Island, planted with a range of aquatic plants, offers peaceful walks down to the millennium fountain.

Hole Park 18

Rolvenden, Cranbrook TN17 4JA. Tel: (01580) 241251

Mr D.G.W. Barham • 4m W of Tenterden, on B2086 between Rolvenden and Benenden • Open April to June, Oct, Mon, Wed; and 14th, 28th April, 5th, 19th May, 2nd, 16th June, 13th, 20th Oct for NGS; all 2 – 6pm. Private visits and parties by appt • Entrance: £3, children under 12 50p ☽ <u>WC</u> ♿ ✎

Situated midway between Sissinghurst and Great Dixter, Hole Park affords the visitor an opportunity to enjoy a peaceful garden of great beauty far away from the crowds and very different from its popular neighbours. The 14-acre gardens were designed and created by the owner's grandfather in the early 1920s, when extensive yew hedges were planted, and these, together with fine trees, broad lawns and old walls, provide the background for herbaceous and mixed plantings as well as pools, statuary and pleasant places in which to wander at will. A new feature is the Millennium water garden. There are splendid views over the beautiful parkland to Rolvenden's famous seventeenth-century postmill and over the Weald of Kent. In the wild garden to the north of the house, daffodils in great variety are followed by flowering shrubs, rhododendrons and azaleas, and the dell is cool and inviting. In May bluebells fill the woodland walk and autumn colours are a speciality, making the garden a sight for all seasons. Nearby is *Great Maytham Hall* (Country Houses Association), said to have inspired *The Secret Garden* [open May to Sept, Wed and Thurs, 2 – 5pm].

Iden Croft Herbs 19

Frittenden Road, Staplehurst TN12 0DH. Tel: (01580) 891432;
Fax: (01580) 892416; E-mail: idencroft.herbs@dial.pipex.com;
Website: www.herbs-uk.com

Rosemary and David Titterington • 10m S of Maidstone. From Staplehurst at Total Garage turn down Frittenden Road. Signed from A229 • Gardens open all year, Mon – Sat, 9am – 5pm. Also March to Sept, Sun and Bank Holiday Mons, 11am – 5pm. (At the time of going to press house on market, so check before travelling.) • Entrance: £2, OAPs £1.50, children (5–15) 50p ○ ◗ ▦ WC ⅍ ⬥ ⌁ ▦ ⚑ ⚲

In these romantic gardens, situated in a quiet backwater near Staplehurst, are four acres of herbs bordered by grass paths and an early Tudor walled garden. The gardens illustrate a variety of plantings and include several demonstration areas to help the planner. There is a special sensory garden suitable for the disabled where texture, smell, shape and colour can be appreciated, and a cottage garden near the refreshment patio demonstrates year-round colour and texture in a small area. A fifteenth-century walled garden is planted with aromatic plants to entice butterflies, bees and insects. The garden has two National Collections: mint and marjoram. An enormous variety of herbs and aromatic plants and seeds is for sale; a new medicinal herb garden was planted last year.

Ightham Mote 20

Ivy Hatch, Sevenoaks TN15 0NT. Tel: (01732) 810378; Fax: (01732) 811029

The National Trust • 6m E of Sevenoaks off A25, 2½ m S of Ightham off A227 • House open • Garden open 24th March to 3rd Nov, daily except Tues and Sat, 10am – 5.30pm (last admission 4.30pm) • Entrance: £5, children £2.50, family ticket £12.50, pre-booked parties of 15 or more £4.20 per person (2001 prices) • Other information: Disabled parking ◑ ◗ ✕ WC ⅍ ▦ ⚑ ⚲

Situated in a wooded cleft of the Kentish Weald, this medieval and Tudor manor house lies in the valley of Dinas Dene, where a stream has been dammed to form small lakes and the moat which surrounds the house. The medieval design of the gardens has evolved over several centuries – the present lawn replaces the stew pond, which was used for breeding fish for the table; further household needs were satisfied with vegetables and herbs for culinary and medicinal purposes, and flowers for decorating and scenting the house. During the nineteenth century the garden emerged as an excellent example of the ideal 'old English' garden, and the Trust is gradually restoring this with extensive replanting. Six acres of woodland walks with fine rhododendrons are re-established and the long border has returned to its former glory.

Ladham House ★ 21

Goudhurst TN17 1DB. Tel: (01580) 212674; Fax: (01580) 212596;

Mr and Mrs Alastair Jessel • 8m E of Tunbridge Wells, NE of Goudhurst off A262 • Open for NGS 21st April, 19th May, 2 – 5.30pm, and by appt for individuals and parties • Entrance: £3, children 50p, £3.50 for private visits • Other information: Teas must be pre-booked ● 🍵 🖼 WC ♿ ⬧ ℀

This Georgian house with additional French features has been in the family for over 100 years and the garden developed over that period. Interesting to see the bog garden, replacing a leaking pond, and the arboretum, replacing the old kitchen garden. The mixed shrub borders are attractive; notable are the magnolias – two M. x *watsonii* over 10 metres and a deep-red-flowering 'Betty Jessel', a seedling from Darjeeling. Amongst the other rarer trees and shrubs are *Cornus kousa*, embothriums, American oaks, *Aesculus parviflora*, *Carpenteria californica* and *Azara serrata*. The arboretum is maturing and has some unusual and interesting trees. Developments continue: the Fountain Garden has been completely reconstructed, the rock garden restored with a waterfall incorporated, a 200 metre Kentish ragstone ha-ha built to the north of the house, and a woodland walk down the side of the park opened up. A new garden planted close to the swimming pool uses tropical and hot-coloured plants.

Leeds Castle Park and Gardens ★ 22

Maidstone ME17 1PL. Tel: (01622) 765400; Fax: (01662) 735616; Website: www.leeds-castle.co.uk

Leeds Castle Foundation • 5m SE of Maidstone on B2163 near M20 junction 8 • Castle opens 11am (10.15am in winter) • Park and gardens open all year, daily, 10am – 5pm (Nov to Feb 3pm). Closed 29th June, 6th July, 25th Dec • Entrance: £8.50, OAPs and students £7, children (4–15) £5.20, family ticket (2 adults and 3 children) £24 (castle, park and gardens £10, OAPs and students £8.50, children (4–15) £6.50, family ticket £29) (2001 prices) ○ 🍵 ✕ 🖼 WC ♿ 🌿 🏪 🍴 ℀

Visit the castle and grounds for its romantic, wooded setting, covering some 500 acres. The woodland garden, with its old and new plantings of shrubs, is especially beautiful in daffodil time. The atmosphere is also much enhanced by wildfowl. The Culpeper Garden, in a secluded area beyond the castle, provides the main interest for the keen gardener. This is not a herb garden as often thought, though a small area does include some herbs, but is named after a seventeenth-century owner, distantly related to the herbalist. Started

in 1980 by Russell Page on a slope overlooking the River Len, and surrounded by high brick walls of stabling and old cottages, the garden already
has an established feeling of old-world charm. A simple pattern of paths lined
with box contains areas of old roses, riotously underplanted with herbaceous
perennials. Old greenhouses have been replanted with peach trees, and
there is an excellent fuchsia display in the summer months. National
Collections of monardas are situated in one corner of the Culpeper Garden.
The spectacular grotto built in 1987 beneath the maze has been much
publicised. The garden is complemented by some rare and attractive birds
in the duckery and aviary, which are well placed amid numerous shrubs and
small trees. The Italian-style terraced Lady Baillie Garden overlooking the
Great Water has stunning sub-tropical plants.

Longacre   23

Perry Wood, Selling, Faversham ME13 9SE. Tel: (01227) 752254

*Dr and Mrs G. Thomas • 5m SE of Faversham. From A2 (M2) take A251 S
signed 'Selling'. Pass White Lion on left, second right, then left, continue for ¼
m. From A252 at Chilham, take road to Selling at Badgers Hill Fruit Farm,
turn left at second crossroads, first right, next left, then right • Garden open for
NGS 21st April, 5th, 6th, 26th May, 9th, 23rd June, 25th, 26th Aug, and at
other times by appt • Entrance: £2, accompanied children free • Other
information: Teas and plants for sale on NGS open days only* ◐ ♥ WC ♨

This is a jewel of a small garden in a tranquil country setting next to Perry
Woods into which the borders of the garden melt. Created entirely by the
present owners, it offers all-year interest of colour and form, replicating in
miniature woodland, alpine and damp areas. There are new flower beds and a
pond with running water. The old nursery is now a gravel garden, which
already looks established after only a few months. There will be further
experiments with the planting here to allow annuals to self-seed. Vegetables
in raised beds are cropping well and trellis around the area supports sun-loving
climbers.

Marle Place Gardens and Gallery ★   24

Brenchley, Tonbridge TN12 7HS. Tel: (01892) 722304; Fax: (01892) 724099

*Mr and Mrs G. Williams • 5m E of Tunbridge Wells, 1m SW of Horsmonden,
W of B2162. Signposted • Open April to 1st Oct, daily, 10am – 5.30pm, and
by appt • Entrance: £4, OAPs and children £3.50 • Other information: Art
exhibitions in gallery throughout season* ◐ ♥ ▥ WC ♿ ♨ ♟ ♻

This 10-acre garden surrounding a seventeenth-century house hidden away in
the byways contains a wide selection of garden features. Close to the house is a
small shady fern garden and a border of several varieties of cistus (at their best
in early June), set off by an old wall furnished with interesting climbers. A
double herbaceous border leads to an area of alliums and ornamental grasses,
also at its peak in June. Near the house is an old ornamental pool garden with a
wildflower bank and aromatic plants, a croquet lawn and several interesting

specimen trees, such as an old *Acer brilliantissimum* and a weeping form of *Ginkgo biloba*. The use of different-coloured foliage hedges as a background to many of the borders illustrates the artistic flair of the owner (her studio is open to garden visitors). Other features include a Victorian gazebo, an Edwardian rockery and two lakes approached by a woodland walk; a red Chinese bridge leads over a boggy area planted with bamboos. A new mosaic terrace has been laid within the blue and yellow border. Areas of wild flowers, both within the garden and in the 10-acre wood of native trees, and several large iron skeletal sculptures of horses and other work by varied artists, plus carved wooden furniture made by the owners' daughter, add to the eclectic charm. A new feature is a *potager* with several varieties of special vegetables.

Mount Ephraim   25

Hernhill, Faversham ME13 9TX. Tel: (01227) 751496; Fax: (01227) 750940; Website: www.mountephraimgardens.co.uk

Mrs M.N. Dawes and Mr and Mrs E.S. Dawes • 6m W of Canterbury, 3m E of Faversham. NE from M2/A2 junction 7. Take A299, and at Duke of Kent pub turn to Hernhill. Garden is through village on left, signposted • Open 15th April to Sept, Mon, Wed, Thurs, Sat, Sun, 1 – 6pm (Bank Holiday weekends 11am – 6pm) • Entrance: £3, children £1, parties £2.50 per person (2001 prices) • Other information: Craft shop Suns only ◑ 🍽 🍴 WC ⬳ 🏤 💡 ✎

Mount Ephraim is remarkable for the variety of its gardens on seven sloping acres with distant views of the Thames Estuary, surrounding fruit orchards and pasture land. Restored after years of neglect from 1950 onwards, it retains much of the original design of the 1800s. It was laid out again in 1912 by William Dawes, including topiary effects and the original rock garden. The house has been in the same family for 300 years. With a backdrop of trees of outstanding shapes and contrasts, it includes rose gardens, a rock garden, a water garden, an arboretum, a small Japanese garden and a lake. Spring bulbs, prunus in blossom and rhododendrons make spring to early June an ideal time to visit, but herbaceous borders and shrubs extend the interest through the seasons North-east of Mount Ephraim is *Busheyfields Nursery*, Herne, with National Collections of *Clematis montana*, *C. chrysocoma* and honeysuckles [open March to Oct, Tues – Sat and Bank Holiday Mons, 10am – 5pm].

Nettlestead Place ★   26

Nettlestead, Maidstone ME18 5HA. Tel: (01622) 812205

Mr and Mrs R.C. Tucker • 6m SW of Maidstone off B2015. Next to Nettlestead Church • Open for NGS 2nd June, 2 – 5.30pm, 10th July, 6 – 8.30pm, 15th Sept, 2 – 5.30pm, and at other times by appt • Entrance: £3 (afternoon opening), £4 (evening opening, inc. wine) ◑ 🍴 WC ⬳

The thirteenth-century manor house is set in a seven-acre plantsman's garden. On entering through the early fourteenth-century gatehouse, an avenue of Irish yews leads into a lawned area edged with a large collection of sun-loving geraniums (155 different cultivars in the garden). The Kentish ragstone walls around three sides of this area are planted with many tender and rare species from Tasmania, Malaysia and Asia, etc., such as *Wattakaka sinensis* (China) and *Viburnum odoratissimum* (Malaysia). There is a small orchard with apples, pears and soft fruit, and a glen garden where the natural spring flowing down the hill is edged with hostas, primulas, dwarf pines, astilbes and shade-loving geraniums. A series of small canals separates the daffodil meadow from the new heather garden, and an 80-metre-long gravel garden planted with rock plants and dwarf bulbs lies along the eastern side of the house, which is clothed with akebia, sophora, fremontodendron and *Rosa* 'Francis A. Lester'. A large sunken pond bounded by a ragstone wall on the southern side provides another sheltered environment for tender plants. A large rose garden has an excellent collection of shrub roses and new plantings of hybrid teas, floribundas, hybrid musks and climbers. The herbaceous garden contains a comprehensive display of plants in a series of island beds, also an arched rose walk with complementary late-flowering clematis leading to a sheltered rose garden of Chinas and Himalayan climbers. There is a diverse collection of shrubs mixed with other plants in a further series of much larger island beds. Hostas and ferns flourish in the shade garden. A planting of trees overlooks a peaceful stretch of the River Medway.

Old Place Farm   27

High Halden, Ashford TN26 3JG. Tel: (01233) 850202

Mr and Mrs J. Eker • 10m SW of Ashford. From A28, opposite Chequers pub in High Halden, take Woodchurch Road and follow for ½ m • Open by appt only • Entrance: £3 ● ☕ WC �& ℺

A four-acre garden surrounding a period house and farm buildings, created since 1968, mainly designed by Anthony du Gard Pasley. The lake of two-thirds of an acre provides a near focus from the house, and an elegant gazebo is an idyllic setting for contemplation. The borders behind have an apricot, gold and cream colour theme offset by blues, purples, silvers and greys. An avenue of *Crataegus prunifolia*, underplanted with white-flowering bulbs from February to May, leads to a fine sheep statue. There is a nut plat, a philadelphus walk and, to provide summer shelter from the sun, two large *Catalpa bignonioides*. A parterre herb garden is linked to a circular brick feature with sundial by an avenue of *Malus* 'Golden Hornet'. A pergola draped with the rose 'New Dawn', white wisteria and purple vines divides the cutting garden from a small *potager*.

Owl House Gardens   28

Lamberhurst TN3 8LY. Tel: (01892) 891290

Estate of the late Maureen, Marchioness of Dufferin and Ava • 6m SE of Tunbridge Wells, S of Lamberhurst off A21. Signposted • Open all year, daily except 25th Dec and 1st Jan, 11am – 6pm • Entrance: £4, children £1 (2001 prices) • Other information: Coaches by appt ○ 🍴 WC �& ⟁ ℘

In 1952 Lady Dufferin fell in love with a cottage which had the crookedest chimney in Kent and was the county's oldest building. In 1522 its tenants paid a yearly rental of one white cockerel to the monks at Bayham Abbey.

During the sixteenth century it was a hiding place for wool smugglers who, at the approach of the law, hooted their warning, hence its name. Within its 16½ acres a beautiful year-round garden was created over the years by the late Lady Dufferin, and is maintained as she left it. Swathes of bluebells and daffodils start the season, followed by camellias, azaleas and rhododendrons. Summer interest is ensured by large numbers of old roses, *R. longicuspis*, 'Bobbie James' and 'Rambling Rector', climbing into the many fine trees; philadelphus and clematis also abound. Statues of owls are dotted about the garden, with seats placed to overlook viewpoints. There is a wisteria temple, a grove of *Parrotia persica*, and four walks: of iris, apple blossom, laburnum and blue hydrangeas. Three lovely water gardens provide a peaceful setting for contemplation.

Penshurst Place and Gardens ★   29

Penshurst, Tonbridge TN11 8DG. Tel: (01892) 870307;
E-mail: enquiries@penshurstplace.com; Website: www.penshurstplace.com

Lord De L'Isle • 5m SW of Tonbridge on B2176, 7m N of Tunbridge Wells off A26 • House open 12 noon – 5.30pm (last admission 5pm) • Garden open weekends in March; April to Oct, daily, 10.30am – 6pm. Garden tours available for parties of 20 or more • Entrance: £4.50, OAPs and students £4, children £3.50, family ticket £13 (house and grounds £6, OAPs and students £5.50, children £4, family £16). Parties of 20 or more £5.30 per person (2001 prices) • Other information: Guide dogs only ◐ 🍽 🏛 WC & ♨ 🏪 🍴 ⚲

The 600-year-old gardens, contemporary with the house, reflect their development under their Tudor owner, Sir Henry Sidney, and the restoration by the present owner, his father and his grandfather. An example is the 640-metre double line of oaks, their planting completed in 1995 as part of a 15-year programme to re-create the historic parkland structure. The many separate enclosures, surrounded by trim and tall yew hedges, offer a wide variety of interesting planting, with continuous displays from spring to early autumn. Just inside the entrance is a garden for the blind, with raised beds of aromatic plants, a small wooden gazebo and the constant music of water splashing on pebbles. The Italian garden with its oval fountain and century-old ginkgo dominates the south front of the magnificent house. Herbaceous borders are teeming with colour. Note also the borders designed by Lanning Roper in the late '60s and the blue and yellow border. Contrast is made by the nut trees and over a dozen different crab apples underplanted with daffodils, myosotis, tulips, bluebells, Lenten lilies, and a magnificent bed of peonies which borders the orchard. Even in late summer the rose garden is colourful with 'Aynsley Dickson' and 'Anna Olivier', and their perfumes mingle with that from mature lavender bushes. A lake and woodland trail have been developed so that the style of design so much enjoyed here by Gertrude Jekyll and Beatrix Farrand is fully recaptured. Two medieval fish ponds have been reclaimed and stocked with fish. Imaginative play area for children.

The Pines Garden 30

Beach Road, St Margaret's Bay CT15 6DZ. Tel: (01304) 852764;
Fax: (01304) 853626; Website: www.pinesgardenandmuseum.co.uk

St Margaret's Bay Trust • 3m NE of Dover off A258, through St Margaret's at Cliffe, just before beach • Open all year, daily, 10am – 5pm • Entrance: £2, children 50p • Other information: Teas and gift shop in St Margaret's Museum opposite, open Easter and May Bank Holidays, and end-May to early Sept, Wed – Sun, 2 – 5pm ○ ⬤ 📠 WC & ⬆ ⚘ 🏛 ℀

It is hard to believe that this well-stocked and perfectly maintained garden was scrubland until 1970. Fred Cleary, founder of St Margaret's Bay Trust, transformed the original six-acre site, known as the Barrack Field, once the home and training ground for soldiers in the Napoleonic Wars. Now the garden is established, with a good variety of trees, flowering shrubs, bulbs and herbaceous plants. The lake is well stocked with fish, and a rockery with a waterfall provides further interest. A bronze statue of Sir Winston Churchill by Oscar Nemon looks across the garden to the famous white cliffs of Dover. A Romany wedding caravan (as used by gypsies of Romney Marsh) stands in the garden, and at the other end there is a seventeenth-century façade from a London Cheapside property, rescued from the Great Fire of London. To celebrate the millennium, Pauline Gould (Fred Cleary's daughter) created a large new bed near the entrance to the garden with perennial plants that have been introduced into Kent for the past few hundred years.

Port Lympne 31

Lympne, Hythe CT21 4PD. Tel: (01303) 264647

Aspinall family • 3m W of Hythe, 18m S of Canterbury on B2067 • House open • Garden open all year, daily, 10am – 5pm (1 hour before dusk in winter) • Entrance: £9.80, OAPs and children £7.80 (house, garden and wild animal park) (2001 prices) ○ ⬤ ✕ 📠 WC ⚘ 🏛 ℀

This is one of those gardens which is hugely enjoyed by some people and leaves others cold. It stands in a 300-acre wild animal park with views across the Channel. The interior of the Lutyens-style house is noted for the murals by Rex Whistler and Spencer Roberts. After a period of distinction in the 1920s and '30s it fell into decay until it was rescued in the 1970s by the late John Aspinall, who wanted the surrounding land for his private wild animal park. He reconstructed the 15-acre garden to something like its original design with advice from experts, including the late Russell Page. Visitors enter down a great stone stairway of 125 steps, flanked by clipped, newly planted yews, to the paved west court with lily pool. Beyond is the lime tree walk and a series of terraces planted with standard fig trees and vines. Everywhere there is fine stone paving and walls with appropriately placed urns, statues from Stowe, etc. There is extensive bedding and use of bedding-out. The late Arthur Hellyer admitted that 'for years it has been fashionable to denigrate Port Lympne' but he admired it; he also waxed lyrical about the beautiful wrought-ironwork by Bainbridge Reynolds.

Riverhill House Gardens 32
Sevenoaks TN15 0RR. Tel: (01732) 458802/452557

Rogers family (correspondence to Mrs John Rogers) • *2m S of Sevenoaks on A225* • *House open to bona fide booked parties only. No children inside house* • *Garden open 29th March to June, Wed, Sun and Bank Holiday Sats and Mons, 12 noon – 6pm* • *Entrance: £3, children 50p (house and garden for parties of 20 or more £4 per person)* • *Other information: Coaches by appt* ● ● ● WC ● ● ●

This was originally one of the great smaller country-house gardens, housing a plantsman's collection of trees and species shrubs as introduced by John Rogers, a keen horticulturist, in the mid-1800s. Massive rhododendrons, many of them species, are topped by a cedar of Lebanon planted in 1815, and azaleas and outstanding underplanting of bulbs make a fine show in spring and early summer. Other features include a wood garden, a rose walk, an orchard with a Wellingtonia planted in 1860, magnolias and much more.

Rock Farm 33
Nettlestead, Gibbs Hill, Maidstone ME18 5HT. Tel: (01622) 812244

Mrs P.A. Corfe • *6m SW of Maidstone. From A26 turn S onto B2015, then turn right 1m S of Wateringbury* • *Open June and July, Wed and Sat, 10am – 5pm for private visits by appt* • *Entrance: £2.50* ● ● WC

This Kentish farmhouse, set on an east-facing slope, is surrounded by a two-acre plantsman's garden. Natural springs supply water for two ponds at different levels and for a small stream whose banks are planted with primulas and other bog plants. The soil is alkaline and there are excellent specimens of ceanothus, a huge *Solanum crispum*, a *Fremontodendron californicum*, a *Magnolia grandiflora* and climbing roses in an old pear tree. The best season is June to July when the large herbaceous border is at its height. An iris border provides a colourful entry to the garden. Of special interest is the *Chionanthus virginicus* or fringe tree. The two ponds are bordered with cupressus of various foliage colour. A *Catalpa bignonioides* 'Aurea' is cut annually to give huge golden leaves, and a *Sequoia sempervirens* is also pruned drastically, resulting in rarely seen new foliage of this coniferous forest tree. A small nursery sells a range of plants seen in the garden.

Scotney Castle Garden ★ 34
Lamberhurst, Tunbridge Wells TN3 8JN. Tel: (01892) 891081;
Fax: (01892) 890110

The National Trust • *8m SE of Tunbridge Wells, 1m S of Lamberhurst on E side of A21* • *Old Castle open May to 12th Sept same times as garden* • *Garden open main season – telephone (0870) 458 4000 for details* • *Entrance: £4.40, children £2.20, family ticket (2 adults and up to 3 children) £11. Pre-booked parties (weekdays only) £3.80 per person (2001 prices)* • *Other information: Possible for wheelchairs but hilly approach* ● WC ● ● ● ●

This is an unusual garden designed in the romantic manner by the Hussey family, following the tradition established by William Kent and using the services of William Gilpin, the artist and landscape gardener, who also advised on the site of the new house, completed in 1843. Of the fourteenth-century castle only one of the four towers remains, plus some of the sixteenth- and seventeenth-century additions. The landscape garden includes smaller garden layouts in the overall area. A formal garden overlooks a quarry garden and the grounds of the old castle enclose a rose garden. Herb garden. Lakeside planting adds an air of informality. Evergreens and deciduous trees provide the mature planting, linking shrubs and plants to give something in flower at every season. Daffodils, magnolias, rhododendrons and azaleas are the most spectacular; also notable are the kalmias and hydrangeas. In a good autumn, the colours are amazing. In some ways the planting seems occasional and haphazard, 'Picturesque' in the true sense, but visit this garden for its setting on a slope that gives fine views of open countryside, and for the romantic eighteenth- to nineteenth-century theme uniting it. A great pity there are no refreshments as there is plenty of space.

Sissinghurst Castle Garden ★★   35

Sissinghurst, Cranbrook TN17 2AB. Tel: infoline (01580) 710701;
Fax: (01580) 713911

The National Trust • 13m S of Maidstone, 2m NE of Cranbrook, 1m E of Sissinghurst on A262 • Garden open main season – telephone (0870) 458 4000 for details. Parties of 11 or more by appt. Timed ticket system in operation, and at peak times visitors may have short wait • Entrance: £6.90, children £3, family £16 (2001 prices) • Other information: Coaches by appt. Picnics beyond car park and in front of castle only. Wheelchairs restricted to two chairs at one time because of narrow, uneven paths; pushchairs not admitted ◑ ⬛ ✕ ▥ WC ♿ ⚘ ⛲

'Profusion, even extravagance and exuberance within the confines of the utmost linear severity', was Vita Sackville-West's description of her design when creating Sissinghurst with her husband Harold Nicolson. It is a romantic garden with seasonal features throughout the year. Certain colour schemes have been followed, as in the purple border, the orange and yellow cottage garden, and the white garden, which is probably the most beautiful garden at Sissinghurst, itself one of the outstanding gardens in the world. The Nicolsons added little to, but saved much of, the Elizabethan mansion. The site was first occupied in the twelfth century, when a moated manor was built where the orchard now stands. The long library and Elizabethan tower are open and the latter is well worth climbing in order to see the perspective of the whole garden and surrounding area. All is kept in immaculate condition, well labelled, with changing vistas at every turn of the winding paths or more formal walks. The rose garden contains many old-fashioned roses as well as flowering shrubs such as *Ceanothus impressus* and *Hydrangea villosa*, which together with iris, clematis and pansies fill the area. There is a thyme lawn leading to the herb garden filled with fragrance and charm. It is a truly magnificent example of Englishness and has had immense influence on garden design because of its structure of separate outdoor rooms within the garden. *Knole* will also interest Vita's fans [park open daily, Lord Sackville's garden on first Wed in every month, May to Sept].

South Hill Farm

36

Hastingleigh, Ashford TN25 5HL. Tel: (01233) 750325

Sir Charles J. Jessel Bt • 6m E of Ashford, on Downs between Hastingleigh and Brabourne • Open by appt only • Entrance: £2, children 25p ● WC &

Originally a Jacobean farmhouse, to which a Georgian south front was added, the house (not open) stands nearly 200 metres above sea level. The two-acre garden, including a ha-ha, was replanned by the owner and his late wife in 1960 and everything has been planted since then, with one or two exceptions such as the lime tree in front of the house. There are around 60 different varieties of clematis, together with various unusual shrubs; also many roses, hydrangeas, hostas and hellebores. Several raised beds, built of flint, were added in 1997 for plants needing well-drained soil. Walls have been added to the kitchen garden, which is entirely organic, and there is a formal water garden. Sculpture in steel and stone adds architectural interest. A garden of considerable charm.

Southover

37

Grove Lane, Hunton, Maidstone ME15 0SE. Tel: (01622) 820876; E-mail: davidway@talk21.com

Mr and Mrs David Way • 6m S of Maidstone between A229 and B2010. From Yalding take Vicarage Road to Hunton. Almost opposite school turn left into Grove Lane; house is about 200yds on the right. From Coxheath turn down Hunton Hill to Hunton; Grove Lane is immediately past the school • Open by appt; groups welcome • Entrance: £2.50, accompanied children free • Other information: Teas on open day only. Wheelchair users must be accompanied ● ➡ & ⬦ ℺

The typical fifteenth-century timber-framed house in the centre of a south-sloping site is surrounded by a garden designed to complement it. Work started in 1980. The foundations of a much larger house were uncovered and planted with hedges to enclose a true garden room. Two ponds, filled in over the centuries, have been redeveloped, and higher up a bank flows with ground-cover plants. Beyond is a wild or conservation area. The spring garden is complemented by an autumn border. Nearer the house are two 'secret' gardens: one, adjoining the house, is a cottage garden planted with roses and scented flowers, the other, similar in size but quite different in atmosphere, is known as the Meditation Garden, recalling memories of visits to gardens abroad. A third garden room has been developed as a *potager*. Impressive herbaceous borders to the south of the house have many unusual plants. Penstemons are a speciality and one border displays over 40 varieties. Other features are a sunken walk in green and white, a damp garden under old oaks and a fern area.

Squerryes Court 38

Westerham TN16 1SJ. Tel: (01959) 562345/563118; Fax: (01959) 565949;
E-mail: squerryes.court@squerryes.co.uk; Website: www.squerryes.co.uk

*Mr and Mrs John Warde • ½ m W of Westerham on A25, near M25 junctions
5 and 6 • House open 1.30 – 5.30pm • Garden open April to Sept, Wed, Sat,
Sun and Bank Holiday Mons, 12 noon – 5.30pm. Parties of 20 or more by
appt any day • Entrance: £3, OAPs £2.50, children (under 14) £1.50, family
ticket (2 adults and 2 children) £7; (house and garden £4.60, OAPs £4.10,
children £2.50, family ticket £10). Reduced rates for pre-booked parties* ◗ ▆
▆ WC ⇦ ♨ ♟

The 20 acres of gardens, laid out around 1700 in the formal Anglo-Dutch style,
were landscaped again in the eighteenth century. The view over the large lake
leads to a gazebo, built around 1740, from where a former member of the
family used to watch his racehorses in training; nearby is a fine old dovecot.
The main feature is the newly restored formal area to the rear of the house; a
1719 print has been used as an outline on which to base the changes. These
reflect the mellow brickwork of the handsome house. Beds, edged with box,
contain lavender, purple sage and santolina. Two long Edwardian borders have
been planted with roses and herbaceous perennials; all are framed by well-
kept yew hedges. There are several other mixed borders and a Victorian
rockery with fine examples of topiary. The woodland garden, currently being
restored, contains rhododendron and azalea shrubberies, which, together
with a broad variety of spring bulbs, makes this a garden for all seasons. Many
fine magnolias around the house and a cenotaph in memory of General Wolfe
(a family friend) complete this most attractive garden. The house is worth a
visit, too, for its collection of paintings. Those with a historical bent will wish
to visit nearby Chartwell (see entry), although this, horticulturally speaking,
has a less interesting garden.

Stoneacre 39

Otham, Maidstone ME15 8RS. Tel: (01622) 862871; Fax: (01622) 862157

*The National Trust • 3m SE of Maidstone, 1m S of A20 from Bearsted, at N
end of Otham • House open • Garden open 6th April to Oct, Wed and Sat, 2 –
6pm (last admission 5pm), and for parties by appt • Entrance: house and
garden £2.50, children £1.25 (2001 prices) • Other information: Disabled
parking at gate. Picnics in car park* ◗ ♞

The Kentish hall house was restored and embellished in the 1920s by Aymer
Vallance, Oxford aesthete, writer and friend of William Morris. After some
years of neglect the garden was restored by Rosemary Alexander, founder of
the English Gardening School. She was helped in her work by old reports on
the gardens and by Graham Stuart Thomas. The result is a charming garden of
borders and lawns within the framework of yew hedges and ragstone walls.
The acre of gardens at the front of the house contains a large ginkgo, a
mulberry, a *Staphylea colchica*, roses and rare plants. At the rear of the house a
grass path leads to the summerhouse and a two-acre wild garden, which

includes apple orchards and three ponds. Plans are underway to add a herb garden, create a Mediterranean area and develop a damp garden. A garden trail, suitable for children, has been devised in conjunction with the Kent Gardens Trust.

Walmer Castle and Gardens 40

Kingsdown Road, Walmer, Deal CT14 7LJ. Tel: (01304) 364288

English Heritage • On coast 2m S of Walmer on A258, off M20 at junction 13 or from M2 to Deal • Castle open • Garden open April to Sept, daily, 10am – 6pm; Oct, daily, 10am – 5pm; Nov, Dec and March, Wed – Sun, 10am – 4pm; Jan, Feb, Sat, Sun, 10am – 4pm. Closed 24th to 26th Dec; also closed when Lord Warden in residence. Telephone in advance of visit to check if open, particularly in winter months and most especially Oct • Entrance: castle and garden £4.80, concessions £3.60, children (5–16) £2.40, family ticket £12. Discount for parties of 11 or more • Other information: Guided garden tours. Wheelchair available. Guide dogs only ◐ 🍴 ✕ 🖼 WC ☕ ✿ 🏛 🖉 ✎

English Heritage is restoring the gardens of this, the official residence of the Warden of the Cinque Ports, to their former status in the early twentieth century. The castle overlooks the sea and the 10-acre gardens are surrounded by shelter belts and meadows. The formal core of the garden consists of three areas. The first is the double herbaceous border which is backed by large crinkle-crankle yew hedges ending in terraces with a croquet lawn. Then there is the traditional kitchen garden with a cut-flower area producing decoration for the castle, and a vegetable area with espaliered apple and pear trees, cold frames and glasshouses. Finally the Queen Mother's Garden, situated in the old walled garden, was redesigned by Penelope Hobhouse to commemorate the 95th birthday of H.M. The Queen Mother. It includes a 95-foot-long formal pond, yew pyramids, box topiary and a mount topped by yew hedges clipped in the shape of a castle. A dry moat is planted with roses and shrubs. An informal woodland walk encircles a wildflower meadow, and there are picnic tables and deck chairs on the oval lawn from which to relax and enjoy it all. The restored glasshouse displays a range of conservatory plants, providing an added attraction in winter and early spring.

Waystrode Manor ★ 41

Spode Lane, Cowden, Tunbridge Wells TN8 7HW. Tel: (01342) 850695

Mrs Jill Wright • 8m W of Tunbridge Wells, 4½ m S of Edenbridge, off B2026 Edenbridge – Hartfield road • Open some Weds and Suns from May to July for NGS • Entrance: £3, children 50p ◐ 🍴 WC ☕ 🖉 🏛

This eight-acre garden on Wealden clay has been developed over the last 30 years and surrounds a beautiful half-timbered sixteenth-century house. An avenue of red-candled horse chestnut trees leads to the house, which is flanked on one side by an old barn supporting wisteria, clematis, actinidia and schizophragma. A stone-flagged area at the rear has herbs growing out of it and, as a central feature, an old mill grinding-wheel planted with low-growing plants. From the house the eye is led via the serpent fountain garden to a small yew-enclosed white garden. A large and decorative two-storey wooden building contains tender and tropical plants. There are several pergolas of wisteria, laburnum and roses. Two small pools connected by a waterfall are crossed by a charming arched bridge. Borders of irises, old roses and geraniums are dotted around, and the whole is complemented by some excellent and unusual specimen trees, such as *Ulmus* x *hollandica* 'Dampieri Aurea', *Abies koreana*, *Betula utilis* var. *jacquemontii* and *Cedrus deodara* 'Pendula'.

Weeks Farm   42

Bedlam Lane, Egerton Forstal, Ashford TN27 9DA. Tel: (01233) 756252

Robin and Monica De Garston • 2½ m E of Headcorn. From Headcorn, take Smarden road, then third turning on left. House is 1½ m on right • Open two Suns for NGS, and for private visits by appt (please telephone evenings) • Entrance: £2 (2001 price) ◐ WC &

The two-acre garden is informally laid out round a typical Kent farmhouse. The prime asset here is a glorious annual display of naturalised spring bulbs, started 30 years ago by the previous owner on a badly drained site, and topped up annually with more bulbs – hyacinths, daffodils and tulips. A new pond, linked to an older one, is generously stocked with fish. The overall effect is much more than a cottage garden, with subtle oriental elements such as bamboos repeated throughout, and for good measure there are two deep mixed borders lining the sweeping drive.

Yalding Organic Gardens   43

Benover Road, Yalding, Maidstone ME18 6EX. Tel/Fax: (01622) 814650

HDRA the organic organisation • 6m SW of Maidstone, ½ m S of Yalding on B2162 • Open May to Sept, Wed – Sun, April and Oct, Sat and Sun only (but open Easter and Bank Holiday Mons), all 10am – 5pm • Entrance: £3, accompanied children free, parties of 14 or more £2.50 (£1 extra for garden tour) ◐ ⬛ ✕ 🍴 WC & 🐕 ♿ ⚲

The pergola of hop poles at the heart of the Yalding links it closely to the surrounding oasts and hop gardens of Kent. The gardens offer a tour of garden style through history, beginning with the natural woodland that once dotted our hills and valleys. Visitors pass through a thirteenth-century apothecary's garden, an Elizabethan Paradise Garden and Tudor knot, an early nineteenth-century cottager's plot, sweeping Edwardian borders and a utilitarian 1950s' allotment before being shown an organic vision of the future. A children's garden completes the tour. A fascinating experience for all the family.

LANCASHIRE

Two-starred gardens are marked on the map with a black square.

Ashton Memorial

Williamson Park, Quernmore Road, Lancaster LA1 1UX. Tel: (01524) 33318;
E-mail: office@williamsonpark.com; Website: www.williamsonpark.com

*E of Lancaster town centre. Signposted • Open daily except 25th, 26th Dec and
1st Jan: April to Sept, 10am – 5pm; Oct to March, 11am – 4pm • Entrance:
park and ground floor of memorial with exhibition free; memorial viewing gallery
50p; butterfly house, mini-beast house, conservation garden and free-flying bird
enclosure £3.25, OAPs £2.75, children £1.75* ○ 🍺 🍽 <u>WC</u> ⏄ 🏪 🔱 ⚲

Ashton Memorial, described by Pevsner as 'the grandest monument in England', stands at the highest point of Williamson Park looking down on the town of Lancaster. There are many views of the surrounding country from various points in the superbly landscaped park. Broad paths run through the grounds, much of which is woodland with an underplanting of rhododendrons and other shrubs. A small lake is spanned by a stone bridge, and nearby a large stairway leads to the huge domed monument. Not far away is the butterfly house and pavilion. Both monument and butterfly house were designed in 1906 by John Belcher in Baroque Revival style.

Catforth Gardens ★ 2

Roots Lane, Catforth, Preston PR4 0JB. Tel: (01772) 690561/690269

Mr and Mrs T.A. Bradshaw, Mr W. Moore and Miss S. Moore • 5m NW of Preston. Turn S off B5269 to Catforth. Roots Lane is S of village. Signposted • Bungalow Garden open mid-March to June, Thurs – Sun and Bank Holiday Mons; Farmhouse and Paddock Gardens open mid-March to Sept, daily, 10.30am – 5pm; and for groups by appt • Entrance: Bungalow Garden £1.25, OAPs £1, children 50p; Farmhouse and Paddock Gardens £1.25, OAPs £1, children 50p ◑ 🍴 WC ⅏ ⬠ 🌿 ⚲

There are three gardens here, separated by two nurseries which stock an excellent range of perennials. *The Bungalow Garden* is informally laid out with grass paths running amongst well-planted beds. Some unusual small trees and shrubs provide height, and a good selection of ferns and grasses gives variety to the foliage, but it is perennials that will impress most. This is the home of a National Collection of geraniums, and the charm and usefulness of the genus is well demonstrated as they are grown in many different situations. Most other perennials are well represented too, flowering throughout the season. Euphorbias, pulmonarias and dicentras are particularly plentiful. There is also a pond surrounded by banks of alpines, and a small woodland area with hydrangeas and dwarf rhododendrons and a new front garden designed as a summer flower and rose garden. *The Farmhouse Garden* was created as a cottage garden. It has a good collection of perennials, sidalceas, phloxes, lythrums and crocosmias, an alpine scree and ponds. Constructed from 1994, the two-acre *Paddock Garden* has now developed into a summer flower garden with long, boldly planted herbaceous borders filled with unusual species and hybrids shading from hot colours to paler hues, three natural water-lily ponds and associated waterside planting, large raised banks planted with sun lovers, and a formal area with roses and complementary herbaceous plants.

Clearbeck House 3

Higher Tatham, Lancaster LA2 8PJ. Tel: (01524) 261029

Peter and Bronwen Osborne • From M6 junction 34 take A683 to Kirkby Lonsdale, turn right on B6480 and follow signposts from Wray village • Open 30th June, 7th July for NGS, 11.30am – 5.30pm. Private visits by appt • Entrance: £1.50, children free ◑ 🍵 WC ⅏ ⬠ 🌿 🌱

Art and water are the two key features of this garden, but there is plenty more in the way of plants and landscaping. The old stone house has a large balcony, from where tea can be taken overlooking the garden. Beneath the balcony is a terrace planted with shrubs and perennials – hebes, geraniums and heathers – and with an unusual glass sculpture. Below the terrace a large irregular lawn has grass paths radiating outwards. One path follows a series of pools planted with water lilies down to the two-acre wildlife lake with its lush margins (47 bird species were noted in a recent year); another leads to a pyramid, the entrance to a small secret garden with its own pool. Beyond a second, raised terrace are fine views over the garden and lake. There is a bog garden surrounding a small natural stream and throughout the garden many shrub roses, grasses and bamboos. But it is the sculpture that fits so well with the natural look of this distinctive garden.

Gawthorpe Hall 4

Padiham, Burnley BB12 8UA. Tel: (01282) 771004; Fax: (01282) 770178

Lancashire County Council (on lease from National Trust) • *2½ m NW of Burnley, N of A671 just E of Padiham town centre* • *Hall open April to Oct, daily except Mon and Fri (but open 16th April and Bank Holiday Mons), 1 – 5pm (last admission 4.30pm)* • *Gardens open all year, 10am – 6pm* • *Entrance: fee (hall £3, children £1.30, family £8; concessions £1.50) (2001 prices)* • *Other information: Refreshments when hall open only* ○ 🍽 🍴 WC ♿ 🐕 🏪 ♨

This garden, though botanically not particularly special, sets off the Eliza-bethan hall. To the front is a formal layout of lawns and gravel paths, and to the rear a parterre by Sir Charles Barry in the form of a sunburst overlooks the River Calder. The woodlands that surround the formal garden are planted with rhododendrons and azaleas and traversed by many walks, with views back to the house and across the valley.

Gresgarth Hall ★★ 5

Caton LA2 9NB. Tel: (01524) 770313; Website: www.arabellalennoxboyd.com

Sir Mark and Lady Lennox-Boyd • *From M6 junction 34 take A683 towards Kirkby Lonsdale, then turn right in Caton village, signed 'Quernmore'* • *Open 14th April, 12th May, 9th June, 14th July, 11th Aug, 8th Sept, 11am – 5pm* • *Entrance: £3* ● 🍽 WC ♿ 🌿 🏪

You expect something special from the garden of such a renowned designer as Arabella Lennox-Boyd, and you will not be disappointed. Over this large area she has experimented with different styles of gardening and produced some superb results – all the more surprising since the weather in this part of northern Lancashire can be harsh. At the front of the house are formal areas – herbaceous borders, protected by yew hedges, to the south a pool and bog garden with a large selection of moisture-lovers, including many ferns. An arboretum contains a large sequoiadendron, acers, lilacs and many other fine specimens, while the walled garden has a happy mix of vegetables, fruit and flowering plants. To the east an attractive terrace and belvedere overlook a rocky beck that rushes through this part of the garden. A Chinese bridge leads to a woodland garden where azaleas, cornus, magnolias and many unusual plants flourish in the light shade. Sculpture, classical and modern, is used creatively throughout. There are woodland walks, a huge variety of plants and so much else that this description can only serve as the briefest of introductions to a fine garden.

Hoghton Tower 6

Hoghton, Preston PR5 0SH. Tel: (01254) 852986; Fax: (01254) 852109

Hoghton Tower Preservation Trust • 5m SE of Preston, mid-way between Preston and Blackburn, on old A675 • House open for guided tours (£3.50, OAPs and students £4, children £2, family ticket £12) • Garden open Bank Holiday Suns and Mons (except Christmas and New Year); July to Sept, Mon – Thurs, 11am – 4pm, Sun, 1 – 5pm. Private tours by arrangement • Entrance: £2 (2001 prices) ◐ ☕ ✕ WC ♿ ⓟ ℚ

Hoghton Tower, a sixteenth-century fortified manor house built of local stone, occupies a hilltop position with good views to all sides and outwards to the surrounding countryside. The house and outbuildings are constructed around two courtyards which, although not qualifying as gardens, are fine spaces. Surrounding the house are three walled gardens. The first, the Wilderness, contains a large lawn and herbaceous borders. The second, the rose garden, has a rectangular lawn flanked on two sides by clipped yews. In the centre is a raised square pond with an elaborate stone fountain. The third is mainly lawn with access to the tops of two crenellated towers. Around the walled gardens runs the Long Walk, which passes under large beech trees, and holly trees (especially weeping hollies) and is planted with shrubs, mainly rhododendrons and azaleas. There is a tradition that Shakespeare lived here during a formative period, and James I knighted a piece of beef 'Sirloin' on 17th August 1617.

Leighton Hall 7

Carnforth LA5 9ST. Tel: (01524) 734474; Fax: (01524) 720357; E-mail: leightonhall@yahoo.co.uk; Website: www.leightonhall.co.uk

Mr R.G. Reynolds • 1m W of Yealand Conyers, signed from M6 junction 35 • Hall open • Gardens open May to Sept, daily except Sat and Mon, 2 – 5pm (Aug, 11.30am – 5pm) • Entrance: (house and garden) £4.50, OAPs £4, children £3, parties of 25 or more £3.50 per person, schools £2.75 per child (2001 prices) • Other information: Dogs in park only, on lead ◐ ☕ 🍽 WC ♿ ⚘ ♿ ⓟ ℚ

Very striking when first seen from the entrance gates, the white stone façade (c. 1822) shines out in its parkland setting with the hills of the Lake District visible beyond. The most interesting area of the gardens, which lie to the west of the house, is the walled garden with its unusual labyrinth in the form of a gravel path running under an old cherry orchard. Opposite is a vegetable garden made in a geometric design with grass paths. There are also herbaceous borders and an aromatic herb garden containing a wide variety of perennials, with climbing roses on the wall behind.

Lindeth Dene ⟨ 8

38 Lindeth Road, Silverdale LA5 0TX. Tel: (01524) 701314

Mrs B.M. Kershaw • 12m N of Lancaster. From M6 junction 35, turn right at Carnforth traffic lights and follow signs to Silverdale. ¼ m after level crossing turn left into Hollins Lane. At T-junction turn right into Lindeth Road and continue to fourth gateway on left • Open by appt • Entrance: £1.50, accompanied children free ● ♨

A garden of one and a quarter acres set in an area of beautiful countryside with fine views over Morecambe Bay. Informal in layout, much of the garden consists of a large limestone rock garden planted with a wide range of perennials and alpines; there are many saxifrages and geraniums, and in the shadier parts (some large mature trees at this end of the garden) hostas, epimediums and varieties of ferns. Close to the house away from the trees are beds containing dwarf conifers and other small shrubs, also a heather garden, stone troughs and an organic kitchen garden. There is much of interest for the plantsman and for anyone looking for planting ideas for a small garden. Be sure to visit the excellent nursery next door, which stocks a large range of plants, including ferns.

Mill Barn ★ 9

Goose Foot Close, Samlesbury Bottoms, Preston PR5 0SS. Tel: (01254) 853300; E-mail: chris@millbarn.globalnet.co.uk

Dr C.J. Mortimer • 6m E of Preston on A677 Blackburn road, turn S into Nabs Head Lane, then Goose Foot Lane • Open 15th, 16th, 22nd, 23rd, 29th, 30th June, all 1 – 5pm, and for parties by appt • Entrance: £1.50, children free • Other information: 'Art and Garden' exhibition 15th, 16th June. Teas and plants for sale on open days ● ➽ WC ♿ ⬗ ♨ ♀ ♋

On the site of an old mill by the River Darwen, this garden has been designed to make the most of its superb setting. A path leads along a high stone embankment overlooking the fast-flowing river. It passes through a series of features: a unique temple to alchemy created from an old sluice gate, a rose-clad pergola, a picturesque ruin constructed to hide a septic tank. Near here a fine 'Paul's Himalayan Musk' rose climbs high up into a tree. Finally there is a rectangular pool set into the wall containing a good variety of water plants and marginals, with a stretch of lawn and an heptagonal summerhouse beyond. A long herbaceous border runs back to the house, containing plants chosen for their contrasting foliage and architectural effects. A bridge crosses the river giving access to a belvedere looking back over the garden. The quarry is becoming a secret garden in a modern style.

Pendle Heritage Centre 10

**Park Hill, Barrowford, Nelson BB9 6JQ. Tel: (01282) 661701;
Fax: (01282) 611718**

*The Heritage Trust for the North West • N of Nelson, near M65 junctions 13
and 14. In Barrowford at A682/B6247 junction • Museum £1, concessions
80p) • Garden open all year, daily except 25th Dec, 10am – 5pm. Parties
welcome by appt • Entrance: Walled garden, barn and woodland £1.20,
concessions 80p* ○ 🍽 ✕ WC ⅙ 🌿 🏛 🔔 ⚲

In the centre of Barrowford among a group of fine old stone buildings (eight
Grade-II-listed) is a walled garden dating from the 1780s. This has been
restored and replanted under the guidance of the NCCPG, using only plants
that were available in the eighteenth century. There are culinary and medicinal herbs and plants that were used in the production of dyes, as well as
traditional varieties of fruit and vegetables. All plants are organically grown in
beds divided by gravel paths and edged in clipped box. A woodland walk takes
the visitor up a steep wooded bank planted with native wild flowers to a
viewing point that looks back over the garden and surrounding countryside
leading to a cruck-frame barn saved and re-erected on the site.

The Ridges 11

Limbrick, Chorley PR6 9EB. Tel: (01257) 279981

*Mr and Mrs J M Barlow • From M61 junction 8 follow signs for Chorley on
A6, then for Cowling and Rivington • Open June and July, Wed and Bank
Holiday Suns and Mons, 11am – 5pm; and by appt at other times • Entrance:
£2.50, children free* ● 🍽 WC ⅙ ⬩ 🌿

In the first area of the garden an herbaceous bed contains hemerocallis and
geraniums, shaded by fruit trees. The seventeenth-century house has French
windows leading onto a small lawn. This is part of the old walled garden; in one
corner is a small pool set within a paved area. A path leads beneath a laburnum
arch and between two large thujas into a separate part, where, in a large
rectangular lawned garden surrounded by woodland, are beds of perennials,
shrubs and trees. There is also a large Victorian glasshouse, a mock ornamental
pond with a central urn, and a water feature with ponds and a stream fringed
with wild flowers and moisture-loving plants.

Rufford Old Hall 12

Rufford, Ormskirk L40 1SG. Tel: (01704) 821254

*The National Trust • 7m NE of Ormskirk, N of Rufford, E of A59 • Hall open
as garden (last admission 4.30pm) • Garden open 23rd March to Oct, Sat –
Wed, 11am – 5.30pm • Entrance: £2 (house and garden £4)* ◑ 🍽 ✕ 🍴 WC
⬩ 🌿 🏛 🔔

The gardens complement the exceptional sixteenth-century timber-framed
house, having been laid out by the Trust in the style of the Victorian/
Edwardian period. On the south are lawns and gravel paths designed in a

formal manner. The many island beds are formal in layout, too, but the shrubs, small trees and herbaceous plants they contain are planted in a more relaxed way. In the centre a path leads from two large topiary squirrels to a beech avenue that extends beyond the garden towards Rufford. There are many mature trees and rhododendrons in this area dating back to the 1820s. To the east of the house by the stables is an attractive cobbled space with climbing plants on the surrounding walls. Look out for the cottage garden to the north side of the house, in which grow many old-fashioned plants enclosed by a rustic wooden fence.

Stonyhurst College 13

Hurst Green, Clitheroe BB7 9PZ. Tel: (01254) 826345

Stonyhurst College • 10m NE of M6 junction 31, just off B6243 Longridge – Clitheroe road on outskirts of Hurst Green • College open 17th July to 27th Aug, daily except Fri • Garden open mid-July to 26th Aug, Sat – Thurs, 1 – 5pm • Entrance: £1 (house and garden £4.50, OAPs and children £3.50) ● ● ● WC ♿

The rather severe stone buildings of Stonyhurst College are surrounded by long-established parkland. Two long rectangular pools flanking the drive date from the seventeenth century. An area of formal gardens to the south of the college is of less interest for the plants than for the stonework which, although in a state of poor repair, is still quite magnificent. Steps lead up to a circular pool, overlooked by an unusual cross-shaped stone building, and down to a gravel terrace with two gazebos placed symmetrically at each end and a fine view across the low connecting wall. Photographs in Gertrude Jekyll's book *Garden Ornament* show Stonyhurst in its former glory; it is hoped that the restoration will achieve something approaching its previous grandeur.

Swiss Cottage 14

8 Hammond Drive, Read, Burnley BB12 7RE. Tel: (01282) 774853

James and Doreen Bowker • 5m NW of Burnley on A671. In Read turn by Pollards Garage into George Lane, then at T-junction left into Hammond Drive • Open for parties by appt • Entrance: £2 per person ●

A modern garden of one and a half acres set on a steeply sloping south-facing site. The west side is backed by mature woodland and planted to enhance the woodland feel. Small trees such as sorbus, salix, acers and birch are here as well as a *Cornus nuttallii*, a particular favourite of the owners. Beneath the trees are rhododendrons, azaleas, camellias and skimmias, while hostas, tiarellas, helle- bores and other shade-lovers fill the remaining space. Close to the centre of the garden a small stream rises and is taken through a series of rock pools bordered by beds of astilbes, irises and calthas; there is also a bed of grasses. The east side of the garden close to the house has irregularly shaped beds meandering down the slope, which is much steeper here. They are mulched with gravel as the owners find that this breaks up the Lancashire clay better than bark or other mulches. Dwarf conifers, alpines and sun-loving perennials like the conditions. The planting is well considered; there is good variety and inspiration here.

Towneley Park 15

Todmorden Road, Burnley BB11 3RQ. Tel: (01282) 424213

Burnley Borough Council • 1½ m SE of Burnley on A671 • Hall open daily except Sat, Mon – Fri, 10am – 5pm, Sun, 12 noon – 5pm. Closed Christmas week • Park open all year, daily during daylight hours • Entrance: free • Other information: Shop in hall ○ 🍵 📦 <u>WC</u> & 🐕 🏛🎹

The hall dates from 1500, but its exterior is largely the work of 1816 to 1820. The frontage looks out over a pond and beyond a ha-ha to open parkland laid out in the late eighteenth century. There are some formal beds to the east of the house planted with bright annuals. Herbaceous plants and shrubs have been chosen for the area around the hall, and the Small Lime Walk has been opened up by removing old rhododendrons, replacing them with a better selection of choice shrubs and ground cover. Further to the east, as well as to the south and west, are extensive woodlands containing many large rhododendrons, and long walks. There is also a museum of local crafts and industries, a nature centre and an aquarium.

Weeping Ash 16

Glazebury, Leigh WA3 5NT. Tel: (01942) 266303 (Bent's Garden Centre)

John Bent • 14m W of Manchester. Turn S off A580 at Greyhound Hotel roundabout onto A574 to Culcheth. Garden is ¼ m further on left • Open Feb to Nov, 3rd Sun in each month, 11am – 5.30pm • Entrance: £2, children free • Other information: Parking, teas, toilet facilities, plants for sale and shop at adjacent garden centre ● 🍵 ✗ <u>WC</u> & 🌿 🏛🎹 ⚘

This garden has been created by a retired nurseryman, so it is only to be expected that a great variety of plants is found here. John Bent has a good collection of small trees, particularly sorbus, and many shrubs, especially roses. The herbaceous border is 90 metres long. There is a large range of perennials, including over 50 hellebores and many bulbs; one large bed is devoted to lilies. But it is his ideas on design that bring so much to the garden. Broad grass paths snake around the mixed beds and small offshoot paths give interesting views back into the main areas. There are views over the whole garden from a ruined Doric temple on a mound – a feature inspired during a visit to Cyprus. Many structures have been created as hosts to climbing plants, the best being a rustic gazebo built entirely from scrapwood, which is now covered by a passion flower and a golden hop.

Woodside 17

Princes Park, Shevington, Wigan WN6 8HY. Tel/Fax: (01257) 255255; E-mail: wseddon@tinyworld.co.uk; www.woodsidegarden.net

Barbara and Bill Seddon • 3m NW of Wigan. From M6 junction 26 or 27 follow signs for Shevington • Open 4th Aug for NGS, 11am – 5pm, and for private visits by appt • Entrance: £2, children free ● 🍵 🌿 ⚘

This is a suburban garden of two thirds of an acre on an attractively undulating site, surrounded by mature trees. Broad grass paths designed to accentuate the landscaping lead round beds of mainly acid-loving plants. There are many azaleas, small rhododendrons, camellias, magnolias, acers and conifers. Of particular note are collections of hostas, peonies and hellebores. An attractive water feature stands at the centre of the garden – a large stone trough with water bubbling up through stones guarded by a pair of bronze geese. There is a well-established herbaceous border which is delightful from mid-June until September, and in August dozens of hydrangeas and three mature *Eucryphia x nymansensis* are in flower. There is also a stone-banked dell excavated at one end of the garden and a waterfall. Everything is exeptionally well kept, and there is a surprising amount to see in what is not a vast garden.

Worden Park   18

Leyland PR25 2DJ. Tel: (01772) 421109

Borough of South Ribble • 4m S of Preston. Take B5253 S from Leyland.
Signposted • Open all year, daily, 8am – dusk • Entrance: free, except first Sat
in June • Other information: Refreshments at craft centre ○ 🍽 ✗ 📖 WC ⑤
🔄 ⊕ ⚲

The gardens are set around part of an old house and a stable block that now contains craft and theatre workshops (the rest of the house was burnt down in the 1940s). The maze is unusual, being made of hornbeam hedges in a circular pattern. A little distance away is a large conservatory with a rockery to one side and a herbaceous border to the other. They face a formal sunken lawned area enclosed by a low balustrade and some fine ironwork gates. Large areas of open parkland surround the gardens, which contain a children's adventure play area, mini golf, a model railway, an ice-house and an arboretum. Areas in the parkland are being developed to attract wildlife. Full events programme (mostly without charge) – telephone for details.

HOW TO FIND THE GARDENS

Directions to each garden are included in the entry. This information has been supplied by the owners and garden Inspectors. It is aimed to be the best available to those travelling by car, and has been compiled to be used in conjunction with a road atlas.

Some gardens can be approached by public transport, but alas these are few and far between. The unreliability of train and bus services makes it unrewarding to include details, particularly as many garden visits are made on Sundays. However, properties that can be reached by public transport feature in National Trust guides and the NGS Yellow Book, which sometimes give details.

LEICESTERSHIRE

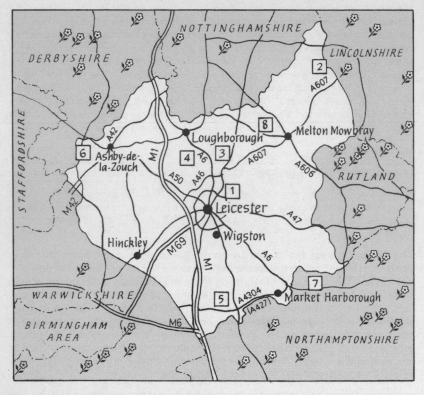

For gardens in Rutland, see pages 356–8.

Beeby Manor ★   1

Beeby LE7 3BL. Tel: (01162) 595238

Mr and Mrs Philip Bland • 5m E of Leicester. Turn off A47 in Thurnby and follow signs through Scraptoft • Open by appt • Entrance: £2 ◑ 🍴 **WC** ♿

Three acres of mature gardens in the form of a series of romantic rooms enclosed by lofty yew hedges, with roses everywhere in soft colours on frames and mellow walls or tumbling through arbours. A parterre, ancient-looking, though only 10 years old, leads to formal lily ponds and exuberant herbaceous borders which are overblown and carefully untidy. A charming Old English garden in the grandest cottage style evokes a bygone age. An arboretum is under development. *Kaye's Garden and Nursery* is nearby on the A607 at 1700 Melton Road, Rearsby [open March to Oct, daily, 10am – 5pm, and Sun, 10am – 12 noon]. The attractively designed garden includes a collection of interesting and unusual hardy plants, herbaceous plants, shrubs and shrub roses.

Belvoir Castle 2

**Belvoir, Grantham, Lincolnshire NG32 1PD. Tel: (01476) 870262;
Email: info@belvoircastle.com; Website: www.belvoircastle.com**

*The Duke of Rutland • 10m NE of Melton Mowbray off A607 by Belvoir.
Signposted • Castle open • Garden open 28th – 31st March, 1st – 7th, 14th,
21st, 28th April; May to Sept, daily; Oct, Sun only; all 11am – 5pm. Open
Bank Holiday Mons. Parties at other times by appt. Spring garden open all year
for pre-booked parties • Entrance: castle and garden £7, OAPs £5.50, children
£3.50, family (2 adults, 2 children) £17. Spring garden £5, OAPs £4.50 per
person for pre-booked parties of 20 to 40 persons (2001 prices)* ◑ ♨ ✕ 🍴 WC
♨ 🔦 ☕

From a distance this castle (pronounced Beaver) has all the appearance of a
medieval fortress, although close to it is clearly a more substantial nineteenth-
century edifice. The house is famous for its rooms by James Wyatt. The mid-
nineteenth-century garden descends from the castle, with fine views of Belvoir
Vale, in a series of terraces and slopes with some small gardens created by
hedging. There are bulbs, early-flowering shrubs and roses, arbours and some
seating, and friendly peacocks. Also available for viewing by pre-booked
parties is the Duchess of Rutland's private woodland garden, known as the
Spring Garden, a delightful informal spot situated in a natural ampitheatre in
the middle of dense woodland. Don't miss the recently restored moss house.
Overall, some people find the site rather municipal in style.

Brinkfields ★ 3

Seagrave LE12 7NH.

*Mr and Mrs John Gennard • Directions on application • Open by written appt
only • Entrance: £2.50* ◖

Three acres, superbly maintained and visually satisfying, which after 30 years are
just coming into the first flush of handsome maturity. Many acid-loving plants are
amazingly robust, defying their clay surroundings. Features include a large rock
garden with alpines and a water feature, an enchanting woodland glade with
meconopsis and rare trilliums, carpets of spring bulbs and many rare specimens
carefully placed together to give of their best. Nothing second-rate here.

Long Close ★ 4

**Main Street, Woodhouse Eaves, Loughborough LE12 8RZ.
Tel: (01509) 890616 (business hours)**

*Mr J.T. Oakland and Miss P. Johnson • S of Loughborough between A6 and
M1 junctions 22 and 23 • Open March to July, Sept to Oct, Mon – Sat,
9.30am – 1pm, 2 – 5.30pm, and for NGS on two Sun afternoons. Private
parties welcome by appt • Entrance: £2.50, children free • Other information:
Tickets for daily visits to be purchased from Pene Crafts gift shop opposite the
garden. Park in adjacent public car park. Teas on NGS open days, and for
parties by arrangement only* ◑ 🍴 WC ♿ ⬨ 🌣 ☕

When Mr and Mrs George Johnson bought Long Close in 1949, they began to restore this five-acre garden, based on the framework and potential left by their predecessor, Colonel Gerald Heygate. Taking advantage of the lime-free loam, they nurtured a large collection of rhododendrons, azaleas and magnolias, which are now in magnificent maturity, adding many camellias and other shrubs and trees. Formal terraces lead to more informal gardens, with winding paths between specimen trees and finally to a natural dappled pool. In spring there are drifts of snowdrops, daffodils and bluebells and in summer prolifically planted herbaceous borders. The present owners have extended the plantings and created a *potager* and penstemon collection in the old walled kitchen garden. A courtyard plays its sheltered part with magnificent wall-covering plants. This is sometimes described as a Cornish garden in Leicestershire due to the many quite tender trees and plants rarely to be found elsewhere so far north. Truly a plantsman's garden. For contrast, stroll along the very old pasture wildflower meadow walk.

Orchards ★ 5

Hall Lane, Walton, Lutterworth LE17 5RP. Tel: (01455) 556958

Mr and Mrs G. Cousins • 8m S of Leicester. Take A5199, turn right for Bruntingthorpe then follow signs for Walton • Open June to Aug, Sun, 2 – 5pm, and at other times by appt • Entrance: £2, children free ◕ ☕ WC ✿

Tucked away behind a modern bungalow, this garden is a success story. There are ideas here that relate to almost any medium-sized plot in town or country – a round pool surrounded by a circle of trees, old brick paths, views through sculpted walks, vistas terminating in unusual artistic arrangements. Most notable is the series of colour-themed gardens full of rare and unusual plants, with views of the countryside beyond.

Paddocks 6

Shelbrook, Ashby-de-la-Zouch LE65 2TU. Tel: (01530) 412606

Mrs Ailsa Jackson • 1½ m W of Ashby-de-la-Zouch on B5003 • Open probably five Sats and Suns, April to Aug, 2 – 5pm, and for parties of 10 or more by appt • Entrance: £1.50, children free ◕ ✕ WC ♿ ✿

A one-acre plantsman's garden and RHS award-winner, created as an exhibition to show the rarely seen to advantage. A National Collection of primulas is closely planted with many new varieties and other unusual plants.

Stoke Albany House 7

Stoke Albany, Market Harborough LE16 8PT. Tel: (01858) 535227

Mr and Mrs Alfred Vinton • 4m E of Market Harborough. Turn S off A427 onto B669. Garden ½ m on left • Open 7th April (Daffodil Sunday), 15th, 22nd, 29th May, 5th, 12th, 19th, 26th June, 3rd, 10th, 17th July, 2 – 4.30pm. Also for parties by appt • Entrance: £2.50, children free • Other information: Teas on Sun only ◕ ♿ ✿ ⚲

A traditional country-house garden set in four acres with picturesque land-scape sweeping beyond. There are fine trees and wide herbaceous borders, striped lawns, and good displays of bulbs in spring and roses in July. The walled grey garden shows splashes of white. The clever avenue of *Nepeta* 'Six Hills Giant' has 'Mme Alfred Carrière' roses skilfully trained over arches, the distances marked with carefully placed urns. A new box parterre filled with roses has been added to the side of the house. Beautifully maintained green-houses. Everything one would expect to see in a perfect English setting.

Wartnaby Gardens ★   8

Wartnaby, Melton Mowbray LE14 3HY. Tel: (01664) 822296

Lord and The Hon. Lady King of Wartnaby • 4m NW of Melton Mowbray. From A606 turn W in Ab Kettleby for Wartnaby • Open 28th April, 19th May, 23rd June, 11am – 4pm, and for parties and individuals by appt (not Weds) • Entrance: £2.50, children free • Other information: Plant fair and picture exhibition on June open day ◑ 🍵 🛍 WC ℘

The garden has delightful little gardens within it, including a white garden, a newly laid-out rose garden, a purple border of shrubs and roses, good herbaceous borders, climbers and old-fashioned roses. Two large pools with primulas, ferns, astilbes and several varieties of willow extend to further pools and woodland planting. There is an arboretum with a good collection of trees and shrub and alongside the drive is a beech hedge laid out in a Grecian pattern. A well-furnished kitchen garden and orchard with arches and a collection of climbing roses and clematis.

SYMBOLS

[NEW] entries new for 2002; ○ open all year; ◐ open most of year; ◑ open during main season; ◕ open rarely and/or by appt; 🍵 teas/light refresh-ments; ✕ meals; 🧺 picnics permitted; WC toilet facilities; <u>WC</u> toilet facilities, inc. disabled; ♿ partly wheelchair-accessible; 🐕 dogs on lead; ℘ plants for sale; 🏪 shop; 🎪 events held; ℀ children-friendly.

POSTCODE PLANTS DATABASE

It is often difficult to find out which plants are local to an area. The Postcode Plants Database locates the names of flowers, trees, butterflies and birds for each of Britain's 26 million home addresses. Simply by typing in the first four characters of their postcode, householders, schools, garden centres and councils, can obtain tailor-made lists of local plants which are both hospitable and garden-worthy. Also included are the names of butterflies and birds most likely to visit gardens in each area. The lists come from innovative software, developed by Royal Mail and *FLORA-for-FAUNA* in conjunction with the Natural History Museum, which searches through hundreds of distribution maps of fauna and flora in the British Isles.

LINCOLNSHIRE

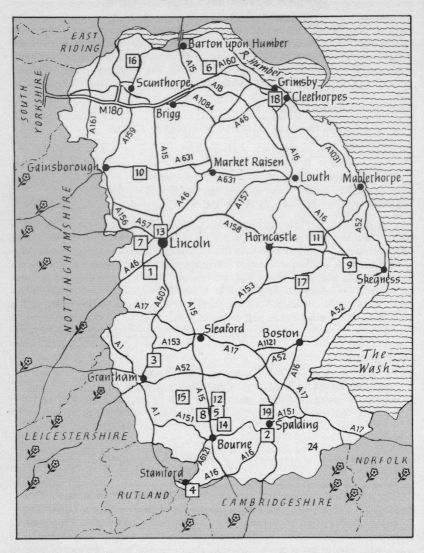

Auburn Hall ★   1

Aubourn, Lincoln LN5 9DZ. Tel: (01522) 788270

Lady Nevile • 7m SW of Lincoln between A46 and A607 • Garden open for charity two or three Suns in early summer, plus June and July, Wed only, 2 – 5.30pm • Entrance: £3, OAPs £2.50 • Other informaion: plants for sale on some days ◑ **WC** ♿

First impressions of the gardens at this lovely red-brick hall (c. 1600) are of spacious simplicity. Glorious undulating lawns and borders sweep through rose arches or along grassy swathes to more lawns and gardens beyond. The enviably deep and diverse borders are carefully planted to give maximum effects of colour, shape and texture. There are also secluded areas in which to linger: the rose garden, the Golden Triangle edged with yew and planted with ornamental crab apple trees and spring bulbs, the ponds and the woodland dell, and a swimming pool surrounded by a late-flowering rose-and-clematis-covered pergola. The nearby church, one of the smallest in Lincolnshire, is also open to visitors on garden open days.

Ayscoughfee Hall, Museum and Gardens 2

Churchgate, Spalding PE11 2RA. Tel: (01775) 725468; Fax: (01775) 762715

South Holland District Council • In centre of Spalding • Hall open March to Oct, daily, 9am – 5pm (Sat opens 10am, Sun 11am), Nov to Feb 2002, Mon – Fri, 9am – 5pm. Closed 25th Dec, 1st Jan • Gardens open all year, daily, 8am – dusk. Closed 25th Dec, 1st Jan • Entrance: free • Other information: Refreshments in main season. Shop in Hall ○ ⬤ ✕ 🛒 WC ♿ ⬙ ♨ ☕ ⚲

The gardens of this late-medieval wool merchant's house are in a beautiful setting next to the River Welland. Entirely enclosed by lovely old walls, they are worth visiting for the bizarrely shaped clipped yew walks, the old rectangular fish pond with fountains, and the fascinating late-medieval red-brick hall, now housing the Museum of South Holland Life, with displays on the history of bulb growing in the Fens. In addition there are good bedding displays, lawns, a pergola and wall shrubs, including a fruiting vine. Nearby is the *Pinchbeck Engine and Land Drainage Museum* – a reminder of how the Fens achieved and maintained their prosperity.

Belton House ★ 3

Belton, Grantham NG32 2LS. Tel: (01476) 566116

The National Trust • 3m N of Grantham off A607 • House open 12.30 – 5pm • Gardens open 23rd March to 3rd Nov, Wed – Sun and Bank Holiday Mons, 11am – 5.30pm (last admission 5pm). Free access to park on foot from Lion Lodge gates all year (closed for special events), but this does not give admittance to house, garden or adventure playground • Entrance: house and gardens £5.60, children £2.80, family ticket £14 ◑ ⬤ ✕ WC ♿ ♨ ☕

The park and gardens are, like the house, composed with perfect harmony and proportion. Serenity, order, and strong architectural conviction are the keynotes. The house itself is superb in its own right, but there are also good views from first-floor windows of the formal gardens and of the East Avenue rising imperiously to the distant Bellmount Tower. The extensive woodland has two lakes, a small canal and noble cedars, and the radiating avenues are an impressive reminder of the late seventeenth- and early eighteenth-century predilection for introducing drama into the landscape, but it is the formal area to the north of the house that makes a visit memorable. The 1870s' Dutch garden is a satisfying composition with pillars of green yew and cushions of golden yew, pale gravel, formal beds cleverly planted and edged with lavender, and generously filled urns. The earlier sunken Italian garden is more reliant on Wyatville's architectural features: a large central pond with a fountain, a lion-headed exedra and, the high point, the superbly restored and replanted orangery. Behind the orangery a little church is glimpsed; it is filled with memorials to generations of Custs, who built the house, and of Brownlows, who created the garden.

Burghley House   4

Stamford PE9 3JY. Tel: (01780) 752451; Fax: (01780) 480125;
Website: www.burghley.co.uk

Burghley House Preservation Trust. Custodian: Lady Victoria Leatham (née Cecil) • ½ m E of Stamford on Barnack road, close to A1. Signposted • House open, daily, April to Oct, 11am — 4.30pm • Sculpture garden and parkland open daily, 10am – 4pm; South Garden open April • Entrance: Free (house £6.80, OAPs £6.30, children (one child per adult) free) • Other information: Limited access for wheelchairs. Dogs in park only, on lead ◑ ☕ ✕ 🍴 WC ♿ ⬧ ⬚ 🏮 ✎

The main attraction at Burghley is the magnificent Elizabethan house with its immense collection of art treasures, built by William Cecil, created Lord Burghley by his Queen. The parkland, landscaped by 'Capability' Brown, is delightful and extensive, even though in the process he swept away the George London Baroque garden of 1700 which had 'canals, rising flights of terraces, ornamental fish-pools, a maze, a vineyard and other conceits'. In addition to creating a large serpentine lake, Brown built a new stable block and an orangery. The finest surviving small building is his recently restored lakeside 'temple', which can be seen while the South Garden is open for its spectacular display of spring flowers in April. Twelve acres of garden have been reclaimed from woodland in recent years and extensively planted with specimen trees and shrubs. This area has an annually changing display of contemporary sculpture alongside a number of permanent site-specific sculptures, one of the most dramatic being a group emerging Excalibur-like from the surface of the lake.

21 Chapel Street   5

Hacconby, Bourne PE10 0UL. Tel: (01778) 570314

Mr and Mrs C. Curtis • 3m N of Bourne off A15, turn E at crossroads to Hacconby • Open 23rd, 24th Feb, 11am – 4pm (snowdrop and hellebore weekend), 7th March, 2 – 6pm, 1st April, 11am – 5pm, 2nd May, 2 – 6pm, 6th June, 5 – 9pm, 4th July, 1st Aug, 5th Sept, 2 – 6pm, 6th Oct, 11am – 5pm; and at other times by appt • Entrance: £1, children (under 16) free ● ☕ 🍴 WC ✎ ✎

The gay and cottagey impression of this village garden has been achieved by minimising lawn area and replacing it with planting space. The circuitous path passes rockeries and scree beds, small trees and shrub roses, rustic arches, troughs and a pond, all exuberantly planted and underplanted to ensure year-round colour, from snowdrops in February to red, yellow and gold herbaceous plants in late summer and asters extending the season into October. There are hundreds of varieties of bulbs, alpines and herbaceous plants here to satisfy both the casual gardener and the seeker of the rare. Over towards the A1 is the collection of plantsman Richard Bish, not open to the public but offering private visits by arrangement (Tel: (01476) 550273).

Croft House   6

Pitmoor Lane, Ulceby, Brigg DN39 6SW. Tel: (01469) 588330

Mr and Mrs P. Sandberg • 9m NW of Grimsby, 7m SE of Barton-upon-Humber on A1077 • Open by appt for NGS, also for individuals and groups • Entrance: £2, children under 12 free • Other information: Refreshments by arrangement and plants for sale on open days ● ☕ ♿ ⊲⊳ 🌿 ♋

Although set within a formal design of high walls, clipped *Lonicera nitida* hedges, a pergola walk and gravel paths, this two-acre garden could not seem less formal. The eclectic planting of old favourites among sought-after varieties gives a refreshingly cottagey air, intensified by flowers allowed to seed freely in the gravel. The interesting variety of areas includes mixed, herbaceous and 'woodland' borders, a heather bed, a rock garden, a grassy meadow, a gravel bed, a kitchen garden and a Victorian vinery.

Doddington Hall   7

Doddington, Lincoln LN6 4RU. Tel: (01522) 694308;
E-mail: fionawatson@doddingtonhall.free-online.co.uk;
Website: www.doddingtonhall.free-online.co.uk

Mr and Mrs A.G. Jarvis • 5m W of Lincoln on B1190 • House and garden open May to Sept • Garden open Feb and April, Sun only; May to Sept, Wed, Sun and Bank Holiday Mons; all 2 – 6pm. Parties at other times by arrangement • Entrance: £2.15, children £1.10 (house and garden £4.50, children £2.25, family £12.50), special rates for disabled in wheelchairs and parties of 20 or more ● ☕ 🍴 WC ♿ 🏧 ♋

The romantic gardens of the Elizabethan house successfully combine many different styles and moods. The simplicity of the gravel, box and lawned courtyard, the formal croquet lawn and the gravel walk along the kitchen garden wall contrasts with the walled west garden with its elaborate parterres of roses, iris and clipped box edging and its borders of herbaceous plants, flag iris and the sound of gently falling water from the fountains. The parterres were restored in Elizabethan style in 1900. Fine eighteenth-century Italian gates open onto a formal yew alley, more old roses and a good wild garden. Here the meandering walks take in a turf maze, a stream, ancient specimens of sweet chestnut, cedar, yew and holly, and the Temple of the Winds built by the present owners. The more recently planted herb garden, pleached hornbeams and dwarf box-edging continue to harmonise the different areas.

Grimsthorpe Castle   8

**Grimsthorpe, Nr Bourne PE10 0NB. Tel: (01778) 591205;
Fax: (01778) 591259; Website: www.grimsthorpe.co.uk**

*Grimsthorpe and Drummond Castle Trust Ltd • 4m NW of Bourne on A151
Colsterworth – Bourne road • Castle open 1pm, last admission 4.30pm • Garden
open April to July, Sept, Thurs, Sun; Aug, Sun – Thurs; all 11am – 6pm •
Entrance: Park and garden £3, OAPs £2, children £1.50 (additional £3.50 for
castle, OAPs £2.75) (2001 prices)* ◐ ⬛ ✕ 🍴 WC ♿ ♨ ▯ ✎

The impressive house, part-medieval, part-Tudor and part-eighteenth-cen-
tury, of Vanbrugh design, is surrounded on three sides by good pleasure
gardens in which 'Capability' Brown had a hand. The Victorian knot garden to
the east of the house has beds of lavender, roses and catmint with edges of
clipped box. To the south are two yew-hedged gardens with topiary, a yew
broad walk and a retreat. Leading to the west terrace is a double yew walk
with classic herbaceous borders; beyond is a shrub rose border and a row of
70-year-old cedars. The yew hedging throughout the garden is superbly
maintained and differs in design from one area to another. Beyond the pleasure
gardens are the arboretum, the wild garden, an unusual geometrically designed kitchen garden with clipped box and bean pergola, and extensive
parkland. Views of the old oak and chestnut avenues and of the parkland
with its lake and Vanbrugh summerhouse are provided by cleverly positioned
vistas and terraces.

Gunby Hall ★   9

Gunby, Spilsby PE23 5SS. Tel: (01909) 486411

*The National Trust • 7m NW of Skegness, 2½ m NW of Burgh-le-Marsh on S of
A158 • Hall and garden open, Wed, 2 – 6pm (last admission 5.30pm) •
Garden open 27th March to Sept, Wed and Thurs, 2 – 6pm. Also Tues and Fri
by written appt to Mr and Mrs J.D. Wrisdale. Coaches and parties pre-book in
writing • Entrance: £2.60, children £1.30 (hall and garden £3.70, children
£1.80) • Other information: Possible for wheelchairs but some gravel paths; no
wheelchair access to hall* ◐ WC ♿ ⬧ ✿ ▯

The early eighteenth-century hall, its walls smothered in fine plants, is set in
parkland with avenues of lime and horse chestnut. The shrub borders, wild
garden, lawns with old cedars and restrained formal front garden of catmint
and lavender beds backed by clipped yew provide a startling contrast to the
main attraction of Gunby – its walled gardens. The dazzling pergola garden
with its apple-tree walkway has a maze of paths leading to beds of old roses, a
herb garden and brimming herbaceous and annual borders. The second walled
area houses an impressive kitchen garden reached after passing more borders
of perfectly arranged herbaceous plants and hybrid musk roses. Backing onto
its wall is another wonderfully classic herbaceous border and, beyond, an early
nineteenth-century long fish pond and orchard complete an altogether enchanting garden.

Hall Farm and Nursery 10

Harpswell, Gainsborough DN21 5UU. Tel: (01427) 668412;
Fax: (01427) 667478; E-mail: nursery@hall-farm.co.uk;
Website: www.hall-farm.co.uk

Mr and Mrs M. Tatam • 7m E of Gainsborough on A631 • Open March to Oct, daily; Nov to Feb, Mon – Fri (and most Sats and Suns – telephone to check); and 1st Sept for NGS (inc. free seed collection); all 10am – 6pm. Also by appt • Entrance: donation to charity • Other information: Coaches by appt. Teas on charity open day only ○ WC ♿ ⌀ 🏮 ☕

This garden combines the formal and the informal in a most imaginative way. The owners' sheer delight in plants, satisfied by their adjoining nursery, is evident everywhere. There are hundreds of varieties of unusual herbaceous plants, roses and shrubs. A santolina-edged rose pergola leads from a decorative paved area to the main garden at the rear of the farmhouse. Here the walled top terrace has steps down to a classic double herbaceous border, a sunken garden with box edging and seasonal bedding, lawns, a rose garden and a large informal pond. A short walk away is an interesting medieval moat. A superb garden to visit in summer.

Harrington Hall 11

Harrington, Spilsby PE23 4NH. Tel: (01790) 754570 (Gardener)

Mr and Mrs D.W.J. Price • 5m E of Horncastle, 2m N of A158 • Open two days in June, two in July, 2 – 5pm • Entrance: £2, children free ● ☕ WC ⌀ ⌀

Red-brick Tudor and eighteenth-century walls provide the perfect backdrop for wall shrubs and a variety of borders. Referred to in Tennyson's 'Maud,' it is hard to imagine that these walled gardens and terrace have changed since then, although they were in fact replanted in the 1950s after wartime vegetable cultivation. The present owners have recently remade the formal one acre vegetable garden with gravel paths, miniature box edging and espalier fruit trees. The tiny church is open to those visiting the garden.

25 High Street 12

Rippingale, Bourne PE10 0SR. Tel: (01778) 440693

Mr and Mrs Beddington • 6m N of Bourne off A15 • Open 16th, 17th Feb in conjunction with Manor Farm, Keisby (see entry)(hellebore and snowdrop Sat and Sun), 11am – 4pm; 5th May, 8th June, 9th June, 2 – 5pm, and at other times by appt • Entrance: £1 each garden, children free • Other information: Refreshments and plants for sale on open days only ● ☕ WC ♿ ⌀ ☕

What at first seems a small informal garden of lawn, borders and island beds in fact provides half and acre of many delightful surprises. There are shady paths and secret corners, a bog garden, ponds, pergola and paved areas, and through a small gate an inspirational vegetable garden complete with fruit cage and rhubarb pots. The assiduous care of the knowledgeable owners ensures a display of unusual herbaceous plants, shrubs and bulbs throughout the year. The February opening is in conjunction with Manor Farm, Keisby (see entries), but in June about 15 gardens are usually open together.

The Lawn   13

Union Road, Lincoln LN1 3BL. Tel: (01522) 873629.

Lincoln City Council • Off Burton Road beside Lincoln Castle • Garden open all year, daily, 9am – 5pm (opens 10am Sat and Sun, closes 4pm Fri, Sat and Sun in winter) • Entrance: free, but charge for parking • Other information: Lincoln Archaeological Centre ○ 🍵 ✕ 🪧 WC & ♿

When Lincoln City Council bought this disused Georgian mental hospital in 1985 they aimed to establish a botanic collection to represent Lincoln's partnership with cities and countries around the world. Central to this is the Sir Joseph Banks conservatory. Here, an excellent use of water, and arrangements of plants in areas corresponding with parts of the world visited by Banks on his three-year voyage with Captain Cook, have made this small area both exotic and interesting. The nearby walled *John Dawber Garden* continues this international theme, with mini-gardens representing England, Germany, China and Australia. The ruins of the medieval *Bishop's Palace* at Lincoln Cathedral have been given new life by Mark Walker's contemporary design for the Walled Terrace Garden. Austerely but delightfully classical, it includes a network of pyramid-shaped hornbeams set among triangles of lawn.

32 Main Street   14

Dyke, Bourne PE10 0AF. Tel: (01778) 422241

Mr and Mrs D. Sellars • 1m N of Bourne, off A15 • Open by appt. Parties especially welcome • Entrance: £1, children 25p ● 🍴 🌿

This small area (30 x 15 metres) is subdivided into tiny compartments allowing an astonishing number of planting schemes. Every available space is crammed with a choice plant, ornament, trough or architectural feature, and careful planning and underplanting ensure continuous colour.

Manor Farm   15

Keisby, Lenton, Bourne PE10 0RZ. Tel: (01476) 585607

Mr and Mrs C.A. Richardson • 9m NW of Bourne, N of A151 between Lenton and Hawthorpe • Open 16th, 17th Feb (snowdrop and hellebore weekend) 11am – 4pm, and 30th June 2 – 5pm, for charity • Entrance: £1.50 ● 🍵 WC & 🌿 ♿

With its artistic planning and colour-harmonisation, this pretty, informal garden is a delight. The tiny paths to the herb garden, pergola and stream meander through the beds and so allow close inspection of the many choice plants, including herbaceous perennials, shrub roses, ramblers, clematis, and a large collection of snowdrops and hellebores. The formal herb garden and wildflower area are designed in 'new naturalism mode', say the owners. A further half an acre is being planted up.

Normanby Hall   16

Normanby Hall Country Park, Normanby, Scunthorpe DN15 9HU.
Tel: (01724) 720588; Fax: (01724) 721248

Run by North Lincolnshire Council • 4m N of Scunthorpe on B1430 • Hall and Farm Museum open April to Oct, daily, 1 – 5pm • Park open all year, daily, 9am – 5pm (up to 9pm in summer). Victorian walled garden open daily except 25th Dec, 1st Jan, 10.30am – 5pm (4pm in winter) • Entrance: £3.50, concessions £2.50, family £9.50, discount for North Lincolnshire residents, season tickets available (2001 prices) ○ 🍽 ✕ 🛍 WC ᣔ ⬠ 🌿 ♿ 🔌 ✎

The parkland and woodland here are extensive, with superb nature trails, rhododendron walks, lakes and an accessible deer park; current plantings reflect the importance of its Victorian heritage. The pleasure grounds, although somewhat reduced, are being replanted. Next to the Regency house are formal rose beds, a new gravel and box parterre, and a lavender-hedged, pastel-themed sunken garden with a fish pond. Further away, however, are two lovely gardens partially enclosed by tall, mellow brick walls and old holly and conifer hedges. The first has four large herbaceous borders planted à la Gertrude Jekyll – cool colours at each end and hot colours in the centre – grass paths and good wall shrubs and climbers. The second, until the mid-1980s a paddling pool, was restored four years ago, with the help of the Heritage Lottery Fund and European Development Fund, as a Victorian kitchen garden, using entirely authentic plants and techniques of the period. Faithfully re-created with peach case, display house and vinery, potting shed and bothy, and using Victorian varieties of fruit, vegetables and flowers, this garden is both beautiful and educational. The garden is run totally organically, employing Victorian techniques. Work continues on the Victorian woodland and the 123-metre-long bog garden in the base of the ha-ha, giving a display of acid-loving trees, shrubs and perennials. Within the grounds is a farm museum which, like the house, has no entrance fee, allowing all the family to find something of interest at a minimal cost.

The Old Rectory   17

Church Lane, East Keal, Spilsby PE23 4AT. Tel: (01790) 752477

Mr and Mrs J. Ward • 12m W of Skegness, 2m SW of Spilsby on A16 • Open 7th April, 16th May, 16th June, 25th August 2 – 5pm, and Thurs by appt. For information on other open times please telephone • Entrance: £1.20, children free ● 🍽 ⬠ 🌿

Nestled on a hillside in the beautiful Wolds, this possibly boasts the best views of all the gardens listed in Lincolnshire. Over the last decade, the owners have kept the many old walls, paved areas and yew hedges, adding new plantings and creating a gorgeous three-quarter-acre garden. There are paths every-where – grass, brick, stone and granite-sett – all meandering from one delight to another. Essentially the garden is cottagey, with lawn kept to a minimum and masses of flowers tumbling over rockeries, ponds, borders and retaining walls. Extensive vegetable garden and orchard and birch and rhododendron walk.

People's Park 18

Welholme Road, Grimsby. Tel: (01472) 323 423 (Ranger Service)

Charity Commission Trust/North-East Lincolnshire Council • Open all year, daily • Entrance: free ○

A large Victorian park with a sizeable, well landscaped lake, many mature trees, a fountain and waterfowl. The greenhouse has some good collections of exotic plants — alpines, succulents and tropical plants and an enclosed area surrounding it contains some choice small shrubs and trees.

Spalding Tropical Forest 19

Glenside North, Pinchbeck, Spalding PE11 3SD. Tel: (01775) 710882

Michael and Judy Mitchell • 2m N of Spalding off A16. Signposted • Tropical Forest open all year, daily except 25th, 26th Dec, 1st Jan, summer 10am – 5.30pm, winter 10am – 4pm • Entrance: £2.45, OAPs £1.99, children (5–16) £1.40, family (2 adults and 2 children) £6 (2001 prices) • Other information: Refreshments from March to Oct only (telephone for opening hours). Plants for sale in Rose Cottage water garden centre ○ 🍽 🛍 WC ♿ 🌳 🏠 ✂

Enclosed by half an acre of glass, the forest, designed by David Stevens, has been arranged into four zones — oriental, tropical, temperate and dry tropical — each with appropriate landscapes and plantings. The use of rock and water is on a grand scale with streams, ponds and cascades. There is even a waterfall to walk through. The careful monitoring of temperature, light and humidity ensures a pleasant environment in which to linger.

GARDENING WEBSITES
Many gardens now have their own websites, and we include these by owners' request. Other useful websites for garden visitors are:
  Duchas: www.heritageireland.ie
  English Heritage: www.english-heritage.org.uk
  Historic Houses Association: www.hha.org.uk
  Historic Royal Palaces: www.hrp.org.uk
  Historic Scotland: www.historic-scotland.gov.uk
  Landmark Trust: www.landmarktrust.org.uk
  National Gardens Scheme: www.ngs.org.uk
  National Trust: www.nationaltrust.org.uk
  National Trust for Scotland: www.nts.org.uk
  Royal Horticultural Society: www.rhs.org.uk
  Welsh Historic Monuments: www.cadw.wales.gov.uk

LIVERPOOL & WIRRAL

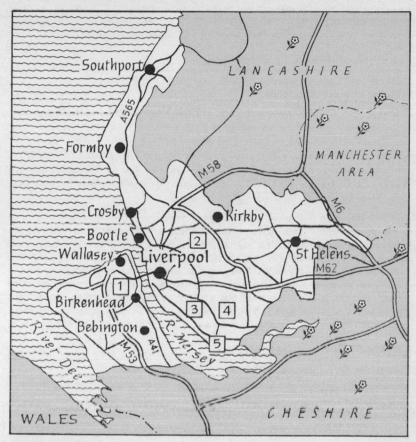

Southport

LANCASHIRE

A565

Formby

M58

*MANCHESTER
AREA*

Crosby

Kirkby

M6

Bootle

2

Wallasey

Liverpool

St Helens

1

M62

Birkenhead

3   4

Bebington

5

M53   A41

R. Mersey

River Dee

WALES

CHESHIRE

Birkenhead Park ★   1

**Birkenhead, Wirral CH62 8BP. Tel: (0151) 647 2366 or
(0151) 652 5197 (Ranger)**

*Metropolitan Borough of Wirral • 1m from centre of Birkenhead, S of A553 •
Open all year, daily, during daylight hours • Entrance: free* ○ **WC** 🚻

Birkenhead Park is rich in history. Opened in 1847, it was the world's first urban
park to be built at public expense. Designed by Joseph Paxton, it was highly
influential in the creation of New York's Central Park. His master-stroke was to
separate 'through' traffic from peripheral traffic on roads meandering around the
perimeter of the park. He also banked up the edges of the lakes to keep them
hidden, and made them sinuous in shape to provide walkers with a constantly
changing view. No subsequent public park has succeeded in fashioning a more

subtle yet masterly landscape. The lake on the eastern side has its well-landscaped banks planted with trees and shrubs; a Swiss-style bridge links two islands, and to one end a fine stone boathouse has recently been restored. The lake in the west part has weeping willows and rhododendrons planted round its edge. Restoration work was enhanced by the award of a £6.6 million grant in 2000.

Croxteth Hall and Country Park   2

Croxteth Hall Lane, Liverpool L12 0HB. Tel: (0151) 228 5311;
Website: www.croxteth.co.uk

Liverpool City Council, Leisure Services • Turn N off A5058 Liverpool ring-road into Muirhead Avenue on NE side of city. Signposted • Hall and Victorian farm also open • Garden open probably 29th March to Sept, daily, 11am – 5pm (winter times on request) • Entrance: grounds free; walled garden £1.05, OAPs and children 55p; all facilities £3.60, OAPs and children £1.80, family ticket (2 adults and 2 children) £9 (2001 prices) • Other information: Dogs in outer park only. Shop in Hall ◐ ● ✕ 🦐 wc ⎱ ♨ 🏛 ⚘

The hall stands in 500 acres of its original parkland, in which there are large areas of woodland and many rhododendrons. The centre of interest to gardeners is the large walled garden to the north of the house. Interpreted as a working Victorian kitchen garden and divided up by gravel paths, this contains a great variety of fruit, vegetables and decorative plants, organically cultivated; espalier fruits are grown against the walls and trained on wire fences, and the south-facing wall has a broad herbaceous border containing a good variety of perennials and ornamental grasses. Several greenhouses and a mushroom house are all open to the visitor, and there is a small herb garden.

Liverpool Botanic Gardens ★   3

Calderstone Park, Liverpool L18 3JD. Tel: (0151) 233 3000

Liverpool City Council, Environmental Services • 4m SE of city centre, S of A562 • Park open all year, daily. Old English garden and Japanese garden open all year, daily except 25th Dec, 8am – 6pm (Oct to March closes 4pm) • Entrance: free • Other information: Dogs in park only ○ ● ✕ 🦐 wc ⎱ ⚘ ⚲

These botanic gardens are a credit to the city council and well repay a visit to enjoy a wide variety of plants in a most attractive setting. Calderstone is essentially a large, well-landscaped park with mature trees, a lake and a rhododendron walk. At its heart, close to the house, is an area of gardens set around the old walled garden. To the front is a long herbaceous border, 20 feet deep, with a range of strong-growing perennials; beyond the flower garden features large clumps of grasses and day lilies and beds of annuals. Overlooking it is a greenhouse containing the national collections of co-diaeum, dracaena and aechmea, many fine orchids, an impressive collection of cacti, and much else besides. To the rear of the greenhouse the Old English flower garden has beds of perennials, bulbs and shrubs set within a formal layout of paths, with a circular lily pool and pergolas bearing clematis, vines, golden hops and honeysuckle at its centre. In the Japanese garden a chain of rocky streams and pools is fringed by acers, pines and clumps of bamboo. Altogether one of the best 'free' gardens in the country.

Reynolds Park Walled Garden 4

Church Road, Woolton, Liverpool L24 OTR. Tel: (0151) 724 2371

Liverpool City Council (controlled by Environmental Services, Calderstone Park) • *4½ m SE of Liverpool city centre. Turn left off A562 up Beaconsfield Road to end and right into Church Road. Park is on left* • *Open 29th March to Sept, Mon – Fri, 10am – 5.30pm* • *Entrance: free* ○

This walled garden has herbaceous borders, large dahlia beds and excellent wall climbers. Other features include a large grass area with mature trees, an unusual clipped yew garden and a small rose garden – all in very good condition, litter-free and maintained by only two staff. East of the city centre in Knowsley, within the 35-acre Victorian Court Hey Park, *The National Wildflower Centre* has demonstration areas of different plantings, including a garden of medicinal plants and herbs, plus a sculpture garden, workshops and activities for children. [Open April to Sept, Wed – Sun and Bank Holiday Mons, Oct to March Wed only, 11am – 4pm.]

Speke Hall 5

The Walk, Liverpool L24 1XD. Tel: (0845) 585702 (Infoline) or (0151) 427 7231

The National Trust • *8m SE of city centre, S of A561. Signposted* • *Hall open – telephone for details of times and prices* • *Garden open all year, daily except Mon (but open Bank Holiday Mons), 11.30am – 5.30pm (closes earlier in winter). Closed 1st Jan, 24th to 26th and 31st Dec* • *Entrance: £2, children £1, family £5* • *Other information: Picnics in orchard only. Self-drive wheelchair available for grounds; accessible path around Stocktons Wood* ○ ▦ ▦ WC ♿ ♨ ⚲ ⚘

The gardens at Speke are neither as old nor as impressive as the Elizabethan hall. They are remarkable, however, for although they are situated amidst the industrial areas of south Liverpool and close to the airport, they seem to be set in the heart of the countryside. In front of the house is a large lawn with shrub borders to the sides containing mainly rhododendrons and hollies. On the side opposite the house a ha-ha allows views to the fields and woodland. A stone bridge leads over a drained moat to the ornate stone entrance of the hall. The moat continues to the west where there is a herbaceous border with a variety of perennials; a large holm oak stands opposite. To the south are new Victorian borders, and a formal rose garden contains fragrant varieties of old-fashioned roses. In the centre of the house is a large cobbled courtyard in which grow two enormous yews. The Trust is continuing to develop many areas of the gardens, and a mid-Victorian-style stream garden has been planted with rhododendrons, azaleas, camellias, ferns and other plants. New beds have been planted on the South Lawn. A minibus service from Speke Hall will take visitors to the tiny garden at *20 Forthlin Road*, former home of Sir Paul McCartney, where the Beatles composed and rehearsed.

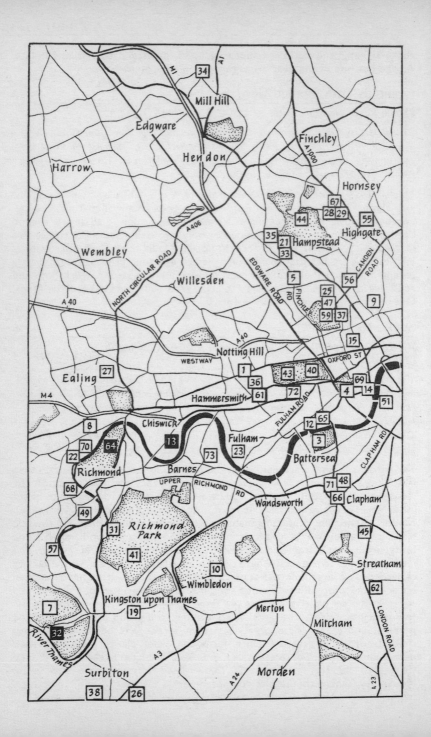

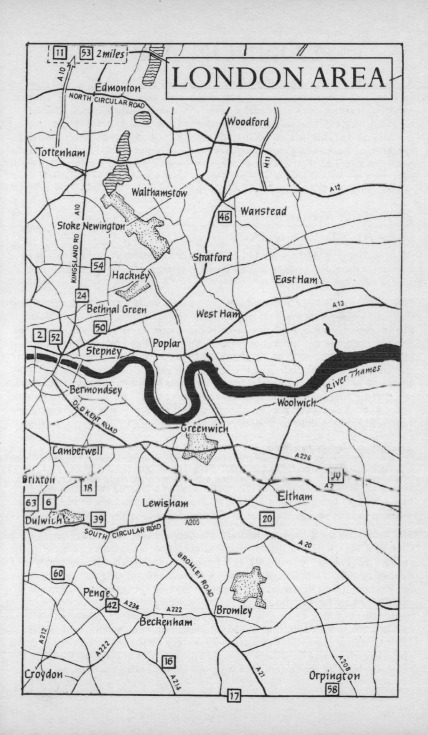

LONDON AREA

A few gardens with Kent and Surrey addresses are included in the London section for convenience, but check these two county sections as another beautiful garden may be nearby. For the same reason check the other neighbouring counties of Buckinghamshire, Essex and Hertfordshire.

At the end of this section we include some of London's most attractive open spaces: City parks and gardens, squares and other retreats. The famous parks justify an entry of their own, but we have listed others of merit with a brief description under 'London's Open Spaces' at the end of this section.

Two-starred gardens are marked on the map with a black square.

29 Addison Avenue   1

London W11 4QS. Tel: (020) 7603 2450

Mr and Mrs D.B. Nicholson • Off Holland Park Avenue, W of tube station. Cars must enter via Norland Square and Queensdale Road • Open 28th July, 2 – 6pm • Entrance: £1.50 ◗

The meticulously kept and well-designed small walled garden of a charming stuccoed villa makes the best use of every inch of space, with a profusion of plants on every surface. A tiny lawn is dominated by a venerable pear tree. Beyond them are perennial borders, slightly raised and formally laid out but informally planted, with an emphasis on phlox and hardy geraniums. To one side of the studio workshop at the end of the garden is a small shade garden, complete with statue. In July the fine wall shrubs *Hydrangea villosa* and *Itea ilicifolia* are at their best, while a rampant *Solanum jasminoides* is in bloom from June to September. The colour themes of the borders (pink, blue and white) and the variegated foliage help to unify the garden.

Barbican Conservatory   2

The Barbican, Silk Street, London EC2Y 8DS. Tel: (020) 7638 4141

City of London • In Barbican Centre, on 3rd floor • Open Sun and Bank Holiday Mons only, 12 noon – 5.30pm. Telephone to confirm opening times as conservatory is sometimes used for conferences • Entrance: free ◗ WC &

The lift to the third floor of the Barbican propels you from the streets of the City to a lush jungle of temperate and semi-tropical plants. Planted in the autumn of 1980–81 using 1600 cubic metres of soil, the conservatory was opened in 1984. Twin *Dicksonia antarctica* grace the main entrance, while a vast banyan tree (*Ficus bengalensis*) in the eastern section threatens to burst through the roof. Many familiar houseplants like *Ficus benjamina* have reached gigantic proportions, and a colossal Swiss cheese plant (*Monstera deliciosa*) produces edible fruits after flowering. The Arid House on the second level, added in 1986, contains epiphyllum and cacti. There are finches in the aviary and the ponds are alive with fish. Another interesting contemporary garden is at the *Broadgate Arena* at the far end of Liverpool Street Station concourse.

Battersea Park 3

Battersea, London SW11 4NJ. Tel: (020) 8871 7530/8800

Wandsworth Borough Council • S side of River Thames, from Chelsea Bridge to Albert Bridge • Open all year, daily, 7am – dusk • Entrance: free, but parking charge ○ 🍽 ✕ 🎒 <u>WC</u> ♿ ⚓ 🏭 🍴 ♿

With half a mile of Thames frontage, the 200-acre park retains many of its original Victorian features, which have been restored with a £6.9 million grant from the Heritage Lottery Fund. The 15-acre boating lake has been revitalised and its banks replanted in keeping with the original Victorian style. Also restored are the remaining features from the Festival of Britain in 1951, including the Russell Page Garden, the Vista Lakes and a new jetty, which connect the park to the Millennium Dome by river. A borehole has been sunk to ensure fresh water at all times and a wildlife management programme put in place: Battersea Park is now one of only two sites in London where herons breed. Visitors can also enjoy the Old English garden, the cascade, the children's zoo, sculptures by Henry Moore and Barbara Hepworth and a modern Buddhist temple. Ancillary to all this are the 1930s' Lakeside café, many sports facilities, and a long and refreshing river view.

Buckingham Palace Garden 4

Westminster, London SW1A 1AA. Tel: (020) 7839 1377; Website: www.the-royal-collection.org.uk

Crown Estate Commissioners • N end of Buckingham Palace Road, on N side beyond Royal Mews and Royal Gallery. Entrance through courtyard to S of Buckingham Palace • Open Aug to Sept (timed tickets from 9.30am – 4.30pm) • Entrance combined with admission to State Rooms: £11, over 60s £9, children under 17 £5.50, family ticket (2 adults, 2 children under 17) £27.50, children under 5 free, group rate (minimum 15 persons) £10 per person • Other information: Advance tickets available via website or by telephone on (020) 7321 2233. Ticket office in Green Park end July to Sept. Coaches must contact Visitor Officer (020) 7839 1377 well in advance NEW ●

From 2001, visitors to the Palace end their tour of the State Rooms along a 450-metre guided route on the south side of the garden, and halfway along the three-acre lake are then directed out into Grosvenor Place. Although they may not roam freely they will be able to marvel at a 39-acre walled garden in central London – part parade ground, part ecological and dendrological oasis and part wildlife habitat. The magnificent trees were planted by William Aiton – head of Kew in the nineteenth century – and latterly by the Royal Family in acts of commemoration. The romantic and naturalistic lake is host to more than 30 types of bird. The visitors' view of Nash's handsome garden front of the palace is a privilege in itself. Time will tell if more access to the garden will be allowed, but this is a first and important step in the right direction.

15A Buckland Crescent ★   5

London NW3 5DH. Tel: (0207) 586 2464

Lady Barbirolli • Near Fitzjohn's Avenue at Swiss Cottage end. 5 min walk from Swiss Cottage tube station and various buses • Open 9th June, 2.30 – 6pm • Entrance: £2, children free. Private visits welcome for parties of 25 and over; please telephone for appt ● & ℘

The strong sense of space and line that musicians often possess is expressed in this dignified third-of-an-acre town garden, in which the ground plan combines flowing unfussy lines and ingenious geometry. Planting is everywhere discriminating, ranging from a functional but decorative vegetable patch to some unusual plants, citrus and other interesting shrubs, including a small bamboo 'grove'. A generous terrace is enhanced by boldly planted urns.

5 Burbage Road   6

Herne Hill, London SE24 9HJ. Tel: (020) 7274 5610

Crawford and Rosemary Lindsay • Close to Half Moon Lane. Nearest station: Herne Hill • Open on special open days for NGS (telephone for information); otherwise by appt only • Entrance: £1.50 ● ☕ ℘

An attractive garden in a tranquil and sheltered setting, with a well-kept lawn, quietly splashing fountain and herb beds. There is year-round interest and a continual introduction of unusual plants; borders are filled with choice arrangements of herbaceous perennials and shrubs, and good use is made of a variety of pots housing climbers, ferns and alpines.

Bushy Park   7

Hampton, Surrey. Tel: (020) 8979 1586

Royal Parks • N of A308 Hampton Court road, between Kingston Bridge and Hampton Court Bridge. Access from Hampton Court or Twickenham. Entrance to Waterhouse Plantation via gate on Hampton Court road • Open all year, daily, 9am – dusk • Entrance: free ○ **WC** ♨

Once a royal hunting ground, the park adjoins Hampton Court (see entry) to the north. The vast avenue of four rows of limes and one of chestnuts planted by Wise for William III created a grand approach to the palace. It was punctuated by a formal basin in which Queen Anne resited the Arethusa fountain (long called the Diana fountain) from the Old Privy Garden. In the *Waterhouse Plantation* paths wind round mass shrub plantings and open onto small lakes and the Longford River with many bridges.

7 The Butts   8

Brentford, Middlesex TW8 8BJ. Tel: (020) 8232 8597

Mrs Susan Sharkey • Off Manor Road and Half Acre (A3002), a short walk from Brentford High Street. Buses 235 and 267. Nearest mainline station Brentford • Open for NGS • Entrance: £2 NEW ● ☕ ℘

A garden designer's garden (27 x 14 metres) cleverly planted with an abundance of foliage plants. It is separated into three sections. Next to the house a terrace has raised beds and strong use of colour. Leading from a plant-festooned pergola to a well-kept lawn framed by box edged beds, the garden opens up and gives a feeling of space, before revealing the final secret area with an original water feature and unusual planting for year-round interest.

Camley Street Natural Park 9

12 Camley Street, London NW1 0PW. Tel: (020) 7833 2311;
Fax: (020) 78332488; E-mail: lwtcamleyst@cix.co.uk;
Website: www.wildlondon.org.uk

London Borough of Camden; managed by London Wildlife Trust • Off Goods Way, near King's Cross railway station • Open all year, Mon – Thurs, 9am – 5pm, Sat and Sun, 11am – 5pm (winter, 10am – 4pm or dusk if earlier) • Entrance: free, but donations welcome ○ � WC ☧ ♿ ⚲

An innovative project created in the early 1980s and now a designated local nature reserve, this is an example of a successful and thriving urban wildlife park and garden created against all the odds. Just over two acres set between the Regent's Canal and the railway, have been landscaped with a large pond and include a visitors' centre with an environmental education classroom. This tranquil space has a fine sighting record of birds and other wildlife. Views of the canal and passing narrow boats are offset somewhat romantically by relics of Victorian industry. The park will remain open throughout the Channel Tunnel rail link works in the area.

Cannizaro Park 10

West Side Common, Wimbledon, London SW19 4UF. Tel: (020) 8946 7349

London Borough of Merton • West Side Common, Wimbledon • Open all year, daily, Mon – Fri, 8am – sunset, Sat, Sun and Bank Holidays, 9am – sunset • Entrance: free • Other information: Teas on summer Suns only. Top garden possible for wheelchairs ○ WC ⚲ ♿ ⚲

Formerly the grounds of Cannizaro House and approached through imposing gates and a formal drive, lined with beautifully kept seasonal bedding. The trees are the principal attraction here: cork oaks, mulberries and sassafras. Some enormous and beautiful beeches, mature red Japanese maples, magnolias and rhododendrons are among the many attractions. At the southern wooded end of the park, Lady Jane's Wood, the main feature is the magnificent and vibrantly colourful azalea dell. In the midst of the trees a secluded picnic area, set with tables, contains – somewhat unexpectedly – a bust of the Emperor Haile Selassie of Ethiopia, who sought refuge in Wimbledon. There is a small aviary, a pretty walled rose garden, an azalea and rhododendron collection and a heather garden. The old garden, a formal garden and the pool are found down a steep slope directly in front of the house, with a wild garden in the same location. A sculpture exhibition is held in the park in June and an open-air theatre season in July and August.

Capel Manor College   11

Bullsmoor Lane, Enfield, Middlesex EN1 4RQ. Tel: (020) 8366 4442;
E-mail: enquiries@capelmanorcollege.freeserve.co.uk;
Website: www.capel.ac.co.uk

*Capel Manor Charitable Corporation • From M25 junction with A10, via
Turkey Street/Bullsmoor Lane. Signposted. Or walk from railway station • Open
April to Oct, daily, 11am – 6pm (last admission 4.30pm), Nov to March, Mon
– Fri (times vary, so telephone before travelling) • Entrance: £4, OAPs £3.50,
children £2. Special prices for show weekends • Other information: Plants for sale
at special events* ○ 💬 📠 ✕ WC 👤 🐕 🏛 👤 ✂

These busy gardens of the well-known horticultural college have several
functions. They show the history of gardening from the sixteenth century
to the present, and also serve as a design centre for the garden industry and as
an instructional venue, with a wide variety of plants, combination planting and
features such as water, paving and buildings. Although inevitably any sense of
unity (such as at nearby Myddelton House – see entry) is lacking, pleasure can
be found in individual features. Sponsors are found each year for the many
small show gardens, such as the Japanese garden and flower arranger's garden.
A large area has been established by *Gardening from Which?* which includes
demonstration plots, an A-Z of shrubs, a theme garden and a low-allergen
garden designed for the National Asthma Campaign by Lucy Huntingdon.
Suitable for a family outing, enhanced by a maze and rare breeds of farm
livestock including Kune-Kune pigs and Clydesdale horses.

Chelsea Physic Garden ★   12

66 Royal Hospital Road, Chelsea, London SW3 4HS. Tel: (020) 7352 5646;
Fax: (020) 737 6910; Website: www.cpgarden.demon.co.uk

*Chelsea Physic Garden Company • Entrance in Swan Walk, off Chelsea
Embankment and, for wheelchair users only, in Royal Hospital Road • Open
April to Oct, Wed, 12 noon – 5pm, Sun, 2 – 6pm; also during Chelsea Flower
Show and Chelsea Festival Week, 12 noon – 5pm. There are some Sun openings
and sales in winter (telephone for details) • Entrance: £4, students, children and
unemployed £2* ◑ 💬 WC 👤 🌱 🏛 👤

Founded in the seventeenth century to train London's apothecary apprentices
in herbal medicine, the Chelsea Physic Garden is still actively involved in
displays of herbal medicine, as well as playing an important botanical role. Its
three and a half acres are well worth visiting, not only for the fascinating range
of medicinal plants, but also for the rare and interesting ones, including trees
like the magnificent olive tree (*Olea europaea*). The garden also houses what is
believed to be one of the earliest rock gardens in Europe, created with basaltic
lava brought back by the botanist Sir Joseph Banks from Iceland in 1772 and
restored in 2001. The main part of the garden is devoted to systematically
ordered beds of plants, but there are also displays associated with the plant
hunters and botanists who have played their part in the development of the
garden, including Banks, Philip Miller, William Hudson and Robert Fortune, as

well as an attractive woodland garden, glasshouses and a Garden of World Medicine showing the use of medicinal plants by tribal peoples. A Pharmaceutical Garden showing plants linked to modern day pharmaceutical drugs was opened for the millennium. National Collection of cistus.

Chiswick House ★★ 13

Burlington Lane, Chiswick, London W4 2RP. Tel: (020) 8995 0508

London Borough of Hounslow and English Heritage • 5m W of central London; entrance on A4 • House open April to Sept, daily, 10am – 6pm (closes 5pm in Oct, 4pm Nov to March). Closed 24th, 25th Dec and 1st to 16th Jan • Gardens open all year, daily, 8.30am – dusk • Entrance: garden free (house £3.30, concessions £2.50, children £1.70) • Other information: Dogs outside Italian garden only ○ ☕ WC & ♨ ⚲

The handsome eighteenth-century gardens, stretching over many acres, with a lake, statues, monuments, bridges and magnificent trees, were created from 1726 and extended by William Kent to complement the Palladian villa built by Lord Burlington in 1729. They are full of splendid vistas, avenues and changes of contour. Drawings of the time show the degree of perfection the English lawn had reached even in the early eighteenth century. The Victorian garden with parterres is now filled with vividly coloured bedding plants in front of the handsome conservatory (both introduced after Kent's day). A large canal-shaped lake has at its southern end a cascade designed by Kent in 1738 to mimic an underground river flowing from a rocky hill. He failed to get the cascade to work. English Heritage has now succeeded, using information from archaeological excavation and from the archives at Chatsworth. English Heritage, in co-operation with the London Borough of Hounslow, plan the complete restoration of the gardens and have received Lottery funding. West of the lake, the oriental plane walk has been restored with holly hedges, re-creating the walk in the manner of the mid-nineteenth century. William Kent's carriage drive and the raised walk that flanked the drive have also been re-created. Although this is not yet open to the public, visitors can walk the length of the *allée* leading from the Burlington Gate to the classical bridge. There is an outstanding camellia collection, with early-nineteenth-century specimens; a new outdoor camellia garden is planned to the south of the Italian garden. Further work is planned in Burlington's Orange Tree Amphitheatre and in the northern and western wildernesses. From about Easter there are two return trips a day by boat from Westminster (telephone (020) 7930 4721).

College Garden and Little Cloister 14

Westminster Abbey, London SW1P 3PA. Tel: (020) 7222 5152; Website: http://www.westminster-abbey.org

Dean and Chapter of Westminster • Entrance via Broad Sanctuary (west end of Abbey) then Dean's Yard, Great Cloister and Fountain Court (signposted) • Garden open all year, Tues to Thurs, 10am – 6pm (Oct to March closes 4pm) • Entrance: suggested donation 20p • Other information: Band concerts (free) July and Aug, Thurs, 12.30 – 2pm as advertised ○ ☕ & ♨

The eleventh-century College Garden (a little over one acre) has been under cultivation for more than 900 years, and therefore qualifies as one of the oldest in England. Originally the source for herbs used in the monastic infirmary of the Benedictine Abbey, it is now a private garden for Abbey staff and members of Westminster School. Landscaping by John Brookes encourages visitors to move towards the south and east, from where some of the best architecture of the Abbey may be viewed. In the south-west corner is a shaded area with a crucifixion group in bronze. Some interesting small gardens with topiary and intensive planting adjoin the buildings to the north of the area. The Little Cloister Garden is a miniature study in green and white, with a fountain and fish pond in the centre. Fine trees throughout and good labelling.

Colville Place   15

London W1.

London Borough of Camden • Between Charlotte Street and Whitfield Street, near Tottenham Court Road • Open all year, daily, 7.30am – dusk • Entrance: free ○ &

Fortunate houses in Colville Place look across a paved path onto a cross between a *hortus conclusus* and a small piazza. This imaginative tiny public garden was created on a bomb site. There is a lawn, a pleasing pergola, fruit trees and, slightly tucked away, a children's play area. Planting is bold, simple and pleasing, with lots of lavender. This seems to be London's nearest equivalent to modern garden design in the public arena, and has great charm.

Dolly's Garden   16

43 Layhams Road, West Wickham, Kent BR4 9HD. Tel: (020) 8462 4196

Mrs Dolly Robertson • Off A232 and A2022. Semi-detached house with small sunken garden in front opposite Wickham Court Farm • Open all year by appt only • Entrance: by donation to collecting box ● WC & ◁

This is a raised vegetable garden purpose-built for the disabled owner with easy access to wide, terraced walkways. She maintains the entire 8 x 23 metres herself, and is pleased to pass on her experiences as a disabled gardener so that others, even if they are wheelchair-bound, may share her joy and interest.

Down House   17

Luxted Road, Downe, Kent BR6 7JT. Tel: (01689) 859119

English Heritage • 2m NE of Biggin Hill off A21 • Open April to Sept, Wed – Sun and Bank Holiday Mon, 10am – 6pm (Oct, 10am – 5pm; 1st Nov to 23rd Dec, 10am – 4pm). Closed 24th Dec to 28th March • Entrance: £5.50, OAPs £4.10, children £2.80. Entry must be pre-booked 12th July to 10th Sept – telephone (01689) 859119 ○ ☕ WC & ♿ ☂ ⚲

Charles Darwin and his family lived at Down House for 40 years from 1842, and his daughter claimed, 'Many gardens are more beautiful and varied but few could have greater charm or repose.' Darwin used the garden, woodland and meadows as his open-air laboratory as he formulated the theories which culminated in his ground-breaking work, *On the Origin of Species*. For visitors one of the most famous features of the garden is his 'sand-walk' or 'thinking path'. The greenhouse where he studied plant growth and pollination has been restored and now houses orchids and carnivorous plants. The nearby $\frac{1}{4}$ –acre kitchen garden, which provided fruit, vegetables and flowers from the vegetable plots as well as material for Darwin's experiments, is being re-created. The flower garden outside the drawing room, now restored to its appearance during the late 1870s, was used by the family as an extra room. Outside, on the lawn, is a 'wormstone' laid out here by Darwin's son Horace in an experiment to measure soil displacement. The estate is home to 170 species of fungi, including rare grassland species such as wax-caps (hygrocybe). There are plans for a Darwin centre/museum next to the house and garden.

66a East Dulwich Road   18

East Dulwich, London SE22 9AT. Tel: (020) 8693 3458;
Email: kevin@edulwich66.fsnet.co.uk

Kevin Wilson • Behind Goose Green, opposite Dulwich swimming baths. Buses 37, 175, 176; underground station East Dulwich (20 mins) • Open by appt; parties welcome • Entrance: £2.50 NEW ● ☕ ♨ WC

The 30-metre-long garden is distinguished by lush planting, ponds, a willow tree and climbing plants used to great advantage. The owner's unique method of festooning may-poles with climbers, head-height seating areas and plant-filled antique hip baths defy all the rules. Large plantings of slug-free hostas and hanging baskets of ferns line the gravel path leading to a decking area, and pots of helxines march up wooden steps. Before reaching the large workroom, a pole with a mirrored top reflects the abundant planting. Decking with a swing and a seating area entice you to the end of this unusual garden.

The Elms   19

13 Wolverton Avenue, Kingston upon Thames, Surrey KT2 7QF.
Tel: (020) 8546 7624

Professor and Mrs R. Rawlings • 1m E of Kingston on A308, 100 metres from Norbiton station. Entrance opposite flats in Manorgate Road • Open 16th, 17th March, 13th, 14th April, 11th, 12th May, 2 – 5pm, and for parties of 10 or more by appt • Entrance: £1.50 ● ☕ ♨

This is a true collector's garden with some rare and unusual plants, featuring rhododendrons, magnolias, camellias, dwarf conifers and a wide range of evergreen and deciduous shrubs. In a very small area (just $16\frac{1}{2}$ x $7\frac{1}{2}$ metres) are small trees, herbaceous ground cover, and a two-level pool with a geyser and well-planted margins; room is even found for plums, pears and soft fruit. The roof garden (open to private visitors only) is an object lesson in the possibilities of such high-level spaces.

Eltham Palace Gardens   20

Court Road, Eltham, London SE9 9QE. Tel: (020) 8294 2548

English Heritage • Near Eltham High Street, $\frac{1}{2}$ m from Eltham railway station (then Bus 161) or $\frac{3}{4}$ m from Mottingham railway station (then Bus 126 or 131) • Palace open as garden • Garden open April to Sept, Wed – Fri, Sun and Bank Holiday Mon, 10am – 6pm (Oct closes 5pm, Nov to March 4pm). Closed 24th to 15th Jan • Entrance: £3.60, OAPs £2.70, children £1.80 (house and garden £6, OAPs £4.50, children £3) ● ● ● WC & ● ● ●

Despite its proximity to Eltham High Street, the approach to Eltham Palace, over the medieval bridge spanning a moat of water lilies and small islands, is a far cry from the city bustle. The palace has one of the oustanding Art Deco interiors in London, though little now remains of the medieval building except the hall. The gardens were laid out in 1936 for Stephen and Virginia Courtauld, and a major programme of garden repair and restoration has started. The rose garden has been replanted using early hybrid tea and hybrid musk varieties, a permanent planting scheme created in the Triangle Garden, and the cascade rock garden restored. Wide paths have been mown in the wild meadows and framed views of the palace opened up on the route from the new car park. Contemporary planting in the spirit of the 1930s' garden has been created in the 120-yard-long South Moat border and White Wood by designer Isabelle Van Groeningen.

Fenton House   21

Hampstead Grove, London NW3 6RT. Tel/Fax: (020) 7435 3471

The National Trust • In centre of Hampstead in Holly Hill behind Heath Street • House open (closes $\frac{1}{2}$ hour earlier than garden) • Garden open 1st to 22nd March, Sat and Sun, 2 – 5pm; 23rd March to 3rd Nov, Sat, Sun and Bank Holiday Mons, 11am – 5pm, Wed – Fri, 2 – 5pm. Parties at other times by appt • Entrance: house and garden £4.30, family ticket £10.50 • Other information: Toilet facilities if house is also visited ● & ● ●

The entrance to the handsome seventeenth-century house and the garden is through the grand iron gate into an avenue of robinias or by a side gate near the yew bower, from which the south garden is seen. The one-and-a-half acre walled garden is formal, with gravel walks and herbaceous borders planted to give some summer-long interest, edged with neatly clipped box. Standard hollies are a feature, and the walls are particularly well planted; note the interesting collection of *Clematis viticella* varieties. The ground drops on several levels to a sunken rose garden and a late-summer/autumn border surrounded by tall yew hedges dividing the formal lawn area from the rose garden. Steps lead down to an ancient orchard delightful in spring with narcissus, fritillaries and bluebells. At one end is the reinstated glasshouse with a herb border by its side (note the two olive trees in pots), at the other the vegetable garden and cutting borders.

The Ferry House   22

**Old Isleworth, Middlesex TW7 6BD. Tel: (020) 8560 6769;
Fax: (020) 8560 0709**

*Lady Caroline Gilmour • 2m W of Kew Bridge, adjacent to Syon Park gates.
Bus 267 from Hammersmith, Bus 37 from Richmond; signed from A315/310 at
Bush Corner. • Open two days in June, 2 – 6pm, for NGS, and for parties by
appt • Entrance: £2.50, OAPs £1.50, children 50p, parties £4 per person for
charity • Other information: Plants sometimes for sale* ● ● WC & ⟨⟩ ⚥

A three-acre garden of exceptional charm on the bend of the Thames opposite
Richmond Old Deer Park, with Kew to the south-east. A terrace commands a
view of a completely unspoilt stretch of the river, framed in spring by white
cherry blossom. The terrace itself, flanked by pleached lime trees, is planted
mainly in white, with a profusion of plants in urns and tubs and splendid
mature climbers on the old brick walls around the house. The borders are full
of old-fashioned roses and other scented flowers, aromatic herbs and variegated and golden shrubs. On one side of the house is a large walled area, to
which the fine old trees of nearby Syon Park provide a backdrop. Here there
are avenues of whitebeam, groups of well-chosen trees and shrubs, winding
paths with shaded seats, wildflower areas and, in spring, carpets of bulbs. Fine
gazebo, attractive vegetable and fruit cage.

Fulham Palace   23

Bishops Avenue, London SW6 6EA. Tel: (020) 7736 3233

*London Borough of Hammersmith and Fulham • Off Fulham Palace Road
down Bishop's Avenue • Museum open March to Oct, Wed – Sun and Bank
Holiday Mons, 2 – 5pm; Nov to Feb 2003, Thurs – Sun, 1 – 4pm • Garden
open all year, daily except 25th Dec, 1st Jan, 8am – dusk. Tours of Palace and
garden every second Sun of the month, 2pm; other tours by appt • Entrance: free
(museum £1, concessions 50p, children free; tours £5) (2001 prices) • Other
information: Plants for sale in nearby nursery. Annual plant sale end April/
early May, 11am – 4pm. Garden walks once a season* ○ ● & ● ● ⚲

The palace, surrounded in its prime by a moat, was the former home of the
Bishops of London; in the seventeenth century Bishop Compton used his
missionaries to help him establish here a collection of shrubs and trees sent
back from America. It is a charming place for a peaceful walk. The museum tells
the story of the site and its garden. The east front of the house looks over
lawns with enormous cedars and other trees, including an ancient evergreen
oak. The ancient holm oak, estimated over 500 years old, has been nominated a
Great Tree of London. The romantic old walled garden contains a very long (if
ruined) vinery built along a curved wall, and an elliptical box-edged herb
garden enclosed by a magnificent old wisteria pergola. Another part has order
beds and an orchard, recently replanted using historic varieties. The small
courtyard at the front of the house (part Henry VII, part Victorian) has
euphorbias, some climbers and other plants and a fountain.

Geffrye Museum Herb Garden 24

**Kingsland Road, London E2 8EA. Tel: (020) 7739 9893/
(020) 7739 8543 (Infoline); Website: www.geffrye-museum.org.uk.**

*Geffrye Museum Trust • 200 metres N of Shoreditch Church. Take underground
to Liverpool St. (Bishopsgate exit) then buses 149 or 242. Buses 243, 242, 67.
Front garden open all year, daily except 1st Jan, 29th March, 24th to 26th Dec;
herb garden open April to Oct, daily except Mon (but open Bank Holiday Mons,
12 noon – 5pm), 10am – 5pm, Sun, 12 noon – 5pm • Entrance: free • Other
information: Guide dogs only* ○ 🐛 ✕ 🍴 <u>WC</u> ♿ 🏛 ⚲ ✎

This enjoyable museum and gardens are on the site of eighteenth-century
almshouses formerly belonging to the Ironmongers' Company. The walled herb
garden entrance is tucked away by the side of the museum. This mature garden
has 170 different herbs, including sweet woodruff, *Asperula odorata* (*Galium
odoratum*), sweet cicely (*Myrrhis odorata*) and buckler-leaf sorrel (*Rumex scutatus*).
Flower beds contain informal, labelled groupings of herbs showing those for
aromatic, culinary, cosmetic, dye, household and medicinal uses. Secluded
arbours with roses and climbing plants surround a delightful fountain. Period
gardens lead from the herb garden and are arranged chronologically to reflect
the museum's main displays of period rooms.

70 Gloucester Crescent 25

London NW1 7EG. Tel/Fax: (020) 7485 6906

*Lucy Gent and Malcolm Turner • Near junction of Gloucester Crescent and
Oval Road 350 yards SW of Camden Town underground • Open by appt –
visitors most welcome • Entrance: £2 (for NGS)* ◐

Mrs Charles Dickens once lived in this end-of-crescent house, and the garden,
with its idiosyncratic shape, is strong on character. The three areas – a square at
the front, a triangle at the side and a wedge at the back – show how a difficult
town site may successfully be exploited. The owner, a garden designer and
author, has created a place of strong geometry and infinite interest. The contrast
with the bustle of Camden Lock around the corner is quite something.

8 Grafton Park Road 26

Worcester Park, Surrey KT4 7HS. Tel: (020) 833 71110

*Robin Green and Ralph Cade • S of A3. From A240 Kingston-Epsom road take
slip road signed 'Worcester Park', turn right at Hogsmill Inn, left at next
junction (Grafton Road). Grafton Park Road is first left • Open for NGS 13th
June, 6 – 9pm; 13th, 14th July, 11am – 6pm, and for private group bookings
(minimum 10 persons) by appt • Entrance: £3 in June, £2 in July, children 50p
• Other information: Refreshments and herbs for sale on NGS open days.
Unsuitable for people unsteady on their feet* [NEW] ◐ 🐛

Brave the journey to deepest Worcester Park, and have fun. This sloping
garden, fifty feet square, has a profusion of colour carefully planted to give each

area maximum impact. The hand-made path and steps wind from raised beds brimming with sun-loving plants and backed by a silver ball fountain or by unusual planting in creative containers. A greenhouse and a vegetable garden edged with seashells fit with surprising ease into this small plot, ending in a colourful beach hut.

1 Grange Park   27

Ealing, London W5 3PL. Tel/Fax: (020) 856 77172;
Email: davidrose.ealing@virgin.net

David Rosewarne and Magie Gray • SW off Ealing Common off Warwick Road. Nearest underground station Ealing Common • Open 5th May, 23rd June for NGS, and by appt to parties of ten or more • Entrance: £2, children free NEW ● ● ㅊ Qe

Hidden in the heart of Ealing is a leafy fairytale garden with a large willow tree centre stage; around its base has been built a willow-cane cave and other secret spaces. One path leads to a twig arch with a large medallion of fir cones as support for morning glory and clematis. A pruned eucalyptus with a tufted top looks down on a small pond surrounded by helxines and campanulas. Imaginative hand-made seats, pots with woven willow bands, plinths with statues and eye-catching objects all reveal David Rosewarne's vision of the garden as an extension of his creativity. *Gunnersbury Park* – the most used and least known of London's public spaces – is nearby. Lottery funds have restored its Italian gardens, William Kent temple and landscape, orangery by Smirke, Japanese garden designed by a Rothschild and Princess Amelia's Bath House. A full report next year.

4 The Grove ★   28

Highgate Village, London N6 6JU.

Mr Cob Stenham • In Highgate Village, off Hampstead Lane • Open 9th June, 2 – 5pm • Entrance: £2, OAPs/children £1 (combined price of £5 and £3 for 2 other gardens open on same day). Other information: Teas may be available at 5 The Grove on open day ●

The seventeenth-century house sits behind a dignified front courtyard, beautifully paved with brick and surrounded by lush plantings of evergreens such as skimmias and ivy grown along the railings, with spring-flowering magnolias in the borders. A side passage brings the visitor through to an outstanding vista: the terrace, with a formal pool surrounded by dramatic planting, is the foreground to an immaculate lawn with well-planted mixed borders. Beyond this is an extensive backdrop to the wooded slopes of Hampstead Heath. An arbour of silver pears overlooks this stunning view, and a ceanothus arch leads down, through a tunnel of *Vitis coignetiae*, to the lower garden. This comprises an orchard with an old mulberry tree and some good statuary. One yew hedge conceals the well-ordered compost/bonfire area, and another balances this to enclose a secret garden dominated by a *Cladrastis lutea*. *Rosa laevigata* 'Cooperi' flourishes on the south wall of the house, and the whole garden, which is beautifully designed and maintained, has exceptional charm. *No. 5 The Grove* and No. 7 (see below), are usually also open on the same day in June.

7 The Grove ★ 29

Highgate Village, London N6 6JU. Tel: (020) 8340 7205

Thomas G. Lyttelton • In Highgate Village, off Hampstead Lane • Open 7th April, 7th June, 29th Sept, 2 – 5.30pm • Entrance: £2, OAPs and children £1 (£5, OAPs and children £3 for all three gardens) • Other information: Teas available on open days in March and Sept and at 5 The Grove on open day in June ● 🍵 🍽 ☕ &. ♋

A half-acre London walled town garden behind a handsome Victorian house of c.1830, splendidly designed by the owner for low maintenance, but with a variety of good planting schemes and ideas. Tunnels, arbours, screens abound, providing inspiration for busy garden-owners who would still like to have an interest outside the house. A series of nineteenth-century brick-built arches across the width of the garden separates it into two compartments. The area near the house is formal with a lawn, the area beyond the screen much less so, with fine compartments and features. Secret paths and unexpected views make this a magical place for children. Much use is made of evergreens and there are some exquisite shrubs, including a row of camellias down one wall and a massive *Hydrangea petiolaris* with a trunk as thick as a boxer's biceps. There are many species and varieties of a particular genus – five varieties of box and even more of ivies, for example. The owner describes it as a green and yellow garden, with glimpses of white and red here and there. The canal feature was restructured and enhanced into a water garden in autumn 1996. No. 4 (see above) and *No. 5 The Grove* are also open on the charity day in June.

Hall Place 30

Bourne Road, Bexley, Kent DA5 1PQ. Tel: (01322) 526574

Bexley Council • Just N of A2 near A2/A223 junction • House open Mon – Sat, 10am – 5pm (4.15pm in winter), Sun, 11am – 6pm (summer only) • Garden open all year, daily, Mon – Fri, 7.30am – dusk, weekends and Bank Holidays, 9am – dusk. Model allotment, parts of nursery and glasshouses open all year, daily except 25th Dec, Mon – Fri, 9am – 6pm (4pm in winter) • Entrance: free ○ 🍽 ✕ 🍽 WC &. ♨ 🏛 🍽 ♋

Surrounding a splendid Jacobean mansion, this is arguably the most interesting and best-kept public garden in south-east London. Although there is a strong emphasis on municipal annual bedding plants like ageratum, *Senecio × hybrida* and African marigolds to provide summer colour, they are used with restraint and good taste, as are the roses in the large classical rose garden. So, too, are the herbaceous plants in two splendid borders separated by a turf *allée* and backed by a characterful old brick wall on one side and a tightly clipped yew hedge on the other. Features include a raised walk overlooking one of Britain's finest topiary gardens, several rich shrubberies, a large and beautifully de-signed patterned herb garden, a rock garden, meandering stretches of the River Cray, a heather garden and acres of lawn studded with evergreen and deciduous trees to provide vistas.

Ham House ★ 31
Ham Street, Richmond, Surrey TW10 7RS. Tel: (020) 8940 1950

The National Trust • On S bank of Thames, W of A307 at Petersham • House and garden open all year, Sat – Wed, garden 11am — 6pm, house 1 — 6pm (or dusk if earlier) • Entrance: £2, children £1, family £5 (house £6, children £3, family £15) • Other information: Parking 400 metres by river, disabled on terrace. Refreshments 23rd March to 3rd Nov, daily, otherwise weekends in Nov, Dec, March ○ ☕ ✕ 🍴 **WC** ♿ 🌿 🏠 🌳 ♒

Seventeenth-century formality predominates in the gardens here. The strongly architectural nature of the wilderness, gravel terraces and parterres of box, lavender and cotton lavender, together with the replicas of seventeenth-century garden furniture, add to the charm of the restoration. The south terrace border has been replanted in formal seventeenth-century style with clipped yew cones, standard hibiscus and pomegranate trees. Pots and tubs copied from seventeenth-century originals decorate the terrace and the grass plats below. The seventeenth-century orangery, the earliest surviving example of its type in the country, is fronted by a walled garden currently being restored as a seventeenth-century kitchen garden, with period fruit, vegetables, flowers and herbs. The wilderness, a popular area, is bounded by a mile of hornbeam hedges enclosing compartments planted with thousands of spring bulbs and summer meadow wild flowers. A ferry across the Thames connects Ham House with Marble Hill (see entry). Nearby is *The Palm Centre* at Ham Central Nursery [open Mon – Fri, 10am – 6pm. Tel: (020) 82556191].

Hampton Court Palace ★★ 32
East Molesey, Surrey KT8 9AU. Tel: (020) 8781 9500; Website: www.hrp.org.uk

Historic Royal Palaces Trust • On A308 at junction of A309 on N side of Hampton Court Bridge over Thames • Palace open • Gardens open all year, daily, dawn – dusk • Entrance: Rose, Wilderness and East Front Gardens free; Maze £2.80, children £1.90; Privy Garden, Sunken Garden and Great Vine £2.80, children £1.90 (free to palace ticket-holders). Afternoon garden tours, including entrance to Privy Garden, weekends only from April to Oct, £5 (£3 to palace ticket-holders); special pre-booked morning tours by arrangement ○ ☕ ✕ 🍴 **WC** ♿ 🚲 🏠 🌳 ♒

The gardens, which provide the setting for the palace, are an exciting and eclectic mixture of styles and tastes, with many different areas of character and interest. They are traditionally famous for the Great Vine, planted in 1768 (probably the oldest in the world) and still producing hundreds of 'Black Hamburg' grapes each year (for sale to the public when harvested in September), and the 1691 maze, the oldest hedge-planted maze in Britain. The Pond Gardens offer a magnificent display of bedding plants, and there is a 1924 knot garden with interlocking bands of dwarf box, thyme, lavender and cotton lavender infilled with bedding plants. On a truly grand scale, the great Fountain Garden, an immense semi-circle of grass and flower beds with a central fountain, is probably the most impressive element, but the Wilderness Garden in spring, with its mass of daffodils and spring-flowering trees has the most charm. The laburnum walk – a tunnel of trained trees with butter-coloured rivulets of flowers in May – off the Wilderness Garden is another great attraction. The former kitchen garden now houses a rose garden. The restored Privy Garden of William III is a spectacular example of the Baroque, with parterres, cutwork, clipped yews and spring and summer displays of seventeenth-century plants. It now forms a magnificent setting for Sir Christopher Wren's south front of the palace and the elaborate gilded ironwork railings by Jean Tijou. Though this restoration has been much praised, it probably does not compare favourably with the design and maintenance of its model, Paleis Het Loo, in the Netherlands. An area of the gardens sometimes missed by visitors is the secluded twentieth-century garden, an area developed originally for the training of apprentices, but now also open to all. It is located just over the canal next to the Fountain Garden (signposted) and is open daily. Too much to see in one day – plan at least two trips; one in spring and one in summer to walk in only part of the 66 acres of gardens and the informal deer park 10 times that size. By-the-by, try taking the boat from Westminster pier down to Hampton Court – the most charming approach to the garden. The park is also the venue for the annual Hampton Court Palace International Flower Show in July. Bushy Park (see entry) lies across Hampton Court Road.

37 Heath Drive   33

London NW3 7SD. Tel: (020) 7435 2419

Mr C. Caplin • Off Finchley Road • Open 12th May, 7th July, 2.30 – 6pm • Entrance: £2, children 50p ● ☕ ♿ ⚑ ✑

A square garden of about one-fifth of an acre with a vast number of plants packed into it. There is an attractive pergola walk and unusual and interesting plants. Lots of abutilons, tree peonies, rhododendrons, palms, broom trees, black and other bamboos, a tamarisk tree, a handkerchief tree, figs and a mulberry tree. Other features of the garden include pools and rockeries, a fruit tree pergola, raised beds and a greenhouse and conservatory for exotics. The garden has an effective compost heap hidden behind a hedge of delightful cut-leaved alder. In the front garden is a highly scented stauntonia flowering in spring, and a very large *Pieris formosa forrestii*.

Highwood Ash   34

Highwood Hill, Mill Hill, London NW7 4EX. Tel (020) 8959 1183

Mr and Mrs Roy Gluckstein • From central London via A41 (Watford Way) to Mill Hill Circus, turn right up Lawrence Street, bear left at top up Highwood Hill. House is at top on right • Open 18th, 19th, May, 2 – 6pm, and May to Sept for groups by appt for charity • Entrance: £2, children 50p • Other information: Refreshments and plants for sale on 18th and 19th May only ● ⬦

This is a surprising country-sized garden in north London – some three and a half acres in all. The house (not open) dates from the sixteenth to the eighteenth centuries, during which time it was home to, amongst others, the noted traveller Celia Fiennes (d. 1741). A spacious lawn takes the eye to boundaries of mature trees with a brick wall on one side fronted by a broad mixed border. On the opposite side are headlands of juniper planned by the late Percy Cane, who helped with the design in its early phases. His main feature was a formal rose garden. Another noted designer, John Brookes, assisted with the late 1980s' water features in the lower garden. Two large pools have imaginative planting at their edges, with an old mulberry over one bank and ornamental trees elsewhere. Behind a copper beech are white-barked birches, *Betula jacquemontii*, partially shielding the Secret Garden with its spring bulbs. Other surprises include a terrace with a raised herb bed and a covered arbour leading to the swimming pool. Rhododendrons and azaleas are a spring feature.

The Hill Garden   35

Inverforth Close, North End Way, London NW3 7EX. Tel: (020) 8455 5183

Corporation of London • From Hampstead past Jack Straw's Castle on road to Golders Green, on left hand side. Inverforth Close is off North End Way (A502) • Open all year, daily, 9am – dusk • Entrance: free ○ 🍵 ✗ WC &

Overgrown in parts, the chief charm here lies in the secluded setting. The pergola, now completely restored, was built between 1906 and 1925 to a design by Thomas H. Mawson to screen Lord Leverhulme's house, The Hill (now known as Inverforth House), from its kitchen gardens and to shield it from people walking on the Heath. It is one of the best examples of its type, with all its columns and timber features intact. The pergola walk and the former kitchen garden have both been replanted. Other features include a large formal lily pond, herbaceous borders, undulating lawns and many shrubs and trees. There are wonderful views across the Heath.

Holland Park   36

Kensington, London W8/W11. Tel: (020) 7471 9813

Royal Borough of Kensington and Chelsea • Between Kensington High Street and Holland Park Avenue, with several entrances • Parking (pay and display) from Abbotsbury Road entrance • Open all year, daily, 7.30am – dusk • Entrance: free ○ 🍵 ✗ 🧺 WC & ⬧ 🍴 ⚲

Most of the famous Holland House was destroyed by bombs in World War II, but the formal gardens, created in 1812 by Lord Holland, have been maintained. The 53-acre park contains some rare trees such as Pyrenean oak, Chinese sweet gum, Himalayan birch, violet willow and the snowdrop tree, which flowers in May. The rose walk has now been replanted with a variety of azaleas. There is a small iris garden round a fountain. Peacocks strut the lawns and drape the walls with their tail feathers, and in the woodland section birds and squirrels find sanctuary from London's noise and traffic. There are excellent children's play areas. In 1991 the charming and beautifully maintained one-acre Kyoto Garden was opened as a permanent souvenir of the Japanese Festival. One of the most pleasant small London parks, although paths and grass can look worn and tired after the busy summer period, and not everyone will admire the bedding plants.

The Holme 37

Inner Circle, Regent's Park, London NW1 4NT.

Crown Estate Commissioners • In Regent's Park, just W of Inner Circle • Open several days for NGS • Entrance: £2.50, children £1 • Other information: Parking in Outer Circle. Refreshments and toilet facilities in café opposite ◑ ♿

A garden designed to enhance the setting of one of the best-positioned houses (by Decimus Burton) in central London, overlooking Heron Island in Regent's Park Lake. Wisely, waterfowl are excluded. A gravel path leads down through a shrubbery towards sweeping lawns and herbaceous beds at the back of the house. A spectacular rock garden with grotto, bridge and waterfall is not to be missed. Find time to sit at some of the many vantage points to admire the mature trees, good planting schemes and views.

239a Hook Road 38

Chessington, Kingston-upon-Thames KT9 1EQ;
Email: derek.st.romaine@virgin.net

Derek and Dawn St Romaine • On Hook road (A243) close to Hook underpass and A3. Opposite recreation ground • Open by appt • Entrance: £2 • Other information: Parking in recreation ground opposite NEW ◑

Created since 1985, this garden of many visual delights reflects the artistic skill of the garden-photographer owner and his wife. Under an *Albizia julibrissin* tree overhanging the curved lawn is the gravel garden and dining area planted with grasses and drought-tolerant plants. Around the circular lawn are standard hollies and box balls act as edging to the wide and effective borders. A circular pond and an L-shaped rose tunnel leads into the *potager*, where thriving vegetables are given designer willow supports, and fruit trees are under-planted with patterns of herbs, vegetables and low hedges. Look out for the picturesque garden shed with its cobwebby windows, which puts in an appearance in many garden photographs.

Horniman Gardens 39

Hornimans Drive, London SE23 3BT. Tel: (020) 8699 8924

Horniman Museum • On South Circular at Lordship Lane/London Road junction • Open all year, daily except 25th Dec, 7.15am – dusk (Sun opens 8am) • Entrance: free • Other information: Horticultural demonstrations March to Sept, first Wed in month, 2.30pm. International music festival end June ○ ☕ 🍴 WC 🍽 ⚲

This charming, rather old-fashioned park has a fine setting, with extensive views over the North Downs, St Paul's and west London, and its attractions include formal bedding, a rose pergola, a bandstand – with a band on summer Sunday afternoons and children's entertainment in August – and a steep hill garden with rocks, stream, conifers, etc. The large and impressive Victorian conservatory was rebuilt recently behind the museum, which does not contain any plants in winter but is used for functions and for the concert series held in spring and autumn. There are two nature trails, one in the gardens and one along a stretch of disused railway line with a pond and wildflower meadow, also an animal enclosure and a new natural history building.

Hyde Park   40

Rangers Lodge, London W2 2UH. Tel: (020) 7298 2100

Royal Parks • Open all year, daily, dawn – midnight • Entrance: free • Other information: Dogs not permitted in rose garden ○ ☕ ✕ WC ᵫ ⬥ 🏛 💡 ☕

A popular retreat from the surrounding streets is the rose garden. This enclosed area has matured well, with plenty of seats from which to admire the colour-coordinated planting in many flower beds. The heavy metal pergola has in part been covered by 'Sander's White Rambler' roses. The plan is to match the growth and flowering times of a range of rambling roses and plant them, together with varieties of clematis, to complement the adjoining flower beds. The meadow area around the police station has a wide variety of native grasses; it is mown in late summer. The dell is currently overgrown but nonetheless a charming enclosed area, with a waterfall, stream, ducks and even a few rabbits. The Holocaust Memorial stone stands close by among a small grove of trees. The seven-mile-long walk in memory of Diana, Princess of Wales, through Kensington Gardens, Hyde Park, Green Park and St James' Park, was opened in 2000.

Isabella Plantation ★   41

Richmond Park, Richmond, Surrey TW10 5HS. Tel: (020) 8948 3209; Fax: (020) 8332 2730

Royal Parks • Richmond Park, Broomfield Hill • Open all year, daily, dawn – dusk • Entrance: free • Other information: Parking in Broomfield Hill car park, Pembroke Lodge, Roehampton Gate, disabled at north entrance by way of Ham Gate. Refreshments at Pembroke Lodge. Toilet facilities in summer only. Motorised wheelchair available weekdays. Telephone to book by 12 noon previous day ○ WC ᵫ ⬥ ☕

The remarkably rich wooded plantation features many fine indigenous forest trees – oaks, beeches and birches – as well as more exotic specimens like magnolias, camellias, witch hazels and styrax trees. The principal glory is the collection of rhododendrons and azaleas, the earliest rhododendron 'Christmas Cheer' blossoming in the New Year, but the garden is at its best from April until June, when the dwarf azaleas and the waterside primulas around the several ponds, streams and a bog garden, are also in flower. The garden is a notable bird sanctuary – nuthatches, tree-creepers, kingfishers, woodpeckers and owls have all been spotted, and herons fish regularly in the ponds. The Waterhouse Plantation in neighbouring Bushy Park (see entry) is also fine.

26 Kenilworth Road 42

Penge SE20 7QG. Tel: (020) 8402 9035

Mr and Mrs S. Clutson • Off A234 Beckenham Road; 10-min walk from Kent House station • Open by appt only • Entrance: £1 ● & ॰

This garden is an inspiration for anyone with active youngsters and little space. Created by a designer, it has a Mediterranean theme, with paved patio, pots and densely planted interesting borders. An olive tree (*Olea europaea*) is the central focus; cardoons and alliums stand tall above woodruff.

Kensington Gardens 43

London W2 2UH. Tel: (020) 7298 2100

Royal Parks • Entrances off Bayswater Road, Kensington Gore and West Carriage Drive, Hyde Park • Palace State Apartments open all year, daily, 10am – 5pm (Nov to Feb closes 4pm). Orangery open daily; for information telephone (020) 7937 9561 • Gardens open all year, daily, 6am (closing time displayed at gate) • Entrance: free (State Apartments £8.80, OAPs/students £6.90, children £6.30, family £26.80 • Other information: Outdoor sculpture sometimes on display at Serpentine Art Gallery, open Mon — Fri ○ ☕ ✕ **WC** & ⬧ ॰

These 274 acres of finest park, adjoining Hyde Park, have their own pleasures, including sculpture by G.F. Watts. Children and older enthusiasts will relish the Peter Pan statue and a whole new imaginative Peter Pan world – a playground in memory of Diana, Princess of Wales, which features a pirate ship, wigwams, a tree house and a splendidly realistic crocodile among its many attractions. The Albert Memorial is a glittering treat, and the elegant Baroque orangery by Hawksmoor and Vanbrugh, with decoration by Grinling Gibbons, is well worth a visit. So, too, is the sunken water garden surrounded by beds of bright seasonal flowers, which can be viewed from 'windows' in a beech walk. From the Broad Walk south to the Albert Memorial, semi-circular flower beds are kept planted against a background of flowering shrubs.

Kenwood 44

Hampstead Lane, London NW3 7JR. Tel: (020) 8348 1286

English Heritage • N side of Hampstead Heath, on Highgate – Hampstead road • House open April to Oct, 10am – 6pm (5pm in Oct); Nov to March, 10am – 4pm. Closed 1st Jan, 24th, 25th Dec • Park open all year, daily, 8am – 8.30pm (winter closes 4.30pm) • Entrance: free • Other information: Parking at West Lodge car park, Hampstead Lane ○ ☕ ✕ ▦ **WC** & ⬧ ⬛ ⬤ ॰

A picturesque landscape laid out by Humphry Repton at the end of the eighteenth century. Vistas, sweeping lawns from the terrace of Kenwood House and views over Hampstead Heath (and London) predominate, and the magnificent mature trees include oak and beech. There are large-scale shrubberies dominated by rhododendrons, and a kitchen garden with walls once heated. Walks follow Repton's original plan. The pasture ground slopes down towards two large lakes. Woods to the south of the lakes fringe the heath side of the pasture ground, with several gates onto the heath itself. It is a good place to walk at any season, but particularly when the trees are turning in autumn, to recall that the lime walk was a favourite of that great gardener of the eighteenth century, Alexander Pope. Look out for the ivy arch which opens out on to the lakes (one of Repton's famous 'surprises') and the sham bridge on the Thousand Pound Pond, which has been faithfully rebuilt with its single upside-down baluster, There is also some worthwhile modern sculpture, including a Henry Moore and a 1953 Barbara Hepworth. On the western side are haymeadows which change colour from May to July; natural regeneration of the ancient woodlands (SSSI) is being encouraged.

Kew Gardens

(see ROYAL BOTANIC GARDENS)

38 Killieser Avenue   45

Streatham Hill, London SW2 4NT. Tel/Fax: (020) 8671 4196

Mrs Winkle Haworth • Off Streatham Hill, near Streatham station. From Sternhold Avenue take second turning right • Open to groups of 5 or more by appt • Entrance: £1.50 ◐ ☕ ✈

This much-visited South London garden is lovingly tended and full of carefully chosen plants and shrubs evoking a romantic atmosphere. Lush and skilful planting divides the garden into two distinct areas where perennials and annuals blend harmoniously — creamy nasturtiums surround bronze fennel, old-fashioned roses, clematis and violas. An obelisk, a rose arch and a water cascade give architectural interest, while box cones beside a delightful rose-clad Gothick arbour introduce visitors to a second level, with a parterre and wall fountain providing an element of formality.

1 Lister Road   46

London E11 3DS. Tel: (020) 8556 8962

Mr Myles Challis • Off Leytonstone High Road, 10-min. walk from underground station. Hills Garage marks corner of Lister Road • Open one Sun for NGS • Entrance: £1 ◐ WC

Here is a garden that will inspire those with the imagination and daring to try planting with tender items. The owner's remarkable flair for assembling sub-tropical and temperate plants evokes a mysterious atmosphere. They include palms, bamboos, daturas, gingers, rice-paper plants and bananas — all achieving their natural size. Many, like the tree ferns, were grown here before they became fashionable. Quite extraordinary, with hardy exotics too, and all jostling for space in just 12 x 6 metres.

London Zoo 47

Regent's Park, London NW1 4RY. Tel: (020) 7722 3333;
Fax: (020) 7586 5743; Website: www.zsl.org; www.londonzoo.co.uk

London Zoo • In Regent's Park to N of Outer Circle. Take Bus 274 from Camden/Baker Street to Prince Albert Road and walk across bridge to main gate; tube to Camden Town/Baker Street; waterbus from Camden Lock or Little Venice • Open all year, daily except 25th Dec, 10am – 5.30pm (4pm in winter) • Entrance: £10, OAPs and students £8.50, children under 15 £7, under-3s free, family ticket £30 • Other information: Car park at zoo or metered parking in Outer Circle. Wheelchairs and buggies available from information kiosk at main gate ○ 💬 ✕ 🍽 WC ♿ ♨ 🍴 ℴ

Hear the dramatic cries of the macaws in the distance as you enter the main gate and notice the mixed carex planted in front of their enclosure. All the enclosures are designed to provide the conditions which the animals need. The keepers choose the most appropriate materials, all grown on site for each species: sand or earth for burrowing animals, hard surfaces for hoofed animals, branches and perches for arboreal species. Note the tree of heaven (1870) with the listed penguin pool built around it, and the old black mulberry (wrongly labelled 'white' a century ago), whose leaves are fed to silk worms. Find time to walk over the timber bridge below the 'stream' of blue slate in the Water-wise Garden. As part of the 'Web of Life' exhibition, housed within the Millennium conservation centre, a native wildlife garden has been created. This includes habitats such as meadows, woodland and hedgerow, along with ideas for a domestic garden including a rockery and a herb garden, showing ways that birds, butterflies and animals can be attracted to a city garden.

4 Macaulay Road 48

Clapham, London SW4 0QX. Tel: (020) 7627 1137

Mrs Diana Ross • Off Clapham Common Northside • Open by appt only • Entrance: £5 per person (10 people min.) inclusive of guided tour ◐

A walled garden (24 x 15 metres) set out on strong, clear lines with formality heightened by box hedges, topiary and lots of pots. A circular lawn is surrounded by dense mixed planting, arches and a pergola. There is a grotto with a fernery around it and many exotic shrubs and herbaceous plants chosen for their handsome foliage. The garden has been designed to look as good in winter as in summer; with a large range of plants, many grey or variegated, the overall effect is of profusion and soft colours.

Marble Hill 49

Richmond Road, Twickenham, Middlesex TW1 2NL. Tel: (020) 8892 5115

English Heritage • S of Richmond Bridge off Richmond Road. Additional access by river launch • House open April to Sept, daily, 10am – 6pm; Oct, daily, 10am – 5pm; Nov to March, Wed – Sun, 10am – 4pm. Closed 1st to 16th Jan,

24th to 26th Dec • Park open all year, daily, 7.30am – dusk • Entrance: £3.30, concessions £2.50, children £1.70 (2001 prices) ○

The gardens, originally laid out in the 1740s for the Countess of Suffolk, are still in the process of being restored by English Heritage and awaiting the result of a Heritage Lottery bid based on the Thames Landscape Strategy – a conservation plan for the whole of this historic area. Alexander Pope, a neighbour of the Countess, took an interest in the layout, and recent excavations have revealed one of the two grottos known to have been constructed. There is an ice-house and a young Sweet Walk. The gardens (if they can be called that, as now they are largely sports pitches and a venue for summer music concerts) lay claim to the largest and probably the oldest black walnut in the country and also the tallest bay willow and Italian alder trees. Then take the ferry to Ham House (see entry) over the river. You can also visit *Strawberry Hill* (eponymous station nearby) where Horace Walpole's 'little Gothick castle' can be seen from Easter to Oct on Sunday afternoons [parties by appt. Tel: (020) 8892 0051].

Mile End Park 50

Mile End Road, London E3. Tel: (020) 7364 5000; Fax: (020) 7364 4449

London Borough of Tower Hamlets • Access from Burdett Road (A1205), St Paul's Way, Mile End Road (A1), Grove Road (A1205). Nearest underground station: Mile End • Park open all year • Entrance: free ○ 🍴 **WC** ♿ ⟐ 🦮 ♺

Publicised as the park for the twenty-first century, this great green lung in the heart of Tower Hamlets has been welcomed by schools, youth clubs and community groups. All have been invited to take part in planting trees – rowans, pines and hornbeams – shrubs and bulbs. Already the green bridge and terraced gardens have established creatively wild planting. Swathes of grasses, euphorbias, sisyrinchium, *Viburnum* x *bodnantense* and galegas are covering the ground to give a mature feeling. Exciting mounds have appeared, one with wide grass steps and a winding path topped by standing stones. Then there are designer ponds and views of the canal with sections set aside for wildlife The recently completed ecology park and arts park, each with its own earth-sheltered building, house various activities throughout the year.

Museum of Garden History 51

Lambeth Palace Road, London SE1 7LB. Tel: (020) 740 8865;
Fax: (020) 7401 8869; Website: www.museumgardenhistory.org.uk

The Tradescant Trust • Lambeth Palace Road, parallel to River Thames on S bank, hard by Lambeth Bridge • Open early Feb to mid-Dec, daily, 10.30am – 5pm • Entrance: Voluntary admission charge £2.50, concessions £2 • Other information: Historic collection of garden tools and artefacts. Courses, exhibitions, lectures, plant fairs and concerts ◔ ☕ **WC** ♿ ✿ 🛍 ♺

The garden in the churchyard was created in 1981. It commemorates the two John Tradescants (father and son), gardeners to Charles I and II, who are buried in a fine tomb in the replica seventeenth-century garden, which contains examples of plants brought back by the Tradescants from their plant-hunting travels in Europe and America in the seventeenth century. Lady Salisbury's knot garden design incorporates some of the Tradescants' imported plants which are now thought of as indigenous to this country. Well-labelled herbs abound amongst pretty perennials, making a delightful backcloth for the table tombs, whilst the walls are clothed in Virginia creeper, ivy, roses and clematis.

Museum of London Nursery Garden 52

The Museum of London, London Wall, London EC2Y 5HN.
Tel: (020) 7600 3699; Fax: (020) 7600 1058

Museum of London • Take underground to St Paul's or Barbican, then follow signs • Open 30th March to Oct, daily, 10am – 5.30pm (Sun opens 12 noon) • Entrance: £5 (annual ticket), OAPs £3 (museum), children free • Other information: Possible for wheelchairs but shallow steps make assistance necessary ◑ ☕ ✕ WC ♿ ♨

Garden designers Colson and Stone totally revamped the internal courtyard in 1990 to coincide with the exhibition of London's gardens, and have transformed an almost lifeless area into a living history of plantsmanship in the City from medieval times to the present day. Legendary names like Henry Russell, who sold striped roses in Westminster, and James Veitch, who sold exotica like the monkey puzzle tree from his nursery in Chelsea, are represented. This tiny roof garden is flanked on four sides by high buildings, yet the designers have still managed to incorporate a tumbling rill and a rock garden.

Myddelton House Gardens ★ 53

Bulls Cross, Enfield, Middlesex EN2 9HG. Tel: (01992) 702200

Lee Valley Regional Park Authority • S of M25 on A10 (junction 25), turn first right into Bullsmoor Lane, left into Bulls Cross; Myddelton House is on right at junction with Turkey Street • Open all year, Mon – Fri, 10am – 4.30pm; also 31st March to Oct, Sun, Bank Holiday Mons, 2 – 5pm. Also open for NGS. Closed Christmas week and Bank Holidays • Entrance: £2, concessions £1.40 • Other information: Teas on Charity Suns only ○ WC ♫ ♟

A magnificent, diverse plant collection set in four acres was built up by the famous E.A. Bowles and is now restored. Splendid spring bulbs, followed by an award-winning iris collection, followed by autumn crocus and impressive varieties of autumn-remontant iris, make this garden a joy all year round. Sternbergia and nerines are but a few of the autumn bulbs, and there is a fine *Crinum moorei* near the old conservatory. This is by no means a municipal garden, and the impressive plant collection is displayed attractively in a well-designed area surrounding the Regency house. The garden is still unified by Bowles's plants and vision and it is worth reading details of his plan, which included a Lunatic Asylum planted with botanical misfits. Other attractions include the carp lake, magnificent wisteria and part of the old London Bridge.

17A Navarino Road 54

Hackney, London E8 1AD. Tel: (020) 7254 5622

John Tordoff • Off London Fields, near Hackney Central station. Buses 30, 38 •
Open by appt for groups of 10 or more • Entrance: £2 for parties of 10 or more
🌓

An imaginative explosion of design occupies just 25 x 8 metres, yet this garden
visit must not be hurried, starting with the Italianate courtyard with its
fountain guarded by white pottery doves – the doves, archways, Mount Fuji,
tea house and mirrored alcove are recycled or made by the owner. Clipped
yews lead to a new perspective – a Japanese garden. Do not miss the seating
area on the right which shares the pool with neighbours. Miniature conifers
and well-placed rocks bring the eye down to the small scale of the design, and
the whole is kept together by the rich green carpet of *Soleirolia soleirolii* (baby's
tears). The clear stream is a haven for many birds. Memorable.

Noel–Baker Peace Garden 55

Elthorne Park, Hazelville Road, London N19.

London Borough of Islington • Entrances to Elthorne Park in Beaumont Road
and Sunnyside Road • Open all year, daily, Mon – Fri, 8am – dusk (Sat opens
9am, Sun, 10am) • Entrance: free • Other information: Toilet facilities in
adjacent playground ○ ♿

This is a small, well-designed formal garden within a London park, created in
1984 in memory of Philip Noel-Baker, winner of the Nobel Peace Prize in 1959.
It is an interesting example of late-twentieth-century garden design and
planting, centering on a water feature and a striking bronze figure (with a
horizontal bronze reflection). Much use is made of brick and York-stone
paving, and raised beds together with lawns; the overall effect is softened and
enlivened by the excellent planting, with many unusual species (e.g. *Feijoa*
sellowiana, Clerodendrum bungei, C. trichotomum). The emphasis is on green, grey
and white, lifted here and there by splashes of colour and linked by the strong
lines of the asymmetrical design. There are several secluded sitting areas. The
garden receives extensive use and support from the local community, and
although the results of limited maintenance are sometimes apparent, the
overall impression is of well-loved amenity. In adjacent *Elthorne Park* is a good
children's playground and a fitness trail.

1F Oval Road 56

Flat 1, 1F Oval Road, London NW1 7EA. Tel (020) 7267 0655

Sheila Jackson • On Oval Road. Nearest tube Camden Town. Buses to Camden
Town or Camden High Street, stops C2 and 274 very near • Open by appt only
• Entrance: £1, children 50p • Other information: Parking difficult, especially on
Suns 🌓

A tiny space squeezed between a tall Victorian house and the Euston railway
line has been transformed into a miniature garden of great charm and

horticultural interest. Despite its small size one needs to walk through and around the garden to explore all the hidden places and vistas, and to appreciate the huge variety of unusual plants. Most of them grow in containers and have thrived this way for years.

Pembridge Cottage 57

10 Strawberry Hill Road, Twickenham TW1 4PT. Tel: (020) 828 78993

Ian and Lydia Sidaway • 1m from Twickenham town centre, approached from Cross Deep or Waldegrave Road. Strawberry Hill station; Buses 33, 110, 267, 281, 290, 490 • Open 16th, 23rd June for NGS, and by appt • Entrance: £1
[NEW] 🍴 ●

A carefully maintained artist's garden which is an excellent example of a green garden without the ubiquitous lawn. Interesting at all seasons, it is designed with recessed areas framed by structural shrubs – bay, elaeagnus, fig, olive, viburnums, box and photinia. Gravel paths are outlined by groups of large river stones. Bamboos, strong ferns and grasses have stylishly planted terracotta pots placed among them. The journey ends at the artist's studio. Ask to see the imaginative scrapbook showing the garden's progress over the past six years, with pictures also of an obvious inspiration, the clipped Luberon garden in France.

Priory Gardens 58

Orpington, Kent. Tel: (020) 8464 3333 ext. 4471

London Borough of Bromley • Off Orpington High Street • Open all year, daily, 7.30am – dusk (weekends and Bank Holidays opens 9.30am) • Entrance: free • Other information: Separate area for dogs ○ 🍴 WC & 🌱

Adjacent to an attractive medieval priory building (now Bromley Museum), this is one of the most tastefully gardened public spaces in outer London, whose documentation dates from 1634. Pre-1939 the gardens were extended in the formal Arts and Crafts style. It has an excellent example of patterned annual bedding, a recently replanted herbaceous garden, a rich rose garden, fine mature trees and shrubs and a refurbished lake.

Regent's Park (and Queen Mary's Rose Garden) ★ 59

Inner Circle, Regent's Park, London NW1. Tel: (020) 7298 2000

Royal Parks • Off Marylebone Road. Many other entrances to park • Open all year, daily, dawn – dusk • Entrance: free • Other information: Dogs in parkland only ○ 🍴 ✕ 🍴 WC & 🌱 ♒

These sedate, well-laid-out and beautifully manicured gardens are justly famous. Playing host to more than 60,000 roses – dominated by hybrid teas and floribundas, although also including old-fashioned, shrub and species roses – the sight and scent of the gardens in high summer is a magnet for thousands of visitors. It must be said, however, that this style of rose garden is not to everyone's taste. The roses are grown with almost military discipline and are in perfect condition. Swagged and garlanded climbers surround the circular rose garden, but the herbaceous borders are also worth visiting, particularly in late July and August, as is the large ornamental lake with its central island. It attracts many varieties of waterfowl, including herons which nest on the island. The Broad Walk (five minutes from the Rose Gardens) between the Inner and Outer Circle towards Cambridge Gate is another exquisitely maintained Victorian-style area of planting. Its side walks are lined with urns and fountains following Nesfield's originals. Cypress lookalikes line the paths. There are 32 ornamental urns and tazzas (shallow bowls) and eight fountains. Nesfield's planting precision has been described as performing the same function as a military band – it provides entertainment for park visitors. Do not miss the charming little St John's Lodge garden. Nearby, at 66 Portland Place, W1 (a short walk from Oxford Circus) is the *Royal Institute of British Architects* (RIBA). The delightful roof garden on the first floor adjoining the café which features gleaming steel containers with clipped box and other architectural foliage plants, and a William Pye fountain, is open to the public during office hours. Another stylish sculpture garden in the area, which also has a café, is to be found at *The Wallace Collection* in Manchester Square.

48 Rommany Road   60

Gipsy Hill, London SE27 9PX.

Dr Belinda Barnes and Ronald Stuart-Moonlight • Off Salters Hill and Gipsy Hill, ½ m from Gipsy Hill mainline station. Buses 3, 322 • Open for NGS, inc. some evenings, and by appt (15 persons max.) • Entrance: £2 ◑

This gem of a garden (10 x 7 metres) was started from scratch in 1995. The owners designed and built every feature – garden walls, paving, pergola and arbour. The careful planting includes climbers such as muehlenbeckia intertwined with *Clematis armandii*. Hostas and ferns flourish in large pots; white-flowered wisteria, a small mulberry tree, *Acacia dealbata* and much more are an object lesson in imaginative planting in a small space.

The Roof Garden   61

99 Kensington High Street, London W8 5ED. Tel: (020) 7937 7994

Virgin Group • In Derry Street off Kensington High Street by lift • Telephone to check gardens open before attempting to visit • Entrance: free ◑ ✕ ◍

A fantasy one-and-a-half-acre garden 30 metres above the ground on the sixth floor of what was Derry and Toms 1938 department store. Listed Grade II by English Heritage and a private members' club with restaurant facilities, the gardens which surround the bar and dining room are also used for functions and conferences. Ralph Hancock designed them to give three distinct illusions – a formal Spanish garden with canal, an English woodland garden and a Tudor garden. The soil is nowhere thicker than a metre, so it is remarkable that more than 500 varieties of trees and shrubs, including palms, figs and vines, survive up here. Ducks swim about in their high-rise ponds, watched over by flamingos, and there is a delightful maze of small paths, bridges and walkways, with peepholes in the outer walls giving glimpses across the city skyline.

The Rookery   62

Streatham Common South, London SW16. Tel: (020) 8671 0994

*Lambeth Council • Streatham High Road (A23), then Streatham Common
South. No entrance by car from Streatham North Crown Lane • Open all year
except 25th Dec, 9am — dusk • Entrance: free • Other information: Dogs on
leads on top terrace only* ○ 🍵 📠 WC ♿ ◔

This surprising garden space up the hill from Streatham High Road was once
part of a private garden. In over a quarter of a mile there is much to enjoy: an
abundantly planted English garden with quiet seating areas, a rock garden and
stream, a small yew-hedged pond area close by a wisteria-clad pergola. The
white garden, at its peak in July, almost rivals Sissinghurst. Further down the
hill through shrubbery-lined paths is a quiet orchard picnic ground. On the
way back up the hill seek out the well – one of the three original wells of
Streatham's spa waters, dating from 1659. A fenced and gated play area with
large paddling pool, much used by local families, is next to the parking area.

167 Rosendale Road   63

West Dulwich, London SE21 8LW. Tel: (020) 876 67846

*Mr and Mrs A Pizzoferro • Off South Circular Road at junction of Rosendale
and Lovelace Roads. Nearest train stations Tulse Hill or West Dulwich • Open
for NGS and at other times by appt • Entrance: £1.50* NEW ● 🌿

The warm colour theme of the front garden gives no hint of the charm to be
found in the small woodland area, the natural winter stream and child-safe
wildlife pond in the back garden. This is a place to visit for ideas: bamboo canes
topped with holed flints; massed perennials and winding bark paths, one of
which leads to an old wooden ladder leaning against a fruit tree; grasses massed
in pots, houseleeks at home in bricks, hostas planted at eye level for inspection, agapanthus and bulbs in pots, are just a few of the visual delights.

Royal Botanic Gardens ★★   64

**Kew, Richmond, Surrey TW9 3AB. Tel: (020) 8940 1171 (24-hour message);
Website: www.kew.org**

*Trustees • Kew Green, S of Kew Bridge • Kew Palace (maintained by Historic
Royal Palaces) closed for refurbishment • Gardens open all year, daily, except
25th Dec and 1st Jan, 9.30am – 4/7.30pm depending on season; glasshouses
close earlier. Guided tours daily from the Victoria Gate visitor centre, 11am and
2pm • Entrance: £6.50 (last hour of admission £4.50), OAPs, students £4.50,
children under 16 free, blind, partially-sighted and essential carers free, season
ticket (for Kew and Wakehurst Place) £24, couples season ticket £43 (2001
prices). Other season tickets and Friends of Kew Membership available. • Other
information: Parking Kew Green/Brentford Gate car park in Ferry Lane. Coach
parking Kew Road. Wheelchairs may be reserved in advance free of charge.
Guide dogs permitted* ○ 🍵 ✕ 📠 WC ♿ ♨ 🍴 ◔

Kew's delightful and varied gardens and grounds of 300 acres have something for everyone. In spring, the flowering cherries, crocuses, daffodils and the fine rock garden; in May and June, the bluebell wood, the lilacs (made famous by the song) and the water-lily house; in summer the Duke's Garden, the rose garden; in autumn bulbs and trees; in winter, the winter-flowering cherries and (indoors) the alpine house. The trees range from ash and birch collections through conifers, eucalyptus and mulberry to walnut. The lake, once a disused gravel pit, has an abundance of wildfowl. Year-round pleasures are Decimus Burton's Palm and Temperate Houses, the Filmy Fern House and the elegant modern Princess of Wales Conservatory (named after Princess Augusta, founder of the Botanic Gardens in 1759) with its computer-controlled microclimates. The huge glasshouses, some of which are kept at tropical temperatures, have their unique collections of exotic and unusual plants, ranging from banana trees to giant water lilies. There is an Evolution House, and Museum No. I (opposite the Palm House) exhibits the Economic Botany collection. The somewhat formal rose garden, the delightful rock garden and the grass and bamboo gardens should not be missed. The Japanese gateway has been completely restored and the area around landscaped. All these buildings and gardens are elements in 'working' Kew, which is primarily a botanic research institution, collecting, conserving and exchanging plants from all over the world. There is another Kew — historic and royal. The palace, now restored to its former glory — externally at any rate — became in 1729 home to Frederick, Prince of Wales. It was he who commissioned the gardens here, his Lord of the Bedchamber, the 3rd Earl of Bute, who created them, and his consort, Princess Augusta, who after Frederick's death commissioned Sir William Chambers to design the splendid buildings which today give Kew its historical hinterland — the three temples dedicated to Aeolus, Arethusa and Bellona, the 1761 orangery, the ruined arch and the pagoda. A relic of an earlier age, the seventeenth-century Queen's Garden beside the palace, has been re-created in period style, and the palace itself is to be refurbished and re-opened. The disabled will find most parts of Kew accessible; indeed there is a Secluded Garden, designed by Anthea Gibson, created with the partially sighted and disabled in mind. (Telephone (020) 8332 5622 for details.) Children will enjoy the imaginative mangrove swamps, Mohave Desert and carnivorous plants in the Princess of Wales Conservatory, and the Palm House with its bananas and Marine Display showing seaweeds and fish from around the world.

Royal Hospital, Chelsea (Ranelagh Gardens)   65

Royal Hospital Road, London SW3 4SR. Tel: (020) 7881 5248

Royal Hospital Chelsea • Through Royal Hospital London Gate in Royal Hospital Road, and through next gate into South Grounds, then through small gate on left • Open all year, daily (except 1st Jan, 25th, 26th Dec, and May and June due to Chelsea Flower Show), Mon – Sat, 10am – 1pm, 2pm – sunset, Sun, 2pm – sunset • Entrance: free ○ WC ⊹ ☗

The elegant and attractive gardens are sited to one side of the Royal Hospital, with over a mile of wide walkways through undulating park-like grass and handsome tree and shrub plantings, and a few perennial and shrub borders.

Formerly the pleasure grounds of Ranelagh, complete with a large rotunda (now demolished) and laid out in formal style, they were redesigned by Gibson in the nineteenth century, turned into allotments for pensioners between the two world wars, and later reconstructed according to Gibson's plan. A summerhouse by Sir John Soane, near the entrance to the garden, houses several seats plus glass cases with a history and a map of the gardens indicating the major trees. These include many species of poplar, birch, beech, holly, cherry, chestnut, lime, oak and so on, with a couple of more exotic ones – the tree of heaven and the maidenhair tree. To one side of the park is the area used to house the Chelsea Flower Show. A long avenue of plane trees marks the western boundary of the gardens.

35 Rudloe Road   66

Clapham, SW12 0DR. Tel: (020) 8673 2437

Judith Sharpe • Off A24 Clapham Common South, directly off Poynders Road (A205 South Circular). Clapham South station is 10-min walk • Open by appt • Entrance: £5 ● WC

This 10 x 6 metre garden is an excellent example of good design and imaginative planting. The Chelsea-winning owner nips and tucks a wide variety of plants with complementary shapes into this small space. Clematis, climbing roses, metallic-leaved phormiums and myrtle share abundant good health. A variety of pots, an antique garden seat and Scottish pebbles complete an unusual garden.

Southwood Lodge   67

33 Kingsley Place, Highgate, London N6 5EA. Tel: (020) 8348 2785

Mr and Mrs Christopher Whittington • Off Southwood Lane, Highgate • Open 19th May, 2 – 6pm, for NGS, and for private visits April to July by appt • Entrance: £1.50, children 50p • Other information: Plants for sale on NGS Suns only ●

An imaginatively designed garden created in 1963 from a much larger, older one, set at the highest part of London with a magnificent view to the east 'as far as the Urals'. In approximately a third of an acre on a fairly steep site, there is much variety of mood and planting. By the house, a densely planted paved area is enclosed on two sides by a high beech hedge, through which steps lead down to a grassy walk planted with shrubs, clematis and herbaceous plants. A wooded area in the lowest part of the garden, with many shade-loving plants, leads up past two pools to the soothing sound of trickling water, and suitable bog plants. Alpines grow in troughs on a low wall.

7 St George's Road ★   68

St Margaret's, Twickenham, Middlesex TW1 1QS. Tel: (020) 8892 3713

Mr and Mrs R. Raworth • Off A316 between Twickenham Bridge and St Margaret's roundabout • Open 2nd June, 16th June, 2 – 6pm, 6th June, 6 –

8pm, and by appt • Entrance: £2, children 50p, evening opening £3 including wine • Other information: Home-made teas and plants for sale on open days only ● 🍴 ⚘

A most successful result of garden design, inspired by Hidcote and Tintinhull on a miniature scale. This is one of the most interesting and impressively maintained private gardens in the west London area and well worth going out of one's way to see. Among its many striking features are impressive hedges of privet, yew, box and hornbeam, which enclose various rooms and a newly planted formal knot garden. Entering through a sunken Mediterranean garden and a sink garden full of interesting small plants, you pass by a rose-covered pergola to an emerald grass carpet, flanked by flower borders backed by old trees in a private park. In one corner is a water feature, a pool with waterside planting and a bog garden surrounded by wooden decking and crossed by a charming bridge. A new parterre gives an air of formality amongst the rare shrubs and containerised plants to interest the plantsperson, who will also be drawn to the large, elegant conservatory on the north-facing wall, with old-fashioned Victorian plants.

St James's Park ★ 69

London SW1A 2BJ. Tel: (020) 7298 2000

Royal Parks • Extends from Buckingham Palace on W to Horse Guards Parade on E, The Mall on N and Birdcage Walk on S • Open all year, daily, 5am – midnight • Entrance: free ○ 🍴 🛍 WC ♿ ⇪ 🚻 ⚘

One of the smaller royal parks but one of the prettiest, though the Garden History Society and the Victorian Society criticise those who have replaced its original path system with 'a crude and quite unplanned overlay' of tarmacked straight lines. It was Henry VIII who turned this swampy field into a pleasure ground and nursery for deer. After the Restoration in 1660, Charles II employed the French garden designer Le Nôtre, who planned the gardens at Versailles, to refashion the park into a garden. Le Nôtre gave advice, via his nephew, Claude Desgots, on a formal canal and included a pitch for King Charles to play the old French game of *paille maille*, a crude form of croquet, which gave its name to neighbouring Pall Mall. Nash remodelled the lake and gardens in 1827–29. The islands are still home to a wide variety of birds.

Syon Park ★ 70

Brentford, Middlesex TW8 8JF. Tel: (020) 8560 0881;
Website: www.syonpark.co.uk

The Duke of Northumberland • 2m W of Kew Bridge, road marked from A315/ 310 at Bush Corner • Telephone for house opening dates, times and entrance charges • Garden open all year, daily except 25th, 26th Dec, 10am – 5.30pm (or dusk if earlier) • Entrance: £3, concessions/children £2.50, family ticket £7 (2001 prices) ○ 🍴 🛍 WC ♿ ⚘ 🏛 🚻 ⚘

The Tudor house, with interiors redesigned by Robert Adam c.1760, is the London seat of the Percy family. The park shows British gardening on a grand scale and is one of the oldest landscapes in the country. A few statistics: 3200 trees here, one in four of which are over 100 years old and about one in seven over 200 years old. There are wonderfully mature oaks and swamp cypresses among the 211 different species in this park landscaped by 'Capability' Brown, but the most glorious asset is the great curving conservatory designed by Charles Fowler, which is said to have inspired Paxton when he was working at Chatsworth. One wing is full of scented flowers, leading to a collection of succulent plants, the other is planted with vines, leading to a fern-covered waterfall; the central part with its renovated dome is not planted as it is used for receptions. The formal garden in front of it has been simplified and now has an austere Italianate feel. The brashly commercial architecture of the garden centre and the crude, unshielded parking area in front of the house have done great damage to the setting, yet the house remains serene and the direct view to the river from it is remarkably untouched. The surrounding park and lakeside walk are of great interest, and a new path was opened in 1999 to allow visitors to walk the complete circuit of the lake. In spite of economic restraints much work has been done in eliminating unsuitable 1960s' planting and in trying to bring the garden closer to Brown's original vision. Wildflower areas are being developed, and the rose garden has been redesigned and replanted with old varieties. One of the glories of Syon has always been the view from the ha-ha across water meadows towards the Thames; here new vistas and the famous axis to the Palm House at Kew are being opened up, and soon it will be possible to see across to the observatory and the pagoda. Much work still needs to be done, but there is a continuing programme for improvement and conservation, including work in the woodland garden, and a new gravel garden planted with grasses and perennials. The future is bright indeed. Nearby *Osterley Park* – 650 acres surrounding the neo-classical villa by Robert Adam – has a farm, ornamental lakes, classical buildings and fine old hills, and is a delightful place for a walk, especially in May when the paddocks and chestnut trees are in flower. [Open all year, daily, 9am – 7.30pm or sunset.]

Trinity Hospice ★ 71

30 Clapham Common North Side, London SW4 0RN. Tel: (020) 7787 1000

Trustees of the Hospice • Off N side of Common • Open for charity 20th, 21st April, 15th, 16th June, 7th, 8th Sept, 2 – 5pm, and by appt at other times • Entrance: £1, children free ● ➤ WC ♿ ⚘ ♨ ⚲

The gardens at Trinity Hospice were created primarily for the benefit of patients, their families and the staff. Stretching over nearly two acres, they are set out on slightly rolling park-like terrain and were designed by John Medhurst and David Foreman of London Landscape Consortium on the principles laid down by Lanning Roper. The latter had originally been asked by the Sainsbury Family Charity Trust to design these gardens on a dilapidated site, but his illness caught up with him before he could do much. The gardens were finished thanks to donations made by his friends and called the Lanning Roper Memorial Garden. Perennials and shrubs predominate, but there is also a wild garden at one end, a large pool with a mobile sculpture by George Rickey and a smaller pool with a water feature by William Pye.

Victoria and Albert Museum (The Pirelli Garden)   72

Cromwell Road, London SW7 2RL.

Cromwell Road, close to South Kensington tube station • Open all year, daily except 24th to 26th Dec, 10am – 5.45pm • Entrance: £5, concessions £3, Friends of the V&A, students and children under 18 free (entrance free after 4.30pm) • Other information: Refreshments during summer only. Music, wine and food tectures, etc. available on Wed evening openings (seaonsal) – telephone (020) 7942 2209 for details ○ WC ♿ ⚙ ▯

This large area within the splendid Victorian pile originally had a large number of cherry trees which had reached the end of their natural life and a big ash tree. At the time, the early 1980s, the then-director of the museum, Sir Roy Strong, had just staged an epoch-making *The Garden* exhibition. Thanks to the sponsorship of Pirelli it was possible to employ two architects, Douglas Childs and Maggie Davies, who produced an elegant design of classic geometry sympathetic to the Italianate style of the museum buildings. The central fountain is floodlit in the evening. On the corner of Cromwell Road and Queen Anne's Gate is *The Natural History Museum Wildlife Garden*, where 1000 trees and 20,000 wild flowers have been planted in an acre site landscaped to re-create British nature sites. [Open April to October for tours and special interest parties (telephone (020) 7938 9461) and on weekdays for school parties (telephone (020) 7938 9090).]

The Wetland Centre   73

Queen Elizabeth's Walk, Barnes, London SW13 9WT. Tel: (020) 8409 4400; E-mail: info@wetlandcentre.org.uk

The Wildfowl and Wetlands Trust • Nearest underground station Hammersmith; Buses 33, 72, 209, 283 from Hammersmith Bus Depot (alight at Red Lion pub) • Open all year, daily, 9.30am – 6pm (5pm in winter) (last admission 1 hour before closing) • Entrance: £6.75, OAPs £5.50, children £4, family ticket £17.50 NEW ○ ➠ ✗ 🖻 WC ♿ ⚙ ▯ ✎

Within 105 acres of the wetlands in an area close to the visitors' centre, three high-profile young garden designers have focused on the theme of sustainability and created gardens to motivate and encourage conservation gardening. The first, designed by Land Arts, has a loosely laid spiralling path of slate curving from the outer edge of the garden to finish in a tight central oval resembling a butterfly's proboscis. Block planting of perennials rich in pollen and scent has been chosen to give interest for the partially sighted and to attract insects. By contrast, Arne Maynard's garden consists of structured formal planting with turf-topped walls formed from split oak logs, radiating across the site in undulating curves. The planting is meadow-like. The third garden is a tongue-in-cheek Bouncing Bomb/Barnes Wallis/Barnes Wetlands, by Cleve West and Johnny Woodford. It is surrounded by cobalt-blue spikes, with a seat resembling sharp teeth. The eye is led to the central pond with the 'bouncing bomb' skimming the surface; reed beds surround the pond and planting is simplified to increase the sculptural impact. Find time to include the Wildfowl and Wetland Trust areas, and look out for the hide with its roof of succulents.

London's Open Spaces

OTHER LONDON PARKS

NW3: *Golders Hill Park*, North End Way, a 36-acre park with a vibrant two-acre flower garden, a water garden and a menagerie.

N19: *Waterlow Park*, Dartmouth Park Hill, has three ponds, tree-lined walkways, mature shrub beds and a terraced garden surrounding historic Lauderdale House, all set on undulating hillside with panoramic views.

E7: *West Ham Park*, Forest Gate, originally a late-eighteenth-century garden rivalling Kew, now a well-maintained 77-acre park with fine trees, Victorian bedding schemes, a rose garden and entertainments for children and adults.

E10: *Lee Valley Regional Park* totals 10,000 acres. Telephone information centre at Waltham Abbey Gardens (01992) 702210.

E16: *Thames Barrier Park*. Exciting new park on Thames at N end of the Barrier, designed by Alain Provost, raised above the river on a plateau. 'Green dock' incorporates hedges cut into waves echoing an impressive water feature. Altogether *nouvelle vague* and fun.

SE9: *Avery Hill Park*, Eltham, is notable for its rose gardens, three giant conservatories and aviary.

SE10: *Greenwich Park*, Greenwich, the oldest enclosed royal park, covering 183 acres, has fine views and historic buildings. Deer park, flower garden, rose and herb gardens, playground and children's entertainments.

SE20: *Crystal Palace Park*, Crystal Palace Park Road, 200 acres surrounding Paxton's resited Crystal Palace created for the Great Exhibition of 1851 (alas burnt down in 1936). Terraces and features remain, and there is plenty of family interest.

SE24: *Brockwell Park*, Tulse Hill, a peaceful and attractive refuge with a walled garden, shrubs, trees, formal bedding and three delightful ponds.

Morden: Just over the border in Surrey is *Morden Hall Park*, a former deer park with ancient haymeadows, waterways and an impressive collection of stables, mills and cottages. Nearby is a garden centre, a city farm (closed Mons except Bank Holidays) and craft workshops (closed Tues).

CITY OF LONDON PARKS AND GARDENS

Although there is inevitably a certain similarity in the design and planning of any group of gardens administered by a public body, those within the City of London (numbering around 150), being principally located on bomb sites, churchyards and former churchyards, perhaps have more variety than might be expected. For tourists and workers these gardens provide a welcome respite from the City traffic, and almost all are provided with lots of benches. *They are open 8am – 7pm or dusk, 7 days a week unless otherwise stated.* An excellent free English Tourist Board leaflet, produced in conjunction with the Corporation of London, *Open Spaces in the City of London*, gives details 📖 ⅗

EC1: *Christchurch – Greyfriars Rose Garden*, Newgate Street. A collection of hybrid teas and climbing roses trained up wooden pillars with rope linking them. *Postman's Park*, Aldersgate Street. Close to St Paul's Cathedral. Formal bedding in the centre with mature trees and shrubs, a small pool with fountain and goldfish, together with tombs and headstones as the area is still a churchyard. An arcade protects the Watts Memorial, a tiled wall commemorating the deeds of those who died in their efforts to save others.

EC2: *Finsbury Circus.* [Closed Oct to March at weekends] The largest public open green space in the City and London's first public park (1606). Apart from the ubiquitous London plane trees, it also boasts the only bowling green in the City, surrounded by low box hedges, bedding plants, shrubs, a drinking fountain and a small bandstand. *St Anne and St Agnes Churchyard*, Gresham Street. [Permanently open] Here the church still stands, alongside the remains of part of London Wall and those of a Roman fort, surrounded by trees and shrubs. *St Botolph-without-Bishopsgate Churchyard*, Bishopsgate. [Permanently open] Apart from the usual planting, there is also a tennis court and a netball court and a former school house, restored in 1952 by the Worshipful Company of Fan Makers to serve as a church hall. *St Mary Aldermanbury*, Love Lane. [Permanently open] Made within the low ruined walls of a Wren church destroyed in the Blitz, the stumps of remaining pillars mark different levels of the garden. A shrubbery encloses a monument to Shakespeare's pals, John Heminge and Henry Condell. There is also a small knot garden. *St Mary Staining*, Oat Lane. [Permanently open] Another patch of grass surrounded by shrubs, roses and benches. A rare opportunity to see a design by the late David Hicks is available at *Salter's Garden*, Fore Street. Hicks before his death ensured that there were benches for office workers and visitors to eat their sandwiches or otherwise relax. Paved areas alternate with grass alleys dividing rectangular box-edged beds. Formally placed obelisks in the beds have been planted with climbing roses and some of the *allées* run below honeysuckle-clad tunnels. Three fountains. *St Alphage Highwalk Garden*, London Wall is nearby [Permanently open]. This roof garden beside London Wall can be reached via the escalator at Moorgate station and consists of a series of raised beds and extensive trellis work. The planting is a mixture of shrubs, climbers and herbaceous plants with an interesting collection of grasses as a centrepiece.

EC3: *Pepys Garden*, Seething Lane. [Open weekdays only, 9am – 5.30pm] A splinter of garden on the site of the Navy Office, where Samuel Pepys lived and worked. A surprising number of trees in a tiny area. *St Dunstan in the East Church Garden*, St Dunstans Hill. The most romantic garden in the City, it has been created within the walls of a Victorian Gothick church which was bombed during World War II. Only the Wren tower survived and was restored. The remaining walls, containing arched windows and doorways, are covered with creepers and climbing plants and the spaces between planted with small trees and shrubs. There is a small fountain surrounded by benches and large tubs with standard fuchsias and bedding plants.

EC4: *Bow Churchyard*, just off Cheapside, will interest US visitors as in its small garden is the statue of Captain John Smith, 'citizen and cord-wainer', who was leader of the first settlers in Virginia. *St Paul's Churchyard*. [Open 6am – 7.30pm] Winding paths surround the back of the Cathedral with welcome shade and a resting place for the weary tourist. Apart from the usual municipal planting, there is a rose garden in the SE corner.

E1: *Portsoken Street Garden*, between Portsoken Street and Goodman's Yard. A tiny oasis with a bubbling fountain, brick walls, small trees and shrubs.

LONDON SQUARES

When this *Guide* first appeared over a generation ago, the squares of London were mostly municipal in appearance, even though the majority of them were in fact private, and their gates firmly locked to visitors except residents or those with a key. Now the story is different as the gardens in the squares get much more attention from professionals as well as amateurs, and for several years now many are open to the public on the second Sunday in June. Some have events such as Punch and Judy shows as well as the opportunity for visitors to buy plants. London has about 400 squares, of which only about 15 per cent are currently open on this one day in the year designated London Garden Square Day, though a few of the others welcome the public more frequently, some on a daily basis. The squares were mostly built in the eighteenth and nineteenth centuries to provide an outlook for the fashionable houses which surrounded them and in not-so-fashionable areas like Pimlico so that the lesser classes could imitate the behaviour of their betters. A few squares still remain the joint property of the owners of houses (and today, flats) round them, the grandest being Belgrave Square built by Basevi in 1825, Cadogan Square and Eaton Square. Other private squares, hardly less grand, include Brompton, Carlyle, Edwardes, Lowndes, Montpelier, Onslow, Pembroke and others to the west of Hyde Park Corner. One enthusiast, Roger Phillips of Eccleston Square, says that in order to keep the squares going for the benefit of the residents and the visual pleasure of others passing by, it is necessary to wage a horrendous battle against potential developers. By contrast, Michael Heseltine has said that 'someone, somewhere, should get a grip' on London squares. There should be tree-planting schemes, seats for the elderly, statues or water features – possibly provided by sponsors.

Amongst gardens which have recently joined the 'open day' scheme are Eaton Square, the Inner and Middle Temple Gardens, Little Venice along the canal, and Portman Square in the West End. For information about the 'open' scheme, tickets and descriptive booklets are available from May by writing with a s.a.e. to London Gardens Squares Day, c/o London Historic Parks and Gardens Trust, Duck Island Cottage, St James Park, London SW1A 2BJ. Further information may be available from English Heritage Customer Services from May (020) 7973 3434. Of the many other squares and 'gardens' open to the public outside the one-day scheme, the following may be worth a visit.

Northern area: Despite its name probably the least romantic is the home of the Bloomsberries, *Bloomsbury Square; Russell Square*, recently restored after a period of neglect; *Queen Square*, with its statue of Queen Charlotte, after whom it is named; *Brunswick Square*, beyond which is the walled garden, usually a haven of peace; *Coram's Fields*, a children's play area open 10am-5pm with *Mecklenburgh Square* adjoining; *Tavistock Square* (quietest in the area); *Woburn Square; Gordon Square*, closed weekends; and *Fitzroy Square*, the work of Sir Geoffrey Jellicoe, not open but viewable. Further north is *Gibson Square* in Islington, with plenty of seats, much grass, fine trees and too many municipal roses.

Central area: *Berkeley Square; Cavendish Square; Grosvenor Square. Phoenix Gardens,* a community-run site with a 20-year lease which shows what can be done by London residents, and, unlike many others, is open 24 hours a day; and *St James's Square* (this is the earliest, begun 1665, and the quietest). *Mount Street Gardens* is a well-hidden leafy retreat much loved by locals while the throng of the city seems to pass it by. Tasteful planting and lofty trees make it the perfect spot to take your ease after shopping. Versailles tubs planted with palms, beds of sugar-pink and white geraniums or other interesting and varied schemes can be enjoyed from dozens of wooden benches donated by those who have enjoyed this garden's charm [Open spring and summer, weekdays, 8am – up to 9.30pm; autumn and winter, 8am – 4.30pm. Suns and Bank Holidays, open from 9am. Free]. Also within walking distance are *St Paul's Churchyard*, *Covent Garden* and *Soho Square*.

Eastern area: *Embankment Gardens*, if rather municipal, are leafy and tranquil. At *Gray's Inn* Field Court is open to the public during weekday lunchtimes in the summer. *Inner and Middle Temple Gardens* stretch up from the Embankment (no entrance here) to Fleet Street. Their fourteenth-century origins are recalled by names of some of the individual squares. The Inner Temple's Great Gardens were extended in the early eighteenth century, with majestic trees, and again in the nineteenth century. The smaller Middle Temple has fine borders and a small rose garden. Alas, the future of these beautiful, historic and unique gardens is in jeopardy because of a plan to build a bridge, with twin towers as high as the dome of St Paul's, on their very doorstep. At *Lincoln's Inn* one of the 'squares', New Hall, is open to the public Mon – Fri, 12 noon – 1.30pm only. The newest square in London is surrounded by offices, not houses. This is *Arundel Great Court*, which may be viewed from The Strand, south of Aldwych and entered from Arundel and Norfolk Streets. To the south is the luxurious courtyard garden of the *Norfolk Hotel*.

Southern area: *Cadogan Place* (above the car park halfway down Sloane Square (to its E) and *Cadogan Square* (to the W) are sometimes open for two or three days in early June for the Chelsea Festival. *Eccleston Square* in Pimlico [Open two or three times for NGS. Tel: (020) 7834 7354 for details] is a three-acre square, run by a committee of residents, and normally reserved for the use of the residents. It has something for everyone – a tennis court, areas for children to play in and a paved patio. It is also of considerable horticultural interest and contributes to the National Collection of ceanothus. More than 400 different roses and 110 different camellias.

OTHER LONDON 'PUBLIC' SPACES

N1: *New River*, a narrow man-made stream and park off Canonbury Road. *St Mary Churchyard Gardens*, Upper Street, opposite the King's Head Theatre.

EC1: *Angel/Upper Street*. Three charming courtyard gardens have been built below the new office block, Regent's House, in Upper Street, just a few metres from the Angel tube exit. Nowhere to sit, but pleasant strolling space. *Bunhill Fields Burial Ground*, between Bunhill Row and City Road. [Open Mon – Fri, 7.30am – 7pm (4pm Oct to March), weekends 9.30am – 4pm] A burial ground, unused since 1853, containing many fine tombs and memorials, including those of William Blake and John Bunyan. Most of the tombs are behind railings, but part of the grounds which were bomb-damaged has been planted with grass, trees and shrubs. Fine planes and a mulberry. *Fortune Street Garden*, NW of the

Barbican between Beech Street and Old Street. *Myddleton Square*, St John Street, which houses St Mark's Church.

EC3: *Trinity Square*, Tower Hill, home to Wyatt's Trinity House.

SE1: The new *Globe Theatre* is to have an Elizabethan knot-garden on its one-acre site. For further details contact Shakespeare Globe Trust, Bear Gardens, London SE1 (Tel: (020) 7928 7710).

SE15: *Centre for Wildlife Gardening*, 28 Marsden Road, near East Dulwich railway station, gives information and sells plants for gardeners who want to attract wildlife. [Open Tues – Thurs and Sun, 11am – 4pm, but telephone first (020) 7252 9186. 🍴 WC ♿ 🐾 ⛪ 🌳]

SE23: *Sydenham Hill Woods*, near Forest Hill railway station. Over 180 species of trees and plants.

SW1: *Whitehall Court*. Parallel to N bank of River Thames, between Horse-guards Avenue, Whitehall Place and Victoria Embankment. A Grade-II-listed garden, owned by Westminster City Council, re-created in 1994. The excellent planting plan takes into account the proximity of heavy traffic along Victoria Embankment and gives occasional views of the River Thames. Cross over Northumberland Place and visit the rest of *Victoria Embankment Gardens*, especially Bryant's small lily pond and Sullivan's Victorian memorial, which are well supported by planting. Maintenance is to a high standard.

W9: *Clifton Nurseries* is a commercial establishment for the sale of plants and garden paraphernalia, but for all that it has the charm of a small enclosed London green space, well worth visiting at all times of year (nearest tube station: Warwick Avenue) WC 🐕 🐾 ⛪. Nearby is *Rembrandt Gardens*, a small municipal triangle by the side of the canal where, if the weather is suitable, the newspaper can be read in pleasant surroundings.

W10: Some London cemeteries have a gardenesque style, or have acquired one over the centuries. *Highgate* is one of the best known. The longest-surviving cemetery still in private ownership is the 77-acre *Kensal Green* in Harrow Road. (Tube to Kensal Green on Bakerloo line or bus No 18. Parking access via West Gate WC ♿ 🐕). It also has more free-standing mausoleums than any other in England – the majority were constructed to the owners' approved designs before being put to use. Several are Grade-II-listed. There are fine trees here as well as grand graves. The company which established Kensal in 1832 aimed to create a spacious park that would complement the fine monuments. They succeeded, and their work is now assisted by subscription-paying 'Friends'. [Open April to Sept, 9am – 5.30pm, Oct to March, 9am – 4pm (Suns and Bank Holidays, 10am – 4pm). Guided tours on Suns at 2pm throughout the year.]

MANCHESTER AREA

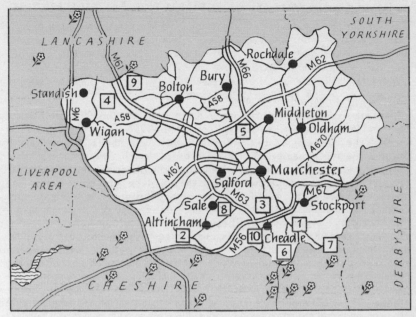

We have included some gardens with Manchester postal addresses in Cheshire for convenience, so it is also worthwhile consulting pages 42–55.

Bramall Hall 1

Bramall Park, Bramhall, Stockport, Cheshire SK7 3NX Tel: (0161) 485 3708; Fax: (0161) 186 6959

Stockport Metropolitan Borough Council • 3m S of Stockport on A5102 between Bramhall and Stockport. Signposted • Hall open April to Sept, daily, 1 – 5pm; Oct to Dec, daily except Mon and 25th, 26th Dec, 1 – 4pm; Jan to March, weekends only • Grounds open all year, daily • Entrance: free (hall £2.95, OAPs and children £2) (2001 prices) ○ 🖪 WC 👤 ⏦ 🧺

The gardens round the magnificent black-and-white timber-framed house are of mixed interest, the best parts being those at a little distance from the front of the house where, in a narrow strip of land, formal beds contain bright annuals and a herbaceous border is enclosed by a hedge. The parkland is another matter. In the valley of a small river broad areas of grassland encircle a number of small lakes. Woods, which contain some very large beech trees, surround the park and hide all sign of the suburbs of Stockport. The riverside walk has banks covered in wild flowers.

Dunham Massey ★ 2

Altrincham, Cheshire WA14 4SJ. Tel: (0161) 941 1025; Fax: (0161) 929 7508

The National Trust • 3m SW of Altrincham off A56 • House open April to 1st Nov, daily except Thurs and Fri, 12 noon – 5pm (last entry 4.30pm) • Garden open April to Oct, daily, 11am – 5.30pm (closes 4.30pm in Oct). Park open all year, daily • Entrance: car park £3, garden £3, house and garden £5 (2001 prices) • Other information: Manual wheelchairs and Batricar available. Dogs in park only, on lead ◑ ☕ ✕ 🛍 WC ♿ ♪ 🏛 ☕

Between the conurbations of Liverpool and Manchester sits the 3000-acre estate of Dunham Massey, where fallow deer still roam free in a 200-acre park. A miraculous survival, the avenues predate the English Landscape School of the eighteenth century. The park is medieval in origin. The broad stretch of water curling round the north and west sides of the house is an Elizabethan moat, and the semi-circular promontory jutting out into the moat was the site of the Elizabethan mount. The house, described as of 'beautifully proportioned austerity', is an eighteenth-century replacement of the Elizabethan mansion. Enough of the formal seventeenth-century Baroque lay-out of the park to the west and the south remained for The Trust to repair and replant the six long avenues which radiate out from a *patte d'oie* in front of a triple row of lime trees each side of the southern forecourt. In the garden proper, becoming known as one of the finest plantsman's gardens in the North-West, other historical layers remain, including an Edwardian parterre planted in purple and gold by the north front of the house, an eighteenth-century orangery and an old well-house. The acid conditions and varied site permit a wide range of shade and moisture-loving plants, all set amongst lawns, mixed borders and woodland. Visitors to the house will find an attractive courtyard in the centre with four beds of shrubs and herbaceous plants.

Fletcher Moss Botanical and Parsonage Gardens ★ 3

Mill Gate Lane, Didsbury M20 2SW. Tel: (0161) 445 4241

Manchester City Council Education Leisure Department • 5m S of Manchester city centre on Mill Gate Lane, S of A5145, close to centre of Didsbury • Open all year, daily, 9am – dusk • Entrance: free ○ ☕ 🛍 WC ♿ ⟐

Much of this well-maintained garden is set on a steep south-facing bank planted with a variety of shrubs, heathers, bulbs, alpines, azaleas and small trees. Rocky streams run down to a water garden and lawned area planted with gunneras and other moisture-lovers. Across some grass tennis courts a large grass area contains specimen trees. Within a short walking distance the more formal Parsonage Gardens, laid out in Victorian times, have lawns, good herbaceous borders, camellias and rhododendrons. Fine trees.

Haigh Hall Gardens 4

Haigh Country Park, Haigh, Wigan WN2 1PE. Tel: (01942) 832895

Metropolitan Borough of Wigan (Department of Leisure) • 2m NE of Wigan, N of B5238. Signposted • Parkland open all year, daily, during daylight hours •

Entrance: free, but parking charge during summer • Other information: Wheelchairs available from information centre. Craft gallery. Children's rides, model village and railway ○ 🍵 WC ⚅ ⬿ ⬛ ℺

The hall is set in the midst of mature parkland, and a short distance to the east are formal gardens, probably of Victorian and Edwardian origin. In an open area of lawn rose beds and specimen shrubs surround an oval pool. Three walled gardens adjoin. The middle one contains a good herbaceous border and a well-stocked shrub border. The second, to the south, has shrubs around the walls and young specimen trees planted in a lawn in the centre; the low wall to the south gives a view across a wild garden with a pond. The third, at the northern end, can only be entered at peak times, and here against the south-facing wall is a cactus house. On the west side a landscaped area has heathers and conifers. The rest of the layout is formal, with roses, yew hedges and lawns and, against the east wall, a border of shrub roses. The arboretum, featuring acers set in woodland, is developing well.

Heaton Hall 5

Heaton Park, Prestwich, Manchester M25 2SW.
Tel: (0161) 236 5244 (Hall enquiries); (0161) 773 1085 (Park enquiries)

Manchester City Council • 4m N of city centre on A576 just S of junction with M66 • House open summer months only • Garden open all year, daily, during daylight hours • Entrance: free, but parking charge on Sun and Bank Holiday Mons • Other information: Some areas possible for wheelchairs but telephone first ○ 🍵 WC ⬿ ⬛ ℺

The hall, designed in 1772 by James Wyatt, was described by Pevsner as 'the finest house of its period in Lancashire'. The 650-acre park, landscaped between 1770 and 1830, contains a number of other neo-classical buildings. To the front of the hall are formal, brightly planted Edwardian gardens. The stables to the west have a small heather garden in front and a large formal rose garden behind. A path leads through a tunnel to an attractive dell of mature trees and many rhododendrons, then follows a stream through a series of pools and waterfalls to a large boating lake. On the Prestwich side of the park small demonstration gardens are enclosed within old walls.

73 Hill Top Avenue 6

Cheadle Hulme, Cheshire SK8 7HZ. Tel: (0161) 486 0055

Mr and Mrs Martin Land • S of city centre. From A34 follow B5094 to Cheadle Hulme. Take 2nd left turn into Gillbent Road, go to end and turn right at roundabout into Church Road, then 2nd left into Hill Top Avenue • Open one day for NGS, and by appt • Entrance: £2, children free NEW 🍵 🌱

A small suburban garden packed with a great deal. Perennials are its mainstay and the variety is huge. A lawn snakes through the length of the garden. To one side is a border in full sun, its soil lightened over the years; it contains delphiniums, campanulas, penstemons, hemerocallis, achilleas and other sun lovers. Shade lovers, including ferns, are grown in the opposite border in heavier soil. Providing colour later in the year are phlox in variety, dahlias, asters and crocosmias. A selection of small shrubs has been chosen for foliage colour, a *Cercis canadensis* 'Forest Pansy', berberis, golden elm (*Ulmus* x *hollandica* 'Dampieri Aurea'), *Salix exigua* and silver elaeagnus. A small pool has a selection of moisture-lovers, and there are shrub roses and clematis. Don't get the impression, however, that this is just an impressive plant collection, for the planting has been planned for its aesthetic effect and the result is a most attractive garden.

Lyme Park ★ 7

Disley, Stockport, Cheshire SK12 2NX. Tel: (01663) 762023/766492;
E-mail: mlyrec@smtp.ntrust.org.uk

The National Trust • 6m SE of Stockport just W of Disley on A6 • Open 30th March to Oct, Fri – Tues, 11am – 5pm, Wed and Thurs, 1 – 5pm; Nov to 20th Dec, Sat and Sun, 12 noon – 3pm. Guided tours by arrangement • Entrance: garden £2.50 (park: pedestrians free, car and occupants £3.50)
🕐 ☕ ✕ 🍴 WC ⌛ ♿ 🏵 ⚑

Lyme Hall, a Palladian-style mansion, is set in spectacular parkland in the foothills of the Pennines with panoramic views of the Cheshire Plains. The 17-acre gardens are of great historic importance, retaining many original features from Tudor and Jacobean times. Lyme Park is regarded as one of the foremost National Trust garden for high-Victorian-style bedding in magnificent formal beds, using many rare and old-fashioned plants such as *Penstemon* 'Rubicunda' (bred at Lyme in 1906). Important features include a well-planted orangery (by Lewis Wyatt, 1814) containing two venerable 150-year-old camellias; a spectacular Dutch garden with a rare example of a *parterre de broderie* using Irish ivy; a fine Gertrude Jekyll-style herbaceous border designed by Graham Stuart Thomas; a wooded ravine garden with a stream and fine collections of rhododendrons, azaleas, ferns and other shade-loving plants; a collection of rare trees and plants associated with the eminent plantsman, the Hon. Vicary Gibbs; a large reflection lake; a 300-year-old lime avenue; extensive lawns and a recently restored Edwardian rose garden. A rare garden designed by Lewis Wyatt (1817) has been re-created and the Sundial Terrace restored.

17 Poplar Grove ★ 8

Sale, MK33 3AX. Tel: (0161) 969 9816;
E-mail: gordoncooke.ceramics@virgin.net

Gordon Cooke • SW of city centre off M60 junction 6. From the A6144 at Brooklands Station turn into Hope Road; Poplar Grove is the 3rd turning on right • Open two days for NGS, and by appt in June • Entrance: £2, children 50p • Other information: Teas on NGS open days only NEW ☕ WC ♨ ℗

That the owner is a landscape gardener and potter is soon evident, for in a suburban setting and a fairly small area he has created a very distinctive garden. A masterstroke was to set the paths at diagonals to the main axis and this, together with the changes in level and varied use of building materials, creates interest throughout. Many of the plants are chosen for their foliage shape and colour: phormiums, thistles, alliums, euphorbias, cordylines, grasses and ferns all contribute to the variety. At one side is an unusual grotto sunk into the ground, with plants growing over the top, which overlooks a long rectangular pool surrounded by pieces of modern sculpture. Other water features, as well as fine ceramics, are spread around the garden. Innovative and inspiring.

Rivington Terraced Gardens   9

Bolton Road, Horwich, Bolton BL6 7SB. Tel: (01204) 691549 (Rivington Information Centre)

United Utilities • 1m NW of Horwich. Follow signs to Rivington from A673 in Horwich or Grimeford. Gardens are 10-min. walk from Rivington Hall and Hall Barn • Open all year, daily • Entrance: free • Other information: Parking, refreshments, toilet facilities at Hall Barn and refreshments, toilet facilities and information at Great House Barn ○ 🍵 🥪 WC ⟁

These are not gardens as such but the remains of gardens built by Lord Leverhulme and designed by Thomas Mawson in the early part of this century. Set mainly in woodland on a steep west-facing hillside, they have fine views across Rivington reservoirs. Particularly impressive is a rocky ravine, the remains of a Japanese garden and the restored pigeon tower. The number and variety of mature trees and rhododendrons indicate that this must once have been a very grand estate. Take care on the steep, sometimes slippery paths.

Wythenshawe Horticultural Centre   10

Wythenshawe Park, Wythenshawe Road M23 0AB. Tel: (0161) 998 2117

Manchester City Council • 7m S of Manchester city centre, $\frac{1}{4}$ m S of M63 junction 9, $\frac{1}{2}$ m SE of M56 junction 3, S of B5167 • Open all year, daily except 25th Dec, 10am – 4pm • Entrance: free ○ 🍵 🥪 WC & 🌿 🏛 🍽

Once this nursery grew bedding stock for the city's parks; now it is a demonstration garden where a large number of different plants can be seen growing. To the right of the entrance a large lawned area runs along a chain of pools planted with many moisture-lovers, including irises and astilbes, in large effective clumps. The developing area, backed by mature woodland, already looks attractive. The Safari Walk through a long array of greenhouses leads past a series of plant collections – cacti, tropical plants, carnivorous plants, a fernery and some unusual displays, including one on rice growing. Behind the greenhouses is an area of demonstration gardens – a heather garden, a pool and rockery, a collection of shrubs and small trees, a well-labelled herbaceous border and a section of dwarf conifers. Another area is devoted to fruit, with many of the bushes and trees grown as cordons.

NEWCASTLE-UPON-TYNE AREA

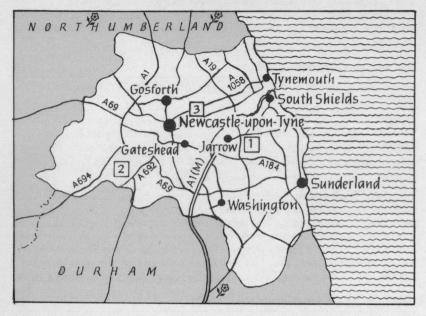

Some gardens have postal addresses in one county and are physically situated in another. If in doubt, a check in the index will direct the reader to the page on which the garden appears.

Bede's World Herb Garden   1

Church Bank, Jarrow, South Tyneside NE32 3DY. Tel: (0191) 489 2106

Bede's World • 8m NE of Gateshead off A185, or S entrance to Tyne Tunnel off A19 • Museum open all year • Garden open daily except Good Friday, April to Oct, 10am – 5.30pm; Nov to Mar, 10am – 4.30pm (Sun all year, 12 noon – 5.30pm). Telephone for details of Christmas openings • Entrance: garden free (museum, Anglo-Saxon farm and garden £4.50, concessions £2.50, family ticket £9) (2001 prices) ○ ☕ WC ♿ 🌿 🏛 ♀

A small garden of great interest to the herbalist, with a wide range of herbs in four sections: culinary, Anglo-Saxon medicinal, aromatic and medicinal. There are also narrow beds in a second part of the garden based on the plans of a medicinal herb garden found at St Gall (c. AD 816), and a bricked area at the top of the garden with seating, planted around with rosemary, lavender and with two banks of herbs below it leading down to the 'St Gall' area. An 'Anglo-Saxon' farm has been developed on adjacent land – an 11-acre site with fields, crops and animals and Anglo-Saxon timber buildings. Some herbs and early vegetable strains will be grown here, together with pond and stream plants and trees of species available at the time of the Venerable Bede (AD 673–735). The adjacent museum building has a courtyard with four raised beds planted in the style of a late-medieval formal garden.

Gibside 2

Burnopfield, Gateshead NE16 6BG. Tel: (01207) 542255

The National Trust • 6m SW of Gateshead, 20m NW of Durham from B6314, off A694 at Rowlands Gill. Signed from A1(M) • Open all year, daily, except Mon (but open Bank Holiday Mons), 10am – 5pm. Closed 25th, 26th Dec • Entrance: summer £3, children £1.50; winter £2 • Other information: Chapel open, service first Sun each month ○ 🍵 📷 WC ⌁ 🏪 🎪

One of the finest eighteenth-century designed landscapes in the North. The fine avenue of mostly Turkey oaks is memorable. The Palladian chapel is surrounded by woods leased to the Forestry Commission. There is a walled kitchen garden dating from the 1730s which is an open space waiting to be filled. Walks have been opened up with views to the ruined hall, orangery and other estate buildings in the grounds. In all, the Trust, assisted by the National Heritage Memorial Fund, has acquired 354 acres to secure the future of this great eighteenth-century landscape garden and protect the chapel setting.

Jesmond Dene 3

Jesmond NE7 7BQ. Tel: (0191) 281 0973; Website: www.newcastle.gov.uk

Newcastle City Council • 1m E of city centre along Jesmond Road • Open all year, daily • Entrance: free • Other information: Parking in Benton Bank. Visitor Centre open at weekends. Café open daily ○ 🍵 📷 WC ♿ ⌁ 🎪 ♀

Presented to the city in 1883 by Lord Armstrong, the famous engineer, and only a mile from the city centre, this steep-sided, thickly wooded dene provides extensive walks in an entirely natural setting, complete with a waterfall, a ruined mill and some fine old buildings. There is a well-run pets' corner, and from Freeman Road the upper park has a children's play area and pond. For a city park, its condition is quite exceptional. Those who want to drive out to the country may like to visit the National Trust's *Cherryburn*, some 11 miles west at Station Road, Mickley, the birthplace of Thomas Bewick, where they can see his splendid engravings and picnic in the garden. Cragside (see entry in Northumberland) was also the creation of Lord Armstrong.

SYMBOLS

[NEW] entries new for 2002; ○ open all year; ◐ open most of year; ◑ open during main season; ● open rarely and/or by appt; 🍵 teas/light refreshments; ✗ meals; 📷 picnics permitted; WC toilet facilities; WC toilet facilities, inc. disabled; ♿ partly wheelchair-accessible; ⌁ dogs on lead; 🌱 plants for sale; 🏪 shop; 🎪 events held; ♀ children-friendly.

NORFOLK

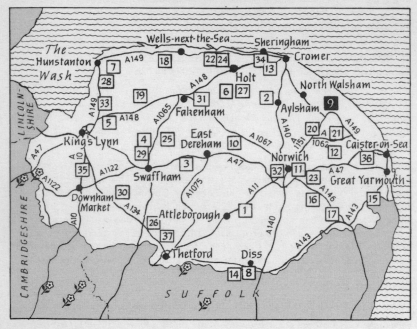

Two-starred gardens are marked on the map with a black square.

Besthorpe Hall ★ 1

Besthorpe, Attleborough N17 2LJ. Tel: (01953) 450300; Fax: (01953) 450308

Mr J.A. Alston • 14m SW of Norwich, 1m E of Attleborough on Bunwell Road. Entrance on right, past church • Open by appt only ● WC &

A pool and fountain occupy the centre of the entrance forecourt. Beyond the house, more pools and fountains are set among lawns skirted by high clematis-hung walls of Tudor brick which form a backdrop to long herbaceous borders. The largest lawn, believed to have been a tilt yard once, has developing topiary, while on another is an enormous and shapely Wellingtonia. There are many other fine trees, among which are paulownias and a variety of birches, acers and magnolias, including the sumptuous *M. delavayi*, and other features include a walled kitchen gardens, a nuttery and a herb garden. A small lake is home to wildfowl, and on another pool lives a pair of black swans. Bearded irises are the June feature. *Peter Beales Roses*, London Road, Attleborough is not far away [open daily, 9am – 5pm (4pm on Sun)].

Blickling Hall ★   2

Aylsham, Norwich NR11 6NF. Tel: (01263) 738030; Fax (01263) 731660;
Website: www.nationaltrust.org.uk

*The National Trust • 15m N of Norwich, 1½ m NW of Aylsham on N side of
B1354 • House open 23rd March to 3rd Nov, Wed − Sun, 1 − 4.30pm •
Garden open 23rd March to July, Wed − Sun and Bank Holiday Mons; Aug,
Tues − Sun; Sept and Oct, Wed − Sun; all 10.15am − 5.15pm; Nov and Dec,
Thurs − Sun, 11am − 4pm; Jan to March, Sat and Sun, 11am − 4pm •
Entrance: £3.80 (house and gardens £6.70) (2001 prices) • Other information:
Picnics in walled garden only. Dogs in park only, on lead* ◐ ☕ ✕ wc ♿
☙ ♨ ♗ ♘

Although the gardens seem so suited to the style and beauty of the Jacobean
house, they consist of a blend of features from the seventeenth to the
twentieth centuries. From the earliest period come the massive yew hedges
flanking the south approach. To the east is the parterre planned by Nesfield
and Wyatt in 1870 with topiary pillars and blocks of yew shaped like grand
pianos. Complicated flower beds were replaced in 1938 with Norah Lindsay's
four large square beds of herbaceous plants in selected colours with surrounding borders of roses edged with catmint. The central pool has a seventeenth-
century fountain. A high retaining wall bounds the southern side, while in the
centre of the eastern side flights of steps mount to the highest terrace with a
central vista through blocks of woodland to the Doric temple of 1730 raised
above parkland beyond. The two blocks are intersected by *allées* in seventeenth-century style planted in 186164 and now replanted using Turkey oak,
lime and beech. On the southern side the orangery of 1782 by Samuel Wyatt
houses half-hardy plants and a 1640s' statue of Hercules by Nicholas Stone. In
the corner of the northern block is the Secret Garden, a remnant of a larger
eighteenth-century garden for which Repton made recommendations, consisting now of a lawn with a central sundial surrounded by high beech hedges.
The shrub border through which it is approached is by Norah Lindsay, who
was also responsible for the planting of the dry moat around the house. North
of the parterre is a raised grassy area, possibly a remnant of the Jacobean
mount; here grows an enormous, sprawling Oriental plane. To the north-west
is landscaped parkland where woods descend to the curving lake formed
before 1729 and later extended. West of the house stand cedars of Lebanon and
a collection of magnolias around a nineteenth-century fountain. Elsewhere in
the park are the Gothick tower of 1773 and the mausoleum of 1796, a pyramid
nearly 14 metres square by Joseph Bonomi. The Trust has now restored the
park to its 1840 limits and replanted 30 acres of the Great Wood.

Bradenham Hall ★   3

Bradenham, Thetford IP25 7QP. Tel: (01362) 687243/687279;
Fax: (01362) 687669.

*Mr and Mrs Christian Allhusen • 8m E of Swaffham, 5m W of East Dereham S
off A47 • Open April to Sept, 2nd, 4th and 5th Suns in month, 2 − 5.30pm,*

and for NGS 28th April, 28th July, 22nd Sept. Coach parties on open days or at other times by written appt (with meals if requested) • *Entrance: £3, children under 12 free* • *Other information: Plant sale 25th Aug* ◑ ☕ WC ♨

The gardens sit near the top of one of Norfolk's highest hills and give a fine view to the south over rolling farmland. The gardens and arboretum comprise about 27 acres and surround a fine early-Georgian brick house (not open). Since the site is windy, the gardens are divided by many yew hedges screening 90 yards of herbaceous borders, backing onto shrubs and the Philosophers' Walk. There is a paved garden and a large old-fashioned rose garden. The other borders contain a plantsman's collection of shrubs, flowers and trees. The house and garden walls are covered with a wide range of shrubs, climbers and fruit. The walled kitchen garden has vegetables, cut flowers and a mixed border backed by laburnums, and there are two glasshouses, an attractive old barn and the new millennium aviary. The arboretum, of about 1000 varieties, is underplanted for spring with fritillaries and large drifts of naturalised daffodils (some 90 selective cultivars). Noted gardeners have described Bradenham as 'exceptional' and 'a must' for visitors.

Bressingham Gardens

(see THE DELL GARDEN and FOGGY BOTTOM)

Castle Acre Priory   4

Castle Acre, King's Lynn PE32 2AF. Tel: (01670) 755394

English Heritage • *5m N of Swaffham, $\frac{1}{4}$ m W of Castle Acre, off A1065* • *Open April to Sept, daily, 10am – 6pm; Oct, daily, 10am – 5pm; Nov to March, Wed – Sun, 10am – 4pm. Closed 24th to 26th Dec and 1st Jan* • *Entrance: £3.50, OAPs £2.60, children £1.80, family ticket £8.80* ○ ☕ ▥ WC ♿ ⬙ ♨ ⚲ Q

This is a walled herb garden divided into four sections containing medicinal, decorative, culinary and strewing herbs. Lavenders line the walls, where there are also three apple trees dating from the sixteenth century. A central circular bed contains a bay tree. The Old Rectory, South Acre (see entry) is nearby, and *West Acre Gardens*, a commercial nursery for rare plants set in a two-acre walled kitchen garden, is about four miles away.

Congham Hall Hotel   5

Lynn Road, Grimston, King's Lynn PE32 1AH. Tel: (01485) 600250; Fax: (01485) 601191; E-mail: reception@conghamhallhotel.co.uk

Mr A. Chantrell, General Manager • *7m NE of King's Lynn. From A149/A148 interchange, follow A148 signed 'Sandringham/Fakenham/Cromer' for 100 metres. Turn right for Grimston. Hotel is $2\frac{1}{2}$ m on left* • *Open April to Sept, daily except Sat. Small parties by arrangement at other times* • *Entrance: free* • *Other information: No coaches* ◑ ☕ ✕ WC ♿ ♨ Q

The hotel, set in 40 acres of parkland with a neat parterre full of bright bedding at the entrance, is listed in the *Good Food Guide*. It merits an entry in this *Guide* for its formal herb garden with about 650 varieties of both culinary and medicinal herbs, each labelled in an eccentric manner, although it also has some herbaceous plantings and pergolas with roses. The herb garden was started some 13 years ago to supply the hotel kitchen, and is thus a working garden. A 'woodery' accommodates the increasing collection of herbs, using timber salvaged from fallen trees instead of rocks.

Corpusty Mill Garden   5

Corpusty, Norwich NR11 6QR. Tel: (01263) 587223

Roger Last • 15 m NW of Norwich, 6 m S of Holt. Turn off B1149 at Corpusty; mill is in centre of village. • Parties only by appt • Entrance: £5 [NEW] ●

This four-acre garden is as unexpected as it is intriguing, gradually revealing itself as a complex series of interlinked spaces, each with a mood and character of its own. The planting is varied and lush with a rich collection of trees, shrubs, herbaceous and water-loving plants. Water is everywhere, in fountains, ponds, a stream, a small lake and a river. Buildings and follies are discovered as the garden unfolds: a long high flint wall inset with heads of Roman emperors; a Gothic arch with knapped flints, and a dark and mysterious four-chambered grotto, built with moss-covered ginger sandstone. Elsewhere, a Gothick ruin with a spiral staircase, a flint humpback bridge and a classical pavilion in the kitchen garden, with ornamental compost containers. A separate area, rich with trees, has been developed as a landscaped meadow. Here a small lake with a raised bank and walkway on one side is dominated by a gunnera. A water-filled cave reveals a figure drowning or rising up from the mud. To the north, the River Bure forms a tranquil natural boundary. By the house a contemporary formal garden, with a stainless steel water column and a central rill and pool, completes a highly eclectic but well-judged sequence of different styles and moods, skilfully blended, within a relatively constricted site.

Courtyard Farm ★   7

Ringstead PE36 5LQ.

Lord Melchett • 16m NE of King's Lynn, 3½ m E of Hunstanton, 2m E of Ringstead, on road crossing Ringstead Common to Chosely and Burnham Market • Open all year, daily • Entrance: free ○ 🐝 ⟨⟩

The primeval gardener was a stone-age farmer who enjoyed the wild flowers that spattered his little fields of ripening grain, and Courtyard Farm harks back to those prehistoric days of marigolds and corncockles. The best time to visit is in July. Take a circular walk through fields of ripening grains and acres of wild flowers – 93 plant species have been identified in the grassland areas, 29 in the cornfields. This is not gardening on a small scale, but it is a most praiseworthy effort to retain our natural heritage of wild and cultivated plants. On many farms the cornflowers have been exterminated as weeds – there are no weeds here! Most heartening.

The Dell Garden, Bressingham
(Bressingham Steam Experience and Garden) ★   8

Bressingham, Diss IP22 2AB. Tel: (01379) 688585;
E-mail: info@bressingham.co.uk; Website: www.blooms-online.com

Mr Alan Bloom • *2½ m W of Diss on A1066* • *Open early April to Oct, daily,*
10am – 5.30pm (closes 4.30pm in Oct) • *Entrance: £7, OAPs £6, children £5,*
under-3s free (including admission to Steam Experience but not rides and Foggy
Bottom) (2001 prices) • *Other information: B&B at Bressingham Hall from*
April to Oct ◑ 💭 ✕ 🍽 WC ☕ 🌸 🏛 🅿 ⚲

Alan Bloom's two passions are on display side by side here – steam engines,
including trains, and fine plants (a superb collection of over 5000 species and
cultivars). The famous island beds, often with cleverly placed snaking flint walls
to provide extra height, are planted with a collection of herbaceous perennials
for continual colour from spring to autumn. Differences in heights and
textures, as well as in the colour of the blossoms, provide rich variety. In
the middle of summer the colours are striking: blue agapanthus and lemon
yellow daisies, fiery crocosmias and rich magenta loosestrifes. Willow, birch
and oak trees give cool shaded patches, and a pool lies at the garden's heart.
New summer and winter gardens have been made at the entrance to the
garden. Entry is through the steam museum where engines and trains chug
away and whistle in the background, but Mr Bloom claims that these nostalgic
sounds do not detract from the peace of the garden. For complete quiet also
visit Adrian Bloom's Foggy Bottom (see entry), a 5-minute walk away – a new
pathway links the two gardens.

East Ruston Old Vicarage ★★   9

East Ruston, Norwich NR12 9HN. Tel: (01692) 650432 (daytime);
Fax: (01692) 651246; E-mail: erov@btinternet.com;
Website: www.e-ruston-oldvicaragegardens.co.uk

Graham Robeson and Alan Gray • *15m NE of Norwich, 4m E of North*
Walsham. Turn off A149 signed 'Walcot, Bacton', then left at T-junction. After
2m, the house is next to the church • *Open 31st March to 25th Oct, Sat, Sun,*
Wed, Fri and Bank Holiday Mons, 2 – 5.30pm, and by appt for coach parties •
Entrance: £3.80, children £1, season tickets £12 ◑ 💭 🍽 WC ☕ 🌸 🅿

This garden has as much to offer in style as in substance, for its twin strengths are
the architectural framework of walls and hedges and an astonishing profusion of
plants. Two Norfolk churches are visible from the garden, and play a funda-
mental role as focal points at the end of skilfully crafted vistas. Within the garden
the value of theatre is not forgotten: tall dark hedges with openings beckon the
visitor on to yet more discoveries: a box parterre and sunken garden, superb
herbaceous borders, a Mediterranean garden and, one of the most striking
elements, a tropical border recently trebled in size and relocated. How rare to
find bananas growing one and a half miles from the North Sea, their leaves intact,
surrounded by equally luxurious foliage of cannas and many other exotics. Rare
plants are everywhere, set in gravel or in borders; because of the garden's

coastal setting, many are semi-hardy, and shrubs from the southern hemisphere are well represented. On the perimeter, a cornfield achieves an astonishing density and brilliance of summer colour, and the garden continues to be developed with apparently limitless energy on the part of the owners. A Desert Wash has mature palms, a large colourful lampranthus, delospermas and self-sown annuals, all left out for winter.

Elsing Hall ★ 10

Elsing, East Dereham NR20 3DX. Tel: (01362) 637224

Mr and Mrs D.H. Cargill • 14m NE of Norwich, 5m NE of East Dereham. Signed off A47 • Open June to Sept, Sun only, 2 – 6pm, and by appt • Entrance: £3, children free ● � ▟ WC ⬠

The romantic appearance of the garden is in complete harmony with the moated half-timbered and flint house which it surrounds. It is rich, lush and unrestrained, and in mid-summer is filled with the scent of the old garden roses which cover the walls and fill the borders. The lawn between the house and the moat has been abandoned to wild orchids; wildfowl nest among the reeds. Both the moat and a nearby stewpond are encircled by moist borders supporting luxuriant growth. On the walls of the kitchen garden grow old roses, many of which seem unique to this place, and more are continually being added. A large variety of trees has been planted, a formal garden developed, and an avenue of ginkgos established.

The Exotic Garden 11

6 Cotman Road, Thorpe, Norwich NR1 4AF. Tel: (01603) 623167; Fax (01603) 617661; Website: www.exoticgarden.com

Mr W.R.S. Giles • In E Norwich off A47 Thorpe road, ¼ m from Norwich Thorpe station. From Yarmouth follow one-way system towards city centre, turn right at traffic lights opposite DEFRA building. New entrance and car park via side entrance of Alan Boswell Insurance, 126 Thorpe Road, next to DEFRA building • Open 7th July to 22nd Sept, Sun only, 1.30 – 5.30 pm, and for private visits of 10 or more by appt • Entrance: £3.50, children free, groups £5 per person (including refreshments) • Other information: Wheelchairs by arrangement ● � ⬠

An exotic garden of half an acre on a south-facing hillside, with tall trees and hedges creating a sheltered microclimate. The unusual collection of plants includes gingers, bananas, aroids and succulents. The garden reaches its peak in high to late summer, when such exotics as cannas and brugmansias are in full bloom. It is also renowned for its use of house plants as bedding plants. Tillandsias may be spotted in the branches of trees which are underplanted with codiaeums, guzmanias and tradescantias. Philodendrons and *Monstera deliciosa* are also used in this way, flourishing in the summer months. There are many flint walls and two raised pools. A feeling of fantasy pervades the whole place, especially in the evening when the various scents are at their headiest. A new half-acre garden has been added for hardy exotics that need far less maintenance and tolerate winter cold.

Fairhaven Woodland and Water Garden ★   12

School Road, South Walsham, Norwich NR13 6DZ. Tel/Fax: (01603) 270449;
E-mail: fairhavengardens@norfolkbroads.com;
Website: www.norfolkbroads.com/fairhaven

The Fairhaven Garden Trust • 9m NE of Norwich. At South Walsham, follow
brown tourist-signs on A47 at junction with B1140 • Open all year, daily except
25th Dec, 10am – 5pm; May to Aug, Wed, Thurs, 10am – 9pm. Guided walks
for parties • Entrance: £3.50, OAPs £3, children £1.25, under 5 free. Season
tickets £12.50 family season ticket £30, wildlife sanctuary £1. Discounts for
parties • Other information: Boat trips available ○ ● ✕ ▦ WC ⅙ ⬥ ℘ ⛁
⚲ ⚲

A garden created in natural woods of oak and alder extending to about 180
acres surrounding the unspoiled (private) South Walsham Inner Broad. Paths
wind among banks of azaleas and large-leaved rhododendrons and lead to the
edge of the broad itself. Much of the area is wet and supports a rich variety of
primulas, especially candelabras, with lysichitums, hostas, astilbes, ligularias
and gunneras of exceptional size merging into the natural vegetation, among
which are many royal ferns and some majestic oaks. Although particularly
colourful during the flowering of the azaleas and rhododendrons in the spring,
the garden gives pleasure at all times of the year if natural beauty is preferred
to man-made sophistication. Three miles of woodland walks with fine views.

Felbrigg Hall ★   13

Felbrigg, Norwich NR11 8PR. Tel: (01263) 837444; Fax: (01263) 837032;
E-mail: afgusr@smtp.ntrust.org.uk

The National Trust • 2m SW of Cromer off A148. Entrance on B1436 • Hall
open as garden, 1 – 5pm (Bank Holiday Mon, 11am – 5pm) • Garden open
23rd March to 3rd Nov, Sat – Wed, 11am – 5.30pm; Walled garden open 18th
July – 30th Aug, 12 noon – 4pm; Park and woodland walks all year, daily,
dawn – dusk • Entrance: £2.30, children £1 (house and gardens £5.90,
children £2.90, parties £4.90 per person) • Other information: Self-drive scooter
available • Garden: ◑ ● ✕ ▦ WC ⅙ ℘ ⛁ ⚲ *Park:* ○ ⬥

The Jacobean house faces south across the park, which is notable for its fine
woods and lakeside walk. William Windham III, the great-grandson of the
builder of the hall, was Humphry Repton's landlord. A ha-ha separates the
park from the lawns of the house, where there is an orangery planted with
camellias. To the north the ground rises and there are specimen trees and
shrubs, including many of North American origin. At some distance to the east
a large walled kitchen garden is now richly planted with a combination of fruit,
vegetables and flowers in a formal design behind clipped hedges; it contains a
vine house and great brick dovecot with a flock of doves. In early autumn there
is a display of many varieties of colchicums: the National Collection is kept
here. The gardens are in immaculate order, and restoration, renewal and
replacement continue at a brisk pace. Sheringham Park (see entry) is nearby.

Foggy Bottom ★   14

Bressingham, Diss IP22 2AA. Tel: (01379) 688585; Website: www.blooms-online.com

Mr and Mrs Adrian Bloom • 2½ m W of Diss on A1066 adjoining The Dell, Bressingham (see entry) and close to Blooms of Bressingham • Open April to Oct, daily except Sat and Mon, 12.30 – 4.30pm. Parties by appt • Entrance: £7, OAPs £6, children £5, under-3s free (includes admission to The Dell Garden and the Steam Experience but not rides) (2001 prices) • Other information: food and toilet facilities available at Blooms of Bressingham ◑ 💺 ✕ 🍽 WC ♿ 🐾 ♨ 💡 ℃

Foggy Bottom is a wicked name for a splendid garden – it sparkles with colour, principally from the excellent collection of gold and blue conifers. The specimens in the old conifer bed are being dispersed to other areas of the garden, and a new all seasons bed has been created. The trees are combined with excellent herbaceous perennials and shrubs planted in bold clumps. Heathers in many colours and shades form cushions of colour throughout the year and numerous grasses have been planted to great effect. Spacious, with marvellous vistas through the islands of trees, a soft lawn for ambling and an attractive woodland glade with a new summerhouse nearby, this is a quiet place, full of brightness, a place to linger before, or after, visiting the Steam Museum and Garden just 300 metres away.

Fritton Lake Countryworld   15

Fritton, Great Yarmouth NR31 9HA. Tel: (01493) 488208

Lord and Lady Somerleyton • 5m SW of Great Yarmouth off A143 • Garden open April to Sept, daily, 10am – 5.30pm • Entrance: £5.30, OAPs £4.80, children £3.90 (includes all attractions except miniature railway 80p, children 60p). Discounts for parties • Other information: Falconry, heavy horses, golf, putting, boats, children's farm, pony rides, miniature tractors, cycle trail and craft workshops ◑ 💺 ✕ 🍽 WC ♿ ♨ 💡 ℃

The large lake remains almost unspoilt and separate from the tea rooms and other commercial attractions of this country park. An unusual feature is a Victorian garden of about half an acre in the gardenesque style with irregular beds surrounded by clipped box hedges and filled with shrubs and herbaceous perennials. In addition to the formal lakeside gardens there are woodland walks and gardens, including the Lost Gardens of Fritton Hall. The Victorian hall was burnt down in 1957 and the gardens left to go wild. They contain a large collection of rhododendrons and azaleas intersected by paths.

The Garden in an Orchard   16

Mill Road, Bergh Apton, Norwich NR15 1BQ. Tel: (01508) 480322

Mr and Mrs R.W. Boardman • 6m SE of Norwich off A146 at Hellington Corner • Open Bank Holiday weekends and several others May to Sept, 11am – 6pm, but check before visiting • Entrance: £1.50 • Other information:

Refreshments on Suns only. Part of Bergh Apton Sculpture Trail 18th, 19th, 26th, 27th May, 1st, 2nd June ● 💺 🍽 WC ⟳ 🌿 🍴

The garden started as a three-and-a-half-acre commercial orchard and over the years has been planted up bit by bit with rare and unusual plants and trees. Narrow paths meander through dense plantings of species roses, giving eye-to-eye contact with their flowers, then open up to similar plantings of herbaceous walks, imbuing the garden with an atmosphere of mystery. Mr Boardman is a professional plantsman and among his rare trees are *Phellodendron amurense, Prunus padus* 'Colorata', *Paulownia tomentosa* and nine species of eucalyptus. *Lonicera ledebourii* catches the eye, along with *Malva sylvestris mauritanica* and many special clematis scrambling through trees. A half-acre wildflower meadow, with a wide range of British flora, is now maturing.

Hales Hall   17

Hales, Loddon NR14 6QW. Tel: (01508) 548395;
E-mail: expert@readsnursery.co.uk

Mr and Mrs Terence Read • 12m SE of Norwich, off A146. Signposted • Open all year, Tues – Sat, 10am – 5pm, Sun and Bank Holiday Mons, 11am – 4pm. Closed 29th March. Guided parties by arrangement • Entrance: £2 (Great Barn and gardens) • Other information: Fifteenth-century thatched Great Barn ○ 🍽 WC ♿ 🌿 🍴 🔍

A moat surrounds the remaining wing of a vast house of the late fifteenth century and a central lawn with well-planted borders and topiary of box and yew backed by high brick walls. Work is continuing on the restoration of the garden after centuries of neglect. A fruit garden has been planted, and there is a pot-grown orchard. The owners specialise in rare and unusual perennial plants, and look after National Collections of citrus, figs and greenhouse grapes. The associated century-old nurseries offer an extensive range of conservatory plants, vines, figs, mulberries, and many peach, apricot, nectarine and greengage varieties.

Holkham Hall ★   18

Wells-next-the-Sea NR23 1AB. Tel: (01328) 710227; Fax: (01328) 711707;
(01328) 711636 (Holkham Nursery Gardens); Website: www.holkham.co.uk

The Earl of Leicester • 23m W of Cromer, 2m W of Wells on A149 • Hall open 28th May to 30th Sept, Sun – Thurs, 1 – 5pm. Also 31st March, 1st April, 5th, 6th May, 2nd, 3rd, 4th June, 25th, 26th Aug; all 11.30am – 5pm • Terrace gardens open 28th May to 30th Sept, Mons – Thurs, 1 – 4.45pm (but closed Bank Holiday Mons). Nursery gardens open daily except 25th, 26th Dec, March to Oct 10am – 5pm (Nov to Feb, 11am – dusk) • Entrance: Terrace and nursery gardens free (hall and bygones museum £8, children £4; either hall or museum separately £5, children £2.50) • Terrace gardens: ◑ 💺 ✕ 🍽 WC ⟳ 🌿 🍺 *Nursery gardens:* ○ 🌿

The vast park, famous for its holm oaks, was laid out originally by William Kent but altered by 'Coke of Norfolk' and the 2nd Earl. On the west side of the house, lawns sweep down to the great lake. The terrace which fronts the south façade was added in 1854, but the scale of the house and park is so large that, from a distance at least, this does not seriously disrupt the vision of the two. The formal beds designed by W.A. Nesfield flank a great fountain representing St George and the Dragon, said to be designed by R. Smith. The nursery gardens, in the original eighteenth-century walled kitchen garden in the grounds, extend to over six acres, subdivided into six areas with perennial borders and the original greenhouses. Alpines, shrubs, perennials, herbs, roses, bedding and house plants are for sale. About five miles away, at South Creake, is another nursery worth visiting, the *Creake Plant Centre*.

Houghton Hall ★ 19

King's Lynn PE31 6UE. Tel: (01485) 528569

The Marquess of Cholmondeley • 13m NE of King's Lynn off A148 • Hall open as garden • Park and gardens open 31st March to 29th Sept, Sun, Thurs and Bank Holiday Mons, 2 – 5.30pm • Entrance: £3.50, children £2 (hall, park and gardens £6, children £3) (2001 prices) ◑ 👽 🗟 WC ♿ 🌿 🏛

One of the most magnificent houses in Britain, built between 1721 and 1735 by Colen Campbell and James Gibbs. The five-acre walled kitchen garden has, over the last few years, been transformed by the present marquess and his enthusiastic head gardener into an exciting and ambitious new garden. A 120-metre-long double herbaceous border, edged with catmint and backed by yew hedges, spans it and there will be a garden room at one end, with a Kent seat closing the view. The rose garden is based on the design of the ceiling in the White Drawing Room. New English and old-fashioned roses, underplanted with lavender, fill the beds and climb over metal arches painted in verdigris, as in Monet's garden. The centrepiece is a sunken pool, flanked by antique statues. There are roses everywhere, and it is said that the scent can be detected as far away as the park. The vegetable and fruit garden is as perfect as the flower garden. Orderly rows of produce supply the house (fifteen varieties of vegetables are available each day during the summer season) with a useful herb border nearby. Wide grass paths are edged with 100 different varieties of cordon apples, 30 varieties of pears, red and white currants in double cordons and fan-trained cherries. These will eventually form tunnels. Blocks of raspberries, gooseberries and hybrid berries and strawberries fill the beds. An ambitious area of pleached hornbeam walks and a water garden with fountain surrounded by topiary are both coming along well.

Hoveton Hall Gardens 20

Wroxham, Norwich NR12 8RJ. Tel: (01603) 782798

Mr and Mrs Andrew Buxton • 9m NE of Norwich, 1m N of Wroxham on A1151 • Open 31st March to 15th Sept, Wed, Fri, Sun and Bank Holiday Mons, plus Thurs in May, all 11am – 5.30pm. Coach parties and tours by arrangement • Entrance: £3.50, wheelchairs £2, children (5–14) £1, season tickets £9.50, family £20 ◑ 👽 🗟 WC ♿ 🌿 🐾

Set in the Norfolk Broads area, the gardens are amply supplied with water and streams. For mid-May and early June the rhododendrons and azaleas, many rare varieties, are spectacular, dominating and scenting the woodland walks. The formal walled garden, planted and enclosed in 1936, with herbaceous borders of that period, is now in the process of additional planting. A delightful gardener's cottage is set picturesquely in one corner, covered in roses. The adjoining walled kitchen garden is a good example of traditional vegetable planting. The entrance to the two walled gardens has an intriguing iron gate in the shape of a spider, hence the formal garden is called the Spider Garden. A water garden, leading to the lake, has good water plants, vast examples of *Gunnera manicata*, peltiphyllums, hostas and fine stands of bamboos. The whole area is laced with streams and interesting bridges, adding calm and reflection at every corner. Birds, both migratory and native, abound.

How Hill Farm ★   21

Ludham, Gt. Yarmouth NR29 5PG. Tel: (01692) 678558

Mr P.D.S. Boardman • 15m NE of Norwich, 1m W of Ludham off A1062. Follow signs to How Hill. Farm Garden S of How Hill • Open probably 19th May, 2 – 5pm. Party visits at other times by arrangement • Entrance: £2, children free ● ● ● WC & ⊕ ⌀

The garden around the farm is comparatively conventional, with a new garden and pond in the old bullock yard and a large Chusan palm planted in a dog cage from which it threatens to escape. Here, too, is a collection of over 100 varieties of *Ilex aquifolium* as well as many rare species of the ilex genus. Over the road in the river valley is a rich combination of exotics mingled with native vegetation. Around a series of pools, banks of azaleas merge into reed beds, rhododendron species rise over thickets of fern, wild grasses skirt groves of the giant *Arundo donax*, with birches, conifers and a collection of 50 different bamboos against a background of a recently created three-acre broad, thick with water lilies. The soil acidity in some places is as low as pH 2.8, other parts varying up to pH 7.5, supporting a wide variety of trees and shrubs.

Kettle Hill ★   22

Blakeney NR25 7PN. Tel: (01263) 741147

Richard and Frances Winch • 11m W of Cromer, just outside Blakeney on B1156 Langham road • Parking • Open for charity 5th Aug, 2 – 6pm • Entrance: £3, children free ● ● WC & ⌀

With the help of Mark Rumary, the owners have transformed this garden into a luxurious and elegant delight. A box-edged rectangular parterre with heart-shaped beds, heightened with topiary spirals and mop heads, reflects their interest in the *Romantic Garden Nursery* at Swannington. A cleverly sited brick wall shelters a long mixed border packed with colour and unusual plants and leads to a circular secret garden. A large lawn, featuring a delightful Gothick summerhouse by George Carter, extends from the house to mature woodland, to which many ornamental trees have been added and which is carpeted in spring with bluebells and naturalised lilies. The walks cut through the wood hold many surprises, but the triumph is the short downward slope to a semi-formal fenced garden full of fragrant shrub roses.

Lake House Water Gardens 23

Brundall, Norwich NR13 5LU. Tel: (01603) 712933

Mr and Mrs Garry Muter • 5m E of Norwich. From A47 roundabout take Brundall turn and turn right at T-junction into Postwick Lane • Open 31st March, 1st April, 5th, 6th May, 11am – 5pm. Private parties by appt • Entrance: £2, children free • Other information: Sale of unusual plants on open days ● ☕ ▤ ⬤ ⬥

Two acres of water gardens set in a steep cleft in the river escarpment. From the top of the hill the gardens fall away to a lily-covered lake at the bottom. They were once part of a 76-acre private estate and arboretum planted about 1880. Plant associations are a feature throughout the garden, reflecting Mrs Muter's talent as a flower arranger. Surrounding the formal areas are drifts of primroses, bluebells and daffodils in season; wild flowers abound. The formal planting has many rare and interesting species: *Zantedeschia* 'Green Goddess' and *Z. aethiopica* 'Crowborough' in a large clump cool down a flamboyant *Hemerocallis* 'Frans Hals'. A wide variety of hardy geraniums blooms in succession and a good collection of hybrid helianthemums awaits those who visit by appointment in June.

Lawn Farm 24

Cley Road, Holt NR25 7DY. Tel: (01263) 713484

Mr and Mrs G.W. Deterding • From Holt take Cley Road opposite King's Head pub in High Street. After 1m, turning is on right after Holt Hall School gates sign posted. • Open April to July by appt • Entrance: £3, children free ● WC ⬥ ⬥

The six-and-a-half acre garden was designed and laid out by the owners in 1987. There are four natural ponds with two planted water gardens, and a very damp wooded area with hydrangeas and azaleas. A completely different atmosphere is to be found in the two medieval flint-walled courtyards; here roses and many interesting and unusual shrubs and climbers flourish in the hot and sheltered microclimate. Mrs Deterding has a magpie's eye for the rare and difficult to find, including a good collection of unusual trees.

Lexham Hall 25

East Lexham, King's Lynn PE32 2QJ. Tel: (01328) 701288/701341; Fax (01328) 700053

Mr and Mrs Neil Foster • 6m N of Swaffham, 2m W of Litcham off B1145 • Open 10th, 24th Feb (for snowdrops), 19th May, 16th June, and May to July mid-week by appt for parties of 20 or more • Entrance: £3, parties £4 per person ● ☕ ▤ WC ⬥ ⬥ ⬥ ⬥

The seventeenth- and eighteenth-century hall sits well amid beautiful parkland with sheep and interesting trees. The ground falls away to the river forming a lake and canals crossed by elegant bridges; the garden was the inspiration of the present owner's mother who, with the help of the late Dame Sylvia Crowe, laid out its bones. Massive yew hedges reveal intimate views of the park, taking the eye to the distance beyond. Wide terracing to the south of the house is well planted and colourful, and a long grass walk edged with herbaceous plants and shrubs progresses to woodland full of rhododendrons, azaleas and spring bulbs. (In early spring, the parkland and adjoining church-yard are awash with snowdrops.) There is a colourful rose garden, and the kitchen garden has an early eighteenth-century crinkle-crankle wall covered with fruit, a cutting border, greenhouses with plants for the house and tender vegetables, the whole a picture of health. A wood to the south, known as the American Gardens, is reputedly planted from seeds collected in America.

Magpies   26

Green Lane, Mundford IP26 5HS. Tel: (01842) 878496

Patricia Cooper • ½ m N of A134 Downham Market – Thetford road at Mundford roundabout, or off A1065 Swaffham road • Open May to July, daily, 12 noon – 5pm; nursery open March to Sept, daily except Wed, 12 noon – 5pm (closed 25th, 26th Aug) • Entrance: £1 (for charity) • Other information: Picnic facilities by arrangements for groups only ◑ WC ዿ ⬧ ⬠

The garden in mid-summer is a living display of vegetable fireworks, but for all that it is a tranquil, subtle place. Shimmering fountains of golden oats (*Stipa gigantea*) are its hallmark. Larches and birches provide a light canopy over irregular island beds boldly planted with perennials. Tall mulleins and evening primroses are mixed with chicories and plume poppies, while the fragrance of jasmine and honeysuckle hangs in the air. It is a real cottage garden composed of informal rooms, each filled to the brim with interesting plants. There is a pond and shady nooks and crannies where you may even chance to see a wandering hedgehog snuffling about under the billowing cranesbills. Many of the excellent, modestly priced plants are for sale. Worth visiting, on the A1065 Swaffham road, is *Lynford Arboretum* and, to the south, Lynford Lakes and Zig-Zag Covert. Lynford Hall, a hotel specialising in organic food, is also nearby.

Mannington Hall ★   27

Saxthorpe, Norwich NR11 7BB. Tel: (01263) 584175

Lord and Lady Walpole • 18m NW of Norwich, 5m SE of Holt, off B1149. Signposted • Open May to Sept, Sun, 12 noon – 5pm; also June to Aug, Wed – Fri, 11am – 5pm • Entrance: £3, OAPs and students £2.50, children free ◑ ☕ 🛍 WC ዿ ⬠ 🏛 🍽 ☕

The romantic appearance of this garden of 20 acres is only matched in Norfolk by Elsing Hall (see entry), where the house is also of the fifteenth century. Lawns run down to the moat, crossed by a drawbridge, to herbaceous borders backed by high walls of brick and flint. The moat also encloses a secret, scented garden in a design derived from one of the ceilings of the house. Outside the moat are borders of flowering shrubs flanking a Doric temple, and beyond are woodlands containing the ruins of a Saxon church and nineteenth-century follies. Within the walls of the former kitchen garden, a series of rose gardens has been planted following the design of gardens from medieval to modern times and featuring roses popular at each period. A twentieth-century rose garden incorporates a planthouse, vegetable plot and children's garden. There are now more than 1500 varieties of roses in the gardens. A lake, woods and meadowland with extensive walks are other features.

Norfolk Lavender   28

Caley Mill, Heacham, King's Lynn PE31 7JE. Tel: (01485) 570384;
Fax: (01485) 571176; E-mail: admin@norfolk-lavender.co.uk

Norfolk Lavender Ltd • 13m N of King's Lynn on A149 • Open all year, daily except 25th, 26th Dec, 1st Jan, 9.30am – 5pm • Entrance: free ○ 🍽 ✕ WC 🚾 ⬇ 🌳 🏛

Fields of lavender, stretching into the distance like giant stripes of corduroy, are a splendid sight in July and August. There is a more intimate display of named lavender (designated as a National Collection) near the Victorian watermill that serves as the visitor centre for this major commercial enterprise. A small herb garden is well tended and labelled, and the beds in the rose garden are lavender-edged. The four-acre fragrant garden has helped to reduce the pressure of visitors, particularly in July and August.

Oak Tree House

{see THE EXOTIC GARDEN)

The Old Rectory   29

South Acre, King's Lynn PE32 2AD. Tel: (01760) 755469;
E-mail: jardann@aol.com

Mr and Mrs Clive Hardcastle • 3m N of Swaffham off A1065, opposite South Acre church • Open for NGS one Sun in June, 2 – 5pm, and from May to July by appt • Entrance: £2.50, private visits £3 ● 🍽 WC ⬇ 🌳

A three-acre garden where a long lawn with mixed herbaceous borders on each side leads the eye past a huge willow tree to a fine view of the eleventh-century Castle Acre Priory (see entry). Clipped topiary peacocks guard the entrance to the herb garden. Box and climbing roses edge the well-tended vegetable garden, with fruit trees trained against the wall. A new box and lavender parterre is being created, running the length of the vegetable garden. To the other side of the lawn, behind a yew hedge, a pool garden leads into a wild area, with specimen shrubs, ancient box trees and many bulbs in spring. Behind the house is the rose garden. The house was the childhood home of Margaret Fountains of *Love among the Butterflies* fame.

Oxburgh Hall 30

Oxborough, King's Lynn PE33 9PS. Tel: (01366) 328258; Fax: (01366) 328066

The National Trust • 7m SW of Swaffham off A134 • House open 23rd March to 3rd Nov, Sat – Wed, 1 – 5pm (Bank Holiday Mons opens 11am) • Garden open 2nd to 17th March, Sat, Sun, 11am – 4pm; 23rd March to 3rd Nov, Sat – Wed (daily in Aug), 11am – 5.30pm • Entrance: £2.80, children £1.40 (hall and garden £5.50, children £2.80, family ticket £14.50) ◑ 🍴 ✕ 🛍 WC ♿ ⬚ ☕

The romantic mellow red-brick manor house seems to float in its rectangular moat above a haze of fringed water lilies. Both house and garden are concealed from view until you have walked past the orchard of quince, plum and greengage trees. Then you look down over the formal parterre, a Victorian copy of a Le Nôtre design consisting of a moderately restrained pattern of beds edged with clipped box hedges, punctuated by clipped tumps of yew. Yellow, red, violet and silver are the colours of the annual bedding – a colourful carpet. Behind a long yew hedge is a narrow border edged with wispy catmint, with carefully repeated clumps of perennials: loosestrife, golden-rod, daisies and mallows. There are some fine trees, and circular walks lead into the park and woodland, full of snowdrops and winter aconites in early spring.

Pensthorpe Waterfowl Park 31

Pensthorpe, Fakenham, Norfolk NR21 0LN. Tel: (01328) 851465; Fax: (01328) 855905; E-mail: enqu@pensthorpe.sagehost.co.uk

Mr Bill Makins • 1m E of Fakenham on A1067 Norwich Fakenham road. Signposted. Open March to Dec, daily; Jan to March, weekends only, all 10am – 5pm (Nov to Jan closes 4.30pm) • Entrance: £4.90, OAPs £4.30, children £2.40. Special rates for parties of 15 or more • Other information: Walk-through aviaries. Children's adventure playground ○ 🍴 ✕ 🛍 WC ♿ ⬚ ☕ ⚲

The 200-acre waterfowl park, already well known for one of Europe's finest collections of endangered and exotic water birds, also has a new feature of considerable interest to gardeners. In 1999 the well-known Dutch designer and plantsman Piet Oudolf was commissioned to create a millennium garden overlooking one of the lakes. Extending to nearly an acre, it is the largest project he has undertaken in the UK. The perennial planting style for which he has become famous is both spectacular and sensitive, blending well into the environment of the park where a traditional English garden would have looked out of place. There are large drifts and clumps of herbaceous plants, interspersed with grasses such as miscanthus and calamagrostis to contrast with other areas of deschampsis and lower-growing sesleria. The early flowering of *Nepeta subsessilis*, a spectacular planting of *Geranium* 'Brookside' and *Filipendula rubra* 'Venusta' ('Magnifica') help ensure that this must be one of the finest plantings of perennials in the country. The garden is at its best in July, August and September, but should not be forgotten through the autumn, especially if your visit coincides with a hoar frost. The darker areas near the water provide excellent growing conditions for drifts of *Lythrum salicaria* 'Stitchflame' and *L.*

'Zigeunerblut'. He has also used substantial plantings of eupatoriums, thalic-
trums and *Veronica* 'Mammuth'. The garden is a paradise for huge numbers of
butterflies, bumble-bees and insects.

The Plantation Garden 32

**4 Earlham Road, Norwich NR2 3DB. Tel: (01603) 621868
(Trust chairman: Mr B.M. Adam); Website: www.plantationgarden.co.uk**

*Plantation Garden Preservation Trust • Entrance off Earlham Road, next to
Beeches Hotel • Open daily April to mid-Oct 9am – 6pm, winter 10am –
4pm. Guided parties by arrangement • Entrance: £1.50 (honesty box),
accompanied children free, guided parties £24 min, special openings £2 per
person* ● � ৬ ♨ ♀

This unusual surviving example of a high-Victorian suburban garden, framed
by mature trees, was created by Henry Trevor in a disused chalk quarry just
outside the medieval walls of Norwich. The first feature in his garden, an
idiosyncratic Gothick fountain over nine metres high, was built in 1857. There
followed terraces with walls in the medieval style (random rubble), built using
an extraordinary conglomeration of materials: industrial waste, locally made
fancy bricks, flint and stone. Flights of steps with Italianate pedestals and
balustrades, a replica rustic bridge (1998), flower beds and woodland paths
combine to make a garden simultaneously typical of its period and the personal
vision of one individual. Conservation and restoration is an on-going process.
It is also an area of ecological interest with birds and lime-loving wild flowers.
Registered Grade II by English Heritage.

Sandringham House ★ 33

Sandringham, King's Lynn PE35 6EN. Tel: (01553) 772675

*H.M. The Queen • 9m NE of King's Lynn on B1440 near Sandringham
Church • House open as garden • Garden and park open Easter to July, early
Aug to Oct, daily, 11am – 4.45pm • Entrance: museum and grounds £5, OAPs
£4, children £3, family £13 (house, museum and grounds £6, OAPs £4.50,
children £3.50, family £15.50) (2001 prices)* ◑ 🍽 ✕ <u>WC</u> ৬ ♨ ▦ ♀ ✑

The house stands among broad lawns with an outer belt of woodland through
which a path runs past plantings of camellias, hydrangeas, cornus, magnolias
and rhododendrons, with some fine specimen trees including *Davidia involucrata*
and *Cercidiphyllum japonicum*. The path passes the magnificent cast- and wrought-
iron Norwich Gates of 1862. In the open lawn are specimen oaks planted by
Queen Victoria and other members of the Royal Family. To the south-west of
the house is the upper lake whose eastern side is built up into a massive rock
garden using blocks of the local carrstone, and now largely planted with dwarf
conifers. Below the rock garden, opening onto the lake, a cavernous grotto
was intended as a boathouse, while above is a small summerhouse built for
Queen Alexandra. There are thick plantings of hostas, agapanthus and various
moisture-loving plants around the margin of the lake. The path passes between
the upper and large lower lakes set in wooded surroundings. To the north of

the house is a garden designed by the late Sir Geoffrey Jellicoe for King George VI: a long series of beds surrounded by box hedges, divided by gravel and grass paths and flanked by avenues of pleached lime, one of which is centred on a gold-plated statue of a Buddhist divinity.

Sheringham Park ★   34

Upper Sheringham NR26 8TB. Tel: (01263) 823778

The National Trust • 4m NE of Holt off A148 • Park open all year, daily, dawn – dusk • Entrance: £2.70 per car inc. parking and all occupants. Coaches £8.10 • Other information: Coaches must pre-book with Warden during rhododendron season. Refreshments available April to Sept only ○ 🍽 🧺 WC ♿ 🐕

Located in a secluded valley at the edge of the Cromer/Holt ridge, close to the sea but protected from its winds by steep wooded hills, house and park, both designed by Humphry Repton, are now the property of the Trust, although the house remains in private occupation. The park is remarkable not only for its great beauty and spectacular views but also for an extensive collection of rhododendrons which thrive in the acid soil. Crowning an eminence is a modern classical temple based on a Repton design and erected to mark the 70th birthday of Mr Thomas Upcher, the last descendant of the original owner to live at Sheringham. This is the most-admired and best-preserved work of Repton.

Stow Hall ★   35

Stow Bardolph, King's Lynn PE34 3HU. Tel: (01366) 383194; E-mail: d.howlett49@fsnet.co.uk

Lady Rose Hare • 2m N of Downham Market, E of A10 • Open 28th Aprl, 26th May, 23rd June for NGS, 2 – 6pm, and for parties by appt • Entrance: £2.50, children free • Other information: Possible for wheelchairs but some gravel paths ● 🍽 🧺 WC ♿ 🐕 🌿 ☕

Majestic plane trees, beeches and cedars of Lebanon, certainly two centuries old, provide a changing backdrop for a garden that is in effect a long series of imaginative and interesting gardens linked by a straight path of red bricks and gravel. The high, warm walls of the old stableyard and the house are swathed in roses and wisteria – this is a paradise for anyone enthralled by old roses. Shrubs more usually seen in milder gardens also have congenial homes in the shelter of these walls – vanilla-scented *Azara microphylla*, white and blue abutilon, sun roses, Californian lilac, and many others. Amble along the path from the house to the nineteenth-century walled kitchen garden and you pass small elegant formal gardens, mixed perennial garden including irises, a Dutch garden, cloisters with more roses, and a croquet lawn. Inside the kitchen garden you will find gnarled apple trees and pear trees, a venerable mulberry, and more roses. A collection of antique apple trees has recently been planted. Everything is carefully maintained. Even if none of this existed, the astounding, self-layering fern-leaved beech would make any visit to Stow Hall worthwhile.

Idiosyncratic planter, Crathes Castle, Scotland

Sundial by Mark Lennox-Boyd, Holker Hall, Cumbria

Enclave designed by Keith Wiley, Garden House, Devon

Mosaic by Maggy Howarth, Gresgarth Hall, Lancashire

The Lance Hattatt Design Garden, Herefordshire

One of Marylyn Abbott's designs at West Green, Hampshire

Eighteenth-century sundial, House of Pitmuies, Scotland

Grass rings by Kathy Swift, The Dower House, Shropshire

Blue tree by Andrew Lawson, The Gothic House, Oxfordshire

Copper willow fountain, Chatsworth, Derbyshire –
nineteenth-century copy of 1695 original

Water feature by Simon Allison, Kiftsgate Court, Gloucestershire

Barbara Hepworth Museum and Sculpture Garden, Cornwall

Thrigby Hall Wildlife Gardens 36
Filby, Great Yarmouth NR29 3DR. Tel: (01493) 369477

*Mr K.J. Sims • 6m NW of Great Yarmouth on A1064. Signposted • Open all
year, daily, 10am – 6pm or dusk • Entrance: £5.90, OAPs £4.90, children (4 –
14) £3.90* ○ ● ▦ WC & ▥ ⚲

The chief attraction here is a collection of Chinese plants arranged to form the
landscape of the willow-pattern plate, complete with pagodas and bridges
across a small lake. Complementing the collection of Asiatic animals, the plants
are those particularly associated with temple gardens and include *Ginkgo biloba*,
Pinus parviflora, *Paeonia suffruticosa*, *Nandina domestica* and *Chimonobambusa quad-
rangularis*, set against a background of willows of many species. Otherwise
Thrigby is a wildlife park with many facilities for children.

Wretham Lodge 37
East Wretham, Thetford IP24 1RL. Tel: (01953) 498997.

*Mr Gordon Alexander • 6m NE of Thetford off A1075. Left by village sign,
right at crossroads, then bear left • Open 31st March, 1st April 11am – 6pm;
30th June 2 — 5pm. Parties by appt • Entrance: £2.50, children free • Other
information: Teas and plants for sale on certain open days only*
● ● WC & ⚘ ⚲

Extensive lawns surround the handsome flint-built former rectory set in its
own walled park; there are wide mixed borders around the house and within
the walled kitchen garden. Roses are massed in informal beds and cover the
high flint walls, and plants worthy of note include espalier and fan-trained fruit
trees, a large indoor fig, and unusual vegetables. A wide grass walk runs
around the park and through mature and recently established trees where
daffodils are naturalised; a long walk among narcissi and bluebells leads to a
grove of flowering trees. Spring sees the flowering of many bulbs, and in
summer the wildflower meadows are a haze of colour. New developments
include a double herbaceous border.

NATIONAL COUNCIL FOR THE CONSERVATION OF PLANTS AND
GARDENS
The NCCPG publishes a *National Plant Collections Directory*. Those interested in
particular families of plants who want to see some of the rarer species and
garden varieties will find this an invaluable publication. The latest edition,
which offers information on about 600 collections comprising more than
50,000 plants and contains articles by holders of the collections, is available
from NCCPG, The Pines, RHS Garden, Wisley, Woking GU3 6QB (Tel:
(01483) 221465; Fax: (01483) 212404; Website: www.nccpg.org.uk. The
2002 edition will be published January or February 2002.

NORTHAMPTONSHIRE

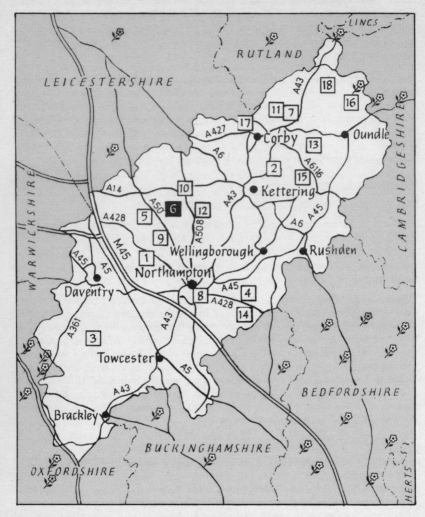

Two-starred gardens are marked on the map with a black square.

Althorp House

Althorp, Northampton NN7 4HQ. Tel: (01604) 770107; Fax: (01604) 770042 (House and Park Office); E-mail: mail@althorp.com; Website: www.althorp.com

Earl Spencer • 6m NW of Northampton on A428 Northampton – Rugby road • House and grounds open July to 30th Aug • Entrance: house and gardens £10, OAPs £8.50, children (5–17) £5 (pre-booked tickets) ● ☕ 🖼 WC ♿ 🧺

The original Elizabethan house was surrounded by formal gardens probably swept away during the fashionable eighteenth-century improvements by the architect Henry Holland, helped by Samuel Lapidge, 'Capability' Brown's assistant. The present gardens were laid out in the 1860s by the architect W.M. Teulon and enclosed by stone walls and balustrades. To the side and rear the gardens are also laid to lawn, although the talented designer Dan Pearson has recently planted beds with a subtle blend of bronze fennel, aconitum, potentillas and *Verbena bonariensis* outside the stable block, which now houses a tasteful shop, and the same restricted palette is used in other borders, harmonising wonderfully with the honey-coloured stone. Because this was the home of Diana, Princess of Wales, its future will inevitably be dedicated to her memory and to those who visit out of respect or curiosity. The Earl, her brother, recognising this, engaged Pearson to produce an unusual memorial – a two-mile walk in the grounds through the park and house to the island where the Princess is buried, leading through a green meadow of long grasses and wild flowers by the lake colonised by 1000 white water lilies, and black swans.

Boughton House Park 2

Kettering NN14 1BJ. Tel: (01536) 515731; E-mail: llt@boughtonhouse.org.uk; Web: www.boughtonhouse.org.uk

The Duke and Duchess of Buccleuch and Queensberry • 2m NW of Kettering off A43, entry via Geddington. Signposted • House open as garden • Garden open Aug to 1st Sept, 2 – 5pm (last admission 4.30pm). Park open May to 1st Sept, daily except Fri, 1 – 5pm. Specialist and educational parties welcome at other times by prior arrangement • Entrance: £1 (house, gardens and park £6, OAPs and children £5) • Other information: Dogs in park only, on lead ◑ ☕ ✕ ▤ WC ♿ ⚘ ♨ ⚑ ⚲

Although with only limited formal gardens remaining, Boughton will be attractive to garden enthusiasts and the whole family. The large sixteenth- and seventeenth- century house, with monastic origins and a strong French influence, contains an extensive collection of paintings and furniture. The magnificent surrounding park, with its lakes and canalised river, and avenues of trees, was laid out by the first Duke of Montagu before 1700 with the help of a Dutch gardener, Van der Meulen, who had experience of reclamation work in the Fens. The second Duke, known as 'John the Planter', added a lake and a colossal network of avenues of elms and limes in the 1730s to an ambitious plan of Bridgeman, though not even 'The Planter' was prepared to carry out the complete network and indeed in 1731 he sacked Bridgeman. Even so the avenues stretched to 23 miles with rides through woods extending another twenty or so. The garden close to the house includes herbaceous borders and some fine planted vases. To the south of the house a small circular rose garden leads on to the outstanding rectangular lily pond, beyond which the walled garden houses a long herbaceous border and well-stocked plant centre. In the 350-acre park are walks and trails, including one for the disabled, and a woodland adventure play area for children.

Canons Ashby House 3

Canons Ashby, Daventry NN11 3SD. Tel: (01327) 860044

The National Trust • 6m S of Daventry off A361 Daventry – Banbury road • House open • Garden open 23rd March to 3rd Nov, Sat – Wed, 11am – 5.30pm, or dusk if earlier (last admission 5pm), (closes 4.30pm, Oct); 9th Nov to 22nd Dec, Sat, Sun, 11am – 3pm, • Entrance: £1, children 50p (house and garden £5.20, children £2.60, family ticket £13. Reductions for pre-booked parties) • Other information: Parking 200 metres from house. Disabled telephone in advance and park near house. Wheelchairs available. Taped braille guide available. Picnics in car park. Dogs in home paddock only, on lead ◑ 💜 WC ♿ ⛾

The brooding, romantic house where Spenser wrote part of *The Faerie Queene* was the first to be rescued by the National Heritage Memorial Fund. The historical framework of the garden has been painstakingly re-created over the past decade by the Trust. Formal, with axial arrangements of paths and grass terraces, high stone walls, lawns and gateways, the design dates almost entirely from the beginning of the eighteenth century; a cedar planted in 1781 survives from the original four. The garden is maturing well, with trees and shrubs beginning to give the required height and scale. Hexagonal beds, part of the later Inigo Trigg's plan of 1901, have been reinstated and feature seasonal bedding. Borders have majestic plants such as acanthus, cardoons and globe artichokes, while the green court contains fine topiary. Old varieties of soft fruit bushes and fruit trees include espaliered pears grown from the original stock planted in 1710 by Edward Dryden, whose family owned the house. The wild gardens are in direct contrast to the formal, carefully maintained terraces at the highest level, from where the eye is irresistibly drawn down the principal vista to the Lion Gates and the fine Baroque gate piers.

Castle Ashby Gardens 4

Castle Ashby, Northampton NN7 1LQ. Tel: (01604) 696187

Earl Compton • 5m E of Northampton, between A45 Northampton – Wellingborough road and A428 Northampton – Bedford road • Gardens open daily, 10am – dusk, with occasional closures when house can be hired as corporate venue. Tours for parties by appt • Entrance: (tickets from machine when entrance unattended) £2.50, OAPs/children £1.50, season tickets £32 (2001 prices) • Other information: Refreshments at tea rooms in village, 400 metres; teas available in garden if pre-booked for coach parties or large groups. Possible for wheelchairs but uneven paths. Farm shop and craft centre in village. Country fair first week in July ○ 🍴 ♿ ⛾ 🍂 ⛾ ⚘

Originally Elizabethan, then a park landscaped by 'Capability' Brown, and later a Matthew Digby Wyatt terrace, Italian garden and arboretum. The house is never open to the public, but there is access to most of the gardens (except the east terrace, although there are good views from near the church) which present a glorious combination of views. A nature walk past mature trees leads over a terracotta bridge and to the 'knucklebone arbour' (sometimes open), a summerhouse with what are probably sheep or deer knuckles set in the floor. Among the wild and naturalised plants are carpets of aconites and snowdrops, winter heliotropes, butterburs, daffodils, bluebells, wood anemones, celandines, bush vetches, wood buttercups and a wide selection of lake and pondside plants. Features include an orangery and archway greenhouses, topiary and well-planted large vases. Restoration of the garden and architectural features is continuing.

Coton Manor Gardens ★   5

Guilsborough, Northampton NN6 8RQ. Tel: (01604) 740219; Fax: (01604) 740838; E-mail: pasleytyler@cotonmanor.fsnet.co.uk; Website: www.cotonmanor.co.uk

Mr and Mrs Ian Pasley-Tyler • 10m NW of Northampton, 11m SE of Rugby near Ravensthorpe Reservoir, signed from A428 and A5199 • Open 29th March to Sept, Tues – Sat, Bank Holiday Mons; Sun, April, May only; all at 12 noon – 5.30pm • Entrance: £4, OAPs £3.50, children £2.50 ◗ ⌷ ✕ WC & ⌷ ⌷ ⌷

Dating from the 1920s, when the original seventeenth-century farmhouse was bought and added to by Mr Pasley-Tyler's grandparents, this is a beautifully maintained garden of exceptional charm, with unexpected vistas at every turn. There is something for everyone here: a most attractive assortment of pelargoniums in pots on the terrace by the house leading to the rose garden, a contrastingly shady woodland garden, a water garden, lush lawns sloping down to a large pond complete with black swans and ornamental ducks, and magnificent mixed borders, particularly striking in July with campanulas and philadelphus. There is a surprise around every corner (do not rub your eyes should you think you see a real crane or flamingo beside the neatly clipped yew hedge – no verdigris imitations here) and strategically placed seats from which to enjoy the views and effects of Mrs Pasley-Tyler's marvellous eye for colour. The garden has continued to develop since the present generation moved into the house in 1991. The Mediteranean bank, rose walk and herb garden are now well established, along with replanting of the rose bank and the midsummer and late summer borders. The bluebell wood is magical in May and the path through the wildflower meadow makes a pleasant walk. A water staircase has just been completed running down between old apple orchards. This garden could not fail to inspire and manages to retain its atmosphere of family involvement. A helpful and interesting booklet and plant list is available; don't miss a visit to the extensive nursery.

Cottesbrooke Hall ★★   6

Cottesbrooke, Northampton NN6 8PF. Tel: (01604) 505808; Fax: (01604) 505619; E-mail: hall@cottesbrooke.co.uk; Website: www.cottesbrookehall.co.uk

Captain and Mrs J. Macdonald-Buchanan • 10m N of Northampton between A5199 and A508 (A14 – A1/M1 link road) • House open as garden, but

Thurs and Bank Holiday Suns and Mons only; also 5th May, 2nd June, 7th July, 4th Aug, 1st Sept • Gardens open May to Sept, Tues, Wed and Fri, 2 – 5.30pm (last admission 5pm). Parties by appt • Entrance: £3, children £1.50, RHS members free (house and gardens £4.50, children £2.25) ◑ 🍵 🖼 WC ♿ 🐾

An excellently maintained formal garden surrounding a fine Queen Anne house, set in a large park (also open) with lakes and a stream, vistas and avenues. Designs by Edward Schultz, Geoffrey Jellicoe, Dame Sylvia Crowe and the late Hon. Lady Macdonald-Buchanan are being continued by the present owners – particularly the planting. The result is a series of delightful enclosed courtyards and gardens around the house with superb borders, urns and statues. Be sure to visit the intriguingly named Dilemma Garden and to examine the Statue Walk. The spinney garden is at its best in spring with bulbs and azaleas. New trees, borders, yew hedges, gates and vistas have recently been added and Philip Astley, formerly head gardener at Hardwick, is beginning to make his mark as certainly here. Beyond the thatched Wendy house the wild garden surrounds a running stream and cascades, with azaleas, rhododendrons, acers, cherries, spring bulbs and wild flowers. The magnolia, cherry and acer collections and the ancient cedars are notable. The house contains fine paintings, including several distinguished Stubbses, and was possibly the model for Jane Austen's Mansfield Park.

Deene Park 7

Corby NN17 3EW. Tel: (01780) 450278/450223

Mr Edmund Brudenell • 6m N of Corby off A43 Kettering – Stamford road • House open • Gardens open 31st March, 1st April, 5th, 6th May, 2nd, 3rd June; then June to Aug, Sun and 26th Aug, all 2 – 5pm. Parties by appt • Entrance: £3, children (10–14) £1.50, accompanied children under 10 free (house and gardens £5, children (10–14) £2.50, accompanied children under 10 free) (2001 prices) • Other information: Picnics in car park ● 🍵 WC ♿ 🚻 ▮

The glory of Deene, which was created by generations of the Brudenell family, is its trees. Fine mature specimens and groups fringe the formal areas and frame tranquil and enchanting views of the parkland and countryside. The main features of the garden are the long borders, old-fashioned roses, parterre and the lake. The parterre, designed by David Hicks, is a particularly fine feature, running along the whole south side of the house. The gardens, parkland, church and house together provide a delightful, interesting and relaxing afternoon for visitors in what was the home of the Earl of Cardigan who led the Charge of the Light Brigade in 1854.

Delapre Abbey 8

London Road, Northampton NN4 8AW. Tel: (01604) 761074

Northampton Borough Council Leisure Department • 1m S of Northampton on A508 • Walled gardens open April to Sept, Mon – Thurs, 9am – 3pm, Fri, 9am – 2.30pm. Park open all year • Entrance: free ◑ WC ♿ 📧 ✎

Largely rebuilt in the seventeenth century, the house, on the site of the former nunnery of St Mary of the Meadow, together with 500 acres of land, passed into public ownership in 1946. With improving standards of maintenance (although some associated buildings are in need of repair), it is still possible to glimpse the hey-day of a lovely garden. Beyond the walled former kitchen garden, well-tended lawns, perennial, annual and rose beds and an eighteenth-century thatched game larder are walks through the wilderness garden with fine trees, shrubberies and lily ponds. There are lakes and a golf course in the park, and at the roadside close to the entrance one of the Queen Eleanor Crosses commemorates the funeral procession in 1290 of Edward I's queen.

Holdenby House Gardens and Falconry Centre 9

Holdenby, Northampton NN6 8DJ. Tel: (01604) 770074;
Fax: (01604) 770962; Website: www.holdenby.com

Mr and Mrs James Lowther • 7m NW of Northampton, signed from A5199 and A428 • House open 1st April, 29th May, 26th Aug, and by appt. Garden and falconry centre open April to Sept, Sun, 1 – 5pm, July and Aug, daily except Sat, 1 – 5pm • Entrance: £3, OAPs £2.50, children £1.75 (house and gardens £5, children £3) • Other information: Meals by appt. Special events Easter, May Day, Whitsun and Aug Bank Hols, 1 – 6pm ◑ 💷 🥐 WC ⬧ ⟁ 🏕 🐾 🐾

Two grassed terraces, a fish pond and the palace forecourt with its original arches remain of the extensive Elizabethan garden which surrounded the vast mansion built by Elizabeth I's chancellor, Sir Christopher Hatton, in the late sixteenth century. The gardens still link the surviving remnant of the house (one-eighth of its former size) to its past, especially the delightful Elizabethan garden, planted in 1980 by the late Rosemary Verey as a miniature replica of Hatton's original centrepiece, using only plants available in the 1580s. Other garden features include the fragrant border (now replanted by Rupert Golby), part of the nineteenth-century garden, the silver border and kitchen garden, the falconry centre, an authentically re-constructed seventeenth-century farmstead and children's amusements.

Kelmarsh Hall ★ 10

Kelmarsh, Northampton NN6 9LU Tel: (01604) 686543

The Kelmarsh Trust • 5m S of Market Harborough, 11m N of Northampton, on A508 near A14 junction 2 • House and garden open 31st March to 1st Sept, Sun and Bank Holiday Mons, 2 – 5pm. Garden open 31st March to 26th Sept, Mon – Thurs, 2 – 5pm • Entrance: £2 (house and garden £3.50, children free) ◑ WC ⬧ 🐾

The Palladian house, designed by James Gibbs and built in 1730, is set in an eighteenth-century landscape and has twentieth-century gardens made by Nancy Lancaster, who was advised by Norah Lindsay in planting the lavish herbaceous borders. The deep terrace on the garden front of the house, designed by Geoffrey Jellicoe, looks out across the lake and has rows of pleached limes on either side. A sunken garden, surrounded by billowing box hedges, is filled with sweetly scented plants in pale pastel colours. The fan-shaped rose garden, filled with old-fashioned roses, looks across a meadow towards the church; a herd of British White Cattle grazes. Early in the year, the garden is rich with spring flowers, from fritillaries naturalised down the drive to large drifts of daffodils in the woodland walk. A great sense of peace pervades this very private garden, and its well-articulated design and sure sense of style are re-emerging as the major features are restored.

Kirby Hall   11

Deene, Corby NN17 5EN. Tel: (01536) 203230

English Heritage • 4m NE of Corby off A43 on road W of Deene • Open April to Sept, daily, 10am – 6pm; Oct, daily, 10am – 5pm; Nov to March, Sat and Sun, 10am – 4pm. Closed 24th to 26th Dec, 1st Jan • Entrance: £3, concessions £2.30, children £1.50 ○ ⚊ ▣ WC ﹠ ⟨⟩ ⏤ ⦿ ℺

The gardens date from at least the period when Sir Christopher Hatton owned the hall in Elizabethan times. However, it was in the late seventeenth century that they achieved considerable fame through the work of the fourth Sir Christopher Hatton, who devoted his energies to the gardens until his death in 1705. In the 1930s the Great Garden was laid out following the pre-war idea of how a Baroque formal garden would have appeared. Since then, following extensive research of the period, the 1930s' garden is being buried and the parterre re-created using a design based on Longleat (see entry in Wiltshire), which will provide a more accurate view of how this garden would have looked in 1686. Over 80 two-metre-high clipped yew cones, holly mopheads and box balls, many placed in oak barrels similar to those used in the Hampton Court restoration, surround the dramatic geometric design of the *gazon coupé* parterre of wide gravel paths and cut-through patterns of lawn. The north border was replanted in 1995 with species following as closely as possible those mentioned by Hatton in his notebooks. These include old varieties of fruit trees – apples, pears and cherries – trained against the walls.

Lamport Hall Garden   12

Lamport, Northampton NN6 9HD. Tel: (01604) 686272; Fax: (01604) 686224; E-mail: admin@lamporthall.co.uk

Lamport Hall Trust • 8m N of Northampton on A508 • Hall open • Garden open 31st March to 6th Oct, Sun and Bank Holiday Mons, 2.15 – 5.15pm (last admission 4pm). Details of other days available on request. Coach parties at any time by arrangement • Entrance: £4, OAPs £3.50, children £2 (house and gardens) (2001 prices) • Other information: Dogs in picnic area only, on lead. Regular programme of events – telephone for details. School study centre and agricultural museum ◐ ⚊ WC ﹠ ⟨⟩ ⦿

The principal façade of the hall is by John Webb and the Smiths of Warwick. The grounds, initially laid out by Gilbert Clarke in 1655, have been restored, and there are now extensive herbaceous and mixed borders and lawns, a lily pond and rose garden. Sir Charles Isham's local ironstone rockery, the home of the first garden gnome, has been painstakingly restored and his box bowers are growing back to their original style. The unusual shell and coral fountain at the centre of the Italian garden is in working order.

Lyveden New Bield 13

Oundle, Peterborough PE8 5AT. Tel/Fax: (01832) 205358

The National Trust • 4m SW of Oundle off A427, 3m E of Brigstock • House, Elizabethan water garden and visitor information room Wed – Sun, 23rd March to 3rd Nov, 10.30am – 5pm; 3rd Nov to March 2003, Sat, Sun, 10.30am – 4pm • Entrance: £2, children £1, family £5 • Other information: Access on foot only, ½ m along farm track. Teas for groups by prior arrangement ● 🍴 WC ◁▷ ♿

This is not a garden, but the remains of an unfinished late-Elizabethan one. Its principal elements were water and sculpted landform, both of which remain largely intact. Part of the canal system survives, as do the ruins of a banqueting house or lodge. The latter is a three-storey building in the shape of an equal-armed cross as a celebration of the Passion of Christ. Alas, there is no planting of the period, though the raised grass terrace with its broad walk is still in place, with turf pyramids at each end. The Trust is undertaking a project to reveal the extensive remains of an elaborate water garden, containing a series of truncated pyramids and circular mounds, surrounded by moats and terraces. Writing in *The Garden*, Stephen Anderton suggests the remains of 'this bare relic' could be developed into something modern and 'truly remarkable'.

The Menagerie 14

Horton, Northampton NN7 2BX. Tel: (01604) 870957 (Leave message for Administrator)

Mr A. Myers • 6m SE of Northampton, on B526 turn left 1m S of Horton into field. Watch out for tiny notice on gate • Open April to Sept, Mon and Thurs, 2 – 5pm, also last Sun of those months, 2 – 6pm • Entrance: £3.50, children £1.50 (2001 prices) ● 🍴 WC ♟

The informal approach through a farm gateway and across uncultivated fields gives no hint of the delights of the fascinating journey beyond. This is a garden still in the making, with formal water gardens and wetlands surrounding the house, an eighteenth-century folly, where Lord Halifax had his private zoo. The house is one of the most important surviving works of Thomas Wright of Durham. The garden created by the late Gervase Jackson-Stops and Ian Kirby is a recent development, attractively sited with views across to where Horton Hall once stood. The central lime avenue, planted in the 1980s, provides a vista to a mount with a spiral path to the obelisk on top. Two hornbeam *allées* end in eighteenth-century ponds with fountains. Two thatched arbours have been built – one circular and classical, the other triangular and Gothick – with newly planted shrubberies designed to hide them from the house. The charming rose garden enclosed by yew hedges was designed by Vernon Russell-Smith in 1989. A most unusual garden, in which most of the plantings are now well established.

The Old Rectory ★   15

Sudborough, Kettering NN14 3BX. Tel: (01832) 733247; Fax: (01832) 733832

Mr and Mrs Anthony Huntington • 7m SE of Corby off A6116 Corby – Thrapston road, A14 junction 12 • Open April to June, Tues, Sat, Sun and Bank Holiday Mons, June to Sept, Tues only, all 10am – 4pm; and by appt. Parties welcome • Entrance: £3 (£4 with tea and biscuits), children under 16 free • Other information: light lunches and evening parties can be arranged ● ● WC & ♨

A delightful three-acre rectory garden in a beautiful stone and thatch village. Much has been accomplished in recent times to develop plantings throughout the year, with a fine collection of hellebores in spring and many containers, especially in summer. Copious planting in the mixed borders, around the pond and many climbers. The *potager*, begun by the late Rosemary Verey and completed by Rupert Golby, is fascinating, with small beds and brick paths leading to a central wrought-iron arbour; standard roses, gooseberries and tents of runner beans and marrows provide vertical features. A small wild garden with interesting trees and a woodland walk along the stream completes the picture, with excellent labelling throughout.

The Prebendal Manor House   16

Nassington, Peterborough PE8 6QG. Tel: (01780) 782575;
E-mail: info@prebendal-manor.demon.co.uk; Web: www.prebendal-manor.co.uk

Mrs Jane Baile • 8m W of Peterborough off A1, in Nassington opposite church • Open May and June, Sun and Wed; July and Aug, Sun, Wed and Thurs; Sept, Sun and Wed; all 1 – 5.30pm • Entrance: £3.50, children £1.50 ◑ ● ● WC & ♨ ♦ ♨

From a window sill of the early thirteenth-century tawny stone house a pair of carved heads gaze down, guardians of the secrets of this ancient place. Scattered around its six acres are reconstructions of various types of medieval gardens. The herber has grass seats, a fig tree and scented plants, while the trellis garden's compartments overspill with poppies and mallows. Concealed by an ancient wall and protected by a fine withy fence is a vegetable patch with broad beans, herbs and wheat, and a new nut walk leads to two fishponds. Patches of wild flowers sit in the lawn; old willows, the other guardians of the manor's secrets, billow silvery in the breeze. The tithe barn contains an interpretative museum display with some look-alike farm tools. The latest addition is a small vineyard near the vegetable patch.

Rockingham Castle Gardens   17

Market Harborough LE16 8TH. Tel: (01536) 770240

Commander James Saunders Watson and family • 2m N of Corby on A6003. Signposted • House open • Garden open April to Sept – telephone for details • Entrance: £3 (castle and gardens £4.50, OAPs £4, children £3, family ticket (2 adults and 2 children) £12.50, parties of 20 or more £4 per person) • Other information: Disabled park near entrance ◑ ● ✕ ● WC & ♦ ♨ ♨ ♨

Rockingham sits on a hilltop fortress site with stunning views of three counties. It has remains from all periods of its 900-year history, with major features ranging from formal seventeenth-century terraces and yew hedges to the romantic wild garden of the nineteenth century. There is a circular rose garden surrounded by a yew hedge and also good herbaceous borders. The wild garden was replanted with advice from Kew Gardens in the late 1960s and includes over 200 species of trees and shrubs. The result is a delightful blend of form, colour, light and shade.

The Walnuts 18

King's Cliffe, Peterborough PE8 6XH. Tel: (01780) 470312;
Fax: (01780) 470071; E-mail: mplwalnuts@aol.com

Mr and Mrs Martin Lawrence. 7m N of Oundle, 7m SW of Stamford, 4m W of Wansford from A1 and A47; last house on left in King's Cliffe on road to Apethorpe • Open April to July, Wed, 2 – 6pm, for NGS one spring weekend and one summer weekday evening, and for groups by appt at other times • Entrance: £2, children free NEW ◑ 🐾 WC ♿ ⬥ 🌿 🔍

Set around a handsome limestone village house, two and a half acres of partly terraced, partly sloping garden lead down to a wood-edged brook, through a well-managed water meadow full of spring wild flowers. In the last ten years, the owners have developed an attractive and apposite country garden, dedicated to promoting wild life, and filled chiefly with shrubs, roses, perennials and bulbs. There is also an ornamental vegetable garden and a child-friendly orchard with a willow tunnel and a sandpit.

GARDEN AND FLOWER SHOWS 2002
- 10th to 12th May: Spring Gardening Show, Malvern
  (Three Counties Showground, Malvern, Worcestershire)
  Ticket hotline: (01684) 584924
- 21st to 24th May: Chelsea Flower Show
  (Royal Hospital, Chelsea, London SW3)
  Ticket hotline: (0870) 906 3780
- 19th to 23rd June: BBC *Gardeners' World* Live
  (National Exhibition Centre, Birmingham)
  Ticket hotline: (0870) 264 5555
- 25th to 27th June, 20th to 22nd Aug: Wisley Flower Show
  (RHS Garden, Wisley, Woking, Surrey)
  Tel: (01483) 224234; Fax: (01483) 211750
- 2nd to 7th July: Hampton Court Flower Show
  (Hampton Court Palace, East Molesey, Surrey)
  Ticket hotline: (0870) 906 3790
- 17th to 21st July: RHS Flower Show, Tatton Park
  (Tatton Park, near Knutsford, Cheshire)
  Ticket hotline: (0870) 906 3810

For details of all these shows, telephone RHS on (020) 7834 4337.

NORTHUMBERLAND

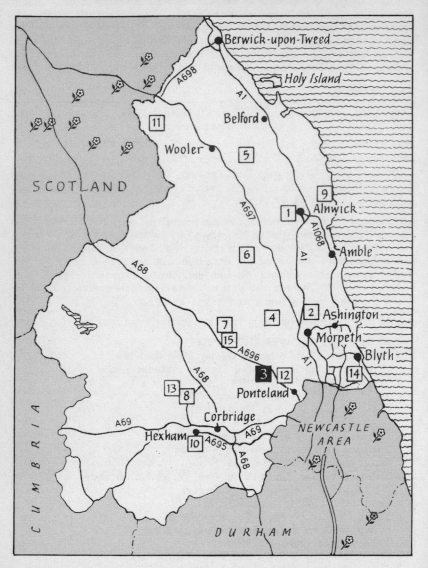

Two-starred gardens are marked on the map with a black square.

Alnwick Castle 1

Alnwick NE66 1NQ. Tel: (01665) 510777 (Mon – Fri), (01655) 511100 (Infoline)

Duke and Duchess of Northumberland • 35m N of Newcastle upon Tyne. Take A1 and turn W at Alnwick. Signposted • Castle open 28th March to Oct • Grounds open, daily, 11am – 5pm or dusk if earlier (last admission 4.15pm). Closed 25th Dec. The Alnwick Garden open all year, daily, 10am – 5pm or dusk if earlier. Closed 25th Dec • Entrance: Grounds £6.75, OAPs/students £5.75, children (5–16) £3.50, family £15.50 (2001 prices). The Alnwick Garden £4, OAPs/students £3.50, accompanied children (16 or under) free. Friends of Alnwick garden £10 membership, family £25 (castle and Alnwick garden £9.50) ◗ ☕ ⊞

Set in a 'Capability' Brown landscape, Alnwick Castle and its grounds has long been open to the public. Although the castle was remodelled in the 1850s, the landscape survives almost intact. But, in 2001, the first stage of a remarkably ambitious and dramatic new garden was completed. Within the twelve-acre Victorian walled former kitchen garden, a giant cascade has been constructed which in effect will become the spine of a new garden. On plan it looks remarkably like a turbine engine. Designed by the Wirtz father and sons team from Belgium, the cascade will send tumbling down a series of 27 weirs over 7000 gallons of water per minute. This will then disappear through four large bell-mouth openings to erupt the other side of a walkway as four huge watery mounds. These then become a vertical flowing wall discharging down the two stone arms of the Grand Cascade, and creating a spectacular vortex at its exit. Along the flow of the cascade, three large central jets propel water 18 feet into the air, with 40 smaller jets rising to 12 feet; along the sides of the cascade 80 jets create a crossfire over the centre of the cascade. Finally, jumping jets fire streams of water over the walkway and into the Grand Basin beyond. The climax of this dynamic flow and contra-flow is a veritable explosion of fountains producing a moving mass of water, 18 feet high at its peak. An underground store of 250,000 gallons enables the cascade to be fed and recycled with filtered water. Cascades are so rare in English gardens that Alnwick will be the first real challenge to Chatsworth's miraculous seventeenth-century precursor, immortally described by Daniel Defoe: 'Out of the mouths of beasts, pipes, urns etc, a whole river descends the slope of a hill a quarter of a mile in length, over steps, with a terrible noise and broken appearance.'

Ashfield 2

Hebron, Morpeth NE61 3LA. Tel: (01670) 515616; Fax: (01670) 511600; E-mail: rona.mcwilliam@virgin.net

Barry and Rona McWilliam • 3m N of Morpeth, 1m E of A1 on C130 S of Hebron • Open all year by impromptu appt • Entrance: £2, children free ● ☕ 🍴 WC ㅊ 🐾 ⚲

The house looks out onto a terrace dense with bulbs and a carpet of alpines, many, including *Androsace lanuginosa*, tumbling over the supporting wall. The lawn slopes gently down beyond, sheltered by beech and prunus hedges and punctuated by small island beds planted with bulbs, shrubs and small trees, including many varieties of sorbus. The owner is a keen plantsman and the five-acre garden reflects his enthusiasm. On the east side is a mixed border, including an area for bog plants. Beyond this is the Three-acre Garden, an expanse of lawn with colourful herbaceous borders, a small pinetum, and beds of shrubs and bulbs. On the west side lies a one-and-a-half-acre woodland deeply planted under mature trees. The woodland walks wind past beds planted with spring bulbs, hellebores, hostas and other shade-loving plants and small trees (sorbus, betulas, acers, etc.). Many plants come from abroad and have been grown from seed, as in the scree-bed, planted with Sino-Himalayan alpines beside the entrance.

Belsay Hall, Castle and Gardens ★★   3

Belsay, Newcastle–upon–Tyne NE20 0DX. Tel: (01661) 881636;
Fax: (01661) 881043

English Heritage • 14m NW of Newcastle on A696 • Hall and castle open •
Gardens open April to Sept, daily, 10am – 6pm; Oct, daily, 10am – 5pm; Nov
to March, daily, 10am – 4pm. Closed 24th to 26th Dec, 1st Jan. Pre-booked
evening tours in summer include joint natural history and gardening tours •
Entrance: £3.90, OAPs £2.90, children £2. Reductions for parties of 11 or more
(2001 prices) • Other information: Advance notice preferred for coaches.
Refreshments Easter to Oct only. Wheelchairs available for loan. Annual NCCPG
plant sale in June ◑ 🍲 ✕ 🖼 WC & ⬦ 🌿 🏛 ♟ ✎

The 30-acre gardens are the creation of two men who between them owned the hall in succession from 1795 to 1933. Sir Charles Monck built the severe neo-classical house with formal terraces leading through woods to a 'garden' inside the quarry from which the house was built. Sir Arthur, his grandson, took over in 1867, adding Victorian features. Both were discerning plantsmen. The result is a well-cared-for collection of rare, mature and exotic specimens in a fascinating sequence. The terrace looks across to massed June rhododendrons. Other areas (flower garden, magnolia terrace, winter garden) lead to woods, a wild meadow and the quarry garden itself. Reminiscent of the ancient Greek quarries in Syracuse, this was carefully contrived and stocked to achieve a wild romantic effect; the sheltered microclimate has resulted in the luxuriant growth of some remarkable and exotic trees and shrubs, dramatically beautiful in the light and shade of the sandstone gorge. Here, among the massive hewn slabs silvered by lichen are memorable corners: the well of a natural amphitheatre, cascading with ferns; stepped rock ledges carpeted with moss; a host of fritillaries naturalised in grass. The winter garden, with its heathers, also has a 28-metre high Douglas fir, and rhododendrons, some of which may bloom as early as December. An unexpected pleasure is the grand croquet lawn on which white-clad figures pleasure themselves with their strange sport. The one-and-a-half-mile Crag Wood walk is a stepped, serpentine path which passes by the lake and through the hanging woods opposite the hall.

Bide-a-Wee Cottage ★ 4

Stanton, Netherwitton, Morpeth NE65 8PR. Tel: (01670) 772262; Website: www.bide-a-wee.co.uk

Mark Robson • 7m NW of Morpeth, 3m SW of Longhorsley, off A697 Morpeth – Coldstream road towards Stanton • Open 27th April to Aug, Sat and Wed, 1.30 – 5pm. Parties by arrangement, except Sun • Entrance: £2 ● ℘

One of the most enchanting and richly planted gardens in the North-East. Combining formal, informal and wild features, it occupies a long-abandoned stone quarry and some of the higher surrounding land. The varied topography, soil and climate allow for a diversity of plants to be grown, from marsh-loving to drought-tolerant species. The beauty of the natural rock faces has been exploited to the maximum and they have been enriched by truly sympathetic planting. As well as being a highly refined plantsman, the owner is also a splendid mason whose stonework has done much to embellish the garden. About 3m N of Morpeth is a well-known garden centre, *Heighley Gate*, open seven days a week, with coffee shop.

Chillingham Castle 5

Chillingham NE66 5NJ. Tel: (01668) 215359/215390; Fax: (01668) 215463

Sir Humphry Wakefield, Bt. • 12m NW of Alnwick between A1 (signposted), A697, B6346 and B6348 • House open • Gardens open May to Sept, Sun, Mon, Wed – Fri, 12 noon – 5pm; and by appt • Entrance: £4.50, OAPs £4, children under 12 free, over 12 £1, parties of 10 or more £3.80 per person. Guided tours £30 ◑ ● WC ℘ ⊞ ⊕ ℺

Since the 1200s this has been and continues to be the family home of the Earls Grey and their relations. Sir Humphry has restored the castle and garden along with the grounds, landscaped in 1828 by Wyatville (of Windsor Castle and Royal Lodge fame). The Elizabethan-style walled garden has been virtually excavated to rediscover its intricate pattern of clipped box and yew (enlivened by scarlet tropaeolum), with rose beds, fountains, a central avenue and a spectacular herbaceous border running the whole length. Outside are lawns and a rock garden, delightful woodland and lakeside walks through drifts of snowdrops, spring displays of daffodils, bluebells and, later, rhododendrons. The medieval castle and mountain views provide a spectacular backdrop.

Cragside House, Garden and Estate 6

Rothbury, Morpeth NE65 7PX. Tel: (01669) 620333; Fax: (01669) 620066; E-mail: ncrvmx@smtp.ntrust.org.uk; Website: nationaltrust.org.uk

The National Trust • 13m SW of Alnwick off A697 between B6341 and B6344 • Estate and gardens open 23rd March to 3rd Nov, daily except Mon (but open Bank Holiday Mons), 10.30am – 7pm (last admission 5pm); 6th Nov to 15th Dec, Wed – Sun, 11am – 4pm • House open 23rd March to 30th Sept, 1 – 5.30pm (last admission 4.30pm), Oct to 3rd Nov, 1 — 4.30pm (last admission 3.30pm) • Entrance: garden and estate £4.40, family (2 adults and 3 children)

£11; house, garden and estate £6.90, family £17.30 • Other information: Main car parks either near to house (with ½ m walk to formal garden) or near formal garden, with further car parks along the estate drive. Visitor centre and Armstrong Exhibition (some distance from garden) with toilet facilities and shop
🕐 ▇ ✕ ▇ WC ♿ ▦ ▮ ✎

Lord Armstrong, one of the greatest of Victorian engineers, clothed this hillside above the Coquet Valley with millions of trees and shrubs as the setting for a house designed by R. Norman Shaw (the first ever lit by hydro-electricity) that was then the wonder of the world. From the car park nearest to the house the path (signposted 'Garden') affords views of the rock gardens below the house. These have been cleared after years of neglect and are now planted with an impressive display of heathers, shrubs and alpines. The path descends sharply into the Debdon gorge, crosses the river by a rustic bridge (magnificent views of the elegant iron bridge soaring above) and climbs through majestic conifers to the clock tower (1864) which overlooks the formal garden. This walled area, laid out in high-Victorian style, is set in three terraces and restoration is continuing. On the upper terrace are rock ferneries, grottos and a small canal. The middle terrace contains the imposing orchard house, with its rotating fruit pots of sixteen types of fruit, to one side of which is a carpet bed (2 x 18 metres) planted with small foliage plants in a formal star-and-diamond pattern typical of the 1870s. Carpet bedding is taken literally at Cragside: two of the beds mirror the design of floor-coverings in the house. In the formal beds some 6000 tulips are planted in autumn for spring colour. On the lower terrace is a cast-iron rose loggia built at Lord Armstrong's works and now planted colourfully. The walk back through the gorge impresses on the visitor the contrasting forces of wild romanticism and industrial technology which influenced this estate in equal measure. Two hundred rare North American coniferous species, given to the Trust by the Royal Botanic Gardens in Edinburgh, have been planted here. The climatic conditions and historic landscape of the property make it an ideal site for a collection of specimen conifers, which include *Abies magnifica* and *Pinus ponderosa*. It has to be said that the replanting and rerouting and all the infrastructure here subtract somewhat from the romance which must have characterised the original. Helpful leaflets.

Herterton House ★   7

Hartington, Cambo, Morpeth NE61 4BN. Tel: (01670) 774278

Frank and Marjorie Lawley • 11m E of Morpeth, 2m N of Cambo off B6342, signed 'Hartington' • Open April to Sept, daily except Tues and Thurs, 1.30 – 5.30pm • Entrance: £2.40, children £1 (under 5 free) (2001 price) ◑ WC ℗

The Lawleys took over this land and near-derelict Elizabethan building, with commanding views over picturesque upland Northumberland, in 1976. With vision and skill they have created four distinct areas. In front, a winter garden with tranquil vistas; alongside, a cloistered 'monastic' knot garden of mainly medicinal, occult and dye-producing herbs; and to the rear, their most impressive achievement, a flower garden with perceptively mingled hardy flowers chosen with an artist's eye. Many are unusual traditional plants (including many species from the wild) that flourish within the newly built sheltering walls. The fourth area, the Fancy Garden, is nearly ready, with the two-storey gazebo already open. A gem of a place.

Hexham Herbs   8

The Chesters Walled Garden, Chollerford, Hexham NE46 4BQ.
Tel: (01434) 681483

Kevin and Susie White • 5m N of Hexham, ½ m W of Chollerford on B6318 • Open March to Oct, daily, 10am – 5pm, reduced hours in winter. Also by appt • Entrance: £1.50, children (under 10) free (2001 prices) • Other information: Ices, cold drinks available. Possible for accompanied wheelchairs, but gravel paths ◑ ⓓ ℘ ⏢

The tall brick walls of the old kitchen garden slope gently south from the very line of Hadrian's Wall, echoing the Roman forts that lie to east and west. Within these ramparts, still with vestiges of the Victorian glasshouses and heating system, the Whites have fashioned a large herb collection (over 900 varieties), including most fittingly a unique Roman garden with plants (myrtle, etc.) identified by archaeologists through pollen analysis. A major feature is the National Collections of thymes and marjorams. A rose garden (over 60 species), extensive herbaceous borders (with some 1500 varieties) and terraced lawns against the architectural backdrop of Norman Shaw's Chesters mansion fill out this splendid intriguing 'fort'. A formal round pool with a fountain is set in a gravelled area with benches and a knot garden laid out in box and yew to William Lawson's design of 1617. A woodland walk with wild flowers and a secluded pond are also open.

Howick Hall ★   9

Howick, Alnwick NE66 3LB. Tel/Fax: (01665) 577285

Lord Howick of Glendale (Howick Trustees Ltd) • 6m NE of Alnwick, 2m N of Longhoughton, off B1339 • Open early April to Oct, daily, 1 – 6pm • Entrance: £2, children and concessions £1 (2001 prices) ◑ **WC** ⓓ

Acquired by the Grey family in 1319, the accident of woodland which sheltered this site from the blasts of the North Sea enabled Lord and Lady Grey to start building a fine collection of tender plants, which would do credit to a Scottish west-coast garden. Although the main house is unoccupied, Stephen Anderton describes the ambience as 'a genial lived-in garden of the best kind'. The lower terrace has a pond and excellent borders and the lawns run down through shrubs to a stream. Winding paths lead through shrubbery or parkland to Silverwood, under whose magnificent trees the visitor passes among numerous fine shrubs and woodland flowers planted by Lord and Lady Grey from 1931, the year of their silver wedding. There are good varieties of rhododendron and azalea, and outstanding species hydrangea (*H. villosa*) apart from other unusual varieties. A large pond-side garden is maturing well, with a great variety of moisture-loving plants making an impressive display. A catalogue of plants would be helpful. This is a plantsperson's garden, but there are many delights for the aesthete, such as the agapanthus of varying blues on the terrace. In early April visitors will be impressed by the spectacular view of drifts of daffodils in the meadow and parkland. One of the signed walks is the Long Walk, a one-and-a-half-mile path to the sea.

Loughbrow House 10

Hexham NE46 1RS. Tel: (01434) 603351; Fax: (01434) 609774

Mrs Kenneth Clark • 20m E of Newcastle, 1m S of Hexham. Take B6306 off Whitley Chapel road and at fork is brick lodge and long drive to house • Open 23rd June, 11th Aug, 2 – 5pm, and by appt at other times • Entrance: £2, children free ● � WC ⚘

There is a large terrace and lawn with inspirational ideas both for plantspersons and those who enjoy original design concepts. On the terrace is an interesting canal. Roses and shrubs. The two large herbaceous borders show the owner's colour concepts to great advantage, and beyond is a woodland garden, maturing well. Kitchen garden. A pond has been constructed and planted and the bog garden extended.

Mindrum 11

Cornhill-on-Tweed TD12 4QN. Tel: (01890) 850246

The Hon. P.J. Fairfax • 14m SW of Berwick-upon-Tweed. From A697 turn onto B6351 at Akeld, join B6352 towards Kirk Yetholm and continue 3m to Mindrum • Open for NGS and by appt • Entrance: £2 • Other information: Teas and plants for sale on open days only ● � WC ⚔ ⚘

From the nineteenth-century house built on flat ground there are fine views to the valley of the Bowmont Water (you can actually see the Scottish Borders to the south), and the creators of the three-acre garden have taken good advantage of the different levels of the site. From the lawn at the side of the house – over 90 metres above sea level – a path leads down a gentle slope to a walled garden with many flowering shrubs, roses and a fine white abutilon. Opposite this, and separated from it by a sage hedge, is a rose garden with yew hedges on the far sides. The path then descends steeply, winding down beside a small stream which tumbles over dramatic rocks into a still pool at the foot of the bank and joins a tributary of the Bowmont Water. The rocky bank above is densely planted with colourful perennials, shrub roses, many varieties of acer and golden yew, irises and candelabra primulas by the water – the whole a feast for the eyes. The tributary is crossed by wooden bridges which lead to the riverside walk. The far bank has rhododendrons, azaleas, acers, and planting still continues.

Northumberland College at Kirkley Hall 12

Ponteland NE20 0AQ. Tel: (01661) 860808; Fax: (01661) 860047

11m NW of Newcastle off A696, right at Ponteland on C151 for 2½ m. Signposted • Open April to Sept, daily, 10am – 3pm • Entrance: free ◐ ▤ ⚘ ▯ ℺

The 10-acre grounds with their three-acre Victorian walled garden form a showcase for all the gardening arts from propagation onwards. Inside the walls are climbers, borders and bedding plants in profusion, all pleasingly grouped. The grounds contain a succession of beds, skilfully shaped to follow the rolling contours of the land, each carefully composed for variety of profile and continuity of colour. Then to the hall with its array of beautifully planted containers on terraces down to a most attractive sunken garden and a wildlife pond. National Collections include beeches.

Nunwick ★   13

Simonburn, Hexham NE48 3AF.

Mrs L.G. Allgood • On B6320 8m NW of Hexham • Open for parties only, by appt in writing • Entrance: £2 • Other information: Teas and toilet facilities on open days only ☕

This is one of the most interesting gardens in a county full of remarkable ones. The house (not open) is described by Pevsner as perfect for its date (1760). It looks out over lawns and parkland, with fine trees which the owners have been meticulous in caring for and replacing when necessary. Walking down to the gardens (when the house was built it was fashionable to place these well away from the park) it is clear that the owners combine a clever sense of colour and shape with an interest in unusual plants. The herbaceous borders are cut back from their sheltering wall to ease maintenance, and there are fine beech hedges and shrub roses to provide shelter on the orchard side. The large Victorian walled kitchen garden is excellently maintained. Mrs Allgood experiments with varieties of vegetables – there were about 12 named potato varieties when our inspector visited. Good flowers, too, along the walks. Behind one wall is a small and elegant orangery containing a camellia over 100 years old. The other fascinating feature is the woodland path to the bog garden (*en route* note the stone wellhead), where the visitor first becomes aware of the owner's passion for hostas. The latter become evident again after crossing one of the rustic bridges over the burn and reaching the eighteenth-century Gothick kennels. Its four rooms, now open to the sky, house a spectacular collection of hostas, and the walls are planted with purple erinus, ivies of many kinds, toadflax and ferns. Trees and plants are well labelled. Back beside the house is a large collection of stone farm troughs with alpines, and a newly installed fountain. It is difficult to do justice in words to the charm of this garden, but it is a 'must' for anyone within miles of Hexham who can arrange an appointment – there will be interest all year round.

Seaton Delaval Hall   14

Seaton Sluice, Whitley Bay NE26 4QR. Tel: (0191) 237 1493/0786

Lord Hastings • 10m NE of Newcastle, ½ m inland from Seaton Sluice on A190 • Parts of house open together with coach house, stables and ice-house • Garden open 6th May, 3rd, 4th June; then Wed and Sun; July and Aug, Wed, Sun and 26th Aug; Sept, Wed, Sun; all 2 – 6pm • Entrance: £3, OAPs £2.50, children £1 ◑ ☕ WC ⚹ ⬦ 🏫 ⚲

The original grounds of this architectural masterpiece by Vanbrugh no doubt matched its magnificence, but little is known save for an early painting showing a swan lake. A notable weeping ash survives from that time, and there is a venerable and impressive rose garden, its beds outlined by box hedges 60 cm high and 30 cm wide. Since 1948 an excellent parterre has been laid out by Jim Russell, now embellished by a large Italianate pond and fountain. An attractive shrubbery (rhododendrons, azaleas, etc.), herbaceous borders and a laburnum walk have been established on the south side towards the fine Norman chapel. Replanting continues and the garden is obviously in good hands.

Wallington ★   15

Cambo, Morpeth NE61 4AR. Tel: (01670) 774283l; Fax: (01670) 774420; Website: www.ntnorth.demon.co.uk

The National Trust • 20m NW of Newcastle off A696 (signed on B6342) • House open April to Oct, daily, except Tues, 1 – 5.30pm (4.30pm in Oct; last admission ½ hour before closing) • Walled garden open April to Oct, daily, 10am – 7pm (Oct 6pm; or dusk if earlier); Nov to March, daily, 10am – 4pm. Grounds open all year, daily, during daylight hours • Entrance: £4.10, children £2.50 (house and grounds £5.70 children £2.85, family £14.25) • Other information: Self-drive scooters and guided tours available ○ 💭 ✗ 🍱 WC ⅃ ⟨⟩ 🌿 🏛 ♀

The handsome house is set in a 100-acre landscape of lawns, terraces (fine views) and flower beds – serene, quiet and essentially English – but it is the walled garden, quite some distance away across the entry road via an attractive woodland walk, which has the most appeal. A rill runs from the pond to narrow lawns fringed with beds on two levels, and climbers cluster in prodigal numbers on the lovely old walls. (Alas, two of the elegant statues that graced the balustrade were stolen and the rest removed for safe-keeping.) The sloping site reveals the layout and invites exploration of the harmonious and generously filled herbaceous border. There is a garden house designed in Tuscan style by Daniel Garrett; the Victorian peach house is now restored, and the spectacular Edwardian conservatory is home to many treasures, with a rich tapestry of colour at every turn. Outside, the walks step down from a classical fountain past beds re-designed by Lady Trevelyan in the 1930s, including notable heathers and many herbaceous perennials. Trees planted by the Duke of Atholl in 1738 include a great larch, the survivor of three, by the China Pond.

NOTTINGHAMSHIRE

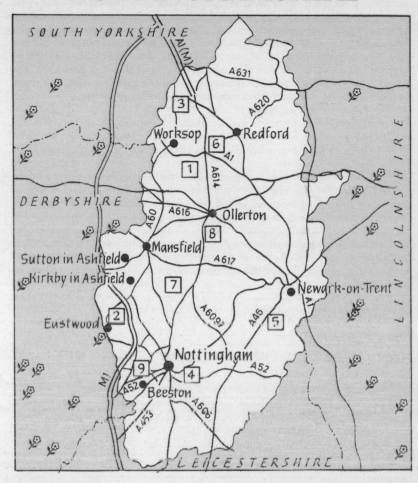

Clumber Park 1

Clumber Estate Office, Clumber Park, Worksop S80 3AZ. Tel: (01909) 476592

The National Trust • 4½ m SE of Worksop off A1 and A57, 11m from M1 junction 30 • Park open all year, daily during daylight hours, except 13th July, 17th Aug, 25th and 26th Dec • Walled kitchen garden open April to Sept, Wed, Thurs, 10.30am – 5.30pm, Sat, Sun and Bank Holiday Mons, 10.30am – 6pm • Entrance: 70p. Vehicle charge for park: cars £3.50, caravans and mini-coaches £4.50 • Other information: Wheelchairs, inc. those for children, available. Bicycles for hire. Chapel open (telephone for details) ○ 🍵 ✕ 📖 <u>WC</u>
♿ 🤲 🌸 🏛 🔦 ⚲

The park of 3800 acres was enclosed from Sherwood Forest in the eighteenth century, and the Dukes of Newcastle had their seat here. The garden was largely the creation of the 9th Earl of Lincoln (subsequently the 2nd Duke of Newcastle) in the second half of the eighteenth century, when he landscaped the park and laid out the pleasure ground, serpentine walks and shrubberies, possibly with advice from his architect Stephen Wright, and his friend and mentor Joseph Spence. Wright designed two temples and a bridge for the lake, which remain today. In 1824 William Sawrey Gilpin arrived on the scene, and created the Italianate terrace to the south of the house, island beds and picturesque walks in the pleasure ground. The two-mile-long lime avenue of 1838 and the Lincoln Terrace (now restored) of 1845 were completed by other hands. From the nineteenth century also are Charles Barry's stable block and clock tower and G. F. Bodley's ornate Gothic chapel built in the pleasure garden. Since the demolition of the great house in 1938 (Barry's being the last in the line), the chapel has become the focus of the garden. The Trust, with contributions from local authorities and the public, purchased the park in 1946 and has kept in good order the wide expanse of park, peaceful woods, open heath and rolling farmland with a superb serpentine lake at its heart. The vinery and palm house have been restocked and the extensive glasshouses (138 metres) are the best and longest in the Trust's properties. The kitchen garden exhibition of late nineteenth-century and early-twentieth-century tools is fascinating and reminds us that modern powered tools have taken much of the heavy work out of gardening. The walled kitchen garden contains an impressive herbaceous border as well as cut-flower, fruit and vegetable and herb borders, a collection of old varieties of apple trees and a working Victorian apiary. The cedar avenue has Atlantic cedars and sweet chestnut trees of breath-taking size.

Felley Priory ★ 2

Underwood NG16 5FL. Tel: (01773) 810230; Fax: (01773) 580440

The Hon. Mrs Chaworth Musters • ½ m from M1 junction 27. Take A608 signed 'Heanor' and 'Derby'. Garden on left • Garden and nursery open all year Tues, Wed and Fri, 9am – 12.30pm; March to Oct, second and fourth Weds in month, 9am – 4pm, and third Sun in month, 11am – 4pm; 14th April, 11am – 4pm for NGS. Also open for groups by appt • Entrance: £2, children free. Other information: NCCPG Plant Fairs 2nd June, 6th Oct, 12 noon – 4pm
🕐 ☕ WC ♿ 🌿 🐕 ♒

Despite the M1 being only half a mile away, the first impression is of a garden with quiet English countryside as a backdrop. The owners have, with the use of hedging, created several gardens within the one, the original ancient walls unifying the parts as well as providing shelter and support for many unusual and slightly tender bulbs, perennials, shrubs and climbers. The rose garden is a glorious sight in full bloom.

Hodsock Priory ★ 3

Blyth, Worksop S81 0TY. Tel: (01909) 591204; Fax: (01909) 591578

Sir Andrew and Lady Buchanan • 6m NE of Worksop, 2m W of A1 at Blyth off B6045 Blyth – Worksop road • Open 2nd Feb to 10th March, daily (weather permitting – telephone before travelling), 10am – 4pm • Entrance: £3, children free • Other information: Coaches must book. Hot refreshments. Dogs in park only ◑ ☕ ✕ WC ⅗ ⌀

An historic five-acre private garden with Grade-I-listed gatehouse c. 1500 and a dry moat, but open only in the winter for the Snowdrop Spectacular, which covers one and a half miles. The part-acid, part-neutral soil allows a wide range of plants, including 30 different ferns, and there is an unusual mix of garden styles. Fine trees include a huge variegated cornus, a very old catalpa (Indian bean), a tulip tree and a swamp cypress, and there is an interesting holm oak hedge. The walks beyond the small lake and bog garden and into the old moat are also accessible to the disabled. Three new arbours have been built, and the working Victorian apiary is now on show.

Holme Pierrepont Hall   4

Radcliffe–on–Trent NG12 2LF. Tel/Fax: (0115) 933 2371;
Website: www.holmepierreponthall.com

Mr and Mrs R. Brackenbury • 5m SE of Nottingham off A52/A6011. Continue past National Water Sports Centre for 1½ m • House open as garden • Garden open 31st March, 1st April, 5th, 6th, 26th, 27th May; then Thurs in June, Wed and Thurs in July, Tues – Thurs in Aug; all 2 – 5.30pm. Parties by appt all year, inc. evening visits • Entrance: £2 (house and garden £4, children £1) ◑ ☕ WC ⅗ ⌀ ⌂

The hall is a medieval brick manor house, but the listed garden and box parterre of 1875 have been restored by the present owners. The parterre is the outstanding feature of the gardens, and the herbaceous borders next to the York-stone path (replacing old rose beds) enhance the courtyard garden further. (The Jacob sheep are friendly lawnmowers.) The owners work hard with improvements and new plantings in this peaceful house and garden and willingly provide ample information. Their innovations include a winter garden, outer east garden, yews, shrubs and roses. Recent years have seen great improvements as the collection of plants, which includes medlars and quinces, matures and increases.

Mill Hill House   5

Elston Lane, East Stoke, Newark NG23 5QJ. Tel: (01636) 525460;
E-mail: millhill@talk21.com; Website: http://come.to/mill.hill.plants&garden

Mr and Mrs R.J. Gregory • 5m SW of Newark. Take A46, turn left into Elston Lane (signed 'Elston') and house is first on right • Open April to Oct, Fri – Sun and Bank Holiday Mons; Oct, Tues, 10am – 5.30pm, and for NGS. Parties and individuals welcome by appt • Entrance: £1.50, accompanied children free • Other information: Parking 100 metres past house in nursery ◑ ▦ WC ⌀ ⌀ ℺

A half-acre cottage garden generously filled with a wide variety of plants provides year-round interest and tranquillity. The garden is well screened from the road and visitors have often commented 'What a beautiful surprise' or 'One of the best kept secrets in Nottinghamshire'. Birds, bees and butterflies have no difficulty in finding it, however. This garden uplifts the spirit as it demonstrates how to overcome the problems of an exposed site. The plants provide a wealth of propagating material for the nursery, and the garden holds a National Collection of berberis.

Morton Hall 6

Ranby, Retford DN22 8HW. Tel: (01777) 702530

Lady Mason • 4m E of Worksop, 4m W of Retford. Entrance on A620/ southbound A1 link road • Open for charity 31st March, 12th May, 2nd June 20th Oct, 2 – 6pm • Entrance: £2.50 per car or £1.50 per person, whichever is least ◐ 🍵 🖳 WC ᕦ ⏛ ⚘ ⚘ ⚲

Within a relatively small park is a fine collection of mature and rare specimen trees and shrubs, planted over 100 years ago by the Mason family, all amateur botanists. The well-stocked nursery next to the gardens was started 30 years ago by Sir Paul and Lady Mason and is run by Mrs McMaster. The soil is sandy and poor but obviously suits the slightly more tender shrubs – romneyas thrive next to the house. Enjoy the rare and unusual and the colours in spring and autumn in this peaceful garden, but do not expect immaculate lawns and flower beds. The forestry walks feature some modern planting by William Mason, the present landowner.

Newstead Abbey ★ 7

Newstead Abbey Park, Nottingham NG15 8GE. Tel: (01623) 455900

Nottingham City Council • 11m N of Nottingham on A60 • Gardens open all year, daily, 9am – dusk, except last Fri in Nov. House with Byron memorabilia open April to Sept, 12 noon – 5pm (last admission 4pm) • Entrance: £4, children £2 ○ 🍵 ✕ 🖳 WC ᕦ ⏛ 🏛 ⚘

Water predominates in this estate which the poet Byron inherited but in which he could rarely afford to live. In most of the extensive and immaculate gardens there is much of interest. The Japanese gardens are justly famous and the rock and fern gardens worth visiting. Indeed, the waterfalls, wildfowl, passageways, grottos and bridges provide plenty of fun for children, but in addition there is an excellent, imaginatively equipped play area with bark mulch for safety. The tropical garden and the monks' stewpond are visually uninteresting but they are of laudable age. It is a pity that the large walled kitchen garden is now a rose garden – rose gardens, however pretty, are commonplace, but large kitchen gardens to the great houses are now rare. The old rose garden, now the iris garden, is in the process of development.

Rufford Country Park 8

Ollerton, Newark NG22 9DF. Tel: (01623) 822944; Fax: (01623) 825919; E-mail: marilyn.louden@nottscc.gov.uk; Website: www.ruffordcraftcentre.org.uk

Nottinghamshire County Council • 9m NE of Mansfield, 2m S of Ollerton on A614 • Rufford Abbey Cistercian area open • Park open all year, daily, dawn – dusk • Entrance: free. Parking charge from April to Dec at weekends and Bank

Holidays, and through school holidays in summer • Other information: Four wheelchairs available for pre-booking. ○ ⬛ ✕ 🍴 <u>WC</u> ♿ ⬥ 🐾 🏛 💡 ℚ

This contains almost everything that might be expected of an important country park, e.g. lake, lime avenues, mature cedars, etc. A visit to the eight themed gardens within the formal gardens is well worthwhile, and there is now a rose garden in front of the abbey ruins. Large areas are managed with wildlife in mind, but ball games are allowed on the lawns beneath cut-leaved beeches and cedars. The Reg Hookway arboretum, established in 1983, has a good collection of oaks and birches – all well labelled.

Wollaton Park   9

Nottingham NG8 2AE. Tel: (0115) 915 3900

Nottingham City Council • W of city centre on A609. From M1 junction 25 take A52, turn left onto A614 and left onto A609 • Natural history museum in hall open Mar to Nov, daily, 11am – 5pm. Closed 24th to 26th Dec, and 1st Jan. Free except small charge on Sun and Bank Holidays • Garden open all year, daily, dawn to dusk • Entrance: free but small charge for parking ○ ⬛ 🍴 <u>WC</u> ♿ ⬥ 🏛 💡

This large park and garden – the setting for Smythson's masterpiece – is surrounded by the city, but because of its size the visitor feels deep in the country, although near the park periphery the roar of traffic dispels that illusion. The polyanthus in spring are spectacular, as is the summer bedding, where castor-oil plants and ornamental cabbages have their place in the schemes. The formal gardens at the top of the hill afford views of huge cedars and holm oaks, lime avenues and the deer in the park.

GUIDANCE ON SYMBOLS

Wheelchair users: The symbol ♿, denoting suitability for wheelchairs, refers to the garden only – if there is a house open, it may or may not be suitable. Additionally, some areas in the garden may not be accessible by wheelchair, or may require assistance.

Dogs: ⬥ indicates that there is somewhere on the premises where dogs may be walked, preferably on a lead. The garden itself is often taboo – parkland, or even the car park, are frequently indicated for the purpose.

Picnics: 🍴 means that picnics are allowed, but usually in certain restricted areas only. It does not give visitors the all-clear to feast where they please!

Children-friendly: the symbol ℚ suggests that there are activities specifically designed for children, such as an adventure playground, or that the garden itself is a place they would instinctively enjoy.

OXFORDSHIRE

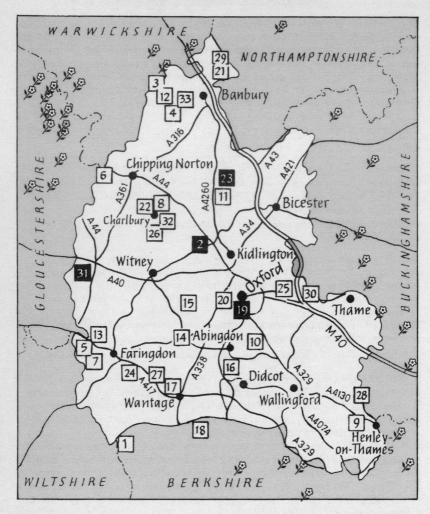

Two-starred gardens are marked on the map with a black square.

Ashdown House 1

Lambourn, Newbury, Berkshire RG16 7RE. Tel: (01488) 72584 (Estate Office)

The National Trust • 9m E of Swindon, 3½ m NW of Lambourn on W side of B4000 • House (hall, stairway and roof) open by guided tour only, Wed – Sat, starting at 2.15, 3.15 and 4.15pm • Garden open April to Oct, Wed and Sat only, 2 – 5pm. Woodlands open all year, Sat – Thurs, dawn – dusk. Parties must pre-book in writing • Woodlands free (house £1.50). No reduction for parties • Other information: Parking 250 metres from house ● 📖 ⅄ ℺

Seen from the main road, the exquisite hunting lodge built by the first Lord Craven for Elizabeth of Bohemia appears to have a tall central section complete with cupola flanked by two lower wings. It is only when the visitor approaches the front entrance that it becomes obvious that the wings are quite separate from the central block. The remains of a large formal park are present in a western lime avenue, and a complementary lime avenue planted in 1970 to the north of the house is maturing well; the avenue west of the parterre has been replanted. A.H. Brookholding-Jones's appropriately intricate parterre was laid out in the 1950s; the avenue west of the parterre has been replanted. In spring thousands of snowdrops, naturalised in the avenue and woodland, are at their showiest.

Blenheim Palace ★★ 2

Woodstock, Oxford OX20 1PX. Tel: (01993) 811091

The Duke of Marlborough • 8m NW of Oxford. At Woodstock on A44 • House open as garden • Park open all year, daily except 25th Dec, from 9am. Garden open mid-March to Oct, 10.30am – 5.30pm (last admission 4.45pm) • Entrance: park only (inc. herb garden, butterfly house, train and nature trail): pedestrians £2, children £1, cars inc. occupants £6. Gardens only £3.50 (house and gardens £9.50, OAPs £7.30, children £4.50) (2001 prices) • Park: ○ 📖 ⅄ ◁ 🍴 ☕ *Garden:* ◐ 🥤 ✕ WC ⅄ ℺

The visitor who walks through Hawksmoor's Triumphal Arch into Blenheim Park sees one of the greatest contrived landscapes in Britain. The architect Vanbrugh employed Bridgeman and Henry Wise, Queen Anne's master gardener and the last of the British formalists. Wise constructed a bastion-walled 'military' garden, laid out kitchen gardens, planted immense elm avenues and linked Vanbrugh's bridge to the sides of the valley. The gardens were ready when the first Duke of Marlborough moved into the palace in 1719. Major alterations were made by the 4th, 5th and 9th Dukes, one of the earliest of which was the grassing-over of Wise's formal gardens by 'Capability' Brown after 1764. Brown also landscaped the park, installing the lake and cascade, and removed Wise's military garden. The gardens include formal areas designed by Achille Duchêne early this century to replace those grassed by Brown. He made formal gardens to the east and west, the latter as two water terraces in the Versailles style. To the east of the palace is the elaborate Italian garden of patterned box and golden yew, interspersed with various seasonal plantings. To the south-west from the terraces are the rose garden and arboretum. From the vast south lawn 'one passes through a magnificent grove of cedars... part shrubberies of laurel and an exedra of box and yew, the whole exemplifying the Victorian pleasure grounds', in the words of the *Oxford Companion*. In 1991, as a contribution to the celebration of the 300th anniversary of the replanting of the maze at Hampton Court, the Duke planted a maze which is maturing well in part of the kitchen garden; in a few years it should provide visitors with a puzzling and pleasurable experience. The former garden centre has been redeveloped as a lavender and herb garden.

Brook Cottage ★ 3

Well Lane, Alkerton, Banbury OX15 6NL. Tel: (01295) 670303/670590

Mrs D. Hodges • 6m NW of Banbury. From A422 Banbury – Stratford-upon-Avon road, turn W signed to Alkerton. With small war memorial on right, turn left into Well Lane and right at fork • Open April to Oct, Mon – Fri, 9am – 6pm. Weekends, evenings and all group visits by appt only • Entrance: £3, OAPs £2, children free • Other information: Refreshments for parties must be pre-booked. DIY tea/coffee/biscuits daily for individual visitors. Unusual plants for sale ◗ ➌ ➍ WC ⬱ ⬧ ℺

A four-acre garden of genuine originality, created since 1964 as a series of interconnecting informal enclosures, all of them intensively planted. It is the work of a plantswoman and an architect who together have embraced Alexander Pope's credo, 'Consult the Genius of the Place in all', for the garden is moulded to the topography of the steeply sloping, west-facing site. Once past the terrace below the house, slivers of paths force visitors into single file, making their emergence onto open lawn above the stream and lower pond all the more exciting. Here, the planting is bold and confident, grouped tellingly in individual clumps or in beds with skilful combinations of colour. In the bog garden a splendidly broad band of foliage plants contrasts with feathery or piercing flower spikes. The hanging garden of shrub roses is the garden's most famous feature in its season, but for those who wish to see a profusion of plants, many of them rare, disposed in a masterly way, Brook Cottage is a living workshop of ideas at all times of year.

Broughton Castle ★ 4

Broughton, Banbury OX15 5EB. Tel: (01295) 276070;
Website: www.broughtoncastle.demon.co.uk

Lord Saye and Sele • 2½ m SW of Banbury on B4035 • Castle open • Garden open 31st March, 1st April, 5th, 6th May; then 19th May to 11th Sept, Wed, Sun and Bank Holiday Mons; also Thurs in July and Aug, all 2 – 5pm. Also by appt for parties all year • Entrance: £4.50, OAPs and students £4, children £2 • Other information: Teas on open days only. Refreshments for parties by arrangement ◗ ➌ ✕ ➍ WC ⬥ ⬱ ⬧ ⌂ ℺

More of a house than a castle, with gardens that are unexpectedly domestic within the confines of the moat. In 1900 there were 14 gardeners, now there is one maintaining the overall splendour. The most important changes were made after 1969 following a visit from Lanning Roper, who suggested opening up the views across the park. There are now two magnificent borders, where great planting skill is evident in the serpentine flows of colour. The west-facing border, backed by the battlement wall, is based on blues and yellows, greys and whites, the other on reds, mauves and blues. On the south side is the walled 'ladies' garden' with box-edged, fleur-de-lys-shaped beds holding floribunda roses. Another wonderful border rises up to the house wall. Everywhere is a profusion of old-fashioned roses and original planting.

Buscot Park ★ 5

Faringdon SN7 8BU. Tel: (01367) 240786; Fax: (01367) 241794;
E-mail: estbuscot@aol.com: Website: www.buscot-park.com

Administered by Lord Faringdon on behalf of The National Trust • On A417
between Lechlade and Faringdon • House open 29th March to 29th Sept, Wed to
Fri, plus several weekends, all 2 – 6pm • Garden open 29th March to 29th Sept
Mon (including Bank Holiday Mons) and Tues, all 2 – 6pm • Entrance: £4,
children £2 (house and grounds £5, children £2.50) • Other information: Teas
available when house open and on Bank Holiday Mons ◑ 🏠 🥤 WC

Although the house was built in 1780, the garden was developed during the
twentieth century. The water-garden-within-a-wood was created by Harold
Peto in 1912; later, avenues linking lake to house were cut through,
branching out from a goose-foot near the house, with fastigiate and weeping
varieties of oak, beech and lime. The Egyptian avenue created by Lord
Faringdon in 1969 is guarded by sphinxes and embellished with Coade-stone
statues copied from an original from Hadrian's Villa. Two new gardens at
allée intersections the Swinging Garden and the Citrus Bowl provide
enclosed areas of great charm. The large walled kitchen garden was rearranged in the mid-1980s, and is now intersected by a pleached avenue of
ostrya (hop hornbeam) and a Judas tree tunnel. Deep borders under the
outside walls have unusual and skilled planting by Tim Rees, mixing old roses
and climbing vegetables (gourds, marrows, beans, cucumbers) which lay
themselves out over the rose bushes after their flowering is over. Walkways
both outside and inside the kitchen garden are between wide borders which
use the exterior and interior walls and trellises as screens. In the latter the
planting by the late Peter Coats and imaginative development by Lord
Faringdon is exceptionally effective. The small garden at *Buscot Old Parsonage*,
also a Trust property, has different opening times.

Chastleton House 6

Chastleton GL56 0SU. Tel: (01608) 674355; Fax: (01608) 674355

The National Trust • 6m NE of Stow-on-the-Wold off A436 • Open 27th March
to 28th Sept, daily, 1 – 5pm (last admission 4pm), 2nd Oct to 2nd Nov, 1 –
4pm (last admission 3pm). Ticket numbers retricted and prospective visitors
strongly advised to telephone in advance. Pre-booked guided tours available
Wed am, price £7 (incl, NT members). Groups of 11 – 25 by prior appt only. •
Entrance: £5.40, children £2.70, family ticket £13.50 (2001 prices) • Other
information: No large coaches. Parking 270 metres from house – telephone for
details of parking for disabled. Braille guide available ◑ 🥤 WC ♿ 🐕

The house was somewhat in disarray when it was in private hands, but the
Trust has sensitively retained the atmosphere of genteel decay. The garden,
which was at its peak in the early twentieth century and survived more or less
intact until the 1960s, has been treated in the same spirit. The impressive
topiary, probably a Victorian re-creation of a seventeenth-century design, still
makes an emphatic statement; the rest provides a pleasant setting for the

enchanted house. The rules of modern croquet were first codified at Chastleton and one of the original lawns has been restored. At *Chastleton Glebe* Prue Leith's garden is usually open one day a year for the NGS.

Clock House 7

Coleshill, Swindon, Wiltshire SN6 7PT. Tel: (01793) 762476

Denny Wickham and Peter Fox • 3½ m SW of Faringdon on B4019 • Open 19th May, 23rd June, 15th Sept, 6th Oct; April to Oct, Thurs; all 2 – 5pm (closes 8pm in June); also by appt • Entrance: £1.50, children free • Other information: Teas in courtyard in fine weather ◕ ☕

Situated on a hillside with inspiring views over the Vale of the White Horse, this exuberant, delightful garden was created by the present owners in the last 40 years in the grounds of Coleshill House (burned, then demolished in the 1950s). The ground-plan of the original house is planted out in box and lavender, to show the layout of walls and windows. The gravel 'rooms' are full of self-sown poppies in June and *Verbena bonariensis* in late July. There is a courtyard with a collection of plants in pots, and a sunny walled garden in the old laundry-yard with roses and mixed planting and a fine greenhouse. The lime avenue at the front of the house sweeps down to the views, and a pond and terrace are sheltered by tall shrubs. The mixed herbaceous borders are filled with interesting and unusual plants. This is an original garden, designed by an artist, with a large collection of plants in imaginative settings.

Gothic House ★ 8

Charlbury, Chipping Norton OX7 3PP, Tel: (01608) 810654

Mr and Mrs Andrew Lawson • In centre of Charlbury on B4022 Witney – Enstone road • Open 7th July, 2 – 6pm, for NGS, and for parties by appt • Entrance £2.50, children 50p ◕

A third-of-an-acre walled town garden, designed by one of the country's leading garden photographers and his sculptress wife. Artistic flair is evident everywhere, from the intriguingly furnished conservatory to the dead tree painted electric-blue. There are different inspirations each year – in 2001 it was a chess-board arrangement of squares set into gravel which included a charming box-edged pool, a wigwam, two thyme squares, naturalistic planting in greys and purples, and an assemblage of pots. An imaginatively planted broad border leads through to the rear garden, which is dignified by espaliered fruit trees alongside a pleached lime walk and has many artful touches. *Objets trouvés* amid the foliage and the whole effect delightful. Briony Lawson's sculptures are everywhere, numbered and for sale. Regular visitors find inspiration here year on year. The garden is open jointly with The Priory (see entry).

Greys Court ★ 9

Rotherfield Greys, Henley-on-Thames RG9 4PG. Tel: (01491) 628529

The National Trust • W of Henley-on-Thames, E of B481. From town centre take A4130 towards Oxford. At Nettlebed mini-roundabout take B481. Signposted to left shortly after Highmoor • House open 27th March to 27th Sept, Wed – Fri and Bank Holiday Mons, 2 – 6pm. Closed 29th March • Gardens open April to Sept, Tues – Sat, and Bank Holiday Mons, 2 – 6pm (last admission 5.30pm). Closed 13th April • Entrance: £3.20, children £1.60, family ticket £8 (house and garden £4.80, children £2.40, family ticket £11.20) • Other information: Plants for sale on certain days only. Picnics in car park only ◐ 🍽 WC & 🍴

The statue symbolising St Fiacre, the protector of gardeners and commemorating Charles Taylor, a former head gardener, stands modestly in this beautiful garden, or several gardens, set against the ruins of a fourteenth-century fortified house. The largest area, an orchard, is divided by lines of morello cherries and parallel hedges of *Rosa mundi*. An ancient wisteria forms a canopy over a walled area, approached on one side through a tunnel of wisterias and *Robinia hispida*. The impeccably kept peony bed and rose garden glow against the ancient walls. Beyond the kitchen garden – now an ornamental garden of unusual vegetables – across the nut avenue, is the grass Archbishop's Maze, interesting for its symbolism. Donkey wheel and restored ice-house open.

The Harcourt Arboretum 10

Nuneham Courtenay, Oxford OX44 9PX. Tel: (01865) 343501; Fax: (01865) 341828

Oxford University Botanic Garden • 6m S of Oxford off A4074 • Open all year except 29th March to 1st April and 22nd Dec to 4th Jan: May to Oct, daily, 10am – 5pm; Nov to April, Mon – Fri, 10am – 4.30pm • Entrance: free, but £2 car parking charge • Other information: No coaches (_) 🚌

The village and church of Nuneham were demolished in the 1670s to make way for a classical landscape to be seen from the house; Oliver Goldsmith's poem *The Deserted Village*, written in 1770, may be based on that upheaval. Horace Walpole, in 1780, described the gardens, designed by 'Capability' Brown and William Mason (the poet-gardener), as the most beautiful in the world. The garden was then full of flowers, not only along the walks, but in carefully planted beds. This 85-acre site, now owned by Oxford University Botanic Garden, dates from 1835 when the Harcourt family, who owned the Nuneham estate at the time, planted a pinetum. Many of those plantings are now magnificent mature specimens underplanted with camellias, rhododendrons, bamboos, magnolias and a collection of acers. There is also a 10-acre bluebell wood and a 22-acre meadow.

Hill Court 11

Tackley. (Enquiries to Court Farm, Tackley, Kidlington OX5 3AQ.
Tel: (01869) 331221)

Mr and Mrs Andrew C. Peake • 9m N of Oxford, off A4260. From Oxford turn opposite Sturdy's Castle; from S turn off at Tackley sign • Open 8th, 9th June, 2 – 6pm • Entrance: £2, children free ● ● WC & ♨

A two-acre, sixteenth-century walled garden formerly attached to the house, which was demolished *c.* 1960. Remains of the manor house, also demolished, can be seen across the park, which dates from 1787. The garden, the design of which was influenced by Russell Page, is unusual because it is terraced uphill from the entrance. The rose beds were removed a decade ago and the sensitive and original planting which replaced them is the work of Rupert Golby.

Home Farm 12

Balscote, Banbury OX15 6JP. Tel: (01295) 738194

Mr and Mrs G.C. Royle • 5m W of Banbury, ½ m off A422 • Open March to Oct by appt, and on NGS open days with other village gardens • Entrance: £2 • Other information: Teas on open days only, otherwise light refreshments if pre-booked ● ● WC & ⬤

This sophisticated hilltop garden of half an acre has been created by the Royles since 1984 from a farmyard on a gently sloping site, with soft pastoral views of grazing sheep. There is nothing mimsy here. Mrs Royle has a firm way of using colour, and the garden is abundantly planted with unusual flowering shrubs, bulbs, herbaceous plants, alpines and roses – designed to give all-year interest, with a special love of coloured or contrasting foliage.

Kelmscott Manor 13

Kelmscott, Lechlade, Gloucestershire GL7 3HJ. Tel: (01367) 252486

The Society of Antiquaries • 2m E of Lechlade in Kelmscott • House open as garden • Garden open April to Sept, Wed, 11am – 1pm, 2 – 5pm, first Sat of July and Aug, and third Sat of each month, 2 – 5pm. Tours for parties by appt on Thurs and Fri • Entrance: house and garden £7, children/students £3.50 ● ● ✕ ▣ WC & ⬤ ⚲

Described by *Country Life* as a magical house in a remarkably unchanged village, its strange atmosphere will be relished by those who are attracted by William Morris in particular, or the Pre-Raphaelite Brotherhood in general. The magazine says the impression one forms of all Morris's gardens is that they had an unruly beauty where weeds might well have been encouraged if they were decorative. Above all the choice of flowers was essentially artistic and romantic because, for him, gardens were places of magic and mystery, fairytale worlds where lovers met under rose-covered arbours. The present owners have tried to re-create some of that romanticism – what Morris himself described as 'a heaven on earth... and such a garden! Close down on the river, a boat house and all things handy.'

Kingston Bagpuize House 14

Kingston Bagpuize, Abingdon OX13 5AX. Tel: (01865) 820259; Fax: (01865) 821659; Website: www.kingstonbagpuizehouse.org.uk

Mr and Mrs Francis Grant • 5½ m W of Abingdon at junction off A415 and A420. At entrance to village, park by large ornamental gates • Open 17th, 24th Feb, 3rd, 17th, 31st March, 1st, 7th, 20th, 21st April, 5th, 6th, 19th May, 3rd, 4th, 9th, 16th, 30th June, 7th, 20th, 21st, 28th July, 4th, 25th, 26th, 28th Aug, 7th, 8th, 11th, 21st, 22nd Sept, 13th Oct, 10th Nov; all 2 – 5pm. Open to groups by appt all year. Guided tours available • Entrance: £2 (house and garden £4, OAPs £3.50, children (5–15) £2.50 • Other information: Home-made teas. Meals available for groups by arrangement ◐ � WC ⚅ ⚘ ♨ ⚑*

Miss Marlie Raphael, an enthusiastic and much-travelled plant collector, owned the seventeenth- and eighteenth-century house from 1939 until her death in 1976. With the help of Sir Harold Hillier and other friends, she created a 15-acre garden with its mind-boggling variety of rare and unusual trees, shrubs and plants. Since inheriting the house in 1995, the present owners have most successfully uncovered and restored much of Miss Rapael's original planting, adding to it with their own complementary and innovative ideas. Within the framework of mellow brick walls and hedges of yew, beech and laurel (and even of senecio!), there is an air of relaxed informality, the plants thriving in the exceptionally fertile greensand soil. An enormous mixed border 10 metres deep is packed with tall perennials, many self-sown, covering a broad spectrum of harmonious colours. At every turn in the three-acre woodland garden are rare and interesting trees and shrubs, including several magnolias. Many of them are quite spectacular, and beneath the jungle canopy are carpets of snowdrops and other bulbs, followed by drifts of geraniums, astrantias, campanulas, vincas, hellebores, lilies and other shade-loving perennials. Along the edge of the Garden Park with its beech avenue, Wellingtonias and other specimen trees, the shrub border reveals yet more rarities. The terrace walk has a growing cistus collection and provides an excellent vantage point from which to enjoy a view of the house and different aspects of the garden, which is planned to give colour and interest throughout the year.

Manor House ★ 15

Stanton Harcourt, Witney OX29 5RJ. Tel: (01865) 881928; Answerphone/Fax: (01865) 880117

Mr and The Hon. Mrs Gascoigne • 9m W of Oxford, 5m SE of Witney off B4449 • House open • Garden open 31st March, 1st, 11th, 14th, 25th, 28th April, 2nd, 5th, 6th, 16th, 19th, 30th May, 2nd, 3rd, 13th, 16th, 27th, 30th June, 11th, 14th, 25th, 28th July, 8th, 11th, 22nd, 25th, 26th Aug, 5th, 8th, 19th, 22nd Sept, all 2 – 6pm • Entrance: £3, OAPs and children under 12 £2 (house and garden £5, OAPs and children £3) ◑ ▬ WC ⚅ ♨

Twelve acres of gardens incorporated in and around the ruins of a fourteenth- and fifteenth-century manor house. An avenue of clipped yew leads from the house to the chapel, and there are herbaceous and rose borders, with clematis, hydrangeas and roses clambering up the magnificent old walls. The kitchen garden has been redesigned as a formal rose garden, using David Austin's New English roses, espaliered apple trees, and a fountain in the middle. The stewponds are sadly low in water, but covered with water lilies in high summer and fringed with water-loving plants, and are crossed by some enchanting old bridges. It would take an army of gardeners to keep this garden immaculate, so enjoy it for its nostalgic atmosphere and history, magnificent walls and urns, and romantic paths winding through nut-walks underplanted with bulbs and primulas in the spring. Don't miss the teas in the medieval kitchens. For contrast, see a completely different kind of garden, more of a museum really, a walled garden laid out as it was in Victorian times, at *Cogges Manor Farm Museum* between Witney and the A40 to the south. All produce is organic. Various events and plenty for the kids, too.

The Mill House   16

Sutton Courtenay, Abingdon OX14 4NH. Tel: (01235) 848219;
Fax: (10235) 848959

Mrs Jane Stevens • 1½ m S of Abingdon off B4016. Leave town over river bridge, entrance gates in main street opposite Fish pub • Open 8th April, 10th June, 23rd Sept, 2 – 6pm, and at other times by appt for parties of 10 or more • Entrance: £2, children £1, under 4 free, parties £4 per person ● ● WC & ℺

Although the stone house behind high walls suggests promise, the romantic experience of the garden cannot be guessed at as the visitor approaches it through the winding main street of the village. Of course, few gardeners have the gift of the Thames in their territory, but the present owner has made remarkable us of it. She had the benefit of a structure laid out by Colonel Peter Laycock, a colleague of Eric Savill, who planted some splendid trees around the ruined paper mill, and she has added highly imaginative touches of her own – like the circles of comfrey. This is a garden to be walked in, sat in and savoured, so do not attempt to rush around the eight and a half acres. There are formal areas on either side of the early Georgian house, but once past these, the wanderer will be lost in a sylvan idyll amongst the water, trees and groves. There are three islands, planted with a mass of wild flowers, and seasonal interest comes from the fine bulbs in spring, old-fashioned roses in summer, and charming autumn colours. For those who like to conjure up dreams of previous owners, Herbert and Margot Asquith lived here before 1916 while he was Prime Minister and entertained all the great figures of the day for Fridays-to-Mondays weekends. The nearby *Manor House*, with a garden by Norah Lindsay, is open once a year, usually mid-May, for the NGS.

Old Church House   17

2 Priory Road, Wantage, Berkshire OX12 9DD. Tel: (01235) 762785

Dr and Mrs Dick Squires • Near Wantage Market Square next to parish church and opposite Vale and Downland Museum • Open April to Oct, Tues – Sat, 10.30am – 4.30pm, Sun, 2 – 5pm. Private visits by appt • Entrance: £1 or donation to charity (tickets available at Museum). Children welcome • Other information: Park in nearby public car park. Refreshments and toilet facilities at Museum ◑ 📚 ♿

An unusual and exciting town garden running down to Letcombe Brook. Dr and Mrs Squires have transformed his childhood garden into a series of rooms leading away from the existing lawns and mature trees. There is a sunken water garden, a Mediterranean garden, a pergola garden and a wild garden, all filled with unusual plants and shrubs, follies and highly imaginative building. It is an inspiration to see what can be achieved in less than three years. Some fascinating documentation shows the development of the planning and the work itself in before-and-after style.

The Old Rectory ★   18

Farnborough, Wantage OX12 8NX. Tel: (01488) 638298

Mr and Mrs Michael Todhunter • 4m SE of Wantage off B4494 • Open 21st April, 12th May, 23rd June, for NGS, 2 – 6pm, and by written appt • Entrance: £2, children free on open days, and £5 by appt • Other information: Teas nearby on charity open days and for parties ● WC ♿ ✿

At nearly 250 metres, and despite being prey to winds from the Downs, this four-acre site has been created over 30 years on a good original structure of large trees and hedges, with magnificent views. Deep, parallel herbaceous borders are backed by yew hedges. The planting by the front of house is subtle and effective, and smaller areas have been laid out for sun- or shade-loving plants. Woodland contrasts with shrubs and lawns, and the fast-growing arboretum now contains over 100 trees. The swimming pool is surrounded by a large *Hydrangea sargentiana* and potted lilies, with mixed roses and clematis around the outside walls. There is a collection of old roses and small-flowered clematis, and wild flowers line the front lawn by the ha-ha. The tennis court has been turned into a *boule à drôme* – a place in the middle to play boule – with four large beds, pretty wrought-iron gates and a gazebo. Those who like John Betjeman's poetry will be interested to know that he lived here from 1945 to 1950 and can look for the ghost of Miss Joan Hunter Dunn in the shrubberies. A John Piper window in the church is in his memory.

Oxford Botanic Garden ★★   19

**Rose Lane, Oxford OX1 4AZ. Tel: (01865) 286690,
E-mail: postmaster@botanic-garden.ox.ac.uk**

University of Oxford • In city centre opposite Magdalen College near bridge • Open all year, daily: April to Sept, 9am – 5pm (glasshouses 10am – 4.30pm); Oct to March, 9am – 4.30pm (glasshouses 10am – 4pm). Closed 29th March and 25th Dec • Entrance: April to Aug £2, children under 12 free; Sept to March by donation to collecting box • Other information: Professional photography and music prohibited ○ 📚 **WC** ♿ ✿ ☕

This is the oldest botanic garden in Britain and one of the most attractive to the general visitor. Nowhere else on earth, it is claimed, are there so many different plants in four and a half acres, 8000 species in all, and representatives of over 90 per cent of families of flowering plants. Founded in 1621 for physicians' herbal requirements, it is surrounded by a high wall and entered through a splendid gateway by Nicholas Stone. One yew survives from the early plantings, and there is a series of beds containing herbaceous and annual plants in systematic and labelled groups. The old walls back beds with tender plants, including roses and clematis. To the left are the greenhouses, modern ones replacing those built in 1670. A rock garden has been renovated, as has the bog garden and late summer/ autumn borders. A National Collection of euphorbias is held here. The site amply justifies its original purpose 'to promote learning and glorify the works of God'. Outside the front entrance is a large rose garden donated by Americans in memory of those university staff who developed penicillin. Several miles away at Nuneham Courtenay (south of the A423) is the Harcourt Arboretum (see entry) opened in 1968. Guided tours of both gardens are held on summer evenings in June, July and August – contact the Botanic Garden for details.

Oxford College Gardens 20

Most colleges are helpful about access to their gardens, although the more private ones, such as the Master's or Fellows', are rarely open. Specific viewing times are difficult to rely on because some colleges prefer not to have visitors in term time or on days when a function is taking place. The best course is to ask at the porter's lodge or to telephone ahead of visit. However, it is fair to say that some Oxford college gardens will always be open to the visitor, by arrangement with porters, even if others are closed on that particular day. Some colleges have a policy of allowing public entrance on official guided tours only and others now make a charge for entry.

Amongst the college gardens of particular interest are the following: *Christ Church*: the War Memorial Gardens on St. Aldate's, with its attractive herbaceous borders, and, just beyond, the rose garden with its water feature, are open daily except 25th Dec (Mon–Sat, 9am – 5.30pm, Sun, 11.30am – 5.30pm). So are the splendid Christ Church Meadows, with the herd of Old English Longhorns resident in summer and autumn months. Most of the other gardens – Masters', Cathedral and Pocock – are open once a year, usually mid-Aug, for the NGS, allowing a sight of the Oriental plane planted in 1636 and of the Cheshire Cat's horse chestnut tree – a reminder of the college's connection with Lewis Carroll. WC ⟨⟩ ☕ *Corpus Christi*: the smallest college, with an attractive small garden overlooking Christ Church Meadow [normally open 1.30 – 4pm]. *Exeter*: Fellows' Garden [open most days, 2 – 5pm] is walled on all sides with part of boundary formed by the old Bodleian Library and Divinity Schools. The mound at the end gives excellent views across Radcliffe Square with the Camera, Church of St Mary the Virgin and All Souls College all clearly visible. Visitors are requested to keep to the paths. Herbaceous borders, shrubs and mature trees. Also the Rector's private garden [open for NGS in conjunction with New College Warden's Garden one Sun in late June/early July, 2 – 5pm]. *Green College*: alas this institution with its environmental name is only open to the public once a year. *Holywell Manor*, part of Balliol: a restful, well-maintained garden of one acre [Open 10.30am – 6.30pm]. *Kellogg College*: an unusual and pleasant inner courtyard with three separate walled gardens at the back situated in Rewley House, Wellington Square [Open all year – telephone (01865) 270360 WC ⟨⟩]. *Lady Margaret Hall*: eight formal

and informal acres, mainly designed by the Victorian architect Blomfield, who was also responsible for some of the buildings. Fine specimen trees and good borders [Open 2 – 6pm or dusk if earlier. All visitors are requested to call at the porter's lodge &]. *Magdalen College*: 100 acres of meadows including a deer park adjacent to the college buildings and Fellows' Garden (open to the public). The water meadows bounded by the River Cherwell and circled by Addison's Walk, named after the eighteenth-century essayist and garden enthusiast, are famous for the display of fritillaries in April [College and gardens open nearly all year, 2 – 6pm (12 noon – 6pm, July to Sept). Refreshments sometimes available ⍩ WC &].
New College: admirers of the writings of Robin Lane Fox will be able to see examples of his plantings, outstanding mixed borders against Oxford city wall, rose borders, cloister garden. The mound was completed in 1649. [Open Easter to Oct at New College Lane Gate, 11am – 5pm; winter at Holywell Gate, 2 – 4pm].
Nuffield: formal gardens in two quadrangles with water features [Open Mon – Fri, 9am – 5pm, but closed Christmas, Easter and August Bank Holiday. No large parties]. *Queen's*: a garden with a fourteenth-century history, today pleasantly modernised. Good herbaceous borders in the Fellows' Garden [Open once a year for charity, but not to casual visitors during year except those on guided tours through the Information Centre]. *Rhodes House*: not a college and not a pretty building but an unexpectedly pleasant garden behind [9am – 5pm weekdays only].
St Catherine's: in the midst of so much ancient charm in garden design it is pleasing to be able to recommend a modern garden (1960–4) created by the distinguished Danish architect Arne Jacobsen (1902–71). Noted for his concern for integrating building and landscape, this is a remarkable example. It has a fine water feature, and John Brookes says that, later in the season, when the water planting is at its best, the canal comes into its own – there is a marvellous transition throughout the building to a little floating platform which gives onto a beautiful three-dimensional concept. [Open except Easter, Aug and Christmas]. *St Hilda's*: five acres of lawns and beds; flood plain meadow with interesting wild flowers [Open one Sun in March, 2 – 5pm for NGS]. *St Hugh's*: an interesting 10-acre garden largely created by Annie Rogers, a Fellow. [All visitors are requested to call at the porter's lodge &]. *St John's*: landscaped in the eighteenth century and still immaculately kept. Striking in spring when bulbs in flower. William Pye has designed a new water sculpture. See also the new Garden Quad, opened in 1993, designed by MacCormac Jamieson & Pritchard and described as 'one of the most important buildings of the 'nineties anywhere in Britain' [Open daily, 1 – 5pm or dusk if earlier. Better to go during the week, rather than at weekends, to avoid crowds &]. *Trinity*: broad sweeping lawns, magnificent herbaceous borders and informal woodland carpeted with bulbs in spring; interesting trees including 1737 catalpa and a splendid fraxinus. [Open daily, 10.30am – 12 noon, 2 – 5pm &]. Trinity Fellows' and President's Gardens, recently developed with choice plants, statuary and fountain [Open for NGS, one Sun in late March or early April and Aug, 2 – 5pm ⍩ WC ⍟]. *Wadham*: herbaceous borders, new 'fragrant' garden, rare and fine old trees [Open 1 – 4.30pm WC &]. *Wolfson*: nine acres designed around modern college buildings by Powell and Moya. Mature beds of perennials and shrubs, formal lawns and mature trees in a peaceful riverside setting. [Open daily, daylight hours WC & ⍟]. *Worcester*: the only true landscaped garden in Oxford, including a lake, made from a swampy area in 1817. Brightly coloured beds in front quad [Open term time 2 – 6pm, vacation 9am – 12 noon and 2 – 6pm.

Organised parties not admitted except by prior written arrangement]. The Provost's Garden, open on special occasions, has a charming rose garden stretching to wooded lakeside walks and orchards. *The University Parks* (a short walk from Rhodes House past the amazing museum): these were laid out in 1864 and are the perfect place for walking in all weathers and across the bridges to Mesopotamia or the Spalding Nature Reserve. The herbaceous border near South Lodge Gate is laid out in colour themes. The borders along the West and North Walks contain a broad collection of shrubs and groundcover plants chosen especially for their drought tolerance, grouped in strong associations to create a focus in the middle distance. The extended pond provides a habitat for moisture-loving plants while Cox's Corner has an emphasis on winter colour. The Parks have a fine collection of mature trees mixed with newer plantings [Open daily, except St Giles Fair on 3rd Sept, 8am – dusk WC &].

Pettifers ★   21

Lower Wardington, Banbury OX17 1RU. Tel: (01295) 750232

Mr J. and The Hon. Mrs Price • 5m NE of Banbury on A361 Daventry Road from M40 junction 11. Opposite Lower Wardington church • Open two days for NGS, 2 – 6pm, and by appt • Entrance: £3 ● & ℺

Created over 15 years, the garden is still evolving but has an air of maturity and peace which stems partly from the stunning view dominating the landscape. Interesting foliage plants ensure plenty of colour all year round. Bold planting of some more unusual plants, and attention to detail – for instance in the elegant patterns made in the paths – make this a garden to linger in now, and to watch mature with pleasure. There is a box-edged herb garden, cutting gardens, a green and white border and borders of old roses.

The Priory   22

Charlbury OX7 3PX. Tel: (01608) 810417

Dr D. El Kabir and others • On B4022 Witney – Enstone road. In Charlbury adjacent to church • Open 7th July, 2 – 6pm • Entrance: £2, children 50p ● ℘

In this formal terraced topiary garden with Italianate features, the owners have aimed to create a poetic and contemplative atmosphere through terraces, parterres, foliage colour schemes, statuary and water features. Over one acre is planted with many unusual specimen trees and shrubs mainly in various 'rooms'. There is a young three-acre arboretum which has about 200 different trees. The garden is open jointly with Gothic House (see entry).

Rousham House ★★   23

Nr Steeple Aston, Bicester OX25 4QX. Tel/Fax: (01869) 347110 or (mobile) (07860) 360407; Website: www.rousham.org

Charles Cottrell-Dormer • 11m N of Oxford, 2m S of Steeple Aston off A4260 and B4030 • House open April to Sept, Wed, Sun and Bank Holiday Mons, 2 – 4.30pm • Garden open all year, daily, 10am – 4.30pm • Entrance: £3, no children under 15 ○ ▓ WC &

This is much admired because William Kent's design of 1738 is effectively frozen in time. Historical enlightenment can be combined with the enchantment of the setting and the use he made of it. In fact, before Kent it was already a famous garden, described by Alexander Pope as 'the prettiest place for water-falls, jetts, ponds, inclosed with beautiful scenes of green and hanging wood, that ever I saw'. Kent's design, influenced perhaps by stage scenery, created a series of effects. There are splendid small buildings and follies, fine sculpture, water and many seats and vantage points. The best way to view the garden is to follow these one by one, in the order Kent intended, and for this a guidebook is necessary. By taking the effects *seriatim*, a feeling for the whole will then gradually emerge. This was also one of the first places where the garden took in the whole estate, 'calling-in' the surrounding countryside, to use Pope's words. Walled gardens next to the house, which pre-date Kent, have been made into a major attraction with herbaceous borders, parterre, rose garden, dovecot and vegetable garden.

Shellingford House   24

Shellingford, Faringdon SN7 7QA. Tel: (01367) 710612

Mr and Mrs Nicholas Johnston • 2m SE of Faringdon off A417 Faringdon – Wantage road A417 • Open one Sun in April for charity and on other days by prior appt ● ● ● WC & ⇦ ⚘ ⚑

This two-acre garden has some eccentric features inspired by the late Robert Heber Percy's Faringdon House, alas no longer open. There is a stream, and orchard, and spring features include fritillaries and bulb carpets. For children there is also a wooden crocodile, gnome garden and other sculpture fantasies, which will soon include a bamboo house. One of the garden rooms is, logically, furnished, weather permitting, with rugs and pictures; it will be interesting to see how far this is taken by other gardeners who have gone mad about rooms.

Shotover House   25

Shotover Estate, Wheatley, Oxford OX33 1QS.

Lt Col Sir John Miller • 6m E of Oxford on A40 (S carriageway) • Open probably April and July for NGS, but check Oxford Times newspaper for dates • Entrance: £1.50, children free • Other information: Possible for wheelchairs but some unsurfaced paths ● ● ● WC & ⇦ ⚘ ⚬

Rare cattle and sheep, including black varieties, greet visitors as they walk from the car park at the end of the drive round to the colonnaded back of the eighteenth-century house (not open). Much is being done to enliven the planting in the formal garden surrounding it and to revive the statuary. From the rear arcade the view is of a long canal ending in a Gothic folly, which can be reached by walking via the pet cemetery and interestingly decorated wooden chalet. From the west front of the house, visitors will enjoy strolling down the long avenues carved out of what was once part of the royal forest of Wychwood. The garden was begun c. 1718 and William Kent was involved in the design in the 1730s, constructing a domed octagonal temple, now ringed by cherry trees, and, on another axis, an obelisk (Kent was working at nearby Rousham (see entry) from 1738). Allow an hour to explore this pleasant park.

The Skippet ★ 26

Mount Skippet, Ramsden, Chipping Norton OX7 3AP. Tel: (01993) 868253

Dr M.A.T. Rogers • 4m N of Witney off B4022 Charlbury road. At crossroads signed Finstock turn E and almost immediately turn right. After 500 metres turn left up no-through-way lane • Open April to Sept by appt • Entrance: £1 for charity ● WC ⬥

Tucked away between the village pond, which he maintains was contructed by the Romans 1700 years ago, and ancient ridge-and-furrow farmland not far from Akeman Street, the owner, a retired research chemist now in his nineties, has developed a two-acre garden of exceptional interest over the last 25 years. It is literally crammed with rare and fascinating plants of every description, in luxuriant herbaceous borders reminiscent of Monet, in rockeries, in greenhouses and in an enormous number of pots and containers of all shapes and sizes. There are exotic and unusual climbers both in the conservatory and all around the largely seventeenth-century house. A courtyard with a profusion of annuals, mostly self-sown, and bulbs in spring, leads to the prolific vegetable garden. Across the lawn, surrounded by a large variety of shrubs, are attractive vistas, and the alpine house contains a collection of treasures. There is an interesting tufa collection, unusual shrubs and trees in the wild garden, a mass of bulbs in the orchard in spring, and snowdrops beside the pond. Most of the plants are labelled, some rare specimens are for sale, and, if you are lucky, Dr Rogers will delight in giving you an enthusiastic and highly informative tour.

Stansfield ★ 27

49 High Street, Stanford-in-the-Vale, Faringdon SN7 8NQ. Tel: (01367) 710340

Mr and Mrs D. Keeble • 16m SW of Oxford, 3½ m SE of Faringdon. Turn off A417 opposite Vale Garage • Open 2nd April, 7th May, 4th June, 2nd July, 6th Aug, 3rd Sept, 10am – 4pm, and by appt; parties and evening visits welcome • Entrance: £1.50 ● 🍴 ♿ ☕

A one-acre-plus plantsman's garden with many island beds and borders, and a large collection of plants for both damp and dry conditions. All-year round interest is provided by a wide use of foliage and seasonal flowers, starting with species spring bulbs – indeed, attention is focused on the number and variety of plants rather than the design and layout, which includes woodland, a grass border, a scree garden and a model vegetable garden. Alpines in sinks and troughs give interest on a smaller scale. Rabbit-proof fencing encloses perforce the entire property.

Stonor Park 28

Stonor, Henley-on-Thames RG9 6HF. Tel/Fax: (01491) 638587

Lord Camoys • 5m N of Henley-on-Thames on B480 • House open • Garden open April to Sept, Sun, Bank Holiday Mons; July to Aug, Wed, Sun; all 2 – 5.30pm. Parties by arrangement, Tues, Wed or Thurs (am and pm) • Entrance: £2.50 (house and gardens £4.50, children under 14 in family parties free) (2001 prices). Party rates on application • Other information: Lunches for parties by arrangement. Wheelchairs by arrangement ◐ ☕ ▦ WC ♿ ♨ ♀

The house, a red-brick, E-shaped Tudor building with twelfth-century origins, is set in a bowl on the side of a hill with open parkland and large trees in front. Behind and to the side of the house on higher land, sheltered against the hill, are flower and vegetable gardens. Lawns lead up to a terrace with pools, stone urns and planting along the steps. The orchard, with its cypresses and espaliered fruit trees, and the lavender hedges are attractive features.

Wardington Manor 29

Wardington, Banbury OX17 1SW. Tel: (01295) 750202/758481;
Fax: (01295) 750805

Lord and Lady Wardington • 5m NE of Banbury off A361 from M40 junction 11 • Open by appt only • Entrance: £4 ◑ ▦ ♿ ⬧

Great lawns spread themselves in front of the Carolean manor house with its wisteria-covered walls. The topiary is impeccable too, and there are attractive borders. Away from the house, the owners have created a flowering shrub walk with interesting ground cover, which leads to a walled area planted with hostas. To the left is a rockery and a large pond with a peripheral walk.

Waterperry Gardens ★ 30

Wheatley, Oxford OX33 1JZ. Tel. (01044) 339220; Fax: (01044) 339003;
Website: www.waterperrygardens.co.uk

9m E of Oxford, 2½ m N of Wheatley off M40 junction 8 from London, or 8A from Birmingham. Signposted • Garden open daily, 9am – 5pm. Closed Christmas and New Year holidays. 18th to 23rd July open only to visitors to Art in Action (enquiries (020) 7381 3192) • Entrance: Nov to March, £1.60; April to Oct, £3.5 0, OAPs £3, children £2 (under 10 free), coach parties (of 20 or more) by appt only, £2.90 per person (2001 prices) • Other information: art and craft gallery. Teashop closed 18th to 23rd July ○ ☕ ✕ WC ♿ ⬧ ♨ ♀ ♞

Waterperry has to be included in this *Guide* although its 20 acres are difficult to categorise. There is a strong educational atmosphere going back to the 1930s when a Miss Havergal opened up a small horticultural school. There is also a commercial garden centre which occupies large areas of the walled garden. The herbaceous nursery stock beds are in the ornamental gardens and form a living catalogue, the plants grown in rows and labelled. Intermixed with this are major features of the old garden, lawns and a substantial herbaceous border – also new beds containing collections of alpines, dwarf conifers, other shrubs and a new rose garden. The south field is a growing area for soft fruit. The clay bank is planted with shade-lovers. Almost all the plants are labelled and the owners describe the place as one where 'the ornamental and the utilitarian live side by side'. The greenhouses in the nursery are interesting too, containing a good stock of houseplants for sale, usually including orchids and tall ficus; another, in the old walled garden, has an enormous citrus tree (it's worth the detour just to catch the scent of blossom) and other Mediterranean specimens, which are not for sale. Several hours need to be spent here to do it justice, especially if the visitor wishes to stroll down the shady path by the little River Thame. A guide is sold at the shop. Several Wheatley gardens are also open in spring for charity, including Shotover House (see entry). A few miles east down the M40 is *Le Manoir aux Quat' Saisons*, in Church Road, Great Milton (off A329 Thame–Stadhampton road). The 12-acre garden surrounding Raymond Blanc's renowned hotel includes an impressive potager, a water garden, Japanese garden, orchard etc. It is open one day for the NGS and can be viewed by patrons.

Westwell Manor ★★   31

Burford OX18 4JT.

Mr and Mrs T.H. Gibson • 10m W of Witney, 2m SW of Burford off A40 • Open 1st July, 2 – 6.30pm • Entrance: £3, children 50p ● WC ✿

Although this garden is open only once a year, it is worth a special effort to see it, both for the originality of its design and for the high standard of its maintenance. At first sight it may appear merely one of the gems of the Cotswold manor genus, but Mrs Gibson has achieved a feeling of modernity by clever touches throughout a series of seemingly conventional rooms – over 20 at the last count. A useful plan (£1) leads the visitor round the six complex acres; more is being taken in to the garden each year. There are too many fine features to list in their entirety – they include good borders, a lavender terrace, sundial garden, vegetable garden, rose garden, fine topiary, a water garden, knot garden, lily pond and so on. Clever design ideas will be found in the alder basket area, moonlight garden, secret garden, two rills lined by a pleached lime *allée* and in a new *pièce d'eau* complete with rowing boat in place of the grass tennis court. There is an interesting wild meadow, and a new copse of native trees beyond the walls..

Wilcote House ★   32

Wilcote, Finstock, Chipping Norton OX7 3DY. Tel: (01993) 868606

The Hon. and Mrs Charles Cecil • 4m N of Witney, 3m S of Charlbury E off B4022 • Open by written appt • Entrance: £2, children free, parties negotiable. • Other information: conducted tours for private parties on weekdays by arrangement ● WC ◁◁

Surrounding and complementing a fine sixteenth- to nineteenth-century Cotswold stone house, the large garden is itself a period piece, with extensive beds of old-fashioned roses and mixed borders and a nearly 40-metre laburnum walk at its best at the end of May. An unusual feature is the large wild garden intersected by grass paths, planted within the last two decades with an increasing selection of trees now beginning to feature, particularly with autumn colour. Mount Skippet (see entry) is nearby.

Wroxton Abbey   33

Wroxton, Banbury OX15 6PX. Tel: (01295) 730551

Wroxton College of Fairleigh Dickinson University of New Jersey, USA • 3m W of Banbury off A422 • House (now used for academic purposes) open only by appt • Grounds open all year, daily, dawn – dusk, but closed for 3 weeks in Aug and late Dec to early Jan • Entrance: free • Other information: Parking in village. Vehicles not permitted in grounds ○

The historical interest of this garden and park is that in 1727 Tilleman Bobart (a pupil of Wise) was commissioned to construct a Renaissance-style garden with canals by the owner of the large Jacobean manor house, the 2nd Baron Guilford. But by the late 1730s his son had this grassed over to convert it to the then-fashionable landscape style, and Sanderson Miller designed some of the garden buildings c. 1740. The present American owners have restored much of this early landscape garden since 1978. On entering the long drive up to the house, it appears to be a conventional park, but beyond are interesting features including a serpentine river, lake, cascade which can be seen from a viewing mount, Chinese bridge, Doric temple, Gothic dovecot and ice-house, all restored from their derelict state. There is a rose garden and a knot garden. The steps have all been renovated. The wire fence has been erected to deter vandals. In all, the grounds cover 56 acres and offer many hours of pleasant walks. A garden guide is available.

GARDENING WEBSITES

Many gardens now have their own websites, and we include those by owners' request. Other useful websites for garden visitors are:

Duchas: www.heritageireland.ie
English Heritage: www.english-heritage.org.uk
Historic Houses Association: www.hha.org.uk
Historic Royal Palaces: www.hrp.org.uk
Historic Scotland: www.historic-scotland.gov.uk
Landmark Trust: www.landmarktrust.org.uk
National Gardens Scheme: www.ngs.org.uk
National Trust: www.nationaltrust.org.uk
National Trust for Scotland: www.nts.org.uk
Royal Horticultural Society: www.rhs.org.uk
Welsh Historic Monuments: www.cadw.wales.gov.uk

RUTLAND

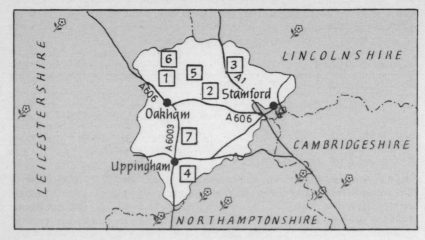

For gardens in Leicestershire, see pages 234–7.

Ashwell House

1

Ashwell, Oakham LE15 7LW. Tel: (01572) 722833

Mr and Mrs S.D. Pettifer • 3m N of Oakham via B668 towards Cottesmore, turn left to Ashwell • Open by appt only • Entrance: £1 ● ☕ **WC** ♿ 🏳

An old walled garden, well planned with combinations to provide all-year colour, together with a well-stocked vegetable garden. There is a wide range of shrubs and perennials in the borders. The pleasure garden has a pavilion in classical style and architectural features by George Carter.

Barnsdale Gardens

2

The Avenue, Exton, Oakham LE15 8AH. Tel: (01572) 813200;
Fax: (01572) 813346; E-mail: office@barnsdalegardens.co.uk;
Website: www.barnsdalegardens.co.uk

Nick and Sue Hamilton • 5m NE of Oakham off A606 • Gardens open March to Oct, daily, 10am – 5pm (last admission 3pm), Sat, Sun and Bank Holiday Mons by ticket only (telephone (01572) 813200), and to groups by appt. Nursery open Nov to Feb, 10am – 4pm • Entrance: £5, children under 16 free, season ticket £12.50 • Other information: Pre-booked wheelchairs available on free loan ◑ ☕ **WC** ♿ 🌱

Here are the show gardens immortalised by the late Geoff Hamilton on *Gardener's World*, impressive in their range and variety. Themes include town and country paradises, modern estate, cottage gardens, allotment, ornamental *potager*, woodland, stream, bog and parterre – all excellent aids to planning or redesigning green spaces. The adjoining nursery, now run by

Hamilton's son and daughter-in-law, sells a wide range of plants propagated from the gardens.

Clipsham House ★ 3

Clipsham, Oakham LE15 7SE. Tel: (01780) 410238

Mr and Mrs R. Wheatley • *10m NE of Oakham, E of A1 Stamford — Grantham road on B668* • *Open for charity in June for parties by appt only* • *Entrance: £3, children free* ● WC &

This romantic three-acre garden is at one with the pretty Regency rectory (1820) set in parkland with fine trees and rolling pasture. The exceptional walled garden, laid out in 1939 and designed by Dame Brenda Colvin, features old-fashioned roses, shrubs with contrasting foliage and hardy perennials in muted colours. An elevated summerhouse with pool gives added dimension, and a pleached hornbeam walk takes the eye to the perfect folly. A mile away is *Clipsham Yew Tree Avenue*, 150 yew trees clipped into topiary which are nearly 200 years old. Enjoy a stroll and discover the anchor, the three bears, the deer, the elephant and other surprises.

Lyddington Bede House 4

Blue Coat Lane, Lyddington LE15 9LZ. Tel: (01572) 822438

English Heritage • *In Lyddington, 7m S of Oakham, 1m E of A6003* • *Open April to Sept, daily, 10am – 6pm (Oct, daily, 10am – 5pm)* • *Entrance: £2.75, OAPs £2.10, children £1.40, under 5s free* • *Other information: Parking off road, 20 metres from entrance via cobbled alley* ◑ ▦ & ♨ ♀ ℺

Originally a medieval palace of the Bishops of Lincoln, the house retains many of its original features; it was later converted into an almshouse. It is set in small gardens among picturesque golden stone cottages and beside the handsome parish church of St Andrew. Situated in a sunny corner at the entrance and backed by walls, the herb garden forms an L-shape, with culinary herbs of the period (about 42 varieties) on the longer side of the L, medicinal herbs (about 20 varieties) on the shorter side. Beds are edged with low box hedging.

The Old Hall 5

Market Overton, Oakham LE15 7PL. Tel: (01572) 767276

Mr and Mrs T. Hart • *6m NE of Oakham, 2m N of Cottesmore off B668* • *Open one day for NGS, 2 – 6pm, and otherwise by appt only* • *Entrance: £2, children 50p (combined admission with The Old Manor House on open day)* ● &

Five acres of softly agreeable grounds. Carefully coloured borders lead from a sunken lawn which falls away gently to distant vistas and a trickling stream; the formal enclosed swimming pool in the walled kitchen garden has views through ornamental gates and avenues of mature trees. There are many interesting focal points, including a raised pond with enchanting tiny frog sculptures that spout from lily leaves into the jaws of a lion mask. The pleached lime screen now coming into its own is elegant and well placed. The whole is at one with its beautiful surroundings of Rutland stone and rolling landscape.

The Old Rectory 6

Teigh, Oakham LE15 7RT. Tel/Fax: (01572) 787681

Mrs D.B. Owen • 5m N of Oakham between Wymondham and Ashwell • Open 9th June, 2 – 6pm, and by appt in April, June and July. Parties welcome • Entrance: £1 ◑ 💷 ⅍ ⬨

A delightful, partially walled garden of three-quarters of an acre. First laid out in the 1950s, the existing garden has evolved from its original design over the last 25 years under the present owners, with much successful thought given to colour and juxtaposition of plants. There is a good show of spring bulbs and blossom, but perhaps the best month is July. Roses are used cleverly, connecting shapes and contrasts of foliage. Fine trees and climbing plants everywhere to complement the mellow walls of the eighteenth-century stone rectory. The special Strawberry-Hill-Gothick church next door is a testament to the grandeur of an earlier incumbent.

10 Wing Road 7

Manton LE15 8SZ. Tel: (01572) 737538

Betty Hunt • 5m SE of Oakham off A6003 • Open by appt only • Entrance: charge ◑

This colourful, densely planted garden, where wild areas successfully combine and contrast with more formal plantings, is the creation of an artist and plant collector who was runner-up in a recent Daily Mail/RHS national competition. It is a narrow, south-facing plot, roughly 55 x 20 metres, sheltered behind a tall hedge of conifers. The exuberant planting of trees, shrubs, perennials and wild flowers reflects her enthusiasm for conservation and wildlife, attracted especially to the pond and woodland, and reflects also the rolling landscape that surrounds the garden.

OPENING DATES AND TIMES

Times of access given are the best available at the moment of going to press, but some may have been changed subsequently. *Note*: In 2002 the late-May Bank Holiday is replaced by the Queen's Jubilee celebrations (1st to 4th June). It may be wise to check with garden owners concerning these particular dates. In the entries, the times given are inclusive: that is, an entry such as May to Sept means that the garden is open from 1st May to 30th Sept inclusive, and 2–5 pm means that entry will be effective during that period. Please note that many owners will open their gardens to visitors by appointment. They will often arrange to give a personally conducted tour on these occasions. Unavoidably some owners cannot give their opening times before we go to press. In such cases we attempt to give the best guidance we can.

SHROPSHIRE

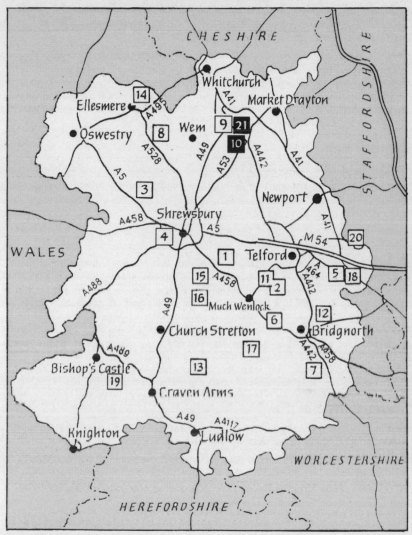

Two-starred gardens are marked on the map with a black square.

Attingham Park 1

Attingham, Shrewsbury SY4 4TP. Tel: (01743) 708162; Fax: (01743) 708175

The National Trust • 4m SE of Shrewsbury. Turn off B4380 at Atcham • House open probably 27th March to Oct, Fri – Tues, 1 – 4.30pm, Bank Holiday

Mons, 11am – 5pm (last admission 4pm). Parties by arrangement • Deer park and grounds open all year except 25th Dec, 8am – 8pm (Nov to Feb closes 5pm) • Entrance: £2, children £1 (house and grounds £4.20, children £2.10, family £10). Party and out-of-hours rates available • Other information: Self-drive electric scooter available by pre-booking ○ 🍴 📷 WC ♿ ⇦ ♨

This is a landscape mainly of large trees and shrubs, including a magnificent grove of Lebanon cedars. A mile-long walk by the River Tern is enlivened by daffodils in spring followed by azaleas and rhododendrons; autumn colour is provided by dogwoods and American thorns. A longer walk through the deer park affords fine views of the house and the Repton landscape. The eighteenth-century orangery has been restored.

Benthall Hall   2

Broseley TF12 5RX. Tel: (01952) 882159

The National Trust • 1m SW of Broseley off B4375, 4m NE of Much Wenlock, 4½ m S of Telford • Part of house open same times as garden • Garden open April to Sept, Wed, Sun and Bank Holiday Mons, 1.30 – 5.30pm. Coaches and parties by arrangement only • Entrance: £2 (house and gardens £3.50) • Other information: Parking 150 metres down road ◑ WC ♿

A small garden containing interesting plants and features, including topiary. George Maw and Robert Bateman both lived in the house and contributed to the garden design and plant collection. The rose garden has fine plants and a small pool and there is a delightful raised scree bed. A good collection of geraniums and ground-cover plants, together with a peony bed, and clematis and roses growing through trees and shrubs, create a pleasant place to stroll through. The old kitchen garden now contains a collection of crab apples, roses, wall plants, etc. In spring daffodils and the crocus introduced by George Maw provide interest, and the large specimens of Scots pine, beech and chestnut are stunning features. A monument to botanical history.

Brownhill House   3

Ruyton XI Towns, Shrewsbury SY4 1LR. Tel: (01939) 261121 Fax: (01939) 260626; E-mail: brownhill@eleventowns.co.uk; Website: www.eleventowns.co.uk

Roger and Yoland Brown • 10m NW of Shrewsbury on B4397 • Open May to Aug by appt, and several times in summer for NGS, 1.30 – 5.30pm • Entrance: £2, children free • Other information: Parking at Bridge Inn 100 metres away. Bed and breakfast accommodation ◐ 🍴 WC 🌿

Out of an impossible north-facing cliff a most unusual and distinctive garden of great variety has been created since 1972. The slope has been transformed from a scrap-covered wilderness into a series of terraces and small gardens connected by over 550 steps that wander up and down the hill through plantings of trees and shrubs, patches of wild flowers and open flower-filled spaces. At the bottom a riverside garden runs from an open lawn to a bog garden. A series of formal terraces includes a laburnum walk, and at the top there are paved areas with a pool, gazebo, parterre, a long walk with herbaceous border, flower beds and a large kitchen garden with glasshouses. Also incorporated into the design are a folly, Thai spirit house, grotto, summer house, large Arabic arch, cascade and a unique design of Menorah. Developments are continuing on the extensive terracing on which grow many of the collection of over 100 varieties of hedera. This is a garden that has to be seen to be believed. A few miles away, just west of the A5 at Kinnerley, is *Hall Farm Nursery*, which has an award-winning selection of herbaceous perennials.

Cruckfield House   4

Shoothill, Ford, Shrewsbury SY5 9NR. Tel/Fax: (01743) 850222

Mr and Mrs G.M. Cobley • 5m W of Shrewsbury off A458. Turn left signed 'Cruckton' • Open probably one Sun in May and one Fri in June and July for NGS, and for groups of 20 or more by appt • Entrance: £3, children £1 (2001 prices) ● ♥ WC ℘ ℀

Sheltered and surrounded by mature trees, the delightful four-acre garden, managed organically for many years, is designed in traditionally English formal style with an abundance of roses and rare peonies in their season as part of the attraction. There are exuberant plantings of shrubs and herbaceous plants, many of them rare or unusual. Specimen trees and a pretty bog area surround a large pond. The ornamental kitchen garden is set off by attractive outbuildings.

David Austin Roses   5

Bowling Green Lane, Albrighton, Wolverhampton WV7 3HB. Tel: (01902) 376300; Fax: (01902) 372142

Mr and Mrs David Austin • 8m NW of Wolverhampton, 6m SE of Shifnal, between A41 and A454. Take Junction 3 off M54 towards Albrighton, turn right at sign 'Roses and Shrubs', then second right • Open all year, Mon – Fri, 9am – 5pm, Sat, Sun and Bank Holiday Mons, 10am – 6pm (closes dusk mid-Oct to mid-March). Closed 24th Dec to 1st Jan • Entrance: free ○ ♥ WC ⅗ ⟁ ℘

David Austin is one of the country's leading rose breeders, so this is an ideal place for inspecting them *en masse*. There are about 900 varieties, including shrub, climbing, species and old roses. For the past 15 years Claire Austin has presided over the hardy plants department, which stocks more than 1000 species and varieties of hardy perennials and grasses. The nursery also has comprehensive selections of irises and peonies, including tree peonies.

The Dower House   6

Morville Hall, Morville, Bridgnorth WV16 5NB. Tel/Fax: (01746) 714407; E-mail: kate@kwswift.demon.co.uk

Dr Katherine Swift • 3m NW of Bridgnorth at A458/B4368 junction, within Morville Hall grounds • Open 3rd April to 29th Sept, Wed, Sun and Bank Holiday Mons, 2 – 6pm; 16th June, 2 – 6pm, with other local gardens for NGS; and at other times, inc. evenings, by appt. Guided tours for parties • Entrance: £2, children under 16 50p, guided tours £2.50 per person • Other information: Parking in churchyard. Special Rose Days in late June/early July. Garden design workshops ◑ ♥ ⅗ ⟁ ℘ ☿ ℀

Starting in 1989, the present owner has transformed a one-and-a-half-acre site within the grounds of Morville Hall, with the aim of relating the history of English gardens in a sequence of separate features: a turf maze, a medieval cloister garden, a knot garden, a seventeenth-century plat and flower beds, a William and Mary canal garden with formal water feature and box-edged *platesbandes*, an eighteenth-century flower garden, a Victorian rose border, a nineteenth-century wilderness and, finally, an ornamental fruit and vegetable garden. Particular attention is given to the use of authentic plants and construction techniques; old roses are a speciality.

Dudmaston 7

Quatt, Bridgnorth WV15 6QN. Tel: (01746) 780866; Fax: (01746) 780744

The National Trust • 4m SE of Bridgnorth on A442 • House open • Garden open April to Sept, Sun – Wed and Bank Holiday Mons, 12 noon – 6pm (last admission 5pm). Special openings for pre-booked parties only, Mons. Estate open free of charge for pedestrian access throughout the year • Entrance: £2.50 (house and garden £4, children £2, family £8) • Other information: Batricar available. Dogs in Dingle only, on lead ◑ 💻 🧺 <u>WC</u> ⑤ ⬥ ⅋ ⚕ ⍝

An eight-acre garden of appeal and interest. Features include a large pool and bog garden, and island beds filled with shrubs, azaleas, rhododendrons, viburnums and good old roses. Large specimen trees, old fruit trees and mature shrubs give the place an established feel. The rock garden has been restored and the Big Pool has attractive plantings. There are two estate walks.

Gate Cottage 8

English Frankton, Ellesmere SY12 0JU. Tel: (01939) 270606

G.W. Nicholson and Kevin Gunnell • 10m N of Shrewsbury on A528. At Cockshutt take road to English Frankton; garden 1m on right • Open 19th May, 2nd June, 1 – 5pm, for NGS, and for parties by appt • Entrance: £2, children 50p • Other information: Teas on charity open days only ◐ 💻 ⬥ ⅋

This garden is changing and developing all the time to accommodate a vast range of plants. Roses and clematis scramble through old fruit trees, and there are many other fine roses along the exterior fence and in the herbaceous borders. Aquatic interest comes from pools and a bog garden with primulas. In the extended area shrubs have been planted for colour effect. Large pebbles create attractive features, and there are unusual brown and black foliage plants and some interesting grasses. The rock and gravel plantings now include an area of hardy carnivorous plants.

Hawkstone Historic Park and Follies 9

Weston–under–Redcastle, Shrewsbury SY4 5UY. Tel: (01939) 200611; Fax (01939) 200311

13m NE of Shrewsbury via A49, 6m SW of Market Drayton on A442 Telford – Whitchurch road. Entrance on road from Hodnet to Weston-under-Redcastle.

Signed from Hodnet • Park open April to June, Sept, Oct, Wed – Sun; July, Aug, daily; all 10.30am – 5pm (last admission 4pm). Closed 6th Jan to 30th March. Dates may vary, telephone to check • Entrance: park £5, OAPs £4, children £3, family (2 adults and 3 children) £14 (peak time 2001 prices). Reduced rates for pre-booked parties ◗ ☕ ✕ 🍽 WC ⬥ 🏛 ☻

In its day Hawkstone was as famous as Stowe and Stourhead, and the grounds have now been returned to their eighteenth-century grandeur and sublimity (the latter was supposed to induce awe if not fear). A series of monuments, now reconstructed, is linked by winding paths and tunnels. Ascending towards the White Tower, the visitor passes the thatched buildings, in one of which was a mechanical hermit famous for his artificial cough (now replaced by a hologram), then a grotto (used to house Santa at Xmas) and a so-called Swiss bridge, a fallen tree across a gorge. Much remains to be done to the Red Castle, which is genuinely medieval. The whole thing is a triumph for all involved, including English Heritage, who rate this Grade I. A walk through the park is approximately three and a half miles, but visitors should be warned that it involves climbing and descending many steps. Nearby are the restored Victorian gardens of *Hawkstone Hall*, open to the public in August.

Hodnet Hall ★★ 10

Hodnet, Market Drayton TF9 3NN. Tel: (01630) 685202; Fax: (01630) 685853

Mr A.E.H. and The Hon. Mrs Heber-Percy • 12m NE of Shrewsbury, 5½ m SW of Market Drayton, at A53/A442 junction • Open April to Sept, Tues – Sun and Bank Holiday Mons, 12 noon – 5pm • Entrance: £3.50, OAPs £3, children £1.50, (2001 prices) ◗ ☕ 🍽 WC ⬥ ⬥ 🏛 ⚘

The 60-acre parkland offers a constant succession of interest, although the greatest effect comes in autumn when the acers, sorbus and birches present their display. The grounds are grouped around a series of lakes and water gardens, home to black swans. This is essentially splendid large-scale parkland planting: magnolias, azaleas, rhododendrons in late spring are followed in summer by fuchsias, astilbes and gunneras, matched with water lilies on the lakes. For the herbaceous gardener there are shrub roses, tree peonies and the more traditional border plants. The working walled kitchen garden is well maintained, and there are also displays of flowers and pot plants grown especially for use in the hall, together with many varieties of fruit and vegetables.

Limeburners 11

Lincoln Hill, Ironbridge, Telford TF8 7NX. Tel: (01952) 433715

Mr and Mrs J.E. Derry • 4m SW of Telford. Turn off B4380 W of Ironbridge at traffic island. Take Church Hill for ½ m; garden on left below Beeches Hospital • Open April to Sept by appt • Entrance: £2, children free ● WC ⬥ ⚘

The garden was started in 1970 with the then not-so-fashionable vision of planting for wildlife. Thirty years on, the mature garden continues to act as a haven for butterflies and birds with its collection of buddleias, nectar-rich flowers and native trees and shrubs of holly, broom, blackthorn, alder and dogwood. Shrub roses abound. The central pool (which looks natural but is man-made) features a waterfall with a stream splashing in. Once a year, usually one Sunday in early August, the grounds of *Meeson Hall*, Great Bolas (Tel: (01952) 812852) are open for charity, 2 – 6pm. They are Victorian in character, with a rose garden, shrubberies and glasshouses.

Lower Hall ★ 12

Worfield, Bridgnorth WV15 5LH. Tel: (01746) 716607; Fax: (01746) 716325

Mr and Mrs C.F. Dumbell • 4m NE of Bridgnorth. Take A454 Wolverhampton/ Bridgnorth road, turn right to Worfield and after village stores and pub turn right • Open 29th, 30th June for charity, 2 – 6pm. Also by appt from for a limited number of horticultural groups • Entrance: £3, children under 12 free • Other information: Access for large coaches difficult. Garden room available for groups (min. 15, max 50) for pre-booked refreshments ● ▆ ✕ WC ⬫ ℘ ℺

This modern four-acre plantsman's garden has been developed by the present owners since 1964, helped originally by the designer Lanning Roper. The courtyard and its fountain are featured in many design books. The walled garden has a magnificent display of roses, clematis and irises in season. Everywhere the use of colour combinations and plant associations is good – a red border, another of white and green giving a cool effect. Roses abound. The water garden is separated from the woodland garden by the River Worfe with two bridges and two weirs. A deck built over the pool exploits the view across to the colourful primula island. The woodland garden includes rare magnolias, a collection of birches with bark interest, acers, cornus and amelanchiers – all-year variety and colour.

Millichope Park 13

Munslow, Craven Arms SY7 9HA. Tel: (01584) 841234

Mr and Mrs L. Bury • 15m SW of Telford, 8m NE of Craven Arms, 11m N of Ludlow on B4368 • Open 6th May and July to Oct, Thurs, 2 – 6pm, for NGS, and for parties by appt • Entrance: £2.50 per person (2001 price) • Other information: Teas on open days only. Picnics in woodland only ● WC ⬫ ℘

The glory of Millichope is its magnificent landscaping, commissioned in the 1760s by a father seeking a fitting memorial to his four sons, all of whom had predeceased him. The main memorial was an elegant Ionic temple now drama- tically sited away from the house across a lake. The present owners have commissioned a fine Chinese-style bridge across one of the gorges, and Mrs Bury has added a set of herbaceous borders disposed in elegant 'rooms' framed by yew hedges. Away from Georgian classicism, romantic wilderness plantings of roses and philadelphus combine to make this a most beautiful park and garden.

Oteley 14

Ellesmere SY12 0PB. Tel: (01691) 622514

Mr and Mrs R.K. Mainwaring • 8m NE of Oswestry, 1m E of Ellesmere near A528/495 junction. From N past the Mere turn left opposite convent • Open 6th

May, 3rd June, 2 – 6pm, and by appt • Entrance: £2, children 50p • Other information: Possible for wheelchairs if dry ● 💺 WC ♿ ⟨⟩ ✿

The magnificent 10-acre garden, set in park and farmland with glimpses of the Mere beyond surrounding trees, has extensive lawns with architectural features, interesting and old handsome trees set about the lawns, a grey/silver border, decorative island beds, rhododendrons, azaleas, roses and shrubs in a gracious setting, with a collection of peonies flowering simultaneously. Herbaceous borders are backed by high walls covered with roses, clematis and other climbing plants; and a folly and a walled kitchen garden provide the finishing touches. All this plus a superlative plant stall.

The Patch   15

Acton Pigott, Acton Burnell, Shrewsbury SY5 7PH. Tel: (01743) 362139

Mrs Margaret Owen • 8m SE of Shrewsbury between A49 and A458. From Acton Burnell take Cressage Road. After ½ m turn left signed Acton Pigott • Open 24th Feb, 11am – 3pm, 31st March, 1st April, 2 – 5pm, 2nd June, 7th July, 2 – 6pm, 29th Sept, 2 – 5pm, and for parties by appt at other times • Entrance: £1.50, children free ● 💺 WC ♿ ✿

Do not be deceived by this half-acre garden – allow time. It is filled with beauties, starting in spring with snowdrops, hellebores, erythroniums, dicentras, trilliums and violas. On into summer go *Paeonia mlokosewitschii* and *P. daurica*, followed by dictamnus, veratrums (National Collections applied for), roses, and National Collections of camassias and epimediums. Other specialities include nerines and schizostylis. The garden is bordered by a broad grassy path, and at its centre lies a white garden. It is graced with tree rarities such as *Eucalyptus pauciflora* spp. *debeuzevillei, Styrax obassia* and *Toona sinensis.*

Preen Manor   16

Church Preen, Church Stretton SY6 7LQ. Tel: (01694) 771207

Mr and Mrs P. Trevor-Jones • 5m W of Much Wenlock on B4371. After 3m turn right for Church Preen and Hughley; after 1½ m turn left for Church Preen, over crossroads. Drive is ½ m on right • Open several dates in summer and autumn for NGS, and by arrangement for parties of 15 or more in June and July only • Entrance: £3, children 50p ● 💺 WC ✿ ⚲

The grounds are blessed with a beautiful south-east aspect facing Wenlock Edge. Despite the attractions of the more formal part of the gardens, it is the wooded landscaped walks beside the pools and natural stream which are the most outstanding feature. Rodgersias, *Primula japonica, Rhododendron ponticum* hybrids and magnificent yews and cedars create a noble setting on the banks which fall away from the former manor house. The formal gardens are akin to a pretty cottage garden with roses, deutzias and violas planted to good effect. Other gardens, including a chess garden, pebble garden and gazebo complete with parrot and cat, demonstrate an esoteric style of gardening which may appeal to some. Slightly east of Preen is *Wenlock Priory* (English Heritage), a large ruin featuring imaginative topiary [open all year].

Ruthall Manor 17

Ruthall Road, Ditton Priors, Bridgnorth WV16 6TN. Tel: (01746) 712608

Mr and Mrs G.T. Clarke • 7m SW of Bridgnorth. Ruthall Road signed near garage, manor garden ¾ m further on • Open by appt and for parties • Entrance: £2 (2001 price) ● ▦ WC ᵬ ⬦

Set below the heights of Abdon Burf, the one-acre garden, designed for ease of maintenance, is now coming to maturity. It offers a mixture of settings, from a delightful old pond planted to great natural effect to more formal plantings near the house, a woodland area and a vegetable garden. There are good examples of well-sited trees and shrubs, mixed with climbers and perennials. New features continue to be added.

Swallow Hayes ★ 18

Rectory Road, Albrighton, Wolverhampton WV7 3EP. Tel: (01902) 372624; E-mail: patedwards70@hotmail.com

Mrs Michael Edwards • 9m SE of Telford, 7m NW of Wolverhampton. Turn off M54 at junction 3, then off A41 into Rectory Road after garden centre • Open one day in mid-Jan (for National Collection of witch hazels), 11am – 4pm, several days in spring and for parties by appt. Telephone for details • Entrance: £2 (on open days), parties £2.50 per person (incl. tea and biscuits), children 10p • Other information: Teas on open days only ● ⬤ ▦ WC ᵬ ⬦ ⚘ ℀

A delightful two-acre modern garden with many design features, colour and foliage contrasts, and a beautiful display of plants, shrubs and trees. Although planted for easy maintenance, it contains nearly 3000 different types of plants (most of which are labelled), and gives year-round interest. The Mediterranean wall has tender plants. Small pools, ferns and a woodland area provide contrast. National Collections of witch hazels and lupins are here, plus an interesting area of small gardens to copy at home, vegetables and fruit trees, nursery stock beds and a hardy geranium trial of over 100 labelled hardy varieties.

Walcot Hall 19

Lydbury North SY7 8AZ. Tel: (01588) 680232; Fax: (01588) 680361; E-mail: enquiries@walcothall.com; Website: www.walcothall.com

Mr C.R.W. Parish • 7m NW of Craven Arms, 3m S of Bishop's Castle, off B4385. Turn left by Powis Arms in Lydbury North • Open 2nd to 4th June, 2 – 6pm, and for groups by appt (min charge £20) • Entrance: £3, children free [NEW] ⬤ ▦ WC ⬦ ⬤

The beautiful setting in the borderland hills enhances this arboretum planted by Lord Clive of India's son. Rhododendrons and azaleas sweep down to pools and are set amid many fine specimen trees. The lake and pools display the fine collection to advantage, enhanced by the lovely vision of Sir William Chambers' clock towers among the rolling hills. Although only open for a short period each year, the arboretum is well worth a visit if in the area to those who particularly enjoy landscape settings.

Weston Park ★ 20

Weston-under-Lizard, Shifnal TF11 8LE. Tel: (01952) 852100;
Website: www.weston-park.com

*Weston Park Enterprises • 6m E of Telford on A5, 7m W of M6 junction 12
and 3m N of M54 junction 3 • House open at 1pm. Extra charge • Garden
open April to Sept (please enquire for days, times and events list) • Entrance:
park and gardens £2.50, OAPs £2, children £1.50 (house, park and gardens
£4, OAPs £3.50, children £2.50)* ◗ 💺 ✕ 🍽 WC ⬦ ⬛ 🕯 ⚭

A distinctive 'Capability' Brown creation covering almost 1000 acres of
delightful woodland planted with rhododendrons and azaleas, together with
beautiful pools. Magnificent trees form a handsome backcloth to many shrubs.
A rose walk leads to the deer park, and the rose garden by the house and the
Italian parterre garden have been restored. The many architectural features –
Temple of Diana, Roman bridge and orangery – were all designed by James
Paine. Children will enjoy the adventure playground, the Weston Park Railway and the pets' corner. Gourmet dinners and open-air events are also on
offer.

Wollerton Old Hall ★★ 21

Wollerton, Hodnet, Market Drayton TF9 3NA. Tel: (01630) 685760 (Daytime)

*John and Lesley Jenkins • 12m NE of Shrewsbury off A53. Brown-signed from
Hodnet and Tern Hill A53/A41 junction • Open 29th March to Aug, Fri, Sun
and Bank Holiday Mons, Sept, Fri, 12 noon – 5pm • Entrance: £3.50, children
£1* ◖ 💺 ✕ WC ♿ ☙ 🕯 ⚭

In design and layout this is a garden in the classic English mode. Within a little
over three acres is a series of beautifully planted rooms, each distinct in
character yet very much part of the whole. This effect is achieved through the
careful positioning of a number of principal and secondary axes upon which the
overall plan of the garden depends. The framework, seemingly a constant, has
on occasion had to change. A wonderful new planting of yews replaced the
former box-edged compartments (struck by the dreaded fungal disease),
creating an all-embracing, deeply green atmosphere. Within the different
garden rooms, contrasts are much in evidence. Fiery borders in the hot
garden, stunning in August, are tempered with cool whites in a scented
garden; openness, in the form of a broad expanse of lawn, contrasts with
the intimacy of a pergola dripping with roses and clematis. But this garden is
not just about plantsmanship and design. It is charged with atmosphere,
enhanced by a number of most appealing structures; in recalling the Arts
and Crafts Movement of the early years of the last century, it is redolent of
many fashionable ones of the present.

SOMERSET

Two-starred gardens are marked on the map with a black square.

Ammerdown House ★   1

Radstock, Bath BA3 5SH.

Mr Andrew Jolliffe • 10m S of Bath, ¹/₂ m off A362 Radstock – Frome road on B3139 • Open for charity 1st April, 6th May, 3rd June, 26th Aug, 11am – 5pm • Entrance: £3, children free • Other information: Pre-booked catering for parties at Ammerdown Study Centre. Tel: (01761) 433709 ● ● WC ◁

The Bath-stone house was designed by James Wyatt, with panoramic views on one side and a garden on the other; the garden was a brilliant conception by Lutyens, who wanted to link the house with the orangery. Walking through the Italianate 'rooms' of yew and sculpture and parterre, one is unaware of the tricks of space that are being played. Massive yew planting, now mature and nearly four metres high, creates enclosed formal areas which lead irresistibly one from another – the spaces between being almost entirely filled with hedging. The originality and grandeur remain, as do some particularly clever details such as the clipped Portugal laurels, honeysuckles trained over wire umbrellas, and ancient lemon verbenas in pots in the orangery and on terraces.

Daffodils, narcissi and cowslips are spring features; fountains and statues add architectural interest at all seasons.

Barford Park ★ 2

Spaxton, Bridgwater TA5 1AG. Tel: (01278) 671269

Mr and Mrs M. Stancomb • 5m W of Bridgwater. From Bridgwater – Spaxton road, turn to Enmore • House open by appt • Garden open for individuals and parties by arrangement from May to Sept • Entrance: £3, children free (house and garden) ● WC & ⬦

This is a garden in the eighteenth-century style developed over the last 32 years, set in parkland and protected by a ha-ha on three sides. After watching the golden orfe darting around the lily pond, stroll down a sweep of lawn to a stand of tall trees. In spring the woodland glade is a carpet of many shades of primulas. The eighteenth-century walled garden is unusually sited in view of the house – a lawn with deep herbaceous borders on each side makes a colourful vista.

Barrington Court Garden ★ 3

Barrington, Ilminster TA19 0NQ. Tel: (01460) 241938

The National Trust • 5m N of Ilminster, on B3168 in Barrington • Garden open March, Oct, Thurs – Sun; April to June, Sept, Sat – Thurs; July, Aug, daily. House open April to Sept, Sat – Thurs, all 11am – 5.30pm (except March, Oct closes 4.30pm) • Entrance: £5.20, children £2.50, family ticket £13, parties of 15 or more, £4.50 by arrangement with visitor services manager (Tel: (01460) 241938) • Other information: Self-drive buggy and wheelchairs available ◑ ⬛ ✕ ▦ & ℺

In 1917, at the end of her career, Gertrude Jekyll planned the planting for the Lyle family, the Trust's first tenants at Barrington, and planning schemes today are based on her original ideas. It ranks among her finest work and is one of the best preserved of her gardens. Set in a park with avenues of mature chestnut trees, the gardens are in the Hidcote style of separate 'rooms'. The lily garden has a central pool with surrounding beds of annuals and perennials planted with a 'hot' theme of oranges, reds and yellows. The white-flowering and silver-leaved plants are seen in the White Garden *à la* Sissinghurst, though this is a Lyle, not a Jekyll, scheme. It is interesting that this was part of the farm before the Lyle lease, and the cattle troughs can still be seen in the beds. Beyond, a pergola (also not Jekyll) supports clematis, wisteria and honeysuckles in profusion. Note the cattle sheds, *c.* 1800, of considerable visual appeal. The vast walled kitchen garden produces a wide variety of fruit and vegetables. Further afield a cider orchard provides raw material for the liquid refreshments.

Cannington College Gardens 4

Cannington, Bridgwater TA5 2LS. Tel: (01278) 655000; Website: www.cannington.ac.uk

Cannington College • 3m NW of Bridgwater on A39 • Open April to Oct, daily, 9am – 5pm, and to parties by appt • Entrance: £2, OAPs and children (5–16)

£1 • Other information: Teas for parties by arrangement. Guide dogs only
◑ ▣ ▧ <u>WC</u> ⅋

The gardens, enclosed within a medieval priory wall surrounding the fifteenth-century Cannington Court, contain one of the largest collections of rare and unusual plants in the South-West, including the National Collections of abutilons, argyranthemums, osteospermums and wisterias. The gardens are planted individually on various botanical themes, including an Australasian Garden and the Bishop's Garden, featuring plants from the eastern Mediterranean. In total, the college gardens cover an area of approximately two-and-a-half acres. The nearby plant centre sells some National Collection species and a range of others.

City of Bath Botanical Gardens 5

Royal Victoria Park, Upper Bristol Road, Bath BA1 2NQ.

City of Bath • In Royal Victoria Park • Open all year, daily, 8.30am – dusk • Entrance: free • Other information: Toilet facilities in park ○ ⬦ ℺

Located in the city's Royal Victoria Park, the botanical gardens were formed in 1887 to house a collection of plants assembled over a lifetime by Mr C.E. Broome of Batheaston, an enthusiastic amateur botanist and plant collector. It has become one of the finest collections, certainly in the West Country, of plants on limestone. To mark the centenary in 1987, the gardens were extended to take in the adjacent Great Dell. The herbaceous border was replanted in 1990. Ongoing improvements to the plant collections and educational aspects received a grant from the Heritage Lottery Fund and developments are afoot in the park.

Claverton Manor 6

Claverton, Bath BA2 7BD. Tel: (01225) 460503

The American Museum • 2m SE of Bath off A36, signed 'American Museum' • Garden open 23rd March to 3rd Nov, daily except Mon, 1 – 5pm; Bank Holiday Suns and Mons, 11am – 5pm. Pre-booked private garden tours by arrangement • Entrance: grounds and galleries: £3.50, children £2. House, grounds and galleries: £6, OAPs £5.50, children £4. Garden tours £3 per person • Other information: Museum and new gallery ◑ ▣ ▧ <u>WC</u> ⬦ ℘ ⛁

The house, designed by Jeffry Wyatville, and garden are set on the side of the valley of the Avon in a stunning position with splendid views from the terrace. The rather stark high walls of the house and the terrace support honeysuckle, clematis and old rose climbers, and fastigiate yews make strong buttress shapes up the south-facing wall. The Colonial Herb Garden is modest in size but the little herbarium is popular for seeds, herbs, tussie-mussies and so on. The Mount Vernon Garden, a colonial interpretation of George Washington's famous garden, with rampant old-fashioned roses, trained pear trees and box and beech hedges, is surrounded by white palings. There is a replica of the octagonal garden house used as a school room for Washington's step-grandchildren. The seven-acre arboretum, which contains a fine collection of exclusively native American trees and shrubs, is believed to be the only one of its kind outside the USA. Labelling is extensive and a map listing trees and shrubs is available. An orchard contains American apple varieties, and there is also a fernery, a cascade and a waterfall.

Clevedon Court   7

Tickenham Road, Clevedon, Bristol BS21 6QU. Tel: (01275) 872257

The National Trust • 1½ m E of Clevedon on B3130. M5 junction 20 • House open • Garden open 31st March to 29th Sept, Wed, Thurs, Sun and Bank Holiday Mons, 2 – 5pm (last admission 4.30pm) • Entrance: £4.50, children £2 (house and garden) (2001 prices) • Other information: Coaches by appt ◑ WC ♋

The fourteenth-century house is magnificently sited with steeply terraced gardens which contain a wide variety of species. The upper terrace is backed by ornamental woodland of ilexes and holm oaks. In the lower garden there are London planes and a mulberry tree said to be 'ancient' in 1822. The Trust suggests that the south-facing terraces may have housed apricots and figs, but they have been replanted with species such as the strawberry tree (*Arbutus unedo*), *Canna iridiflora*, palms, myrtles, fuchsias, a Judas tree and fine magnolias (best in spring) which flourish in the sheltered microclimate. Nearby is *Passiflora*, Lampley Road, Kingston Seymour (Tel: (01934) 877255), a nursery with over 200 species of seeds and plants available [open Mon – Sat, 9am – 1pm, 2 – 5pm].

Cothay Manor ★★   8

Greenham, Wellington TA21 0JR. Tel: (01823) 672283; Fax: (01823) 672345

Mr and Mrs Alastair Robb • 5m W of Wellington. From west (M5 junction 27) take signed A38 signed 'Wellington', then after 3½ m turn left to Greenham. From north (junction 26) take Wellington exit; at roundabout take A38 signed 'Exeter'. After 3½ m turn right to Greenham (1½ m) and right again on left-hand corner at bottom of hill. House is 1m further, always keeping left • House open for parties by appt • Garden open May to Sept, Wed, Thurs, Sun and Bank Holiday Mons, and for NGS 24th June, 29th July, all 2 – 6pm • Entrance: £3.50 • Other information: Coaches by appt ● 🍴 WC ♿ ❀ 🛍 🕯

The house is reputed to be one of the finest small medieval manors in the country, and its outstanding garden appears integral to the house, each a natural extension of the other. In fact the gardens seen today were laid out only in the 1920s. They have been redesigned and replanted over the last few years, within the original yew hedges which constitute a serene seventeenth-century promenade complete with 'conversation' arbours. Surrounding meadows, planted with specimen trees, shrubs and spring bulbs, lead on to herbaceous borders, a cottage garden and a magical white garden. There is also a bog garden. Masterly planting is evident everywhere, exuberance balanced by restraint, as the owners are never afraid to repeat a theme within an enclosed space. Particularly unusual is the effective way that complementary greys and mauves flow into the house walls. Plants propagated from the garden are for sale. If you are heading back to Taunton, 3m south-west is *Broadleigh Gardens Nursery* [open Mon – Fri only], where bulbs and herbaceous plants may be ordered after viewing them in flower in the garden. The 100-yard-long Walk of the Unicorn, an avenue of *Robina pseudoacia* 'Umbraculifera' underplanted with *Nepeta* 'Six Hills Giant', is a wonderful sight in May when a thousand white tulips appear in bloom through the catmint.

Crowe Hall ★   9

Widcombe Hill, Bath BA2 6AR. Tel: (01225) 310322

Mr John Barratt • Behind Bath Spa station off A36 within walking distance of station • Open 21st April, 12th May, 9th June, 14th July, 2 – 6pm, and for parties by appt • Entrance: £2, children £1 ● ▮ ◈

These gardens, which extend to 11 acres on the hillside above Widcombe, are some of the most mysterious and beautiful in Bath. Through the gates is an intriguing view of a drive, portico and terrace, and once inside the grounds few gardens in the area offer so many surprises and delights. The owner describes it as an island of classical simplicity surrounded by romantic wilderness. Around the Regency-style house are Italianate terraces, a pond, grottos, tunnels, woods, glades, kitchen gardens and a long walkway with a stone statue facing a stunning view of Prior Park (see entry). Vistas and views are a feature of this steeply banked garden, where down one walk you suddenly come upon the roof of the fifteenth-century church of St Thomas à Becket. The loss of 20 trees in storms is regarded as an improvement by the owner because new vistas have opened up. Beyond the restored grotto is a meadow garden and an amusing garden dedicated to Hercules, with a theatrically ferocious hero. This garden has been redesigned, and Hercules now appears in a mosaic pool as well as on dry land. Magnificent trees include mulberries, beeches and limes. The charming little enclosed Sauce Garden, with its trelliswork and canal-like pool, was created in 1995, and the 1852 greenhouse has been restored to its former glory. For its stunning setting in the meadows above and facing away from Bath and for the romantic ambience Crowe Hall is an experience not to be missed.

Dunster Castle ★   10

Dunster, Minehead TA24 6SL. Tel: (01643) 821314; Fax: (01643) 823000; E-mail: wdugen@smtp.ntrust.org.uk

The National Trust • 3m SE of Minehead on A39 • Castle open Sat – Wed • Garden and park open daily, 10am – 5pm (28th Sept to Dec, 11am – 4pm) (last admission ½ hour before closing). For Christmas details telephone (01643) 823004 • Entrance: £3, children under 16 £1.50, family ticket (2 adults and 3 children) £7.50 (castle, garden and park £6.20, children under 16 £3.10, family ticket £15.50, pre-booked parties £5.20 per person) • Other information: Self-drive batricar and volunteer-driven multi-seater available ○ **WC** ᕦ ♿ ☕ ☞

The Luttrell family, who had lived here since the fourteenth century, gave the castle and gardens to the Trust in 1976. A fine border of rare shrubs surrounds a lawn by the keep and is well worth the steep climb to view. On the formal terraces below and along the river thrives a variety of sub-tropical plants, camellias and azaleas. Thousands of bulbs have been planted, and after the daffodils and snowdrops come fine displays of forsythias, camellias and early rhododendrons. There is a National Collection of arbutus and a huge 18-metre *Magnolia campbellii*. Views stretch across to Exmoor, the Quantocks and the Bristol Channel. The park totals 28 acres in all.

East Lambrook Manor Gardens ★   11

South Petherton TA13 5HH. Tel: (01460) 240328; Fax: (01460) 242344;
E-mail: enquiries@eastlambrook.com; Website: www.eastlambrook.com

Robert and Marianne Williams • 3m SW of Martock off A303, 2m NE of South Petherton • Open Feb to Oct, daily, 10am – 5pm • Entrance: £2.95, OAPs, students, groups £2.50, children £1 (2001 prices) • Other information: Art gallery open throughout summer ◐ 💻 ✕ 🍴 WC ♨ ♿ 🔔 ⚲

Margery Fish established the garden for endangered species, and it still houses a remarkable collection of plants, many of which she saved from extinction. Thanks to the previous owner, Andrew Norton, the National Collection of geraniums (cranesbill) species and cultivars also remains here. An extensive restoration programme was started by the present owners and their head gardener, Mark Stainer, in 1999, with the aim of improving historically important areas of the Grade-I-listed garden, famous not only for its plants but also for its controlled luxuriance of growth, colour and scent. This will include restoring the green garden, replacing the pudding trees and clearing the top terraces and the colosseum. The eventual plan is to follow Margery Fish's interest in medicinal herbs and create an enclosed herb garden, which will also incorporate a return to her vegetable garden. The nursery has been restored to Margery Fish's original site and the National Collection of geraniums has a new display bed.

The Georgian Garden   12

Gravel Walk, Bath BA1 2EW. Tel: (01225) 477752;
E-mail: costume_enquiries@bathnes.gov.uk

Heritage Services, Bath and North East Somerset • Entrance on Gravel Walk • Open May to Oct, Mon – Fri except Bank Holiday Mons, 9am – 4.30pm • Entrance: free • Other information: Parking in Charlotte Street, a short walk across Royal Victoria Park. Toilet facilities in park ◐

Anyone interested in seeing how a Georgian town garden looked should not miss the fully restored garden behind The Circus. Designed to be seen from the house, the garden plan is based on excavations conducted by the Bath Archaeological Trust of the original garden, laid out in the 1760s. Surprisingly simple, there is no grass but instead a bed of yellow gravel edged with stone paving. Three flower beds are on a central axis. The planting sets out to show how a Georgian garden might have evolved between 1760 and 1836. Boxrimmed borders are planted starkly with scented varieties of phlox, stocks, asters and a good deal of love-lies-bleeding; honeysuckle clings to a central white pole. An eye-catcher is a curious bench copied from an eighteenth-century original. Another pleasant garden in Bath is at the *Holburne Museum*, Great Pulteney Street. Meanwhile, if you are looking for garden tools, pots or, indeed, anything 'from a trowel to a 50-foot fountain', it may be worth seeking out David Bridgewater at *Heather Cottage*, Lansdown, Bath (Tel: (01225) 463435), who will also search for specific items if he does not stock them.

Greencombe ★★ 13

Porlock TA24 8NU. Tel: (01643) 862363

Greencombe Garden Trust (Miss Joan Loraine) • 7½ m W of Minehead, ½ m W of Porlock off B3225 • Open April to July, and Oct to Nov, Sat – Wed, 2 – 6pm • Entrance: £4, children 50p • Other information: Coaches by arrangement
◑ ☕ WC ♿ ✿ 🔍

Created in 1946 by Horace Stroud, this garden has been extended by the present owner over the last 30 years. Overlooking the Bristol Channel, set on a hillside where the sun cannot penetrate for nearly two months in the winter, it glows with colour. The formal lawns and beds round the house are immaculate. Roses, lilies, hydrangeas, maples and camellias thrive. By contrast the woodland area, terraced on the hillside, provides a nature walk of great interest; here a wide variety of rhododendrons and azaleas flowers in the shelter of mature trees, and ferns and woodland plants also flourish. No sprays or chemicals are used in the cultivation of this completely organic garden, which contains National Collections of erythroniums, gaultherias, polystichums and vacciniums.

Hadspen Garden and Nursery ★★ 14

Castle Cary BA7 7NG. Tel/Fax: (01749) 813707

Mr N.A. Hobhouse and N. and S. Pope • 3½ m NW of Wincanton, 2m SE of Castle Cary on A371 • Open March to 1st Oct, Thurs – Sun and Bank Holiday Mons, 10am – 5pm • Entrance: £3, children 50p • Other information: Coaches by arrangement ◑ ☕ 🛍 WC ♿ ✿ 🔍

Here is the classic English walled garden set in parkland, but completely transformed under the present regime. The basic plan was devised by Margaret Hobhouse in the Victorian gardening 'boom' days, to provide a setting for the eighteenth-century hamstone Hobhouse home. Over the years the garden became overgrown and formless, with an interval in the 1960s when Penelope Hobhouse endeavoured to restore some order. Over the last few years it has been reclaimed by Nori and Sandra Pope, who have retained the best of the original plan and embellished it with a variety of new plantings. Their thing is colour – bold, innovative, thought-provoking colour. Indeed, you could say it is their trademark. The borders, therefore, are colour-co-ordinated season by season, from white and pale through a subtle spectrum to very dark shades and then black. Other features include a lily pond, shrub walks, a curved walled garden and a wildflower meadow. Hostas are a speciality; they, and other high-class plants, are for sale in the nursery.

Hestercombe Gardens ★ 15

Cheddon Fitzpaine, Taunton TA2 8LG. Tel: (01823) 413923;
Fax: (01823) 413747; Website: www.hestercombegardens.com

HGP Ltd/Somerset County Council • 4m NE of Taunton off A361, just N of Cheddon Fitzpaine. Signposted • Garden open all year, daily, 10am – 6pm (last admission 5pm). Parties by written appt only • Entrance: £4, OAPs £3.80, children (5–15) £1, under 5 free (2001 prices) • Other information: Coaches by arrangement ○ 🍽 🛒 WC ♿ ⟨⟩ 🌿 🏛 ⚲

This is a superb product of the collaboration between Edwin Lutyens and Gertrude Jekyll, blending the formal art of architecture with the art of plants. *The Oxford Companion* describes it as Lutyens at his best in the detailed design of steps, pools, walls, paving and seating. The rills, pergola and orangery are also fine examples of his work. To the north of the house is the Combe, laid out two centuries earlier than the main gardens and a unique example of eighteenth-century pleasure grounds unchanged until the timber was felled in the 1960s. Visitors are now able to see the eighteenth-century parkland designed between 1750 and 1786 by Coplestone Warre Bampfylde, and his (restored) Great Cascade; he also designed the cascade from the lake at Stourhead (see entry in Wiltshire). He described Hestercombe's as one 'that will rivet you to the spot with admiration'. This ambitious restoration of a Grade-I-listed landscape is likely to continue for a further five years, and will form a 35-acre landscape garden in its own right. The restoration of the Victorian terrace is now completed, including the fountain, and a programme is underway to restore the Victorian shrubbery in the style of William Robinson, c. 1880. Be sure to see the Doric temple, the mausoleum, the rebuilt witch's hut as well as the Gothic alcove, which commands views of Taunton Vale. Tim Richardson writes of the remarkable way in which the gentleness of Bampfylde's vision has endured. There is still a sense of nature enhanced rather than transformed, with the set pieces so well sited and spaced that they seem to relax into the natural setting. A major reassessment and restoration of Jekyll's planting is underway and the formal garden will be completely replanted, as close as possible to her original plans, in time for the garden's centenary in 2004.

Jasmine Cottage 16

26 Channel Road, Clevedon BS21 7BY. Tel: (01275) 871850;
Website: www.bologrew.pwp.blueyonder.co.uk

Mr and Mrs Michael Redgrave • 12m W of Bristol. From M5 junction 20, take road to seafront, continue N on B3124 and turn right at St Mary's church • Open by appt May to Aug, daily • Entrance: £1.50, children free • Other information: Plants for sale in nursery ● WC ♿ 🌿

Here is something for everyone: old-fashioned roses, climbers, mixed shrubs, herbaceous borders, island beds, a pergola walk and a vegetable garden – all crammed into one-third of an acre. An inspiration for suburban enthusiasts, especially as it is only about 100 metres from the sea. The rectangular shape is cleverly disguised, with island beds in one area, and a pond enclosed by a hedge over three and a half metres high and cut annually. Through the hedge is the so-called cottage garden with unusual climbers, including *Rhodochiton atrosanguineum* and *Dregea sinensis*.

Lady Farm ★   17

Chelwood, Bristol BS18 4NN. Tel: (01761) 490770.
Website: http://wkweb5.cableinet.co.uk/bologrew

Malcolm and Judy Pearce • 9m S of Bristol on A368, ½ m E of Chelwood roundabout (A37/A368) • Open for parties by appt • Entrance: £4, children free but under 14s not encouraged ◑ 💺 WC

Set on the side of a valley and covering approximately six acres, this is an essential visit for anyone interested in the changing face of gardening. Here is the pioneering continental style set down in the English countryside. Water is an essential part of the garden. A spring-fed water course with marginal planting and waterfalls flows into a lake with adjacent rock features, then flows on down to join a further lake, made by damming a stream in the valley bottom, where lakeside and woodland walks are being developed. But the greatest excitement is reserved for the sunny slopes on the other side of the waterfall. One slope is planted as a steppe garden, peaking from April to June, with rhythmical clumps of foliage plants and splashes of colour from spring bulbs and strong-hued summer flowers. Another slope has a large area of perennial prairie planting, with substantial large groups of heleniums, achilleas, rudbeckias, eupatoriums and the like, and many ornamental grasses; this is at its most colourful from July to October. Elsewhere are wildflower meadow areas, a meandering walk of birch species underplanted with hostas, hellebores, alliums and grasses. A new formal garden has a thatched summer house and herbaceous perennials, in rich plum and purple shades, in a four-square design with a circle in the centre. From there a path leads through a formal topiary garden. This is a garden with a future, and one for all seasons.

Lower Severalls   18

Crewkerne TA18 7NX. Tel: (01460) 73234; Fax: (01460) 76105

Mary Cooper • 1½ m NE of Crewkerne off A30 • Open March to 14th Oct, Mon – Wed, Fri, Sat, 10am – 5pm, and May to June also Sun, 2 – 5pm • Entrance: £2 • Other information: Coaches by appt. Teas for pre-arranged parties only. Plants for sale in nursery ◑ 🍴 WC ♿ 🐾

A typical cottage garden of some two and a half acres with herbaceous borders against the stone-walled house. The garden extends through stone pillars which make a frame for the view of the valley over lawn and varied shrubs and a bog garden. Additional features include arches made from recycled farm machinery, and a 'dogwood basket' (woven cornus growing in a circle with a large structure forming the handle). Water gardens, fed from a spring in adjacent farmland, have been created, together with a wadi or dry garden built up to form a windbreak for a sheltered valley.

Lytes Cary Manor 19

Charlton Mackrell, Somerton TA11 7HU. Tel: (01458) 224471/(01985) 843600

The National Trust • *2½ m NE of Ilchester, signed from A303* • *Open 23rd March to Oct, Mon, Wed and Sat; June, July, Aug, Mon, Wed, Fri, Sat, all 2 – 6pm or dusk if earlier (last admission 5.30pm)* • *Entrance: £4.60, children £2* ◑ wc ᕕ ♨ ℺

Once the house of the medieval herbalist Henry Lyte, the main feature is a long, wide border which has been replanted in line with Graham Stuart Thomas's original design, with a mixture of roses, shrubs and herbaceous plants. There are also pleasing lawns with hedges in Elizabethan style and some topiary, as well as a large orchard with naturalised bulbs and mown walks with a central sundial. A little over 5 miles to the west, at Langport, is the legendary nursery *Kelways*, a leading grower of peonies (Tel: (01458) 250521). [Open daily, weekdays 9am-5pm, Sat 10am-5pm, Sun 10am-4pm.]

Manor Farm 20

Middle Chinnock, Crewkerne TA18 7PN. Tel: (01935) 881895;
E-mail: AJ@simonjohnson.co.uk

Simon and Antonia Johnson • *5m W of Yeovil off A30* • *Open 6th May, 16th June, 2 – 6pm, and by appt* • *Entrance: £2, children free* ◑ ▆ wc ᕕ ⟁ ℺

Despite being the recent creation of the owner, designer Simon Johnson, the garden succeeds in making the visitor feel that it could always have been here, and that its scale and proportion are right for both the site and the family life that goes on in and around it. The hamstone farmhouse has architectural distinction without being grand, and this is reflected in the garden spaces. There is a traditional framework of stone walls and hedges – yew and hornbeam – allowing areas for plants and colours, for architectural austerity and lush wildness, for fruit- and vegetable-growing. Contrasts appear throughout, and everywhere are seats from which to take in the views of the landscape beyond the garden. Despite its air of timelessness and maturity, the garden is still evolving, with structures and new plantings appearing as time and funds allow, including a walled garden surrounding a renovated cottage, and a pond complete with an island.

The Manor House ★ 21

Walton-in-Gordano, Clevedon BS21 7AN. Tel: (01275) 872067;
E-mail: simon.wills@tesco.net

Mr and Mrs C. Wills and Mr and Mrs S. Wills • *2m NE of Clevedon on N side of B3124 Clevedon – Portishead road* • *Open for NGS May and June,*

Thurs, 10am – 4pm, 1st July, 2 – 6pm, and by appt all year • *Entrance: £2, children under 14 free* ◕ **WC** ♿

A truly remarkable garden, created behind a largely early-eighteenth-century farmhouse by the present owners over the past 20 years. Expanding on the plantings, mostly of trees, which remain from the eighteenth century onwards, it definitely *vaut le détour*. Ornamental trees, shrubs, herbaceous plants and bulbs are used to give form and colour throughout the year, particularly in autumn. The informal design disguises the thought and knowledge that lie behind the sensitive planting of a seemingly endless variety of specimen trees, some of them grown from seeds brought back by the Wills from their travels to Chile, Nepal and elsewhere. South of the house, the white and silver beds retain something of their original layout. A formal pool garden, hedged with yew, contains rectangular pools and fountains framed by an explosion of delicate pinks, blues, white and silver. The owners have given a new and different meaning to the term plantsman's garden, combining scholarship with an eye for light and shade, texture, form and understated colour to make a visit a deeply satisfying experience.

Milton Lodge ★   22

Wells BA5 3AQ. Tel: (01749) 672168

Mr D.C. Tudway Quilter • ½ *m N of Wells. From A39 Wells – Bristol road turn N up Old Bristol Road* • *Open Easter to Oct, Tues, Wed, Sun and Bank Holiday Mons, 2 – 5pm* • *Entrance: £2.50, children under 14 free* • *Other information: Parties and coaches by special arrangement. Teas on Sun and Bank Holiday Mons only* ◑ **WC** ✿ ⛪

The Grade-II-listed terraced garden, replanted by the present owner in the 1960s, is cultivated down the side of a hill overlooking the Vale of Avalon, affording a magnificent view of Wells Cathedral. A wide variety of plants, all suitable for the alkaline soil, provides a succession of colours and interest from March to October. Many fine trees can be seen in the garden and in the seven-acre arboretum opposite the entrance to the car park

Montacute House ★   23

Montacute TA15 6XP. Tel: (01935) 823289; Fax: (01935) 826921

The National Trust • *4m W of Yeovil. Signposted from A3088 and A303 near Ilchester* • *House open 23rd March to 3rd Nov, daily except Tues, 12 noon – 5.30pm (last admission 5pm)* • *Park and garden open all year: 23rd March to 3rd Nov, daily except Tues, 11am – 5.30pm (or dusk if earlier); 6th Nov to March 2003 Wed – Sun, 11.30am – 4pm (or dusk if earlier)* • *Entrance: March to Nov, garden and park £3.40, children £1.50; Nov to March 2003, £2, children £1 (house, garden and park £6.20, children £3, family £15)* • *Other information: Picnics in designated areas only. Dogs in park only, on lead. Plants for sale April to Sept* ○ 🍽 ✕ ♿ ⛪ ♨ ♞

This Elizabethan garden of grass lawns surrounded by clipped yews set in terraces is a triumph of formality. The surrealism of the topiary, which some claim was inspired by a dramatic snowfall, adds immensely to the effect. A large water feature has replaced the original Elizabethan high circular mount, and there is a charming raised walk, two original pavilions and an arcaded garden house probably devised by Lord Curzon during his tenancy, when he lived here, first with Elinor Glyn. Colour is provided by herbaceous borders from mid-summer. The gardens are surrounded by graceful parklands giving vistas and an impression of space. A new avenue of 72 limes is now established.

2 Old Tarnwell 24

Upper Stanton Drew BS39 4EA. Tel: (01275) 333146

Mr and Mrs K. Payne • 6m S of Bristol, W of Pensford between A368 and B3130 • Open June and July for small groups by appt • Entrance: £2 ◑

An astonishingly interesting and praiseworthy garden, tiny in scale but highly imaginative in the use of colour and texture and packed with ideas for owners of small plots. Three beds in the front garden use yellow as the dominant colour. The rear garden manages to include a tiny trickling pool enclosed by rampant clematis and climbing plants.

Prior Park Landscape Garden★ 25

Ralph Allen Drive, Bath BA2 5AH. Tel: (01225) 833422 (General Enquiries)

The National Trust • No parking at garden or nearby; catch Badgerline bus from city centre or walk up A3062 from Widcombe • Open Feb to Nov, Wed – Mon, 12 noon – 5.30pm (16th April to Sept opens 11am); Dec to Jan 2002, Fri – Sun, 12 noon – dusk. Closed 14th, 15th April, 25th, 26th Dec and 1st Jan • Entrance: £4, children £2 (£1 discount, on production of ticket, for those arriving by public transport or pre-booked coach) • Other information: Small area for disabled parking (must be pre-booked), with limited access for disabled ◑ 🚌 <u>WC</u> ♿ 🍴 ☕

This remarkable restoration by the Trust, when completed, will have transformed Prior Park. The Palladian mansion, designed by the architect John Wood from 1735 for Bath's leading entrepreneur and philanthropist Ralph Allen, dominates the steeply sloping landscape and provides stunning views of the city. While the mansion is owned and used by Prior Park College and is not open to the public, the grounds below are well worth the circular walk (allow 1½ hours) from the entrance gate off Ralph Allen Drive. Allen landscaped and planted continuously over a period of 30 years from 1734 to 1764, helped by several gardeners, notably 'Capability' Brown, who eliminated areas of formality. Alexander Pope inspired the area known as the Wilderness, which includes a Rococo sham bridge and the ruins of Mrs Allen's grotto (full restoration of the Wilderness is ongoing). The walk continues from the mansion viewpoint down the east side of the valley to the lakes and the Palladian bridge of 1755, returning by the west side of the valley via the Rock Gate. Undoubtedly two-star are the views – sensitively created by the Trust – of the Palladian bridge, the mansion from the bridge and the city of Bath.

Sherborne Garden 26

Pear Tree House, Litton BA3 4PP. Tel: (01761) 241220

Mr and Mrs J. Southwell • 15m S of Bristol, 7½ m N of Wells on B3114, ¼ m beyond Litton and The Kings Arms • Open 4th June to 24th Sept, Mon and occasional Suns, 11am – 6pm, and other days by appt • Entrance: £2, children free ● ☕ 🏺 WC & ⬧ ⬧ ⬧

A large, rather surreal garden that displays a very personal choice of specimen trees, grasses and water garden features in a four-and-a-half-acre site reclaimed from farmland. It is an interesting example of how natural pasture land may be tamed and surface water channelled into ponds. The owners are compulsive tree people who since 1963 have planted hundreds of native and exotic trees, expanding the original cottage garden and paddock into a mini-arboretum. The garden now boasts a one-acre spinney of native species, a pinetum, nut hedges, a collection of species roses, gravel beds with collections of giant and miniature grasses and about 150 varieties of hemerocallis, a Prickly Wood that offers 100 varieties of holly, and a collection of over 250 ferns. Most trees and plants are clearly labelled.

Ston Easton Park ★ 27

Ston Easton, Bath BA3 4DF. Tel: (01761) 241631;
E-mail: stoneastonpark@stoneaston.co.uk; Website: www.stoneaston.co.uk

Andrew Davis • 11m SW of Bath, 6m NE of Wells on A39 • Open by appt only • Entrance: free • Other information: Teas and toilet facilities in hotel ● ☕ ✕ WC

The Grade-I-listed Palladian house is set in a park replanned and replanted by Humphry Repton in 1792–93. A suitably impressive drive winds past old stables to the plain Palladian magnificence of the house. The glory is the view from inside the great Saloon, or from Repton's terrace immediately outside, over the River Norr with a bridge and cascades. Repton made a Red Book with his proposals for improvement, and Penelope Hobhouse worked with the previous owners on the restoration of the park to his plans. Beyond the terrace are wide lawns, woods, cedars, beeches, oaks, willows and some newly planted yew hedges. The vast kitchen garden, with its glasshouses, cutting garden and metres of beautifully presented fruit and vegetables, now has a rose garden, recently completed with the help of Mrs Hobhouse. It took seven years to repair the kitchen garden walls, three and a half years for each side. It is worth making an appointment to visit this historic place – the house is a Relais and Châteaux Hotel.

Tintinhull House Garden ★ 28

Farm Street, Tintinhull, Yeovil BA22 9PZ. Tel: (01935) 822545;
E-mail: wtifxs@smtp.ntrust.org.uk

The National Trust • 5m NW of Yeovil, ½ m S of A303. Signposted • Open 23rd March to 29th Sept, Wed – Sun and Bank Holiday Mons, 12 noon – 6pm • Entrance: £3.80, children £1.80 • Other information: Disabled parking by arrangement ◑ ☕

A relatively small modern garden, barely two acres, which achieves an impression of greater size with a series of vistas created under the influence of Hidcote. Developed from the 1930s by Phyllis Reiss, it was later in the care of Penelope Hobhouse. The Eagle Court near the house has fine borders and passes on to a small white garden; from here, an opening leads to the stylish kitchen garden with orchard beyond. The pool garden is particularly splendid, with its 'hot' and 'cool' borders. The Cedar Court has some old trees, including a yew said to be 400 years old. In order to retain the charm of a private garden the wide variety of plants is not labelled, but an inventory is available for interested visitors.

Wayford Manor ★   29

Crewkerne TA18 8QG. Tel: (01460) 73253; Fax: (01460) 76365

Mr and Mrs R.L. Goffe • 3m SW of Crewkerne off B3165 at Clapton • Open 5th, 6th, 19th May, 2nd, 16th June, 2 – 6pm, and for parties by appt • Entrance: £2, children 50p ● ● WC ⬦ ᵂ

A well-maintained garden of flowering shrubs and trees complementing a fine manor house dating from the thirteenth century with Elizabethan and Victorian additions. This is a fine example of the work of Harold Peto, who redesigned the garden in 1902. The formal upper terrace with yew hedges and topiary fronting the house leads down to the next level, a walled garden with rose and herbaceous beds, lawns and gravel paths. It descends again to a rockery and a grass tennis court enclosed on three sides by a yew hedge. Below is a large area or informal, partly wild garden with extensive plantings of mature trees and shrubs, including rare and colourful maples, cornus, magnolias, rhododendrons and spring bulbs. Water features throughout, from a spring-fed pond on the top terrace through streams and ponds at all levels. The millennium project was the replacement of a timber pergola by a stone-pillared one to complement the loggia designed by Peto.

William Herschel Museum and Star Vault   30

19 New King Street, Bath BA1 2BL. Tel: (01225) 311342/446865,
Website: www.bath.preservation-trust.org.uk

Trustees of the Museum • On New King Street close to Queen's Square and Green Park Station • Museum open • Garden open March to Oct, daily, 2 – 5pm; Nov to Feb, Sat and Sun, 2 – 5pm. Closed 13th April • Entrance: £3.50, children under 18 £2, family (2 adults and up to 4 children) £7.50 ● WC ⬛ ᵠ ᵠ

This is one of the smaller and more fascinating museums, from whose garden William Herschel discovered the planet Uranus in 1781. Over the years the garden has suffered from neglect, but replanting has re-created a charming small town garden such as might well have existed in Herschel's time

Windmill Cottage   31

Hillside Road, Backwell BS48 3BL. Tel: (01275) 463492

Mr and Mrs Alan Harwood • 8m SW of Bristol on A370. Cottage is 10-min walk up Hillside Road, single-track lane. Park in Backwell and New Inn

(telephone for special arrangements for disabled etc.) • *Open to groups May to Oct by appt* • *Entrance: £2* ● ⬛ WC ⬥ ⌘

A wooded background to a rocky hill site facing north is hardly the best place for a garden, but the owners have accepted the challenge and over several years have achieved a remarkable result. Interspersed with a range of shrubs and grasses, beds of varying shape and content climb the hill. A pretty pool area, a dry stream and scree beds are reached by winding grass paths and lead on to an unfolding progression of unusual plants in strong but blended colours. A pergola is home to a variety of roses and honeysuckles, and a magnificent 'Etoile de Hollande' rose covers the cottage wall. A rare *Holboellia latifolia* survives the winters. Clematis abound, blue and white ones bedecking the ruined windmill overseen by the donkey in its orchid and wildflower patch.

Woodborough 32

Porlock Weir TA24 8NZ. Tel: (01643) 862406

Mr and Mrs R.D. Milne • *6m W of Minehead. From A39 at Porlock take B3225 towards Porlock Weir. At Porlock Vale House on right, take left tarmac lane uphill immediately opposite. Garden first on right* • *Open by appt only* • *Entrance: £2, children under 10 free* • *Other information: No coaches* ● ⬟

This fascinating garden created on a steep (1 in 4) hillside has magnificent views over Porlock Bay. The wide variety of shrubs includes some of the lesser-known hybrid rhododendrons and a number of Ghent azaleas. A bog garden and two pools add interest over a longer season. The owners will happily share with visitors their hard-won experience in garden restoration and their battle with the dreaded honey fungus.

A TOTALLY INDEPENDENT PUBLICATION

The *Guide* makes no charge for entries, which are written by our own inspectors. The factual details are supplied by owners. This is a totally independent publication and its only revenue comes from sales of copies in bookshops.

NATIONAL COUNCIL FOR THE CONSERVATION OF PLANTS AND GARDENS

The NCCPG publishes a *National Plant Collections Directory*. Those interested in particular families of plants who want to see some of the rarer species and garden varieties will find this an invaluable publication. The latest edition, which offers information on about 600 collections comprising more than 50,000 plants and contains articles by holders of the collections, is available from NCCPG, The Pines, RHS Garden, Wisley, Woking GU3 6QB (Tel: (01483) 221465; Fax: (01483) 212404; Website: www.nccpg.org.uk. The 2002 edition will be published January or February 2002.

STAFFORDSHIRE

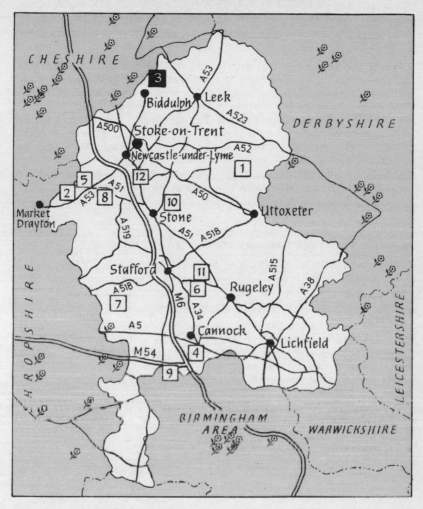

Two-starred gardens are marked on the map with a black square.

Alton Towers ★ 1

Alton ST10 4DB. Tel: (08705) 204060; Website: www.altontowers.com

Alton Towers • From N take M6 junction 16 or M1 junction 28, from S take M6 junction 15 or M1 junction 23A. Signposted • Theme park, ruins and grounds open all year, daily, 9.30am – 5pm, 6pm or 7pm (1 hour before rides open until 1 hour after they close). Telephone for opening times Nov to mid-

March (when probably grounds only open) • Entrance: mid-March to 1st Nov (theme park and grounds) £22, OAPs £12, children (4–12) £18, family season ticket £70. Towers Two ticket allows second day at Park for £10. Party rates available (2001 peak-time prices; telephone to check premium and off-peak prices) ○ 🍽 ✕ 🛍 WC ♿ 🚻 🅿 🐾

This fantastic garden of ornamental architecture was one of the last great follies, created in the early nineteenth century. W.A. Nesfield was active here (one of his parterres is still *in situ* though in need of restoration). It contains many beautiful and unusual features, including the Chinese pagoda fountain, a copy of the To Ho pagoda in Canton. The enormous rock garden is planted with a range of conifers, acers and sedums. The fine conservatory houses geraniums etc. according to the season, and the terraces have rose and herbaceous borders. There is a Dutch garden, Her Ladyship's Garden featuring yew and rose beds, the Italian garden, a yew-arch walkway and woodland walks. Water adds further beauty and interest. In addition, there are all the attractions of the theme park.

Arbour Cottage 2

Napley, Market Drayton, Shropshire TF9 4AJ. Tel: (01630) 672852

Mr and Mrs D.K. Hewitt • 4m NE of Market Drayton. From A53 take B5415 signed 'Woore.' In $1\frac{3}{4}$ m turn left at telephone box • Open several days in April, May and June, 2 – 5.30pm, for NGS, and at other times by appt. Parties welcome • Entrance: £2.50, children 50p ● 🍽 WC ♿ 🐾

The owners have established a two-acre garden of wide-ranging interest and year-round colour in an area of countryside beauty with many species of trees. There are peonies, grasses, bamboos, etc. and tender specimens such as New Zealand flax. A collection of shrub roses and alpines, screes and rockeries. Plenty here for the plantsman, including a large greenhouse with tropical plants, some for sale.

Biddulph Grange Garden ★★ 3

**Grange Road, Biddulph, Stoke–on–Trent ST8 7SD.
Tel: (01782) 517999 (Garden Office)**

The National Trust • $3\frac{1}{2}$ m SE of Congleton, 7m N of Stoke-on-Trent. Access from A527 Biddulph/Congleton road • Open 23rd March to 3rd Nov, Wed – Fri (but closed Good Friday), 12 noon – 5.30pm, Sat, Sun and Bank Holiday Mons, 11am – 5.30pm (or dusk if earlier); 11th Nov to 22nd Dec, Sat and Sun, 12 noon – 4pm (or dusk if earlier). Guided tours by appt only • Entrance: £4.50, children £2.40, family £11.50, parties of 15 or more £3.80 per person; Nov and Dec free • Other information: Limited wheelchair access ◐ 🍽 WC 🐾 🚻

This is one of the most remarkable and innovative gardens of the nineteenth century. There is an Egyptian garden with a pyramid and obelisks of clipped yew. The Chinese garden has a joss house, a golden water buffalo overlooking a dragon parterre, a watch tower and a temple reflected in a calm pool. In front of the house terraces descend to a lily pond. The Stumpery demonstrates an innovative Victorian way to display suitable plants. The verbena, araucaria and rose parterres and the Shelter House and Dahlia Walk (with over 600 dahlias) have now been restored just as they were in the middle of the nineteenth century. A courageous effort was the felling and replanting of the fine, long Wellingtonia avenue. In all, one of the country's most unusual gardening rediscoveries and restorations – it should not be missed.

12 Darges Lane   4

Great Wyrley, Walsall WS6 6LE. Tel: (01922) 415064

Mrs A. Hackett • 2m SE of Cannock. From A5 (Churchbridge junction) take A34 towards Walsall. First turning on right over brow of hill. House on right on corner of Cherrington Drive • Open 28th April, 2 – 6pm, 26th June, 6.30 – 9.30pm, 1st Sept, 2 – 6pm, and by appt • Entrance: £1.50 • Other information: Plants for sale on open days, and March to Sept third Mon in month ● ● ●

A quarter-acre garden on two levels, attractively laid out, well stocked and of great interest to plantsmen. Fine trees and large variety of shrubs and foliage plants are the background to a comprehensive collection of flowering plants and small shrubs, some unusual, even rare. A National Collection of lamiums is here. There are borders and island beds, and a small water garden. Every inch is used to grow or set off the plants, and there is year-round appeal for flower arrangers. The overall effect is attractive as well as enticing to the plant lover. Plants for sale include some more unusual ones.

The Dorothy Clive Garden ★   5

Willoughbridge, Market Drayton, Shropshire TF9 4EU. Tel: (01630) 647237

Willoughbridge Garden Trust • 7m NE of Market Drayton, 1m E of Woore on A51 between Nantwich and Stone • Open April to Oct, daily, 10am – 5.30pm • Entrance: £3.20, OAPs £2.70, children (11–16) £1, under 11 free (2001 prices) • Other information: Disabled parking ● ● ✕ ● WC & ● ●

Created by the late Colonel Clive in memory of his wife, with the help of distinguished gardeners including the late John Codrington, this garden has wide appeal in terms both of design and inspired planting. The guide identifies the highlights season by season. These include the rhododendrons and azaleas in the quarry garden and the pool with the scree garden rising on the hillside above it. In spring there are unusual bulbs and primulas, in summer colourful shrubs, unusual perennials and many conifers; other trees provide autumn colour. The scree garden must give gardeners many good ideas. The garden has been extended, and new features include a laburnum arch with roses and other climbers, and a small pool with a bog garden.

The Garth   6

2 Broc Hill Way, Milford, Stafford ST17 0UB. Tel: (01785) 661182

Mr and Mrs David Wright • 4½ m SE of Stafford. On A513 Stafford – Rugeley road, at Barley Mow turn right, then left after ½ m • Open 2nd, 23rd June, 2 – 6pm, and by appt for parties • Entrance: £2, children free ● ● WC ● ● ●

This half-acre garden surrounded by countryside contains specialist areas which should give inspiration and ideas to any gardener. The visitor moves down the different levels to discover old caves at the bottom of the slope. The range of plants includes six unusual beeches, 20 different ferns, 30 different clematis, magnolias, rhododendrons, pulmonarias, hostas, azaleas, penstemons and astilbes, berberis, fothergillas, garryas, amelanchiers and *Holodiscus discolor*, all planted to provide foliage interest and colour combinations. Archways are covered with roses and loniceras, and in the herbaceous borders are heathers, campanulas and osteospermums. There is also a pool and a bog garden.

Little Onn Hall   7

Church Eaton, Stafford ST20 0AU. Tel: (01785) 840154

Mrs I.H. Kidson • 6m SW of Stafford, 2m S of Church Eaton, midway between A5 and A518 • Open by appt only • Entrance: £3, children 50p ● ☕ 🍽 WC ♿ ⬥ ♨

The driveway to this six-acre garden is flanked by long herbaceous borders backed by yew hedges. The large rose garden contains standards, shrub and hybrid teas. An unusual-shaped pool known as the Dog Bone is planted with water lilies; bog plants reside elsewhere in the medieval moat, a delightful feature. Since 1971 the present owner has been planting new trees and is trying to maintain the original design by Thomas H. Mawson. Many rhododendrons, spring bulbs and large beeches and conifers ensure colour for a long season. Some eight miles north-west, at Offley Brook, Eccleshall, is *Heath House*, where the varied and interesting garden contains a wide selection of unusual plants. [Open for NGS and by appt – telephone (01785) 280318.]

Manor Cottage   8

Chapel Chorlton, Newcastle-under-Lyme ST5 5JN. Tel: (01782) 680206

Mrs Joyce Heywood • 6m SW of Newcastle-under-Lyme. From A51 Nantwich – Stone road turn behind Cock Inn at Stableford. House on village green • Open Bank Holiday Mons, and by appt • Entrance: £1.50, children 50p ● ☕ WC ♿ ⬥ ✿

This two-thirds-of-an-acre garden has been created by the present owner over several years and is beautifully designed for year-long interest with excellent colour combinations and varieties of foliage, including many variegated forms. It is a flower arranger's paradise, with a wide range including collections of ferns, geraniums, hellebores, grasses and hostas. Small paths lead to surprises round each corner, and there are roses climbing through old fruit trees, a broad range of conifers and a good alpine area. Unusual plants are continuously being introduced.

Moseley Old Hall   9

**Moseley Old Hall Lane, Fordhouses, Wolverhampton WV10 7HY.
Tel: (01902) 782808; Fax: (01902) 782808**

The National Trust • 4m N of Wolverhampton. From S on M6 and M54 take junction 1 to Wolverhampton. From N on M6 take junction 11 then A460. Coaches must use A460 • House opens same dates as but ¹/₂ hour later than garden • Garden open 23rd March to 3rd Nov, Wed, Sat, Sun; also Bank Holiday Mons and Tues following, 12 noon – 5pm; Nov to 15th Dec, Sun only, 2 – 4pm • Entrance: £4.10, children £2.05, family ticket (2 adults and 3 children) £10.25; groups of 15 or more £3.50 per person (house and garden) ❶ ☕ 🍽 WC ♿ ⚑ 🌿 🎁 ☕

Around the Elizabethan house where Charles II hid after the Battle of Worcester is a garden mainly for the specialist interested in old species, as all are seventeenth century except for a few fruit trees. The knot garden is from a design of 1640 by The Rev. Walter Stonehouse. A wooden arbour is covered with clematis and *Vitis vinifera* 'Purpurea'. Fruit trees include a mulberry, medlars and a morello cherry. The walled garden has topiary and herbaceous borders, and fritillaries grow in the nut walk. There is a small herb garden and boles for bees. It is interesting to see plants grown in times past to provide dyes and for cleansing and medicinal purposes.

Oulton House   10

Oulton, Stone ST15 8UR. Tel: (01785) 813556

Mr and Mrs W.A. Fairbairn • 8m N of Stafford, ½ m NE of Stone. From Stone take Oulton road and after Oulton village sign turn left. After houses turn right up long drive • Open April to July by appt • Entrance: £2, children 75p ❶ ☕ 🍽 WC 🌿 ☕

This three-acre garden with fine views, surrounded by parkland, has been developed by the present owner over more than 20 years. A range of large trees provides shelter. The conservatory contains vines, camellias and roses. Herbaceous borders are distinguished by interesting colour combinations and a wide range of plants, including geraniums, delphiniums, euphorbias and astrantias. Old shrub roses abound, and a grey-and-silver border by the house has clematis and roses climbing its walls. A new border features yellow, blue and white perennials, including superb delphiniums, and the bank behind is covered with ivies, loniceras and roses. There is also a rhododendron walk, a large rockery, a patio area, a golden corner, a white area, and a large vegetable and fruit garden. Although not a weed-tree garden, there is plenty to delight the eye; it is hoped it may be open more often as the borders contain a mass of snowdrops and tulips which must be a delight to see in spring and early summer.

Rode Hall

(see Cheshire)

Shugborough ★   11

Milford, Stafford ST17 0XB. Tel: (01889) 881388; Fax: (01889) 881323; Website: www.staffordshire.gov.uk

Staffordshire County Council/The National Trust • 6m E of Stafford on A513 • House, museum and Park Farm open • Garden open 30th March to 29th Sept, Tues – Sun, 11am – 5pm (but open Bank Holiday Mons); Oct, Sun only. Open for pre-booked parties all year from 10.30am • Entrance: £2 per vehicle to parkland, gardens, picnic area, walks and trails. Voyager tickets to house, museum and farm £8, concessions £6, family £18 (2001 prices) • Other information: Batricars available. Dogs in park only, on lead ◑ ◙ ✕ 🖗 WC & 🏧 ♀

Shugborough is of interest to garden historians because Thomas Wright of Durham worked here. Many of the buildings and monuments are ascribed to James 'Athenian' Stuart and were built for Thomas Anson from the 1740s onwards. These are some of the earliest examples of English neo-classicism, and there is also an early example of Chinoiserie based on a sketch made by one of the officers on Admiral Anson's voyage round the world. *The Oxford Companion* suggests that the buildings were 'randomly scattered', but another view is that they were put in place as 'hidden architectural treasures' to surprise. As for the garden, the Victorian layout with terraces by Nesfield was revitalised for the Trust in the mid-1960s by Graham Stuart Thomas, who also worked on the Edwardian-style rose garden. Seasonal attractions include azaleas, rhododendrons and a fine herbaceous border. The first stage of a major tree-planting scheme has begun with over 1000 young oaks, the aim being to restore Shugborough to its original eighteenth-century layout with more hedgerows and wooded areas. There is also a woodland walk, and guided tours of the garden are available.

Trentham Gardens   12

Stone Road, Trentham, Stoke-on-Trent ST4 8JG. Tel: (01782) 657341

Trentham Leisure Ltd • On A34 S of Stoke-on-Trent. 2m from M6 junction 15 • Open early April to early Oct, daily, 10am – 6pm (telephone to check dates) • Entrance: £1, concessions and children 50p • Other information: Conference centre adjacent ◑ ◙ 🖗 WC & ⬦ ♀ ℚ

The 750 acres of parkland were designed by 'Capability' Brown. Nesfield added a large Italian garden and Sir Charles Barry laid out formal gardens for the Duke of Sutherland. The gardens have been greatly simplified but still retain many features, such as Brown's large lake (on which one can now enjoy waterskiing). There is a rose garden, a good selection of shrubs including hebes, potentillas and buddleias, and magnificent trees alongside the River Trent, which flows through the gardens, and in the woodland area by the lake. A good place for a family day out, as there are picnic areas and a play area. However, the buildings and hundreds of acres of parkland have been neglected and at the time of going to press are still awaiting planning permission for a major refurbishment by the new owners.

SUFFOLK

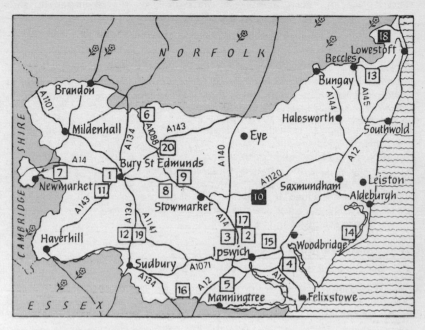

Some gardens have postal addresses in one county and are physically situated in another. If in doubt, a check in the index will direct the reader to the page on which the garden appears.

Two-starred gardens are marked on the map with a black square.

Abbey Gardens 1

Bury St Edmunds. Website: www.stedmunds.gov.uk

Borough of St Edmundsbury • In town centre • Open all year, daily, 9am – dusk • Entrance: free ○ 🍽 ✕ 📷 WC ♿ ⏱ ☘ 🛒 🔋 ✎

This is a most surprising garden. In 945 the Benedictines founded the Abbey, which undoubtedly had gardens for herbs and vegetables. The abbey ruins (it was dissolved in 1539) form the extraordinary 'bones' of the present-day landscape; if for no other reason, visit the place to see the great walls, like some extraordinary geological feature, now dissolving into flinty stumps. Then think forward 900 years and bring to mind that one Nathaniel Hodson actually formed a botanic garden on this site in 1821. The present arrangement of formal beds on the site of the Great Court of the abbey mirrors his garden, of which perhaps only a few trees remain. The planting in the formal garden may be bright – lots of begonias and busy lizzies in summer – but in its way it is the modern equivalent of Hodson's choice. You will learn more about the history of the gardens by asking for the excellent free leaflet at the Bowling Green office; there is also a leaflet about the small 'medieval' herb garden. So this is a special place, of historical interest, much used by the townspeople, and certainly worth a visit when you are in the town.

Barham Hall ★ 2

Church Lane, Barham, Ipswich IP6 0QF. Tel: (01473) 830055

Mr and Mrs Richard Burrows • *5m NW of Ipswich off A14 (A45). Take third turning to Claydon, ½ m up Church Lane* • *Open 24th March, 30th June for charity, 2 – 5pm* • *Entrance: £2* ● ➊ WC ♿ ✿

The garden, seven acres in all, includes a water garden and lake surrounded by bog plants, a woodland shrub garden, many herbaceous borders and a collection of Victorian roses, all kept to the highest standard. The whole impression is of immaculate care and attention to detail, achieved during the past 10 years, with extensive remodelling over the past five. In 2000 a new border and a water canal were added. If the perfection of maintenance will not make you green with envy you must see this garden – if it does, go anyway to see the Henry Moore sculpture in the church.

Blakenham Woodland Garden 3

Little Blakenham, Ipswich. Tel: (07760) 342131

4m NW of Ipswich, 1m off B1113. Signed from The Beeches in Little Blakenham, 1m off old A1100 (now B1113) • *Open March to June, daily except Sat, 1 – 5pm. Parties welcome by appt* • *Entrance: £1* ◑

Set in five acres of bluebell wood, planted with a huge variety of ornamental trees and flowering shrubs, Blakenham is at its best in spring, full of cornus, azaleas, magnolias, camellias and rhododendrons, followed later by roses, hydrangeas and abutilons. As summer advances it gets more overgrown, which only adds to its charm. Grass paths wind through and one can sit on one of the many seats, listening to the birds in perfect peace.

Bucklesham Hall ★ 4

Bucklesham, Ipswich IP10 0AY. Tel: (01473) 659263

Mr and Mrs D.R. Brightwell • *6m SE of Ipswich, ½ m E of Bucklesham. Entrance opposite and N of primary school* • *Open by appt* • *Entrance: £3* • *Other information: Coaches by appt. Refreshments by arrangement* ● ➊ ▦ ♿ ✈ ✿ ♟

The great interest of Bucklesham is how these seven acres of interlocking gardens, terraces and lakes have been created from scratch since 1973 by the previous owners and added to and further improved by the present owners since 1994. A Monet-type bridge was built in 1999 with a waterfall falling between two lakes. A 16-step water staircase has also been made so that the water flows from an island lake into the streams. Round the house are secret gardens so packed with flowers that no weed could survive; beds of old-fashioned roses overflow their borders, and a courtyard garden has been created with the use of every kind of container. Descending terraces of lawns, ponds and streams lead to the woodland and beyond; round each corner is a new vista. Skill, wide horticultural knowledge and imagination have resulted in a remarkable display of plants, shrubs and trees.

East Bergholt Place 5

East Bergholt, CO7 6UP. Tel/Fax: (01206) 299224;
E-mail: placeforplants@martex.net

Mr and Mrs Rupert Eley • 8m SW of Ipswich, 2m E of A12 on B1070 • Open March to Oct, daily, 10am – 5pm. Closed 31st March • Entrance: £2.50, children free ◑ 🍽 WC ⅄ ⚘

The garden was originally laid out between 1900 and 1914 by Charles Eley, the present owner's great-grandfather, and many of the existing plants originate from the great plant collector George Forrest. The 15 acres are an interesting blend of the formal and informal, and are particularly lovely in the spring. The yew topiary and terrace area are linked to undulating informal walks by water features, including a pool and stream. The large collection of rare specimen trees and shrubs includes many camellias, magnolias and rhododendrons. There is an extensive plant centre in the attractive walled garden.

Euston Hall ★ 6

Thetford, Norfolk IP24 2QP. Tel: (01842) 766366

The Duke and Duchess of Grafton • 3m S of Thetford on A1088 • House open as garden • Garden open 6th June to 26th Sept, Thurs, plus 30th June and 1st Sept, all2.30 – 5pm • Entrance: £3, OAPs £2.50, children £1 (under 5 free), parties of 12 or more £2.50 per person; Gardens only £1 (2001 prices) ◑ ☕ WC ⅄ ⛪

Fronted by terraces, the hall stands among extensive lawns and parkland along a winding river, the work of William Kent in the 1740s (followed by 'Capability' Brown), as are the splendid domed temple isolated on an eminence to the east and the pretty garden house in the formal garden by the house, which as been developed by the present Duke. The pleasure grounds, laid out in the seventeenth century by John Evelyn, have grown into a forest of yew, but straight rides trace out the original formal layout. Also from this period are the stone gate piers which, together with the remnants of a great avenue, mark the original approach to the house. A small lake reflects the house across the park, and there are many fine specimen trees and a wealth of shrub roses.

Garden House 7

Brookside, Moulton, Newmarket CB8 8SG. Tel: 01638 750283

Mr and Mrs J. Maskelyne • 3m E of Newmarket on B1085 in Moulton village • Open for charity and for parties by appt April to July • Entrance: £2 ◑ ☕ WC ⅄

A midsummer afternoon; an English village quaint with time; the gentle rustle of the leaves in a soft breeze; exotic perfumes wafting over the green; a quiet murmuring of voices wondering what that rose might be, or where might we get such-and-such a clematis. Bliss. And this is the kind of relaxing, near-perfect garden we all want to live in, a veritable, vibrant pot-pourri. There are too many plants to mention, arrayed in beds and borders, but the principals are old roses and clematis. There is a stunning *Carpenteria californica*, and overhead a variegated maple (not everyone's favourite, but here just right). Sages and geraniums, delphiniums and day lilies, all fitting into place and all looking healthy and happy. In spring the hellebores and epimediums in the shaded nooks are a joy. The summer colour combinations are subtle and immaculate: creams and dark crimsons, lilacs and blues. Not to be missed, especially in mid-summer, when you can linger for afternoon tea on the patio.

Garden House Farm   8

Rattlesden Road, Drinkstone, Bury St Edmunds IP30 9TN. Tel: (01449) 736434; E-mail: gardenhousefarm@dial.pipex.com

Mr and Mrs Hans Seiffer • 8m E of Bury St Edmunds, 3m SW of Woolpit off A14; from Woolpit follow signs to Drinkstone Green • Open Easter to Sept, Wed, 2 – 5pm, plus 23rd June, 2 – 6pm, and at other times by appt • Entrance £2.50 ● 🍽 ㅩ

Formerly the display gardens of Barcocks Nursery, there are now 11 acres of hedge-lined gardens, each with its own character. The summer garden, planted with many old-fashioned roses and exuberant herbaceous perennials, contrasts with a fiery-coloured foliage and flower garden. In the formal secret garden paths radiate from a central pond. There is also a winter garden, a lake, large woodland areas filled with rare and unusual plants and many fine trees. The house offers B&B.

Haughley Park ★   9

Stowmarket IP14 3JY. Tel: (01359) 240701

Mr R.J. Williams • 4m NW of Stowmarket, signed 'Haughley Park' (not 'Haughley') on A14 • House open by appt • Garden open 28th April, 5th May (Bluebell Suns), and May to Sept, Tues, 2 – 5.30pm • Entrance: £2, children £1 • Other information: Coaches by appt. Teas provided on Bluebell Suns ● 🍴 WC ㅩ 🐕 🌿 ☕

A hundred acres of rolling parkland at the heart of 100 more acres of woodland surround the seventeenth-century Jacobean mansion. Unexpected secret gardens with clipped hedges or flint and brick walls hide immaculate flower beds, climbers and flowering shrubs; each garden has its own character. The main lawn is surrounded by herbaceous borders, with a splendid lime avenue at the end drawing the eye across many miles of open countryside. Rhododendrons, azaleas and camellias grow on soil which is, unexpectedly for Suffolk, lime-free. The trees include a splendid *Davidia involucrata*, a 12-metre-wide magnolia and a flourishing oak over nine metres in girth, reputed to be 1000 years old. Beyond are the walled kitchen garden, the greenhouses and the shrubbery. In spring the broad rides and walks through the ancient woodland reveal not only the newly planted trees, specimen rhododendrons and other ornamental shrubs, but 10 acres of bluebells, two acres of lilies-of-the-valley and half a mile of mauve *ponticum* rhododendrons.

Helmingham Hall Gardens ★★ 10

Stowmarket IP14 6EF. Tel: (01473) 890363 (Contact Jane Tresidder); Website: www.helmingham.com

Lord Tollemache • 9m N of Ipswich on B1077 • Open 28th April to 8th Sept, Sun, 2 – 6pm; also Wed, 2 – 5pm, for parties and individuals by prior appt • Entrance: £3.75, children £2, parties of 30 or more £3.25 per person (Wed parties £3.75 per person) • Other information: Safari rides to see deer, Highland cattle and Soay sheep ● ▊ ▊ WC ♿ ⬦ ✿ ♨ ♥

Nineteen generations of Tollemaches have lived here, and though there have been many changes over the past five centuries the property retains a strong Elizabethan atmosphere. The double-moated Tudor mansion house of great splendour and charm, built of warm red brick, stands in a 400-acre deer park. A nineteenth-century parterre, edged with a magnificent spring border, leads to the Elizabethan kitchen garden which is surrounded by the Saxon moat with banks covered in daffodils. Within the walls the kitchen garden has been transformed into an enchanting *potager* most subtly planted; the meticulously maintained herbaceous borders and old-fashioned roses surround beds of vegetables separated by arched tunnels of sweet peas and runner beans. Beyond is a meadow garden and, leading from it, a yew walk with philadelphus and shade-loving plants. On the other side of the hall, framed by a yew hedge, is an historical knot and herb garden with a magnificent collection of shrub roses underplanted with campanulas and hardy geraniums. All the plants are chosen to be contemporary with the house. Some 7 miles to the north, off the A140 at Wetheringsett, *Park Green Nurseries* stock over 300 varieties of hostas [open March to Sept, daily, 10am – 5pm].

Ickworth Park and Gardens 11

Horringer, Nr Bury St Edmunds IP29 5QE. Tel: (01284) 735270

The National Trust • 3m SW of Bury St Edmunds; signposted • Park open daily (except 25th Dec), dawn to dusk • Garden open Jan to 3rd Nov, daily, 10am – 5pm (Jan to March closes 4pm), 23rd March to 3rd Nov, 4th Nov to Dec, Mon – Fri, 10am – 4pm • Entrance: £2.70, children 80p ○ ▊ ✕ ▊ WC ♿ ✿ ♥ ♨

The vast park, girdled by woodland, is in part the work of Lancelot 'Capability' Brown and provides a formidable setting for the late eighteenth-century house. At first the building is not obvious, but the great rotunda soon looms large, and the monster stands revealed, grandiose and gaunt, with vast curving wings, dominating the gardens which surround it. A formal garden, in the Italian style, lies to the south of the house. It features many Mediterranean species and provides an intriguing point of contrast to the thoroughly bucolic, English landscape of the grazed parkland beyond its boundary wall. Within the

Italian garden, there is box everywhere (the property holds the National Collection of buxus). Bands of Jerusalem sage and catmint, and bedded-out scarlet pelargoniums, provide occasional colour. Hidden behind the clipped hedges you can discover a series of hidden gardens – spring, silver and gold – and the extraordinary stumpery complete with bits of the Giant's Causeway, signalling one of the other stupendous creations of Ickworth's builder, the fourth Earl of Bristol (also Bishop of Derry): his Mussenden Temple at Downhill, on the north coast of Northern Ireland. The park and woods at Ickworth contain many other delights, including an ornamental canal and summerhouse which pre-date the house, a recently planted vineyard, miles of way-marked woodland walks, and a deer enclosure complete with hide.

Melford Hall   12

Long Melford, Sudbury CO10 9AA. Tel: (01787) 880286

The National Trust • 14m S of Bury St Edmunds, 3m N of Sudbury, in village, W of A134 • Hall open with special Beatrix Potter exhibition • Garden open 23rd March to 28th April, Sat, Sun and Bank Holiday Mon; May to Sept, Wed – Sun and Bank Holiday Mon; 1st Oct to 3rd Nov, Sat and Sun; all 2 – 5.30pm • Entrance: principal rooms and garden £4.50 • Other information: Disabled driven to hall. Wheelchairs provided. Stannah stairlift to first floor. Picnics in car park only. Dogs in park only, on lead ◑ 🍽 WC �& ℺

The magnificent sixteenth-century house of mellow red brick is set in a park and formal gardens. A plan by Samuel Pierse of 1613 shows that the park was separated from the hall by a walled enclosure, outside which was the moat; part of this is now the sunken garden. The avenue at the side of the house has been replanted with oaks grown from acorns taken from the existing trees. The octagonal brick pavilion on the north side of the path, a rare and beautiful example of Tudor architecture, overlooks the village green and the herbaceous borders inside the garden, which are being restored to their original Victorian and Edwardian design and planting. Outside the pavilion clipped box hedges and a bowling-green terrace lead past dense shrubbery. The garden has many good specimen trees, including the rare *Xanthoceras sorbifolium*. Great domes of box punctuate the lawns, and an interesting detail is the arrangement of yew hedges to the north of the house. Outside the walls are topiary figures. Round the pond and fountain are beds originally planted with herbs in 1937 and now being gradually improved.

North Cove Hall ★   13

North Cove, Beccles NR34 7PH. Tel: (01502) 476631

Mr and Mrs B. Blower • 3½ m E of Beccles, 50 metres off A146 Lowestoft road • Open one day for NGS, and by appt • Entrance: £2, children free ◑ 🍽 WC �& ⏁ ℘ ℺

Climbing roses adorn this sunny Georgian house set in lawns surrounded by mature park trees. The walled garden partly encloses the half-acre pond studded with water lilies and bordered by majestic *Gunnera manicata, Taxodium ascendens* 'Nutans', a group of *Betula jacquemontii* and *Alnus glutinosa* 'Imperialis'. A small stream with waterfalls has recently been constructed and planted. Inside the walls are herbaceous and shrub borders, pergolas and the kitchen garden, and there is a small scree garden. Outside are woodland walks among mature trees and various younger conifers. About 10 miles south of Beccles is *Woottons* of Wenhaston, a small garden of one acre attached to a nursery run by Mr Loftus, well laid-out and labelled, and full of rare and unusual plants.

The Old Rectory   14

Orford, Woodbridge IP12 2NN. Tel: (01394) 450063

Mr and Mrs Tim Fargher • 10m E of Woodbridge. Take B1084 Woodbridge – Orford road. Old Rectory on left behind church • Open mid-June to mid-July, Mon – Fri, 10am – 4pm, Sat, 10am – 12 noon, by appt only • Entrance: £4, OAPs and children £2 • Other information: Parking for disabled only. Visitors asked to make themselves known to gardener, Mr Denny ☺

This extensive five-acre garden, tucked behind Orford church, is immaculate, secluded and unexpected. It was designed for the owners' parents by Lanning Roper, with additions by Mark Rumary, and its beautifully planned borders and vistas surround the house, which has a large conservatory.

Playford Hall   15

Playford, Ipswich IP6 9DX. Tel: (01473) 622509

Mr and Mrs Richard Innes • 3m NE of Ipswich, 1m N of A1214 between Ipswich and Woodbridge, on edge of Playford • Open by appt only • Entrance: £5 ☺ 🍵 ⟨⟩

A beautiful moated Elizabethan house set in 10 acres of outstanding gardens. Trees, lawns and a lake surround the house, with yew hedges dividing herbaceous and shrub borders full of unusual plants. Roses cascade over the house and moat walls, and there is also a pergola rose garden underplanted with lavender and other old favourites. The orchard contains a small vegetable and herb garden.

The Priory ★   16

Stoke by Nayland CO6 4RL. Tel: (01206) 262216

Mr and Mrs Henry Engleheart • 8m SE of Sudbury on B1068 • Open 19th May, 23rd June, 2 – 6pm • Entrance: £3, children free ☺ 🍽 WC ♿ ⟨⟩ ☂ ☕

An exceptional nine-acre garden, with fine views over Constable country. Around the house is a splendid selection of plants and roses in terraces and mixed borders. Lawns slope down to a series of six small lakes, planted with a mass of water plants and water lilies. A Chinese bridge links to a tea pavilion by one of the lakes. In the spring rhododendrons and azaleas ring the lakes under large trees. A garden of mixed planting in the walled garden leads into the greenhouse/conservatory, with its colourful collection of tender plants.

Shrubland Park ★ 17

**Coddenham, Ipswich IP6 9QQ. Tel: (01473) 830221;
Fax: (01473) 832202 (Estate Office)**

Lord de Saumarez • 4m N of Ipswich. Turn off A140/A14 interchange slip road towards Ipswich and turn to Barham • Open March to Sept, Sun and Bank Holiday Mons, 2 – 5pm. Guided tours for parties of 10 or more at other times by appt • Entrance: £3, OAPs and children £2 ◕ WC

The magnificence of the hall is reflected in the Victorian gardens, laid out by Sir Charles Barry and later modified by William Robinson. They are amongst the most important of their type remaining in England. From the upper terrace outside the house visitors descend by a stunning cascade of a hundred steps and terraces to a garden of formal beds, fountain and eye-catcher loggia. Beyond is the wild garden, which merges into the woods and is bordered by the park with its many fine trees, some reputed to be 800 years old. The gardens are punctuated by a series of enchanting follies, ranging from a Swiss chalet to an alpine rockery and magnificent conservatory. The box maze is now established and growing well, and the old dell garden undergoes slow restoration. The hot wall has been totally restored: pointed, refurbished and replanted back and front.

Somerleyton Hall and Gardens ★★ 18

**Somerleyton, Lowestoft NR32 5QQ. Tel: (01502) 730224
(732950 during opening hours); Website: www.somerleyton.co.uk**

Lord and Lady Somerleyton • 8m SW of Great Yarmouth, 5m NW of Lowestoft on B1074. Signposted • House open 1 – 5pm. Telephone for details of running times of miniature railway • Gardens open 31st March to 29th Sept, Thurs, Sun and Bank Holiday Mons; July and Aug, Tues, Wed, Thurs, Sun and Bank Holiday Mon, 12.30 – 5.30pm. Private tours of hall and gardens for parties by arrangement with the administrator • Entrance: £5.20, OAPs £5, children £2.60, family (2 adults and 2 children 5–16) £14.60, parties of 20 or more rates on application (2001 prices). Check prices and opening details on website
◑ ✕ WC ♿

The former Jacobean house was extensively rebuilt in the mid-nineteenth century by Sir Morton Peto as a grand Italianate palace, and the gardens splendidly reflect this magnificence with 12 acres of formal gardens, a beautiful walled garden, an aviary, a loggia and a winter garden surrounding a sunken garden displaying statues from the original nineteenth-century winter garden. Special features include the 1846 William Nesfield yew hedge maze and the 90-metre-long iron pergola covered in wisteria, vines and roses. Not to be missed are the extraordinary peach cases and ridge-and-furrow greenhouses designed by Sir Joseph Paxton, now containing peaches, grapes and a rich variety of tender plants. The Victorian kitchen garden and a museum of 'bygone' gardening equipment are being developed.

Sun House ★ 19

Hall Street, Long Melford, Sudbury CO10 9HZ. Tel: (01787) 378252

Mr and Mrs J. Thompson • 3m N of Sudbury. In centre of Long Melford opposite Cock and Bell and next to Swags and Bows shop • Open by appt only • Entrance: £2.50 ◑ ℗

The gardens consist of a large central section created over the past decade. They have a notable false acacia tree, a stone courtyard with formal pond near the house and a small, less formal pond at the far end. Weathered statues and busts make strong focal points, as do weeping pear and birch in mixed shrub and herbaceous borders. Over 100 clematis wind through old apple trees or grow against the mellow brick walls of the 'secret' garden. Old roses, lilies, peonies and irises are contained in neat box-edged beds within this new garden, with its colonnaded summerhouse and lion wall fountain. Compost heap and tool area are cunningly disguised by a flint wall, complete with shell mosaic; ferns and ivy add romantic enchantment to this recently created 'ruin'. The garden cottage is available for B&B.

Wyken Hall ★ 20

Stanton, Bury St Edmunds IP31 2DW. Tel: (01359) 250287/250240

Sir Kenneth and Lady Carlisle • 9m NE of Bury St Edmunds on A143. Leave A143 between Ixworth and Stanton. Signed 'Wyken Vineyards' • Garden open April to Oct, every day except Sat 2 – 6pm • Entrance: £2.50, OAPs £1.50, children under 12 free • Other information: Vineyard ◑ 🍵 ✕ <u>WC</u> ⟨ ℗ 🏬 ℺

This outstanding garden covers four acres, most of which have been planted in the last twenty years. It is divided into a series of rooms, starting with the wild garden and winter garden, which leads into the south and woodland garden, and so into the dell. Mown paths meander between shrubs and into the newly planted copper beech maze next to the nuttery and gazebo. Then to the rose garden, enclosed on three sides by a hornbeam hedge and on the fourth by a rose-laden pergola. Beyond the wall are the knot and herb gardens, separated by yew hedges and designed by Arabella Lennox-Boyd. An 'edible garden' and a kitchen garden have been planted to the north of the house, and there is a new pond just beyond the garden. The whole place is remarkable for its colours and scents, particularly in high summer. An eccentric dog kennel, a chapel (with armchair), a contemplation garden and a curious veranda with rocking chairs might be described as the 'personal touches' of Lady Carlisle.

SYMBOLS

NEW entries new for 2002; ○ open all year; ◑ open most of year; ◐ open during main season; ◕ open rarely and/or by appt; 🍵 teas/light refreshments; ✕ meals; 🧺picnics permitted; WC toilet facilities; <u>WC</u> toilet facilities, inc. disabled; ⟨ partly wheelchair-accessible; ⟨⟩ dogs on lead; ℗ plants for sale; 🏬 shop; 🎪 events held; ℺ children-friendly.

SURREY

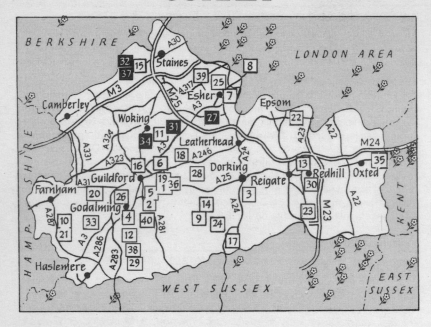

We have included some gardens with Surrey postal addresses in the London section for convenience. So before planning a day out in Surrey it is worth consulting pages 250–288.

Two-starred gardens are marked on the map with a black square.

Albury Park Gardens ★   1

Albury, Guildford GU5 9BB. Tel: (01483) 202964; Fax: (01483) 205013

Trustees of the Albury Estate/Country Houses Association Ltd • 5m SE of Guildford. Turn off A25 onto A248 (signed Albury). After ¼ m, turn left and entrance immediately left • House open as grounds • Grounds open May to Sept, Wed and Thurs, 2 – 5pm • Entrance: £2.50 ● ☕ ♿

John Evelyn designed the 14 acres of pleasure grounds in the mid-seventeenth century. Two dramatic terraces, a quarter of a mile long, extend across the grounds. A tunnel entrance in the upper terrace leads through the hillside to a semi-circular pond which was originally fed by water from the Silent Pool; the bathhouse on the lower level is dated 1676. In the grounds are about 70 different species of trees, a lake and a small canal. The gardens around the house have impressive trees, a bank of azaleas and a formal rose garden. On one of his rural rides in 1882, Cobbett described the gardens as 'without exception the prettiest in England; that is to say, that I ever saw in England'.

Barnett Hill 2

Wonersh, Guildford GU5 ORF. Tel: (01483) 893361

Barnett Hill Conference Centre Ltd • Leave Guildford on A281 S towards Horsham. After 1½ m cross railway bridge and turn left at Shalford village green for Wonersh. Continue for 1½ m and turn left signed 'Conference Centre'. Entrance at top of hill on right • Open 19th May, 2 – 5.30pm • Entrance: £2.50, children under 14 free ● ➍ ▧ WC ◁▷ ✿ ℺

The attractive house was built in 1906 by the grandson of Thomas Cook, founder of the firm of travel agents. On a 26-acre site with 10 acres of formal and planted gardens he employed 14 gardeners. Now there are three. After World War II, Mrs Cook gave the property to the British Red Cross for eventual use as a training and conference centre. The garden stands on a levelled hilltop with the ground falling away on all sides, giving panoramic views. There is an azalea walk and banks of mature rhododendrons, a formal sunken garden with a fish pool, a charming period Wendy house, a new area with grasses, specimen trees and a woodland walk. On open days a band plays on the wide lawn and other entertainment is laid on for visitors, as well as an extensive plant sale with many unusual plants.

Brook Lodge Farm Cottage 3

Blackbrook, Dorking RH5 4DT. Tel: (01306) 888368

Mrs Basil Kingham • 1m S of Dorking. From A24 turn left in Mill Road for Leigh and Brockham, then left at T-junction. Garden is short distance on left • Open monthly through summer for NGS, and for private visits by appt • Entrance: £2, children free NEW ● ➍ WC ♿ ✿ ▯

The present owner created this immaculately kept plantsman's garden 50 years ago, the emphasis being on plant associations and foliage. Now mature trees shelter flowering shrubs, clematis, roses, herbaceous and tender plants, and towering specimen conifers. The fruit and vegetable gardens lead to a heated greenhouse full of tender flowering plants and the gardener's cottage garden.

Busbridge Lakes 4

Hambledon Road, Godalming GU8 4AY. Tel: (01483) 421955;
Fax: (01483) 421955; Website: www.busbridgelakes.co.uk

Mr and Mrs Douetil • 1½ m S of Godalming off B2130 Hambledon road • Open 29th March, 1st to 7th April, 5th, 6th, 26th, 27th May, 18th to 26th Aug, 10.30am – 5.30pm; pre-booked parties any day April to Sept by arrangement • Entrance: £3.80, OAPs and children £2.80, under-5s free • Other information: Refreshments at weekends and on Bank Holidays only ● ➍ ▧ WC ♿ ⚒ ℺

Parkland was created here in the 1650s and the grounds were landscaped in 1750 by Philip Webb MP. It is now a Grade-IIA-Heritage garden. Beside the largest of the three lakes stands an early-nineteenth-century Gothick boat-house, recently restored, with delicate blind windows, a room with a fireplace and two verandahs. At the end of the lake, what appears to be a bridge, multi-arched and built of rocks, proves to be an illusion. Huge plane trees dominate the lakeside; the 30-metre Restoration chestnuts, probably planted in 1660, may be the tallest in England. Tulip trees (*Liriodendron tulipifera*) and a fine cedar of Lebanon stand near the orchard; a sequoia towers above the house. Across the canal lake is a hermit's cave, excavated in 1756 as a tomb for the then owner's wife and two of their children. Further up, a late-eighteenth-century Doric temple with two porticos has recently been restored; below it a grotto contains the spring which feeds the lakes. There are peacocks on the lawns, and the site abounds with attractive, rare and endangered species of ducks, geese, swans and pheasants, all flourishing – as are the gardens. 2m SW of Godalming on the A3100 is *Secretts Garden Centre*, Portsmouth Road, Milford (Tel: (01483) 426633), where the plants for sale are placed in imaginatively designed garden settings.

Chilworth Manor ★ 5

Chilworth, Guildford GU4 8NL. Tel: (01483) 561414

Lady Heald • 3m SE of Guildford on A248. Turn off in Chilworth up Blacksmiths Lane • House open on garden open days only • Garden open one weekend in April, May, June and July, 2 – 6pm, and by appt • Entrance: £2 (house £1.50), children free • Other information: Teas on open days only
● WC ㅊ ⬳

A lovely old garden, particularly in spring and summer, but something to see all the year round. Laid out in the eighteenth century, a walled garden was carved in three tiers out of the side of the hill by Sarah, Duchess of Marlborough. The high walls, backed by wisteria, shelter many fine plants, a herbaceous border, lavender walk and shrubs. There is also a woodland area with magnolias, rhododendrons, azaleas, an oak tree reputed to be 400 years old and a Judas tree. There are candelabra primulas along the stream and golden carp in the monastic stewponds. The house (originally built in AD900 as a monastery) is decorated by various Surrey flower clubs in turn. The ideal time to visit is on a day warm enough to sit on one of the strategically placed seats so as to absorb the atmosphere created by time past and time present.

Clandon Park 6

West Clandon, Guildford GU4 7RQ. Tel: (01483) 222482; Fax: (01483) 223479

The National Trust • 3m E of Guildford on A247 at West Clandon; or take A3 to Ripley then join A247 via B2215 • House open April to Oct, Tues – Thurs, Sun, Good Friday and Bank Holiday Mons, 11am – 5pm (last admission 4.30pm). Parties, Tues – Thurs only, must book • Garden open all year, daily during daylight hours • Entrance: free (house £6, children £3, family £15, parties of 15 or more £5 per person, combined ticket with Hatchlands (see entry) £9) • Other information: Disabled parking near front of house. Dogs in picnic area only, on lead ○ ☕ ✕ 🖼 WC ㅊ 🎗 🍷

Clandon was built by the Venetian architect Giacomo Leoni in the early 1730s for the 2nd Lord Onslow, whose family still owns the park although the house and garden are owned by the National Trust. The seven-acre garden is on a hillside and gives a fine view of the lake. An interesting feature is the Maori meeting house, known as 'Hinemihi', brought from New Zealand over 100 years ago by the then Lord Onslow. Note also the grotto, parterre and herbaceous border, and the bedding and colours in the sunken Dutch garden. In Gomshall, three miles further east on the A25, is *The Conservatory*, where a fine range of well-established and young plants is on display and for sale. [Open all year, daily except Christmas and Easter, 10am – 5pm. Tel: (01483) 203019.]

Claremont Landscape Garden ★   7

Portsmouth Road, Esher KT10 9JG. Tel: (01372) 467806

The National Trust • E of A307, just S of Esher • House (not NT) and Belvedere open – telephone for details • Garden open Jan to March, daily except Mon, 10am – 5pm; April to Oct, Mon – Fri, 10am – 6pm, Sat, Sun and Bank Holiday Mons, 10am – 7pm; Nov to March, daily except Mons, 10am – 5pm or sunset if earlier (last admission ½ hour before closing) but closed 25th Dec, 1st Jan. Coach parties must book • Entrance: £3.70, children £1.85, family (2 adults and 2 children) £9.25, pre-booked parties £3.20 per person • Other information: Dogs, Nov to March only, on lead ○ ☕ ✕ 🍴 WC ♿ ⛪ ☗

The Oxford Companion describes this as one of the most significant historic landscapes in the country. The great landscape designers of the eighteenth century each adapted it in turn for the owner, the immensely wealthy man who eventually became Duke of Newcastle. He bought the house from Sir John Vanbrugh, who also designed the belvedere for him (the views from the top are amazing). The Duke employed Bridgeman in 1716, then Kent in the 1730s; the latter adapted the garden to create picturesque settings, evoking various moods, and also enlarged the pond to make the lake, with pavilion (recently restored). When the Duke died, Clive of India purchased the estate. He brought in 'Capability' Brown, who also designed the house and, in typical form, diverted the London-Portsmouth road to improve the viewpoints, the most striking of which is the grass amphitheatre. In the nineteenth century it was a favourite retreat of Queen Victoria and her younger son. The 50 acres restored by the Trust are only part of the original estate, which was broken up in 1922 when part of the house became a school. A useful leaflet describes the various contributions to the park, which will appeal to everyone with its sensitive reconstruction of the eighteenth-century English style, even if it has nothing specific to offer the plantsperson, except perhaps the camellia terrace. A few miles east, in Leatherhead Road, Chessington, *Chessington Nursery* (Tel: (01372) 744490) offers a wide range of plants for both house and garden, attractively displayed. [Open all year, daily, 9am – 6pm (10am – 4pm on Sun).]

Coombe Wood ★ 8

The Water Gardens, Warren Road, Kingston Hill, Kingston upon Thames KT2 7LF.

The Water Garden's Residents' Association • From Kingston take A308 (Kingston Hill) towards London. About 1½ m on right, turn right into Warren Road • Open probably open twice for NGS. Write for details • Entrance: £2.50, OAPs £1.50, children 50p (2001 prices) ◑ ⑤

Now an unusual and historic Japanese water garden, this was the original site of Veitch's famous nursery, to which the owner's eldest son, resident in Japan, sent hundreds of plants for commercial development in the 1860s. At the turn of the century more oriental plants arrived from Ernest Wilson's expeditions to China. When the nursery was sold in 1914, General Sir Arthur Paget and his wife, who lived next door, bought the two acres containing the stream and a pond, which they incorporated within their own Japanese-style garden, saving many Veitch plantings. The Paget estate changed hands again, and today part is a residential development of 10 acres, of which the water gardens form a most beautiful area. The Japanese features have been retained and improved. First-rate and well-restored bridges, tea house, etc. in the Japanese style induce a sense of excitement for visitors exploring the winding paths, as the maturity of the planting creates a full woodland effect. The rhododendrons are a particular attraction and include many exotic species, introduced by and named for Wilson. Note also the fine magnolias, camellias and Japanese maples, which show to advantage at the spring and autumn openings, and the blue hydrangeas are a remarkable sight. There are many unusual trees. The upkeep is above average. (Note: the NGS calls these The Watergardens, Kingston-upon-Thames.)

Coverwood Lakes, Garden and Farm 9

Peaslake Road, Ewhurst, Cranleigh GU6 7NT. Tel: (01306) 731103; Fax: (01306) 731299 / 731158; E-mail: metsoncoverwood@supanet.com

Mrs C.G. Metson and Mr and Mrs N. Metson • 7m SW of Dorking, 6m SE of Guildford, ½ m S of Peaslake off A25 • Gardens and farm open 14th, 21st, 28th April, 5th, 12th, 19th, 26th May, 2 – 6pm; 20th Oct, 11am – 4.30pm • Entrance: £2.50, children £1 (share to NGS). Large or private parties by prior arrangement • Other information: Home-made teas available on April and May open days, hot soup and sandwiches on Oct open day ◑ ☕ WC ⑤ ♨ ⑨ ⚲

The original gardens were designed in 1910 by a rich Edwardian businessman. Now it is a woodland estate surrounding four lakes, the water for which comes from the natural springs in the bog garden. Each lake has a different character, from the towering rhododendrons reflected in the calm water of the highest to the largest alongside the arboretum. This was planted early in 1990 and contains 100 different kinds of trees, which are prospering in this natural setting. Bordering the paths are a great many varieties of hostas, trilliums and candelabra primulas, and lilies-of-the-valley form a carpet below a dazzling display of rhododendrons and azaleas. There is a marked trail to see pedigree Poll Hereford cattle, sheep, horses and wonderful views.

Crosswater Farm 10

Millais Nurseries, Crosswater Lane, Churt, Farnham GU10 2JN.
Tel: (01252) 792698; Fax: (01252) 792526;
E-mail: sales@rhododendrons.co.uk; Website: www.rhododendrons.co.uk

Mr and Mrs E.G. Millais • *6m SE of Farnham, 6m NW of Haslemere, ½ m N of Churt off A287. Signed 'Millais Nurseries'* • *Open 27th April to 14th June, daily, 10am – 5pm (6th, May, 3rd, 4th June for charity)* • *Entrance: £2, children free* • *Other information: Teas on charity open days only* ◑ 🍴 WC & ⚘ 🎋 ♿

These six acres of woodland gardens were begun in 1946 by the present owners, who specialise in azaleas and rhododendrons and have assembled an exceptional international collection. Among the mature and some more recent plantings are rare species collected in the Himalayas and hybrids raised by them, including *Rhododendron* 'High Summer'. The plants are labelled and most are available from the adjoining nursery, which grows more than 750 different varieties. There is also an excellent collection of sorbus trees. The surrounding garden features a stream, ponds and attractive companion plantings including young species, some being the first to be grown outside the Himalayas.

Dunsborough Park 11

Ripley, Woking GU23 6AL. Tel: (01483) 225366

Baron and Baroness Sweerts de Landas Wyborgh • *3m NE of Guildford. Take A247 or A3 to Ripley. Entrance across Ripley Green* • *Open by appt* • *Entrance: £2.50, children £1.25* ◑ WC

The ten-acre garden of the Georgian house has recently been restored as a showplace for the owners' extensive collection of statuary. Herbaceous borders lead to the extensive walled gardens, now redesigned as pleasure gardens; a row of ginkgo trees, grown originally for sale, became too big to move and now forms an unusual feature. A hidden garden encloses an ancient mulberry. At the end of the water garden the bridge, with its belvedere, is now accessible, and the fine Victorian glasshouses have been restored. The Antique Garden Ornament Centre is open by appointment. For those who wish to see more sculpture in a 'garden' setting, the English Heritage Grade II* *Brookwood Cemetery*, near Woking, opened in mid-Victorian times, is said to be Europe's largest (2000 acres).

Feathercombe Gardens 12

Feathercombe, Hambledon, Godalming GU8 4DP. Tel: (01483) 860264/860257

The Campbell and Murray families • *4m S of Godalming, E of Hydestile – Hambledon road* • *Open several days in May for NGS, 2 – 6pm, and by appt* • *Entrance: £2.50, children 50p (2001 prices)* ◑ 🍴 WC & ⬦ ♿

The garden is notable for its good display of rhododendrons and azaleas, yew topiary and tree heaths, and for the fine views across three counties. The original design of 1910 was by Eric Parker, whose wife Ruth was one of Ludwig

Messel's daughters; there were strong links between Feathercombe and the Messel garden at Nymans in West Sussex (see entry).

Gatton Park 13

Reigate RH2 0TW. Tel: (01737) 645826/644968; Fax: (01737) 642294; Website: www.gatton-park.org.uk

The Royal Alexandra and Albert School • 3m NE of Reigate. From A23, NE of junction with A25, turn left into Rocky Lane. Entrance is almost 1m on left • Open: Feb to Oct, 1st Sun each month, 1 – 5 pm • Entrance: £2 ◑ ▐ WC ◁

The Domesday Book records a manor and deer park at Gatton. In the fifteenth century it became a rotten borough: a diminutive town hall still stands opposite the impressive portico, which is all that remains of the Italianate mansion, burnt down in 1934 and rebuilt in plainer style in 1937. There are magnificent cedars and sequoias around the house, and ancient oaks below in the parkland. In the eighteenth century, 'Capability' Brown swept away earlier formal gardens and created the 28-acre lake as well as a chain of smaller ones, the parkland, woods and vistas, enhancing the spectacular setting on the North Downs. This was one of his larger commissions, for which he was paid £3000. In the late Victorian and Edwardian eras Jeremiah Colman, the mustard magnate, developed the gardens, building a dramatic rock and water garden on a slope, with Pulhamite pools, massive rocks and curving steps. This has been restored and is now shaded by yews and appropriately planted. Colman also created a Japanese garden with interlacing pools and paths and waterside plants; now restored, it is overlooked by a thatched tea house. Future plans include the restoration of the lakes, extensive stone-walled kitchen gardens and dry arch.

Goddards 14

Abinger Common, Dorking RH5 6JH. Tel: (01306) 730871 (Ticket bookings during office hours)

The Landmark Trust • From Guildford take A25 Dorking Road E. At Wotton take right turn for Abinger Common. House on green opposite Victorian well • Open 3rd April to 30th Oct, Wed only, 2 – 6pm, strictly by appt • Entrance: £3 • Other information: Limited parking, must be booked ◑ WC

Sir Edwin Lutyens designed the house originally in 1898 as a home of rest for ladies of small means. He planned it around a courtyard garden, facing slightly west of south and overlooked by all the principal rooms – in effect an outdoor room. Gertrude Jekyll collaborated on the structure of the garden, which remains intact. A dipping well in the centre, providing water for the plants, is surrounded by paved paths, low walls, curved beds and a raised sundial. There are flower borders under the windows and vines and wisteria grow against the house walls. Architectural yew hedges enclose the formal gardens around the house, and yew arches give vistas over lawns, a ha-ha and across a meadow to a curving backdrop of woods. The house, part of the Landmark Trust Scheme, may be rented for self-catering holidays.

Great Fosters 15

**Stroude Road, Egham TW20 9UR. Tel: (01784) 433822; Fax: (01784) 472455;
E-mail: enquiries@greatfosters.co.uk; Website: www.greatfosters.co.uk**

*Great Fosters (1931) Ltd • Off M25 junction 13, 1m S of Egham. From railway
station follow Manorcroft Road into Stroude Road and continue 1m. Hotel on
left • Open all year, daily during daylight hours • Entrance: free • Other
information: Refreshments and toilet facilities in hotel* ○ ✗ WC ⅙

Built in the late sixteenth century, possibly as a Windsor Forest hunting lodge,
the house has been a hotel since 1929. The Grade-II garden, developed in 1918,
has recently been restored. Behind the hotel, a long, paved terrace gives views
of a wide semi-circular lawn and a lime avenue truncated at the far end by the
M25. Steps lead down to four knot gardens with box edging, topiary and
statues surrounding a sixteenth-century sundial, the whole outlined by a U-
shaped Saxon moat. Wisteria drapes the Japanese bridge, which arches over
the moat and leads to a pergola underplanted with lavender. A circular,
sunken rose garden with an octet of steps down to a lily pool and fountain is
bordered by rose arches and a paved path and surrounded by yew. Two square
iris and peony gardens, also enclosed by yew hedges, are on a more intimate
scale. At the side of the hotel a vista garden with serpentine yew hedges is
developing. An orangery has been built at the southern end, and orange trees
in containers stand on the terrace in summer.

Guildford Castle Gardens 16

Castle Street, Guildford GU1 3TU. Tel: (01483) 505050

*Guildford Corporation • From High Street walk through arches into Tunsgate.
Castle opposite at far end • Castle keep open 10am – 5pm. Admission charge •
Gardens open all year, daily, dawn – dusk • Entrance: free* ○ 🍴 ⬧ 🅿 ♿

This ruined keep built by William the Conqueror (close to the present city
centre) once formed part of the garden of a private house bought by Guildford
Corporation in 1885. Clever use has been made of the original moat. A path
runs around the bottom, and shaped beds, retaining their interesting Victorian
designs, are cut into the sloping turfed sides. They are bedded out for
spectacular spring and summer displays with much the same plants as the
Victorians would have used. There are plenty of seats. A tunnel, its damp,
shady approach brightly planted, leads up to a bandstand and a bowling green
with attractive borders and clipped hedges.

Hannah Peschar Sculpture Garden 17

**Black and White Cottage, Standon Lane, Ockley RH5 5QR.
Tel: (01306) 627269; Fax: (01306) 627662; E-mail: hpeschar@easynet.co.uk;
Website: www.hannahpescharsculpture.com**

*Hannah Peschar • 6m S of Dorking, 1m SW of Ockley off A24. Follow signs
'Golf and Country Club'. Entrance on right in Standon Lane 400 metres past
low bridge over stream • Open May to Oct, Fri and Sat, 11am – 6pm, Sun and*

Bank Holiday Mons, 2 – 5pm; other days, except Mon, by appt only • Entrance:
£7, OAPs £5, children under 16 £4 • Other information: Refreshments and
meals for parties by arrangement only. Details of lecture tours, party and school
visits on request ◐ 🍴 WC も ⊲⊳ ℺

The heart of this garden was part of the Leith Vale Estate, planted with
rhododendrons and camellias, and later belonged to Dick Trotter, a former
treasurer of the RHS; it had been neglected for many years when the present
owners arrived. The garden was opened in 1984 and has been extended and
redesigned on informal lines with woodland, streams, lakes and grassed areas.
Planting is architectural and large scale to provide a background for the
display, for sale, of contemporary sculpture.

Hatchlands Park   18

East Clandon, Guildford GU4 7RT. Tel: (01483) 222482

The National Trust • 5m NE of Guildford, E of East Clandon, N of A246 •
House and garden open April to Oct, Tues – Thurs, Sun and Bank Holiday
Mons, also Fri in Aug, 2 – 5.30pm (last admission 5pm); park walks and
grounds open April to Oct, daily, 11am – 6pm. Parties Tues – Thurs •
Entrance: park walks £2.50 (house, garden and walks £6, family £15, parties of
15 or more (by arrangement) £5 per person, combined ticket with Clandon (see
entry) £9) ◐ ☕ ✕ 🍴 WC も ⊞ ♀

The restoration of these gardens has been successfully completed and the
Gertrude Jekyll garden re-created most effectively with herbaceous planting
and roses. Beside the garden is a magnificent 200-year-old London plane tree,
temple and ice-house. A wildflower meadow is left uncut until July. The
Italianate garden at the front has been returned to its original Reptonian
design of lawns and vistas. The park has also been restored to Reptonian
principles, and there are three woodland walks to enjoy, including a bluebell
wood.

Heathfield   19

Heath Lane, Albury Heath, Nr Guildford GU5 9DD. Tel: (01483) 202139

Mr and Mrs M. Demetriadi • 5m SE of Guildford. From A25 take A248; turn
1st left into New Road. 1st left into Park Road, 1st right into Heath Lane •
Open 7th, 14th July, 10am – 5pm, 24th July, 6 – 8.30pm, and by appt •
Entrance £2.50, children free NEW ◐ ☕ WC も ⊲⊳ ♨ ℺

Amazingly, Mrs Demetriadi created this 1¼ -acre garden of hedged rooms in a
single year (1996), on the site of a former rhododendron nursery. Curved
borders combine unusual plants, and old friends surround a pool, a slate-lined
stream, a bog garden and a rockery. The circular plan herb garden has beds
neatly edged in variegated box; opposite is a decorative vegetable patch and
fruit garden. An arch leads from the hot, dry Mediterranean garden to a cool
fernery and a lovely wildflower meadow.

Hethersett   20

Littleworth Cross, Seale, Farnham GU10 1JL.

Lady Adam Gordon • 4m E of Farnham, S of Hog's Back (A31). 1½ m from Seale Church on Elstead road, or 1m N of B3001 on Seale Road • Open one day for NGS, 2 – 6pm • Entrance: £2, children free (2001 prices) ● ◁▷ ℘ ℀

This magical 25-acre woodland garden, rarely open, was created at the end of the nineteenth century by H.A. Mangles, an early hybridiser of rhododendrons. Under mature trees, many of his hybrids and species have grown as tall as trees themselves, intermingling with shrubs and varieties of ground cover. In clearings there are splashes of colourful azaleas, and a circular walk, with intersecting paths and seats at intervals, guides the visitor through the wood.

High Meadow   21

Tilford Road, Churt, Farnham GU10 2LN. Tel: (01428) 606129

Mr and Mrs John Humphries • 3m N of Hindhead. Take A287 from Hindhead then fork right to Tilford. House nearly 2m on right • Open 25th, 26th Aug, 2 – 5pm. Parties by appt • Entrance: £2, children free • Other information: Parking and toilet facilities at Avalon PYO farm on left past turning to house. Disabled parking in drive to house ◑ ● ℘

As the name suggests, this garden is situated high on a meadowside protected by a series of hedges of beech, holly and cupressus. A small terrace is overlooked by a pergola with a variety of climbers. Unusually shaped beds surround grass of putting-green quality and contain a wealth of colour-coordinated shrubs, roses and herbaceous plants cleverly graded by height. There is a small pool set in a rock garden, a bog plant section, a rockery and a small peat garden. A plantsman's garden.

Knightsmead   22

Rickman Hill Road, Chipstead CR5 3LB. Tel: (01737) 551694

Mrs C. Jones and Miss C. Collins • 1m SW of Coulsdon, 3m SE of Banstead, off B2032 • Open two days in May, 2 – 5.30pm, and by appt • Entrance: £2, accompanied children 50p ● ● WC ℘

When the present owners came here over a decade ago, the half-acre garden was overshadowed by vast Lawson cypresses. Now there are shrub roses and clematis, with arcs of smaller trees underplanted with spring bulbs and woodland plants such as erythroniums, trilliums and pure-colour-bred hellebores. A graceful 18-metre Deodar cedar dominates this well-designed plantsman's garden, and a lily pond, rose arch and beds of shrubs and perennials give year-round interest. On heavy clay soil, a bog garden, peat bed and limestone scree provide ideal conditions for choice plants. Walls support climbers and a conservatory extends the range. New pergola and water feature.

Langshott Manor 23

Langshott, Horley RH6 9LN. Tel: (01293) 786680; Fax: (01293) 783905

Mr and Mrs Peter Hinchcliffe • 4m N of Crawley. From Horley on A23 turn right at Chequers Hotel roundabout into Ladbroke Road and continue about 1m. Manor is on right • Open all year • Entrance: free ○ ⬤ ✗ WC ㅤ& ㅤ⬥ ㅤ⦿

This beautifully restored Grade-II Elizabethan manor house, draped in roses, clematis and a huge *Magnolia grandiflora*, is tucked away down a country lane; it is now a hotel. The peaceful setting is enhanced by a garden whose design complements the house. A sunken rose garden with borders edged in box contains an interesting star-shaped brick-and-tile feature with roses growing up a central pillar. The terrace of mellow stone and brick is edged with lavender. A pleached lime avenue curves around one side of the croquet lawn, and a hornbeam pergola leads from the entrance drive down towards it. A small orchard of old varieties of fruit on dwarf rooting stock contains a turf seat and a colourful mixed bed of herbs and salad plants. There is also a small lake with swans, cygnets and ducks and a rustic stone bridge separating the birds' domain from the ornamental part, planted with water lilies and moisture-loving plants.

Leith Hill Rhododendron Wood 24

Tanhurst Lane, Coldharbour. Tel/Fax: (01306) 712711/712153

The National Trust • 5m S of Dorking. Take Coldharbour Road and continue to Leith Hill. At next junction keep right, then fork left. Wood immediately on left • Leith Hill Tower open 29th March to Sept, Wed, 10 – 5pm, Sat, Sun and Bank Holidays, 11am – 5pm (last admission 4.30pm). Also weekends Oct to March, 11am – 3.30pm (last admission 3pm). Closed 25th Dec • Rhododendron wood open all year, daily, during daylight hours • Entrance: £1.50 per car for wood • Other information: Light refreshments when tower open ○ 📖 & ⬥

The wood was originally part of the estate of Leith Hill Place, once the home of the composer Ralph Vaughan Williams. Beside the car park is an extensive picnic area, and below this the rhododendrons and azaleas are a blaze of colour in April and May. There has been some replanting and the paths have been improved. An immense tulip tree, *Liriodendron tulipifera*, can be seen in the field beyond, and there are spectacular views. Further on, the mature trees create a shady area for rhododendrons in soft colours.

Little Lodge 25

Watts Road, Thames Ditton KT7 0BX. Tel: (020) 8339 0931

Mr and Mrs Peter Hickman • From London take A3. In Thames Ditton village follow High Street down Watts Road. Griggs Hill Green is on left, house is opposite library • 9th June, 11.30am – 6pm, 12th June, 6.30 – 9pm and by appt • Entrance: £2, children free ⬤ ⬤ & ⬥ ⬥

The house rests comfortably in its own lush surround. A pond and wild planting with formal topiary beds in the front garden give little hint of the large cottage garden behind the house. Outside the house is a paved suntrap with a wide variety of containers and unusual plants. The densely covered house walls make this a perfect seating area. The main lawned area has herbaceous borders and island beds with secret spots defined by yew hedges and bamboo screens. A vegetable garden with raised well-stocked beds adds to the charm of this much-visited garden.

Loseley Park ★ 26

Compton, Guildford GU3 1HS. Tel: (01483) 304440; Fax: (01483) 302036; E-mail: enquiries@loseley.park.com; Website: www.loseley-park.com

Mr and Mrs M.G. More-Molyneux • 3m SW of Guildford, W of A3, off B3000 • House open June to Aug, Wed – Sun and Bank Holiday Mons, 1pm – 5pm • Garden open 6th May to 29th Sept, Wed – Sun and Bank Holiday Mons, 11am – 5pm • Entrance: £3, OAPs/disabled £2.50, children £1.50 (house and garden £3, OAPs/disabled £3.50, children £3) (2001 prices) ◑ 🍽 ✕ <u>WC</u> ♻   🐾

The Elizabethan house is surrounded by parkland. Hidden away at the side of the house, the vast walled garden has been transformed: based on a Gertrude Jekyll design, five gardens have been created, each with their own theme and character. The old mulberry is still there and a medlar with a group of palms. An enchanting rose garden with low box hedges is filled with old-fashioned roses, carefully labelled; box balls and circles emphasise the design, while pillars of roses and hollies give height. Along one side is an arcade of vine and clematis. A herb garden displays culinary, medicinal and ornamental herbs in triangular beds and others used in cosmetics, lotions and dyes, all well labelled. Quartets of domed acacias stand at the intersections of the main paths, and golden malus (crab apple) form a square avenue in the fruit and flower garden, which is planted in bold fiery colours. In contrast, the fountain garden is planted with white and silver flowers and foliage to create a romantic atmosphere. Future plans include a wildflower meadow. The moat walk shelters a long border of sun-loving plants, including yuccas (don't step back while admiring them). Near the entrance to the garden are an ancient wisteria and a good herbaceous border.

Painshill Landscape Garden ★★ 27

Portsmouth Road, Cobham KT11 1JE. Tel: (01932) 868113 (Information) or (01932) 864674 (Opening times); Fax: (01932) 868001; E-mail: enquiries@fsbusiness.co.uk; Website: www.painshill.co.uk

Painshill Park Trust • From M25 junction 10, take A3 and A245. W of Cobham. Entrance 200 metres from A245/A307 roundabout • Garden open all year, April to Oct, daily except Mon (but open Bank Holiday Mons), 10.30am – 6pm (last admission 4.30pm); Nov to March, daily except Mon and Fri, 11am – 4pm (last admission 3pm) or dusk if earlier. Closed 25th, 26th Dec. Parties of 10 or more by appt • Entrance: £4.50, concessions £4, children (5–16) £2.

*Children under 16 must be accompanied. School parties welcome • Other
information: Wheelchairs and electric buggies available by prior booking for
disabled* ☀ 🍽 🛍 <u>WC</u> ♿ 🎁 ⚘

The Hon. Charles Hamilton created Painshill – contemporary with Stowe and
Stourhead – between 1738 and 1773, when it was sold after he ran out of funds.
The garden was well maintained until World War II, then in 1948 it was sold off in
lots and all but lost. Between 1974 and 1980 Elmbridge Council bought up most
of the land; the following year the Painshill Park Trust was formed and began the
task of restoration. The landscaped park, which now covers 160 acres, was
designed around a serpentine 14-acre lake fed from the River Mole by a
spectacular waterwheel. The restored Chinese bridge, opened in 1988, leads
to an island and a magical grotto, still being restored, the main chamber of which
is 12 metres across, hung with stalactites and lined with shards of glistening
felspar. The mausoleum, near the river, was depicted on one of the plates of
Catherine the Great's Wedgwood 'Frog Service'; a further reach of the lake
reflects an abbey ruin. The focal point of the garden is the elegant Gothick
temple on higher ground. It is approached across a grassed 'amphitheatre'
encircled by formal eighteenth-century-style shrubberies. A dramatic blue and
white Turkish tent with a gold coronet stands on a plateau among informal
plantings. In the distance is the Gothick tower. The great cedar of Lebanon, 36½
metres high and with a girth of 10 metres, is reputedly the largest in Europe. The
vineyard has been replanted on a southern slope as it was in Charles Hamilton's
day. Much has been achieved, and the Trust has plans to complete the restoration
of the grotto and rebuild more of the original features, including the 'missing'
Temple of Bacchus. Painshill needs 80,000 visitors annually to meet running
costs, and the capital costs of completing the project will be the subject of fund-
raising appeals for some years to come.

Polesden Lacey ★   28

**Great Bookham, Dorking RH5 6BD. Tel: (01372) 452048/458203 (Infoline);
Fax: (01372) 452023**

*The National Trust • 5m NW of Dorking, 2m S of Great Bookham off A246
Leatherhead – Guildford road • House open 31st March to 4th Nov, Wed –
Sun, 1 – 5pm and Bank Holiday Mons, 11am – 5pm (last admission ½ hour
before closing) • Grounds open all year, daily, 11am – 6pm, or dusk if earlier
(last admission 5pm) • Entrance: £4, family ticket £10 (house and grounds £7,
family ticket £17.50, pre-booked parties of 15 or more £6 per person) • Other
information: Parking 150 metres away. Disabled parking area. Batricar
available on pre-booked basis. Braille guide available. Picnics and dogs permitted
outside formal garden only. Open-air theatre and concerts mid-June to early July*
○ 🍽 ✕ 🛍 <u>WC</u> ♿ ⟨⟩ ⚘ 🎁 ⚘

This 30-acre garden has grown up over several centuries. Richard Brinsley
Sheridan, the dramatist who owned the house for over 20 years, lengthened
the Long Walk before he died here in 1816. The present house was built a few
years later by Cubitt in the Greek classical manner for an owner who made
extensive alterations and planted over 20,000 trees. In the Edwardian era the

society hostess Mrs Greville laid out the formal walled gardens; her tomb stands near the house in the centre of a lawn surrounded by yew hedges. The garden was further developed early in the twentieth century and given to the Trust in 1944. The walled rose garden is in four square compartments divided by paths and arched over by wooden pergolas, and the area is dominated by a water tower covered with an ancient Chinese wisteria. Small gardens of peonies, bearded irises and beds of different kinds of lavender lead to a winter garden overshadowed by ironwood trees (*Parrotia persica*), a long herbaceous border and a sunken garden. A fragrant evergreen *Clematis armandii*, flowering in April, grows on the wall of the house. A detailed garden guide is available. Stunning walks through the landscape of the North Downs have been constructed on the estate, including one suitable for wheelchairs.

Ramster   29

Chiddingfold, Godalming GU8 4SN. Tel: (01428) 654167

Mr and Mrs P. Gunn • NE of Haslemere, $1\frac{1}{2}$ m S of Chiddingfold on A283 • Open 13th April to 7th July, daily, 11am – 5pm, and for parties by appt • Entrance: £3, children free • Other information: Teas daily in May, and on weekend open days. Possible for wheelchairs in dry weather only ◑ ☕ ▩ WC 占 ⬦ ✿ ℺

Owned by the same family for over 70 years, there are 20 acres of peaceful woodland with views of lakes and hillsides filled with colour and interest. Planting includes Californian redwoods, cedars, firs, camellias, rhododendrons and azaleas, plus the rarer *Styrax obassia*, *Tetracentron sinense* and *Kalopanax pictus*. A camellia garden, magnolia bed and widespread bluebells and daffodils ensure that flowers are on view throughout the spring. A notable feature is an avenue of *Acer palmatum* 'Dissectum'.

Red Oaks   30

Redhill Common, Redhill RH1 6JN Tel: (01737) 764425

Brian and Prue Moray • Take A25 from Reigate towards Redhill for 1m. Turn right at war memorial into Hatchlands Road, then immediately left in to Blackstone Hill • Open 23rd June, 14th July, 11am – 5pm • Entrance: £2, children free NEW ☕ ☕ WC 占 ✿ ℺

A steep walk leads up to this garden, but it is worth the effort. The owners must spend every waking moment in their beautifully presented, well thought-out $\frac{2}{3}$ acre, arranged around a stone Victorian house. A conservatory shelters a collection of unusual pelargoniums. Borders of good plants are colour themed: the circular cobbled courtyard, for example, in blues and yellows, while beyond the convincingly naturalistic pond and stream, a deep border in reds and purples, and others in shades of pink and blue hide a circular sunken garden with drystone walls, backed by a catenary of white roses. The fence behind the neat, flourishing kitchen garden supports a striking display of blue clematis and golden roses.

RHS Garden Wisley ★★   31

Wisley, Woking GU23 6QB. Tel: (01483) 224234; Website: www.rhs.org.uk

*Royal Horticultural Society • 20m SW of London, 7m NE of Guildford, on A3.
Signed from M25 junction 10 south. Trains to West Byfleet or Woking; taxi
service usually available at stations • Garden open Mon – Fri, 10am – sunset
(6pm during British Summer Time); Sat, Sun, 9am – 4.30pm (6pm during
British Summer Time); (Sun for RHS members and a guest only) • Entrance: by
membership or £5, children (6–16) £2, under 6 free; companion for wheelchair-
bound or blind visitor free (2001 prices) • Other information: Disabled and
shaded parking* ○ 🍽 ✕ 🛍 <u>WC</u> ♿ 🐾 ♨ 🎈 ☕

Wisley Garden was presented to the Royal Horticultural Society in 1903 by Sir
Thomas Hanbury, who created the famous La Mortola garden in Italy. The
Society's first major development was the rock garden, a fashionable feature at
the time, sections of which were reconstructed in the 1980s. The laboratory,
built in 1916 in Tudor style, is the hub of the Society's advisory service to
members: identifying plants, answering queries on pests and diseases and
gardening problems. Talks and demonstrations of gardening techniques are
given, informative walks conducted, and a training programme run for
students. The combination of learning and pleasure is the essence of Wisley,
as well over half a million visitors discover each year as they explore the 240
acres. The Broadwalk, between double mixed borders, each over 120 metres x
5½ metres, leads to a new Country Garden designed by Penelope Hobhouse,
to the rose gardens and onwards to Battleston Hill and East Battleston, with
azaleas, rhododendrons, hydrangeas and lilies. Over the crest of the hill, on the
southern slope, is the Mediterranean garden, planted since the Great Storm of
1987 and, beyond it, the Portsmouth Field. Here the Society, as the leading
international trials institution, holds trials of plants, flowers and vegetables,
including, every year, delphiniums, sweet peas and dahlias. To the west the 32-
acre Jubilee Arboretum encircles the Fruit Field, where growing trees can be
compared. In 1980 displays of hedging and ground cover were planted between
the arboretum and the glasshouses to compare rates of growth. The temperate
house, the central section of the main glasshouse, has been completely
redesigned: at one end is a curved area for subjects preferring arid conditions;
at the other end a water feature with plants enjoying moisture, and in the
centre a circular seasonal display area. The orchid house is naturalistic, with a
stream and bridge. Nearby the popular model gardens include a display of
bonsai and prize-winning gardens transported from the Chelsea Flower Show;
others display herbs, fruit and vegetables – 1000 varieties of top, bush and soft
fruit are grown. The peaceful pinetum, the riverside walk and the new heather
garden in Howard's Field lie beyond the restaurant. The lakes nearby have
been enlarged to be more natural, with planting mainly for winter effect. Sir
Geoffrey Jellicoe designed the canal and loggia in front of the laboratory.
Martin Lane Fox and the garden staff have transformed the walled garden – a
sun trap which now shelters Italian cypresses, Chusan palms, tree ferns and a
host of tender plants. Beyond the rockery along the lower path through the
trees are new, dramatic meadow-style borders, each 11 metres deep and 146

metres long, designed by the Dutch garden designer and plantsman Piet Oudolf. An avenue of *Cornus Kousa* var. *chinesis* and shrubs backs herbaceous perennials and grasses planted in diagonal drifts to give a ribbon effect. At the top is the staff millennium project, a fruit mount; step-over apples grow round the base and the spiral path is bordered by blackberries and vines. From the top there is a spectacular view of the Surrey countryside. A reading room is near the restaurant, and the bookshop should be visited. Wisley is acclaimed by gardeners throughout the world, but you do not have to be a keen gardener to appreciate its virtues.

The Savill Garden (Windsor Great Park) ★★ 32

Wick Lane, Englefield Green TW20 0UU. Tel: (01753) 847518

Administered by the Crown Estate Commissioners • 5m S of Windsor. From A30, turn into Wick Road and follow signs, or follow signs from Englefield Green • Open daily: March to Oct, 10am – 6pm; Nov to Feb, 10am – 4pm. Closed 25th, 26th Dec • Entrance: £3 – £5 (seasonal), OAPs/parties £2.50 – £4.50 (seasonal), accompanied children under 16 free (2001 prices). Guided tours available ○ ▣ ✕ WC ᕳ ✿ ⌂ ⊕ ⚲

A particularly fine woodland garden covering some 35 acres, it contains a wide range of rhododendrons, camellias, magnolias, hydrangeas and a great variety of other trees and shrubs producing a wealth of colour throughout the seasons. A wonderful collection of hostas and ferns flourishes in the shadier areas. Meconopsis and primulas are splendid in June, while lilies are the highlight of high summer and the tweedy autumn colours are almost as satisfying in their mellowness as the jauntier spring hues. A more formal area is devoted to modern roses, herbaceous borders, a range of alpines and an interesting and attractive dry garden. An imposing temperate house was opened in 1995; on fine days the whole of one of its walls can be raised so that the garden continues into the house. Tender subjects – tree ferns, mimosas, eucryphias and delicate shrubs – are arranged in tiered beds and underplanted with exotics. Metal obelisks support non-hardy climbers: *Lapageria rosea* is on the main wall. The minimum temperature maintained in the $36\frac{1}{2}$ x 18-metre glasshouse is only 2°C (38°F), easily achieved in a conservatory.

Street House 33

The Street, Thursley, Godalming GU8 6QE. Tel: (01252) 703216

Mr and Mrs B.M. Francis • 6m SW of Godalming, just W of A3 between Milford and Hindhead, near road junction in Thursley • Open several times April to July for charity (telephone for details). Private parties welcome by appt • Entrance: £2, children 50p • Other information: Parking on recreation ground, behind house from A3 ◑ ▣ WC ᕳ ⊲⊳ ✿ ⚲

Sir Edwin Lutyens spent his early years at this listed Regency house, and it was said that he first met Gertrude Jekyll here. There are three separate gardens around the house. A walled garden is full of interesting plants, trees and shrubs, including an immense false acacia (*Robinia pseudoacacia*), a Japanese snowball tree (*Viburnum plicatum* 'Sterile') and *Rubus* 'Benenden'. The main lawn is surrounded by shrubs with a curving backdrop of fine limes, while the lower lawn is framed by dazzling rhododendrons and azaleas and has splendid views. There is an unusual astrological feature constructed with Bargate-stone unearthed from the garden and local ironstone.

Sutton Place ★★   34

Guildford GU4 7QV. Tel: (01483) 504455

Sutton Place Foundation • 3m N of Guildford off A3 • Open by appt for pre-booked parties, but property up for sale, so essential to check ● ● WC &

Henry VIII gave Sutton Place to Sir Richard Weston in the early sixteenth century and it remained in the family until this century. Paul Getty lived here in the 1960s and '70s; in 1980 Stanley Seeger, the oil magnate, arrived and commissioned the late Sir Geoffrey Jellicoe to design a new garden on a grand scale; in 1986 Sutton Place was sold again and the gardens closed. Now the new owner, Sutton Place Foundation, has reopened the mansion and the gardens. The restoration and development of Jellicoe's series of gardens have been successfully achieved and some areas replanned. There is a new rose garden in soft colours with a central arbour, the beds divided like a cake and edged with box. The walls are clothed in climbers and the borders punctuated by conical yews. A long rose arch separates it from a *potager*. Beyond the wall a Jellicoe path with false perspective passes huge decorative urns bought from Mentmore. Thoughtfully surrounded by yew hedges is Ben Nicolson's 'White Wall' sculpture. The Ellipse Garden is approached by curving paths through a shrubbery planned to give scent throughout the year; in the centre is a pool with a funereal fountain bordered by an ellipse of pleached hornbeams. As well as a camellia garden and an 18-acre woodland garden going down to the River Wey, there is an orchard of different varieties of apples, pears and plums, underplanted with daffodils. Across the south front of the house is a vast lawn with mature trees, including a magnificent Atlas cedar, its branches sweeping the ground; a dramatic Victorian fountain has been placed as the focal point of a yew bauble avenue leading from the mansion. Citrus trees grow in boxes in front of the house, with herbaceous borders on either side, one in hot and one in cool colours. High-arching pleached limes lead to Jellicoe's two-storey summerhouse, designed to balance a sixteenth-century one in the old walled garden. His Paradise Garden, now prosaically renamed the East Walled Garden, is a delight of rose arbours around little fountain pools, curving brick paths, tall laburnum arches and mixed planting. A moat with water lilies divides it from the house. Jellicoe's secret moss garden has gone, and now the enormous, central plane tree, with its welcome circular seat, stands on a square lawn with borders planted in purples and blues. The pool garden has a silver and old gold scheme and a Gertrude Jekyll shelter. At the front of the house, beyond a double avenue of American oaks, is a vast lake designed by Jellicoe in the shape of a foetus, part of his allegorical theme.

Titsey Place   35

Titsey Hill, Oxted RH8 0SD. Tel: (01273) 407077/407056 (Information line);
Fax: (01273) 478995. Website: www.titsey.com

Trustees of the Titsey Foundation • 9m W of Sevenoaks. Leave M25 at junction 6.
From A25 E of Oxted, turn left into Limpsfield (signed Warlingham). At end of
High Street fork left into Blue House Lane and first right into Water Lane • House
open • Garden open 1st April, 6th May, then 15th May to Sept, daily, 1 – 5pm,
(last admission 4pm) • Entrance: £2, children £1 (house and garden £4.50, no
concession for children) • Other information: Parking through park near walled
garden, or by gate for woodland walks with long walk to garden ● ● **WC**

The recently restored 18-acre gardens and grounds have been in the same
family for 400 years. The walls of the one-acre Victorian kitchen garden were
damaged by a World War II bomb and now, rebuilt, support espaliered fruit
behind deep borders of old-fashioned roses and annuals. The garden is divided
classically at crossing points, two ironwork gazebos giving height in the
centre. Box-edged beds are filled with vegetables, salad crops, herbs and
100 varieties of tomatoes, raised from unusual varieties of seed collected from
all over the world. There are strawberries too, and flowers for cutting.
Against the south wall greenhouses shelter collections of alstroemerias,
pelargoniums and unusual varieties of tomatoes and peaches. The central
glasshouse displays exotic and more familiar plants in pots, and from here the
central path leads out into the gardens. An unusual knot border stretches
across the front of the house, and below it herbaceous borders curve round a
fountain. An ancient yew guards old gravestones. Two modern rose gardens
are attractively planned, but the colour schemes are unappealing. Magnificent
mature trees dominate the lawns, which lead down to two lakes divided by a
bridge and a cascade; the larger lake has an island, and a stream has been
planted with marginals. Two woodland walks are open, free, all the year.

Vale End   36

Albury, Guildford GU5 9BE. Tel/Fax: (01483) 202296;
Email: daphne@dfoulsham.freeserve.co.uk

Mr and Mrs J. Foulsham • 4½ m SE of Guildford. From Albury take A248 W
for ¼ m • Open 20th June, 6 – 9pm (£3.50 incl. wine; picnickers welcome),
16th June, 28th, 29th July, 10am – 5pm • Entrance: £2.50, children free
● ● ● **WC** ⬦ ⬦ ⬦

In an idyllic setting with views of a mill pond backed by woodland, this one-
acre walled garden is arranged on different levels. The sloping lawn is
bordered by old roses and old favourites as well as less familiar perennials.
The terrace in front of the house is a sun trap, the border filled with subjects
that thrive in hot, dry conditions. Beyond a yew hedge, a cool area is shaded by
a spreading magnolia, and above, edging a walk, stand clipped yew boxes and a
catenary of posts and rope swags, festooned with roses, wisteria and vines. An
attractive courtyard is hidden behind the house. Up a flight of steps, level with
the roof, is a fruit, vegetable and herb garden.

The Valley Gardens (Windsor Great Park) ★★ 37

Wick Road, Englefield Green TW20 0VU. Tel: (01753) 860222

Administered by the Crown Estate Commissioners • 5m S of Windsor. From A30 turn into Wick Road and follow signs for Savill Garden (1m to W) and drive to car park adjoining Valley Gardens, avoiding a 2m round walk • Open all year, daily, 8am – 7pm or dusk if earlier. Possible closure if weather inclement • Entrance: car and occupants £3.50 (£5 April, May, Oct) (10p, 20p, 50p and £1 coins only) (2001 price) • Other information: Refreshments and plants for sale at Savill Garden (see entry) ○ WC ⬦ ℅

One of Britain's most discriminating and experienced garden visitors, the late Arthur Hellyer, suggested that the Valley Gardens are among the best examples of the 'natural' gardening style in England. With hardly any artefacts or attempts to introduce architectural features, they are merely a tract of undulating grassland (on the north side of Virginia Water) divided by several shallow valleys, that has been enriched by the introduction of a fine collection of trees and shrubs. They were started by the royal gardener Sir Eric Savill, when he ran out of room in the Savill Garden, to continue making 'natural' landscapes. One of the valleys is filled with deciduous azaleas. In another, the Punchbowl, evergreen azaleas rise in tiers below a canopy of maples. Notable too are collections of flowering cherries, a garden of heathers which amply demonstrates their ability to provide colour during all seasons, and one of the world's most extensive collections of hollies. Lovers of formal gardening might be forgiven for suggesting that the Valley Gardens have something of that rather too open, amorphous, scrupulously kept feel found in America. *Virginia Water Lake*, off the A30, adjacent to the junction with the A329, was a grand eighteenth-century ornamental addition to Windsor Great Park created by the Duke of Cumberland, who became its ranger in 1746. It had dams, rockwork, a cascade and grotto. There was a fake 'Mandarin yacht', a Chinese pavilion and a Gothick belvedere with a mighty single-arch bridge spanning the water. Alas, almost all have disappeared, but the woodland and the lovely one-and-a-half-mile lake, full of fish and wildfowl, survive, and there is still a colonnade of Roman pillars and a nine-metre waterfall.

Vann 38

Hambledon, Godalming GU8 4EF. Tel: (01428) 683413; E-mail: mary@caroe.com

Mrs M.B. Caroe • 11m S of Guildford, 6m S of Godalming. Take A283 to Wormley, turn left at Hambledon crossroads into Vann Lane and continue for 2m • Open for NGS, and April to Sept by appt. Groups by written arrangement • Entrance: £3, children 50p • Other information: Refreshments for parties by prior arrangement and on some open days only. Toilet facilities at weekends only. Limited access for wheelchairs. Plants for sale at weekends only ◑ 🍵 WC ⬦

The Grade-II-listed house (not open), standing in lawns, dates from 1542 (the name derives from the word 'fen'). The oldest part of the garden is at the front, enclosed by clipped yew hedges, divided by paths and planted in cottage-garden style. Behind the house a stone pergola (W.D. Caröe 1907), underplanted with shade lovers, strides out towards an old field pond. The woodland water garden was designed with Gertrude Jekyll, who supplied the plants in 1911. It has a winding stream, crossed and recrossed by Bargate-stone paths and swathed in lush planting; above the pond a narrow, stone-walled stream is enclosed by a yew walk. A serpentine crinkle-crankle wall supports fruit trees, and there are double borders in the vegetable garden and island beds in the orchard.

The Walled Garden 39

**Sunbury Park, Thames Street, Sunbury–on–Thames.
Tel: (01784) 451499 (Community Services)**

Spelthorne Borough Council • In Sunbury-on-Thames via B375 Thames Street. Entrance through car park • Open all year, daily except 25th Dec, 8am – dusk • Entrance: free • Other information: Wheelchair available on request ○ **WC** &

The original house was built for a courtier of Elizabeth I, and the hearth return for 1664 shows it, with its 27 hearths, to have been the largest domestic building in Sunbury. A later house was pulled down in 1946 and the site bought by Surrey County Council; the local borough council began to develop the walled garden in 1985. A pergola leads to beds of roses of the Victorian era. Adding interest are knot gardens of lavender and box, parterres, modern roses and island beds of plants from all over the world. There are climbers against the walls and gates which lead through to Sunbury Park. During the summer, exhibitions of sculpture, paintings, etc. are on view and a band plays at published times.

Winkworth Arboretum 40

**Hascombe Road, Godalming GU8 4AD. Tel: (01483) 208477;
Fax: (01483) 208252; Website: www.cornuswweb.co.uk**

The National Trust • 2m SE of Godalming, E of B2130. Signposted • Open all year, daily, dawn dusk (but may be closed in bad weather, especially high winds) • Entrance: £3.50, children (5–16) £1.75, family (2 adults, 2 children and one other family member) £8.50, cyclists and public transport users 50% discount, carers free. Pre-booked guided tours available • Other information: Coaches must pre-book. Disabled parking. Possible for wheelchairs but some steps and steep paths ○ ▆ ▆ **WC** ◁▷ ▦ ♁

Winkworth is open 365 days of the year, so is a great place to take the family for a walk on Christmas Day or any other. A new brochure celebrates 50 years of Trust ownership. The 60 plant families and 150 genera grown here provide variety and interest throughout the year. In the spring there are slopes carpeted in bluebells, then azaleas, rhododendrons, cherries, and in the autumn sorbus, liquidambars, acers and nyssas. The arboretum contains a National Collection of whitebeams. The hillside setting and two lakes give pleasing views from almost all of the site. The boathouse is a tranquil resting place with balcony views over the water. Nearby, in Hambledon, *Oakhurst Cottage*, a small timber-framed cottage restored and furnished as a simple dwelling in the 1800s, has a delightful cottage garden with a variety of contemporary plants [open strictly by appointment with Witley Common Information Centre. Tel: (01428) 683207].

Wisley

(see RHS GARDEN)

SUSSEX, EAST

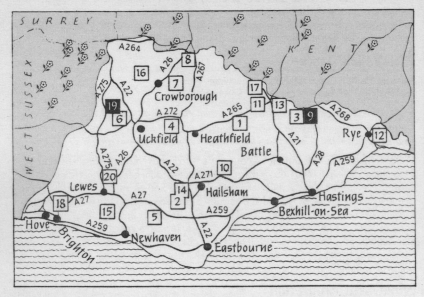

Two-starred gardens are marked on the map with a black square.

Bateman's 1

Burwash, Etchingham TN19 7DS. Tel: (01435) 882302; Fax: (01435) 882811

The National Trust • 10m SE of Tunbridge Wells, 6m SW of A21/A265 junction, ½ m S of Burwash off A265 • House and mill (which grinds flour most Sats in open season) open, 11am – 5pm (last admission 4.30pm) • Garden open 23rd March to 3rd Nov – telephone (0870) 458 4000 for details • Entrance: £5.00, children £2.50, family £12.75, pre-booked parties of 15 or more £4.25 per person (house, mill and garden) • Other information: Picnics in area provided. Dog creche available ◐ ⬛ ✕ 🖼 WC ♿ 🌿 🏛 🍴

Kipling may be more screened than read these days, but his home from 1902 to 1936 is much visited. The house was built in 1634 and the rooms and study remain as they were during the period when he wrote many of his best-known works. Much of the garden was his doing and contains formal lawns with yew hedges, a rose garden and pond, a wild garden, and, on the right as you descend from the car park, an exceptional herb garden. Not far away in Rottingdean is the *Grange Museum* [open weekdays, 10am – 4pm and Sun, 2 – 4pm], opposite which are two acres of garden, formerly part of the house the Kiplings rented on their return from India. These *Kipling Gardens* are open on weekdays.

Bates Green Farm 2

Arlington, Polegate BN26 6SH. Tel: (01323) 482039

Mrs Carolyn McCutchan • 7m NW of Eastbourne, 2½ m SW of A22, 2m S of Michelham Priory (see entry) at Upper Dicker. Approach Arlington passing Old Oak Inn on right, continue for 350 metres, turn right along small lane. Signposted • Open April to Oct, for NGS and by appt • Entrance: £2 ● ● WC & ⚘

Successful and original groupings of plants express the owner's flair for using colour and foliage to create atmosphere and effect. Overall this might be described as a 'plantsman's artistic garden'. A splendid mature oak isolated after the '87 hurricane has been underplanted with foliage plants rejoicing in the dappled shade. Bark paths interweave between the planting and under the young trees. The warm and sheltered area of the former vegetable garden has colour-themed borders of sun-loving plants and foliage contrast. A serpentine path leads from the front of the old farmhouse to the pond where water-loving plants are skilfully grouped. Views from the pond are of the adjoining woodland where there are delightful walks in the bluebell season.

Brickwall 3

Northiam, Rye TN31 6NL. Tel: (01797) 253388

The Frewen Educational Trust • 9m N of Hastings, on B2088 Rye road • House open • Garden open July, Aug, Wed and all Bank Holiday Mons, 2 – 5pm • Entrance: £4, children under 10 free • Other information: Coaches by appt ● WC & ⚘ ⚘

This is an interesting example of a Stuart garden, and care has been taken to use the plants, such as day lilies, bergamots, *Lychnis chalcedonica*, Cheddar pinks and columbines, chosen by Jane Frewen when she was making and planting it between 1680 and 1720. There are two old mulberries, groups of clipped yew, and a superb pleached beech walk. A striking modern addition is the Chess Garden with green and golden yew chessmen in iron frames, set in squares of white and black limestone chips. Great Dixter (see entry) is not far away.

Cabbages and Kings ★ 4

Wilderness Farm, Hadlow Down, Uckfield TN22 4HU. Tel: (01825) 830552; Fax: (01825) 830736; Website: www.ckings.co.uk

Ryl and Andrew Nowell • 4m E of Uckfield, ½ m S of Hadlow Down off A272 at Wilderness Lane • Open 29th March to Sept, Thurs – Mon and Bank Holiday Mons, 10.30am – 5.30pm, but telephone in advance to check. Also by appt • Entrance: £4, OAPs £3.50 • Other information: Guided talks and tea for parties by arrangement ● ● WC & ⚘ ⚘

This imaginative contemporary garden, notable for the strength and originality of its layout, is the work of designer Ryl Nowell. A windswept east-facing slope has been stunningly transformed into a series of small terraced gardens which embrace and enhance subtle water features, urns, statuary, a swimming pool and trelliswork. The garden opens out to the beautiful landscape of the High Weald beyond, and the difficult transition from garden to countryside has been skilfully achieved with soft colours and balanced planting. Nearer to the buildings richer colours in the plants and more exotic foliage effects set off the fine detail of the paving and the warmth of the brickwork. The 13-acre flower meadow has been opened up with mown walks, and there is a permanent undercover exhibition on garden design.

Charleston   5

Firle, Lewes BN8 6LL. Tel: (01323) 811265/811626;
E-mail: info@charleston.org.uk; Website: www.charleston.org.uk

The Charleston Trust • 6m E of Lewes on A27 • House open (guided tours Wed – Sat) • Garden open April to Oct, Wed – Sat, 2 – 6pm (July and Aug, 11.30am – 6pm); Sun and Bank Holiday Mons, 2 – 6pm (last admission 5pm) • Entrance: £2, children £1 (farmhouse and garden £6, children £3.50) ◑ ☕
WC ఉ ✿ ▦ ☕ ⚲

Created by artists of the Bloomsbury Group, this is a delightful example of a garden fashioned during the 1920s by an idiosyncratic group of highly creative people. The walled garden has been meticulously restored through painstaking research and from the memories of people who visited when Vanessa Bell and Duncan Grant lived at the farmhouse and of those like Angelica Garnett and Quentin Bell who spent their childhood there.

Clinton Lodge ★   6

Fletching, Uckfield TN22 3ST. Tel: (01825) 722952

Mr and Mrs Hugh Collum • 4m W of Uckfield from A272. Turn N at Piltdown and continue 1½ m to Fletching. House is in main street surrounded by yew hedge • Open 16th, 17th, 26th June, 5th July, 2nd Aug, 2 – 5.30pm, and for private parties by appt • Entrance: £3.50. Minimum agreed entrance fee for parties ◐ ☕ WC ✿

The house was enlarged by the Earl of Sheffield for his daughter, who married Henry Clinton, one of the three generals of Waterloo. The eighteenth-century façade is set in a tree-lined lawn, flanked by a newly created canal, and overlooking parkland. The 1987 storm removed the old oaks but these have been replanted in a Repton-style landscape leading to a tall stone pillar on the hill. The garden itself is of about six acres of clay soil divided into areas by period. The Elizabethan herb garden has camomile paths and turf seats, and four knot gardens. The Victorian era is represented by a tall white, yellow and blue herbaceous border; the Pre-Raphaelites by an *allée* of white roses, clematis, purple vines and lilies; the twentieth century by an unusual swimming pool garden encircled by an arcade of apples. A wildflower meadow is reached through an avenue lined with fastigiate hornbeams, and a pleached lime avenue leads to the medieval herb garden and a *potager*. An enclosed garden of old and English roses is trained at nose-height to enjoy the scent.

Cobblers 7

Mount Pleasant, Tollwood Road, Jarvis Brook, Crowborough TN6 2ND.
Tel: (01892) 655969

*Martin and Barbara Furniss • On A26 at Crowborough Cross take B2100
towards Crowborough and Jarvis Brook station. At second crossroads take
Tollwood Road • Open several days May to Sept for NGS, all 2 – 5pm •
Entrance: £4 (inc. home-made tea), children £1* ◐ ◖ ✕ <u>WC</u> ᕃ ⟁ ⌇

Martin Furniss, an architect, created the garden from a wilderness round the
sixteenth-century farmhouse nearly 35 years ago. He is fascinated by the
architectural forms of plants and this is reflected in the inspired planting of
over 2000 species and varieties in settings ranging from a terrace filled with rock
plants and alpines to magnificent mixed borders and beds and, at the lowest part
of the garden, a rhododendron walk. The water garden is full of surprises and
delights. The different areas are bound together visually by ingenious brick
paths and stone steps, and enhanced by the creation of vistas in all directions. The
many strategically placed seats were designed and made by the owner.

Crown House 8

Eridge Green, Tunbridge Wells TN3 9JU. Tel: (01892) 864389

*Major L. Cave • 5m NE of Crowborough, 3m SW of Tunbridge Wells off A26.
In Eridge take Rotherfield turn S, and house first on right, 300 metres from bus
stop • Open for NGS 6th, 7th July and by appt May to Oct; small parties
welcome • Entrance: £2, children under 14 free* ◐ ◖ WC ᕃ ⌇ 🏛

This gently sloping one-and-a-half-acre garden contains several different areas.
At the front of the house are lily ponds surrounded by rare shrubs; on the east side
the principal lawn is dominated by a raised, round bed which has at its centrepiece
an umbrella of old-fashioned musk roses, surrounded by *Spiraea japonica* 'Gold-
flame' and nepetas. On the south side are two more lily ponds, an alpine garden
leading to a grass walk, which is flanked on one side by a herbaceous border and on
the other by a heather garden. The walk ends in a paved seating area enclosed by a
trellis of roses and sweet peas surrounding an ornamental pond with fountain. On
the east side is an arboretum and a croquet lawn, on the south-west and west sides
a formal rose garden, a herb garden and a rose walk leading to a further lawn and
shrubbery. Panoramic views of the surrounding countryside.

Great Dixter ★★ 9

Dixter Road, Northiam, Rye TN31 6PH. Tel: (01797) 252878;
Fax: (01797) 252879; E-mail: office@greatdixter.co.uk;
Website: www.greatdixter.co.uk

*Christopher Lloyd and Olivia Eller • 10m N of Hastings, ½ m N of Northiam.
Turn off A28 at Northiam post office • House open • Garden open April to mid-
Oct, daily except Mon (but open Bank Holiday Mons), 2 – 5pm • Entrance:
£4.50, children £1 (house and garden £6, children £1.50) (2001 prices)* ◐ 🏵
<u>WC</u> ᕃ ⌇ 🏛 ⌕

One of the best-known gardens in Britain surrounds the fifteenth-century house bought in 1920 by Nathaniel Lloyd and restored by Lutyens. The sunken garden was designed and constructed by Mr Lloyd, and his son Christopher has continued his family's great gardening tradition, backed up by a strong team under head gardener Fergus Garrett. Within the series of gardens is to be found fine topiary, a magnificent mixed long border, and an exotic garden, spectacular in autumn; the latest development is a pebble mosaic of two reclining dachshunds. Throughout the complex of gardens are pockets of wild flowers, and spring at Great Dixter is famous for the huge drifts of naturalised bulbs. Another feature is the use of theme plants such as forget-me-nots and verbena, which have, as Christopher Lloyd has written, a unifying role and are threaded through the borders. This is truly a plantsman's garden, but also a joy for anyone who enjoys gardening in the finest tradition. Over the past decade, when many might have thought of him as an established pioneer of the British garden, Lloyd has made it clear that he regards his life's work as being to coax new and exciting effects out of plants of all kinds, employing his wizardry with colour, shape and texture to create idiosyncratic and unforgettable plantings. To see what this means, visit Dixter.

Herstmonceux Castle   10

Hailsham BN27 1RN. Tel: (01323) 833816; Fax: (01323) 834499;
E-mail: c_dennett@isc.queensu.ac.uk; Website: www.herstmonceux-castle.com

Queen's University (Canada) • 14m N of Eastbourne, off A271 Hailsham – Bexhill road • Open 29th March to 27th Oct, daily, 10am – 6pm (last admission 5pm), but check before travelling • Entrance: £4, children (under 15) £3, children (under 5) free, concessions £3, family ticket £11 ◑ 💬 🍴 WC ⬖ 🌣 ♨ ▥ 🍵

The approach to the impressive fifteenth-century castle is past the science centre housed in the erstwhile observatory buildings. The path continues alongside the moat and under gnarled but stately 300-year-old sweet chestnuts. The garden proper is contained within yew hedges (some castellated) and ancient walls comprising a knot garden, a herb garden, rose gardens and herbaceous borders. An orchard has been planted with old varieties of fruit trees. A woodland area with azalea walk and lake includes a folly garden. In all, 550 acres of woodland and gardens, including a nature trail.

King John's Lodge   11

Sheepstreet Lane, Etchingham TN19 7AZ. Tel: (01580) 819232;
Fax: (01580) 819562

Mr and Mrs R.A. Cunningham • 10m NW of Hastings, 2m SW of A21/A265 junction. In Etchingham, turn into Church Lane leading to Sheepstreet Lane • Open April to Sept, daily, 11am – 6pm, and by appt • Entrance: £3, children free • Other information: Shop selling statuary ◑ 🍴 WC &

This romantic four-acre garden has been developed since the present owners came here more than a decade ago. The 80s' hurricane removed sixty per cent of the mature trees, leaving some rhododendrons, a small number of formal and informal water features and a wild garden incorporating bulbs in spring and roses in summer. Main borders include softly coloured old roses and herbaceous plantings. The Secret Garden leads to an attractive garden house, which then passes through a meadow to a barn covered in roses and honeysuckle. The historic Jacobean house forms a delightful backdrop. The garden has been increased to feature a large pond near the wild garden, with a bridge leading to a shaded garden and on through gates to the parkland with its many fine trees.

Lamb House   12

West Street, Rye TN31 7ES. Tel: (01892) 890651; Fax (01892) 890110

The National Trust • In centre of Rye, in West Street, facing W end of church • House open • Garden open 3rd April to Oct, Wed and Sat, 2 – 6pm (last admission 5.30pm) • Entrance: house and garden £2.60, children £1.30, family £6.50, groups £2.20 per person (2001 prices) • Other information: No parking near house ◐

Although the author Henry James professed to have no horticultural knowledge, with help from Alfred Parsons he left a town garden of charm and interest. An oasis of calm in this crowded town, there are unusual trees and shrubs, vegetable and herb gardens and herbaceous plantings enclosed within the one-acre walled garden.

Merriment Gardens ★   13

Hawkhurst Road, Hurst Green TN19 7RA. Tel: (01580) 860666;
Fax: (01580)) 860324; E-mail: markbuchele@beeb.net;
Website: www.merriments.co.uk

Mr and Mrs Mark Buchele and Mr David Weeks • 7m N of Battle, on A229 (formerly A265) between Hawkhurst and Hurst Green • Open April to 10th Oct, daily, 10am – 5pm • Entrance: £3.50, children £2 ◐ ⬛ ✕ WC & ⬳ ⚘ 🍴

The extravagant planting of the swirling beds and waterside areas of this sloping garden reveals the growth potential and indicates the appropriate placing of plants. Tall, rustling ornamental grasses, dramatic shrubs grown for foliage effect, skilled combinations of form and colour, extensive exotic and indigenous tree planting, make this a garden of ideas and inspiration. A few years ago it was a field. Innovative ideas have included a yellow/orange border at the far end of the garden. In late summer, the golden colours of over-two-metre-tall *Rudbeckia laciniata* and the equally tall *Helianthus salicifolius* complement the glowing tones of autumnal leaves. In mid- to late summer also, the new, brightly painted Monet pergola rises amidst the jewelled colours of clematis, nasturtiums, dahlias and rudbeckias, with the ruby foliage of *Ricinus communis* 'Carmencita' against the uprights. A recent development is a gravel garden using blue flowers.

Michelham Priory ★   14

Upper Dicker, Hailsham BN27 3QS. Tel: (01323) 844224

Sussex Past • 10m N of Eastbourne off A22 and A27. Signposted • House, museum and gardens open March to July, Sept to Oct, Wed – Sun and Bank Holiday Mons, 10.30am – 5pm (closes 4pm in March and Oct); Aug, daily,

10.30am – 5.30pm • Entrance: £4.80, OAPs and students £4.20, children (5–15) £2.50, family (2 adults and 2 children) £12.20. Rates available for pre-booked parties of 20 or more • Other information: Working watermill and museum ◑ 💻 ✕ 🖺 wc ♿ ⚘ 🏛 ⛽ ✎

Initially, the main horticultural interest of this historic monastic site – more a Tudor manor than a monastery – was the physic garden, but every visit reveals new areas of interest within the moated site of the old priory. The stewponds have been re-excavated and fringed with exotic waterside plants, particularly those with dramatic foliage. The widely sweeping herbaceous border is planted in swathes of bold colour and form and leads into new areas of mixed planting alongside the moat and adjoining the buildings. A fine ornamental *potager* of vegetables, flowers and central pergola lies behind the walls of a yew hedge. Young liquidambars and catalpas are gaining strength and enliven the foreground to the more natural moatside planting. A cloister garden in the well courtyard, inspired by illustrations of medieval 'Mary' gardens, includes an arbour, turf seat and raised beds for medicinal plants.

Monk's House ★ 15

Rodmell, Lewes BN7 3HF. Tel: (01892) 890651; Fax: (01892) 890110

The National Trust • 4m S of Lewes off old A275, now C7. In Rodmell follow signs to church and continue 400 metres to house • House open • Garden open 3rd April to Oct, Wed and Sat, 2 – 5.30pm (last admission 5pm), and Thurs for pre-booked parties • Entrance: £2.60, children £1.30, family £6.50 (2001 prices) ◑ wc ✎

The cottage home of Virginia and Leonard Woolf from 1919 until his death in 1969. There are three ponds, one in dewpond style. An orchard, underplanted with spring and autumn bulbs, contains a comprehensive collection of daffodils, and Leonard's vegetable area is still thriving. Flint stone walls and yew hedges frame the more formal herbaceous areas, leading to a typical Sussex flint church at the bottom of the garden. The one-and-three-quarter-acre garden is a mixture of chalk and clay, nurturing a wide variety of species. Among the interesting specimen trees are *Salix hastata* 'Wehrhahnii', Chinese lanterns over six metres tall, *Magnolia liliiflora*, walnut, mulberry and an Indian bean.

Moorlands 16

Friar's Gate, Crowborough TN6 1XF. Tel: (01892) 652474

Dr and Mrs Steven Smith • 2m N of Crowborough on St John's Road to Friar's Gate or turn left off B2188 at Friar's Gate onto road signed 'Narrow road to Crowborough and Horder Centre for Arthritis' • Open April to 1st Oct, Wed, 11am – 5pm, and 9th May, 14th July, 2 – 6pm • Entrance: £3, children free ◑ 💻 🖺 wc ⬦ ⚘ ✎

It is fifty years since work commenced on this fine wetland garden in the Ashdown Forest. Over the years a handsome terrace has been made by the house, its flatness contrasting sharply with the precipitous slope behind and the undulating slopes down to the river and ponds below. In spring, the ponds and waterside are fringed with primulas, irises, lysichitons, rheums and rodgersias, backed by azaleas and rhododendrons and set among more unusual shrubs and trees. Autumn colour is provided by the rich red tones of liquidambar and scarlet oak, set against the russet foliage of a group of larches. From the riverside walk visitors can look back at the garden across its own lush valley.

Pashley Manor ★ 17

Ticehurst TN5 7HE. Tel: (01580) 200888

Mr and Mrs James A. Sellick • 10m SE of Tunbridge Wells on B2099 between Ticehurst and A21. Signposted • Open probably April to Sept, Tues – Thurs, Sat and Bank Holiday Mons, 11am – 5pm. Coach parties by appt only • Entrance: £6, OAPs £5 ◗ ➍ ➦ WC ふ ℘ 曲 ♀

Pashley Manor is a Grade-I-listed Tudor timber-framed ironmaster's house of 1550 with a George I rear elevation dated 1720, standing in some eight acres of formal garden, being completely renovated with advice from Antony du Gard Pasley. The planting is subtle, with emphasis on colour and form, pale colours blending with the carefully chosen foliage. From the terrace and over the magnificent fountain there is a view of the Mad Jack Fuller obelisk at Brightling Beacon several miles away. A series of enclosed gardens is surrounded by beautiful eighteenth-century walls. Grass paths, some concealing the original Victorian gravel beneath, lead through camellia and rhododendron shrubberies. A large fountain, and the natural springs which feed a series of ponds falling away from the house and medieval moat, ensure that the sound of falling water is heard over most of the garden. Access to a small island with classical temple is by a decorative iron bridge. A golden garden has been created, and other projects include an extensive planting of tulips to complement the Tulip Festival held in May; an avenue of pleached pear trees underplanted with box so arranged as to give a view through to magnificent hydrangeas; and a garden of old-fashioned roses to complement the Summer Flower Festival held in June. In the new 1½-acre garden to the south-east of the old walled garden, ample herbaceous borders designed by Antony du Gard Pasley are planted with strong colours and sculptural plants for late-summer flowering.

Royal Pavilion Gardens 18

Brighton BN1 1EE. Tel: (01273) 290900; Fax: (01273) 292871; Website: www.royalpavilion.brighton.co.uk

Brighton & Hove Council • In central Brighton • Royal Pavilion open June to Sept, daily, 10am – 6pm; Oct to May, daily except 25th, 26th Dec, 10am – 5pm • Garden open all year, daily • Entrance: gardens free (Royal Pavilion £5.20, concessions £3.75, children under 16 £3.20) (2001 prices) ○ ➍ ➦ WC ふ 曲 ♀ ⚲

The gardens surrounding the Royal Pavilion have been restored to their original Regency splendour, closely following John Nash's plans of the 1820s. Nash conceived the building and grounds as a unity, and his vision will be fully realised as the plants and shrubs continue to flourish and mature.

The beds are of mixed shrubs and herbaceous plants, a combination first applied in the Regency period. Species and varieties have been selected to conform as closely as possible to the original lists of plants supplied to the Prince Regent (later King George IV). The gardens and grounds reflect the great revolution in landscape gardening that began in the 1730s, when straight lines and symmetrical shapes were banished, and in their place appeared curving paths and 'natural' groups of trees and shrubs undulating gracefully over the lawn. As visitors pass through the grounds, the magical Royal Pavilion is disclosed by a succession of varying views through the shrubs and thickets.

Sheffield Park Garden ★★   19

Sheffield Park TN22 3QX. Tel: (01825) 790231; Fax: (01825) 791264; Website: www.nationaltrust.org.uk/regions/kentesussex

The National Trust • 5m NW of Uckfield, midway between East Grinstead and Lewes E of A275. Bus connects with Bluebell Railway which links with Connex South Central services • Garden open Jan to Feb, weekends, 10.30am – 4pm; March to Oct, Tues – Sun and Bank Holiday Mons, 10.30am – 6pm; Nov to Dec, Tues – Sun, 10.30am – 4pm (last admissions 1 hour before closing) • Entrance: £4.60, children £2.30, family ticket, £11.50, pre-booked parties £4 per person, children £2 • Other information: Teas at Oak Hall. Wheelchairs and self-drive powered vehicles available ◐ 🍴 ✕ <u>WC</u> & ♨ 🏛 ♿ ⚬

A 120-acre landscape garden and arboretum with two lakes (later extended to four, in an inverted-T formation below the house) created by 'Capability' Brown for the Earl of Sheffield in 1776. Repton worked here in 1789, and a waterfall and cascades were added later. Between 1909 and 1934 a collection of trees and shrubs notable for their autumn colour was planted, including many specimens of *Nyssa sylvatica*. These and other fine specimen trees, particularly North American varieties, provide good all-year-round interest. The Trust aims to plant 9000 new trees and shrubs over the next five years to repair storm damage. Features include good water lilies in the lakes, the Queen's Walk and, in autumn, two borders of the Chinese *Gentiana sino-ornata* of amazing colour. Three new beds of brightly coloured azaleas include varieties recently rediscovered, expanding the National Collection of Ghent azaleas.

Wellingham Herb Garden   20

Wellingham Lane, Nr Lewes BN7 58SW. Tel: (01435) 883187

Grant Brickell • 2m N of Lewes off A26 • Open Easter to Sept, Sat and Sun, 10.30am – 5.30pm • Entrance: free ◐ & ♨

Enclosed within a walled garden is a delightful and aromatic herb garden, created since 1992. Herbs are displayed in four main box-edged beds. The walls are clothed with fruit, including medlars, and accompanied by old roses and perfumed shrubs.

SUSSEX, WEST

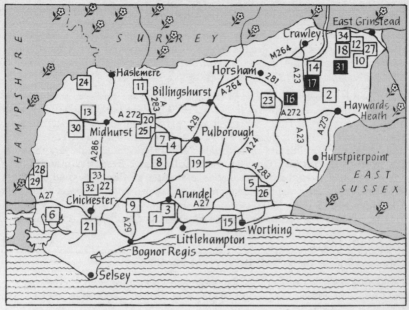

Two-starred gardens are marked on the map with a black square.

Berri Court

1

Yapton, Arundel BN18 OED. Tel: (01243) 551663

Mr and Mrs J.C. Turner • 8m E of Chichester, 5m SW of Arundel on B2233, in Yapton between post office and Black Dog pub • Open some days during summer – check local press for details. Groups by arrangement • Entrance: £2, children free ● ● WC ⅃ ﹪ ℺

A series of sheltered gardens within a one-and-a-half-acre garden of great interest to plant enthusiasts. A mass of daffodils flowers in spring, with the azaleas and rhododendrons. The borders have an impressive display of herbaceous plants and many varieties of shrubs and climbing roses. Around the house are magnificent *Magnolia grandiflora*, *Drimys winteri* and *Clematis rehderiana*. Elsewhere, *Clematis* x *jackmanii* clambers through trees, and different varieties of eucalyptus are grown throughout the garden. The vigorous *Rosa glauca* (syn. *Rosa rubrifolia*) provides spectacular foliage colour contrast, and *Tropaeolum speciosum* create splashes of vermilion through the borders.

Borde Hill Garden ★ 2

Balcombe Road, Haywards Heath RH16 1XP. Tel: (01444) 450326;
Fax: (01444) 440427; E-mail: info@bordehill.co.uk

Borde Hill Gardens Ltd • 1½ m N of Haywards Heath on Balcombe – Haywards Heath road • House open to groups by appt • Garden open all year, daily, 10am – 6pm; guided tours by arrangement • Entrance: £5.50, children £3, family ticket £15, family season ticket £35 ○ ♥ ✕ ➦ WC ᕼ ⬠ ⋎ 🏛 🍴 ⋒

Described by *Country Life* as one of the country's great gardens, here is a rich variety of all-season colour set in 200 acres of parkland and bluebell-carpeted woods. Planted from 1893 with trees and shrubs from China, Asia, Tasmania, the Andes and Europe, there are award-winning collections of azaleas, rhododendrons, magnolias and camellias, including the popular cultivars raised at Borde Hill before 1939, 'Donation' and 'Salutation'. Extensive new planting has taken place, with rose, herbaceous and water gardens designed by Robin Williams, plus an ongoing 'Garden Renaissance' using a grant from the Heritage Lottery Fund. Attractions include coarse fishing, children's fishing, Pirates adventure playground, extensive woodland walks and lakes.

Burpham Place 3

Burpham, Arundel BN18 9RH. Tel: (01903) 884833

Elizabeth Woodhouse • ½ m S of Arundel, turn off A27 Arundel – Worthing road and continue for 2m through Wepham to Burpham • Open by appt • Entrance: charge ◑

The owner, a RHS medallist in botanical illustration, has turned her attention to garden design consultancy, and her artist's eye shows to full effect in her own garden of just under an acre. The form and colour of each plant are minutely thought through. Steeply sloping to the foot of the South Downs (a ramblers' paradise), the garden is arranged in three tranches. Two circular layers with wide, colourful beds lead to a third, wild area. This runs down to a pond and folly through masses of self-seeding verbascum.

Champs Hill 4

Coldwaltham, Pulborough RH20 1LY. Tel: (01798) 831868

Mr and Mrs D. Bowerman • 2m S of Pulborough. From A29 at Coldwaltham turn W towards Fittleworth. Garden is 300 metres on right • Open 10th, 17th, 24th March, 5th, 12th, 19th May, 4th, 11th, 18th Aug, Wed, 11am – 4pm (Sun 2 – 6pm). Private parties welcome – please telephone • Entrance: £2.50, children free ◑ ♥ WC ᕼ ⋎

This fascinating heathland garden, with over 300 varieties of heather grown alongside dwarf conifers and other interesting plants, is complemented by spectacular views of the Arun Valley and South Downs. The heathers are best viewed in March and August, but a walk in May through the 27 acres of natural woodland interplanted with a wealth of rhododendron and azalea species is a real bonus, and sculptures and a trickling stream add to the appeal.

Chantry Green House 5

Church Street, Steyning BN44 3YB. Tel: (01903) 814824

Mr R.S. Forrow and Mrs J.B. McNeil • 8m N of Worthing, 10m NW of Brighton off A283. From Steyning High Street, opposite White Horse Inn, turn into Church Street. House is 150 metres on left • Open 15th, 16th June, 2 – 5pm • Entrance: £2, children 50p • Other information: Parking in Fletchers Croft car park opposite church ● ⊲◈ ♋

A sheltered and well-maintained one-acre town garden with some interesting features – a water garden, a kitchen garden, an American garden and an arboretum with unusual trees, including *Liriodendron tulipifera* 'Aureomarginatum', *Lagerstroemia indica*, the crape myrtle, and *Eriobotrya japonica*, the Japanese loquat. In a corner, an old wall fountain is the focus of a shady area planted with ferns and hostas. Also of note are the many varieties of cistus.

Chidmere House 6

Chidham Lane, Chidham, Chichester PO18 8TD. Tel: (01243) 572287/573096

Mr T. Baxendale • 4m E of Emsworth, 6m W of Chichester, S of A259. Turn right at southern end of Chidham • Open one Sun and Mon in spring and summer for NGS, and by appt, 2 – 6pm • Entrance: £2, children free ● WC �& ⊲◈

The Tudor house (not open) is excitingly situated next to Chidmere Pond, so much so that the well-filled greenhouse which borders the mere almost feels like a houseboat. The garden was laid out in 1930–36 by the present owner's father, and is divided into separate compartments by tall hedges of hornbeam and yew. Flowering cherries, sheets of daffodils and bluebells ensure that it is spectacular in the spring. There are other fine flowering trees, while the house supports a Banksia rose and two wisterias. Later, the roses, a fine herbaceous border, a tulip tree and *Taxodium distichum* demand attention.

Coates Manor 7

Fittleworth, Pulborough RH20 1ES. Tel: (01798) 865356

Mrs G.H. Thorp • 3m W of Pulborough, ½ m S of Fittleworth off B2138 • Open 20th Oct, 11am – 5pm, and by appt • Entrance: £2, children 20p ● ▦ WC ♋

This one-acre garden has an abundance of trees and shrubs carefully chosen to give long-term pleasure. There are ferns, grasses such as *Stipa gigantea* like frozen waterfalls, *Phlomis italica* and *P. chrysophylla*, blue and white agapanthus, and many specimen trees chosen for their foliage, berries or autumn colour. A small paved walled garden has *Clerodendrum trichotomum*, clematis, phlox and other scented flowers. The owner, who has lived here for over 35 years, is particularly interested in colour contrasts and light and shade, and goes to considerable lengths to find the best species available. Look out for a variegated ivy contrasting well with *Cotinus coggygria* 'Notcutt's Variety' on a wall by the house; a mature copper beech tree stands nearby. The delightful Elizabethan house is partly covered in variegated ivy and euonymus, linking it with the surrounding countryside.

Cooke's House ★   8

West Burton, Pulborough RH20 1HD. Tel: (01798) 831353

Miss J.B. Courtauld • 5m SW of Pulborough. Turn W off A29 at foot of Bury Hill and continue for ¾ m • Open 14th to 21st May, 1 – 5pm, and by appt • Entrance: £2, children under 14 free ● ◉ 🏠 WC ❖ ♿

This delightful garden, surrounding an Elizabethan house (not open) with views of wooded downs, has the components of a great garden in miniature, each section perfectly articulated to vistas leading the eye beyond. There is a tiny paved Gertrude Jekyll garden and herb garden, a meadow filled in spring with cowslips, and an orchard. Yew topiary of cubes, cones and birds about to take flight is overlooked by a stone heraldic lion. Steps lead up to a path between borders of tulips, yielding later to herbaceous plants. Shrubs are underplanted with snake's-head fritillaries, Solomon's seal and bluebells. Notable too are the Judas tree, tulip tree and magnolias.

Denmans ★   9

Fontwell, Arundel BN18 0SU. Tel: (01243) 542808; Fax: (01243) 544064
Email: denmans@cwcom.net; Website: www.denmans-garden.co.uk

John Brookes • 5m E of Chichester. Turn S off A27, W of Fontwell racecourse • Open March to Oct, daily, 9am – 5pm • Entrance: £2.95, OAPs £2.65, children over 4 £1.75, parties of 15 or more £2.50 per person if pre-booked (2001 prices) ◑ ◉ ✕ WC ❖ ♿ 🏠

Described by Penelope Hobhouse as 'a really important garden'. John Brookes, one of Britain's most influential designers. moved here in 1980 and now owns the garden. The whole site relies for its drama on foliage plants – even in spring, in spite of the early flowering bulbs, one comes away with one's mind full of euphorbias, yuccas, phormiums and mounds of clipped box. The centre of the garden is a 'river' of pebbles and gravel against which the leaves of thistles and bamboo show up dramatically. There are some choice tulips and other spring bulbs, interesting primulas and spring-flowering shrubs, including a *Stachyurus praecox*. The walled garden contains many old roses as well as a herb garden and perennials and is at its finest in late June and July. Outside the house is the South Garden. Very tender species are planted in another gravel area near a circular pond. In late summer a large border of *Romneya coulteri*, the Californian tree poppy, is at its best, while autumn and winter interest are given by the stems of willow and cornus, and by the leaves of *Parrotia persica* and staphylea, the bladder nut.

Duckyls   10

Sharpthorne, East Grinstead RH19 4LP. Tel/Fax: (01342) 811038;
E-mail: HMTDUCKYLS@aol.com

Lady Taylor • 4m SW of East Grinstead, 6m E of Crawley. Take B2028 S at Turners Hill and fork left after 1m to W Hoathly. Turn left at sign to Gravetye Manor (see entry) on right • Open April to May, 2 – 6pm, and for small parties by appt • Entrance: £3, children £1 ● ◉ WC ♿

These 14 acres of terraced and hilly garden, with breathtaking views of woods and Weir Wood Reservoir, are established with rhododendrons and azaleas among carpets of bluebells and daffodils. The rose garden, containing vegetables and the white Rugosa rose 'Blanche Double de Coubert', is now a parterre garden with some beds underplanted with irises. There are ponds and a bog garden with gunnera and philadelphus. Some interesting new trees are maturing near the house. The woods are occupied by a small flock of Soay sheep. Only a portion of the garden is maintained to the same standard as that around the house, yet the place stays immensely attractive.

Frith Hill   11

Northchapel, Petworth GU28 9JE. Tel: (01428) 707531; Fax: (01428) 708183

Mr and Mrs P. Warne • 8m NE of Midhurst, 7m N of Petworth on A283. In Northchapel turn E into Pipers Lane by Deep Well Inn; after ¾ m turn left into bridleway past Peacocks Farm • Open six times a year for charity (send s.a.e. for further details) and for parties of 10 or more by appt • Entrance: £2.50, children free ● ● WC ♿ ☞ ⚭

This one-acre garden of variety and charm surrounds a brick-and-tile-hung house and relates effortlessly to the countryside beyond, with surprises in every corner. The first walled garden has a huge herbaceous border to the north and leads to another walled area with an arbour and old-fashioned roses enclosed by clipped box, then proceeds in shade past a quince through a gate to splendid views of the rolling weald. Overlooking the view is a third garden with a paved area and beside the gazebo a shady white garden with massed *Rugosa* roses ('Blanche Double de Coubert'), water bubbling over a millstone, and a herb garden with alliums, mallows and almost black opium poppies as well as culinary herbs. There are also massive white ramblers, lilies, good hydrangeas and interesting pots everywhere. A millennium pond faces views of the rolling Weald.

Goodwood House and Sculpture Park

(see SCULPTURE AT GOODWOOD)

Gravetye Manor   12

Vowels Lane, East Grinstead RH19 4LJ. Tel: (01342) 810567

Mr P. Herbert • 4m S of East Grinstead between M23 and A22. By M23, take exit 10 onto A264 towards East Grinstead. After 2m, at roundabout, take 3rd exit on B2028. 1m after Turners Hill turn left and follow signs • Open all year to hotel and restaurant guests; perimeter footpath only for public on Tues and Fri • Entrance: free • Other information: Parking in drive in lay-by before gates. Hotel restaurant open to non-residents for lunch and dinner, but reservations essential. Toilet facilities for hotel and restaurant guests only ●

This historically important garden has been carefully restored in the style pioneered here by William Robinson. The area around the hotel (which can only be visited by guests or visitors having lunch or dinner) can be viewed from a public footpath which passes through wildflower meadows to the north and south. There are several large shrubs and trees – parrotias, rhododendrons and pines – which may be part of the original planting. The path to the west edged with hydrangeas and large camellias leads down through a wooded area to a large lake, continues along the lake and completes the circumnavigation back to the entrance. For those interested in the Robinsonian doctrine, it is well worth giving yourself a treat, either by spending a night at Gravetye or simply going for a meal, though do not plan a visit without asking about prices and availability beforehand. For a complete contrast, not far away is *Birch Farm Nursery*, open all year for the sale of Ingwersen's renowned alpines – 1800 different varieties (formerly part of the original Robinson estate).

Hammerwood House   13

Iping, Midhurst GU29 0PF. Tel: (01730) 813635

The Hon Mrs Lakin • 3m W of Midhurst, 1m N of A272 • Open 14th, 21st May, 2 – 5.30pm • Entrance: £2.50, children free ● ▭ WC ᚻ ⟨⟩ ⚘ ⚭

This is a peaceful country garden, formerly part of a Regency vicarage, planted with care and a fine eye for good plants. Although the rhododendrons and azaleas give it its most spectacular flowering season, there are some splendid camellias, magnolias, cornus and other specimen trees. Across a meadow from the main garden is the woodland walk by a stream. Wild flowers abound.

High Beeches Gardens ★   14

Handcross RH17 6HQ. Tel: (01444) 400589; (01444) 401543.
E-mail: office@highbeeches.com; Website: www.highbeeches.com

High Beeches Gardens Conservation Trust • 5m S of Crawley, 1m E of Handcross, S of B2110 • Open March to June, Sept and Oct, daily except Wed, 1 – 5pm. Event days 1st April, 6th May, 3rd June, 18th Aug, 13th Oct, 10.30am – 5pm • Entrance: £4.50, accompanied children under 14 free. Guided parties of 10 or more by appt any day or time, £5 per person with lunches etc. by arrangement ◑ ▭ ▩ WC ⚘

This is an important woodland and water garden of over 20 acres where the visitor will find a continually extended collection of rare trees and shrubs. Originally designed by Colonel Loder in 1906, the garden was influenced by John Millais (son of the painter Sir John Everett Millais), by Arthur Soames of Sheffield Park and by William Robinson. The collection is well labelled. The woodland, carpeted with bluebells and other wild flowers, extends over a series of valleys, often with ponds and streams. There are plenty of benches from which to enjoy the different woodland pictures. Rhododendrons, amelanchiers and magnolias are splendid in spring, and autumn colour is particularly fine. Plants to seek out, amongst a wide collection, include *Cyclamen hederifolium* flowing over the roots of a tall oak tree near Centre Pond, adding to an explosion of autumn colour; *Disanthus cercidifolius*, a little-known shrub, its bluish-green round leaves attractive from spring until they colour brilliantly in autumn; and an attractive small tree, *Elaeagnus angustifolia* 'Quicksilver'. The National Collection of stewartias is here.

Highdown 15

Littlehampton Road, Goring-by-Sea BN12 6PE. Tel: (01903) 501054

Worthing Borough Council • 3m W of Worthing, N of A259 • Open April to Sept, Mon – Fri, 10am – 6pm, Sat, Sun and Bank Holidays, 10am – 6pm; Oct to March, Mon – Fri, 10am – 4.30pm (4pm Dec to Jan) • Entrance: free – donation box • Other information: Refreshments at peak times only. Toilet facilities available to wheelchair users only with key ○ 🍴 WC ♿ ☕

Gardeners everywhere, but particularly those who garden on chalk, must be grateful to Worthing Council for their continuing high standard of care for Sir Frederick Stern's chosen site in 1910 in and around a bare chalk pit donated to Worthing in 1968. The season starts with a mass of hellebores; narcissi and cowslips follow, and then peonies and iris. Brilliant scarlet anemones are naturalised in the grass; later there will be agapanthus, eremurus and autumn crocus. And these are just the flowers. There are also fine specimen trees – davidia, arbutus and cornus – and many shrubs, including roses, ceanothus, kolkwitzia and laburnum, with buddleia and paulownia to follow. Dramatic banks of pittosporum are a striking feature. Highdown is a plantsman's garden – it doesn't have a lot of shape – and unfortunately there are few labels. There is, however, an explanatory display at the entrance.

Leonardslee Gardens ★★ 16

Lower Beeding, Horsham RH13 6PP. Tel: (01403) 891212; Fax: (01403) 891305; E-mail: gardens@leonardslee.com; Website: www.leonardslee.com

The Loder family • 4m SW of Handcross and M23 on B2110/A281 • Open April to Oct, daily, 9.30am – 6pm • Entrance: April: £5, May: weekdays £6 weekends £7, June to Oct: £5, children £3. Season tickets £14 • Other information: Victorian motor car collection ◑ 🍴 ✕ 🍴 WC 🐕 ♿ 🏠 ☕

The garden was enlarged by Sir Edmund Loder, who raised the famous *Rhododendron* 'Loderi' hybrids, with their huge scented flowers. This 240-acre valley with its seven lakes, its collection of rhododendrons (some are 190 years old), azaleas, camellias, acers, magnolias, snowdrop tree and other shrubs, and sweeps of bluebells, combines to form a beautiful landscape in a peaceful setting. Wallabies (used as mowing machines) have lived semi-wild in parts of the valley for over 100 years. The immense scale and the mature trees give the garden a special quality. In the late afternoon and early evening light the colours of the rhododendrons and azaleas glow and their heady scent fills the air. The rock garden has ferns and Kurume azaleas in perfect small scale. Nor should visitors miss the excellent bonsai exhibition, the alpine house with 400 species of alpines including lewisias and other miniatures, the temperate greenhouse with banana, *Ceanothus thyrsiflorus repens* like a blue umbrella, and the miniature landscape of the 'Behind the Doll's House' exhibition. Selehurst (see entry) is opposite.

Nymans ★★ 17

Handcross, Haywards Heath RH17 6EB. Tel: (01444) 40032/0016/00157;
Fax: (01444) 400253

*The National Trust • 4m S of Crawley. At southern end of Handcross, off A23/
M23 and A279. Signposted • House open as garden end March to Oct, 11am
— 4.30pm • Garden open March to Oct, Wed – Sun (but open Bank Holiday
Mons), 11am – 6pm or dusk if earlier (last admission 5.30pm); Nov to Feb,
weekends only, weather permitting (telephone for details) • Entrance: house and
garden £6, children £3, family £15, parties of 15 or more £5 per person. Joint
ticket available with Standen (see entry) Wed – Fri only, £9 • Other information:
Coaches must pre-book. Batricar, wheelchairs and braille/audio guide available
on free loan. Map of wheelchair route available* 🕐 ☕ ✕ 🛍 WC ♿ 🌳 🧺 🌷

An historic collection of trees, shrubs and plants in a beautifully structured
setting, full of outstanding and almost theatrical effects: sheets of white narcissi
under sorbus trees, a circle of camellias around a lawn with an urn in the centre, a
vista down a lime avenue with a 'prospect' at the end and several borders of great
splendour. Originally started by Ludwig Messel in 1890, it was continued by his
son Leonard and daughter-in-law Maud, and then by his granddaughter, Anne,
Countess of Rosse. Although the garden was given to the Trust in 1954, Lady
Rosse continued to live there until her death in 1992. The library, drawing room
and walled garden have been preserved and opened to the public. These rooms
lead out to the forecourt and a knot garden. The picturesque ruins of the original
building (built c. 1928 to resemble a medieval manor house and largely destroyed
by fire in 1947) are planted with clipped yew and other topiary. The Messel
creations include a pinetum, a sunken garden with a stone loggia, a laurel walk, a
croquet lawn, a heather garden, roses in beds and over arbours, and magnificent
herbaceous borders. Some of these areas can be viewed from on high, from the
Mound. Bedding is always beautifully done and the whole is exceptionally well
maintained. *Magnolia* x *loebneri* 'Leonard Messel' and *Eucryphia* x *nymansensis* were
both raised at Nymans. An exhibition of garden history situated within the garden
is a recent welcome addition. On the opposite side of the road is the Rough, a wild
garden. Overall, there are many fine, rare, well-labelled trees and only the very
sharp-eyed could spot signs today of the hurricane which cut such a swathe
through the South Weald in 1987. The Trust also have in hand some 600 acres of
park. This is one of the most outstanding gardens in an area of interesting ones.

Orchards 18

Off Wallage Lane, Rowfant, Crawley RH10 4NJ. Tel: (01342) 718280;
E-mail: penelope.hellyer@hellyers.co.uk; Website: www.hellyers.co.uk

*Penelope S. Hellyer • 4m E of Crawley. From Turners Hill crossroads, turn N on
B2028 for 1½ m, left into Wallage Lane, and after ¼ m right immediately after
railway bridge, up farm track • Open March to Oct, Wed – Sat, 10am – 4pm;
Mon and Tues by prior appt only • Entrance: £2.50, accompanied children free
• Other information: Practical gardening workshops held throughout the year —
send s.a.e. for details* 🕐 ☕ 🛍 WC 🌳 🌷

The late Arthur Hellyer acquired this 7½-acre plot of south-facing land in 1934. Working on the site at weekends only, he and his wife camped out in a small wooden hut while building their house and, initially, developing a market garden. Full use has been made of the sloping terrain. Viewed from the house, an open area with magnificent conifers on either side leads down to a small pond with lush marginal plantings of *Gunnera manicata*. Mainly a woodland garden, *Juniperus recurva* var. *coxii*, liquidambar, *Picea omorika* (Serbian spruce) and *Liriodendron tulipifera*, the tulip tree, are just a few of the striking mature specimen trees to be found here. Penelope, the Hellyers' daughter, now runs the small nursery and is restoring and maintaining the garden with the help of her husband. They have added a herb and vegetable garden. Sadly, much of the variegated willow avenue has now died and is due to be replaced. Beneath an old apple tree is a meadow planted with wild flowers, including orchids. Snowdrops, *Helleborus orientalis* and *Scilla messeniaca* herald the spring, followed by thousands of daffodils and spring-flowering shrubs. The herbaceous and shrub plantings include hardy geraniums and alliums, buddleias, weigelas, philadelphus and ribes. The borders are planted for a long season, taking interest into the late autumn with many different asters. Numerous camellias, a bluebell wood, apple orchards, rhododendrons, conifers and a heather border make this a year-round garden.

Parham House and Gardens ★   19

Nr Pulborough RH20 4HS. Tel: (01903) 742021/744888;
Fax: (01903) 746557/744888 (Information line);
E-mail: enquiries@parhaminsussex.co.uk; Website: www.parhaminsussex.co.uk

4m SE of Pulborough on A283, equidistant from A24 and A29 • House open as garden but 2 – 6pm (last admission 5pm) • Garden open 31st March to Oct, Wed, Thurs, Sun and Bank Holiday Mons, 12 noon – 6pm (last admission 5pm); also 13th, 14th July for garden weekend, and 7th, 8th Sept for flower-arranging weekend. Private parties and guided tours on other days • Entrance: £3.50, children 50p, season ticket £22.50 (house and garden £5.50, OAPs £4.50, children £1, family £11, season ticket £32.50). Pre-booked parties per person: unguided of 20 or more £4.50; guided of 30 or more £6.50 (2001 prices) • Other information: Advance notice required for wheelchairs ◑ ☕ ▥
WC ♿ ⇔ ⌓ 🚻 🌳 ✕

Set in the heart of a medieval deer park on the slopes of the South Downs, the award-winning gardens of this Elizabethan house are approached through Fountain Court. A broad gravelled path leads down a gentle slope through a wrought-iron gate guarded by a pair of Istrian stone lions to a walled garden of about four acres, which retains the original quadrant layout divided by broad walks and includes an orchard and teak walk-through greenhouse. In 1982 the walled garden was redesigned, retaining its character and atmosphere; the borders were replanted to give interest for many months, with shrubs as well as herbaceous plants. Recent additions are a *potager*, a rose garden and a green border, planted along the outer west wall, and a lavender garden. In one corner is an enchanting miniature house with its own garden, a delight for both children and adults. The pleasure grounds of about seven acres provide lawns and walks under stately trees to the lake, with views over the cricket ground to the South Downs. Veronica's brick and turf maze is a feature here. This is a garden for all seasons, and in spring it is dominated by the splendid 'sacred' grove of 'Mount Fuji' white-flowering cherry, over 50 years old.

Petworth House ★   20

Petworth GU28 0AE. Tel: (01798) 342207; Fax: (01798) 342963; Website: www.nationaltrust.org.uk

The National Trust • 6½ m E of Midhurst on A272 in Petworth • House open 23rd March to 3rd Nov, Sat – Wed (but open 29th March), 11am – 5.30pm • Pleasure Ground open 9th, 10th, 16th, 17th March, 12 noon – 4pm, 23rd March to 3rd Nov, Sat – Wed (but open 29th March), 11am – 6pm. Deer park open all year, daily, 8am – dusk • Entrance: £7, children £4, family £18. Pre-booked parties of 15 or more £6.50 per person (house and grounds). Deer park free • Other information: Parking ½ m N of Petworth on A283. Disabled visitors by arrangement, special parking available. Refreshments only on days house open • Pleasure Ground: ◑ ☕ ✕ 🖼 WC ᇰ ⛪ 🔱 *Deer park:* ○

Petworth is a stately palace, with one of the finest late-seventeenth-century interiors in England. The house sits in a magnificent park. Its deer park grew from a small enclosure for fruit and vegetables in the sixteenth century to its present size of 705 acres over centuries, and is enclosed by an impressive five-mile-long stone wall. George London worked here at the end of the eighteenth century. So did 'Capability' Brown from 1751–63 for the 2nd Lord Egremont, modifying the contours of the ground, planting cedars and many other trees and constructing the serpentine lake in front of the house. It was one of Brown's earliest designs, planned while he was still at Stowe (see entry in Buckinghamshire). Turner painted fine views of the park (as well as the interior of the house) and it is interesting to see these and have them in one's mind when strolling around the park, as Turner himself must have done many times while staying at Petworth. This is not a garden for the botanist, but it is a splendid experience, all year round, for any lover of man's improvements upon nature, and the individual trees and shrubs, including Japanese maples and rhododendrons, deserve close study. Majestic veteran trees now tower over wildflower meadows and ornamental shrubs, providing interest throughout the year. It is worth noting that at the turn of the century Petworth had over two dozen gardeners (they were always counted in dozens). Far fewer staff have, since the storms of 1987 and 1990, planted in the region of 40,000 trees.

Rymans   21

Apuldram, Dell Quay, Chichester PO20 7EG. Tel: (01243) 783147

Mrs Suzanna Gayford • 1m SW of Chichester. Turn off A259 (old A27) at sign to Dell Quay, Apuldram, garden on left • Open two days for NGS, and by appt • Entrance: £2, children 50p ◑ 🖼 WC ᇰ 🐾 ◑

Previously owned by Lady Anne Phillimore, a member of the Dorrien-Smith family of the famous Tresco Abbey Gardens, Isles of Scilly (see entry in Cornwall), the garden holds a number of plants with Tresco connections. Surrounding a fifteenth-century house with mellow Ventnor-stone exterior, the garden is being developed by the present owner. A walled garden filled with flowering shrubs and roses, including *Rosa chinensis* 'Mutabilis', and furnished with a new pergola leads to a modern architectural water feature. The paddock opposite the old stables is now planted with a selection of trees, and two wildflower glades. Seen from within the walled garden an avenue of black poplars, *Populus nigra*, stretches beyond a magnificent wrought-iron gate to nearby twelfth-century Apuldram church. Planted with massed daffodils, the avenue is a picture in springtime.

Sculpture at Goodwood ★ 22

Goodwood, Chichester PO18 0QP. Tel: (01243) 538449; Fax: (01243) 581853; Web: www.sculpture-org.uk

Mr and Mrs Wilfred Cass • 7m N of Chichester, 3m S of East Dean, between A286 and A285 (telephone (01243) 77114 for directions) • Open April to Nov, Thurs – Sat, 10.30am – 4.30pm • Entrance: £10, students and children £6
◑ WC ♿ ♨

Twenty acres of woodland have been shaped to provide a finer setting for British contemporary sculpture than any indoor gallery. The quality of the work is outstanding; the trees act as screens, giving each piece its own stage, and sometimes opening to give a backdrop of the Sussex countryside. Beautiful new gates by Wendy Ramshaw herald the entrance to the park, while at the end of one walk the spire of Chichester cathedral is borrowed sculpture of the most majestic kind, flanked at present by Tony Cragg's bronze 'Pillars of Salt'. Pieces, mostly for sale, vary as works are commissioned to provide about twenty new works a year. It is worth following the directions of the printed guide on a tour of the wood – at present the visitor begins walking down to a gallery designed by architect Craig Downie. Sir Anthony Caro's Piranesian steel tower, a mass of girders and stairs, William Furlong's 'Walls of Sound' emitting birdsong, Jon Isherwood's granite pillars, Ellis O'Connell's bronze 'Unfold' like an intricate mantle and Charlotte Mayer's feathery bronze 'Pharus 2001' are some of the more recent pieces on show.

Selehurst 23

Lower Beeding, Horsham RH13 6PR. Tel: (01403) 891501

Mr and Mrs M. Prideaux • 4½ m SE of Horsham on A281, opposite Leonardslee (see entry) • Open 12th May, 1 – 5pm • Entrance: £3 ◑ 💷 🛍
WC ♿ ♨

The 20-acre woodland garden is now emerging as a romantic landscape garden in the skilful hands of garden designer and novelist Sue Prideaux. Near the house a 30-metre rose and laburnum tunnel is underplanted with ferns, phormiums, artichokes and hostas in a striking tapestry of foliage. The Italian border has purple old-fashioned roses and darkest delphiniums. A box-patterned herb knot is scented with lilies and moss roses. The walled garden shelters a huge white wisteria and herbaceous borders, the woodland a collection of tender scented rhododendrons and specimen trees, including the tallest eucalyptus in the kingdom, according to the late Alan Mitchell. A series of ponds linked by waterfalls leads ultimately to Pope's Vale, a green theatre with urns and a spring-fed tear-drop pond. A Gothick folly tower is being decorated with shells, while the Chinese pavilion on the water is planted with black bamboo and cloud-pruned myrtles; gold dragons fly through the red lacquer interior.

Shulbrede Priory   24

Linchmere, Haslemere, Surrey GU27 3NQ. Tel: (01428) 653049

Laura Ponsonby and Ian and Kate Russell • 2m SW of Haslemere off B2131 •
Open 26th May, 2nd, 3rd June, 25th, 26th Aug, 2 – 6pm, and by appt •
Entrance: house and garden £3, children £1, parties (maximum 30) £4 per
person (guided tour included) ● ▣ ▤ WC & ◁

Originally an Augustinian priory, twelfth-century Shulbrede became the home of Lord Ponsonby, a writer and former pacifist MP early in the twentieth century. He and his wife Dorothea created a garden here which delighted Dorothea's father, Sir Hubert Parry, the composer and Director of the Royal College of Music, who often visited Shulbrede and composed the *Shulbrede Tunes* for piano. Their grand-daughter, Laura Ponsonby, continues to improve the garden. Cottage-style borders are seen and smelt from the house, a sunken garden gives an Italianate air, a waterside walk in the wild garden inspires a sense of mystery, and vast yew hedges enclose a series of individual gardens planted to great effect. A gem on the Sussex/Surrey borders.

Somerset Lodge   25

North Street, Petworth GU28 0DG. Tel: (01798) 343842

Mr and Mrs R. Harris • 6½ m E of Midhurst on A272 in Petworth, 100 metres
N of church • Open some days in early June, 12 noon – 6pm, and for parties by
appt • Entrance: £1.50, children 50p ● ▣ WC ◁ ☙ ◷

This seventeenth-century house near Petworth House (see entry), has a steeply sloping garden with splendid views towards the North Downs. In just over a decade the present owners, retired architects, have transformed an ancient orchard by creating different elements on several levels. An abundance of clearly labelled roses includes *Rosa mundi* (*R. gallica* 'Versicolor') and *R. moyesii* planted with *Clematis* 'Mrs Cholmondeley'. Herbaceous borders, a wild garden leading to an impeccable vegetable garden, ponds and a gazebo contribute to the peaceful yet exuberant atmosphere. The superb woodwork has been designed and built by Mr Harris.

St Mary's House   26

Bramber BN44 3WE. Tel: (01903) 816205

Peter Thorogood • 8m NE of Worthing off A283 in Bramber, 1m E of Steyning •
Open April to Sept, Thurs, Sun and Bank Holiday Mons, 2 – 6pm (last tour

5pm). Parties by appt daily, 9am – 6pm, except during public open times. Secret Gardens open May to Sept, first Sun in month; tours 2.30pm, 3.30pm, 4.30pm • Entrance: formal gardens £3, children 50p; Secret Gardens £2 extra, children free (house and formal gardens £5, concessions £4.50, children £2) ◑ ◙ WC ♿ ♨ ♀

Around the fifteenth-century timber-framed house, the established formal gardens contain topiary in the shapes of animals and birds. There is also a mysterious ivy-clad Monks' Walk and an exceptional example of the living fossil tree, *Ginkgo biloba*. The adjacent Victorian Secret Gardens are currently being restored. Originally laid out in the 1890s, the pleasure and kitchen gardens have been 'asleep' for the last 50 years. Clearance has revealed that one of the three Victorian glasshouses has survived intact, as well as a magnificent 40-metre fruit wall, a rare circular orchard, heated pits with their stove-house, and a Boulton and Paul potting shed with its apple store. Plans for restoration include the re-creation of herbaceous borders, fruit-wall planting, the re-establishment of a woodland area as a nature reserve, the creation of a wildflower meadow and a small lake for wildfowl, and the conversion of the potting shed into a rural museum. Two magnificent herbaceous borders were designed by students on the Intermediate Diploma Garden Design course at Brinsbury College, Pulborough.

Standen 27

East Grinstead RH19 4NE. Tel: (01342) 323029; Fax: (01342) 316424; E-mail: sstpro@smtp.ntrust.org.uk;

The National Trust • 2m S of East Grinstead signed from A22 at Felbridge, and from B2110 • House open days as garden March to Nov, 12.30 – 4pm • Garden open 28th March to 4th Nov, Wed – Sun and Bank Holiday Mons, 11am – 6pm; 9th Nov to 16th Dec, Fri – Sun, 11am – 3pm • Entrance: £3, children £1.50 (house and garden £5.50, children £2.75, family £13.75); joint ticket available with Nymans (see entry) Wed – Fri only, £9, children £4.50 • Other information: Picnics in picnic area only. Dogs in woodland walks only ◑ ◙ ✕ ☕ WC ♨ ♀ ♿

The Philip Webb house and estate have close connections with Morris and Co., and the garden reflects much of the Arts and Crafts period of the latter part of the nineteenth century. It is made up of a succession of small, very English gardens, and the helpful leaflet lists 12 different areas or features, including bamboo and rose gardens. Perhaps the most outstanding is the little quarry (with its restored bridge), which has survived as a Victorian fernery. There are good views from this hillside garden across the Medway Valley. Two walks are described in the leaflet, but these can be muddy.

Stansted Park Victorian Walled Garden 28

Rowlands Castle, Hampshire PO9 6DX. Tel: (023) 9241 3090

7m W of Chichester, 2m N of Westbourne, off B2149 • Garden centre and walled gardens open May to Oct, daily, 10am – 5pm (Sun 10.30am – 5pm) • Entrance: free ◑ ◙ WC ♨ ♿

Now a garden centre, the Victorian glasshouses, conservatories and complex of walled gardens, and the circular well-head garden in the arboretum, have recently been restored. The Garden in Mind in the Lower Walled Garden is unaffected (see entry below).

Stansted Park: The Garden in Mind 29

Rowlands Castle, Hampshire PO9 6DX. Tel: (023) 9241 2265

7m W of Chichester, 2m N of Westbourne, off B2149. Signposted. In Lower Walled Garden of Stanstead House • Open all year, daily, 1 – 5pm, and by appt • Entrance: £3.50, OAPs £3, children £2, family ticket (2 adults, 3 children) £9, groups £30 ◑ ℘

Ivan Hicks is now widely known for his imaginative work at Groombridge (see entry in Kent) and elsewhere, but his intriguing design in what was a walled kitchen garden, incorporating old iron, wood and stone objects, remains as a shrine for the Sunday afternoon *cognoscenti*. Lilies grow in a room with a telephone, bed, wardrobe and fireplace, a chair is perched in the air, a pair of legs is all that is left of someone who has dived into a dell of ferns. Underworlds and overworlds, a source of inspiration and a thought-provoking place.

Trotton Old Rectory 30

Trotton, Petersfield GU31 5EN. Tel: (01730) 813612

Captain and Mrs John Pilley • 3m W of Midhurst on A272 • Open for parties by appt • Entrance: £3 ◕

Set in the pretty Rother valley, the one-and-a-half-acre garden consists of several different areas of varying shapes and sizes, each with its own character. Many are lavishly planted, and they are separated from each other by hedges of yew, holly and beech as well as a trellis screen and walls. To the north of the house are newly planted pleached limes and box, to the south a terrace leads out into a formal rose garden. This is planted with attractive pink and white roses, contrasting with the old roses in the circular rosarium in the garden beyond, which is surrounded by mixed borders where lavender, delphiniums, campanulas and many other plants provide a riot of colour. A restful enclosure dominated by a venerable oak has gunneras, clipped yew and a lawn speckled with bulbs in spring to give variations of texture and shades of green; against the hedge are the graves of family pets. Another garden surrounds the croquet lawn. To the east of the house at a lower level is a large pond surrounded by clumps of handsome *Iris ensata*. Linking the different areas are walks lined with shrubs and hostas, hemerocallis and lilies.

Wakehurst Place Garden and Millennium Seed Bank ★★ 31

Ardingly, Haywards Heath RH17 6TN. Tel: (01444) 894066 (Infoline); Website: www.kew.org

The Royal Botanic Gardens, Kew• 7m N of Haywards Heath on B2028. From London take A(M)23, A272, B2028 or A22, B2110 • Part of house open •

Garden open all year, daily, except 25th Dec and 1st Jan: Nov to Jan, 10am –
4pm; Feb, 10am – 5pm; March and Oct, 10am – 6pm; April to Sept, 10am –
7pm (last admission ½ hour before closing). Guided walks available 11.30am
and 2.30pm Sat, Sun and Bank Holiday Mons • Entrance: £6.50, OAPs,
students and UB40 £4.50, children (under 12) free. Season tickets and Friends
of Kew membership available ○ 🍽 ✕ 🖻 WC ⑆ ♨ 🏛 🔦 ⚲

Dating from Norman times, the estate was bought by Gerald W.E. Loder
(Lord Wakehurst) in 1903. He spent 33 years developing the gardens, a work
carried on by Sir Henry Price. The gardens have been managed by the Royal
Botanic Gardens, Kew, since 1965. They have a fine collection of hardy plants
arranged geographically and display four comprehensive National Collections
– betulas, hypericums, nothofagus and skimmias. Unique is the glade planted
with species growing at over 3000 metres in the Himalayas. A plantation of
Japanese irises is part of the extensive and fascinating water gardens. There
are two walled gardens, one given over to colourful bedding schemes, the
other to herbaceous borders, delightfully planted in subtle shades. Wakehurst is a place for the botanist, plantsman and garden lover, offering features
of year-round interest, particularly the winter garden which bursts into
colour about late November. The Wellcome Trust Millennium Building,
home to an international seed bank and interactive public exhibition, opened
in 2000 – futuristic and even slightly sinister in appearance, the design and
presentation are masterly.

Weald and Downland Open Air Museum   32

Singleton, Chichester PO18 0EU. Tel: (01243) 811348;
E-mail: wealddown@mistral.co.uk; Website: www.wealddown.co.uk

Weald & Downland Open Air Museum • 5m N of Chichester on A286 • Open
March to Oct, daily, 10.30am – 6pm (last admission 5pm); Nov to Feb, Wed, Sat
and Sun, 10.30am – 4pm • Entrance: £7, children £4, under-5s free, family (2
adults and 2 children) £17, OAPs £6.50 (2001 prices) ○ 🍽 🖻 WC ◁▷ ♨ 🏛 🔦 ⚲

Set in the heart of the South Downs, the main exhibits of this museum
(founded in 1967) are over 45 traditional buildings, ranging from medieval
to Victorian, rescued from certain destruction, restored and rebuilt on the
museum's countryside site. Complementing the buildings, seven historic
gardens have been researched and planted to demonstrate the changes and
consistencies in ordinary domestic gardens from the early 1400s to 1900. The
earliest garden has only a few plants, including wild garlic and edible weeds
such as fat hen. A complete medieval farmstead has been re-created around
Bayleaf Farmhouse, and the replica fifteenth-century garden is required to
fulfil the gastronomic and medical needs of six adults, their children and
servants from beds over four metres long and a metre wide. By the Victorian
era, represented by a typical cottage garden of the period, the gardens were
not only practical but showed the introduction of flowers for their beauty
alone. A delightful, educational experience for those keen to experience
period husbandry.

West Dean Gardens ★ 33

West Dean, Chichester PO18 0QZ. Tel: (01243) 818210; Fax: (01243) 811342; E-mail: gardens@westdean.org.uk; Website: www.westdean.org.uk

Edward James Foundation • 5m N of Chichester on A286 • Open March to Oct, daily, 11am – 5pm (May to Sept opens 10.30am; last admission 4.30pm). Groups by appt only • Entrance: £4.50, OAPs £4, children £2. Pre-booked parties of 20 or more £4 per person ◑ 🍽 ✕ 🍴 WC & ⚘ 🏤 🛈

There have been gardens here since 1622; in 1836 a number of rare trees were mentioned by J.L. Loudon, and in 1891 William James bought the property and Harold Peto designed the magnificent 100-metre-long pergola. The advent of Jim Buckland as head gardener has resulted in another burst of activity, with the laying out of new paths and much new planting. The restored pergola has roses, clematis and honeysuckle and is underplanted with pulmonarias, ferns, the attractive double primula 'Marie Crousse' and dicentras in quantity, followed by hostas and alchemillas. The south side of the pergola is planted with sun-loving Mediterranean plants. At one end is a stone pavilion, at the other a sunken garden with beds of glowing tulips and wallflowers in spring. A woodland walk has a collection of flowering trees and shrubs. At the westerly end of the garden the rustic summerhouse has been restored with moss walls, seaweed decorations, a heather ceiling and a thatched roof. Particularly noteworthy, however, is the walled garden with a large collection of trained fruit trees, three large herbaceous borders, and a large vegetable and cut-flower garden – the *Victorian Kitchen Garden* come to life. An extensive range of Victorian glasshouses, with displays of flowers, ferns, peaches, figs and melons, together with a circular thatched apple store, makes this whole area especially memorable. It is all immaculately maintained. The house (now an Arts and Crafts college) and its gardens are surrounded by parkland, and it is possible to follow a marked path of two and a quarter miles to *St Roche's Arboretum*, which has a good collection of rare trees and shrubs.

Yew Tree Cottage ★ 34

Turner's Hill Road, Crawley Down RH10 4EY. Tel: (01342) 714633

Mrs Hudson • 1m S of A264 between Crawley and East Grinstead. On Down Lane (B2028) opposite Grange Farm entrance, turn right and cottage is second of semi-detached on left • House open for small parties, 50p extra per person • Garden open by appt for small parties • Entrance: £1.50, children free ● ⚘

A plantsman's delight and an encouragement to all with small gardens; it is not surprising that this third-of-an-acre plot has been a prizewinner. Changes to reduce maintenance include the use of gravel and the introduction of drought-resistant plants. Inspired by the Dutch designer Piet Oudolf, a number of grasses have been added, such as the low-growing, feathery *Stipa tenacissima*, which has proved most successful. To the rear of the house a mature quince, underplanted with hellebores, stands over a well, while the borders are bursting with colour and unusual plants. *Cornus kousa, Veronica virginica*, Miss Willmott's Ghost, the pink-flowered bronze elderflower, lysimachia, and a range of hellebores and astrantias are but a few of the interesting plants in this exceptional garden.

WARWICKSHIRE

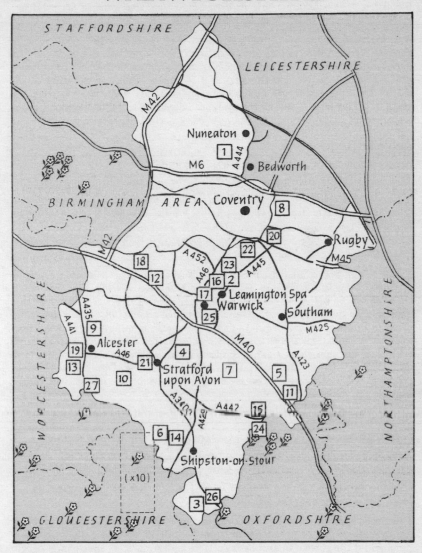

STAFFORDSHIRE

LEICESTERSHIRE

M42

Nuneaton

1 A444

M6 Bedworth

BIRMINGHAM AREA Coventry 8

M42 20

A452 22 Rugby

18 23 M45

12 A46 16 2 A445

17 Leamington Spa

Warwick Southam

25 M425

A435 A441 9 Alcester

A46 A423

19 4

13 21 Stratford

27 10 upon Avon 7 5

A34(?) 11

A429 A447 15

6 14 24

Shipston-on-Stour

(x10)

3 26

GLOUCESTERSHIRE OXFORDSHIRE

WORCESTERSHIRE

NORTHAMPTONSHIRE

Arbury Hall ★   1

Arbury, Nuneaton CV10 7PT. Tel: (024) 7638 2804

Viscount and Viscountess Daventry • 10m N of Coventry, $3\frac{1}{2}$ m SW of Nuneaton off B4102 Fillongley/Nuneaton road • House and garden open 31st

March, 1st April, 5th, 6th May, 2nd, 3rd June, 25th, 26th Aug, 2 – 6pm (last admission 5pm) • *Entrance: £4, children £2.50 (hall and gardens £6, children £3.50, family £14* ● ● ✕ ▤ WC �& ⬙ ▥ ❂

A formal rose garden and climbing roses are features of this delightful, peaceful garden, distinguished also by the lakes with their wildfowl, the parkland, the drive and the bluebell woods. Especially memorable are the pollarded limes, the old walled garden and the beautiful old trees. Bulbs at the start of the season are followed by rhododendrons and azaleas, then roses in June and autumn colour from trees and shrubs. A canal system was installed years ago as a method of transport.

Avon Cottage   2

Ashow, Kenilworth CV8 2LE. Tel: (01926) 512850

Neil Collett • *5m NE of Warwick, 1½ m E of Kenilworth. From A452 Kenilworth – Leamington road turn onto B4115 (signed to Ashow and Stoneleigh), after ¼ m turn right into Ashow and right again. Continue to end of Ashow. Cottage is beside church* • *Open 25th, 26th May, 29th, 30th June, 24th to 26th Aug* • *Entrance: £2, children 50p* • *Other information: Refreshments and toilet facilities available in village club on Suns* ● ℘ ℺

A delightful one-and-a-half-acre garden surrounding a picturesque eighteenth-century listed cottage in a lovely riverside setting. The owner, a landscape architect, has worked organically to protect valuable wildlife habitats, and sensitive use of reclaimed materials and varied plantings provide interest all year round. There are riotous mixed herbaceous borders, with vegetables and herbs growing among the flowers, an orchard area with domestic and water fowl, a rhododendron walkway, a collection of old-fashioned shrub roses and masses of daffodils in spring. Don't leave without crossing the footbridge to the twelfth-century church, or you will miss a sensational view of the garden.

Barton House ★   3

Barton-on-the-Heath, Moreton-in-Marsh GL56 0PJ. Tel: (01608) 674303

Mr and Mrs I.H.B. Cathie • *6m S of Shipston-on-Stour off A3400, 4m E of Moreton-in-Marsh off A44* • *Open for NGS 2nd June, 2 – 6pm, and for parties by appt* • *Entrance: £2.50, children £1* • *Other information: Refreshments in coach house on open day* ● ● WC �& ℘

This six-acre garden around a manor house by Inigo Jones (not open) has many varied features and surprises. Borders of rhododendrons greet the visitor, and throughout the garden an excellent collection of American, species and hybrid types provides a long flowering period. A secret garden planted for colour and form has magnolias, maples with camellias, pieris, crinodendrons, euphorbias and geraniums for ground cover. Viewing points have been made to enjoy the surrounding countryside, and there are some fine mature Scots pines, Wellingtonias and Douglas firs. Other features are a catalpa walk, a collection of moutan tree peonies, (*Paeonia suffruticosa*), a rose garden with beds of individual colours surrounding an oblong lily pool, a Himalayan garden, a Japanese garden, herbaceous and shrub beds, statues, archways and a copy of the portico of St Paul's, Covent Garden. There are many rare specimens plus National Collections of nothofagus and stewartias, and masses of spring bulbs. A paved roundel in the centre of the walled kitchen garden is surrounded by plants. The ornate cast-iron atrium from the Royal Exchange in Threadneedle Street forms the roof of the orangery. A vineyard has been planted to commemorate the millennium. Also worth seeing is *Whichford Pottery* off the other side of the A3400 [open all year, daily except Sun]. Although not a garden, it is inspirational for its design ideas as well as its stylish pots.

Charlecote Park   4

Charlecote, Wellesbourne, Warwick CV35 9ER. Tel: (01789) 470277;
E-mail: charlecote@smtp.ntrust.org.uk

The National Trust • 5m E of Stratford-upon-Avon, 1m W of Wellesbourne • House open as garden • Garden open 3rd March to 3rd Nov, Fri – Tues, 12 noon – 5pm • Grounds open 11am – 6pm. Parties by appt • Entrance: house and garden £5.80, children £2.90, family ticket £14.50 • Other information: Braille guide available ◑ ▟ ✕ ▤ WC ⅍ ⇗ ℘ ⊞ ⓞ ℺

Home of Lucy family since the thirteenth century. The pink brick gatehouse is the only remnant of the early Tudor house left untouched. The park was laid out by 'Capability' Brown, who was directed not to destroy the avenues of elms (later eliminated by Dutch elm disease). The orangery is now a restaurant, a parterre has been re-instated, the wild garden is interesting and the cascade will attract those who like water features – these include a pond in the small wilderness garden, full of wildlife. The Shakespeare border has plants which feature in the plays, ranging from herbs to quince and medlar, old roses and carnations. A courtyard garden has been designed in front of the house.

The Coach House   5

Bitham Hall, Avon Dassett CV47 2AH. Tel: (01295) 090255

Mr and Mrs C.J. Rice • 7m N of Banbury off B4100, leave M40 junction 12 at Gaydon, or from Leamington take A462 to join Banbury road. 3 m after Gaydon turn left to Avon Dassett. Entrance to garden on hill. Parking on hill and in village • Open for NGS, and by appt • Entrance: £1.50, children free [NEW] ▟ WC ⇗ ℘ ℺

These two acres, set on sloping ground overlooking Edgehill, originally formed part of a Victorian garden, and are now planted for year-round interest, with many varieties of trees, shrubs, climbers and perennials. Walls give shelter to tender plants. Two areas are devoted to bush and cordon fruit trees and vegetables, and there is also a wet garden. The woodland has well-established trees and some 70 young native trees, underplanted with new shrubs, including camellias, rhododendrons and peonies. Flowering bulbs and primroses give spring interest.

Compton Scorpion Farm 6

Ilmington, Shipston-on-Stour CV36 4PJ. Tel: (01608) 682552

Mrs T.M. Karlsen • 8m S of Stratford-upon-Avon, 4m NW of Shipston-on-Stour off A3400. Take left fork uphill at Ilmington village hall. After 1½ m turn left down steep narrow lane and house is on left • Open all year, Mon, 2 – 5pm, and by appt • Entrance: £2, children free ● ⬦ ℆

One of the most stunning views in the county unfolds as you drive along the ridge from Ilmington towards this farmhouse, which in 1989 was surrounded by a mere meadow, sloping steeply towards the house. The owner has worked wonders, from the small walled garden behind the house aiming at Jekyll-inspired single colour schemes, to the rose-encrusted slope up beyond and the rabbit-proof vegetable garden around the old sheep shed. A spring-fed pond has been established in the orchard. In countryside as beautiful as this you could say that she started with an advantage, but the stylish planting is all her own. Combine with a visit to Ilmington Manor (see entry).

Compton Verney 7

Near Kineton CV35 9HZ. Tel: (01926) 645500

9m SE of Warwick, via M40 junctions 12 or 15, on B4086 Kineton – Wellesbourne road S of Fosse Way • Grounds open all year, daily • Entrance: free ○ WC ⬥ ℆

Compton Verney art gallery will open to the public in 2003. In 2002 the site will be 'under construction', so telephone for details of new art projects, children's activities and events. The park, landscaped by Capability Brown, includes a lake, a cedar of Lebanon and an avenue of Wellingtonias.

Coombe Country Park 8

Brinklow Road, Binley, Coventry CV3 2TL. Tel: (024) 7645 3720 (Ranger Service)

Just E of Coventry on B4027 • Open all year, daily, 7.30am – dusk • Entrance: free but parking charge ○ � ✗ ▣ WC ᶑ ⬦ ⬥ ⬥ ℆

Nearly 400 acres of beautiful parkland including woodland and lakeside walks, all-weather pathways, wildflower meadows and historic gardens by William Andrews Nesfield and William Miller. There are also the remains of a duck decoy and an arboretum. Facilities include an information centre, a history video, a wildlife discovery centre, a bird hide and play areas.

Coughton Court ★ 9

Alcester B49 5JA. Tel: (01789) 400777; Fax: (01789) 765544

Mrs C. Throckmorton • 8m NW of Stratford-upon-Avon, 2m N of Alcester on A435 • House open • Garden open 23rd March to September, Wed – Sun and Bank Holiday Mons; Aug, Tues – Sun; 1st to 27th Oct, Sat and Sun only, all 11am – 5.30pm. Closed 29th March, 22nd June, 21st July. Parties by appt •

Entrance: £6.95, children £3.45 (under 5 free), family ticket £21.45, (house and garden £9.45, children £4.75 (under 5 free), family ticket £29.25) ◑ ➡ ✕ ▤ WC & ◁ ✍ 🏛 ♨ ⚲

The grounds complement the mid-sixteenth-century house and include a variety of gardens both formal and informal. The main garden, courtyard and walled garden were designed by Christina Williams. The redesigned orchard contains many old local varieties and there is also a chef's herb garden. The large lawn is bordered by cloistered lime walks, while a peaceful stroll beside the River Arrow reveals willows, wild garlic, ferns, hellebores and native trees and shrubs. In spring there is a bluebell wood and many bulbs to enjoy. A second lake has been drained to form a bog garden. One of the finest features is the large walled garden with 'hot' and 'cold' herbaceous borders dedicated to Professor d'Abreu – Mrs Throckmorton's father – containing a superb display of plants to give colour and interest through the seasons. The red and white gardens are surrounded by hornbeam hedges being trained to provide windows. In the rose labyrinth masses of roses and clematis grow over arches and pedestals, with herbaceous underplanting. In the early summer garden wisteria is trained over raised hoops with peonies beneath, and pale colours change to deeper shades of blue and red. The architectural features are also good. A pond and fountain is surrounded by benches and planted in green and white as a peaceful place for contemplation.

Elm Close   10

Binton Road, Welford-on-Avon CV37 8PT. Tel: (01789) 750793

Mr and Mrs E.W. Dyer • 5m SW of Stratford-upon-Avon on B439. Turn left after 4½ m to Welford • Open for NGS, and by appt • Entrance: £2, children free ● WC ✍

A relatively small garden filled with fresh ideas and a wide range of plants. Clematis (over 300) are trained over pergolas and climb through trees and shrubs, and there are dwarf conifers, a rock garden, hellebores, a pool, alpine troughs, raised beds and an excellent variety of bulbs. Herbaceous plants and shrubs, including a wealth of peonies, cornus and magnolias, provide interest and colour throughout the year.

Farnborough Hall   11

Farnborough, Banbury, Oxfordshire OX17 1DU. Tel: (01295) 690002

The National Trust/Mr and Mrs Holbech • 5m N of Banbury, ½ m W off A423 or 1½ m E off B4100 • House open • Grounds open April to Sept, Wed and Sat, and 5th, 6th May; terrace walk only open Thurs and Fri; all 2 – 6pm (last admission 5.30pm) • Entrance: garden and terrace walk £1.70, children 85p; terrace walk only £1, children 50p (house and grounds £3.40, children £1.70) ◑ WC & ◁ ⚲

The house has been in the same family since 1684. It was reconstructed in the eighteenth century with fine Rococo plasterwork and the grounds were improved in the 1740s with the aid of Sanderson Miller, the architect, landscape gardener and dilettante who lived at nearby Radway. Climbing gently along the ridge looking towards Edgehill is the fine S-shaped terrace walk built by William Holbech in order to greet his brother on the adjoining property. *The Oxford Companion* describes it as a majestic concept marking the movement towards the great landscaped parks at the end of the eighteenth century. There are two temples along the walk and an obelisk at the end. The trees are beeches, sycamores and limes. Beyond the cedar tree is part of the site of the former orangery, a rose garden, and a yew walk with steps at the end leading into a field, where there is a seat with a fine view over the river and towards Edgehill. The cascade fountain suppresses the otherwise-invasive hum of the M40. A uniquely interesting site.

Hickecroft 12

Mill Lane, Rowington CV35 7DQ. Tel: (01564) 782384

Mr and Mrs Pitts • 6m NW of Warwick, 15m SE of Birmingham on B4439 between Hockley Heath and Hatton. Turn into Finwood Road (signed 'Lowsonford') at Rowington crossroads and first left into Mill Lane • Private visits by societies or individuals welcome by appt • Entrance: £2.50, children 50p ◐ WC ♿

This well-designed garden uses hedges to divide the different sections, and there are surprises round most of the corners. A woodland garden with fritillaries and trilliums is matched by a good range of grasses and geraniums, and a new water feature contains bog plants. The owners' flair shows itself in their use of colour contrasts, topiary, paths made of a range of different materials, and trees planted at strategic points with roses growing up through them. There is also an orchard with daffodils to enjoy.

The Hiller Garden 13

Dunnington Heath Farm, Alcester B49 5PD. Tel: (01789) 772771

Mr and Mrs R. Beach • 9m W of Stratford-upon-Avon, 3m S of Alcester at former A441/A435 junction, now B4088 • Open all year, daily, 10am – 5pm • Entrance: free ○ ☕ ✗ WC ♿ ⋈ ⌘ ⌂

An established two-acre garden with year-round interest. Large beds of herbaceous perennials with frequent new introductions enable visitors to the garden centre to see mature, well-labelled plants in good colour combinations and so judge their suitability for personal use. The garden also embraces an extensive rose garden, which includes more than 200 varieties and has a Victorian rose area as its centrepiece. The owners' adjacent private garden is also open for pre-booked visits by horticultural societies.

Ilmington Manor 14

Ilmington, Shipston–on–Stour CV36 4LA. Tel: (01608) 682230

Mr D. Flower and Lady Flower • 4m NW of Shipston-on-Stour, 8m S of Stratford-upon-Avon • Open for NGS 7th April, 12th May, 16th June, 2 – 6pm, for NGS and by appt. Other gardens in village may be open on 7th April. Parties welcome • Entrance: £2, children free ◐ ☕ WC ♿ ⋈ ⌘

Created from an orchard in 1919, this is now a mature garden full of surprises with a strong formal design; there is also much to interest the plantsperson. To the right of the drive is a paved pond enlivened by many fish, including enormous koi; thyme of many varieties ornament the stones, and aromatic climbers scent the air. Next, a walk by the pillar border presents an unusual combination of shrubs and herbaceous plants in colour groups. Then, up stone steps, is the formal rose garden and the long double border planted with old and modern shrub roses and herbaceous plants. The so-called Dutch garden is really an informal cottage garden with a profuse mixture of colour. There is much more – a trough garden, iris and foliage beds, a rock garden and, in the spring, plenty of daffodils and crocus. A charming gazebo has a vast green unicorn standing guard behind, and new plants and trees are still being added.

Ivy Lodge ★ 15

Radway CV35 0UE. Tel: (01295) 670371/670580

Mr M. Dunne • 14m SE of Stratford-upon-Avon, 7m NW of Banbury via B4100 and B4086 • Open by appt only • Entrance: £1.50, OAPs £1, children free ● ➊ 🏠 WC & ⬦

Radway nestles below Edgehill, and the garden of Ivy Lodge runs back across the former battlefield. Above on the skyline can be seen the mock castle by Sanderson Miller, who lived in the village. The previous owner developed a splendid 'natural' garden with bulbs and blossom in spring, in summer an outstanding number of old roses, many rambling through the trees, and in autumn, wonderful October colours. Nearer the mock-Gothic house are interesting plants and two attractive beds.

Jephson Gardens 16

Leamington Spa CV32 4AD.

Tel: (01926) 450000 (Amenities Department, Warwick District Council)

Warwick District Council • In Leamington Spa, main entrance off Parade • Open all year, daily, 8am (9am Sun and Bank Holidays) – dusk • Entrance: free • Other information: Parking in Newbold Terrace ○ ➊ WC & ⬦

The spa town has always made a great effort to provide floral displays in its streets, and this vibrancy can also be enjoyed at its peak in the intensive bedding-out of the principal formal public garden. It is fine enough to be listed by English Heritage and, besides flowers, contains a remarkable collection of trees. Leamington has a string of parks and gardens running along the River Leam right across the town – an almost unique piece of town planning of a century ago. It is possible to walk their length: Mill Gardens, Jephson Gardens, Pump Room Gardens, York Promenade and Victoria Park. There are some fine listed examples of Victorian iron bridges, as well as earlier stone ones. On the outskirts of nearby Kenilworth is the ruined *Kenilworth Castle*, whose reconstructed Tudor garden is worth a visit in memory of what it once was.

The Master's Garden 17

Lord Leycester Hospital, Warwick CV34 4BH.
Tel: (01926) 491422 (Contact: Susan Rhodes)

Board of Governors of Lord Leycester Hospital • In High Street • Open end
March to Sept, daily except Mon (but open Bank Holiday Mons), 10am –
4.30pm • Entrance: £1 ◐ ☕

The restoration work of this garden is remarkable. Old cobbles from the summerhouse have been relaid in the new circular house with its thatched roof of Norfolk reeds, and archways dating from the 1850s have been copied to support roses, clematis and other climbers. A brick pathway through the centre of the garden repeats the feathered pattern. The 150-year old pleached lime avenue remains, and on the walls is a fig tree, along with gooseberries and redcurrants. An eighteenth-century dovecot has been converted into a gazebo, and a pineapple frame is to be restored. A circular herb garden has a sundial at its centre, and there is a vegetable and fruit area. Through the seasons the borders are filled with 4000 tulips and various perennials. A twelfth-century Norman arch leads into the other half of the garden, which includes a Victorian rock garden, shrubs, roses and perennials.

Packwood House ★ 18

Lapworth, Solihull B94 6AT. Tel: (01564) 782024

The National Trust • 11m SE of central Birmingham, 2m E of Hockley Heath
on A3400 • House open 6th March to 3rd Nov, Wed – Sun, Good Fri and
Bank Holiday Mons, 12 noon – 4.30pm • Garden open 6th March to 3rd Nov,
Wed – Sun, Good Fri and Bank Holiday Mons, 11am – 4.30pm (May to Sept
closes 5.30pm) (last admission ½ hour before closing). Parties of 15 or more by
written arrangement • Entrance: £2.50, children £1.25 (house and garden
£5.20, children £2.60, family £13) • Other information: Picnic site opposite
main gates. Combined entry ticket with Baddesley Clinton – see below ◐ ☕
▦ WC ♿ ⏚ ⚐ ⚲

Hidden away in a rather suburban part of Warwickshire, this garden is notable for its intact layout, dating from the sixteenth and seventeenth centuries when the original house was built. There are courtyards, terraces and brick gazebos. Even more remarkable is the almost surreal yew garden, unique in design. Tradition claims that it represents the Sermon on the Mount, but in fact the 'Apostles' were planted in the 1850s as a four-square pattern round an orchard. Never mind, the result is now homogeneous. A spiral 'mount' of yew and box is a delightful illusion; note also the clever use of brick. G. Baron Ash, who gave the property to the Trust, made a sunken garden in the 1930s and restored earlier design features. He also introduced colourful border planting, and now the gardens are worth seeing at all seasons of the year. In spring drifts of daffodils follow the snowdrops and bluebells carpet the copse, while shrubs flower on red-brick walls. The herbaceous border, the sunken garden, the terrace beds and climbing roses and honeysuckle are a riot of colour in summer, and autumn brings changes in foliage. The head gardener, who moved here from Powis Castle in 2000, is clearing and replanting some beds and slowly restoring the walled kitchen garden after many years of neglect. It promises to be splendid. There is a combined entry ticket with nearby *Baddesley Clinton,* visited particularly by those who enjoy the restaurant. The medieval moated manor house has a walled garden containing herbaceous borders, climbers, herbs and greenhouses, and there are pleasant walks round the lake, a wilderness walk and a discovery trail quiz for the young.

Ragley Hall   19

Alcester B49 5NJ. Tel: (01789) 762090; E-mail: ragley.hall@virginnet.co.uk; Website: www.ragleyhall.com

Marquess and Marchioness of Hertford • 8m W of Stratford-upon-Avon, 1m S of Alcester off A435 • House open as garden, but 12 noon – 5pm • Park and garden open 28th March to 29th Sept, Thurs – Sun, and daily during summer school holidays, all 10am – 6pm • Entrance: £5, concessions £4, children £4 (house, park and garden, £6, concessions £5, children £4.50 • Other information: Dogs in park only, on lead ◑ 🍽 ✕ 🖼 **WC** ♿ 🏛 🍴 🌂

The 27 acres of formal and informal gardens date from the 1870s and include some now vast trees — blue cedar, picea, abies and Wellingtonia. Near the house (the scene of a great range of entertainments) is a border of unusual and tender perennials and, beyond, the rose garden with beds of individual varieties. There are also roses on the pillars of the house. There is a 'fumpery' with ferns, rhododendrons, hydrangeas and foxgloves. The Secret Garden has a central fountain and beds of herbaceous plants. A new bog garden is planted with gunneras, primulas and astilbes to encourage wild life, and a meadow contains wild flowers, orchids and fritillaries. There are lovely views of the surrounding parkland and pleasant walks through woodland and around the lake. Children will enjoy an adventure area. A yew walk is to become a topiary area, and overall there is steady development across this very large property.

Ryton Organic Gardens   20

Ryton-on-Dunsmore, Coventry CV8 3LG. Tel: (024) 7630 3517. Website: www.hdra.org.uk

HDRA – the organic organisation • 7m NE of Leamington Spa, 5m SE of Coventry. Turn off A45 onto Wolston road • Open all year, daily except Christmas period, 9am – 5pm • Entrance: £3, accompanied children free, parties of 14 or more £2.50 per person (50p extra for guided tour) (2001 prices) • Other information: Guide dogs only ◯ 🍽 ✕ 🖼 **WC** ♿ 🌱 🏛 🍴 🌂

Ryton was set up in 1985 to be a centre of excellence for organic horticulture. Since then the 10 acres have been steadily developed, in a beautifully land-scaped setting, to provide a wide range of inspirational and educational displays of herbs, roses, unusual vegetables, fruit, wildlife gardening and plants for bees. The individual gardens include demonstrations of organic methods of looking after soil, and of pest and disease control. There are also gardens for the visually impaired and those with other special needs, and a children's play area with a growing willow structure that invites exploration. At the centre of the garden is a vibrant display of herbaceous perennials in an informal drift of form and colour. The most recent additions are a garden for the enthusiastic cook, a highly acclaimed Paradise Garden created in memory of the late Geoff Hamilton by award-winning designer Isabelle van Groeningen, a recycled garden and a children's trail. Events and courses are held throughout the year.

The Shakespeare Houses and Their Gardens 21

Stratford–upon–Avon. Tel: (01789) 204016; Fax: (01789) 296083; E–mail: info@shakespeare.org.uk; Website: www.shakespeare.org.uk

Shakespeare Birthplace Trust • Located in Stratford-upon-Avon and surrounding area • All properties open all year except 23rd to 26th Dec. Opening and closing times vary – times and prices on application • Other information: Parking on site at Anne Hathaway's Cottage and Mary Arden's House, otherwise in town car parks. Restaurant/tea shop at Hall's Croft and café and picnic area at Mary Arden's House ○ WC 🚻 ♿ ⚭ 🏧 ♨

Some claim that little is known about Shakespeare and less still about his gardens. The Trust has made them interesting adjuncts to the houses. They include: *The Birthplace Garden*, a small informal collection of over 100 trees, herbs, plants and flowers mentioned by the Bard. *Mary Arden's House*, the front a *mélange* of box, roses and flowers, the rear a stretch of lawn with a wild garden beyond. Country museum with tools, etc. *Anne Hathaway's Cottage*: a typical English cottage garden dating from the end of the nineteenth century, including a small garden with varieties of Victorian vegetables, and a nearby tree garden with examples of those mentioned in the *Works*, where a circular yew maze was planted in 2001 based on an Elizabethan model. Garden centre with plants and herbs for sale grown by the Trust's gardeners, and a small display of Victorian and Edwardian garden tools. *Nash's House and New Place*: the house Shakespeare bought for his retirement, demolished in the eighteenth century; the foundations are planted with a garden beyond which, it is suggested, his orchard and kitchen garden lay. Reconstructed Elizabethan knot garden with oak palisade and 'tunnel' or 'pleached bower' of that time. *Hall's Croft*: a walled garden, including a herbal bed, bearing little resemblance to its probable form in the period when it was owned by the Bard's son-in-law. All the above are Trust houses and fee-charged. Beyond the knot garden is the *Great Garden* with free access. Also free are *Bancroft Gardens* in front of the Theatre and the long stretch owned by the Royal Shakespeare Theatre, along the River Avon between the Swan Theatre and the church where Shakespeare is buried.

Stoneleigh Abbey 22

Kenilworth CV8 2LF. Tel: (01926) 858535; Fax: (01926) 850724; E–mail: enquiries@stoneleighabbey.org; Web: www.stoneleighabbey.org

Stoneleigh Abbey Ltd (Charitable Trust) • 4m N of Leamington Spa, 5m NE of Warwick, 7m S of Coventry, off M40 junction. Turn off A46 onto B4113, then

follow signs to Ashow; entrance on right between two lodges • *Opening from 1st May. Please telephone for details* • *Other information: Dogs allowed in park only, on lead* ◑ 💭 🍴 WC 💡

Over the last four years, extensive restoration by the charitable trust in which ownership was vested in 1997 has included the Baroque west wing of the abbey and its grand state rooms, the fourteenth-century gatehouse, the conservatory overlooking the River Avon, and the early-nineteenth-century stables and riding school. From now on it will be the turn of the park and gardens which will be made accessible as one of Humphry Repton's most imaginative and picturesque landscape plans is gradually reinstated. The estate was the focus in 1809 of one of his finest and largest Red Books. Not all Repton's proposals were executed, but under his aegis the Avon was widened, a stone bridge built, an inspirational reflective pool created to mirror the south façade, and next to it, as counterpoint, a weir built to churn the waters of the river. Later hands responsible for shaping the landscape included a pupil of Wyatville, C.S. Smith, who in the 1810s and 1820s provided many of the buildings in the park, and Percy Cane who, in the twentieth century, restored and replanted the western terrace. W.S. Nesfield's strident Italianate garden, created overnight for a visit by Queen Victoria in 1858, may be left as a footnote in gardening history, but a new herbal parterre has been planted in the manner of Nesfield in front of the west wing.

University of Warwick 23

Gibbet Hill Road, Coventry CV4 7AL. Tel: (02476) 524189 (Estate Office)

Warwick University • *Nearer to Coventry than Warwick, most direct access is off A46 signed 'University of Warwick/Stoneleigh' just S of Coventry* • *Open all year. Term dates: 7th Jan to 16th March, 22nd April to 29th June, 1st Oct to 8th Dec* • *Entrance: free* ○ 💭 ✕ WC ♿

The university buildings have been the subject of early controversy but their impact has been mellowed by clever landscaping, including creation of new sports fields south of Gibbet Hill Road, the plantings of many trees and the use of bedding schemes. Interesting in a smaller space is a wisteria-covered pergola in the social sciences quadrangle. Formal gardens are being created, and around the arts centre and at sites across the university is a sculpture trail which features work by Richard Deacon, Liliane Ljin, Keir Smith, Bettina Furne and William Pye *et al.* The university now has five lakes with a wetlands environment and nature reserve. There are several walks through and around the extensive grounds.

Upton House ★ 24

Banbury, Oxfordshire OX15 6HT. Tel: (01295) 670266; Fax: (01295) 670266; E-mail: vuplan@smtp.ntrust.org.uk; Website: www.ntrustsevern.org.uk

The National Trust • *12m SE of Stratford-upon-Avon, 7m NW of Banbury on A422* • *House open (timed tickets at peak times)* • *Garden open 23rd March to 3rd Nov, Sat, Sun and Bank Holiday Mons, 11 – 5pm, Mon – Wed, 12.30 –*

5pm, (last admission 4.30pm). Closed Thurs and Fri but open Good Friday; Garden and restaurant open 9th Nov to 15th Dec, 12 noon – 4pm. Parties of 15 or more and evening guided tours by arrangement • Entrance: £2.70 (house £5.50, children £2.70). No reductions for parties (2001 prices) • Other information: Coaches by arrangement with property manager. Possible for wheelchairs in parts but very steep in places. Motorised buggy with driver available for access to and from lower garden ◐ 💌 WC 🌳 ♨ 🍷

The house itself, which dates from 1695, contains a fine collection of paintings including three superb Stubbs. More interesting to the garden visitor is that it stands on limestone, over 210 metres above sea level on Edgehill, near the site of the famous battle. Below a great lawn, the garden descends in a series of long terraces, along one end of which an impressive flight of stone steps leads down to the large lake. In the centre of the terraced area is a huge sloping vegetable garden, well labelled to indicate varieties. The grand scale of the plan is the main interest, but there are many unusual plants, particularly perennials and bog plants, and the National Collection of Michaelmas daisies is here. This is a fine example of terraced gardening, beautifully maintained by the Trust. *The National Herb Centre*, with small display gardens, good herb nursery, research glasshouses, exhibition and herb bistro, is nearby on B4100 at Warmington [open March to Dec, daily from 9.30am. Tel: (01295) 690999].

Warwick Castle ★ 25

Warwick CV34 4QU. Tel: (0870) 442 2000; Website: www.warwick-castle.co.uk

The Tussauds Group • In Warwick • Castle open • Grounds open all year, daily except 25th Dec, 10am – 6pm (Nov to March closes 5pm) • Entrance: Peak period (12th May to 9th Sept) £11.50, OAPs £8.20, children (4-16) £6.75, family ticket (2 adults and 2 children) £30 (2001 prices). Reduced rates at off-peak periods ◯ 💌 ✕ 🍴 WC ♿ ♨ 🍷 ☕

The castle stands on the banks of the River Avon, surrounded by 60 acres of beautiful grounds landscaped by 'Capability' Brown. He had previously been in employment as gardener to Lord Cobham at Stowe, but after the latter's death in 1749 decided to take on commissions of his own. His work at Warwick Castle for the first Earl (Francis Greville) is thought to have been his first independent commission, for which he received much praise, encouragement and publicity. He removed the old formal garden outside the wall and shaped the grounds to frame a view using an array of magnificent trees, notably cedars of Lebanon. In 1753 he began to landscape the courtyard, removing steps, filling in parts of the yard and making a coachway to surround the large level lawn. He then worked on the creation of the park on the other side of the eleventh-century mound. In 1779, when Brown's remodelling was barely 20 years old, the 2nd Earl embarked on a grandiose scheme of expansion which involved demolishing several streets in the town. In 1786 he constructed the conservatory at the top of Pageant Field, which today houses a replica of the famous Warwick Vase. From here visitors can view the panorama before them – the Peacock Garden and the tree-lined lawn of Pageant Field which meanders down to the gently sloping banks of the River Avon. On the other side of the castle entrance is the Victorian rose garden re-created in 1986 from Robert Marnock's designs of 1868. Also in the town is The Master's Garden (see entry) at Lord Leycester Hospital. The castle itself is ★★.

Wheelwright House 26

Long Compton CV36 5LE. Tel: (01608) 684478

Richard and Suzanne Shacklock • 6m S of Shipston-on-Stour on A3400. At S end of Long Compton take road signed 'Little Compton' and continue 300 metres. House on left • Open by appt only • Entrance: £2, children free • Other information: Teas for parties by prior arrangement ● WC & ⟨⟩ ✿ ℺

The central feature of this attractive one-acre garden surrounding the early eighteenth-century Cotswold stone house is a natural stream, with little waterfalls, distinctive bridges and banks covered in moisture-loving plants. In nine years the owners have created a garden with a variety of moods, aspects and colour themes, containing many interesting and unusual plants. There is a formal lily pond with surrounding rose pergola, a woodland garden, shady areas with ferns, hostas and pulmonarias, a Mediterranean garden in a sheltered sunny spot, a collection of pots, and several mixed borders designed for year-round colour. Seats are strategically placed to enjoy the various vistas. The garden continues to develop: the latest project just completed is a box wheel in the front garden accompanied by a topiary wheelwright. Barton House (see entry) is nearby.

Woodpeckers ★ 27

The Bank, Marlcliff, Bidford–on–Avon B50 4NT. Tel: (01789) 773416

Dr and Mrs A.J. Cox • 7m SW of Stratford-upon-Avon off B4085 between Bidford and Cleeve Prior • Open by appt • Entrance: £3, children free • Other information: Wheelchair users must be accompanied ● ☕ ▦ ▩ ℘

This two-and-a-half-acre garden, planned for year-round interest, contains a wide range of design and planting ideas, and blends well with the surrounding countryside. A small arboretum with a wide selection of choice trees provide contrast in form and colour. Moving around the garden, there are many surprises — a collection of old roses, with clematis climbing through; a small potager with archways covered with apple trees at the corners; colourful and unusual herbs and vegetables. A knot garden has been created from three varieties of box. Other features are topiary, an ivy arbour with statue, a fern border, a white and apricot bed, several island beds with splendid ranges of colour and plants, a Mediterranean garden, a cactus and succulent greenhouse and a round greenhouse for tender plants including mimosas, abutilons, salvias and clematis. The terrace has a range of troughs and alpine plants, and there is a delightful pool and bog garden. A belvedere of framed English oak affords fine views of the garden, including a wildflower area in spring. A new two-storey oak building with a balcony overlooks the arboretum and rose garden.

WILTSHIRE

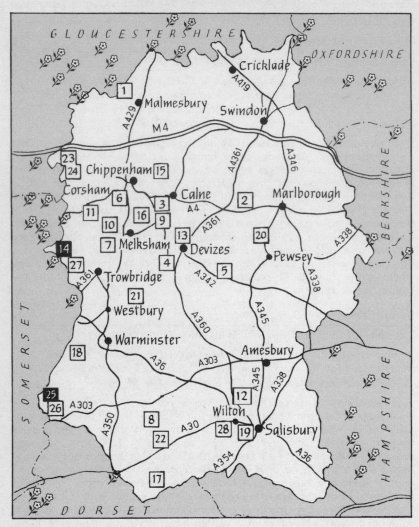

Two-starred gardens are marked on the map with a black square.

The Abbey House Gardens ★   1

**Malmesbury SN16 9AS. Tel: (01666) 822212; Fax: (01666) 822782;
E-mail: abbeyhousegarden@aol.com**

*Barbara and Ian Pollard • In town centre next to Abbey • Open 21st March to
21st Oct, daily, 11am – 6pm, and to groups by appt • Entrance: £5, OAPs/*

students £4.50, children (5–15) £2 • *Other information: RHS members free March and Oct. Free car park close to garden* ◗ 🍴 🖼 WC ᒀ ♨ 🔦 ♿

A remarkable five-acre garden, created in only five years. The owners' passion and enthusiasm are reflected in the exuberant design planting schemes. The setting around a late-Tudor house beside the abbey is unique, the effect overwhelming, with thousands of roses (the largest private collection in the country), an enormous arcade-encircled herb garden, a generously proportioned laburnum tunnel and many other triumphs. Also included are a Celtic cross knot garden echoing its historic surroundings, huge herbaceous borders in riotous colours, water features, a river and woodland walk (with kingfishers and water voles if you are lucky), rhododendrons, and a bog garden with an exceptional display of meconopsis in spring. The season starts with a dazzling display of thousands of tulips and continues right through to the autumn. As well as clematis and climbing roses, there is a large and interesting variety of fruit trees around an arcade, with sweet peas for added colour, a foliage walk and a maple walk. Another interesting display of sculpture will appear in 2002.

Avebury Manor   2

Marlborough SN8 1RF. Tel (01672) 539250

The National Trust • *6m W of Marlborough, 1m N of A4 Bath road on A4361. Manor on N side of High Street, behind church* • *House open Tues, Wed, Sun and Bank Holiday Mons, 2 – 5.30pm* • *Garden open April to Oct, daily except Mon and Thurs (but open Bank Holiday Mons), 11am – 5.30pm* • *Entrance £2.50, children £1.20 (house and garden £3.50, children £1.70) (2001 prices)* • *Other information: Parking in outer village. Alexander Keiller Museum, New Barn Gallery exhibition, refreshments and shop adjacent* ◗ WC ᒀ

The house and gardens were purchased by the Trust in 1991. The much-altered house has monastic origins with notable Queen Anne alternations. The rose garden in the shadow of the church tower is a fragrant delight, herbaceous borders are set neatly behind low box hedging, and there is a splendid lavender walk at the main entrance to the house, which on the south-west is framed by lawns and topiary. The orchard has been replanted with old apple varieties from Wiltshire. The topiary garden pond has been restored and its box hedges are in the design of overlapping diamonds, inspired by a plaster ceiling in the house.

Bowood House and Gardens ★   3

Bowood House, Derry Hill, Calne SN11 0LZ. Tel: (01249) 812102; Website: www.bowood-house.co.uk

The Marquis and Marchioness of Lansdowne • *8m S of M4 junction 17, 4½ m W of Calne, 5m SE of Chippenham. Off A4 in Derry Hill. Separate rhododendron walks off A342 Chippenham – Devizes road midway between Derry Hill and Sandy Lane* • *House open* • *Garden and pleasure grounds open 23rd March to 3rd Nov, daily, 11am – 6pm or dusk if earlier. Rhododendron walks open daily end April to early June (depending on flowering season)* • *Entrance:*

House and gardens £6.05, OAPs £5, children £3.85, rhododendron walks £3.30 extra, children free ◑ ☕ ✕ 🗎 WC ♿ �️ 💡 ⚲

The house and its pleasure grounds cover over 100 acres and lie in the centre of 'Capability' Brown's enormous park. Other splendours include a tranquil lake, arboretum and pinetum, Doric temple, cascade waterfall and hermit's cave. Thousands of bulbs bloom in spring. The Robert Adam orangery (converted into a gallery) is particularly fine, and in front of it are formal Bath-stone terraces with rose beds, standard roses and fastigiate yews. *Fremontodendron californicum* flourishes on the Italianate terrace. The upper terrace was laid out in 1817 and the present fountains were added in 1839. In the twentieth century, when elaborate bedding schemes became too time-consuming, the parterre was planted with hybrid tea roses, thus blurring the edges. Mary Keen advised replacing the grass paths with gravel and compensating for the loss of green by putting box hedges around the beds. New planting has ensured that the flowering season starts almost three months earlier than it used to. In the nineteenth century it was the aim of every garden to be 'as clean as a drawing room', and Bowood is now in this class once again. The rhododendron walks are situated in a separate 50-acre area, which is only open when the rhododendrons are flowering. Robert Adam's mausoleum (a little gem well worth a visit) is in this area.

Broadleas Garden   4

Broadleas, Devizes SN10 5JQ. Tel: (01380) 722035

Lady Anne Cowdray/Broadleas Garden Charitable Trust • 1m S of Devizes on A360. Signed from Devizes town centre • Open April to Oct, Sun, Wed, Thurs, 2 – 6pm • Entrance: £3, children under 12 £1. Parties of 10 or more £2.50 • Other information: Coaches must use Devizes town centre approach. Teas on Suns until end of Aug only ◑ ☕ WC ⟨▷ 🌿

This garden was bought just after World War II and started from nothing by Lady Anne Cowdray in a combe below Devizes. Mature and semi-mature magnolias grow on each side of a steep dell. As good as any Cornish garden, it is stuffed with fine things that one would think too tender for these parts. Large specimens of everything (much of it now over 40 years old) – *Paulownia fargesii*, *Parrotia persica*, all manner of magnolias, azaleas, hydrangeas, hostas, lilies and trilliums of rare and notable species. There has also been much planting in recent years, including many rhododendrons and camellias. It is a garden of tireless perfectionism, at its most stunning in spring when sheets of bulbs stretch out beneath the flowering trees. Rarely seen in such quantities for instance are the erythroniums or dog-tooth violets. Many of the more unusual plants, both shrubs and perennials, are grown for sale at Broadleas. There is also a woodland walk, a sunken rose garden and a silver border. This is serious plantsmanship and dendrology.

Chiffchaffs

(see Dorset)

Clock House
(see Oxfordshire)

Conock Manor 5
Conock, Devizes SN10 3QQ.

Mr and Mrs Bonar Sykes • 5m SE of Devizes, Nr Chirton off A342 • Open 20th May, 2 – 6pm • Entrance: £2.50, children under 16 free • Other information: cream teas available ● & ♨ ♋

Set between distant views of Marlborough Downs and Salisbury Plain, the Georgian house looks out over lawns with specimen trees, ha-has and a recently planted arboretum. From a Reptonesque thatched dairy near the house, a long brick wall and mixed shrub border lead to the stable block, in early Gothic-Revival style, with a copper-domed cupola. Beyond, yew and beech hedges and brick walls frame unusual trees and shrubs, a small kitchen garden and 1930s' shrub walk. Beech forms attractive bays and box makes clipped balls. Notable are the pleached limes and a magnolia garden including malus, sorbus, prunus and many eucalyptus. There is also a woodland walk, and a small new arboretum of unusual trees.

Corsham Court 6
Corsham SN13 0BZ. Tel: (01249) 701610

James Methuen-Campbell • 4m W of Chippenham on A4 • House open • Garden open Jan to 19th March, Sat and Sun, 2 – 4.30pm; 20th March to Sept, daily except Mon (but open Bank Holiday Mons), 2 – 5.30pm; Oct and Nov, Sat and Sun, 2 – 4.30pm (last admission ½ hour before closing). Closed Dec. Also open by appt for parties of 15 or more • Entrance: £2, OAPs £1.50, children £1, garden season tickets £10 (house and garden: £5, OAPs £4.50, children £2.50, parties £4.50 per person) ● ● WC & ♋

Approaching from Chippenham, look out for a glimpse of this house on your left, once framed by an avenue of elms now replaced by some lime trees. The house, which has a fine collection of pictures and furniture, is surrounded by a landscape of 'Capability' Brown's devising finished off by Humphry Repton (the lake and boat-house particularly). It is an example of this kind of gardening at its best. Rare and exotic trees look entirely at home: black walnuts, Californian redwoods, cedars, Wellingtonias, and the most astonishing layered Oriental plane tree, shading beeches, oaks, sycamores and Spanish chestnuts. There are 340 species of trees and 75,000 daffodils in the 20-acre arboretum. The Bath House designed by Brown leads out into a small enclosed flower garden with catalpa trees. Repton's roses trained over metal arches encircling a round pond are a rare surviving example of the elegance of early-nineteenth-century flower gardens. Here the flower borders contain the unusual *Clerodendrum trichotomum* and enormous iron supports for roses and *Clematis x jackmanii*. A box-edged garden, a hornbeam *allée*, urns, arbours and seats add further elegant touches.

The Courts Garden 7

Holt, Trowbridge BA14 6RR. Tel: (01225) 782340;
E-mail: wcoaxh@smtp.ntrust.org.uk

The National Trust • 3m SW of Melksham, 3m N of Trowbridge, 2½ m E of Bradford-on-Avon on B3107 • Open 24th March to 13th Oct, daily except Sat, 12 noon – 5.30pm, and out of season by appt • Entrance: £4, children £2 • Other information: Parking at village hall ◐ & ♿ ♖

The eighteenth-century house is set in formal areas of garden which give place to wild, bog and orchard gardens beyond. Created by Sir George Hastings in 1900–1911, there are many lawns, much topiary, beguiling nooks and lots of good Edwardian features such as stone walls and paths, hedges, lily ponds and terraces. A garden in the Hidcote mould, it is being substantially restored under the care of the present head gardener. The large terrace has been rebuilt and replanted; the lower pond has been restored and will be replanted. There are some superb specimen trees. A large part of the garden is given over to wild flowers, with close-cut pathways winding through. Three miles away is Europe's biggest provider of chalk-tolerant plants, specialising in foxgloves, *The Botanic Nursery*, on A36 towards Bath, just past Atworth.

Fonthill House 8

Tisbury, Salisbury SP3 5SA. Tel: (Estate Office) (01747) 87020

Lord and Lady Margadale • 12m W of Salisbury, E of Hindon on B3089. Entrance is S of Fonthill Bishop, on farm road over bridge and through deer park • Parking • Open one day April, May, June, July for charity, 2 – 6pm; telephone for details • Entrance: £2, children free ● ▆ WC & ♿ ♖ ♖

The 1970s' neo-Georgian house, built on the site of a demolished Detmar Blow masterpiece on the estate, stands at the head of a combe with fine views and is backed by mature beech and oak trees. Throughout this woodland grow camellias and rhododendrons and, in spring, a carpet of bluebells. The façade of the house is framed by new planting. The charm and isolation of the place add to its magic, particularly in spring when the woodland is a mass of colour. Five acres in all. For children, there is a heated swimming pool open from mid-May.

The Garden Lodge 9

Chittoe, Chippenham SN15 2EW. Tel: (01380) 850314;
E-mail: Juliet-wilmot@zeronet.co.uk

Mrs Juliet Wilmot • Off A342 mid-way between Chippenham and Devizes, take small road signed 'Chittoe and Spye Park' (dead end). House is 1m on right behind brick wall • Open by appt only • Entrance: £3 ● WC &

The inspiration, design, ability and devoted hard work of the owner has transformed this site from a wilderness into a remarkable garden, laid out within the original brick walls of a Victorian vegetable garden. A series of terraces intersected by a large pond lead into an amphitheatre with a rill and a central area planted with 'Sander's White Rambler' roses. Clematis and roses abound. The mature wooded backdrop sets off the various terraces to their best advantage; on one is a brick clock let into the grass, another leads into a yew crinkum-crankum walk with a meandering cut grass path, and on to a small summerhouse complete with an ingenious snakes-and-ladders game. On the house a yellow *banksiae* rose competes for wall space with a splendid white wisteria.

Great Chalfield Manor 10

Melksham, Wilts SN2 8NJ. Tel: (01225) 782239; Fax: (01225) 783379

The National Trust • 3m SW of Melksham off A350 and B3107 via Broughton Gifford Common • Open 2nd April to Oct, Tues – Thurs, 12noon – 5pm for groups, and by appt • Entrance: £4 ◖ **WC** ♨

The moated fifteenth-century house and its surroundings were restored by Robert Fuller in the early 1900s, and given to the Trust forty years later. He employed Sir Harold Brakspear as his architect, and Alfred Parsons designed the gardens to complement the house; Brakspear also contributed a gazebo. The spacious lawns are broken up by vast jelly-mould yew shapes, and have substantial borders. There are some splendid old-fashioned and rambling roses. Good views open up from the moat walk and, nearby, a shrubbery is managed as a semi-natural area with woodland plants.

Hazelbury Manor 11

Box, Corsham SN13 8LB. Tel: (01225) 812088

5m SW of Chippenham. From Box take A365 towards Melksham, turn left onto B3109, next left, and right immediately into private drive • Open one weekend for NGS, and by appt • Entrance: £2.80, OAPs £2, children £1, under 6 free ◖ **WC** ♿ ⚘

The extensive formal gardens, surrounding a sprawling Elizabethan house, are undergoing restoration based on evidence from old photographs. The rock garden at the front of the house is impressive, although it could not be called in keeping with the house and makes as big a twentieth-century statement as the earlier Edwardian garden. The formal garden has a large lawn, with a chess set and other topiary sculpture, banked up on either side by high walks between clipped beeches. In spring the *allées* are carpeted with polyanthus, cowslips and wallflowers. Mammoth herbaceous borders blaze in summer. Other features include a beautiful arched laburnum walk, a lime walk and terraced alpine garden.

Heale Gardens ★ 12

Middle Woodford, Salisbury SP4 6NT. Tel: (01722) 782504

Mr and Mrs Guy Rasch • 4m N of Salisbury between A360 and A345 • Gardens open Tues – Sun and Bank Holiday Mons, 10am – 5pm. Snowdrop Sundays 3rd and 10th Feb • Entrance: £3.25, children (5–15) £1.50, under-5s free ○ ☕ 🛍 **WC** ♿ ⚘ 🏛

This is an idyllic garden with mature yew hedges, much of it designed by Harold Peto. A tributary of the Avon meanders through, providing the perfect boundary and obvious site for the sealing-wax red Japanese bridge and the thatched tea-house which straddles the water. This was made in 1910 with the help of four Japanese gardeners and extends under the shade of *Magnolia* x *soulangeana* along the boggy banks planted with bog arums, *Rodgersia aesculifolia*, candelabra primulas and irises. There are two terraces immediately beside the house. One is rampant with alchemilla, spurges and irises; the other has two stone lily ponds and two small borders given height by nearly three-metre-high wooden pyramids bearing roses, clematis and honeysuckles. The Long Border contains roses backed by a simple but effective rustic trellis, and also many interesting herbaceous plants; behind it is a border of musk roses. The walled kitchen garden is possibly the most successful part, achieving a satisfying marriage between practicality and pleasure. The formal nature of rows of vegetables is made into a feature, and plots are divided by espaliered fruit trees forming an apple and pear tunnel, and by pergolas and hedges. The wonderful flint-and-brick wall provides protection for many plants including *Cytisus battandieri* and an ancient fig. This is a walled garden where one is encouraged to linger on the seats and in the shaded arbours and enjoy and admire the extraordinary tranquillity of the place. Look out for the ancient mulberry, the very old *Cercidiphyllum japonicum* (the second tallest known in Europe), and the *Magnolia grandiflora*. The plant centre is comprehensive and the shop appeals to the discerning. Unique wrought-iron plant supports can be bought here.

Home Covert ★ 13

Roundway, Devizes SN10 2JA. Tel: (01380) 723407

Mr and Mrs John Phillips • 1m N of Devizes. Turn off A361 on edge of built-up area NE of town, signed 'Roundway'. In Roundway turn left towards Rowde. House is ¾ m on left. Signposted • Open one day for NGS, and by appt. Guided parties (12–40 persons) welcome • Entrance: £2.50, children free • Other information: Teas and plants for sale on charity open days only ● ☕ ⬟

This garden, developed in the 1960s, has been created by the present owners out of amenity woodlands of the now-demolished Roundway House. In front of the house is a large lawn on a plateau edged with grasses, herbaceous plants and alpines producing colour throughout the year. Beyond this, grass pathways meander through a collection of trees and rare shrubs. A steep path drops from the plateau to a water garden, lake, waterfall and bog garden, rich with colour from bog primulas and other moisture-loving plants, and shaded by fine specimen trees. Excellent collections of hostas and hydrangeas are scattered informally throughout, and roses and clematis scramble over walks and through trees. Described as 'a botanical madhouse', this garden offers wonderful contrasts.

Iford Manor ★★ 14

Bradford–on–Avon BA15 2BA. Tel: (01225) 863146

Mrs Cartwright-Hignett • 2m S of Bradford-on-Avon off B3109, 7m SE of Bath via A36. Signposted • Open April, Sun; May to Sept, Tues – Thurs, Sat, Sun and Bank Holiday Mons; Oct, Sun; all 2 – 5pm. Other times and parties by appt • Entrance: £3, OAPs, students and children over 10 £2.50. Children under 10 admitted Tues – Thurs only • Other information: Teas May to Sept, Sat, Sun and Bank Holiday Mons only ◑ ☕ WC ⬦ 🍽

Harold Peto found himself a near-ideal house in the steep valley through which the River Frome slides langorously towards Bath. The topography lends itself to the strong architectural framework favoured by Peto and the creation of areas of entirely differing moods. The overriding intention is Italianate with a preponderance of cypresses, junipers, box and yew, punctuated at every turn by sarcophagi, urns, terracotta, marble seats and statues, columns, fountains and loggias. In a different vein is a meadow of naturalised bulbs, most spectacularly martagon lilies. A path leads from here to the cloisters – an Italian-Romanesque building of Harold Peto's confection made with fragments collected from Italy. From here one can admire the whole, and the breath-taking valley and the walled kitchen garden on the other side. Perhaps somewhat incongruously, at the top of the garden, is a Japanese area, pleasantly done. Westwood Manor (see entry) is nearby.

Kellaways   15

Chippenham SN15 4LR. Tel: (01249) 740203

Miss J.A. Hoskins • 3m NE of Chippenham off B4069 on East Tytherton road • Open by appt • Entrance: £2, children 20p ◑ ☕

June is a rewarding month to visit because of the old roses which, cleverly underplanted, predominate throughout. Winter is another outstanding time, because of the profusion of winter-flowering shrubs. The seventeenth-century Cotswold-stone house has a stone terrace on the walled garden side bursting with thyme and wild strawberries. The clemency of the walls means that the owner can grow joyous things like sun roses, *Carpenteria californica* and other frailties. A serious cottage garden. Nearby, at Cold Aston, is *Special Plants Nursery*, famous for many rarities [open March to Sept. 10.30am – 4pm] Its garden is open for the NGS on a few days May to Sept, and by appt – telephone (01225) 891686.

Lacock Abbey   16

Lacock, Chippenham SN15 2LG. Tel: (01249) 730227

The National Trust • 3m S of Chippenham off A350 • Abbey open 30th March to 3rd Nov, daily except Tues, 1 – 5pm. Closed 29th March • Grounds, cloisters and Museum of Photography open 16th March to 3rd Nov, daily, 11am – 5.30pm. Closed 29th March, 21st to 29th Dec • Entrance: grounds, cloisters and museum £4, children £2.40, family £11.30 (abbey, grounds, cloisters and museum £6.20, children £3.40, family £16.80, parties £5.70 per person, children £2.80) • Other information: Refreshments and shop in village. Batricar available ◑ 🍴 ♿ ♻

The thirteenth-century abbey, set in meadows beside the River Avon, was turned into a private house by Sir William Sharington after the Dissolution, and was gothicised by John Ivory Talbot in the eighteenth century. The romantic Victorian woodland garden is best viewed in spring when sheets of crocuses, daffodils, and later, fritillaries, replace the large drifts of snowdrops and aconites. Lady Elisabeth's Rose Garden, originally created for the mother of William Henry Fox-Talbot, inventor of photography, has been re-created from the original photograph of 1840, which is probably the earliest known photograph of a garden. Fox-Talbot was also an eminent botanist, and planted many unusual trees which can still be seen today, including specimens of the American black walnut, the Judas tree and the swamp cypress. His walled 'Botanic Garden', once fallen into use as allotments, has reopened after restoration. An eighteenth-century grotto will also be restored. The Abbey also featured in the Harry Potter film.

Larmer Tree Gardens 17

Rushmore Estate, Tollard Royal, Salisbury SP5 5PT. Tel: (01725) 516228; Fax: Tel: (01725) 516449; Email: larmer.tree@rushmore-estate.co.uk

Mr W. Gronow Davis • 16m SW of Salisbury, 7m SE of Shaftesbury off B3081. Signposted • Open Easter to Oct, Sun – Fri, 11am – 6pm (closed July), but check before travelling • Entrance: £3.75, concessions and groups £2.75. Discount entry available with Chettle House (see entry in Dorset) • Other information: Tea rooms and shop closed July and Oct ◑ 🍽 ✕ 🗺 WC ♿ 🌿 🏧 🔦 🐾

The 12 acres were first laid out in 1880 by General Pitt-Rivers for the enjoyment of the local populace. They contain a unique collection of buildings, including a Roman temple, an open-air theatre, a colonial-style tea pavilion and Nepalese rooms, introduced by the General as points of interest for those with small knowledge of the outside world. The buildings surround the main lawn, off which radiate laurel-hedged rides forming small enclosed areas intended for picnickers. The aim in restoring the gardens was that they continue to be a place of entertainment: regular concerts, theatrical events and festivals are held throughout the summer and local bands play on the stage most Sundays. There are stunning views northwards to the Cranborne Chase and southwards to the Solent.

Longleat 18

Warminster BA12 7NW. Tel: (01985) 844400

The Marquess of Bath • 3m SW of Warminster, 4½ m SE of Frome on A362 • House open • Garden open all year, daily except 25th Dec, 10am – 5.30pm (Nov to March closes 4pm) • Entrance: £2, OAPs and children £1, coaches free (house extra) (2001 prices) • Other information: Helicopter landing pad available by prior request ○ 🍽 ✕ 🗺 WC ♿ ✈ 🔦 🐾

This garden has been rearranged and developed by most of the great names in English landscape history. There is nothing left to show today of the two earliest gardens here, the Elizabethan one and that created by London and Wise in the 1680s-1690s, which must have been one of the most elaborate ever made in England. Sadly it was barely half a century before 'Capability'

Brown ironed out the formality and created a chain of lakes set amongst clumps of trees and hanging woods, best admired today from 'Heaven's Gate'. The park was slightly altered by Repton in 1804 and added to in the 1870s when it became fashionable to collect exotic trees such as Wellingtonias and monkey puzzles and to make groves of rhododendrons and azaleas. It remains both beautiful and rewarding for all who delight in trees. In this century the fortunes of the garden came under the guiding hand of Russell Page. The nineteenth-century formal garden in front of the orangery to the north of the house was simplified and improved upon by him to great effect, although, alas, most of his work has since been swept away. The orangery itself is a dream of wisteria and lemon-scented verbenas. A quarter of a mile to the south there is a pleasure walk in a developing arboretum, with many spring bulbs and wild flowers. To the immediate west of the house the small private garden is not open to the public. Lord Bath says this was designed by Lawrence Fleming in 1965 around the two commas within the yin and yang symbols: bulbs and fruit trees in the first and a lily pond in the second. There is a large dovecot in one corner – inspired by the turrets on the roof of the house. Elsewhere, the safari park and other attractions are available to visitors. The amazing Lord Bath planted the world's longest hedge at Longleat in 1975, and new ones are currently at various stages of growth, from the Sun Maze and Lunar Labyrinth to the east of the house to the Love Labyrinth in front of the orangery. Future examples of the genre will encompass a variety of styles and materials.

Mompesson House   19

The Close, Salisbury SP1 2EL. Tel: (01722) 335659

The National Trust • In city centre, N of Choristers' Green in Cathedral Close • House and Garden open 23rd March to 29th Sept, Sat – Wed, 12 noon – 5.30pm and Fri, 31st March (last admission 5pm); • Entrance: 80p (house and garden £3.90, children £1.95, parties £3.40 per person) • Other information: Charge for parking in the Close. Teas when house open. NT shop nearby ◑ ☕ WC ♿ ⌖

If visiting Salisbury, the Cathedral and the Close are a must, and if you have been fortunate enough to find a parking space, take time also to visit this small walled garden, which is in the Old English style. Its reposeful atmosphere is very refreshing. Summer is best, with the old-fashioned roses in bloom, but it is attractive throughout the open season.

Oare House ★   20

Oare, Marlborough SN8 4JQ. Tel: (01672) 562613

Mr H. Keswick • 2m N of Pewsey on A345 • Open 28th April, 14th July, 2 – 6pm • Entrance: £2, children 20p ◑ ☕ WC ♿ ⌖

The 1740 house was extended by Clough Williams-Ellis in the 1920s and the garden created from 1920 to 1960 by two successive owners, Sir Geoffrey Fry and Henry Keswick. The house is seen as the backdrop to a cathedral-like nave of limes, a worthy overture to many good things. The main garden is approached through a wisteria-covered pergola enlivened by a lily pond and tinkling fountain. Great yew hedges enclose a 'library' garden, from which an elegant loggia (where splendid teas are served on open days) can be spied along a formal axis of pleached limes. Below is a long, corridor-like secret garden, known as the Slip, where good brick walls have been used for interesting planting. The lawns to the west of the house are very much in the grand manner. The eye rises over an immaculate lawn to the sweep of the Marlborough Downs seen at the end of a woodland ride. Substantial borders on either side of this lawn lead down to a swimming pool of equally grand proportions flanked by great herbaceous borders, one all gold achilleas and heleniums and the other filled with dahlias. In the impressive kitchen garden fruit and vegetables are arranged around the edge in purposeful manner behind their lavender hedges, espalier fruit trees and shrub roses. The two axial paths are magnificent: one is dominated entirely by white roses, while in the other a mossy gravel path threads its way through a stunning tunnel of herbaceous plants with yellow and white violas spilling out beneath clumps of richly coloured phlox and heleniums of many varieties. This is a garden worth every mile of a long detour.

The Old Vicarage ★ 21

Edington, Westbury BA13 4QF. Tel/Fax: (01380) 830512

J.N. d'Arcy • *4m NE of Westbury on B3098 to West Lavington. Signposted* • *Open once for charity in mid-June, and by appt* • *Entrance: £3.50, children free (includes other neighbouring gardens)* • *Other information: Parking in church car park* ● ● WC & ⬧ ◯

Every year new discoveries mark the travels of this peripatetic gardener, who has created a varied, scented garden on a two-and-a-half-acre escarpment set high on the north side of Salisbury Plain. To be shown round by Mr d'Arcy is a treat as he mixes wit with erudition. Swags of clematis, cistus and mahonias enliven the plain faade of the former vicarage, where a wide lawn – croquet of course – leads to a meadow artful with wild flowers beneath rare varieties of chestnut, sorbus and maple. National Collection of evening primroses gives pleasure after dusk. Stunning views towards Edington Church lift the visitor's eyes through well-planted vistas. Dividing the garden is a dense yew hedge, only 17 years old, which is clipped so that the base gets the light. 'For a mature hedge it is agreeably slim,' he says. An *allée* of fastigate hornbeams points the view towards Devizes. Newly built brick walls create rooms and shelter exotic plants and trees, and a base of natural greensand over clay and a mulch from elaborate bays of compost ensure vigorous plants. Waves of *Phlomis bovei* mark the hot garden, while a sunken garden to the rear of the house is cool and romantically planted round a 15-metre well. Nepetas, a particular passion, run riot. Towards the end of the tour a gravel bed is a sea of agapanthus and eryngium, and everywhere seedlings push through the gravel – phlomis, dierama, *Acanthus discoridis* and *Oenothera caespitosa* 'Marginata', an unusual evening primrose with white flowers. The strong salvia, *S. darcyi*, is a souvenir of his Mexican tour – 400 species there.

Old Wardour Castle 22

Tisbury, Salisbury SP3 6RR. Tel: (01747) 870487

English Heritage • 2m SW of Tisbury, off A30 • Open April to Sept, daily, 10am – 6pm; Oct, daily, 10am – 5pm; 1st Nov to 28th March, Wed – Sun, 10am – 1pm and 2 – 4pm; closed 24th to 26th Dec, 1st Jan • Entrance: £2.50, concessions £1.90, children £1.30 ○ 🍵 🛍 WC 🚻 ♿ 🚼 ♨ 🐕

In a picture-book setting, the ruins of this fourteenth-century castle stand overlooking a lake and surrounded by woodland. The gardens and park were laid out in the eighteenth century when the nearby New Wardour Castle was built, and remnants of this landscape can still be seen in some fine trees and shrubs. There is a pavilion in Gothic style and a picturesque grotto built of stone, brick and plaster by Josiah Lane, a noted creator of rockwork grottos in Wiltshire in the eighteenth century. Paths and tunnels twist between ancient-looking weathered rocks containing nooks and alcoves. Notable among the trees are a stand of yews around 400 years old, Atlas Mountain cedars of between 150 and 200 years old, and a mighty cedar of Lebanon.

Pound Hill House 23

West Kington, Chippenham SN14 7JG. Tel: (01249) 782781; Fax: (01249) 782953; E-mail: pound.hill.garden@virgin.net

Mr and Mrs Philip Stockitt • 8m W of Chippenham, 2m NE of Marshfield between A420 and M4 • Open Feb to Oct, daily, 2 – 5pm, and for parties by arrangement • Entrance: £2.50 • Other information: Plants for sale in adjacent plant centre open, daily except Jan, 10am – 5pm ◐ 🍵 WC 🚻 ♿ 🐕

A Cotswold garden in two acres around a sixteenth-century stone house. The viewer takes in the effect from the yard through to an 'old-fashioned rose garden' (planted and labelled David Austin roses) leading to a Victorian vegetable garden with espaliered fruit trees, then through a wisteria, rose and clematis tunnel, culminating in a statue. Beyond there is an orchard, a Cotswold garden with topiary, yew-screened tennis court, herbaceous border and drystone walls showing off 'Ballerina' roses, topiary and two trelliswork obelisks. A water garden, with many shade-loving as well as moisture-loving plants, is surrounded by yew hedging to create another small garden. A walk area, using *Betula utilis* var. *jacquemontii*, underplanted with *Pulmonaria officinalis* 'Sissinghurst White' and tulips, leads on to a rose walk lined with clipped sweet chestnuts and planted with old-fashioned roses. The courtyard has many interesting planters. The nursery sells progenies from 2000 varieties of rarer plants as well as roses, topiary and specimen plants.

Ridleys Cheer 24

Mountain Bower, Chippenham SN14 7AJ. Tel: (01225) 891204

Mr and Mrs Antony Young • 8m W of Chippenham off A420. Turn N at Shoe, take second left, then first right • Open 7th April, 19th May, 16th June, 7th July, 2 – 6pm. Parties welcome by appt • Entrance: £2, children under 14 free.

£3 per person for group visits • Other information: Picnics in meadow only, from 1pm ● ⬛ ✕ 🛆 WC & 🌱 ♀

The garden, created over the past 20 years, covers some three acres, two of which hold a young and interesting arboretum, and there is also a three-acre wildflower meadow. The garden is on two levels, connected by a broad flight of steps and a grass walk, and contains many fine examples of rarer shrubs and trees. The shrub roses, including over 100 species and hybrids seldom encountered, are a major summer feature. There is a small *potager*, and a recent addition is a small gravel garden in box and yew outside the conservatory. Autumn colour is given by a growing number of maples, beeches, tulip trees, oaks and zelkovas. In the main, this in an informal garden, full of appeal for plantsmen, who can derive much information from the knowledgeable owners. A small nursery sells trees, shrubs and perennials, many of them unusual. Pound Hill House (see entry) is nearby.

Stourhead ★★   25

Stourton, Warminster BA12 6QF. Tel/Fax: (01747) 841152;
E-mail: wstest@smtp.ntrust.org.uk; Website: www.nationaltrust.org.uk

The National Trust • 3m NW of Mere (A303) at Stourton off B3092 • House open 23rd March to 3rd Nov, daily except Thurs and Fri, 12 noon – 5.30pm or dusk if earlier (last admission 5pm) • Gardens open all year, daily, 9am – 7pm (or dusk if earlier) • Entrance: House or garden, March to Nov: £4.90, children (5–16) £2.70, family ticket £12.30; garden only, Nov to Feb, £3.80, children £1.85, family ticket £9.20; house and garden £8.70, children £4.10, family ticket £20 • Other information: Refreshments in restaurant or at Spread Eagle Inn at garden entrance. Wheelchairs available. Buggy service from car park in peak season. Dogs Nov to Feb only ○ ⬛ 🛆 WC & 🌱 ⚏ 🍴 ♀

An outstanding example of an English landscape garden, designed by Henry Hoare II between 1741 and 1780, a paragon in its day and almost the greatest surviving garden of its kind. The sequence of arcadian images is revealed gradually if one follows a route anti-clockwise around the lake, having come from the house along the top route, so seeing the lake from above. Each experience is doubly inspiring: visitors glimpse classical temples across the lake, almost unattainable and mirage-like, and when they reach their goal some other vision always attracts the eye – the boat-house, Temple of Flora, turf bridge, Temple of Apollo, rock bridge, cascade (these two are tucked away and very surprising), Pantheon, Gothic rustic cottage and grotto. The view from the Temple of Apollo (1765) was described by Horace Walpole as 'one of the most picturesque scenes in the world', by which he meant that it was as fine as a painting. To gain a better idea of how these buildings would have looked had the surrounding planting remained as it was originally, take a walk by Turner's Paddock Lake below the cascade. Between 1791 and 1838 Hoare's grandson Richard Colt Hoare planted many new species, particularly from America, including tulip trees, swamp cypresses and Indian bean trees. He also introduced *Rhododendron ponticum*. From 1894 the 6th baronet added to these with the latest kinds of hybrid rhododendrons and scented azaleas, and a large number of copper beeches and conifers, such as the Japanese white pine, Sitka spruce and Californian nutmeg, of which many are record-sized specimens. In the early nineteenth century Stourhead boasted one of the best collections of pelargoniums in the world, over 600 varieties. The latest effort to emulate Richard Colt Hoare's interests consists of over 100 varieties of pelargoniums in a 1910 lean-to greenhouse. Especially wonderful in winter when the garden is quiet, and more views are afforded through the bare trees.

Stourton House Flower Garden ★ 26

Stourton House, Stourton, Warminster BA12 6QF. Tel: (01747) 840417

Elizabeth Bullivant • 3m NW of Mere (A303) off B3092. Follow signs to Stourhead and park in Stourhead car park, follow blue signs to 'Stourton House Garden' • Open April to Nov, Wed, Thurs, Sun and Bank Holiday Mons, 11am – 6pm (or dusk if earlier), and for parties of 12 or more on other days by arrangement • Entrance: charge ◑ ♨ ✕ WC ㅅ ⌯ 🧺 ☙

This colourful five-acre garden contains treasures in friendly, small spaces: a wild, a woodland and a secret garden, and delphinium and rose walks. Seats abound. Rare plants and imaginative designs are everywhere; there are 270 different varieties of hydrangea, many species of magnolia, unusual daffodils and camellias; euphorbias, chocolate plants and a profusion of flowers for drying. A switchback hedge of Leyland cypress encloses a herbaceous garden of island beds, lavishly planted, and a lily pond with many carnivorous plants and a great urn full of flowers. All-year-round interest.

Westwood Manor 27

Bradford–on–Avon BA15 2AF. Tel: (01225) 863374; Fax: (01225) 867316

The National Trust • 5m SE of Bath, 1½ m SW of Bradford-on-Avon off B3109. In Westwood beside church • Open 31st March to 29th Sept, Sun, Tues and Wed, 2 – 5pm, and at other times for parties of up to 20 by written appt with s.a.e. • Entrance: £4. No reduction for children or OAPs ◑

Turning from the Italianate glories of Iford Manor (see entry) one mile away, topiarists and others might like to contemplate the dense green geometry of the garden here. There are no flowers, other than the lilies in the pond set into the lawn and the swathes of wisteria on the wall leading to the entrance. A small garden links the ancient barns to the medieval manor house which the yew hedges enfold and enclose. This simple design looks centuries-old but dates from the early part of the twentieth century, when Mr Edgar Lister purchased and restored the house and created and designed the garden, both of which he later left to the Trust. The late James Lees-Milne wrote that the exquisite manor in its present form 'was his [Lister's] creation and should be his memorial'. It must be emphasised that the garden should be visited as an adjunct and a complement to the house, which is lived in and administered by the Trust's tenant.

Wilton House ★   28

Wilton, Salisbury SP2 0BJ. Tel: (01722) 746720;
E-mail: tourism@wiltonhouse.com; Website: www.wiltonhouse.com

The Earl of Pembroke • 3m W of Salisbury on A30 • House open • Grounds
open 29th March to Oct, daily, 10.30am – 5.30pm (last admission 4.30pm) •
Entrance: £4, children £3 (house, grounds and exhibition areas £9.25, OAPs
£7.50, children (5–15) £5, parties £6 per person, family ticket £22) • Other
information: Plants for sale in garden centre

◐ ⬤ ✕ 🗑 WC ♿ 🅿 ⛪ ☕ ⚲

The first garden the visitor sees, in the north courtyard, was designed by
David Vickery in 1971. It incorporates formal pleached limes in a rectangular
layout, the geometry being further emphasised by a box parterre infilled with
lavender and a central, torrential fountain which provides a cool haven in
summer. It has created a green space with immense style which manages to
answer the architecture of the house. A wrought-iron gate adjoining the
courtyard leads to the east front with wall-trained shrubs and extensive
herbaceous borders. Looking to the south, the Palladian bridge built in
1737 spanning the River Nadder is a focal point. Beside this stands a fine
golden oak, *Quercus robur* 'Concordia', raised and grafted in 1843 at a nursery in
Ghent. Going east along the broad gravel walk among many specimen trees set
in eighteenth-century landscaped parkland, the visitor reaches the walled rose
garden containing a large collection of old-fashioned English roses. This adjoins
a pergola clothed with climbing plants and a water garden containing roses,
aquatic species and ornamental fish. Beyond is the Whispering Seat with its
unusual acoustic properties and a loggia facing the statue from the Arundel
collection, all enclosed by a short avenue of *Quercus ilex*, with the river a
glistening vista in the distance. Within the central courtyard of the house, the
current (17th) Earl has completed the fourth new garden (visible but not
visitable) where, echoing designs from the central, ninth-century Venetian
wellhead, a border of cotton lavender encloses quadrants of clipped box
hedge. For children there is fun and excitement in a large adventure playground; for historians, interest in searching out those parts of the garden
which show the work of Isaac de Caus (c. 1632), the 8th Earl, the 9th 'Architect
Earl', Sir William Chambers and James Wyatt (1801). Tree-trail leaflet available. Nearby is *Philipps House*, Dinton (Tel: (01985) 843600), a National Trust
house by Wyatville c. 1816, open all year with 100-acre *Dinton Park*. The house
(ground floor only) is open 4th April to Oct, Mon, 1 – 5pm and Sat, 9am – 1pm.
Walks in the park and woodland start from the car park.

WORCESTERSHIRE

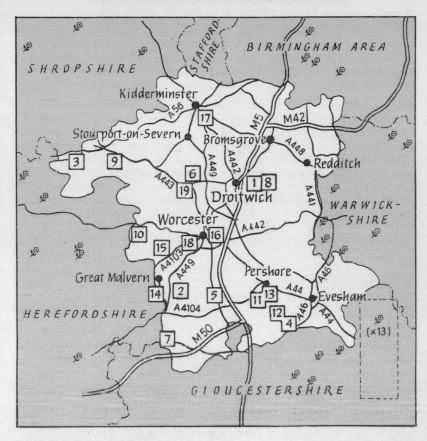

24 Alexander Avenue

1

Droitwich WR9 8NH. Tel: (01905) 774907

*David and Malley Terry • Take M5 exit 5 or 6, then A38 • Open 28th April,
9th June, 14th July for NGS, and by appt • Entrance: £2* ◐ & ⚘

This 40 x 10m garden is a lesson in what can be done in a small space and a short
time. The present owners moved here in the winter of 1995 and have turned a
barren patch of grass into a paradise. High hedges obscure the views of
neighbouring houses, and through them climb some of the 100 clematis the
garden grows. The borders are stuffed with a dazzling array of interesting
plants, many of them rare; most shrubs have climbers growing through them.
There is a fine collection of ferns, and alpines grow in many old stone troughs
or the gravel bed in front of the house. A garden of immaculate artistry.

Barnard's Green House 2

10 Poolbrook Road, Barnard's Green, Great Malvern WR14 3NQ.
Tel: (01684) 574446

Mr and Mrs Philip Nicholls • Just E of Great Malvern at B4211/B4208 junction • Open April to Sept, Thurs, 2 – 6pm, 10th March, 23rd June for NGS, and at other times by appt • Entrance: £2, children free ◐ ☕ WC ⓓ ⌾ ⓖ ⌇

Wide, well-kept lawns surround a Grade-II-listed house dating from 1635, and among many fine trees are two mature cedars. Elsewhere established yew and box hedges contribute both structure and style to what is, in terms of design and atmosphere, a period piece. Of particular interest is the immaculate vegetable garden, laid out with a series of fine herring-bone brick paths and containing a splendid glasshouse and a series of cold frames. In the centre is a new rose-covered gazebo known as the Millennium Dome to which a newly commissioned statue, entitled 'Looking to the Future', is pointing. Mrs Nicholls is a plantswoman so the formal herbaceous borders and new rockery contain many unusual specimens. These, together with winding paths, a rose garden, a small pond and woodland area, complete this quintessentially English garden.

Burford House Gardens ★ 3

Tenbury Wells WR15 8HQ. Tel: (01584) 810777; Fax: (01584) 810673

Mr C. Chesshire • 19m SW of Kidderminster, 1m W of Tenbury Wells on A456; 8m S of Ludlow via A49 and A456 • Open all year, daily, 10am – 5pm • Entrance: £3.50, children £1. Parties of 10 or more by prior arrangement £3 per person • Other information: Plants for sale, especially clematis, at Treasures garden centre opposite ○ ☕ ✕ ▦ WC ⓓ ⌾ ⌂ ⓖ ⌇

The redesigns undertaken over the last five or so years by the present owner are coming to maturity, and, as in the past, this is now a garden worth a lengthy detour. The re-opening of the vista from the front of the Georgian house is superb. Plantings of echinaceas, heleniums and hemorocallis, and of course, the clematis for which the garden was originally famed, form part of the imaginative schemes. The restoration of the eighteenth-century bridge across the River Teme (to commemorate the late John Treasure who began the garden) has resulted in new areas of garden beyond the original. Billowing softer plantings drift in between mulberry and other fruit trees.

Conderton Manor ★ 4

Conderton, Tewkesbury GL20 7PR. Tel: (01386) 725389;
E-mail: carrs.conderton@virgin.net

Mr and Mrs William Carr • 8m SW of Evesham, 5½ m NE of Tewkesbury between A46 and B4079. Opposite Yew Tree Inn in Conderton • Open for NGS and by appt • Entrance: £4 • Other information: Refreshments at Yew Tree Inn. Toilet facilities by arrangement ◐ WC ⓓ

The seven-acre garden of this fine seventeenth-century manor house has spectacular views. Completely restructured over the last ten years, it has an attractive parterre containing foliage plants on the terrace, an old vegetable garden transformed with rose arches and mixed borders, and a 135-metre-long border with unusual shrubs. The quarry garden and bog bank includes cornus and salix for winter stem colour with ferns and primulas for the summer. The vistas through the box walk, cider apple avenue and the fountain garden are quite magnificent. The whole garden is planted with many unusual trees, the owner's special interest. A garden for all seasons.

Croome Park 5

High Green, Severn Stoke WR8 9JS. Tel: (01905) 371006; Fax: (01905 371090; E-mail: croome@smtp.ntrust.org.uk

The National Trust • 8m S of Worcester, E of A38 and M5 • Gardens open 24th March to 3rd Nov, Fri – Mon, 11am – 5pm (last admission 4.30pm). Guided tours by prior application in writing • Entrance: Gardens £3.40, children £1.70, family £8.50. Pre-booked guided tours available (inc. NT members) • Other information: For disabled access, telephone in advance
❶ 🖶 WC ⟨⟩ ℺

The Trust describes Croome as the first complete landscape designed by 'Capability' Brown, the one which made his reputation. The elegant park buildings and other structures are mostly by Robert Adam and James Wyatt. 670 acres of the park were acquired with substantial grant aid from the Heritage Lottery Fund and a substantial donation from Royal & SunAlliance, and the 10-year restoration plan included dredging the water features, clearance and replanting of the garden and parkland.

Eastgrove Cottage Garden Nursery ★ 6

Sankyns Green, Shrawley, Little Witley WR6 6LQ. Tel: (01299) 896389; Website: www.eastgrove.co.uk

Malcolm and Carol Skinner • 8m NW of Worcester on road between Shrawley (B4196) and Great Witley (A443) • Open 18th April to July, Thurs – Sun and Bank Holiday Mons, then 5th Sept to 12th Oct, Thurs – Sat, all 2 – 5pm. Closed Aug • Entrance: £2, children free **❶ WC** ♿ ⚘ ℺

This delightful cottage garden with a profusion of colour has been carefully planted to give each plant maximum impact, the interaction of variegated foliage and strongly coloured shrubs creating backdrops for a variety of perennials. A collection of flowers and foliage by the front door, looking stunningly casual, turns out to be all in pots. The brick paths lead through areas of clever colour combinations. The romantic Secret Garden, concentrating on pinks, mauves, silver and strong burgundy, leads into the Great Wall of China, a raised bed stuffed with sun lovers and backed by old apple trees – a different atmosphere altogether. The arboretum, now extended, is artistically planted to give maximum effect to the variously coloured foliage. A wide range of well-grown, less usual plants is for sale, all propagated at the nursery.

Eastnor Castle 7

Eastnor, Ledbury HR8 1RL. Tel: (01531) 633160; Fax: (01531) 631776

Eastnor Estate • 8m SW of Great Malvern, 2m E of Ledbury on A438 • Castle open selected days for collections of armour, tapestries and fine art • Garden open 31st March to 6th Oct, Sun; July and Aug, daily except Sat; also Bank Holiday Mons; all 11am – 5pm (last admission 4.30pm) • Entrance: £3, children £2 (house and garden £5, children £3) • Other information: Refreshments on castle open days ◑ ☕ ✕ 🗽 WC ♿ ⌗ ⌗ ⚘ ⌗ ⚑ ⚲

Essentially an arboretum, Eastnor has one of the best nineteenth-century plantings in the country. It is worth visiting early in the year for the display of spring bulbs. The house is an early-nineteenth-century castle in medieval style by Sir Robert Smirke, surrounded by grounds now brought under control as an extensive restoration and replanting plan gathers momentum. A path around the lake gives striking views of the castle, although an area of the water is covered in summer with 'Pattypans', *Nuphar lutea*, the common yellow water lily, and around the edges are clumps of khaki shelters which, by day, partially conceal the common cold fisherman. There is a great variety of both conifers and broad-leaved trees. Paths have been kept clear, and the keen tree enthusiast will enjoy the long walks in the woodland. From time to time the park is the venue for a variety of large events, craft fairs, Land Rover and mountain bike rallies.

Hanbury Hall 8

School Road, Hanbury, Droitwich WR9 7EA. Tel: (01527) 821214; Fax: (01527) 821251; E-mail: hanbury@smtp.ntrust.org.uk; Website: www.ntrustsevern.org.uk

The National Trust • 4½ m E of Droitwich, 1m N of B4090, 6m S of Bromsgrove, 1½ m W of B4091 • House and garden open 24th March to Oct, Sun – Wed, 1.30 – 5pm • Entrance: £2.90 (house and garden £4.60, children £2.30, family ticket £11.50) • Other information: Batricar available ◑ ☕ ✕ 🗽 WC ♿ ⌗ ⚘ ⌗ ⚑ ⚲

The Trust has restored much of the early eighteenth-century garden design by George London. The formal garden, typical of the period, comprises a sunken box-edged parterre, a fruit orchard and a wilderness. Structural additions include two summerhouses, two timber bowling-green pavilions and an obelisk. Lawns spread round to the orangery, which houses citrus trees. Further on a cedar walk leads to a fine ice-house. An almost three-metre pond has its fountains operated by solar panel.

Kyre Park 9

Kyre, Tenbury Wells WR15 8RP. Tel: (01885) 410247

Mr and Mrs J. Sellers • 22m SW of Kidderminster, 4m S of Tenbury Wells, 7m N of Bromyard off B4214 • Open Feb to Dec, daily, 11am – 6pm • Entrance: £2, children 50p ◑ ☕ ✕ 🗽 WC ♿ ⌗ ⚘ ⚲

To describe this as a garden is somewhat misleading. More accurately it should be seen as a mid-eighteenth-century landscaped pleasure ground and shrubbery. It extends to some 29 acres and includes a number of Georgian features, not least winding lakes, waterfalls, rapids and romantically placed ruins. The old tunnel leading into the grotto has been restored and a new tower built. Of particular interest are National Collections of hardy ferns – cystopteris, dryopteris, polypodiums and thelypteris – which form a major part of the plantings. Tithe Barn (now Toy City) and Norman dovecote.

Lakeside   10

Gaines Road, Whitbourne, Worcester WR6 5RD. Tel: (01886) 821119

Mr D. Gueroult • 9m W of Worcester off A44. Turn left at county boundary sign, signed 'Linley Green' (ignore sign to Whitbourne) • Open by appt for parties of 10 or more • Entrance: £2.50, children free ● ▆ WC

The first glimpse of this six-acre garden is a moment of sheer delight: a dramatic vista of the lake at the bottom of a steep grassy slope. The main part of the garden lies within the walls of what was the fruit garden of Gaines House nearby and consists of mixed beds and borders with many unusual plants, including bulbs and climbers. The main lake – complete with fountain – is the largest of three medieval stewponds. A small pinetum is maturing well, as is a large bog garden. A short woodland walk, bordered with ferns and different varieties of holly, leads to the attractive lakeside walk. Don't miss the view from the top of the heather garden.

The Manor House   11

Birlingham, Pershore WR10 3AF. Tel: (01386) 750005

Mr and Mrs D. Williams-Thomas • 8m W of Evesham, 2m SW of Pershore, off A4104 in Birlingham • Open 9th, 13th, 16th, 20th, 23rd, 27th June; all 11am – 5pm • Entrance: £2.50, children free • Other information: Rare plant fair 9th June, entrance £3 ● ▆ ▆ WC ৬ ৬

The charm here lies in the successful blend of spacious, informal areas, made up of sweeping lawns, wide, well-stocked borders and splendid views over open countryside, with more enclosed, formal gardens where a sense of secrecy and intimacy is maintained. Notable is a partly walled white garden where old brick paths weave amongst massed plantings of roses, hardy geraniums and campanulas complemented by grey-foliage plants. On the south side of the house an expanse of lawn carries the eye over a ha-ha and meadow to the river, a view echoed from the windows of a pretty little summerhouse retreat. Mature trees and hedges, climbing roses and free-flowering clematis give an air of tranquillity.

Overbury Court ★   12

Overbury, Tewkesbury, Gloucestershire GL20 7NP.
24hr Answerphone/Fax: (01386) 725528; Website: www.overbury.org.uk

Mr and Mrs Bruce Bossom • 9m SW of Evesham, 5m NE of Tewkesbury, 2½ m N of Teddington (A46/A435) roundabout • Open by appt only • Entrance: £2, children free ● ৬

The south side of this magnificent Georgian house boasts a fine stone terrace overlooking a great sweep of formal lawns with hundreds of metres of clipped hedges, specimen clipped yews and a formal pool. To the east, the lawn is framed by a silver and gold border designed by Peter Coats with a crinkle-crankle edging of golden gravel, leading to a gazebo overlooking the road and the country to the south. On the west the frame is completed by more hedging and a sunken garden of attractively underplanted species roses leading to the west side of the house. There, under enormous plane trees, a stream winds its way from a grotto over vast lawns, falling gently into pools before disappearing underground. Elsewhere, shrub and flower borders and aged cherries merge and blend into the adjacent churchyard. Everything speaks of a continuity rare today. Conderton Manor (see entry) is nearby.

Pershore College 13

'Avonbank', Pershore WR10 3JP. Tel: (01386) 552443

7m SE of M5 junction 7, 1m E of Pershore on A44 • Gardens open 1st June for College Open Day, 10am – 5pm, and weekdays by appt for large parties • Entrance: £1, coaches £50 on open day ● ▤ WC ⅃ ✿ ⌂ ▯

The grounds are working areas designed with an educational bias, and include 'model gardens' created by students, and a variety of specialist gardens. There is also an arboretum, orchards, automated glasshouses and a hardy plant production nursery and plant centre. The RHS Pershore Centre is on the campus, and the Alpine Garden Society has its national HQ here; the college also holds a National Collection of penstemons and philadelphus.

The Picton Garden 14

Old Court Nurseries, Colwall, Great Malvern WR13 6QE. Tel: (01684) 540416; E-mail: picton@dircon.co.uk; Website: www.autumnasters.co.uk

Mr and Mrs P. Picton • 3m SW of Great Malvern on B4218 • Garden open Aug, Wed – Sun; Sept, daily; 1st to 13th Oct, daily, 17th to 31st Oct, Wed – Sun; all 11am – 5pm • Old Court Nurseries open as garden, plus May to July, Wed, Sun • Entrance: £2, children under 15 free (2001 prices) ◑ ✿

A one-and-a-half-acre plantsman's garden on the site of Ernest Ballard's Old Court Nurseries. A large collection of herbaceous perennials ensures plenty of late summer interest, while shrubs and shade beds create year-round diversity. The National Collection of Michaelmas daisies is here, growing in every imaginable variety, notably as the dominant force in the former alpine and rose gardens. Another interesting garden close by is *Caves Folly Nursery* in Evandine Lane, off Colwall Green, B4218 between Malvern and Ledbury. The well-established nursery, devoted to organic plants, is open Thurs-Sat 10am-5pm all year; the garden is open twice for NGS and group visits are welcome at other times (Tel: (01684) 540631).

Shuttifield Cottage 15

Birchwood, Storridge, Malvern WR13 5HA. Tel: (01886) 884243

Angela and David Judge • 8m SW of Worcester off A4103. Turn right opposite Storridge church to Birchwood. After 1¼ m turn left down tarmac drive. Park on road and walk down this drive • Open 21st April, 6th May, 3rd, 23rd June, 7th July, 4th Aug, 15th Sept, all 2 – 5pm, and at other times by appt • Entrance: £2.50, children free ● ● 🖉

Lawns lead down the sloping site in a succession of pleasure and interest, past borders and beds planted with shrubs and flowering plants – many of them unusual – to the rose garden. This has space for a large collection of old varieties to spread, sprawl, climb and bloom abundantly in what is almost a secret garden. Beyond is a 20-acre wood carpeted with wood anemones and bluebells. In other parts are colour-themed beds, splendid trees, herbaceous plants, a woodland walk, a vegetable garden, a deer park and ponds. The planning and planting are skilful, the effect is natural and unstudied.

Spetchley Park 16

Spetchley, Worcester WR5 1RS. Tel: (01905) 345224/213

Trustees of Spetchley Gardens Charitable Trust • 3m E of Worcester on A422 • Open April to Sept, Tues – Fri and Bank Holiday Mons, 11am – 5pm, Sun, 2 – 5pm. Closed other Mons and all Sats • Entrance: £3.50, children £1.80 ◑ ● WC &

For gardens which are, after all, of considerable size, there is an alluring intimacy about the grounds of Spetchley Park. Linked romantically with Ellen Willmott, whose sister Rose Berkeley was responsible for the gardens in her day, they retain a wonderful sense of the past. Mellow brick walls, clipped yew hedges hiding secret enclosures, unfolding walks and vistas, antique statues and an ornate fountain are but a few of the delights to be discovered. Fine trees abound, as does interesting planting, including drift after drift of the handsome *Lilium martagon* along the walk to the horse pool in summer. Within the old kitchen garden, a new development, part sunken, shows great promise.

Stone House Cottage Gardens ★ 17

Stone, Kidderminster DY10 4BG. Tel: (01562) 69902; Fax: (01562) 69960; E-mail: Louisa@shcn.co.uk

Mr and Mrs James Arbuthnott • 2m SE of Kidderminster via A448 • Open March to Sept, Wed – Sat and Bank Holiday Mons, 10am – 5.30pm, Oct to March by appt • Entrance: £2.50, children free ◑ WC & 🖉

The garden has been created since 1974, and looking round it now, it is difficult to believe that the whole area was once flat and bare. The owners have skilfully built towers and follies to create small intimate areas and at the same time provide homes for many unusual climbers and shrubs. Yew hedges break up the area to give a vista with a tower at the end, covered with wisteria, roses and clematis. Hardly anywhere does a climber grow in isolation – something will be scrambling up it, usually a small late-flowering clematis. Raised beds are full to overflowing, shrubs and unusual herbaceous plants mingle happily. In a grassed area shrubs are making good specimens. In June during two evenings of music the towers have a secondary purpose as platforms for wind ensembles. You are invited to picnic in the garden for a modest fee – the effect is akin to non-pretentious Glyndebourne transplanted to San Gimignano. At other times you may ascend the towers to view the garden as a whole for the price of a donation to the Mother Theresa charity. Not far away, north of Kidderminster, is *Bodenham Arboretum*. At Wolverley follow brown signs along B4189. Open April to mid-November, daily, 11 am – 5pm; winter months weekends and Bank Holidays only. (Tel: (01562) 852444).

21 Swinton Lane 18

Worcester WR2 4JP. Tel: (01905) 422265

Mr A. Poulton • 1½ m W of city centre off Bransford road (B4485) from St Johns to Rushwick. Turn left between Portobello pub and Worcester golf course • Open by appt only • Entrance: £2 ● ⅏

Behind the 1930s' house, in a space no greater than one third of an acre, the owners have created a most imaginatively planned, splendidly planted, atmospheric garden. Clever use of divisions, hedges, trees, shrubs and trelliswork has resulted in distinct areas or enclosures, notably a beautifully conceived and executed silver and white garden, designed for all-year interest, a hot late-summer border and an area devoted to shade-loving plants. Throughout, herbaceous borders are supplemented with pot-grown, tender perennials, which are moved in and out of key positions according to flowering season.

Witley Court 19

Worcester Road, Great Witley, Worcester WR6 6JT. Tel: (01299) 896636

English Heritage • 10m NW of Worcester on A433 • Open April to Oct, daily, 10am – 6pm (5pm in Oct); Nov to March 2003, Wed – Sun, 10am – 4pm. Closed 25th, 26th Dec, 1st Jan. Evening guided tours available by appt • Entrance: £3.80, OAPs £2.90, children £1.90, family ticket £9.50 • Other information: Disabled parking available ● ⬛ 🐌 WC & ⬧ ⬛ ⬤

Witley Court is an early Jacobean manor house which in the nineteenth century was turned into a vast Italianate mansion, with porticoes by John Nash. It is now a spectacular ruin. The elaborate gardens, William Nesfield's 'Monster Work', still contain immense stone fountains. Gravel walks lead around the lake and through woodland to the house and the skeleton of the formal Victorian gardens, which it is hoped will soon be restored. The Jerwood Foundation Sculpture Park is being created here in the North Park, with Elizabeth Frink's 'The Walking Man' as its first permanent installation. Other sculptures have followed, including three by Michael Ayrton and one each by Lynn Chadwick, Antony Gormley and Kenneth Armitage. The landscape architects Colvin and Moggridge are creating spaces within the restored nineteenth-century wilderness to house the sculpture; they are also involved in new plantings in the Governor's Garden.

YORKSHIRE (N. & E. RIDING)

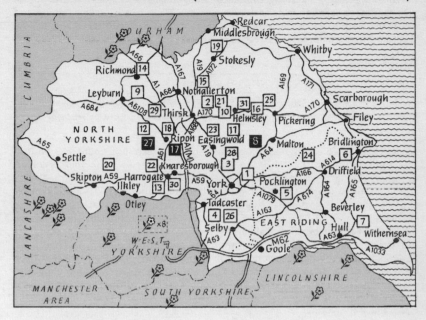

Two-starred gardens are marked on the map with a black square.

Aldby Park ★   1

Buttercrambe, York YO41 1XU. Tel (01759) 371398

Mr and Mrs G.M.V. Winn • 7m NW of York off A166 Bridlington road. Turn left at sign to Buttercrambe and continue ½ m past Gate Helmsley • Open one Sun for charity, and by appt • Entrance: £2, children £1 • Other information: Teas and other refreshments on open days only. Plants for sale in adjacent nursery ● ➘ ➤ WC ᶑ ☜ ✿

The fine 1726 house stands on a wooded hillside site which includes the mound and dry moat of King Edwin's seventh-century castle. The original terraced garden was created by Thomas Knowlton in 1746. In 1964 Mr Winn, who had known and loved the pre-war garden as a child, took over the house, and with a single gardener began the huge task of restoring what was by then a jungle to the garden we see today. The result is a triumph – a truly romantic garden which lifts the heart as it reveals itself to you. A glimpse through ornamental trees leads to a grassy terrace around a mound, decked on the sunny side with day lilies, yuccas and agapanthus. Pale colours contrast with the dark yews and box and range from white and yellow to silver and pink. In shady areas electric-blue geraniums take over, and a band of hostas flourishes free of slugs, thanks to hungry hedgehogs. Golden elders, *Hypericum* 'Hidcote' and corkscrew hazels add interest. Now a steep drop to the river is revealed, and the path leads down to a grassy walk along the water's edge, where kingcups and primulas glow and dark ferns thrive. On the water are black swans, greylag geese and ducks. Back up towards the house, a 'Kiftsgate' rose has smothered a large yew tree, and fine shrub roses, selected for looks and fragrance, abound.

Arden Hall 2

Hawnby, York YO62 5LS. Tel: (01439) 798348

Earl and Countess of Mexborough • 11m NE of Thirsk, 9m NW of Helmsley off B1257 • Open two or three times a year for charities, and possibly by prior appt to suitably interested parties • Entrance: charge ☾

Formerly the site of a Benedictine convent, the house (not open) was built in the eighteenth century, and the gardens are a series of formal terraces, dominated by a massive yew hedge at least 250 years old. A natural spring supplies four gallons of water a minute, a bonus imaginatively developed under the direction of gardener Stephen Mead. A formal Italianate pond is fed through a series of rills in stone troughs which pass through the terraces. An 800-feet-long laburnum walk and splendid borders have been made by the old croquet lawn. A 1920s' swimming pool (too cold for use) has been converted into a wildlife-oriented pond which flows into a stream and then a series of pools disappearing down the valley. The valley has abundant wild plants, especially wood garlic, and the philosophy of Stephen Mead is to progress from the naturally informal environment – an 'Arden' indeed.

Beningbrough Hall and Gardens 3

Shipton-by-Beningbrough, York YO30 1DD. Tel: (01904) 470666; Fax (01904) 470002

The National Trust • 8m NW of York off A19 York – Thirsk road at Shipton • House open 12 noon – 5pm (last admission 4.30pm), with National Portrait Gallery loan exhibition • Gardens open 23rd March to 3rd Nov, Sat – Wed, and Good Friday; also Fri in July and Aug; all 11am – 5.30pm (last admission 4.30pm) • Entrance: gardens and exhibitions £3.60, children £1.80, family £9 (house, gardens and exhibitions £5.20, children £2.60, family £13). Party rates available and discount ticket for cyclists • Other information: Picnics in walled garden only ◑ 🍽 ✕ WC ♿ 🌿 ♨ 🍴 🌳

The main formal garden, comprising geometrically patterned parterres, was laid out at the time the house was built in 1716, but was replaced during the late eighteenth century by sweeping lawns and specimen trees, part of an estate of 365 acres. This is essentially a pleasure garden with an historic framework, amongst which considerable recent planting has been integrated. The wilderness and two privy gardens have been restored to the original standards, and there is a nineteenth-century American garden and a Victorian conservatory. The main border has been planted as part of a three-stage redevelopment project. New planting has brought the walled garden back to life, including more than 5000 lavender plants, flowers for cutting, blocks of vegetables, and soft fruit, with vegetables surplus to the restaurant requirements sold in the shop.

Bolton Percy Churchyard   4

Bolton Percy, York YO23 7BA.

7½ m SW of York, 5m E of Tadcaster. Open all year, daily • Entrance: donation welcome ○

The enthusiasm of Roger Brook has brought a wilderness under control in the splendid one-acre village churchyard, and it is now in all respects a paradise of garden plants growing in the new perennial style of gardening, with limited maintenance required – a lesson for churchwardens the country over. Roger Brook is now converting *Wordsborough Cemetery* near Barnsley on the same principles.

Burnby Hall Gardens and Museum ★   5

The Balk, Pocklington, East Riding YO42 2QF. Tel: (01759) 302068

Stewart's Burnby Hall Gardens and Museum Trust • 13m E of York off A1079 in Pocklington • Open 31st March to Sept, daily, 10am – 6pm • Entrance: £2.40, OAPs £1.90, children (5–15) £1, under 5 free. Parties of 20 or more £1.50 per person (2001 prices) ◑ 🍽 🍴 WC ♿ 🌿 🏛 🌳

When the gardens were established on eight acres of open farmland in 1904 by Major Stewart, the original ponds, which covered two acres, were constructed for fishing, but in 1935 they were converted to water-lily cultivation. The large collection of hardy water lilies here forms part of the National Collection. They may be seen from June to mid-September in a normal year, and in July and August the two lakes are covered in blooms from 80 different varieties.

Burton Agnes Hall   6

Burton Agnes, Driffield, East Riding YO25 4NB. Tel: (01262) 490324; Website: www.burton-agnes.com

Mrs Susan Cunliffe-Lister/Burton Agnes Preservation Trust Ltd • 5m S of Bridlington, 5m NE of Great Driffield on A166 • House open • Garden open April to Oct, daily, 11am – 5pm • Entrance: £2.40 (hall and garden £4.80, OAPs £4.30) ◑ 🍽 ✕ 🍴 WC ♿ 🐕 🌿 🏛 🌳

The beautiful Elizabethan hall – designed by Robert Smythson, master mason to Elizabeth I and builder of Longleat and Hardwick – is approached through the gatehouse archway, up a wide gravel drive flanked by rows of fig-shaped yew hedges, with lawns beyond. Little evidence remains of the garden's history, any former flower planting in sight of the hall having succumbed to lawn on all sides. However, the walls of the former enormous kitchen garden conceal a riot of colour (including campanulas, thymes, clematis, hardy geraniums and old roses). The *potager* of vegetables and herbs supplies the needs of the household. There are two herbaceous borders, a scented garden, a jungle of bamboos and giant exotic species, and a maze. A series of large-scale games (including chess, draughts and snakes and ladders) is laid out on paving at the end of the walled garden. Behind the hall is a woodland garden and a one-mile arboretum walk. Adjoining is the English Heritage *Burton Agnes Manor House*, a rare example of a Norman house open 'any reasonable time'.

Burton Constable Hall 7

Burton Constable, Hull, East Riding HU11 4LN. Tel: (01964) 562400

Burton Constable Foundation • 7½ m NE of Hull off A165 • Hall open 1 – 5pm (last admission 4.15pm) • Grounds open 31st March to Oct, Sat – Thurs, 12.30 – 5pm. Parties at any time by arrangement • Entrance: £1, children 50p (hall and grounds £5, OAPs £4.50, children £2, family ticket £11, parties please call for details) ◑ ☕ ▨ WC & ⬀ ⛪ ⚲

The fine Elizabethan house is surrounded by parkland laid out in the 1770s by 'Capability' Brown, whose plans can still be seen. His 20 acres of lakes are spanned by a good stone bridge, and while not all his trees have survived they are being replaced by new plantings, still in their infancy. Around the house is a four-acre garden with a handsome eighteenth-century orangery, statuary and borders. This is one of the grandest establishments in the North-East, and with the help of a £3.5m endowment from the National Heritage Memorial Fund should soon regain its former glory.

Castle Howard ★★ 8

York YO60 7DA. Tel: (01653) 648444 ext. 220; Fax: (01653) 648501; E-mail: house@castlehoward.co.uk; Website: www.castlehoward.co.uk

Castle Howard Estates Ltd • 17m NE of York, 5m SW of Malton off A64 • House open • Garden open 15th March to 3rd Nov, daily, 10am – 4.30pm. Special tours of woodland garden and rose gardens available for pre-booked parties • Entrance: £4.50, children (4–16) £2.50, (house, gardens and grounds £7.50, OAPs £6.75, children (4–16) £4.50) (2001 prices). Special rates for garden tours on request • Other information: Dogs permitted, on lead ◑ ☕ ✕ ▨ WC & ⬀ ✿ ⛪ ⚲ ⚲

Described as one of the finest examples of the heroic age of English landscape architecture, the house and grounds were first designed by Sir John Vanbrugh, assisted by Nicholas Hawksmoor. This architectural framework still basically exists, although in recent times features have been added, for example the impressive fountains designed by Nesfield. Although known principally as a fine landscape with remarkable park and buildings, there is also much for the garden lover. It holds one of the largest collections of old-fashioned and species roses in Europe, with the soil of the two gardens having been completely replaced in recent years and 2000 new roses planted. Ray Wood and the adjacent area accommodate fine collections of magnolias, rhododendrons, sorbus and vacciniums, an adjunct to the newly extended arboretum, which will soon be one of the largest and most important in the country. A new association has been formed between the Royal Botanic Gardens, Kew and Castle Howard to manage the wood. Most of the plants are well labelled

Constable Burton Hall 9

Leyburn, North Yorkshire DL8 5LJ. Tel: (01677) 450428

Mr Charles Wyvill • 16m NW of Ripon, 3m E of Leyburn on A684 • Open mid-March to mid-Oct, daily, 9am – 6pm • Entrance: £2.50, OAPs £2, children 50p (honesty box) ◐ 🍴 WC ⚲ ⟳ 🏵 ℺

In a walled and wooded parkland setting is a perfect Palladian mansion designed by John Carr of York in 1768. Built in beautiful honey-coloured sandstone, it rises from the lawns shaded by fine mature cedars. The owners have made a great effort to replant and develop. A delightful terraced woodland garden of lilies, ferns, hardy shrubs, roses and wild flowers drops down to a lake enhanced by an eighteenth-century bridge (no access). Near to the entrance drive are a stream and rock garden, and a new lily pond has been added. This substantial garden is a pleasure to visit because, after placing their entry coins in the honesty box, visitors can follow the numbered directional arrows using the concise notes to pass from one area of the garden to another (a technique that many other gardens could use with advantage). Surprises abound, such as *Lilium monadelphum* (yellow Turk's cap) in profusion and many mad climbers and shade-loving ground-cover plants. Several grand borders and a herbaceous garden have replaced the old formal rose garden. A fine morning or afternoon outing at all times of year.

Duncombe Park 10

Helmsley, North Yorkshire YO62 5EB. Tel: (01439) 770213/771115 (during open hours); Fax: (01439) 771114; E-mail: sally@duncombepark.com; Website: www.duncombepark.com

Lord Feversham • 12m E of Thirsk, 1m SW of Helmsley off A170 • House and garden open probably Easter to Oct – telephone for details. Parkland Centre and National Nature Reserve also open • Entrance: parkland and country walks £2; grounds £4; house and grounds £6. Discounts for pre-booked parties visiting house and grounds (2001 prices) • Other information: Parking at Parkland Centre. Alternative entrance for wheelchair users ◐ 🍴 ✗ WC ⚲ 🏛 🏵 ℺

Home of the Duncombes for 300 years, the mansion has recently been restored as a family home by Lord Feversham. Its 35-acre garden, set in 300 acres of dramatic parkland, dates from c. 1715 and was described by Sacheverell Sitwell as 'the supreme masterpiece of the art of the landscape gardener'. Impressive are the tree-lined terraces, classical temples, statues and vast expanses of lawn. The magnificent trees, mostly dating from the original eighteenth-century planting, include the tallest ash and lime trees, according to the *Guinness Book of Records*. The ha-has is one of the earliest ever built, pre-dating Bridgeman's at Stowe (see entry in Buckinghamshire). There is also a yew walk and an orangery.

Fountains Abbey

(see STUDLEY ROYAL AND FOUNTAINS ABBEY)

Gilling Castle   11

Gilling East, North Yorkshire YO62 4HP. Tel: (01439) 788238

*The Right Reverend The Abbot of Ampleforth • 20m N of York on B1363 York –
Helmsley road • Great chamber and entrance hall of castle open during term only
• Garden open daily, 10am – 4pm • Entrance: £1.50, children free ○*

A lovely garden in outstanding scenery. The terraces have been constructed on
the south-facing side, four of them tumbling down the slope from an expansive
lawn at the top. Many old-fashioned flowers grow in the borders, with a
backdrop of majestic trees.

Hackfall Wood   12

Grewelthorpe, North Yorkshire.

*Woodland Trust • 6m NW of Ripon off A6108, between Grewelthorpe and
Masham • Open all year, daily • Entrance: free ○ ⬦*

The site is a spectacular gorge cut out by the River Ure. Now battered by neglect,
this romantic woodland garden, painted by Turner and praised by Wordsworth,
was laid out by William Aislabie between 1750 and 1765 as a counterpoint to the
splendour of Studley Royal (see entry) created by his father. In the 112 acres of
entirely overgrown semi-natural scenery, paths lead to a pool, a grotto and a
number of small Arcadian ruins. The crumbling banqueting hall commands
magnificent views over the gorge. Restoration of the paths, sometimes soggy,
is underway. Spring sees masses of flowering wild garlic and bluebells, and tall
ferns flourish in late summer amid beech, Turkey oak, elder and elm.

Harlow Carr Botanical Gardens
(RHS Garden Harlow Carr) ★   13

**Crag Lane, Harrogate, North Yorkshire HG3 1QB. Tel: (01423) 565418;
Fax: (01423) 530663; Website: www.harlowcarr.fsnet.co.uk**

*Royal Horticultural Society • 1½ m W of Harrogate on B6162 Otley road •
Open all year, daily, 9.30am – 6pm (dusk if earlier) • Entrance: £4.50, OAPs
£3.50, accompanied children under 11 free. Parties of 20 or more £3.50,
children under 11 free (2001 prices) • Other information: Manual and electric
wheelchairs for loan. Guide dogs only ○ 🍽 ✕ 🖼 WC ♿ 🐾 ⬦ ❦*

The 68-acre site, established in 1949 by the Northern Horticultural Society,
(which merged with the Royal Horticultural Society in July 2001) as a centre
for garden plant trials, now also provides a wide range of horticultural courses
for amateurs. It is said that if a plant prospers here it will grow anywhere in the
North. The garden hosts National Collections of heather and rhubarb cultivars
as well as those of dryopteris and polypodium ferns, and there are many
rhododendrons and alpines. The streamside planting boasts one of the best
collections of moisture-loving plants in the north of England. There is also a
fine alpine house and two extensive rock gardens.

Millgate House ★   14

Richmond, North Yorkshire DL10 4JN. Tel: (01748) 823571;
Fax: (01748) 850701; Website: www.millgatehouse.com

Austin Lynch and Tim Culkin • In Richmond, in corner of Market Square opposite Barclays Bank • Open mid-March to mid-Oct, daily, 10am – 5.30pm, and at other times by appt • Entrance: £1.50 ◑ ♀

This small but outstanding award-winning town garden is walled on two sides, with the continuous sound of waterfalls on the River Swale in the background. Clematis, roses and jasmine jostle for place against the walls. Hostas and ferns are at the roots of the rose 'Boule de Neige', while 'Maigold' hangs in fragrant swags from the Regency balcony that runs across the first floor of the house. The lower garden houses over 28 varieties of roses, the clematis list is equally spectacular, and there is a specialist collection of hostas. A jewel offering plenty of ideas for the small garden.

Mount Grace Priory   15

Staddle Bridge, Northallerton, North Yorkshire DL6 3JG. Tel: (01609) 883494

English Heritage • 12m N of Thirsk, 7m NE of Northallerton on A19 • Open April to Sept, daily, 10am – 6pm; Oct, daily, 10am – 5pm; Nov to 28th March, Wed – Sun, 10am – 1pm, 2 – 4pm (last admission 3.30pm; closed 24th to 26th Dec, 1st Jan • Entrance: £2.90, concessions £2.20, children £1.50 (2001 prices) ◔ ▆ ▆ WC ♨ ⚖ ♀ ✂

The ruins of the priory guest house, incorporated into a seventeenth-century manor, were combined in 1900–1901 with a larger house which is an important example of the Arts and Crafts Movement. The monks' cells in the monastery were occupied from 1398 to the dissolution in 1539, and each cell had its own garden. Some have been replanted, with the latest crop of herbs illustrating varieties used for medicinal purposes. The design of the cell-garden is in the form of paths and raised beds. A low box hedge surrounds the central bed, which is filled with blocks of herbs; every second year these follow a different theme. The one-acre early-twentieth-century garden of stepped terraces falling away from the house is being re-created, with rock plants spilling over the edges. There are shrubberies and narrow borders and a Japanese garden with ponds, colourful maples, rhododendrons and azaleas.

Nawton Tower ★   16

Highfield Lane, Nawton, York YO62 7TU. Tel: (01439) 771218

Mrs Sylvia Ward • 14½ m E of Thirsk, 2½ m NE of Helmsley, off A170 Scarborough road. In Nawton and Beadlam, turn left up Highfield Lane for 2m • Open May and June, weekends only, 2 – 6pm, and at other times by appt • Entrance: £1.50, children 75p ● ⟨⟩ ♨ ✂

This remarkable, atmospheric 12-acre garden on the edge of the North York Moors was created during the 1930s by the Earl of Feversham. It consists of a series of formal grassy walks between living tapestries woven from a masterly selection of trees, rhododendrons, azaleas and old shrub roses. Every junction from the central walk leads to a fresh surprise: a statue on a pedimented gazebo as the focal point of another pathway; a yew-hedged topiary garden; a quiet contemplative clearing with a silent stone fountain at its centre. A magical experience.

Newby Hall and Gardens ★★ 17

Ripon, North Yorkshire HG4 5AE. Tel: (01423) 322583; Fax: (01423) 324452

R. Compton • 4m SE of Ripon on B6265, 3m W of A1 • Open April to Sept, daily except Mon (but open Bank Holiday Mons), 11am – 5.30pm • Entrance: £5, OAPs £4, children £3.50 (house and gardens £6.80, OAPs £5.80, children £4) (2001 prices) • Other information: Wheelchairs provided. Dogs in area adjacent to picnic area only ◑ ♨ ✕ 🖼 <u>WC</u> ♿ 🌳 🏺 🌡 ⚘

The much-loved home of the Compton family, who have restored this famous Adam house to its original beauty and have renovated and developed 25 acres of award-winning gardens. Some features remain from the eighteenth century, such as the east-to-west walk marked by Venetian statuary and backed by yew and purple plum. The south face has long wide green slopes down to the River Ure, with herbaceous borders on either side backed by clipped hedges and flowering shrubs. Cross-walks lead to smaller gardens full of interest. These include species roses and tropical, autumn, rock and stepped water gardens, as well as a fine woodland area attributed to Ellen Willmott. A National Collection of cornus is here. There is also a garden restaurant, a children's adventure garden and a miniature railway. Events such as craft fairs are held in the summer, with special admission prices. The Newby plant stall is operated in conjunction with *Oland Plants*, a nursery and garden five miles west of Ripon on B6265.

Norton Conyers 18

Ripon, North Yorkshire HG4 5EQ. Tel: (01765) 640333

Sir James and Lady Graham • 4m N of Ripon, near Wath. From A1 turn off at Baldersby flyover, take A61 to Ripon and turn right to Melmerby • House open as garden, but 2 – 5pm (admission charge) • Open 19th May to 1st Sept, Sun; 8th to 13th July, daily; and Bank Holiday Suns and Mons; all 12 noon – 5pm. Also open Thurs throughout the year, 10am – 4pm (but telephone beforehand to check). Parties at other times by appt • Entrance: free, though donations welcome • Other information: Plants, especially hardy plants, for sale. PYO fruit during summer ◑ WC ♿ ⬆ 🌡

The lure of both house and garden lies with the past, especially the association of the house with Charlotte Brontë, who made it one of the models for Thornfield Hall in *Jane Eyre*. The eighteenth-century walled garden, with its orangery and herbaceous borders, covers two and a half acres. The plantings are modest but pleasant and give an historic feel.

Ormesby Hall 19

Ormesby, Middlesbrough TS7 9AS. Tel: (01642) 324188; Fax: (01642) 300937

The National Trust • 3m SE of Middlesbrough, W of A171 • Open 24th March to 3rd Nov, telephone for details • Entrance: £2.20, children £1 (house, garden, railway and exhibitions £3.70, children £1.80). Party rates available • Other information: Disabled parking near house. Braille guide available. Dogs on leads, in park only ◑ ☕ WC & ⛪ 🔦 ✂

There have been recent developments in the gardens, including the re-introduction of the original ironwork fencing, and the planting of many new bulbs and shrubs. The main rose beds have been renewed, and further ground cover is taking place in the Holly Walk. A new glasshouse will help with the propagation of plants for the garden and the sales shop. Spring and summer mini garden guides are available, and the head gardener officiates at garden tours on the last Thursday of the month. The hall itself is licensed for wedding ceremonies, and the stable block is used by the local mounted police.

Parcevall Hall Gardens ★ 20

Skyreholme, Skipton, North Yorkshire BD23 6DE. Tel: (01756) 720311;
E-mail: info@parcevallhallgardens.co.uk;
Website: www.parcevallhallgardens.co.uk

Walsingham College (Yorkshire Properties) Ltd • 10m NE of Skipton, 1m NE of Appletreewick off B6265 Pateley Bridge – Skipton road • Open April to Oct, daily, 10am – 6pm; in winter by appt; also open for charity • Entrance: £3, children 50p • Other information: Teas available – for opening times telephone (01756) 720630. Picnics in orchard only ◑ ☕ 🏪 WC ⟨⟩ ✤ ✂

A garden of interest to the plantsperson all year round, many of Sir William Milner's treasures having survived years of neglect. Much of the garden has been renovated – and each year another area is restored, currently the old rose garden. There are red borders, an extended woodland walk, fish ponds and a rock garden. A fine range of rhododendrons, many originally collected in China, still thrive in the walk here. It is worth a visit just to enjoy the spectacular views of Simon's Seat and Wharfedale from the terrace.

Rievaulx Terrace and Temples ★ 21

Rievaulx, Helmsley, North Yorkshire YO6 5LJ. Tel: (01439) 798340

The National Trust • 10m E of Thirsk, 2½ m NW of Helmsley on B1257 • Open probably 23rd March to 3rd Nov, daily, 10.30am – 6pm (April and Oct 5pm). Ionic temple closed 1 – 2pm • Entrance: £3.30, children £1.50, family ticket (2 adults and up to 3 children) £8 • Other information: Coach park. Possible for wheelchairs but steps to temples. Electric runaround available for pre-booking; one manual wheelchair also available. Exhibition of landscape design in basement of Ionic temple ◑ 🏪 WC & ⟨⟩ ⛪ 🔦 ✂

This is a unique example of the eighteenth-century passion for the romantic and the picturesque – that is, making landscape look like a picture. The work was done at the behest of the third Thomas Duncombe around 1754 and consists of a half-mile-long serpentine grass terrace high above Ryedale with fine views of the great ruins of one of the finest of all of Britain's Cistercian abbeys. At one end is a Palladian Ionic temple-cum-banqueting-house with furniture by William Kent and elaborate ceilings. At the other is a Tuscan temple with a raised platform, from which are views to the Rye Valley. The concept is wonderfully achieved. Those who want to see flowers will have to concentrate their attention on the grass bank below the terrace which is managed for wildflower content – fine displays of cowslips, primroses, orchids, violets, bird's foot trefoils, ladies' bedstraws, etc. There is also blossom throughout the spring season, such as cherry (bird and wild), blackthorn, rowan, whitebeam, elder and lilac.

Ripley Castle

22

Ripley, Harrogate, North Yorkshire HG3 3AY. Tel: (01423) 770152; Fax (01423) 771745; E-mail: enquiries@ripleycastle.co.uk; Website: www.ripleycastle.co.uk

Sir Thomas Ingilby, Bt • 3½ m N of Harrogate off A61 Harrogate – Ripon road • Castle open Sept – May, Tues, Thurs, Sat, Sun; June to Aug, daily; all 10.30am – 3pm • Garden open all year, daily , 10am – 5pm • Entrance: £3, OAPs £2.50, children £1.50. Parties of 25 or more £2.50 per person • Other information: Guide dogs only ◑ 🍴 ✕ 🏪 WC & 🌷 🏛 🏺 ⚲

The mid-eighteenth-century 'Capability' Brown landscape with formal gardens has been developed by Peter Aram for a family that has lived here since the fourteenth century. The formal areas have been completely restored and the huge herbaceous borders – a total of 110 metres long – are amongst the most spectacular in the north of England. Other features include a lake with an attractive Victorian iron bridge, an eighteenth-century orangery and summer-houses. There are magnificent specimen trees. A woodland walk leads to a temple with fine views, and a lakeside walk takes the visitor through the deer park. Extensive plantings of a rich variety of spring-flowering bulbs have been made to complement a National Collection of hyacinths here, and the tropical plant collection formerly owned by Hull University at Cottingham Botanical Gardens is now at Ripley and is open to the public in the restored listed greenhouses. The vegetable garden has rare species adopted from the Henry Doubleday Research Association. Nearby, at the arts centre in Knaresbor-ough, is a 'garden of the senses' designed for *Henshaw's College* for children with disabilities. Telephone (01423) 886451 for details.

Shandy Hall

23

Coxwold, York YO61 4AD. Tel: (01347) 868465; Fax: (01347) 868465; Website: www.shandy-hall.org.uk

The Laurence Sterne Trust • 18m N of York, 7m SE of Thirsk. From York, take A19 towards Thirsk, turn off to Easingwold and follow signs to Coxwold. From crossroads go 150 metres past church • House open May to Sept, Wed, 2 –

4.30pm and Sun, 2.30 – 4.30pm • Garden open May to Sept, daily except Sat, 11am – 4.30pm • Entrance: £2.50 (house and garden £4.50, children £1.50) • Other information: Refreshments in village nearby. Permanent Sterne exhibition. Art and pottery gallery ◑ WC ᴦ ✆ 🏛

A delightful small-scale, three-part garden, full of year-round interest, surrounds the pretty fifteenth-century cottage in which Laurence Sterne wrote *Tristram Shandy* during the 1760s. In the Barn Garden, borders of herbaceous plants and shrub roses enfold on three sides, with a view out to Byland Abbey and the North York Moors beyond. The Old Garden is approached through a small orchard where some of the gnarled trees are covered with climbing roses. A wide selection of old-fashioned roses in raised beds against drystone walls is interspersed with herbaceous planting in which careful thought is given to plant associations for colour and form. The foliage of a silver poplar provides a perfect backdrop for shrub roses such as 'Kassel', 'Fantin-Latour' and 'La Reine Victoria'. The third section is a surprise garden, created within a long-abandoned adjacent quarry and devoted mainly to a wonderful display of wild flowers underplanted with bulbs. Starting in the spring with narcissi and then bluebells, the tree-fringed quarry garden changes colour through the year, from yellow to blue to pink, then purple (in July) and on to a deep bosky green, punctuated by clematis and climbing roses, before moving into autumn colours. Four magnificent ash trees form a centrepiece, and grassy paths wind through its undulations, past rustic seats and bowers.

Sledmere House 24

Sledmere, Great Driffield, East Riding YO25 3XG. Tel: (01377) 236637; Fax: (01377) 236500; E-mail: sledmerehouse@aol.com

Sir Tatton Sykes, Bt • 9m NW of Great Driffield off A166. Signposted • House open • Garden open 29th March to 2nd April; then 4th May to 29th Sept. Closed Mon and Sat, but open Bank Holiday Mons, 11.30am – 4.30pm • Entrance: £2, children £1 (house, park and garden £4.50, OAPs £4, children £2) ◑ ✗ 🖥 WC ᴦ ✆ 🏛 ◉ ✎

A listed garden, Sledmere is among the best-preserved of 'Capability' Brown's landscape schemes. Dating from the 1770s, it clearly reveals his characteristic belting and clumping of trees and carefully controlled diagonal vistas to distant 'eye-catchers'. His use of a ha-ha allows the park to flow up to the windows of the house (whence it is best seen) across extensive tree-planted lawns. To the rear of the house is a well-stocked herbaceous border and a knot garden. The eighteenth-century walled gardens, now grassed over and planted mainly with roses and herbaceous plants, are entered through a small but attractive rose garden set off by garden urns.

Sleightholme Dale Lodge 25

Fadmoor, Kirbymoorside, North Yorkshire YO62 7JG. Tel: (01751) 431942

Dr and Mrs O. James • 20m NE of Thirsk, 3m N of Kirbymoorside, 1m from Fadmoor off A170 Thirsk – Scarborough road • Open by written appt and a few days for NGS and NHS • Entrance: £2, children 50p ◑ WC ◁▷

This garden occupies a unique position on the side of a wooded valley opening onto the moors. In the spring it is a blaze of blossom, wild daffodils and azaleas, and through the summer the walled garden, which runs steeply up the hill to the north, is breathtaking in the colour and exuberance of the parallel borders. This is described as 'a gardeners' garden' and there are many rare plants to be seen, notably meconopsis. Descending terraces, built at the beginning of the century to the south of the house, have deep shrubberies. The lowest of them is a grass platform separated from the meadow beyond by a ha-ha. A fine series of steps runs down through the terraces.

Stillingfleet Lodge ★   26

Stillingfleet, York YO19 6HP. Tel/Fax: (01904) 728506;
E-mail: Vanessa.cook@still-lodge.freeserve.co.uk;
Website: www.stillingfleetlodgenurseries.co.uk

Mr and Mrs J. Cook • 6m S of York. From A19 York – Selby road take B1222 signed Sherburn in Elmet. In Stillingfleet turn opposite church. Garden at end of lane • Open for Pulmonaria Day on 21st April, 1.30 – 5.30pm; May and June, Wed, Fri; July to Sept, Wed, 1 – 4pm; and 12th May, 23rd June, 1.30 – 5.30pm for NGS • Entrance: £2, children free • Other information: Parking and plants for sale at nursery ◕ WC ♨

An eclectic and most attractive garden has been unfolding here since the owners started developing their windswept plot sloping down to the River Fleet in 1974. Vanessa Cook is a notable plantswoman with an instinctive feeling for both naturalistic and formal planting styles. The wilder areas which include a meadow, a grassy walk dominated by beehives and wild flowers, and a large pool generously fringed with exotic and native species have no quarrel with the magnificently ordered double herbaceous borders, furnished with trees, shrubs and many bulbs for year-long colour interest. Many climbing roses and clematis, and a good use of foliage plants in soft colours, give the garden a romantic feel. A National Collection of pulmonarias is here. The nursery, well stocked with unusual plants, is also well worth a visit. [Open April to mid-Oct, Tues, Wed, Fri, Sat, 10am – 4pm.]

Studley Royal and Fountains Abbey ★★   27

Ripon, North Yorkshire HG4 3DY. Tel: (01765) 608888;
Website: www.fountainsabbey.org.uk

The National Trust • 2m SW of Ripon, 9m N of Harrogate. Follow Fountains Abbey sign off B6265 Ripon – Pateley Bridge road • Deer park open all year during daylight hours. Abbey and garden open all year, daily except 24th, 25th Dec and Fri from Nov to Jan: April to Sept, 10am – 6pm; Oct to March, 10am – 4pm or dusk if earlier (last admission 1 hour before closing). Free guided tours April to Oct, daily • Entrance: Deer park free. Abbey and garden £4.80, children £2.50, family ticket £12. Special rates for pre-booked coach parties • Other information: Parking free at main visitor centre car park but £2 at Studley park (pay-and-display, NT members free). Self-drive powered runarounds available by prior booking ○ ☕ ✕ WC ♿ ⇦ 🏛 ♨ ⚲

The gardens of Studley Royal were created by John Aislabie, who had been Chancellor of the Exchequer but whose finances were 'ruined' by the South Sea Bubble in 1720; he retired here to his estate in 1722 and worked until his death in 1742 to make the finest water garden in the country. The lakes, grotto springs, formal canal and water features, plus buildings such as the Temple of Piety, turn what is essentially a landscape with large trees and sweeping lawns into one of the most stunning of green gardens. The views from Colen Campbell's Banqueting House must also be savoured. Furthermore, there is its intimate and dramatic landscape relationship with Fountains Abbey, the largest and most complete Cistercian foundation in Europe, described by *The Oxford Companion* as probably the noblest monastic ruin in Christendom. This can be seen in the distance from the 'surprise view', through a door in a small building. Restoration of Anne Boleyn's seat, a timber gazebo with a fine view, is now complete. A further £3–4 million is required to continue the programme of restoration, including the repair of river banks, fords and bridges, the restoration of Fountains Hall and Abbey Mill, and an on-going programme of woodland management and tree planting. Tent Hill, a once-lost area of the garden, is also now open. Muniment and archaeological researches have brought to light hidden features of the past, including evidence of a major garden dating from the reign of Charles II.

Sutton Park ★   28

Sutton-in-the-Forest, York YO61 1DP. Tel: (01347) 810249/811239;
Fax: (01347) 811251; E-mail: suttonpark@fsbdial.co.uk;
Website: www.statelyhome.co.uk

Sir Reginald and Lady Sheffield • 8m N of York on B1363 • House open April to Sept, Sun and Wed, also 29th March to 1st April and all Bank Holiday Mons, 1.30 – 5pm. Private parties by appt at other times • Gardens open April to Sept, daily, 11am – 5pm • Entrance: £2.50, children 50p (house and gardens £5, OAPs £4, children £2.50, parties (min. 15) £5.50 per person) (2001 prices) • Other information: Coaches by appt (£4 per person). Specialist plant fair 2nd June ◑ 💻 WC ♿ 👤 ✎

The distinguished English garden designer, Percy Cane, came in 1962 to this Georgian house and its terraced site with views over parkland said to have been moulded by 'Capability' Brown. Cane started the elegant planting which has been most carefully expanded by the present owners. There are several fine features on the terraces – a tall beech hedge curved to take a marble seat, ironwork gazebos, and everywhere soft stone. The woodland walk leads to a temple. A water feature has been created in the old walled garden, and the herb garden and fernery are also recent additions.

Thorp Perrow Arboretum and
The Falcons at Thorp Perrow ★   29

Bedale, North Yorkshire DL8 2PR. Tel: (01677) 425323;
E-mail: louise@thorpperrow.freeserve.co.uk; Website: www.thorpperrow.com

Sir John Ropner, Bt • 10m N of Ripon, 2m S of Bedale, signed off B6268 Masham road • Arboretum open all year, daily, dawn – dusk • Entrance: £5,

OAPs and concessions £3.75, children (4–16) £2.75, family tickets £14 and £18 • Other information: Electric wheelchair available ○ ☕ 🍴 WC ♿ ⬦ 🌱 ♨ 💡 ☕

The arboretum was established many years ago and has one of the finest collections of trees in the north of England, containing over 2000 species. Within the 85 acres is a Victorian pinetum, sixteenth-century woodland and National Collections of ash, limes and walnuts. You can follow the tree trail, the nature trail or simply amble at your own leisure. Thousands of naturalised daffodils and bluebells in spring, glorious wild flowers in summer and stunning autumn colour. There are new plantings and continual improvements in the arboretum. Falconry demonstrations and children's trail.

Valley Gardens ★ 30

Valley Drive, Harrogate, North Yorkshire. Tel: (01423) 500600

Harrogate Borough Council • In centre of Harrogate; main entrance near Pump Room Museum and Mercer Art Gallery • Open all year, daily during daylight hours • Entrance: free ○ ☕ 🍴 WC ♿ ⬦ 💡 ☕

One of the best-known public gardens in the north of England, laid out earlier this century at the time Harrogate was fashionable as a spa. The restored Sun Pavilion is available for events, and there are several sporting and children's activities on offer. The standard of formal bedding remains high, and a fine dahlia border display is an annual feature.

Wytherstone House 31

Pockley, York YO62 7TE. Tel: (01439) 770012; Fax: (01439) 770468

Lady Clarissa Collin • 15m E of Thirsk, 2½ m NE of Helmsley off A170. In Pockley, past church • Open for individuals and parties by appt • Entrance: £2.50 ◐ ☕ 🍴 WC 🌱

A large and expanding plantsman's garden created from a green-field site over the course of 30 years, with a wide range of rare shrubs, perennials and roses. It consists of a series of interlinked compartments, each with its own character. The spring garden has a tapestry of azaleas and rhododendrons and newly installed peat terracing. Next to the spring garden is a rock garden with some rare alpines. A sunken garden of mixed shrubs and herbaceous plants, enclosed by tall beech hedges, leads through to other delights beyond, past a newly planted arboretum and pond to a woodland walk. Back in the conservatory garden, climbing roses smother trees, and fine herbaceous plants and old roses create borders full of interest and colour, along with plants not normally thought to be hardy in the North of England, such as *Melianthus major*, thriving and flowering year after year.

YORKSHIRE (S. & W. AREA)

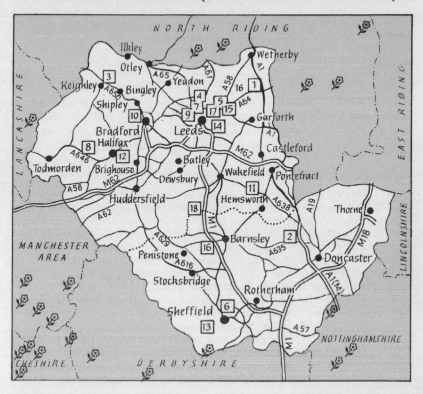

Bramham Park ★ 1

Wetherby LS23 6ND. Tel: (01937) 846000/846002; Fax: (01937) 846001;
Website: www.bramhampark.co.uk

Mr G. Lane Fox • 10m NE of Leeds, 15m SW of York, 5m S of Wetherby just off northbound A1 • House open by written appt only • Garden open April to Sept, daily, 10.30am – 5.30pm (closed for horse trials, please telephone for dates) • Entrance: £4, OAPs/children £2, under 5s free. Reduced rates for parties of 20 or more ◑ 🪑 <u>WC</u> ♿

Created by Robert Benson after the style of Le Nôtre nearly 300 years ago, this is one of the few formal landscape gardens in the French style to survive in this country. Although a great storm early in 1962 caused extensive damage to trees and avenues, the original concept has been maintained and the layout restored. Apart from their unique design, the gardens also have a substantial rose garden providing summer-long colour, and an interesting herbaceous border. However, it is the splendid architectural features (such as the Gothic pavilion) with trees and water, that are outstanding. Mary Keen calls it 'forest gardening' – a genre practised by generations of the owner's family. In 1991 the remains of a massive eighteenth-century cascade were found. Apparently the family of the day had a change of mind, so they carefully grassed it over without ever starting to build a pond at the bottom of the valley.

Brodsworth Hall 2

Brodsworth, Doncaster DN5 7XJ. Tel: (01302) 722598; Fax: (01302) 337165

English Heritage • 5m NW of Doncaster. Access from A1(M) junction 37 off A635 • House and garden open March to 4th Nov, Tues – Sun and Bank Holiday Mon, 12 noon – 6pm (house opens 1pm). Garden also open winter, Sat and Sun, 11am — 4pm; telephone for details • Entrance: summer £2.60, concessions £2, children £1.30; winter £1.60, OAPs £1.20, children 80p (hall and gardens £5, OAPs £3.80, children £2.50) ◑ ☕ ✕ 🍴 WC ♿ 🚻 ♀ ⚲

The 15 acres were designed and planted when the Italianate house was being built in the mid-1860s on a site with many fine established trees. It also featured a long, deep quarry dating from the eighteenth century. Main features in the garden are tamed evergreen shrubberies and a border where trimmed shrubs are underplanted with Japanese anemones, day lilies, aconites, ferns and fuchsias. Beyond, around a marble fountain, an intricate bedding scheme uses the original shapes cut in the lawn. Trees overhanging the old quarry shade a maze of walkways and bridges in fine rockwork; these offer vistas into the recently restored fern dell. This Rocky Fern Dell, cooled by an elegant cascade, is planted with period ferns, shrubs, bulbs, herbaceous perennials and dwarf conifers. It has been re-created thanks to the historic collection built up by the late Wing Commander Baker and donated to Brodsworth in 2000 by his widow. This part of the garden, including the rose garden, is undergoing further restoration and planting. The lawns are rich in natural flora. A collection of the Portland group of roses has been planted here, along with other historic roses, and a large herbaceous border provides a fine backdrop.

East Riddlesden Hall 3

Bradford Road, Keighley, Bradford BD20 5EL. Tel: (01535) 607075; Fax: (01535) 691462

The National Trust • 1m NE of Keighley off B6265, 3m NW of Bingley • House open • Garden open 23rd March to 3rd Nov, Sat, 1 – 5pm; Sun, Tues and Wed, 12 noon – 5pm. Also open Good Friday, Bank Holiday Mons and Mons in July, Aug. Parties must pre-booked • Entrance: £3.60, accompanied children £1.90, family ticket £8.90 ◑ ☕ WC ♿ ◁▷ 🚻 ♀ ⚲

In spring, the garden designed by Graham Stuart Thomas is dotted with primroses, violas and 'Baby Moon' narcissi. A fragrant medicial herb border leads into a small walled garden, which in summer is filled with honeysuckles, roses, lavenders, clematis, herbaceous perennials and mophead acacias. The Orchard Garden, opened in April 2000 (the inspiration of one of the gardeners) has been planted with Yorkshire apple trees; spring bulbs and wild flowers act as a changing carpet of colour from season to season.

Golden Acre Park ★ 4

Otley Road, Leeds. Tel: (0113) 246 3504

Leeds City Council • NW of Leeds off A660 Leeds – Otley road at approach to Bramhope • Open all year, daily, during daylight hours • Entrance: free ○ ➰ WC ⑂ ⟁ ⬚

Until 1945, when it was purchased by Leeds Corporation for £18,500, this was a privately owned pleasure park. Since then it has been developed as an important public park and minor botanic garden. It stands on a pleasant undulating site leading down to a lake, and has an extensive tree collection. Rhododendrons are a feature, together with alpine plants both in the rock garden and the alpine house. The park is noted for its fine collection of sempervivums and heathers. Demonstration plots are maintained where instruction is provided for home gardeners; the quality of planting and vegetables improves annually.

Harewood House ★ 5

Harewood, Leeds LS17 9LQ. Tel: (0113) 218 1010; Fax: (0113) 218 1002; E-mail: business@harewood.org; Website: www.harewood.org

The Earl and Countess of Harewood • 7m N of Leeds on A61 • House open, 11am – 4.30pm • Grounds open 8th March to Oct, daily; Nov to mid-Dec, Sat and Sun, all 10am – 6pm (or dusk if earlier) • Entrance: Terrace Gallery, Bird Garden and grounds £6.25, OAPs £5.25, children £3.50, freedom ticket £8, OAPs £7, children £5; family Harewood Card £60 (2001 prices) • Other information: Art gallery. Regular garden tours and talks programme ◐ ➰ ✕ ⬚ WC ⟁ ⌁ ⬚ ☕ ⚲

Originally laid out in the 1770s by 'Capability' Brown, the gardens and park retain many of his characteristic features, most notably a majestic lake and a well-wooded horizon. Sir Charles Barry's 1840s' terrace contains formal parterres and fountains, herbaceous borders and bedding. The terrace has been restored, the intricate patterns of the parterre have been re-created to Barry's original designs after decades under grass, and the West Garden on the upper terrace was given an elegant new design by the late David Hicks. Nineteenth-century rhododendrons enrich the edge of the lake, other features in this woodland setting are a vaguely Japanese bog garden housing a good collection of hostas below the lake's cascade. Parkland, excellently maintained with trees and shrubs, is being further replanted. Children will enjoy the bird garden and the adventure playgrounds.

Hillsborough Walled Garden 6

Middlewood Road, Sheffield S6 4HD. Tel: (0114) 281 2167

Hillsborough Community Development Trust • Adjacent to Hillsborough Library • Garden open Mon – Fri, 9am – 5pm, weekends by appt, closed Bank Holidays • Entrance: free but donations welcome • Other information: Parking for disabled only ○ ➰ ⬚ WC ⟁ ⌁ ☕ ⚲

The site embraces four different gardens: a wildlife area, a lawn with herbaceous borders, a woodland glade and a formal garden with raised beds for easy use by disabled gardeners. There are many architectural features, and varied gardens including a herb, a vegetable and nursery garden, a Victorian heated garden and a garden for the visually handicapped. Planned, created and run by the community, this is not just an area to look at and enjoy, but everyone is encouraged to help with its upkeep – tools are available on site and plants always welcomed.

The Hollies Park ★ 7

Weetwood Lane, Leeds LS16 5NZ. Tel: (0113) 247 8361
(Parks and Countryside)

Leeds City Council • In NW Leeds, off A660 Leeds – Otley road • Open all year, daily, during daylight hours • Entrance: free ○ 🐌 **WC** ⬦

The original layout is Victorian, and the gardens were given to Leeds Corporation in 1921 by the Brown family in memory of a son killed during World War I. The fine informal, largely woodland garden features woody plants, especially rhododendrons. Ferns flourish throughout the gardens and a varied collection of hydrangeas provides late summer colour. Many slightly tender subjects thrive in the pleasant microclimate. Several National Collections are held here, including those of hemerocallis, hostas and deutzias, and probably the most comprehensive philadelphus collection in Europe.

Land Farm 8

Colden, Hebden Bridge, Calderdale HA7 7PJ. Tel: (01422) 842260

Mr and Mrs J. Williams • 3½ m NE of Todmorden, off A646 between Sowerby Bridge and Todmorden. Call at visitor centre in Hebden Bridge for map • Open May to Aug, Sat, Sun and Bank Holiday Mons, 10am – 5pm. Parties welcome • Entrance: £3 ◐ ✗ **WC** ⬦ 🌿 🏛 🌶

A four-acre garden created by the owners on a north-facing site 300 metres up in the Pennines. Designed as a low-maintenance garden, it nevertheless contains a wide diversity of shrubs, herbaceous plants and alpines. A woodland garden has rhododendrons and cornus underplanted with herbaceous plants. *Tropaeolum speciosum* runs in glorious riot through parts of the garden. There is also an art gallery in the former barn.

30 Latchmere Road 9

Leeds LS16 5DF. Tel: (0113) 275 1261

Mr and Mrs Joe Brown • NW of Leeds off A6120 (ring road to Bradford). Turn up Fillingfir Drive, right at postbox, then left into Latchmere Road • Open for horticultural societies, garden clubs and tourist parties by appt only • Entrance: £2, children 50p • Other information: No parking in Latchmere Road ◕ 🌣 **WC** 🌿

A garden of exceptional merit created from scratch over the last 30 years, and a good example of inspired design on a small scale. Herbaceous plants, ferns, climbers and shrubs all contribute to a series of mini-features through which the visitor passes in a controlled circuit of the garden. These include a clematis collection, sink gardens, pools, a patio and an alpine garden. The different levels and all the paving, retaining walls and steps have been built by the owners from local stone.

Lister Park   10

Keighley Road, Bradford. Tel: (01274) 751535

City of Bradford Metropolitan Council • 1½ m N of Bradford centre (Forster Square) on A650 Bradford – Keighley road • Open all year, daily, during daylight hours • Entrance: free • Other information: Cartwright Hall, City Art Gallery and Museum open all year, daily except Mon ○ 💽 ✕ WC ⭘ ⬀ ⬤ ⚲

A pleasant city park with an old botanical garden which is currently being restored through a Heritage-Lottery-funded grant. There is an attractive formal bedding display in front of the Cartwright Hall and an interesting floral clock: a rare example of Victorian ingenuity. The latest phase of restoration includes a new garden reflecting the simplicity of Mughal design, a symmetrical synthesis of Islamic and Hindu styles, which was completed in summer 2000.

Nostell Priory   11

Doncaster Road, Nostell, Wakefield WF4 1QE. Tel: (01924) 863892

The National Trust • 6m SE of Wakefield on A638 • House open 23rd March to 3rd Nov, Wed – Sun, plus 29th March and Bank Holiday Mons, 1 – 5.30pm • Garden open 2nd to 17th March, 11am – 4pm; 23rd March to 3rd Nov, Wed – Sun, plus 29th March and Bank Holiday Mons; 9th Nov to 15th Dec, Sat and Sun; all 11am – 4.30pm • Entrance: £2.50, children £1.20 (house and garden £4.50, children £2.20, family £11) • Other information: Batricar available. Special events and fairs (separate charge) ◑ 💽 🛍 WC ⭘ ⬛ ⬤ ⚲

The dark, brooding eighteenth-century mansion by Robert Adam sits in open parkland with an attractive lake and a variety of well-established trees. A fine rose garden is the main gardening feature, together with extensive lakeside gardens planted with magnolias and rhododendrons, a summerhouse, a Gothick archway and a cock-fighting pit. One of the most attractive Gothick buildings, with later additions by Robert Adam, has been restored.

People's Park   12

Hopwood Lane, Halifax. Tel: (01422) 359454;
Website: www.calderdale.gov.uk/fttourism/parks/peoples/html

Metropolitan Borough of Calderdale • Open daily, dawn – dusk • Entrance: free ○ 🛍 WC ⭘ ⬀ ⬤ ⚲

A gift by Francis Crossley to the town, this is a good example of a Victorian park. Designed by Joseph Paxton, it was opened on 14th August 1857, and in

1874 a bandstand was added. Queen Victoria presented two swans to the park in 1861. The pavilion was designed by Stokes and has a statue of Crossley by Joseph Durham. The statues on the terrace are by Francesco Bienaime. Restoration of the park, including the water features and the pavilion, and new landscaping, is now almost complete, and the atmosphere is being rejuvenated with a varied events programme and community involvement.

Sheffield Botanical Gardens 13

Sheffield S10 2LN. Tel/Fax: (0114) 267 6496; E-mail: pwc.scc@virgin.net; Website: www.sbg.org.uk

Sheffield Council • ½ m from A625, 1½ m SW of city centre • Open all year, daily except 25th Dec, 10am – dusk • Entrance: free ○ ⬤ ✕ 🍽 WC ♿ 🌱 ♨ 🔦 ☕

These historic gardens (opened in 1836) are popular with visitors for the peace and seclusion of 19 sheltered acres so close to the city centre. Facilities have been improved by the conversion of the erstwhile curator's house into a tearoom/restaurant. This is just one of many proposals to be supported by a Heritage Lottery Fund award of £5.6m, with a further £1.25m being raised by the Friends of the Botanical Gardens and the Botanical Gardens Trust. The jewels in the crown – the impressive glass pavilions – are now being refurbished. These are linked by unusual glass corridors, which will be reinstated; the 90-metre linear glasshouse displaying temperate plant collections from around the world will open in the summer of 2002. The project continues until 2004, and other work-in-progress includes the restoration of the unique bear pit, the Pan statue and the fossil tree, and the extension of existing plant collections.

Temple Newsam Park 14

Leeds LS15 0AE. Tel: (0113) 264 5535

Leeds City Council • 3m E of Leeds, signed off A63/A6120 ring road junction • House open daily except Mon, 10.30am – 6.15pm (house closed for refurbishment during 2002) • Park open all year, daily, 9am – dusk; National Collections open Mon – Fri, 11am – 3pm, Sat and Sun, 11am – 2pm • Entrance: free ○ ⬤ WC ♿ 🌱

A pleasant oasis surrounded by urban Leeds. Set in the remnants of a 'Capability' Brown landscape of the 1760s (much reduced by a golf course and open-cast mining) is a wide diversity of gardens. Around the house are an Italian paved garden and a Jacobean-style parterre surrounded by pleached lime walks. A rhododendron and azalea walk leads to small ponds with a bog garden and arboretum, beyond which is a large walled rose garden and greenhouses containing collections of ivies, cacti and some rather dashing climbing pelargoniums. National Collections of delphiniums, phlox and asters are held here. Also within the large walled garden are traditional herbaceous borders considered to be amongst the best in England.

Tropical World ★ 15

Roundhay Park, Roundhay, Leeds LS8 2ER. Tel: (0113) 266 1850; Fax: (0113) 237 0077; Website: www.leeds.gov.uk

Leeds City Council • S of A6120 northern ring, off A58 Roundhay Road from city centre • Open all year, daily, except 25th Dec, 10am – dusk • Entrance: £2, children (8–15) £1, under 8s free, Leeds card holders free (2001 prices) • Other information: Dogs in park only, on lead ○ 🍽 ✕ 🛍 <u>WC</u> ♿ 🏛 🍴 ♋

The intensively cultivated canal gardens area was formerly the kitchen and ornamental gardens of the Nicholson family, who sold the site to the Leeds Corporation in 1871. The extensive parkland with its fine trees is an extravagant setting for the pure horticultural extravaganza of the canal gardens with their formal bedding and generous collections. The exotic houses have the largest collection outside Kew, with exotic butterflies and birds. Waterfalls and pools are surrounded by tropical plants, and the arid house holds a large collection of cacti and succulents. There is an underwater world of plants and fish, an insect house and a nocturnal house where bush babies, monkeys and other animals can be seen. A day out for all the family.

Wentworth Castle Gardens ★ 16

Lowe Lane, Stainborough, Barnsley S75 3ET. Tel: (01226) 731269

Barnsley Metropolitan Borough Council • 3m SW of Barnsley off M1 junction 37, 2m along minor roads signed 'Oxspring, Gilroyd and Northern College' • Gardens open, mainly for guided tours, mid-April to June, Tues – Thurs and selected Suns; Thurs, July and Aug, selected dates in Oct. Telephone for details ● WC ᐧ🐾

One of the most exciting gardens in Yorkshire, laid out mainly under the direction of William Wentworth between 1739 and 1791, which is currently undergoing a complete review of its activities. As we go to press, the anticipated award of a Heritage Lottery Fund grant which would shape the restoration of the pleasure gardens, parkland and walled garden has still not been made. Barnsley Council's development package is in conjunction with the Northern College (which owns and occupies the house). The castle holds National Collections of species magnolias and species rhododendrons; there are also extensive new plantings of camellias, especially the *C.* x *williamsii* hybrids, which also have National Collection status. The eighteenth-century landscape has been designated Grade I by English Heritage. Among the many features are a three-quarter-mile-long serpentine lake, monuments to Queen Anne and Lady Mary Wortley Montagu, and the stunning Gothick folly of Stainborough Castle, constructed on the highest point of the estate, which forms a fitting dramatic climax to the gardens. Noise from the M1 in the valley is the only intrusion.

York Gate ★   17

**Back Church Lane, Adel, Leeds LS16 8DW. Tel: (0113) 267 8240;
Website: www.gardeners-grbs.org.uk**

*The Gardeners' Royal Benevolent Society • Off A660 Leeds – Otley road, behind
Adel Church • Open May to Aug, Thurs, Sun, 2 – 5pm (and at other times –
telephone or visit website for details) • Entrance: £3, children free • Other
information: Coaches by appt only* ◐ **WC**

A garden created by the Spencer family and bequeathed by the late Sybil
Spencer to the Gardeners' Royal Benevolent Society. Bought by the Spencers
in 1951, this was a bleak farmhouse and unpromising area of land. When her
husband died, her son took over the design and in a tragically short life he
achieved a garden of rare delight, using local stone, cobble stones and gravel to
create a structure of impeccable taste and style and great horticultural
interest. As to the design, the late Arthur Hellyer remarked on its debt to
Hidcote, but noted that many of the ideas used there in 10 acres are here
confined to barely one. He also commented on the clever use of architectural
features and topiary. 'This is a garden made for discovery,' he said, as 'from no
vantage point is it possible to see the whole... Nor is any route of exploration
specially indicated.' It is also a plantsperson's garden, maintaining a quality
collection arranged in clearly defined model features. These include an extraordinary miniature pinetum, fern and peony borders, and an exquisite
silver and white border, now showing a hint of pink.

Yorkshire Sculpture Park   18

**Bretton Hall, West Bretton, Wakefield WF4 4LG. Tel: (01924) 830302;
Fax: (01924) 830044; E-mail: office@ysp.co.uk**

*Yorkshire Sculpture Park, Independent Charitable Trust • 6m NW of Barnsley,
6m SW of Wakefield at West Bretton. Leave M1 at junction 38 • Open all year,
daily, except 24th, 25th, 31st Dec: summer, 10am – 6pm, winter, 10am – 4pm
• Entrance: free but donation welcomed. Parking £1.50 per car • Other
information: Coaches by prior arrangement. Access Sculpture Trail suitable for
wheelchairs. Information Centre, caf and two indoor galleries* ○ ▆ ✗ ▆ **WC**
♿ ⬦ ⬚ ⬚ ⬚

Britain's first permanent sculpture park was established in 1977, and is now
considered to be one of Europe's leading open-air galleries. The Palladian-style
house and its 500 acres of formal gardens, woods, lakes and parkland provide a
fine setting for temporary and permanent exhibitions. The layout makes it
possible to view sculpture in garden as well as 'public' settings that demand a
more monumental approach by the sculptor. The park hosts temporary
exhibitions by sculptors from many parts of the world, as well as rotating
its own permanent collection to other site.

IRELAND

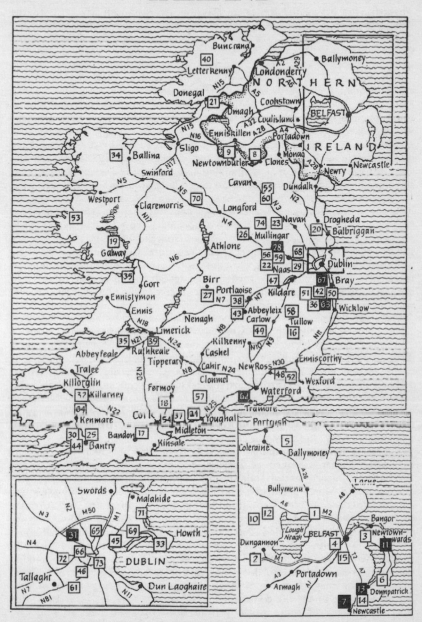

Two-starred gardens are marked on the map with a black square.

A Renaissance for Irish Gardens

Anybody who has visited Ireland in the last ten years will have noticed the enormous increase of interest in plants and gardens, garden visiting and garden-based events. Garden tourism has become an important part of the flow of visitors visitor flow between April and October. For those who come from Britain there is the added bonus of a wide range of plants readily available for sale.

This increase in the popularity of gardening is also reflected in the ever-rising membership of gardening clubs and societies, notably the Irish Garden Plant Society. To match this growth in interest, there has been an explosion in the number of new garden centres throughout the country (currently over 430 outlets to service a smallish population – and still rising). Plant sales have rocketed to such an extent that exports of plants to the British market have diminished in order to keep the home market supplied. Rarer are the specialist nurseries, but that is changing also, and there are some very good small producers now opening for retail sales – long overdue and very welcome.

Of course, the Irish climate is temperate, wet and windy, but the range and diversity of the plant population of Irish gardens can be quite astonishing to the first-time visitor. Many gardens boast extraordinary growth rates, so fine specimens of exotic trees and shrubs are to be found from the colder north to the sultry gardens of the south coast. The gardens of Waterford, Cork and Kerry are justly renowned for their collections. For those who love the challenge of champion trees there are many to see in gardens throughout the country; a survey is in progress. Deciduous trees and conifers alike thrive in the humidity and protection of gardens like Kilmacurragh, Mount Usher, Annes Grove and Fota.

Many people consider Mount Stewart to be one of the finest gardens anywhere in these islands, while Castlewellan's wonderful arboretum is a joy to visit, boasting many rarities both tender and tough. Killruddery in Wicklow, a distinguished seventeenth-century landscape inspired by André Le Nôtre, is hardly known, while its neighbour, Powerscourt, is probably the most visited and best-known of all. Its formal gardens and mature arboretum in the splendid setting of the Wicklow hills, though sullied now by the conversion of its great house ruin into a modern shopping mall complete with escalator, still manage to offer Victorian splendour to garden visitors. Many small private gardens are open occasionally, and they too are much visited.

A driving force in contemporary Irish gardening has been the recently completed Great Gardens of Ireland Restoration Programme, initiated through the Department of Tourism in Dublin and administered by the Irish Tourist Board, which prompted over 1500 garden owners to apply for grant aid. An expert committee then sifted through these applications, and a process of detailed evaluation resulted in some of the most important historic landscapes and gardens receiving financial help. The programme provided some IR£4m of European Regional Development Fund monies, matched 50/50 by garden owners, and the result has been a large pool of money for much-needed works in great gardens and demesnes throughout the Republic of Ireland. Thanks to the imaginative use of these EU funds, and the huge imput of local people working under the community employment schemes associated with the grant, many of these gardens have been brought back to life. The programme has been very successful, raising awareness of these beautiful places, generating employment, re-instating the head gardener/garden manager system employing professional horticulturists. It has resulted in conservation and restoration works in 26 gardens, at a cost totalling some IR£12-15m.

Many newly enhanced gardens are now open, such as Ballindoolin House, Ballinlough Castle, Enniscoe House, Kylemore Abbey, Larchill, Loughcrew House, Marlay Park and Strokestown Park. Others like Belvedere House, which had floundered for years as forgotten gardens and needed major reappraisal and help, received it through the Great Gardens scheme.

Other historic gardens helped by the scheme were already open and well known but over the years had slipped into varying degrees of tiredness, dilapidation, decay or ruin. Their owners, hard-pressed to keep them up to scratch, responded enthusiastically to the invitation to apply for funding. Wonderful places like the Talbot Botanical Garden within Malahide Castle's demesne, Creagh's romantic waterside garden in west Cork (now closed and sold on), Birr Castle's demesne and formal Edwardian garden, Bantry House's terraced Italianate gardens in their spectacular natural setting, have had their faces washed and their curves smartened, while the fine bones of others have been fleshed out with new plantings. All have begun to smile happily again.

NORTHERN IRELAND

The National Trust Ulster Gardens Scheme runs private gardens openings on special days and by appointment. For a list of gardens opening in 2002 telephone (02897) 510721.

Antrim Castle Gardens   1

Randalstown Road, Co. Antrim BT41 4LH. Tel: (028) 9442 8000;
Fax (028) 9446 0360; E-mail: clotworthy@antrim.gov.uk;
Website: www.antrim.gov.uk

Antrim Borough Council Arts and Heritage Service • Access from A6 Randalstown Road • Grounds open all year, daily, 9.30am – dusk. Guided tours for parties at any time by arrangement • Entrance: Individuals free. Small groups £2, concessions £1; groups of 40 or more £1 per person; school parties 50p per child • Other information: Refreshments by arrangement for groups. Interpretative display in Clotworthy Arts Centre ○ 🍴 **WC** ♿ 🔦

A rare example of a demesne where the main elements survive as laid out for a late-seventeenth-century castle (now demolished). The canals, connected by a cascade, are lined with clipped lime and hornbeam hedges. Paths crisscross through the wooded wilderness, the main avenue of which leads to an airy clearing with a round pond reflecting sky and trees. Following a restoration project, a large parterre has been planted with varieties known in the seventeenth century and is set off by a quincunx grove of standard hornbeam (new) and an immense yew hedge (old). The adjacent Anglo-Norman motte retains its spiral path; access can be gained by collecting a key from the arts centre (£5 refundable deposit), and it is worth a climb to the top to see the lower course of the Sixmilewater river, the centre of the town of Antrim, and the 37-acre ornamental site below – a fraction of a once-vast estate stretching as far as the eye could see.

The Argory   2

Moy, Dungannon, Co. Tyrone BT71 6NA. Tel: (028) 8778 4753; Fax: (028) 8778 9598

The National Trust • 4m NE of Moy, 3m from M1 junction 14 • House open • Grounds and garden open all year, daily: Oct to April 2003, 10am – 4pm, May to Sept, 10am – 8pm • Entrance: £4, children £2 (includes guided tour of house). Parking charge £2 • Other information: Coaches must use M1 junction 13 because of weight restrictions. Parking 100 metres from house ◐ ▆ ▩ WC ⬦ ⬦ ⬦ ⬦ ⬦

The lawns of the pleasure ground slope down past yew arbours to two pavilions, one a pump house, the other a garden house. Beyond, the visitor can walk under pollarded limes along the banks of the Blackwater River, and there are other woodland walks in this tranquil landscape. A splash of summer colour near the house attracts the eye to a pretty, enclosed early-nineteenth-century sundial garden of box-edged rose beds. There is a new riverside walk of 1½ miles.

Ballywalter Park   3

Ballywalter Nr Newtownards, Co. Down BT22 2PAN. Tel: (028) 4275 8264; Fax: (028) 4275 8818; E-mail: bd@dunleath-estates.co.uk

Dunleath Estates • 20m E of Belfast, 10m SE of Newtownards off B5 between Greyabbey and Ballywalter. Turn right at T-junction facing gates and follow wall to entrance on left opposite farm • Open by appt only. Please telephone Mon – Fri between 9am and 1pm • Entrance: house or garden £4 each (house and garden £7) • Other information: PYO in season ◑

The fine mid-nineteenth-century Italianate house by the architect Lanyon, with an elegant conservatory wing, was praised by Sir John Betjeman. The surrounding grounds are an amalgam of two earlier 'landscaped' demesnes, embellished for the present house with a rock garden around a stream with bridges, also by Lanyon. The notable rhododendron collection is sheltered by mature trees throughout the park. A rose pergola and restored glasshouse decorate the walled garden.

Belfast Botanic Gardens Park   4

Stranmillis Road, Belfast City BT9 5BJ. Tel/Fax: (028) 9032 4902

Belfast City Council Parks Department • Between Queen's University and Ulster Museum, Stranmillis. Buses 69, 84 and 85 • Open all year, daily, 7.30am – dusk. Palm House and Tropical Ravine, summer, weekdays, 10am – 5pm, weekends and public holidays, 2 – 5pm (closes 4pm in winter). Guided tours and parties at any time by arrangement • Entrance: free. Guided tours £10 • Other information: Refreshments in Ulster Museum ○ ▩ WC ⬦ ▇

Established in 1828, this became a public park in 1895. As well as two magnificent double herbaceous borders and a rose garden with 8000 roses, there are two other reasons to visit this otherwise unexceptional park – the curvilinear iron and glass conservatory (1839–52), and one of the finest Victorian glasshouses (Richard Turner built only the wings; the dome is by Young of Edinburgh, restored in the 1970s). It contains a finely displayed collection of tropical plants, while massed pot plants are changed throughout the seasons in a cooler wing. The restored Tropical Ravine House is the greater delight, a perfect piece of 'High Victoriana' with ferns, bananas, lush tropical vines and tree ferns, goldfish in the Amazon lily pond, and a waterfall worked with a chain-pull. Marvellous, evocative of crinoline days.

Benvarden 5

Ballybogey, Ballymoney, Co. Antrim BT53 6NN. Tel: (028) 2074 1331; Fax (028) 2074 1955

Mr and Mrs Hugh Montgomery • 4m E of Coleraine off B67. Signposted • Open June to Aug, Tues – Sun and Bank Holiday Mons, 1.30 – 5.30pm, and at other times by appt • Entrance: £2.50 ◑ ➽ WC ⅋ ⌗ ⌀

The walled garden has a curved and brick-faced three-metre high wall, lined with old espalier-trained apple and pear trees and focused on a round goldfish pond and fountain. Vertical interest is achieved by climbers scrambling over former glasshouse frames, beneath which seats are provided. The adjoining one-acre traditional kitchen garden is in full production and contains melon and tomato houses, potting sheds and gardener's bothy, fruit trees and box hedges. The eighteenth-century house is set in lawns where the visitor can wander along the banks of the Bush River, which is spanned at this point by an elegant Victorian iron bridge, 36 metres long, leading to a pond surrounded by yews, rhododendrons and azaleas.

Castle Ward 6

Strangford, Downpatrick, Co. Down BT30 7LS. Tel: (028) 4488 1204; Fax: (028) 4488 1729; E-mail: ucwest@smtp.ntrust.org.uk

The National Trust • 7m NE of Downpatrick, 1½ m W of Strangford on A25, on S shore of Strangford Lough. Entrance by Ballyculter Lodge • House open – telephone for details • Estate, gardens and grounds open Oct to April, daily, 11am – 4pm, May to Sept, 10am – 8pm • Entrance: Parking charge £3 (£1 when house and other facilities closed) ○ ➽ ✕ ▨ WC ⅋ ⬦ ⬛ ⬤

Beautifully situated on a peninsula near the mouth of Strangford Lough, the landscape park enhances the 1760s' house with its classical west front and Gothick east front. Both house and decorative Lady Anne's Temple command the heights; below lie an impressive canal and yew walks, features retained from the gardens of a previous early-eighteenth-century house. The sunken Windsor Garden has lost much of its intricate bedding but there are colourful borders containing an interesting range of plants, some quite rare, leading to the rockery and a sentinel row of cordylines and Florence Court yews.

Castlewellan National Arboretum ★★   7

Castlewellan, Co. Down BT31 9BU. Tel: (028) 4477 8664; Fax (028) 4477 1762

Forest Service, Dept of Agriculture (Northern Ireland) • 25m S of Belfast, 4m NW of Newcastle, in Castlewellan • Open all year, daily • Entrance: cars £3.80, minibuses £10, coaches £25 (2001 prices) • Other information: Disabled parking. Refreshments in summer only. Caravan and camping ground in park
○ 🛍 WC & ⬧ ♻

The walled garden, now called the Annesley Garden, contains an outstanding collection of mature trees and shrubs, many planted before in the late nineteenth century by the Earl Annesley. Original specimens of some of Castlewellan's cultivars thrive here, in fine condition. In the spring and summer there are many rhododendrons in bloom, and scarlet Chilean fire bushes (*Embothrium coccineum*). In mid-summer, the snow-carpet consists of the fallen petals of an unequalled collection of eucryphias. In all, there are 34 champion specimen trees in one area of just nine acres: *Cupressus macrocarpa* 'Lutea', *Dacrycarpus dacrydioides* (syn. *Podocarpus dacrydioides*), *Dacrydium colensoi*, *Juniperus recurva* and *Picea breweriana*. The garden has 15 southern-hemisphere broad-leaved champions, including *Pittosporum tenuifolium*, *Crinodendron hookerianum*, *Eucryphia cordifolia*. Half of these specimens are also thought to be the oldest examples in cultivation. Apart from the trees there are rhododendrons, bulbs, herbaceous borders, a fragrant garden, a small glasshouse display range with canaries, as well as topiary of Irish yew and, in summer, an impressive show of tropaeolum. The 12-acre walled garden has a formal axis, with an herbaceous border and two restored fountain pools with water lilies. Beyond the walls the arboretum extends for a further 85 acres in the Forest Park, planted with heathers, dwarf conifers and birch, and flowering trees (malus, prunus, etc.). Signposted walks lead into the forest and round the magnificent lake within the Forest Park. A major new piece of landscaping, the largest and longest hedge maze in the world, represents the path to peace in Northern Ireland. Castlewellan is well known for the golden Leyland cypress that came from here – don't be dismayed, the arboretum contains many more wonderful plants, some unique, all in their prime. You will not see decrepit trees here – the maintenance and labelling are exceptionally good. Red squirrels all year. A programme of restorative regeneration is under way, including the reinstatement of the 'lost vista' of the Mourne Mountains from the viewing terrace.

Crom Estate   8

Newtownbutler, Fermanagh BT92 8AP. Tel: (028) 6773 8174; (028) 6773 8118 (Visitor Centre); E–mail: ucromw@smtp.ntrust.org.uk

The National Trust • 3m W of Newtownbutler on Crom road, signed from Lisnaskea and Newtownbutler • Estate open 17th March to Sept, daily, 10am – 6pm (but Suns opens 12 noon, July and Aug closes 8pm) • Entrance: £3 parking charge for cars and boats • Other information: Batricar available. Visitor Centre with jetty to allow cruiser access. Boat hire available. Castle not owned by Trust – please respect areas marked 'Private' ◐ 🍴 🛍 WC & ⬧ 🏛 ♻ ✎

Although no formal gardens remain, many lovely walks can be enjoyed at this heavily wooded lough shore and island demesne, including a beautiful rhododendron walk in the American Garden, which also has fine specimens of azaleas and magnolias, at their peak in April and May. The autumn colours are spectacular, and a pair of ancient and venerable yew trees must be visited. The aim is to keep up the estate as a nature conservation site. Cross the White Bridge to Inisherk Island and survey the naturally picturesque landscape enhanced by W.S. Gilpin in the 1830s for the present house. The many interesting estate buildings, such as the boat house, the tea house and the island folly, Crichton Tower, are used as eye-catchers and surprises, and the local church and ruins of the seventeenth-century Old Castle are incorporated into the vistas.

Florence Court 9

Florencecourt, Enniskillen, Co. Fermanagh BT92 1DB. Tel: (028) 6634 8249; Fax (028) 6634 8873

The National Trust • 8m SW of Enniskillen, via A4 Sligo road and A32 Swanlinbar road, 4m from Marble Arch Caves • House open April, May and Sept, Sat, Sun and Bank Holiday Mons; June to Aug, daily except Tues; all 1 – 6pm • Estate open all year, daily, Oct to April, 10am – 4pm, May to Sept, 10am – 8pm. Closed 25th Dec • Entrance: Forest Park and Pleasure Gardens £2.50 per car (house £3.50, children £1.75, family ticket £8.50, parties £3 per person) • Other information: Batricar available ○ ◑ ✕ 🖼 WC ♿ ⇔ 🎁 🌂 ♋

The original, the mother of all Irish yews (*Taxus baccata* 'Fastigiata'), still grows in the original garden site – accessible by well-marked woodland paths and about a quarter of a mile from the splendid mansion at Florence Court, although strong shoes are essential (especially in rainy season) if you wish to pay your respects to the venerable 250-year-old tree. Well worth the walk, the gravel path allows glimpses of the mountains and the handsome 'Brownian' park in front of the house. Some fine weeping beeches, Japanese maples and old rhododendrons grow in the pleasure grounds. Other features include an icehouse, a water-driven saw mill and a restored summerhouse, an eel bridge and a hydraulic ram. The three-acre walled garden, including the listed Rose Cottage and Gate Lodges, has recently been acquired by the Trust. The nearby caves are worth visiting too, making a rewarding day out.

28 Killyfaddy Road 10

Magherafelt, Co. Londonderry BT45 6EX. Tel: (028) 7963 2180

Ann Buchanan • 10m NE of Cookstown off A31. From Magherafelt, take Moneymore road. After ¼ m Killyfaddy Road is second on left opposite filling station. Gardens 1m further along, both sides of road • Open all year, Tues – Sat, 1 – 5pm, and by appt • Entrance: donation to charity ◑ 🖼 WC 🌿 ♋

An acre of informal country garden created over nearly three decades, densely planted with an extensive range of herbaceous perennials plus trees, shrubs, alpines, fruit, vegetables and a small orchard. The 'wild' garden in a separate site across the road has woodland and shade areas and a wildlife pond with associated bog plants.

Mount Stewart ★★ 11

Greyabbey, Newtownards, Co. Down BT22 2AD. Tel: (02842) 788387/788487;
Fax: (02842) 788569; E-mail: umsest@smtp.ntrust.org.uk

*The National Trust • 15m E of Belfast, 5m SE of Newtownards on A20 Portaferry
road • House open different times – telephone for details • Lakeside gardens and
walk open Oct to April, 10am – 4pm, May to Sept, 10am – 8pm. Formal garden
open 16th to 18th, 23rd, 24th, 29th to 31st March; then April to Sept, daily; Oct to
March, Sat and Sun; all 11am – 5pm • Entrance: £3.75, children £2, family
£8.50, parties £3.50 per person • Other information: Parking 300 metres away.
Two pre-bookable battery wheelchairs available* ◑ ➌ ✕ ▦ WC ♿ ⬃ ⬚ ♟

Of all Ireland's gardens this is the one not to miss. Any adjective that evokes
beauty can be applied to it, and it's fun too. In the gardens fronting of the
eighteenth- and nineteenth-century house is a collection of statuary depicting
British political and public figures as dodos, monkeys and boars. The planting
here is formal, with rectangular beds of hot and cool colours. Beyond in the
informal gardens are mature trees and shrubs – a botanical collection with few
equals, planted with great panache and maintained with outstanding attention
to detail. Spires of giant lilies (cardiocrinums), aspiring eucalyptus, banks of
rhododendrons, ferns and blue poppies, rivers of candelabra primulas, and much
more. Walk along the lakeside path to the hill that affords a view over the lake to
the house. Rare tender shrubs such as *Metrosideros umbellatus* flourish here outside
the walled family cemetery. Leading from it is the Jubilee Avenue and its statue of
a white stag. Mount Stewart should be seen several times during the year truly to
savour its rich tapestry of plants and water, buildings and trees. The Temple of
the Winds, James 'Athenian' Stuart's banqueting hall of 1782–5, is memorable.

Moyola Park 12

Castledawson, Magherafelt, Co. Londonderry BT45 8ED. Tel: (028) 7946 8606

*Lord Moyola • 3m NE of Magherafelt, 3m W from NW shore of Loch Neagh, in
Castledawson. Main entrance in Bridge Street • Open certain days in May or
June by appt for groups and societies • Entrance: £2 per person* ◕ WC ♿

The imposing mid-eighteenth-century house surrounded by lawns sits above
the Moyola River; behind is a succession of beautifully planted woodland
compartments merging above and beside its banks, enhanced by tall old trees.
Planting is interesting throughout the seasons, beginning with swathes of
daffodils, followed by camellias and rhododendrons, then giving way to the
paler shades of old roses, meconopsis and primulas. Numerous specimen trees
and shrubs planted since the 1960s serve as a backdrop within the glades.

Rowallane Garden ★★ 13

Saintfield, Ballynahinch, Co. Down BT24 7LH. Tel: (028) 9751 0131;
Fax (028) 9751 1242

*The National Trust • ½ m S of Saintfield on A7 Belfast – Downpatrick road •
Open April to Oct, Mon – Fri, 10.30am – 6pm, Sat and Sun, 12 noon – 6pm;*

Nov to March 2003, Mon – Fri, 10.30am – 5pm. Closed 24th Dec to 1st Jan •
Entrance: £3, children £1.25, family ticket £7, parties £2 per person ○ 🍵 📷
WC ♿ ⬦ 🌱

While famous as a 52-acre rhododendron garden and certainly excellent in this regard, Rowallane has much more to interest keen gardeners. In summer, the walled garden blossoms in lemon and blue, while hoherias scatter their white petals in the wind and in secluded places a pocket-handkerchief tree blows. There is a restored Victorian bandstand (music-filled on some summer weekends) and a rock garden with primulas, meconopsis, heathers, etc. Any season will be interesting, and for the real enthusiast there are rhododendron species and cultivars in bloom from October to August. A National Collection of large-flowered penstemons is here. A feature is made of *Hypericum* 'Rowallane' at the entrance to the walled garden; within are the original plant of *Viburnum plicatum* 'Rowallane' and the original *Chaenomeles* x *superba* 'Rowallane'. The wildflower meadows are becoming famed for such comparative rarities as wild orchids, and as the garden is almost organic in cultivation, wildlife abounds.

Seaforde   14

Downpatrick, Co. Down BT30 8PG. Tel: (028) 4481 1225;
Fax: (028) 4481 1370; Website: www.seafordegardens.com

Mr Patrick and Lady Anthea Forde • 22m S of Belfast on A24 Belfast –
Newcastle road • Garden open all year except 25th Dec to 1st Jan, Mon – Sat,
10am – 5pm, Sun, 1 – 6pm (Nov to Feb, Mon – Fri only) • Entrance: £2.50,
children £1.50 ○ 🍵 ✕ 📷 WC ♿ 🌱 🛍 ℗

The fine landscaped park can be glimpsed on the way to the vast walled garden, half of which is a commercial nursery with the attraction of a butterfly house displaying a collection of tropical plants. The other half is an ornamental garden bedecked in late summer with blooms of eucryphia that make up a National Collection. The hornbeam maze has a rose-clad arbour at the centre, the vantage point for which is a 1992 Mogul tower. Beyond the walled garden is the Pheasantry, a verdant valley enclosed by mature trees, full of note-worthy plants collected over many years and still expanding.

Sir Thomas and Lady Dixon Park   15

Upper Malone Road, Belfast. Tel: (028) 906 11506 / 903 20802

Belfast Park Department • S of Belfast city centre, on Upper Malone Road •
Open all year, daily (walled garden, 8am – sunset) • Entrance: free ○ 🍵 WC
♿ ⬦ ℗

This 128-acre park, presented to the City of Belfast in 1959, is part of a demesne established in the eighteenth century. The main feature today is the International Rose Trial area, where some 20,000 rose bushes can been seen in carefully labelled beds following the contours of the park. One display has old varieties demonstrating the history of the rose. In 2000 the park was awarded a Plaque of Merit from the World Federation of Rose Societies. Elsewhere there are riverside meadows by the River Lagan, a walled garden, international camellia trials and a Japanese garden constructed in 1990. A secluded children's playground and band performances during the summer make it enjoyable for all the family.

THE REPUBLIC OF IRELAND

The year 2002 will see the Euro become the only currency in the Republic. We have therefore translated the entrance charges to the gardens into Euros which we have rounded up or down – for example IR£2 has been rounded down to a clean E2.50 rather than being quoted as E2.54 (its exact conversion rate at the time of our going to press) and IR£1.50 has been rounded up to E2 from its true equivalent of E1.90. Individual owners will obviously make their own decisions about whether to round up or down or to charge precise decimal points of Euros. So our entrance charges are guidance not gospel.

Altamont   16

Tullow, Co. Carlow. Tel: (503) 59128

Duchas – the Heritage Service • 19km SE of Carlow, 8km S of Tullow, off Tullow-Bunclody road (N80/81) near Ballon • Telephone for opening times and details • Entrance: E2.50, OAPs E2, students E1.50, children E1.50, family E6.50, groups E2 per person • Other information: Garden centre. Coaches welcome ◗ WC ⑆ ⌖

The lily-filled lake, surrounded by fine, mature trees, forms a backdrop for a gently sloping lawn. A central walkway formally planted with Irish yews and roses leads from the house to the lake. There is a beautiful fern-leaved beech, and other ancient beeches form the Nun's Walk. A long walk through the demesne leads to the River Slaney with diversions to a bog garden, through an Ice-Age glen of ancient oaks undercarpeted with bluebells. The late owner Mrs North's passion for trees, old-fashioned roses and unusual plants is evident. Hopefully the garden will be kept in the spirit she intended. A flower border in her memory was planted two years ago.

Amergen   17

Walshestown, Ovens, Co. Cork. Tel: (21) 7331326

Mrs Christine Fehily • Take N22 Cork – Killarney road, 9km W of Cork, turn right at Dan Sheahan's pub, follow road to crossroads, turn right into cul-de-sac for about 1.5km. Garden on right • Open for parties by appt • Entrance: E4.50 ◗ ▦ WC ⑆ ⌖

A plantsman's garden in a beautiful setting overlooking the valley of the River Lee. Behind the house is a modest arboretum that merges into mixed borders interspersed with informal lawns. The driveway divides the main garden from a slope thickly planted with shrubs and trees. Paths meander through this area, where lush *Geranium maderense* and handsome dogwoods vividly demonstrate the mildness of the Cork climate. Many tender plants can be grown outdoors, including *Melianthus major, Acacia melanoxylon* and correa, so interesting and unusual shrubs and perennials − *Viburnum harryanum, Mimulus aurantiacus* − abound. The garden, started only in the early '80s, is an object lesson in informality and variety.

Annes Grove 18

Castletownroche, Near Mallow, Co. Cork. Tel/Fax: (22) 26145

Mr and Mrs F.P. Grove Annesley • 2.5km N of Castletownroche, between Fermoy and Mallow • Open 17th March to Sept, Mon − Sat, 10am − 5pm, Sun, 1 − 6pm, and at other times by appt • Entrance: E4, OAPs and students E2.50, children E1.50. Reductions for pre-booked parties ◑ ▣ WC ♿ ⬦ ♟ ♐

This is an archetypal 'Robinsonian' (alias wild) garden. Rhododendron species and cultivars arch over and spill towards the pathways, carpeting them with fallen blossoms. Steep, sometimes slippery paths descend at various places into the valley of the Awbeg river (which inspired Edmund Spenser). The statuesque conifers planted in the valley make a colourful tapestry behind the river garden, with mimulus, day lilies and candelabra primroses in profusion. The glory of Annes Grove is, however, the collection of rhododendron species, many of them introduced through subscription to Kingdon Ward expeditions. Visitors may spot hidden surprises − a superb *Juniperus recurva* 'Castlewellan', a mature pocket-handkerchief tree (*Davidia involucrata*) and other exotic flowering trees.

Ardcarraig ★ 19

Oranswell, Bushypark, Co. Galway. Tel: (91) 524336

Mrs Lorna MacMahon • From Galway − Oughterard road, take second left past Glenlo Abbey Hotel; garden is on left • Open 22nd May, 10am − 9pm, and by appt • Entrance: E4, parties of 15 or more E3.50 per person • Other information: Refreshments and plants for sale on open day only ◕ WC

In front of the house is a collage of heathers and conifers, with spring and autumn-flowering bulbs; ordinary but attractive. Beside it is a formal, sunken garden, with a pergola covered by clematis and a terracotta *pithoi* as the focal point; handsome, but not unusual. The path then enters a wild hazel wood carpeted with bluebells, ramsons and ferns; nature's garden. A clearing ablaze with scented azaleas in spring and roses and geraniums in summer is the first surprise. The path winds on to a pool surrounded by blue Himalayan poppies, hostas and candelabra primulas. And on... to a bubbling peat-stained stream that chatters over granite rocks to a bog garden with heathers and skunk cabbage, to a stunning tranquil Japanese hill and pool garden in which a snow-viewing granite lantern sits by a pool, while the boulder beyond suggests Mount Fuji. And on... to Harry's Garden, the newest part, started in 1997, full of plants given to Lorna in memory of her late husband, and planted (with a pick!) among the natural granite boulders.

Ardgillan Castle and Garden   20

**Balbriggan, Co. Dublin. Tel: (1) 849 2212 (Castle), (1) 849 2324 (Garden);
Fax: (353) 1 849 2786**

*Fingal County Council Parks • 24km N of Dublin, between Balbriggan and
Skerries. Signposted off N1 • Castle open all year, daily except Mon (but open
Bank Holiday Mons and Mons in July and Aug). Closed 23rd Dec to 2nd Jan •
Park and gardens open all year, daily except 25th Dec, 10am – 5pm (Feb, March,
6pm; April, Oct to Dec, 7pm; May, Sept, 8pm; June to Aug, 9pm). Conducted
tours June to Aug, Thurs, 3.30pm • Entrance: free but guided tours E2 (castle
tours E4, concessions E2.50, family ticket E8.50)* ○ 💭 ✕ 🍴 **WC** & ♿

The approach to the castle is one of the most spectacular in Ireland, with views
northwards along the coast to the Carlingford and Mourne mountains, and the
castle itself nestled in a hollow. The castle was built in 1738 by the Revd Robert
Taylor. It now houses an eclectic assortment of eighteenth- and nineteenth-
century furniture, and an important collection of seventeenth-century 'Down
Survey' maps of Ireland. The demesne today covers about 194 acres, and within
it are various gardens. A fine Victorian conservatory rescued from another
house has been re-erected and is now the centrepiece of the formal rose
garden. In the walled garden a unique, free-standing low brick wall with niches
is a source of much discussion by visitors – is it a fruit wall, or were the niches
for bee skeps? Whatever its original use, it is now planted with fruit. A good
mixture of shrubs, perennials, herbs, rock plants, salad vegetables and fruit
adorn its beds, borders and walls. Many of the beds were created recently and
are not part of the original layout, but they contain some choice plants. The
garden has been grant-aided under the Great Gardens of Ireland Restoration
Programme for remedial work on its woodland paths, rose garden (now
planted with Edwardian and Victorian cultivars) and a small garden museum,
and to provide some new plant stock to extend its collection. A National
Collection of potentillas is held here. Don't miss the ice-house, a short way
along the woodland walk.

Ardnamona   21

Lough Eske, Co. Donegal. Tel: (73) 22650; Fax: (73) 22819

*Kieran and Amabel Clarke • On NW shore of Lough Eske, approached from
Donegal, following signs for Harvey's Point • Open Jan to June, 10am – 8pm,
July to Dec, by appt • Entrance: E2.50* ○ **WC** ♿ ♿

William Robinson would have been proud of this garden created by the
Wallaces between 1880 and 1932. Ardnamona is wild gardening at its most
exuberant and refined. Imagine a Himalayan mountain slope cloaked with
primeval rhododendron forest, 18 metres tall, with a carpet of fallen leaves
underfoot embroidered in discarded flowers – you are close to imagining
Ardnamona. The rhododendrons are mainly over 100 years old, and they
proclaim their age with proud clean trunks, coloured from cinnamon to
purple, and canopies well beyond reach. Opened in 1992, this garden (once
neglected, now again cared for) will welcome visitors – bed and breakfast is

offered in the house. Rhododendron enthusiasts will need little more encouragement than the prospect of being in paradise.

Ballindoolin House and Garden 22

Carbury, via Edenderry, Co. Kildare. Tel: (405) 31430

The Molony family • 5km N of Edenderry on R401. Also signposted from N4 between Enfield and Kinnegad • House open; guided tours only (extra charge) • Open May to Sept, daily except Mon, 12 noon – 6pm, and by appt at other times • Entrance: E5, children over 5 E2.50 NEW ◑ ✗ WC ♿ ⚲ ▥

A medium-sized demesne surrounding an 1821 Georgian house which still retains its original interior and furnishings. Some of the farmyard buildings and outhouses still await repair, but the two-acre walled garden has been restored under the Great Gardens of Ireland Restoration Programme. It has aged espaliered apple trees in various stages of decrepitude, which have been carefully kept and are charming, setting the atmosphere for the garden. A melon-pit ruin has also been conserved. The soil is rich and fertile, and the old borders have been beautifully replanted with a wide range of herbaceous perennials, roses and herbs. Every year the new plantings get better and better, and a good variety of vegetables and fruit thrive once again in the warm microclimate, providing much of the produce for the restaurant. The wonderfully preserved walls include a high, brick-lined south-facing fruit wall, which has also been replanted. Outside the walled garden a path leads past a quirky little rockery towards the trefoil-shaped dovecote, on to the lime kiln, the 'Iron Age' mound and the woodland walk, where a long beech avenue leads into the woods and back towards the house.

Ballinlough Castle Gardens 23

Clonmellon, Co. Westmeath. Tel: (46) 33135; Fax: (46) 33331

Sir John and Lady Nugent • On N52 between Kells and Mullingar, 5km from Clonmellon • Open May to Sept, Thurs – Sat, 12 noon – 6pm, Sun and Bank Holiday Mons, 2 – 6pm. Closed 1st to 14th Aug. Check opening times before travelling • Entrance: E5, concessions E4, group rates on application NEW ◖ ☕ ✗ WC ♿ ⚲ ⚲

The gardens, woods and lakes have recently been restored under the Great Gardens of Ireland Restoration Programme. The present castle dates from the seventeenth century, with eighteenth- and nineteenth-century additions, but the history of the site goes way back into antiquity. The long avenue through the demesne hints at good things to come, and as the house comes into view on its mound above the two lakes it is truly delightful. The arched gateway into the first of several walled enclosures leads to a new formal pool, mature trees and flowering shrubs, and on to double herbaceous borders. Lady Nugent has filled the gardens with choice plants, fruit, herbs and vegetables, some old, many newly planted and all well cared for. Sir John and the garden staff have become proficient under-gardeners, and a real team spirit is evident. The formality of the walled gardens gives way to free-style wild plantings along the woodland paths, leading down to two rock bridges, a summerhouse, and a planted rockery and glade. A walk around the lake is rewarded by the view from the far side, where the castle seems to float above the water's edge. Swans have recolonised the lakes, and other creatures are settling in again.

Ballymaloe Cookery School Gardens 24

Shanagarry, Co. Cork. Tel: (21) 46 46785; Fax: (21) 46 46909

Tim and Darina Allen • 36km E of Cork, between Cloyne and Ballycotton • Open April to Sept, daily, 10am – 6pm. Guided tours for parties by arrangement • Entrance: E5 • Other information: Booking for groups essential ◑ ☕ 🍴 WC ♿ ⬙

Take the bones of an old Quaker garden and begin afresh – that is what Darina Allen has done at Kinoith (and she hasn't finished yet). The antique beech hedges are being clipped again, and within their shelter are compartments, each one different and refreshing. The first is the flower garden with short herbaceous borders, and beside a small pool is a summerhouse, the floor of which is patterned with shards of Delft. Beyond is the herb garden, where dwarf box hedges delineate a formal pattern of beds planted mainly with culinary herbs. These compartments can be enjoyed from ground level and also from a viewing platform. The pool garden lies outside the old hedges, and has an incomplete folly. A double herbaceous border, planted in 1996, leads to a plain garden house with Gothic windows. 'Please do not touch my insides' is a friendly piece of advice, for the interior of this unassuming building is decorated with myriad shells. The organic vegetable garden appeals directly to the eye with its tapestry of vegetables and edible flowers.

Bantry House and Gardens 25

Bantry, Co. Cork. Tel: (27) 50047; Fax: (27) 50795;
E-mail: info@bantryhouse.ie; Website: www.bantryhouse.ie

Mr and Mrs E. Shelswell-White • On outskirts of Bantry on Cork road • House open • Gardens open March to Oct, daily, 9am – 6pm • Entrance: E4, children free, (house and garden E9.50, concessions and students E8, children free) • Other information: Annual music festival, last week in June (house closed) – telephone for details NEW ◑ ☕ ✕ WC ♿ ⬙ 🌿 🏛

Bantry House is worth a visit to see the house in its setting, quite apart from its magnificent garden. The gardens were created from 1844 to 1867 while in the ownership of the second Earl of Bantry, Richard White, who also built up an impressive art collection as a result of his Grand Tour travels. His artistic ambitions drove him to develop the house and its setting, so formal parterres, terraces and beds were laid out around the house; behind is his amazing staircase of a hundred steps stretching up the steep hillside. Those who reach the top are rewarded with the most stunning view of the house and gardens below and Bantry Bay sweeping out to the broad Atlantic beyond. Statues, urns and balustrading encircle and embellish the gardens, all now restored under the

Great Gardens of Ireland Restoration Programme. Copies of original terracotta urns which punctuate the great flight of steps are filled with tender plants. There is a definite Italian air about the place – and its warm humid climate has inevitably influenced the plants that will grow there towards Japanese and Chinese wisterias, magnolias, myrtles, *Trachelospermum jasminoides* – the lakeside gardens of Como and Maggiore spring to mind here. The extensive programme of restoration and replanting is impressive, for instance the rose parterre to the west of the house facing the loggia, but the unpredictable Irish climate can be a cruel test of plantsmanship.

Belvedere 26

Mullingar, Co. Westmeath. Tel: (44) 49060; Fax: (44) 49002

Westmeath County Council • 8km S of Mullingar on N52 Tullamore road • House and garden open all year, daily; May to Aug, Mon – Fri, 9.30am – 6pm, Sat, Sun and Bank Holiday Mons, 10.30am – 7.00pm; Sept, Oct, 10.30am – 6.30pm; Nov to April, 10.30am – 4.30pm (last admission 1 hour before closing times) • Entrance: E5.50, children E3.50, family E13.50 ○ ▣ ✕ WC ♿ ⬥ 🌿 ⛪ ☕ ✎

The eighteenth-century hunting lodge, formal garden, Victorian walled garden and landscaped park, extending over 160 acres on the shores of Lough Ennell, have been restored thanks to a IR£5.7 million grant. There are fine views of the lough and islands from the terraces which drop in steps to the water. The Jealous Wall is one of those typically Gothick-Irish follies, built in 1750 to separate squabbling brothers. It looks antique and is impressive. There are also 6km of trails and a children's play area. An exhibition in the restored stables relates the story of the Wicked Earl and the Mary Molesworth scandal, the history of the estate and its restoration. Its real glory is the eighteenth-century parkland, follies – including Thomas Wright's Gothick arch – and woods.

Birr Castle Demesne ★ 27

Birr, Co. Offaly. Tel: (509) 20336; Website. www.birrcastle.com

The Earl and Countess of Rosse • 130km SW of Dublin, 38km S of Athlone, on N52 in Birr • Demesne open all year, daily 9am – 6pm (winter 10am – 5pm). Guided tours by arrangement • Entrance: E6.50, OAPs and students E4.50, children E3, family E15.50, parties of 25 or more E4.50 per person • Other information. Parking outside castle gates. Exhibition daily. Picnics in walled garden only. Castle not open. Historic Science Centre ○ ▣ 📖 WC ♿ ⬥ 🌿 ⛪ ☕

The Victorian Gothic castle dominates vistas which strike through the park and at whose centre is the restored 'Leviathan' (the Great Telescope which made Birr famous in the last century and which operates regularly throughout the day). Around, in profusion, are rare trees and shrubs, many raised from seed received from central China in the 1930s. Over one of the rivers is a beautiful suspension bridge, and hidden amongst laurels is a Victorian fernery with recently restored water-works. Evergreen conifers, golden willows, carpets of daffodils, and world-record box hedges, magnolias in the river garden, a cherry avenue and the original plant of *Paeonia* 'Anne Rosse' are mere selections of the many attractions. Recent improvements carried out under the Great Gardens of Ireland Restoration Programme include the restoration of the formal gardens, repairs to bridges, lake dredging and new plantings throughout the demesne.

Butterstream ★★ 28

Trim, Co. Meath. Tel: (46) 36017; Fax: (46) 31702

Jim Reynolds • Write for directions • Open April to Sept, daily, 11am – 6pm • Entrance: E4 ◗ 🦽 WC ♨

Like all the best gardens, this is a single-handed work of art. A series of compartments, containing different arrangements of plants, varies from a formal box-hedged garden of old roses and lilies to an informal gold garden carpeted with ferns and hostas. In the main garden a selection of choice herbaceous perennials in an island bed encircled by wide borders processes through the summer from whites and blues to yellows and reds – phlox, kniphofia, lobelia, macleaya and allium are just a few of the genera represented. A formal pool, replete with water lilies and carp, is flagged in Liscannor stone, and large terracotta pots of box topiary stand sentinel. A view across the rich pastures of adjoining farmland adds to the sense of a Tuscan villa garden. The large tennis lawn has a restrained gallery of clematis, deep purple hedges and a rustic summerhouse. New features include a Gothick pavilion, a small laburnum archway skirted by box and a maturing yew obelisk still caged in its wooden trellis. Twin canals of immense length and elegant proportions have been added and the garden continues to be developed with great enthusiasm and style.

Coolcarrigan House and Gardens 29

Naas, Co. Kildare. Tel: (45) 863 512/834 1141; Fax: (45) 834 41400

Mr and Mrs Wilson-Wright • 17.5km N of Naas, 14.5km W of Clane on minor road. Signposted • Open April to Aug, Mon – Fri, by appt only • Entrance: E5 • Other information: Lunch or dinner for groups (12 – 30) only, by prior arrangement [NEW] ◖ ✕ WC ♿ ♨

The Victorian house (occasionally open) was built in 1838. The 10-acre gardens are mainly planted with shrubs and trees. The large and much-admired collection of rare and unusual trees and shrubs was formed with the advice of Sir Harold Hillier many years ago; they are dotted about the lawns in informal style as specimens. A large and well-maintained Victorian greenhouse dominates the main garden, and a fine herbaceous border fronted by an immaculate lawn completes the picture.

Derreen ★ 30

Lauragh, Killarney, Co. Kerry. Tel: (64) 83588

The Hon. David Bigham • 24km SW of Kenmare on R571 road along S of Kenmare Bay, towards Healy Pass • Open April to Sept, daily, 11am – 6pm •

Entrance: E4, children E2 • Other information: Picnics on lawn near car park only ◑ 🍵 🏠 WC ♿ ℗

The broad sweep of plush lawn and the bald outcroppings of rock by the house do not prepare visitors for the lushness of the walks which weave through native woodlands and palisades of jade-stemmed bamboo. The evocatively named King's Oozy – a path that has a hankering to be a river – leads to a grove of tall, archaic tree-ferns (*Dicksonia antarctica*) with socks of filmy ferns. Wellies are the plantsman's only requirement to enjoy the large collection of rhododendrons that shelter among clipped entanglements of *Gaultheria shallon*. This is probably one of the wettest places in these islands, a fact you're reminded of by the lushness (and midges in season).

The Dillon Garden ★★ 31

45 Sandford Road, Ranelagh, Dublin 6; Website: www.dillongarden.com

Helen and Val Dillon • 10-min. drive or ½-hour walk from city centre in a cul-de-sac off Sandford Road just after Merton Road and church • Open March, daily; April to June, Sun only; July and Aug, daily; Sept, Sun only; all 2 – 6pm. Parties (min 15) at any time by written appt • Entrance: E5 • Other information: Possible for wheelchairs but limited access ◑ WC ℗

Within a walled rectangular garden, typical of Dublin's Georgian town houses, Helen Dillon has created one of the best designed and planted gardens in Ireland. As a central foil there is a wide canal and a series of formal pools set in limestone paving enhancing the colourful embroidery of the borders. Exploration reveals a necklace of secret rooms with raised beds for rarities, such as lady's slipper orchids or double-flowered *Trillium grandiflorum*. On the sunken terrace, terracotta pots sprout more rare plants. Clumps of *Dierama pulcherrimum* arch over the sphinxes, and a small alpine house and conservatory shelter the choicest species – *Lapageria rosea*, prize-winning ferns, alpines and bulbs. The mixed borders of shrubs and herbaceous perennials are changeful, each season revealing unusual plants and exciting colour combinations. One border is planted predominantly with reds ('hot' colours), both in flowers and foliage, and the opposite one is 'cool', blues and whites. Yellows cluster under the apple tree in the corner.

Dunloe Castle Gardens 32

Hotel Dunloe Castle, Beaufort, Killarney, Co. Kerry. Tel: (64) 44111

Killarney Hotels Ltd • 6km W of Killarney, off Killorglin Road. Signposted • Open early May to Sept, but opening date varies – check with hotel. Parties by appt only • Entrance: individuals free, parties E63.40 per coach • Other information: Toilet facilities in hotel ◑ 🍵 ✗ WC

On a superb site facing the Gap of Dunloe lie the imposing buildings of the Hotel Dunloe Castle, opened in 1965, surrounded by acres of parkland and gardens with magnificent and unusual trees and shrubs. Visitors and hotel guests may wander freely and appreciate the well-kept lawns and colourful planting, the walled garden and the ruined fort of Dunloe Castle. The more serious garden visitor will spot such tender specimens as *Eriobotrya deflexa*, *Glyptostrobus pensilis*, *Banksia marginata* and *Telopea oreades* with the aid of the plan and catalogue compiled by Roy Lancaster. Plantings of 1920 have been continually added to and the whole is impeccably maintained. Plants, however, are becoming crowded and tough decisions will have to be made in the near future to allow the choicest to achieve their full potential.

Earlscliffe ★ 33

Baron's Brae, Ceanchor Road, Baily, Co. Dublin. Tel: (1) 832 2556;
Fax: (1) 832 3021; E-mail: davidrobinson@eircom.net;
Website: www.earlscliffe.com

Dr David Robinson • 8km NE of city centre on Howth. At end of Ceanchor Road, enter through last gate on left signed 'Baron's Brae' • Open for parties by appt only • Entrance: prices on application ◐ WC

This garden is perched on the cliffs looking south over Dublin Bay (a view to rival the Bay of Naples) on the southern side of the Hill of Howth, a peninsula almost encircled by sea. Severe frost is rare and there is an almost constant breeze – just what the most tender species need. The collection of plants in these six acres is astonishing. A memorable forest of *Echium pininana*, the spire-shaped, blue-blossomed bugloss from the Canary Isles, is naturalised here. An octopus-like weeping cedar groping a thicket of the Chatham Islands daisy-bushes (*Olearia* 'Henry Travers'), a grove of bananas that flower and fruit, and waxy yellow-blossomed heathers from South Africa greet the visitor. Many eucalyptus species thrive, not to mention the cupressus-like *Callitris rhomboidea* and the gigantic *Hebe* 'Lavender Queen'. Dr Robinson's garden philosophy may disturb the ecologically minded because, with impunity, he uses chemicals (principally glyphosate) to control weeds (*Echium pininana* is not one).

Enniscoe House Gardens 34

Castlehill, Crossmolina, via Ballina, Co. Mayo. Tel: (96) 31112; Fax: (96) 31773;
E-mail: mail@enniscoe.com

Mrs Susan Kellett • After Ballina, turn sharp left in Crossmolina at statue, and drive for 4km on R315 (Pontoon and Castlebar road). Gates and signs on left • Open April to Sept, daily except Mon, 2 – 6pm, and at other times by appt • Entrance: E5, children E1.50 • Other information: Check if tea room open before travelling (none other nearby) NEW ◑ 💺 WC ♿ ⬙ 🏛

Set near the shores of Loch Conn, the estate dates from the seventeenth century, the picturesque house (now a country house hotel with good fishing and cuisine) from the eighteenth. The surrounding landscape is beautiful and unspoilt. The pleasure grounds were developed in the 1870s, but the woods may be a remnant of original woodland taken into ownership in the 1600s and managed ever since. The walled gardens were derelict from the 1950s until the present owner received grant aid from the Great Gardens of Ireland Restoration Programme. The ornamental garden within the old walls has been faithfully restored to its Edwardian origins, and today is bright with annual bedding and borders filled with perennials and shrubs. The paths are smartly gravelled, the box hedging trim and the lawns settling down. The old fruit and vegetable garden linked to it by a fern-draped rustic arch is now being taken in hand as an organic market garden.

An Féar Gorta (Tea and Garden Rooms) 35

Ballyvaghan, Co. Clare. Tel: (65) 707 7157; Fax: (65) 707 7127;
E-mail: kaodonoghue@ireland.com

Catherine and Brendan O'Donoghue • In Ballyvaghan, on sea-front • Open June to mid-Sept, Mon – Sat, 11am – 5.30pm • Entrance: free ◑ ▆ WC ♿

The Burren, John Betjeman's 'Stony seaboard, far and foreign ...', is this simple garden's dramatic backdrop. Catmint spills over the native limestone, shrubby cinquefoils sparkle in the sun, butterfly bushes burst with blossom and are a-flutter with insects. There are several compartments, in front of and behind the traditional cottages, all different but each one filled with shrubs and perennials that thrive by the edge of the sea. A conservatory contains other joys, including the red banana passion flower (*Passiflora antioquiensis*) and, appropriately, the cup-and-saucer vine (*Cobaea scandens*). You can sit under their shade, sipping tea and eating scrumptious cakes, enjoying the view.

Fernhill Gardens 36

Sandyford, Co. Dublin. Tel: (1) 295 6000

Mrs Sally Walker • 13km S of city centre on R117 Dublin – Enniskerry road • Open March to Sept, Tues – Sat, 11am – 5pm, Sun, 2 – 6pm, Bank Holiday Mons, 11am – 5pm • Entrance: E5, OAPs E4, children E3 (under 5 free) ◑ ▩
WC ⚲

The garden is situated on the eastern slope of the Dublin Mountains and has a laurel lawn, some fine nineteenth-century plantings and an excellent flowering specimen of *Michelia doltsopa*. The plantings of rhododendron species and culti-vars provide spectacles of colour from early spring into mid-summer; many of the more tender rhododendrons flourish here. The walkways through the wooded areas wind steeply past many other shrubs – pieris and camellias are also outstanding. There is a rock garden and a water garden near the house, and drifts of daffodils in the spring. In the summer there are the roses and a good collection of herbaceous plants, many as underplanting through the woodland.

Fota Arboretum ★ 37

Fota Trust, Carrigtohill, Co. Cork. Tel: (21) 4812728;
Website: www.zenith.ie/fota

Duchas – The Heritage Service • 15.5km E of Cork, on Cobh road • Arboretum open all year, daily, 10am – 5pm (Sun opens 11am) • Entrance: free for arboretum. Automatic pay barrier to car park • Other information: Refreshments and shop in wildlife park ◑ WC ♿ ⬧

Perhaps the wonders of Fota are best appreciated in summer when the obvious distractions like camellias, embothriums, drimys, pieris and most of the rhododendrons have finished flowering. There is no lack of colour: the walls sparkle with abutilons and cestrums, and the myrtles take on a pinkish hue. *Davidia involucrata* may be bereft of handkerchiefs, but admire instead the elaborate flowers of *Magnolia* x *wieseneri*, or the frothy white blooms of *Eucalyptus delegatensis*. Now is the time to appreciate the complicated growth of the Chilean hazel, the immense canopy of the fern-leaved beech, a perfect *Pinus montezumae* and the marvellous bark of the stone pine. Note the wickedly spiny species of colletia and the elegance of *Restio subverticillatus*, then spend a few minutes in the cool fernery. Storm damage in the winter of 1997 depleted the collection and provided new planting opportunities.

Garinish Island

(see ILNACULLIN)

Gash Gardens   38

Castletown, Mountrath, Co. Laois. Tel: (502) 32247; Fax: (502) 32857

The Keenan family • S of Mountrath, 1km off N7 Dublin – Limerick road. Signposted • Open May to Oct, daily, 10am – 5pm (Sun opens 2pm). Groups welcome by appt • Entrance: E4.50 • Other information: Children not admitted
NEW ◗ ⚘

Developed by the late Noel Keenan and now lovingly looked after by his daughter Mary, this is a plantsman's garden full of treasures. Water features include a lily pond, a stream garden, a cascade and a bog garden. There is also an extensive scree and rock garden, a riverside walk, a beech walk and a laburnum arch. This garden deserves to be better known.

Georgian House and Garden   39

2 Pery Square, Limerick. Tel: (61) 314130; Fax: (61) 310130;
Website: www.georgianhouseandgarden@eircom.net

Limerick Civic Trust • In Limerick • House and garden open all year, Mon – Fri, 10am – 4.30pm and weekends by appt • Entrance: E3.50
NEW ○ WC ♿ ♨ ⚐

A handsome early-nineteenth-century town house in a terrace overlooking the public gardens of Pery Square has recently been conserved and renovated. The garden at the rear, enclosed by high brick walls and backed by the coach house, has been restored to complement the house. It comprises a central lawn, surrounded by neatly maintained wall borders planted with favourites of the era that give interest throughout the year.

Glenveagh Castle ★   40

Glenveagh National Park, Churchill, Letterkenny, Co. Donegal.
Tel: (74) 37088/37090/37262; Fax: (74) 37072

National Parks and Wildlife Service • 24km NW of Letterkenny • Castle open, E2.50 • Garden open 16th March to 3rd Nov, 10am – 5pm, and at other times by appt • Entrance: E2.50, OAPs and parties per person E2, students and children E1.50 • Other information: Parking at visitor centre. Access to garden and castle by official mini-coaches only ◑ ⬛ ✕ WC

The centrepiece of the Glenveagh National Park is the garden surrounding the castle, which is set beside a mountain lough encircled by high, peat-blanketed mountains in the middle of windswept moorlands – a most unpromising site. But surprises are countless. The lower lawn garden has fringing shrubberies and, beyond, steep pathways wind through oak woods in which grow scented white-flowered rhododendrons and numerous other tender shrubs. Terraced enclosures with terracotta pots or plants and sculptures are encountered unexpectedly. The *jardin potager* at the castle has rank upon rank of old Irish vegetables, ornamental vegetables and flowering herbs. This is a paradise for plantsmen and gardeners keen on seeing fine and unusual specimens. Linger, and walk the mountain sides, then take the last bus back to the remarkable heather-roofed visitor centre with its imaginative landscaping.

Glin Castle Gardens   41

Glin, Co. Limerick. Tel: (68) 34173/34112; Fax: (68) 34364;
E-mail: knight@iol.ie; Website: www.glincastle.com

Madam Fitzgerald and the Knight of Glin • 48km W of Limerick on N69 • Garden open by appt only • Entrance: E4 (E2.50 per person for parties) • Other information: Accommodation available ◑ WC ♿

The formal garden could not be simpler, with its lawns and two domed bays flanking a path to a sundial and an elegant *Parrotia persica*, beyond which is a meadow with daffodils and a woodland with fine old trees. Magnolias and bluebells bring their spring flowering, and in early summer rhododendrons are still providing a splash of colour, in contrast to the cool tones of a large *Abutilon vitifolium*, while the grey walls of the castle are relieved by climbing plants. An outstanding feature is the walled garden on a steep slope, with its mathematically neat rows of vegetables and herbs, figs, fruit, roses and clematis, a castellated henhouse, a rustic temple with marble incumbent, and a lovely view across the Shannon over the walls and undulating slate roofs of the old battlemented, cobblestoned stableyard. If you like kitchen gardens, Glin's will please you.

Graigueconna ★   42

Old Connaught, Bray, Co. Wicklow. Tel: (1) 282 2273 (1) 282 2273

Mr and Mrs John Brown • 19km SE of Dublin city centre. Take N11, then slip road to Bray and turn right at traffic lights. From S take N11 towards Dublin, then slip road signed 'Bray/Enniskerry Rathmichael'. Turn left for Graigueconna • Open May to July, 9am – 6pm, by appt only for parties of four or more; and for Wicklow Gardens Festival • Entrance: E4.50 per person • Other information: Coffee provided for small groups by arrangement ● WC ♿ ✿

This three-acre garden was created early this century by Lewis Meredith, who wrote *Rock gardens – how to make and maintain them* (1906), one of the earliest 'text books' on this topic. His rock garden lies hidden at the end of a specially laid railway track along which rocks were trundled. Today, this track is a grassy path, punctuated by Irish yews and lined with excellent mixed borders of herbaceous perennials and shrubs. The rock garden, while intact, is planted for easier maintenance with ground-cover species, bulbs and ferns, along with many interesting southern-hemisphere shrubs. There are numerous 'old' roses on the walls and in shrubberies. Near the house are tender and unusual plants, throughout the borders are uncommon herbaceous perennials, while the conservatory houses tender southern-hemisphere species and a collection of arisaema. The whole place is painstakingly cared for.

Heywood Garden   43

Ballinakill, Co. Laois. Tel: (502) 33563

Duchas – The Heritage Service • 5km SE of Abbeyleix. Turn E in Abbeyleix signed Ballinakill. Outside Ballinakill • Open all year, daily, during daylight hours • Entrance: free ○ ⅊ ⏖

Edwin Lutyens' walled garden with pergola and lawns is acknowledged as his finest small-scale work in Ireland. It is a gem, now restored close to its original state as far as the walls and ornaments are concerned. On the driveway leading towards the school buildings is an eighteenth-century folly. Heywood has now been recognised as a heritage garden of historic and architectural importance.

Ilnacullin (Garinish Island) ★   44

Glengarriff, Co. Cork. Tel: (27) 63040; Fax: (27) 63149; Website: www.heritageireland.ie

Duchas – The Heritage Service • On island in Bantry Bay • Open March and Oct, Mon – Sat, 10am – 4.30pm, Sun, 1 – 5pm; April to June and Sept, Mon – Sat, 10am – 6.30pm, Sun, 12 noon – 6.30pm; July and Aug, Mon – Sat, 9.30am – 6.30pm, Sun, 11am – 6.30pm (last landing 1 hour before closing) • Entrance: E4, OAPs E2.50, students and children E1.50, family E9.50, parties of 20 or more ◑ ▆ ▤ WC ⅊ ⏖

The boat trip across the sheltered inlets of Bantry Bay past sun-bathing seals, with views of the Caha Mountains, is doubly rewarding; landing at the slipway you gain entrance to one of Ireland's gardening jewels, begun in the early 1900s. Most visitors cluster around the Casita – an Italianate garden – and reflecting pool, designed by Harold Peto, to enjoy (on clear days) spectacular scenery, and some quite indifferent annual bedding. But walk beyond, to the Temple of the Winds, through shrubberies filled with plants usually confined indoors, tree ferns, southern-hemisphere conifers, rhododendron species and cultivars. A flight of stone steps leads to the Martello tower, and thence the path returns to the walled garden with its double-sided herbaceous border.

Irish National War Memorial   45

Islandbridge, Dublin 8.

Duchas – The Heritage Service • In Islandbridge • Open all year, daily except 25th Dec, during daylight hours • Entrance: free ○ ⅊

Sir Edwin Lutyens' Irish gardens (see also entry for Heywood) are not nearly as well known as his English ones. This memorial garden (1938, dedicated 1988), restored and planted anew, is typical of his reserved, calm style, with sunken rose gardens, a simple altar stone, colonnades and formal plantings of trees. In the bookroom are volumes with the names of Irish men and women who died in World War I.

Iveagh Gardens   46

Clonmel Street, Dublin 2. Tel: (1) 6613111

Duchas – The Heritage Service • Access via Clonmel Street or National Concert Hall, Earlsfort Terrace • Open all year, Mon – Sat, 8.30am – 6pm, Sun and Bank Holiday Mons, 10am – 6pm (closes earlier Oct to March) • Entrance: free • Other information: Wheelchairs via Clonmel Street entrance only ○ ⅊ ⋞⫤

Ranked among the finest and least known of Dublin's parks and gardens, they were designed by Ninian Niven in 1863 and include a rustic grotto, a cascade, fountains, a maze, a rosarium, archery grounds, a wilderness and woodlands. An ongoing programme of restoration is underway, and many of the highlights of the gardens have already been restored, including the fountains, the cascade, the rosarium and the maze.

The Japanese Garden   47

Irish National Stud, Tully, Kildare, Co. Kildare. Tel: (45) 521617/522963; Fax: (45) 522964

Irish National Stud • 40km SW of Dublin, 1.5km off M/N7 outside Kildare • Garden open 11th Feb to 11th Nov, daily, 9.30am – 6pm. Guided tours available • Entrance: by combined ticket for Japanese Garden, St Fiachra's Garden, Irish National Stud and Horse Museum E7.50, OAPs and students E6, children E4, family (2 adults and 4 children under 12) E18 • Other information: Picnics in car park only. Lego area for children ↻ ⧫ ✕ WC ⋞⫤ ⸚

Devised by Colonel William Hall-Walker (later Lord Wavertree), a wealthy Scotsman of a famous brewery family, and laid out 1906–10 by the Japanese Elda and his son Minoru, the gardens, symbolising the 'Life of Man'. This is not a plantsman's garden, and few of the plants are Japanese; to be sure there are some excellent old maples, but many of the trees and shrubs are clipped and shaped beyond reason. The overshadowing Scots pines are exquisite. A pathway meanders through artificial caves into a watery stream, past the tranquil ponds and on to the weeping trees of the grave. Beautiful stone lanterns grace the site, which is in the style of a Japanese tea garden. New in 1999 was the creation of *St Fiachra's Garden*, 'a garden in commemoration of the Patron Saint of Gardeners in his home country of Ireland' as the National Stud puts it.

John F. Kennedy Arboretum 48

New Ross, Co. Wexford. Tel: (51) 388171

Duchas – The Heritage Service • 8km S of New Ross • Arboretum open all year, daily except 25th Dec and 29th March: April, 10am – 6.30pm; May to Aug, 10am – 8pm; Sept, 10am – 6.30pm; Oct to March, 10am – 5pm • Entrance: E2.50, OAPs E2, students and children E1.50, family E6.50 (2001 prices) • Other information: Refreshments available mid-March to Oct, sometimes Suns only. Visitor Centre with Kennedy memorial and video ○ 🍽 🛍 WC ♿ ⇪ 🛒 ⚲

A spacious modern arboretum laid out in botanical sequence with rides; from the summit of a nearby hill is a superb panorama not only of the arboretum but also of parts of six counties. Best to begin at the viewpoint – turn left just beyond the main entrance and drive to the summit car park to see the layout. At the arboretum be prepared for a long walk; fortunately those not keen on gardening tend to linger near the café so that the distant reaches are quiet and empty. Planting began in the 1960s, and now 4500 different trees and shrubs are growing, ranging from conifers to flowering shrubs. Most species are represented by several specimens, and keen plantsmen can take their time examining the groups. A colourful planting of dwarf conifers is on the western side, a small lake on the east. While primarily a scientific collection, the arboretum is now achieving an established reputation.

Kilfane Glen and Waterfall 49

Thomastown, Co. Kilkenny. Tel: (56) 24558; Fax: (56) 27491; Website: www.NicholasMosse.com

Mrs Susan Mosse • 19km SE of Kilkenny, 6.5km N of Thomastown, signed off N9 • Open April to June, Sun, 2 – 6pm; July and Aug, daily, 11am – 6pm; Sept, Sun, 2 – 6pm, and at other times by appt • Entrance: E5, OAPs E4.50, children E4, family E13 ◑ 🍽 🛍 WC 🐾 ⚲

This romantic woodland garden dates from 1790, when the glen was designed to display nature in all her terrifying beauty, *à la* Wordsworth. It has the requisite romantic traits including a hermit's grotto, a *cottage orné* and a waterfall, so that present-day visitors can enjoy the beauties just as their predecessors did under the tuition of the gentry of Kilfane House. A good leaflet with a suggested walk tells the reader when to feel the *frisson*.

Killruddery ★ 50

Bray, Co. Wicklow. Tel: (1) 286 3405; Fax: (1) 276 0577; Tel/Fax: (1) 286 2777 (Administrator); Website: www.killruddery.com

The Earl and Countess of Meath • 23km S of Dublin, just beyond Bray. Follow signs off roundabout on Bray/Greystones road. From N11 (1st exit for Bray travelling N; 3rd exit for Bray/Greystones travelling S) follow signs off roundabout • House open May, June and Sept, daily, 1 – 5pm with conducted tours, and at other dates and times for pre-arranged parties • Garden open April to Sept, daily, 1 – 5pm. Guided tours for parties of 20 or more by appt •

Entrance: E4.45, OAPs/students E3.20, children E1.30 (house and garden E7, OAPs/students E4.45, children E1.90, parties of 20 or more E4.50 per person). All children must be accompanied • Other information: Teas and meals for groups by arrangement ◑ WC ☙ ⚬

Killruddery is unique in having the most extensive early formal gardens, still in their original style, surviving in Ireland, dating largely from the seventeenth century with nineteenth-century embellishments. The joy of the garden is the formal hedging, known as 'The Angles', set beside the formal canals which lead to a ride into the distant hills. There is a collection of nineteenth-century French cast statuary, a sylvan theatre created in bay, and a fountain pool enclosed in a beech hedge. The fine nineteenth-century conservatory has been completely re-roofed, its original Turner dome put back and its unique collection of statues conserved; the marble statuary within has been restored. The garden deserves to be better known. Nearby is the *National Gardens Exhibition Centre* at Kilquade, a one-stop shop for gardeners and individual gardens created by different designers.

Kilmacurragh   51

Kilbride, Rathdrum, Co. Wicklow. Tel: (1) 647 3000; Fax: (1) 836 0080

Duchas – The Heritage Service • 48km S of Dublin, 8km S of Wicklow off N11. Turn right at Old Tap pub. After 1m turn left at T-junction. Entrance through gateway with curved granite wall and sequoiadendrons • Opening dates and prices: for details write to Duchas – The Heritage Service, or telephone (1) 6613111 ●

This garden is rated highly because of its atmosphere and magnificent ancient plants. It was created by Thomas Acton in the mid- to late-nineteenth century. Behind the derelict eyesore of a house there was an incomparable avenue composed of alternating Irish yews and crimson rhododendrons, although in recent years there has been much storm damage. Beyond, paths wind through the arboretum under mighty rhododendrons. The trees include many unequalled specimens – rare conifers abound. If you can, visit it when crocus blossom is in the meadow, when the rhododendron flowers are tumbling down, at any time for elegant decrepitude. The garden is now managed, as Thomas Acton always wished, as an adjunct to the National Botanic Gardens, Glasnevin (see entry).

Kilmokea   52

Great Island, Campile, Co. Wexford. Tel: (51) 388109; Fax: (51) 388776; E-mail: kilmokea@indigo.ie; Website: www.kilmokea.com

Mark and Emma Hewlett • 13km S of New Ross, 0.5km off R733 New Ross – Ballyhack road towards River Barrow • Open March to Oct, 10am – 6pm, Tues – Sun • Entrance: E5, accompanied children under 16 E2.50 ◑ ☕ ✗ WC ⬦ ✿ ⌂ ⚬

The gardens of the rectory, developed over the past 45 years, have matured splendidly in the gentle microclimate of Waterford Harbour. The contrast between the formal and the informal is marvellously displayed here. It is impossible to decide which is the more inspired – a series of enclosed gardens featuring an herbaceous border, topiary and an Italian garden, etc., or the more recently developed woodland garden, which was started on the site of an old mill and where the smaller and rarer rhododendrons, candelabra primulas and tender shrubs excel beneath a canopy of conifers and exotic trees, alongside a stream and its falls. The influence of Peto is discernible, the imaginative hand of the previous owners, the Prices, is paramount. Now the garden has been restored and many rare and tender plants added. Admire also the pergolas, gazebos and boardwalks.

Kylemore Abbey   53

Connemara, Co. Galway. Tel: (95) 41146; Fax: (95) 41145;
E-mail: info@kylemoreabbey.ie; Website: www.kylemoreabbey.com

Benedictine Nuns • On N59 9.5km N of Letterfrack • Open Easter to Oct, daily, 10.30am – 4.30pm. Abbey open all year (except Christmas week and Good Friday), 9am – 5.30pm • Entrance to walled garden E6.50, family ticket E12.75, concessions and groups (minimum 10 persons) E4. (garden and abbey E10, family ticket E20, concessions and groups (minimum 10 persons) E6.50)
[NEW] ◑ 🍴 WC ♿ ♿

Set in spectacular Connemara landscape, the 1860s' Scottish Baronial house is reflected in a lake and backed by tree-covered mountains. The trees are some of the hundreds planted by the original owner, Mitchell Henry, who also established an elaborate six-acre walled garden in a clement spot a mile away from the house. Kylemore Castle became Kylemore Abbey when it was bought by Benedictine nuns in the 1920s. A portion of the walled garden was maintained for many years, but it had become overgrown and the buildings dilapidated until the nuns, aided by a Great Gardens of Ireland Restoration Programme grant, decided in 1995 to restore the walled garden to its late-nineteenth-century splendour and to conserve the buildings. Half the garden has become again an ornamental flower garden, containing typical annual beds in lawns, the other half was a fruit and vegetable garden, now fully replanted. The two areas are separated by a tree-lined stream. Restoration of the 21 glasshouses in a handsome range has begun. The head gardener's house (sadly not lived in), bothy, toolshed and lime kiln (from which the heat for the glasshouses was piped) are on view, and traditional Victorian favourites and exotic plants can be enjoyed once more.

Lakemount ★   54

Barnavara Hill, Glanmire, Co. Cork. Tel/Fax: (86) 811 0241

Brian Cross • 8km E of Cork off R639, at top of Barnavara Hill above Glanmire • Open April to Sept, daily, 2.30 – 5pm, and by appt • Entrance: E5 ◑

A skilfully designed and immaculately maintained two-acre hillside garden, with rhododendrons, azaleas and camellias in spring and a wealth of summer interest and colour, especially from hydrangeas. There are paved areas on different levels, a poolhouse and planthouse with exotics such as *Lochroma cassia* and tibouchina, while to the rear of the house a lawn slopes gently from a rock garden to beds with a mixed planting of trees, shrubs and herbaceous plants. This is an evolving garden with many unusual plantings, most recently in the old orchard and in meadows now filled with wild flowers fringed with rare trees and shrubs. A large pond has also been added.

Lakeview 55

Mullagh, Co. Cavan. Tel: (46) 42480; Fax: (46) 42406; E-mail: jshack@indigo.ie; Website: www.lakeviewgardens.net

Daphne and Jonathan Shackleton • 2km W of Mullagh on Virginia road • Open May to Sept, Fri – Sun and Bank Holiday Mons, 2 — 6pm, and at other times by appt • Entrance: E4.50 • Other information: Rare and special plants fair 12th May NEW ● ⬛ WC ♿ ☸

This charming old walled garden slopes downhill beside the house which over-looks natural wildflower meadows and Mullagh Lake. Rescued in the last few years, the traditional path layout and old apples trees form a framework to different areas, each crammed with a superb collection of thriving plants. An ornamental vegetable garden and cottage garden beds end the long double herbaceous border, and a yellow and lemon herbaceous border is a feature of the summer months. Seasonal interest evolves in luxuriant wall borders and in a small woodland. Many of the plants growing in the garden are for sale in the nursery.

Larchill Arcadian Gardens 56

Kilcock, Co. Kildare. Tel: (1) 628 7354; Fax: (1) 628 4580; E-mail: delascasas@indigo.ie

Michael and Louisa de las Casas • 8km from Kilcock on Dunslaughlin Road• Open May to Aug, daily, and Sept, Sat, Sun, 12 noon – 6pm, • Entrance: E5.50, children E3.50, family ticket (2 adults, 3 children) E15, groups by arrangement NEW ● 🍴 ⬛ WC ♿ ☸ 🎠

The modest mid-eighteenth-century house overlooks a tree-lined parkland landscape, which initially appears commonplace. However, a circulatory walk through the trees leads to several unique rustic follies, including the Fox's Earth and a sham fort on an island in the lake (no longer used for mock sea battles but by resting wild fowl). Rare breeds of cattle graze in the park, and other rare domestic breeds live in the attractive farmyard. Contemporary design and colourful planting in the walled garden near the house provide a bright area of contrast to the calming greens of the parkland. The follies have been conserved, the lake flooded and the entire site restored with the aid of a grant from the Great Gardens of Ireland Restoration Programme.

Lismore Castle Gardens 57

Lismore, Co. Waterford. Tel: (58) 54424; Fax: (58) 54896; E-mail: lismoreestates@eircom.net; Website: www.lismorecastle.com

The Duke and Duchess of Devonshire • 57.5km SW of Waterford in Lismore • Open 30th March to 29th Sept, daily, 1.45 – 4.45pm (opens 11am July, Aug) • Entrance: E4, children under 16 E2. Parties of 20 or more during working

hours E3.50 per person, children E1.75 • Other information: Toilet facilities, inc. disabled, nearby ◑ 📖 ⬸ ℀

The situation of the castle overlooking the River Blackwater is stunning. There are two gardens linked by the gatehouse entrance: the upper, reached by a stairway in the gatehouse, leads to a terrace with vegetables and flowers, a reduced glasshouse by Joseph Paxton (with an interesting ridge-and-furrow roof) and a fine view from the main axis to the church spire emphasised by a new herbaceous border. In the lower garden, several steps down from the gatehouse, are a few meritricious plants, but the principal feature, an ancient yew walk, is wonderful. Contemporary sculpture on show includes an Antony Gormley. Edmund Spenser is said to have written *The Fairie Queene* here, and it is the Irish home of the Duke and Duchess of Devonshire, who have Chatsworth (see entry in Derbyshire) to console them in England.

Lisnavagh   58

Rathvilly, Co. Carlow. Tel: (503) 61104; Website: www.lisnavagh.com

Lord and Lady Rathdonnell • 2.5km SE of Rathvilly off N81. Signposted • Open by appt only • Entrance: E4, children E2 (2001 prices) ◐ WC & ℘

Originally designed by Daniel Robertson in the 1850s with panoramic views of the Wicklow hills and Mount Leinster, the 10-acre gardens have a wonderful array of majestic trees and shrubs, including magnificent rhododendrons, azaleas, camellias, embothriums and many unusual plants, as well as some spectacular Irish yews. They also boast a large walled garden with peacocks strutting amongst the old fruit trees, mixed borders and a small rock garden. There are endless woodland walks with all sorts of wildlife.

Lodge Park Walled Garden   59

Straffan, Co. Kildare. Tel: (1) 62 88412; Fax: (1) 62 73477;
E-mail: garden@steam-museum; Website: www.steam-museum.ie

Mr and Mrs Robert Guinness • 20km N of Dublin. Take N4 to Maynooth or Lucan or N7 to Kill. Follow signs to Straffan and steam museum, 1.5km from village • Open June and July, Tues – Fri and Sun, 2.30 – 6pm, Aug, Tues – Fri, 2.30 – 5.30pm, and at other times by appt • Entrance: E4 NEW ◐ ☕ WC & ℘ 🏛

The two-acre walled garden dates from the late eighteenth century and provided produce and flowers for the house. The present owners have been restoring it over a number of years, adding their own personal touches to the layout. It is filled with a great assortment of rare flowering plants, herbs, salad crops and fruit and is beautifully kept – the potting shed must be the most perfect example of its kind of cleanliness and order. The lack of commerciality is refreshing, and despite being relatively unknown its high standards mark it out as a gardener's garden.

Loughcrew Historic Gardens 60

Oldcastle, Co. Meath. Tel: (49) 854 1922; Fax (49) 854 1722;
E-mail: info@loughcrew.com; Website: www.loughcrew.com

Mr and Mrs Charles Naper • 85km NW of Dublin off N3, 5m from Oldcastle off Mullingar road • Open 17th to 31st March, 12 noon – 4pm; April to Sept daily, 12 noon – 6pm; Oct to 16th March, 2003, Sat, Sun and Bank Holiday Mons, 12 noon – 4pm • Entrance: E4.50, OAPs E4, children E2.50, family ticket E15.50 NEW ○ ● ● WC & ⬦ ✎ ● ● ●

An extraordinary survival of a seventeenth-century demesne, retaining many of its features through the waxing and waning of the family fortunes. The remarkable yew walk dates from the mid-1660s and has few rivals for the beauty and girth of its individual trees. The lime avenue runs down in a straight and elegant sweep to an ancient burial ground. The tower house alone is worth a visit. A massive centre motte is the focal point of the garden; behind it a huge cedar spews a water cascade from its base into a dark pool. This 'devil's cauldron' has been planted in fiery colours and terminates the main herbaceous border. A yew parterre fronts the site of the ruined seventeenth-century longhouse, where a carved wooden doorframe echoes the original. A slender and elegant canal flows parallel to the replanted herbaceous border, which itself skirts the outside of the old walled garden. Many of the original features of the garden and pleasure ground have been repaired, restored or unashamedly reinvented. The atmosphere of the whole place is one of considerable antiquity blended with an artistic approach in its recent improvements. Where else in Europe would the ruined portico of a burnt-down great house be re-erected as a folly? Loughcrew is one of the 26 gardens that are worthy recipients of the Great Gardens of Ireland Restoration Programme.

Marlay Park 61

Grange Road, Rathfarnham, Co. Dublin 18. Tel: (1) 4934059; Fax: (1) 493 3546;
E-mail: dshannon@dlrcoco.ie; Website: www.irishtabletop.com

Dun Laoghaire-Rathdown County Council • In Rathfarnham, signposted on Brehon Road/Grange Road • House by appt • Park open, all year, dawn – dusk. Walled garden, April to Sept, Tues – Sun, 12 noon – 5pm • Entrance: Park free, walled garden E3.17, children E1.90 NEW ○ ● WC & ⬦ ● ● ●

The extensive 200 acre public park under the Dublin mountains, with the Little Dargle River running through, contains a lake, lawns and fine old trees. Once the demesne of the La Touche banking family, the late-eighteenth-century house has recently been sensitively restored for public use. The adjacent large walled garden has also been restored with the aid of a grant from the Great Gardens of Ireland Restoration Programme. The garden was traditionally divided into three parts, two of which are on view. On entering through the head gardener's house, the central position is taken by an attractive Regency-style ornamental flower garden, containing colourful flowerbeds of mixed bedding fashionable in that era. Features of interest, such as a shrubbery, an orangery, a rustic summerhouse and a fountain embellish the site. Another section of the walled garden contains a large kitchen garden, set out in a traditional early-nineteenth-century manner, containing vegetables and fruit known to have been grown at that time, many now rare.

Mount Congreve ★★ 62

Kilmeaden, Co. Waterford. Tel: (51) 384115 (Office)

Mr Ambrose Congreve • Write for directions • Open all year, Mon – Fri, 9am – 5pm, strictly by appt for cognoscenti and dendrologists only. Closed Bank Holiday Mons • Entrance: E12.70 per person for visits organised by travel agents who specially ask for conducted tours. Individuals may go round by themselves without charge, provided they have permission from office. No children under 12 ◑ WC

In emulation of Exbury, the owner has amassed an unequalled collection of rhododendron, camellia and magnolia species and cultivars, with many other trees as icing on the cake. It is a staggering collection which cannot be described adequately in a single entry: 100 acres of shrubs, mass upon mass, since every cultivar is planted in groups. In addition to the flowering shrub collections, which include Mount Congreve hybrids, there are many other splendours, including a whole series of surprises, one of the most spectacular being a pagoda at the base of 25-metre cliffs. Highlights are memorable. In early March a forest of *Magnolia campbellii* offers pink to white goblets to the rooks. A languid walled garden has a fine eighteenth-century vinery and range of glasshouses. In the borders is an extensive collection of herbaceous plants arranged in order of monthly flowering – May to July, a large arrangement for August, plus a border for September and October – an unusual idea. There is far too much here to appreciate in one visit and it is satisfying to know the garden will eventually be left to the nation with a trust for maintenance for the first 25 years.

Mount Usher ★★ 63

Ashford, Co. Wicklow. Tel: (404) 40116/40205/40483; Fax: (404) 40205; E-mail: mount-usher.gardens@indigo.ie; Website: www.mount-usher-gardens.com

Mrs Madelaine Jay • 80km S of Dublin, 6.5km NW of Wicklow, on N11 at Ashford • Open 17th March to Oct, daily, 10.30am – 6pm • Entrance: E5, OAPs, students and children E4. Special rates for parties of 20 or more. Guided tours (E30) must be pre-booked ◑ ☕ ✕ WC ♿ ⬛ ♀

The Vartry River flows through this exquisite garden over weirs and under bridges which allow visitors to meander through the collections. It is a plant-lovers' paradise. *Pinus montezumae* is always first port of call, a shimmering tree, magnificent when the bluebells are in flower. Throughout are drifts of rhododendrons, fine trees and shrubs, including many that are difficult to cultivate outdoors in other parts of Britain and Ireland. The grove of eucalyptus at the lower end of the valley is memorable; a kiwi-fruit vine (*Actinidia chinensis*) cloaks the piers of a bridge, and beside the tennis court is the gigantic original *Eucryphia* x *nymansensis* 'Mount Usher'. In spring, bulbs, magnolias, a procession of rhododendrons and camellias, in summer eucryphias and leptospermums, in autumn russet and crimson leaves falling from maples – a garden for all seasons.

Muckross House and Gardens ★   64

Killarney National Park, Killarney, Co. Kerry. Tel: (64) 31947/31440

National Parks and Wildlife Service • 6.5km S of Killarney on N71 Kenmare road • House open. Admission charge • Gardens open all year, daily • Entrance: free ○ 🍴 ✕ WC ⅊ ⏚ ⏛

The garden around the house is almost incidental to the spectacle of the lakes and mountains of Killarney; indeed, it is principally renowned as a viewing area for the wild grandeur of the mountains. The lawns sweep to clumps of old rhododendrons and Scots pines, and there is a huge natural rock garden. Quiet corners abound along the lough-shore walks, and anyone interested in trees and shrubs is strongly recommended to head for the recently developed arboretum area (it can be reached by car easily – follow the signpost – and is a short walk from the house). There, good specimen trees surround a wooden pergola of imaginative design, and there are plantings of tender shrubs in the wild, shaded woods beyond, which, with their unique flora and ancient yews and the almost immortal strawberry trees (*Arbutus unedo*), are enticing. Useful guidebook. This is a place to spend a whole day or more.

National Botanic Gardens, Glasnevin ★   65

Glasnevin, Dublin 9. Tel: (1) 837 4388; Fax: (1) 836 0080;
E-mail: nbg@indigo.ie

Duchas – The Heritage Service • 1.5km N of city centre on Botanic Road close to cemetery • Open all year, daily except 25th Dec, summer, 9am – 6pm, winter, 10am – 4.30pm (Sun opens 11am). Opening times for glasshouses posted at entrance • Entrance: free ○ 🍴 ✕ WC ⅊ ⏚ ⏛ ⏛

This historic garden is changing yearly. Gone is its Victorian atmosphere. The plant collections and glasshouses are undergoing restoration and renewal. Interesting new planting schemes near the entrance and around the Curvilinear Range are helping to expunge the tired image, although major building developments mean disruption in large sections of the gardens. In the winter, the glasshouses are worth visiting; by spring there are daffodil-crowded lawns and flowering cherries; the summer highlight is the double, curving herbaceous border, and in autumn the fruit-laden trees and russet foliage can be magical. The Turner Conservatory (1843–69), the finest in Ireland, has been restored and planted with cycads and related plants, with south-east Asian rhododendrons (sect. Vireya) and plants from the South African fynbos and dry temperate areas of Australia and South America. Glasnevin is undoubtedly worth visiting, especially by gardeners with a strong interest in shrubs and perennials; soil conditions preclude large-scale rhododendron planting. The alpine house contains, in season, collections of plants of considerable interest. Highlights are hard to enumerate, but a few outstanding plants may be mentioned: *Zelkova carpinifolia* (especially in winter a marvellously architectural tree); the ancient wisteria on the Chain Tent (*c.* 1836); the weeping Atlas cedar (*Cedrus atlantica* 'Pendula'); Chusan palms planted in 1870; orchids; *Parrotia persica* (near entrance, wonderful in February and October); and of course 'The Last Rose of Summer'. The gardens hold National Collections of *Potentilla fruticosa* and garryas.

The Phoenix Park 66

Dublin 8. Tel: (1) 8213021; Fax: (1) 8205584

Duchas – The Heritage Service • N of River Liffey. From city centre follow signs to 'The West', or take No. 10 bus to Phoenix Park • Open all year, daily, 7am – 11pm • Entrance: free • Other information: Guided tours of àras an Uachtar in (residence of President of Ireland), Sats from 9.45am from visitor centre
○ 💺 ✕ 🍴 WC ⅏ ⬧ ♨

This is the largest enclosed park in any European city, replete with a herd of fallow deer, some splendid monuments and great houses, most of which are accessible to the public by request. There is a new information centre a short distance from the Phoenix monument, which has been relocated to its original position on the main avenue. The planting is large-scale – the avenues of horse chestnuts, limes and beeches are spectacular in blossom and in autumn, and gas lights twinkle at night the whole way along the ceremonial avenue. The People's Garden, near the main city entrance, is the only part where there is intensive gardening, but the park is a place to be lost in among the hawthorns and the wild flowers.

Powerscourt ★ 67

Enniskerry, Co. Wicklow. Tel: (1) 204 6000; Fax: (1) 204 6900;
E-mail: gardens@powerscourt.ie; www.powerscourt.ie

Slazenger family • 19km S of Dublin, just outside Enniskerry • House open, with exhibition on history of estate and gardens • Gardens open all year, daily except 25th, 26th Dec, 9.30am – 5.30pm (Nov to Feb closes dusk) • Entrance: E6, OAPs and students E5, children (5–16) E3, under 5 free. Separate charge for waterfall (not part of garden) (house and garden E8, OAPs/students E6.50, children E4) ○ 💺 ✕ 🍴 WC ⅏ ⬧ ⚘ 🏛 ♨ ⚲

This is a 'grand garden', a massive statement of the triumph of art over the natural landscape. In its present form, with an amphitheatre of terraces and great central axis (mid-nineteenth century), it is largely the design of the inimitable Daniel Robertson. In some ways it is beyond compare – the axis formed by the ceremonial stairway leading down to the Triton Pond and jet, and stretching beyond to the Great Sugarloaf Mountain, is justly famous. We recommend that you walk along the terrace towards the Pepperpot, and on through the mature conifers which Lord Powerscourt collected. The Pepperpot tower has been restored and visitors can climb it to view 'the killing hollow' and the North American specimen trees in the tower valley. A treetrail, devised by the late Alan Mitchell, has recently been opened, and will amuse dedicated dendrophiles (purchase the book when you get the entrance ticket). Wander on to the edge of the pond and look up along the stairway past the monumental terraces to the faade of the house. That's the view of Powerscourt that is breathtaking – a man-made amphitheatre guarded by winged horses. Statuary and the famous perspective gate, an avenue of monkey puzzles and a beech wood along the avenue add to the glory.

Primrose Hill ★ 68

Lucan, Co. Dublin. Tel: (1) 628 0373

Mrs Cicely and Mr Robin Hall • 13km W of city centre off N4. Turn right signed 'Lucan', drive through village and, after Garda (police) station, take steep, narrow Primrose Lane on left. Continue to top and through black gateway • House open • Garden open Feb, daily, 2pm – dusk, June to July, daily, 2 – 6pm, and at other times by appt • Entrance: E4 ◑ 🍴 **WC** ♨

The garden is approached up a beech avenue, flanked by a developing three-acre arboretum. The garden itself is not much bigger than one acre, yet it succeeds in housing a fine collection of snowdrops – the biggest and certainly the most named collection, including some of their own 'Primrose Hill' seedlings, glorious in flower. It is unusual for a garden to boast that February is its best month – but undoubtedly it is here, starting the visiting season; to return in late spring and summer when the borders are in full colour is an added joy. The herbaceous plants are lovingly cared for and planted in humus-rich compost in large clumps, giving a generous effect to the borders. Irises are high on the priority list, and so are lobelias (two named ones originated here), lilies, kniphofias and, of course, *Primula auricula* 'Old Irish Blue', plus many others.

45 Sandford Road, Dublin

(see THE DILLON GARDEN)

St Anne's Park 69

Raheny, Dublin 3. Tel: (1) 672 3292; Fax: (1) 670 7332; E-mail: parks@dublincorp.ie; Website: www.dublincorp.ie

Dublin Corporation, Mount Prospect Avenue • Park open all year. Rose Garden at best in June, July • Entrance: free NEW ○ 🍴 **WC** ♿ 🐕 🎎 ♨

The park was once the grounds to a grand Victorian mansion, long since demolished but retaining many features of the gardens and fine mature trees. The establishment of the rose garden was inspired by the memory of the vigorous pinky-white Bourbon rose, 'Souvenir de St Anne's', which was discovered in the gardens. The main reason for visiting the large public park today is to see the outstanding display of roses in the 14-acre rose garden where thousands of blooms, from old-fashioned shrub roses to modern hybrid teas, floribundas, climbers and patio miniatures, flourish. The height of the season coincides with the Rose Festival held each July. A new rose, called 'Stardust Memory' and raised in Co. Carlow, was introduced during the 2001 Festival.

Strokestown Park   70

Strokestown, Co. Roscommon. Tel: (78) 33013; Fax: (78) 33712; E-mail: info@strokestownpark.ie; Website: www.strokestownpark.ie

The Westward Group • 23km W of Longford on N5 • House open • Park open April to Oct, daily, 11am – 5.30pm. Parties by arrangement • Entrance: park free; garden E5.71, concessions E4.57; house, museum and garden E11.53, concessions E9.78 • Other information: Restaurant and toilet facilities at Famine Museum ◑ ♨ ✕ ▥ WC ♿ ⬦ ⚘ ⛪ ☕ ☞

The neo-Palladian house, entered from one of the broadest streets in Ireland, was purchased in 1979 by a local company, who put in motion a restoration plan involving the refurbishment of the house, the replanting of the remaining parkland and the creation of new gardens within the old walls. In the five-acre garden is one of the largest double herbaceous borders in these islands, resplendent from the top – silver, blue and white – to the bottom – purple, red and yellow – and repeated for much of its 146 metres. Handsome gates (from Rockingham near Boyle) have been restored and re-erected, the pool and the pergola completed, a yew and beech hedge planted. The old summer-house is close by the new maze and croquet lawn. A rose garden, a wildflower meadow and a fern walk are the latest achievements. The two-acre Georgian walled fruit and vegetable garden, the 1780 vinery, the 1740 banqueting folly and the Regency gazebo tower have all been restored.

Talbot Botanic Garden ★   71

**Malahide Castle, Malahide, Co. Dublin.
Tel: (1) 846 2456; (1) 890 5629 (Parks Department, Dublin)**

Fingal County Council • 16km N of Dublin in Malahide • Castle open • Garden open May to Sept, daily, 2 – 5pm, and to groups by appt. Conducted tour of walled garden, Wed, 2pm • Entrance: E3.50, groups E2.50 per person ◑ ♨ ✕ ▥ WC ♿ ⛪

A 22-acre botanic garden within the 290-acre estate of Malahide with the castle centre stage. The castle was home to the Talbot family for 800 years until the death of Lord Milo Talbot in 1973; in 1976 the estate was acquired by the local authority. The garden is in two sections – the 18-acre West Lawn area of non-ericaceous plants, and a four-acre walled garden of more tender plants. with an emphasis on southern-hemisphere species. Genera well represented are pittosporum, euphorbia, azara, berberis, magnolia, pseudopanax and a National Collection of olearias.

Trinity College Botanic Garden   72

Palmerston Park, Dublin 6. Tel: (1) 497 2070

School of Botany, Trinity College, Dublin • Adjacent to Palmerston Park, near Ranelagh, Dublin • Open all year, daily, Mon – Fri, 9am – 5pm, preferably by appt • Entrance: free ○ ♿

This is essentially a research garden, but there is a small arboretum, order (family) beds and a collection of Irish native plants, including many national rarities, as well as some glasshouses; a fragment of *Todea barbara* from a plant donated in 1892 grows in one glasshouse. Also a collection of saxifrages, the rare Mauritius bluebell (*Nesocodon mauritianus*) and rare species recently collected from the Pitcairn group of islands. *Melianthus major* flowers well every year, and there are good specimens of *Betula utilis* 'Trinity College' and *Sorbus hibernica*.

Trinity College, Dublin 73

Dublin 2. Tel: (1) 608 1724 (Enquiries Office)

Entrances in College Green and Nassau Street. Vehicular access at Lincoln Place Gate • Open all year, daily, 8am – 12 midnight • Entrance: free ○

This 40-acre urban campus contains an eclectic collection of trees in an impressive architectural setting – 600 of them, illustrating what may be grown successfully in town. The most notable are the pair of *Acer macrophyllum* in Library Square, which probably originate from the earliest introduction by David Douglas; one is the largest in Europe. There are also good specimens of *Trachycarpus fortunei*, *Tilia mongolica*, *Betula ermanii*, *Ostrya carpinifolia* and *Sorbus sargentiana*. Lanning Roper devised planting schemes for parts of the campus, and there are low-maintenance shrubberies associated with new buildings. Some interesting modern sculptures, and a handsome campanile (1855). Building work is causing some disruption.

Tullynally Castle 74

Castlepollard, Co. Westmeath. Tel: (44) 61159; Fax: (44) 61856;
E-mail: tpakenham@eircom.ie

Thomas Pakenham • 1.5km NW of Castlepollard on R395 Granard road • Castle open • Grounds open May to Aug, daily, 2 – 6pm, and at other times by appt • Entrance: E4.50, children E1.50 ◑ ➜ ✕ 🧺 <u>WC</u> & ⟨⟩ 🌿 🏬 ⚘

The elaborate early-eighteenth-century formal garden of canals and basins was succeeded by romantic parkland and pleasure grounds in the best Reptonian manner. They encompass two artificial lakes and a grotto of fantastic eroded limestone from nearby Lough Derravaragh. The present owner has added new features: a Gothick summerhouse, a Chinese garden complete with pagoda and a Tibetan garden of waterfalls and ponds. Walled gardens beyond have extensive flower borders and an avenue of memorable 200-year-old yews. The energetic can undertake a mile-long walk through woodland encircling the park, which offers splendid views of the castle.

SYMBOLS
[NEW] entries new for 2002; ○ open all year; ◐ open most of year; ◑ open during main season; ◕ open rarely and/or by appt; ➜ teas/light refreshments; ✕ meals; 🧺 picnics permitted; **WC** toilet facilities; <u>WC</u> toilet facilities, inc. disabled; & partly wheelchair-accessible; ⟨⟩ dogs on lead; 🌿 plants for sale; 🏬 shop; ⚘ events held; ⚭ children-friendly.

SCOTLAND

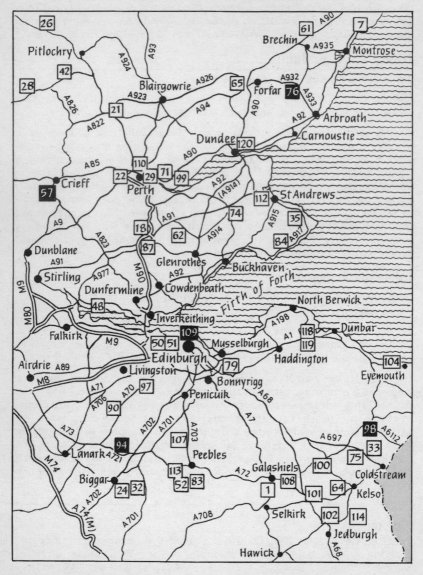

Two-starred gardens are marked on the maps with a black square.

(S.E. & S.W.)

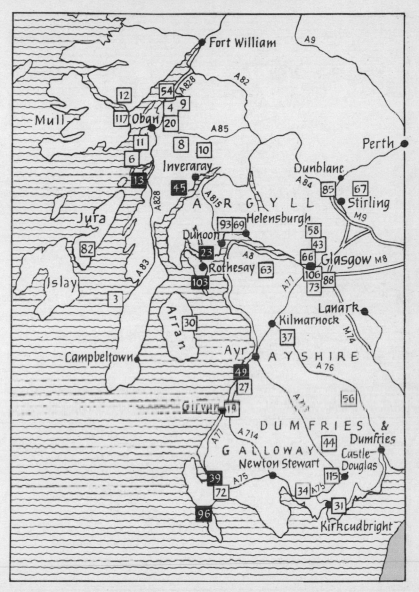

SCOTLAND

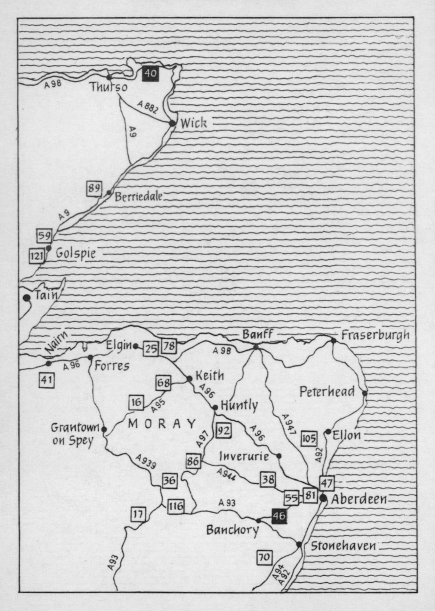

(N.E. & N.W.)

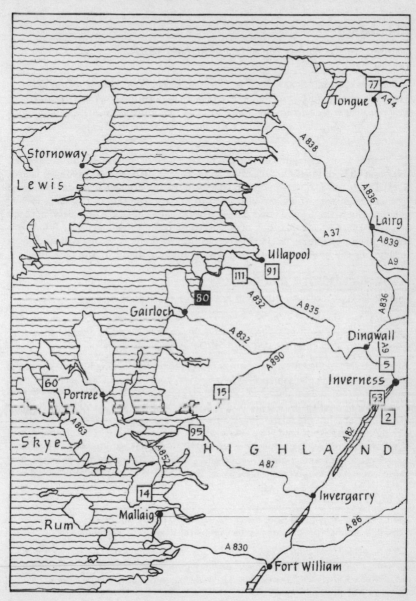

SCOTLAND

Abbotsford 1

Melrose, Scottish Borders TD6 9BQ. Tel: (01896) 752043; Fax: (01896) 752916

Dame Jean Maxwell-Scott • 1m S of Galashiels, 3m W of Melrose on A6091, turn SW onto B6360. Just S of A72 • House open 18th March to Oct, daily, 9.30am – 5pm (March to May and Oct, 2 – 5pm only on Suns) • Garden open June to Oct, daily, 9.30am – 5pm • Entrance: £4, children £2, parties £3 per person, children £1.50 (2001 prices) ◑ 🍵 ▥ WC ♿ ▥ ⚲

Sir Walter Scott's magnificent house astride a river valley was built between 1817 and 1821 to satisfy his yearning to become a laird, and its garden is rich in Scottish allusions. A yew hedge to the south of the house has medallions inset from an old cross, which was also used to make a fountain in the same formal garden. The River Tweed flows past the house, and there are fine views across a stretch of garden. Herbaceous beds lead to a Gothic-type fern house filled with other plants beside ferns. However, dedicated Scott scholars will find most interest in the house, amongst historical relics collected by the laird himself.

Abriachan Garden and Nursery 2

Loch Ness Side, Inverness, Highland IV3 8LA. Tel: (01463) 861232

Mr and Mrs Davidson • 9m S of Inverness off B862 on main Loch Ness road; ignore side roads signed 'Abriachan' • Open Feb to Nov, daily, 9am – dusk • Entrance: £2 (collecting box) NEW ○ 🍵 ✕ ▥ WC ⬥ ⚘ ⚲

Although this is officially a retail nursery, it is also a fascinating hillside garden of over four acres – a plantsman's joy with paved viewing areas and secluded seats from which to contemplate the ever-mysterious Loch Ness. The clever terracing of the beds ensures that plants are seen from every angle and level, and one cannot resist climbing onwards and upwards along the network of paths meandering into the woodland. The owners have obviously worked very hard, and the planting content is comprehensive and professional, ranging from bog plants to gravel lovers and alpines, especially primulas, meconopsis, gentians and campanulas. Enticingly, the majority of the plants on view are also for sale.

Achamore Gardens ★ 3

Isle of Gigha, Argyll and Bute PA41 7AD. Tel: (01583) 505267; E-mail: william@isle-of-gigha.co.uk; Website: www.isle-of-gigha.co.uk

Mr and Mrs Derek Holt • Take A83 to Tayinloan then ferry to Gigha • Open all year, daily, but at time of going to press property on market, so check before travelling • Entrance: £2, children £1, collecting box • Other information: Refreshments at hotel ○ WC ⬥

An amazing idea to create such a superb garden on the Isle of Gigha. The journey there is via most beautiful countryside finishing up with the ferry trip, surrounded by squawking sea birds. In 1944 Sir James Horlick purchased the whole island with the sole purpose of creating a garden in which to grow the rare and the unusual. This was accomplished with the advice of James Russell, and the overall effect is tropical. A delightful woodland landscape was planted with a vast collection from around the world. Few gardens outside the national botanic collections can claim such diversity and rarity. The rhododendrons are unsurpassed in variety, quality and sheer visual magnitude, with fine specimens of tender species such as *R. lindleyii*, *R. fragrantissimum*, and *R. macabeanum*, and there are many varieties of camellias, cordylines, primulas and Asiatic exotica. A great number of genera are represented by very good specimens, thriving in Gigha's mildness. There is a fine *Pinus montezumae* in the walled garden; drifts of Asiatic primulas feature around the especially pretty woodland pond. Gigha is a must, a Mecca for the keen plantsman and avid gardener.

Achnacloich 4

Connel, Oban, Argyll and Bute PA37 1PR. Tel: (01631) 710221

Mrs T.E. Nelson • 3m E of Connel off A85 • Open 25th March to Oct, daily, 10am – 6pm • Entrance: £1.50, OAPs £1, children free ◗ & ⬦

A small castellated Scottish baronial house beautifully situated above the loch on a rocky cliff, with fine views to Loch Etive and the surrounding countryside. A curved drive sweeps past massed bulbs in spring, and later there are azaleas and fine Japanese maples; autumn colour is good throughout the garden. The natural woodland with its interlinked glades is beautiful in spring with bluebells, primroses and wood anemones, while other gaps are planted with primulas, magnolias, rare shrubs and rhododendrons. There are two water gardens, and the garden walks have been extended, taking in an oak wood planted with large-leaved rhododendrons.

Allangrange 5

**Munlochy, Black Isle, Ross and Cromarty, Highland IV0 0NZ.
Tel: (01463) 811249**

Major and Mrs A. Cameron • 5m N of Inverness, signed from A9 • Open several days during summer for charity, 2 – 5.30pm, and at other times by appt • Entrance: £2, children 20p (2001 prices) ◗ ▣ WC & ⬦ ✿ ⊞

A most attractive garden which spills down the hillside in a series of descending terraces merging naturally with the rolling agricultural landscape of the Black Isle. The formal part incorporates white and mauve gardens, many old and shrub roses, tree peonies and a small corner for plants of variegated foliage. In July climbing Himalayan roses, including *Rosa filipes* 'Kiftsgate', make a spectacular display. There is also a small pool garden, and to the rear of the house a woodland garden with unusual rhododendrons, primulas, meconopsis and *Cardiocrinum giganteum*. The hand of an accomplished flower painter, Elizabeth Cameron, shows itself everywhere.

An Cala   6

Easdale, Isle of Seil, Argyll PA34 4RF. Tel: (01852) 300237

*Mrs Sheila Downie • 16m SW of Oban. Signed to Easdale on B844 off A816
Oban – Campbelltown road • Open April to Oct, daily, 10am – 6pm •
Entrance: £1.50* ◐ ⊲◊ ℀

A little jewel of under five acres designed in the 1930s in front of a row of old
distillery cottages, nestling into the surrounding cliffs. The stream, with its
ponds and little waterfall, is an essential element in a series of different spaces
filled with sophisticated colour. This is how azaleas and rhododendrons should
be planted on the small scale – enhancing rather than dominating the picture.
Local slate paths invite the visitor into each well-planned corner. Just over the
gate, in a different world, are ocean and islands.

Arbuthnott House   7

Laurencekirk, Kincardineshire AB30 1PA. Tel: (01561) 361226

*The Viscount of Arbuthnott • 22m S of Aberdeen, 3m from Inverbervie on B967
between A90 (A94) and A92 • Garden open all year, daily, 9am – 5pm •
Entrance: £2, children £1 • Other information: Refreshments available at Grassic
Gibbon Centre in village* ○ **WC**

The enclosed garden dates from the late seventeenth century and with the
policies is contained within the valley of the Bervie Water. The entrance drive
is flanked by rhododendrons and the verges are full of primroses and celandines in spring. The drive crosses a fine bridge topped by imposing urns before
reaching the house set high on a promontory, with most of the garden sloping
steeply to the river. The design is unusual in that it has always been treated as
an extension of the house, rather than being laid out at some distance. The
sloping part has four grassed terraces and this pattern is dissected by diagonal
grassed walks radiating out in a manner reminiscent of the Union Jack. This
fixed structure creates long garden 'rooms' and vistas as the garden is
explored. Although the garden plan is very old, much of today's mature
planting was done by Lady Arbuthnott in the 1920s, and this is continued by
the present Lady Arbuthnott. Herbaceous borders, old roses, shrub roses and
ramblers, shrubs underplanted with hostas, primulas, meconopsis and lilies,
lilacs and viburnums provide colour throughout the summer. A metal stag for
target practice stands at the bottom of the slope by the lade (millstream).

Ardanaiseig Garden and Hotel   8

**Kilchrenan, Argyll and Bute PA35 1HE. Tel: (01866) 833333;
E–mail: ardanaiseig@clara.net; Website: www.ardanaiseig–hotel.com**

*4m E of Kilchrenan on B845 • Open April to Oct, 9am – 8pm • Entrance: by
collection box at car park £2, OAPs and children free • Other information:
Refreshments at hotel. No children under 8* ◐ ▆ ✗ **WC** ⊲◊ ℀

A picturesque 10-mile drive from Taynuilt down the peninsular makes a fitting
introduction to this traditional Argyll garden. Attractive slate paths guide the

visitor round 20 acres of well-planted woodland set behind an 1834 baronial house, now a comfortable hotel, with lovely views across Loch Awe. The species and hybrid rhododendrons are particularly fine. Note the unusual curved walls of the walled garden.

Ardchattan Priory 9

Oban, Argyll and Bute PA37 1RQ. Tel: (01796) 481355; Fax: (01796) 481211; Website: www.gardens-of-argyll.co.uk

10m NE of Oban. Cross Connel Bridge on A828 N and turn first right to Ardchattan • *Open 28th March to 30th Oct, daily, 9am – 6pm* • *Entrance: £2* ◑ WC & ⬗ ℀

A charming garden with spectacular views over Loch Etive. The extensive lawn to the front of the house is surrounded by herbaceous, rose and shrub borders and a rockery. Either side of the drive, the wild garden is full of roses, shrubs and ornamental trees. The garden surrounds a priory (now a private house) founded by the Valescaullian Order in 1230. The ruined chapel and its early graveyard are open with the garden.

Ardkinglas Woodland Garden 10

Cairndow, Argyll and Bute PA26 8BH. Tel: (01499) 600261; Website: www.ardkinglas.com

Mr John Noble • *On A83 Loch Lomond – Inveraray road. Signposted* • *Open all year, daily, during daylight hours* • *Entrance: charge, children under 16 free*
○ 🍴 🍂 WC ⬗ 🌿 🏛 ℀

The reclamation of these 25 acres continues to gather momentum with an ambitious programme of conservation aimed at rejuvenating and diversifying the historic plant collection. Selective felling and the eradication of undesirable regeneration have begun to restore a sense of balance and atmosphere to this dramatic landscape setting above the shores of Loch Fyne. There are panoramic views from the gazebo (linger to read the literary quotations inscribed within) The next generation of plants is well and truly established amongst bluebells and ferns. A further area has new footpaths and a bridge over the River Kinglas giving access to a seventeenth-century mill. The garden contains five champion trees including the 'mightiest conifer in Europe', a silver fir (*Abies alba*) with a girth in excess of 10 metres, and the tallest tree in Britain measured by plumb line, a grand fir (*Abies grandis*) at just over 67 metres.

Ardmaddy Castle 11

By Oban, Argyll PA34 4QY. Tel/Fax: (01852) 300353; E-mail: c.m.struthers@lineone.net

Mr and Mrs Charles Struthers • *13m SW of Oban. Signed from B844 to Easdale along narrow road* • *Open all year, daily, 9am – dusk* • *Entrance: £2*
○ 🍂 WC & ⬗ 🌿 ℀

The handsome but modest fifteenth-century castle, with steps up to its *piano nobile*, faces both ways – outwards with wide views to the islands and the sea, inwards on the garden side towards steep surrounding woods and a formal walled garden. In the eighteenth century Armaddy marked the western extent of the Earl of Breadalbane's estate, enabling him to ride from one side of Scotland to the other on his own land – until all was gambled away in the early twentieth century. The walled garden set below the castle has traditional box hedge compartments and an increasing collection of herbaceous plants and flowering shrubs and trees as well as an immaculate vegetable section. A water garden with two ponds, and a woodland garden with walks add further interest. There is always a good selection of home-grown plants and vegetables (in season) on sale.

Ardtornish 12

Lochaline, Morvern, Oban, Highland PA34 5UZ.
Tel: (01967) 421288 (Estate Office)

Mrs John Raven • 30m SW of Corran. From Corran ferry, 9m SW of Fort William, cross to Morvern and take route left on A861 towards Lochaline, then left on A884. Gardens 2m before Lochaline on left • Open April to Oct, daily, 10am – 4.30pm • Entrance: £3, children free. Collecting box • Other information: 14 self-catering units available, 5 in house ◑ ⬦ ⌀ ⚲

A plantsman's garden with a particularly fine and extensive collection of unusual shrubs, deciduous trees and rhododendrons set against a background of conifers, a loch and outstanding Highland scenery. The gardens have developed over the past 100 years or more following the first house on the site, established by a distiller from London in the 1860s. They are on a steeply sloping site and rainfall is heavy. Mrs Raven's late husband wrote a book, *The Botanist's Garden* (now republished), about their other garden, Docwra's Manor (see entry in Cambridgeshire), and he assisted his wife to follow in her parents' footsteps in trying to establish a plantsman's paradise here. Apart from the area around the house, there is a pleasing air of informality about the gardens, which include Bob's Glen with *Rhododendron thomsonii* and *R. prattii*, a larger glen with still more species and hybrid rhododendrons, and a kitchen garden under separate management nearby, where plants are for sale.

Arduaine Garden ★★ 13

Oban, Argyll and Bute PA34 4XQ. Tel/Fax: (01852) 200366

The National Trust for Scotland • On A816, 20m S of Oban, 17m N of Lochgilphead. Joint entrance with Loch Melfort Hotel • Open all year, daily, 9.30am – sunset • Entrance: £3, concessions and children £2 • Other information: Refreshments at hotel adjacent ○ 🏠 **WC** ♿

Arduaine – popularly pronounced Ardoony, but properly Ardooan – was conceived and planted in the early 1900s by James Arthur Campbell, possibly with advice from his friend Osgood Mackenzie, creator of Inverewe Garden (see entry). The Essex nurserymen Edmund and Harry Wright restored the garden after they acquired it in 1971 and gave it to the Trust in 1992. It consists of an outstanding 20 acres on a promontory bounded by Loch Melfort and the

Sound of Jura, climatically favoured by the North Atlantic Drift or Gulf Stream – make the effort to climb to the high viewing point to enjoy the panorama. Although its fame rests largely on its outstanding rhododendrons, azaleas, magnolias and other rare trees and shrubs (the rhododendron species collection ranks high in importance in Scotland), the garden has far more than botanical interest to offer. Trees and shrubs, some over a hundred years old and thickly underplanted, tower overhead as they, and visitors, climb the glen, while at the lower level hostas, ferns, candelabra primulas and other more modest flowers and foliage cluster around lawns and along the sides of the watercourses.

Armadale Castle Gardens 14

Armadale, Sleat, Isle of Skye IV45 8RS. Tel: (01471) 844305; Website: www.cland.demon.co.uk

Clan Donald Lands Trust • 14m S of Broadford at S end of Skye, close to Mallaig ferry • Visitor Centre open 29th March to Oct • Garden open all year, daily, 9.30am – 5.30pm • Entrance: £4, concessions £3 • Other information: Guided tours with head gardener available. Two electric wheelchairs available ○ ➽ ✕ 🐟 WC ♿ ⟐ 🌵 🏭 🔦 ⚲

This fine garden is so well groomed that it has almost the atmosphere of a city park. The cultivated areas have been sympathetically developed to include pond gardens with scree planting, a long herbaceous border with raised walk behind the ruined castle, lawns with ornamental trees and a romantic garden planted within one of the ruined sections of Armadale Castle. Surrounding the cultivated area are four miles of nature trails set within 50 acres of woodland and wildflower meadows. Although Armadale is further north than Moscow, the climate is warm and everywhere there are inspiring views up Loch Nevis to Mallaig and Knoydart. Allow plenty of time to get here: the 14-mile approach road is single-track in places and every oncoming driver must be acknowledged and thanked. The *Museum of the Isles*, located within the garden, is included in the admission charge and worth visiting.

Attadale 15

Strathcarron, Wester Ross, Ross-shire IV54 8YX. Tel: (01520) 722217; Fax: (01520) 722546; Website: www.attadale.com

Mr and Mrs Ewen Macpherson • 15m NE of Kyle of Lochalsh, on A890 between Strathcarron and Skye • Open April to Oct, daily except Sun, 10am – 5.30pm • Entrance: £3, children £1 • Other information: Honesty box, maps and leaflets inside gate. Disabled parking. Light refreshments and meals available at Carron Restaurant 1½ m away ◑ 🐟 WC ♿ ⟐ 🌵 ⚲

The car park is 50 yards from the garden down the prettiest drive. Inside the gate a stream and ponds all along one side are beautifully planted with candelabra primulas, iris, giant gunneras and bamboos. A bridge over a waterfall links the water garden with the upper rhododendron walk, commanding views of the sea and hills. Sculpture from Zimbabwe and a bronze by

Bridget McCrum are reflected in the ponds. The formal kitchen garden is planted, Villandry-style, with squares of different coloured vegetables and herbs; behind it are recently rediscovered shrubs planted by the Schroder family a century ago. A woodland walk has been reclaimed and replanted with drifts of meconopsis and shade-loving plants, and stone paths lead down to a dell of old rhododendrons surrounded by rocky cliffs. From there the visitor emerges into an area of shrub and ornamental tree plantings ending in a more formal sunken garden. The king of the garden is undoubtedly the 150-year-old laburnum next to the ha-ha, and the owners have now given him over 2000 new subjects planted throughout the garden. Many of the plants, particularly meconopsis and primulas, are for sale. The house (not open) was built in 1755. Visitors are advised to wear waterproof shoes.

Ballindalloch Castle   16

Grantown-on-Spey, Banffshire, Highland AB37 9AX. Tel: (01807) 500205; Fax: (01807) 500210; Website: www.ballindallochcastle.co.uk

Mrs Oliver MacPherson-Grant Russell • Halfway between Grantown-on-Spey and Keith on A95. Signposted • Castle open • Garden open 29th March to Sept, daily, 10.30am – 5pm, and at other times by appt • Entrance: grounds £2 (castle and gardens £5.20) • Other information: Dog-walking area ◑ 💯 🏛
WC ♿ ⌀ 🌱 🏛 💡 ⚲

What a pleasure to find a garden of this scale and calibre set in the magnificent Spey valley. The most attractive feature is undoubtedly the 1937 rock garden, which comes tumbling down the hillside onto the most impressive lawn in the land. It takes three men two days to mow and edge it. The owners have completely renovated all the borders over the last few years and landscaped the old walled garden into a rose and fountain garden. The daffodil season and the river/woodland walks are particularly lovely. A small parterre at the side of the house shows how stunning humble nepeta and *Alchemilla mollis* can be when all else is eaten by the deer, and the walled garden has been transformed with a splendid rose garden.

Balmoral Castle   17

Ballater, Aberdeenshire AB35 5TB. Tel: (013397) 42334/5 (Estates Office); Fax: (013397) 42034; E-mail: info@balmoralcastle.com

H.M. The Queen • 6m W of Ballater on A93 at Crathie • Castle ballroom and carriage exhibitions open • Gardens and grounds open mid-April to end-July, daily, 10am – 5pm • Entrance: £4.50, OAPs £3.50, children (5–16) £1, under 5 free ◑ 💯 🏛 WC ♿ ⌀ 🌱 🏛 💡 ⚲

Balmoral, the personal home of Her Majesty the Queen in Scotland, is Gaelic for 'majestic dwelling'. There had been earlier castles on the same site before the estate was purchased in 1852 by Prince Albert, consort to Queen Victoria. She called Balmoral 'this dear paradise', and she and the Prince immediately began making a three-acre garden about the castle and planting the grounds with rare coniferous and broad-leaved forest trees. Queen Mary added the sunken rose garden in 1932, and since 1953 the Queen and Prince Philip have made other improvements and extensions, the latest being the water garden, created in 1979 close to Queen Victoria's garden cottage. There are herbaceous borders, but generally the gardens are natural in style. Throughout the grounds statues and cairns have been erected in memory of Queen Victoria's family and their descendants, and specimen trees labelled with the names of the visiting dignitaries who planted them.

The Bank House 18

Glenfarg, Perth and Kinross PH2 9N7. Tel: (01577) 830275

Mr and Mrs C.B. Lascelles • 10m SW of Perth off B996 between M90 junctions 8 and 9. In Glenfarg, 50 metres along Ladeside, by Glenfarg Hotel • Open by appt • Entrance: £5 ● 🖿 ⑁ ⟨⟩

The main garden is approached through a paved area with additional planting above low retaining walls. An apple-and-clematis tunnel leads the visitor onwards to large curved beds set into lawns on a gently sloping site. A horse-shoe-shaped yew hedge underplanted with yellow archangel and star of Bethlehem is a fine spring feature; bulbs and early-flowering herbaceous plants carry the display through to summer. The owners have built up an eclectic collection of rare and unusual plants of much merit, and these are grown to perfection using organic gardening techniques. The careful planting, with great regard to colour and form, makes for an instructive visit. A smaller garden across the street, with a 'flowform cascade' water feature and a 'yin and yang' circular bed, may be visited at any time. Ornamental trees have been planted in a field, where a pond has been created and a wildflower meadow sown.

Bargany 19

Girvan, South Ayrshire KA26 9QL. Tel: (01465) 871249

John Dalrymple-Hamilton • 18m SW of Ayr off B734 Girvan – Dailly road • Open May only, Sat — Mon, 10am – 5pm • Entrance: £2, children under 12 free 🖙 🖿 ⑁ ⟨⟩ ⩊ ⑁

This is a woodland garden, densely planted with splendid ancient rhododendrons, azaleas, fine trees and conifers. Wonderfully diverse paths make for a relaxed stroll round a charming lily pond, rock garden and walled garden.

Barguillean's 'Angus Garden' 20

Taynuilt, Argyll and Bute PA35 1JS. Tel: (01866) 822048;
Fax: (01866) 822652

Mr Sam S. MacDonald • 5m SE of Oban, 3m SW of Taynuilt. Take minor road to Kilmore off A85 at Taynuilt Hotel • Open all year, daily, dawn — dusk. Parties welcome by prior appt in writing • Entrance: £2, children free ◐ 🖿 ⟨⟩

Set on a Highland hillside overlooking a lochan with views to Ben Cruachan, this is a nine-acre woodland garden with no formal paths or borders, but with areas of established rhododendrons, azaleas and conifers and some rare trees and shrubs. It is interesting to compare the new planting, combining modern rhododendron hybrids from the north-west of the United States within native birch and oak woodland, with established rhododendron gardens of the west coast. Described by its owner as a place of tranquillity and love, it was created by Betty Macdonald in memory of her writer/journalist son, killed in Cyprus during the 1956 troubles.

Beatrix Potter Garden 21

Birnam, Perth and Kinross PH8 0DS. Tel: (01350) 727674 (Birnam Institute); E-mail: birnaminst@aol.com

Perthshire and Kinross Council • 13m NW of Perth in Birnam, at centre of short loop diversion from A9 • Open all year, daily except 25th Dec, 1st Jan • Entrance: free • Other information: Refreshments and shop at new Birnam Institute nearby, plus Beatrix Potter exhibition (£1 charge, children 50p)

○ 🍵 🍴 WC & 🖼 🏛 💡 ℺

The garden displays bronze sculptures of animals in their natural surroundings, as they were first observed by Beatrix Potter before she humanised them into her enduringly famous characters. Only on an ornamental roadside gate donated by Frederick Warne, holder of copyright to the author's work, do we find Peter Rabbit in the blue jacket so familiar to his fans. In her diaries Beatrix Potter reveals that some of her characters were based upon people she met in the Birnam area during her many visits.

Bell's Cherrybank Gardens and
Scottish National Heather Collection ★ 22

Bell's Cherrybank Centre, Cherrybank, Perth PH2 0PF. Tel: (01738) 627330; Fax: (01738) 472823

Guinness UDV • Off A93 in southern outskirts of Perth, approx 1m from Broxden roundabout • Open 29th March to 1st April, May to Sept, Mon – Sat, 10am – 5pm, Sun, 11am – 5pm; Oct to April by appt • Entrance: £3, children free • Other information: Guide dogs only ◐ 🍵 WC & 🌿 🏛 💡 ℺

This modern garden surrounding commercial offices is in fact two gardens, the first laid out in the early 1970s, plus the Scottish National Collection of heathers, begun in 1983. Their aim is to have the world's largest collection – there are now over 900 varieties, all in superb condition. Other plant collections are well maintained and beautifully designed. Interest is sustained throughout the total of 18 acres by water features, modern sculptures, pleasant vistas, a tiny putting green, tubular bells and an aviary. The children's play area includes a roundabout for wheelchair-bound children. The Bell's Pride of Perth Exhibition is also on the site.

Benmore Botanic Garden ★★ 23

Dunoon, Argyll, Argyll and Bute PA23 8QU. Tel: (01369) 706261; Fax: (01369) 706369

Royal Botanic Garden Edinburgh • At Dunoon, 7m S of A885/A816 junction. Signposted • Open March to Oct, daily, 10am – 6pm, and at other times by appt • Entrance: £3, concessions £2.50, children £1, family £7. Season tickets inc. Dawyck and Logan Botanic Gardens (see entries) available ◑ � ✕ 🖳 WC ⟨⟩ ⌖ 🏠 ⍟ ℺

This specialist garden of the Royal Botanic Garden Edinburgh is a magnificent mountainside garden set in the dramatic location of the Cowal Peninsula. It is world-famous for its collections of flowering trees and shrubs. From Britain's finest avenue of giant redwoods (*Sequoiadendron giganteum*) planted in 1863, a variety of trails spreads out. More than 250 species of rhododendron and an extensive magnolia collection provide a positive array of colour on the hillside beside the River Eachaig. Other features include the formal garden with memorials and stately conifers, the Glen Massan arboretum with some of the tallest trees in Scotland, and an informal pond. A short climb leads to a stunning viewpoint looking out across the garden, Strath Eck and the Holy Loch to the Firth of Clyde and beyond.

Biggar Park ★ 24

Biggar, South Lanarkshire ML12 6JS. Tel: (01899) 220185

Capt. and Mrs David Barnes • 30m SW of Edinburgh at S end of Biggar on A702 • Open May to July by appt. Parties welcome by appt • Entrance: £2 • Other information: Teas by arrangement ◑ 🖳 WC ⌖ ⟨⟩

A Japanese garden of tranquillity welcomes the visitor to this well-planned 10-acre plantsman's garden. The efficient labelling adds greatly to the enjoyment when walking through the woodland and the small arboretum and admiring the well-planted ornamental pond, all carefully designed to give year-round interest. This starts with a stunning display of daffodils, followed by glades of meconopsis, rhododendrons and azaleas in early summer before the huge herbaceous borders burst into colour. The centrepiece, however, must be the outstanding walled garden, reached through a fine rockery bank beside the eighteenth-century mansion house. The view through the wrought-iron gate stretches the length of a 45-metre double herbaceous border, attractively backed by swags of thick ornamental rope hanging from rose 'pillars', whilst either side is divided into intensively planted sections intersected by pleasing grass paths and plots of fruit and vegetables.

Blackhills House 25

Lhanbryde, Elgin, Moray IV30 8QU. Tel: (01343) 842223; E-mail: info@blackhills.org.uk; Website: www.blackhills.co.uk

Mr and Mrs John Christie • 4m E of Elgin off A96. Take B9103 southwards, then minor road • Open 26th, 31st May, and by appt at other times • Entrance: £2, children free • Other information: Teas on open days only ◑ ▮ WC ⌖ ⟨⟩ ⌖ ⍟ ℺

The east coast of Scotland is not, with a few exceptions, noted for its rhododendron gardens, but this garden in the Laich of Moray should be visited for its collection of species rhododendrons in early May and late May for hybrids. Both sorts are spread under tree cover in a steep-sided valley with many fine specimen trees. These include a davidia, a Japanese red cedar (*Cryptomeria japonica*), Brewer's weeping spruce and a golden chestnut (*Chrysolepis chrysophylla*) – a rare chestnut relative from North America. The finest rhododendrons are those in the subsections Falconera, Grandia and Taliensia, but the genus is well represented as a whole. The wooded valley opens to reveal two lakes with plantings of maples and other Asiatic plants. Mr Thomas North Christie, who was responsible for the early planting in the 1920s, corresponded at length and exchanged the latest introductions with his neighbour the Brodie of Brodie.

Blair Castle ★ 26

Blair Athol, Pitlochry, Perthshire PH18 5TL. Tel: (01796) 481207;
E-mail: office@blair-castle.co.uk

The Manager, The Blair Charitable Trust • 35m N of Perth on A9 2m N at Blair Atholl. Signposted • House open as garden • Open April to Oct, daily, 10am – 6pm (last entry 5pm), and Nov to March by appt • Entrance: £2, children £1, OAPs/students £1, family ticket £5. House and grounds £6.25, children £4, OAPs/students £5.25, family ticket £18 NEW ○ 💽 ✕ 🖼 WC ⅃ ⬦ 🏛 🚻 ⚲

Magical and blazing white, the castle remains one of Scotland's most important, most visited and best presented historic houses in private hands. The magnificent 2,500-acre managed park and landscape were begun in 1730 by the 2nd Duke of Atholl in the French manner, with geometrically patterned avenues and walks radiating out from the castle. His most important legacy was the nine-acre walled Hercules Garden of 1758, named after the life-size lead statue by John Cheere which overlooks it. It is unique, not only for its scale, but also for the fact that it contains extensive water features. A series of delightful ponds, planted islands and peninsulas form a central axis from which fruit tree orchards – faithfully reproduced, but without the original underplanting of fruit and vegetables – slope gently upwards to herbaceous borders, yew buttresses and elegant gravel walks backed by the original eighteenth-century walls. A charming apple-store museum, a gardener's cottage, statuary, an ogee-roofed pavilion and a Chinoiserie bridge all add to the beauty of this unusual garden in its splendid Highland setting.

Blairquhan 27

Maybole, South Ayrshire KA19 7LZ. Tel: (01655) 770239;
E-mail: enquiries@blairquhan.co.uk

James Hunter Blair • 12m S of Ayr, 7m SE of Maybole on B7045. Signposted • House open • Garden open 13th July to 11th Aug, daily except Mon, 1.30 – 4.45pm (last admission 4.15pm) • Entrance: £5, OAPs £4, children £3 (house and garden) ● 💽 🖼 WC ⅃ ⬦ ⚘ 🏛 🚻 ⚲

The castle is approached by a three-mile drive along the River Girvan, giving good opportunities to admire the extensive wood and parkland. The three-acre walled garden has been redesigned with ornamental planting, and there is an 1860 pinetum.

Bolfracks   28

Aberfeldy, Perth and Kinross PH15 2EX. Tel: (01887) 820207

Mr J.D. Hutchison • 2m W of Aberfeldy on A827 towards Loch Tay • Open: April to Oct, daily, 10am – 6pm • Entrance: £2.50, children free (honesty box at gate) ◑ WC ⚲ ⚲

There has been a garden on this site for 200 years, but the present garden was started by the owner's parents in the 1920s and reshaped by him over the last 20 years. Three acres of plantsman's garden are well laid out within a walled enclosure and demonstrate the potential of an exposed hillside site with a northerly aspect. Astounding views over the Tay Valley are matched by the garden's own interesting features, including peat walls and a stream garden. There are masses of fine bulbs in spring and good autumn colour. Gentians, meconopsis, ericaceous plants and celmisias do well on this soil. The walled garden contains a collection of old and modern shrub roses and rambling roses.

Branklyn Garden ★   29

116 Dundee Road, Perth, Perth and Kinross PH2 7BB. Tel: (01738) 625535

The National Trust for Scotland • ½ m from Friarton Bridge on A90, then A859 to Perth • Open March to Oct, daily, 9.30am – sunset • Entrance: £2.50, OAPs and children £1.70, family £6.65. Pre-booked parties of 20 or more £2 per person • Other information: Parking ¼ m from gate. Coaches and disabled parking at gate. Possible for wheelchairs but some paths too narrow ◑ 🍴 WC ⚲ 🍴 ☕

John and Dorothy Renton created this garden nearly within sight and certainly within sound of the centre of Perth. Work commenced in 1922, and in 1955 Dorothy was awarded the Veitch Memorial Medal by the Royal Horticultural Society. The National Trust for Scotland took over the garden in 1968, after the death of Dorothy in 1966 and of her husband the following year. It extends to nearly two acres, the main interest being its Sino-Himalayan alpine and ericaceous plants and magnificent scree/rock gardens. There is also a splendid collection of dwarf rhododendrons. Essential work continues to maintain Branklyn's rightful reputation as an outstanding plantsman's garden. It is impossible to describe all the fascinating things to be found here, from the fine trees to the comprehensive collection of dwarf and smaller rhododendrons, the meconopsis to the notholirions. This is a garden that repays many visits.

Brodick Castle ★ 30

Isle of Arran, North Ayrshire KA27 8HY. Tel: (01770) 302202; Fax: (01770) 302312

The National Trust for Scotland • On Isle of Arran, 2m N of Brodick. Ferry from Ardrossan or Kintyre • Gardens and country park usually open all year, daily, 9.30am – sunset, but advisable to check. • Entrance: £2.50, concessions £1.75, parties of 20 or more £2 per person (castle and gardens £6, concession £4, pre-booked parties of 20 or more £4.80 per person) (2001 prices) • Other information: Wheelchair available ○ 🍽 ✕ 🛍 WC ◁ ♿ 🏧 🍵 ⚲

High above the shores of the Firth of Clyde and guarding the approaches to Western Scotland is a castle of locally quarried sandstone. The garden was an overgrown jungle of rhododendrons until it was restored by the Duchess of Montrose after World War I. She was much helped after 1930 when her daughter married John Boscawen of Tresco Abbey (see entry in Cornwall). Many trees and plants arrived at that time by boat from Tresco in the Scillies; others came from subscriptions to the second generation of great plant-hunters like Kingdon-Ward and, in particular, George Forrest, one of the greatest of all collectors. Plants from the Himalayas, Burma, China and South America, normally considered tender, flourish in the mild climate. There is a good display of primulas in the bog garden. The walled formal garden to the east of the castle is over 250 years old and has recently been restored as an Edwardian garden with herbaceous plants, annuals and roses. It is impossible to list all the treasures of the woodland garden, but perhaps the most surprising is the huge size of the specimens in the lower rhododendron walk, where *R. sinogrande* are found with leaves up to 60 centimetres long. Opposite Brodick on the W side of the island, 5 miles north of Blackwaterfoot is *Dougarie Lodge*, an impressive castellated terrace garden created in 1905 to celebrate the marriage of Mary Louise, daughter of the 12th Duke of Hamilton to the 6th Duke of Montrose. A fine plantsman's garden with a good range of semi-hardy trees and plants, and lovely views towards the Mull of Kintyre. [Open one day in summer for SGS and by appt; telephone Mr and Mrs Gibbs on (01475) 337355 for details.]

Broughton House ★ 31

12 High Street, Kirkcudbright, Dumfries and Galloway DG6 4JX. Tel: (01557) 330437; Fax: (01557) 330437; E-mail: fscott@nts.org.uk

The National Trust for Scotland • 28m SW of Dumfries. Take A75 from Dumfries past Castle Douglas, then 1m past Bridge of Dee take A711 to Kirkcudbright. Signposted • Open April to Oct, daily, 1 – 5.30pm (July and Aug opens 11am Mon – Sat, 11am Sun) (last admission 4.45pm). Telephone or fax for winter opening hours. Pre-booked parties may be admitted outside opening hours • Entrance: £3.50, OAPs £2.50, family £9.50 ◐ WC 🍵 ⚲

Created by an artist, E.A. Hornel, who lived here from 1901 to 1933, this fascinating garden reflects an interest in oriental art following his visit to Japan, and incorporates both Japanese and Scottish features. After his death the house became a museum and its surroundings were gradually restored. The garden starts with a sunken courtyard, beyond which is a pleasant hybrid, a cross between 'fantasy Japan and fantasy old-world cottage garden'. Japanese cherries blossom over skilful low-level planting in the sunken courtyard, and further down are all the elements of a much larger garden: rose parterre, pergola, glasshouse, box hedges and herbaceous borders, all looking remarkably uncrowded. Charming lily pools have flat stepping stones and dramatic boulders, and are fed by an immense rainwater tank. At the end of the long central walk, beyond a hedge, is the River Dee with its mudflats and saltings.

Broughton Place   32

Broughton, Biggar, Scottish Borders ML12 6HJ. Tel: (01899) 830234

*Buchanan-Dunlop family, Mr and Mrs R.C. Carr, H. Graham and G. Reilly •
29m SW of Edinburgh, just N of Broughton on A701 Edinburgh – Moffat road.
Follow signs for Broughton Gallery • Garden open 24th March to 30th Sept,
daily except Wed, 10.30am – 6pm • Entrance: by donation to collection box •
Other information: Alternative entrance for wheelchairs* ◐ WC ﹠ ⚘ ﬧ

Winding up the towering eighteenth-century beech avenue, you come to the magnificent turreted modern mansion designed by Sir Basil Spence, cushioned into the surrounding Tweeddale hills. Although nearly 300 metres above sea level, the effects of frosts are limited by the hillside location. Jane and Graham Buchanan-Dunlop have a thriving art gallery, and it is through this that the visitor gains entry into the charming three-acre garden. Meandering paths lead up and down well-kept borders full of rare and interesting plants, mainly herbaceous perennials.

Bughtrig   33

**Leitholm, Coldstream, Berwickshire, Scottish Borders TD12 4JP.
Tel: (01890) 840678**

*Major General and The Hon. Mrs Charles Ramsay • 5m N of Coldstream, ¼ m
E of Leitholm on B6461 • Open 15th June to 15th Sept, daily, 11am – 5pm •
Entrance: £2, children under 18 £1, inc. donation to SGS • Other information:
Special arrangements for bona fide parties to garden, and occasionally to house.
Sometimes possible for parties of up to 8 persons to stay in house* ◐ ﬧ ⬠

Bughtrig has been owned by just three families since the fourteenth century. The traditional Scottish family garden was designed for amenity and support for the larder, but unusually is hedged rather than walled and close to the house. Its two-and-a-half acres contain an interesting combination of herbaceous perennials, shrubs, annuals, vegetables and fruit, surrounded by fine specimen trees which provide remarkable shelter.

Cally Gardens and Nursery 34

**Gatehouse of Fleet, Castle Douglas, Dumfries and Galloway DG7 2DJ.
Fax and Infoline: (01557) 815029**

*Mr Michael Wickenden • 30m SW of Dumfries via A75. Take Gatehouse
turning and turn left through Cally Palace Hotel gateway. Signposted • Open
14th April to Sept, Tues – Fri, 2 – 5.30pm, Sat and Sun, 10am – 5.30pm •
Entrance: £1.50, children under 13 free* ◑ WC ふ ⬦ ⊌

Three hundred Glasgow children 'dug for Victory' here in World War II and
the gardens have flourished since the present owner arrived. A specialist
nursery in the two-and-three-quarter-acre, eighteenth-century walled garden
has large beds of herbaceous plants and many unusual varieties, well worth a
visit by plant lovers. There is a impressive collection of perennial geraniums,
kniphofias, crocosmias and others – 3500 varieties in all. Ninety-five per cent
of the plants in the sales area are propagated on the premises, some from seed
collected abroad or sent in botanic garden exchanges, and a changing selection
of several hundred is available pot-grown. A favourite with visitors is the
spread of meconopsis (Himalayan blue poppies) when in season in early June.
The Cally Oak Woods which surround the nursery have nature trails. Catalogue available (3 x 1st-class stamps).

Cambo Estate Gardens 35

**Kingsbarns, St Andrews, Fife KY16 8QD. Tel: (01333) 450313;
Fax: (01333) 450987; E-mail: cambohouse@cs.com;
Website: www.camboestate.com**

*Mr and Mrs P. Erskine • 6m SE of St Andrews on A917 between Kingsbarns
and Crail • Open all year, daily, 10am – dusk • Entrance: £2.50, children free*
○ ▓ WC ふ ⬦ ⊌

The two-and-a-half-acre walled garden is bisected by the Cambo burn, the
focal point, crossed by rose-hung iron bridges; the sound of running water
adds to the relaxing atmosphere. This is a very productive garden with a new
potager in one section. There are ornamental beds of herbaceous plants, a mass
of roses, and many different shrubs. A section of the original glasshouses is still
in good condition and fully used. In early spring, the snowdrops are spectacular
– over 120 specialist kinds. A lilac walk of 26 varieties makes a visit in May
worthwhile, and from then until September there is plenty of colour and
interest. A woodland garden is being developed.

Candacraig Garden and Nursery 36

Strathdon, Aberdeenshire AB36 8XT. Tel: (01975) 651226

*26m SW of Huntly. Take A97 Huntly – Dinnet road then A944 (formerly B973)
Strathdon – Tomintoul road • Open May to Sept, daily, 10am – 5pm, Sat and Sun,
10am – 6pm, and at other times by appt • Entrance: by donation* ◑ ▓ WC ふ ⊌ ⬧

At an altitude of 300 metres this old walled garden dates from 1820 and
covers a three-acre sheltered site in upper Donside. It features a wild garden

with an established wildflower meadow and a natural clay-lined pond, and a cottage garden brimful of interesting plants. Display beds of primulas and meconopsis make a great show in June. In the main central walk the herbaceous borders were refurbished in 2001. There is also a Victorian summerhouse in Gothic style which houses exhibitions during the summer months and, for readers so inclined, serves as the local registry office and marriage room. A wide range of plants is available for sale and by mail order.

Carnell ★   37

Hurlford, Kilmarnock, South Ayrshire KA1 5JS. Tel: (01563) 884236; Fax: (01563) 884407

Mr and Mrs J.R. Findlay and Mr James Findlay • 4m SE of Kilmarnock, NW of Mauchline on A76, $1\frac{1}{2}$ m off A719 • Open probably 28th July, 2 – 5.30pm. Private parties by appt • Entrance: £2.50, children under 12 free (2001 prices) • Other information: Sixteenth-century pele tower ● ● ● WC & ◁ ▷ ● ●

Eighty years ago this was a limestone quarry – now it is an exquisite example of 90 metres of linear herbaceous borders facing a rectangular pool with informal planting as a contrast on the opposite bank. There is a phlox and shrub border, an interesting rock garden and a walled garden. Burmese and Japanese features include a Chinese gazebo and Burmese dragons, all mementos of Commander Findlay's travels. Climbing the slope behind the pavilion in the south-east corner is the rock garden. The garden adjacent to the house has long herbaceous borders and a shrub and lily collection. The entrance to the demesne is through an archway bedecked with a 'Kiftsgate' rose.

Castle Fraser   38

Sauchen, Inverurie, Aberdeenshire AB51 7LD. Tel: (01330) 833463

The National Trust for Scotland • 15m NW of Aberdeen, off B993 near Kemnay • Castle open Easter; May to Sept, daily; Oct, weekends • Garden open all year, daily, 9am – 6pm • Entrance: £2, concessions £1.30, parties £1.60 per person, school parties £1 per child (castle and garden £5, concessions £3.50, family £12, parties £4 per person, school parties £1 per child) (2001 prices) • Other information: Dogs on dog trail only ○ ● ✕ ● WC & ● ● ●

The grounds – the setting for one of the most spectacular of the castles of Mar – consist of a late seventeenth-/early eighteenth-century designed landscape with eighteenth-century agricultural developments; the work of Thomas White (1794) was followed by 'natural-style' improvements of c. 1800. The deep, south-facing herbaceous border restored in 1959 by James Russell, and the planting in the walled garden designed by Eric Robson along traditional lines in the 1970s, are being substantially renewed to their original schemes. There are excellent views to and from the castle, and extensive walks in the grounds include superb views of the stunning castle in its parkland setting and outwards to nearby hills, notably Bennachie.

Castle Kennedy and Lochinch Gardens ★★ 39

Stranraer, Wigtownshire, Dumfries and Galloway DG9 8BX.
Tel: (01776) 702024; E-mail: ckg@stair-estates.soc.co.uk

The Earl of Stair and the Countess of Stair • 5m E of Stranraer on A75 • Open Easter to Sept, daily, 10am – 5pm • Entrance: £3, OAPs £2, children £1. Discount for parties of 20 or more (2001 prices) ◑ ◙ ▨ WC ௯ ⬙ ℘ ⚒ ℺

One of Scotland's most famous gardens, set on a peninsula between two lochs and well worth a visit for its sheer 75-acre magnificence and spectacular spring colour. The gardens were originally laid out in 1730 around the ruins of his castle home by Field Marshal the 2nd Earl of Stair, who used his unoccupied dragoons to effect a major remoulding of the landscape, combining large formal swathes of mown grassland with massive formal gardens, criss-crossed by avenues and *allées* of large specimen trees. The garden is internationally famous for its pinetum, for its good variety of tender trees and for its species rhododendrons, including many of Sir Joseph Hooker's original introductions from his Himalayan expeditions. The monkey-puzzle avenue, now sadly a little tattered, was once the finest in the world; there is also an avenue of noble firs and another of hollies underplanted with embothriums and eucryphias. An impressive two-acre circular lily pond puts everyone else's in their proper place, and a good walk from this brings you back to the ruined castle and its walled garden, well planted with themed borders.

Castle of Mey ★★ 40

Thurso, Caithness, Highland KW14 8XH.

The Queen Elizabeth Castle of Mey Trust • 1½ m from Mey on A836 • Open probably two days in July, one day in Sept for SGS. Telephone (0131) 229 1870 or (01955) 621697 for details • Entrance: £2, OAPs and children under 12, £1 (2001 prices) ◑

The castle dates from the late sixteenth century and was renovated by H.M. The Queen Mother in 1955. Gardening would not be possible in such an exposed position without the protection of the 'Great Wall of Mey'. Within the walled garden, she has collected her favourite flowers; many were gifts and have special meaning. The personal private feeling pervades the whole garden, which is especially well planted and well maintained. The colour schemes are very good, blending the garden with the vast natural panorama within which it is situated.

Cawdor Castle ★ 41

Cawdor, Nairn, Highland IV12 5RD. Tel: (01667) 404615;
Fax: (01667) 404674; E-mail: info@cawdorcastle.com;
Website: www.cawdorcastle.com

The Dowager Countess Cawdor • Between Inverness and Nairn on B9090 off A96 • Castle open • Garden open May to 13th Oct, daily, 10am – 5.30pm • Entrance: £3.20 (castle and garden £6.10, OAPs £5.10, children £3.30. Family ticket (2 adults and up to 5 children) £18. Parties of 20 or more £5.30 per person) ◑ 💬 ✕ 📷 wc ♿ 🏧 💡 ☎

Frequently referred to as one of the Highland's most romantic castles and steeped in history, Cawdor Castle is a fourteenth-century keep with seventeenth- and nineteenth-century additions. The surrounding parkland is handsome and well kept, though not in the grand tradition of classic landscapes. To the side of the castle is the formal garden, where recently added wrought-iron arches frame extensive herbaceous borders, a peony border, a very old hedge of mixed varieties of *Rosa pimpinellifolia* (the Scots or Burnet rose), a rose tunnel, old apple trees with climbing roses, interesting shrubs and lilies. An abundance of lavender and pinks completes a rather Edwardian atmosphere. The castle wall shelters exochordas, *Abutilon vitifolium*, *Carpenteria californica* and *Rosa banksiae*. Pillar-box red seats create an unusual note in this splendidly flowery place, but the owner likes them. The walled garden below the castle has been restored with a holly maze, a thistle garden, a laburnum walk and a white garden. The latter is a 'Paradise garden', preceded by Earth represented as a knot garden, and between the two lies Purgatory. There are fine views everywhere of the castle, the park and the surrounding countryside, which one can enjoy more actively by walking one of the five nature trails, varying in length from half a mile to five miles. Further developments include the Auchindoune gardens, where Arabella Lennox-Boyd helped with the planting.

Clan Donald Visitor Centre

(see ARMADALE CASTLE GARDENS)

Cluny House ★   42

Aberfeldy, Perth and Kinross PH15 2JT. Tel: (01887) 820795;
E-mail: matcluny@aol.com

Mr J. and Mrs W. Mattingley • 32m NW of Perth. N of Aberfeldy, over Wade's Bridge, take A827 Weem – Strathtay road. House signed in 3m • Open March to Oct, daily, 10am – 6pm • Entrance: £2.50, children free ◑ 📷 ⚒ 💬 ☎

Unlike most other gardens, this is as truly wild as one can find – friendly weeds grow unchecked for fear of disturbing the National Collection of Asiatic primulas. Sheltered slopes create a moist microclimate where all the plants flourish abundantly, including a Wellingtonia with the British near-record girth of over 10 metres. In the superb woodland garden many of the plants were propagated from seed acquired by Mrs Mattingley's father on the Ludlow/Sherriff expedition to Bhutan in 1948. Special treats are the carpets of bulbs, trilliums and meconopsis, a fine selection of Japanese acers, *Prunus serrula*, hundreds of different rhododendrons, *Cardiocrinum giganteum*, massive lysichitons and many fine specimen trees. The garden is managed on strictly organic principles, and it is delightful to see native wild flowers and garden plants growing together in harmony and profusion.

Colzium Lennox Estate 43

Kilsyth, Glasgow G65 0PY. Tel: (01236) 828150

*North Lanarkshire Council • 14m NE of Glasgow, ½ m E of Kilsyth on A803 •
House and museum open by appt • Estate open all year, daily. Walled garden
open April to Sept, daily, 12 noon – 7pm; Oct to March, Sat and Sun only, 12
noon – 4pm • Entrance: free* ○ 🍴 ♨ <u>WC</u> ⚹

An outstanding collection of conifers, including dwarf cultivars, and rare trees
in a beautifully designed large walled garden. Everything is well labelled and
immaculately maintained; even gravel paths are raked. There are also 100
varieties each of snowdrops and crocuses. Other attractions include a seventeenth-century ice-house, a glen walk, a fifteenth-century tower house, an
arboretum, a curling pond and a clock theatre.

Corsock House 44

**Corsock, Castle Douglas, Dumfries and Galloway DG7 3NJ.
Tel: (01644) 440250**

*Mr and Mrs M.L. Ingall • 10m N of Castle Douglas on A712. Signed from
A75 onto B794 • Open by appt • Entrance: £2, children 50p • Other
information: Refreshments on open day* ●

A most attractive 20-acre woodland garden with exceptionally fine plantings
both of trees (*Fagus sylvatica*, Wellingtonia, oak, Douglas fir, cercidiphyllum,
acer) and of rhododendrons (*R. thomsonii, lacteum, loderi, prattii, sutchuenense*). The
knowledgeable owner has contributed most imaginatively to the layout of the
gardens over the last 40 years, creating glades, planting vistas of azaleas and
personally building a temple and *trompe-l'œil* bridge which give the gardens a
classical atmosphere. An impressive highlight is the large water garden, again
cleverly laid out and with the water-edge plantings set off by a background of
mature trees with good autumn colour.

Crarae Garden ★★ 45

Minard, Inveraray, Argyll and Bute PA32 8YA. Tel: (01546) 886614/886388

Crarae Gardens Charitable Trust • 11m SW of Inveraray on A83

> Crarae, one of the most important of Scottish gardens, was forced to close
> in June 2001 due to lack of resources. We have reprinted opposite last year's
> entry from the *Guide* to remind everyone just how remarkable is this
> 'Himalayan ravine' which is threatened with permanent closure. The
> National Trust for Scotland is attempting to step into the breach but
> naturally they have to be sure of an endowment sufficient to guarantee the
> continuity of the garden. At the time of going to press, £1m had been raised
> towards the rescue operation, leaving a further £500,000 to be found. The
> *Guide* invites its readers to send donations to the Trust, 28 Charlotte
> Square, Edinburgh EH2 4ET, and to visit Crarae in 2002 if it is saved.

The gardens at Crarae were originally planned by Grace, Lady Campbell in the early part of last century, possibly inspired by her nephew Reginald Farrer, the famous traveller and plant collector. Subsequently her son, Sir George Campbell (1894–1967), spent many years creating this superb Himalayan ravine set in a Highland glen. Using surplus seed from the great plant expeditions, numerous gifts from knowledgeable friends and the shared expertise of a network of famous horticulturists, Sir George planted a variety of rare trees (his first love), together with exotic shrubs and species rhododendrons, which now form great canopies above the winding paths. These, together with many other plants from the temperate world, make a magnificent spectacle of colour and differing perspectives, the whole enlivened by splendid torrents and waterfalls. The autumn colouring of sorbus, acers, liriodendrons, prunus, cotoneasters and berberis is one of the great features of the garden, which contains a National Collection of nothofagus. Another 50 acres of research arboretum opened in late 2000.

Crathes Castle Garden ★★ 46

Crathes Castle, Banchory, Aberdeenshire AB31 5QJ. Tel: (01330) 844525

The National Trust for Scotland • 3m E of Banchory, 15m SW of Aberdeen on A93 • Castle open April to Sept, daily, 10.30am – 5.30pm (timed entry system; last admission 4.45pm), Oct, daily, 10.30am – 4.30pm (last admission 3.45pm). Other times by appt • Garden and grounds open all year, daily, 9am – dusk • Entrance: castle, garden and grounds £7, OAPs/children/concessions £5. Pre-booked parties of 20 or more £5.20 per person, concessions £5 (2001 prices) • Other information: Parking 400 metres from gardens (charge for non-Trust members). Dogs on nature trail in grounds only ○ ● ✕ 🖼 WC ⅙ ✿ ♿ ⚱

The romantic castle, set in flowing lawns, dates from 1596, and looks much as it did in the mid-eighteenth century. There is no record of how the garden looked then, although the splendid yew topiary of 1702 survives. Sir James Burnett, who inherited the estate, was a keen collector, his wife an inspired herbaceous garden designer, and the garden today reflects their achievements. In all there are eight gardens, each with a different character and varied planting schemes. The terraces and sloping terrain increase the dramatic effect. Rare shrubs reflect Burnett's interest in the Far East. Splendid wide herbaceous borders with clever plant associations were Lady Burnett's creation, the most famous of which is the white border. There are many specialist areas, such as the trough garden; the large greenhouses contain a National Collection of Malmaison carnations. Extensive wild gardens and grounds with picnic areas, with 10 miles of marked trails. Often compared to Hidcote but with evident inspiration from Jekyll.

Cruickshank Botanic Garden 47

St Machar Drive, Aberdeen AB24 3UU. Tel: (01224) 272704

The Cruickshank Trust and University of Aberdeen • 1½ m N of city centre in Old Aberdeen. Entrance in Chanonry. Signposted • Open all year, Mon – Fri,

9am – 4.30pm; also May to Sept, Sat and Sun, 2 – 5pm • Entrance: free. Children must be accompanied by adult ○ ᕕ ᐊᗺ ᑫ

Endowed by Miss Anne H. Cruickshank in 1898 to cater for teaching and research in botany at the University of Aberdeen and for the public good, the original six acres were designed by George Nicholson of Kew. That layout disappeared with World War I. The long wall, herbaceous border and sunken garden date from 1920 but much reverted to vegetable cultivation during World War II. In 1970 the garden was extended and a new rock garden made. A terrace garden was added by the long wall in 1980, a new rose garden completed in 1986 and the peat walls restored in 1988. The rock garden, with a series of connecting pools, has interesting alpines, bulbs and dwarf shrubs. A small woodland area is rich in meconopsis, primulas, rhododendrons and hellebores. Proximity to the North Sea does not permit good growth of large conifers, with the exception of dawn redwood and *Pinus radiata*, but there are fine species lilacs, witch hazels, and the long wall shelters more tender exotics. The total area of the present garden is 11 acres, of which four acres are planted as an arboretum – this is reached by a path from the summit of the rock gardens.

Culross Palace   48

Culross, Dunfermline, Fife KY12 8JH. Tel: (01383) 880359; Fax: (01383) 882675; Email: cwhite@nts.org.uk; Website: www.nts.org.uk

The National Trust for Scotland • 12m W of Forth Bridge off A985 • Open April to Sept, daily, 10am – 5pm, Oct, Sat, Sun, 1 – 5pm • Entrance: palace and garden £5, OAPs £4, family ticket (2 adults and 3 children) £14 (2001 prices) ◑ ☕ ✕ 🗎 <u>WC</u> ᕕ 🌿 🏛 🛡 ᑫ

A small area packed full of fascinating plants and features, including the old poultry breed, the Scots Dumpy. The atmosphere of the seventeenth-century garden is evoked by the crushed-shell paths, and great attention paid to detail – clay watering cans, plants in baskets and hurdles, bee skeps in wall niches. On the walled terrace a kitchen and ornamental garden of the period is planted with an abundance of fruit, vegetables and herbs. Head gardener Mark Jeffrey describes this as a historical showpiece which runs on organic principles; the walled area contains truly old-fashioned vegetables which flourish in a relatively frost-free environment.

Culzean Castle and Country Park ★★   49

Maybole, South Ayrshire KA19 8LE. Tel: (01655) 884400; Fax: (01655) 884522

The National Trust for Scotland • 12m S of Ayr on A719 coast road • Castle open • Gardens and country park open April to Oct, daily, 10.30am – 5.30pm • Entrance: £4, OAPs/children £3, parties £3.50 per person (castle, grounds and country park £8, concessions £6, family ticket £20, groups £6.50 per person) (2001 prices) ◑ ☕ ✕ 🗎 <u>WC</u> ᕕ ᐊᗺ 🌿 🏛 🛡

Over 200,000 people a year visit Culzean, regarded by many as the flagship of The National Trust for Scotland. The castle was originally a medieval fortified house atop the Ayrshire cliffs, but was extensively restructured by Robert Adam from 1777 in what has become known as his 'Culzean' style. This is reflected in the many fine architectural features scattered throughout the grounds, and in particular the handsome home farm courtyard, now a visitor centre. Restoration work continues. A major undertaking was the consolidation and partial rebuilding of Robert Adam's unique viaduct. The camellia house, a picturesque 1818 glasshouse, has been beautifully restored to its original use as an orangery, and the fountain in the garden below the castle has been repaired and replumbed. The Swan Pond buildings have been conserved and repaired along with the beautiful bridge to the north. The restored pagoda is now spectacular, the vinery in the south walled garden has also been restored, and the Dolphin House turned into an environmental education centre for school visits. The country-park landscape covers 563 acres with a network of woodland and cliff-top paths; the gardens themselves occupy a spacious 30 acres and include all the traditional elements of a grand garden at the turn of the century, the main elements being a fine fountained pleasure garden and a vast walled garden with herbaceous and vegetable plantings.

Dalmeny: The House 50

South Queensferry, Edinburgh EH30 9TQ. Tel: (0131) 331 1888

The grounds around the house open July and Aug, Sun, Mon, Tues, 2 – 5.30pm. Parties by arrangement at other times • Entrance: grounds free. House (with collection) £4, OAPs £3.50, students £3, children (10–16) £2, under 10 free. Parties of 20 or more £3 per person during opening hours ● ● WC & ⬦ ●

Some one and a half miles from Mons Hill (see below) is the Garden Valley and other ornamental areas close to the house. They feature rhododendrons, azaleas and specimen trees, and are worth seeing if the house itself is to be visited.

Dalmeny: The Park 51

Mons Hill, Dalmeny Estate, South Queensferry, Edinburgh. Tel: (0131) 331 1888

The Earl of Rosebery • 7m W of Edinburgh city centre off A90. • Mons Hill open for charity one Sun late Feb/early March, depending on snowdrops • Entrance: £2, children free ● ●

Mons Hill is a partially wooded hill of semi-natural hardwoods with several acres of wild snowdrops and outstanding views (weather permitting) towards the Pentland Hills, Edinburgh and the Firth of Forth. The snowdrops are over a quarter of a mile uphill from the car park and must be seen to be believed, although Wellington boots are recommended. There is no possibility of taking wheelchairs or vehicles up the hill.

Dawyck Botanic Garden ★ 52

Stobo, Peeblesshire, Scottish Borders EH45 9JU. Tel: (01721) 760254;
Fax: (01721) 760214; Website: www.rbge.org.uk

Royal Botanic Garden Edinburgh • 20m SW of Edinburgh, 8m SW of Peebles on B712 • Open 14th Feb to 15th Nov, daily, 10am (closing times vary), and at other times by appt • Entrance: £3, concessions £2.50, children £1, family £7. Season tickets inc. Logan and Younger Botanic Gardens (see entries) available • Other information: Guide dogs only ◑ ● ▮ WC ℗ ⚏

This is a specialist garden of the Royal Botanic Garden Edinburgh (see entry). With over 300 years of tree planting, Dawyck is one of the world's finest arboretums; its collections include rare Chinese conifers and the unique Dawyck beech. At the entrance is the formal azalea terrace which leads the visitor into Scrape Glen, and from here paths cross the slopes of Scrape Hill, with the burn tumbling down under the Swiss bridge in the middle of the glen. The mature specimen trees stand majestically, towering above a variety of flowering trees and shrubs. From further up the hill there are magnificent views of the garden, including the beech walk with its tree-top outlook. In the Heron Wood is the first cryptogamic sanctuary and reserve for non-flowering plants; illustrated panels provide details of the essential role played by these plants. The fine stonework and terracing on bridges, balustrades and urns was produced by Italian craftsmen in the 1820s.

Dochfour Estate 53

Dochfour, Inverness, Highland IV3 8GY. Tel: (01463) 861218 (Estate Office);
Fax: (01463) 861366; E-mail: admin@dochfour.co.uk

Hon A.J. Baillie • 6m SW of Inverness on A82 • Open April to Sept, Mon – Fri, 10am – 5pm • Entrance: £1.50, OAPs and children 50p • Other information: PYO in season ◑ & ●

The estate is bounded by the River Ness to the east, and overlooked by steeply rising hills providing a dramatic backdrop to the extensive walled kitchen gardens. The formal landscaped gardens are contained within high yew hedges clipped at intervals to provide spectacular views of the loch below. There are large areas of rhododendrons, terraces of daffodils, vast grass parterres and magnificent trees.

Druimavuic House Gardens 54

Appin, Argyll and Bute PA38 4BQ. Tel: (01631) 730242

Mr and Mrs Newman Burberry • 4m S of Appin on A828 Oban – Fort William road, turn L at new road bridge. Signposted • Open April to June, daily, 10am – 6pm • Entrance: £1, children free ◑ ▮ ⬧ ℗

A romantic site which was begun after World War I but has now been replanted and cultivated by its dedicated owners. The humorous and descriptive guide states that 'the real architect of Druimavuic Gardens is Nature', but they have certainly embellished her work most successfully. The stream garden makes an immediate impact with colourful clumps of many varieties of primulas (*florindae, vialii* and 'Inverewe') and meconopsis mixed in with other varied spring plantings. The well-planted woodland garden has lovely open oil-painting views of cattle watering in the loch below. There is an excellent working kitchen garden with strawberries grown at eye level.

Drum Castle   55

Drumoak, by Banchory, Aberdeenshire AB31 5EY. Tel: (01330) 811204;
E-mail: drum@nts.org.uk; Website: www.drum-castle.org.uk

The National Trust for Scotland • 10m W of Aberdeen, 3m W of Peterculter, off A93 • Garden open April to Sept, daily, 10am – 6pm; Oct, Sat and Sun, 10am – 5.30pm. Grounds open all year, daily, 9.30am – sunset • Entrance: grounds free, garden only £1 (castle, garden and grounds £6, children and concessions £4.50; parties of 20 or more £4.50 per person (2001 prices) • Garden: ◑ ☕ 🍴 WC ♿ ஓ ♨ ⌖ *Grounds:* ○ ⬩ ⚲

Within the old walled garden of the castle, the Trust has established a 'garden of historic roses' which was officially opened in June 1991 as part of its Diamond Jubilee celebrations. The four quadrants of the garden are designed and planted with roses and herbaceous or other plants appropriate to the seventeenth, eighteenth, nineteenth and twentieth centuries. The central feature is a copy of the gazebo at Tyninghame, East Lothian (see entry), and a small garden house in one corner, now restored, acts as an interpretative centre. The grounds around the castle also contain interesting conifers, spacious lawns and walks in the Old Wood of Drum, a SSSI.

Drumlanrig Castle   56

Thornhill, Dumfries and Galloway DG3 4AQ. Tel: (01848) 330248/600283;
Fax: (01848) 331682; E-mail: bre@drumlanrigcastle.org.uk;
Website: www.drumlanrigcastle.org.uk

The Duke of Buccleuch • 16m SW of M74 Junction 14, 18m NW of Dumfries, 3m N of Thornhill on A76, between A77 and A75 Signposted • Castle open 27th April to 8th Sept Mon – Sat, 11am – 4pm, Sun, 12 noon – 4pm (closed 12th to 23rd Aug) • Garden and country park open 27th April to 30th Sept, daily, 11am – 5pm • Entrance: £3 (extra charge for house) NEW ◑ ☕ ✕ 🍴 WC ♿ ♨ ⚲

Built in the late seventeenth century by William Douglas, 1st Duke of Queensberry, Drumlanrig is one of Scotland's finest and most palatial residences. The formal terraces and parterres around and below the house reflect this contemporary 'grand manner', in a magnificent setting. The parterres were first restored to their former glory in the Victorian era by two of the foremost designers of their day, Charles M'Intosh and David Thomson who, in the fashion of the time, introduced a variety of foreign plants and shrubs as well as many of the exotic conifers still thriving in the woodland walk today. These include one of the oldest Douglas firs in the UK, the tallest weeping beech (*Fagus sylvatica* 'Pendula') and an early fan-trained *Ginkgo biloba*. A charming heather-rooted pavilion in the woodland walk overlooks the tumbling Marr burn. The gardens were simplified during the two world wars and are now being beautifully restored again. The four parterres, all with different plants and colour themes, are stunning seen from the 220-yard-long terrace above; the Shawl Parterre in particular has a pretty design using circles, ovals and hearts. Annuals are used on an impressive scale: 2000 pink and white begonias, 2000 *Cineraria (Senecio)* 'Silver Dust' and 1000 antirrhinums.

Drummond Castle Gardens★★ 57

Muthill, Crieff, Perth and Kinross PH5 2AA. Tel: (01764) 681257;
Fax: (01764) 681550; E-mail: thegardens@drummondcastle.sol.co.uk

Grimsthorpe and Drummond Castle Trust Ltd • 2m S of Crieff on A822 • Open 29th March to 1st April; then May to Oct, daily; all 2 – 6pm (last admission 5pm) • Entrance: £3.50, OAPs £2.50, children £1.50 ◗ **WC** ⬧ ❂

The gardens were first laid out in 1630 by John Drummond, 2nd Earl of Perth. Next to the fine castle, across a courtyard, is the house and below both is the great parterre garden with, at its centre, the famous sundial made by the master mason to Charles I. When the garden was revived by Lewis Kennedy from 1818 to 1860, he achieved what *The Oxford Companion* calls 'the re-creation of an idea of the seventeenth-century Scottish garden' with stunning effect. The long St Andrew's cross design has Italian, French and Dutch influences. Beautiful white marble Italian statuary is set in arbours along the southern borders. The fruit and vegetable gardens and glasshouses should also be visited.

Dun Ard 58

Main Street, Fintry, Stirlingshire G63 0XE. Tel: (01360) 860369.

Mr Alastair Morton and Mr Niall Manning • 17m SW of Stirling. 17m N of Glasgow on B822 • Open by appt only • Entrance: free ●

An exceptionally well-planned organic garden incorporating many of the most stimulating elements of contemporary horticultural design, all carved out of a sloping three-acre field. Areas of exuberant planting are interspersed with minimalist, restful or wild areas, so that visitors are always ready for the next surprise as they climb ever onward and upward, culminating at a sandstone pyramid with a bird's-eye view over the whole garden, the valley and the mountains beyond. All the features sought after by today's gardeners are here – a *potager*, an early garden, a rose parterre, a bulb meadow, a still pool enclosed by a beech hedge, a bog garden, a formal pleached hornbeam avenue and, best of all, a late garden planted in hot colours in the increasingly popular continental matrix style, combining wild and herbaceous patchwork planting, viewed in all its deliciousness from a smart decking platform.

Dunrobin Castle Gardens ★ 59

Golspie, Sutherland, Highland KW10 6SF. Tel: (01408) 633177/633268;
Fax: (01408) 634081

The Sutherland Trust • 1m NE of Golspie on A9 • Castle open • Garden open April to 15th Oct, Mon – Sat, 10.30am – 4.30pm, Sun, 12noon – 4.30pm;

Jun to Sept, daily, 10.30am – 5.30pm; (Suns in June and Sept opens 12 noon)
• *Entrance: £6, OAPs and children £4.50, students £5, family £17, parties*
£5.50 per person, OAPs and children £3. British school parties free ◑ ☕ ✕ 📷
WC ♿ ♨

These Victorian formal gardens were designed in the grand French style to
echo the architecture of Dunrobin Castle, which rises high above them and
looks out over the Moray Firth. They were created by the architect Sir
Charles Barry in 1850. Descending the stone terraces, one can see the round
garden (evocative of the Scottish shield, perhaps), grove, parterre and
herbaceous borders laid out beneath. The round ponds, all with fountains,
are a particular feature, together with the wrought-iron Westminster gates.
Roses have been replaced with hardy geraniums, antirrhinums, and *Potentilla
fruticosa* 'Abbotswood'; the interest continues from tulips in spring through to
the autumn-flowering lilies. An eighteenth-century summerhouse, converted
into a museum in the nineteenth century, is now also open to the public and
well worth seeing. Other developments include the removal of the shrubbery and its replacement by 20 wooden pyramids covered in roses, clematis
and sweet peas and interplanted with small ornamental trees to continue the
French style visible elsewhere. In the policies there are many woodland
walks.

Dunvegan Castle   60

Isle of Skye IV55 8WF. Tel: (01470) 521206; Fax: (01470) 521205;
E-mail: info@dunvegancastle.com

MacLeod Estate • *14m NW of Portree, beyond A850/A863 junction* • *Castle
open* • *Garden open all year, daily, 10am – 5.30pm (Nov to mid-March closes
4pm)* • *Entrance: £3.80, children £2 (castle and gardens £5.50, concessions £5,
children £3) (2001 prices)* ○ ☕ ✕ 📷 WC ⬦ ♿ ♨ ♿

A superb backcloth for the castle which stands on the shores of Loch
Dunvegan, the gardens have three areas of interest. First, a round garden
with a boxwood parterre of 16 triangular beds, three mixed borders for
summer show and a fern house. Second, an expanding woodland waterfall dell,
which carries the season on past rhododendron time. The meconopsis and
giant cardiocrinums are breathtaking in this setting, but note also tiny
maidenhair ferns, native woodsage and other treasures. Third, an exciting
two-acre walled garden, created by head gardener Thomas Shephard on a
long-derelict site and open to the public since 1998. Laid out on a formal plan,
the four quarters each have a focus of interest: a lawn with a sorbus avenue; a
raised pool with gravel surround pierced by plants; a triangle with an internal
yew triangle; and an unusual stepped 'temple' evocative of Mayan architecture.
The surrounding paths spill over with helianthemums, cistus and other
Mediterranean plants. Non-gardeners can take an exciting boat trip to the
nearby seal colony – on a calm day.

Edzell Castle ★ 61

Edzell, Brechin, Angus DD9 7UE. Tel: (01356) 648631

Historic Scotland • 6m N of Brechin. Take A90 (A94) and after 2m fork left on B966 • Ruins open (closed Thurs pm and Fri in winter) • Garden open April to Sept, Mon – Sat, 9.30am – 6.30pm; Sun, 9.30am – 6.30pm; Oct to March, Mon – Sat, 9.30am – 4.30pm, Sun, 2 – 4.30pm (last admission ½ hour before closing) • Entrance: £2.80, OAPs and UB40 holders £2, children (5–16) £1, under 5 free) ○ 🐚 WC ♿ ⬇ 🌿 ⚏ 🏮 ⚲

In 1604 Sir David Lindsay made a remarkable small walled garden at his fortress at Edzell; as reconstructed, it gives us a clear idea of how his garden might have looked in its heyday. By the time they came into the custody of H.M. Office of Works in 1932, the garden and castle had lain in ruins for over 150 years. Although the plantings date from the 1930s, they are elaborate examples in the manner of the period of the early seventeenth century. Meticulously kept parterres of box, lawn, and bedding are contained within the original walls of unique and curious design. There are 43 panels of alternating chequered niches and sculptured symbolic figures with large recesses below for flowers. The whole is laid out to be viewed from a corner garden-house and the windows of the now-ruined castle. Edzell itself is a good example of an ordered Victorian Scottish Highland village, with shops, a tea room and two hotels.

Falkland Palace Garden 62

Falkland, Fife KY7 7BU. Tel: (01337) 857397

The National Trust for Scotland • 11m N of Kirkcaldy via A92 and A912. M90 junction 8 from Forth Road Bridge • Palace open as garden (last tour of palace 4.30pm) • Garden open April to Oct, Mon – Sat, 11am – 5.30pm, Sun, 1.30 – 5.30pm (June to Aug opens 11am weekdays) • Entrance: £2.50, OAPs and children £1.70 (palace and garden £5, OAPs and children £3.50) (2001 prices) • Other information: Parking 100 metres from palace. Toilet facilities in town car park and next to NTS shop ◑ 🐚 WC ⚏

This was originally the garden at the sixteenth-century palace, which was the hunting lodge for the Stuart monarchs. Kings and queens from James II to Charles II enjoyed the Fife landscape and the grounds of the Renaissance palace. During World War II the garden was a 'Dig for Victory' effort and was thereafter remodelled by the landscape designer Percy Cane. The palace itself lends a gracious and dignified atmosphere to this three-acre garden. The shrub island borders are now fully mature and provide a good illustration of how to break up large areas of lawn. The main herbaceous border, recently replanted, runs the full depth of the garden and is maturing well, and there is a memorable narrow border filled with delphiniums. In addition, visitors can see the royal tennis court (i.e. real tennis) where occasional competitions of this old game are still staged, and an outdoor chequers game near the herb garden. There is also an orchard. Note the interesting village houses nearby.

Finlaystone 63

Langbank, Renfrewshire PA14 6TJ. Tel/Fax: (01475) 540285;
E-mail: info@finlaystone.co.uk; Website: www.finlaystone.co.uk

Mr George Gordon MacMillan of MacMillan • 8m W of Glasgow Airport, on A8 W of Langbank • Old Kitchen open by appt • Garden open all year, daily, 10.30am – 5pm • Entrance: £3, OAPs and children £2 • Other information: Doll museum and Celtic exhibition in visitor centre. Play area ○ 🍵 🍴 WC
&. ⟨⊲⟩ 🏛 ⚓ ℗

Designed in 1900 and enhanced and tended over the last 50 years by the late Lady MacMillan, much respected *doyenne* of Scottish gardens, and her family, this spacious garden is imaginatively laid out over 10 acres, with a further 70 acres of mature woodland walks. There are large, elegant lawns framed by long herbaceous borders, interesting shrubberies and mature copper beeches looking down over the River Clyde. John Knox's tree, a Celtic paving 'maze', a paved fragrant garden and a bog garden are added attractions. A walled garden is planted in the shape of a Celtic ring cross.

Floors Castle 64

Roxburghe Estate Offices, Kelso, Roxburghshire, TD5 7SF. Tel: (01573) 223333; Fax: (01573) 226056; Website: www.floorscastle.com

The Duke of Roxburghe • Well signposted on the outskirts of Kelso • Open 28th March – 27th Oct, 10am – 4.30pm • Entrance to house and garden: £5.50, OAPs/students £4.50, children £3.25, family ticket £15 ○ 🍵 ✕ 🍴 WC &.
⟨⊲⟩ 🐾 🏛 ⚓

Floors Castle is, architecturally, one of Scotland's grandest country houses – a real swagger castle – magnificently situated with glorious views across a huge sweep of open parkland. The walled kitchen garden of 1857 is of equally stately proportions and contains the classic mix of glasshouses, herbaceous borders, fruit, vegetables and annuals. The borders – long, broad and packed with colour – have a backing of chain swags covered with the bright pink rose 'American Pillar'. The large children's playground is conveniently, but not aesthetically, sited within the walled garden. Recent additions are a woodland garden and a two-acre parterre, designed in the French style and featuring the intertwined initials of the present Duke and Duchess. Much use has been made of traditional box, with contrast and highlighting provided by *Euonymus fortunei* 'Emerald 'n' Gold'.

Glamis Castle 65

Glamis, Forfar, Angus DD8 1RJ. Tel: (01307) 840393; Fax (01307) 840733; E-mail: admin@glamis-castle.co.uk; Website: www.glamis-castle.co.uk

The Earl of Strathmore and Kinghorne • 5m W of Forfar on A94 • Castle open, guided tours • Garden open April to Oct, daily, 10.30am – 5.30pm (last admission 4.45pm) • Entrance: £3.20, OAPs, students and children (5–16) £2,

disabled persons free (castle and grounds £6.50, OAPs and students £4.80,
children (5–16) £3.20, family ticket £18). Reductions for parties of 20 or more
◑ ☕ ✕ 🗎 WC ♿ ⬦ 🌳 🏛 🍽 🦮

At the end of a long, tree-lined avenue and against the backdrop of mountain
and moorland, the turrets and spires of Glamis Castle beckon the visitor.
Although much older, the park was landscaped in the 1790s by a garden
designer working under the influence of 'Capability' Brown, and the avenue
was replanted about 1820. On the lawn near the castle is an intriguing Baroque
sundial, six and a half metres tall and with a face for every week of the year. On
the east side of the castle a two-acre Italian garden consists of high yew hedges,
herbaceous borders, fountain and seventeenth-century-style gazebos, and the
creation of this quiet haven is commemorated by an engraved stone. The
pinetum, planted c.1870, is now open to visitors. Glamis was the childhood
home of H.M. The Queen Mother.

Glasgow Botanic Gardens   66

730 Great Western Road, Glasgow G12 0UE. Tel: (0141) 334 2422;
Fax: (0141) 339 6964

Glasgow City Council • Near city centre on corner of Great Western Road and
Queen Margaret Drive • Open all year, daily, 7am – dusk. Kibble Palace
Glasshouse open 10am – 4.45pm (4.15pm in winter). Main range open 10am
– 4.45pm (closes 4.15pm in winter) • Entrance: free ○ ☕ 🗎 WC ♿ ⬦
🍽 🦮

A pleasant afternoon's walk with well-maintained herbaceous, shrub and
annual borders. A greatly extended herb garden is in the process of being
developed and will include a unique Scottish Garden containing plants
endemic to Scotland with explanatory labels on how these plants have
been utilised over centuries. The chief attraction, and well worth visiting, is
the Victorian Kibble Palace. This glasshouse, built in 1872, houses temperate
plants interspersed with classic marble statuary. In the nearby tropical
glasshouses are displays of orchids and the National Collection of species
begonias, also cacti and economic plants – all meticulously maintained. The
Arid Adaptations house has on display some of the most bizarre plants in
the world; the unique development of island plants is also demonstrated
here.

14 Glebe Crescent   67

Tillicoultry, Stirling, Perthshire FK13 6PB. Tel: (01259) 750484

Mrs Joy McCorgray • 8m W of Stirling on A91 at east end of village; signed by
yellow arrow at Glebe Crescent • Open for SGS, and by appt • Entrance: £2,
children free [NEW] ☕ 🌳

This delightful half-acre plantsman's garden is designed to fill every corner
with a different plant setting and thus a different 'feel'. Clever terracing of the
natural slope ensures that the garden does not seem unduly overcrowded and
yet, believe it or not, there is a Japanese koi carp pool, a collection of bonsai, a

perfumed garden, a formal courtyard area, a conifer lawn, over 40 ornamental grasses and a woodland area with a large collection of rare ferns, arisaemas, hellebores and trilliums. Our inspector particularly admired the unusual *Cercidiphyllum japonicum* 'Ruby' and the variegated angelica tree (*Aralia elata* 'Aureovariegata') but most people covet the beautiful umbrella pine (*Pinus pinea*). As if this wasn't enough, the owner has won first prize in the council garden competition for hanging baskets, and comments: 'There's a lot squashed into this garden'. Indeed there is.

Glen Grant Garden 68

Rothes, Aberlour, Moray AB38 7BS. Tel: (01542) 783318

Glen Grant Distillery • 10m SE of Elgin on A941, on main roundabout in Rothes • Open April to Oct, daily: Mon – Sat, 10am – 4pm, Sun, 12.30 – 4pm; Nov to mid-March by appt • Entrance: garden and distillery £2.50 (inc. £2 voucher redeemable against purchase of 70cl bottle of whisky) • Other information: Distillery tours ◑ WC & ℘

It is hard to believe that you are further north than Moscow in this sheltered glen, originally laid out in 1886 by Major James Grant when he inherited the family business. It has been well restored with exact replicas of the original rustic bridges, waterside paths and his heather-thatched dram hut. Excellent descriptive leaflet and plant list.

Glenarn ★ 69

Rhu, Helensburgh, Dunbartonshire G84 8LL. Tel: (01436) 820493; Fax: (0141) 2216834

Michael and Sue Thornley • On A814 between Helensburgh and Garelochhead. Go up Pier Road to Glenarn Road • Open 21st March to 21st Sept, daily, dawn – dusk • Entrance: £2, OAPs/children £1 • Other information: Refreshments on certain open days only ◑ 🍴 ⬤ ℘ ℺

Established in the 1920s by the Gibson family, this is a very special woodland garden. An earlier Victorian garden had been fed by the famous plant expeditions. Well-kept paths meander round a 10-acre sheltered bowl, sometimes tunnelling under superb giant species rhododendrons (including a *falconeri* grown from seed supplied by Hooker in 1849), sometimes allowing a glorious vista across the garden to the Clyde estuary, and sometimes stopping the visitor short to gaze with unstinted admiration at 12-metre magnolias, pieris, olearias, eucryphias and hoherias. The owners, both professional architects, acquired Glenarn some years ago and with almost no help are successfully replanting and restoring where necessary, whilst retaining the special atmosphere created by such magnificent growth. The rock garden falls steeply down past the daffodil lawn to the house with its tall, twisting chimney pots; work is continuing to expose the quarry face and restore the scree bed.

Glenbervie House 70

Drumlithie, Stonehaven, Kincardineshire AB39 3YA. Tel: (01569) 740226

*Mrs C.S. MacPhie • 8m NE of Laurencekirk, 6m from Stonehaven off A90
Laurencekirk – Stonehaven road. On minor road 3m W of Drumlithie • Open
one day for charity, and by appt • Entrance: £2, children 80p (2001 prices)*
◐ ◪ ▨ WC ⌘

Two very different gardens may be enjoyed here – a traditional Scottish walled
garden on a slope, and a woodland garden by a stream. Occupying one wall of
an enclosed garden is a fine example of a Victorian conservatory, with a great
diversity of pot plants and climbers on the walls. Elsewhere in the walled area
is a typical mix of herbaceous plants, fruit, vegetables and summer bedding.
There are many shrub and old roses, and on walls and pillars a variety of
climbing and rambler roses. Spring brings good displays of bulbs, and the
woodland garden with its drifts of primulas, ferns and interesting shrubs is
beautiful in early summer. There are fine trees near the house.

Glendoick Gardens ★ 71

**Glendoick, Glencarse, Perth and Kinross PH2 7NS. Tel: (01738) 860205
(Nursery); (01738) 860260 (Garden Centre); Website: www.glendoick.com**

*Mr and Mrs Peter Cox and Kenneth Cox • 8m E of Perth, 14m SW of Dundee
on A90 • Open probably two Suns in May for SGS, and for parties by appt in
May • Entrance: £2, children under 5 free (2001 price) •* ◐ ◪ WC ♿ ⌘ ⊞

One of the world's most comprehensive collections of rhododendrons is
contained within the grounds of a fine Georgian mansion associated with
Bonnie Prince Charlie, who is reputed to have visited the Laird of Glendoick
one dark night in 1745. The plant collection was started by the late Euan H.M.
Cox, and the present owners planted an arboretum in 1993 in memory of the
100th anniversary of his birth. They continue to visit the East in search of
new varieties and grow a wide range of hybrids and new cultivars from
elsewhere. The woodland garden, which has also been extended, is full of
naturalised wild plants as well as introductions. Roy Lancaster says this
garden is a focal point for all who believe that plant exploration in its
noblest sense is alive and well. The garden centre includes hybrid test beds of
new varieties on show.

Glenwhan Garden 72

**Dunragit, Stranraer, Wigtownshire, Dumfries and Galloway DG9 8PH.
Tel/Fax: (01581) 400222**

*Mr and Mrs Knott • 7m E of Stranraer, 1m off A75 at Dunragit. Signposted •
Open April to Sept, daily, 10am – 5pm, and by appt. Evening visits by
arrangement • Entrance: £3, OAPs £2.50, children £1, toddlers free, family rate
£8.50, season ticket £10, conducted tours for parties of 20 or more £15 • Other
information: Picnics permitted on request. Dogs strictly on leads (dog-walking
area). Plants for sale in nursery* ◐ ◪ ✕ ▨ WC ♿ ◁ ⌘ ⊞ ⛲

This exciting 12-acre garden has commanding views over Luce Bay and the Mull of Galloway, and is set in an area of natural beauty with many rocky outcrops. Because of the Gulf Stream and consequent mild climate, exotic plants thrive amongst the huge collections of trees, shrubs and plants. Seats and walkways abound in the maze of hilly plantings, mostly overlooking the central lakes and bog gardens. Collections, whether of genera, reminders of friends or particular themes of interest, are to be seen everywhere. The garden continues to expand and mature. There are enchanting woodland walks where species rhododendrons flourish amongst many different kinds of primulas.

Greenbank Garden ★ 73

Flenders Road, Clarkston, Glasgow G76 8RB. Tel: (0141) 639 3281

The National Trust for Scotland • From Clarkston Toll in S Glasgow take Mearns Road for 1m. Signposted • Open all year, daily except 1st, 2nd Jan and 25th, 26th Dec, 9.30am – sunset • Entrance: £3.15, concessions and children £2.10 • Other information: Refreshments in summer only. Catering for parties and guided tours by arrangement. Dogs in woodland only, on lead ○ 🍵 🧺 WC ♿ ⚲ 🏛 ⛲

The large old walled garden of an eighteenth-century house has been divided into many sections, offering imaginative practical demonstrations to illustrate the design and planting of small gardens. The colour combinations are especially good. All the plants are in good condition and admirably labelled. An old hard tennis court in the corner has been converted into a spacious and pleasant area full of ideas for disabled and infirm gardeners, with raised beds and a waist-high running-water pond. Wheelchair access to the glasshouse and potting shed allows disabled people to attend classes and work here. Woodland walks are filled with spring bulbs and shrubs and there are usually Highland cattle in the paddock.

Hill of Tarvit Mansion–House 74

Cupar, Fife KY15 5PB. Tel/Fax: (01334) 653127

The National Trust for Scotland • 2½ m S of Cupar off A916 • House open 29th March to 1st April, May, June, Sept and weekends in Oct, 1.30 – 5.30pm; July and August 11am – 5.30pm (last admission 4.45pm) • Grounds open all year, daily, 9.30am – sunset • Entrance: £2, children and concessions £1 (honesty box); (house and grounds £5, children and concessions £4, family ticket (2 adults and up to 6 children) £14, parties of 20 or more £4 per person), (2001 prices) • Other information: Shop and tea room open from 12.30pm daily ○ 🍵 🧺 WC ♿ ⚲ 🏛 ⛲ ⚲

The garden surrounds the charming Edwardian mansion designed in 1906 for a Dundee financier by Sir Robert Lorimer, who also laid out the grounds to the south of the house. The views over Fife are particularly fine. There is a lovely rose garden. Good-size borders are filled with an attractive variety of perennials, annuals and heaths, and the grounds as a whole contain many unusual ornamental trees and shrubs now reaching maturity. The plantings are regularly upgraded to include newer and more unusual specimens. A good garden for amateurs and keen plantspersons. A massive two-day plant sale is held the first weekend in October – there is no entry charge, and the public queue at the gate well before the opening.

The Hirsel   75

Coldstream, Berwickshire TD12 4LP. Tel/Fax: (01890) 882834

The Earl of Home • 9m NE of Kelso, 15m SW of Berwick-on-Tweed, W of Coldstream on A697 • Grounds open all year, daily during daylight hours • Entrance: parking charge £2 per car • Other information: Craft workshops
○ ⬤ ✕ 🖼 WC ♿ ⬇ 🏬 ⚕

The house is not open, but at all seasons of the year the grounds have much of interest and enjoyment for the visitor who values the peace and ever-changing beauty of the countryside. There is something here for the ornithologist, botanist, geologist, forester, zoologist, historian and archaeologist. In spring, snowdrops and aconites and then acres of daffodils herald the coming summer as the birds, resident and migrant, of which 169 have been definitely identified within the estate boundaries, start busying themselves around their nesting sites. In May and June the rhododendron wood, Dundock, is justly famous for its kaleidoscopic colouring and breathtaking scents. Rose beds, herbaceous and shrub borders follow through the summer. In October and November, the leaves turning on trees and shrubs provide attractive autumn colouring, and hundreds of duck, geese and gulls make the lake their nightly home. In winter the same trees are stark but magnificent in their skeletal forms against storm clouds and sunsets.

House of Pitmuies ★★   76

Guthrie, By Forfar, Angus DD8 2SN. Tel/Fax: (01241) 828245

Mrs Farquhar Ogilvie • 1½ m W of Friockheim, on A932 • House open for parties by appt • Garden open April to Oct, daily, 10am – 5pm, and at other times by appt • Entrance: £2.50 by collection box • Other information: Teas by arrangement for parties visiting house ◑ 🖼 WC ⬇ ⚘

In the grounds of an attractive eighteenth-century house and courtyard, these beautiful walled gardens lead down towards a small river with an informal riverside walk and two unusual buildings – a turreted dovecot and a Gothick wash-house. There are rhododendron glades with unusual trees and shrubs, but pride of place must go to the spectacular semi-formal gardens behind the house, where exquisite old-fashioned roses and a series of long borders containing a dramatic and superbly composed palette of massed delphiniums and other herbaceous perennials in June and July constitute one of the most memorable displays of its type to be found in Scotland.

House of Tongue ★ 77

Tongue, Lairg, Sutherland, Highland IV27 4XH. Tel: (01847) 611209

The Countess of Sutherland • 1m N of Tongue off A838 • Open 3rd Aug, 2 – 6pm for charity, and at other times by appt • Entrance: £2.50, children under 12 50p ● ﹠ ◁◁ ℺

Sheltered from wind and salt by tall trees, this walled garden is a haven in an otherwise-exposed environment. Adjoining the seventeenth-century house, it is laid out after the traditional Scottish acre, with gravel and grass walks between herbaceous beds, hedged vegetable plots and orchard. A stepped beech-hedged walk leads up to a high terrace which commands a fine view over the Kyle of Tongue. The centrepiece of the garden is Lord Reay's sundial (1714), a sculpted obelisk of unusual design.

Innes House Garden 78

Elgin, Moray IV30 3NF. Tel: (01343) 842410

Mr and Mrs Mark Tennant • 5m E of Elgin, off A96 on B9103 Lossiemouth road • Open to parties by appt only • Entrance: By donation ●

An extensive ornamental garden divided into compartments, the whole framed by a wide variety of mature and interesting trees. The gardens were partially replanned and reorientated by the present owner's great-grandmother in 1912, when yew hedges were planted, providing a central walk. A charming garden has been created on the site of the original chapel. The large trees are a major feature of the property – 47 varieties are represented, many estimated to be over 200 years old, including rare oaks, Californian Madroña (*Arbutus menziesii*) and Chinese beech. A complete tree list is available.

Inveresk Lodge and Village Gardens 79

Musselburgh, East Lothian EH21 8BQ. Tel: (0131) 665 1855

Various owners inc. The National Trust for Scotland (Lodge) • 6m E of Edinburgh, S of Musselburgh via A6124 • Lodge garden open all year, Mon – Fri, 10am – 4.30pm, Sat and Sun, 2 – 5pm (closed Sat, Oct to March • Entrance: Lodge £2 (honesty box), other gardens £1.50 each • Other information: Privately owned gardens in village open several days for SGS with teas ○ ▦ WC ﹠ ♀ ℺

The large seventeenth-century house in the village of Inveresk is situated on a gently sloping site. The garden has been completely remade since it came under the ownership of the Trust. No attempt has been made to re-create a period style: it is 'modern' in most respects, semi-formal, well planted and well maintained, and offering a wide selection of plants flowering from spring through autumn. The high stone retaining walls support a wide range of climbers, and the south-facing slope permits more unusual plants to be grown; a particularly good border devoted to shrub roses was designed by Graham Stuart Thomas. There is a large conservatory with some good hardy ornamentals and an aviary. The village itself is a unique, unspoilt example of eighteenth-century villa development, with houses dating from the late seventeenth and early eighteenth centuries. All have well-laid-out gardens enclosed by high walls and containing a wide range of shrubs and trees as well as some unusual plants. One, *Catherine Lodge*, in two acres, contains many unusual mature trees underplanted with large drifts of snowdrops, crocus and daffodils. Much of the layout, with its traditional herbaceous borders surrounding an old grass tennis court, has remained the same since the early part of this century. In the large vegetable garden, by contrast, many changes have been made: although vegetables are still grown in profusion, some of the beds have been given over to roses and a large wildlife pond has been created. The other, *Shepherd House*, is a one-acre plantsman's garden, full of surprises and constantly being developed, with interesting water features, an alpine wall, a *potager*, an old-fashioned rose border, a shade garden, a parterre and herb gardens, all planted to capacity so as not to allow room for weeds.

Inverewe Garden ★★ 80

Poolewe, Ross and Cromarty, Highland IV22 2LG. Tel: (01445) 781200

The National Trust for Scotland • 6m NE of Gairloch on A832 • Garden open all year, daily, 9.30am – 9pm (closes 5pm Oct to March) • Entrance: £5, concessions £3.50, parties £4 per person, senior parties £3.20 per person, family ticket £12.80 (2001 prices) • Other information: Restaurant and shop open 15th March to Oct only ○ 🍵 ✕ WC ᠔ 🌲 🏛

This garden is spectacular. Created from 1865 on the shores of the sea loch, Loch Ewe, it covers the entire Am Ploc Ard peninsular. Planned as a wild garden around one dwarf willow on peat and sandstone, it has been developed as a series of walks through herbaceous and rock gardens, a wet valley, a rhododendron walk and a curved vegetable garden and orchard. It is a plantsman's garden (labelling is discreet), containing many tender species from Australia, New Zealand, China and the Americas, sheltered by mature beech and pine trees. New Zealand plants include the National Collections of olearias and ourisias. The garden is well tended and way-marked. Note: midge-repellent is advisable and on sale at the main desk.

Johnston Gardens 81

Viewfield Road, Aberdeen. Tel: (01224) 522734

Aberdeen City Council • In Aberdeen, ½ m S of Queens Road (A944 to Alford), ¼ m W of junction with ring road • Open all year, daily, 8am – 1 hour before dusk • Entrance: free ○ 🍴 WC ᠔ ❀

When Johnston House was demolished and the grounds sold for redevelopment, it was impossible to utilise the deepest area of the ravine. This was converted into a water and rock garden by the City of Aberdeen Parks and Recreation Department. The result is a congenial oasis of trees, shrubs and mature rhododendrons surrounding a small lake complete with an island, bridges and resident waterfowl. The rock and scree gardens contain some interesting alpine plants.

Jura House 82

Ardfin, Isle of Jura, Argyll and Bute PA60 7XX. Tel: Peter Cool (01496) 820315

Riley-Smith family • On Jura, 5m SE of ferry terminal off A846. Vehicle ferries from Kennacraig by Tarbert to Port Askaig, Islay, and from Islay to Feolin, Jura • Open all year, daily, 9am – 5pm • Entrance: £2.50, children (5-16) £1 (collecting box) • Other information: Teas available June to Aug, Mon – Fri only. Possible for wheelchairs but sloping gravel paths. Booklet available, 50p ○ 🍵 🥗 WC ⅃ 🦽 ♨ ℺

A circular walk around the Jura House estate illustrates the rich natural history and geology of the island. Starting from the car park, the visitor walks through native woodland and follows the fuchsia-clad banks of the burn to where it plunges into a ravine, filled with ferns and lichens, over the raised beach to the sea. Spectacular views of the Islay coast accompany the steep path down to the shore. Dykes and rock formations are home to wild scree plants and scrubby trees, and here is an example of machair – dune grassland. After the climb back up the cliff, signs guide the visitor to the garden proper. This organic walled garden is a sheltered haven with many unusual plants, including a collection of Australasian origin. Linger awhile before continuing on the woodland path back to the lodge.

Kailzie Gardens ★ 83

Peebles, Peeblesshire, Scottish Borders EH45 9HT. Tel/Fax: (01721) 720007

Lady Angela Buchan-Hepburn • 2½ m SE of Peebles on B7062 • Garden and trout pond open all year, daily (in winter, during daylight hours) • Entrance 13th April to mid-Oct: £2.50, children (5–14) 75p, groups £2.20 per person; mid-Oct to mid-March, honesty box, groups 85p per person; snowdrop days, as advertised • Other information: Gallery open probably late March to mid-Oct. Holiday cottage available ○ ✗ 🥗 WC ⅃ ♨ 🏛 ♨ ℺

'A Pleasure Garden' is the description in one of the advertisements for Kailzie (pronounced Kailie), and very apt it is too. The gardens of 17 acres are situated in a particularly attractive area of the beautiful Tweed Valley and are surrounded by breathtaking views. The old mansion was pulled down in 1962 and the vast walled garden, which still houses the magnificent greenhouse, has been transformed by the present owner from vegetables to a garden of meandering lawns and island beds full of interesting shrubs and plants. There are many surprises, including snowdrops in drifts in February and March, a choice flower area, secret gardens, loving seats invitingly placed under garlanded arbours and several thoughtfully sited pieces of statuary. A magnificent fountain at the end of the herbaceous borders leads on to woods and stately trees, and from here you may stroll down the Major's Walk, lined with laburnum and underplanted with rhododendrons, azaleas, blue poppies and primulas. There is also a small duck pond and a fishing pond.

Kellie Castle   84

Pittenweem, Fife KY10 2RF. Tel: (01333) 720271

The National Trust for Scotland • 3m NW of Pittenweem on B9171 towards Arncroach • Castle open 13th April to Sept, daily; Oct, Sat and Sun, all 1.30 – 5.30pm (last admission 4.45pm) • Garden and grounds open all year, daily, 9.30am – sunset • Entrance: £2, children £1 (castle and garden extra charge) • Other information: Parking 100 metres, closer for disabled. Refreshments, toilet facilities (not disabled) and shop when castle open only ○ 🍷 🛍 WC ♿ 🏛 🔦 ♋

The garden appears to be seventeenth century in plan, embellished by Professor James Lorimer and his family in late Victorian times. Entered by a door in a high wall, the one-and-a-half acres inspire dreams within every gardener's reach. Simple borders, such as one of catmint, capture the imagination as hundreds of bees and butterflies work the flowers. Areas of lawn are edged with box hedges, roses on arches and trellises abound. In one corner, behind a trellis, is a small romantic garden within a garden. A large, green-painted commemorative seat designed by Hew Lorimer provides focal interest at the end of one of the main walks. The head gardener has established a collection of old and unusual vegetable varieties employing only organic gardening methods. Outside the walled garden, mown walks wind through woodland which in late spring is a haze of wild garlic.

Kilbryde Castle   85

Dunblane, Perthshire FK15 9NF. Tel: (01786) 824897

Sir James Campbell • 9m NW of Stirling, off A820 Dunblane – Doune road • Open 26th May, 2 – 5pm, for charity, and by appt • Entrance: £2, OAPs and children £1.50; non-open day charge £3 • Other information: Plants for sale on open days only ◗

The 20-acre garden was created by the present owner's father and mother, whose passions were rhododendrons, azaleas, clematis and bulbs. The garden is in two parts – a partly walled upper garden with island beds full of colour on a south-facing slope, and a lovely woodland garden on either bank of a stream well planted with rhododendrons and azaleas under a canopy of mature trees. The best time to visit is spring, particularly the end of May.

Kildrummy Castle Gardens ★   86

Alford, Aberdeenshire AB33 8RA. Tel: (01975) 571203/571277

Kildrummy Castle Garden Trust • 2m SW of Mossat, 10m W of Alford, 17m SW of Huntly. Take A944 from Alford, following signs to Kildrummy, and turn left onto A97. From Huntly turn right on to A97 • Open April to Oct, daily,

10am – 5pm • Entrance: £2, children (5–16) free (2001 prices) • Other information: Cars park inside hotel main entrance, coaches in delivery entrance. Woodland walks and children's play area ❶ 🍽 🏷 WC ♿ ⬤ 🐾 🛍 ✂

The gardens are set in a deep ravine between the ruins of a thirteenth-century castle and a Tudor-style house, now a hotel. The rock garden, by Backhouse of York (1904), occupies the site of the quarry which provided the stone for the castle. The narrowest part of the ravine is crossed by a copy of the towering fourteenth-century Auld Brig O'Balgownie (Old Aberdeen Bridge) built by Colonel Ogston in 1900. This affords a spectacular bird's-eye view of both sides of the water garden commissioned from a firm of Japanese landscape gardeners in the same period; Backhouse continued the planting. In April the reflections in the still water of pools increase the impact of the luxuriant *Lysichiton americanus*, and later come primulas, Nepalese poppies and a notable *Schizophragma hydrangeoides*. There are also fine maples, rhododendron species and hybrids, oaks and conifers. Although a severe frost pocket, the garden can grow embothriums, dieramas and other choice plants. The garden is especially beautiful in autumn with colchicums in flower and acers in brilliant leaf.

Kinross House Gardens 87

Kinross, Kinross-shire KY13 8ET. Fax: (01597) 863372;
E-mail: jm@kinrosshouse.com

Mr James Montgomery • 13m N of Dunfermline, E of M90, in Kinross • Open May to Sept, daily, 10am – 7pm • Entrance: £2, children 50p ❶ ♿ ✂

Four acres of walled garden, all beautifully maintained, surround the mansion designed in the 1680s and restored early this century. The walls, surmounted by fine statuary, have decorative gates. This is a formal garden of spacious lawn, clipped hedging, herbaceous borders, some with colour themes, and rose borders round the fountain. There are yew hedges in interesting shapes, with well-placed seating for those in a contemplative mood or wishing to view Loch Leven Castle on the nearby island. It was here that Mary Queen of Scots was imprisoned in 1567; though it has no garden, it would be churlish not to walk to the pier to make the short boat trip to its sombre walls.

Kittoch Mill 88

Busby Road, Carmunnock, Glasgow G76 9BJ. Tel: (07980) 320235

Margaret and Les Watson • 4m NW of East Kilbride, on B759 Busby – Carmunnock road • Open for groups by appt • Entrance: £50 per group (maximum 20 people) ◖

This charming small garden, created by the owners and set above the mill-stream waterfall adjacent to a SSSI, includes a woodland walk and Japanese-style garden. It includes among its attractions a good collection of hostas, ligularias and anthemis.

Langwell House   89

Berriedale, Caithness, Highland KW7 6HE. Tel: (01593) 751237 or (01593) 751278 (Head Gardener); E-mail: Robert@welbeck2.freeserve.co.uk

The Lady Anne Bentinck • 2m E of Berriedale off A9 • Open two days in Aug and Sept for NGS, and by appt • Entrance: £2 ● WC & ⊲⊳ ⌘ ℺

A lovely traditional two-acre walled garden. It has a sadly short season, due to the fact that it is almost as far to the north-east as it is possible to go, but inspires commensurate interest and admiration as a result. The cruciform layout lends itself to dramatic 64-metre-long herbaceous borders specialising in plants that are not only colourful but also manage to thrive in these conditions. They are framed by yew hedges, behind which lie vegetable and fruit sections – all immaculately maintained.

Lawhead Croft   90

Tarbrax, West Calder, West Lothian EH55 8LW.

Sue and Hector Riddell • 12m SW of Balerno, 6m NE of Carnwath on A70 towards Tarbrax • Open for charity June to Sept, daily, at any reasonable time, and for parties by written appt only • Entrance: £2, children 20p • Other information: No coaches down farm road (no turning room) ◑ 🍴 &

Nearly 300 metres up in the midst of the bleak Lanarkshire moors, the present owners have planted hedges and laboriously carved out a luxuriant garden. Grass walks lead from one interesting border to another, full of unusual plants. Colour associations and leaf contrasts are carefully thought out. There is an enchanting series of garden rooms, all with a different theme. Great ideas include an excellent bonsai collection. Recently most of the vegetable garden has been swept away and replanted in a great sweep of curved, tiered and circular beds of spectacular and original design.

Leckmelm Shrubbery and Arboretum   91

Little Leckmelm House, Lochbroom, Ullapool, Ross-shire, Highland.

Mr and Mrs Peter Troughton • 4m S of Ullapool on A835 • Open April to Sept, daily, 10am – 6pm • Entrance: £1.50 ◑ ⊲⊳

Situated on the shore of Loch Broom and warmed by the Gulf Stream, the 10-acre arboretum is full of fine specie rhododendrons and mature trees, various shrubs and bamboos. Originally planted in 1870, it was abandoned for 50 years in the 1930s until reclamation started in 1984, and is now restored to its former Victorian glory. Note particularly the venerable old weeping beech whose spread covers at least a third of an acre, and the largest *Chamaecyparis lawsoniana* 'Wisselii' in Europe. A map and planting plan are available in the car park. N of Ullapool off A835 at Achiltibuie, *The Hydroponicum* demonstrates the innovative and effective method of growing a vast number of sub-tropical and exotic plants, herbs and vegetables without soil in bubble-wrap solar-heated glasshouses. [Open 10am – 5pm, Easter to 30th Sept.]

Leith Hall and Gardens ★ 92

Huntly, Aberdeenshire AB54 4NQ. Tel: (01464) 831216; Fax: (01464) 831594; E-mail: lpadgett@nts.org.uk; Website: www.nts.org.uk

The National Trust for Scotland • 34m NW of Aberdeen, 1m W of Kennethmont on B9002 • Hall open inc. exhibition 2nd to 5th April; May to Sept, daily; Oct, weekends; all 1.30 – 5.30pm (last admission 4.45pm) • Garden and grounds open all year, daily, 9.30am – dusk • Entrance: £2, OAPs and children £1.30, pre-booked parties of 20 or more £1.60 per person (hall and gardens £6, OAPs and children £4.50, pre-booked parties of 20 or more £4 per person) (2001 prices) • Other information: Dogs outside walled garden only ○ 🍵 🏠 WC 🐾

The gardens are being restored and it is the old garden, remote from the house, that offers the greatest pleasure to the enthusiast. This comprises a series of small gardens, sheltered by walls and hedges, rising on a gentle slope from the west drive. It includes long borders and a large, well-stocked rock garden with a stream and gravel paths. The simple, romantic design allows a tremendous display of flowers during the whole of summer and early autumn; especially fine are magenta *Geranium psilostemon* and an entire border of solid catmint. There are no courtyards and no dominating architecture, just massive plantings of perennials and the odd rarity amongst the rocks. The circular moon gate at the top of the garden leads to the old turnpike road. Woodland walks throughout the designed landscape take in ponds and views down the garden.

Linn Botanic Gardens 93

Cove, Helensburgh, Dunbartonshire, Argyll and Bute G84 0NR. Tel: (01436) 842242

Mr J.H.K. Taggart • 6m S of Garelochhead, ¾ m N of Cove on shore of Loch Long • Open all year, daily, dawn – dusk • Entrance: £3, OAPs £2.50, students and teenagers £2, accompanied children 12 and under free • Other information: Entirely unsuitable for wheelchairs and prams. Light refreshments for organised tours. Plants for sale in adjacent nursery ○ 🏠 WC 🐾

The garden has been developed in its present form since 1971 (the villa dates from the 1860s), with thousands of unusual, exotic and rare plants. Water is a constant presence: in the extensive water garden, in formal ponds and fountains, in the glen with its tumbling waterfall, and, beyond the garden, in the views down to the Firth of Clyde from the terrace. There are also herbaceous borders, a rockery and a cliff garden. A one-kilometre signed route takes visitors through all parts of the garden; a useful leaflet is available.

Little Sparta ★★ 94

Dunsyre, Lanark, South Lanarkshire ML11 8NG.

Dr Ian Hamilton Finlay • Turn off A721 at Newbiggin for Dunsyre. 1m W of Dunsyre turn up unmarked farm track signed 'Stonypath, Little Sparta'. Alternatively take A702 from Edinburgh, turning off at Dolphinton; road signposted to Dunsyre • Open probably mid-June to Sept, Fri and Sun, 2 – 5pm • Entrance: free, but donation to Little Sparta Trust welcome ●

Described by Sir Roy Strong as the most original contemporary garden in the country, the garden is now mercifully open to the public once more. On arrival at the gate to the property a beautifully carved wooden sign greets the visitor, giving a hint of the fine craft that combines with the art of this admired sculptor. Hamilton Finlay believes that a garden should both appeal to all the senses and provoke thought, both serious and trivial, and he has therefore revived the art of emblematic gardening which died out in Britain in the seventeenth century, although his personal philosophy is inspired more closely by the eighteenth-century poet-gardeners Alexander Pope and William Shenstone. He has achieved an international reputation in the process. It is impossible to describe Little Sparta briefly, except to say that he has transformed a sizeable hill farmstead 1000 feet above sea level in the Pentland Hills (starting in 1996 with the idea of establishing a testing-ground for his sculptures) into a garden full of classical inscriptions and images, allusions and symbols. Not all are easily understood or interpreted – *n'importe*, as this is a garden, not a crossword puzzle.

Lochalsh Woodland Garden (Balmacara Estate)   95

Lochalsh House, Balmacara, Kyle, Ross-shire, Highland IV40 8DN.
Tel: (01599) 566325; Fax: (01599) 566359; E-mail: iturnbull@nts.org.uk

The National Trust for Scotland • 3m E of Kyle of Lochalsh off A87 • Open all year, daily, 9am – dusk • Entrance: £2, children £1 • Other information: Parking off A87 with ½ m walk to garden, closer parking by prior arrangement
○ 🪧 WC ⬦ ⚲

The garden is approached down the wooded road through the village of Glaick on the lochside. From there, across the water, rise the magnificent mountains of Skye and Knoydart. Woodland planting on this steep-sided, 11-acre site began in 1887 around Lochalsh House, and the canopy of beeches, larches, oaks and pines is now outstanding. Ornamental plantings began in the late 1950s with large-leaved rhododendrons, followed from the 1980s to the present day by shrubs from China, Japan, the Himalayas and Australasia. Paths created through the woods give a choice of walks. Alongside these and in glades, logs have been used to build curved, raised beds for plantings which include hydrangeas, fuchsias, bamboos and ferns.

Logan Botanic Garden ★★   96

Port Logan, Stranraer, Wigtownshire, Dumfries and Galloway DG9 9ND.
Tel: (01776) 860231; Fax: (01776) 860333; Website: www.nbge.org.uk

Royal Botanic Garden Edinburgh • 14m S of Stranraer, off B7065. Signposted • Open March to Oct, daily, 9.30am – 6pm, and at other times by arrangement • Entrance: £3, concessions £2.50, children £1, family ticket £7. Local membership scheme, inc. Dawyck and Benmore Botanic Gardens (see entries), available • Other information: Discovery Centre and Sound Alive guided tours. Guide dogs only ◑ ☕ ✕ WC 🌢 🏬

This is a regional garden of the Royal Botanic Garden Edinburgh (see entry). In the far south-west of Scotland on a peninsula washed by the Gulf Stream, Logan's mild climate allows a fine collection of exotic plants to be grown in the open. Flourishing here are beautiful specimens from South and Central America, Southern Africa, Australasia and the Mediterranean which survive outside in few other British gardens. Throughout the summer it is ablaze with colour. One of the best Scottish collections of tender perennials includes diascias, fuchsias and salvias. As the season progresses rhododendrons, primulas, meconopsis and other acid-loving plants come into bloom on the peat walls, a feature first developed here. The walled garden was established over 100 years ago and contains many smaller gardens. Major features are the water garden with the original cabbage palms and tree ferns, and the terrace garden framed by an avenue of Chusan palms. The woodland garden is wild by contrast, with glades of eucalyptus and magnolias surrounded by many unusual flowering trees and shrubs. All in all, a fascinating tour of exotic plant collections native to the southern hemisphere.

Malleny Garden 97

Balerno, Edinburgh EH14 7AF. Tel: (0131) 449 2283;
E-mail: pdeacon@nts.org.uk; Website: www.nts.org.uk

The National Trust for Scotland • In Balerno, off A70 Edinburgh – Lanark road • Open all year, daily, 9.30am – 7pm (Nov to March closes 4pm) • Entrance: £2, OAPs/children £1 ○ 🏠 WC & 🌿

Aptly described as The National Trust for Scotland's secret garden, Malleny seems an old and valued friend soon after meeting and reflects the thoughtful planning by the head gardener and his talented wife. An impressive Deodar cedar reigns over this three-acre walled garden, assisted by a square of early seventeenth-century clipped yews and by yew hedges. As well as containing a National Collection of nineteenth-century shrub roses and a permanent display from the Scottish Bonsai Association, Malleny's four metre wide herbaceous borders are superb, as is the large glasshouse containing a summer display of flowering plants. Don't forget to admire the attractive herb and ornamental vegetable garden, laid out in traditional manner.

Manderston ★★ 98

Duns, Scottish Borders TD11 3PP. Tel: (01361) 883450; Fax: (01361) 882010;
E-mail: palmer@manderston.co.uk; Website: www.manderston.co.uk

Lord Palmer • 2m E of Duns on A6105 • House open • Gardens open mid-May to Sept, Sun and Thurs, and 27th May, 26th Aug, 2 – dusk. Also for parties at any time of year by appt • Entrance: £6, children £3 (house and garden), gardens only £3.50, children £1.50. Reduced rate for parties of 20 or more (2001 prices) ● 🍴 🏠 WC & 🔺 🍴 🌿

One of the last great classic houses to be built in Britain, Manderston was modelled on Robert Adam's Kedleston Hall (see entry in Derbyshire). It was described in 1905 as a 'charming mansion inexhaustible in its attractions', and this might equally well apply to the gardens, which remain an impressive example of gardening on the grand scale. Four magnificent formal terraces planted in Edwardian style overlook a narrow serpentine lake, and a Chinoiserie bridging dam tempts one over to the woodland garden on the far side, thus elegantly effecting the transition from formal to informal. The woodland garden has an outstanding collection of azaleas and rhododendrons, and is at its best in May. The formal walled gardens to the north of the house are a lasting tribute to the very best of the Edwardian era, when 24 gardeners were employed to do what two now accomplish to the same immaculately high standard. Gilded gates open on to a panorama of colourful planting on different levels, with fountains, statuary and a charming rose pergola all complementing each other. Even the greenhouses were given lavish treatment, with the walls created from lumps of limestone to resemble an exotic planted grotto. Fifty-six acres of formal and informal beauty.

Megginch Castle   99

Errol, Perthshire PH2 7SW. Tel: (01821) 642222; Fax: (01821) 642708

Lady Strange • 8m E of Perth off A85 Perth – Dundee road • Open April to Oct, daily, 2 – 5.30pm • Entrance: £2.50, children over 5 £1 ◑ 🍴 ♿ ⌁ 💡 ⚬

Originally a fifteenth-century tower house (not open), Megginch, meaning Beautiful Island, was considerably restructured by Robert Adam in 1790 and by successive generations, and this gives the gardens and the Gothick courtyard of 1806 a timeless atmosphere. A fountain parterre to the west of the house is of particular interest for its yew and variegated holly topiary, including an unusual yew crown planted to commemorate Queen Victoria's Jubilee. There are four clumps of thousand-year-old yews, at 22 metres the highest in Scotland. Try and visit Megginch during August when a stunning 110-metre double border – the length of the eighteenth-century walled garden – is a glorious blaze of annual plantings. So many dahlias can rarely have been displayed. An adjacent sixteenth-century walled area contains an interesting astrological garden with plants relevant to each sign. Peacocks abound.

Mellerstain ★   100

Gordon, Berwickshire TD3 6LG. Tel: (01573) 410225; Fax: (01573) 410636

The Earl of Haddington • 6m NW of Kelso off A6089 • House open (extra charge) • Garden open 29th March to 1st April, then May to Sept, daily except Sat, 12.30 – 5pm (last admission 4.30pm), and to parties of 20 or more at other times by appt • Entrance: £2, children free (house and garden £5, OAPs and students £4.50, children £2, parties £4.50 per person) • Other information: Craft gallery ◑ ☕ ✕ 🍴 <u>WC</u> ♿ ⌁ 🐾 🏛

The house is a rare example of the work of the Adam family; both William and his son Robert worked on the building. The garden is formal, composed of dignified terraces, balustraded and 'lightly' planted with climbers and simple topiary, because even when labour was plentiful there were a mere six gardeners employed. The great glory of the garden is the landscape, complete with lake and woodlands in the style of Brown and Repton, but redesigned early this century by Sir Reginald Blomfield. The view of the Cheviot Hills from the terraces is one of the finest to be found in this lovely area of the Scottish Borders. Mellerstain is a must for lovers of the formal, 'arranged' landscape.

Mertoun 101

St Boswells, Roxburghshire, Scottish Borders TD6 0EA. Tel: (01835) 823236

The Duke of Sutherland • 8m SE of Galashiels, 2m NE of St Boswells on B6404 • Open April to Sept, Sat, Sun and Bank Holiday Mons, 2 – 6pm • Entrance: £2, OAPs £1.50, children (under 14) 50p ◕ WC ♿

Overlooking the Tweed and with Mertoun House in the background, this is a lovely garden in which to wander and admire the mature specimen trees, azaleas and daffodils, and the most attractive ornamental pond flanked by a good herbaceous border. The focal point is the immaculate three-acre walled garden, which is everything a proper kitchen garden should be. Walking up from a 1567 dovecot, thought to be the oldest in the county, through a healthy orchard, the visitor reaches the box hedges, raised beds and glasshouses of the main area. Vegetables, herbs and bright flowers for the house vie for attention with figs and peaches in the well-stocked glasshouses.

Monteviot 102

Jedburgh, Scottish Borders TD8 6TJ. Tel: (01835) 830380 (mornings)

5m NE of Jedburgh. Turn off A68 onto B6400 to Nisbet. Entrance second turn on right • Open April to Oct, daily, 12 noon – 5pm. Parties book with Administrator • Entrance: £2, children under 16 free. (2001 prices) • Other information: Refreshments at Harestanes Countryside Visitor Centre, ½ m ◑ WC ♿

The river garden running down to the River Teviot has been extensively replanted with herbaceous perennials and shrubs to a more informal design. Beside it, the semi-enclosed terraced rose gardens overlooking the river have a large collection of hybrid teas, floribundas and shrub roses. The pinetum is full of unusual trees, and nearby a water garden has been created, planted with hybrid rhododendrons and azaleas. A circular route has been laid out around the gardens, and there are fine views.

Mount Stuart ★★ 103

Rothesay, Isle of Bute. Argyll and Bute PA20 9LR. Tel: (01700) 503877

Mount Stuart Trust • Ferry from Wemyss Bay. 5½ m S of Rothesay ferry terminal on A844 • House open as garden, 11am – 4.30pm (last admission 3.45pm) • Garden open May to Sept, daily except Tues and Thurs, 10am – 6pm Guided tours available • Entrance: £3.50, OAPs £3, children £2 (house and garden £6.50, OAPs £5, children £2.50). Party discounts available ◑ ✕ WC ♿

Incorporated in the 300 acres of designed landscape and waymarked woodland walks, there is a wealth of horticultural interest, and one of the most elegant drives in the country. The gardens contain a considerable mature pinetum of 1860 and a magnificent old lime tree avenue leading to the shore, but on the whole they have been restored and augmented over the last decade by the late John Bute and his wife Jennifer. In conjunction with the Royal Botanic Garden Edinburgh, 100 acres have also been set aside to grow endangered conifer species from all over the world, in order to create a seedbank for the future. Rock gardens provide decorative features near the house, but the two most important elements are the kitchen garden and the 'Wee' garden. The latter is actually eight acres of mixed and exotic plantings with emphasis on species from the southern hemisphere. It is set in the mildest part of the grounds and grows some of the most tender plants to be found outside the glasshouse, some flourishing to unusual size. The kitchen garden has been designed as an ornamental *potager* by the late Rosemary Verey and includes herb gardens, trellised fruit enclosure, fan-trained plum trees and mixed beech hedges. Set in the middle is the Pavilion glasshouse planted with rare flora from SE Asia. One of Scotland's finest gardens.

Netherbyres 104

Eyemouth, Berwickshire, Scottish Borders TD14 5SE. Tel: (018907) 50337

Colonel S.J. Furness • 8m NW of Berwick-upon-Tweed, ¼ m from Eyemouth on A1107 • Open twice yearly in April and July for charity and April to Sept for small parties by appt • Entrance: £2, children £1 ● &

Although the Victorian conservatory and vineries were demolished to make way for a modern house and conservatory, the garden is worth seeing for the unique elliptical walls, built before 1750. The present layout dates from the 1860s, and constitutes one of the few Scottish walled gardens with a traditional mix of fruit, flowers and vegetables still fully cultivated on traditional lines. A central gazebo and a shrub border have been added.

Pitmedden Garden ★ 105

Pitmedden Village, Ellon, Aberdeenshire AB41 7PD. Tel: (01651) 842352; Fax: (01651) 843188

The National Trust for Scotland • 14m N of Aberdeen. 1m W of Pitmedden, 1m N of Udny on A920 • Gardens open May to Sept, daily, 10am – 5.30pm (last admission 5pm) • Entrance: £5, concession £4, parties £4, children £4, family ticket £14 • Other information: Coaches please book. Wheelchairs supplied. Museum of farming life ◑ ● ● WC & �’ ⌸

The Great Garden exhibits the taste of seventeenth-century garden-makers and their love of patterns made to be viewed from above. The rectangular parterre garden is enclosed by high terraces on three sides and by a wall on the fourth. Simple topiary and box hedging abound. The south- and west-facing walls, lined by fine herbaceous borders, are covered by a great variety of old apple trees in both fan and espalier styles, producing nearly one ton of fruit at the end of the season. Ornamental patterns are cut in box on a grand scale, infilled with 20,000 annuals. The overall impact is striking when viewed from the original ogivally roofed stone pavilion at the north of the garden or when walking along the terraces. When the Trust acquired Pitmedden in 1952 all that survived was the masonry, and since nothing remained of the original design, contemporary seventeenth-century plans for the garden at the Palace of Holyrood in Edinburgh were used in re-creating what is seen today.

Pollok House 106

Pollokshaws Road, Glasgow G43 1AT. Tel: (0141) 616 6410

The National Trust for Scotland • 3½ m S of city centre. In Pollokshaws take A736. Signposted • House and gallery open • Garden open all year except 25th Dec and 1st Jan, daily except Sat, 10am – 5pm • Entrance: free (house £4)
○ ▬ ✕ ▦ WC ⅋ ⬧ ⬧ ⬧ ☙

A visit to Pollok House offers a full day's entertainment. Next to the house is a lovely formal terrace of box parterres. There are borders near the water and a nineteenth-century woodland garden on the ridge nearby. Stone gazebos with ogee roofs. The house holds the Stirling Maxwell collection of European paintings, and in the grounds, famous for their bluebells in spring, is The Burrell Collection, one of the world's finest modern galleries, housing decorative and fine arts. The building was designed to complement the woodland, and the parkland around is beautifully planted and maintained.

Portmore ★ 107

Eddleston, Peebleshire, Scottish Borders EH45 8QU. Tel: (01721) 730296

Mr and Mrs D.L. Reid • ½ m N of Eddleston, on A703 Peebles – Edinburgh road • Open for SGS in mid-July, and for parties by appt • Entrance: £2.50
● ▬ WC ⬧

It is a joy to see an old neglected estate brought lovingly back to life. The long drive winds up through woods, fields and little lochs to the Edwardian mansion which proudly overlooks the rolling acres. Parterres have recently been planted at the far side of the house, and shrub-filled woodland walks are being planned. The wonder of the place is the large walled garden designed and replanted by Chrissy Reid with great taste and flair – she cares particularly about colours and the effect at the entrance is magical. The soft mixture of pale greens, blues, mauves and white delights the eye in the herbaceous borders and leads the gaze to the greenhouses stuffed full of geraniums, pelargoniums, streptocarpus, fuchsias, etc. Leading off these there is an enchanting cool, dripping Victorian Italian grotto, fern-filled. The remainder of the garden is divided into squares of *potagers*, herb gardens, cherry walks, rose gardens, all surmounted with wonderful wrought-iron arches. Even the luxurious-looking fruit is protected by wire held up by three elegant arches.

Priorwood Garden 108

Melrose, Ettrick and Lauderdale, Scottish Borders TD6 9PX.
Tel: (01896) 822493

The National Trust for Scotland • On A6091 in Melrose • Open April to 24th Dec, Mon – Sat, 10am – 5.30pm, Sun, 1.30 – 5.30pm (closes 4pm Oct to Dec) • Entrance: by donation £2, OAPs £1 ◑ ▬ ⅋ ⬧ ⬧ ⬧ ⬧ ☙

Purchased by The National Trust for Scotland in 1974, this was originally the walled garden belonging to Priorwood House, now Melrose Youth Hostel. The garden has been developed for the production of dried flowers, and by drying them in dessicants – as the ancient Egyptians did – the range of plants has been greatly increased to include some 700 varieties of annual and herbaceous plants. There is also an orchard, which has been designed to show the development of the apple tree in Britain, and a woodland area. The eighteenth-century garden walls are complemented by ornamental ironwork thought to be the work of Lutyens.

Royal Botanic Garden Edinburgh ★★ 109

Inverleith Row, Edinburgh EH3 5LR. Tel: (0131) 552 7171;
Fax: (0131) 248 2901

1m N of city centre at Inverleith. Signposted • Open all year, daily except 25th Dec and 1st Jan, 9.30am – 4pm (up to 7pm depending on season). Garden tours operate April to Sept, daily, 11am and 2pm from West Gate • Entrance: free, voluntary contributions invited • Other information: Exhibition hall and Inverleith House gallery open. Guide dogs only ○ 🍽 ✕ WC & 🌿 🏠 🟡 🌂

Set on a hillside with magnificent panoramic views of the city, the Royal Botanic Garden Edinburgh is one of the finest botanic gardens in the world; arguably the finest garden, physically, of its type in Britain. Established in the seventeenth century on an area the size of a tennis court, it now extends to 75 acres. Rhododendrons and azaleas abound, and in spring their stunning flowers provide a blaze of colour and intriguing scents. The world-renowned rock garden is spanned by a long bridge over the stream. In summer, marsh orchids, lilies, saxifrages and bell-shaped campanulas give brilliant colour. There are also peat and woodland gardens and a stunning herbaceous border. The arboretum sweeps along the garden's southern boundary. A relatively recent addition is the Pringle Chinese Collection on the south-facing slope of Inverleith Hill, which includes a spectacular wild-water ravine crossed by bridges, tumbling down into a tranquil pond at the bottom of the hillside. A T'ing (pavilion) provides an ideal place to relax. The Glasshouse Experience, featuring Britain's tallest palm house, leads the visitor on a trail of discovery through the temperate and tropical regions of the world, featuring passion flowers, cycads (some over 200 years old) and species that provide everyday necessities such as food, clothes and medicine.

Scone Palace Gardens 110

Perth, Perth and Kinross PH2 6BD. Tel: (01738) 552300.
Website: www.scone-palace.co.uk

The Earl and Countess of Mansfield • Just outside Perth on A93 Perth – Braemar road • Palace and grounds open April to Oct, daily, 9.30am – 5.15pm (last admission 4.45pm) • Entrance: £3.10, OAPs/students £2.50, children £1.70 (palace and gardens £6.20, OAPs/students £5.30, children £3.60, family £20; groups of 20 or more: £5.30, OAPs/Students £4.60, children £3.10)
◑ 🍽 ✕ 🧺 WC & 🔺 🏠 🟡 🌂

The 100 acres of gardens, surrounding the site of Macbeth's ancient city of Scone, include the famous nineteenth-century pinetum with magnificent towering trees and *Sequoia giganteum* over 48 metres tall. Since 1977 a second pinetum has been planted, and there is also an acer collection, a butterfly garden, a 30-metre-long laburnum pergola and a beech maze designed by Adrian Fisher, opened in 1998, which comprises 2000 beech trees in the shape of the Murray Star. Taking their turn in season are spectacularly massed daffodils, a primrose drive, rhododendrons and azaleas. The renowned explorer/plant collector, David Douglas, born at Scone, supplied the garden with many of his discoveries, and one of his original firs survives. His life is marked by an exhibition in the palace. There are always orchids in flower within the palace, the Earl of Mansfield having the largest collection in the country. It is also worth travelling 7m further north to marvel at the *Meikleour Beech Hedge*, now 30 metres high and a quarter of a mile long, beside the A93. Legend has it that men who planted it in 1745 were called away to fight and not one returned alive from the battle of Culloden.

Sea View   111

Durnamuck, Dundonnell, Ross-shire IV23 2QZ. Tel: (01854) 633317;
Fax: (01854) 633370; E-mail: simone@smokedsalmon.uk.com:
Website: www.smokedsalmon.uk.com/garden

Mr and Mrs Ian Nelson • 20m NW of Braemore, off A832 Dundonnell –
Gairloch road. Turn at Badcaul. Signposted • Garden open May to Sept, daily,
10am – 6pm, and by appt at other times • Entrance: £1 ◗ ⌙ ⌘

This half-acre garden, started in 1990 on the shores of Little Loch Broom, has been carved out of an inhospitable environment. The paucity of soil, only 8 inches deep, has been enriched with tons of manure and the use of raised beds, and in spite of the inherent difficulties an enchanting, varied and densely planted garden has been achieved. Among the many interesting plants is the *Rhododendron* 'Elizabeth Lockhart' with beautiful deep red new leaves, *R. camtschaticum*, grey-leaved *Olearia ilicifolia*, hebes, red-flowered *Jasminum beesianum*, flowering *Pittosporum tenuifolium* 'Tom Thumb', *Pseudowintera colorata* (the New Zealand pepper tree) and phormiums. A heather bed, rockery banks and bed, orchard, bog area and pond, the whole surrounded by hedges of escallonia, fuchsia and griselinia, complete the picture.

St Andrew's Botanic Garden   112

Cannongate, St Andrews KY16 8RT. Tel: (01334) 476452/477178,
Fax: (01334) 476452; E-mail: st-and-bg@cwcom.net;
Website: www.st-and.ac.uk/standrews/botanic/

Fife Council • ½ m from town centre, signed in Cannongate • Open all year,
daily, 10am – 7pm (closes 4pm Oct to April) • Entrance: £2, OAPs/children (5–
16) £1 ○ ⬛ ▤ WC ⌘ ⌘

On its present site the garden dates from 1960, covering 18 acres along the Kinness Burn; in 1987 it was leased by the University to the local council.

Although the botanical collections are now increasingly adapted for low maintenance, the areas of specialised planting remain excellent. Visitors will find something of interest all year; even in winter a pleasant afternoon may be spent in the greenhouses among the arid, alpine and temperate-zone plants. The pond and rockery are particularly attractive, and the order beds are a valuable educational aid, rarely seen elsewhere. There are good collections of cotoneasters, sorbus and berberis, and stunning clumps of *Lathraea clandestina*.

Stobo Castle Water Gardens   113

**Peebles, Scottish Borders EH45 8NY. Tel: (01721) 760245;
Fax: (01721) 760319; E-mail: hugh.Seymour@btinternet.com**

*Hugh and Charles Seymour • 6m SW of Peebles on B712, 12m E of Biggar •
Open by appt, but advisable to confirm in writing in addition to telephoning •
Entrance: £2, children free* ◐ ⬦

The enduring appeal of water is exemplified here; the planting, although most attractive, takes second place to the visual impact of clear water flowing down a series of cascades and waterfalls. Japanese bridges and stepping stones invite frequent crossings from side to side, and peaceful rills stray from the main torrent to create one huge water garden. In fine landscape-garden tradition, man has contrived to manipulate nature – in this case a large earth dam across a steep valley – into something of classical delight. The dam was faced with stone to create a magnificent waterfall and the resulting flow is impressive even in dry summers. The lovely mature trees, such as *Cercidiphyllum japonicum*, *Kalopanax pictus* var. *maximowiczii* and many Japanese maple varieties, obviously date from this period, which ended with the outbreak of World War I.

Teviot Water Garden   114

**Kirkbank House, Eckford, Kelso, Scottish Borders TD5 8LE.
Tel: (01835) 850734/253**

*Mr and Mrs Denis Wilson • Between Kelso and Jedburgh on A698 • Open April
to Sept, daily, 10am – 5pm, and by appt at other times • Entrance: free*
◑ ☕ ✕ WC ⬦ ⌖ 🏛 ⛽ ⚲

Created over the years from a stony riverside field, these gardens occupy a spectacular position on a steep north-west-facing bank of the River Teviot. A series of terraces linked by waterfalls displays a wide range of plants, giving a varied show throughout the summer months. Aquatic plants are a speciality, but this intimate and tranquil garden also contains a selection of choice perennials, grasses, ferns and bamboos. The shop stocks plants and other items needed by the water garden enthusiast, from fish to pumps and liners. A visit to the coffee shop and smokery completes the outing.

Threave Garden and Estate ★ 115

Stewartry, Castle Douglas, Dumfries and Galloway DG7 1RX.
Tel: (01556) 502575

The National Trust for Scotland • 1m W of Castle Douglas off A75 • Open all year, daily, 9.30am – dusk (walled garden and glasshouses close 5pm) • Entrance: £4.40, OAPs and children £2.90, family (2 adults, up to 6 children) £11.70, parties £3.50 per person, school parties £1 per child • Other information: Exhibition in visitor and countryside centre, March to Dec, daily
○ ☕ ✕ 🖙 WC ⚄ 🌿 ⚒ ⚐ ☌

The Threave estate, which extends to 1500 acres, includes the famous 65-acre garden which has been used as a school of horticulture since 1960 and caters for trainee gardeners. Numerous perennials, annuals, trees and shrubs are used in imaginative ways and maintained by the resident horticultural students. For the visitor the principal interest is the working walled garden with its range of glasshouses, vegetables, orchard and wall-trained fruit. This may be contrasted with the less formal woodland and rock gardens, heath garden and arboretum. The garden is famous for its collection of daffodils, complemented in spring by rhododendrons and flowering trees and shrubs.

Tillypronie 116

Tarland, Aboyne, Aberdeenshire AB34 4XX. Tel: (013398) 81238;
E-mail: Philip.astor@tillypronie.com

The Hon. Philip Astor • 4½ m W of Tarland via A97 Dinnet – Huntly road • Open 9th June, 25th Aug for charity, 2 – 5pm • Entrance: £2, children £1
◑ ☕ WC ⚄ ⚓ 🌿 ☌

Set on the south-facing slope of a hill at over 300 metres above sea level, this is a cold garden, but shelter belts dating from the mid-1800s ensure that a wide range of plants can be grown; more shelter planting was added from 1925 to 1951. The overall layout was completed in the 1920s, the work of George Dillistone of Tunbridge Wells. The terraces below the house date from the same period and support narrow herbaceous borders. The house walls provide shelter for less hardy climbers, and trained *Buddleia davidii* cultivars make a good display in August. Curved stone steps lead between extensive heather gardens to lawns sweeping down to the ponds with their colourful plantings of astilbes, filipendulas, lysichitons, primulas and ferns. Azaleas and rhododendrons feature strongly in June, and there are fine specimens of *Picea breweriana* and many other conifers and an area devoted to dwarf varieties. Spectacular views end with the Grampians on the horizon.

Torosay Castle and Gardens 117

Craignure, Isle of Mull, Argyll and Bute PA65 6AY. Tel: (01680) 812421;
Fax: (01680) 812470

Mr Christopher James • 1½ m S from Craignure. Steamer 6 times daily April to Oct (2 to 4 times daily Nov to March) from Oban to Craignure. Motor boat during high season. Miniature steam railway from Craignure ferry. Or take Lochaline to Fishnish ferry, then travel 7m S on A849 • Castle open, April to mid-Oct, 10.30am – 5pm • Garden open all year, daily, 9am – 7pm (or dusk in winter) • Entrance: £5, OAPs and students £4, children £1.75 (castle and gardens) ○ 💬 🍽 WC ♿ ⏏ 🐾 🏛

The house in baronial castle style by Bryce (1858) is complemented by a formal Italianate main garden based on a series of descending terraces with an unusual statue walk. This features one of the richest collections of Italian Rococo statuary in Britain and alone justifies the crossing from Oban to Mull. Vaguely reminiscent of Powis Castle (see entry in Wales), it makes a dramatic contrast with the rugged island scenery. The peripheral gardens around the formal terraces are also a contrast – an informal water garden and Japanese garden looking out over Duart Bay, and a small rock garden. Rhododendrons and azaleas are a feature but less important than in other west-coast gardens, and there is a collection of Australian and New Zealand trees and shrubs. A major 15-year restoration is under way, and 2000 species and cultivars have been planted over the past five years. Outside the main garden, the owners, in conjunction with the Royal Botanic Garden Edinburgh, have created a five-acre Chilean wood and are underplanting another two-acre wood with plants from the collection of the late Jim Russell.

Tyninghame House ★   118

Tyninghame, East Linton, East Lothian EH42 1XW.

Tyninghame Gardens Ltd • 25m E of Edinburgh between Haddington and Dunbar. N of A1, 2m E of A198 • Open 12th May, 7th July for charity, 1 – 5pm • Entrance: £2 ● 💬 WC ⏏ 🐾

Tyninghame is renowned for the gardens created by the Dowager Lady Haddington from 1947 onwards, which have been described as of 'ravishing beauty'. They consist of a formal rose garden, terraces, a secret garden, an Italian garden and an area of woodland. When her husband died in 1986, her son reluctantly sold the house, but those who worried about the garden's future need not have feared, as the conversion and addition of two houses was handled by Kit Martin with great sensitivity. The garden is close to the sea, with fine views in all directions, and those who are able to visit it on the open days will have a rare opportunity of seeing how the unique character has been maintained, perhaps enhanced, by the architectural changes around it, and by the dedicated work of Mrs Timothy Clifford and others.

Tyninghame Walled Garden   119

Dunbar, East Lothian EH42 1XW. Tel: (01620) 860559

Mr and Mrs Charles Gwyn • 25m E of Edinburgh N of A1. Take turning to North Berwick and Tyninghame on A198; after 1m turn right through archway • Open two day for SGS, and by appt, 1 – 5pm • Entrance: £2, children free [NEW] ● ♿

The heated brick walls and gateways here date from 1760, making it one of the earliest walled gardens in Scotland. The name, however, does not perhaps do justice to the treasury of specialist trees and plants contained within its immaculate four and a half acres. The clean-cut layout (redesigned in the 1960s by James Russell) is best viewed from the delightful 1832 camellia house attached to the main house beside a magnificent *Magnolia grandiflora*. Straight ahead stretches a grass *allée* of clipped yew walls, niched to offset eight classical statues and centred on a Florentine fountain. This *allée* divides the entire garden lengthways; the transverse paths consist of a rose pergola and a well-planted rose walk. As well as extensive borders of mixed planting, there is also a spacious lawned *potager* and an eye-catching collection of bearded irises. The two outstanding areas are the almost monastic espaliered apple-tree walk, 90 metres long, with Bacchus and Diana as the focal points at either end, and the comprehensive collection of mature exotic and unusual trees, too numerous to mention. On the whole of the right-hand side of the garden they have been cleverly underplanted with huge sweeping beds.

University of Dundee Botanic Garden 120

Riverside Drive, Dundee DD2 1QH. Tel: (01382) 647190

University of Dundee • 2½ m from city centre on A90 Perth road. Signposted • Open March to Oct, Mon – Sun, 10am – 4.30pm; Nov – Feb, 10am – 3.30pm • Entrance: £2, OAPs £1, children £1, family ticket (2 adults and 2 children) £5 ● ➤ ✕ 🍴 WC & 🌿 🏛 ♀

Founded in 1971 as a source of plant material for teaching and research purposes, the 23-acre garden has always been open to the public for their pleasure. The planting around the glasshouse and large pond near the entrance is extremely attractive and reminiscent of a private rather than a botanic garden. The large area beyond has plants grouped according to region or habitat, including many Scottish natives; though mainly composed of trees and shrubs, the artistic layout ensures plenty to see of interest as well as beauty. The glasshouse is brimful of fine specimens, from tropical to temperate zones, from rainforest to desert – a pleasure whatever the weather is like outside. In all, a very varied 23 acres.

West Drummuie Garden 121

West Drummuie, Golspie, Sutherland, Highland KW10 6TA. Tel: (01408) 633493

Mrs Elizabeth Woollcombe • 1m S of Golspie off A9. At white milestone, turn up hill and bear right at fork to last house • Open mid-April to early Oct by appt only • Entrance: donations welcome • Other information: No coaches please ● 🌿

A smallish and beautiful private garden, on a steeply sloping hillside overlooking the Dornoch Firth, which combines a variety of plants, woodland and water. It needed to be sheltered by hedges and tall shrubs and to be rabbit-proof, but after nearly 30 years it is mature in a way that is unusual in such a location. The garden is complementary to the house and produces vegetables, fruit, firewood and free-ranging bantams which help keep the hostas slug-free.

WALES

Two-starred gardens are marked on the map with a black square.

Aberglasney 1

Llangathen, Llandeilo, Carmarthenshire SA32 8QH. Tel/Fax: (01558) 668998; E-mail: info@aberglasney.org.uk; Website: www.aberglasney.org.uk

Aberglasney Restoration Trust • 3m W of Llandeilo on A40. Turn S at Broak Oak junction • Open all year; April to Oct, daily, 10am – 6pm (last entry 5pm); telephone for winter opening details • Entrance: £5, OAPs £4, children and disabled £2.50, family ticket £12 ◑ ➤ ✗ 🍴 WC & 🌢 ℀

Here are gardens lost in time. Records for Aberglasney go back to the mid-fifteenth century, when mention was made of nine gardens, orchards and vineyards. Around 1600 the Bishop of St David's bought the estate to turn it into a private palace, and it is probably he who built the gatehouse and the marvellous cloister garden. To the side of the ruined house is a yew tunnel unique in Britain. After many years of neglect the gardens are being restored with great care and attention to detail. The large upper walled garden was designed by Penelope Hobhouse to complement the historic site, and the lower walled garden is home to vegetables, herbs and plants grown for cutting. The wooded area known as Bishop Rudd's Walk has fine collections of rare and unusual woodland plants. Pigeon House Wood is a natural, unspoilt area where you may sit in the shade of splendid beech trees and other woodland planting. The restoration of the formal cloister garden, devoted to plants typically grown in an early-seventeenth-century garden, was completed in 2001.

Ashford House 2

Talybont-on-Usk, Brecon, Powys LD3 7YR. Tel: (01874) 676271

Mr and Mrs Anderson • 6m SE of Brecon, 1m E of Talybont on B4588 • Open April to Sept, Tues, 2 – 6pm, and by appt • Entrance: £2, children free ◑ ➤ 🍴 WC & ⬥ 🌢 ℀

About one acre with a further three acres of woodland and wild garden. The walled garden has a good selection of shrubs and herbaceous plants and long raised beds with an fine collection of alpines – one of the owners' interests. The wild garden, interplanted recently with rhododendrons and other shrubs, contains a healthy wild pool with frogs and dragonflies. Mrs Anderson propagates plants for sale.

Bodnant Garden ★★ 3

Tal-y-Cafn, Colwyn Bay, Conwy LL28 5RE. Tel: (01492) 650460; Website: www.oxalis.co.uk/bodnant

The National Trust • 8m S of Llandudno, just off A470 • Garden open mid-March to Oct, daily, 10am – 5pm (last admission 4.30pm) • Entrance: £5.20, children £2.60 • Other information: Parking 50 metres from garden. Plant centre (not NT) adjacent ◑ ➤ ✗ WC & 🌢 🏛 🌢

One of the finest gardens in the country, not only for the magnificent collections of rhododendrons, camellias and magnolias but also for its beautiful setting above the River Conwy and extensive views of the Snowdon range. The garden, which covers 80 acres, has many interesting features, the best-known being the laburnum arch, which in late May and early June is an overwhelming mass of bloom. Others include the lily terrace, the curved and stepped pergola, the canal terrace, Pin Mill and the dell garden. In the dell is the tallest redwood in the country, the 45-metre *Sequoia sempervirens*. These, together with the outstanding autumn colours, make it a garden for all seasons. The whole effect was created by four generations of the Aberconway family (who bought Bodnant in 1874), aided by three generations of the Puddle family as head gardeners.

Bodrhyddan 4

Rhuddlan, Denbighshire LL18 5SB. Tel: (01745) 590414

Lord Langford • 4m SE of Rhyl. Take A5151 Rhuddlan – Dyserth road and turn left. Signposted • House open • Garden open June to Sept, Tues and Thurs, 2 – 5.30pm • Entrance: £4, children under 16 £2 (house and garden) ◖ ☕ WC 㧖

The main feature here is a box-edged parterre laid out by William Andrews Nesfield, the father of the renowned William Eden Nesfield, who designed the 1875 alterations to the house. Other points of interest are clipped yew paths and, to the north-west, the Pleasance, part of a larger area known on very old maps as the Grove. This is probably because it embraces St Mary's Well, revered since pagan times and covered now by a 1612 Inigo Jones pavilion, said to have been used for clandestine marriages. The two-acre Pleasance, originally a Victorian shrubbery, has been restored; it has four ponds, fine mature trees and many new plantings, and an additional area is being developed as a wild garden, picnic spot and new walk.

Bodysgallen Hall ★ 5

Llandudno, Gwynedd LL30 1RS. Tel: (01492) 584466;
E-mail: info@bodysgallen.com; Website: www.bodysgallen.com

Historic House Hotels • 2m S of Llandudno. At A55/A470 junction turn onto A470 towards Llandudno. Hall is 1m on right • Open all year, daily • Entrance: free to guests using hotel facilities • Other information: Refreshments in hotel ○

The Garden has written that 'there can be few better living examples of early seventeenth-century gardens anywhere in England and Wales'. Both house and gardens have been restored to a high standard. The limestone outcrops provide an interesting array of rockeries and terraces; major features include a parterre sympathetically planted with herbs, and a formal walled rose garden. The fine trees and shrubs include a medlar and a mulberry, and woodland walks add a further dimension to a magnificent award-winning garden. A few miles further south, off the A470, is *Bryn Meifod*, where the garden is closed for a period, but the celebrated nursery is still open. Telephone (01492) 580875 for opening times.

Brynmelyn 6

Cymerau Isaf, Ffestiniog, Gwynedd LL41 4BN. Tel: (01766) 762684

Mr and Mrs A.S. Taylor • 8m E of Porthmadog, 2m SW of Ffestiniog on A496 • Open April to Aug, 10am – 1pm, 2 – 5pm. Telephone in advance, before

10am or after 9pm • Entrance: collecting box • Other information: Parking in lay-by opposite junction to Manod ($^{1}\!/_{2}$ m to garden along path at lower gate bearing right after garage) ◗

An interesting garden, not only for its range of plant material, but also for its wild mountainside setting. It lends itself well to the overall informal style, and includes a nature reserve and woodland.

Bryn-y-Bont   7

Nantmor, Beddgelert, Caernarfon, Gwynedd LL55 4YG. Tel: (01766) 890448

Miss J. Entwisle • 6m NE of Porthmadog, 2$^{1}\!/_{2}$ m S of Beddgelert. Turn left over Aberglaslyn Bridge onto A4085. After 500 metres turn left up hill marked 'Nantmor'; house is second on right • Open by appt and for pre-booked parties • Entrance: £1.50, children free, parties £2.50 (including tea) ● 🍵 WC ⬧ 🌿 ॐ

The well-designed two-acre garden has been created from a bracken-strewn hillside since 1978, taking full advantage of the south-facing view over Glaslyn Vale. Mixed borders, a small pond and a bog garden, and rhododendron beds give way to a woodland area where trees and shrubs are being introduced to make a small arboretum and an environmentally friendly haven for wildlife.

Cae Hir ★   8

Cribyn, Lampeter, Ceredigion SA48 7NG. Tel: (01570) 470839

Mr W. Akkermans • From Lampeter take A482 towards Aberaeron. After 5m at Temple Bar take B4337 signed Llanybydder. House is 2m on left • Open daily except Mon (but open Bank Holiday Mons), 1 – 6pm • Entrance: £2.50, OAPs £2, children 50p ◐ 🍵 🍽 WC ⬧ ⬧ 🌿 🔦 ॐ

The aim of the gardener (a Dutch plantsman) to create a balance between the natural and the cultivated has been triumphantly achieved. Six acres of sheer delight, from colour-themed sub-gardens and a bonsai enclosure to wildflower bog areas. Fine views and plenty of seating.

Cefn Bere   9

Cae Deintur, Dolgellau, Gwynedd LL40 2YS. Tel: (01341) 422768

Mr and Mrs Maldwyn Thomas • N of A496 Barmouth road (not bypass). From Dolgellau, turn left (towards Barmouth) at top of main bridge, turn right within 100 metres, then second right behind school. Continue up hill to left-hand bend; house is fourth on right • Open spring, summer and autumn by appt only • Entrance: by donation to collecting box ◑

This relatively small garden has a diverse plant collection, including an array of old-fashioned roses, amassed over the last 40 years. Planted informally within a formal framework, it is a delight to amateur and professional gardeners alike. The alpine house, bulb and peat frames, and troughs are a fine sight.

Cefn Onn Park   10

Cardiff, South Glamorgan.

*Cardiff City Council • From city centre take A469 under M4. Turn first right
then left opposite Lisvane Station. From elsewhere, at M4 junction 32, turn S of
A470. Take first left to T-junction, turn right, left at church, left at T-pass
under M4, first right then left opposite Lisvane Station • Open all year, daily,
during daylight hours • Entrance: free* ○ WC ⑤ ⟨⟩

This park retains a little of the formality common in such areas, with straight
gravelled paths running through the centre, but there are no large areas of
bedding plants – rather, large areas of informally planted azaleas and rhododendrons. Colour and perfume, layer upon layer, reach up into the upper storey of
trees, which can only be appreciated by standing on the bank opposite in order
to see them at all. The camellias and magnolias here have also become trees,
rather than shrubs, and the visitor may have to guard against a cricked neck
trying to see everything. It may also be a little dull once the rhododendrons are
over. If in the city on Sat, 10am – 12 noon or Tues, 1 – 3pm, call in at *Cardiff
Horticultural Society Demonstration Garden*, which has about 200 herbs.

Centre for Alternative Technology   11

Machynlleth, Powys SY20 9AZ. Tel: (01654) 705950; Fax: (01654) 702782; E-mail: help@catinfo.demon.co.uk; Website: www.cat.org.uk

*C.A.T. • 3m N of Machynlleth on A487. Also access by water-balanced cliff
railway, Easter to Oct • Open all year, daily except 25th Dec and mid-Jan, 10am
– 5.30pm (4pm in winter) • Entrance: £7, OAPs, claimants and students £5,
children £3.60, family ticket (2 adults and up to 4 children) £26 (2001 prices).
Discounts for arrival by public transport or bicycle • Other information: Parking
inc. coaches at base of site, but for elderly and disabled at top of steep drive.
Guide dogs only* ○ ☻ ✕ ▤ WC ⑤ ⟨ ⬛ ⚑ ⚲

High in a former slate quarry, and at the heart of the environmentally friendly
community here, is the most exciting garden. Compactly laid out, using natural
and recycled materials to form harmoniously shaped raised beds, ponds and
walks, the garden is vibrant (in June) with colour and insect life drawn to the
organically grown flowers and companion-planted vegetables. There are suggestions, too, for urban gardeners and displays of land reclamation, wildlife gardening, composting, weed and pest control. Wind turbines and solar fountains in
different sizes and designs could be considered unusual, if highly functional,
garden sculptures. Whether you want to experience the world of the worm in
the underground mole hole, or wander gently by one of the lakes, be sure not to
miss the view from the balcony of the water-balanced railway. A new information
centre has been built from rammed earth and insulated with sheep's wool.

Chirk Castle ★   12

Chirk, Wrexham, Clwyd LL14 5AF. Tel: (01691) 777701

*The National Trust • 10m SW of Wrexham, 2m W of Chirk off A5, 1½ m up
private drive • Castle open as gardens but 12 noon – 5pm (last admission 4.30pm)*

• *Gardens open Feb, Sat and Sun (telephone to check times), 12 noon – 4pm; then 23rd March to 3rd Nov, daily except Mon and Tues (but open Bank Holiday Mondays, 11am – 6pm (last admission 5pm); Oct, Nov, Wed – Sun, 11am – 5pm (last admission 4.30pm)* • *Entrance: £3.30, children £1.65 (less in Feb) (castle and garden £5.60, children £2.80, family ticket £13.80)* • *Other information: Parking 350 metres from garden; courtesy coach offers transport* ○ 🍴 ✕ 🛍 WC ♿ 🎁 ⛲ ♣

The castle, its walls now covered with climbing plants, dates from 1300 and is set in an eighteenth-century landscaped park. Six acres of trees and flowering shrubs, including rhododendrons and azaleas, were mostly planted by Lady Margaret Myddleton; they contrast with the yews in the formal garden, which were planted in the 1870s by Richard Biddulph. The rose garden contains mainly old cluster-flowered (floribunda) roses. From the terrace, with its fine views over Shropshire and Cheshire, the visitor passes to the classical pavilion, then along a lime tree avenue to a statue of Hercules. There is interesting nineteenth-century topiary, a rockery and an old hawk house, and a pleasure-ground wood to stroll in. Chirk is described by the Trust as a 'family' garden.

Clyne Gardens ★★ 13

Blackpill, Swansea, West Glamorgan SA3 5AR. Tel: (01792) 401737

Swansea City Council • *From Swansea take A4067 Mumbles road and turn right at Woodman Roast Inn* • *Open all year, daily, 8am – dusk. Telephone for details of garden tours* • *Entrance: free* • *Other information: Refreshments in May only. Rare plants sale in May* ○ 🛍 WC ⛲ ⛲

Fifty acres of well-kept woodland garden to interest everyone from the beginner to the more knowledgeable. Near the entrance gates is a planting of young magnolias and a variety of rhododendrons and azaleas; this leads on to a magnificent group of large-leaved rhododendrons. The garden holds a National Collection of the rhododendron section Falconera, but even these tree-like specimens are looked down upon by *Magnolia campbellii*. Clearly defined paths lead the visitor through other areas where National Collections of rhododendron section Triflora, pieris and enkianthus flourish; the perfume from *Rhododendron fragrantissimum* is heady and unforgettable. The bog garden is a prehistoric forest of *Gunnera manicata* linked by a colourful ribbon of primulas to the lake and waterfall spanned by a Japanese bridge. Many more rare and interesting trees and shrubs are there for the discerning.

Colby Woodland Garden 14

Stepaside, Amroth, Narberth, Pembrokeshire SA67 8PP. Tel: (01834) 811885

The National Trust • *10m SW of St Clear, near Amroth on Carmarthen Bay off A477* • *Open all year, daily, 10am – 5pm; walled garden 11am – 5pm. Guided walks available with head gardener* • *Entrance: £2.80, children £1.40, family ticket £7, parties of 15 or more £2.30 per person, children £1.15* • *Other information: Facilities open 23rd March to 3rd Nov; Plant fair – telephone for details. Parking 50 metres from garden; disabled parking closer. Coaches welcome. Gallery* ○ 🍴 🛍 WC ⛲ 🌼 🎁 ⛲

This early-nineteenth-century estate garden round a Nash-style house is now mainly woodland with some formal gardens. The walled garden is planted informally for ornamental effect. The woodland garden has many rhododendrons and some interesting trees. A new hydrangea bed gives further summer interest. Delightful autumn colour.

Cwm-Pibau   15

New Moat, Clarbeston Road, Haverfordwest, Pembrokeshire SA63 4RE. Tel: (01437) 532454

Mrs Drew • 10m NE of Haverfordwest. Take A40 through Robeston Wathen, turn left on B4313, follow signs to New Moat. 3m from Clarbeston Road on outskirts of New Moat, take concealed drive on left and continue for ½ m, keeping left • Open by appt for charity • Entrance: £2 ●

Created by the owner since 1978, the garden has as a background mature woodland, and the long driveway is a difficult uphill walk (although on charity days it is possible to get a lift down and back to the car). Rhododendrons have been planted along the side of the drive, which leads to lawns and herbaceous plantings near the house. Paths are then signposted down through five acres of shrub plantings and along a stream fringed with moisture-lovers. This area is still young, but leads on to five more acres of woodland planted with embothriums, rhododendrons and rare shrubs.

The Dingle ★   16

Welshpool, Powys SY21 9JD. Tel: (01938) 555145

Mr and Mrs Roy Joseph • 3m NW of Welshpool. Take A490 for 1m to Llanfyllin then turn left signed 'Dingle Nursery' or 'Frochas'. After 1½ m fork left • Open all year, daily, except Tues and 25th Dec to 2nd Jan, 9am – 5pm • Entrance: £1.50 for charity, children free • Other information: Possible for wheelchairs but steep in places ○ 🏛 WC ♿ ⌖ ✿ ♋

Set on the steep slopes of a verdant Welsh valley, this garden is more a woodland creation of over 4000 carefully chosen trees and shrubs. The owners began by damming the stream (the dingle) that flows through the site, and have created two large pools which now set off the garden superbly. There is a grove of acers, with many other interesting specimens such *Davidia involucrata* and many different pittosporums. The real treat has to remain the nursery, which is worth driving many, many miles to reach.

Dolwen ★   17

Cefn Coch, Llanrhaeadr-ym-Mochnant, Powys SY10 0BU. Tel: (01691) 780411

J. Marriott and B. Yarwood • 14m W of Oswestry, on B4580 Oswestry – Llanrhaeadr road. Turn sharp right in Llanrhaeadr at Three Tuns Inn • Open probably May to Aug, Fri and last Sun in the month, 2 – 4.30pm. Groups welcome by appt • Entrance: £2 ◐ 🍵 🏛 WC ♿ ⌖ ✿ 🏺 ♨ ♋

A dramatic woodland and water garden situated high in the Berwyn hills with splendid views. What started as a small cottage garden was extended by the previous owner to two-and-a-half acres, with the extra land used to great advantage. Striking plants in the water areas include *Salix fargesii* and *S. udensis* 'Sekka', but she was careful not to overplant the margins of the three ponds, which she referred to as 'The Lake District'. Large boulders are sited imaginatively, and contemporary sculpture adds charm in unexpected places; so do the bridges, some of which have unusual origins. As well as shrubs and climbing roses, there are wonderful trees. Many of the uncommon plants here were supplied by the *Crug Farm Nursery* near Caernarfon.

Donadea Lodge 18

Babell, Flintshire CH8 8QD. Tel: (01352) 720204

Mr and Mrs Patrick Beaumont • 8m E of St Asaph. Turn off A541 Mold – Denbigh road at Afonwen, signed 'Babell', and at T-junction turn left; or take A55 then B5122 to Caerwys and third turn on left • Open May to July by appt • Entrance: £2, children 20p ● WC & ℘

The garden demonstrates what creative design can achieve on a very long site. On one side an avenue of mature lime trees is a fine feature in its own right. The other side is a mixed border of bays and small islands, each with its own restrained and carefully thought-out colour scheme, often achieved using unusual plants in unexpected but entirely effective combinations. A particular feature is the use of roses and clematis.

Dyffryn Gardens ★ 19

St Nicholas, Cardiff, Vale of Glamorgan CF5 6SU. Tel: (029) 2059 3328; E-mail: GFDonovan@valeofglamorgan.gov.uk; Website: www.dyffryngardens.org.uk

Vale of Glamorgan Council • 4m SW of Cardiff on A4232 turn S on A4050 and W to A48 • Open all year, daily, 10am – dusk • Entrance: £3, OAPs and children £2, family £6.50 ○ 🍽 🎁 WC & ⟨⟩ ℘ 🏛 ♿

What is happening at Dyffryn, one of Wales's largest landscape gardens and also one of its best-kept secrets, is one of the Heritage Lottery Fund's most intelligent acts of garden funding. With the help of a huge grant – some £6.15 million – Thomas Mawson's 1904 plans for the distinguished horticulturist Reginald Cory are to be used as the basis for a full-scale restoration over the first three years of the new century. Major projects are the reinstatement of the lake and the restoration of the walled kitchen garden and its magnificent glasshouse. Arguably one of the most important gardens of the Edwardian era, here are herbaceous borders on an heroic scale, croquet and archery lawns, panel gardens, rose gardens, a heather bank, a rockery, an arboretum and a series of themed garden rooms, including the Pompeian Garden with a Grade-II-listed garden building open to the public.

Erddig ★ 20

Wrexham, Clwyd LL13 0YT. Tel: (01978) 355314

The National Trust • 2m S of Wrexham off A525 • House open 12 noon – 5pm (closes 4pm from 1st Oct) • Garden open 31st March to Nov, daily except Thurs

and Fri, 11am – 6pm (closes 5pm from 1st Oct). Conducted tours for parties by prior arrangement • Entrance: £3.40, children £1.70, pre-booked parties of 15 or more £2.70 per person, family (2 adults and 2 children) £8.50 (house and garden £6.60, children £3.30, family ticket £16.50, pre-booked parties £5.30 per person) • Other information: Parking 200 metres from garden. Wheelchairs provided. Dogs in grounds only, on lead ◑ 💻 ✕ <u>WC</u> ♿ ⚘ ⬚ ♨

The gardens, a rare example of early-eighteenth-century formal design, were almost lost along with the house, but have now been carefully restored. The large walled garden contains varieties of fruit trees known to have been grown there during that period, and there is a canal garden and fish pool. South of the canal walk is a Victorian flower garden, and later Victorian additions include the parterre and yew walk. A National Collection of ivies is here, also a narcissus collection. Apple Day is celebrated at Erddig in October.

Farchynys Cottage 21

Bontddu, Gwynedd LL42 1TN. Tel: (01341) 430245

Mrs G. Townshend • 4m W of Dolgellau on A496 Dolgellau – Barmouth road. After Bontddu on right. Signposted • Open April to 30th June, daily except Sat and Wed, 2.30pm – 6pm • Entrance: £1.50 ◑

This woodland garden overlooking the Mawddach estuary is set in natural oak and conifer woodland. There is much new planting, but azaleas, rhododendrons and magnolias are well established and repay a spring visit. A small sculpture garden has been established.

Foxbrush 22

Aber Pwll, Port Dinorwic, Gwynedd LL56 4JZ. Tel: (01248) 670463

Mr and Mrs B.S. Osborne • 3m SW of Bangor on B4507 (old Caernarfon road) N of A487. Avoiding new bypass, enter village. House on left after high estate wall, opposite layby. Signed 'Felinheli' • Open by appt only • Entrance: £1.50, children free • Other information: Cottage museum ◑ 💻 ▦ WC ♿ ⬙ ⚘

A private three-acre plantswoman's garden, created single-handedly from a wilderness on the site of a sixteenth-century mill. Narrow paths meander through romantic plantings of rare treasures and sudden surprises, over bridges and under tunnels of laburnum and a 14-metre rose and clematis pergola, past herbaceous borders, a croquet lawn, a river and ponds. Although essentially a spring garden (despite ferocious flooding), it is much admired throughout the summer, too. *Crug Farm Nursery,* Caernarfon, is nearby.

Glansevern Hall Gardens 23

Berriew, Welshpool, Powys SY21 8AH. Tel: (01686) 640200

G.E and M.B Thomas • From Welshpool take A483 S. After 5m entrance on left by bridge over River Rhiew • Open May to Sept, Fri, Sat and Bank Holiday Mons, 12 noon – 6pm • Entrance: £3, OAPs £2, children free ◑ 💻 ▦ WC ♿ ⬙ ⚘ ⬚ ⚬

The mature 18-acre garden is set in a wider parkland on the banks of the River Severn, and is noted for its range of unusual trees. A four-acre lake has islands where swans, ducks and other waterfowl breed. The streams, which form a water garden and feed the lake, are planted along the banks with moisture-loving plants and shrubs. A large area of lawn contains mature trees and herbaceous borders. Notable too are the fountain with its surround and walk festooned with wisteria, the restored rockery and grotto, the walled garden and the rose gardens.

Hilton Court ★ 24

Roch, Haverfordwest, Pembrokeshire SA62 6AE. Tel: (01437) 710262; Fax: (01437) 711074; Website: www.hiltongardensandcrafts.co.uk

Mr and Mrs Peter Lynch • 6m NW of Haverfordwest off A487 St Davids road. About ¾ m beyond Simpson Cross signed on left • Open all year, daily: Feb, 10.30am – 4pm; March to Aug, 10am – 5.30pm; Sept, 10.30am – 5pm; Oct to Dec, daily, 10.30am – 4pm. Closed Jan • Entrance: £1 ◑ ☕ ✕ **WC** ♨ 🏛

The garden has been developed by the present owners within the framework of the nine-acre grounds of an old estate, the house dating from 1735. Several lakes have been formed and the main water areas can be viewed from the decking area next to the teashop. The woodland walk is 200 years old. The garden is associated with a delightful garden centre arranged in a novel way so that plants are located near others that require similar conditions. Stone outbuildings house craft workshops. The drive to the gardens has views over the cliffs and shoreline of St Bride's Bay. The coast is subject to the gales off the Irish Sea and so a feature of the nursery is a selection of plants that can withstand both wind and salt spray. Aquatic plants are also a speciality.

Llanerchaeron 25

Aberaeron, Ceredigion SA48 8DG. Tel: (01545) 570200; Fax: (01545) 571759

The National Trust • 16m SW of Aberystwyth, 2m E of Aberaeron off A482 • House open as garden • Garden open 23rd March to 3rd Nov, Wed – Sun and Bank Holiday Mons, 11am – 5pm. Guided tours July to Sept, Thurs, 2pm (£1 extra). Parkland open all year, dawn – dusk • Entrance: £4, children £2. Pre-booked parties £3.20 per person, children £1.60 • Other information: ◑ 🍴 **WC** ♿ ♨ ⚕

The Trust acquired this rare survivor of an intact Welsh gentleman's estate complete with a Nash house and its 12 acres of garden, including two walled gardens, in 1989. 2002 will see the opening of the house after extensive restoration and refurbishment. The home farm gardens and grounds have been open while the restoration was in progress. Nash's villa of 1794 – 1796 – set in the beautiful Aeron valley – is the most complete example of his early work. Llanerchaeron was built as a self-sufficient estate with its own dairy, laundry, brewery and salting house contained with a service courtyard, and home farm buildings ranging from stables to threshing barn. Today it is a working organic farm; the two restored walled gardens produce home-grown fruit and herbs as well as housing a re-created rose parterre. There are extensive walks around the estate and parkland.

Maenan Hall 26

Llanrwst, Gwynedd LL26 0UL. Tel: (01492) 640441

The Hon. Mr and Mrs Christopher McLaren • 2m N of Llanrwst on E side of A470, ¼ m S of Maenan Abbey Hotel • Open 19th May, 18th Aug for charity, 10.30am – 5.30pm (last admission 4.30pm) • Entrance: £2, children £1 ● ▭ ▩ WC ♿ ⬧ ✿ ♨

Created in 1956 by the late Christabel, Lady Aberconway are formal gardens surrounding the Elizabethan and Queen Anne house, with less formal gardens in the mature woodland beyond. The present owners have extended the planting of ornamental trees and shrubs in both settings. Azaleas, rhododendrons and camellias, the latter situated in a dell at the base of a cliff, make a spring visit rewarding, while a large number of eucryphias are spectacular in late summer. This is a garden with many distinctive aspects.

Museum of Welsh Life and St Fagans Castle Gardens ★ 27

St Fagans, Cardiff, South Glamorgan CF5 6XB. Tel: (029) 2057 3500; Fax: (029) 2057 3490

National Museum of Wales • Near M4 junction 33. Signposted • Open all year, daily, 10am – 5 or 6pm • Entrance: free ○ ▭ ✕ ▩ WC ♿ ⬧ ⬚ ♨ ♨

An historic garden with terraces, herb and knot gardens, a hornbeam tunnel, an old grove of mulberry trees and a vinery. The Rosery of 1900 has been restored with the original varieties. Mature trees, both coniferous and broad-leaved, are an impresssive feature, as are the broad high terraces with massive stone walls hosting many climbing plants. Beneath are large fish ponds containing carp, bream and tench, traditionally farmed over the years to feed the household. In the grounds rhododendrons are underplanted with spring bulbs. The range of glasshouses is in poor condition, but plans for a complete restoration are in hand. Elsewhere the restoration and replanting of the formal gardens continue to reflect the Edwardian spirit. Gardens attached to re-erected buildings from all over Wales are also being developed to re-create the differences in social status and period, using traditional horticultural techniques, tools and vegetable varieties.

National Botanic Garden of Wales 28

Middleton Hall, Llanarthne, Carmarthenshire SA32 8HG.
Tel: (01558) 667132/667134, (01558) 668768 (Infoline);
Website: www.gardenofwales.org.uk

Trustees, NBGW • 8m E of Carmarthen, 7m W of Llandeilo off A48(M) • Open all year, daily, 10am – 6pm (last admission 1 hour before closing) • Entrance: £6.50, concessions £5, children £3. Family £16 (2001 prices) ● ▭ WC ♨

The vast new £43-million garden, supported by £22 million from the Millennium Commission, is located at the Regency estate of Middleton Hall, deep in the beautiful Towy valley. Its scale and purpose is summed up in its centre-piece, the Great Glasshouse, a stunning 91-metre-long 'teardrop' structure designed by architects Foster and Partners. Within the world's largest single-span glasshouse, visitors can walk through and wonder at plants, landscapes and waterfalls normally found in threatened Mediterranean environments. A 300-metre-long broadwalk of herbaceous plants and flowers leads through the middle of the garden, passing the unique double-walled garden and towards the Wallace Garden, which demonstrates the history of plant genetics. Visitors can also explore a necklace of three lakes, features of the late-eighteenth-century water park, where plants cultivated in slate beds adjoin the natural setting of gentle Welsh countryside, parkland and grassland; Paxton's View, site of the former mansion, offers a panorama down the valley. There is also an environmental Energy Zone. The promotional material gives lavish praise to the whole project, but admits it will take time to reach maturity.

Pant-yr-Holiad ★ 29

Rhydlewis, Llandysul, Ceredigion SA44 5ST. Tel: (01239) 851493

Mr and Mrs G. Taylor • 12m NE of Cardigan. Take A487 coast road to Brynhoffnant, then B4334 towards Rhydlewis for 1m, turn left and garden is second left • Open two Suns in spring for NGS, and at other times for pre-booked parties by appt • Entrance: £2.50, children £1 ● 💻 WC ♔

This five-acre woodland garden, created by the owners since 1971, was started in an area of natural woodland backing onto the farmhouse. Since then hundreds of rhododendrons (species and hybrids) have been planted along the banks. Acers, eucalyptus, eucryphias and many other rare and unusual trees have now reached maturity, and the paths wander in and around to give something to please the eye wherever the visitor may care to look. A stream runs through the middle of the garden, creating a boggy area which is home to iris and primulas, numerous species of ferns and a *Rhododendron macabeanum*. A fairly recent addition is a summer walk, along which slate-edged beds are filled with herbaceous plants, including a collection of penstemons. A small pergola has a rose-embowered seat from which the lovely view over the valley may be enjoyed, and the remainder of the walk is beneath arches of climbing roses. Nearer the house is a walled garden, alpine beds, a series of pools for ornamental waterfowl and a *potager*-style kitchen garden. Not far away, within a mile or two of the coast at Llangrannog, is *Pigeonsford Walled Garden*, an interesting example of an old garden being reclaimed, about half-a-mile's walk from the nursery of the same name. [Open Easter, then May to Sept, Wed – Sun and Bank Holiday Mons, 10am – 6pm (Tel: (01239) 654360).]

Pencarreg ★ 30

Glyn Garth, Menai Bridge, Gwynedd LL59 5NS. Tel: (01248) 713545

Miss G. Jones • 1½ m NE of A545 Menai Bridge towards Beaumaris. Glan y Menai drive is turning on right, Pencarreg 100 metres on right • Open all year by appt • Entrance: charity box • Other information: Parking in lay-by on main road, limited parking in courtyard for small cars and disabled ● 💻 WC

This beautiful garden, with a wealth of species planted for all-year interest, has colour achieved by the use of common and unusual shrubs. A small stream creates another sympathetically exploited feature. The garden ends at the cliff edge and this, too, has been skilfully planted. The views are remarkable.

Penlan–Uchaf Farm Gardens 31

Gwaun Valley, Fishguard, Pembrokeshire SA65 9UA. Tel: (01348) 881388

Mr and Mrs Vaughan • 7m SE of Fishguard, 3m S Of Newport. From Fishguard take B4313 Narberth road and after 4m turn left signed 'Cwm Gwaun/Gwaun Valley (Pontvane)'. From Newport take Gwaun Valley road. Next to Sychpant Forest car park • Open 24th March to early Nov (weather permitting), daily, 9am – dusk • Entrance: £2, children 50p, disabled persons and children under 3 free • Other information: Cars carrying wheelchairs may set down at main garden. Up to 22-seater coaches and minibuses permitted ◗ ▆ ▆ WC ૯ ⏏ ✿ ℺

A medium-sized garden on a hillside near the top of the Gwaun Valley. The drive is very steep, but the view from the tea room is worth the effort. This is a young garden but the owners, realising that its position will make many trees and shrubs an impossibility, have chosen alpines and herbaceous borders and planted a 27-metre pergola with sweet peas. There are some 30,000 spring bulbs, and fuchsias, geraniums and annuals give plenty of colour later. A raised herb garden, suitable for wheelchair visitors and the blind, contains more than 100 different herbs and wild flowers, and there is also an extra-sensory area.

Penpergwm Lodge 32

Abergavenny, Monmouthshire NP7 9AS. Tel/Fax: (01873) 840208;
E-mail: penpergwmplants@amk.com; Website: www.penplants.com

Mrs C. Boyle • 2½ m SE of Abergavenny off B4598 Usk road. Turn left opposite King of Prussia Inn. Entrance 300 metres on left • Open April to Sept, Thurs – Sun, 2 – 6pm • Entrance: £2 (2001 price) • Other information: Teas on Sats and Suns only ◗ ▆ WC ૯ ⏏ ✿ ▯ ℺

This spacious three-acre garden forms the centrepiece for an established and successful school of gardening, which offers day-long gardening workshops. Broad south-facing terraces command views over wide expanses of lawn well screened by mature trees and shrubs. A vine pergola makes a bold statement and provides a visual link with the house, while a recently planted formal garden of yew and box creates a delightful and effective enclosure. Old-fashioned roses, herbaceous perennials and an imaginative vegetable garden contribute interest throughout the season. The nursery sells unusual plants.

Penrhyn Castle ★ 33

Bangor, Gwynedd LL57 4HN. Tel: (01248) 353084; Fax: (01248) 371281

The National Trust • 1m E of Bangor on A5122 • Castle open 12 noon – 5pm (July to Aug opens 11am) • Garden open 23rd March to 3rd Nov, daily except Tues, 11am – 5.30pm (July and Aug opens 10am) • Entrance: £4, children £2 (castle and garden £6, children £3, family ticket £15, parties £5 per person) • Other information: Golf buggy available if pre-booked ◗ ▆ ▆ WC ૯ ⏏ ▥ ▯

The large garden covers 48 acres with some fine specimen trees, shrubs and a Victorian walled garden in terraces with pools, lawns and a wild garden. Although the original house dated from the eighteenth century, the gardens are very much early Victorian, contemporary with the present castle designed by Thomas Hopper. A giant tree fern, which will dwarf any children who visit, has been sent from Tasmania to take its place in a specialist collection that also includes another giant, gunnera, and the Australian bottle brush plant. These can be found in the spectacular bog garden beyond the walled garden.

Picton Castle ★ 34

Haverfordwest, Pembrokeshire SA62 4AS. Tel: (01437) 751326

Picton Castle Trust • 4m SE of Haverfordwest off A40. Signposted • Castle open for conducted tours April to Sept. Telephone for details • Garden open April to Oct, daily except Mon (but open Bank Holiday Mons), 10.30am – 5pm • Entrance: gardens and gallery £3.95, OAPs £3.75, children £1.95 (castle, gardens and gallery £4.95, OAPs £4.75, children £1.95) ◑ 💬 ✕ 🖻 WC ⚅ ⬠ 🌿 🎪 🍽 ☕*

The grounds extend over nearly 40 acres, with woodland walks among massive oaks and giant redwoods. Rarities include the biggest *Rhododendron* 'Old Port' in existence and a metasequoia, a deciduous conifer presumed extinct but rediscovered in China in 1941. In June all these wondrously exotic shrubs reach their full splendour. In the walled garden are herb borders and summer-flowering plants, with a central pond and fountain creating a cool and calming atmosphere.

Plantasia 35

Parc Tawe, Swansea SA1 2AL. Tel: (01792) 474555;
Website: www.plantasia.org

Swansea City Council • Signed from city centre • Open all year, daily except Mon (but open Bank Holiday Mons), 10am – 5pm • Entrance: £2.50, concessions £1.75 ○ 💬 WC ⚅ 🍽 ☕*

A hothouse of over 1600 square metres divided into three zones – arid, tropical and humid – it contains over 5000 plants on permanent display from cacti to orchids. The tropical house is alive with monkeys, snakes, lizards, fish, insects and butterflies.

Plas Brondanw Gardens ★ 36

Llanfrothen, Penrhyndeudraeth, Gwynedd LL48 6SW. Tel: (07880) 766741

5m NE of Porthmadog between Llanfrothen and Croesor • Open all year, daily, 9am – 5pm • Entrance: £1.50, children 25p ○ WC

This garden, in the grounds of the house given to Sir Clough Williams-Ellis by his father, is quite separate from the village of Portmeirion (see entry), and was created by the architect over a period of 70 years. His main objective was to provide a series of dramatic and romantic prospects inspired by the great gardens of Italy; it includes architectural features, such as the orangery.

Visitors should walk up the avenue that leads past a dramatic chasm to the folly, from which there is a fine view of Snowdon — indeed mountains are visible from the end of every vista. Williams-Ellis made a prodigious investment in hedging and topiary (mostly yew) and the present head gardener has calculated that the former, if laid flat, would cover four acres. Hydrangeas and ferns flourish in the damp climate.

Plas Newydd ★ 37

Llanfairpwll, Anglesey LL61 6DQ. Tel: (01248) 714795; Fax: (01248) 713673; E-mail: ppnmsn@smtp.ntrust.org.uk

The National Trust • 4m SW of Menai Bridge, 2m S of Llanfairpwll via A5 • House with military museum open as gardens, 12 noon – 5pm • Garden open 23rd March to Oct, daily except Thurs and Fri, 11am – 5.30pm (last admission 5pm). Rhododendron garden open April to early June only. Guided tours by arrangement • Entrance: £2.50, children £1.25 (house and gardens £4.80, children £2.40, family £11, pre-booked parties of 15 or more £3.70 per person) (2001 prices) • Other information: Parking ¼ m from garden. A minibus offers a complimentary service between the car park and house on request, and a 'shuttle' service in the garden ◐ ⬛ ✕ 🍽 WC ♿ ⚘ 🏛 ☕ ⚲

The eighteenth-century house by James Wyatt is worth visiting, mainly to see Rex Whistler's largest painting. Humphry Repton's suggestion of 'plantations... to soften a bleak country and shelter the ground from violent winds' has resulted in an informal open-plan garden, with shrub plantings in the lawns and parkland, which slopes down to the Menai Straits and frames the view of the Snowdonia peaks. There is a formal Italian-style garden to the front of the house. A new arbour has replaced a conservatory on the top terrace with a tufa mound, from which water falls to a pool on the bottom terrace. The pool has a new Italianate fountain to add to the overall Mediterranean effect of this formal area within the parkland. The influence of the Gulf Stream enables the successful cultivation of many frost-tender shrubs, and a special rhododendron garden is open in the spring when the gardens are at their best, although they are expertly tended throughout the year. Major restoration of the Italianate terrace garden continues and includes the building of a deep grotto and the replanting of the mixed borders. The marine and woodland paths along the Menai Straits have also been restored. Summer brings displays of hydrangeas, while autumn colour appears in the ever-changing arboretum of southern-hemisphere trees and shrubs, and wild flowers appear in their seasons. There is an adventure trail for children. An historical cruise, a boat trip on the Menai Strait, one of the most scenic and romantic waterways in Europe, operates during normal opening times (additional cost).

Plas Penhelig ★ 38

Aberdovey, Gwynedd LL35 0NA. Tel: (01654) 767676; Fax: (01654) 767783

Gordon Bates • 11m SW of Machynlleth on A43. At Aberdovey, between two railway bridges • Open all year, daily, 2.30 – 5.30pm • Entrance: £2.50, children £1, for charity ◐ ⬛ ✕ WC ⚲

A traditional Edwardian estate garden of seven acres, reclaimed over the past 20 years, includes an informal garden with lawns, terraces, pools, fountains, an orchard, a rock garden and herbaceous borders. Spring bulbs, azaleas, rhododendrons, magnolias, euphorbias, roses and some mature tree heathers of immense size command admiration. The jewel is the half-acre formal walled garden, including over 80 square metres of glass with nectarines and peaches. The house is now a hotel. Some 3m E of Aberdovey is *Panteidal Garden Nursery*, a 150-acre landscape nursery and garden which specialises in sub-tropical or Mediterranean-type plants. Scrubland area and cottage garden. [Open 2 days for NGS, and by appt (Tel: 01654 767322). Organic shop and restaurant open daily, 9am – 5.30pm.]

Plas-yn-Rhiw 39

Pwllheli, Gwynedd LL53 8AB. Tel: (01758) 780219

The National Trust • Near tip of Lleyn Peninsular. 16m SW of Pwllheli, take A499 and B4413. Signposted at Botwnnog • House open (numbers limited) • Garden and snowdrop wood open some weekends Jan and Feb (telephone to check). Garden open 23rd March to 13th May, daily except Tues; Oct, Sat and Sun only, plus 21st to 25th Oct; all 12 noon – 5pm (last admission 4.30pm) • Entrance: £2, children £1; garden and snowdrop wood £2.50; house and garden £3.20, children £1.60, family ticket £8. Pre-booked evening parties £1.40 extra per person • Other information: Parking 80 metres from garden. No coaches ◑ WC

This is essentially a cottage garden, laid out around a partly medieval manor house on the west shore of Hell's Mouth Bay. Flowering trees and shrubs, rhododendrons, camellias and magnolias are divided by formal box hedges and grass paths extending to three quarters of an acre. A snowdrop wood stands on high ground above the garden.

Portmeirion ★ 40

Penrhyndeudraeth, Gwynedd LL48 6ET. Tel: (01766) 770228 (Hotel Reception)

2m SE of Porthmadog near A487 • Open all year, daily except 25th Dec, 9.30am – 5.30pm • Entrance: £4.50, OAPs £3.60, children £2.25, under 5 free, family (2 adults and 2 children) £12, season ticket £35 (2001 prices) • Other information: Parking at top of village. Difficult for wheelchairs as steep in places ○ ✕ WC

Architect Sir Clough Williams-Ellis's wild essay into the picturesque is a triumph of eclecticism, with Gothick, Renaissance and Victorian buildings arranged as an Italianate village around a harbour and set in 70 acres of sub-tropical woodlands criss-crossed by paths. This light opera is played out against the backdrop of the Cambrian mountains and the vast empty sweep of estuary sands. The gentle humour of the architecture extends to the plantings in both horizontal and vertical planes – in the formal gardens and in the wild luxuriance which clings to the rocky crags. Portmeirion provides one of Britain's most stimulating objects for an excursion, and during the period of the June festival in nearby Criccieth there are other good gardens open in the district. Write for details (with s.a.e.) to Criccieth Festival Office, PO Box 3, 52 High Street, Criccieth LL52 0BW.

Post House Gardens   41

Cwmbach, Whitland, Carmarthenshire SA34 0DR. Tel: (01994) 484213

Mrs Jo Kenaghan • 10m NW of Carmarthen off A40. Take B4298 through Meidrim, then centre lane signed 'Llanboidy', turn right at crossroads signed 'Blaenwaun', right again at next crossroads to Cwmbach • Open by appt May and June • Entrance: £2.50 ◐ 🍴 **WC**

Some five acres of woodland valley garden, begun in 1978, wind along the bank of the River Sien along paths leading through shrubberies to a large pool. A sloping path leads to higher levels, then meanders between shrubberies housing many species and hybrid rhododendrons, and on through a rose garden planted with old roses. There is also an easier path at mid-garden level which gives a good view of the shrubberies. Above the pond a summerhouse provides seating from which to admire *Rosa* 'Paul's Himalayan Musk', now rampant through and over adjacent trees; several other seats give views of different areas. Near the entrance the range of well-known and unusual plants, which together with the wild flowers and wooded background make up this interesting garden. Many of the rhododendrons, other shrubs and trees are grown from seed.

Powis Castle and Garden ★★   42

Welshpool, Powys SY21 8RF. Tel: (01938) 554338; Fax: (01938) 554336; E-mail: ppcmsa@smtp.ntrust.org.uk

The National Trust • ¾ m S of Welshpool on A483. Signposted • Castle open, 1 – 5pm • Garden open 23rd March to 30th June, daily except Mon and Tues (but open Bank Holiday Mons); July and Aug, daily except Mon (but open Bank Holiday Mon); Sept to 3rd Nov, daily except Mon and Tues; all 11am – 6pm (last admission half hour before closing) • Entrance: £5, children (5–16) £2.50, under 5 free, family ticket (2 adults and 3 children) £12.50, parties £4 per person (castle, garden and museum £7.50, children (5–16) £3.75, under 5 free, family £18.75, parties £6.50 per person) • Other information: Events programme and guided tours of garden – telephone for details (01938) 551920. Picnics in park outside garden only. Problematic for wheelchairs and pushchairs as very steep with steps ◑ 🍱 ✕ **WC** 🐾 ♿ 🔦

The garden was originally laid out at the turn of the seventeenth century based on formal designs attributed to William Winde. The most notable features are the broad hanging terraces, interestingly planted and with huge clipped yews. The terraces are inspired by those of the palace at St Germain-en-Laye near Paris, where the 1st Marquis of Powis joined James II in exile in 1689. On the second terrace, above the orangery, are fine urns and statuary by van Nost's workshop stand in front of the deeply recessed brick alcoves of the aviary. The late-eighteenth-century changes to the garden as a result of the English landscape style are attributed to William Emes. Advantage was taken of the many micro-climates to develop the ornamental plantings during the nineteenth century, and the kitchen garden of the lower garden was transformed into a formal flower garden in 1911 by Lady Violet, wife of the 4th Earl. Unusual and tender plants and climbers now prosper in the shelter of the walls and hedges. The planting schemes are superb. The box-edged terraces have notable displays of clematis and pittosporums; in season *Abutilon vitifolium* 'Tennant's White' matched with *Rosa banksiae* 'Lutea' and R. 'Gloire de Dijon' are inspiring, the collection of ceanothus cloaking the terraces magnificent; in late summer the eucryphias repeat the performance. The more recent gardens below, lying towards the Severn valley, are set in hues of purple and burgundy, with arches of vines continuing the formality in enclosed hedged rooms. The basket-weave terracotta pots continue to be planted with a masterly touch. This garden is not for the faint-hearted because it is very steep, but it is well worth the effort to relish the views which are as fine as any, anywhere. There is also a good collection of old roses.

Singleton Botanic Gardens ★   43

Singleton Park, Swansea, West Glamorgan SA2 8QD. Tel: (01792) 302420

Swansea City Council • In Swansea. Entrance in Gower Road • Open all year, daily, 9am – 6pm (4.30pm in winter) • Entrance: free • Other information: Refreshments during Aug only ○ WC &

A four-and-a-half-acre garden with herbaceous borders, rockeries, rose beds and an interesting collection of trees and shrubs, including tapestry hedges using a variety of different shrubs. Newly erected temperate and tropical glasshouses contain an extensive range of rare and unusual plants, including orchids, bromeliads and epiphytes.

Stammers Gardens ★   44

Stammers Road, Saundersfoot, Pembrokeshire SA69 9HH. Tel: (01834) 813766

Mr and Mrs B. Sly • 2m N of Tenby off A478. In Saundersfoot, turn right immediately after Post Office into Stammers Road. Garden is 200 metres on right • Open Easter to Oct, daily except Sat, 10.30am – 5pm • Entrance: £3.50, OAPs £3, accompanied children free ◐ ☕ WC ⇦

A pleasant surprise nestling in the heart of a typical Welsh seaside resort. Now extending to some seven acres, the gardens were first established in the late 1970s, so they have an air of maturity and are being carefully restored, extended and replanted by the present owners. The shrubberies, ponds, stream, woodland and arboretum will be added to with a new bog garden. Refreshments can be taken while gazing out over Carmarthen Bay.

Tredegar House   45

Newport, Gwent NP10 8YW. Tel: (01633) 815880

Newport County Borough Council • 3m S of Newport. Signed from A48 and M4 junction 28 • Open 29th March to Sept, Wed – Sun, 11.30am – 4pm. Park open daily, dawn – dusk • Entrance: free; house £4.95, OAPs £3.65, children £2.25, family £12.95 (2001 prices) • Other information: Dogs in park only, on lead ◐ ☕ ✕ ▥ WC & ⇦ ⛪ ♗ ◕

One of the finest Restoration houses in the country with a remarkable interior containing pictures from Dulwich and furniture from the V&A. The reason for it being in this *Guide* is that researchers in the Orangery Garden discovered physical evidence of a unique piece of archaeology: a late-seventeenth-century mineral parterre, using coal and brick dust, coloured sands and sea shells. It is the first to be re-created in this country and well worth seeing.

Tretower Court   46

Tretower, Crickhowell, Powys NP8 1RF. Tel: (01874) 730279

Cadw: Welsh Historic Monuments • 3m NW of Crickhowell off A479. Signed from Tretower village • Open March to 26th Oct at various times and prices (telephone for details) ◑ WC ♿

This late-medieval house is set in the beautiful Usk valley; an earlier castle stands across an open meadow to the rear. Stretching south from the Court is a charming re-creation of a mid-fifteenth-century pleasure garden in a design faithful to the period. Planted in 1991, it is maturing well. Try to time your visit to take in one of the entertaining talks on medieval gardens which it is hoped will take place weekly from June to early August.

Upton Castle   47

Cosheston, Pembroke Dock, Pembrokeshire SA72 4SE. Tel: (01646) 651782; E-mail: enquiries@carewcastle.pembrokeshirecoast.org.uk; Website: www.pembrokeshirecoast.org.uk

Canon and Mrs H.J.N. Skelton • 2m NE of Pembroke off A477. In Cosheston turn right. Castle signed on left • Open April to Oct, daily except Sat, 10am – 5pm, but check before travelling • Entrance: £1.20, children 60p, family £3. Season tickets available • Other information: Approach roads very narrow. No coaches ◑ 📖 ⬧ ♿

The grounds of the part-thirteenth-century castle were planted as a garden in the 1930s with a large collection of rhododendrons and camellia species and hybrids of the period. These have grown into large mature specimens to which the Pembrokeshire Coast National Park, which has a management agreement with the owners, has added new cultivars. Large specimens of redwood, drimys and chestnut-leaved oak, embothriums and a particularly magnificent *Magnolia campbellii*, planted in 1936, are among the 250 or more kinds of trees and shrubs growing in the grounds. A walk through the woods leads down to the Carew River. The old walled garden is now mostly grass, with fruit and vegetables and two greenhouses. There are also formal terraces with herbaceous borders and rose beds, and a medieval chapel.

Veddw House   48

Devauden, Monmouthshire NP16 6PH. Tel: (01291) 650836; E-mail: Chawes@veddw.freeserve.co.uk; Website: www.oxalis.co.uk/gf/veddw.html

Anne Wareham and Charles Hawes • 5m NW of Chepstow off B4293. In Devauden, signed from pub on green • Open 7th April to 29th Sept, Sun and

Bank Holiday Mons, 2 – 5pm, and for parties afternoon or evening by appt •
Entrance: £2.50, children £1 ● 🏠 WC 🐾 🌱 ℺

Situated on a sheltered slope near the Wye Valley, framed by old beech woods
and with views in all directions, this garden is the product of over a decade of
enthusiastic labour by the owners. There are two acres of flower garden and
meadow and two acres of woodland where the trees are embellished by
decorative plaques and quotations. The generously planted borders include
many unusual varieties, and around every corner is something of interest – a
magnolia walk, a cotoneaster walk with rampant rambler roses growing
through it, a philadelphus border. In front of the house four rectangular beds
are punctuated by balls of clipped evergreens; nearby is a grey border of
eucalyptus, cistus and buddleia. The formal vegetable garden with its fruit cage
is enclosed by borders of old scented roses and 40 varieties of clematis on trellis
and arches. From here an arch leads into the orchard and the meadow, full of
bulbs in spring and grasses and wild flowers in summer. Behind the house the
ground slopes steeply upwards, with paths and steps leading to viewpoints. A
new garden is being created here, with yew hedges enclosing a formal garden
planted with cornfield annuals, a garden of only two hedges, and two spaces, one
with reflecting pool, which are not yet complete. Overlooking these gardens is
another fascinating parterre, where box hedges form compartments replicating
the 1824 tithe map of the area. The spaces between are filled with a variety of
grasses. Further up still is a hazel coppice and the wood with its superb old beech
trees, sorbus and hornbeam. Detailed guide and plant list available.

Winllan   49

Talsarn, Lampeter, Ceredigion SA48 8QE. Tel: (01570) 470612

Mr and Mrs Ian Callan • 16m S of Aberystwyth, 8m N of Lampeter on B4342 •
Open for NGS May and June, daily, 2 – 6pm, July and Aug by appt only • Entrance:
£2, children 50p, under 12 free • Other information: Coaches by appt only ● 🏠 ◁◻

The six-acre garden has been created by the owners mainly as a haven for the
wildlife which is disappearing so rapidly countrywide. After 25 years, the
garden is home to over 200 species of wild flowers, including seven of wild
orchid, and more appear all the time; these in turn attract the butterflies
which thrive on the rich flora of the meadow. Similarly, dragonflies in their
season enliven the pond. A small area was planted up as a woodland with some
35 species of mainly native trees in 1982; this again has its attendant wild
flowers and birds. Beyond the wood is a haymeadow, and along the length of
the garden the river creates another habitat. Although there is a small area of
conventional garden, the emphasis is on native wild plants. Visitors receive
personal attention from the owners.

Wyndcliffe Court   50

St Arvans, Chepstow, Monmouthshire NP16 6EY. Tel: (01291) 622352

Mr and Mrs H.A.P. Clay • Off Wye Valley road from Chepstow • Open 3rd June
for NGS, and by appt for private parties • Entrance: £2 • Other information:
Garden only accessible for wheelchairs on terrace ● 🏠 WC ⭐ ◁◻ 🌱 ℺

A garden conceived in the Arts and Crafts tradition and largely unchanged since its creation in 1922. From a broad paved terrace, two flights of steps descend to the topiary terrace with its semi-circular pool; the topiary yew drums are matched by ten rectangular beds of annuals. The next level is a bowling green (with clock golf, too). Beyond the charming summerhouse is a sunken garden with a long rectangular pool. Long herbaceous borders lead to the large walled vegetable garden, much of it devoted to flowers and shrubs. There are several fine specimen trees and old fruit trees. David Wheeler of *Hortus* says, 'Wyndcliffe remains secure in a romantic time warp, swathed in roses and old-world fragrance, the essence of the life of a country garden.' Fine views of the Severn estuary and its two bridges.

Ynyshir Hall   51

Eglwysfach, Machynlleth, Powys SY20 8TA. Tel: (01654) 781209; Fax: (01654) 781366; E-mail: info@ynyshir_hall.co.uk; Website: www.ynyshir_hall.co.uk

Mr and Mrs R. Reen • 13m NE of Aberystwyth off A487 Machynlleth road. Signed in Eglwysfach • Open May, daily • Entrance: £1 • Other information: Refreshments and toilet facilities in hotel ○ ◆ ✗ WC ⬧

Although the house (now a hotel) was once owned by Queen Victoria, the 12 acres of gardens were not really developed and extensively planted until they fell into the hands of William Mappin, who owned the Hall from 1930–70. During this time many unusual trees were planted and the grounds land-scaped. Water played an important part in the garden, and the present owners have discovered pools and a water course which are being cleared and replanted. The trees, now nearing maturity, are fine specimens which create a noble background for a variety of rhododendrons, azaleas, camellias and other shrubs. When the garden was open all year, early visitors were able to see massed plantings of daffodils and fritillaries, moving on to magnolias and other later-flowering shrubs, finishing the season with autumn colour from the maples. There is a famous 'Ironstone tree' dating from the period when Queen Victoria used to visit. The 500 acres of woodland round the house were given by Mappin to the RSPB.

WELSH HISTORIC GARDENS TRUST
Formed in 1989, the Trust has since created a network throughout Wales. The membership has topped 600 and apart from national projects invol-ving the Trust office, the branches undertake projects locally. Its national aims are to initiate and assist in the conservation of gardens, parks and designed landscapes that are of historic, cultural and aesthetic impor-tance in the Welsh Heritage, and to raise public awareness. The address to contact is: Tyleri, Talybont, Ceredigion SY24 5ER (Tel/Fax: (01970) 832268).

CHANNEL ISLANDS

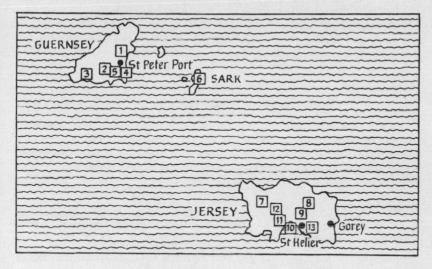

GUERNSEY AND SARK

Candie Gardens   1

Candie Road, St Peter Port, Guernsey GY1 1UG. Tel: (01481) 720904

States of Guernsey • In St Peter Port, off Candie Road • Open all year, daily, 8am – sunset (5pm in winter) • Entrance: free • Other information: Teas, toilet facilities, (inc. disabled), shop and events in Guernsey Museum and Art Gallery
○ ⬤ ✕ 🗑 WC ♿ ⬦ 🏛 ⚱

Situated on a slope overlooking the harbour at St Peter Port, there are wonderful views over the islands of Herm and Sark from the gardens. Created over 100 years ago, they contain statues of Queen Victoria and Victor Hugo, who lived on Guernsey in exile from 1855 to 1871. The Lower Gardens used to be the walled fruit and vegetable garden of Candie House (now the Priaulx Library) but were remodelled as a public garden in 1887. A rare surviving example of a Victorian public flower garden, they have been sympathetically restored. Guernsey's mild climate and the shelter afforded by the garden walls has enabled many varieties of exotic plants from all over the world to be grown, including a magnificent *Phoenix canariensis* (Canary palm) considered to be the largest in the British Isles, a huge *Gingko biloba*, camellias, rhododendrons, ferns, aquatics and a South African bulb collection which originated in the late nineteenth century. The gardens also contain herbaceous borders and two 1792 show glasshouses in an excellent state of preservation. The Guernsey Museum and Art Gallery, built around an original Victorian bandstand, and the Priaulx Reference and Genealogical Library are here.

The Hermitage 2

**Les Maindonnaux, St Martin GY4 6AH. Tel: (01481) 235256 or
Guernsey Tourist Information (01481) 723552**

*Mr and Mrs J. Webb • 1½ m S of St Peter Port • Open one or two days a year
and for private parties by appt • Entrance: £2.50* ◐ WC ♿

Dating from the 1750s, the house is surrounded by about three acres of
landscaped gardens, dominated by a very tall Monterey cypress some 200 years
old. From this vantage point visitors can view a small lake surrounded by giant
gunneras, ligularias and other moisture-loving plants, fed by freshwater
springs to the obvious enjoyment of the resident ducks and moorhens. Nearby
azaleas, rhododendrons, camellias and fuchsias grow in abundance in a woodland setting. A walled garden offers shelter to fine specimens of *Cestrum elegans,
Clethra arborea, Clianthus puniceus, Crinodendron hookerianum*, giant echiums and
many other unusual shrubs and perennials.

Mille Fleurs 3

**Rue du Bordage, St Pierre du Bois GY7 9DW. Tel/Fax: (01481) 263911;
Website: www.millefleurs.co.uk**

*Mr and Mrs D. Russell • 6m SW of St Peter Port. 100 metres down lane from Rue de
Quanteraine/Rue du Bordage junction • Open one or two days a year and for parties
by appt • Entrance: £3 • Other information: Self-catering cottages available* ◐

Natural country gardens of some three acres set in a peaceful, wooded
conservation valley. The areas around the house and holiday cottages are a
profusion of roses, clematis, penstemons and other herbaceous perennials,
with sweetly scented honeysuckle and jasmine framing arches and doorways.
Paths flanked by lilies, lavender and other fragrant plants meander down to the
bottom of the valley, where more tender, sub-tropical plants, such as bananas,
cannas and palms, flourish in the sheltered microclimate. A natural spring
feeds into two ponds surrounded by mature tree ferns and giant gunneras
amid huge stands of arum lilies. A large mature fig tree and a host of terracotta
pots brimming with red pelargoniums and cordylines, together with banks of
crocosmias, phormiums and euphorbias, lend a Mediterranean feel to the
swimming-pool area.

La Petite Vallée 4

St Peter Port GY1 2TE. Tel: (01481) 238866

*Mrs Jennifer Monachan • 2m S of central St Peter Port • Open occasionally for
charity days. See local paper or tourist information office. (Tel: (01481) 726611)*
NEW ◐

This is a garden full of surprises and excitement, since it reflects the enthusiasm and passions that the owner has lavished on this three-acre valley
going down towards the sea. Wildflower meadows, shrubberies, rose gardens,
a folly, a stream, along with herb, water and terrace gardens all flow into each
other with effortless ease. One of the best in the Channel Islands.

Sausmarez Manor Exotic Woodland Garden   5

St Martins, Guernsey GY4 6SG. Tel: (01481) 235571

Mr Peter de Sausmarez • 1½ m S of St Peter Port, off Fort Road • Manor open mid-week in summer • Garden open all year, daily, 10.30am – 5.30pm (or dusk if earlier). Guided tours for parties by appt • Entrance: £3, OAPs/children £2.50, disabled persons and babies free • Other information: Rare plant sale 28th May. Doll's house collection. Pitch and putt course. Sculpture park, ride-on trains ○ 🍵 WC ⅏ 🏧 🍵

Set around two small lakes in an ancient wood is a garden which has been crammed with the unusual and rare to give an exotic feel. It is strewn with plants from many parts of the world, particularly the sub-tropics and the Mediterranean, which survive in Guernsey's mellow maritime climate. Collections of yuccas, ferns, camellias (over 300), bamboos, hebes, bananas, echiums, lilies, palm trees, fuchsias, as well as hydrangeas, hostas, azaleas, pittosporums, clematis, rhododendrons, cyclamens, impatiens, giant grasses etc., all jostle with indigenous wild flowers. No pesticides are used so wildlife flourishes and appears in season. Also here is the Art Park, showing around 200 pieces of sculpture by about 90 British, European, African, American and local artists.

La Seigneurie   6

Sark GY9. Tel: (01481) 832345 (Sark Tourism); Fax: (01481) 832628; Website: www.sark-tourism.com

Seigneur Mr J.M. Beaumont • ½ m NW of Creux Harbour, Sark • Open 25th March to 11th Oct, Mon – Fri, 10am – 5pm, and Sats July to Sept for charity • Entrance: £1.20, children 60p ◑ WC ⅏ ⚲

The grounds and walled garden of La Seigneurie, the residence of the Seigneurs of Sark, are beautifully maintained. Visit in spring and early summer for the camellias, azaleas and rhododendrons, later for roses, old-fashioned annuals, and in autumn for the glowing colours of dahlias and fuchsias. The walled garden contains clematis, geraniums, lapagerias, abutilons, osteospermums and many sub-tropical and tender plants. There is a *potager*, a wild pond area, a restored Victorian greenhouse with vines and bougainvilleas, a hedge maze for children, and a small outdoor museum with antique cannons. The Gothick *colombier* (the dovecot being the prerogative of the lord of the manor) may still be seen behind the house.

JERSEY

Creux Baillot Cottage   7

le Chemin des Garennes,St Ouen JE3 2FE. Tel: (01534) 482191; Email: judith.queree@jersey-mail.co.uk; Website: www.judith.queree.freewebspace.com

Judith Quérée • 1/4 m N of St Ouen. Location map provided or directions given when booking made • Open May to Sept, 11am and 2pm (or by arrangement) by appt only for conducted tours • Entrance £3.50 NEW ● 🌿

This garden, largely laid out as a cottage garden, belongs to a dedicated plantsperson. With 1700 different species and cultivars, it is a living encyclopaedia of the rare and unusual crammed into a 3/4–acre site in a secluded valley. To name but a few, there are 105 different clematis, 25 species of corydalis, eight types of tree ferns. It is an unusual feature with a charming sculpture, a curtain of chains for climbers, a raised walkway through a bog garden with a small wooden boat and a collection of anchors to lend a nautical and humorous touch to a serious garden.

Domaine Des Vaux   8

La Rue de Bas, St Lawrence JE3 1JG.

Mr and Mrs Marcus Binney • 2m N of St Helier • Open one Sun, 2 – 5pm, for charity (check with Jersey Tourist Board (01534) 500700). Private parties by prior arrangement with owners in writing • Entrance: £3.50 ● ▧ WC ⬦ ◉

Marcus Binney, architectural correspondent of *The Times*, has a passion for the preservation of architecture and landscape, and these tastes are very much reflected in his and his wife Anne's delightful garden. It is in two completely contrasting parts. The top is a formal Italianate garden, set around and above a sunken rectangular lawn, and the borders here are a riot of unusual and familiar perennials and shrubs. This perfect formal garden was created by the previous generation, Sir George and Lady Binney, and designed by Walter Ison who created the strong architectural form. Lady Binney planted with an eye for colour in foliage as much as in flowers, as is evidenced by the grey and silver borders facing the yellow, gold and bronze ones. The Binneys have planted a small formal herb garden on a triangular theme and have created a *jardinire* and a pair of long flower borders. The lower garden is a semi-wild and quite steep valley with a string of ponds connected by a stream. In spring the valley and wood are at their best, with a carpet of wild Jersey narcissi under camellias, azaleas and rhododendrons. A magnificent *Magnolia campbellii* has reached maturity and flowers abundantly in March. Of particular note are the camellias in both gardens and an interesting collection of conifers, and other trees planted to give year-round foliage colour in a small arboretum. A newly created Mediterranean Garden stands at the top of the valley with a collection of planted pots which reflect the colours of the south of France and Italy.

Eric Young Orchid Foundation   9

Victoria Village, Trinity JE3 5HH. Tel: (01534) 861963

The Eric Young Charitable Trust • 1½ m N of St Helier • Open all year except 1st Jan, 25th, 26th Dec, Thurs – Sat, 10am – 4pm • Entrance: £2.50, OAPs £1.50, students £1.50, children £1 • Other information: Light refreshments available from cold drinks machine. Plants for sale, when available ○ ▧ ▧ WC ⬦

This exquisite collection, described as 'the finest private collection of orchids in Europe, possibly the world', was built up by the late Eric Young, who came to Jersey after World War II. In 1958 he merged his own collection with that of a Sanders nursery which was closing down, and continued to acquire new plants. The purpose-built centre, which has won many awards, consists of five growing houses and a landscaped display area where visitors may view these exotic flowers in close detail. From November to April there are cymbidiums, paphiopedilums, odontoglossums and calanthes, from May to June cattleyas, miltonias and odontoglossums and from June to October, phalaenopsis, miltonias and odontoglossums. (The beauty of these flowers is inversely proportional to the difficulties of their names.) Meanwhile, those wishing to see native orchids in season may find a walk in Les Blanches Banques, the sand dunes behind St Ouen's Bay, rewarding.

Howard Davis Park 10

St Saviour.

In St Helier, between St Clement's Road and Don Road • Open all year, daily: Oct to March, 8.30am – 4.30pm; April to May, 8am – 8pm; June to Sept, 8am – 10pm • Entrance: free (charge for bandstand seats) ○ ◆✕ ▦ WC & ♀ ℀

Given by T.B. Davis, a great benefactor of the island, in memory of his son who was killed in World War I, this is the most famous of Jersey's public gardens. Colourful sub-tropical trees and plants flourish here, and the bandstand is the venue for an excellent variety of live entertainment from May to September. Other public parks in St Helier are Parade Gardens, off Parade Place, and Victoria Park, off St Aubins Road/Cheapside. Both contain interesting statues.

Jersey Lavender 11

Rue du Pont Marquet, St Brelade JE3 8DS. Tel: (01534) 742933; Fax: (01534) 745613; E-mail: jerseylavender@cocaldial.com; Website: www.jerseylavender.co.uk

David and Elizabeth Christie • 3m W of St Helier near Pont Marquet Country Park • Open 20th May to 21st Sept, Mon – Sat, 10am – 5pm • Entrance: £2.75, children free ◐ ◆ ✕ ▦ WC & ⬆ ℘ ⛪

This lavender farm was started in 1983 and now covers nine acres. Visitors are invited to walk around the main fields, planted with five varieties of lavender, to enjoy their different colours and scents. Harvesting is done by hand, starting in late June, and the distillation and perfume-bottling processes may also be seen. There is an extensive garden of herbs, including a National Collection of lavenders and a collection of 75 different species of bamboos.

Jersey Zoological Park 12

Les Augres Manor, Trinity JE3 5BP. Tel: (01534) 860000

Durell Wildlife Conservation Trust • 2½ m NW of St Helier on B361 • Open daily except 25th Dec, 9.30am – 6pm (last admission dusk) • Entrance: £9, OAPs £7.50, children £6.50. Parties of 10 or more £2 less per person ○ ◆ ✕ ▦ WC & ⬆ ♀ ℀

Over 100 rare and endangered species of animals reside within the 31 acres of parkland and water gardens. The late author and naturalist Gerald Durrel founded the Zoo as a sanctuary forty years ago. Today Sumatran orangutans,

Andean bears and Montserrat orioles, rescued from beneath the smouldering volcano, live in lush, spacious environments, which closely replicate their native habitats. Madagascar lemurs and tiny lion tamarins from Brazil live free in the Zoo's woodland, leaping through the trees. The group of five western lowland gorillas is led by the male silverback Ya Kwanza, an impressive male weighing 26 stone.

Samarès Manor 13

St Clement JE2 6QW. Tel: (01534) 870551; Fax: (01534) 768949

Vincent Obbard • *2m E of St Helier* • *Manor (guided tours daily except Sun, am. £1.95 extra) open* • *Garden open 3rd April to 16th Oct, daily, 10am – 5pm* • *Entrance: £4.20, OAPs £3.50, children £1.90, under 5 free (2001 prices)* • *Other information: Craft centre* ◑ ☕ ✕ 🍴 WC ﾖ 🐾 ⌂ 🔦

The name Samarès is derived from the French for salt marsh, and indeed sea salt was once extracted from marshy land nearby. It is not known who built the existing manor house, which has passed through many owners, but the grounds have developed gradually. By 1680 they were famed for their trees. The present garden was the work of Sir James Knott, who bought the property in 1924 and had it developed, employing 40 gardeners, at a cost of £100,000. Two quite different gardens here: a herb garden specialising in culinary and medicinal herbs in a partially walled garden leading to a lakeside area, and a Japanese garden. Of particular note are the camellias, the *Taxodium distichum* in the lake and the rocks imported from Cumberland.

GARDEN AND FLOWER SHOWS 2002

- 10th to 12th May: Spring Gardening Show, Malvern
  (Three Counties Showground, Malvern, Worcestershire)
  Ticket hotline: (01684) 584924
- 21st to 24th May: Chelsea Flower Show
  (Royal Hospital, Chelsea, London SW3)
  Ticket hotline: (0870) 906 3780
- 19th to 23rd June: BBC *Gardeners' World* Live
  (National Exhibition Centre, Birmingham)
  Ticket hotline: (0870) 264 5555
- 25th to 27th June, 20th to 22nd Aug: Wisley Flower Show
  (RHS Garden, Wisley, Woking, Surrey)
  Tel: (01483) 224234; Fax: (01483) 211750
- 2nd to 7th July: Hampton Court Flower Show
  (Hampton Court Palace, East Molesey, Surrey)
  Ticket hotline: (0870) 906 3790
- 17th to 21st July: RHS Flower Show, Tatton Park
  (Tatton Park, near Knutsford, Cheshire)
  Ticket hotline: (0870) 906 3810

For details of all these shows, telephone RHS on (020) 7834 4337.

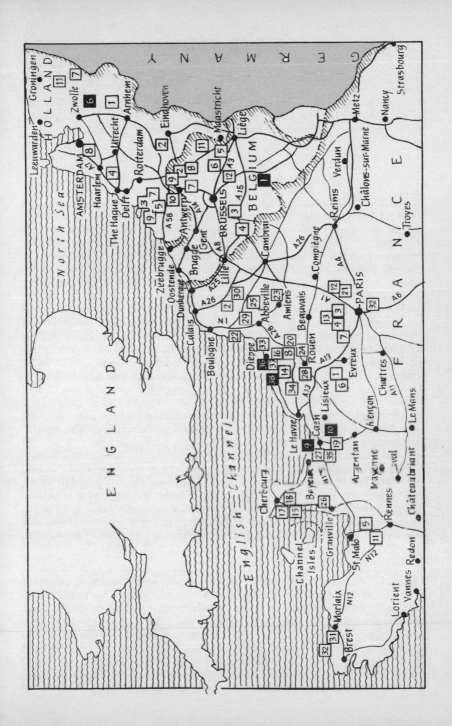

EUROPE

Throughout the *Guide* two-starred gardens are marked on the maps with a bold square.

For some years the *Guide* has included a selection of gardens in Europe, concentrating on those which are a reasonable distance from the Channel ports or some other points of entry such as a Eurostar station.

FRANCE

Paris Gardens

Central Paris: *The Tuileries Garden* near the Louvre (being restored, including *Le Jardin du Carrousel*. Christopher Bradley-Hole in his description has written that the Wirtz family 'have used yew hedges, planted in an extensive *patte d'oie* converging on the Arc de Triomphe, to make sense of some of the disparate geometry of the site'); *Parc Monceau* on Boul. de Courcelles (nineteenth-century nannyland); *The Luxembourg Gardens* on the Left Bank (*grandeur ancienne*); *The Fondation Cartier* has a gallery and garden for *'l'art contemporain'* at 261 boulevard Raspail (Tel: 42.18.56.51). Here Patrick Blanc has created a spectacular jungle-like hanging garden above the entrance which links the boulevard trees to the Fondation's rear garden; *Jardin de Plantes* also on the Left Bank, Pont d'Austerlitz; *Place des Vosges*, which landscape architect Gordon Haynes calls 'a masterpiece' of design and an excellent venue for picnics purchased in rue St Antoine and rue Birague to the south. An exhibition was held in 2000 at *Bagatelle* near the Trianon and this may be a regular event; there is also an elegant rose garden there.

Inner suburbs: *Parc André Citroën* (the most exciting modern park in Paris); *Jardin Albert Kahn* at Boulogne Billancourt (several gardens including an authentic Japanese garden); *Fondation Cartier Sculpture Garden* in Jovy-en-Jonas (20 minutes by train or RER line B. Good café).

Outer suburbs: *Parc Caillebotte*, Yerres, near Orly (garden of the painter who launched Monet); *Roseraie de L'Hay les Roses* (famous rose garden in the corner of a large municipal park near Orly); *La Bagatelle* on the edge of the Bois de Boulogne in Neuilly (perhaps the most elegant display of roses in the world).

Ile de France: *Château de St Jean de Beauregard* at Les Ulys (one of the best *potagers*), which hosts an annual plant fair (telephone 1.60.12.00.01 for details).

Shows

Two other major garden events are held every year within reasonable distance of Paris. Les Journées des Plants de Courson is held every May and October (now in its eighteenth year) in the seventeenth-century Château de Courson, 35km south of Paris. Dubbed the 'French Chelsea', this is an international plant sale with exhibitors and nurserymen from all over Europe, organised by the château owners, Patrice and Hélène Fustier, who were awarded the RHS Gold Veitch medal in 1993. To reach Courson from Paris, take the train (line C 'RER') from Alma, Les Invalides or Austerlitz stations to Breuillet or Bruyéres-Le-Châtel on Dourden route (first four carriages of train only), then shuttle bus or taxi from Breuillet to Courson (6km). For 2002 dates and prices, telephone 1.64.58.90. Further south, 185km from Paris, the Festival des Jardins, now in its eleventh year, takes place at the Château de Chaumont. Dozens of miniature gardens are on show, created by designers from all over the world. The festival runs from mid-June to mid-October. There is a regular train service from Austerliz to Chaumont-sur-Loire, sometimes having to change at Blois. For further information and prices, telephone 1.48.04.84.59.

Arboretum d'Harcourt 1

27800 Harcourt, Normandie. Tel: 2.32.46.29.70; Fax: 2.32.46.53.38

Open daily except Tues: March to 14th June, 2pm – 6pm, 15th June to 14th Sept, 10.30am – 6.30pm, 15th Sept to 14th Nov, 2pm – 6pm

A nine-hectare arboretum set in a 94-hectare forest, started in 1802 and including many fine trees from North America.

Botanica 2

79 rue de Fruges

62130 Hernicourt-Sauricourt. Tel: 3.21.04.04.03
Open March to Oct, Thurs – Sun, 10am – 5pm

A beautifully landscaped garden with fine trees and good collections of herbaceous perennials. Landscaped lake with rustic bridge.

Chantilly ★ 3

60500 Chantilly. Tel: 3.44.62.62.62; Fax: 3.44.62.62.61

Open all year, daily, 10am – 6pm. 45-minute train around the park available, with commentary in French and English.

Acknowledged as one of André Le Nôtre's greatest creations, notable for its magnificent scale and water features.

Château d'Ambleville 4

95710 Bray-et-Lû. Tel: 1.34.67.71.34

Open April to 15th Oct, Sat, Sun and public holidays, 10.30 – 6.30pm

Italian gardens created between the two world wars, expressed as terraces, topiary and water.

Château de la Ballue 5

35560 Bazouges-la-Prouse, Brittany. Tel: 2.99.97.47.86; Fax: 2.99.97.47.70; Website: www.laballue.com

Open 15th April to 15th Oct, daily, 1 – 5.30pm, and in winter by appt

A series of theatrical gardens in the Baroque or Mannerist style of the sixteenth and seventeenth centuries, created in 1973 and now restored.

Château de Beaumesnil ★ 6

27410 Beaumesnil. Tel/Fax: 2.32.44.40.09

Open April to Oct, daily, except Mon, 10am – 12 noon, 2 – 6pm

Designed by La Quintinye in 1640 and extensively remodelled in the eighteenth century. Features include a formal garden, an unusual labyrinth and lakeside walks.

Château de Bizy 7

27200 Vernon. Tel: 2.32.51.00.82; Fax: 2.32.21.66.54

Open April to Oct, daily, except Mon, 10am – 12 noon, 2 – 6pm

Surrounding the nineteenth-century château, a series of elaborate cascades, fountains and statuary, lime and yew walks and an attractive park.

Château de Bosmelet 8

76720 Auffay. Tel: 2.35.32.81.07; Fax: 2.35.32.84.62

Garden open for groups all year, 1 – 7pm. Potager open May to Oct, daily except Tues and Thurs

A re-creation of the classical French design laid out in 1715 by Le Colinet, first gardener to André Le Nôtre at Versailles, and including an ancient lime avenue and a fine ornamental kitchen garden.

Château de Brécy ★★ 9

14480 St Gabriel–Brécy. Tel/Fax: 2.31.80.11.48

Open April to 2nd Nov, Tues, Thurs and Sun, 2.30 – 6.30pm, and for groups at other times by appt

A seventeenth-century garden laid out on five terraces in the Italian style in the 1650s – sophisticated, architectural and compact.

Château de Canon ★★ 10

14270 Mézidon. Tel: 2.31.20.05.07/2.31.28.77.04; Fax: 2.31.20.65.17

Open July to Oct, daily, 2 – 7pm

Unchanged since the mid-eighteenth century, a combination of French and English picturesque styles, including an Anglo-Chinese garden.

Château de Caradeuc 11

35190 Bécherel, Brittany. Tel: 2.99.66.77.76

Open April to June, Sept and Oct, weekends; July to Aug, daily, 2.30pm – 6pm

A garden restored in the traditional French manner in the late nineteenth century, distinguished by *allées*, vistas, statues and monuments.

Château de Compiègne ★ 12

60200 Compiègne. Tel: 3.44.38.47.00; Fax: 3.44.38.47.01

Open all year, daily except Tues and public holidays, 10am – 6pm

An important restoration project, noted especially for the magnificent vista and trellis-covered walk commissioned by Napoleon to complement a garden dating originally from the reign of Louis XV.

Château de Corbeil-Cerf 13

60110 Corbeil-Cerf. Tel: 3.44.52.02.43

Open by appt to groups only

A series of rides cut through the forest surrounding the château, with a formal area to the north and four other modern gardens.

Château de Galleville ★ 14

76560 Douderville, Normandie. Tel: 2.35.96.52.40

Open May to Oct for groups by appt. Guided visits mid-July to Aug

An elegant contemporary design uniting the seventeenth-century château with its garden and magnificent park.

Château de Martinvast 15

50690 Martinvast. Tel: 2.33.52.02.23

Open all year, Sat, Sun and public holidays, 2 – 7pm, by written appt only

A wooded park created in the English manner in 1820, with extensive water features, complementing the Gothick château.

Château de Miromesnil 16

Tourville sur Arques, 76550 Offranville. Tel/Fax: 2.35.85.02.80

Open May to mid-Oct, daily, except Tues, 2 – 6pm

A garden notable for its connection with Guy de Maupassant, magnificent beech wood and charming traditional *potager*.

Château de Nacqueville 17

50460 Urville–Nacqueville, Nr Cherbourg, Manche. Tel: 2.33.03.01.02

Open all year, Tues and Fri. Guided visits only, hourly from 2pm to 5pm

A park in the English style, created in the 1830s, damaged in World War II and now restored, set in a green valley sheltered by wooded escarpments.

Château de Vauville 18

50440 Beaumont-Hague, E. Cherbourg. Tel: 2.33.52.71.41; Fax: 2.33.52.72.31

Open July and Aug, daily. Guided visits only hourly from 2.30pm to 5.30pm

A post-war garden, informal in its style and Mediterranean in its planting, specialising in exotic and succulent plants arranged in a series of 'green rooms'.

Château de Vendeuvre 19

14170 Saint-Pierre-sur-Dives.

Open May to Sept, daily; March, April, Nov, Dec, weekends and public holidays; all 10am – 6pm

A classical château and lake and many contemporary ideas, including new plantings and intriguing architectural and water features.

Clos du Coudray 20

76850 Etaimpuis, Normandie. Tel: 2.35.34.96.85

Open Easter to 1st Nov, Thurs – Sun, 10am – 7pm

Thousands of different plant species grouped into 22 distinctive areas within clipped hedges or meandering paths – a succession of delightful surprises.

Ermenonville (Parc Jean-Jacques Rousseau) ★ 21

1 rue Ren de Girardin, 60950 Ermenonville. Tel: 3.44.54.01.58; Fax: 3.44.54.04.96

Open Easter to Oct, Sat and Sun; June to Sept, daily except Tues, all 1.30 – 7pm

A natural landscape of grass, trees and water embellished with statues and follies in the Stowe/Painshill tradition and indelibly associated with the great philosopher.

Herbarium des Remparts 22

80230 St Valéry-sur-Somme. Tel: 3.22.26.90.72

Open May to 15th Nov, daily, 10am – 12 noon, 3 – 6pm

A well-laid-out collection of medicinal, aromatic and culinary herbs and other plants useful to man, within the walls of an old convent garden.

Les Hortillonages 23

54 Boulevard Beauville, 80000 Amiens. Tel: 3.22.92.12.18

Open April to Oct, daily, 2 – between 5 and 8pm, depending on season

Unique. Small electric boats take visitors around these former vegetable gardens (filled now with flowers), intersected by numerous small canals. Striking views of Amiens Cathedral.

Jardin d'Angélique 24

**Hameau du Pigrard, Route de Lyons, 76520 Montmain, Normandie.
Tel: 2.35.79.08.12**

Open 15th April to Oct, daily, 10am – 7pm

A small garden dedicated to the beauty of life in memory of a lost daughter, filled with roses and perennials in a subtle combination of scents and colours, plus a newer, more formal garden.

Jardins de Maizicourt 25

80370 Maizicourt. Tel: 3.22.32.69.64

Open May to Oct, June and Sept, daily, 2 – 6pm

Clipped box hedges, herbaceous borders and old roses, all planted with impeccable taste. The small church over the garden wall is worth visiting, (key with garden owner).

Jardin de Plantbessin 26

14490 Castillon, Calvados, Nr Bayeux. Tel: 2.31.92.56.03; Fax: 2.31.22.70.09

Open 15th May to 1st June, Mon – Sat; 2nd June to 14th July, daily; 15th July to 15th Oct, Mon – Sat, all 2.30 – 6pm

A delightful setting for a fine nursery, laid out in garden 'rooms', including herbaceous borders and water, Japanese and herb gardens – a plantsman's delight.

Jardin des Plantes, Caen 27

Rue Desmoneux, 14000 Caen. Tel: 2.31.30.432.63

Open all year, daily, 8am – between 5.30 and 7.30pm, (Suns and public holidays open 2pm). Tropical greenhouses, 2 – 5pm • Entrance: free

A pleasant public garden founded in 1736, with a park added in 1805 – fine trees, rare shrubs, plant order beds, a rock garden and a pond.

Jardin des Plantes, Rouen 28

**114 ter avenue des Martyrs de la Résistance, 76100 Rouen.
Tel: 2.35.72.36.36/2.32.18.21.30; Fax: 2.35.72.34.55**

Open all year, daily, 8am – between 5.15 and 7.45pm. Greenhouses 8 – 11am, 1.30 – 4.30pm • Entrance: free

A well-maintained eight-hectare park with interesting plants, attractive greenhouses and order beds.

Jardins de Valloires 29

80120 Argoules. Tel: 3.22.23.53.55

Open 13th March to 3rd Nov, daily, 10am – 5pm (closes 6.30pm, May to Sept)

Designed by one of France's foremost garden designers, Gilles Clément. Evoking the peace and contemplation of its monastic past, spacious lawns, subdued flower combinations, a rosery and a cloister furnished with yew columns and a parterre, a water garden and a garden of the five senses.

Jardin de Yves Gosse de Gorre 30

2 rue du bois, 62270 Séricourt. Tel: 3.21.03.64.42

Open April to Oct, Tues – Sat, 9am – 12 noon, 2 – 6pm

Good collection of species roses, chosen especially for their colourful heps, together with amusing topiary, and colour-themed rooms.

Jardin Exotique 31

Roscoff, 29680 Brittany. Tel: 2.98.61.29.19 (summer); Fax: 2.98.61.12.34

Open all year, daily: Feb, Dec, times vary but always open 2 – 5.30pm; May to Oct, mornings and 2 – 5.30pm; Feb, Mar, Nov, Dec, closed Tues

The giant echiums are spectacular. Over 2000 species of exotic plants grown in an informal seaside setting, fringing paths, pools, waterfalls and rocky outcrops.

Jardin Georges Delaselle 32

29253 Ile de Batz, Finistre, Brittany. Tel: 2.98.61.75.65

Open April to Sept, daily

A late-nineteenth-century plantsman's garden sheltered, nurtured and now restored, with many palms and exotics from the southern hemisphere complementing the Bronze Age tombs and excellent modern sculptures.

Jardins et Pépinières de Cotelle 33

76370 Derchigny–Graincourt. Tel: 2.35.83.61.38; Fax: 2.35.04.06.00

Open late April to mid-Nov, Mon – Sat, 10am – 12 noon and 2 – 5pm; occasionally open Suns, May, June, Oct

A garden created by a nurseryman and his painter wife around their nursery of unusual plants.

Manoir du Fay ★ 34

Rue du Grand Fay, 76190 Yvetot, Normandie. Tel: 2.35.56.24.73

Open May to Oct, one Sun per month, 2 – 6pm, and by appt

Behind a seventeenth-century manor house, a *potager* re-created in the traditional manner using entirely organic principles.

Parc et Jardins du Château d'Harcourt 35

14220 Thury–Harcourt. Tel: 2.31.79.65.41 or 2.31.79.72.05

Open April and Oct, Sun and public holidays, May to Sept, daily, all 2.30 – 6.30pm

A dazzling spring and summer garden with a profusion of flowers laid out with consummate artistry on a sloping site: a world away from the dramatic ruins of château destroyed in World War II and its 70 hectares of park and gardens.

Parc Floral des Moutiers ★★ 36

76119 Varengeville-sur-Mer. Tel: 2.35.85.10.02; Fax: 2.35.85.46.98

Open mid-March to mid-Nov, and for groups by appt

A Lutyens garden with Jekyll undertones surrounding a characterful house, combining formality, exuberant planting and archetypal architectural features in a satisfying Anglo-French alliance.

Shamrock 37

route du Manoir d'Ango, 76119 Varengeville-sur-Mer. Tel: 2.35.04.02.33; Fax: 2.35.85.30.20

Open July to Oct, Fri, Sat, Sun and public holidays, 10am – 12 noon, 2.30pm – 6pm

Possibly the largest collection of hydrangeas in the world, with over 6000 different species and varieties brought together by Corinne Malet.

Le Vasterival ★★ 38

76119 St-Marguerite-sur-Mer. Tel: 2.35.85.12.05

Open by appt only

A garden created since 1957 by an outstanding plantswoman, the Princess Sturdza, informal in layout, immaculately cultivated, fascinating at any season.

BELGIUM

Brussels Gardens

Brussels itself has a number of gardens open at all times, including *Abbaye de la Cambre, Bois de la Cambre,* the *Jean Massart Experimental Garden, Parc Leopold* on rue Belliard and the park in the City Centre. Other gardens include *Parc Tenbosch* (with outstanding trees) on chausseé de Vleurgat, and *Maison d'Erasme,* 31 rue du Chapitre Anderlecht. *Parc Solvay* on chaussée de la Hulpe and *Jardins du Museé van Buuren,* 41 rue Leo Errera are in the south of the city. Ten kilometres north of Brussels is the *National Botanic Garden,* open daily 9am – sunset. Once a year, usually in April/May, the King of Belgium opens the conservatories in the *Laeken Royal Palace* on the northern outskirts of the city.

Annevoie ★★ 1

5537 Annevoie-Rouillon, Anhee.

Open April to Oct, daily, 9.30am – 6.30pm

An historically important garden, created in the mid-eighteenth century with elements borrowed from the Italian, French and English styles, linked by a network of water features, including some spectacular fountains, fine urns and statues and superb trees.

Arboretum Kalmthout 2

Heuvel 2, B–2920 Kalmthout. Tel: 3.666.6741; Fax: 3.666.3396

Open 15th March to 15th Nov, daily, 10am – 5pm

The largest dendrological collection in Belgium, a 10-acre arboretum of outstanding quality with many collections of rare and unusual trees and shrubs.

Château d'Attre ★ 3

Avenue du Château, 7941 Attre, Brugelette. Tel: 32.68.45.44.60

Open by appt only: April to Oct, Sat, Sun; July, Aug, daily, except Wed; all 10am – 12 noon, 2 – 6pm

A picturesque 28-hectare park with magnificent old trees and interesting follies and garden building.

Château de Belœil 4

rue du Château, Belœil, près Mons. Tel: 32.69.68.96.55

Open April to Oct, Sat, Sun; July, Aug, daily except Wed; all 10am – 6pm

An exceptional garden with a great six-hectare lake flanked by garden characterful 'rooms', plus 10km of spectacular hedges and other foliage features.

Château de Hex 5

B–3870 Heers. Tel: 12.74.73.41; Fax: 12.74.49.87

Open 15th, 16th June and 28th, 29th Sept, all 10am – 6pm

Five hectares of formal garden set in 60 hectares of English-style park, all in a beautiful natural site, with a huge collection of old roses and a traditional *potager*.

Château de Leeuwergem ★ 6

B–9620 Zottegem. Tel: 93.60.08.73; Fax: 93.61.01.38

Open May to 1st Oct by appt only

A park with a rare eighteenth-century *théâtre de verdure* (still in regular use), and formal gardens laid out in 1702 in the French classical style – a splendid counterpoint to the spare simplicity of the château.

Château Fort d'Ecaussinnes (Le Potager) 7

Rue de Seneffe, 7191 Ecaussinnes–Lalaing. Tel/Fax: 67.44.24.90

Open all year, daily except Mon; Easter to 1st Nov, 10am – 8pm, 2nd Nov to Easter, 8am – 4pm

A seventeenth-century walled ornamental *potager* across a private road from the medieval castle, reputedly the first garden in Belgium to be listed.

Château s'Gravenwezel   8

2970 s'Gravenwezel, Schilde. Tel: 36.58.14.70; Fax: 36.58.37.81

A 40-hectare formal park surrounding an ancient castle, reinvigorated by leading designer Jacques Wirtz with wide walks, extensive tree planting and the restoration of the eighteenth-century garden plan in the English landscape style, plus an attractive botanical garden and a redesigned walled garden.

Hof ter Weyden   9

Greefstraat 1, 2910 Essen. Tel: 36.77.22.74

Open 12th, 13th May, 10am – 6pm

Three distinctive planting areas surrounding an old farmhouse and its historic barn: a formal rose garden, an architectural garden divided by hedges, and an orchard, with a double row of poplars and a lake linking the garden with the countryside.

Park van Beervelde   10

Beervelde-Dorp 75, B-9080 Lochristi. Tel: 93.55.55.40

Open 11th, 12th May and 12th, 13th Oct, by appt

A 20-hectare arboretum and garden in the English landscape style, with a spectacular flowering of Ghent azaleas in May.

Rekem Garden ★   11

Achter St Pieter 24, 3621 Rekem-Lanaken. Tel: 89.71.46.92

A small, immaculately maintained garden sheltered by fine hedges, with an unusual central pavilion of *Cornus mas* and distinctive areas planted with an artist's eye for design and colour.

Vlaamse Toontuinen (Flemish Show Gardens)   12

1 Houtmarkt, Hoegaarden 3320. Tel: 16.76.78.43/16.76.56.39; Fax: 16.76.79.19

Within a walled park, a permanent exhibition of 22 different types of gardens, all designed by landscape architects and professional gardeners, plus nature trails, a sculpture exhibition and horticultural displays.

NETHERLANDS

Broekstraat 17 ★   1

6999 De Hummelo. Tel: 314.38.1120; Fax: 314.38.1199

The highly original creation of one of the gurus of the contemporary Dutch style of naturalistic gardening, Piet Oudolf, and his wife Anja, displaying the masterly orchestration of nature that won him the top prize at Chelsea 2000.

Huys de Dohm 2

De Doom 48–50, 6419 CX Heerlen. Tel: 45.571.0470

Open 1st, 2nd, 8th, 9th, 15th, 16th June, 10am – 5pm

Restored since 1980 as a series of outdoor rooms, including double herbaceous borders, a delightful *potager* and topiary, white, water and wild gardens, reflecting the character of the small, ancient castle and its hunting lodge.

De Kempenhof 3

Zuiverseweg 4, 4357 NM Domburg. Tel: 118.58.16.47

Open 6th, 7th July, and by appt

A two-hectare garden focused on a splendid all-season double herbaceous border, with island beds, roses, hellebores and an avenue planted with ornamental grasses for additional seasonal interest.

Leiden Botanic Garden ★ 4

Hortus Botanicus, Rapenburg 73, Leiden. Tel: 71.527.7249

Open April to Sept, Mon – Sat, Oct to March 2003, Mon – Fri, all 9am – 5pm

Clusius's late-sixteenth-century garden reconstructed as the original, with 60 beds and ancient trees, plus a general garden with other features of interest.

Middelburg Garden ★ 5

Seisdam 22, 4331 NT Middelburg. Tel: 118.62.85.74

A superlative small town garden, where well-trimmed hedges and evergreens form the background for three abundant herbaceous borders, a small iris avenue, old roses and an oasis of verdant shade.

Paleis Het Loo, National Museum ★★ 6

Koninklijk Park 1, 7315 JA Apeldoorn. Tel: 55.577.2400; Fax: 55.521.9983

Open all year, daily except Mon (but open Bank Holiday Mons), 10am – 5pm

William Prince of Orange's magnificent formal garden of 1684, transformed into a landscape park, then destroyed and now triumphantly restored to its original design, including a sunken garden, parterres, elaborate water conceits, an upper garden with a curved colonnade, and delightful gardens near the palace.

Priona Gardens 7

Schnineslootweg 13, Schninesloot. Tel: 523.68.17.34

Open 30th April to Sept, Tues to Sat, 12 noon – 5pm, Sun, 2 – 6pm

The naturalistic garden of Henk Gerritsen, combining artistry and a profound knowledge of wild flowers and their habitats.

Slot der Nisse 8

Dorpsplein 4443 AE, Nisse. Tel: 113.64.94.69

Open 6th, 7th July, and by appt

A modern garden for the coachhouse of a demolished castle – delightful ingredients include a lovely herb garden, a natural pond, double white borders, an orchard, a spring avenue with medlars, and fine views.

J.P. Thijsse–Park 9

Prins Bernhardlaan 8, Amstelveen, Amsterdam. Tel: 205.40.42.65

A public 'new-wave' park created post-war and devoted to plants that grow in the wild, with large and varied groups of plants creating an entirely natural feeling, all connected by a long and narrow meandering pond.

De Tintelhof 10

Golsteinseweg 24, 4351 SC Veere. Tel: 118.61.45.20

Open 6th, 7th July, and by appt

A garden of well-balanced herbaceous borders, many old and modern roses in a frame of trimmed hedges and clipped evergreens, and a contrasting area of woodland, all sensitively integrated into its surroundings.

Ton ter Linden Gardens 11

Achterma 20, 7963 PM Ruinen. Tel: 522.47.26.55

Open 30th April to 1st Oct, Tues – Sun, 10am – 5pm

A magical meadow-like garden in the new Dutch style contrived by one of the acknowledged masters of the art.

Specialist Lists

Arboretums

Many of the gardens in the *Guide* are extensively treed, and this list concentrates on mature arboretums, in which the trees are labelled.

Bedfordshire *Luton Hoo, Swiss Garden*
Birmingham *University of Birmingham Botanic Garden*
Cheshire *Cholmondeley Castle, Ness, Tatton*
Cornwall *Pencarrow*
Cumbria *Holker, Muncaster Castle*
Derbyshire *Chatsworth, Derby Arboretum*
Devon *Bicton College, Bicton Park*
Dorset *Deans Court, Forde Abbey, Melbury House, Minterne*
Durham *Bowes Museum*
Essex *Cracknells, Saling Hall*
Gloucestershire *Batsford, Westonbirt*
Hampshire *Nunwell House, Sir Harold Hillier Gardens and Arboretum*
Herefordshire *Hergest Croft*
Hertfordshire *Beale Arboretum*
Kent *Bedgebury, Belmont, Emmetts, Ladham House, Riverhill House*
London Area *Cannizaro Park, Isabella Plantation, Royal Botanic Gardens Kew*
Manchester Area *Haigh Hall*
Norfolk *Holkham Hall*
Oxfordshire *Harcourt Arboretum*
Suffolk *The Rookery*
Surrey *Coverwood, RHS Wisley, Winkworth*
Sussex, East *Sheffield Park*
Sussex, West *High Beeches, Leonardslee, Nymans, Wakehurst Place, West Dean*
Warwickshire *Arbury Hall*
Wiltshire *Bowood, Broadleas, Corsham Court*
Worcestershire *Eastnor Castle*
Yorkshire, North *Castle Howard, Thorp Perrow*
Yorkshire, South & West *Temple Newsam, Wentworth*
Ireland *Brook Hall, Castlewellan, Fota, John F. Kennedy Arboretum*
Scotland *Castle Kennedy, Cruickshank Botanic, Leckmelm Shrubbery, Monteviot*
Wales *Dyffryn Botanic Garden*

Herb Gardens

Many gardeners now grow herbs for the kitchen, and this listing is mainly devoted to those who make an ornamental feature of the necessity, though some may be purely ornamental.

Bedfordshire *Toddington Manor*
Bristol *Goldney Hall*
Cambridgeshire *Emmanuel College Cambridge*
Cheshire *Cheshire Herbs, Little Moreton Hall, Norton Priory*

Cumbria *Acorn Bank, Brantwood, Levens*
Derbyshire *Hardwick Hall, Herb Garden*
Dorset *Cranborne Manor, Edmondsham House, The Manor House, Sandford Orcas*
Essex *Fanners Green, Tye Farm*
Gloucestershire *Alderley Grange, Barnsley House, Hullasey House, Painswick, Sudeley*
Hampshire *Gilbert White's House, Hollington Herbs, Tudor House Museum*
Hertfordshire *Hatfield, Knebworth*
Kent *Iden Croft, Leeds Castle, Long Barn, Marle Place, Scotney, Sissinghurst, Stoneacre*
Lancashire *Leighton Hall*
Lincolnshire *Doddington, Gunby*
London Area *Chelsea Physic, Hall Place, Museum of Garden History, 7 St Georges Road*
Newcastle Area *Bede's World*
Norfolk *Besthorpe Hall, Congham Hall, Norfolk Lavender*
Northamptonshire *Hill Farm, Holdenby House*
Northumberland *Herterton House, Hexham Herbs*
Nottinghamshire *Rufford Country Park*
Oxfordshire *Blenheim*
Somerset *Gaulden Manor*
Suffolk *Helmingham*
Surrey *RHS Wisley*
Sussex, East *Bateman's, Clinton Lodge, Crown House, Michelham Priory, Wellingham*
Sussex West *Parham House*
Wiltshire *Abbey House Gardens, Broadleas*
Yorkshire, North *Harlow Carr*
Scotland *Falkland Palace, Kailzie, Malleny Garden, Monteviot*
Wales *Bodysgallen Hall, Pant-yr-Holiad, Penlan-Uchaf*
Channel Islands *Sausmarez Manor, Guernsey*

Herbaceous Borders

There was a time when every worthwhile garden had to have one, but now the fashionable thing is 'grasses'. None the less, these borders are the glory of the British garden, and we select some of the best, though this does not mean there are no great and good ones elsewhere.

Buckinghamshire *Cliveden*
Cambridgeshire *Anglesey Abbey*
Cheshire *Arley Hall, Tatton*
Cornwall *Lanhydrock*
Cumbria *Sizergh*
Devon *Arlington Court, Castle Drogo, Coleton Fishacre, Killerton, Knightshayes*
Dorset *Stour House*
Gloucestershire *Hidcote, Rodmarton*
Hampshire *Bramdean House*
Kent *Sissinghurst*
Lincolnshire *Gunby*
Manchester Area *Dunham Massey*
Norfolk *Blickling, Felbrigg, Oxburgh*

Northumberland *Wallington*
Somerset *Barrington Court, Lytes Cary, Montacute*
Staffordshire *Shugborough*
Suffolk *Melford Hall*
Sussex, West *Nymans*
Warwickshire *Packwood*
Wiltshire *The Courts*
Yorkshire, North *Beningbrough Hall*
Wales *National Botanic Garden of Wales, Powis Castle*

Japanese and Chinese Gardens

The influence of the oriental on British gardening tastes goes back some while, so we only list here those gardens which have a fairly full-blown connection with the Far East.

Cheshire *Tatton Park*
Cornwall *Japanese Garden and Bonsai Nursery*
Dorset *Compton Acres*
Hertfordshire *Japanese Garden*
Kent *Mount Ephraim*
London Area *Capel Manor, Holland Park (Kyoto Garden), 8 Lower Merton Rise, 17 Navarino Road*
Nottinghamshire *Newstead Abbey, The Pureland Japanese Garden (North Clifton. Tel: (01777 228567)*
Rutland *Barnsdale*
Surrey *Coombe Wood*
Wiltshire *Heale, Wilton*
Yorkshire, West *Harewood*
Ireland *Japanese Garden*
Scotland *Arbigland, Gorstain Cottage Garden (Taynuilt. Tel: (01866) 822831/822375)*

Mazes

These are not, as they once were, relics of the past, but are now found in many shapes and sizes all over the country.

Birmingham *Castle Bromwich Hall Gardens*
Buckinghamshire *Chenies Manor*
Cheshire *Tatton*
Cornwall *Glendurgan*
Derbyshire *Chatsworth*
Essex *Bridge End Gardens, Turf Maze*
Hampshire and the Isle of White *Barton Manor*
Hertfordshire *Hatfield, Knebworth*
Kent *Groombridge Place, Hever, Leeds Castle*
Lancashire *Worden Park*
Liverpool *Speke Hall*
London Area *Capel Manor, Crystal Palace Park, Hampton Court*
Oxfordshire *Blenheim, Greys Court*

Suffolk *Somerleyton Hall, Wyken Hall*
Sussex, West *Parham House*
Wiltshire *Longleat*
Yorkshire, North *Burton Agnes Hall*
Ireland *Carnfunnock Country Park*
Scotland *Cawdor Castle, Finlaystone, Scone Palace*
Channel Islands *La Seigneurie*

Organic Gardens

Some of those listed are 'instructional', while others are included because their owners follow the philosophy by spurning the use of chemicals, etc.

Bedfordshire *The Lodge*
Devon *Fardel Manor*
Dorset *Dean's Court, Edmondsham House*
Gloucestershire *Snowshill Manor*
Hertfordshire *Hatfield*
Kent *South Hill Farm, Yalding*
Lancashire *Pendle Heritage Centre*
Liverpool *Croxteth Hall*
Somerset *Greencombe*
Surrey *Titsey Place*
Warwickshire *Avon Cottage, Ryton Organic*
Ireland *Ballymaloe Cookery School, Creagh*
Scotland *Bank House, Carnell, Kellie Castle*
Wales *Centre for Alternative Technology*
France *Manoir du Fay*

Rock Gardens

An unusual taste for the modern gardener, so many of those listed are historic, though not necessarily anachronisms for that.

Bedfordshire *Luton Hoo*
Cheshire *Arley Hall, Cholmondeley Castle, Tatton*
Cornwall *Pencarrow*
Derbyshire *Chatsworth*
Dorset *Forde Abbey*
Hampshire *Exbury Gardens*
Kent *Mount Ephraim*
Norfolk *Sandringham*
Northamptonshire *Lamport Hall*
Northumberland *Bide-a-Wee Cottage, Chillingham Castle*
Warwickshire *Warwick Castle*
Worcestershire *Spetchley Park*
Yorkshire, North *Newby Hall*
Scotland *Manderston, Torosay*

Rose Gardens

Most of the entries are for rose gardens, though some may be included because they have a number of unusual varieties although not a rose garden as such. It is hoped that owners of listed gardens have labelled their rose varieties. Many beautiful roses will of course be found in other gardens not listed here. The Royal National Rose Society publishes a free leaflet on *Rose Gardens toVisit*, covering the UK and Ireland.

Bedfordshire *Luton Hoo*
Berkshire *Folly Farm*
Birmingham *Botanical Gardens and Glasshouses, University Botanic*
Buckinghamshire *Chicheley, Cliveden, Manor House Bledlow*
Cambridgeshire *Elton Hall, St John's College Cambridge*
Cheshire *Bridgemere, Cholmondeley Castle, Ness, Tatton, Tirley Garth*
Cumbria *Dalemain, Graythwaite Hall, Holker*
Derbyshire *Haddon, Kedleston, 210 Nottingham Road*
Devon *Docton Mill, Rosemoor*
Dorset *Cranborne Manor, Friars Way, Weston House*
Durham *Raby Castle, University of Durham Botanic, Westholme Hall*
Essex *Saling Hall, RHS Hyde Hall*
Gloucestershire *Abbotswood, Hunts Court, Kiftsgate Court, Misarden Park, Painswick, Stancombe, Sudeley*
Hampshire *Exbury, Fairfield House, Gilbert White's House, Mottisfont, Northcourt, Ventnor Botanic*
Herefordshire *Hergest Croft, How Caple*
Hertfordshire *Benington Lordship, Gardens of the Rose, Hatfield*
Kent *Chartwell, Emmetts, Godinton, Goodnestone Park, Hever, Leeds Castle, Mount Ephraim, Penshurst, Scotney, Sissinghurst, Squerryes Court*
Leicestershire *Belvoir*
Lincolnshire *Ayscoughfee Hall, Burghley, Doddington, Hall Farm*
Liverpool *Speke Hall*
London Area *Avery Hill Park, Cannizaro Park, Capel Manor, Fenton House, Gunnersbury Park, Hall Place, Hampton Court Palace, Priory Gardens, Queen Mary's Rose Garden, Royal Botanic Kew, Syon Park*
Manchester Area *Heaton Hall*
Norfolk *Norfolk Lavender, Mannington Hall*
Northamptonshire *Boughton, Holdenby, Kelmarsh, Rockingham Castle*
Northumberland *Belsay Hall, Chillingham, Hexham Herbs*
Nottinghamshire *Holme Pierrepoint Hall*
Oxfordshire *Blenheim, Brook Cottage, Greys Court, Oxford Botanic, Rousham, Stonor Park*
Rutland *Ashwell House, Old Manor House*
Shropshire *Benthall Hall, David Austin Roses, Dower House, Hodnet, Paddocks, Weston Park*
Somerset *Gaulden Manor*
Staffordshire *Eccleshall Castle, Shugborough, Trentham*
Suffolk *Euston Hall, Helmingham, Somerleyton*
Surrey *Albury Park, Mansion, Loseley Park, Polesden Lacey, RHS Wisley, The Walled Garden*

Sussex, East *Crown House*
Sussex, West *Apuldram Roses, Duckyls, Hammerwood House, Nymans, Parham*
Warwickshire *Arbury Hall, Farnborough, Ilmington Manor, Ragley, Ryton, Warwick Castle*
Wiltshire *Abbey House Gardens, Avebury Manor, Bowood, Broadleas, Corsham Court, Heale Garden, Iford Manor, Longleat, Pound Hill House, Wilton*
Worcestershire *Eastnor Castle, Spetchley Park*
Yorkshire, North & East *Castle Howard, Newby Hall, Norton Conyers*
Yorkshire, South & West *Bramham Park, Nostell Priory, Temple Newsam*
Ireland *St Anne's Rose Garden*
Scotland *Cawdor, Drum, Dunrobin, Hill of Tarvit, Hirsel, Malleny Gardens, Manderston, Monteviot, Tyninghame*
Wales *Bodysgallen Hall*

Sculpture Gardens

Many of the gardens in the *Guide* have sculpture, but those listed have ornamental features as their primary purpose.

Cornwall *Barbara Hepworth Museum*
Cumbria *Grizedale Sculpture Trail (Forestry Commission)*
Devon *Castle Drogo, The Mythic Garden (Stone Lane Gardens, Chagford)*
Gloucestershire *Westonbirt Arboretum*
Hampshire *Garden Gallery*
Kent *Druidstone Artpark, Honey Hill, Canterbury*
Leicestershire *Belvoir Castle Artpark, Grantham*
London *Holland Park (to March 2001)*
Norfolk *Sculpture Trail, Bergh Apton village, May and June (Tel: (01508) 521298)*
Nottinghamshire *Boots Millennium Sculpture Garden (Tel: (0115) 9593090)*
Republic of Ireland *Shekina Sculpture Garden, Glenmalure, Co. Wicklow (Write for appt.)*
Suffolk *Hillwatering (Bury St Edmunds. Tel: (01359) 258948)*
Surrey *Dunsborough Park, Hannah Peschar Gallery*
Sussex, West *Boldhorns Park, Rusper (Tel: (Groups by appt only Tel: (01293) 871575), Borde Hill, Goodwood*
Wiltshire *Roche Court (East Winterslow)*
Worcestershire *Witley Court*
Yorkshire, South & West *Yorkshire Sculpture Park*
Scotland *Little Sparta*
Channel Islands *Sausmarez Manor*

Index

An * indicates that the garden or nursery is mentioned in the text of another garden entry; # means that only garden names, addresses and contact details, with perhaps a very brief description, are given; *col. ill.* refers to a photograph in the colour insert.